AMERICA

tenth edition

AMERICA
A Narrative History

David Emory Shi

George Brown Tindall

W. W. NORTON & COMPANY, INC.
New York • London

W. W. Norton & Company has been independent since its founding in 1923, when William Warder Norton and Mary D. Herter Norton first published lectures delivered at the People's Institute, the adult education division of New York City's Cooper Union. The firm soon expanded its program beyond the Institute, publishing books by celebrated academics from America and abroad. By midcentury, the two major pillars of Norton's publishing program—trade books and college texts—were firmly established. In the 1950s, the Norton family transferred control of the company to its employees, and today—with a staff of four hundred and a comparable number of trade, college, and professional titles published each year—W. W. Norton & Company stands as the largest and oldest publishing house owned wholly by its employees.

Copyright © 2016, 2013, 2010, 2007, 2004, 1999, 1996, 1992, 1988, 1984 by W. W. Norton & Company, Inc.

All rights reserved
Printed in the United States of America

Editor: Jon Durbin
Associate Editors: Justin Cahill and Scott Sugarman
Project Editors: Melissa Atkin and Linda Feldman
Editorial Assistant: Travis Carr
Managing Editor, College: Marian Johnson
Managing Editor, College Digital Media: Kim Yi
Production Manager: Ashley Horna
Media Editor: Laura Wilk
Media Project Editor: Penelope Lin
Media Editorial Assistant: Chris Hillyer
Marketing Manager, History: Sarah England
Design Director: Hope Goodell-Miller
Photo Editor: Stephanie Romeo
Permissions Manager: Megan Jackson
Composition: Jouve North America
Manufacturing: Quad Graphics Taunton

Permission to use copyrighted material is included on page A165.

Library of Congress Cataloging-in-Publication Data

Shi, David E. Tindall, George Brown.
  America: a narrative history / David Emory Shi, George Brown Tindall.
Tenth edition. New York: W. W. Norton & Company, 2016.
  Includes index.
LCCN 2015036484
  ISBN 9780393265934 (hardcover)
LCSH: United States—History—Textbooks.
LCC E178.1 .T55 2017 DDC 973—dc23 LC record available at http://lccn.loc.gov/2015036484

W. W. Norton & Company, Inc., 500 Fifth Avenue, New York, NY 10110-0017
wwnorton.com
W. W. Norton & Company Ltd., Castle House, 75/76 Wells Street, London W1T 3QT
1 2 3 4 5 6 7 8 9 0

FOR
MY WIFE,
ANGELA HALFACRE SHI

DAVID E. SHI is a professor of history and the president emeritus of Furman University. He is the author of several books on American cultural history, including the award-winning *The Simple Life: Plain Living and High Thinking in American Culture* and *Facing Facts: Realism in American Thought and Culture, 1850–1920.*

GEORGE B. TINDALL, recently of the University of North Carolina, Chapel Hill, was an award-winning historian of the South with a number of major books to his credit, including *The Emergence of the New South, 1913–1945* and *The Disruption of the Solid South.*

CONTENTS

PART SIX MODERN AMERICA 895

MAPS

PREFACE

This Tenth Edition of *America: A Narrative History* seeks to improve upon a textbook grounded in a compelling narrative history of the American experience. From the start of our collaboration in 1984, George Tindall and I strove to write an engaging book focused on political and economic developments but animated by colorful characters, informed by balanced analysis and social texture, and guided by the unfolding of key events. Those classic principles, combined with a handy format and low price, have helped make *America: A Narrative History* one of the most popular and well-respected American history textbooks.

This Tenth Edition of *America* features a number of important changes designed to make the text more teachable and classroom-friendly. Chief among them are major structural changes, including the joining of several chapters to reduce the overall number from thirty-four to thirty-two as well as the resequencing of several chapters to make the narrative flow more smoothly for students. Major organizational changes include:

- New Chapter 6, *Strengthening the New Nation*, combines *Shaping a Federal Union* and *The Federalist Era* from previous editions to better integrate the events after the Revolution.
- New Chapter 19, *Political Stalemate and Rural Revolt, 1865–1900* combines *The Emergence of Urban America* and *Gilded Age Politics and Agrarian Revolt* from previous editions to connect the clash of urban and rural cultures.

In terms of content changes, the overarching theme of the new edition is the importance of the culture of everyday life in understanding American history. While an introductory textbook must necessarily focus on major political, constitutional, diplomatic, economic, and social changes, it is also important to understand how ordinary people managed everyday concerns: housing, jobs, food, recreation, religion, and entertainment.

I have looked to broaden the political narrative by incorporating more social and cultural history into the text, primarily using the refreshed and expanded coverage of the culture of everyday life as the main vehicle for doing so. Key new discussions include:

- Chapter 1, *The Collision of Cultures*, features new material about Native American religious beliefs and practices as well as aspects of everyday life.
- Chapter 2, *England's Colonies*, provides additional insights into the status of indentured servants and slavery in the colonies.
- Chapter 3, *Colonial Ways of Life,* includes a new portrait of Antonio, an enslaved African brutalized by his Dutch owner in Maryland in the mid-seventeenth century. There is also new material about colonial houses, taverns, diets, and the competition among American colonists for British luxury goods in the 1760s and 1770s.
- Chapter 4, *From Colonies to States,* has more material on the non importation efforts (boycotts of British goods imported into America) led by ordinary Americans. It also includes new material about the conversion of farmers into soldiers after the shooting at Lexington and Concord.
- Chapter 5, *The American Revolution, 1776–1783*, includes more material about slaves who took advantage of the war to escape or join the British forces, and about the ways in which women, Native Americans, and slaves became engaged in the war effort.
- Chapter 6, *Strengthening the New Nation,* includes more about Shays's Rebellion and other expressions of agrarian discontent across the nation that occurred after the Revolution, and more on how women, Native Americans, and slaves figured into the thinking of the Founding Fathers during the Constitutional Convention in 1787.
- Chapter 7, *The Early Republic, 1800–1815*, has new material on the way in which the War of 1812 affected slavery/blacks.
- Chapter 8, *The Emergence of a Market Economy, 1815–1850*, includes new discussions of the emergence of the cotton culture in the South, the nature of farming, canals, boats, and steamship travel, and the plight of the Irish fleeing the famine at home and heading to America.
- Chapter 9, *Nationalism and Sectionalism, 1815–1828*, more fully fleshes out the role of labor advocates and unions in helping to forge what would become the Jacksonian movement.
- Chapter 10, *The Jacksonian Era, 1828–1840*, describes the effects of the Panic of 1837 and the ensuing depression on the working poor.
- Chapter 11, *The South, Slavery, and King Cotton, 1800–1860*, has substantial new material related to slavery, cotton, and everyday life within African American society. There is also a new discussion of a New Orleans slave uprising led by Charles Deslondes in 1811, the largest slave revolt in American history.

- Chapter 12, *Religion, Romanticism, and Reform, 1800–1860*, includes enriched treatment of the revivalism of the Second Great Awakening, a rewritten discussion of Mormonism, and a new section on Sylvester Graham and his health reform movement (Grahamism).
- Chapter 13, *Western Expansion, 1830-1848*, is enlivened by textured portraits of John Fremont and Sam Houston and a much fuller profile of James K. Polk.
- Chapter 15, *The War of the Union, 1861–1865*, includes new material about the social history of the Civil War, including more material on the everyday life of common soldiers, rioting in opposition to the military draft, and backwoods violence rarely included in discussions of the war, such as the summary of the execution of thirteen Unionists in Madison County, North Carolina.
- Chapter 16, *The Era of Reconstruction, 1865–1877*, has more material about former slaves—from their perspective. It also includes new examples of the ways in which the Freedmen's Bureau helped negotiate labor contracts between white planters and freedmen.
- Chapter 17, *Business and Labor in the Industrial Era, 1860–1900*, discusses the emergence of a new middle class during the Gilded Age, and includes substantially revised material on women's and labor history.
- Chapter 18, *The New South and the New West, 1865–1900*, includes a rewritten section on the emergence of new racial segregation in the South, and also new material about the everyday realities of Western expansion.
- Chapter 21, *The Progressive Era, 1890–1920*, includes new sections on the attitudes of Theodore Roosevelt and Woodrow Wilson concerning race.
- Chapter 22, *America and the Great War, 1914–1920*, now discusses the war's social effects in the United States, with special attention to women, blacks, and Mexican Americans. There is also new material about the grim nature of trench warfare.
- Chapter 23, *A Clash of Cultures, 1920–1929*, includes new material on the consumer culture, women's history, and revised material on the Harlem Renaissance with a new profile of Zora Neale Hurston. There are also fresh treatments of the impact of the radio, automobiles, cinema, and airplanes.
- Chapter 26, *The Second World War, 1933–1945*, includes new material about the social effects of the war at home, including the wartime experience of Mexican Americans.
- Chapter 27, *The Cold War and the Fair Deal, 1945–1952*, includes new coverage of George Kennan's role in inspiring the containment doctrine, women industrial workers, and also the efforts of Latinos to gain equal rights in the aftermath of World War II.

- Chapter 28, *Cold War America, 1950-1959*, features enhanced treatments of the emerging civil rights movement.
- Chapter 29, *A New Frontier and a Great Society, 1960–1968*, includes a new portrait of Fannie Lou Hamer, a black Mississippi activist, in the section on the early civil rights movements.
- Chapter 30, *Rebellion and Reaction, 1960s and 1970s*, includes new material on the women's movement, Mexican Americans, and Native Americans.
- Chapter 32, *Twenty-First-Century America, 1993–Present*, features developments in the twenty-first century—the presidency of Barack Obama , the killing of al Qaeda leader Osama bin Laden, the emergence of the Tea Party and the Occupy Wall Street movements—as well as the stagnant economy in the aftermath of the Great Recession.

In addition, I have incorporated throughout this edition fresh insights from important new scholarly works dealing with many significant topics. Whether you consider yourself a political, social, cultural, or economic historian, you'll find new material to consider and share with your students.

As part of making the new editions even more teachable and classroom friendly, the new Tenth Edition of *America: A Narrative History* also makes history an immersive experience through its innovative pedagogy and digital resources. Norton InQuizitive for History—Norton's groundbreaking, formative, and adaptive new learning program—enables both students and instructors to assess learning progress at the individual and classroom level. The Norton Coursepack provides an array of support materials—free to instructors—who adopt the text for integration into their local learning-management system. The Norton Coursepack includes valuable assessment and skill-building activities like new primary source exercises, guided reading exercises, review quizzes, and interactive map resources. In addition, we've created new Office Hours videos that help students understand the Focus Questions and make history relevant for them (see pages xxv–xxvii for information about student and instructor resources).

MEDIA RESOURCES FOR INSTRUCTORS AND STUDENTS

America's new student resources are designed to make them better readers, guiding them through the narrative while at the same time developing their critical thinking and history skills.

The comprehensive ancillary package features a groundbreaking new formative and adaptive system, as well as innovative interactive resources, including maps and primary sources, to help students master the Focus Questions in each chapter and continue to strengthen the skills they need to do the work of historians. Norton is unique in partnering exclusively with subject-matter experts who teach the course to author these resources. As a result, instructors have all of the course materials they need to successfully manage their U.S. history survey course, whether they are teaching face-to-face, online, or in a hybrid setting.

INSTRUCTOR RESOURCES

LEARNING MANAGEMENT SYSTEM NORTON COURSEPACKS: STRONG ASSESSMENT AND LECTURE TOOLS

- **New! Office Hour Videos:** These segments feature David Shi speaking for 90 seconds on the Focus Questions of each chapter. There are over 100 of these new video segments.
- **New! Primary Source Exercises:** These activities feature several primary sources with multiple-choice and short essay questions to encourage close reading and analysis.
- **Guided Reading Exercises:** These exercises are designed by P. Scott Corbett (Ventura College) to help students learn how to read a textbook and, more important, comprehend what they are reading. The reading exercises instill a three-step Note-Summarize-Assess pedagogy. Exercises are based on actual passages from the textbook, and sample feedback is provided to model responses.
- **Interactive iMaps:** These interactive tools challenge students to better understand the nature of change over time by allowing them to explore the different layers of the maps from the book. Follow-up map worksheets help build geography skills by allowing students to test their knowledge by labeling.
- **Review Quizzes:** Multiple-choice, true/false, and chronological-sequence questions allow students to test their knowledge of the chapter content and identify where they need to focus their attention to better understand difficult concepts.
- **Primary Sources:** Over 400 primary source documents and images are available on the Student Site that accompanies *America: A Narrative History*, Tenth Edition. Instructors and students can use these resources for assignments and further research on each chapter.

- **Norton American History Digital Archive:** The Digital Archive offers roughly 2,000 images and audio and video files spanning American history. The comprehensive collection provides endless opportunities to enhance lecture presentations, build new assignments, and expand your students' comprehension through visual history and artifacts. From government documents, to personal artifacts, this collection enhances students' understanding of history.

INSTRUCTOR'S MANUAL

The Instructor's Manual for *America: A Narrative History*, Tenth Edition, is designed to help instructors prepare lectures and exams. The Instructor's Manual contains detailed chapter outlines, lecture ideas, in-class activities, discussion questions, as well as chapter concept maps.

TEST BANK

The Test Bank contains over 2,000 multiple-choice, true/false, and essay questions. This edition of the Test Bank has been completely revised for content and accuracy. All test questions are now aligned with Bloom's Taxonomy for greater ease of assessment.

LECTURE POWERPOINT SLIDES

These ready-made presentations provide comprehensive outlines of each chapter, as well as discussion prompts to encourage student comprehension and engagement.

STUDENT RESOURCES

NEW! NORTON INQUIZITIVE FOR HISTORY

This groundbreaking formative, adaptive learning tool improves student understanding of the Focus Questions in each chapter. Students receive personalized quiz questions on the topics with which they need the most help. Questions range from vocabulary and concepts to interactive maps and primary sources that challenge students to begin developing the skills necessary to do the work of a historian. Engaging game-like elements motivate students as they learn. As a result, students come to class better prepared to participate in discussions and activities.

NEW! STUDENT SITE

wwnorton.com/college/history/America10

Free and open to all students, Norton Student Site includes additional resources and tools to ensure they come to class prepared and ready to actively participate.

- **Office Hour Videos:** These segments feature David Shi speaking for 90 seconds on the Focus Questions of each chapter. There are over 100 of these new video segments.
- **iMaps:** Interactive maps challenge students to explore change over time by navigating the different layers of the maps from the book. Practice worksheets help students build their geography skills by labeling the locations.
- **Online Reader:** The online reader offers a diverse collection of primary source readings for use in assignments and activities.

PRIMARY SOURCE READERS TO ACCOMPANY *AMERICA: A NARRATIVE HISTORY*

- **New** sixth edition of *For the Record: A Documentary History of America*, by David E. Shi and Holly A. Mayer (Duquesne University), is the perfect companion reader for *America: A Narrative History*. *For the Record* now has 250 primary-source readings from diaries, journals, newspaper articles, speeches, government documents, and novels, including a number of readings that highlight the substantially updated theme of African American history in this new edition of *America*. If you haven't scanned *For the Record* in a while, now would be a good time to take a look.
- **New Norton Mix: American History** enables instructors to build their own custom reader from a database of nearly 300 primary- and secondary-source selections. The custom readings can be packaged as a standalone reader or integrated with chapters from *America* into a custom textbook.

ACKNOWLEDGMENTS

This Tenth Edition of *America: A Narrative History* has been a team effort. Several professors who have become specialists in teaching the introductory survey course helped create the test bank, interactive media, and primary source exercises:

Erik Anderson, San Antonio College
Melissa Weinbrenner, Northeast Texas College
Mark Goldman, Tallahassee Community College

Brian McKnight, University of Virginia at Wise
Laura Farkas, Ivy Tech College–West Lafayette
Jon Lee, San Antonio College

The quality and range of reviews on this project were truly exceptional. The book and its accompanying media components were greatly influenced by the thoughts and ideas of numerous instructors.

Milan Andrejevich, Ivy Tech College–South Bend
Evan Bennett, Florida Atlantic University
Laura Bergstrom, Ivy Tech College–Sellersburg
Keith Berry, Hillsborough Community College
Albert Broussard, Texas A&M, College Station
Blanche Brick, Blinn College
Cory Burger, Ivy Tech College–Terre Haute

Brian Cervantez, Tarrant County College–Northwest Campus
Michael L. Collins, Midwestern State University
Lee Cowan, Tarrant County College
Thomas A. DeBlack, Arkansas Tech University
Scott Derr, Ivy Tech College–Bloomington
S. Matthew DeSpain, Rose State College
Michael Downs, Tarrant County College–Northeast Campus

Shannon Duffy, Southwest Texas State University

Karen Dunn-Haley, University of California, Davis

Stephen D. Engle, Florida Atlantic University

Laura Farkas, Ivy Tech College–West Lafayette

David Haney, Austin Community College

Andrew Hollinger, Tarrant County College–Southeast Campus

Frances Jacobson, Tidewater Community College

Robert MacDonald, Ivy Tech College–Lafayette

Richard McCaslin, University of North Texas–Denton

Suzanne McFadden, Austin Community College

Joel McMahon, Kennesaw State University

Greg Miller, Hillsborough Community College

Catherine Parzynski, Montgomery County Community College

R. Lynn Rainard, Tidewater Community College

Hazel Ramos, Glendale Community College

Nicole Ribianszky, Georgia Gwinnett College

Allen Smith, Ivy Tech College–Indianapolis

Bruce Solheim, Citrus College

Mark Stanley, University of North Texas–Denton

Melissa Weinbrenner, Northeast Texas College

As always, my colleagues at W. W. Norton shared with me their dedicated expertise and their poise amid tight deadlines, especially Jon Durbin, Justin Cahill, Melissa Atkin, Linda Feldman, Travis Carr, Ashley Horna, Laura Wilk, Chris Hillyer, Sarah England, Hope Goodell Miller, Stephanie Romeo, Marne Evans, John Gould, Heather Laskey, and Donna Ranieri.

In addition, Jim Stewart, a patient friend and consummate editor, helped winnow my wordiness.

Finally, I have dedicated this Tenth Edition of *America* to Angela Halfacre Shi, my radiant wife who makes the present as fascinating as the past.

AMERICA

part one

A NOT-SO- "NEW" WORLD

History is filled with ironies. Luck and accidents—the unexpected and unplanned happenings of life—often shape events more than intentions. Long before Christopher Columbus lucked upon the Caribbean Sea and an unexpected continent in his effort to find a westward passage to the Indies (east Asia), the native peoples he mislabeled "Indians" had occupied and transformed the lands of the Western Hemisphere (also called the Americas—North, Central, and South).

Initially, everyone in what came to be called America came from somewhere else. By 1492, when Columbus began his voyage west from Spain across an uncharted ocean, there were millions of Native Americans living in the Western Hemisphere. The "New World" he found was *new* only to the Europeans who began exploring, conquering, and exploiting the region at the end of the fifteenth century.

Over thousands of years, Native American peoples had developed highly sophisticated societies. Some were rooted in agriculture; others focused on trade or the conquest of others. Many Native Americans were healthier, better fed, and lived longer than Europeans, but they and their cultures were almost destroyed by the arrival of Europeans and Africans. As the two different societies—European and Native American—collided, each having its own distinct heritage and worldview, Indian peoples were exploited, infected, enslaved, displaced, and exterminated.

Yet the conventional story of invasion and occupation oversimplifies the complex process by which Indians, Europeans, and Africans interacted in the colonial period. The Native Americans, also called First Peoples, were more than passive victims of European power; they were also trading partners and military allies of the transatlantic newcomers. They became neighbors and advisers, religious converts and loving spouses. As such, they participated actively in the creation of the new society known as America.

The Europeans who risked their lives to settle in the Western Hemisphere were themselves a diverse lot. Young and old, men and women, they came from Spain, Portugal, France, the British Isles, the Netherlands (Holland), Scandinavia, Italy, and the German states (Germany would not become a united nation until the mid–nineteenth century).

A variety of motives inspired Europeans to undertake the often-harrowing transatlantic voyage. Some were fortune seekers lusting for gold, silver, and spices. Others were passionate Christians eager to create kingdoms of God in the New World. Still others were adventurers, convicts, debtors, servants, landless peasants, and political or religious exiles. Many were simply seeking opportunities for a better way of life. A settler in Pennsylvania noted that "poor people of all kinds can here get three times the wages for their labor than they can in England."

Yet such wages never attracted sufficient numbers of workers to keep up with the rapidly expanding colonial economies, so Europeans early in the seventeenth century turned to Africa for their labor needs. In 1619, a Dutch warship brought the first twenty Africans to the English settlement at James-town, near the coast of Virginia, and exchanged that human cargo for food and supplies.

This first of many transactions involving enslaved people in British America would transform American society in ways that no one at the time envisioned. Few Europeans during the colonial era saw the contradiction between the promise of freedom in America for themselves and the bondage of slavery for Africans and Indians.

The intermingling of people, cultures, plants, animals, germs, and diseases from the continents of Africa, Europe, and the Western Hemisphere gave colo-nial American society its distinctive vitality and variety. In turn, the diversity of the environment and the varying climate spawned different economies and patterns of living in the various regions of North America. As the original set-tlements grew into prosperous and populous colonies, the transplanted Euro-peans had to create new communities and political systems to manage growth and control rising tensions.

At the same time, bitter rivalries among the Spanish, French, English, and Dutch triggered costly wars in Europe and around the world. The monarchs of Europe struggled to manage often-unruly colonies, which, they discovered, played crucial roles in their frequent wars.

Many of the colonists had brought with them to America a feisty indepen-dence, which led them to resent government interference in their affairs. A British official in North Carolina reported that the colonists were "without any Law or Order. Impudence is so very high, as to be past bearing." The Amer-icans and their British rulers maintained an uneasy partnership throughout the seventeenth century. But as the royal authorities tightened their control during the mid–eighteenth century, they met resistance from colonists, which exploded into revolution.

1

The Collision of Cultures

De Soto and the Incas This 1596 color engraving shows Spanish conquistador Hernando de Soto's first encounter with King Atahualpa of the Inca Empire. Although artist Theodor de Bry never set foot in North America, his engravings helped shape European perceptions of Native Americans in the sixteenth century.

America was born in melting ice. Tens of thousands of years ago, during a long period known as the Ice Age, vast glaciers some two miles thick inched their way southward from the Arctic Circle at the top of the globe. Their awesome power crushed hills, rerouted rivers, and scraped bare all the land in their path.

Vast glacial ice sheets eventually covered much of North America—Canada, Alaska, the Upper Midwest, New England, Montana, and Washington. Then, as the continent's climate began to warm, the ice started to melt, year after year, century after century. So much of the world's water was bound up in glacial ice that the slow melt ultimately caused sea levels to rise more than 400 feet.

As the ice sheets receded, they left behind in the Midwest a thick blanket of fertile topsoil that had been scoured from Canada and pushed down the continent, creating what would become the world's richest farmland. The shrinking glaciers also opened valley pathways for the first immigrants to begin a process of crossing the continent.

The American past belongs to many different peoples. Debate still rages about when and how humans first arrived in North America. Until recently, archaeologists and anthropologists had assumed that ancient peoples, risk-takers from northeast Asia, clothed in animal hides and furs, began following big game animals across the Bering Strait, a sixty-mile-wide waterway that now connects the Arctic and Pacific Oceans. During the Ice Age, however, the Bering Strait was dry—a vast treeless, windswept landmass (Beringia) that served as a wide, inviting bridge connecting eastern Siberia with Alaska. The oldest place in the Bering region with traces of early human activity is Broken

focus questions

1. Why were there so many diverse societies in the Americas before Europeans arrived?

2. What were the major developments in Europe that enabled the Age of Exploration?

3. How were the Spanish able to conquer and colonize the Americas?

4. How did the Columbian Exchange between the "Old" and "New" Worlds affect both societies?

5. In what ways did the Spanish form of colonization shape North American history?

THE FIRST MIGRATION

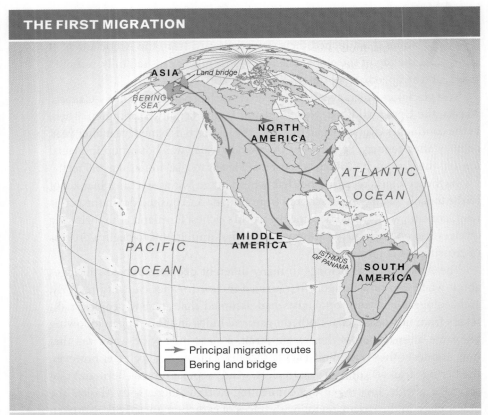

- When did people first cross the Bering Sea? What evidence have archaeologists and anthropologists found from the lives of the first people in America?
- Why did those people travel to North America?

Mammoth, a 14,000-year-old site in central Alaska where the first aboriginal peoples, called Paleo-Indians (Old Indians), arrived in North America. More recently, archaeologists in central Texas unearthed evidence of people dating back almost 16,000 years.

Over hundreds of years, as the climate kept warming and the glaciers continued to melt, small hunting groups, carrying their few possessions with them, crossed into Alaska and then fanned out during the summers southward across the entire Western Hemisphere, from the Arctic Circle to the tip of South America. Some of them may also have traveled by boats hugging the coast. One major land pathway followed the Pacific coast while the other used an open land corridor between two ice sheets east of the Rocky Mountains.

Paleo-Indians were risk-taking pioneers, skilled hunters and gatherers who moved in search of large grazing mammals, rabbits, whales, seals, fish, and wild plants, berries, nuts, roots, and seeds. As they moved southward toward warmer weather, they trekked across the prairies and the plains, encountering massive animals unlike any found there today: mastodons, giant sloths, camels, bison (buffalos), lions, saber-toothed tigers, cheetahs, and giant wolves, beavers, and bears.

Recent archaeological discoveries in Pennsylvania, Virginia, and Chile, however, suggest that prehistoric humans may have arrived much earlier from various parts of Asia—and some may even have crossed the Atlantic Ocean from southwestern Europe. Regardless of when humans first set foot in North America, the continent eventually became a crossroads for various adventurous peoples from around the world: Europeans, Africans, Asians, and others, all bringing with them distinctive backgrounds, cultures, technologies, religions, and motivations that helped form the multicultural society known as America.

EARLY CULTURES IN AMERICA

Archaeologists have labeled the earliest humans in North America the *Clovis* peoples, named after a site in New Mexico where ancient hunters around 9500 B.C.E. (before the Common Era) killed tusked woolly mammoths using distinctive "Clovis" stone spearheads. They also used a wooden device called an *atlatl*, which gave them added leverage to hurl spears farther and more accurately. Over many centuries, as the climate warmed, days grew hotter and many of the largest mammals—mammoths, mastodons, giant bison, and single-hump camels—died and grew extinct.

Skeletal remains of Paleo-Indians reveal that the women were much smaller than the men, who were bold, aggressive, and hypermasculine. More than half of the male skeletons show signs of injuries caused by violence. Four out of ten have fractured skulls. The physical evidence is clear: Paleo-Indian men assaulted and killed each other with regularity.

Over time, the ancient Indians adapted to their diverse environments—coastal forests, grassy plains, southwestern deserts, eastern woodlands. Some continued to hunt large animals; others fished and trapped small game. Some gathered wild plants and herbs and collected acorns and seeds; others farmed. Many did some of each.

Contrary to the romantic myth of early Indian civilizations living in perfect harmony with nature and one another, they in fact often engaged in warfare, exploited the environment by burning large wooded areas to plant fields, and overhunted large game animals. They also mastered the use of fire; improved technology such as spear points, basketry, and pottery; and developed their own nature-centered religions.

By about 5000 B.C.E., Native Americans had adapted to the warmer climate by transforming themselves into farming societies. Agriculture provided reliable, nutritious food, which accelerated population growth and enabled a once nomadic (wandering) people to settle down in villages. Indigenous peoples became expert at growing the plants that would become the primary food crops of the entire hemisphere, chiefly **maize** (corn), beans, and squash, but also chili peppers, avocados, and pumpkins. Many of them also grew cotton. The annual cultivation of such crops enabled Indian societies to grow larger and more complex, with their own distinctive social, economic, and political institutions.

THE MAYAS, INCAS, AND MEXICA

Around 1500 B.C.E., farming towns first appeared in what is now Mexico. Agriculture supported the development of sophisticated communities complete with gigantic temple-topped pyramids, palaces, and bridges in Middle

Mayan society A fresco depicting the social divisions of Mayan society. A Mayan lord, at the center, receives offerings.

America (*Mesoamerica*, what is now Mexico and Central America, where North and South America meet). The Mayas, who dominated Central America for more than 600 years, developed a rich written language and elaborate works of art. They also used sophisticated mathematics and astronomy to create a yearly calendar more accurate than the one the Europeans were using at the time of Columbus.

THE INCAS   Much farther south, as many as 12 million people speaking at least twenty different languages made up the sprawling Inca Empire. By the fifteenth century, the Incas' vast realm stretched some 2,500 miles along the Andes Mountains in the western part of South America. The mountainous Inca Empire featured irrigated farms, enduring stone buildings, and interconnected networks of roads made of stone.

THE MEXICA (AZTECS)   During the twelfth century, the **Mexica** (Me-SHEE-ka)—whom Europeans later called Aztecs ("People from Aztlán," the place they claimed as their original homeland)—began drifting southward

Aztec sacrifices to the gods Renowned for their military prowess, Aztecs preferred to capture and then sacrifice their enemies.

from northwest Mexico. Disciplined, determined, and energetic, they eventually took control of the sweeping valley of central Mexico, where they started building the city of Tenochtitlán in 1325 on an island in Lake Tetzcoco, the site of present-day Mexico City. Tenochtitlán would become one of the largest cities in the world.

Warfare was a sacred ritual for the Mexica, but it was a peculiar sort of fighting. The Mexica fought with wooden swords intended to wound rather than kill, since they wanted captives to sacrifice to the gods and to work as slaves. Gradually, the Mexica conquered many of the neighboring societies, forcing them to pay tribute (taxes) in goods and services and developing a thriving trade in gold, silver, copper, and pearls as well as agricultural products. Towering stone temples, broad paved avenues, thriving marketplaces, and some 70,000 adobe huts dominated the dazzling capital city of Tenochtitlán.

When the Spanish invaded Mexico in 1519, they found a vast **Aztec Empire** connected by a network of roads serving 371 city-states organized into thirty-eight provinces. As their empire had expanded across central and southern Mexico, the Aztecs had developed elaborate urban societies supported by detailed legal systems; efficient new farming techniques, including irrigated fields and engineering marvels; and a complicated political structure. Their arts were flourishing; their architecture was magnificent.

Aztec rulers were invested with godlike qualities, and nobles, priests, and warrior-heroes dominated the social order. The emperor lived in a huge palace; the aristocracy lived in large stone dwellings, practiced polygamy (multiple wives), and were exempt from manual labor.

Like most agricultural peoples, the Mexica were intensely spiritual. Their religious beliefs focused on the interconnection between nature and human life and the sacredness of natural elements—the sun, moon, stars, rain, mountains, rivers, and animals. To please the gods, especially Huitzilopochtli, the Lord of the Sun, and bring good harvests and victory in battle, the Mexica, like most Mesoamericans, regularly offered live human sacrifices—captives, slaves, women, and children—by the thousands.

In elaborate weekly rituals, blood-stained priests used stone knives to cut out the beating hearts of sacrificial victims and ceremonially offered them to the sun god to help his fight against the darkness of the night; without the blood from human hearts, he would be vanquished by the darkness. The heads of the victims were then displayed on a towering skull rack in the central plaza. The constant need for more human sacrifices fed the Mexica's relentless warfare against other indigenous groups. A Mexica song celebrated their warrior code: "Proud of itself is the city of Mexico-Tenochtitlán. Here no one fears to die in war. This is our glory."

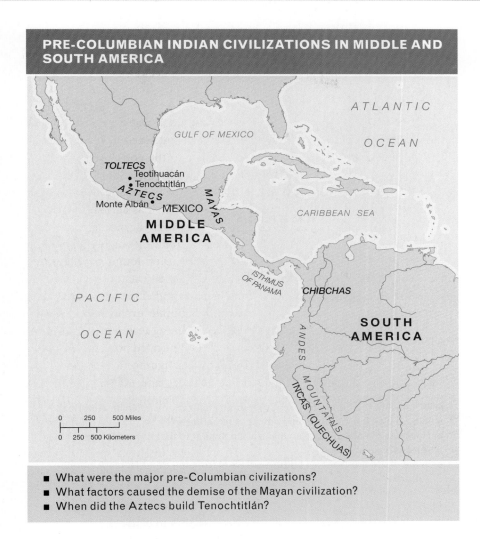

PRE-COLUMBIAN INDIAN CIVILIZATIONS IN MIDDLE AND SOUTH AMERICA

- What were the major pre-Columbian civilizations?
- What factors caused the demise of the Mayan civilization?
- When did the Aztecs build Tenochtitlán?

NORTH AMERICAN CIVILIZATIONS

Many indigenous societies existed north of Mexico, in the present-day United States. They shared several basic spiritual myths and social beliefs, including the sacredness of land and animals (animism); the necessity of communal living; and the importance of collective labor, communal food, and respect for elders. Native Americans did not worship a single god but believed in many "spirits." To the Sioux, the ruling spirit was Wakan Tanka, the Great Spirit, who ruled over all the other spirits. The Navajo believed in the Holy People: Sky, Earth, Moon, Sun, Thunders, Winds, and Changing Woman.

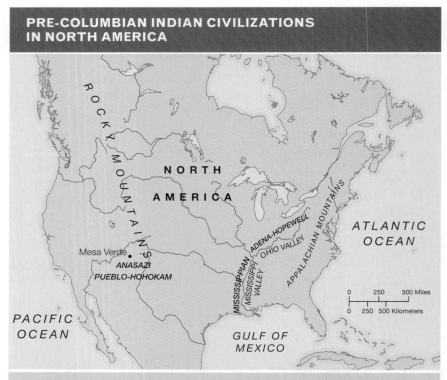

PRE-COLUMBIAN INDIAN CIVILIZATIONS IN NORTH AMERICA

- What were the dominant pre-Columbian civilizations in North America?
- Where was the Adena-Hopewell culture centered?
- How was the Mississippian civilization similar to that of the Mayans or the Aztecs?
- What made the Anasazi culture different from the other North American cultures?

Many societies believed in ghosts, the spirits of dead people who acted as bodyguards in battle. War dances the night before a battle invited the spirits to join the combat.

For all of their similarities, the indigenous peoples of North America developed in different ways at different times and in different places, often as strangers unaware of each other. In North America alone, there were probably 10 million native people organized into 240 different societies speaking many different languages when the Europeans first arrived in the early sixteenth century.

Native Americans owned land in common rather than separately, and they had well-defined social roles. Men were hunters, warriors, and leaders. Women tended children, made clothes, blankets, jewelry, and pottery; dried animal skins, wove baskets, built and packed tipis; and gathered, grew, and cooked food. Indians often lived together in extended family groups in a lodge or tipi (a Sioux word meaning "dwelling"). The tipis were mobile homes made of buffalo skins. Their designs had a spiritual significance. The round floor represented the earth, the walls symbolized the sky, and the supporting poles served as pathways from the human world to the spiritual world.

THE SOUTHWEST   The dry Southwest (what is now Arizona, New Mexico, Nevada, and Utah) hosted corn-growing societies, elements of which exist today and heirs to which (the Hopis, Zunis, and others) still live in the multistory adobe (sunbaked mud) cliff-side villages (called *pueblos* by the Spanish) erected by their ancient ancestors. About 500 C.E. (Common Era), the native Hohokam ("those who have vanished") people migrated from Mexico northward to southern and central Arizona, where they built hundreds of miles

Cliff dwellings Ruins of Anasazi cliff dwellings in Mesa Verde National Park, Colorado.

of irrigation canals to water crops. They also crafted decorative pottery and turquoise jewelry, and constructed temple mounds (earthen pyramids used for sacred ceremonies). Perhaps because of prolonged drought, the Hohokam society disappeared during the fifteenth century.

The most widespread and best known of the Southwest pueblo cultures were the Anasazi (Ancient Ones). They developed extensive settlements in the Four Corners region where the modern-day states of Arizona, New Mexico, Colorado, and Utah meet. Unlike the Aztecs and Incas, Anasazi society was remarkable for *not* having a rigid class structure. The religious leaders and warriors worked much as the rest of the people did. The Anasazi engaged in warfare only as a means of self-defense. (*Hopi* means "Peaceful People.") Environmental factors shaped Anasazi culture and eventually caused its decline. Toward the end of the thirteenth century, a lengthy drought and the aggressiveness of Indian peoples migrating from the north led to the disappearance of Anasazi society.

THE NORTHWEST   Along the narrow coastal strip running up the heavily forested northwest Pacific coast, from northern California to Alaska, where shellfish, salmon, seals, whales, deer, and edible wild plants were abundant, there was little need for farming. In fact, many of the Pacific Northwest peoples, such as the Haida, Kwakiutl, and Nootka, needed to work only two days to provide enough food for a week. Because of plentiful food and thriving trade networks, the Native American population was larger and more concentrated than in other regions.

Such social density enabled the Pacific coast peoples to develop intricate religious rituals and sophisticated woodworking skills. They carved towering totem poles featuring decorative figures of animals and other symbolic characters. For shelter, they built large, earthen-floored, cedar-plank houses up to 100 feet long, where whole groups of families lived together. They also created sturdy, oceangoing canoes carved out of red cedar tree trunks—some large enough to carry fifty people. Socially, the Indian bands along the northwest Pacific coast were divided into slaves, commoners, and chiefs. Warfare usually occurred as a means to acquire slaves.

THE GREAT PLAINS   The many different peoples living on the Great Plains (Plains Indians), a vast, flat land of cold winters and hot summers west of the Mississippi River, and in the Great Basin (present-day Utah and Nevada) included the Arapaho, Blackfeet, Cheyenne, Comanche, Crow, Apache, and Sioux. As nomadic hunter-gatherers, they tracked enormous herds of bison across a sea of grassland, collecting seeds, nuts, roots, and berries as they roamed. At the center of most hunter-gatherer religions is the animistic idea that the hunted animal is a willing sacrifice provided by the gods (spirits). To ensure a successful hunt, these nomadic peoples performed sacred rites of gratitude beforehand. Once a buffalo herd was spotted, the hunters would set fires to drive the stampeding animals over cliffs.

THE MISSISSIPPIANS East of the Great Plains, in the vast wood-lands from the Mississippi River to the Atlantic Ocean, several "mound-building" cultures flourished as predominantly agricultural societies. Between 800 B.C.E. and 400 C.E., the Adena and later the Hopewell peoples (both names derive from the archaeological sites in Ohio) developed communities along rivers in the Ohio Valley. The Adena-Hopewell cultures focused on agri-culture, growing corn, squash, beans, and sunflowers, as well as tobacco for smoking. They left behind enormous earthworks and 200 elaborate **burial mounds** shaped like great snakes, birds, and other animals, several of which were nearly a quarter mile long. Artifacts buried in the mounds have revealed a complex social structure featuring a specialized division of labor, whereby

Great Serpent Mound At over 1,300 feet in length and three feet high, this snake-shaped burial mound in Adams County, Ohio, is the largest of its kind in the world.

different groups performed different tasks for the benefit of the society as a whole. Some were fisher folk; others were farmers, hunters, artists, cooks, and mothers.

Like the Adena, the Hopewell also developed an extensive trading network from the Gulf of Mexico to Canada, exchanging exquisite carvings, metalwork, pearls, seashells, copper ornaments, and jewelry. By the sixth century, however, the Hopewell culture disappeared, giving way to a new phase of Native American development east of the Mississippi River, the Mississippian culture, which flourished from 800 to 1500 C.E.

The Mississippians, centered in the southern Mississippi Valley, were also mound-building and corn-growing peoples led by chieftains. They grew corn, beans, squash, and sunflowers, and they built substantial towns around central plazas and temples. The Mississippian peoples, the most powerful of which were the Natchez, developed a far-flung trading network that extended to the Rocky Mountains. Their ability to grow large amounts of corn each year in the fertile flood plains of rivers spurred rapid population growth around regional centers.

CAHOKIA The largest of these advanced regional centers, called *chiefdoms*, was **Cahokia** (1050–1250 C.E.), in southwest Illinois, just a few miles across the Mississippi River from what is now St. Louis, Missouri. There the Mississippians constructed an intricately planned farming settlement with monumental public buildings, spacious ceremonial plazas, and more than 100 flat-topped earthen pyramids with thatch-roofed temples on top.

Over the years, the Cahokians cut whole forests to create their huge village and to protect it with a two-mile-long stockade built of 15,000 oak and hickory logs twenty-one feet tall. At the height of its influence, prosperous Cahokia hosted 15,000 people on some 3,200 acres, making it the largest city north of Mexico. Outlying towns and farming settlements ranged up to fifty miles in all directions.

Cahokia, however, vanished after 1250 and its people dispersed. What caused its collapse remains a mystery, but environmental changes are the most likely reason. The overcutting of trees may have set in motion ecological changes that doomed the community when a massive earthquake struck around 1200 C.E. The loss of trees led to widespread flooding and the erosion of topsoil that finally forced people to seek better lands. As Cahokia disappeared, however, its former residents carried with them its cultural traditions and spread its advanced ways of life to other areas across the Midwest and into what is now the American South.

EASTERN WOODLANDS PEOPLES

After the collapse of Cahokia, the **Eastern Woodlands peoples** rose to dominance along the Atlantic seaboard from Maine to Florida and along the Gulf coast to Louisiana. They included three regional groups distinguished by their different languages: the Algonquian, the Iroquoian, and the Muskogean. These were the societies the Europeans would first encounter when they arrived in North America.

THE ALGONQUIANS The Algonquian-speaking peoples stretched from the New England seaboard to lands along the Great Lakes and into the Upper Midwest and south to New Jersey, Virginia, and the Carolinas. They constructed no great mounds or temple-topped pyramids. Most Algonquians lived in small, round shelters called *wigwams* or multifamily longhouses. Their villages typically ranged in size from 500 to 2,000 people, but they often moved their villages with the seasons.

The Algonquians along the Atlantic coast were skilled at fishing and gathering shellfish; the inland Algonquians excelled at hunting deer, moose, elk, bears, bobcats, and mountain lions. They often traveled the region's waterways using canoes made of hollowed-out tree trunks (dugouts) or birch bark.

All of the Algonquians foraged for wild food (nuts, berries, and fruits) and practiced agriculture to some extent, regularly burning dense forests to improve soil fertility and provide grazing room for deer. To prepare their vegetable gardens, women broke up the ground with hoes tipped with clam shells or the shoulder blades from deer. In the spring, they planted corn, beans, and squash in mounds. As the cornstalks rose, the tendrils from the

Algonquian in war paint From the notebook of English settler John White, this sketch depicts a Native American chieftain.

climbing bean plants wrapped around them for support. Once the crops ripened, women made a nutritious mixed meal of *succotash*, combining corn, beans, and squash.

THE IROQUOIANS West and south of the Algonquians were the powerful Iroquoian-speaking peoples (including the Seneca, Onondaga, Mohawk, Oneida, and Cayuga nations, as well as the Cherokee and Tuscarora), whose lands spread from upstate New York southward through Pennsylvania and into the upland regions of the Carolinas and Georgia. The Iroquois were farmer/hunters who lived together in extended family groups (clans), sharing bark-covered *longhouses* in towns of 3,000 or more people. The oldest woman in each longhouse was deemed the "clan mother" of the residents. Villages were surrounded by *palisades*, tall fences made of trees intended to fend off attackers. Their most important crops were corn and squash, both of which figure prominently in Iroquois mythology.

Unlike the Algonquian culture, in which men were dominant, women held the key leadership roles in the Iroquoian culture. As an Iroquois elder explained, "In our society, women are the center of all things. Nature, we believe, has given women the ability to create; therefore it is only natural that women be in positions of power to protect this function."

Men and women were not treated as equals. Rather, the two genders operated in two separate social domains. No woman could be a chief; no man could head a clan. Women selected the chiefs, controlled the distribution of property, and planted and harvested the crops. After marriage, the man moved in with the wife's family. In part, the Iroquoian matriarchy reflected the frequent absence of Iroquois men, who as skilled hunters and traders traveled extensively for long periods, requiring women to take charge of domestic life.

War between rival groups of Native Americans, especially the Algonquians and Iroquois, was commonplace, usually as a means of settling feuds or gaining slaves. Success in fighting was a warrior's highest honor. As a Cherokee explained in the eighteenth century, "We cannot live without war. Should we make peace with the Tuscaroras, we must immediately look out for some other nation with whom we can engage in our beloved occupation."

EASTERN WOODLANDS INDIANS The third major Native American group in the Eastern Woodlands included the southern peoples along the Gulf coast who spoke the Muskogean language: the Creeks, Chickasaws, and Choctaws. Like the Iroquois, they were often matrilineal societies, meaning that ancestry was traced only through the mother's line, but they had a more rigid class structure. The Muskogeans lived in towns arranged around a central plaza. In the region along the coast of the Gulf of Mexico, many of their thatch-roofed houses had no walls because of the hot, humid summers.

Over thousands of years, the native North Americans had displayed remarkable resilience, adapting to the uncertainties of frequent warfare, changing climate, and varying environments. They would display similar resilience in the face of the challenges created by the arrival of Europeans.

EUROPEAN VISIONS OF AMERICA

The European exploration of the Western Hemisphere resulted from several key developments during the fifteenth century. In Europe, dramatic intellectual changes and scientific discoveries transformed religion, warfare, family life, and the economy. In addition, the resurgence of old vices—greed, conquest, exploitation, oppression, racism, and slavery—would help fuel European expansion abroad.

A severe population decline caused by warfare, famine, and plagues (the Black Death) left once-great noble estates without enough agricultural workers to maintain them. By the end of the fifteenth century, medieval feudalism's static agrarian social system, in which serfs worked for local nobles in exchange for living on and farming the land, began to disintegrate. People were no longer forced to remain in the same locality and keep the same social status in which they were born. A new "middle class" of profit-hungry bankers, merchants, and investors emerged. They were committed to a more dynamic commercial economy fueled by innovations in banking, currency, accounting, and insurance.

The growing trade-based economy in Europe freed monarchs from their dependence on feudal nobles, enabling them to unify the scattered cities ruled by princes (principalities) into large kingdoms with stronger, more centralized governments. The rise of towns, cities, and a merchant class provided kings and queens with new tax revenues, and the once dominant nobility was gradually displaced by powerful new merchants, bankers, and monarchs.

THE RENAISSANCE   At the same time, the rediscovery of ancient Greek and Roman writings about representative government (republics) spurred an intellectual revolution known as the *Renaissance* (rebirth). Educated people throughout Europe began to challenge prevailing beliefs as well as the absolute authority of rulers and churchmen. They discussed controversial new ideas about politics, religion, and science; engaged in scientific research; and unleashed their artistic creativity.

The Renaissance also brought the practical application of new ideas that sparked the Age of Exploration. New knowledge and new technologies made possible the construction of larger sailing ships capable of oceanic voyages. The development of more-accurate magnetic compasses, maps, and navigational instruments such as *astrolabes* and *quadrants* helped sailors determine their ship's location. The fifteenth and sixteenth centuries also brought the invention of gunpowder, cannons, and firearms—and the printing press.

THE RISE OF GLOBAL TRADE By 1500, trade between western European nations and the Middle East, Africa, and Asia was flourishing. The Portuguese, blessed with expert sailors and fast, three-masted ships called *caravels*, took the lead, roaming along the west coast of Africa collecting grains, gold, ivory, spices, and slaves. Eventually, these mariners continued all the way around Africa in search of the fabled Indies (India and Southeast Asia), and continued on to China and Japan, where they found what they had dreamed about: spices, silk cloth, and other exotic trade goods.

By the end of the fifteenth century, four powerful nations had emerged in western Europe: England, France, Portugal, and Spain. The marriage of King Ferdinand of Aragon and Queen Isabella of Castile in 1469 led to the unification of their two kingdoms into a single new nation, Spain. The Spanish king and queen were Christian expansionists eager to spread the Catholic faith to peoples around the world. On January 1, 1492, after nearly eight centuries of religious warfare between Spanish Christians and Moorish Muslims on the Iberian Peninsula, Ferdinand and Isabella declared victory for Catholicism at Granada, the last Muslim stronghold. The Christian monarchs gave the defeated Muslims, and soon thereafter, the Jews living in Spain and Portugal (called Sephardi), the same desperate choice: convert to Catholicism or leave.

The forced exile of Muslims and Jews was one of the many factors that prompted Europe's involvement in global expansion. Other factors—urbanization, world trade, the rise of centralized nations, plus advances in knowledge, technology, and firepower—combined with natural human curiosity, greed, and religious zeal to spur the exploration and conquest of the Western Hemisphere. Beginning in the late fifteenth century, Europeans set in motion the events that, as one historian has observed, would bind together "four continents, three races, and a great diversity of regional parts."

THE VOYAGES OF COLUMBUS

These were the circumstances that led Christopher Columbus to pursue his own dream of finding a route to the Indies west across the Atlantic. Born in Genoa, Italy, in 1451, the son of a weaver, Columbus took to the sea at an early age, teaching himself geography, navigation, and Latin. By the 1480s, he was eager to spread Christianity across the globe and win glory and riches. The tall, red-haired Columbus eventually persuaded Ferdinand and Isabella to finance his voyage. They agreed to award him a one-tenth share of any riches he gathered; they would keep the rest.

CROSSING THE ATLANTIC On August 3, 1492, Columbus and a crew of ninety men and boys, mostly from Spain but from seven other nations as well, set sail on three tiny ships, the *Santa María*, the *Pinta*, and the *Niña*, respectively about sixty, fifty-five, and fifty feet long. They traveled first to Lisbon, Portugal, and then headed west. For weeks they journeyed across the open sea, hoping with each dawn to sight the shore of Asia, only to be disappointed. By early October, the worried sailors rebelled at the "madness" of sailing blindly and forced Columbus to promise that they would turn back if land were not sighted within three days.

Then, at dawn on October 12, a sailor named Rodrigo, on watch atop the masthead, yelled, "Tierra! Tierra!" ("Land! Land!"). He had spotted a small island in the Bahamas east of Florida that Columbus named San Salvador (Blessed Savior). Columbus mistakenly assumed that they must be near the Indies, so he called the island people "Indios." At every encounter with these peaceful native people, known as Tainos or Arawaks, his first question was whether they had any gold. If they did, the Spaniards seized it; if they did not, the Europeans forced them to search for it.

The Arawaks, unable to understand or repel the strange visitors, welcomed the Europeans by offering gifts of food, water, and parrots. Columbus described them as "well-built, with good bodies, and handsome features. Their hair is short and coarse, almost like the hairs of a horse's tail." He marveled that they "would make fine servants," boasting that "with fifty men we could subjugate them all and make them do whatever we want." Thus began the typical

Christopher Columbus A portrait by Sebastiano del Piombo, ca. 1519.

European bias displayed toward the Indians: they were inferior peoples worthy of being exploited and enslaved.

EXPLORING THE CARIBBEAN   After leaving San Salvador, Columbus continued to search for a passage to the Indies. He went ashore in Cuba, sword in one hand, cross in the other, exclaiming that this is the "most beautiful land human eyes have ever beheld." After a few weeks, he sailed eastward to the island he named Hispaniola (now Haiti and the Dominican Republic). There he found indigenous people who wore gold jewelry and introduced him to smoking tobacco.

At the end of 1492, Columbus, still convinced he had reached an outer island of Japan, sailed back to Spain after leaving about forty men on Hispan-

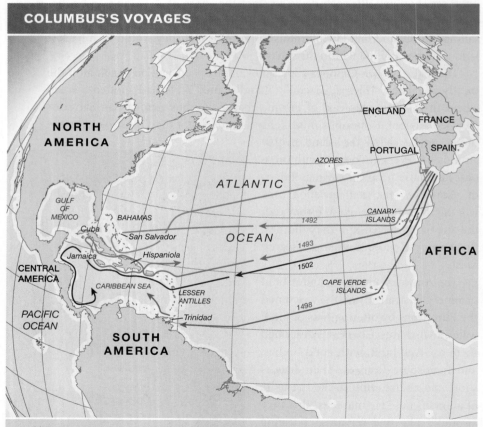

COLUMBUS'S VOYAGES

- How many voyages did Columbus make to the Americas?
- What is the origin of the name for the Caribbean Sea?
- What happened to the colony that Columbus left on Hispaniola in 1493?

iola and capturing a dozen Arawaks to present as gifts to the Spanish king and queen. Upon reaching Spain, he received a hero's welcome as he excitedly told people about the "new world" he had discovered. He promised Ferdinand and Isabella that his discoveries would provide them "as much gold as they need . . . and as many slaves as they ask."

Thanks to the newly invented printing press, news of Columbus's path-breaking voyage spread rapidly across Europe. The Spanish monarchs told Columbus to prepare for a second voyage, instructing him to "treat the Indians very well and lovingly and abstain from doing them any injury." Columbus and his men would repeatedly defy this order.

Spain worked quickly to secure its legal claim to the New World. With the help of the Spanish-born pope, Alexander VI, Spain and Portugal signed the Treaty of Tordesillas (1494). With the stroke of a pen, it divided the non-Christian world, giving most of the Western Hemisphere to Spain, while Africa and what would become Brazil were granted to Portugal. In practice, this meant that while Spain developed its American empire in the sixteenth century, Portugal would provide it with enslaved African laborers.

The Treaty of Tordesillas was a remarkable illustration of the Catholic worldview and the power of the papacy. Pope Alexander's effort to give Spain, his homeland of less than 7 million people, control over virtually the entire Western Hemisphere, reflected his desire to convert all the native peoples to Catholicism and to "train them in good morals." This missionary impulse of the Catholic Church joined with the quest for gold and silver among the explorers to drive the efforts of Columbus and others to lay claim to the as yet unknown boundaries of the New World.

In 1493, Columbus returned across the Atlantic with seventeen ships and 1,400 men. Also on board were Catholic priests eager to convert the native peoples to Christianity. Upon his arrival back in Hispaniola, Columbus discovered that the men he had left behind had lost their senses, raping women, robbing villages, and, as Columbus's son later added, "committing a thousand excesses for which they were mortally hated by the Indians."

The Europeans also carried with them to the Americas a range of infectious diseases—smallpox, measles, typhus—that would prove disastrous for the indigenous peoples, who had no natural immunities to them. The Spaniards found little gold, so they loaded their ships with hundreds of enslaved Indians to be sold in Europe, half of whom died during the voyage to Spain.

NAMING AMERICA Columbus would make two more voyages to the Caribbean. To the end of his life, he insisted that he had discovered the outlying parts of Asia, not a new continent. By one of history's greatest ironies, this led Europeans to name the New World not for Columbus but for another Italian sailor-explorer, astronomer Amerigo Vespucci.

In 1499, with the support of Portugal's monarchy, Vespucci sailed across the Atlantic, landing first at Brazil and then sailing along 3,000 miles of the South American coastline in hope of finding a passage to Asia. In the end, Vespucci reported that South America was so large that it must be a *new* continent rather than Asia. In 1507, a German mapmaker paid tribute to Vespucci's navigational skills by labeling the New World using a variant of his first name: America.

PROFESSIONAL EXPLORERS News of the remarkable voyages of Columbus and Vespucci raced across Europe and stimulated other expeditions to the Western Hemisphere. Over the next two centuries, Spain, Portugal, France, Britain, the Netherlands, and Russia dispatched ships and claimed territory in the Americas by "right of discovery."

The first explorer to sight the North American continent was John Cabot, an Italian sponsored by King Henry VII of England. His landfall in 1497 at what the king called "the new founde lande," in present-day Canada, gave England the basis for a later claim to all of North America. During the early sixteenth century, however, the English grew so preoccupied with internal divisions and war with France that they failed to follow up on Cabot's discoveries.

Lusting for gold and sudden riches, the Spanish still sought a passage from the Atlantic to the Pacific to reach Asia. In 1505, a Spanish ship unloaded pigs and goats in Puerto Rico, intending them to grow and multiply in anticipation of settling a colony there. Puerto Rico would be the first European settlement on what would become, in 1902, a territory of the United States of America.

In 1519, Ferdinand Magellan, a Portuguese sea captain hired by the Spanish, discovered the strait at the southern tip of South America that now bears his name. Magellan then kept sailing north and west across the Pacific Ocean, making landfall on the island of Guam and, eventually, the Philippines, where indigenous people killed him. Surviving crew members made their way back to Spain, arriving in 1522. Their dramatic accounts of the voyage around the world quickened Spanish interest in global exploration.

RELIGIOUS CONFLICT IN EUROPE

At the same time that explorers were crossing the Atlantic, powerful religious conflicts were tearing Europe apart in ways that would greatly influence settlement in the New World.

When Columbus sailed west in 1492, all of Europe acknowledged the thousand-year-old supremacy of the Roman Catholic Church and its pope in Rome. The brutal efforts of the Spanish to convert native peoples to **Roman Catholicism** illustrated the murderous intensity with which European Christians embraced religious life in the sixteenth century. Spiritual concerns inspired, comforted, and united them. People fervently believed in heaven and hell, devils and witches, demons and angels, magic and miracles. And they were willing to kill and die for their beliefs.

MARTIN LUTHER

The enforced unity of Catholic Europe began to crack in 1517, when Martin Luther, a thirty-three-year-old German priest who taught at the University of Wittenburg, changed the course of history by launching what became known as the **Protestant Reformation**.

Luther was a genuine spiritual revolutionary who undermined the authority of the Catholic Church by showing that many of its officials were corrupt. He called the pope "the greatest thief and robber that has appeared or can appear on earth" and denounced the Catholic Church as "the kingdom of sin, death, and hell."

LUTHER'S BELIEFS Luther especially criticized the sale of *indulgences* (whereby priests would forgive sins in exchange for money or goods). God alone, through Christ, he insisted, offered people salvation; people could not earn it through their good deeds or buy it from priests. Salvation, in other words, resulted from belief. "Christ is the only Savior. One does not save oneself." As Luther exclaimed, "By faith alone are you saved!"

Luther tried to democratize Christianity by centering faith on the individual believer rather than in the authority of the church and its priests. He urged believers to read the Bible themselves rather than blindly follow the dictates of Catholic priests and the distant pope. The people, he claimed, represented a "priesthood of all believers," perhaps his most revolutionary idea. To help Germans be their own "priests," Luther produced the first Bible in a German translation, and he reassured Christians that God was not an angry judge but a forgiving father.

THE CATHOLIC REACTION Lutheranism exploded Catholic assumptions and certainties like a bomb. Angry Catholic officials lashed out at Luther's "dangerous doctrines." Luther fought back with equal fury, declaring that he was "born to war." When Pope Leo X expelled Luther (a "wild boar") from the Catholic Church in 1521 and sentenced him to death, civil war erupted throughout the German principalities. Amid the fighting, a powerful German prince protected Luther from the Church's wrath.

What had begun as a fierce religious drama now became a political reformation, too. Luther was no longer simply an outspoken priest; he was a spiritual revolutionary, a folk hero, and a political prophet, encouraging German princes and dukes to separate themselves from the Italian papacy.

The wars of the Reformation were especially brutal conflicts involving tortures and burnings of believers from both sides of the religious divide. A settlement between warring Lutherans and Catholics did not come until 1555, when each prince was allowed by the Treaty of Augsburg to determine the religion of his subjects.

JOHN CALVIN

Soon after Martin Luther began his revolt against the shortcomings of Catholicism, Swiss Protestants also challenged papal authority. They were led by John Calvin (1509–1564), a brilliant French scholar who had fled Catholic France to more tolerant Geneva and brought the Swiss city under the sway of his powerful beliefs.

CALVINISM   In his great theological work, *The Institutes of the Christian Religion* (1536), Calvin set forth a stern doctrine. All Christians, he taught, were damned by Adam's original sin, but Christ's sacrifice on the cross made possible the redemption of those whom God "elected" to be saved and thus had "predestined" to salvation from the beginning of time.

Intoxicated by godliness, Calvin insisted that a true Christian life practiced strict morality and hard work. Moreover, he taught that God valued every form of work, however lowly it might be. Calvin also permitted church members a share in the governance through a body of elders and ministers called the presbytery. Calvin's doctrines formed the basis for the German Reformed Church, the Dutch Reformed Church, the Presbyterians in Scotland, some of the Puritans in England (and, eventually, in America), and the Huguenots in France.

CALVIN'S IMPACT   Through these and other Protestant groups, John Calvin exerted a greater influence upon religious belief and practice in the English colonies than did any other leader of the Reformation. His insistence on the freedom of individual believers, as well as his recognition that monarchs and political officials were sinful like everyone else, helped contribute to the evolving ideas of representative democracy, whereby the people elected their rulers, and of the importance of separating church power from state (governmental) power.

THE PROTESTANT REVOLUTION

Even though the Catholic Church launched an aggressive Counter-Reformation, the Protestant revolt continued to spread rapidly during the sixteenth century. Most of northern Germany, along with Scandinavia, became Lutheran; the areas that did so often called themselves the "Protesting Estates," from which came the label "Protestants."

The Reformation thus formed in part a theological dispute, in part a political movement, and in part a catalyst for social change, civil strife, and imperial warfare. Throughout the sixteenth and seventeenth centuries, Catholics and Protestants persecuted, imprisoned, tortured, and killed each other in large numbers in Europe—and in the Americas.

Every major international conflict involved, to some extent, a religious holy war between Catholic and Protestant nations. Equally important, the Protestant worldview, with its emphasis on the freedom of the individual conscience and personal Bible reading, would play a major role in the colonization of America.

THE REFORMATION IN ENGLAND In England, the Reformation followed a unique course, blending aspects of Protestantism with Catholicism. The Church of England, or the Anglican Church, emerged through a gradual process of integrating Calvinism with English Catholicism. In early modern England, the church and government were united and mutually supportive. The monarchy required people to attend religious services and to pay taxes to support the church. The English rulers also supervised the church officials: two archbishops, twenty-six bishops, and thousands of parish clergy. The royal rulers often instructed religious leaders to preach sermons in support of particular government policies. As one English king explained, "People are governed by the pulpit more than the sword in time of peace."

KING HENRY VIII Purely political reasons initially led to the rejection of papal authority in England. Brilliant and energetic Henry VIII ruled between 1509 and 1547. The second monarch of the Tudor dynasty, he had won from the pope the title Defender of the Faith for refuting Martin Luther's rebellious ideas. Henry's marriage to Catherine of Aragon, his brother's widow, had produced no male heir, however, and for him to marry again required that he convince the pope to annul, or cancel, his marriage. Catherine, however, was the aunt of Charles V, king of Spain and ruler of the Holy Roman Empire, whose support was vital to the church in Rome.

The pope refused to grant an annulment. Henry angrily responded by severing England's nearly 900-year-old connection with the Catholic Church. He then named a new archbishop of Canterbury, who granted the annulment, thus freeing Henry to marry his mistress, the lively Anne Boleyn.

In one of history's greatest ironies, Anne Boleyn gave birth not to the male heir that Henry demanded but to a remarkable daughter named Elizabeth. The disappointed king took vengeance on his wife. He accused her of adultery, ordered her beheaded, and declared the infant Elizabeth a bastard. Yet Elizabeth received a first-rate education and grew up to be quick-witted and nimble, cunning and courageous.

THE REIGN OF ELIZABETH After the bloody reigns of her Protestant half brother, Edward VI, and her Catholic half sister, Mary I, she ascended the throne in 1558, at the age of twenty-five. Over the next forty-five years, Elizabeth proved to be the greatest female ruler in history. Her long reign over the troubled island kingdom was punctuated by frequent political turmoil, religious strife between Protestants and Catholics, economic crises, and foreign wars. Yet Queen Elizabeth came to rule confidently over England's golden age.

Born into a traditionally man's world and given a traditionally man's role, Elizabeth could not be a Catholic, for her birth was illegitimate. During her long reign, from 1558 to 1603, therefore, the Church of England became Protestant, but in its own way. The Anglican organizational structure, centered on bishops and archbishops, remained much the same as the Roman Catholic Church, but the church service changed; the clergy were permitted to marry; and the pope's authority was no longer recognized.

THE SPANISH EMPIRE

During the sixteenth century, Spain was creating the world's most powerful empire at the same time it was trying to repress the Protestant Reformation. At its height, Spain controlled much of Europe, most of the Americas, parts of Africa, and various trading outposts in Asia.

But it was the gold and silver looted from the Americas that fueled Spain's "Golden Empire." By plundering, conquering, and colonizing the Americas and converting and enslaving its inhabitants, the Spanish planted Christianity in the Western Hemisphere and gained the resources to rule the world.

SPAIN IN THE CARIBBEAN The Caribbean Sea served as the gateway through which Spanish power entered the Americas. After establishing colonies on Hispaniola, including Santo Domingo, which became the capital of the West Indies, the Spanish proceeded eastward to Puerto Rico (1508) and westward to Cuba (1511–1514). Their motives, as one soldier explained, were "to serve God and the king, and also to get rich."

Bartolomé de Las Casas (1474–1566), a Catholic priest whose father sailed with Columbus, described the native Cubans as generally peaceful people who lived in large communal wood buildings roofed with palm fronds. "Marriage laws," he explained, "are non-existent: men and women alike choose their mates and leave them as they please, without offense, jealousy, or anger."

Native Cubans wore colorful feathers on their heads, fashioned bead necklaces from fish bones and shells, and "put no value on gold and other precious things." They lived lives of simple sufficiency, relying solely on nature for their basic needs.

Las Casas noted with regret that the Spaniards "committed irreparable crimes against the Indians." Soldiers "thought nothing of knifing Indians by tens and twenties and of cutting off slices of them to test the sharpness of their blades." Cuban men were forced to work full-time in the mountains digging for gold while their wives stayed behind to tend vast fields of *cassava*, a starchy root vegetable known as the "bread of the tropics."

Within a few years after the arrival of Europeans, most of the Indians throughout the Caribbean had died. Disunity everywhere—civil disorder, rebellion, and tribal warfare—left them vulnerable to foreign conquest. Attacks by well-armed soldiers and deadly germs from Europe overwhelmed entire Indian societies.

A CLASH OF CULTURES

The often-violent relationship between the Spanish and Indians involved more than a clash between different peoples. It also involved contrasting forms of technological development. The Indians of Mexico used wooden canoes for transportation, while the Europeans crossed the ocean in heavily armed sailing vessels. The Spanish, with their steel swords, firearms, explosives, and armor, terrified most Indians, whose arrows and tomahawks were seldom a match for guns, cannons, and warhorses. A Spanish priest in Florida observed that gunpowder "frightens the most valiant and courageous Indian and renders him slave to the white man's command."

The Europeans enjoyed other cultural advantages. Before their arrival, for example, the only domesticated four-legged animals in North America were dogs and llamas. The Spanish brought with them strange beasts: horses, pigs, sheep, and cattle. Horses provided greater speed in battle and gave the Spanish a decided psychological advantage. "The most essential thing in new lands is horses," reported one Spanish soldier. "They instill the greatest fear in the enemy and make the Indians respect the leaders of the army." Even more feared among the Indians were the fighting dogs that the Spanish used to guard their camps.

CORTÉS'S CONQUEST   The most dramatic European conquest on the North American mainland occurred in Mexico. On February 18, 1519, thirty-four-year-old Hernán Cortés, driven by dreams of gold and glory, set sail for Mexico from Cuba. His fleet of eleven ships carried nearly 600 soldiers and sailors. Also on board were 200 indigenous Cubans, sixteen horses, and cannons.

After the invaders landed on the coast of the Gulf of Mexico, Cortés convinced the Totomacs, a society conquered by the Mexica, to join his assault against the dominant Mexica, their hated rivals. To prevent any of his heavily armed and helmeted soldiers, called *conquistadores* (conquerors), from retreating or deserting, Cortés had the ships dismantled.

Conquistadores were then widely recognized as the best soldiers in the world, loyal to the monarchy and the Catholic Church. They received no pay; they were pitiless professional warriors willing to risk their lives for a share in the expected plunder. One conquistador explained that he went to America "to serve God and His Majesty, to give light to those who were in darkness, and to grow rich, as men desire to do."

With his small army, cannons, horses, and Indian allies, Cortés brashly set out to conquer the sprawling Mexica (Aztec) Empire, which extended from central Mexico to what is today Guatemala. The nearly 200-mile march of Cortés's army through the mountains to the magnificent Mexica capital of Tenochtitlán (modern Mexico City) took nearly three months. Along the way, Cortés used treachery and terror to intimidate and then recruit the native peoples, most of whom had been conquered earlier by the Mexica.

After entering the city of Cholula, home to the largest pyramid in the Americas (as well as 40,000 people), Cortés learned of a plot to ambush his army. He turned the tables on his hosts by inviting the local chieftains and nobles to the city's ceremonial plaza to talk and exchange gifts. When they arrived, however, the Spanish and their Indian allies, the Tlaxcalans, killed the leaders as well as thousands of other Cholulans.

SPANISH INVADERS   As Cortés and his invading army continued their march across Mexico, they heard fabulous accounts of the carefully planned Mexica city of Tenochtitlán. With some 200,000 inhabitants, it was larger than most European cities. Graced by wide canals and bridges, stunning gardens, and formidable stone pyramids, the lake-encircled city and its stone buildings seemed impregnable.

One of the Spanish conquistadores described their first glimpse of the great capital city: "Gazing on such wonderful sights we did not know what to say or whether what appeared before us was real; for on the one hand there were great cities and in the lake ever so many more, and the lake itself was crowded with canoes, and in the causeway were many bridges at intervals, and in front of us stood the great City of Mexico, and we—we did not number even four hundred soldiers!"

Yet the vastly outnumbered Spanish made the most of their assets—their fighting experience, superior weapons, numerous Indian allies, and an aggressive sense of religious and racial superiority. Through a combination of threats and deceptions, the invaders entered Tenochtitlán peacefully and captured the

Cortés in Mexico Page from the *Lienzo de Tlaxcala*, a historical narrative from the sixteenth century. The scene, in which Cortés is shown seated on a throne, depicts the arrival of the Spanish in Tlaxcala.

emperor, Montezuma II. Cortés explained to the emperor why the invasion was necessary: "We Spaniards have a disease of the heart that only gold can cure." Montezuma submitted in part because he mistook Cortés for a god.

After taking the Mexicas' gold and silver, sending 20 percent of it to the Spanish king (referred to as "the royal fifth"), and dividing the rest among themselves, the Spanish forced the native Mexicans to mine more of the precious metals.

Then, in the spring of 1520, disgruntled Mexica decided that Montezuma was a traitor. They rebelled, stoned him to death, and, armed only with swords and wicker shields, they attacked the conquistadores. Forced to retreat, the Spaniards lost about a third of their men.

The Spaniards' 20,000 Indian allies remained loyal, however, and Cortés's forces gradually regrouped. They surrounded the imperial city ("the most beautiful city in the world," said Cortés) for eighty-five days, cutting off its access to water and food and allowing a highly infectious smallpox epidemic to devastate the inhabitants. Bernal Diaz del Castillo, a Spanish soldier, recalled that "God saw fit to send the Indians small pox." One of the Mexica reported that the smallpox "spread over the people as great destruction. Some it covered on all parts—their faces, their heads, their breasts, and so on. There was great havoc. Very many died of it. . . . They could not move; they could not stir."

For three months, the Mexica bravely defended their capital. Then the siege came to a bloody end. The ravages of smallpox and the support of thousands of anti-Aztec Indians help explain how such a small force of determined Spaniards was able to vanquish a proud nation of nearly 1 million people.

After the Aztecs surrendered, a merciless Cortés ordered the leaders hanged and the priests devoured by dogs. He reported that, in the end, 117,000 Aztecs were killed.

In two years, Cortés and his disciplined army and Indian allies had conquered a fabled empire that had taken centuries to develop. Cortés became the first governor of New Spain and began replacing the Mexica leaders with Spanish bureaucrats and church officials. The Spanish conquest of Mexico established the model for waves of plundering conquistadores to follow. Within twenty years, Spain had established a vast empire in the New World.

In 1531, Francisco Pizarro led a band of conquistadores down the Pacific coast of South America from Panama toward Peru, where they brutally subdued the huge Inca Empire. The Spanish invaders seized Inca palaces, took royal women as mistresses and wives, and looted the empire of its gold and

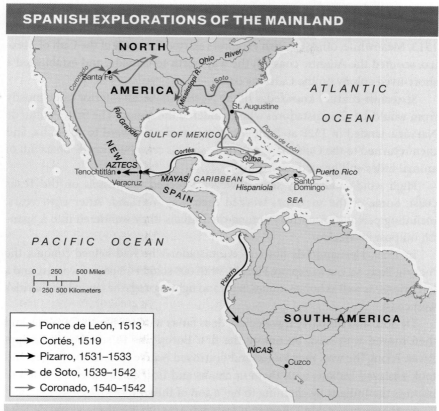

SPANISH EXPLORATIONS OF THE MAINLAND

NORTH AMERICA

ATLANTIC OCEAN

Ohio River

Coronado
Santa Fe

Mississippi R.

de Soto

St. Augustine

Rio Grande

GULF OF MEXICO

Ponce de León

NEW

Cortés

AZTECS

Cuba

Tenochtitlán

Veracruz

Puerto Rico

MAYAS   CARIBBEAN

Santo Domingo

Hispaniola

SPAIN

SEA

PACIFIC OCEAN

0   250   500 Miles

0 250 500 Kilometers

Pizarro

SOUTH AMERICA

INCAS

Cuzco

→ Ponce de León, 1513
→ Cortés, 1519
→ Pizarro, 1531–1533
→ de Soto, 1539–1542
→ Coronado, 1540–1542

- What were the Spanish conquistadores' goals for exploring the Americas?
- How did Cortés conquer the Aztecs?
- Why did the Spanish first explore North America, and why did they establish St. Augustine, the first European settlement in what would become the United States?

silver. From Peru, Spain extended its control southward through Chile by about 1553 and north, to present-day Colombia, by 1538.

SPANISH EXPLORERS Throughout the sixteenth century, the Spanish expanded their control over much of North America, bullying and brutalizing, looting and destroying the native peoples, then forcing them to work the mines and plantations in return for learning the Spanish language and embracing the Catholic religion.

Juan Ponce de León, then governor of Puerto Rico, made the earliest-known exploration of what the Spanish called La Florida—the Land of Flowers—in 1513. Meanwhile, other Spanish explorers skirted the coast of the Gulf of Mexico, scouted the Atlantic coast all the way north to Canada, and established a short-lived colony on the Carolina coast.

Sixteenth-century knowledge of the North American interior came mostly from would-be conquistadores who plundered the region. The first, Pánfilo de Narváez, landed in 1528 at Tampa Bay, marched northward to Alabama, and then returned to the Gulf coast, where he and his crew built crude boats out of animal hides and headed for Mexico.

High winds and heavy seas, however, wrecked the vessels on the Texas coast. Some of the survivors worked their way overland. After *eight* years, including periods of captivity among the Indians, they wandered into a Spanish outpost in Mexico.

In 1539, Hernando de Soto, a conquistador who had helped conquer the Incas in Peru, set out to explore Florida. With 600 soldiers, a pair of women, and a few priests, as well as horses, mules, pigs, and fighting dogs, he landed on Florida's west coast.

De Soto and his party traveled north as far as western North Carolina, and then moved westward, becoming the first Europeans to see the Mississippi River. Along the way, they looted and destroyed Native American villages, and took enslaved Indians with them in chains and iron collars. De Soto tried to impress the Indians by claiming to be "a son of the sun."

In the spring of 1542, having wandered America for three years, de Soto died near Natchez, Mississippi. The next year, the survivors among his party floated down the Mississippi River, and 311 of the original adventurers found their way to Spanish Mexico. They left behind them a trail of infectious diseases which continued to ravage the Indians for years thereafter.

In 1540, Francisco Vázquez de Coronado led an expedition of 1,500 Spaniards and Indian allies, 1,000 horses, 500 cattle, and 5,000 sheep northward into New Mexico and northeast as far as present-day Kansas.

NEW SPAIN The Spanish established provinces in North America not so much as commercial enterprises but as protective buffers to defend their empire in Mexico and South America. They were concerned about French traders infiltrating from Louisiana, English settlers crossing into Florida, and Russian seal hunters wandering down the California coast.

As the sixteenth century unfolded, the Spanish shifted from looting the native peoples to enslaving them. To reward the crusading conquistadores,

Spain transferred to America a medieval socioeconomic system known as the *encomienda*, whereby favored army officers were given huge parcels of land. They were to provide the Indians with protection in exchange for "tribute"— goods and labor, tending farms or mining for gold and silver.

New Spain therefore developed a society of extremes: wealthy *encomenderos* and powerful priests at one end of the spectrum, and Indians held in poverty at the other. The Spaniards used brute force to ensure that Indians accepted their new role as serfs. Nuño de Guzman, a conquistador who became the governor of a Mexican province, loved to watch his massive fighting dog tear apart rebellious Indians. After a Spaniard talked back to him, he had the man nailed to a post by his tongue.

A CATHOLIC EMPIRE The Spanish (and later the French) launched a massive effort to convert the Indians (deeming them "heathens") into Catholic servants. During the sixteenth century, hundreds of priests fanned out across New Spain (and, later, New France).

Many of the Catholic missionaries decided that the Indians of Mexico could be converted only by force. "Though they seem to be a simple people," a Spanish priest declared in 1562, "they are up to all sorts of mischief, and

Missionaries in the "New World" A Spanish mission in New Mexico, established to spread the Catholic faith among the indigenous peoples.

are obstinately attached to the rituals and ceremonies of their forefathers. The whole land is certainly damned, and without compulsion, they will never speak the [religious] truth." By the end of the sixteenth century, there were more than 300 monasteries or missions in New Spain, and Catholicism had become a major instrument of Spanish imperialism.

Some Spanish officials criticized the forced conversion of Indians and the *encomienda* system. In 1514, the Catholic priest Bartolomé de Las Casas resolved to spend the rest of his life aiding the Indians. He gave away his land in Hispaniola, freed his slaves, and began urging the Spanish to change their approach: "Everything done to the Indians thus far," he claimed, "was unjust and tyrannical."

Las Casas spent the next fifty years advocating better treatment for indigenous people. He was officially named "Protector of the Indians." Las Casas insisted that the Indians be converted to Catholicism only through "peaceful and reasonable" means. His courageous efforts aroused furious opposition, however. Most colonizers believed, as a Spanish bishop in Mexico declared in 1585, that the Indians must be "ruled, governed, and guided" to Christianity "by fear more than by love."

A leading Spanish scholar, Juan Ginés de Sepúlveda, directly challenged Las Casas's cry for justice. Indians, he claimed, are as inferior "as children are to adults, as women are to men, as different from Spaniards as cruel people are from mild people."

Over time, however, Las Casas convinced the monarchy and the Catholic Church to issue new rules calling for better treatment of the Indians in New Spain. At Las Casas's urging, Pope Paul III declared that Indians were human beings deserving of respect and Christian salvation. Still, the use of "fire and the sword" continued, and angry colonists on Hispaniola banished Las Casas.

On returning to Spain, Las Casas said, "I left Christ in the Indies not once, but a thousand times beaten, afflicted, insulted and crucified by those Spaniards who destroy and ravage the Indians." In 1564, two years before his death, he bleakly predicted that "God will wreak his fury and anger against Spain some day for the unjust wars waged against the Indians."

THE COLUMBIAN EXCHANGE

The first European contacts with the Western Hemisphere began the **Columbian Exchange** (also called the Great Biological Exchange), a worldwide transfer of plants, animals, and diseases that ultimately worked in favor of the Europeans at the expense of the indigenous peoples.

The plants and animals of the two worlds differed more than the peoples and their ways of life. Europeans had never encountered iguanas, bison, cougars, armadillos, opossums, sloths, tapirs, anacondas, condors, or hummingbirds. Nor had the Native Americans seen horses, cattle, pigs, sheep, goats, chickens, and rats, which soon flooded the Americas.

THE EXCHANGE OF PLANTS AND FOODS The exchange of plant life between the Western Hemisphere and Europe/Africa transformed the diets of both regions. Before Columbus's voyage, three foods were unknown in Europe: maize (corn), potatoes (sweet and white), and many kinds of beans (snap, kidney, lima, and others). The white potato, although commonly called Irish, is actually native to South America. Explorers brought it back to Europe, where it thrived.

Other Western Hemisphere food plants included peanuts, squash, peppers, tomatoes, pumpkins, pineapples, sassafras, papayas, guavas, avocados, cacao (the source of chocolate), and chicle (for chewing gum). Europeans in turn introduced rice, wheat, barley, oats, wine grapes, melons, coffee, olives, bananas, "Kentucky" bluegrass, daisies, and dandelions to the Americas.

In this biological exchange, the food plants were more complementary than competitive. Corn flourished almost anywhere. The new food crops transferred from the Americas helped spur a dramatic increase in the European population that in turn helped provide the restless, adventurous young people who would colonize the New World.

AN EXCHANGE OF DISEASES The most significant aspect of the biological exchange, however, was not food crops but the transmission of **infectious diseases**. During the three centuries after Columbus's first voyage, Europeans and enslaved Africans brought with them deadly diseases that Native Americans had never encountered: smallpox, typhus, diphtheria, bubonic plague, malaria, yellow fever, and cholera.

The results were catastrophic. Far more Indians—tens of millions—died from infections than from combat. Smallpox was an especially ghastly killer. In central Mexico alone, some 8 million people, perhaps a third of the entire Indian population, died of smallpox within a decade of the arrival of the Spanish. A Spanish explorer noted that half the Indians died from smallpox and "blamed us." Often there were not enough survivors to bury the dead; Europeans arrived at villages to discover only rotting corpses strewn everywhere.

Unable to explain or cure the diseases, Native American chieftains and religious leaders often lost their stature—and their lives, as they were

Smallpox Aztec victims of the 1538 smallpox epidemic are covered in shrouds (center) as two others lie dying (at right).

usually the first to meet the Spanish and thus were the first infected. As a consequence of losing their leaders, the indigenous peoples were less capable of resisting the European invaders. Many Europeans, however, interpreted such epidemics as diseases sent by God to punish those who resisted conversion to Christianity.

The Spanish in North America

Throughout the sixteenth century, no European power other than Spain held more than a brief foothold in what would become the United States. By the time the English established Jamestown in Virginia in 1607, the Spanish had already explored the Smoky Mountains and the Great Plains, and established colonies in the Southwest and Florida.

Spain had the advantage not only of having arrived first but also of having stumbled onto those regions that would produce the quickest profits. While France and England were preoccupied with political disputes and religious conflicts, Spain had forged an intense national unity that enabled it to dominate Europe as well as the New World.

St. Augustine

The first Spanish outpost in the continental United States emerged in response to the French. In the 1560s, spirited French Protestants (called Huguenots) established France's first American colonies, one on the coast of what became South Carolina and the other in Florida. They did not last long.

In 1565, the Spanish founded St. Augustine, on the Atlantic coast of Florida. It became the first European town in the present-day United States. It included a fort, church, hospital, fish market, and more than 100 shops and houses—all built decades before the first English settlements in America.

In September 1565, Spanish soldiers from St. Augustine assaulted Fort Caroline, the French Huguenot colony in northeastern Florida, and hanged all the men over age fifteen. The Spanish commander notified his Catholic king that he had killed all the French he "had found [in Fort Caroline] because . . . they were scattering the odious Lutheran doctrine in these Provinces." Later, when survivors from a shipwrecked French fleet washed ashore on Florida beaches after a hurricane, the Spanish commander told them they must abandon Protestantism and swear their allegiance to Catholicism. When they refused, he killed 245 of them.

The Spanish Southwest

The Spanish eventually established other permanent settlements in what are now New Mexico, Texas, and California. From the outset, in sharp contrast to the later English experience, the Spanish settlements were sparsely populated, inadequately supplied, and dreadfully poor. These northernmost regions of New Spain were so far from the capital in Mexico City that they were regularly neglected.

The Spanish colonies in America were extensions of the monarchy's absolute power. Democratic ideals and notions of equal treatment were nonexistent; people were expected to follow orders. There was no freedom of speech or religion or movement, no local elections, no real self-government. The military officers, bureaucrats, wealthy landowners, and priests appointed by the king to govern New Spain regulated every detail of colonial life. Settlers could not travel within the colonies without official permission.

NEW MEXICO The land that would later be called **New Mexico** was the first center of Catholic missionary activity in the American Southwest. In 1595, Juan de Oñate, the rich son of a Spanish mining family in Mexico, whose wife was a descendant of both Cortés and Montezuma II, received a land grant for *El Norte*, the mostly desert territory north of Mexico above the Rio Grande—Texas, New Mexico, Arizona, California, and parts of Colorado. Over the next three years, he recruited an army of colonists willing to move north with him: soldier-settlers and hundreds of Mexican Indians and *mestizos* (the offspring of Spanish and indigenous parents).

In 1598, the caravan of colonists, including women, children, and 7,000 cattle, horses, goats, and sheep, began moving north from the mountains above Mexico City across the harsh desert landscape of parched mesas, plateaus, and canyons enlivened by lush river valleys. "O God! What a lonely land!" one of the footsore travelers wrote to relatives in Mexico City.

Upon crossing the Rio Grande at what became El Paso, Texas, Oñate claimed the entire region for the Spanish monarchy. Indians who resisted were killed. A priest recorded that Oñate "had butchered many Indians, human blood has been shed, and he has committed thefts, sackings, and other atrocities."

After walking more than 800 miles in seven months, along ancient Indian footpaths that the Spanish settlers called the *Camino Real* (royal road), they established the colony of New Mexico, the farthest outpost of New Spain. The Spanish called the local Indians "Pueblos" (a Spanish word meaning village) for the city-like aspect of their terraced, multistoried buildings, sometimes chiseled into the walls of cliffs. They also dug out underground chambers called *kivas*, where they held religious ceremonies and stored sacred objects such as prayer sticks and feathered masks.

The Pueblos (mostly Hopis and Zunis) were farmers who used irrigation to water their crops. They were also skilled at making clay pottery and woven baskets. Some of the Native Americans wore buffalo skins, most wore decorative cotton blankets. "Their corn and vegetables," Oñate reported, "are the best and largest to be found anywhere in the world." Most of their customs resembled those practiced by the Mexicans. "Their government," he noted, "is one of complete freedom, for although they have chieftains, they obey them badly and in few matters."

Unlike the later English colonists in America, the Spanish officials did not view Native Americans as *racially* inferior. Instead, they believed that the Indians were "burdened" by *culturally* inferior ways of life. The Spanish government never intended to establish large colonies of Spanish immigrants in America.

The goal of Spanish colonialism was to force the Native Americans to adopt the Spanish way of life, from Catholicism to modes of dress, speech, work, and conduct. Oñate, New Mexico's first governor, told the Pueblos that if they embraced Catholicism and followed his orders, they would receive "an eternal life of great bliss" instead of "cruel and everlasting torment."

Oñate soon discovered that there was no gold or silver in New Mexico. Nor was there enough corn and beans to feed the Spanish invaders, who had to be resupplied by expensive caravans traveling for months from Mexico City.

Cultural conflict This Peruvian illustration, from a 1612–1615 manuscript by Felipe Guamán Poma de Ayala, shows a Dominican Catholic friar forcing a native woman to weave.

So eventually Oñate established a system that forced the Indians to pay annual tributes (taxes) to the Spanish authorities in the form of a yard of cloth and a bushel of corn each year.

CATHOLIC MISSIONS Once it became evident that New Mexico had little gold, the Spanish focused their attention on religious conversion. Priests established Catholic missions where Indians were forced to work the fields they had once owned and perform personal tasks for the priests and soldiers, cooking, cleaning, and even providing sexual favors. Soldiers and priests used whips to herd the Indians to church services and to punish them for not working hard enough. A French visitor to a mission reported that it "reminded us of a . . . West Indian [slave] colony."

After about ten years, a mission would be secularized, stripped of its religious role. Its lands would be divided among the converted Indians, the mission chapel would become a parish church, and the inhabitants would be given full Spanish citizenship—including the privilege of paying taxes. The soldiers who were sent to protect the missions were housed in *presidios*, or forts; their families and the merchants accompanying them lived in adjacent villages.

Some Indian peoples welcomed the Spanish missionaries as "powerful witches" capable of easing their burdens. Others tried to use the European invaders as allies against rival Indian groups. Still others rebelled. Before the end of New Mexico's first year, in December 1598, the Acoma Pueblos revolted, killing eleven soldiers.

Oñate's response to the rebellion was brutal. Over three days, Spanish soldiers destroyed the entire pueblo, killing 500 Pueblo men and 300 women and children. Survivors were enslaved. Twenty-four Pueblo men had one foot cut off to frighten others and keep them from escaping or resisting. Children were taken from their parents into a Catholic mission, where, Oñate remarked, "they may attain the knowledge of God and the salvation of their souls."

THE MESTIZO FACTOR Spanish women were prohibited from traveling to the New World unless they were married and accompanied by a husband. This policy had unexpected consequences. There were so few Spanish women in North America that soldiers and settlers often married Native Americans or otherwise fathered mestizos.

By the eighteenth century, mestizos were a majority in Mexico and New Mexico. Such widespread intermarriage and interbreeding led the Spanish to adopt a more inclusive social outlook toward the Indians than the English later did in their colonies along the Atlantic coast. Once most colonial officials were mestizo themselves, they were less likely to belittle the Indians. At the same time, many Native Americans falsely claimed to be mestizo as a means of improving their status and avoiding having to pay annual tribute.

THE PUEBLO REVOLT The Spanish presence in New Mexico expanded slowly. In 1608, the government decided to turn New Mexico into a royal province and moved its capital to Santa Fe ("Holy Faith" in Spanish), the first permanent seat of government in the present-day United States. By 1630, there were fifty Catholic churches and monasteries in New Mexico as well as some 3,000 Spaniards. Roman Catholic missionaries in New Mexico claimed that 86,000 Pueblos had been converted to Christianity during the seventeenth century.

In fact, however, resentment among the Indians had increased as the Spanish stripped them of their ancestral ways of life. In 1680, a charismatic Indian spiritual leader named Popé (meaning "Ripe Plantings") organized a massive rebellion. The Spanish claimed that he had cast a magical spell over his people, making "them crazy."

The Indians, painted for war, burned Catholic churches, tortured, mutilated, and executed priests; destroyed all relics of Christianity; and forced the 2,400 survivors to flee the region in humiliation, eventually making their way to El Paso. The entire province of New Mexico was again in Indian hands. The Spanish governor reported that the Pueblos "are very happy without religion or Spaniards."

The Pueblo Revolt of 1680 was the greatest defeat that Indians ever inflicted on European efforts to conquer the New World. It took twelve years and four military assaults for the Spanish to reestablish control over New Mexico.

HORSES AND THE GREAT PLAINS

Another major consequence of the Pueblo Revolt was the opportunity it gave Indian rebels to gain possession of thousands of Spanish horses (Spanish authorities had made it illegal for Indians to ride or own horses). Stealing horses became one of the most honored ways for warriors to prove their courage.

HORSES AND INDIAN CULTURE The Pueblos established a thriving horse trade with the Navajos, Apaches, and others. By 1690, horses were in Texas. They soon spread across the Great Plains, the vast rolling grasslands extending from the Missouri Valley in the east to the base of the Rocky Mountains in the west.

Prior to the arrival of European horses, Indians hunted on foot and used dogs as their beasts of burden. Dogs are carnivores, however, and it was always difficult to find enough meat to feed them.

The introduction of the horse changed everything. Horses provided the Plains Indians with a new source of mobility and power. The vast grasslands of the Great Plains were the perfect environment for horses, since the prairies offered plenty of forage for grazing animals. Horses could also haul up to seven times as much weight as dogs, and their speed and endurance made the indigenous people much more effective hunters and warriors. On the Great Plains, an Indian family's status reflected the number of horses it owned.

By the late seventeenth century, Native American horsemen were fighting the Spaniards on more equal terms. This helps explain why the Indians of the Southwest and Texas, unlike the Indians in Mexico, were able to sustain their

Plains Indians The horse-stealing raid depicted in this hide painting demonstrates the essential role horses played in Plains life.

cultures for the next 300 years: on horseback, they were among the most fearsome fighters in the world.

BISON HUNTING Horses transformed the economy and ecology of the Great Plains. The Arapaho, Cheyenne, Comanche, Kiowa, and Sioux reinvented themselves as horse-centered cultures. They left their traditional woodland villages on the fringes of the plains and became nomadic bison (buffalo) hunters. A male bison could weigh over a ton and stand five feet tall at the shoulder.

Indians used virtually every part of the bison they killed: meat for food; hides for clothing, shoes, bedding, and shelter; muscles and tendons for thread and bowstrings; intestines for containers; bones for tools; horns for eating utensils; hair for headdresses; and dung for fuel. They used tongues for hair brushes and tails for fly swatters. One scholar has referred to the bison as the "tribal department store."

The night after a successful hunt, the Indians would stage a festival feast, with singing and dancing throughout the night. To preserve meat for later, it would be cut into long strips and hung over wooden racks to dry in the sun or over a fire. The dried meat was called jerky. Tougher cuts of buffalo meat would be pounded with a mallet and mixed with fat and berries to make *pemmican.*

Horses eased some of the physical burdens on women, but also imposed new demands. Women and girls tended to the horses, butchered and dried the bison meat, and tanned the hides. As the value of the bison hides grew, Indian hunters began practicing polygamy, primarily for economic reasons: more wives could process more bison carcasses. The rising value of wives eventually led Plains Indians to raid other tribes in search of captive brides.

The introduction of horses into the Great Plains was a mixed blessing. The horse brought prosperity and mobility to the Plains Indians but also triggered more conflict among them. Over time, the Indians on horseback eventually killed more bison than the herds could replace. Further, horses competed with the bison for food, often depleting the prairie grass. And, as Indians on horses traveled greater distances and encountered more people, infectious diseases spread more widely. Still, by 1800, a white trader in Texas would observe that "this is a delightful country, and were it not for perpetual wars, the natives might be the happiest people on earth."

HISPANIC AMERICA

Spanish culture etched a lasting imprint upon American ways of life. Spain's colonial presence in the Americas lasted more than three centuries, much longer than either England's or France's.

New Spain was centered in Mexico, but its borders extended from Florida to Alaska. Hispanic place-names—San Francisco, Los Angeles, Tucson, Santa Fe, San Antonio, and St. Augustine—survive to this day, as do Hispanic influences in art, architecture, literature, music, law, and cuisine.

The Spanish encounters with Indians and their diverse cultures produced a two-way exchange by which the contrasting societies blended, coexisted, and interacted. Even when locked in mortal conflict and driven by hostility and mutual suspicion, the two cultures necessarily affected each other. In other words, New Spain, while savaged by violence, coercion, and intolerance, eventually produced a mutual accommodation with Native Americans that enabled two living traditions to persist side by side. The Spanish introduced cattle, horses, sheep, and goats to Texas, New Mexico, and California, as well as such words as *rodeo, bronco,* and *ranch* (*rancho*), and the names of four states: California, Colorado, Florida, and Nevada.

CHALLENGES TO THE SPANISH EMPIRE

Catholic Spain's successful conquests in the Western Hemisphere spurred Portugal, France, England, and the Netherlands (Holland) to begin their own exploration and exploitation of the New World.

The French were the first to pose a serious threat. Spanish treasure ships sailing home from Mexico, Peru, and the Caribbean offered tempting targets for French pirates. In 1524, the French king sent Italian Giovanni da Verrazano westward across the Atlantic. Upon sighting land (probably at Cape Fear, North Carolina), Verrazano ranged along the coast as far north as Maine. On a second voyage, in 1528, he was killed by Carib Indians.

NEW FRANCE Unlike the Verrazano voyages, those of Jacques Cartier, beginning in the next decade, led to the first French effort at colonization in North America. During three voyages, Cartier explored the Gulf of St. Lawrence and ventured up the St. Lawrence River, now the boundary between Canada and New York. Twice he got as far as present-day Montreal, and twice he wintered at the site of Quebec, near which a short-lived French colony appeared in 1541–1542.

France after midcentury, however, plunged into religious civil wars, and the colonization of Canada had to await the coming of Samuel de Champlain, "the Father of New France," after 1600. Champlain would lead twenty-seven expeditions from France to Canada during a thirty-seven-year period.

THE DUTCH REVOLT From the mid-1500s, greater threats to Spanish power in the New World arose from the Dutch and the English. In 1566, the Netherlands included seventeen provinces. The fragmented nation had passed by inheritance to the Spanish king in 1555, but the Dutch spurned Catholicism and had become largely Protestant (mostly Calvinists making up what was called the Dutch Reformed Church). During the second half of the sixteenth century, the Dutch began a series of sporadic rebellions against Spanish Catholic rule.

A long, bloody struggle for political independence and religious freedom ensued in which Protestant England aided the Dutch. The Dutch revolt, as much a civil war as a war for national independence, was not a single cohesive event but rather a series of different uprisings in different provinces at different times. Each province had its own institutions, laws, and rights. Although seven provinces joined together to form the Dutch Republic, the Spanish did not officially recognize the independence of the entire Netherlands until 1648.

ENGLISH, FRENCH, AND DUTCH EXPLORATIONS

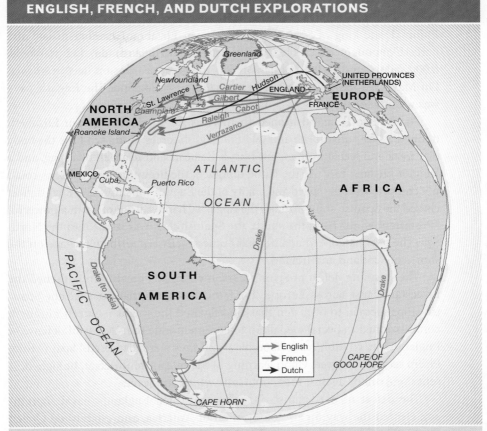

- Who were the first European explorers to rival Spanish dominance in the New World, and why did they cross the Atlantic?
- Why was the defeat of the Spanish Armada important to the history of English exploration?
- What was the significance of the voyages of Gilbert and Raleigh?

THE DEFEAT OF THE ARMADA Almost from the beginning of the Protestant revolt in the Netherlands, the Dutch captured Spanish treasure ships in the Atlantic and carried on illegal trade with Spain's colonies. While England's strong, skillful Queen Elizabeth steered a tortuous course to avoid open war with Spain, she encouraged both Dutch and English privateers to attack Spanish ships and their colonies in America.

The English raids on Spanish ships continued for some twenty years before open war erupted between the two nations. Determined to conquer England, Philip II, the king of Spain who was Queen Elizabeth's brother-in-law and fiercest opponent, assembled the massive **Spanish Armada**: 132 warships, 8,000 sailors, and 18,000 soldiers. It was the greatest invasion fleet in history. On May 28, 1588, the Armada began sailing for England. The English navy was waiting for them.

As the two fleets positioned themselves for the battle, Queen Elizabeth donned a silver breastplate and told the English forces, "I know I have the body of a weak and feeble woman, but I have the heart and stomach of a king, and a King of England too." As the battle unfolded, the heavy Spanish galleons could not compete with the speed and agility of the English warships. The English fleet chased the Spanish ships through the English Channel. Caught up in a powerful "Protestant wind" from the south, the Spanish fleet was swept into the North Sea. The decimated Armada limped home, finally scattering wreckage on the shores of Scotland and Ireland.

The stunning defeat of Spain's fearsome Armada greatly strengthened the Protestant cause across Europe. The ferocious storm that smashed the Spanish ships seemed to be a sign that God favored the English. Queen Elizabeth commissioned a special medallion to commemorate the successful defense of England. The citation read, "God blew and they were dispersed." Spain's King Philip seemed to agree. Upon learning of the catastrophic defeat, he sighed, "I sent the Armada against men, not God's winds and waves."

The defeat of the Spanish Armada confirmed England's naval supremacy, cleared the way for its colonization of America, and established Queen Elizabeth's stature as a great ruler. Although she had many suitors eager to marry her, she refused to divide her power. She would have "but one mistress [England] and no master." Eager to live and die a virgin, she married herself to the fate of England. By the end of the sixteenth century, Elizabethan England had begun an epic transformation from a poor, humiliated, and isolated nation into a mighty global empire.

ENGLISH EXPLORATION OF AMERICA

English efforts to colonize America began a few years before the great battle with the Spanish Armada. They were driven by a desire to weaken Spain's control over the Americas. In 1578, Queen Elizabeth had given Sir Humphrey Gilbert permission to establish a colony in the "remote heathen and barbarous lands" of America.

Gilbert's group set out in 1583, intending to settle near Narragansett Bay (in present-day Rhode Island). They instead landed in fogbound Newfoundland (Canada). With winter approaching and his largest vessels lost, Gilbert and the colonists returned home. While in transit, however, his ship vanished, and he was never seen again.

The next year, Queen Elizabeth asked Sir Walter Raleigh, Gilbert's much younger half-brother, to organize a colonizing mission. Raleigh's expedition discovered the Outer Banks of North Carolina and landed at Roanoke Island. One of the colonists reported that "the soile is the most plentifull, sweete, fruitfull and wholesome of all the worlde." In fact, however, the sandy soil of the Outer Banks was not good for farming. Raleigh named the area Virginia, in honor of childless Queen Elizabeth, the presumably "Virgin Queen," as she once described herself.

After several false starts, Raleigh in 1587 sponsored another expedition of about 100 colonists, including 26 women and children, led by Governor John White. White spent a month on Roanoke Island and then returned to England for supplies, leaving behind his daughter Elinor and his granddaughter Virginia Dare, the first English child born in the New World.

The English in Virginia The arrival of English explorers on the Outer Banks, with Roanoke Island at left.

White's journey back to Virginia was delayed because of the naval war with Spain. When he finally returned, in 1590, the Roanoke outpost had been abandoned and pillaged, much of it having been burned by a lightning-ignited fire. The rude cabins had been dismantled and removed, suggesting that the colonists had left intentionally. On a post at the entrance to the village, someone had carved the word "CROATOAN," leading White to conclude that the settlers had set out for the island of that name some 50 miles south, where friendly Indians lived.

The "lost colonists" were never found. They may have been killed by Indians or Spaniards. The most recent evidence indicates that the "Lost Colony" suffered from a horrible drought that prevented the colonists from growing enough food to survive. While some may have gone south, the main body of colonists appears to have gone north, to the southern shores of Chesapeake Bay, as they had talked of doing, and lived there for some years until they were killed by local Indians.

There were no English colonists in North America when Queen Elizabeth died in 1603. The Spanish controlled the only colonial outposts on the continent. But that was about to change. Inspired by the success of the Spanish in exploiting the New World, and emboldened by their defeat of the Spanish Armada in 1588, the English—as well as the French and the Dutch—would soon develop American colonial empires of their own.

NEW SPAIN IN DECLINE

During the one and a half centuries after 1492, the Spanish developed the most extensive, rich, and envied empire the world had ever known. It spanned southern Europe and the Netherlands, much of the Western Hemisphere, and parts of Asia.

The monarchy financed its imperial ambitions with riches looted from the Americas. Between 1545 and 1660, the Spanish forced Native Americans and Africans to mine 7 million pounds of silver in the New World, twice as much silver as existed in all of Europe in 1492. The massive amounts of silver and gold from the New World led Spanish kings to mobilize huge armies and the naval armada in an effort to conquer all of Protestant Europe.

Yet the Spanish rulers overreached themselves. The widespread religious wars of the sixteenth and seventeenth centuries killed millions, created intense anti-Spanish feelings among the English and the Dutch, and eventually helped bankrupt the Spanish government. At the same time, the Spanish Empire grew so vast that its sprawling size and complexity eventually led to its disintegration.

During the sixteenth century, New Spain gradually developed into a settled society with the same rigid class structure of the home country. From the outset, the Spanish in the Americas behaved more like occupying rulers than permanent settlers, carefully regulating every detail of colonial administration and life.

New Spain was an extractive empire, less interested in creating self-sustaining colonial communities than in taking gold, silver, and copper while enslaving the indigenous peoples and converting them to Christianity. Spain never encouraged vast numbers of settlers to populate New Spain, and, with few exceptions, those who did travel to the New World rarely wanted to make a living off the land; they instead wanted to live off the labor of the native population.

For three centuries after Columbus arrived in the New World, the Spanish explorers, conquistadores, and priests imposed Catholicism on the native peoples as well as a cruel system of economic exploitation and dependence. That system created terrible disparities in wealth, education, and opportunity that would trigger repeated revolts and political instability. As Bartolomé de Las Casas concluded, "The Spaniards have shown not the slightest consideration for these people, treating them (and I speak from first-hand experience, having been there from the outset) . . . as piles of dung in the middle of the road. They have had as little concern for their souls as for their bodies."

CHAPTER REVIEW

SUMMARY

- **Native American Societies**   Hunter-gatherers came across the Bering Strait by foot and settled the length and breadth of the Americas, forming groups with diverse cultures, languages, and lifestyles. Global warming enabled an agricultural revolution, particularly of *maize*, that allowed former hunter-gather peoples to settle and build empires, such as that of the *Mexica*, whose *Aztec Empire* included subjugated peoples and a vast system of trade and tribute. Some North American peoples developed an elaborate continental trading network and impressive cities like *Cahokia*; their *burial mounds* reveal a complex and stratified social organization. The *Eastern Woodlands peoples* that the Europeans would first encounter included both patriarchal and matriarchal societies as well as extensive language-based alliances. The Algonquian, Iroquoian, and Muskogean were among the major Indian nations. Warfare was an important cultural component, leading to shifting rivalries and alliances among tribes and with European settlers.

- **Age of Exploration**   By the 1490s, Europeans were experiencing a renewed curiosity about the world. Warfare, plagues, and famine undermined the old agricultural feudal system in Europe, and in its place arose a middle class that monarchs could tax. Powerful new nations replaced the land estates and cities ruled by princes. Scientific and technological advances led to the creation of better maps and navigation techniques, as well as new weapons and ships. Navies became the critical component of global trade and world power. When the Spanish began to colonize the New World, the conversion of Indians to Roman Catholicism was important, but the search for gold and silver was primary. The rivalries of the *Protestant Reformation* in Europe shaped the course of conquest in the Americas.

- **Conquering and Colonizing the Americas**   Spanish *conquistadores* such as Hernán Cortés were able to exploit their advantages in military technology, including steel, gunpowder, and domesticated animals such as the horse, in order to conquer the powerful Aztec and Inca Empires. European diseases, first introduced by Columbus, did even more to ensure Spanish victories. The Spanish *encomienda* system demanded goods and labor from their new subjects. As the Indian population declined, the Spanish began to import enslaved Africans.

- **Columbian Exchange**   Contact between the Old World and the New resulted in the *Columbian Exchange*, sometimes called the Great Biological Exchange. Crops such as *maize*, beans, and potatoes became staples in the Old World. Native peoples incorporated into their culture such Eurasian animals as the horse and pig. But the invaders also carried *infectious diseases* that set off pandemics of smallpox, plague, and other illnesses to which Indians had no immunity. The Americas were depopulated and cultures destroyed.

- **Spanish Legacy**   Spain left a lasting legacy in the borderlands from California to Florida. Catholic missionaries contributed to the destruction of the old ways of life by exterminating "heathen" beliefs in the Southwest, a practice that led to open rebellion in *New Mexico* in 1598 and 1680. Spain's rival European nation-states began competing for gold and glory in the New World. England's defeat of the *Spanish Armada* cleared the path for English dominance in North America.

CHRONOLOGY

by 12,000 B.C.E.	Humans have migrated to the Americas
5000 B.C.E.	Agricultural revolution begins in Mexico
1050–1250 C.E.	The city of Cahokia flourishes in North America
1325	Mexica (Aztec) Empire founded in Central Mexico
1492	Columbus makes his first voyage of discovery in the Americas
1503	Spaniards bring first African slaves to the Americas
1517	Martin Luther launches the Protestant Reformation
1519	Cortés begins the Spanish conquest of Mexico
1531	Pizarro subdues the Inca Empire in South America for Spain
1565	Spaniards found St. Augustine, the first permanent European outpost in the present-day United States
1584–1587	Raleigh's Roanoke Island venture
1588	The English navy defeats the Spanish Armada
1680	Pueblo Revolt

KEY TERMS

maize p. 8

Mexica p. 9

Aztec Empire p. 10

burial mounds p. 15

Cahokia p. 16

Eastern Woodlands peoples p. 17

Roman Catholicism p. 25

Protestant Reformation p. 25

conquistadores p. 30

encomienda p. 35

Columbian Exchange p. 36

infectious diseases p. 37

New Mexico p. 40

Spanish Armada p. 48

 INQUIZITIVE

Go to InQuizitive to see what you've learned—and learn what you've missed—with personalized feedback along the way.

2 England's Colonies

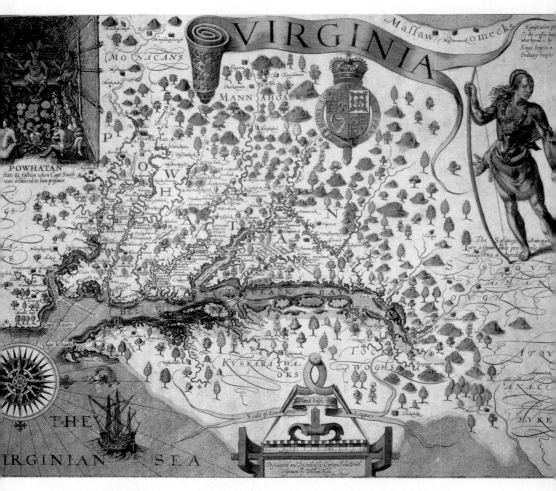

"Ould Virginia" As one of the earliest explorers and settlers of the Jamestown colony, John Smith put his intimate knowledge of the region to use by creating this seventeenth-century map of Virginia. In the upper right hand corner is a warrior of the Susquehannock, whom Smith called a "G[i]ant-like people."

O ver the centuries, the island nation of England had developed political practices and governing principles quite different from those on the continent of Europe. England's parliamentary monarchy was unique among European governments. It began with the Magna Carta (Great Charter) of 1215, a statement of fundamental rights and liberties that nobles forced the king to approve. The Magna Carta established the basic principle that everyone was equal before the law, and no person—not even a king or queen—was above the law.

Much more than the absolute monarchs of France and Spain, English rulers shared power with the nobility and a lesser aristocracy, known as the *gentry*, whose representatives formed the legislature known as Parliament, made up of the House of Lords and the House of Commons. The most important power allocated to Parliament was the authority to impose taxes. By controlling government tax revenue, Parliament exercised great leverage over the monarchy.

RELIGIOUS CONFLICT AND WAR

When Queen Elizabeth, who never married, died in 1603 without a child of her own to inherit the throne, James VI of Scotland, her distant cousin, became King James I of England. While Elizabeth had ruled through constitutional authority, James ominously claimed to govern by "divine right," which meant he answered only to God.

James I confronted a divided Church of England, with the reform-minded **Puritans** in one camp and the Anglican establishment, headed by the

focus questions

1. What motivated England to establish American colonies?

2. What were the characteristics of the English colonies in the Chesapeake region, the Carolinas, the middle colonies—Pennsylvania, New York, New Jersey, and Delaware—and New England prior to 1700?

3. In what ways did the English colonists and Native Americans adapt to each other's presence?

4. What role did indentured servants and the development of slavery play in colonial America?

5. How did the English colonies become the most populous and powerful region in North America by 1700?

archbishop and bishops, in the other. In seventeenth-century England, those who criticized or abandoned the Anglican Church were called *Dissenters*. The Puritans were dissenters who believed that the Church of England needed further "purifying." They demanded that all "papist" (Roman Catholic) rituals be eliminated. No use of holy water. No organ music. No elegant robes (then called vestments). No jeweled gold crosses. No worship of saints. No kneeling for communion. No tyrannical bishops and archbishops.

The Puritans wanted to simplify religion to its basics: people worshipping God in plain, self-governing congregations without all the formal trappings of Catholic and Anglican ceremonies and wealth. They had hoped the new king would support their efforts, but James I instead sought to banish them from England.

Some Puritans eventually decided that the Church of England was so corrupt and corrupting that it should simply be abandoned, so they created their own congregations separate from the Anglican churches, thus earning the name *Separatists*.

Such rebelliousness infuriated the leaders of the Church of England, who required people by law to attend Anglican church services. During the late sixteenth century, the Separatists (also called *Nonconformists*) were "hunted and persecuted on every side." English authorities imprisoned Separatist leaders, three of whom were hanged. In 1604, James I vowed to make the Separatists "conform or I will hurry them out of the land or do worse." Many Separatists left England to escape persecution, and some, who would eventually be known as Pilgrims, decided to sail for America.

James's son, Charles I, succeeded his father in 1625 and proved to be an even more stubborn defender of absolute royal power: he raised taxes without consulting the House of Commons and House of Lords, harassed the Puritans, and took the shocking step of disbanding Parliament from 1629 to 1640.

The monarchy went too far, however, when it forced Anglican forms of worship on Presbyterian Scots. In 1638, Scotland rose in revolt, and in 1640, King Charles, desperate for money to fund his army and save his skin, revived Parliament, ordering its members to raise taxes for the defense of his kingdom against the rampaging Scots. Parliament, led by militant Puritans, refused.

In 1642, when the king tried to arrest five members of Parliament, a bloody civil war erupted in England between Royalists and Parliamentarians, leading many New England Puritans to return home to fight against the Royalist army. In 1646, parliamentary forces led by Oliver Cromwell captured King Charles and, in an unprecedented public trial, convicted him of high treason and contempt of Parliament, labeling him a "tyrant, traitor, murderer, and public enemy." He was beheaded in 1649. As it turned out, however, the Puritans had killed a king, but they had not slain the monarchy.

Oliver Cromwell, the Puritan leader of the parliamentary coup, ruled over England like a military dictator, calling himself Lord Protector. He outlawed Roman Catholics and Anglicans, but his dictatorship fed growing resentment. Many Royalists, called *Cavaliers*, escaped by sailing to Virginia. After Cromwell's death in 1658, the army allowed new elections for Parliament and in 1660 supported the Restoration of the monarchy under young Charles II, eldest son of the executed king.

Unlike his father, King Charles II agreed to rule jointly with Parliament. His younger brother, the Duke of York (who became James II upon succeeding to the throne in 1685), was more rigid. He openly embraced Catholicism in Protestant England, had political opponents murdered or imprisoned, defied Parliament, and appointed Roman Catholics to key positions.

The Execution of Charles I Flemish artist John Weesop witnessed the king's execution and painted this gruesome scene from memory. He was so disgusted by "a country where they cut off their king's head" that he refused to visit England again.

The English people tolerated James II's rule so long as they expected one of his Protestant daughters, Mary or Anne, to succeed him. In 1688, however, the birth of a royal son who would be raised in the Roman Catholic tradition stirred a revolt. Determined to prevent a Catholic monarchy, political, religious, and military leaders urged the king's Protestant daughter, Mary Stuart, and her Protestant husband, the ruling Dutch prince, William III of Orange, to displace James II and assume the English throne as joint husband and wife monarchs. When William landed in England with a Dutch army, King James II, not wanting to lose his head, fled to France.

Amid this dramatic transfer of power, which soon became known as the Glorious Revolution, Parliament reasserted its right to counterbalance the authority of the monarchy. Kings and queens could no longer suspend Parliament, create armies, or impose taxes without Parliament's consent. The monarchy would henceforth derive its power not from God but from the people.

AMERICAN COLONIES

PEOPLE AND PROFITS During these eventful years, all but one of England's North American colonies—Georgia—were founded. From the outset, English colonization differed significantly from the Spanish pattern, in which all aspects of colonial life were regulated by the government.

The English government treated its original American colonies much like it dealt with neighboring Ireland. The Irish had been conquered by the English during the reign of Queen Elizabeth. England thereafter extended its control over the Catholic Irish through the "planting" of new Protestant settlements in Ireland called *plantations*. By confiscating Irish lands and repopulating them with English and Scottish Protestants, the government sought to reduce the influence of Roman Catholicism and smother any rebellious nationalism in conquered Ireland. In time, the English would impose their rule and religion upon the Native Americans as they had been imposed upon the Irish.

England envied the riches taken from the New World by Spain, especially the enormous amounts of gold and silver. However, the English colonies in America were quite different from the Spanish colonies. Spanish settlements were royal expeditions; much of the wealth and lands the Spanish accumulated in the Americas became the property of the monarchs who funded the conquistadores. In contrast, English colonization in the Americas was led by two different groups that sometimes overlapped: those seeking freedom from religious persecution, both Protestants and Catholics, and those seeking land and wealth.

In addition, English colonies in America were private business ventures or collective religious experiments rather than government enterprises. And they were expensive. Few individuals were wealthy enough to finance a colony over a long period.

Those Englishmen interested in colonization thus banded together to share the financial risks of starting colonies in the "American wilderness." Investors purchased shares of stock to form **joint-stock companies**. That way, large amounts of money could be raised and, if a colony failed, no single investor would suffer the whole loss. If a colony succeeded, the profits would be shared among the investors.

Yet while English monarchs did not fund the colonial expeditions, they did grant the royal charters (legal authorization) needed to launch them. The joint-stock companies represented the most important organizational innovation of the Age of Exploration, and they provided the first instruments of English colonization in America.

SELF-SUSTAINING COLONIES The English settlements in America were much more compact than those in New Spain, and the native peoples along the Atlantic coast were less numerous, more scattered, and less wealthy than the Mexica and the Incas.

Unlike the male-dominated French and Spanish colonies, where fur traders and conquistadores often lived among the Indians and intermarried, most English settlers viewed the Indians as devilish threats to be removed as they created family-based agricultural and trading communities.

England's colonies were also much more populous than the Spanish and French colonies in North America. In 1660, there were 58,000 colonists in New England and along the Chesapeake Bay compared with 3,000 in New France and 5,000 in Dutch New Netherland. By 1750, English colonists (male and female) still outnumbered the French (mostly male) nearly 20 to 1 (1.3 million to 70,000), whereas in the northern areas of New Spain, the lands that became Texas, New Mexico, Arizona, Florida, and California, there were only 20,000 Spaniards.

The English government and individual investors had two primary goals for their American colonies: (1) to provide valuable raw materials such as timber for shipbuilding, tobacco for smoking, and fur pelts for hats and coats; and (2) to develop a thriving consumer market for English manufactured goods. To populate the colonies, the English encouraged social rebels (including convicts), religious dissenters, and the homeless and landless to migrate to America, thereby reducing social and economic tensions at home.

By far, the most powerful enticement to colonists was to offer them land and the promise of a better way of life—what came to be called the American dream. Land, plentiful and cheap, was English America's miraculous treasure—once it was taken from the Native Americans. What virtually all of the diverse immigrants shared was the courage to risk everything for a new life of adventure in America. In the process of discovering a New World of opportunities and dangers, they also discovered and recreated themselves as Americans.

THE LANDLESS ENGLISH During the late sixteenth century, England experienced a population explosion that outstripped its economy's ability to support the surplus of landless workers. Many of those poor laborers would find their way to America. An additional social strain for the English poor was the *enclosure* of farmlands on which peasants had lived and worked for generations. As trade in woolen products grew, landlords decided to "enclose" farmlands and evict the farmworkers in favor of grazing sheep.

The enclosure movement of the sixteenth century, coupled with the rising population, generated the great number of beggars and vagrants who wandered across England during the late sixteenth century and gained immortality in the line from the Mother Goose tale: "Hark, hark, the dogs do bark. The beggars have come to town."

The problems created by this uprooted peasant population provided a compelling reason to send many of them abroad to colonies in America and the Caribbean. As the Reverend Richard Hakluyt, an English geographer, explained, "Valiant youths rusting [from] lack of employment" would flourish in the New World and produce crops and materials that would enrich England.

VIRGINIA   In 1606, King James I chartered a joint-stock enterprise called the Virginia Company. It was owned by merchant investors (including the wealthiest merchant in London) seeking to profit from the gold and silver they hoped to find in America. King James also gave the Virginia Company a spiritual mission by ordering the settlers to take the "Christian religion" to the Indians, who "live in darkness and miserable ignorance of the true knowledge and worship of God."

In 1607, the Virginia Company sent to America three tiny ships carrying about 100 men and boys. In May, after five storm-tossed months at sea, they reached Chesapeake Bay, which extends 200 miles from north to south along the present-day states of Virginia and Maryland. To avoid Spanish raiders, the English colonists chose to settle about forty miles inland along a large river with a northwest bend. They called the river the James, in honor of the Catholic king, and named their first settlement James Fort, later renamed Jamestown.

On a low-lying island surrounded by boggy salt marshes swarming with malaria-infested mosquitoes, the sea-weary colonists built a fort with thatched huts and a church. They had come to America overflowing with misperceptions. They expected to find gold, friendly Indians, and easy living. Instead they found disease, drought, starvation, violence, and death. Virtually every colonist fell ill within a year after arriving in Virginia as they moved into a new disease environment against which they had no natural immunities.

Summers in Virginia were much hotter and more humid than in England. The early settlers also struggled to find enough to eat, for most of them were either poor townsmen unfamiliar with farming or "gentleman" adventurers who despised manual labor. "A more damned crew hell never vomited," said the president of the Virginia Company.

The leaders of the company expected the Native Americans to submit to the authority of the colonists. They were wrong. The 14,000 Indians living along the Virginia coast were dominated by the **Powhatan Confederacy**. Powhatan, as the English called him, was the supreme chief of several hundred villages (of about 100 people each) organized into thirty chiefdoms in eastern Virginia.

At the time, the Powhatan Confederacy may have been the most powerful group of native peoples along the entire Atlantic coast. Focused on raising corn, they lived in oval-shaped houses framed with bent saplings and covered with bark or mats. Their walled villages included forts, buildings for storing corn, and temples.

Chief Powhatan (his proper name was Wahunsenacawh) lived in an imposing lodge on the York River not far from Jamestown, where he was protected by forty bodyguards and supported by a hundred wives. Colonist John Smith reported that the chieftain "sat covered with a great robe, made of raccoon skins, and all the tails hanging by," flanked by "two rows of men, and behind them as many women, with all their heads and shoulders painted red."

The Powhatans, Smith reported, were "generally tall and straight," "very ingenious," and handsome, the black hair on their heads half shaven and half grown long. Some adorned their heads with feathers and chains hanging from their pierced ears. Many painted their bodies. Unlike the English, only a few grew beards. During the winter, they wore fur skins and in the summer were mostly naked, covered only by grasses or leaves.

In simple huts made of saplings and bark, the Powhatans lived together in family clusters. Some villages had 20 such huts; others had 200. The Powhatan men, Smith stressed, went to great pains never to engage in "woman's work." When they were not hunting, fishing, or fighting, they sat around watching the "women and children do the rest of the work," gardening, making baskets and pottery, cooking, and "all the rest."

Powhatan was as much an imperialist as the English or Spanish. He forced the chieftains of rival peoples he had conquered to give him corn. Upon learning of the English settlement at Jamestown, he planned to impose his will on the "Strangers" as well. When Powhatans happened upon a group of Englishmen stealing their corn, they killed all seventeen of them, stuffing their mouths with ears of corn.

The inexperienced colonists found a match for Chief Powhatan in John Smith, a canny, iron-willed twenty-seven-year-old mercenary (soldier for hire) who arrived the next year with more colonists. The Virginia Company, impressed by Smith's exploits in foreign wars, had appointed him a member of the council to manage the new colony in America.

It was a wise decision. Of the original 105 settlers, only 38 survived the first nine months. At one point, said Smith, all their food was gone, "all help abandoned, each hour expecting the fury of the savages." After recognizing their "desperate extremity," the Powhatans brought corn to rescue the starving strangers.

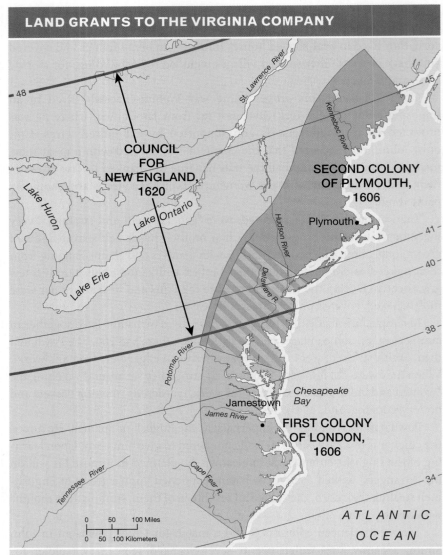

LAND GRANTS TO THE VIRGINIA COMPANY

- What did stockholders of the Virginia Company hope to gain from the first two English colonies in North America?
- How were the first English settlements different from the Spanish settlements in North America?
- What were the major differences between Jamestown and Plymouth?

Thereafter, Smith imposed strict military discipline and forced all to work long days in the fields. He also bargained effectively with the Indians. Through his dictatorial efforts, Jamestown survived. But it was not easy. As he explained, the quarreling colonists were a sorry lot, "ten times more fit to spoil a commonwealth than . . . to begin one."

When no gold or silver was discovered near Jamestown, the Virginia Company shifted its money-making efforts to the sale of land, which would rise in value as the colony grew in population. The company recruited hundreds of new investors and settlers with promises that Virginia would "make them rich."

The influx of settlers nearly overwhelmed the struggling colony. During the winter of 1609–1610, the colony's food supply again ran out, and most of the English colonists died of disease or starvation. Desperate settlers consumed their horses, cats, and dogs, then rats and mice. A few even ate their leather shoes and boots and the starch in their shirt collars. One hungry man killed, salted, and ate his pregnant wife. Horrified by such cannibalism, his fellow colonists tortured and executed him. But the cannibalism continued

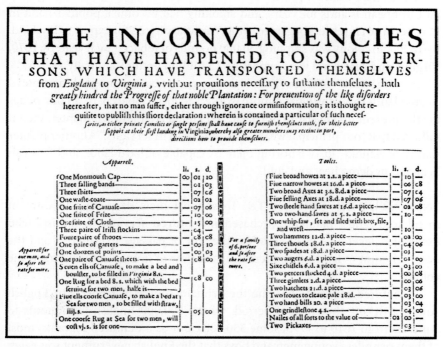

Colonial necessities A list of supplies recommended to new settlers by the Virginia Company in 1622.

as the starvation worsened. "So great was our famine," Smith wrote, "that a savage we slew and buried, the poorer sort [of colonists] took him up again and ate him."

In June 1610, as the surviving colonists prepared to abandon Jamestown and return to England, a new governor, Lord De La Warr, arrived with three ships and 150 men. They established new settlements upstream at Henrico (Richmond) and two more downstream, near the mouth of the James River.

It was a critical turning point for the colony. After Lord De La Warr returned to England in 1611, Sir Thomas Gates took charge of the Virginia settlements and imposed a strict system of laws. The penalties for running away included shooting, hanging, and burning. When a man was caught stealing oatmeal, the authorities thrust a long needle through his tongue, chained him to a tree, and let him starve to death as a grisly example to the community. Gates also ordered the colonists to attend church services on Thursdays and Sundays. Religious uniformity became an essential instrument of public policy and civil duty in colonial Virginia.

Over the next several years, the Jamestown colony limped along until at last the settlers found a profitable crop: **tobacco**. The plant had been grown on Caribbean islands for years, and smoking had become a popular habit in Europe. In 1612, settlers began growing Virginia tobacco for export to England. By 1620, the colony was shipping 50,000 pounds of tobacco each year; by 1670, Virginia and Maryland were exporting 15 million pounds annually.

As large-scale tobacco growing emerged, farmers needed additional cleared lands for planting and more workers to grow tobacco. If "all our riches for the present do consist in Tobacco," explained a Jamestown planter, then it followed that "our principal wealth . . . consisteth in servants." Another planter said they wanted "lusty laboring men . . . capable of hard labor, and that can bear and undergo heat and cold."

INDENTURED SERVANTS To support their deepening investment in tobacco lands, planters purchased **indentured servants** (colonists who exchanged several years of labor for the cost of passage to America and the eventual grant of land), thus increasing the flow of immigrant workers to the colony.

Indentured servitude became the primary source of laborers in English America during the colonial period. Of the 500,000 English immigrants to America from 1610 to 1775, some 350,000 came as indentured servants, most of them penniless young men and boys that the English government was eager to be rid of. In the 1630s, the gender ratio in Virginia was 6 men to every woman; by the 1650s it had dropped to 3 to 1.

Not all indentured servants came to the colonies voluntarily. Many homeless children in London were "kid-napped" and sold into servitude in America. In addition, Parliament in 1717 declared that convicts could avoid prison or the hangman by relocating to the colonies, and some 30,000 made their way to the New World.

Newspapers in American ports announced the arrival of indentured servants for sale. One advertisement noted a shipload of "healthy indented men and women servants . . . a variety of tradesmen, good farmers, stout laborers . . . whose indentures will be disposed of, on reasonable terms, for cash."

Buyers of workers preferred the strongest young men and the most attractive women. Those who were sick or older proved harder to sell, and often they were added to a sale as a "bonus." Some middlemen would buy the whole shipload of servants and then load them on wagons to sell in outlying communities. While most men labored on farms or plantations, young indentured women tended to work as household servants, learning the skills of spinning, sewing, cooking, and cleaning.

Once in America, servants were provided food and a bed, but life was harsh and their rights were limited. Masters could sell or loan or rent servants to others without their permission. Marriage required the master's permission. Masters could whip servants or chain them in iron collars and extend their length of service as penalty for bad behavior or for running away.

Being indentured was almost like being a slave, but servants, unlike slaves, could file a complaint about abuse with the local court. Elizabeth Sprigs, for example, a servant in Maryland, reported of her "toiling day and night, and then [being] tied up and whipped to that degree you would not beat an animal, scarce [fed] anything but Indian corn and salt."

The most important difference between servanthood and slavery was that it did not last a lifetime. When the indenture ended, usually after four to seven years, the servant could claim the "freedom dues" set by custom and law: tools, clothing, food, and, on occasion, small tracts of land.

Some former servants did very well. In 1629, seven members of the Virginia legislature were former indentured servants, and fifteen served in the Maryland Assembly in 1637. Such opportunities were much less common in England or Europe, giving people even more reasons to travel to America.

POCAHONTAS   One of the most remarkable Powhatans was Pocahontas, the favorite daughter of Chief Powhatan. In 1607, then only eleven years old, she figured in perhaps the best-known story of the settlement, her plea for the life of John Smith, who had gotten into trouble by trespassing on Powhatan's

Pocahontas Shown here in European dress; by 1616, Pocahontas was known as "Lady Rebecca."

territory. Smith was wounded and readied for execution. At that point, according to Smith, Pocahontas made a dramatic appeal for his life, convincing her father to release him in exchange for muskets, hatchets, beads, and trinkets.

Schoolchildren still learn the story of Pocahontas and John Smith, but through the years the story's facts have become distorted or even falsified. Pocahontas and John Smith were friends, not Disney lovers. Moreover, the Indian princess saved Smith on more than one occasion, before she herself was kidnapped by English settlers in an effort to blackmail Powhatan, her powerful father.

Pocahontas, however, surprised her English captors by choosing to join them. She embraced Christianity, was baptized and renamed Rebecca, and fell in love with John Rolfe, a twenty-eight-year-old widower who introduced tobacco to Jamestown. After their marriage, they moved in 1616 with their infant son, Thomas, to London. There the young princess drew excited attention from the royal family and curious Londoners. But just a few months after arriving, Rebecca, only twenty years old, contracted a lung disease and died.

THE VIRGINIA COMPANY PROSPERS In 1618, Sir Edwin Sandys, a prominent member of Parliament, became head of the Virginia Company and created a new policy to attract more colonists to Virginia when he announced the **headright** (land grant) program: any male English colonist who bought a share in the company and could pay for passage to Virginia could have fifty acres upon arrival, and fifty more for each servant he brought along.

The Virginia Company also promised that the settlers would have all the "rights of Englishmen," including an elected legislature to advise the colonial governor, arguing that "every man will more willingly obey laws to which he has yielded his consent." This was a crucial development, for the English had long enjoyed the broadest civil liberties and the least intrusive government in Europe. Now the colonists in Virginia were to have the same rights.

By 1619, the settlement had outgrown James Fort and was formally renamed Jamestown. The same year, a ship with ninety young women aboard arrived. Men rushed to claim them as wives by providing 125 pounds of tobacco to cover the cost of each transatlantic passage.

Also in 1619, a Dutch ship called the *White Lion* stopped at Jamestown and unloaded "20 Negars," the first enslaved Africans known to have reached English America. Thus began an inhumane system that would grow rapidly while spurring dramatic economic growth, sowing moral corruption, and generating horrific suffering for African Americans.

By 1624, some 14,000 English men, women, and children had migrated to Jamestown, although only 1,132 had survived or stayed, and many of them were in "a sickly and desperate state." In that year, an English court dissolved the struggling Virginia Company, and "weak and miserable" Virginia became a royal colony.

STRANGE NEWS

FROM

VIRGINIA;

Being a full and true

ACCOUNT

OF THE

LIFE and DEATH

OF

Nathanael Bacon Esquire,

Who was the only Cause and Original of all the late Troubles in that COUNTRY.

With a full Relation of all the Accidents which have happened in the late War there between the Christians and Indians.

LONDON,
Printed for *William Harris,* next door to the Turn-Stile without *Moor-gate.* 1677.

News of the rebellion A pamphlet printed in London provided details about Bacon's Rebellion.

The settlers were now free to own property and start businesses. Their governors, however, would thereafter be appointed by the king. Sir William Berkeley, who arrived as the royal governor in 1642, presided over the colony's rapid growth for most of the next thirty-five years. Tobacco prices surged, and wealthy planters began to dominate social and political life.

BACON'S REBELLION The relentless stream of new settlers into Virginia exerted constant pressure on Indian lands and created growing social tensions among whites. The largest planters in the colony sought to live like the wealthy "English gentlemen" who owned huge estates in the English countryside. In Virginia, these men acquired the most fertile land along the coast and rivers, compelling freed servants to become farmworkers or forcing them inland in order to gain their own farms. In either case, the poorest Virginians found themselves at a disadvantage. By 1676, one fourth of the free white men were landless. They roamed the countryside, squatting on private property, working at odd jobs, poaching game, and struggling to survive.

The simmering tensions among the landless colonists contributed to the tangled events that came to be called **Bacon's Rebellion**. The royal governor,

William Berkeley, noted that "poor, indebted, discontented, and armed" Virginia colonists were ripe for rebellion. The discontent erupted when a squabble over hogs between a white planter and Native Americans on the Potomac River led to the murder of the planter's herdsman and, in turn, to retaliation by frontier vigilantes, who killed some two dozen Indians. When five native chieftains were later murdered, enraged Indians took revenge on frontier settlements.

Scattered attacks continued southward to the James River, where Nathaniel Bacon's overseer was killed. In 1676, when Governor Berkeley refused to take action against the Indian raiders, Bacon defied the governor's authority by assuming command of a rebel group of more than 1,000 men determined to terrorize the "protected and darling Indians." Bacon said he would kill all the Indians in Virginia and promised to free any servants and slaves who joined him.

Bacon's Rebellion quickly became a battle of landless servants, small farmers, and even some slaves against Virginia's wealthiest planters and political leaders. Bacon's ruthless assaults against peaceful Indians and his greed for power and land (rather than any commitment to democratic principles) sparked his conflict with the governing authorities and the planter elite.

For his part, Governor Berkeley opposed Bacon's plan to destroy the Indians not because he liked Indians but because he didn't want warfare to disrupt the profitable deerskin trade the colonists enjoyed with the Native Americans. Bacon, whose ragtag "army" had now dwindled to a few hundred, issued a "Declaration of the People of Virginia" accusing Berkeley of corruption and attempted to take the governor into custody. Berkeley's forces resisted—feebly—and Bacon's men burned Jamestown in frustration.

Bacon, however, could not celebrate the victory long; he fell ill and died a month later. With Bacon dead, the rebellion gradually disintegrated. Governor Berkeley had twenty-three of the rebels hanged. For such severity, the king denounced Berkeley as a "fool" and recalled him to England, where he died within a year.

MARYLAND In 1634, ten years after Virginia became a royal colony, a neighboring settlement appeared on the northern shore of Chesapeake Bay. Named Maryland in honor of English queen Henrietta Maria, its 12 million acres were granted to Sir George Calvert, Lord Baltimore, by King Charles I. It became the first *proprietary* colony—that is, it was owned by an individual, not by a joint-stock company.

Calvert had long been one of the king's favorites. In 1619, he was appointed one of two royal secretaries of state for the nation. Forced to resign after a

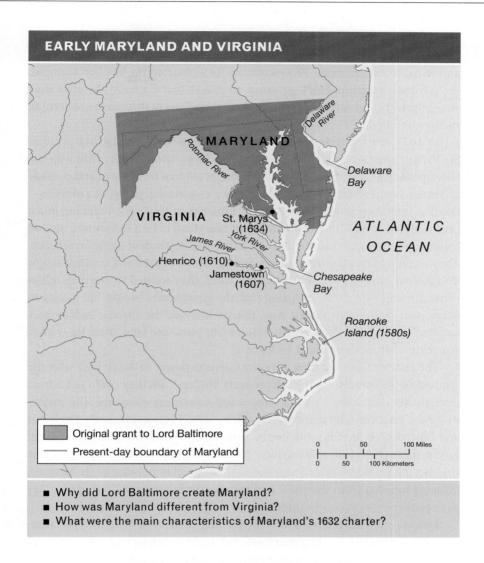

EARLY MARYLAND AND VIRGINIA

MARYLAND

Delaware
River

Potomac River

Delaware
Bay

VIRGINIA   St. Marys
(1634)

ATLANTIC
OCEAN

James River

York River

Henrico (1610)

Jamestown
(1607)

Chesapeake
Bay

Roanoke
Island (1580s)

Original grant to Lord Baltimore

Present-day boundary of Maryland

0   50   100 Miles

0   50   100 Kilometers

- Why did Lord Baltimore create Maryland?
- How was Maryland different from Virginia?
- What were the main characteristics of Maryland's 1632 charter?

squabble with the king's powerful advisers, Calvert used the occasion of his resignation to announce that he had converted from Anglicanism to Catholicism.

Thereafter, Calvert persistently asked the new king, James II, to grant him a charter for an American colony to the north of Virginia. However, Calvert died before the king could act on his request, so the charter was awarded to his son, Cecilius Calvert, the second Lord Baltimore, who actually founded the colony.

Calvert wanted Maryland to be a refuge for English Catholics, a persecuted minority in Anglican England. Yet he also wanted the colony to be profitable and to avoid antagonizing Protestants, so he instructed his brother, Leonard, the colony's first proprietary governor, to ensure that Catholic colonists worship in private and remain "silent upon all occasions of discourse concerning matters of religion."

In 1634, the Calverts planted the first settlement in coastal Maryland at St. Marys, near the mouth of the Potomac River, about eighty miles up the Chesapeake Bay from Jamestown. They sought to learn from the mistakes made at Jamestown. First, they recruited a more committed group of colonists— families intending to stay in the colony rather than single men seeking quick profits. Second, the Calverts did not want Maryland to be a colony of scattered farms and settlements like Virginia, or to become dependent solely on tobacco. They wanted to create a more diversified agriculture and build fortified towns designed to promote social interaction. Third, they wanted to avoid extremes of wealth and poverty by ensuring that the government would "do justice to every man" without partiality. And, fourth, to avoid the chronic Indian wars suffered in Virginia, the Calverts resolved to purchase land from the Native Americans rather than take it by force.

The charter from the king gave the Calverts power to make laws with the consent of the *freemen* (that is, all property holders). Yet they could not attract enough Roman Catholics to develop a self-sustaining economy. The majority of the servants who came to the colony were Protestants, both Anglicans and Puritans. To recruit servants and settlers, the Calverts offered them small farms, most of which grew tobacco. Unlike Virginia, which struggled for its first twenty years, Maryland succeeded more quickly because of its focus on growing tobacco from the start. Its long coastline along the Chesapeake Bay gave planters easy access to shipping.

Despite the Calverts' caution "concerning matters of religion," sectarian squabbles impeded the Maryland colony's early development. When Oliver Cromwell and the Puritans took control in England after the Civil War, Cecilius Calvert, a Catholic like his father, feared he might lose the colony. To avoid such a catastrophe, he wrote the Toleration Act (1649), which welcomed all Christians, regardless of their denomination or beliefs. (It also promised to execute anyone who denied the divinity of Jesus.)

Lord Baltimore convinced the Maryland legislature to pass the Toleration Act in the hope that it would protect the Catholic minority in Maryland. But it did not work. Protestants in Maryland seized control of the government, deprived Lord Baltimore of his governing rights, and rescinded the Toleration

Act in 1654, only to see it reinstituted three years later by Oliver Cromwell. The act deservedly stands as a landmark to human liberty, even though it was enacted more out of expediency than conviction.

The once-persecuted Puritans had become persecutors themselves, at one point driving Lord Baltimore out of his own colony. Were it not for its success in growing tobacco, Maryland may well have disintegrated. In 1692, following the Glorious Revolution in England, Catholicism was banned in Maryland. Only after the American Revolution would Marylanders again be guaranteed religious freedom.

SETTLING NEW ENGLAND

Unlike Maryland and Virginia, the New England colonies were initially intended to be self-governing religious utopias based on the teachings of John Calvin. Dedham, Massachusetts, for example, was founded in the 1630s by English Puritans who signed a written agreement promising to live together in peace and harmony while giving complete obedience to God. The New England settlers were not indentured servants as in the Chesapeake but were mostly middle-class families that could pay their own way across the Atlantic. Most male settlers were small farmers, merchants, seamen, or fishermen. New England also attracted more women than did the southern colonies.

Although its soil was not as fertile as that of the Chesapeake region and its growing season was much shorter, New England was a healthier place to live. Because of its colder climate, settlers avoided the infectious diseases like malaria that ravaged the southern colonies. During the seventeenth century, only 21,000 colonists arrived in New England, compared with the 120,000 who went to the Chesapeake Bay colonies. But by 1700, New England's thriving white population exceeded that of Maryland and Virginia.

The Pilgrims and Puritans who arrived in Massachusetts in the 1620s were on a divine mission to create a model Christian society. In the new land, these self-described "saints" intended to purify their churches of all Catholic and Anglican rituals and enact a code of laws and a government structure based upon biblical principles. Unlike the Anglican Church, which allowed anyone, including sinners, to join, the Puritans would limit membership in their churches only to saints—those who had been chosen by God for salvation. They also sought to stamp out gambling, swearing, and Sabbath breaking. Such holy settlements, they hoped, would provide a beacon of righteousness for a wicked England to emulate.

PLYMOUTH The first permanent English settlement in New England was established by Separatists who were forced to leave England because of their refusal to worship in Anglican churches. The Separatist saints demanded that each congregation govern itself rather than be ruled by a bureaucracy of bishops and archbishops. Separatists had first gathered in Scrooby, an English village, only to be forced out, resettling in the English town of Boston before many of them left England for Holland, where, over time, they worried that their children were becoming Dutch.

In September 1620, about 100 women, men, and children, some of whom were called "Strangers" rather than Separatists because they were not part of the religious group, crammed aboard the tiny *Mayflower*, a leaky vessel only 100 feet long, and headed across the Atlantic bound for the Virginia colony, where they had obtained permission to settle. Storms, however, blew the ship off course to Cape Cod, just south of what became Boston, Massachusetts. "Being thus arrived at safe harbor, and brought safe to land," William Bradford wrote, "they fell upon their knees and blessed the God of Heaven who had brought them over the vast and furious ocean."

Crossing the Atlantic Sailors on a sixteenth-century oceangoing vessel navigating by the stars.

Since they were outside the jurisdiction of any organized government, the forty-one Separatists on board the *Mayflower* signed the **Mayflower Compact**, a covenant (group contract) to form a church. The civil government grew out of the church government, and the members of each were identical. The signers of the Mayflower Compact at first met as the General Court of Plymouth Plantation, like a town meeting, which chose the governor and his

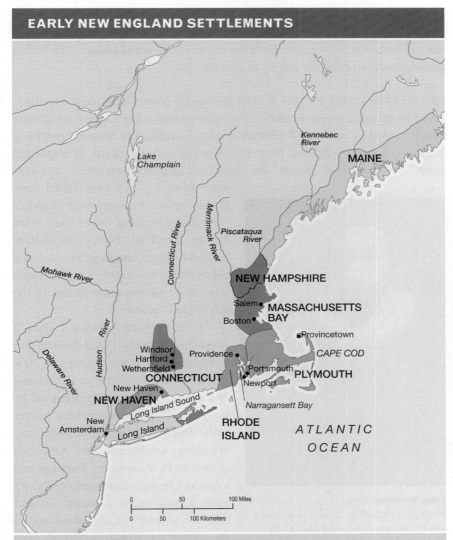

EARLY NEW ENGLAND SETTLEMENTS

- Why did Pilgrims found the Plymouth colony?
- How were the settlers of the Massachusetts Bay Colony different from those of Plymouth?
- What was the origin of the Rhode Island colony?

assistants (or council). Other property owners were later admitted as members, or "freemen," but only church members were eligible to join the General Court. Eventually, as the colony grew, the General Court became a legislative body of elected representatives from the various towns.

The Plymouth colonists settled in a deserted Wampanoag Indian village that had been devastated by smallpox. The Pilgrims named their hillside colony Plymouth, after the English port from which they had embarked. They, too, experienced a difficult "starving time" as had the early Jamestown colonists. During the first winter, half of the Pilgrims died, including thirteen of the eighteen married women. Only the discovery of stored Indian corn buried underground enabled the colony to survive.

MASSACHUSETTS BAY The Plymouth colony was soon overshadowed by its much larger neighbor, the Massachusetts Bay Colony, which was also intended to be a holy Protestant commonwealth. The Massachusetts Bay Puritans, however, differed from the Pilgrims and Anglicans in important ways. They wanted to "purify" the Church of England from within, not separate from it. They were called *Congregationalists* because their churches were self-governing rather than ruled by an Anglican bishop in distant England. Their congregations limited membership to "visible saints"—those who could demonstrate receipt of the gift of God's grace.

In 1629, King Charles I gave a royal charter to the Massachusetts Bay Company, which was planted in New England the following year. It consisted of a group of Calvinist Puritans led by John Winthrop, a prosperous lawyer with intense religious convictions. Winthrop wanted the new American colony to be a haven for Puritans and a model Christian community—"a city upon a hill," as he declared. To that end, he shrewdly took advantage of an oversight in the company charter: it did not require that the joint-stock

John Winthrop The first governor of the Massachusetts Bay Colony, in whose vision the colony would be as "a city upon a hill."

company maintain its home office in England. Winthrop's group took the royal charter with them, thereby transferring government authority from London to Massachusetts, where they hoped to govern themselves.

Winthrop was a strong leader, virtually a dictator, who believed that the government should enforce religious beliefs and ensure social stability. He and the Puritans had no toleration for other religious views in New England. Catholics, Anglicans, Quakers, and Baptists were punished, imprisoned, banished, and sometimes executed.

Even Puritans who spoke out against religious or political policies were quickly condemned. For example, Anne Hutchinson, the strong-willed, intelligent wife of a prominent merchant, raised thirteen children and hosted meetings in her Boston home to discuss sermons.

Soon, however, the discussions turned into large gatherings at which Hutchinson shared her strong feelings about religious matters. According to one participant, she "preaches better Gospel than any of your black coats [male ministers]." Blessed with vast biblical knowledge and a quick wit, Hutchinson claimed to know which of her neighbors had truly been saved and which were damned, including ministers. She quickly was viewed as a "dangerous" woman.

A pregnant Hutchinson was hauled before the all-male General Court in 1637 for trying to "undermine the Kingdom of Christ," and for two days she sparred on equal terms with the Puritan leaders. Her ability to cite chapter-and-verse biblical defenses of her actions led an exasperated Governor Winthrop to explode: "We are your judges, and not you ours. . . . We do not mean to discourse [debate] with those of your sex." He told Hutchinson that she had "stepped out of your place" as a woman in a man's world. As the trial continued, an overwrought Hutchinson was eventually lured into convicting herself by claiming direct revelations from God—blasphemy in the eyes of Puritans.

The Trial of Anne Hutchinson In this nineteenth-century wood engraving, Anne Hutchinson stands her ground against charges of heresy from the all-male leaders of Puritan Boston.

In 1638, Winthrop and the General Court banished the pregnant Hutchinson as a "leper" not fit for "our society." She initially resettled with her family and about sixty followers on an island south of Providence, Rhode Island. The hard journey took its toll, however. Hutchinson grew sick, and her baby was stillborn, leading her critics in Massachusetts Bay to claim that the "monstrous birth" was God's way of punishing her. Hutchinson's spirits never recovered. After her husband's death, in 1642, she moved near New Amsterdam (New York City), which was then under Dutch control. The following year, she and six of her children were massacred by Indians. Her murder, wrote a spiteful John Winthrop, was "a special manifestation of divine justice."

REPRESENTATIVE GOVERNMENT The transfer of the Massachusetts Bay Colony's royal charter, whereby an English trading company evolved into a provincial government, was a unique venture in colonization. Unlike "Old" England, New England had no powerful lords or bishops, kings or queens. The Massachusetts General Court, wherein power rested under the royal charter, consisted of all the shareholders (property owners who were also called freemen). At first, the freemen had no power except to choose "assistants," who in turn elected the governor and deputy governor. In 1634, however, the freemen turned themselves into the General Court, with two or three deputies to represent each town.

A final stage in the democratization of the Massachusetts Bay government came in 1644, when the General Court organized itself like the English Parliament, with a House of Assistants, corresponding roughly to the House of Lords, and a House of Deputies, corresponding to the House of Commons. All decisions had to be ratified by a majority in each house.

The Puritans who had fled religious persecution ensured that their liberties in America were spelled out and protected. Over time, membership in a Puritan church replaced the purchase of stock as the means of becoming a freeman, or voter, in Massachusetts Bay.

RHODE ISLAND More by accident than design, the Massachusetts Bay Colony became the staging area for other New England colonies created by people dissatisfied with Puritan control. Young Roger Williams (1603–1683), who had arrived from England in 1631, was among the first to cause problems, precisely because he was the purest of Puritans—a Separatist. He criticized Puritans for not completely cutting ties to the "whorish" Church of England.

Where John Winthrop cherished strict governmental and clerical authority, Williams stubbornly championed individual liberty and criticized the way the Indians were being shoved aside. The combative Williams posed a radical question: If one's salvation depends solely upon God's grace, as John Calvin had argued, why bother to have churches at all? Why not give individuals the right to worship God in their own way?

In Williams's view, true *puritanism* required complete separation of church and state and freedom from all coercion in matters of faith. "Forced worship," he declared, "stinks in God's nostrils."

Such "dangerous opinions" led Governor Winthrop and the General Court to banish Williams to England. Before authorities could ship him back,

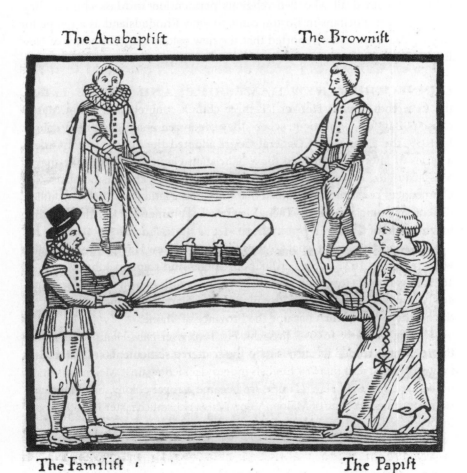

The diversity of English Protestantism Religious quarrels among the Puritans led to the founding of new colonies. In this seventeenth-century cartoon, four Englishmen, each representing a faction in opposition to the established Church of England, are shown fighting over the Bible.

however, he slipped away during a blizzard and found shelter among the Narragansett Indians. In 1636, he bought land from the Indians and established a town he named Providence, at the head of Narragansett Bay, the first permanent settlement in Rhode Island and the first in America to allow complete freedom of religion.

From the beginning, Rhode Island was the most democratic of the colonies, governed by the heads of households rather than by church members. Newcomers could be admitted to full citizenship by a majority vote, and the colony welcomed all who fled religious persecution in Massachusetts Bay. For their part, Puritans in Boston came to view Rhode Island as a refuge for rogues. A Dutch visitor reported that the new colony was "the sewer of New England. All the cranks of New England retire there."

CONNECTICUT, NEW HAMPSHIRE, AND MAINE In 1636, the Reverend Thomas Hooker led three church congregations from Massachusetts Bay to Connecticut, where they organized a self-governing colony. In 1639, the Connecticut General Court adopted the Fundamental Orders, a series of laws that provided for a "Christian Commonwealth" like that of Massachusetts, except that voting was not limited to church members. The Connecticut constitution specified that the Congregational churches would be the colony's official religion. The governor was commanded to rule according to "the word of God."

To the north, most of what are now the states of New Hampshire and Maine was granted in 1622 to Sir Ferdinando Gorges and Captain John Mason. In 1629, Mason and Gorges divided their territory, with Mason taking the southern part, which he named the Province of New Hampshire, and Gorges taking the northern part, which became the Province of Maine.

During the early 1640s, Massachusetts took over New Hampshire, and in the 1650s it extended its authority to the scattered settlements in Maine. This led to lawsuits, and in 1678 English judges decided against Massachusetts in both cases. In 1679, New Hampshire became a royal colony, but Massachusetts continued to control Maine. A new Massachusetts charter in 1691 finally incorporated Maine into Massachusetts.

THE ENGLISH CIVIL WAR IN AMERICA

By 1640, English settlers in New England and around Chesapeake Bay had established two great beachheads on the Atlantic coast, with the Dutch colony of New Netherland in between. After 1640, however, the struggle between king and Parliament in England diverted attention from colonization, and migration to America dwindled for more than twenty years. During the English Civil War (1642–1651) and Oliver Cromwell's Puritan dictatorship (1653–1658), the struggling colonies were left pretty much alone by the mother country.

In 1643, Massachusetts Bay, Plymouth, Connecticut, and New Haven—formed the New England Confederation to provide joint defense against the Dutch, French, and Indians. In some ways, the confederation behaved like a nation unto itself. It made treaties, and in 1653 it declared war against the Dutch, who were accused of inciting Indian attacks. Massachusetts, far from the scene of trouble, failed to cooperate, greatly weakening the confederation.

Virginia and Maryland also defied Cromwell's dictatorship. Virginia burgesses (legislators) in 1649 denounced the Puritans' execution of King Charles and claimed that his son, Charles II, was the lawful king. The colony grew rapidly during its years of independent government before reverting to royal control when William Berkeley returned as governor in 1660 after the monarchy was restored in England.

Cromwell allowed the colonies great flexibility but was not indifferent to Britain's North American empire. He fought trade wars with the Dutch, and his navy harassed England's traditional enemy, Catholic Spain, in the Caribbean. In 1655, a British force wrested Jamaica from Spanish control.

The Restoration of King Charles II in 1660 led to an equally painless reinstatement of previous governments in the colonies. Agents hastily dispatched by the colonies won reconfirmation of the Massachusetts charter in 1662 and the very first royal charters for Connecticut and Rhode Island in 1662 and 1663. All three remained self-governing corporations. Plymouth still had no charter, but it went unmolested. New Haven, however, was absorbed into Connecticut.

THE RESTORATION IN THE COLONIES

The Restoration of Charles II to the British throne in 1660 revived interest among the English in colonial expansion. Within twelve years, the English would conquer New Netherland and settle Carolina. In the middle region, formerly claimed by the Dutch, four new colonies emerged: New York, New Jersey, Pennsylvania, and Delaware. The new colonies were awarded by the king to men (proprietors) who had remained loyal to the monarchy during the civil war. In 1663, for example, Charles II granted Carolina to eight prominent supporters, who became lords proprietor (owners) of the region.

THE CAROLINAS From the start, the southernmost mainland colony in the seventeenth century consisted of two widely separated areas that eventually became two different Carolina colonies, North and South. The northernmost part, called Albemarle, had been settled in the 1650s by colonists from Virginia. For half a century, Albemarle remained an isolated cluster of farms along the shores of Albemarle Sound.

The eight lords proprietor focused on more-promising sites in southern Carolina. To speed their efforts to generate profits, they recruited experienced

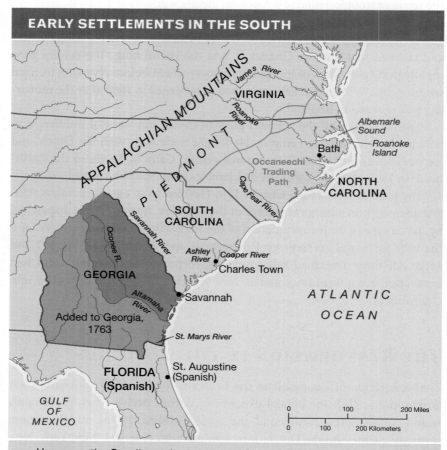

EARLY SETTLEMENTS IN THE SOUTH

- How were the Carolina colonies created?
- What were the impediments to settling North Carolina?
- How did the lords proprietor settle South Carolina?
- What were the major items traded by settlers in South Carolina?

English planters from the tiny Caribbean island of Barbados, the oldest, richest, and most heavily populated colony in English America.

The English in Barbados had developed a hugely profitable sugar plantation system based on the hard labor of enslaved Africans. The "king sugar" colony, the easternmost island in the West Indies, was dominated by a few extraordinarily wealthy planters who exercised powerful political influence in the mother country. The renowned philosopher John Locke reported that the English planters on Barbados "endeavored to rule all."

They also worked their slaves to death; the mortality rate for both slaves and whites in Barbados was twice that in Virginia, forcing English planters on the island to buy huge numbers of additional slaves each year as replacements. By 1670, however, all available land on Barbados had been claimed, and the sons and grandsons of the planter elite were forced to look elsewhere to find estates of their own. They seized the chance to settle South Carolina and bring the Barbadian plantation system to the new colony.

The first English colonists arrived in South Carolina in 1669 at Charles Town (later named Charleston). Over the next twenty years, half the South Carolina colonists came from Barbados and other island colonies in the Caribbean, such as Nevis, St. Kitts, and Jamaica. In a reference to Barbados and the other Caribbean colonies, John Yeamans, an Englishman in Carolina, explained in 1666 that "these settlements have been made and upheld by Negroes and without constant supplies of them cannot subsist."

From the start, South Carolina was a slave-based colony. In their efforts to recruit slaveholding planters, the lords proprietor placed advertisements like the following in the Barbados newspaper: "To the owner of every negro man or slave brought thither [to Carolina] within the first year, 20 acres, and for every woman negro or slave, 10 acres; and all men negroes or slaves after that time and within the first five years, 10 acres; and for every woman negro or slave, 5 acres."

Planters from the Caribbean colonies brought enormous numbers of enslaved Africans to Carolina to clear land, plant crops, and herd cattle. Carolina, a Swiss immigrant said, "looks more like a negro country than like a country settled by white people."

The government of Carolina grew out of a unique documents, the Fundamental Constitutions of Carolina, drafted by one of the eight proprietors, Lord Anthony Ashley Cooper, with the help of his secretary, John Locke. Its provisions for a formal titled nobility encouraged awarding large land grants to prominent Englishmen. From the beginning, however, headrights were given to every immigrant who could pay for passage across the Atlantic. The Fundamental Constitutions granted religious toleration, which gave Carolina a greater degree of religious freedom (extending to Jews and "heathens") than England or any other colony except Rhode Island.

In 1712, the Carolina colony was formally divided in two: North and South. After rebelling against the lords proprietor, South Carolina became a royal colony in 1719. North Carolina remained under the proprietors' rule until 1729, when it, too, became a royal colony.

Rice became the dominant commercial crop in coastal South Carolina because it was perfectly suited to the hot, humid growing conditions. Rice, like sugarcane and tobacco, was a labor-intensive crop, and planters preferred enslaved Africans to work their plantations, in part because west Africans had been growing rice for generations. Both Carolinas also had huge forests of yellow pine trees that provided lumber and other key materials for shipbuilding. The sticky resin from pine trees could be boiled to make tar, which was needed to waterproof the seams of wooden ships (which is why North Carolinians came to be called Tar Heels).

ENSLAVING INDIANS   One of the quickest ways to make money in the early years of Carolina's development was through trade with local Indians. In the late seventeenth century, English merchants began traveling southward

The Broiling of Their Fish over the Flame In this drawing by John White, Algonquian men in North Carolina broil fish, a dietary staple of coastal societies.

from Virginia into the Piedmont region of Carolina, where they developed a prosperous commerce in deerskins with the Catawbas. Between 1699 and 1715, Carolina exported to England an average of 54,000 deerskins per year, where they were transformed into leather gloves, belts, hats, work aprons, and book bindings.

The growing trade in deerskins entwined Indians in a dependent relationship with Europeans that would prove disastrous to their traditional ways of life. English traders quickly became interested in buying enslaved Indians as well as deerskins. They gave Indians goods, firearms, and rum as payment for their capturing rivals to be sold as slaves.

The profitability of captive Indian workers prompted a frenzy of slaving activity among English settlers. As many as 50,000 Indians, mostly women and children, were sold as slaves in Charles Town between 1670 and 1715. More enslaved Indians were exported during that period than Africans were imported, and thousands of others were sold to "slavers" who took them to islands in the West Indies through New England ports.

The growing trade in enslaved Native Americans triggered bitter struggles between rival Indian nations and helped ignite unprecedented colonial violence. In 1712, the Tuscaroras of North Carolina attacked German and English colonists who had encroached upon their land. North Carolina authorities appealed to South Carolina for aid, and the colony, eager for more slaves, dispatched two expeditions made up mostly of Indian allies—Yamasees,

Cherokee chiefs A print depicting seven Cherokee chieftains taken from Carolina to England in 1730.

Cherokees, Creeks, and Catawbas. They destroyed a Tuscarora town, executed 162 male warriors, and took 392 women and children captive for sale in Charles Town. The surviving Tuscaroras fled north, where they joined the Iroquois.

The Tuscarora War in North Carolina sparked more conflict in South Carolina. The Yamasees felt betrayed when white traders paid them less for their Tuscarora captives than they wanted. What made this shortfall so acute was that the Yamasees owed debts to traders totaling 100,000 deerskins. To recover their debts, white traders cheated Yamasees, confiscated their lands, and began enslaving their women and children. In April 1715, the enraged Yamasees attacked coastal plantations and killed more than 100 whites.

The governor mobilized all white and black men to defend the colony; other colonies supplied weapons. But it wasn't until the governor bribed the Cherokees to join them that the Yamasee War ended—in 1717. The defeated Yamasees fled to Spanish-controlled Florida. By then, hundreds of whites had been killed and dozens of plantations destroyed and abandoned. To prevent another conflict, the colonial government outlawed all private trading with Indians.

The end of the Yamasee War did not stop infighting among the Indians, however. For the next ten years or so, the Creeks and Cherokees engaged in a costly blood feud, much to the delight of the English. One Carolinian explained that their challenge was to figure out "how to hold both [tribes] as our friends, for some time, and assist them in cutting one another's throats without offending either. This is the game we intend to play if possible." Between 1700 and 1730, the indigenous population in the Carolinas dwindled from 15,000 to just 4,000.

THE MIDDLE COLONIES AND GEORGIA

The area between New England and the Chesapeake—Maryland and Virginia—included the "middle colonies" of New York, New Jersey, Delaware, and Pennsylvania that were intially controlled by the Netherlands. By 1670, the mostly Protestant Dutch had the largest merchant fleet in the world and the highest standard of living. They controlled northern European commerce and had become one of the most diverse and tolerant societies in Europe—and England's most ferocious competitor in international commerce.

NEW NETHERLAND BECOMES NEW YORK In London, King Charles II decided to pluck out that old Dutch thorn in the side of the English colonies in America: New Netherland. The Dutch colony was older than New

England. The Dutch East India Company (organized in 1602) had hired an English sea captain, Henry Hudson, to explore America in hopes of finding a northwest passage to the spice-rich Indies. Sailing along the coast of North America in 1609, Hudson crossed Delaware Bay and then sailed up the river eventually named for him in what is now New York State. The Hudson River would become one of the most strategically important waterways in all of America, wide and deep enough for oceangoing vessels to travel far north into the interior of the colony, where valuable furs were acquired from Indians.

Like Virginia and Massachusetts, New Netherland was created as a profit-making enterprise. And like the French, the Dutch were interested mainly in the fur trade, as the European demand for beaver hats created huge profits. In 1610, the Dutch established fur-trading posts on Manhattan Island and upriver at Fort Orange (later called Albany).

In 1626, the Dutch governor purchased Manhattan (an Indian word meaning "island of many hills") from the Indians for 60 gilders, or about $1,000 in current values. The Dutch then built a fort and a fur-trading post at the lower end of the island. The village of New Amsterdam (eventually New York City), which grew up around the fort and expanded north to Wall Street, where the Dutch built a defensive wall, became the capital of New Netherland.

New Netherland was a corporate colony governed by the newly organized Dutch West India Company. It controlled political life, appointing the colony's governor and advisory council and not allowing any form of legislature. All commerce with the Netherlands had to be carried in the company's ships, and the company controlled the beaver trade with the Indians.

In 1629, the Dutch West India Company decided that it needed more settlers outside Manhattan to help protect New Amsterdam, the colony's "front door" at the mouth of the Hudson River, from possible Indian attack. To encourage settlers to move into the surrounding countryside, it awarded wealthy individuals a large estate called a *patroonship* in exchange for peopling it with fifty adults within four years. Like a feudal lord, the *patroon* provided cattle, tools, and buildings. His tenants, in turn, paid him rent, used his gristmill for grinding flour, gave him first option to purchase surplus crops, and submitted to a court he established.

These arrangements amounted to transplanting the feudal manor to the New World, and it met with as little success as similar efforts in Maryland and South Carolina. Most settlers, wanting their own farms, took advantage of the company's provision that they could have as farms (*bouweries*) all the lands they could improve.

Dutch settlements gradually emerged wherever fur pelts might be found. In 1638, a Swedish trading company established Fort Christina at the site of

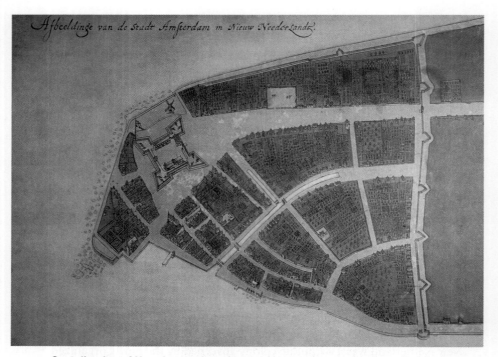

Castello plan of New Amsterdam A map of New Amsterdam in 1660, shortly before the English took the colony from the Dutch and christened it New York City.

present-day Wilmington, Delaware, and scattered settlements up and down the Delaware River. The Dutch in 1655 took control of New Sweden.

Unlike most of the other European colonies in the Americas, the Dutch embraced ethnic and religious diversity. In 1579, the treaty creating the Dutch Republic declared that "everyone shall remain free in religion and . . . no one may be persecuted or investigated because of religion."

Both the Dutch Republic and New Netherland welcomed exiles from the constant religious strife in Europe: Spanish and German Jews, French Protestants (Huguenots), English Puritans, and Catholics. There were even Muslims in New Amsterdam, where eighteen different languages were spoken.

In September 1654, a French ship arrived in New Amsterdam harbor carrying twenty-three *Sephardim*, Jews of Spanish-Portuguese descent. They had come seeking refuge from Portuguese-controlled Brazil and were the first Jewish settlers to arrive in North America.

The anti-Semitic colonial governor, Peter Stuyvesant, refused to accept them, however. Dutch officials overruled him, pointing out that it would

Jewish heritage in colonial America A seventeenth-century Jewish cemetery in New York City.

be "unreasonable and unfair" to refuse to provide Jews a safe haven. They reminded Stuyvesant that some of the West India Company shareholders in the Netherlands were Jews. They told him that they wanted to "allow everyone to have his own belief, as long as he behaves quietly and legally, gives no offense to his neighbor, and does not oppose the government."

It would not be until the late seventeenth century that Jews could worship in public, however. Such restrictions help explain why the American Jewish community grew so slowly. In 1773, more than 100 years after the first Jewish refugees arrived, Jews represented only one tenth of 1 percent of the entire colonial population. Not until the nineteenth century would the American Jewish community experience dramatic growth.

The Dutch West India Company tolerated Jews, but its priority was making profits. In 1626, the company began importing enslaved Africans to meet its labor shortage. By the 1650s, New Amsterdam had one of the largest slave markets in America, although most of the African slaves sold there were sent to Virginia and Maryland.

The extraordinary success of the Dutch economy also proved to be its downfall, however. Like imperial Spain, the Dutch Empire expanded too rapidly. The Dutch dominated European trade with China, India, Africa, Brazil, and the Caribbean, but they could not control their far-flung possessions. It did not take long for European rivals to exploit the sprawling empire's weak points. By the mid–seventeenth century, England and the Netherlands were locked in ferocious commercial warfare.

The New Netherland governors were mostly stubborn autocrats, either corrupt or inept, and especially clumsy at Indian relations. They depended upon a small army for defense, and the residents of Manhattan, many of whom were not Dutch, were often contemptuous of the government. In 1664, the diverse colonists showed almost total indifference when Governor Peter Stuyvesant called them to defend the colony against a threatening English fleet. Stuyvesant finally surrendered the colony without firing a shot.

The English conquest of New Netherland had been led by James Stuart, Duke of York, who would become King James II. Upon the capture of New Amsterdam, his brother, King Charles II, granted the entire Dutch region to him. The Dutch, however, negotiated an unusual surrender agreement that allowed New Netherlanders to retain their property, churches, language, and local officials. The English renamed both New Netherland and the city of New Amsterdam as New York, in honor of James, the Duke of York.

NEW JERSEY Shortly after the conquest of New Netherland, the Duke of York granted the lands between the Hudson and Delaware Rivers to Sir George Carteret and Lord John Berkeley (brother of Virginia's governor) and named the territory for Carteret's native Jersey, an island in the English Channel. In 1676, by mutual agreement, the new colony was divided into East and West Jersey, with Carteret taking the east and Berkeley the west. Finally, in 1682, Carteret sold out to a group of investors.

New settlements gradually arose in East Jersey. Disaffected Puritans from New Haven founded Newark, Carteret's brother brought a group to found Elizabethtown (named for Queen Elizabeth), and a group of Scots founded Perth Amboy. In the west, facing the Delaware River, a scattering of Swedes, Finns, and Dutch remained, but they were soon overwhelmed by swarms of English and Welsh Quakers, as well as German and Scots-Irish settlers. In 1702, East and West Jersey were united as the single royal colony of New Jersey.

PENNSYLVANIA The Quakers, as the Society of Friends was called (because they believed that no one could know Christ without "quaking and trembling"), became the most controversial of the radical religious groups that emerged from the turbulence of the English Civil War. Founded in England in 1647 by George Fox, a saintly roving preacher who often traveled

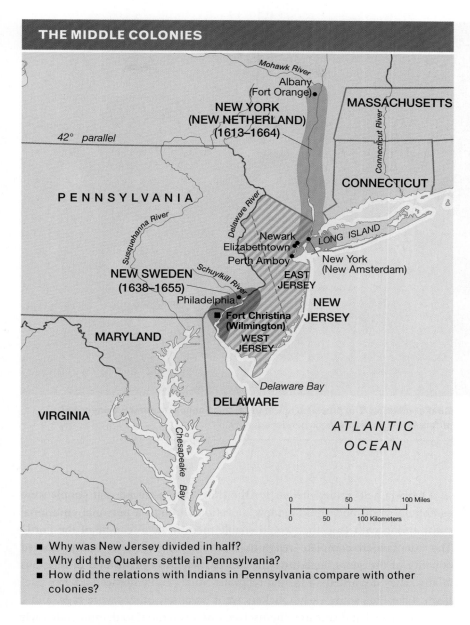

THE MIDDLE COLONIES

Mohawk River

Albany
(Fort Orange)

NEW YORK
(NEW NETHERLAND)
(1613–1664)

MASSACHUSETTS

Connecticut River

42° parallel

CONNECTICUT

PENNSYLVANIA

Delaware River

Susquehanna River

Newark
Elizabethtown
Perth Amboy

LONG ISLAND

New York
(New Amsterdam)

NEW SWEDEN
(1638–1655)

Schuylkill River

EAST
JERSEY

Philadelphia

NEW

Fort Christina
(Wilmington)

JERSEY

MARYLAND

WEST
JERSEY

Delaware Bay

DELAWARE

VIRGINIA

Chesapeake Bay

ATLANTIC
OCEAN

0   50   100 Miles

0   50   100 Kilometers

- Why was New Jersey divided in half?
- Why did the Quakers settle in Pennsylvania?
- How did the relations with Indians in Pennsylvania compare with other colonies?

barefoot, the Friends rebelled against *all* forms of political and religious authority, including salaried ministers, military service, and paying taxes. They insisted that everyone, not just a select few, could experience "God's free gospel," a personal revelation from God, what they called the "Inner Light" of the Holy Spirit.

Quaker meeting The presence of women at this Friends meeting is evidence of progressive Quaker views on gender equality.

Quakers held radical beliefs for the time: they believed that people were essentially good and could achieve salvation through a personal emotional communion with God that would enable them to be a "candle of the Lord." They demanded complete religious freedom for everyone and promoted equality of the sexes, including the full participation of women in religious affairs. They discarded all formal religious rituals and embraced a fierce pacifism. Like Fox, some early Quakers went barefoot, others wore rags, and a few went naked and smeared themselves with excrement to demonstrate their "primitive" commitment to Christ.

The Quakers suffered often violent abuse for their odd behavior because their beliefs were so threatening to the social and religious order. Quakers would gather outside Anglican or Congregational churches, where one of them would try to "outpreach" the minister inside. Authorities accused them of disrupting "peace and order" and undermining "religion, Church order, and the state." New England Puritans banned, tortured, and executed them.

Quakers were especially hated because they refused to acknowledge the supremacy of Puritanism. So that Quakers could be more readily recognized and jailed, they were defaced by the authorities in New England. Their nostrils were slit, their ears lopped off, their tongues pierced by a red-hot rod, or their foreheads branded with the letter H, for "heretic."

But the Quakers kept coming. In fact, the Friends often sought out such abuse and martyrdom as a sign of their intense Christian commitment. Mary Dyer, a follower of Anne Hutchinson who was banned from Massachusetts, later became a Quaker and returned to the colony to visit jailed Quakers. She was eventually arrested and sentenced to death. At the last minute, however, her son convinced the court to release her—against her wishes—on the condition that she relocate to Rhode Island.

In April 1660, however, Dyer went back to Massachusetts in a suicidal effort to protest the "wicked [anti-Quaker] law against God's people and offer up her life there." The mother of six was again sentenced to death. "The will of the Lord be done," she said. "Yea, joyfully shall I go." She was hanged.

The settling of English Quakers in West Jersey encouraged other Friends to migrate, especially to the Delaware River side of the colony, where William Penn's Quaker commonwealth, the colony of Pennsylvania, soon arose. Penn, the son of wealthy Admiral Sir William Penn, had attended Oxford University, from which he was expelled for criticizing the university's requirement that students attend daily chapel services. His furious father banished his rebellious son from their home.

The younger Penn lived in France for two years, then studied law before moving to Ireland to manage the family's estates. There the twenty-two-year-old Penn was arrested in 1666 for attending a Quaker meeting. Much to the chagrin of his parents, he became a Quaker and was arrested several times for his religious convictions.

Upon his father's death, Penn inherited a fortune, including a huge tract of land in America, which the king urged him to settle as a means of ridding England of Quakers. The land was named, at the king's insistence, for Penn's father—Pennsylvania (literally, "Penn's Woods"), and it was larger than England itself. Penn aggressively encouraged people of different religions from different countries to settle in his new colony, which he called a "holy experiment," for he hoped that people of all faiths and nations would live together in harmony.

By the end of 1681, thousands of immigrants had responded to Penn's offer, and a bustling town was emerging at the junction of the Schuylkill and Delaware Rivers. Penn called it Philadelphia (meaning "City of Brotherly Love").

The relations between the Native Americans and the Pennsylvania Quakers were unusually good because of the Quakers' friendliness and Penn's policy of purchasing land titles from the Native Americans. For some fifty years the settlers and the Native Americans lived in peace.

The colony's government, which rested on three Frames of Government drafted by Penn, resembled that of other proprietary colonies except that the freemen (property owners) elected the council members as well as the assembly. The governor had no veto, although Penn, as proprietor, did. Penn hoped to show that a colonial government could operate in accordance with Quaker principles, that it could maintain peace and order, and that religion could flourish without government support and with absolute freedom of conscience.

Over time, however, the Quakers struggled to forge a harmonious colony. In Pennsylvania's first ten years, it went through six governors. A disappointed Penn wrote from London: "Pray stop those scurvy quarrels that break out to the disgrace of the province."

DELAWARE   In 1682, the Duke of York granted Penn the area of Delaware, another part of the former Dutch territory (which had been New Sweden before being acquired by the Dutch in 1655). At first, Delaware—taking its name from the Delaware River, which had been named to honor Thomas West (Baron De La Warr), Virginia's first colonial governor—became part of Pennsylvania, but after 1704 it was granted the right to choose its own assembly. From then until the American Revolution, Delaware had a separate assembly but shared Pennsylvania's governor.

GEORGIA   Georgia was the last of the English colonies to be established. In 1732, King George II gave the land between the Savannah and Altamaha Rivers to twenty-one English trustees appointed to govern the Province of Georgia, named in honor of the king. In two respects, Georgia was unique among the colonies: it was to provide a military buffer protecting the Carolinas against Spanish-controlled Florida and to serve as a social experiment bringing together settlers from different countries and religions, many of them refugees, debtors, or "miserable wretches" making up the "worthy poor." General James E. Oglethorpe, a prominent member of Parliament, was appointed to head the colony designed to provide a haven for the "poor children and other poor that pester the streets of London."

Savannah, Georgia The earliest-known view of Savannah, Georgia (1734). The town's layout was carefully planned.

In 1733, colonists founded Savannah on the Atlantic coast near the mouth of the Savannah River. The town, designed by Oglethorpe, featured a grid of crisscrossing roads graced by numerous parks. Protestant refugees from Austria began to arrive in 1734, followed by Germans and German-speaking Moravians and Swiss. The addition of Welsh, Highland Scots, Sephardic Jews, and others gave the early colony a diverse character like that of Charleston, South Carolina.

As a buffer against Spanish Florida, the Georgia colony succeeded, but as a social experiment creating a "common man's utopia," it failed. Initially, landholdings were limited to 500 acres to promote economic equality. Liquor was banned, as were lawyers, and the importation of slaves was forbidden. But the idealistic rules soon collapsed as the colony struggled to become self-sufficient. The regulations against rum and slavery were widely disregarded and finally abandoned.

In 1754, Georgia became a royal colony. It developed slowly over the next decade but grew rapidly after 1763. Georgians exported rice, lumber, beef, and pork, and they carried on a profitable trade with the islands in the West Indies. Almost unintentionally, the colony became an economic success and a slave-centered society.

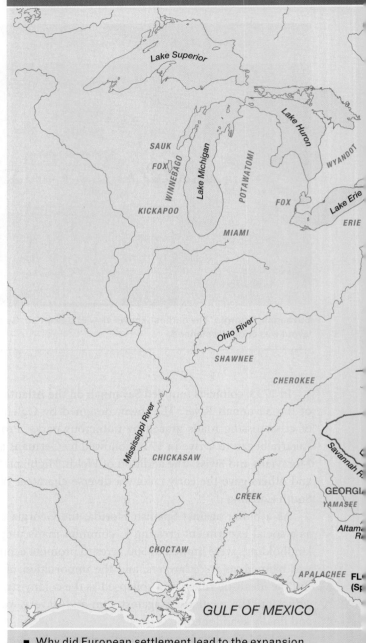

Lake Superior

Lake Michigan

Lake Huron

Lake Erie

SAUK

FOX

WINNEBAGO

POTAWATOMI

WYANDOT

FOX

KICKAPOO

ERIE

MIAMI

Ohio River

SHAWNEE

CHEROKEE

Mississippi River

Savannah R.

CHICKASAW

CREEK

GEORGI

YAMASEE

Altam
R

CHOCTAW

APALACHEE FL
(Sp

GULF OF MEXICO

- Why did European settlement lead to the expansion
  of hostilities among the Indians?
- What were the consequences of the trade and commerce
  between the English settlers and the southern indigenous
  peoples?
- How were the relationships between the settlers and the
  members of the Iroquois League different from those between
  settlers and tribes in other regions?

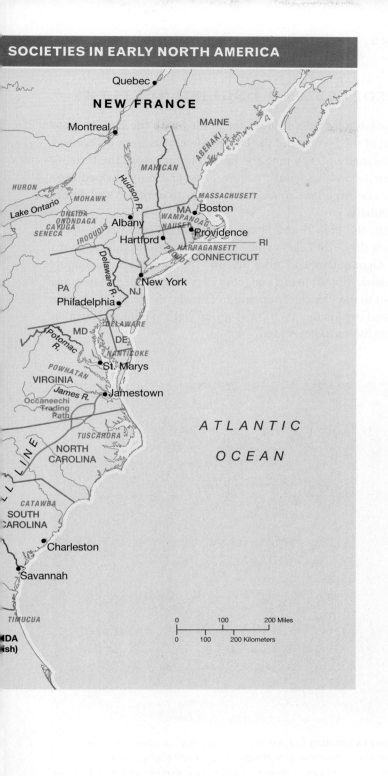

SOCIETIES IN EARLY NORTH AMERICA

Quebec

NEW FRANCE

Montreal

MAINE

ABENAKI

MAHICAN

HURON

Hudson R.

MASSACHUSETT

Lake Ontario

MOHAWK

MA

Boston

ONEIDA
ONONDAGA
CAYUGA
SENECA

WAMPANOAG

Albany

NAUSET

IROQUOIS

Hartford

Providence

RI

NARRAGANSETT

CONNECTICUT

PEQUOT

Delaware R.

New York

PA

NJ

Philadelphia

DELAWARE

Potomac R.

MD

DE

NANTICOKE

St. Marys

POWHATAN

VIRGINIA

James R.

Jamestown

Occaneechi
Trading
Path

TUSCARORA

LINE

**NORTH
CAROLINA**

ATLANTIC

OCEAN

CATAWBA

**SOUTH
CAROLINA**

Charleston

Savannah

TIMUCUA

DA
ish)

| 0 | 100 | 200 Miles |

| 0 | 100 | 200 Kilometers |

NATIVE PEOPLES AND ENGLISH SETTLERS

Most English colonists adopted a strategy for dealing with the Indians quite different from that of the French and the Dutch. Merchants from France and the Netherlands focused on exploiting the profitable fur trade. The thriving commerce in animal skins—especially beaver, otter, and deer—helped spur exploration of the vast American continent. It also both enriched and devastated the lives of Indians.

To get fur pelts, the French and Dutch built trading outposts in upper New York and along the Great Lakes, where they established friendly relations with the Hurons, Algonquians, and other Indians. The Hurons and Algonquians also sought French support in their ongoing wars with the mighty Iroquois nations. In contrast to the French experience in Canada, the English colonists were more interested in pursuing their "God-given" right to hunt and farm on Indian lands and to fish in Indian waters.

Algonquian ceremony celebrating harvest As with most Native Americans, the Algonquians' dependence on nature for survival shaped their religious beliefs.

NATIVE AMERICANS AND CHRISTIANITY The New England Puritans aggressively tried to convert Native Americans to Christianity and "civilized" living. They insisted that Indian converts abandon their religion, language, clothes, names, and villages, and forced them to move to what were called "praying towns" to separate them from their "heathen" brethren. One reason that Roger Williams of Rhode Island was considered so dangerous by the Puritan leaders was his insistence that all faiths—including those of the Indians—should be treated equally. He labeled efforts by governments to impose Puritanism on everyone "soul rape."

THE PEQUOT WAR Indians in the English colonies who fought to keep their lands were forced out or killed. New England Puritans, like the English colonists in Virginia, viewed Indians as demonic savages, "barbarous creatures," and "merciless and cruel heathens." As one colonist asserted, Indians had no place in a "new England."

In 1636, settlers in Massachusetts accused a Pequot of murdering a colonist; the English took revenge by burning a Pequot village. As the Indians fled, the Puritans killed them—men, women, and children. The militia commander declared that God had guided his actions "to smite our Enemies . . . and give us their land for an Inheritance."

Sassacus, the Pequot chief, organized the survivors and counterattacked. During the ensuing Pequot War of 1637, the colonists and their Narragansett allies set fire to an Indian village near West Mystic, in the Connecticut Valley, and killed those who tried to escape. William Bradford, the governor of Plymouth, admitted that it was "a fearful sight" to see the Indians "frying in the fire and the streams of blood quenching" the flames, but "the victory seemed a sweet sacrifice" delivered by God.

Under the terms of the Treaty of Hartford (1638), the Pequot Nation was dissolved. Refugees fled in all directions. Sassacus escaped to the Mohawks in New York, with whom he pleaded to spare his life. They did not. In fact, they sent his scalp to the English as a peace offering.

KING PHILIP'S WAR After the Pequot War, relations between colonists and Indians improved somewhat, but the continuing influx of English settlers and the decline of the beaver population eventually reduced the Native Americans to poverty. By 1675, the Indians and English settlers had come to fear each other deeply.

The era of peaceful coexistence came to a bloody end during the last quarter of the seventeenth century. Native American leaders, especially the chief of the Wampanoags, Metacomet (known to the colonists as King Philip), resented English efforts to convert Indians to Christianity. In the fall of 1674, John Sassamon, a Christian Indian who had graduated from Harvard College, warned the English that the Wampanoags were preparing for war.

A few months later, Sassamon was found dead in a frozen pond. Colonial authorities convicted three Wampanoags of murder and hanged them. Enraged Wampanoag warriors then burned Puritan farms on June 20, 1675. Three days later, an Englishman shot a Wampanoag; the Wampanoags retaliated by ambushing and beheading a group of Puritans.

The shocking violence on both sides soon spun out of control in what came to be called **King Philip's War**, or Metacomet's War. The brutal fighting resulted in more deaths and destruction in New England in proportion to the population than any American conflict since, including the Civil War. Vengeful bands of warriors destroyed twelve towns and attacked forty others.

Within a year, colonists conducted a surprise attack that killed 300 Narragansett warriors and 400 women and children. The Narragansetts retaliated by destroying Providence, Rhode Island, and threatening Boston itself, prompting a prominent minister to call it "the saddest time with New England that was ever known."

King Philip's War A 1772 engraving by Paul Revere depicts Metacomet (King Philip), leader of the Wampanoags.

The situation grew so desperate that the colonies passed America's first conscription laws, drafting into the militia all males between the ages of sixteen and sixty. In the summer of 1676, Metacomet's wife and only son were captured, leading the chieftain to cry: "My heart breaks; now I am ready to die."

In the end, staggering casualties and shortages of food and ammunition wore down the Naragansetts. Some surrendered; many succumbed to disease, and others fled to the west. Those who remained were forced into villages supervised by English officials. Metacomet initially escaped, only to be hunted down and killed. The victorious colonists marched his severed head to Plymouth, where it stayed atop a pole for twenty years. Metacomet's wife and son were sold into slavery in the Caribbean. By the end of King Philip's War, three quarters of the Indians in New England had been killed.

THE IROQUOIS LEAGUE The same combination of forces that wiped out the Indian populations of New England and the Carolinas affected the native peoples around New York City and the lower Hudson Valley. The inability of Indian groups to unite effectively against the Europeans, as well as their vulnerability to infectious diseases, doomed them to conquest and exploitation.

In the interior of New York, however, a different situation arose. There, sometime before 1600, the Iroquois nations—Seneca, Cayuga, Onondaga, Oneida, and Mohawk—had been convinced by Hiawatha, a Mohawk, to forge an alliance.

The **Iroquois League**, known to its members as the *Haudenosaunee*, or Great Peace, became so strong that the outnumbered Dutch and, later, English traders, were forced to work with them to acquire beaver pelts. By the early seventeenth century, a council of some fifty sachems (chieftains) oversaw the 12,000 members of the Iroquois League. Its capital was Onondaga, a bustling town a few miles south of what later became Syracuse, New York.

The League was governed by a remarkable constitution, called the Great Law of Peace, which had three main principles: peace, equity, and justice. Each person was to be a shareholder in the wealth of the nation. The constitution

Wampum belt These valued belts were woven and exchanged to certify treaties or record transactions.

established a Great Council of fifty male *royaneh* (religious–political leaders), each representing one of the female-led clans of the Iroquois nations. The Great Law of Peace gave essential power to the people. It insisted that every time the royaneh dealt with "an especially important matter or a great emergency," they had to "submit the matter to the decision of their people," both men and women, for their consent.

The search for furs and captives led Iroquois war parties to range widely across what is today eastern North America. They gained control over a huge area from the St. Lawrence River to Tennessee and from Maine to Michigan. For more than twenty years, warfare raged across the Great Lakes region between the Iroquois (supported by Dutch and English fur traders) and the Algonquians and Hurons (and their French allies).

In the 1690s, the French and their Indian allies destroyed Iroquois crops and villages, infected them with smallpox, and reduced the male population by more than a third. Facing extermination, the Iroquois made peace with the French in 1701. During the first half of the eighteenth century, they stayed out of the almost constant wars between the two European powers, which enabled them to play the English off against the French while creating a thriving fur trade for themselves.

SLAVERY IN THE COLONIES

SLAVERY IN NORTH AMERICA By 1700, enslaved Africans made up 11 percent of the total American population (slaves would comprise more than 20 percent by 1770). But slavery differed greatly from region to region. Africans were a tiny minority in New England (about 2 percent). Because there were no large plantations in New England and fewer slaves were owned, "family slavery" prevailed, with masters and slaves usually living under the same roof.

Slavery was much more prevalent in the Chesapeake colonies and the Carolinas. By 1730, the black slave population in Virginia and Maryland had become the first in the Western Hemisphere to achieve a self-sustaining rate of population growth. By 1750, about 80 percent of the African American slaves in the Chesapeake Bay region, for example, had been born there.

SLAVERY'S AFRICAN ROOTS The transport of African captives across the Atlantic to the Americas was the largest forced migration in world history. More than 10 million people eventually made the terrifying journey to the Western Hemisphere, the vast majority of them going to Portuguese Brazil or Caribbean sugar islands such as Barbados and Jamaica.

JUST ARRIVED,
THE SEARSDALE, Capt. REED,
with one hundred thirty-nine healthy
SERVANTS,
Men, women, and boys,
Among which are many tradefmen, viz.
SMITHS, bricklayers, plaifterers, fhoemakers, houfe-carpenters and joiners, weavers, barbers and perukemakers, a clerk, a hatter, a rope-maker, a plumber, a glazier, a taylor, a printer, a bookbinder, a painter, a matuamaker, feveral femp-ftreffes, and others ; there are alfo farmers, waggoners, and other country labourers. The fale will commence on *Wednefday* the 10th of *October*, at *Leeds* town, on *Rappahannock*. A reafonable credit will be allowed, giving bond with approved fecurity, to
THOMAS HODGE.

Indentured servants An advertisement for indentured servants from the *Virginia Gazette*, October 4, 1779.

Enslaved Africans spoke as many as fifty different languages and worshipped many different gods. Some had lived in large kingdoms and others in dispersed villages. In their homelands, Africans had preyed upon other Africans for centuries. Warfare was almost constant, as rival tribes conquered, kidnapped, enslaved, and sold one another.

Slavery in Africa, however, was less brutal than in the Americas. In Africa, slaves lived with their captors, and their children were not automatically enslaved. The involvement of Europeans in transatlantic slavery, whereby captives were sold and shipped to other nations, was much worse.

During the seventeenth and eighteenth centuries, African slave traders brought captives to dozens of "slave forts" along the West African coast owned by virtually every European nation: Sweden, Denmark, France, Great Britain, the Netherlands, and Portugal. After languishing for weeks or months, the captured Africans were one day led down tunnels to waiting ships owned by

European slave traders. As one of them remembered, "it was a most horrible scene; there was nothing to be heard but rattling of chains, smacking of whips, and groans and cries of our fellow men."

Once purchased, the captives were branded on the back or buttocks with a company mark, chained, and loaded onto mostly British-owned slave ships. They were packed below deck and subjected to a four-week to six-month trans-atlantic voyage, known as the **Middle Passage** because it served as the middle leg of the so-called *triangular trade* in which British ships traveled on the first leg to West Africa, where they exchanged rum, clothing, and guns for slaves. The slaves then were taken on the second leg of the triangle to American ports, where the ships were loaded with commodities and timber before returning to

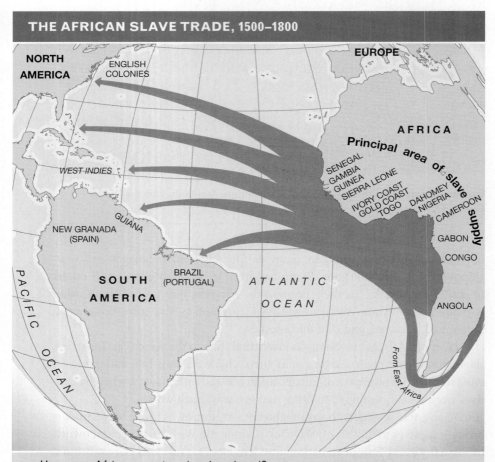

THE AFRICAN SLAVE TRADE, 1500–1800

- How were Africans captured and enslaved?
- Describe how captive Africans were treated during the Middle Passage.
- How did enslaved African Americans create a new culture in the colonies?

Britain and Europe on the final of the three legs of the triangular trade. By the mid–eighteenth century, Britain was the largest slaving nation in the world.

One in six African captives died during the Middle Passage to America, and slave revolts aboard the floating prisons were not uncommon. Yet many of the English engaged in slave trafficking considered their work highly respectable. "What a glorious and advantageous trade this is," wrote slave trader James Houston. "It is the hinge on which all the trade of this globe moves."

The rapid growth of slavery in the Western Hemisphere was driven by high profits and justified by a widespread racism that viewed Africans as beasts of burden rather than human beings. Once in America, Africans were treated as property (chattel), herded in chains to public slave auctions, and sold to the highest bidder.

On large southern plantations that grew tobacco, sugarcane, or rice, groups of slaves were organized into work gangs supervised by black "drivers" and white overseers. The slaves were often quartered in barracks, fed like livestock, and issued ill-fitting work clothes and shoes so uncomfortable that many preferred to go barefoot. Colonial laws allowed whites to use brutal means to discipline slaves. They were whipped, branded, shackled, castrated, or sold

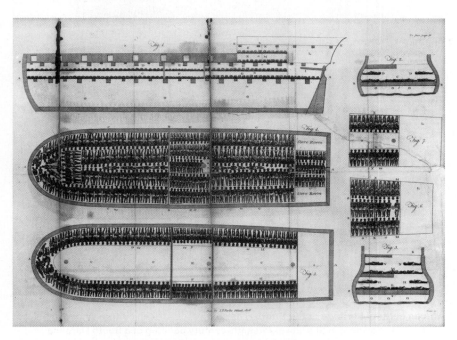

Slave ship One in six Africans died while crossing the Atlantic in ships like this one, from an American diagram ca. 1808.

away, often to the Caribbean islands, where few survived the harsh working conditions of harvesting sugarcane.

Enslaved Africans, however, found ingenious ways to cope. Some rebelled against their captors by resisting work orders, sabotaging crops and stealing tools, faking illness or injury, or running away. If caught, runaways faced terrible punishment. They also faced uncertain freedom. Where would they run *to* in a society ruled by whites and governed by racism?

SLAVE CULTURE   In the process of being forced into lives of bondage in a new world, Africans from diverse homelands forged a new identity as African Americans. At the same time, they wove into American culture many strands of their heritage, including new words such as *tabby, tote, goober, yam,* and *banana*, as well as the names of the Coosaw, Pee Dee, and Wando Rivers.

African cultural heritage in the South   The survival of African culture among enslaved Americans is evident in this late eighteenth-century painting of a South Carolina plantation. The musical instruments and pottery are of African origin (probably Yoruban).

More significant were African influences upon American music, folklore, and religious practices. Slaves often used songs, stories, and religious preachings to circulate coded messages expressing their distaste for masters or overseers. The fundamental theme of slave religion, adapted from the Christianity that was forced upon them, was deliverance: God would eventually free them and open the gates to heaven's promised land.

THRIVING COLONIES

By the early eighteenth century, the English colonies in the New World had outstripped those of both the French and the Spanish. English America, both the mainland colonies and those in the Caribbean, had become the most populous, prosperous, and powerful of the European empires in the Americas. On average, American colonists were better fed, clothed, and housed than their counterparts in Europe.

Yet the English colonization of North America included failures as well as successes. Many settlers found hard labor, desperation, and an early death in the New World. Others flourished only because they were able to exploit Indians, indentured servants, or Africans.

The English colonists enjoyed crucial advantages over their European rivals. While the tightly controlled colonial empires of Spain and France stifled innovation, the English colonies were organized as profit-making enterprises with a minimum of royal control. Where New Spain was dominated by wealthy men who controlled vast estates and often intended to return to Spain, many English colonists ventured to America because, for them, life in England had grown intolerable. The leaders of the Dutch and non-Puritan English colonies, unlike the Spanish and French, welcomed people from a variety of nationalities and religions who came in search of a new life. Perhaps most important, the English colonies enjoyed a greater degree of self-government, which made them more dynamic and creative than their French and Spanish counterparts.

Throughout the seventeenth century, geography reinforced England's emphasis on the concentrated settlements of its American colonies. The farthest western expansion of English settlement stopped at the eastern slopes of the Appalachian Mountains. To the east lay the wide expanse of ocean, which served as a highway for the transport of people, ideas, commerce, and ways of life from Europe to America. But the ocean also served as a barrier that separated old ideas from new, allowing the English colonies to evolve in a "new world"—while developing new ideas about economic freedom and political liberties that would flower later in the eighteenth century.

CHAPTER REVIEW

SUMMARY

- **English Background** England's colonization of North America differed from that of its European rivals. While chartered by the Crown, English colonization was funded by *joint-stock companies*, groups of investors eager for profits. Their colonial governments reflected the English model of a two-house Parliament and long-cherished civil liberties. The colonization of the eastern seaboard of North America occurred at a time of religious and political turmoil in England, strongly affecting colonial culture and development.

- **English Settlers and Colonization** The early years of Jamestown and Plymouth were grim. In time, *tobacco* flourished, and its success also paved the way for a slave-based economy in the South. Sugar and rice plantations developed in the proprietary Carolina colonies, which operated with minimal royal intrusion. Family farms and a mixed economy characterized the middle and New England colonies. Religion was the primary motivation for the founding of several colonies. *Puritans* drafted the *Mayflower Compact* and founded Massachusetts Bay Colony as a Christian commonwealth. Rhode Island was established by Roger Williams, a religious dissenter from Massachusetts. Maryland was founded as a refuge for English Catholics. William Penn, a Quaker, founded Pennsylvania and invited Europe's persecuted religious sects to his colony. The Dutch allowed members of all faiths to settle in New Netherland.

- **Indian Relations** Trade with the *Powhatan Confederacy* in Virginia enabled Jamestown to survive its early years, but brutal armed conflicts such as *Bacon's Rebellion* occurred as settlers invaded Indian lands. Puritans retaliated against Indian resistance in the Pequot War of 1637 and in *King Philip's War* from 1675 to 1676. Among the principal colonial leaders, only Roger Williams and William Penn treated Indians as equals. The powerful *Iroquois League* played the European powers against one another to control territories.

- **Indentured Servants and Slaves** The colonies increasingly relied on *indentured servants*, immigrants who signed contracts (indentures) that required them to work for several years upon arriving in America. By the end of the seventeenth century, enslaved Africans had become the primary form of labor in the Chesapeake. The demand for slaves in the sugar plantations of the West Indies drove European slave traders to organize the transport of Africans via the dreaded *Middle Passage* across the Atlantic. African cultures fused with others in the Americas to create a native-born African American culture.

- **Thriving English Colonies** By 1700, England had become a great trading empire. English America was the most populous and prosperous region of North

America. Minimal royal interference in the proprietary for-profit colonies and widespread landownership encouraged settlers to put down roots. Religious diversity attracted a variety of investors and settlers.

CHRONOLOGY

1603	James I takes the throne of England
1607	The Virginia Company establishes Jamestown
1612	John Rolfe begins growing tobacco for export in Virginia
1619	First Africans arrive in English America
1620	The Plymouth colony founded by Pilgrims; Mayflower Compact
1626	The Dutch purchase Manhattan from Indians
1630	Massachusetts Bay Colony is founded by Puritans
1634	Settlement of Maryland begins
1637	The Pequot War in New England
1642–1651	The English Civil War (Puritans versus Royalists)
1649	The Toleration Act in Maryland
1660	Restoration of English Monarchy
1664	English take control of New Amsterdam (New York City)
1669	Charles Town is founded in the Carolina colony
1675–1676	King Philip's War in New England
1676	Bacon's Rebellion in Virginia
1681	Pennsylvania is established
1733	Georgia is founded

KEY TERMS

Puritans p. 55

joint-stock companies p. 58

Powhatan Confederacy p. 60

tobacco p. 64

indentured servants p. 64

headright p. 66

Bacon's Rebellion p. 67

Mayflower Compact p. 73

King Philip's War p. 98

Iroquois League p. 99

Middle Passage p. 102

 INQUIZITIVE

Go to InQuizitive to see what you've learned—and learn what you've missed—with personalized feedback along the way.

3 Colonial Ways of Life

The artisans of Boston (1766) While fishing, shipbuilding, and maritime trade dominated New England economies, many young men entered apprenticeships, learning a trade from a master craftsman in the hopes of becoming blacksmiths, carpenters, gunsmiths, printers, candlemakers, leather tanners, and more.

The process of carving a new civilization out of an abundant "New World" involved often-violent encounters among European, African, and Indian cultures. War, duplicity, displacement, and enslavement were the tragic results. Yet on another level, the process of transforming the American continent was a story of blending and accommodation, of diverse peoples and resilient cultures engaged in the everyday tasks of building homes, planting crops, trading goods, raising families, enforcing laws, and worshipping their gods. Those who colonized America during the seventeenth and eighteenth centuries were part of a massive social migration occurring throughout Europe and Africa. Everywhere, it seemed, people were in motion—moving from farms to villages, from villages to cities, and from homelands to colonies.

Most English and European settlers were responding to powerful social and economic forces. Rapid population growth and the rise of commercial agriculture squeezed poor farmworkers off the land and into cities like London, Edinburgh, Dublin, and Paris, where they struggled to survive. That most Europeans in the seventeenth and eighteenth centuries were desperately poor helps explain why so many were willing to risk their lives by migrating to the American colonies. Others sought political security or religious freedom. A tragic exception was the Africans, who were captured and transported to new lands against their will.

Those who initially settled in colonial America were mostly young (more than half were under twenty-five), male, single, and poor, and almost half were

focus questions

1. What were the major factors that contributed to the demographic changes in the English colonies during the eighteenth century?

2. What roles did women play in the English colonies?

3. What were the differences and similarities between the societies and economies of the southern, middle, and New England colonies?

4. How did race-based slavery develop during the seventeenth century, and in what ways did this impact the social and economic development of colonial America?

5. In what ways did the Enlightenment and Great Awakening impact American thought?

indentured servants or slaves. During the eighteenth century, England would transport some 50,000 convicts to the North American colonies to relieve overcrowded jails and provide needed workers. Once in America, many of the newcomers kept moving within and across colonies in search of better lands or new business opportunities, such as trading with the native peoples who controlled the profitable fur trade. This extraordinary mosaic of adventurous people created America's enduring institutions and values, as well as its distinctive spirit and restless energy.

THE SHAPE OF EARLY AMERICA

Life in early America was hard and often short. Many in the first wave of American colonists died of disease or starvation; others were killed by Native Americans. The average **death rate** in the first years of settlement was 50 percent. Once colonial life became more settled and secure, however, the colonies grew rapidly. On average, the American population doubled every twenty-five years during the colonial period. By 1750, the number of colonists had passed 1 million; by 1775, it approached 2.5 million. By comparison, the combined population of England, Scotland, and Ireland in 1750 was 6.5 million.

POPULATION GROWTH Benjamin Franklin, a keen observer of life in the new country, said that the extraordinary growth in the colonial population came about because land was plentiful and cheap, and laborers were scarce and expensive. The opposite conditions prevailed in Europe. It suffered from overpopulation and expensive farmland. From this reversal of conditions flowed many of the changes that European culture underwent during the colonization of America—not the least being that more land and good fortune lured enterprising immigrants and led settlers to replenish the earth with large families. Once in the colonies, settlers tended to have large families, in part because farm children could lend a hand in the fields.

Colonists tended to marry and start families at an earlier age than in Europe. In England, the average age at marriage for women was twenty-five or twenty-six; in America, it dropped to twenty. Men in the colonies also married at a younger age. The **birth rate** rose accordingly, since women who married earlier had time for about two additional pregnancies during their childbearing years. On average, a married woman had a child every two to three years before menopause. Some women had as many as 20 pregnancies over their lifetime, making for large families. Benjamin Franklin, for example, had sixteen brothers and sisters.

Birthing children, however, was also dangerous, since most babies were delivered at home in often unsanitary conditions and harsh weather. Miscarriages were common. Between 25 and 50 percent of women died during birthing or soon thereafter, and almost a quarter of all babies did not survive infancy, especially during the early stages of a colonial settlement. Each year, more deaths occurred among young children than any other age group.

Disease and epidemics were rampant in colonial America. In 1713, Boston minister Cotton Mather lost three of his children and his wife to a measles epidemic. (Mather lost eight of fifteen children in their first year of life.) Martha Custis, the Virginia widow who married George Washington, had four children during her first marriage, all of whom died young, at ages two, three, sixteen, and seventeen.

Overall, however, mortality rates in the colonies were lower than in Europe. Because fertile land was plentiful, famine seldom occurred after the early years of settlement, and, although the winters were more severe than in England, firewood was abundant.

The average age in the new nation in 1790 was sixteen years; because the colonial population was younger on the whole, Americans, as a group, were less susceptible to disease than were Europeans. Colonists' longevity reflected

Colonial farm This plan of a newly cleared farm shows how trees were cut down and the stumps left to rot.

the different living conditions in America. The majority of colonists lived in sparsely populated settlements and were less likely to be exposed to infectious diseases. That began to change, of course, as colonial cities grew larger and more congested, and trade and travel increased. By the mid–eighteenth century, the colonies were beginning to see levels of contagion much like those in the cities of Europe.

WOMEN IN THE COLONIES

In contrast to the colonies of New Spain and New France, English America had far more women, which largely explains the difference in population growth rates among the European empires competing in the Americas. More women did not mean more equality, however. Most colonists brought to America deeply rooted convictions about the inferiority of women. As one New England minister stressed, "the woman is a weak creature not endowed with [the] strength and constancy of mind [of men]."

Women, as had been true for centuries, were expected to focus their time and talents on what was then called the "domestic sphere." They were to obey and serve their husbands, nurture their children, and maintain their households. Governor John Winthrop insisted that a "true wife" would find contentment only "in subjection to her husband's authority." The wife's role, said another Puritan, was "to guide the house etc. and not guide the husband." A wife should view her spouse with "a noble but generous Fear, which proceeds from Love."

Women in most colonies could not vote, hold office, attend schools or colleges, bring lawsuits, sign contracts, or become ministers. Divorces were usually granted only for desertion or "cruel and barbarous treatment," and no matter who was named the "guilty party," the father received custody of the children. A Pennsylvania court did see fit to send a man to prison for throwing a loaf of hard bread at his wife, "which occasioned her Death in a short Time."

"**WOMEN'S WORK**" Virtually every member of a household, regardless of age or gender, worked, and no one was expected to work harder than women. As John Cotton, a Boston minister, admitted in 1699, "women are creatures without which there is no Comfortable living for a man." Women who failed to perform the work expected of them were punished as if they were servants or slaves. In 1643, Margaret Page of Salem, Massachusetts, was jailed "for being a lazy, idle, loitering person."

During the eighteenth century, **women's work** typically involved activities in the house, garden, and fields. Unmarried women often worked outside their home. Many moved into other households to help with children or to make clothes. Others stayed at home but took in children or spun thread into yarn to exchange for cloth. Still others hired themselves out as apprentices to learn a skilled trade or craft. Throughout colonial America, there were women silversmiths, blacksmiths, shoemakers, sailmakers, shopkeepers, and mill owners. Other women operated laundries or bakeries. Technically, any money earned by a married woman was the property of her husband.

Farm women usually rose and prepared breakfast by sunrise and went to bed soon after dark. They were responsible for building the fire and hauling water from a well or creek. They fed and watered the livestock, woke the children, churned butter, tended the garden, prepared lunch (the main meal of the

The First, Second, and Last Scene of Mortality Prudence Punderson's needlework (ca. 1776) shows the domestic path, from cradle to coffin, followed by most affluent colonial women.

day), played with the children, worked the garden again, prepared dinner, milked the cows, got the children ready for bed, and cleaned the kitchen before retiring. Women also combed, spun, spooled, wove, and bleached wool for clothing; knitted linen and cotton, hemmed sheets, pieced quilts; made candles and soap; chopped wood, hauled water, mopped floors, and washed clothes. Female indentured servants in the southern colonies commonly worked as field hands, weeding, hoeing, and harvesting.

Meals in colonial America differed according to ethnic groups. The English focused their diet on boiled or broiled meats—venison, mutton, beef, and pork. Meals were often cooked in one large cast iron pot, combining "stew meat" with potatoes and vegetables which were then smothered with butter and seasoned with salt. Puddings made of bread or plums were the favorite dessert, while beer with just a little alcohol content was the most common beverage, even for children and infants. Cooking was usually done over a large open fireplace. The greatest accidental killer of women was kitchen fires that ignited long dresses.

One of the most lucrative trades among colonial women was the oldest: prostitution. Many servants took up prostitution after their indenture was fulfilled, and the colonial port cities had thriving brothels. They catered to sailors and soldiers, but men from all walks of life, married and unmarried, frequented what were called "bawdy houses," or, in Puritan Boston, "disorderly houses." Virginia's William Byrd, perhaps the wealthiest man in the colony, complained in his diary that he had walked the streets of Williamsburg trying to "pick up a Whore, but could not find one."

Local authorities frowned on such activities. In Massachusetts, convicted prostitutes were stripped to the waist, tied to the back of a cart, and whipped as it moved through the town. In South Carolina, several elected public officials were dismissed because they were caught "lying with wenches." New York City officials ordered raids on brothels in 1753. Some two dozen "ladies of pleasure" were arrested, and five of them were subjected to a public whipping. Some enslaved women whose owners expected sexual favors turned the tables by demanding compensation.

On occasion, circumstances forced women to exercise leadership outside the domestic sphere. Such was the case with South Carolinian Elizabeth Lucas Pinckney (1722–1793). Born in the West Indies, raised on the island of Antigua, and educated in England, "Eliza" moved with her family to Charleston, South Carolina, at age fifteen, when her father, George Lucas, inherited three plantations. The following year, however, Lucas, a British army officer and colonial administrator, was called back to Antigua, leaving Eliza to care for her ailing mother and younger sister—and to manage three plantations worked by slaves. She wrote a friend in England, "I have the business of three plantations to transact, which requires much writing and more business and fatigue . . . [but] by rising early I find I can go through much business."

Eliza loved the "vegetable world," and experimented with several crops before focusing on *indigo*, a West Indian plant that produced a much-coveted blue dye for coloring fabric, especially military uniforms. Indigo made her family a fortune, as it did for many other plantation owners on the Carolina coast. In 1744, she married Charles Pinckney, a widower twice her age, who was speaker of the South Carolina Assembly. She made him promise that she could continue to manage the plantation.

As Eliza began raising children, she "resolved to make a good wife to my dear husband . . . a good mother to my children . . . a good mistress to my servants [making] their lives as comfortable as I can." She also pledged "not to be luxurious or extravagant in the management of my table [family budget] and family on the one hand, nor niggardly and covetous, or too anxiously concerned about it on the other."

In the towns, women commonly served as tavern hostesses and shop-keepers and occasionally worked as doctors, printers, upholsterers, painters, and silversmiths. Often, these women were widows carrying on their dead husbands' trade or business, and they became accustomed to some measure of social authority in a "man's world."

WOMEN AND RELIGION   During the colonial era, no denomination allowed women to be ordained as ministers. Only the Quakers let women hold church offices and preach (exhort) in public. Puritans cited biblical passages claiming that God required "virtuous" women to submit to male authority and remain "silent" in congregational matters. Governor John Winthrop demanded that women "not meddle in such things as are proper for men" to manage.

Women who challenged ministerial authority were usually prosecuted and punished. Yet by the eighteenth century, as is true today, women made up the overwhelming majority of church members. Their disproportionate atten-dance at church services and revivals worried many ministers, since a femi-nized church was presumed to be a church in decline.

In 1692, the influential Boston minister Cotton Mather observed that there "are far more Godly Women in the world than there are Godly Men." In explaining this phenomenon, Mather put a new twist on the old notion of women being the weaker sex. He argued that the pain associated with child-birth, which had long been interpreted as the penalty women paid for Eve's sinfulness, was in part what drove women "more frequently, & the more fer-vently" to commit their lives to Christ.

In colonial America, the religious roles of black women were quite dif-ferent from those of their white counterparts. In most West African tribes, women were not subordinate to men and frequently served as priests and cult leaders. Although some enslaved Africans had been exposed to Christianity or Islam in Africa, most of them tried to sustain their traditional African religion once they arrived in the colonies.

In America, black women (and men) were often excluded from church membership for fear that Christianized slaves might seek to gain their free-dom. To clarify the situation, Virginia in 1667 passed a law specifying that children of slaves would be slaves even if they had been baptized as Christians.

Over time, the colonial environment did generate slight improvements in the status of women. The acute shortage of women in the early years made them more highly valued than they were in Europe, and the Puritan emphasis on a well-ordered family life led to laws protecting wives from physical abuse and allowing for divorce. In addition, colonial laws gave wives greater control over property that they had contributed to a marriage or that was left after a husband's death. But the age-old notion of female subordination and domesticity remained firmly entrenched in colonial America. As a Massachusetts boy maintained in 1662, the superior aspect of life was "masculine and eternal; the feminine inferior and mortal."

SOCIETY AND ECONOMY IN THE SOUTHERN COLONIES

As the southern colonies matured, inequalities of wealth became more visible, and social life grew more divided. The use of enslaved Indians and Africans to grow and process the crops most in demand in Europe generated enormous wealth for a few large landowners and their families. Socially, the planters and merchants increasingly became a class apart from the "common folk." They dominated the legislatures, bought luxury goods from London and Paris, and built brick mansions with formal gardens—all the while looking down upon their social "inferiors," both white and black.

Warm weather and plentiful rainfall enabled the southern colonies to grow the **staple crops** (most profitable; also called cash crops) valued by the mother country: tobacco, rice, sugarcane, and indigo. Virginia, as King Charles I put it, was "founded upon smoke." Tobacco production soared during the seventeenth century. "In Virginia and Maryland," wrote a royal official in 1629, "tobacco . . . is our All, and indeed leaves no room for anything else."

The same was true for rice cultivation in South Carolina and Georgia. Using only hand tools, slaves transformed the coastal landscapes, removing trees from swamps and wetlands infested with snakes, alligators, and mosquitos. They then created a system of floodgates to allow workers to drain or flood the fields as needed. Over time, the rice planters became the wealthiest group in the British colonies. As plantations grew in size, the demand for enslaved laborers, first Native Americans, and later Africans, rose dramatically.

The first English immigrants to Virginia and Maryland (the Chesapeake colonies) built primitive one-room huts with dirt floors and little privacy. They provided limited protection from the cold and wind and rotted quickly. A visitor to Virginia in 1622 reported that the colony's huts "were the worst I ever saw." Eventually, colonists built sparsely furnished cabins on stone or brick foundations roofed with thatched straw. The spaces between the log timbers were "chinked" with "wattle and daub"—a mix of mud, sand, straw, and wooden stakes that when dried formed a sturdy wall or seam. There were few furnishings in most colonial homes. Because most of the huts or cabins were

Virginia plantation wharf Southern colonial plantations were often constructed along rivers, with easy access to oceangoing vessels, as shown on this 1730 tobacco label.

too small for beds, residents slept on the floor and used blankets to keep warm. Rarely did they have glass to fill windows. Instead, they simply used wooden shutters to cover the openings.

SOCIETY AND ECONOMY IN NEW ENGLAND

Environmental, social, and economic factors contributed to the remarkable diversity among the early American colonies. New England was quite different from the southern and middle Atlantic regions: more-governed by religious concerns, less focused on commercial agriculture, more-engaged in trade, and much less involved with slavery.

TOWNSHIPS Whenever New England towns were founded, the first public structure built was usually a church. By law, every town had to collect taxes to support a church, and every resident—whether a church member or not—was required to attend midweek and Sunday religious services. The average New Englander heard 7,000 sermons in a lifetime.

The Puritans believed that God had created a *covenant*, or contract, in which people formed a congregation for common worship. This led to the idea of people joining together to form governments, but the principles of democracy were not part of Puritan political thought. Puritan leaders sought to do the will of God, not to follow the will of the people, and the ultimate source of authority was not majority rule but the Bible as interpreted by ministers and magistrates (political leaders).

Unlike the settlers in the southern colonies or in Dutch New York, few New England colonists received huge tracts of land. *Township grants* were usually awarded to organized groups of settlers, often already gathered into a church congregation. They would request from the General Court a "town" (what elsewhere was commonly called a township). They then divided the land according to a rough principle of equity. Those who invested more or had larger families or greater status might receive more land, while the town retained some pasture and woodland in common and held other tracts for later arrivals.

DWELLINGS AND DAILY LIFE The first colonists in New England initially lived in caves, tents, or cabins, but they soon built simple wood-frame

Housing in colonial New England This frame house, built in the 1670s, belonged to Rebecca Nurse, one of the women hanged as a witch in Salem Village in 1692.

houses. The roofs were steeply pitched to reduce the buildup of snow and were covered with thatched grasses or reeds. By the end of the seventeenth century, most New England homes were plain but sturdy dwellings centered on a fireplace. Some had glass windows brought from England. Interior walls were often plastered and whitewashed, but it was not until the eighteenth century that the exteriors of most houses were painted, usually a deep "Indian" red. The interiors were dark, illuminated by candles or oil lamps, both of which were expensive; out of practicality, most people usually went to sleep soon after sunset.

Family life revolved around the main room on the ground floor, called the hall, where meals were cooked in a large fireplace and where the family lived most of the time (hence, they came to be called *living* rooms). Food would be served at a table of rough-hewn planks, called the board. The father was sometimes referred to as the "chair man" because he sat in the only chair (the origin of the term *chairman of the board*). The rest of the family usually stood or sat on stools or benches and ate with their hands and wooden spoons. Forks were not introduced until the eighteenth century. A typical meal consisted of corn, boiled meat, and vegetables washed down with beer, cider, rum, or milk. Cornbread was a daily favorite, as was cornmeal mush, known as hasty pudding.

THE NEW ENGLAND ECONOMY   Early New England farmers and their families led hard lives. Clearing rocks from the glacier-scoured soil might require sixty days of hard labor per acre. The growing season was short, and no staple crops for sale in markets grew in the harsh climate. The crops and livestock were those familiar to the English countryside: wheat, barley, oats, some cattle, pigs, and sheep.

Many New Englanders turned to the sea for their livelihood. Codfish had been a regular element of the European diet for centuries, and the waters off the New England coast had the heaviest concentrations of cod in the world. Whales, too, abounded in New England waters. They supplied oil for lighting and lubrication, as well as ambergris, a waxy substance used in the manufacture of perfumes.

New Englanders exported dried fish to Europe, with lesser grades going to the West Indies as food for slaves. The thriving fishing industry encouraged the development of shipbuilding, and the growing experience and expertise at seafaring spurred transatlantic commerce. Rising incomes and a booming trade with Britain and Europe soon brought a taste for luxury goods in New England that clashed with the Puritan ideal of plain living and high thinking. In 1714, a worried Puritan deplored the "great extravagance that people are fallen into, far beyond their circumstances, in their purchases, buildings, families, expenses, apparel, generally in the whole way of living."

SHIPBUILDING The abundant forests of New England represented a source of enormous wealth. Old-growth trees were especially prized for use as ships' masts and spars (on which sails were attached). Early on, the British government claimed the tallest and straightest American trees, mostly white pines and oaks, for use by the Royal Navy. At the same time, British officials encouraged the colonists to develop their own shipbuilding industry. American-built ships quickly became known for their quality and price. It was much less expensive to purchase ships built in America than to transport American timber to Britain for ship construction, especially since a large ship might require as many as 2,000 trees. Nearly a third of all British ships were made in the colonies.

Profitable fisheries Catching, curing, and drying codfish in Newfoundland in the early 1700s. For centuries, the rich fishing grounds of the North Atlantic provided New Englanders with a prosperous industry.

TRADE By the end of the seventeenth century, the New England colonies had become part of a complex North Atlantic commercial network, trading not only with the British Isles and the British West Indies but also—often illegally—with Spain, France, Portugal, the Netherlands, and their colonies.

Trade in New England and the middle colonies differed from that in the South in two respects: their lack of staple crops to exchange for English goods was a relative disadvantage, but the success of shipping and commercial enterprises worked in their favor. After 1660, to protect its agriculture and fisheries, the English government placed prohibitive duties (taxes) on fish, flour, wheat, and meat, while leaving the door open to timber, furs, and whale oil, products in great demand in the home country. Between 1698 and 1717, New England and New York bought more from England than they exported to it, creating an unfavorable trade balance, as more of their coins went out than came in.

These circumstances gave rise to the **triangular trade**, in which New Englanders, for example, shipped rum to the west coast of Africa, where it was

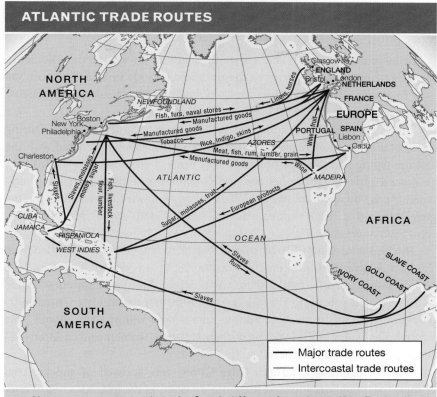

ATLANTIC TRADE ROUTES

Glasgow
ENGLAND
Bristol London
NETHERLANDS
FRANCE

NORTH
AMERICA

NEWFOUNDLAND
Linens, horses
EUROPE

Fish, furs, naval stores
Manufactured goods

New York Boston
Manufactured goods
PORTUGAL SPAIN
Philadelphia
Tobacco
Rice, indigo, skins
Lisbon
Cadiz

Charleston
Meat, fish, rum, lumber, grain
AZORES
Manufactured goods

Wine, fruit

Slaves, molasses, money, sugar
flour, lumber
Fish, livestock
ATLANTIC
MADEIRA

Wine

Sugar, molasses, fruit
European products

AFRICA
CUBA
JAMAICA
HISPANIOLA
OCEAN
WEST INDIES
Slaves
Rum

Slaves

SLAVE COAST
GOLD COAST
IVORY COAST

SOUTH
AMERICA

Slaves

—— Major trade routes
—— Intercoastal trade routes

- How was overseas trade in the South different from that in New England and the middle colonies?
- What was the "triangular trade"?
- What were North America's most important exports?

exchanged for slaves; took the enslaved Africans to the West Indies to sell; and returned home with various West Indian commodities, including molasses, from which New Englanders then manufactured rum. In another version, they shipped provisions to the West Indies, carried sugar and molasses to England, and returned with goods manufactured in Europe.

THE DEVIL IN NEW ENGLAND The Puritans who settled New England were religious fundamentalists who looked to the Bible for authority and inspiration. They read the Bible daily and memorized much of it. Yet at times, religious zeal could get out of hand. The strains of Massachusetts's transition from Puritan utopia to royal colony reached a tragic climax in 1692 amid the witchcraft hysteria at Salem Village, some fifteen miles north of Boston.

Belief in witchcraft was widespread throughout Europe and the colonies in the seventeenth century. Prior to the dramatic episode in Salem, almost 300 New Englanders (mostly middle-aged women) had been accused of practicing witchcraft, and more than 30 had been hanged.

The Salem episode was unique in its scope and intensity, however. During the winter of 1691–1692, several adolescent girls became fascinated with the fortune telling and voodoo practiced by Tituba, a slave from Barbados. The entranced girls began to behave oddly—shouting, barking, crawling, and twitching for no apparent reason. When asked who was tormenting them, the girls replied that three women—Tituba, Sarah Good, and Sarah Osborne— were Satan's servants.

The Reverend Samuel Parris, whose daughter claimed to be bewitched, beat Tituba, his slave, until she confessed. Authorities then arrested Tituba and the other accused women. Two of them were hanged, but not before they named other supposed witches in the village and more young girls experienced inexplicable fits. Soon the wild accusations spread, and within a few months, the Salem Village jail was filled with more than 150 men, women, and children—all accused of practicing witchcraft.

When a prominent farmer, Giles Corey, was accused of supernatural crimes, his neighbors lowered him into an open grave, placed a board over his body, and began loading it with heavy boulders to force a confession. After three days of such abuse, the defiant old man finally succumbed, having muttered only two words: "more weight!" By denying guilt and choosing death, Corey ensured that his estate would go to his son rather than be confiscated by the government. That convicted witches forfeited their property, which was then put up for sale, revealed the practical benefits and self-interested motives behind some of the accusations.

As the allegations and executions multiplied, leaders of the Massachusetts Bay Colony began to worry that the witch hunts were out of control. The governor finally intervened when his own wife was accused of serving the devil. He disbanded the special court in Salem and ordered the remaining suspects released, including Tituba, who had languished in jail for thirteen months.

By then, nineteen people (including some men married to women who had been convicted) had been hanged—all justified by the Biblical verse that tells believers not to "suffer a witch to live." A year after it had begun, the witchcraft frenzy was finally over.

What explains Salem's mass hysteria? It may have represented nothing more than theatrical adolescents trying to enliven the dreary routine of everyday life. Some historians have stressed that most of the accused witches were women, many of whom had in some way defied the traditional roles assigned to females.

Still another interpretation suggests that the accusations may have reflected the panicky atmosphere caused by frequent Indian attacks occurring just north of Salem, along New England's northern frontier. Some of the accusing girls had seen their families killed by Indians.

Whatever its actual causes, the witchcraft controversy also reflected the peculiar social tensions and personal feuds in Salem Village. Late in 1692, as the hysteria subsided, several girls were traveling through nearby Ipswich when they encountered an old woman. "A witch!" they shouted and began writhing as if possessed. But the people of Ipswich showed no interest, and the "bewitched" girls picked themselves up and continued on their way.

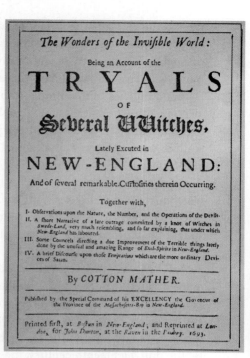

The Wonders of the Invisible World Title page of the 1693 London edition of Cotton Mather's account of the Salem witchcraft trials. Mather, a prominent Boston minister, warned his congregation that the devil's legions were assaulting New England.

SOCIETY AND ECONOMY IN THE MIDDLE COLONIES

Both geographically and culturally, the middle colonies (New York, New Jersey, Pennsylvania, Delaware, and Maryland) stood between New England and the South. They reflected the diversity of colonial life and foreshadowed the pluralism of the future nation.

AN ECONOMIC MIX The middle colonies produced surpluses of foodstuffs for export to the slave-based plantations of the South and the West Indies: wheat, barley, oats, and other grains, flour, and livestock. Three great rivers—the Hudson, the Delaware, and the Susquehanna—and their tributaries provided access to the backcountry of Pennsylvania and New York, which opened up a rich fur trade with Native Americans. The region's bustling commerce thus rivaled that of New England.

Land policies in the middle colonies followed the *headright* system prevalent in the Chesapeake colonies. In New York, the early royal governors continued the Dutch device of the patroonship, granting to influential men (called "patroons") vast estates on Long Island and throughout the Hudson and Mohawk Valleys north of New York City. The patroons controlled large domains farmed by tenants (renters) who paid fees to use the landlords' mills, warehouses, smokehouses, and docks. With free land available elsewhere, however, New York's population languished, and the new waves of immigrants sought the promised land of Pennsylvania.

AN ETHNIC MIX   In the makeup of their population, the middle colonies differed from both New England's Puritan settlements and the biracial plantation colonies to the south. In New York and New Jersey, Dutch culture and language lingered. Along the Delaware River near Philadelphia, the first settlers—Swedes and Finns—were overwhelmed by an influx of Europeans. By the mid–eighteenth century, the middle colonies were the fastest-growing region in North America.

The Germans came to America (primarily Pennsylvania) mainly from the Rhineland region of Europe, which had suffered from brutal religious wars that pitted Protestants against Catholics. William Penn's recruiting brochures in German translation circulated throughout central Europe, and his promise of religious freedom appealed to many persecuted sects, especially the Mennonites, German Baptists whose beliefs resembled those of the Quakers.

In 1683, a group of Mennonites founded Germantown, near Philadelphia. They represented the first wave of German migrants, a large proportion of whom paid their way as indentured servants, or "redemptioners." The large numbers of penniless German immigrants during the eighteenth century alarmed many English colonists. Benjamin Franklin worried that the Germans "will soon . . . outnumber us."

Throughout the eighteenth century, the Scots-Irish moved still farther out into the Pennsylvania backcountry. ("Scotch-Irish" is the more common but inaccurate name for the Scots-Irish, a mostly Presbyterian population transplanted from Scotland to northern Ireland by the English government a century earlier to give Catholic Ireland a more Protestant tone.).

Land was the great magnet attracting the poor Scots-Irish immigrants. They were, said a recruiting agent, "full of expectation to have land for nothing" and

MAJOR IMMIGRANT GROUPS IN COLONIAL AMERICA

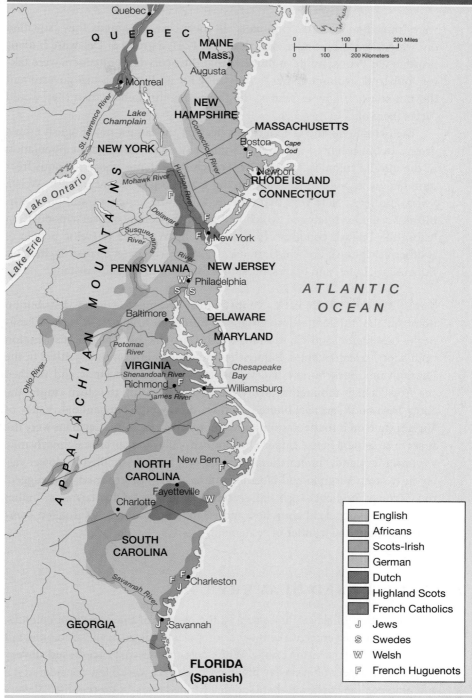

QUEBEC
- Quebec
- Montreal
- Lake Champlain
- St. Lawrence River

MAINE (Mass.)
- Augusta

NEW HAMPSHIRE
- Connecticut River

MASSACHUSETTS
- Boston
- Cape Cod
- Newport
- Lake Ontario
- Lake Erie

NEW YORK
- Mohawk River
- Hudson River
- Delaware River
- Susquehanna River
- New York

RHODE ISLAND
CONNECTICUT

APPALACHIAN MOUNTAINS

PENNSYLVANIA
- Philadelphia

NEW JERSEY

DELAWARE
- Baltimore

MARYLAND
- Potomac River

VIRGINIA
- Shenandoah River
- Richmond
- James River
- Williamsburg
- Chesapeake Bay
- Ohio River

ATLANTIC OCEAN

NORTH CAROLINA
- New Bern
- Fayetteville
- Charlotte

SOUTH CAROLINA
- Charleston
- Savannah River

GEORGIA
- Savannah

FLORIDA (Spanish)

Scale: 0 — 100 — 200 Miles / 0 — 100 — 200 Kilometers

Legend:
- English
- Africans
- Scots-Irish
- German
- Dutch
- Highland Scots
- French Catholics
- J Jews
- S Swedes
- W Welsh
- F French Huguenots

- What attracted German immigrants to the middle colonies?
- Why did the Scots-Irish spread across the Appalachian backcountry?
- Where did the first Jews settle in America? How were they received?

were "unwilling to be disappointed." In most cases, the lands they "squatted on" were claimed by Native Americans. In 1741, a group of Delaware Indians protested to Pennsylvania authorities that the Scots-Irish intruders were taking "our land" without giving "us anything for it." If the colonial government did not stop the flow of whites, the Delawares threatened, then they would "drive them off."

The Scots-Irish and the Germans became the largest non-English ethnic groups in the colonies. Other ethnic minorities also enriched the population in the middle colonies: Huguenots (French Protestants whose religious freedom had been revoked in 1685, forcing many to leave France), Irish, Welsh, Swiss, and Jews. New York had inherited from the Dutch a tradition of ethnic and religious tolerance, which had given the colony a diverse population before the English conquest: French-speaking Walloons (a Celtic people of southern Belgium), French, Germans, Danes, Portuguese, Spaniards, Italians, Bohemians, Poles, and others, including some New England Puritans.

THE BACKCOUNTRY Pennsylvania became the great distribution point for the different ethnic groups of European origin, just as the Chesapeake Bay region and Charleston, South Carolina, became the distribution points for African peoples. Before the mid–eighteenth century, settlers in the Pennsylvania backcountry had trespassed across Indian lands and reached the Appalachian mountain range. Rather than crossing the steep ridges, the Scots-Irish and Germans filtered southward down the Shenandoah Valley of Virginia and on into the Carolina and Georgia backcountry. Germans were the first white settlers in the Upper Shenandoah Valley in southern Pennsylvania, western Maryland, and northern Virginia, and Scots-Irish filled the lower valley in western Virginia and North Carolina. Feisty, determined, and rugged, the German and Scots-Irish settlers built cabins and tended farms on Indian lands, built evangelical churches, and established contentious isolated communities along the frontier of settlement.

RACE-BASED SLAVERY

The institution of slavery is central to the history of the American colonies. During the late seventeenth century, slavery was legalized in all the colonies but was most prevalent in the South. White colonists viewed **race-based slavery** as a normal aspect of everyday life in an imperfect world; few considered it a moral issue. They believed that God determined one's "station in life." Slavery was therefore not a social evil but a "personal misfortune" dictated by God. Not until the late eighteenth century did large numbers of white Europeans and Americans begin to raise ethical questions about slavery.

Initially, during the seventeenth century, many of the first Africans in America were treated like indentured servants, with a limited term of service, after which they gained their freedom. Antonio, an African, arrived in Jamestown during the early 1620s and worked as a servant for fourteen years before gaining his freedom. He thereafter married an African woman, changed his name to Anthony Johnson, and developed a substantial farm of his own along the Virginia shore.

Until the mid–seventeenth century, no laws in the colonies specified the meaning and scope of the word "slavery." Gradually, however, *life-long* slavery for blacks became the custom—and the law—of the land. By the 1660s, colonial legislatures had begun to legalize the institution of race-based slavery, with detailed **slave codes** regulating most aspects of their lives. The South Carolina code, for example, defined all "Negroes, Mulattoes, and Indians" sold into bondage as slaves for life, as were the children born of enslaved mothers.

In 1667, the Virginia legislature declared that slaves could not serve on juries, travel without permission, or gather in groups of more than two or three. Some colonies even prohibited owners from freeing their slaves (manumission). The codes allowed owners to punish slaves by whipping them, slitting their noses, cutting their ankle cords, castrating men, or killing them. In 1713, a South Carolina planter punished a slave by closing him up in a tiny coffin to die, only to have his son slip in a knife so that he could kill himself rather than await suffocation.

COLOR PREJUDICE   More than a century before the English arrived in America, the Portuguese and Spanish had established a global trade in enslaved Africans (in Spanish, the word *negro* means "black"). While English settlers often enslaved Indian captives, as had the Spanish and Portuguese before them, the Europeans did not enslave other Europeans who were captured in warfare. Color was the crucial difference, or at least the crucial rationalization used to justify the institution of slavery and its hellish brutalities.

The English associated the color black with darkness and evil. To them, the different appearance, behavior, and customs of Africans and Native Americans represented savagery and heathenism. Colonial Virginians justified slavery by convincing themselves that blacks (and Indians) were naturally lazy, treacherous, and stupid, among other shortcomings.

COLONIAL SLAVERY During the seventeenth and eighteenth centuries, the profitable sugar-based economies of the French and British West Indies and Portuguese Brazil had the greatest demand for enslaved Africans, as sugar became valued almost as much as gold or silver. By 1675, the island colonies in the Caribbean had more than 100,000 slaves, while slaves in the American colonies numbered about 5,000. The profits generated by sugar colonies in the Caribbean were greater than all of the commerce in the American mainland colonies.

As tobacco, rice, and indigo crops became more established in Maryland, Virginia, and the Carolinas, however, the number of African slaves in those colonies grew enormously. At the same time, the flow of white indentured servants from Britain and Europe to America was slowing. Between 1700 and 1709, only 1,500 indentured servants arrived in the American colonies; 9,000 enslaved Africans arrived during the same period. Until the eighteenth century, English immigrants made up 90 percent of the American colonists. After 1700, the largest number of new arrivals were enslaved Africans who totaled more than all European immigrants combined.

The shifting popularity of black slaves over white servants reflected the growing industry of slave trading. In the late seventeenth century, the profitability of African slavery led dozens of new slave trading companies to emerge, both in Europe and America, thus expanding the availability of enslaved Africans and lowering the price. American colonists preferred slaves because they were officially viewed as property with no civil rights, and they (and their offspring) were servants for life, not for a fixed number of years. Africans were preferred over enslaved Indians because they could not escape easily in a land where they stood out because of their dark skin. In short, African slaves offered a better investment for colonial Americans.

THE MARKET IN SLAVES Once a slave ship arrived at an American port, Africans in chains, not knowing any English, would be auctioned to the highest bidder, who would cart them off to begin lifelong work for a complete stranger. They were usually forbidden to use their former languages, practice African religions, or to sustain their native cultures. With only rare exceptions, slaves were allowed to own nothing.

Enslaved Africans were used in virtually all aspects of the expanding colonial economy. The vast majority worked on farms or plantations, often performing strenuous labor from dawn to dusk in oppressive heat and humidity. As Jedidiah Morse, a prominent Charleston minister, admitted in the late eighteenth century, "No white man, to speak generally, ever thinks of settling a farm, and improving it for himself, without negroes."

During the eighteenth century, the demand for slaves soared in the southern colonies. By 1750, there were almost 250,000 slaves in British America. The vast majority resided in Virginia and Maryland, about 150,000 compared with 60,000 in South Carolina and Georgia.

As the number of slaves grew, so, too, did the breadth of their talents and expertise. Over time, slaves became skilled artisans: blacksmiths, carpenters, bricklayers. Many enslaved women worked as household servants and midwives. Typically, the first wave of enslaved Africans lived five years after arriving in America. Eight of the thirty-two slaves that John Mercer brought to his Virginia plantation in the early eighteenth century died in their first year.

SLAVE ABUSE AND RESISTANCE Colonial laws allowed whites to use brutal means to discipline and control their slaves. They were whipped, branded, castrated, or sold away, often to the Caribbean islands, where working conditions were even worse. A 1669 Virginia law declared that accidentally killing a slave who was being whipped or beaten was not a serious crime. During a three-year period, a South Carolina overseer whipped five slaves to death. William Byrd II, a wealthy Virginia planter, confessed that the "unhappy effect of owning many Negroes is the necessity of being severe."

Colonial newspapers were sprinkled with notices about runaway slaves. A Georgia slave owner asked readers to be on the lookout for "a negro fellow named Mingo, about 40 years old, and his wife Quante, a sensible wench about 20 with her child, a boy about 3 years old, all this country born."

In a few cases, slaves organized armed rebellions in which they stole weapons, burned and looted plantations, and occasionally killed their captors. In the late summer of 1739, some twenty slaves attacked a store in Stono, South Carolina, south of Charleston. Led by a slave named Jemmy, they killed the owner, seized weapons, and headed south toward freedom in Spanish Florida, gathering more recruits along the way. Within a few days, the slaves had roamed over fifteen miles and killed twenty-five whites. The growing army of slaves marched in military formation, waving banners, beating drums, and freeing more slaves as they moved southward. Then the militia caught up with them. Most of the rebels were killed, and in the weeks that followed, sixty more were captured by enraged planters who "cut off their heads and set them up at every Mile Post."

The **Stono Rebellion** so frightened white planters that they convinced the colonial assembly to pass the so-called Negro Act of 1740, which called for more oversight of slave activities and harsher punishments for rebellious behavior. It also reduced the penalty for a white killing a slave to a minor offense and banned slaves from testifying in courts.

SLAVERY IN NEW YORK CITY In contrast to the experience of slaves in the southern colonies, most slaves in the northern colonies lived in towns or cities, and their urban environs gave them more opportunities to move about. New York City had more slaves than any other American city. By 1740, it was second only to Charleston in the percentage of slaves in its population.

As the number of slaves increased in the congested city, racial fears and tensions mounted—and occasionally exploded. In 1712, several dozen slaves revolted; they started fires and then used swords, axes, and guns to kill whites as they attempted to fight the fires. Called out to restore order, the militia captured twenty-seven slaves. Six committed suicide, and the rest were executed; some were burned alive. New York officials thereafter passed their own black code that strictly regulated slave behavior.

The harsh regulations did not prevent another major racial incident. In the bitterly cold March of 1741, city dwellers worried about a series of suspicious

Slavery in New Amsterdam (1642) The significance of African slaves to the colonial economy is the focus of this engraving of the Dutch colony New Amsterdam, later known as New York City.

fires, including one at the governor's house. Their worst fear was that the fires were set by slaves. "The Negroes are rising!" shouted terrified whites.

The frantic city council launched an intense investigation to find the "villains." Mary Burton, a sixteen-year-old white indentured servant, told authorities that slaves and poor whites were plotting to "burn the whole town" and kill the white men. The plotters were supposedly led by John Hughson, a white trafficker in stolen goods who owned the tavern where Mary Burton worked. His wife, two slaves, and a prostitute were charged as co-conspirators. Despite their denials, all were convicted and hanged. Within weeks, more than half of the adult male slaves in the city were in jail. What came to be called the Conspiracy of 1741 finally ended after seventeen slaves and four whites were hanged; thirteen more blacks were burned at the stake, while many more were deported.

Such organized rebellions were rare, however, in large part because the likelihood of success was so small and the punishments so severe. Much more common were subtler forms of resistance and accommodation adopted by enslaved Africans—stealing food, breaking tools, destroying crops, feigning illness, etc.

COLONIAL CITIES

Throughout the seventeenth and eighteenth centuries, the American colonies were mostly populated by farmers or farmworkers. But a handful of cities blossomed into dynamic urban centers of political and social life. Economic opportunity drove most city dwellers. In New York City, for example, a visitor said the "art of getting money" dominated everything the residents did.

Colonial cities hugged the coastline or, like Philadelphia, sprang up on rivers large enough to handle oceangoing vessels. Never comprising more than 10 percent of the colonial population, the large coastal cities had a disproportionate influence on commerce, politics, society, and culture. By the end of the colonial period, Philadelphia, with some 30,000 people, was the largest city in the colonies, and New York City, with about 25,000, ranked second. Boston numbered 16,000; Charleston, South Carolina, 12,000; and Newport, Rhode Island, 11,000.

THE SOCIAL AND POLITICAL ORDER The urban social elite was dominated by wealthy merchants and property owners served by a middle class of shop owners, innkeepers, and skilled craftsmen. Almost two thirds of urban male workers were artisans—people who made their living at

The Rapalje Children John Durand painted the children of a wealthy Brooklyn merchant wearing clothing typical of upper-crust urban society.

handicrafts. They included carpenters and coopers (barrel makers), shoemakers and tailors, silversmiths and blacksmiths, sailmakers, stonemasons, weavers, and potters. At the bottom of the social order were sailors, manual laborers, servants, and slaves.

Colonial cities were busy, crowded, and dangerous. Epidemics such as cholera, malaria, and yellow fever were common. The use of open fireplaces for heating caused frequent fires that in turn led to the development of fire companies. Rising crime and violence required increased policing of neighborhoods by sheriffs and local militias.

Colonists also were concerned about the poor and homeless. The number of Boston's poor receiving aid from colonial authorities rose from 500 in 1700 to 4,000 in 1736; in New York City, the number rose from 250 in 1698 to 5,000 in the 1770s. Those designated "helpless" among the destitute poor, especially the disabled, elderly, widows, and orphans, were often provided money, food, clothing, and fuel. In some towns, "poorhouses" were built to house the homeless poor and provide them with jobs.

THE URBAN WEB Overland travel in the colonies was initially by horse or by foot. Inns and taverns (also called public houses, or pubs) were especially important since travel at night was treacherous—and Americans loved to drink. (During the colonial period, it was said that when the Spanish settled an area, they would first build a church; the Dutch would first erect a fort; and the English would first construct a tavern.) In 1690, Boston alone had fifty-four taverns, half of them operated by women.

Colonial taverns and inns were places to eat, relax, read a newspaper, play cards, gossip, and conduct business. And, of course, they were the most popular places to drink alcoholic beverages: beer, hard cider, and rum, which became the favored drink. But ministers and magistrates began to worry that the pubs were promoting drunkenness and social rebelliousness. Not only

Taverns A tobacconist's business card from 1770 captures men talking in a
Philadelphia tavern while they drink ale and smoke pipes.

were poor whites drinking heavily, but also Indians, which, one governor told
the assembly, would have "fatal consequences to the Government."

Early in the eighteenth century, ministers succeeded in passing an anti-
tavern law in Massachusetts Bay Colony. Called the Act against Intemperance,
Immorality, and Profaneness, it was directed at taverns that had become "nurseries of intemperance." It tightened the process of issuing licenses for the sale
of liquor, eliminated fiddle-playing in pubs, called for the public posting of the
names of "common drunkards," and banned the sale of rum and brandy, the
most potent beverages.

After a few years, however, the law was rarely enforced, and the concerns
about taverns and drinking continued. In 1726, a Bostonian declared that "the
abuse of strong Drink is becoming Epidemical among us, and it is very justly
Supposed . . . that the Multiplication of Taverns has contributed not a little to
this Excess of Riot and Debauchery." The failed 1712 law was the last legislative
effort to restrict alcohol consumption before the Revolution.

By the end of the seventeenth century, there were more taverns in America
than any other business. Indeed, taverns became the most important social
institution in the colonies—and the most democratic. They were places where
rich and poor often intermingled, and by the mid–eighteenth century, they
would become the gathering places for protests against British rule.

Long-distance communication was a more complicated matter. Postal service in the seventeenth century was almost nonexistent—people gave letters to travelers or sea captains in hopes they would be delivered. Under a parliamentary law of 1710, the postmaster of London named a deputy in charge of the colonies, and a postal system eventually encompassed most of the Atlantic Seaboard, providing the colonies with an effective means of communication that would prove crucial in the growing controversy with Great Britain.

More reliable mail delivery spurred the growing popularity of newspapers. Before 1745, twenty-two newspapers had been started: seven in New England, ten in the middle colonies, and five in the South. An important landmark in the development of freedom of the press was John Peter Zenger's 1735 trial for publishing criticisms of New York's royal governor in his newspaper, the *New-York Weekly Journal*. English common law held that one might be punished for libel, or criticism that fostered "an ill opinion of the government." Zenger's lawyer claimed that the editor had published the truth. The jury agreed and found the editor not guilty.

THE ENLIGHTENMENT IN AMERICA

The most significant of the new European ideas circulating in eighteenth-century America grew out of a burst of innovative intellectual activity known as the **Enlightenment**, a profound breakthrough in understanding human society and the natural world. The Enlightenment celebrated rational inquiry, scientific research, and individual freedom. Enlightened people were those who sought the truth, wherever it might lead, rather than remain content with believing ideas and dogmas passed down through the ages or taken from the Bible.

Immanuel Kant, the eighteenth-century German philosopher, summed up the Enlightenment point of view by saying: "Dare to know! Have the courage to use your own understanding." He and others used the power of reason to analyze the workings of nature, and they employed new tools like microscopes and telescopes to engage in close observation, scientific experimentation, and precise mathematical calculation.

THE AGE OF REASON The Enlightenment, often called the Age of Reason, was triggered when the ancient view that the earth was at the center of the universe was challenged by the controversial, heliocentric (sun-centered) solar system described in 1533 by Nicolaus Copernicus, a Polish astronomer and Catholic priest. His theory that the earth orbits the sun was scorned by Catholic officials before it was confirmed by other scientists.

In 1687, Englishman Isaac Newton (1642–1727) announced his transformational theory of the earth's gravitational pull. Using both scientific experiments and mathematics, especially calculus, Newton challenged biblical notions of the world's workings by depicting a changing, dynamic universe moving in accordance with natural laws that could be grasped by human reason and explained by mathematics. He implied that natural laws (rather than God) govern all things, from the orbits of the planets to the effects of gravity to the science of human relations: politics, economics, and society.

Some enlightened people, called **Deists**, carried Newton's scientific outlook to its logical conclusion, claiming that God created the world and designed its "natural laws," and that these laws governed the operation of the universe. In other words, Deists insisted that God planned the universe and set it in motion, but no longer interacted directly with the earth and its people. So the rational God of the Deists was nothing like the intervening (providential) God of the Christian tradition, to whom believers prayed for daily guidance and direct support.

Evil, according to the Deists, resulted not from humanity's inherent *sinfulness* as outlined in the Bible but from human *ignorance* of the rational laws of nature. Therefore, the best way to improve both society and human nature, according to Deists such as Thomas Jefferson and Benjamin Franklin, was by cultivating Reason, which was the highest Virtue. (Enlightenment thinkers often capitalized both words.) By using education, reason, and scientific analysis, societies were bound to improve their knowledge as well as their quality of life.

Faith in human progress was thus one of the most important beliefs of the Enlightenment. Equally important was the enlightened notion of political freedom. Both Jefferson and Franklin were intrigued by the English political philosopher John Locke (1632–1704), who maintained that "natural law" called for a government resting on the consent of the governed and respecting the "natural rights" of all. This idea would later influence colonial leaders' efforts to justify a revolution.

THE AMERICAN ENLIGHTENMENT Benjamin Franklin epitomized the Enlightenment. Born in Boston in 1706, Franklin left home at the age of seventeen, bound for Philadelphia. Six years later, he bought a print shop where he edited and published the *Pennsylvania Gazette*, one of the leading newspapers in the colonies. When he was twenty-six, he published *Poor

Benjamin Franklin A champion of rational thinking and common sense behavior, Franklin was an inventor, philosopher, entrepreneur, and statesman.

Richard's Almanack, a collection of seasonal weather forecasts, puzzles, household tips, and witty sayings. Before he retired from business at the age of forty-two, Franklin had founded a public library, started a fire company, helped create what became the University of Pennsylvania, and organized a debating club that grew into the American Philosophical Society.

Franklin was devoted to scientific investigation. Skeptical and curious, pragmatic and irreverent, he was an inventive genius. His wide-ranging experiments encompassed the fields of medicine, meteorology, geology, astronomy, and physics, among others. He developed the Franklin stove, the lightning rod, bifocal spectacles, and a glass harmonica.

Although raised as a Presbyterian, Franklin became a Deist who prized science and reason. He questioned the divinity of Jesus and the assumption that the Bible was truly the word of God. Like the European Deists, Franklin came to believe in a God that had created a universe directed by natural laws. For Franklin and others, to be "enlightened" meant developing the confidence and capacity to think for oneself, to think critically rather than simply accepting what tradition dictated as truth.

EDUCATION IN THE COLONIES White colonial Americans were among the most literate people in the world. Almost 90 percent of men (more than in England) could read. For the colonists at large, education in the traditional ideas and manners of society—even literacy itself—remained primarily the responsibility of family and church. The modern concept of free public education would not be fully embraced until the nineteenth century. Yet colonists were concerned from the beginning that steps needed to be taken to educate their young.

The Puritan emphasis on reading Scripture, which all Protestants shared to some degree, led to the emphasis on literacy. In 1647, the Massachusetts Bay Colony required every town to support a grammar school (a "Latin school" that could prepare a student for college).

The Dutch in New Netherland were as interested in education as the New England Puritans. In Pennsylvania, the Quakers established private schools. In the southern colonies, however, schools were rare. The wealthiest southern planters and merchants sent their children to England for schooling or hired tutors.

THE GREAT AWAKENING

The growing popularity of Enlightenment rationalism posed a direct threat to traditional religious life in Europe and America. But Christianity has always shown remarkable resilience in the face of challenging new ideas. This was certainly true in the early eighteenth century, when the American colonies experienced a widespread revival of spiritual zeal designed to restore the primacy of emotion in the religious realm.

A   In *Adam's* Fall We Sinned all.

B   Thy Life to Mend This *Book* Attend.

C   The *Cat* doth play And after flay.

D   A *Dog* will bite A Thief at night.

E   An *Eagles* flight Is out of fight.

F   The Idle *Fool* Is whipt at School.

Colonial education A page from the rhymed alphabet of *The New England Primer*, a popular American textbook first published in the 1680s.

Between 1700 and 1750, when the controversial ideas of the Enlightenment were circulating among the best-educated colonists, hundreds of new Christian congregations were founded. Most Americans (85 percent) lived in colonies with an "established" church, meaning that the colonial government officially endorsed—and collected taxes to support—a single official denomination.

The Church of England, also known as Anglicanism, was the established church in Virginia, Maryland, Delaware, and the Carolinas. Puritan Congregationalism was the official faith in most of New England. In New York, Anglicanism vied with the Dutch Reformed Church for control. Pennsylvania had no single state-supported church, but Quakers dominated the legislative assembly. New Jersey and Rhode Island had no official denomination and hosted numerous Christian splinter groups.

Most colonies organized religious life on the basis of local parishes, which defined their theological boundaries and defended them against people who did not hold to the same faith. In colonies with official tax-supported religions, people of other faiths could not preach without the permission of the parish. In the 1730s and 1740s, the parish system was thrown into turmoil by the arrival of outspoken traveling evangelists, called *itinerants*, who claimed that most of the local parish ministers were incompetent. In their emotionally charged sermons, the itinerants, several of whom were white women and African Americans, insisted that Christians must be "reborn" in their convictions and behavior.

REVIVALISM   During the early 1730s, worries about the erosion of religious fervor helped spark a series of emotional revivals known as the **Great Awakening**. The revivals quickly spread up and down the Atlantic coast. Every social class, ethnic group, and region that participated was swept up in the ecstasy of renewed spiritual passion. In the process, the revivals divided congregations, towns, and families, and fueled the growth of new denominations, especially the Baptists and Methodists. A skeptical Benjamin Franklin admitted that the Awakening was having a profound effect on social life: "Never did the people show so great a willingness to attend sermons. Religion is become the subject of most conversation."

Jonathan Edwards One of the foremost preachers of the Great Awakening, Edwards dramatically described the torments that awaited sinners in the afterlife.

JONATHAN EDWARDS   In 1734–1735, a remarkable spiritual transformation occurred in the congregation of Jonathan Edwards, a prominent Congregationalist minister in the western Massachusetts town of Northampton. One of America's most brilliant philosophers and theologians, Edwards had entered Yale College in 1716, at age thirteen, and graduated at the top of his class four years later.

When Edwards arrived in Northampton in 1727, he was shocked by the town's lack of religious conviction. He claimed that the young people of Northampton were preoccupied with sinful pleasures; they indulged in "lewd practices" that "corrupted others."

He warned that Christians had become dangerously obsessed with making and spending money, and that the new ideas associated with the Enlightenment were eroding the importance of religious life.

To counteract the secularizing forces of the Enlightenment, Edwards rushed to restore the emotional side of religion. "Our people," he said, "do not so much need to have their heads stored [with new scientific knowledge] as to have their hearts touched [with spiritual intensity]."

Edwards was fiery and charismatic. His vivid descriptions of the sufferings of hell and the delights of heaven helped rekindle spiritual intensity among his congregants. By 1735, he could report that "the town seemed to be full of the presence of God; it never was so full of love, nor of joy." To judge the power of the religious awakening, he thought, one need only observe that "it was no longer the Tavern" that drew local crowds, "but the Minister's House."

In 1741, Edwards delivered his most famous sermon, "Sinners in the Hands of an Angry God." It was designed in part to frighten people into seeking salvation. Edwards reminded the congregation that hell is real and that God "holds you over the pit of hell, much as one holds a spider, or some loathsome insect, over the fire, abhors you, and is dreadfully provoked. . . . He looks upon you as worthy of nothing else, but to be cast into the fire." When he finished, he had to wait several minutes for the agitated congregants to quiet down before he led them in a closing hymn.

GEORGE WHITEFIELD The most celebrated promoter of the Great Awakening was a young English minister, George Whitefield, whose reputation as a spellbinding evangelist preceded him to the colonies. Congregations were lifeless, he claimed, "because dead men preach to them." Too many ministers were "slothful shepherds and dumb dogs."

Whitefield set out to restore the fires of religious intensity in America. In the autumn of 1739, the twenty-five-year-old evangelist began a fourteen-month tour, preaching to huge crowds from Maine to Georgia. His critics were as fervent as his admirers. A disgusted

George Whitefield The English minister's dramatic eloquence roused Americans, inspiring many to experience a religious rebirth.

Bostonian described a revival meeting's theatrics: "The meeting was carried on with . . . some screaming out in Distress and Anguish . . . some again jumping up and down . . . some lying along on the floor. . . . The whole with a very great Noise, to be heard at a Mile's Distance, and continued almost the whole night."

The short, thin, cross-eyed Whitefield enthralled audiences with his golden voice, flamboyant style, and unparalleled eloquence. His sermons produced electric effects. Even Benjamin Franklin, a confirmed rationalist who went to see Whitefield preach in Philadelphia, was so excited by the fiery sermon that he emptied his pockets into the collection plate.

Whitefield urged his listeners to experience a "new birth"—a sudden, emotional moment of conversion and salvation. By the end of his sermon, one listener reported, the entire congregation was "in utmost Confusion, some crying out, some laughing, and Bliss still roaring to them to come to Christ, as they answered, I will, I will, I'm coming, I'm coming."

RADICAL EVANGELISTS Edwards and Whitefield inspired many imitators, the most radical of whom carried emotional evangelism to extremes, stirring up women as well as those at the bottom of society—laborers, seamen, servants, slaves, and landless farm folk—and ordaining their own ministers.

William Tennent, an Irish-born Presbyterian revivalist, charged that many local ministers were "cold and sapless," afraid to "thrust the nail of terror into sleeping souls." Tennent's oldest son, Gilbert, also an evangelist, defended his aggressive tactics by explaining that he and other traveling preachers invaded parishes only when the local minister showed no interest in the "Getting of Grace and Growing in it."

The Tennents urged people to renounce their ministers and pursue salvation on their own. They also attacked the excesses of the wealthy and powerful. Worried members of the colonial elite charged that the radical revivalists were spreading "anarchy, levelling, and dissolution."

Equally unsettling to the elite was the Reverend James Davenport, the most radical of the revivalists, who urged Christians to renounce "ratio-

Singing Procession in 1740 This engraving depicts a characteristic New England singing procession at the height of the Great Awakening.

nalist" ministers influenced by the Enlightenment and become the agents of their own salvation through a purely emotional conversion experience. A Connecticut minister warned that Davenport and other extremists were "frightening people out of their senses" rather than offering reasonable sermons.

In 1743, in New London, Connecticut, Davenport attracted a huge crowd by building a bonfire and encouraging people to burn their fancy clothes and rationalist books. A few weeks later, the unstable Davenport reversed himself and called his rantings "enthusiastical and delusive."

WOMEN AND REVIVALS

The Great Awakening's most controversial element was the emergence of women who defied the biblical ban against women speaking in religious services. Scores of women served as lay exhorters, including Sarah Haggar Osborne, a Rhode Island schoolteacher who organized prayer meetings that eventually included men and women, black and white. When concerned ministers told her to stop, she refused to "shut my mouth and doors and creep into obscurity."

Similarly, in western Massachusetts, Bathsheba Kingsley stole her husband's horse to spread the gospel among her rural neighbors because she had received "immediate revelations from heaven." When her husband tried to intervene, she pummeled him with "hard words and blows," praying loudly that he "go quick to hell." Jonathan Edwards denounced Kingsley as a "brawling woman" who should "keep chiefly at home." For all of the turbulence created by the revivals, however, churches, even the more democratic Baptist and Methodist congregations, remained male bastions of political authority.

A CHANGING RELIGIOUS LANDSCAPE The Great Awakening made religion intensely personal by creating both a deep sense of spiritual guilt and an intense yearning for redemption. Yet it also undermined many of the established churches by emphasizing that all individuals, regardless of wealth or social status, could receive God's grace without the guidance of ministers. Denominations became bitterly divided as "Old Light" conservatives criticized disruptive and democratic revivalism and sparred with "New Light" evangelicals who delighted in provoking emotional outbursts among their listeners and celebrating individual freedom in matters of faith. Jonathan Edwards, for one, regretted the emergence of warring factions. We are "like two armies," he said, "separated and drawn up in battle array, ready to fight one another."

New England religious life would never be the same, as Puritanism disintegrated amid the intense warfare over the revivals of the Great Awakening.

The Puritan ideal of religious uniformity was shattered. The crusty Connecticut Old Light minister, Isaac Stiles, denounced the "intrusion of choice into spiritual matters" and charged that the "multitudes were seriously, soberly, and solemnly out of their wits" in their embrace of ultra-emotional religion. John Henry Goetschius, a Dutch Reformed evangelist, shot back that Stiles and other Old Lights were simply determined to "impose on many people, against their will, their old, rotten, and stinking routine religion."

In Anglican Virginia, some fifty Baptist evangelists were jailed for disturbing the peace during the Great Awakening. New England subsequently attracted more and more Baptists, Presbyterians, Anglicans, and other denominations, while the revival frenzy scored its most lasting victories along the western frontier of the middle and southern colonies.

In the more sedate churches of Boston, the principle of rational or enlightened religion gained the upper hand in a reaction against the excesses of revivalistic emotion. Boston ministers such as Charles Chauncey and Jonathan Mayhew found Puritan theology too cold and forbidding. To them, the Calvinist concept that people could be forever damned by predestination was irrational. They embraced many insights drawn from Enlightenment rationalism, arguing that God created laws of nature which people could discover and exploit.

RELIGIOUS COLLEGES   In reaction to taunts that "born-again" revivalist ministers lacked learning, the Awakening gave rise to denominational colleges that became the distinctive characteristic of American higher education. The three colleges already in existence had religious origins: Harvard College, founded in 1636 because the Puritans dreaded "to leave an illiterate ministry to the church when our present ministers shall lie in the dust"; the College of William and Mary, created in 1693 to strengthen the Anglican ministry; and Yale College, set up in 1701 to educate the Puritans of Connecticut, who believed that Harvard was drifting from the strictest orthodoxy. The College of New Jersey, later Princeton University, was founded by Presbyterians in 1746.

In close succession came King's College (1754) in New York, later renamed Columbia University, an Anglican institution; the College of Rhode Island (1764), later called Brown University, which was Baptist; Queens College (1766), later known as Rutgers, which was Dutch Reformed; and Dartmouth College (1769), which was Congregationalist and the outgrowth of a school for Indians.

THE HEART VERSUS THE HEAD   Like a ferocious fire that burned intensely before dying out, the Great Awakening subsided by 1750. The emotional

Awakening, like its counterpart, the rational Enlightenment, influenced the forces leading to the revolution against Great Britain and set in motion powerful currents that still flow in American life.

Ministers could no longer control the direction of religious life, as more and more people took charge of their own spirituality and new denominations sprouted like mushrooms. The Awakening implanted in American culture the evangelical impulse and the emotional appeal of revivalism, weakened the status of the old-fashioned clergy and state-supported churches, and encouraged believers to exercise their own individual judgment. By encouraging the proliferation of denominations, it heightened the need for toleration of dissent.

In some respects, however, the warring Awakening and the Enlightenment, one stressing the urgings of the spirit and the other celebrating the cold logic of reason, led by different roads to similar ends. Both movements spread across the mainland colonies and thereby helped bind them together. Both emphasized the power and right of individual decision-making, and both aroused hopes that America would become the promised land in which people might attain the perfection of piety or reason, if not both.

By urging believers to exercise their own spiritual judgment, revivals weakened the authority of the established churches and their ministers, just as colonial resentment of British economic regulations would later weaken the colonists' loyalty to the king. As such, the Great Awakening and the Enlightenment helped nurture a growing commitment to individual freedom and resistance to authority that would play a key role in the rebellion against British "tyranny" in 1776.

CHAPTER REVIEW

SUMMARY

- **Colonial Demographics**   Cheap land lured poor immigrants to America. The initial shortage of women eventually gave way to a more equal gender ratio and a tendency to earlier marriage than in Europe, leading to higher *birth rates* and larger families. People also lived longer on average in the colonies than in Europe. The lower *death rates* led to rapid population growth in the colonies.

- **Women in the Colonies**   English colonists brought their traditional beliefs and prejudices with them to America, including convictions about the inferiority of women. Colonial women remained largely confined to *women's work* in the house, yard, and field. Over time, though, necessity created new opportunities for women outside their traditional roles.

- **Colonial Differences**   A thriving colonial trading economy sent raw materials such as fish, timber, and furs to England in return for manufactured goods. The expanding economy created new wealth and a rise in the consumption of European goods, and it fostered the expansion of slavery. Agriculture diversified: tobacco was the *staple crop* in Virginia, rice in the Carolinas. Plantation agriculture based on slavery became entrenched in the South. New England's prosperous shipping industry created a profitable *triangular trade* among Africa, America, and England. By 1790, German, Scots-Irish, Welsh, and Irish immigrants, as well as other European ethnic groups, had settled in the middle colonies, along with Quakers, Jews, Huguenots, and Mennonites.

- **Race-Based Slavery**   Deep-rooted prejudice led to *race-based slavery*. Africans were considered "heathens" whose supposed inferiority entitled white Americans to use them for slaves. Africans brought diverse skills to help build America's economy. The use of African slaves was concentrated in the South, where landowners used them to produce lucrative staple crops, such as tobacco, rice, and indigo. But slaves lived in cities, too, especially New York. As the slave population increased, race relations grew more tense, and *slave codes* were created to regulate the movement of enslaved people. Sporadic slave uprisings, such as the *Stono Rebellion*, occurred in both the North and South.

- **The Enlightenment and the Great Awakening**   Printing presses, education, and city life created a flow of new ideas that circulated via long-distance travel, tavern life, the postal service, and newspapers. The attitudes of the *Enlightenment* were transported along international trade routes. Sir Isaac Newton's scientific discoveries culminated in the belief that Reason could improve society. Benjamin Franklin, who believed that people could shape their own destinies, became the face of the Enlightenment in America. *Deism* expressed the religious views of the Age of Reason. By the 1730s, a revival of faith, the *Great Awakening*, swept through the colonies. New congregations formed as evangelists insisted that Christians be "reborn." Individualism, not orthodoxy, was stressed in this first popular religious movement in America's history.

CHRONOLOGY

1619	First Africans arrive at Jamestown
1636	Harvard College is established
1667	Virginia enacts slave code declaring that enslaved children who were baptized as Christians remained slaves
1692	Salem witchcraft trials
1730s–1740s	Great Awakening
1735	John Peter Zenger is tried for seditious libel
1739	Stono Rebellion
	George Whitefield preaches his first sermon in America, in Philadelphia
1741	Jonathan Edwards preaches "Sinners in the Hands of an Angry God"

KEY TERMS

death rate p. 110

birth rate p. 110

women's work p. 112

staple crops p. 116

triangular trade p. 120

race-based slavery p. 126

slave codes p. 127

Stono Rebellion p. 129

Enlightenment p. 134

Deists p. 135

Great Awakening p. 138

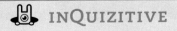 INQUIZITIVE

Go to InQuizitive to see what you've learned—and learn what you've missed—with personalized feedback along the way.

4 From Colonies to States

Boston Tea Party Disguised as Native Americans, a swarm of Patriots boarded three British ships and dumped more than 300 chests of East India Company tea into Boston Harbor.

Four great European naval powers—Spain, France, England, and the Netherlands (Holland)—created colonies in North America during the sixteenth and seventeenth centuries as part of their larger fight for global supremacy. Throughout the eighteenth century, wars raged across Europe, mostly pitting the Catholic nations of France and Spain against Protestant Great Britain and the Netherlands. The conflicts increasingly spread to the Americas, and by the middle of the eighteenth century, North America had become a primary battleground, involving both colonists and Native Americans allied with different European powers.

Spain's sparsely populated settlements in the borderlands north of Mexico were small and weak compared to those in the British colonies. The Spanish had failed to create colonies with robust economies. Instead, Spain emphasized the conversion of native peoples to Catholicism, prohibited manufacturing within its colonies, strictly limited trade with the Native Americans, and searched—in vain—for gold.

The French and British colonies developed a thriving trade with Native Americans at the same time that the fierce rivalry between Great Britain and France gradually shifted the balance of power in Europe. By the end of the eighteenth century, Spain and the Netherlands would be in decline, leaving France and Great Britain to fight for dominance. The nearly constant warfare led Great Britain to tighten its control over the American colonies to raise the funds needed to combat France and Spain. Tensions over the British effort to preserve its empire at the expense of American freedoms would lead first to rebellion and eventually to revolution.

focus questions

1. What were the similarities and differences in the way that the British and French empires administered their colonies before 1763?

2. What were some of the effects of the French and Indian War? How did it change relations among the European powers in North America?

3. In what ways did the British try to strengthen their control over the colonies after the French and Indian War? How did the colonies respond?

4. What were the underlying factors in the events of the 1770s that led the colonies to declare their independence from Britain?

COMPETING NEIGHBORS

The French established colonies in North America at the same time as the English. The bitter rivalry between Great Britain and France fed France's desire to challenge the English presence in the Americas by establishing Catholic settlements in the Caribbean, Canada, and the region west of the Appalachian Mountains. Yet the French never invested the people or resources in North America that the English did. During the 1660s, the population of New France was less than that of the tiny English colony of Rhode Island. By the mid-eighteenth century, the residents of New France numbered less than 5 percent of British Americans.

NEW FRANCE

The actual settlement of New France began in 1605, when soldier-explorer Samuel de Champlain, the "Father of New France," founded Port-Royal in Acadia, along the eastern Canadian coast. Three years later, Champlain established Quebec, to the west, along the St. Lawrence River (*Quebec* is an Algonquian word meaning "where the river narrows"). Champlain was the first European to explore and map the Great Lakes.

Champlain in New France Samuel de Champlain firing at a group of Iroquois, killing two chieftains (1609).

Until his death in 1635, Champlain governed New France on behalf of trading companies exploiting the fur trade with the Indians. The trading companies sponsored Champlain's voyages in hopes of creating a prosperous commercial colony. In 1627, however, the French government ordered that only Catholics could live in New France. This restriction stunted its growth—as did the harsh winter climate. As a consequence, the number of French who colonized Canada was *much* smaller than the number of British, Dutch, and Spanish colonists in other North American colonies.

Champlain knew that the outnumbered French could survive only by befriending the native peoples. To that end, he dispatched young trappers and traders to live with the indigenous peoples, learn their languages and customs, marry native women, and serve as ambassadors of New France. Many of these hardy woodsmen were *coureurs des bois* (runners of the woods), who pushed into the forested regions around the Great Lakes and developed a thriving fur trade.

In 1663, French King Louis XIV changed struggling New France into a royal colony led by a governor-general who modeled his rule after that of the absolute monarchy. New France was fully subject to the French king. The French colonists had no political rights or elected legislature, and public meetings could not be held without official permission.

To solidify New France, the king dispatched soldiers and settlers during the 1660s, including shiploads of young women, known as the King's Daughters, to be wives for the mostly male colonists. Louis XIV also awarded large grants of land, called *seigneuries*, to lure aristocratic settlers. The poorest farmers usually rented land from the *seigneur*.

Yet none of these efforts transformed New France from being essentially a fur-trading outpost. Only about 40,000 French immigrants came to the Western Hemisphere during the seventeenth and eighteenth centuries, even though the population of France was three times that of Spain. By 1750, when the British colonists in North America numbered about 1.5 million, the total French population was 70,000.

From their Canadian outposts along the Great Lakes, French explorers in the early 1670s moved southward down the Mississippi River to the Gulf of Mexico. Louis Jolliet, a fur trader born in Quebec, teamed with Father Jacques Marquette, a Jesuit priest fluent in Indian languages, to explore the Wisconsin River south to the Mississippi River. Traveling in canoes, they paddled south to within 400 miles of the Gulf of Mexico, where they turned back for fear of encountering Spanish soldiers.

Other French explorers followed. In 1682, René-Robert Cavelier, sieur de La Salle, organized an expedition that started in Montreal, crossed the Great Lakes, and made it all the way down the Mississippi River to the Gulf

THE FRENCH IN NORTH AMERICA

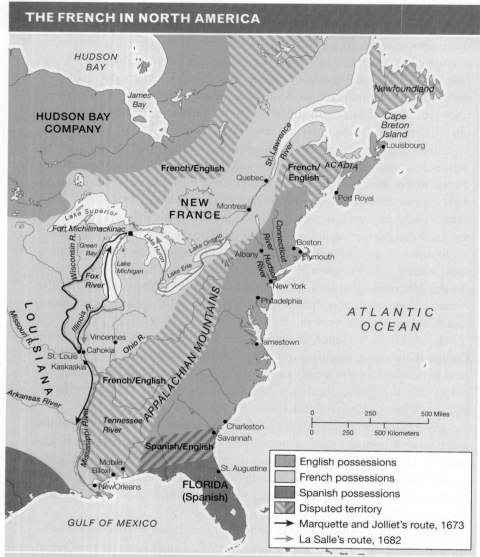

■ Where were the largest French settlements in North America?
■ How were they different from the Spanish and English colonies?
■ Describe the French colonization of the Louisiana Territory.

of Mexico, the first European to do so. La Salle, who learned seven different Indian languages, hoped to create a string of fur-trading posts along the entire length of the river. Near what is today Venice, Mississippi, he buried an engraved plate and erected a cross, claiming for France the vast Ohio and Mississippi Valleys—all the way to the Rocky Mountains. He named the entire region Louisiana, after King Louis XIV.

Settlement of the Louisiana Territory finally began in 1699, when the French established a colony near Biloxi, Mississippi. The main settlement then moved to Mobile Bay and, in 1710, to the present site of Mobile, Alabama.

For nearly fifty years, the driving force in Louisiana was Jean-Baptiste Le Moyne, sieur de Bienville. Sometimes called the Father of Louisiana, he served periodically as governor, and in 1718 he founded New Orleans, which shortly thereafter became the capital of the sprawling Louisiana colony encompassing much of the interior of the entire North American continent.

New France had one important advantage over its British rival: access

Jesuits in New France Founded in 1539, the Jesuits sought to convert Indians to Catholicism, in part to make them more reliable trading partners and military allies.

to the great inland rivers that led to the heartland of the continent and the pelts of fur-bearing animals: beaver, otter, and mink. In the Illinois region, French settlers began farming the fertile soil, while Jesuits established missions to convert the Indians at places such as Terre Haute ("High Land," in what is now Indiana) and Des Moines ("Of the Monks," in present-day Iowa—the name probably shortened from Rivière des Moines, or "River of the Monks").

THE BRITISH COLONIAL SYSTEM

The diverse British colonies in North America were quite different from those of New France. The colonial governments typically were headed by a royal governor or proprietor who could appoint and remove officials, command the militia, and grant pardons to people convicted of crimes.

The British colonies, unlike the Spanish, French, or Dutch colonies, had *elected* legislatures; the "lower" houses were chosen by popular vote. Like Parliament, the assemblies controlled the budget and could pass laws and regulations. Most colonial assemblies exercised influence over the royal governors by paying their salaries. Unlike in New France, self-government in British America was expected and cherished.

MERCANTILISM The English Civil War during the 1640s sharply reduced the flow of money and people to America and created great confusion regarding colonial policies. It also forced English Americans to take sides in the conflict between Royalists and Puritans.

The 1651 victory of Oliver Cromwell's Puritan army over the monarchy had direct effects in the colonies. As England's new ruler, Cromwell embraced **mercantilism**, a political and economic policy adopted by most European monarchs during the seventeenth century. In a mercantile system, the government controlled all economic activities in an effort to strengthen national power. Key industries were regulated, taxed, or "subsidized" (supported by payments from the government). People with specialized skills or knowledge of new industrial technologies, such as textile machinery, were not allowed to leave the country.

Mercantilism also supported the creation of global empires. Colonies, it was assumed, enriched the mother country in several ways: (1) by providing silver and gold as well as the raw materials (furs, fish, grains, timber, sugar, tobacco, indigo, tar, etc.) needed to supply food, build ships, and produce goods; (2) by creating a captive market of colonial consumers who would be forced to buy goods created in the home country; (3) by relieving social tensions and political unrest in the home country, because colonies could absorb the growing numbers of poor, unemployed, and imprisoned; and, (4) by not producing goods that would compete with those produced in the home country.

NAVIGATION ACTS Such mercantilist assumptions prompted Oliver Cromwell to adopt the first in a series of **Navigation Acts** intended to increase control over its colonial economies. The Navigation Act of 1651 required that all goods going to and from the colonies be carried *only* in British-owned ships built in Britain. The law was intended to hurt the Dutch, who had developed a flourishing business shipping goods between America and Europe. Dutch shippers charged much less to transport goods than did the English, and they actively encouraged smuggling in the American colonies as a means of defying the Navigation Acts. By 1652, England and the Netherlands were at war—the first of three naval conflicts that erupted between 1652 and 1674 involving the two Protestant rivals.

After the monarchy was restored to power in 1660, the new Royalist Parliament passed the Navigation Act of 1660, which specified that certain colonial products such as tobacco were to be shipped *only* to England or other colonies. The Navigation Act of 1663, called the Staples Act, required that *all* shipments of goods from Europe to America must first stop in Britain to be offloaded and taxed before being sent on to the colonies.

By 1700, the English had surpassed the Dutch as the world's leading maritime power, and most products sent to and from America via Europe and Africa were carried in British ships. What the English government did not predict or fully understand was that the mercantile system would arouse resentment in the colonies.

COLONIAL RESENTMENT   Colonial merchants and shippers loudly complained about the Navigation Acts, but the English government refused to lift its restrictions. New England, which shipped 90 percent of all American exports, was particularly hard hit. In 1678, a defiant Massachusetts legislature declared that the Navigation Acts had no legal standing. In 1684,

Boston from the southeast This view of eighteenth-century Boston shows the importance of shipping and its regulation in the colonies.

King Charles II tried to teach the rebellious colonists a lesson by revoking the royal charter for Massachusetts.

The following year, King Charles II died and was succeeded by his brother, King James II, the first Catholic monarch in more than 100 years. To demonstrate his power over Americans, the new king reorganized the New England colonies into a single royal supercolony called the Dominion of New England.

In 1686, the newly appointed royal governor, the authoritarian Sir Edmund Andros, arrived in Boston to take control of the Dominion. Andros stripped New Englanders of their civil rights, imposed new taxes as well as the Anglican religion, ignored town governments, strictly enforced the Navigation Acts, and punished smugglers who tried to avoid regulation altogether.

THE GLORIOUS REVOLUTION

In 1688, the Dominion of New England added the former Dutch provinces of New York, East Jersey, and West Jersey to its control, just a few months before the **Glorious Revolution** erupted in England in December. The revolution was called "Glorious" because it took place with little bloodshed. James II was forced to flee to France and was replaced by the king's Protestant daughter Mary and her Protestant husband William III, the ruling Dutch Prince.

William III and Mary II would rule as constitutional monarchs, their powers limited by the Parliament. The new king and queen soon issued a religious Toleration Act and a Bill of Rights to ensure that there never again would be an absolute monarchy in England.

In 1689, Americans in Boston staged their own revolution upon learning of the transfer of power in London. A group of merchants, ministers, and militiamen (citizen-soldiers) arrested Governor Andros and his aides and removed Massachusetts Bay Colony from the new Dominion of New England. Within a few weeks, the other colonies that had been absorbed into the Dominion also restored their independence.

William and Mary allowed all the colonies to regain their former status except Massachusetts Bay and Plymouth, which after some delay were united under a new charter in 1691 as the royal colony of Massachusetts Bay.

William and Mary, however, were determined to crack down on American smuggling and rebelliousness. They appointed new royal governors in Massachusetts, New York, and Maryland. In Massachusetts, the governor was given authority to veto acts of the colonial assembly, and he removed the requirement that only church members could vote in elections.

JOHN LOCKE ON REVOLUTION The Glorious Revolution in England had significant long-term effects on American history in that the removal of King James II revealed that a hated monarch could be deposed according to constitutional principles. The long-standing geographical designation "Great Britain" for the united kingdoms of England, Scotland, and Wales would soon be revived as the nation's official name.

A powerful justification for revolution appeared in 1690 when the English philosopher John Locke published his *Two Treatises on Government*, which had an enormous impact on political thought in the colonies. Locke rejected the "divine" right of monarchs to govern with absolute power. He also insisted that people are endowed with **natural rights** to life, liberty, and property. Locke noted that it was the need to protect those natural rights that led people to establish governments in the first place. When rulers failed to protect the property and lives of their subjects, Locke argued, the people had the right—in extreme cases—to overthrow the monarch and change the government.

An Emerging Colonial System

In early 1689, New Yorkers sent a message to King William thanking him for delivering England from "tyranny, popery, and slavery." Many colonists were disappointed, however, when the king cracked down on American smugglers. The Act to Prevent Frauds and Abuses of 1696 required colonial royal governors to enforce the Navigation Acts, allowed customs officials in America to use "writs of assistance" (general search warrants that did not have to specify the place to be searched), and ordered that accused smugglers be tried in royal *admiralty* courts (because juries in colonial courts rarely convicted their peers). Admiralty cases were decided by judges appointed by the royal governors.

Soon, however, British efforts to enforce the Navigation Acts waned. King George I (r. 1714–1727) and George II (r. 1727–1760), German princes who were descendants of James I, showed much less interest in enforcing colonial trade laws. Robert Walpole, the long-serving prime minister (1721–1742) and lord of the treasury, decided that the American colonies should be left alone to export needed raw materials (timber, tobacco, rice, indigo) and to buy various manufactured goods from the mother country.

Under Walpole's leadership, Britain followed a policy of "a wise and salutary neglect" of the Navigation Acts and gave the colonies greater freedom to pursue their economic interests. What Walpole did not realize was that such **salutary neglect** would create among many colonists an independent attitude that would eventually blossom into revolution.

THE HABIT OF SELF-GOVERNMENT Government within the American colonies evolved without plan during the eighteenth century as the colonial assemblies acquired powers, particularly with respect to government appointments, that Parliament had yet to exercise itself.

The English colonies in America, unlike New France and New Spain, benefited from elected legislative assemblies. Whether called the House of Burgesses (Virginia), Delegates (Maryland), Representatives (Massachusetts), or simply the assembly, the "lower" houses were chosen by popular vote. Only male property owners could vote, based upon the notion that only men who held a tangible "stake in society" could vote responsibly. Because property holding was much more widespread in America than in Europe, a greater proportion of the men could vote and hold office in the colonies. Members of the colonial assemblies tended to be wealthy, prominent figures, but there were exceptions. One unsympathetic colonist observed in 1744 that the New Jersey Assembly "was chiefly composed of mechanicks and ignorant wretches; obstinate to the last degree."

The most profound political trend during the early eighteenth century was the growing power exercised by the colonial assemblies. Like Parliament, the assemblies controlled the budget through their vote on taxes and expenditures, and they held the power to initiate legislation. Most of the colonial assemblies also exerted leverage on the royal governors by controlling their salaries. Throughout the eighteenth century the assemblies expanded their power and influence, sometimes in conflict with the governors, sometimes in harmony with them. Self-government in America became first a habit, then a "right." By the mid–eighteenth century, the American colonies had become largely self-governing.

WARFARE IN THE COLONIES

The Glorious Revolution of 1688 transformed relations among the great powers of Europe. Protestants William and Mary, for example, were passionate foes of Catholic France's Louis XIV. King William organized an alliance of European nations against the French in a transatlantic war known in the American colonies as King William's War (1689–1697).

It was the first of four major wars fought in Europe and the colonies over the next seventy-four years. In each case, Britain and its European allies fought against Catholic France or Spain and their allies. By the end of the eighteenth century, the struggle between the British and the French would shift the balance of power in Europe.

In all four of the wars except the last, the Seven Years' War, battles in the North American colonies were but a sideshow accompanying massive warfare in Europe. Although the wars involved many nations, including Indians who fought on both sides, the conflicts centered on the intense struggle for supremacy between the British and the French, a struggle that ended up profoundly shifting the international balance of power among the great powers of Europe.

The prolonged warfare during the eighteenth century had a devastating effect on New England, especially Massachusetts, for it was closest to the battlefields of French Canada. The wars also reshaped Britain's relationship with America. Great Britain emerged from the wars in 1763 as the most powerful nation in the world. Thereafter, international commerce became increasingly essential to the expanding British Empire, thus making the American colonies even more strategically significant.

THE FRENCH AND INDIAN WAR The most important conflict between Britain and France in North America was the **French and Indian War** (1754–1763), globally known as the **Seven Years' War**. Unlike the earlier wars, the French and Indian War started in America and ended with a decisive victory. It was sparked by French and British competition for the ancestral Indian lands in the vast Ohio Valley, and the stakes were high. Whoever controlled the "Ohio Country" would control the entire continent because of the Ohio and Mississippi Rivers.

To defend their interests in the Ohio Country, the French pushed south from Canada and built forts in the region. When Virginia's British governor learned of the forts, he sent an ambitious twenty-two-year-old militia officer, Major George Washington, to warn the French to leave. Washington made his way on foot and by horseback, canoe, and raft more than 450 miles to Fort Le Boeuf (just south of Lake Erie, in northwest Pennsylvania) in late 1753, only to be rudely rebuffed by the French.

A few months later, in the spring of 1754, Washington, now a lieutenant colonel, went back to the Ohio Country with 150 volunteer soldiers and Indian allies. They planned to build a fort where the Allegheny, Monongahela, and Ohio Rivers converged (where the city of Pittsburgh later developed). The so-called Forks of the Ohio was the key strategic gateway to the vast western territory west of the Appalachian Mountains, and both sides were determined to control it.

After two months of difficult travel through densely forested, hilly terrain, Washington learned that French soldiers had beaten him to the site and built Fort Duquesne in western Pennsylvania. Washington decided to camp about forty miles from the fort. The next day, the Virginians ambushed a French scouting party, killing ten soldiers, including the commander—the first fatalities in what would become the French and Indian War.

Washington and his troops, reinforced by more Virginians and British soldiers dispatched from South Carolina, hastily constructed a tiny circular stockade at Great Meadows in western Pennsylvania. They called it Fort Necessity. Washington remarked that the valley provided "a charming field for an encounter," but there was nothing charming about the battle that erupted when a large French force attacked in a rainstorm on July 3, 1754.

After the day-long, lopsided Battle of Great Meadows, Washington surrendered, having seen a third of his 300 men killed or wounded. The French and their Indian allies lost only three men. The French commander then forced Washington to surrender his French prisoners and admit that he had "assassi-

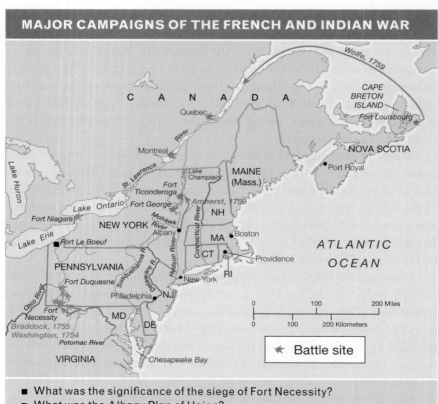

MAJOR CAMPAIGNS OF THE FRENCH AND INDIAN WAR

* Battle site

- What was the significance of the siege of Fort Necessity?
- What was the Albany Plan of Union?
- What led to the British victory over France in North America in 1759?

nated" the group of French soldiers at the earlier encounter. On July 4, 1754, Washington and the defeated Virginians began trudging home. Most of them, he noted, "are almost naked, and scarcely a man has either shoes, stockings, or hat."

France was now in undisputed control of the Ohio Country. Washington's bungled expedition not only had failed to oust the French; it had triggered a massive world war. As a British politician exclaimed, "the volley fired by a young Virginian in the backwoods of America set the world on fire."

THE ALBANY PLAN British officials, worried about war with the French and their Indian allies, urgently called a meeting of the northern colonies as far south as Maryland. Twenty-one representatives from seven colonies gathered in Albany, New York. It was the first time that a large group of colonial delegates had met to take joint action.

At the urging of Pennsylvania's Benjamin Franklin, the Albany Congress (June 19–July 11, 1754) approved the **Albany Plan of Union**. It called for eleven colonies to band together, headed by a president appointed by the king. Each colonial assembly would send two to seven delegates to a "grand council,"

The first American political cartoon Benjamin Franklin's plea to the colonies to unite against the French in 1754 would become popular again twenty years later, when the colonies faced a different threat.

which would have legislative powers. The Union would have jurisdiction over Indian affairs.

The Albany Plan of Union was too radical for the time, however. British officials and the colonial legislatures, eager to maintain their powers, wanted simply a military alliance against Indian attacks, so they rejected the Albany Plan. Benjamin Franklin later maintained that the Plan of Union, had it been adopted, may have postponed or eliminated the eventual need for a full-scale colonial revolution. Franklin's proposal, however, did have a lasting significance in that it would be the model for the form of governance (Articles of Confederation) created by the new American nation in 1777.

WAR IN NORTH AMERICA   With the failure of the Albany Plan, the British government decided to force a showdown with the "presumptuous" French in North America. In June 1755, a British fleet captured the French forts protecting Acadia, a colony of New France along the Atlantic coast of Canada. The British then expelled 11,500 Acadians, the Catholic French residents. Hundreds of them eventually found their way to French Louisiana, where they became known as Cajuns (the name derived from *Acadians*).

In 1755, the British government sent 1,000 soldiers to dislodge the French from the Ohio Country. The arrival of unprecedented numbers of "redcoat" soldiers on American soil would change the dynamics of British North America. Although the colonists endorsed the use of force against the French, they later would oppose the use of British soldiers to enforce colonial regulations.

BRADDOCK'S DEFEAT   The British commander in chief in America, General Edward Braddock, was a stubborn, overconfident officer who refused to recruit large numbers of Indian allies. Braddock viewed Indians with open contempt, telling those willing to fight with him that he would not reward them with land for doing so: "No savage should inherit the land." His dismissal of the Indians and his ignorance of unconventional warfare in American forests would prove fatal. Neither he nor his Irish troops had any experience fighting in the wilderness.

With the addition of some American militiamen, including George Washington as a volunteer officer, Braddock's force left northern Virginia to confront the French, hacking a 125-mile-long road west through the rugged Allegheny Mountains toward Fort Duquesne.

On July 9, 1755, as the British neared the fort, they were ambushed by French soldiers, Canadian militiamen, and Indians. The British troops, dressed in impractical bright-red wool uniforms in the summer heat, suffered shocking losses. Braddock was mortally wounded and would die three days later. Washington, his coat riddled by four bullets, helped lead a hasty retreat.

What came to be called the Battle of Monongahela was one of the worst British defeats in history. The French and Indians killed 63 of 86 British officers, 914 out of 1,373 soldiers, and captured the British cannons and supplies. Twelve of the wounded British soldiers left behind on the battlefield were stripped and burned alive by Indians. A devastated Washington wrote his brother that the British army had "been scandalously beaten by a trifling body of men." The vaunted redcoats "broke & run as sheep pursued by hounds," but the Virginians, he noted, "behaved like Men and died like Soldiers."

A WORLD WAR While Braddock's stunning defeat sent shock waves through the colonies, Indians allied with the French began attacking American farms throughout western Pennsylvania, Maryland, and Virginia, killing, scalping, or capturing hun-

From La Roque's *Encyclopedie des Voyages* An Iroquois warrior in an eighteenth-century French engraving.

dreds of men, women, and children. Desperate to respond, the Pennsylvania provincial government offered 130 Spanish dollars for each male Indian scalp and 50 dollars for female scalps.

Indians and colonists killed each other mercilessly throughout 1755 and 1756 during the French and Indian War. It was not until May 1756, however, that Protestant Britain and Catholic France formally declared war in Europe. The first truly "world war," the Seven Years' War in Europe and the French and Indian War in North America would eventually be fought on four continents and three oceans around the globe. In the end, it would redraw the political map of the world.

The onset of war brought into office a new British government, with William Pitt as prime minister. His exceptional ability and self-assurance matched his towering ego. "I know that I can save England and no one else can," he announced. Pitt assembled a huge force of 45,000 British troops and American militiamen, and in August 1759, they captured the French forts near the Canadian border at Ticonderoga, Crown Point, and Niagara.

THE BATTLE OF QUEBEC In 1759, the French and Indian War reached its climax with a series of British triumphs on land and at sea. The most decisive victory was at Quebec, the hilltop fortress city and the capital of French Canada. During the dark of night, some 4,500 British troops scaled the cliffs above the St. Lawrence River and at dawn surprised the unprepared French defenders in a battle that lasted only ten minutes. The French retreated, only to surrender four days later.

The Battle of Quebec was the turning point in the war. Thereafter, the conflict in North America diminished although the fighting dragged on until 1763. In the South, fighting flared up between the Carolina settlers and the Cherokee Nation. A force of British regulars and colonial militia broke Cherokee resistance in 1761.

A NEW BRITISH KING Meanwhile, the Seven Years' War played out around the globe. In Europe, huge armies ravaged each other. Hundreds of towns and cities were plundered and more than a million people killed.

George III The young king of a victorious empire.

On October 25, 1760, British King George II arose at 6 A.M., drank his morning chocolate milk, and suddenly died on his toilet as the result of a ruptured artery. His death shocked the nation and brought an untested new king to the throne.

George II's inexperienced successor was his twenty-two-year-old grandson, George III, who was despised by his grandfather. Although initially shy and insecure, the young king, the first in his German royal family to be born and raised in England, was an unabashed patriot: "I glory in the name of Britain." He became a strong-willed leader who oversaw the military defeat of France and Spain in the Seven Years' War. The Treaty of Paris, which ended the war, made Great Britain the ruler of an enormous world empire. The American colonists celebrated the great British victories with as much excitement and pride as did Londoners.

THE TREATY OF PARIS (1763) In the **Treaty of Paris**, signed in February 1763, Britain took control of many important French colonies around the world, including several incredibly profitable "sugar island" colonies in the West Indies, most of the French colonies in India, and all of France's North American possessions east of the Mississippi River: all of Canada and what was then called Spanish Florida (including much of present-day Alabama and Mississippi). As compensation, the treaty gave Spain control over the vast Louisiana Territory, including New Orleans and all French land west of the Mississippi River. The loss of Louisiana left France with no territory on the North American continent. British Americans were delighted with the outcome of the war. As a New England minister declared, Great Britain had reached the "summit of earthly grandeur and glory."

Britain's spectacular military success created massive challenges, however. The national debt doubled during the war, and the new cost of maintaining the sprawling North American empire, including the permanent stationing of British soldiers in the colonies, was staggering. In winning a huge global empire, British leaders developed what one historian has called an "arrogant triumphalism," which led them to tighten—and ultimately lose—their control over the Indians and colonists in North America.

MANAGING A NEW EMPIRE No sooner was the Treaty of Paris signed than King George III and his cabinet, working through Parliament, began strictly enforcing economic regulations on the American colonies to help reduce the crushing national debt caused by the war. During and after the war, the British government increased taxes in Britain to fund the military expenses. In 1763, the average British citizen paid twenty-six times as much in taxes each year as the average American colonist paid. With that in mind, British leaders thought it only fair that the Americans should pay more of the expenses for administering and defending the colonies.

Many Americans disagreed, however, arguing that the various Navigation Acts restricting their economic activity were already a form of tax on them. The tension between the British need for greater revenue from the colonies and the Americans' defense of their rights and liberties set in motion a chain of events that would lead to revolution and independence. "It is truly a miserable thing," said a Connecticut minister in December 1763, "that we no sooner leave fighting our neighbors, the French, but we must fall to quarreling among ourselves."

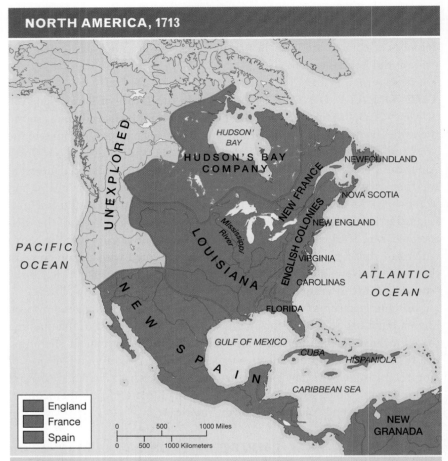

NORTH AMERICA, 1713

HUDSON BAY

HUDSON'S BAY COMPANY

UNEXPLORED

NEWFOUNDLAND

NOVA SCOTIA

NEW FRANCE

NEW ENGLAND

Mississippi River

LOUISIANA

PACIFIC OCEAN

ENGLISH COLONIES

VIRGINIA

CAROLINAS

ATLANTIC OCEAN

FLORIDA

N E W   S P A I N

GULF OF MEXICO

CUBA

HISPANIOLA

CARIBBEAN SEA

NEW GRANADA

England
France
Spain

0   500   1000 Miles

0   500   1000 Kilometers

- ■ What events led to the first clashes between the French and the British in the late seventeenth century?
- ■ Why did New England suffer more than other regions of North America during the wars of the eighteenth century?
- ■ What were the long-term financial, military, and political consequences of the wars between France and Britain?

PONTIAC'S REBELLION After the war, colonists began squabbling over Indian-owned land west of the Appalachian Mountains that the French had ceded to the British in the Treaty of Paris. Native American leaders, none of whom attended the meetings leading to the treaty, were shocked to learn that the French had "given" their ancestral lands to the British. Ohio Indians

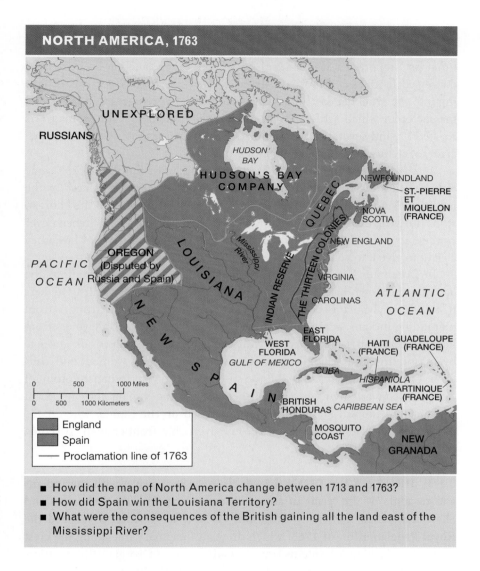

NORTH AMERICA, 1763

UNEXPLORED

RUSSIANS

HUDSON BAY

HUDSON'S BAY COMPANY

QUEBEC

NEWFOUNDLAND

ST.-PIERRE ET MIQUELON (FRANCE)

NOVA SCOTIA

NEW ENGLAND

Mississippi River

LOUISIANA

INDIAN RESERVE

THE THIRTEEN COLONIES

VIRGINIA

CAROLINAS

OREGON (Disputed by Russia and Spain)

PACIFIC OCEAN

NEW SPAIN

ATLANTIC OCEAN

EAST FLORIDA

WEST FLORIDA

GULF OF MEXICO

HAITI (FRANCE)

GUADELOUPE (FRANCE)

CUBA

HISPANIOLA

MARTINIQUE (FRANCE)

BRITISH HONDURAS   CARIBBEAN SEA

MOSQUITO COAST

NEW GRANADA

0   500   1000 Miles
0   500   1000 Kilometers

■ England
■ Spain
── Proclamation line of 1763

- How did the map of North America change between 1713 and 1763?
- How did Spain win the Louisiana Territory?
- What were the consequences of the British gaining all the land east of the Mississippi River?

complained to British army officers that "as soon as you conquered the French, you did not care how you treated us." One chieftain claimed that the British had treated them "like slaves."

The Indians fought back in the spring of 1763, capturing most of the British forts around the Great Lakes and in the Ohio Valley. "Never was panic more general," reported the *Pennsylvania Gazette*, "than that of the Back[woods] Inhabitants, whose terrors at this time exceed that followed on the defeat of General Braddock."

Native Americans raided colonial settlements in Pennsylvania, Maryland, and Virginia, destroying farms and killing thousands. "Every day, for some time past," reported a Marylander, "has offered the melancholy scene of poor distressed families . . . who have deserted their plantations, for fear of falling into the cruel hands of our savage enemies." The refugees told of terrible massacres in which settlers "were most cruelly butchered; the woman was roasted . . . and several of the men had awls thrust in their eyes, and spears, arrows, pitchforks, etc., sticking in their bodies."

The widespread Indian attacks in the spring and summer of 1763 came to be called **Pontiac's Rebellion** because of the prominent role played by the inspiring Ottawa chieftain who sought to unify several tribes in the effort to stop American expansion. Pontiac told a British official that the "French never conquered us, neither did they purchase a foot of our Country, nor have they a right to give it to you."

In December 1763, a group of frontier ruffians in Pennsylvania took the law into their own hands. Outraged at the unwillingness of pacifist Quakers in the Pennsylvania assembly to protect white settlers on the frontier from marauding Indians, a group called the Paxton Boys, Scots-Irish farmers from Paxton, near Harrisburg, armed with tomahawks and rifles, took revenge by massacring and scalping peaceful Conestogas—men, women, and children. Then they threatened to kill the so-called Moravian Indians, a group of Christian converts living near Bethlehem. When the Indians took refuge in Philadelphia, some 1,500 Paxton Boys marched on the capital, where Benjamin Franklin helped persuade the ungovernable frontiersmen to return home.

THE PROCLAMATION LINE To help keep peace with the Indians and to abide by the terms of an earlier agreement with the Delawares and Shawnees, called the Treaty of Easton (1758), King George III issued the **Royal Proclamation of 1763**, which drew an imaginary line along the crest of the Appalachian Mountains from Canada south to Georgia. White settlers ("our loving subjects") were forbidden to go west of the line in order to ensure that the Indians would not be "molested or disturbed" on their ancestral lands.

For the first time, American territorial expansion was to be controlled by royal officials. In practice, the proclamation line ended the activities of speculators buying huge tracts of Indian lands but did not keep land-hungry settlers from pushing across the steep Appalachian ridges into Indian country. By 1767, an Indian chief was complaining that whites were "making more encroachments on their Country than ever they had before."

REGULATING THE COLONIES

As Britain tightened its hold over the colonies after 1763, Americans reminded Parliament that their original charters guaranteed that they should be treated as if they were English citizens, with all the rights and liberties protected by the nation's constitutional traditions. Such arguments, however, fell on deaf ears in Parliament. As one member explained, the British were determined "to make North America pay [for] its own army."

GRENVILLE'S COLONIAL POLICY Just as the Proclamation of 1763 was being drafted, a new British government led by George Grenville began to grapple with the huge debts the government had accumulated during the war along with the added expenses of maintaining troops in America. Grenville insisted that the Americans, whom he called the "least taxed people in the world," must pay for the soldiers defending them. He also resented the large number of American merchants who engaged in smuggling to avoid paying British taxes on imported goods. Grenville ordered colonial officials to tighten enforcement of the Navigation Acts and sent warships to capture smugglers who, if caught, would be tried in new military courts rather than civilian jury trials.

THE SUGAR ACT Grenville's effort to enforce the various Navigation Acts posed a serious threat to New England's prosperity. Distilling rum out of molasses, a sweet syrup made from sugarcane, had become quite profitable, especially if the molasses could be smuggled in from Caribbean islands still controlled by the French.

To generate more money from the colonies, Grenville put through the American Revenue Act of 1764, commonly known as the Sugar Act, which cut the tax on molasses in half. Doing so, he believed, would reduce the temptation to smuggle French molasses or to bribe royal customs officers. But the Sugar Act also added new *duties* (taxes) on other goods (sugar, wines, coffee, spices) imported into America. The new revenues generated by the Sugar Act, Grenville estimated, would help pay for "the necessary expenses of defending, protecting, and securing, the said colonies."

With the Sugar Act, Parliament, for the first time, adopted a policy designed to raise *revenues* from the colonies and not merely to *regulate* trade with other nations. Colonists claimed that the Sugar Act taxed them without their consent, since they had no elected representatives in Parliament. British officials argued, however, that Parliament's power was absolute and indivisible. If the Americans accepted parliamentary authority in *any* area, they had to accept its authority in *every* area. In the end, however, the controversial new sugar tax did not produce more revenue for Great Britain; the cost of enforcing it was four times greater than the revenue it generated.

THE CURRENCY ACT   Americans equally hated another of Grenville's new regulatory measures, the Currency Act of 1764, which prohibited the colonies from coining or printing money, while requiring that all payments for British goods imported into the colonies must be in gold or silver coins or in a commodity like tobacco. The colonies had long faced a chronic shortage of "hard" money (gold and silver coins, called *specie*), which kept flowing overseas to pay debts in England.

To address the lack of specie, many colonies issued their own paper money, which could not be used in other colonies. British creditors feared payment in a currency of such fluctuating value. To alleviate their fears, Grenville implemented the Currency Act. By banning paper money, it caused the value of existing paper money to plummet. As a Philadelphia newspaper complained, "The Times are Dreadful, Dismal, Doleful, Dolorous, and DOLLAR-LESS."

THE STAMP ACT   Prime Minister Grenville excelled at doing the wrong thing—repeatedly. In 1765, for example, he persuaded Parliament to pass the Quartering Act, which required Americans to feed and house British troops. Most Americans saw no need for so many British soldiers in colonial cities. If the British were there to defend against Indians, why weren't they positioned closer to the Indians?

Some colonists decided that the Quartering Act was actually an effort to use British soldiers to bully the Americans. William Knox, a British colonial official, admitted as much in 1763 when he said that the "main purpose" of keeping an army in America was "to secure the dependence of the colonies on Great Britain."

Yet Grenville aggravated colonial concerns by pushing through an even more controversial measure. On February 13, 1765, Parliament passed the **Stamp Act**, which required colonists to purchase stamped paper for virtually every possible use: newspapers, pamphlets, bonds, leases, deeds, licenses, insurance policies, college diplomas, even playing cards. The requirement was to go into effect November 1. The Stamp Act was the first effort by Parliament to place a tax directly on American goods and services rather than levying an "external" tax on imports and exports. Not a single colony supported the new measure.

THE WHIG POINT OF VIEW   Grenville's colonial policies outraged many Americans, especially those living in the large port cities: Boston, New York, Philadelphia, and Charleston. Unwittingly, the prime minister had stirred up a storm of protest and set in motion a violent debate about the proper relationship between Great Britain and her colonies. In the late eighteenth century, the Americans who opposed British policies began to call themselves Patriots or *Whigs*, a name earlier applied to British critics of royal power. In turn, Whigs labeled the king and his "corrupt" government ministers and Parliamentary supporters as *Tories*, a term of abuse meaning friends of the king.

In 1764 and 1765, Whigs felt that Grenville was violating their rights in several ways. A professional army was usually a weapon used by tyrants, and now, with the French defeated and Canada solidly under British control, thousands of British soldiers remained in America. Were the troops there to protect the colonists or to scare them into obedience?

Whigs also argued that British citizens had the right to be taxed only by their elected representatives in Parliament, but Americans had no such representatives. British leaders countered that the colonists enjoyed **virtual representation** in Parliament. William Pitt, a staunch supporter of American rights in Parliament, dismissed Grenville's concept of virtual representation as "the most contemptible idea that ever entered into the head of a man." Many others, in both Britain and America, agreed. Sir Francis Bernard, the royal governor of Massachusetts, correctly predicted that the new stamp tax "would cause a great Alarm & meet much Opposition" in the colonies.

PROTESTS IN THE COLONIES   The Stamp Act aroused fierce resentment and resistance. A New Yorker wrote that "this single stroke has lost Great Britain the affection of all her colonies." In a flood of pamphlets, speeches, resolutions, and street protests, critics repeated a slogan familiar to Americans: "No taxation without representation [in Parliament]."

Protesters, calling themselves **Sons of Liberty**, emerged in every colony, often meeting beneath "liberty trees"—in Boston a great elm, in Charleston, South Carolina, a live oak. In New York City, the Sons of Liberty erected "liberty poles" as symbols of their resistance. In Virginia, Patrick Henry convinced the assembly to pass the "Stamp Act Resolutions," which asserted yet again that the colonists could not be taxed without being first consulted by the British government or represented in Parliament by their own elected members.

THE NONIMPORTATION MOVEMENT   Americans opposed to the Stamp Act knew that the most powerful form of leverage they had against

Opposition to the Stamp Act In protest of the Stamp Act, which was to take effect the next day, the *Pennsylvania Journal* printed a skull and crossbones on its masthead.

the British was economic. To put pressure on the British government and show that the colonists themselves had not become "dependent" on Britain's "empire of goods," Patriots by the thousands between 1767 and 1770 signed what were called nonimportation agreements, pledging not to buy or consume any British goods.

The nonimportation movement of the 1760s and 1770s united Whigs from different communities and different colonies. It also enabled women to play a significant role resisting Britain's colonial policies. Calling themselves **Daughters of Liberty**, many colonial women stopped buying imported British clothes. They also quit drinking British tea in order to "save this abused Country from Ruin and Slavery." Using herbs and flowers, they made "Liberty Tea" instead.

The Daughters of Liberty also participated in public "spinning bees," whereby they would gather in the town square to weave and spin yarn and wool into fabric, known as "homespun." In 1769 the *Boston Evening Post* reported that the "industry and frugality of American ladies" were enabling "the political salvation of a whole continent."

Patriots saw the effort to boycott British products as a way to restore their own virtue. A Rhode Islander declared that a primary cause of America's problems was the "luxury and extravagance" brought on by their freewheeling purchases of British goods. The nonimportation movement would help Americans restore "our frugality, industry, and simplicity of manners." A Boston minister claimed that those who could not do without British luxury goods and be satisfied with "plainness and simplicity" did not deserve to be American citizens.

COLONIAL UNITY The boycotts worked; imports of British goods fell by 40 percent. At the same time, the Virginia House of Burgesses struck the first official blow against the Stamp Act with the Virginia Resolves, a series of resolutions inspired by the fiery Patrick Henry. Virginians, Henry declared, were entitled to all the rights of Englishmen, and Englishmen could be taxed only by their own elected representatives. Because Virginians had no elected representatives in Parliament, they could only be taxed by the Virginia

The Repeal, or The Funeral Procession of Miss Americ-Stamp This 1766 cartoon shows Grenville carrying the dead Stamp Act in its coffin. In the background, trade with America starts up again.

legislature. Newspapers spread the Virginia Resolves throughout the colonies, and other colonial assemblies hastened to follow Virginia's example. "No taxation without representation" became the echoing rally cry for American Whigs.

In 1765, the Massachusetts House of Representatives invited the other colonial assemblies to send delegates to New York City to discuss their opposition to the Stamp Act. Nine responded, and from October 7–25, 1765, the Stamp Act Congress formulated a Declaration of the Rights and Grievances of the Colonies. The delegates insisted that they would accept no taxes being "imposed on them" without "their own consent, given personally, or by their representatives." Grenville responded by denouncing his colonial critics as "ungrateful" for all of the benefits provided them by the British government.

REPEAL OF THE STAMP ACT The storm over the Stamp Act had scarcely erupted before Grenville was out of office. He had lost the confidence of the king, who replaced him with Lord Rockingham in July 1765. Then, in mid-August 1765, nearly three months before the Stamp Act was to take effect, a Boston mob plundered the homes of the royal lieutenant governor, Thomas Hutchinson, and the official in charge of enforcing the stamp tax. Thoroughly shaken, the Boston stamp agent resigned, and other stamp agents throughout the colonies were hounded out of office.

The growing violence in America and the success of the nonimportation movement convinced Rockingham that the Stamp Act was a mistake. In February 1766, a humiliated Parliament repealed it. To save face, Parliament passed the Declaratory Act, which asserted its power to govern the colonies "in all cases whatsoever."

The repeal of the Stamp Act set off excited demonstrations throughout the colonies. Sally Franklin wrote to her father Benjamin in Europe that Philadelphia's church bells were rung and bonfires were built. "I never heard so much noise in my life," she noted.

THE TOWNSHEND ACTS In July 1766, King George III replaced Lord Rockingham with William Pitt, the former prime minister who had exercised heroic leadership during the Seven Years' War. For a time, the guiding force in the Pitt ministry was the witty but reckless Charles Townshend, the treasury chief whose "abilities were superior to those of all men," said a colleague, "and his judgment [common sense] below that of any man."

In 1767, Townshend pushed through Parliament his ill-fated plan to generate more colonial revenue. A few months later, he died at age forty-two, leaving behind a bitter legacy: the **Townshend Acts**. The Revenue Act of 1767, which taxed colonial imports of glass, lead, paint, paper, and tea, was the most hated. It posed an even more severe threat than Grenville's taxes had, for Townshend planned to use the new tax revenues to pay the salaries of the royal governors in the colonies. Until that point, the colonial assemblies paid the salaries, thus giving them some leverage over them. John Adams observed that Townshend's plan would make the royal governor "independent of the people" and disrupt "that balance of power which is essential to all free governments." Writing in the *Boston Gazette*, Adams insisted that such "an INDEPENDENT ruler, [is] a MONSTER in a free state."

DISCONTENT ON THE FRONTIER

Some colonists had little interest in the disputes over British regulatory policy raging along the seaboard. Parts of the backcountry stirred with quarrels that had nothing to do with the Stamp and Townshend Acts. Rival claims to lands east of Lake Champlain pitted New York against New Hampshire. Eventually the residents of the disputed area would form their own state of Vermont, created in 1777 although not recognized as a member of the Union until 1791.

In the south, frontiersmen in South Carolina issued a rising chorus of complaints about the lack of colonial protection—from horse thieves, cattle rustlers, and Indians. Backcountry residents organized societies, called Regulators, to administer vigilante justice in the region, and refused to pay taxes until they gained effective government. In 1769, the assembly finally set up six circuit courts in the region but without responding to the backcountry's demand for representation in the legislative assemblies.

In North Carolina the protest was less over the lack of government than over the abuses and extortion by appointees from the eastern part of the colony. Western farmers felt especially oppressed by the government's refusal either to issue paper money or to accept produce in payment of taxes, and in 1766 they organized to resist. Efforts of these Regulators to stop seizures of property and other court proceedings led to more disorders and the enactment of a bill that made the rioters guilty of treason. That the Regulators tended to be Baptists, Methodists, and Presbyterians who preached plain living, while the coastal elite tended to be Anglicans who paraded their wealth, injected a religious and social element into the squabbles.

In the spring of 1771, North Carolina's royal governor William Tryon led 1,200 militiamen into battle against Regulators. There his forces defeated some

2,000 ill-organized Regulators in the Battle of Alamance, in which eight were killed on each side. Tryon's men then ranged through the backcountry, forcing some 6,500 Piedmont settlers to sign an oath of allegiance to the king.

These disputes and revolts within the colonies illustrate the diversity of opinion and outlook among Americans on the eve of the Revolution. Colonists were of many minds about many things, including British rule, but also differed with one another over how best to protest against particular grievances.

THE CRISIS GROWS

The Townshend Acts surprised and angered many colonists. As American rage bubbled over, Samuel Adams of Boston, one of the most radical rebels, decided that a small group of determined Whigs could generate a mass movement. "It does not take a majority to prevail," Adams insisted, "but rather an irate, tireless minority, keen on setting brushfires of freedom in the minds of men."

Early in 1768, Adams and Boston attorney James Otis Jr. convinced the Massachusetts assembly to circulate a letter they had written to the other colonies. It restated the illegality of taxation without representation in Parliament and invited the support of other colonies. British officials ordered the Massachusetts assembly to withdraw the letter. They refused, and the king ordered the assembly dissolved.

In response to an appeal by the royal governor of Massachusetts, 3,000 British troops were sent to Boston in October 1768 to maintain order. **Loyalists**, as the Americans who supported the king and Parliament were often called, welcomed the soldiers; **Patriots**, those rebelling against British authority, viewed the British troops as an occupation force. Meanwhile, in London the king appointed still another new chief minister, Frederick, Lord North, in January 1770.

Samuel Adams Adams was the fiery organizer of the Sons of Liberty.

THE FIRST BLOODSHED In 1765, Benjamin Franklin had predicted that although British soldiers sent to America would "not find a rebellion; they may indeed make one." The growing tensions between rebellious Americans and British troops triggered several violent incidents. The first, called the Battle at Golden Hill, occurred in New York City, where "Liberty Boys" kept erecting "liberty poles," only to see British soldiers knock them down. The soldiers, called "lobsterbacks" or "redcoats" because of their bright red uniforms, also began posting signs declaring that the Sons of Liberty were "the real enemies of society."

On January, 18, 1770, a group of Patriots captured two British soldiers. Soon, an angry crowd formed around the twenty British soldiers sent to rescue their comrades. The outnumbered soldiers retreated. When they reached Golden Hill, more soldiers arrived. At that point, the redcoats turned on the crowd pursuing them. An officer yelled: "Draw your bayonets and cut your way through them!" They attacked the crowd, and in the confusion, several on both sides were seriously hurt.

The next day, more brawls erupted. Once the British soldiers left the scene, the Sons of Liberty erected another liberty pole which bore the inscription: "Liberty and Property." The first blood had been shed in the growing conflict over American liberties, and it was soon followed by more violence.

THE BOSTON MASSACRE Massachusetts had long been the center of resistance to British authority. In Boston, the presence of thousands of British soldiers had become a constant source of irritation. Crowds frequently heckled the soldiers, many of whom earned the abuse by harassing and intimidating Americans.

On the evening of March 5, 1770, two dozen Boston rowdies—teens, Irishmen, blacks, and sailors—began taunting and throwing icicles at Hugh White, a British soldier guarding the Custom House. Someone rang the town fire bell, drawing a larger crowd to the scene as the taunting continued: "Kill him, kill him, knock him down. Fire, damn you, fire, you dare not fire!"

A squad of soldiers arrived to help White, but the surly crowd surrounded them. When someone knocked a soldier down, he arose and fired his musket. Others joined in. When the smoke cleared, five people lay dead or dying, and eight more were wounded. The first one killed, or so the story goes, was Crispus Attucks, a former slave who worked at the docks.

The so-called **Boston Massacre** sent shock waves throughout the colonies and all the way to London. Virtually the entire city of Boston attended the funerals for the deceased. Only the decision to postpone the trial of the British

The Bloody Massacre Paul Revere's engraving of the Boston Massacre (1770).

soldiers for six months allowed the tensions to subside. At the same time, the impact of the colonial boycott of British products persuaded Lord North to modify the Townshend Acts.

Late in April 1770, Parliament repealed all the Townshend duties except for the tea tax, which the king wanted to keep as a symbol of Parliament's authority. Colonial discontent subsided for two years thereafter. The redcoats left Boston, but remained in Canada, and the British navy still patrolled the New England coast.

THE GASPÉE INCIDENT In June 1772, a naval incident further eroded the colonies' fragile relationship with the mother country. Near Warwick, Rhode Island, the HMS *Gaspée*, a British warship, ran aground while chasing suspected American smugglers. Its hungry crew seized local sheep, hogs, and chickens from local farms. An enraged crowd, some of them dressed as Mohawk Indians, then boarded the *Gaspée*, shot the captain, removed the crew, looted the ship, and then burned it.

The *Gaspée* incident symbolized the intensity of anti-British feelings among growing numbers of Americans. When the British tried to take the suspects to London for trial, Patriots organized in protest. Thomas Jefferson said that it was the threat of transporting Americans for trials in Britain that reignited anti-British activities in Virginia.

In response to the *Gaspée* incident, Samuel Adams organized the **Committee of Correspondence**, which issued a statement of American rights and grievances and invited other towns to do the same. Similar committees sprang up across Massachusetts and in other colonies, forming a unified network of resistance. "The flame is kindled and like lightning it catches from soul to soul," reported Abigail Adams, the high-spirited wife of future president John Adams. By 1772, Thomas Hutchinson, now the royal governor of Massachusetts, could tell the colonial assembly that the choice facing Americans was stark: they must choose between obeying "the supreme authority of Parliament" and "total independence."

THE BOSTON TEA PARTY The new British prime minister, Lord North, soon provided the spark to transform resentment into rebellion. In 1773, he tried to bail out the struggling East India Company, which had in its British warehouses some 17 million pounds of tea that it desperately needed to sell before it rotted. Parliament passed the Tea Act of 1773 to allow the company to send its tea directly to America without paying any taxes. British tea merchants could thereby undercut the prices charged by their American competitors, most of whom were smugglers who bought tea from the Dutch. At the same time, King George III told Lord North to "compel obedience" in the colonies.

In Massachusetts, the Committees of Correspondence, backed by Boston merchants, alerted colonists that the British government was trying to purchase colonial submission with cheap tea. The reduction in the price of tea was a clever trick to make colonists accept taxation without consent. In Boston, furious Americans decided that their passion for liberty outweighed their love for tea. On December 16, 1773, scores of Patriots disguised as Indians boarded three British ships in Boston Harbor and dumped overboard 342 chests filled with 46 tons of East India Company tea.

The **Boston Tea Party** pushed British officials to the breaking point. The destruction of so much valuable tea convinced the king and his advisers that a forceful response was required. "The colonists must either submit or triumph," George III wrote to Lord North, who decided to make an example of Boston to the rest of the colonies. "We are now to establish our authority [over the colonies]," North said, "or give it up entirely."

THE COERCIVE ACTS In 1774, Lord North convinced Parliament to punish rebellious Boston by enacting a cluster of harsh laws, called the **Coercive Acts** (Americans renamed them the "Intolerable" Acts). The Boston Port Act closed the Boston harbor until the city paid for the lost tea. A new Quartering Act ordered colonists to provide lodging for British soldiers. The Impartial Administration of Justice Act said that any royal official accused of a major crime would be tried back in Great Britain rather than in the colony.

Finally, the Massachusetts Government Act gave the royal governor the authority to appoint the colony's legislative council, which until then had been elected by the people, as well as judges and sheriffs. It also ordered that no town meeting could be held without the royal governor's consent. In May, Lieutenant-General Thomas Gage, commander in chief of British forces in North America, was named governor of Massachusetts and assumed command of the British soldiers who had returned to Boston.

The Intolerable Acts shocked colonists. No one had expected such a severe reaction to the Boston Tea Party. Many towns held meetings in violation of

The Able Doctor, or America Swallowing the Bitter Draught This 1774 engraving shows Lord North, the Boston Port Act in his pocket, pouring tea down America's throat and America spitting it back.

the new laws, and voters elected their own unauthorized provincial legislative assembly—which ordered town governments to quit paying taxes to the royal governor. By August 1774, Patriots across Massachusetts had essentially taken control of local governments. They also began stockpiling weapons and gunpowder in anticipation of an eventual clash with British troops.

Elsewhere, colonists rallied to help Boston, raising money, sending supplies, and boycotting, as well as burning or dumping British tea. In Williamsburg, when the Virginia assembly met in May, a member of the Committee of Correspondence, Thomas Jefferson, suggested that June 1, the effective date of the Boston Port Act, become an official day of fasting and prayer in Virginia.

The royal governor responded by dissolving the assembly, whose members then retired to the Raleigh Tavern where they decided to form a Continental Congress to represent all the colonies more effectively in the confrontation with Britain. As Samuel Savage, a Connecticut colonist wrote May 1774, the conflict had come down to a single question: "Whether we shall or shall not be governed by a British Parliament."

THE FIRST CONTINENTAL CONGRESS On September 5, 1774, the fifty-five delegates making up the First Continental Congress assembled in Philadelphia. It was the first time that all of the colonies had met to coordinate policies. Over seven weeks, the Congress endorsed the Suffolk Resolves, which urged Massachusetts to resist British tyranny with force. The Congress then adopted a Declaration of American Rights, which proclaimed once again the rights of Americans as British citizens and denied Parliament's authority to regulate internal colonial affairs. "We demand no new rights," said the Congress. "We ask only for peace, liberty, and security."

Finally, the Congress adopted the Continental Association of 1774, which recommended that every colony organize committees to enforce a new and complete boycott of all imported British goods, a dramatic step that would be followed by a refusal to send American goods (exports) to Britain. If the ideal of republican virtue meant anything, it meant the sacrificing of self-interest for the public good. The Association was designed to show that Americans could deny themselves the "baubles of Britain" in order to demonstrate their commitment to colonial liberties and constitutional rights.

The county and city committees forming the Continental Association became the organizational network for the resistance movement. Seven thousand men across the colonies served on the local committees, and many more women helped put the boycotts into practice. The committees required colonists to sign an oath refusing to purchase British goods. In East Haddam, Connecticut, a Loyalist doctor was tarred, feathered, and rubbed with pig dung. Such violent incidents led Loyalists to claim that it was better to be a slave to the king than to a Patriot mob.

Thousands of ordinary men and women participated in the boycott of British goods, and their sacrifices on behalf of colonial liberties provided the momentum leading to revolution. It was common people who enforced the boycott, volunteered in Patriot militia units, attended town meetings, and ousted royal officials. As the people of Pittsfield, Massachusetts, declared in a petition, "We have always believed that the people are the fountain of power."

The growing rebellion against "British tyranny" now extended well beyond simple grievances over taxation. Patriots decided that there was a *conspiracy* against their liberties at work in London. In Boston, an increasingly nervous General Gage requested that more British troops be sent to suppress the growing rebellion. Mercy Otis Warren wrote that most Americans still balked "at the idea of drawing the sword against the nation from whence she [America] derived her origin." She feared, however, that Britain was poised "to plunge her dagger into the bosom of her affectionate offspring."

LAST-MINUTE COMPROMISE   In London, King George fumed. He wrote Lord North that "blows must decide" whether the Americans "are to be subject to this country or independent." In early 1775, Parliament declared that Massachusetts was officially "in rebellion" and prohibited the New England colonies from trading with any nation outside the British Empire. On February 27, 1775, Lord North issued the Conciliatory Propositions, which offered to resolve the festering dispute by eliminating all taxes on any colony that voluntarily paid both its share for military defense and the salaries of the royal governors. In other words, North was asking the colonies to tax themselves. By the time the Conciliatory Propositions arrived in America, shooting had already started.

BOLD TALK OF WAR   While most of the Patriots believed that Britain would back down, Patrick Henry of Virginia dramatically declared that war was unavoidable. The twenty-nine-year-old Henry, a farmer and storekeeper turned lawyer, claimed that the colonies "have done everything that could be done to avert the storm which is now coming on," but their efforts had been met only by "violence and insult." Freedom, the defiant Henry shouted, could be bought only with blood. If forced to choose, he supposedly shouted, "give me liberty"—then paused dramatically, clenched his fist as if it held a dagger, and plunged it into his chest—"or give me death." Loyalists shouted "Treason!" amid the applause.

As Henry predicted, events quickly moved toward armed conflict. By mid-1775, the king and Parliament had effectively lost control; they could neither persuade nor force the Patriots to accept new regulations and revenue measures. In Boston, General Gage warned that armed conflict would unleash the "horrors of civil war." But Lord Sandwich, head of the British navy, dismissed the rebels as "raw, undisciplined, cowardly men" without an army or navy. Major John Pitcairn, a British army officer, agreed, writing from Boston that "one active campaign, a smart action, and burning two or three of their towns, will set everything to rights."

Patrick Henry of Virginia Henry famously declared "Give me Liberty, or give me Death!"

LEXINGTON AND CONCORD

Major Pitcairn soon had his chance to quash the rebel resistance. On April 14, 1775, the British army in Boston received secret orders to stop the "open rebellion" in Massachusetts. General Gage had decided to arrest rebel leaders such as Samuel Adams and seize the militia's gunpowder stored at Concord, sixteen miles northwest of Boston.

After dark on April 18, some 800 British soldiers secretly boarded boats and crossed the Charles River to Cambridge, then set out westward on foot to Lexington, a town about eleven miles away. When Patriots got wind of the plan, Paul Revere and William Dawes mounted their horses for their famous "midnight ride" to warn the rebel leaders that the British were coming.

In the gray dawn light of April 19, an advance unit of 238 redcoats found American Captain John Parker and about seventy "Minutemen" (Patriot militia who could assemble at a "minute's" notice), lined up on the Lexington town square, while dozens of villagers watched.

Parker and his men intended only a silent protest, but Major Pitcairn rode onto the Lexington Green, swinging his sword and yelling, "Disperse, you damned rebels! You dogs, run!" The outnumbered militiamen were backing away when someone fired. The British soldiers shot at the Minutemen, then charged them with bayonets, leaving eight dead and ten wounded. Jonathan

Harrington, a militiaman who was shot in the back, managed to crawl across the Green, only to die on his doorstep.

The British officers quickly brought their men under control and led them to Concord, where they destroyed hidden military supplies. While marching out of the town, they encountered American riflemen at the North Bridge. Shots were fired, and a dozen or so British soldiers were killed or wounded. More important, the short skirmish and ringing church bells alerted rebel farmers, ministers, craftsmen, and merchants from nearby communities to grab their muskets. They were, as one of them said, determined to "be free or die."

By noon, the British began a ragged retreat back to Lexington. Less than a mile out of Concord, they suffered the first of many ambushes. The narrow road turned into a gauntlet of death as rebel marksmen fired on the British troops from behind stone walls, trees, barns, and houses. "It was a day full of horror," one of the soldiers recalled. "The Patriots seemed maddened."

During the fighting along the road leading to Lexington, a British soldier was searching a house for rebel snipers when he ran into twenty-five-year-old Patriot James Hayward, a school teacher. The redcoat pointed his musket at the American and said, "Stop, you're a dead man." Hayward raised his weapon

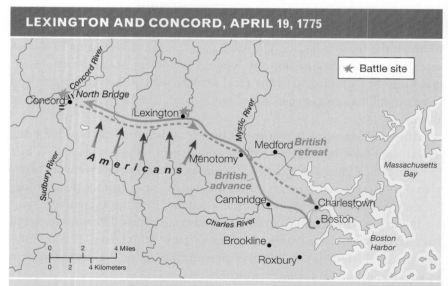

LEXINGTON AND CONCORD, APRIL 19, 1775

- Describe the clash between British soldiers and American militiamen on Lexington Green.
- Why did the Americans' tactics along the road between Concord, Lexington, and Boston succeed?
- Why did the British march on Concord in the first place?

The Battle of Lexington Amos Doolittle's impression of the Battle of Lexington as shooting begins between the Royal Marines and the Minutemen.

and answered, "So are you." They fired simultaneously. The British soldier died instantly, and Hayward succumbed to a head wound eight hours later.

By nightfall, the redcoat survivors were safely back in Boston, having suffered three times as many dead and wounded as the Americans. A British general reported that the colonists had earned his respect: "Whoever looks upon them as an irregular mob will find himself much mistaken."

Until the Battles of Lexington and Concord, both sides had mistakenly assumed that the other would back down when confronted with deadly force. Instead, the clash of arms turned a resistance movement into a war of rebellion. Masses of ordinary people were determined to fight for their freedoms against a British parliament and king bent on denying them their civil and legal rights. In Virginia, Thomas Jefferson reported that the news from Concord and Lexington had unleashed "a frenzy of revenge [against the British]" among "all ranks of people."

THE SPREADING CONFLICT

On June 15, 1775, the Second Continental Congress unanimously selected forty-three-year-old George Washington to lead a new national army. His service in the French and Indian War had made him one of the few experienced

American officers, and he was admired for his success as a planter, surveyor, and land speculator, as well as for his service in the Virginia legislature and the Continental Congress. Perhaps more important, he *looked* like a leader. Tall and strong, Washington was a superb horseman and fearless fighter.

Washington humbly accepted the responsibility of leading the American war effort, but refused to be paid. A few weeks later, Mercy Otis Warren wrote a friend in London that Washington was "a man whose military abilities & public & private virtue place him in the first class of the Good & the Brave."

THE BATTLE OF BUNKER HILL On Saturday, June 17, the very day that George Washington was named commander in chief, Patriot militiamen engaged British forces in their first major clash, the Battle of Bunker Hill (adjoining Breed's Hill was the battle's actual location).

In an effort to strengthen their control over the area around Boston, some 2,400 British troops based in the city boarded boats and crossed over the Charles River to the Charlestown Peninsula, where they formed lines and advanced up Breed's Hill in tight formation through waist-high grass and across pasture fences, as the American defenders watched from behind their earthworks.

View of the Attack on Bunker Hill The Battle of Bunker Hill and the burning of Charlestown Peninsula.

The militiamen, mostly farmers, waited until the redcoats had come within thirty paces, then loosed a volley that shattered the front ranks. The British attacked again, but the Patriot riflemen forced them to retreat a second time. During the third British assault, the colonists ran out of gunpowder and retreated in panic and confusion. "I jumped over the walls," Peter Brown remembered, "and ran for about half a mile while [musket] balls flew like hailstones and cannons roared like thunder."

The British took the high ground but were too tired to pursue the rebels. They had suffered 1,054 casualties, over twice the American losses. "A dearly bought victory," reported British general Henry Clinton; "another such would have ruined us." There followed a nine-month stalemate around Boston, with each side hoping for a negotiated settlement. Abigail Adams reported that the Patriots still living in Boston, where the British army governed by martial law, were being treated "like abject slaves under the most cruel and despotic of tyrants."

"OPEN AND AVOWED ENEMIES" Three weeks after the Battle of Bunker Hill, in July 1775, the Continental Congress sent the king the Olive Branch Petition, urging him to negotiate with his rebellious colonies. When the petition reached London, however, King George refused to look at it. On August 22, he denounced the Americans as "open and avowed enemies." His arrogant dismissal of the Olive Branch Petition convinced Abigail Adams that war was now certain: "the die is cast . . . the sword is now our only, yet dreadful, alternative."

OUTRIGHT REBELLION Resistance had grown into outright rebellion, but few Patriots were ready to call for American independence. They still considered themselves British subjects. When the Second Continental Congress convened at Philadelphia on May 10, 1775, most of the delegates still wanted Parliament to restore their rights so that they could resume being loyal British colonists.

Meanwhile, the British army in Boston was under siege by militia units and small groups of musket-toting men who had arrived from across New England to join the rebellion. They were still farmers, not trained soldiers, and the uprising was not yet an army; it lacked an organized command structure and effective support system. The Patriots also lacked training, discipline, cannons, muskets, bullets, gunpowder, and blankets. What they did have was a growing sense of confidence and resolve. As a Massachusetts Patriot said, "Our all is at stake. Death and devastation are the instant consequences of delay. Every moment is infinitely precious."

With each passing day, war fever infected more and more colonists. "Oh that I were a soldier!" John Adams wrote home to Abigail from Philadelphia. "I will be. I am reading military books. Everybody must, and will, and shall be a soldier." On the very day that Congress met, the British Fort Ticonderoga, on Lake Champlain in upstate New York near the Canadian border, fell to a Patriot force of "Green Mountain Boys" led by Ethan Allen of Vermont and Massachusetts volunteers under Benedict Arnold. Two days later, the Patriots captured a smaller British fort at Crown Point, north of Ticonderoga.

INDEPENDENCE

The Revolutionary War was well underway in January 1776 when Thomas Paine, a recently arrived thirty-nine-year-old English emigrant who had found work as a radical journalist in Philadelphia, provided the Patriot cause with a stirring pamphlet titled **Common Sense**. Until it appeared, colonial grievances had been mainly directed at Parliament. Paine, however, directly attacked the British monarchy by openly appealing to the "passions and feelings of mankind."

The "common sense" of the matter, Paine stressed, was that King George III had caused the rebellion and had ordered the savage and cruel denial of American rights. "Even brutes do not devour their young," he wrote, "nor savages make war upon their families." Yet Britain, the mother of America, was doing just that. Americans, Paine urged, should abandon the British monarchy: "The blood of the slain, the weeping voice of nature cries, 'tis time to part."

It was Paine who helped convince Americans that independence was not unrealistic, it was inevitable. Only by declaring independence, he predicted, could the colonists gain the crucial support of France and Spain: "The cause of America is in great measure the cause of all mankind." The rest of the world would welcome and embrace an independent America; it would be the "glory of the earth." Paine concluded that the "sun had never shined on a cause of greater worth." He insisted that "we have it in our power to begin the world over again."

Within three months, more than 150,000 copies of Paine's stirring pamphlet were circulating throughout the colonies and around the world, an enormous number for the time. "*Common Sense* is working a powerful change in the minds of men," George Washington reported.

BREAKING THE BONDS OF EMPIRE *Common Sense* inspired the colonial population from Massachusetts to Georgia and helped convince British subjects still loyal to the king to embrace the radical notion of independence. "Without the pen of Paine," remembered John Adams, "the sword of Washington would have been wielded in vain." During the spring and summer of 1776, some ninety local governments, towns and colonial legislatures, issued declarations of independence from Great Britain.

Momentum for independence was building in the Continental Congress, too, but success was by no means assured. In Congress, John Dickinson of Pennsylvania urged delay. On June 1, he warned that independence was a dangerous step since America had no national government or European allies. But his was a lone voice of caution.

In June 1776, one by one, the colonies authorized their delegates in the Continental Congress to take the final step. On June 7, Richard Henry Lee of Virginia moved "that these United Colonies are, and of right ought to be, free and independent states." Lee's resolution passed on July 2, a date that John Adams predicted would "be the most memorable" in the history of America.

The coming revolution The Continental Congress votes for independence, July 2, 1776.

The more memorable date, however, became July 4, 1776, when the Congress formally adopted the **Declaration of Independence**. A few delegates refused to sign the momentous document; others, said John Adams, "signed with regret . . . and with many doubts." Most, however, signed wholeheartedly, knowing full well that by doing so they were likely to be hanged if captured by British troops. Benjamin Franklin acknowledged how high the stakes were: "Well, Gentlemen," he told the Congress, "we must now hang together, or we shall most assuredly hang separately."

The Declaration of Independence The Declaration in its most frequently reproduced form, an 1823 engraving by William J. Stone.

JEFFERSON'S DECLARATION   In Philadelphia in June 1776, thirty-three-year-old Thomas Jefferson, a brilliant Virginia attorney and planter serving in the Continental Congress, drafted a statement of independence that John Adams and Benjamin Franklin then edited, followed by the members of Congress themselves.

The Declaration of Independence was crucially important not simply because it marked the creation of a new nation but because of the ideals it expressed and the grievances it listed. It insisted that certain truths were self-evident, that "all men are created equal and independent" and have the right to create governments of their own choosing. Governments, in Thomas Jefferson's words, derive "their just powers from the consent of the people," who are entitled to "alter or abolish" those governments when rulers deny citizens their "unalienable rights" to "life, liberty, and the pursuit of happiness." Because King George III was trying to impose "an absolute tyranny over these states," the "Representatives of the United States of America" declared the thirteen "United Colonies" to be "Free and Independent States."

THE CONTRADICTIONS OF FREEDOM   Once the Continental Congress chose independence, the members set about revising Thomas Jefferson's draft declaration before sending it to London. Southern representatives insisted on deleting the slave-owning Jefferson's section criticizing George III for perpetuating the African slave trade. In doing so, they revealed the major contradiction at work in the movement for independence: the rhetoric of freedom that animated the Revolution did not apply to America's original sin, the widespread system of slavery that fueled the southern economy. Slavery was the absence of liberty, yet few Americans confronted the inconsistency of their protests in defense of freedom—for whites.

In 1764, a group of slaves in Charleston watching a demonstration against British tyranny by white Sons of Liberty got caught up in the energies of the moment and began chanting "freedom, freedom, freedom." But that was not at all what southern planters wanted for African Americans. In 1774, when a group of slaves killed four whites in a desperate attempt to gain their own freedom from tyranny, Georgia planters responded by capturing the rebels and burning them alive.

The Harvard-educated lawyer James Otis was one of the few Whigs who demanded freedom for blacks and women. In 1764, he had argued in a widely circulated pamphlet that "the colonists, black and white, born here, are free British subjects, and entitled to all the essential civil rights of such." He even went so far as to suggest that slavery itself should be ended, since "all men . . . white or black" were "by the law of nature freeborn."

Otis also asked, "Are not women born as free as men? Would it not be infamous to assert that the ladies are all slaves by nature?" His sister, Mercy Otis Warren, became a tireless advocate of American resistance to British "tyranny" through her poems, pamphlets, and plays. In a letter to a friend, she noted that British officials needed to realize that America's "daughters are politicians and patriots and will aid the good work [of resistance] with their female efforts."

In 1765, John Adams had snarled that he and other colonists angered by British actions would not "be their slaves." Actual slaves insisted on independence too. In 1773, a group of enslaved African Americans in Boston appealed to the royal governor of Massachusetts to free them just as white Americans were defending their freedoms against British tyranny. In many respects, the slaves argued, they had a more compelling case for liberty: "We have no property, We have no wives! No children! No city! No country!"

A few months later, a group of four Boston slaves addressed a public letter to the town government in which they referred to the hypocrisy of slaveholders who protested against British regulations and taxes. "We expect great things from men who have made such a noble stand against the designs of their fellow-men to enslave them," they noted. But freedom in 1776 was a celebration to which slaves were not invited. In 1775 the prominent South Carolinian William Henry Drayton expressed his horror that "impertinent" slaves were claiming "that the present contest [with Great Britain] was for obliging us to give them liberty."

George Washington himself acknowledged the contradictory aspects of the Revolutionary movement when he warned that the alternative to declaring independence was to become "tame and abject slaves, as the blacks we rule over with such arbitrary sway [absolute power]." Washington and other slaveholders at the head of the Revolutionary movement, such as Thomas Jefferson, were in part

I am very affectionately your Friend
Phillis Wheatley
Boston March 21. 1774.

Phillis Wheatley An autographed portrait of America's first African American poet.

so resistant to "British tyranny" because they witnessed every day what actual slavery was like—for the blacks under their control.

A morally perplexed Jefferson admitted the hypocrisy of slave-owning revolutionaries. "Southerners," he wrote to a French friend, are "jealous of their own liberties but trampling on those of others." Such inconsistency was not lost on others. Phillis Wheatley, the first African American writer to see her poetry published in America, highlighted the "absurdity" of white colonists claiming their freedom while continuing to exercise "oppressive power" over enslaved Africans.

"WE ALWAYS HAD GOVERNED OURSELVES" Historians still debate the causes of the American Revolution. Americans in 1775–1776 were not desperately poor: overall, they probably enjoyed a higher standard of living than most other societies and lived under the freest institutions in the world. Their diet was better than that of Europeans, as was their average life span. In addition, the percentage of free property owners in the thirteen American colonies was higher than in Britain or Europe. As the wealthy Charlestonian Charles Pinckney remarked a few years later, Americans, by which he meant white Americans, were "more equal in their circumstances than the people of any other Country." At the same time, the new taxes forced on Americans after 1763 were not as great as those imposed on the British people. It is also important to remember that many American colonists, perhaps as many as half, were indifferent, hesitant, or actively opposed to rebellion.

So why did the Americans revolt at all? Historians have highlighted many factors: the clumsy British efforts to tighten their regulation of colonial trade, the restrictions on colonists eager to acquire western lands, the growing tax burden, the mounting debts to British merchants, the lack of American representation in Parliament, and the role of radicals such as Samuel Adams and Patrick Henry in stirring up anti-British feelings.

Yet colonists sought liberty from British "tyranny" for reasons that were not so selfless or noble. Many of the New Englanders and New Yorkers most critical of tighter British regulations were smugglers. Boston merchant John Hancock, for example, embraced the Patriot cause in part because he was a wealthy smuggler. Paying more British taxes would have cost him a fortune. Likewise, South Carolina's Henry Laurens and Virginia's Landon Carter, both prosperous planters, worried that the British might abolish slavery.

Overall, however, what Americans most feared and resented were the British efforts to constrict their civil liberties, thereby denying their rights as British citizens. As Hugh Williamson, a Pennsylvania physician, explained, the

Revolution resulted not from "trifling or imaginary" injustices but from "gross and palpable" violations of American rights that had thrown "the miserable colonists" into the "pit of despotism."

Yet how did the American colonies, the most diverse society in the world, divided by nationality and class, develop such a unified resistance? Although most were of English heritage, there were many other peoples represented: Scots, Irish, Scots-Irish, Welsh, Germans, Dutch, Swedes, Finns, Swiss, French, and Jews, as well as growing numbers of Africans and diminishing numbers of Native Americans. In 1774, Thomas Hutchinson, the royal governor of Massachusetts, assured British officials that "a union of the Colonies was utterly impracticable" because the colonists "were greatly divided among themselves in every colony." He predicted that rebellious Americans would ultimately "*submit*, and that they *must*, and moreover would, *soon.*"

Hutchinson was wrong, of course. What most Americans—regardless of their backgrounds—had come to share by 1775 was a defiant attachment to the civil rights and legal processes guaranteed by the English constitutional tradition. This new outlook rooted in the defense of sacred constitutional principles made the Revolution conceivable, armed resistance made it possible, and independence, ultimately, made it achievable.

The outlook of the revolutionaries was founded on the shared political principle that all citizens were equal and independent, and that all governmental authority had to be based on the consent of those governed and longstanding constitutional principles. This "republican ideal" was the crucial force transforming a prolonged effort to preserve old rights and liberties enjoyed by British citizens into a movement to create an independent nation. As John Adams explained, Americans by 1776 had lost their "affection for England" because British officials were conspiring to strip them of their cherished liberties.

With their declaration of independence, the revolutionaries—men and women, farmers, artisans, mechanics, sailors, merchants, tavern owners, and shopkeepers—had at last become determined to develop their own society. Most Patriots still spoke the same language and worshipped the same God as the British, but they no longer thought the same way. Americans wanted to trade freely with the world and to expand what Jefferson called their "empire of liberty" westward, across the Appalachian Mountains.

Perhaps the last word on the complex causes of the Revolution should belong to Levi Preston, a Minuteman from Danvers, Massachusetts. Asked late in life about the British efforts to impose new taxes and regulations on the colonists, Preston responded by asking his young interviewer, "What were they? Oppressions? I didn't feel them." He was then asked, "What, were you not oppressed by the Stamp Act?" Preston replied that he "never saw one of those stamps . . . I am certain I never paid a penny for one of them." What about the tax on tea? "Tea-tax! I never drank a drop of the stuff; the boys threw it all overboard." His interviewer finally asked why he decided to fight for independence. "Young man," Preston explained, "what we meant in going for those redcoats was this: we always had governed ourselves, and we always meant to. They didn't mean we should."

CHAPTER REVIEW

SUMMARY

- **British and French Colonies**   New France followed the Spanish model of absolute power in governing its far-flung trading outposts. On the other hand, Great Britain's policy of *salutary neglect* allowed the colonies a large degree of self-government, until the British government's decision to rigidly enforce its policy of *mercantilism*, as seen in such measures as the *Navigation Acts*, became a means to enrich its global empire. The *Glorious Revolution* in Great Britain inspired new political philosophies that challenged the divine right of kings with the *natural rights* of free men.

- **The French and Indian War**   Four European wars affected America between 1689 and 1763 as the British and French, joined by their allies, fought throughout the world. Early in the French and Indian War, worried colonies created the *Albany Plan of Union*, which formed an early blueprint for an independent American government. *The Seven Years' War*, known as the *French and Indian War* (1754–1763) in the colonies, eventually was won by the British. In the *Treaty of Paris* in 1763, France lost all its North American possessions, Britain gained Canada and Florida, and Spain acquired the vast Louisiana Territory. The Indians fought to regain control of their ancestral lands in *Pontiac's Rebellion*, and Great Britain, weary of war, negotiated peace in the *Royal Proclamation of 1763*.

- **British Colonial Policy**   After the French and Indian War, the British government was saddled with an enormous debt. To reduce that burden, Prime Minister George Grenville implemented various taxes to compel colonists to pay for their own defense. Colonists resisted, claiming that they could not be taxed by Parliament because they were not represented in Parliament. British officials countered that the colonists had *virtual representation* in Parliament, since each member was supposed to represent his district as well as the Empire as a whole. Colonial reaction to the *Stamp Act* of 1765 was the first intimation of real trouble for British authorities. Conflicts between Whigs and Tories intensified when the *Townshend Acts* imposed additional taxes. The *Sons of Liberty* and the *Daughters of Liberty* mobilized resistance, particularly through boycotts of British goods.

- **Road to the American Revolution**   But the crisis worsened. Spontaneous resistance led to the *Boston Massacre*; organized protesters later staged the *Boston Tea Party*. The British response to the events in Boston, called the *Coercive Acts*, sparked further violence between *Patriots* and *Loyalists*. The First Continental Congress formed *Committees of Correspondence* to organize and spread resistance. Thomas Paine's pamphlet *Common Sense* helped kindle revolutionary fervor and plant the seed of independence, and the Continental Congress delivered its *Declaration of Independence*.

CHRONOLOGY

1651	First Navigation Act passed by Parliament
1688–1689	Glorious Revolution
1756–1763	French and Indian War
1763	Pontiac's Rebellion begins
	Treaty of Paris ends French and Indian War
	Royal Proclamation
1765	Stamp Act; Stamp Act Congress
1766	Repeal of the Stamp Act
1767	Townshend Acts
1770	Boston Massacre
1773	Tea Act; Boston Tea Party
1774	Coercive Acts
1775	Military conflict at Lexington and Concord
1776	Thomas Paine publishes *Common Sense*
	Continental Congress declares independence

KEY TERMS

mercantilism p. 152

Navigation Acts p. 152

Glorious Revolution p. 154

natural rights p. 155

salutary neglect p. 155

French and Indian War (Seven Years' War) p. 157

Albany Plan of Union p. 159

Treaty of Paris (1763) p. 163

Pontiac's Rebellion p. 166

Royal Proclamation of 1763 p. 166

Stamp Act p. 168

virtual representation p. 169

Sons of Liberty p. 169

Daughters of Liberty p. 170

Townshend Acts p. 173

Loyalists p. 174

Patriots p. 174

Boston Massacre p. 175

Committee of Correspondence p. 177

Boston Tea Party p. 177

Coercive Acts p. 178

Common Sense p. 186

Declaration of Independence p. 188

 INQUIZITIVE

Go to InQuizitive to see what you've learned—and learn what you've missed—with personalized feedback along the way.

part two

BUILDING A NATION

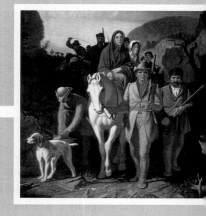

The signing of the Declaration of Independence in July 1776 thrilled the rebellious colonists and forced other Americans to make a hard choice: to remain loyal subjects of King George III and thus traitors to the new United States of America, or to embrace the rebellion and become traitors to Great Britain. It was one thing for Patriot leaders to declare independence and quite another to win it on the battlefield. The odds greatly favored the British; fewer than half of the colonists were Patriots who *actively* supported the Revolution, and many others—the

Loyalists—fought against it. The thirteen independent states had new, untested governments, and General George Washington found himself in charge of an inexperienced and poorly equipped army of amateurs facing the world's greatest military power.

Yet the Revolutionaries would persevere and prevail. As a military leader, Washington proved to be more dogged than brilliant, a general famous for his courage and composure—even in the face of adversity. He had extensive knowledge of the nation's geography and used it to his advantage against the British. Even more important to the Revolutionary cause was the decision by the French (and later the Spanish and Dutch) to join the war against Britain. The Franco-American military alliance, negotiated in 1778, was the decisive turning point in the war. In 1783, after eight years of sporadic fighting and heavy human and financial losses, the British gave up the fight and their American colonies.

While fighting the British, the Patriots also had to create new governments for themselves. Quite different colonies suddenly became coequal states. The deeply ingrained resentment of British imperial rule led the Americans to give more power to the individual states than to the weak new national government, called the Confederation. As Thomas Jefferson declared, "Virginia is my country."

Such powerful local ties help explain why the Articles of Confederation, the original constitution organizing the thirteen states into a loose confederation, provided only minimal national authority when it was finally ratified by the states in 1781. Final power to make and execute laws remained with the states.

After the Revolutionary War, the flimsy political bonds authorized by the Articles of Confederation could not meet the needs of the new nation. This realization led to the calling of the Constitutional Convention in 1787. The process of drafting and approving the new constitution generated a heated debate about the respective powers granted to the states and the national government, a debate that became the central theme of American political thought.

The Revolution also helped reshape American society. What would be the role of women, African Americans, and Native Americans in the new nation? How would the different economies of the various regions of the new United States be developed? Who would control access to the vast Native American ancestral lands to the west of the original thirteen states? How would the United States of America relate to the other nations of the world?

These questions gave birth to the first national political parties in the United States. During the 1790s, the Federalist party, led by George Washington, John Adams, and Alexander Hamilton, and the Democratic-Republican party, led by Thomas Jefferson and James Madison, furiously debated the political and economic future of the new nation.

With Jefferson's election as president in 1800, the Republicans gained the upper hand in national politics and would remain dominant for the next quarter century. In the process, they presided over a maturing republic that aggressively expanded westward at the expense of the Native Americans, embraced industrial development, engaged in a second war with Great Britain, and witnessed growing tensions between North and South over slavery.

5

The American Revolution
1776–1783

The Death of General Mercer at the Battle of Princeton (ca. 1789–1831) After the American victory at Trenton, New Jersey, George Washington (center, on horseback) launched a surprise attack on the British at the Battle of Princeton. The Americans won the battle, but one of the casualties was Washington's close friend, General Hugh Mercer (bottom), whose death created a rallying symbol for the Revolution.

F ew Europeans thought the upstart American Revolutionaries could win a war against the world's richest and most powerful empire— and, indeed, the Americans did lose most of the major battles in the Revolutionary War. But they outlasted the British, eventually forcing them to end the war and grant independence to the United States of America.

This stunning result reflected the tenacity of the Patriots as well as the difficulties the British faced in fighting a transatlantic war 3,000 miles from home. It took five to ten weeks for orders from the government in London to reach British commanders in America, and often they were out of date by the time they arrived. The British also had to adjust to the often unorthodox American ways of warfare. They discovered that Patriots were willing to fight at night, in the cold, in the woods, and in the rain and snow.

What began as a war for independence became both a *civil war* between Americans (Patriots/Whigs versus Loyalists/Tories), joined by their Indian allies, and a *world war* involving numerous "allied" European nations. The crucial development was the ability of the United States to forge military alliances with France, Spain, and the Netherlands, all of which were eager to humble Great Britain and seize its colonies around the world. Those nations provided the Revolutionaries with desperately needed money, supplies, soldiers, and warships. The French and Spanish also sent a combined fleet of warships to the English Channel—forcing much of the Royal Navy to remain at home, thus weakening the British effort to blockade American ports.

The war for independence unleashed unexpected social and political changes, as it required "common people" to take a more active role in governments at all

focus questions

1. What challenges faced the British and American military leaders in fighting the Revolutionary War?

2. What were some of the key turning points in the Revolutionary War? How did they change the direction of the war?

3. In what ways did the American Revolution function as a civil war?

4. How was the Revolutionary War an "engine" for political and social change?

5. How did the Revolutionary War impact African Americans, women, and Native Americans?

levels—local, state, and national. After all, as the Declaration of Independence asserted, governments derive "their just powers from the consent of the governed." The common people readily took advantage of their new opportunities. In Virginia, voters in 1776 elected a new state legislature that, as an observer noted, "was composed of men not quite so well dressed, nor so politely educated, nor so highly born" as had been the case in the past.

Mobilizing for War

The British Empire sent some 35,000 soldiers and half of its huge navy across the Atlantic to put down the American rebellion. The British also hired foreign soldiers (mercenaries), as some 30,000 Germans served in the British armies in America. Most were from the German state of Hesse-Cassel—thus they became known to Americans as **Hessians**.

The British also recruited American Loyalists, Native Americans, and African Americans to fight on their behalf, but there were never as many willing to join them as they had hoped. Further, the British faced a formidable challenge in supplying their large army and navy in America. They initially assumed that there would be enough food for their troops and plenty of forage for their horses in America. As the war ground on, however, most of the supplies had to come from Britain. The war in America became terribly expensive and eventually demoralizing to the British people, as it dragged on year after year costing more and more in lives and money.

The British government under Lord North also never had a consistent war strategy. Initially, the British focused on blockading New England's seaports to strangle American commerce. When that failed, British military leaders sought to destroy George Washington's Continental army in New York. Despite their initial success in driving the Americans out of the city, the British commanders failed to pursue and eliminate the retreating Continental army. They next tried to drive a wedge between New England and New York, splitting the colonies in two. That too would fail, leading to the final British strategy: moving their main army into the southern colonies in hopes of rallying Loyalists in the region.

THE CONTINENTAL ARMY While the Patriots had the advantage of fighting on their home ground, they also had to create an army and navy from scratch, and with little money to do so. Recruiting, supplying, equipping, training, and paying soldiers and sailors were monumental challenges.

Before the war, **citizen-soldiers** (militiamen) were primarily civilians summoned from their farms and shops to defend their communities. Once the danger passed, the militiamen quickly dispersed and returned to their homes or farms. Many militiamen were unreliable and ungovernable. They "come in, you cannot tell how," General Washington said in exasperation, "go, you cannot tell when, and act, you cannot tell where, consume your provisions, exhaust your stores [supplies], and leave you at last at a critical moment."

Once the war started, Washington knew that militiamen alone could not win against veteran British and German soldiers. He needed a professional army with full-time soldiers. While recruiting fighters, General Washington was pleased to see that the men from different colonies were developing a national (or "continental") viewpoint, in which they thought of themselves as fighting for a new *nation*, not just protecting their particular communities like militiamen. Washington thus decided to call it the *Continental army*. About half of the 200,000 Americans who served in the war were in the Continental army. They were mostly young, single, relatively poor farmers, laborers, or indentured servants.

What the Continental army needed most at the start of the war were capable officers, intensive training, modern weapons, and multiyear enlistment contracts. The Revolutionary soldiers also needed strict discipline, for they had no room for error against the British. As Washington began whipping his new army into shape, those who violated the rules were jailed, flogged, or sent packing. Some deserters were hanged.

Many Patriots who had not fought in the French and Indian War found army life unbearable and combat horrifying. As General Nathanael Greene, a Rhode Island Quaker who abandoned the pacifism of his religion for the war effort and became Washington's ablest commander, pointed out, few Patriots had ever engaged in mortal combat, and they were hard-pressed to "stand the shocking scenes of war, to march over dead men, to hear without concern the groans of the wounded."

Desertions grew as the war dragged on. At times, Washington could put only a few thousand men in the field. Eventually, to recruit more soldiers, Congress was forced to provide more generous enticements, such as land grants and cash bonuses, in exchange for recruits agreeing to serve in the Continental army for the duration of the war.

PROBLEMS OF FINANCE AND SUPPLY Financing the Revolution was much harder for the new American nation than it was for Great Britain. Lacking the power to impose taxes, the Confederation Congress could only *ask* the states to provide funds for the national government. Yet the states rarely provided their expected share of the war's expenses, and the Continental Congress reluctantly had to allow the Patriot armies to take supplies directly from farmers in return for written promises of future payment.

George Washington at Princeton
Commissioned for Independence
Hall in Philadelphia, this 1779 painting
by Charles Willson Peale portrays
Washington as the hero of the Battle of
Princeton.

In a predominantly agricultural society, like America, turning farmers into soldiers hurt the national economy. William Hooper, a North Carolinian who signed the Declaration of Independence, grumbled that "a soldier made is a farmer lost." In April 1776, the Continental Congress had ended Britain's trade regulations by opening American ports to the ships of all nations. Soon, however, British warships set up blockades around America's major coastal cities.

Many states found a ready source of revenue in the sale of abandoned Loyalist homes, farms, and plantations. Nevertheless, Congress and the states still fell short of funding the war's cost and were forced to print more and more paper money, which eroded its value. At the start of the fighting there were no uniforms for the soldiers and sailors, and weapons were "as various as their costumes." Most weapons and ammunition were acquired either by capturing British supplies or by importing them from France, a government all too glad to help the Patriots fight its arch-enemy.

NATIVE AMERICANS AND THE REVOLUTION Both the British and Americans recruited Indians to fight with them, but the British were far more successful, largely because they had longstanding relationships with chieftains and they promised to protect Indian lands. The peoples making up the Iroquois League split their allegiances, with most Mohawks, Onondagas, Cayugas, and Senecas, led by Mohawk Joseph Brant and Seneca Old Smoke, joining the British, and most Oneidas and Tuscaroras supporting the Patriots. The Cherokees also joined the British in hopes of driving out American settlers who had taken their lands.

Most Indians in New England tried to remain neutral or sided with the Patriots. The Stockbridge Indians in Massachusetts, mostly Mahicans, formed a company of Minutemen who fought alongside Patriot units. They pledged that "wherever your armies go, there we will go; you shall always find us by your side; and if providence calls us to sacrifice our lives in the field of battle, we will fall where you fall, and lay our bones by yours." Yet however much the British or Americans claimed Native Americans as allies, most Indians engaged in the war as a means of protecting themselves and their own interests.

DISASTER IN CANADA In July 1775, the Continental Congress authorized an ill-planned military expedition in Canada against Quebec, in the vain hope of rallying support among the French Canadians. One Patriot detachment, under General Richard Montgomery, a former British army officer, headed toward Quebec by way of Lake Champlain along the New York–Canadian border; another, under General Benedict Arnold, struggled westward toward Quebec through the dense Maine woods.

The Americans arrived outside Quebec in September, tired, exhausted, and hungry. A silent killer then ambushed them: smallpox. As the deadly virus raced through the American camp, General Montgomery faced a brutal dilemma. Most of his soldiers had signed up for short tours of duty, and many were scheduled for discharge at the end of the year. Because of the impending departure of his men, Montgomery could not afford to wait until spring for the smallpox to subside. Seeing little choice but to fight, he ordered an attack on the British forces defending Quebec during a blizzard, on December 31, 1775.

The American assault was a disaster. Montgomery was killed early in the battle, and Benedict Arnold was seriously wounded. More than 400 Americans were taken prisoner. The rest of the Patriot force retreated to its camp outside the walled city and appealed to the Continental Congress for reinforcements. Smallpox spread throughout the American army, and Arnold warned George Washington in February 1776 that the runaway disease would soon bring "the entire ruin of the Army." The British, sensing weakness, attacked the American camp and sent the ragtag Patriots on a frantic retreat up the St. Lawrence River to the American-held city of Montreal, and eventually back to New York and New England.

By the summer of 1776, the American Revolutionaries had come to realize that their quest for independence would be neither short nor easy, for the king and Parliament were determined to smash the revolt and restore their empire. George Washington confessed to his brother that his efforts to form an effective American army out of "the great mixture of troops" were filled with "difficulties and distresses." Most of the New England soldiers—farmers, sailors, fishermen, and a few former slaves—were, he said, "an exceeding[ly] dirty and nasty people." Units from Pennsylvania, Washington added, did not "know more of a Rifle than my horse."

WASHINGTON'S NARROW ESCAPE   On July 2, 1776, the day the Continental Congress voted for independence, a huge army of British redcoats came ashore on undefended Staten Island, across New York City's harbor from Manhattan. By late August, two thirds of the entire British army, veterans of many campaigns around the world, were camped on Staten Island. They were the first wave in an effort to end the war quickly with a decisive victory.

For the next several weeks, while more ships, supplies, and troops landed and prepared for action, General William Howe and his older brother, Admiral Richard Howe, both of whom sympathized with American grievances but felt strongly that the rebellion must be put down, met with Patriot leaders in an effort to negotiate a settlement of the revolution. Their orders from London told them to "make peace if possible" and then wage "war if peace was out of the question."

After the negotiations failed, on August 22, 1776, a massive British fleet of 427 ships carrying 32,000 troops, including 8,000 hired German soldiers, began landing on Long Island near New York City. It was the largest seaborne military expedition in history to that point. "I could not believe my eyes," recalled a Pennsylvania militiaman. "I declare that I thought all London was afloat."

Meanwhile, George Washington, after ousting the British from Boston, had moved his forces to defensive positions around New York City in February 1776. He still struggled to raise an army powerful enough to match the British. During the winter and spring, he could gather only about 19,000 poorly trained militiamen and recruits. Nor did he have any warships to defend a city surrounded by rivers and bays. It was too small a force to defend New York from the expected British invasion, but the Continental Congress insisted that the strategic city be defended. As John Adams explained, New York was the "key to the whole continent."

Although a veteran of frontier fighting, Washington had never commanded a large force or supervised artillery (cannon) units. As he confessed to the Continental Congress, he had no "experience to move [armies] on a large scale" and had only "limited . . . knowledge . . . in military matters." Washington was still learning the art of generalship, and the British invasion of New York taught him some costly and painful lessons.

The new American army suffered a humiliating defeat at the Battle of Long Island as the British invaders perfectly executed their assault. An American officer noted that the fighting on Long Island was nothing but "fright, disgrace, and confusion." As General Washington watched the British advance, he sighed: "Good God! What brave fellows I must this day lose." In the face of steadily advancing ranks of British soldiers with bayonet-tipped muskets, many of the untested American defenders and their officers panicked. The smoke and chaos of battle disoriented the Patriots. Over the next week of intense fighting, the confused, disorganized, undisciplined, and indecisive Americans steadily gave ground. Only a timely rainstorm and heroic efforts by experienced boatmen enabled the retreating Americans to cross the harbor from Brooklyn to Manhattan during the night of August 29.

Had Howe's British army moved more quickly in pursuing the retreating Patriots, it could have trapped Washington's entire force and ended the Revolution. But the British rested as the main American army, joined by Patriot civilians, made a miraculous escape from Manhattan over the next several weeks. They crossed the Hudson River and retreated with furious urgency into New Jersey and then over the Delaware River into eastern Pennsylvania. A New Jersey resident reported that the retreating Americans "marched two abreast, looked ragged, some without a shoe to their feet, and most of them wrapped in blankets." Thousands had been captured during the New York campaign, and hundreds more deserted, eager to go home ahead of their British pursuers.

General Washington was "wearied almost to death" by one of the greatest chases in military history as the ragged remnants of his army outraced their British pursuers over 170 miles in two months. "In one thing only" did the British fail, reported an observer; "they could not run as fast as their Foe." A British general predicted a quick victory in the war. The Americans, he claimed, would "never again stand before us in the field. Everything seems to be over with them."

The situation was bleak in the fall of 1776. New York City became the headquarters of both the Royal Navy and the British army. Local Loyalists (Tories) in New York City and New Jersey excitedly welcomed the British occupation. "Hundreds in this colony are against us," a New York City Patriot wrote to John Adams. "Tories openly express their sentiments in favor of the enemy."

By December 1776, the American Revolution was near collapse. A British officer reported that many "rebels" were "without shoes or stockings, and several were observed to have only linen drawers . . . without any proper shirt. They must suffer extremely" in the winter weather. Indeed, the Continental Army was shrinking before Washington's eyes. He had only 3,000 men left by Christmas. Unless a new army could be raised quickly, he warned, "I think the game is pretty near up."

Then, almost miraculously, help emerged from an unexpected source: the English-born war correspondent, Thomas Paine. Having opened the eventful year of 1776 with his inspiring pamphlet *Common Sense*, Paine now composed *The American Crisis*, in which he wrote these stirring lines:

> These are the times that try men's souls: The summer soldier and the sunshine patriot will, in this crisis, shrink from the service of his country; but he that stands it NOW deserves the love and thanks of man and woman. Tyranny, like Hell, is not easily conquered. Yet we have this consolation with us, that the harder the conflict, the more glorious the triumph.

Paine's rousing pamphlet boosted Patriot morale. Out of the disastrous defeat came major changes in the way the Continental Congress managed the war. On December 27, 1776, it gave General Washington "large powers" to strengthen the war effort, including the ability to offer army recruits cash, land, clothing, and blankets.

In December 1776, General William Howe, commander in chief of the British forces, decided that the war with America was all but won. He then casually settled down with his "flashing blonde" Loyalist mistress (twenty-five-year-old Elizabeth Loring, the wife of a New England Tory) to wait out the winter in New York City. (Eighteenth-century armies rarely fought during the

Thomas Paine's *Common Sense* Thomas Paine's inspiring pamphlet was originally published anonymously because the British viewed it as treasonous.

winter months.) One American general concluded that Howe "shut his eyes, fought his battles, drank his bottle and had his little whore."

A DESPERATE GAMBLE George Washington, however, was not ready to hibernate for the winter. The morale of his men and the hopes of the nation, he decided, required "some brilliant stroke" of good news after the devastating defeats around New York City. So the normally cautious Washington grew bold out of necessity, launching a desperate gamble to achieve a much-needed victory before more of his soldiers decided to leave the army and return home.

On Christmas night 1776, Washington led some 2,400 men, packed into forty-foot-long boats, from Pennsylvania across the icy Delaware into New Jersey. A blizzard of sleet and snow helped cloak their movements on the frigid night. Near dawn, at Trenton, the Americans surprised 1,500 sleeping Hessians, attacking them from three sides. An American sergeant said his "blood chill'd to see such horror and distress, blood mingling together, the dying groans. . . . The sight was too much to bear."

The **Battle of Trenton** was a total rout, from which only 500 Hessians escaped. Just two of Washington's men were killed. The American commander had been in the thick of the battle, urging his men forward: "Press on! Press on, boys!"

A week later, General Washington and the Americans again crossed the Delaware and won another battle in New Jersey, at Princeton, before taking shelter at Morristown, in the hills of northern New Jersey. A British officer muttered that the Americans had "become a formidable enemy."

The surprising victories at Princeton and Trenton saved the cause of independence and shifted the war's momentum, as a fresh wave of inspired Americans signed up to serve in Washington's army. A British officer recognized that the victories at Trenton and Princeton would "revive the dropping spirits of the rebels and increase their force." The military successes in New Jersey also revived Patriot confidence in George Washington's leadership. British war correspondents claimed that he was more talented than any of their own commanders. Yet although the "dark days" of the autumn of 1776 were over, unexpected challenges quickly chilled the Patriots' excitement.

WINTER IN MORRISTOWN During the record-cold winter in early 1777, George Washington's ragged army again nearly disintegrated as six-month enlistment contracts expired and deserters fled the hardships caused by the brutal weather, inadequate food, and widespread disease. One soldier recalled that "we were absolutely, literally starved. . . . I saw several of the men roast their old shoes and eat them."

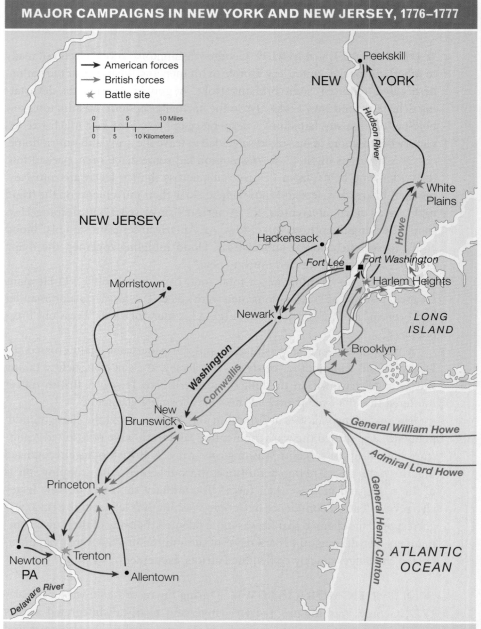

MAJOR CAMPAIGNS IN NEW YORK AND NEW JERSEY, 1776–1777

- Why did General Washington lead his army from Brooklyn to Manhattan and from there to New Jersey?
- How could the British army commander, General William Howe, have ended the rebellion in New York?
- What is the significance of the Battle of Trenton?

Smallpox and other diseases continued to cause more casualties among the American armies than combat. By 1777, Washington had come to view smallpox with greater dread than "the Sword of the Enemy." On any given day, a fourth of the American troops were deemed unfit for duty, usually because of smallpox.

The threat was so great that in early 1777 Washington ordered a mass inoculation, which he managed to keep secret from the British. Inoculating an entire army was a risky undertaking in the eighteenth century, but it paid off. The successful inoculation of the American army marks one of Washington's greatest strategic accomplishments of the war.

Only about 1,000 Patriots stayed with Washington through the brutal Morristown winter. With the spring thaw, however, recruits began arriving to claim the bounty of $20 and 100 acres of land offered by Congress to those who would enlist for three years or for the duration of the conflict, if less. Having cobbled together some 9,000 regular troops, Washington began skirmishing with the British forces in northern New Jersey.

A STRATEGY OF EVASION   General Howe had been making his own plans, however, and so had other British officers. Howe hoped to maneuver the American army into fighting a single "decisive action" that the superior British forces would surely win—and thereby end the war in one glorious engagement.

George Washington, however, refused to take the bait. The fighting around New York City had shown him that his outmanned army almost certainly could not defeat the British in a large open battle. The only way to beat them, he decided, was to evade the main British army, carefully select when and where to attack, and, in the end, wear down the enemy forces and their will to fight on. Washington was willing to concede control of major cities like New York to the British, for it was his army, "not defenseless towns, [that] they have to subdue."

So the Americans in the Revolution did not have to win large battles; they simply had to avoid losing the war. Britain, on the other hand, could win only by destroying the American will to resist. With each passing year, it became more difficult—and expensive—for the British to supply their large army and navy in America. Over time, the British government and people would tire of the human and financial toll of conducting a prolonged war across the Atlantic.

AMERICAN SOCIETY AT WAR

The Revolution was as much a ruthless civil war among Americans (including the Native American peoples allied with both sides) as it was a prolonged struggle against Great Britain. The necessity of choosing sides divided families and friends, towns and cities.

Benjamin Franklin's illegitimate son, William, for example, was the royal governor of New Jersey. An ardent Loyalist, he sided with Great Britain in the war. His Patriot father later removed him from his will. Similarly, eighteen-year-old Bostonian Lucy Flucker defied her Loyalist father's wishes and married bookseller Henry Knox in 1774. (Knox would become an American general.) Lucy's estranged family fled with the British army when it left Boston in 1776, and she never saw them again. "I have lost my father, mother, brother, and sister, entirely lost them," she wrote.

The colonists were generally divided into three groups: Patriots, who formed the Continental army and fought in state militias; Loyalists, or Tories, as the Patriots mockingly called them; and, a less committed middle group that sought to remain neutral but were eventually swayed by the better organized and more energetic Patriots. Loyalists may have represented 20 percent of the American population, but Patriots were the largest of the three groups.

Some Americans (like Benedict Arnold) switched sides during the war. Both the Patriots and the British, once they took control of a city or community, would often require the residents to swear an oath of loyalty to their cause. In Pennsylvania, Patriots tied a rope around the neck of John Stevens, a Loyalist, and dragged him behind a canoe in the Susquehanna River because he refused to sign a loyalty oath.

Where the Patriots rejected the monarchy, the Loyalists, whom George Washington called "abominable pests of society," viewed the Revolution as an act of treason. The British Empire, they felt, was much more likely than an independent America to protect them from foreign foes and enable them to prosper.

Loyalists were most numerous in the seaport cities, especially New York City and Philadelphia, as well as the Carolinas, but they came from all walks of life. Governors, judges, and other royal officials were almost all Loyalists; most Anglican ministers also preferred the mother country, as did many Anglican worshippers. In the backcountry of New York and across the Carolinas, many small farmers who had largely been unaffected by the controversies over British efforts to tighten colonial regulations rallied to the British side. More New York men joined Loyalist regiments than the Continental army. Many Loyalists calculated that the Revolution would fail or feared that it would result in mob rule. In few places, however, were there enough Loyalists to assume control without the support of British troops.

The Loyalists did not want to "dissolve the political bands" with Britain, as the Declaration of Independence demanded. Instead, as some 700 of them in New York City said in a petition to British officials, they "steadily and uniformly opposed" this "most unnatural, unprovoked Rebellion." Jacob Bailey

Four Soldiers (ca. 1781) This illustration drawn by a French lieutenant captures the varied uniforms worn by Patriot forces in the war (left to right): a black soldier (freed for joining the 1st Rhode Island Regiment), a New England militiaman, a frontiersman, and a French soldier.

of Massachusetts dismissed the Patriots as a "set of surly & savage beings who have power in their hands and murder in their hearts."

In few places, however, were there enough Loyalists to assume control of areas or communities without the presence of British troops. The British were repeatedly frustrated by both the failure of Loyalists to materialize in strength and the collapse of Loyalist militia units once British troops departed. Because Patriot militias quickly returned whenever the British left an area, any Loyalists in the region faced a difficult choice: either accompany the British and leave behind their property or stay and face the wrath of the Patriots. Even more disheartening was what one British officer called "the licentiousness of the [Loyalist] troops, who committed every species of rapine and plunder" and thereby converted potential friends to enemies.

The Patriots, both moderates and radicals, supported the war because they realized that the only way to protect their liberty was to separate themselves from British control. Patriots also wanted to establish an American republic, a unique form of government that would convert them from being *subjects* of a king to being *citizens* in a republic with the power to elect their own government and pursue their own economic interests. "We have it in our power," wrote Thomas Paine, "to begin the world over again. . . . The birthday of a new world is at hand."

SETBACKS FOR THE BRITISH (1777)

In 1777, a carefully conceived but poorly executed British plan to defeat the "American rebellion" involved a three-pronged assault on the state of New York. By gaining control of that important state, the British planned to split America in two, cutting off New England from the rest of the colonies.

The complicated plan called for a British army, based in Canada and led by General John Burgoyne, to advance southward from Quebec via Lake Champlain to the Hudson River. At the same time, another British force would move eastward from Oswego, in western New York. General William Howe, meanwhile, would lead a third British army up the Hudson River from New York City. All three advancing armies would eventually converge in central New York and wipe out any remaining Patriot resistance.

The three British armies, however, failed in their execution—and in their communications with one another. At the last minute, Howe changed his mind and decided to move his army south from New York City to attack the Patriot capital, Philadelphia. General Washington withdrew most of his men from New Jersey to meet the British threat in Pennsylvania while other American units banded together in upstate New York to deal with the British threat there.

On September 11, 1777, at Brandywine Creek, southwest of Philadelphia, the British overpowered Washington's army and occupied Philadelphia, then the largest and wealthiest American city. The members of the Continental Congress were forced to flee the city. Battered but still intact, Washington and his army withdrew to winter quarters twenty miles away at Valley Forge, while Howe and his men remained in the relative comfort of Philadelphia.

General John Burgoyne Commander of Britain's northern forces. Burgoyne and most of his troops surrendered to the Americans at Saratoga on October 17, 1777.

THE CAMPAIGN OF 1777

Meanwhile, in northern New York, a second British army had stumbled into an American trap. In June, an overconfident General Burgoyne (nicknamed

"General Swagger") had led his mistress and 7,000 soldiers southward from Canada toward New York's Lake Champlain.

The American commander in northern New York was General Horatio Gates. Thirty-two years earlier, in 1745, he and Burgoyne had served as officers in the same British regiment. Now they were commanding opposing armies. As Burgoyne's army pushed deeper into New York, it became harder to get food and supplies from Canada. Short of wagons and carts, the advance slowed to a snail's pace in the dense forests and swamps, thereby allowing the Americans to spring a trap.

The outnumbered but more mobile Patriots had the benefit of fighting in familiar territory. They inflicted two serious defeats on the British forces in August 1777. At Oriskany on August 6, Patriot militiamen, mostly local German American farmers and their Indian allies, withstood an ambush by Loyalists and Indians and gained time for Patriot reinforcements to arrive at nearby Fort Stanwix, which had been besieged by British soldiers. When the British demanded the fort's surrender, General Gates rejected the offer "with disdain," saying that the fort would be defended to the "last extremity." As the days passed, the Iroquois deserted the British army, leading the British commander to order a withdrawal. As a result, the strategic Mohawk Valley running across central New York was secured by the Patriot forces.

To the east, at Bennington, Vermont, on August 16, New England militiamen, led by Colonel John Stark, decimated a detachment of Hessians and Loyalists. Stark had pledged that morning, "We'll beat them before night, or Molly Stark will be a widow."

As Patriot militiamen converged from across central New York, Burgoyne pulled his dispirited forces back to the village of Saratoga, near the Hudson River. In the ensuing, three-week-long **Battles of Saratoga**, Gates's army surrounded the British forces, cutting off their supply lines. Desperate for food and ammunition, the British failed twice to break through the encircling Americans. "Thus ended all our hopes of victory," noted a British officer.

The trapped Burgoyne surrendered on October 17, 1777, turning over 5,800 troops, 7,000 muskets, and forty-two brass cannons to Gates. In London, King George fell "into agonies on hearing the account" of Burgoyne's defeat. William Pitt, the former British prime minister, made a shocking prediction to Parliament after the defeat: *"You cannot conquer America."*

ALLIANCE WITH FRANCE   The surprising American victory at Saratoga was a strategic turning point because it convinced the French, who had lost four wars to the British in the previous eighty years, to sign two crucial treaties that created an American **alliance with France**.

Under the Treaty of Amity and Commerce, France officially recognized the new United States and offered important trading privileges to American ships. Under the Treaty of Alliance, both parties agreed, first, that if France entered the war, both countries would fight until American independence was won; second, that neither would conclude a "truce or peace" without "the formal consent of the other"; and, third, that each would guarantee the other's possessions in America "from the present time and forever against all other powers." France further agreed not to seek Canada or other British possessions on the mainland of North America.

In the end, the intervention of the French army and navy determined the outcome of the war. The Americans would also form important alliances with the Spanish (1779) and the Dutch (1781), but neither provided as much support as the French.

After the British defeat at Saratoga and the news of the French alliance with the United States, Parliament tried to end the war by granting all the demands that the Americans had made before they declared independence. But the Continental Congress would not negotiate until Britain officially recognized American independence and withdrew its military forces. King George refused.

1778: Both Sides Regroup

VALLEY FORGE AND STALEMATE For George Washington's army at **Valley Forge**, near Philadelphia, the winter of 1777–1778 was a time of intense suffering and unrelenting cold, hunger, and disease. Some soldiers lacked shoes and blankets, and their makeshift log-and-mud huts offered little protection from the chilling winds. By February, 7,000 troops were too ill for duty. More than 2,500 soldiers died at Valley Forge; another 1,000 deserted. Fifty officers resigned on one December day, and several hundred more left before winter's end. Desperate for relief, Washington sent troops across New Jersey, Delaware, and the Eastern Shore of Maryland to confiscate horses, cattle, and hogs in exchange for "receipts" promising future payment.

By March 1778, the troops at Valley Forge saw their strength restored. Their improved health enabled Washington to begin a rigorous training program. Because few of the American officers had any formal military training, their troops lacked leadership, discipline, and skills. To remedy this defect, Washington turned to an energetic Prussian soldier of fortune, Friedrich Wilhelm, baron von Steuben, who used an interpreter and frequent profanity to instruct the troops in the fundamentals of close-order drill.

Valley Forge During the harsh winter of 1777–1778, Washington's army battled starvation, disease, and freezing temperatures.

Steuben was one of several foreign volunteers who joined the American army at Valley Forge. Another was a nineteen-year-old, red-haired French orphan named Gilbert du Motier, Marquis de Lafayette. A wealthy idealist excited by the American cause ("I was crazy [with desire] to wear a uniform," he said), Lafayette offered to serve in the Continental army for no pay in exchange for being named a general.

Washington was initially skeptical of the young French aristocrat, but Lafayette soon became the commander in chief's most trusted aide. Washington noted that Lafayette possessed "a large share of bravery and military ardor." The young French general also proved to be an able diplomat in helping to forge the military alliance with France (there are forty cities, seven counties, and a private college named for Lafayette across the United States).

The Continental army's morale rose when the Continental Congress promised extra pay and bonuses after the war, and it rose again with the news of the military alliance with France. In the spring of 1778, British forces withdrew from Pennsylvania to New York City, with the American army in hot pursuit. Once the British were back in Manhattan, Washington's army encamped at

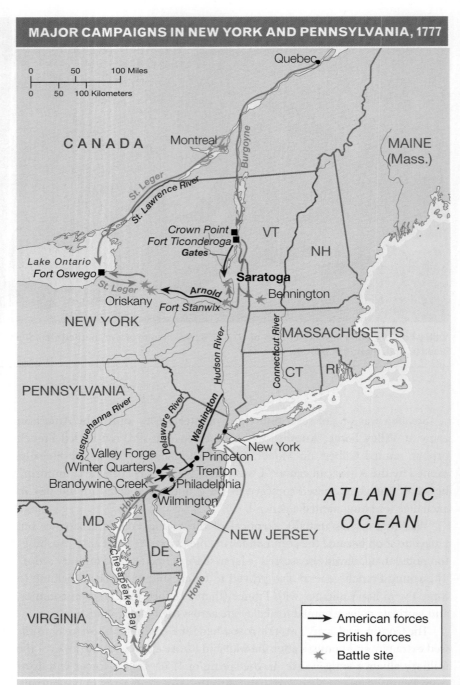

MAJOR CAMPAIGNS IN NEW YORK AND PENNSYLVANIA, 1777

0   50   100 Miles

0   50   100 Kilometers

Quebec

CANADA   Montreal

St. Lawrence River

Burgoyne

St. Leger

MAINE
(Mass.)

Crown Point
Fort Ticonderoga   VT
Gates

NH

Lake Ontario
Fort Oswego

St. Leger

Saratoga

Arnold   Bennington

Oriskany   Fort Stanwix

NEW YORK

Hudson River

Connecticut River

MASSACHUSETTS

CT   RI

PENNSYLVANIA

Susquehanna River

Delaware River

Washington

New York

Valley Forge
(Winter Quarters)

Princeton

Trenton

Brandywine Creek

Philadelphia

Howe

Wilmington

ATLANTIC
OCEAN

MD

NEW JERSEY

DE

Chesapeake Bay

Howe

VIRGINIA

→ American forces

→ British forces

✳ Battle site

■ What were the consequences of Burgoyne's strategy of dividing the colonies by invading upstate New York from Canada?

■ How did life in the American winter camp at Valley Forge transform the army?

■ Why were the Battles of Saratoga a turning point in the American Revolution?

nearby White Plains, north of the city. From that time on, the combat in the north settled into a long stalemate.

WAR IN THE WEST The Revolution had created two wars. In addition to the main conflict between armies in the east, a frontier guerrilla war of terror and vengeance pitted Indians and Loyalists against isolated Patriot settlers along the northern and western frontiers. In the Ohio Valley, as well as western New York and Pennsylvania, the British urged frontier Loyalists and their Indian allies to raid farm settlements and offered to pay bounties for American scalps.

Joseph Brant This 1786 portrait of Thayendanegea (Joseph Brant) by Gilbert Stuart features the Mohawk leader who fought against the Americans in the Revolution.

To end the English-led attacks, early in 1778 George Rogers Clark took 175 Patriot frontiersmen on flatboats down the Ohio River. On the evening of July 4, the Americans captured English-controlled Kaskaskia, in present-day Illinois. Then, without bloodshed, Clark took Cahokia (in Illinois across the Mississippi River from St. Louis) and Vincennes (in present-day Indiana).

After the British retook Vincennes, Clark led his men (almost half of them French volunteers) across icy rivers and flooded prairies, sometimes in water neck-deep, and prepared to attack the British garrison. Clark's rugged frontiersmen, called Rangers, captured five Indians carrying American scalps. Clark ordered his men to kill the Indians in sight of the fort. After watching the terrible executions, the British surrendered.

While Clark's Rangers were in the Indiana territory, a much larger U.S. military force moved against Iroquois strongholds in western New York, where Loyalists (Tories) and their Indian allies had been terrorizing frontier settlements. These Iroquois attacks, led by Mohawk chief Joseph Brant, had killed hundreds of Patriot militiamen.

In response, George Washington sent 4,000 men under General John Sullivan to crush "the hostile tribes" and "the most mischievous of the Tories." At Newton, New York, on August 29, 1779, Sullivan's soldiers destroyed about forty Seneca and Cayuga villages, which broke the power of the Iroquois Confederacy for all time.

In the Kentucky territory, the legendary frontiersman Daniel Boone and his small band of settlers repeatedly clashed with the Shawnees and their British and Loyalist allies. In 1778, Boone and some thirty men, aided by their

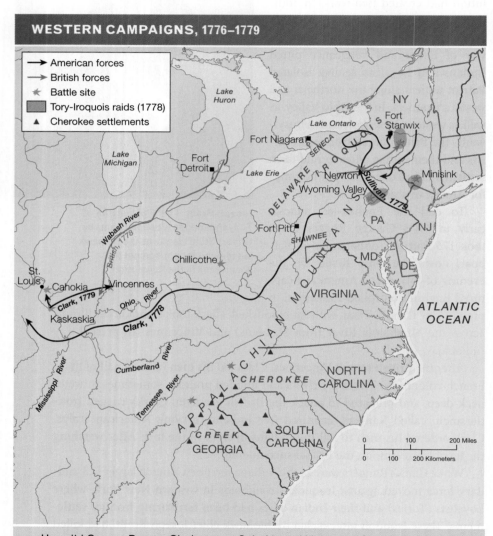

WESTERN CAMPAIGNS, 1776–1779

- ■ How did George Rogers Clark secure Cahokia and Vincennes?
- ■ Why did the American army destroy Iroquois villages in 1779?
- ■ Why were the skirmishes between settlers and Indian tribes significant for the future of the trans-Appalachian frontier?

wives and children, held off an assault by more than 400 Indians at Boonesborough. Later, Boone himself was twice shot and twice captured. Indians killed two of his sons, a brother, and two brothers-in-law. His daughter was captured, and another brother was wounded four times.

In early 1776, a delegation of northern Indians—Shawnees, Delawares, and Mohawks—had talked the Cherokees into attacking frontier settlements in Virginia and the Carolinas. Swift retaliation had followed as Carolina militiamen, led by Andrew Pickens, burned dozens of Cherokee villages. By weakening the major Indian tribes along the frontier, the American Revolution cleared the way for white settlers to seize Indian lands after the war.

THE WAR MOVES SOUTH

In late 1778, the British launched their southern strategy, built on the assumption that large numbers of Loyalists in the Carolinas, Virginia, and Georgia would join the British cause. Once the British gained control of the southern colonies, they would have the shrinking United States pinched between Canada and a British-controlled South.

In December 1778, General Sir Henry Clinton, the new commander in chief of British forces in America, sent 3,000 redcoats, Hessians, and Loyalists to take the port city of Savannah, on the southeast Georgia coast, and roll northeast from there. The plan was to enlist support from local Loyalists and the Cherokees, led by Chief Dragging Canoe, who promised to leave the ground "dark and bloody."

BRITISH MOMENTUM Initially, Clinton's southern strategy worked. Within twenty months, the British and their allies had defeated three American armies, seized the strategic port cities of Savannah and Charleston, South Carolina; occupied Georgia and much of South Carolina; and killed, wounded, or captured some 7,000 American soldiers. The success of the "southern campaign" led Lord George Germain, the British official in London overseeing the war, to predict a "speedy and happy termination of the American war."

Germain's optimistic prediction, however, fell victim to three developments: first, the Loyalist strength in the South was weaker than estimated; second, the British effort to unleash Indian attacks convinced many undecided backcountry settlers to join the Patriot side; and, third, some British and Loyalist soldiers behaved so harshly that they drove Loyalists to switch sides.

WAR IN THE CAROLINAS The Carolina campaign took a major turn when British forces, led brilliantly by Generals Clinton and Charles

Cornwallis, bottled up an entire American army on the Charleston Peninsula. Benjamin Lincoln, the U.S. commander, begged local planters to arm their slaves and let them join the defense of the city, but the slaveholders refused. Prominent South Carolina leaders then used their control of local militia units to prevent Lincoln and his Continental army from escaping the British invasion.

On May 12, 1780, General Lincoln surrendered Charleston and its 5,500 defenders. It was the single greatest Patriot loss of the war. Soon thereafter, General Cornwallis, in charge of the British troops in the South, defeated a much larger American force led by General Horatio Gates at Camden, South Carolina.

Cornwallis had Georgia and most of South Carolina under British control by 1780. Then he made a tactical blunder by sending lieutenants into the Carolina countryside to organize Loyalist fighters to root out Patriots. In doing so, they mercilessly burned homes and hacked to death surrendering rebels. Their behavior alienated many poor rural folk who had been neutral. Francis Kinlock, a Loyalist, warned a British official that "the lower sort of people, who were in many parts . . . originally attached to the British government, have suffered so severely and been so frequently deceived, that Great Britain now has a hundred enemies where it had one before."

In mid-1780, small bands of Patriots based in the swamps and forests of South Carolina launched a successful series of hit-and-run raids. Led by colorful fighters such as Francis Marion, "the Swamp Fox," and Thomas Sumter, "the Carolina Gamecock," the Patriot guerrillas gradually wore down British confidence and morale. By August 1780, the British commanders were forced to admit that South Carolina was "in an absolute state of rebellion" against them.

Warfare in the Carolinas was especially brutal. Patriots fought Loyalists who were neighbors of each other. Both sides looted farms and plantations and tortured, scalped, and executed prisoners. Families were fractured by divided loyalties. Fathers fought sons and brothers killed brothers.

Edward Lacey, a young South Carolina Patriot who commanded a militia unit, had to tie his Tory father to a bedstead to prevent him from informing the British of his whereabouts. Chilling violence occurred on both sides. In Virginia, the planter Charles Lynch set up vigilante courts to punish Loyalists by "lynching" them—which in this case meant whipping them. Others were tarred and feathered.

In the Carolinas and Georgia, British army commanders encouraged their poorly disciplined Loyalist allies to wage a scorched-earth war of terror, arson, and intimidation. "In a civil war," the British general Charles

Cornwallis declared, "there is no admitting of neutral characteristics." He urged his commanders to use the "most *vigorous* measures to *extinguish the rebellion.*"

Tory militiamen took civilian hostages, assaulted women and children, burned houses and churches, stole property, bayoneted wounded Patriots, and tortured and executed unarmed prisoners. Vengeful Patriots responded in kind. When Georgia Loyalist Thomas "Burnfoot" Brown refused to join the revolutionary side, a mob of Patriots bludgeoned him, took his scalp, tarred his legs, and then held his feet over a fire, costing him several toes. Brown thereafter conducted a personal war of vengeance. After a battle near Augusta, Georgia, Brown ordered Loyalists to hang thirteen Patriot prisoners from a staircase banister.

THE BATTLE OF KINGS MOUNTAIN   Cornwallis's two most cold-blooded cavalry officers, Sir Banastre Tarleton and Major Patrick Ferguson, who were in charge of training Loyalist militiamen, eventually overreached themselves. The British officers often let their men burn Patriot farms, liberate slaves, and destroy livestock. Major Ferguson sealed his doom when he threatened to march over the Blue Ridge Mountains, hang the mostly Scots-Irish Presbyterian Patriot leaders ("backwater barbarians"), and destroy their frontier farms. Instead, the feisty "overmountain men" from southwestern Virginia and western North and South Carolina (including "Tennesseans"), all of them experienced hunters and riflemen who had often fought Cherokees, went hunting for Ferguson and his army of Carolina Loyalists in late September 1780.

On October 7, the two sides clashed near Kings Mountain, a heavily wooded ridge along the border between North Carolina and South Carolina. In a ferocious hour-long battle, Patriot sharpshooters, told by an officer to "shout like hell and fight like devils," devastated the Loyalist troops.

Major Ferguson had boasted beforehand that "all the rebels in hell could not push him off" Kings Mountain. By the end of the battle, his lifeless body was riddled with seven bullet holes. Seven hundred Loyalists were captured, twenty-five of whom were later hanged. "The division among the people is much greater than I imagined," an American officer wrote to one of General Washington's aides. The Patriots and Loyalists, he said, "persecute each other with . . . savage fury."

As with so many confrontations during the war in the South, the Battle of Kings Mountain resembled an extended family feud. Seventy-four sets of brothers fought on opposite sides, and twenty-nine sets of fathers and sons.

After the battle, Patriot Captain James Withrow refused to help his Loyalist brother-in-law, who had been badly wounded, and left him to die on the battlefield. When Withrow's wife learned how her husband had treated her brother, she asked for a separation.

Five brothers in the Goforth family from Rutherford County, North Carolina, fought at Kings Mountain; three were Loyalists, two were Patriots. Only one of them survived. Two of the brothers, Preston and John Preston, fighting on opposite sides, recognized each other during the battle, took deadly aim as if in a duel, and fired simultaneously, killing each other.

The American victory in the Battle of Kings Mountain was crucial because it undermined the British strategy in the South. Thomas Jefferson later said that the battle was "the turn of the tide of success." After Kings Mountain, the British forces under Cornwallis were forced to retreat to South Carolina and found it virtually impossible to recruit more Loyalists.

SOUTHERN RETREAT In late 1780, the Continental Congress chose a new commander for the American army in the South: General Nathanael Greene, "the fighting Quaker" of Rhode Island. A former blacksmith blessed with unflagging persistence, he was bold and daring, and well-suited to a drawn-out war.

Greene arrived in Charlotte, North Carolina, to find himself in charge of a "shadow army." The 2,200 troops lacked everything "necessary either for the Comfort or Convenience of Soldiers." Greene wrote General Washington that the situation was "dismal, and truly distressing." Yet he also knew that if he could not create a victorious army, the whole South would be "re-annexed" to Britain.

Like Washington, Greene adopted a hit-and-run strategy. From Charlotte, he moved his army eastward while sending General Daniel Morgan, one of the heroes of the Battles of Saratoga, a heavy-drinking, fist-fighting wagonmaster, with about 700 riflemen on a sweep to the west of Cornwallis's headquarters at Winnsboro, South Carolina.

On January 17, 1781, Morgan's force took up positions near Cowpens, an area of cattle pastures in northern South Carolina about twenty-five miles from Kings Mountain. There he lured Sir Banastre Tarleton's army into an elaborate trap. Tarleton, known for his bravery but hated for his brutality, rushed his men forward, "running at us as if they intended to eat us up," only to be ambushed by Morgan's cavalry. Tarleton escaped, but 110 British soldiers were killed and more than 700 were taken prisoner.

Cowpens was the most complete victory for the American side in the Revolution and was one of the few times that Patriots won a battle in which the two sides were evenly matched. When General Cornwallis learned of the American victory, he was so furiously disappointed that he snapped his ceremonial sword in two, saying that the news "broke my heart."

After the victory at Cowpens, Morgan's army moved into North Carolina and linked up with Greene's troops. Greene lured Cornwallis's starving British army north, then attacked the redcoats at Guilford Courthouse (near what became Greensboro, North Carolina) on March 15, 1781.

The Americans lost the Battle of Guilford Courthouse but inflicted such heavy losses that Cornwallis left behind his wounded and marched his weary men toward Wilmington, on the North Carolina coast, to lick their wounds and take on supplies from British ships. The British commander reported that the Americans had "fought like demons."

Greene then resolved to go back into South Carolina, hoping to lure Cornwallis after him or force the British to give up the state. Greene connected with local guerrilla bands led by Francis Marion, Andrew Pickens, and Thomas Sumter. By targeting outlying British units and picking them off one by one, the guerrillas eventually forced the British back into Charleston and Savannah. George Washington praised Greene for having done "great things with little means."

A War of Endurance

During 1780, the Revolutionary War became a contest of endurance, and the Americans held the advantage in time, men, and supplies. They knew they could outlast the British as long as they avoided a catastrophic defeat. "We fight, get beat, rise, and fight again," General Greene said.

THE VIRGINIA CAMPAIGN By September 1781, the Americans had narrowed British control in the South to Charleston and Savannah, although local Patriots and Loyalists would continue to battle each other for more than a year in the backcountry, where there was "nothing but murder and devastation in every quarter," Greene said.

Meanwhile, Cornwallis had pushed his army northward from Wilmington. Before the Carolinas could be subdued, he had decided that Virginia must be eliminated as a source of American reinforcements and supplies.

In May 1781, the British marched into Virginia. There, Benedict Arnold, the former American general whom the British had bribed to switch sides in the war, was eager to strike at the Americans. Arnold had earlier plotted to sell out his former American command of West Point, a critically important

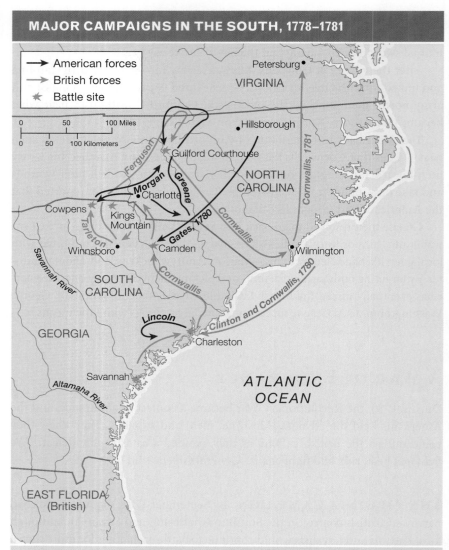

MAJOR CAMPAIGNS IN THE SOUTH, 1778–1781

- American forces
- British forces
- ✳ Battle site

- ■ Why did the British suddenly shift their military campaign to the South in 1778?
- ■ Why were the battles at Savannah and Charleston major victories for the British?
- ■ How did General Nathanael Greene undermine British control of the Lower South?

fortress on the Hudson River north of New York City. Only the lucky capture of a British spy, Major John André, had exposed Arnold's plot. Warned that his plan had been discovered, Arnold joined the British, while the Americans hanged André as a spy.

YORKTOWN When Cornwallis and his army joined Arnold's at Petersburg, Virginia, their combined forces totaled 7,200 men. As the Americans approached, Cornwallis picked Yorktown, a small tobacco port between the York and James Rivers on the Chesapeake Bay, as his base of operations. He was not worried about an American attack, since General Washington's main force seemed preoccupied hundreds of miles away with the British occupation of New York City, and the British navy still controlled American waters.

YORKTOWN, 1781

In July 1780, the French had finally managed to land 6,000 soldiers at Newport, Rhode Island, but they had been bottled up there for a year, blockaded by the British fleet. As long as the British navy maintained supremacy along the coast, the Americans could not hope to win the war.

In May 1781, however, the elements for a combined French-American action suddenly fell into place. As Cornwallis's army moved into Virginia, Washington persuaded the commander of the French army in Rhode Island to join in an attack on the British in New York City.

Before they could strike, however, word came from the Caribbean that Admiral François-Joseph-Paul de Grasse was headed for the Chesapeake Bay with his large fleet of French warships and some 3,000 soldiers. The unexpected news led General Washington to change his strategy. He immediately began moving his army briskly south toward Yorktown. At the same time, French ships slipped out of the British blockade at Newport and also headed south. Somehow, in an age when communications were difficult, the French and Americans coordinated a complex plan to join naval and army forces and destroy the main British army. Success depended on the French fleet getting to the Chesapeake Bay off the coast of Virginia before the British navy did.

On August 30, Admiral de Grasse's twenty-four warships won the race to Yorktown, and French troops landed to join the Americans. On September 6, the day after a British fleet appeared, de Grasse attacked and forced the British navy to abandon Cornwallis's surrounded army, leaving him with no way to get fresh food and supplies. De Grasse then sent ships up the Chesapeake to ferry down the soldiers who were marching south from New York,

Surrender of Lord Cornwallis The artist, John Trumball, completed his painting of the pivotal British surrender at Yorktown in 1781.

bringing the combined American and French armies to 19,000 men—more than double the size of Cornwallis's army.

The **Battle of Yorktown** began on September 28. The American and French troops soon closed off Cornwallis's last escape route and began bombarding the British with cannons. They held out for three grim weeks before running out of food and suffering from widespread disease.

On October 17, 1781, a glum Cornwallis surrendered. Two days later, the British forces marched out and laid down their weapons. Cornwallis himself claimed to be too ill to participate. His report to the British commander in chief in New York was painfully brief: "I have the mortification to inform your Excellency that I have been forced to surrender the troops under my command." Among Cornwallis's surrendered army were five of Thomas Jefferson's former slaves and two owned by George Washington.

THE TREATY OF PARIS (1783)

The war was not yet over. The British still controlled New York City, Charleston, and Savannah, and British ships still blockaded other American ports, but any lingering British hopes of a military victory vanished at Yorktown. In

London, Lord North reacted to the news as if he had "taken a ball [bullet] in the breast." The shaken prime minister exclaimed: "Oh God, it is all over."

In December 1781, King George decided against sending more troops to America. On February 27, 1782, Parliament voted to begin negotiations to end the war, and on March 20, Lord North resigned. In part, the British leaders chose peace in America so that they could concentrate on their continuing global war with France and Spain.

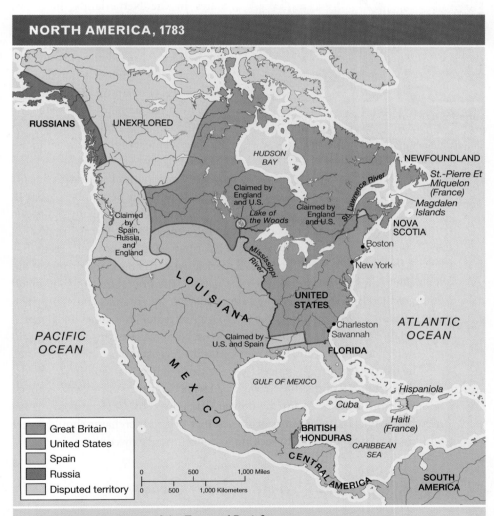

NORTH AMERICA, 1783

- What were the terms of the Treaty of Paris?
- Why might the ambiguities in the treaty's language have led to conflicts among the Americans, the Spanish, and the British?

American Commissioners of the Preliminary Peace Negotiations with Great Britain An unfinished painting from 1782 by Benjamin West. From left, John Jay, John Adams, Benjamin Franklin, Henry Laurens, and Franklin's grandson William Temple Franklin.

A NEGOTIATED PEACE Upon learning of the British decision to negotiate, the Continental Congress named a group of prominent Americans to go to Paris to discuss terms with the British. They included John Adams, who was then representing the United States in the Netherlands; John Jay, minister (ambassador) to Spain; and Benjamin Franklin, already in France. The cranky John Adams was an odd choice since, as Thomas Jefferson said, "He hates [Benjamin] Franklin, he hates John Jay, he hates the French, he hates the English." In the end, Franklin and Jay did most of the work leading to the peace treaty.

The negotiations dragged on for months until, on September 3, 1783, the Treaty of Paris was finally signed. Its provisions were surprisingly favorable to the United States. Great Britain recognized the independence of the thirteen former colonies and—surprisingly—agreed that the Mississippi River was America's western boundary, thereby more than doubling the territory of the new nation. The boundaries of the United States created by the treaty covered some 900,000 square miles, most of which were *west* of the Proclamation Line of 1763, a vast region long inhabited by Indians and often referred to as *trans-Appalachia*. Native Americans were given no role in the negotiations, and they were by far the biggest losers in the final treaty.

The treaty's unclear references to America's northern and southern borders would be a source of dispute for years. Florida, as it turned out, passed back to Spain from Britain. As for the prewar debts owed by Americans to British merchants, the U.S. negotiators promised that British merchants should "meet with no legal impediment" in seeking to collect money owed them.

War as an Engine of Change

Like all major wars, the American war for independence had unexpected effects on political, economic, and social life. The long war upset traditional social relationships and affected the lives of people who had long been discriminated against—African Americans, women, and Indians. In important ways, then, the Revolution was an engine for political experimentation and social change. It ignited a prolonged debate about what new forms of government would best serve the new American republic.

REPUBLICAN IDEOLOGY American Revolutionaries embraced a **republican ideology** instead of the aristocratic or monarchical outlook that had long dominated Europe. The new American republic was not a democracy in the purest sense of the word. In ancient Greece, the Athenians had practiced *direct democracy*, which meant that citizens voted on all major decisions affecting them. The new United States, however, was technically a *representative democracy*, in which property-holding white men governed themselves through the concept of republicanism, whereby they elected representatives, or legislators, to make key decisions on their behalf. As Thomas Paine observed, representative democracy had many advantages over monarchies, one of which was greater transparency: "Whatever are its excellencies and defects, they are visible to all."

To preserve the delicate balance between liberty and power in the new republic, Revolutionary leaders believed that they must protect the rights of individuals and states from being violated by the national government. The war for independence thus sparked a wave of new **state constitutions** that remains unique in history. Not only was a new nation coming into being as a result of the Revolutionary War, but new state-level governments were also being created, all of which were designed to reflect the principles of the republican ideology limiting the powers of government so as to protect the rights of the people.

STATE GOVERNMENTS Most of the political experimentation between 1776 and 1787 occurred at the state level in the form of written constitutions in which the people granted limited authority to their governments. The first state constitutions created state governments during the War of Independence much like the colonial governments, but with *elected* governors and senates instead of royally *appointed* governors and councils. Most of the constitutions also included a bill of rights that protected freedom of speech, trial by jury, freedom from self-incrimination, and the like. Most also limited the powers of governors and strengthened the powers of the legislatures.

THE ARTICLES OF CONFEDERATION Once the colonies had declared their independence in 1776, the Patriots needed to form a *national* government as well. Before March 1781, the Continental Congress had exercised emergency powers without any legal or official authority.

Plans for a permanent form of government emerged quickly. As early as July 1776, a committee appointed by the Continental Congress had produced a draft constitution called the *Articles of Confederation and Perpetual Union*. When the **Articles of Confederation** finally were ratified in March 1781, they essentially legalized the way things had been operating since independence had been declared.

The Confederation government reflected the long-standing fears of monarchy by not allowing for a president or chief executive. In the Confederation government, Congress was given full power over foreign affairs and disputes between the states. But it had no national courts and no power to enforce its resolutions and ordinances. It could not levy taxes, and its budgetary needs depended on requisitions from the states, which state legislatures often ignored.

The states were in no mood to create a strong central government. The Confederation Congress, in fact, had less power than the colonists had once accepted in the British Parliament, because it could not regulate interstate and foreign commerce. For certain important acts, moreover, a "special majority" in the Confederation Congress was required. Nine states had to approve measures dealing with war, treaties, coinage, finances, and the army and navy. Unanimous approval from the states was needed both to impose tariffs (often called "duties," or taxes) on imports and to amend the Articles.

For all its weaknesses, however, the Confederation government represented the most practical structure for the new nation. After all, the Revolution on the battlefields had yet to be won, and an America besieged by British armies and warships could not risk divisive debates over the distribution of power. The new state governments were not willing in 1776 to create a strong national government that might threaten their liberties.

EXPANSION OF POLITICAL PARTICIPATION The new political opportunities afforded by the creation of state governments led more ordinary citizens to participate than ever before. Property qualifications for voting, which already allowed an overwhelming majority of white men to vote, were lowered after 1776 as a result of the Revolutionary fervor. As a group of farmers explained, "no man can be free and independent" unless he possesses "a voice . . . in the most important officers in the legislature." In Pennsylvania, Delaware, North Carolina, and Georgia, any male taxpayer could vote, regardless of how much, if any, property they owned. Farmers, tradesmen, and shopkeepers were soon elected to state legislatures. In general, a higher percentage of American males could vote in the late eighteenth and early nineteenth century than could their counterparts in Great Britain.

THE SOCIAL REVOLUTION

What did the Revolution mean to those workers, servants, farmers, and freed slaves who participated? Many hoped that the Revolution would remove, not reinforce, the elite's traditional political and social advantages. Wealthy Patriots, on the other hand, would have been content to replace royal officials with the rich, the wellborn, and the able—and let it go at that.

In the end, the new republic's social fabric and political culture were visibly different after the war. The energy created by the concepts of liberty, equality, and democracy changed the dynamics of American social and political life in ways that people could not have imagined in 1776.

THE EXODUS OF LOYALISTS   The Loyalists were hurt the most by the brutal civil war embedded within the Revolutionary War. They suffered greatly for their stubborn loyalty to King George III and for their refusal to pledge allegiance to the new United States. During and after the Revolution, their property was confiscated, and many Loyalists were assaulted, brutalized, and executed by Patriots (and vice versa).

After the American victory at Yorktown, tens of thousands of panicked Loyalists made their way to seaports to board British ships and flee the United States. Thousands of African Americans, mostly runaway slaves, also flocked to New York City, Charleston, and Savannah, with many of their angry owners in hot pursuit. Boston King, a runaway, said he saw white slave owners grabbing their escaped slaves "in the streets of New York, or even dragging them out of their beds."

General Guy Carleton, the commander in chief of British forces in North America, organized the mass evacuation after the war. He intentionally violated the provisions of the Treaty of Paris by refusing to return slaves to their owners, defiantly telling a furious George Washington that his slaves from Mount Vernon had already escaped and boarded British ships bound for Canada.

Some 80,000 desperate refugees—white Loyalists, free blacks, freed slaves, and Native Americans who had allied with the British—dispersed throughout the British Empire, changing it in the process. Among the refugees who resettled in Canada were 3,500 former slaves who had been given their freedom in exchange for joining the British army. Some 2,000 freed blacks opted to go to Sierra Leone, where British abolitionists helped them create an experimental colony called Freetown.

About 12,000 Georgia and South Carolina Loyalists, including thousands of their slaves (the British granted freedom only to the slaves of Patriots),

***The Fate of the Loyalists* (1783)** After the Revolution, many Loyalists fled to British colonies in the Caribbean and Canada. This British cartoon shows Patriots, depicted as "savages let[ting] loose," mercilessly hanging and scalping Loyalists.

went to British-controlled East Florida, only to see their new home handed over to Spain in 1783. Spanish authorities gave them a hard choice: swear allegiance to the Spanish king and convert to Catholicism or leave. Most of them left.

Some of the doubly displaced Loyalists sneaked back into the United States, but most went to British islands in the Caribbean. "We are all cast off," complained one embittered Loyalist. "I shall ever tho' remember with satisfaction that it was not I deserted my King [George III], but my King that deserted me." The largest number of Loyalist exiles landed in Canada, where royal officials wanted them to displace the earlier French presence.

The departure of so many Loyalists from America was one of the most important social consequences of the Revolution. Their confiscated homes, lands, and vacated jobs created new social, economic, and political opportunities for Patriots. In Paris, however, the Americans negotiating the peace treaty agreed that the Continental Congress would "earnestly recommend" to the states that the confiscated property be restored, although it rarely was.

FREEDOM OF RELIGION The Revolution also tested traditional religious loyalties and set in motion important changes in the relationship

Religious development The Congregational Church developed a national presence in the early nineteenth century. Lemuel Haynes, depicted here, was its first African American minister.

between church and government. Before the Revolution, Americans *tolerated* religious dissent; after the Revolution, Americans insisted on complete *freedom* of religion as embodied in the principle of separation of church and state.

The Anglican Church, established as the official religion in five colonies and parts of two others, was especially vulnerable to changes prompted by the war. Anglicans tended to be pro-British, and non-Anglicans, notably Baptists and Methodists, outnumbered Anglicans in all states except Virginia. All but Virginia eliminated tax support for the church before the fighting was over, and Virginia did so soon afterward. Although Anglicanism survived in the form of the new Episcopal Church, it never regained its pre-Revolutionary stature.

In 1776, the Virginia Declaration of Rights guaranteed the free exercise of religion, and in 1786 the **Virginia Statute of Religious Freedom** (written by Thomas Jefferson) declared that "no man shall be compelled to frequent or support any religious worship, place or ministry whatsoever" and "that all men shall be free to profess, and by argument to maintain, their opinions in matters of religion." These statutes, and the Revolutionary ideology that justified them, helped shape the course that religious life would take in the new United States: diverse and voluntary rather than monolithic and enforced by the government.

SLAVES AND THE REVOLUTION

The sharpest irony of the American Revolution is that Great Britain offered enslaved blacks more opportunities for freedom than did the United States. In November 1775, the British royal governor of Virginia, John Murray (Lord Dunmore), himself a slave owner, announced that all slaves and indentured servants would gain their freedom if they joined the Loyalist cause. Within a month, the British had attracted more than 300 former servants and slaves to what came to be called the "Ethiopian Regiment." The number soon grew to almost 1,000 males and twice as many women and children. One former slave renamed himself "British Freedom."

Another runaway who joined the all-black Ethiopian Regiment was Harry Washington, one of George Washington's slaves. In his new role as soldier, he wore a uniform embroidered with the motto, "Liberty to Slaves." Washington's farm manager wrote the general that all his slaves "would leave us if they believed they could make their escape," for "liberty is sweet."

The British recruitment of slaves outraged George Washington, Thomas Jefferson, and other white plantation owners in Virginia, where 40 percent of the population was black. Washington predicted that if Dunmore's efforts were "not crushed" soon, the number of slaves joining the British army would "increase as a Snow ball by Rolling."

Jefferson expressed the same concerns after twenty-three slaves escaped from his plantation outside Charlottesville. Jefferson eventually reclaimed six of them, only to sell them for their "disloyalty." Another Virginia planter captured a fifteen-year-old girl who tried to join the British army, lashed her eighty times with his whip, and then poured hot coals on her wounds.

SOUTHERN BACKLASH   In the end, the British policy of recruiting slaves backfired. The "terrifying" prospect of British troops arming slaves persuaded many fence-straddling southerners to join the Patriot cause. Edward Rutledge of South Carolina said that the British decision to arm slaves did more to create "an eternal separation between Great Britain and the colonies than any other expedient." For Rutledge and many other southern whites, the Revolution became primarily a war to defend slavery. In 1775, Thomas Jeremiah, a free black, was convicted and executed in Charleston, South Carolina, for telling slaves that British troops were coming "to help the poor Negroes."

In response to the British recruitment of enslaved African Americans, at the end of 1775 a desperate General Washington authorized the enlistment of free blacks—but not slaves—into the American army. In February 1776, however, southern representatives convinced the Continental Congress to instruct General Washington to enlist no more African Americans, free or enslaved. Two states, South Carolina and Georgia, refused to allow any blacks to serve in the Patriot forces. As the American war effort struggled, however, some states ignored southern wishes. Massachusetts organized two all-black army units, and Rhode Island organized one, which also included Native Americans.

About 5,000 African Americans fought on the Patriot side, and most of them were free blacks from northern states. The white Belknap family of Framingham, Massachusetts, freed their African American slave Peter Salem so that he might enlist in the Massachusetts militia. Salem was with the Minutemen at Concord in 1775 and also fought alongside other blacks at the Battles of Bunker Hill and Saratoga. Another former slave who fought at Bunker Hill, Salem Poor, was commended after the battle for being a "Brave & gallant Soldier" who "behaved like an experienced officer, as well as an excellent soldier."

Overall, the British army, which liberated 20,000 enslaved blacks during the war, was a far greater instrument of emancipation than the American forces. Most of the newly freed blacks found their way to Canada or to British colonies on Caribbean islands.

While thousands of free blacks and runaway slaves fought in the war, the vast majority of African Americans did not choose sides so much as they chose freedom. Several hundred thousand enslaved blacks, mostly in the southern states, took advantage of the disruptions caused by the war to seize their freedom.

In the North, which had far fewer slaves than the South, the ideals of liberty and freedom led most states to end slavery, either during the war or shortly afterward. But those same ideals had little to no impact in the southern states. These contrasting attitudes toward slavery would continue to shape the political disputes of the young nation.

THE STATUS OF WOMEN The ideal of liberty spawned by the Revolution applied to the status of women as much as to that of African Americans. The legal status of women was governed by British common law, which essentially treated them like children, limiting their roles to child rearing and maintaining the household. Women could not vote or hold office. Few had access to formal education. Boys were taught to read and write; girls were taught to read and sew. Most New England women in the eighteenth century could not write their own names. Until married, women were subject to the dictates of their fathers.

Once a woman married, she essentially became the property of her husband, and her property became his. A married woman had no right to buy, sell, or manage property. Technically, any wages a wife earned belonged to the husband. Women could not sign contracts, file lawsuits, or testify in court. A husband could beat and even rape his wife without fearing legal action. Divorces were extremely difficult to obtain.

Yet the Revolution offered women new opportunities for independence and public service. Women in many communities made clothing for soldiers and organized fund-raising efforts. Others became camp followers, traveling and camping with the soldiers, often with their children in tow. The women in the army camps cooked meals, washed clothes, nursed wounds, and, on occasion, took part in battle. In 1777, some 400 armed women mobilized to defend Pittsfield, Vermont. The men of the town had gone off to fight when a band of Loyalists and Indians approached the village. In a day-long battle, the women held off the attackers until help arrived.

A few women disguised their gender and fought as ordinary soldiers. An exceptional case was Deborah Sampson, who joined a Massachusetts regiment as "Robert Shurtleff" and served from 1781 to 1783 by the "artful concealment" of her gender. She was wounded twice, leading Congress to declare after the war that she was the highest "example of female heroism, fidelity, and courage."

Perhaps the feistiest of the fighting women was Georgian Nancy Hart, a tall, red-haired cousin of American general Daniel Morgan and a skilled hunter (local Native Americans called her "War Woman"). When a group of Loyalists accused her of helping a Patriot escape, she didn't deny the charge. Instead, she shot two of them, then held the others at gunpoint until her husband arrived. Her husband, so the story goes, wanted to shoot the remaining Tories, but she insisted on hanging them instead.

WOMEN AND LIBERTY America's war against Great Britain led some women to demand their own independence. Early in the Revolutionary struggle, Abigail Adams, one of the most learned, spirited, and independent women of the time, wrote to her husband, John: "In the new Code of Laws which I suppose it will be necessary for you to make, I desire you would remember the Ladies. . . . Do not put such unlimited power into the hands of the Husbands." Since men were "Naturally Tyrannical," she wrote, "why then, not put it out of the power of the vicious and the Lawless to use us with cruelty and indignity with impunity." Otherwise, "if particular care and attention is not paid to the Ladies we are determined to foment a Rebellion, and will not hold ourselves bound by any Laws in which we have no voice, or Representation."

John Adams could not help but "laugh" at his wife's radical proposals for female equality. While surprised that women might be dissatisfied, he insisted on retaining the traditional

Abigail Adams Abigail Adams, wife of John Adams, in a 1766 portrait. Though an ardent Patriot, Adams and other women like her saw disappointingly few changes in women's rights emerging in the new United States.

privileges enjoyed by males: "Depend upon it, we know better than to repeal our Masculine systems." If women were to be granted equality, he warned, then "children and apprentices" and "Indians and Negroes" would also demand equal rights and freedoms.

Thomas Jefferson shared Adams's stance. In his view, there was no place in the new American republic for female political participation. Women should not "wrinkle their foreheads with politics" but instead "soothe and calm the minds of their husbands." Improvements in the status of women would have to wait. New Yorker Margaret Livingston admitted as much in 1776 when she wrote that "our Sex are *doomed* to be obedient [to men] at every stage of life so that we shan't be great gainers by this contest [the Revolutionary War]."

NATIVE AMERICANS AND THE REVOLUTION Most Native Americans sought to remain neutral in the war, but both British and American agents urged the chiefs to fight on their side. The result was chaos. Indians on both sides attacked villages, burned crops, and killed civilians.

During and after the war, the new American government assured its Indian allies that it would respect their lands and their rights. But many white Americans used the disruptions of war to destroy and displace Native Americans. Once the war ended and independence was secured, there was no peace for the Indians. By the end of the eighteenth century, land-hungry Americans were again pushing into Indian territories on the western frontier.

THE EMERGENCE OF AN AMERICAN CULTURE

On July 2, 1776, when the Second Continental Congress had resolved "that these United Colonies are, and of right ought to be, free and independent states," John Adams had written Abigail that future generations would remember that date as their "day of deliverance." People, he predicted, would celebrate the occasion with "pomp and parade, with shows, games, sports, guns, bells, bonfires and illuminations [fireworks] from one end of this continent to the other, from this time forward, forever more." Adams got everything right but the date. As luck would have it, July 4, the date the Declaration of Independence was approved, became Independence Day rather than July 2, when independence was formally declared.

The celebration of Independence Day quickly became the most important public ritual in the United States. People from all walks of life suspended their normal routine in order to devote a day to parades, patriotic speeches, and fireworks displays. In the process, the infant republic began to create its own myth of national identity. "What a day!" exclaimed the editor of the *Southern Patriot* in 1815. "What happiness, what emotion, what virtuous triumph must fill the bosoms of Americans!"

American nationalism embodied a stirring idea. This new nation was not rooted in antiquity. Its people, except for the Native Americans, had not inhabited it over many centuries, nor was there any notion of a common ethnic descent. "The American national consciousness," one observer wrote, "is not a voice crying out of the depth of the dark past, but is proudly a product of the enlightened present, setting its face resolutely toward the future."

Many people, at least since the time of the Pilgrims, had thought of the "New World" as singled out for a special identity, a special mission assigned by God. John Adams proclaimed the opening of America "a grand scheme and design in Providence for the illumination and the emancipation of the slavish part of mankind all over the earth."

This sense of providential mission provided much of the energy for America's development as a new national republic. From the democratic rhetoric of

Thomas Jefferson to the pragmatism of George Washington to heady toasts bellowed in South Carolina taverns, patriots everywhere claimed a special role for American leadership in history. The first mission was to gain independence. Now, people believed, God was guiding the United States to lead the world toward greater liberty and equality. Benjamin Rush, a Philadelphia doctor and scientist, issued a prophetic statement in 1787: "The American war is over: but this is far from being the case with the American Revolution. On the contrary, but the first act of the great drama is closed."

CHAPTER REVIEW

SUMMARY

- **Military Challenges** In 1776 the British had the mightiest army and navy in the world, and they supplemented their military might by hiring professional German soldiers called *Hessians* to help put down the American Revolution. The Americans had to create an army—the Continental army—from scratch. George Washington realized that the Americans had to turn unreliable *citizen-soldiers* into a disciplined fighting force and try to wage a long, costly war, staking that the British army was fighting thousands of miles from its home base and would eventually cut its losses and give up.

- **Turning Points** After forcing the British to evacuate Boston, the American army suffered a string of defeats before George Washington surprised the Hessians at the *Battle of Trenton* at the end of 1776. The victory bolstered American morale and prompted more enlistments in the Continental Army. The French were likely allies for the colonies from the beginning of the conflict because they resented their losses to Britain in the Seven Years' War. After the British defeat at the *Battles of Saratoga*, the colonies brokered an *alliance with France*. Washington's ability to hold his ragged forces together, despite daily desertions and two especially difficult winters in Morristown and *Valley Forge*, was another major turning point. The British lost support on the frontier and in the southern colonies when terrorist tactics backfired. The Battle of Kings Mountain drove the British into retreat, and French supplies and the French fleet helped tip the balance and ensure the American victory at the *Battle of Yorktown*.

- **Civil War** The American Revolution was also a civil war, dividing families and communities. There were at least 100,000 Loyalists in the colonies. They included royal officials, Anglican ministers, wealthy southern planters, and the elite in large seaport cities; they also included many humble people, especially recent immigrants. After the hostilities ended, many Loyalists, including slaves who had fled plantations to support the British cause, left for Canada, the West Indies, or England.

- **A Political and Social Revolution** The American Revolution disrupted and transformed traditional class and social relationships. American Revolutionaries embraced a *republican ideology*, and more white men gained the right to vote as property requirements were removed. But fears of a monarchy being reestablished led colonists to vest power in the states rather than in a national government under the *Articles of Confederation*. New *state constitutions* instituted more elected positions, and most included bills of rights that protected individual liberties. The *Virginia Statute of Religious Freedom* led the way in guaranteeing the separation of church and state, and religious toleration was transformed into religious freedom.

- **African Americans, Women, and Native Americans**   Northern states began to free slaves, but southern states were reluctant. Although many women had undertaken nontraditional roles during the war, afterward they remained largely confined to the domestic sphere, with no changes to their legal or political status. The Revolution had catastrophic effects on Native Americans, regardless of which side they had allied with during the war. American settlers seized Native American land, often in violation of existing treaties.

CHRONOLOGY

1776	British forces seize New York City
	General Washington's troops defeat British forces at the Battle of Trenton
	States begin writing new constitutions
1777	American forces defeat British in a series of battles at Saratoga
1778	Americans and French form a military alliance
	George Rogers Clark's militia defeats British troops in Mississippi Valley
	American forces defeat the Iroquois Confederacy at Newtown, New York
1780	Patriots defeat Loyalists at the Battle of Kings Mountain
1781	British invasion of southern colonies turned back at the Battles of Cowpens and Guilford Courthouse
	American and French forces defeat British at Yorktown, Virginia
	Articles of Confederation are ratified
	Continental Congress becomes Confederation Congress
1783	Treaty of Paris is signed, formally ending Revolutionary War
1786	Virginia adopts the Statute of Religious Freedom

KEY TERMS

Hessians p. 202

citizen-soldiers p. 202

Battle of Trenton (1776) p. 209

Battles of Saratoga (1777) p. 215

alliance with France p. 215

Valley Forge (1777–1778) p. 216

Battle of Yorktown (1781) p. 228

republican ideology p. 231

state constitutions p. 231

Articles of Confederation p. 232

Virginia Statute of Religious Freedom (1786) p. 235

 INQUIZITIVE

Go to InQuizitive to see what you've learned—and learn what you've missed—with personalized feedback along the way.

6 Strengthening the New Nation

Washington as a Statesman at the Constitutional Convention **(1856)** This painting by Junius Brutus Stearns is one of the earliest depictions of the drafting of the Constitution, capturing the moment after the convention members, including George Washington (right), completed the final draft.

During the 1780s, the United States of America was rapidly emerging from its colonial past as the lone large republic in an unstable world dominated by monarchies. It was distinctive in that it was born out of a conflict over ideas, principles, and ideals rather than from centuries-old shared racial or ancestral bonds, as in Europe and elsewhere.

America was a democratic republic "brought forth" by certain self-evident political ideals—that people should govern themselves, that people should have an equal opportunity to prosper, and that governments exist to protect liberty and promote the public good. Those ideals were captured in lasting phrases: All men are created equal. Liberty and justice for all. *E pluribus unum* ("Out of many, one"—the phrase on the official seal of the United States). How Americans understood, applied, and violated these ideals shaped the new nation's development after 1783.

POWER TO THE PEOPLE

The American Revolution created not only an independent new republic but also a different conception of politics than prevailed in Europe. What Americans most feared in the late eighteenth century was the governmental abuse of power. Memories of the tyranny of King George III, his prime ministers, and royal colonial governors were still raw and frightful. Freedom from such

focus questions

1. What are the strengths and weaknesses of the Articles of Confederation? How did they contribute to the creation of a new U.S. constitution in 1787?

2. What political innovations did the 1787 Constitutional Convention develop for the new nation?

3. What were the debates surrounding the ratification of the Constitution? How were they resolved?

4. In what ways did the Federalists' vision for the United States differ from that of their Republican opponents during the 1790s?

5. How did the attitudes toward Great Britain and France shape American politics in the late eighteenth century?

arbitrary power had been the ideal guiding the American Revolution, while the freedom to "pursue happiness" became the ideal driving the new nation.

To ensure their new freedoms, the Revolutionaries wrestled with a fundamental question: what is the proper role and scope of government? In answering that question, they eventually developed new ways to divide and balance power among the various branches of government so as to manage the tensions between ensuring liberty and maintaining order.

But even with victory in the war, America was a nation in name only. The quest for true nationhood after the Revolution was the most significant political transformation in modern history, for Americans would insist that sovereignty (ultimate power) resided not with a king or an aristocracy but with "the people," the mass of ordinary citizens.

FORGING A NEW NATION   The unlikely American victory in the Revolutionary War stunned the world, but the Patriots had little time to celebrate. As Alexander Hamilton, a brilliant young army officer turned congressman, noted in 1783, "We have now happily concluded the great work of independence, but much remains to be done to reach the fruits of it."

The transition from war to peace was neither simple nor easy. America was independent but it was not yet a self-sustaining nation. In fact, the Declaration of Independence never mentioned the word *nation*. Its official title was "the unanimous Declaration of the thirteen united States of America."

During the war, James Madison of Virginia predicted that the Confederation government would be only temporary. "The present Union will but little survive the present war," he wrote. The states must recognize, he continued, "the necessity of the Union during the war" and "its probable dissolution after it."

Forging a new *nation* out of a *confederation* of thirteen rebellious colonies-turned-"free-and-independent" states posed huge challenges, not the least of which was managing what George Washington called a "deranged" economy, suffocating in war-related debts. The accumulated war debt was $160 million, a huge amount at the time, amounting to the total national budget over the twenty years from 1790 to 1810. Such financial stress made for trying times in the first years of the American republic.

The period from the drafting of the Declaration of Independence in 1776, through the creation of the new federal constitution in 1787, and ending with the election of Thomas Jefferson as president in 1800, was fraught with instability and tension. From the start, the new nation experienced growing political divisions, economic distress, and foreign troubles.

Three fundamental questions shaped political debate during the last quarter of the eighteenth century. Where would sovereignty reside in the new nation? What was the proper relationship of the states to each other and to the national government? And what was required for the new republic to flourish as an independent nation? The efforts to answer those questions created powerful tensions that continue to complicate American life.

THE CONFEDERATION GOVERNMENT

Young John Quincy Adams, a future president, called the years between 1783 and 1787 the "Critical Period" when American leaders developed sharp differences about economic policies, international relations, and the proper relationship of the states to the national government. Debates over those key issues unexpectedly gave birth to the nation's first political parties and, to this day, continue to influence the American experiment in **federalism** (the sharing of power among national, state, and local governments).

After the war, many Patriots who had feared government power and criticized British officials for abusing it now directed their attacks against the new state and national governments. In 1783, after Congress ran out of money, some army officers, upset at not being paid, had threatened to march on Congress and take over the government. Alexander Hamilton reported that the unpaid soldiers had become "a mob rather than an army, without clothing, without pay, without provisions [food], without morals, without discipline." Only George Washington's intervention stopped the rebellious officers from confronting Congress. At the same time, state legislatures desperate for funds to pay off their war debts sparked unrest and riots by raising taxes.

The often violent clashes between the working poor and the state governments were a great disappointment to Washington, John Adams, and other Revolutionary leaders. For them and others disillusioned by the surge of "democratic" rebelliousness, the Critical Period was a time of hopes frustrated, a story shaded by regret at the absence of national loyalty and international respect. The weaknesses of the Articles of Confederation in dealing with the postwar turmoil led political leaders to design an entirely new national constitution and federal government.

A LOOSE ALLIANCE OF STATES The **Articles of Confederation**, formally approved in 1781, had created a loose alliance (confederation) of thirteen independent and often squabbling and ungovernable states. The states were united only in theory; in practice, each state government acted on its own. The first major provision of the Articles insisted that "each state retains its sovereignty, freedom, and independence."

The weak national government under the Articles had only one component, a one-house legislature. There was no national president, no executive branch, no separate national judiciary (court system). State legislatures, not voters, appointed the members of the Confederation Congress, in which each state, regardless of size or population, had one vote. This meant that Rhode Island, with 68,000 people, had the same power in the Confederation Congress as Virginia, the largest and most prosperous state, with more than 747,000 inhabitants.

George Washington called the Confederation "a half-starved, limping government." It could neither regulate trade, nor create taxes to pay off the country's large war debts. It could approve treaties with other nations but had no power to enforce their terms. It could call for raising an army but could not force men to fill the ranks.

The Congress, in short, could not enforce its own laws, and its budget relied on undependable "voluntary" contributions from the states. In 1782, for example, the Confederation asked the states to provide $8 million for the national government; they sent $420,000. The lack of state support forced the Confederation Congress to print paper money, called Continentals, whose value plummeted to two cents on the dollar as more and more were printed, leading to the joking phrase, "Not worth a Continental." Virtually no gold and silver coins remained in circulation; they had all gone abroad to purchase items for the war.

The Confederation government ran up a budget deficit every year of its existence. It was even hard to find people to serve in such a weak congress. And people openly doubted the stability of the new American republic. As John Adams wrote to Thomas Jefferson, "The Union is still to me an Object of as much Anxiety as ever independence was."

Yet in spite of its limitations, the Confederation Congress survived the war years while laying important foundations for the new national government. The Articles of Confederation were crucially important in supporting the political concept of *republicanism* (representative democracy), which meant that America would be governed not by kings or queens or nobles but "by the authority of the people," whose elected representatives would make decisions on their behalf. The Confederation Congress also created the national government's first executive departments and formulated the basic principles of land distribution and territorial government that would guide America's westward expansion.

LAND POLICY   In ending the Revolutionary War and transferring Britain's North American colonies to America, the Treaty of Paris doubled the size of the United States, extending the nation's western boundary to the Mississippi River. Under the Articles of Confederation, land not included within the

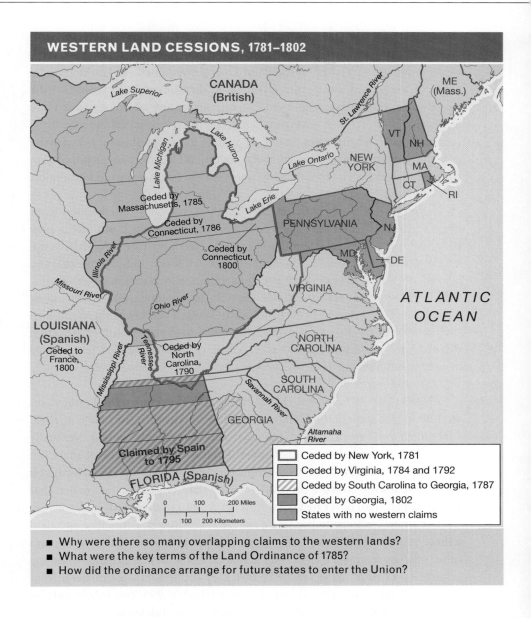

WESTERN LAND CESSIONS, 1781–1802

CANADA (British)

ME (Mass.)

Lake Superior

Lake Michigan

Lake Huron

Lake Ontario

VT

NH

NEW YORK

MA

CT

RI

Ceded by Massachusetts, 1785

Lake Erie

PENNSYLVANIA

NJ

Ceded by Connecticut, 1786

Ceded by Connecticut, 1800

MD

DE

Illinois River

Missouri River

Ohio River

VIRGINIA

ATLANTIC OCEAN

LOUISIANA (Spanish)
Ceded to France, 1800

Mississippi River

Tennessee River

Ceded by North Carolina, 1790

NORTH CAROLINA

SOUTH CAROLINA

Savannah River

GEORGIA

Altamaha River

Claimed by Spain to 1795

FLORIDA (Spanish)

0   100   200 Miles
0   100   200 Kilometers

☐ Ceded by New York, 1781
☐ Ceded by Virginia, 1784 and 1792
▨ Ceded by South Carolina to Georgia, 1787
■ Ceded by Georgia, 1802
■ States with no western claims

- Why were there so many overlapping claims to the western lands?
- What were the key terms of the Land Ordinance of 1785?
- How did the ordinance arrange for future states to enter the Union?

boundaries of the thirteen original states became *public domain*, owned and administered by the national government.

Between 1784 and 1787, the Confederation Congress created three major ordinances (policies) detailing how the government-owned lands in the West would be surveyed, sold, and developed. These ordinances rank among the

Confederation's greatest achievements—and among the most important in American history.

Thomas Jefferson drafted the Land Ordinance Act of 1784, which urged states to drop their competing claims to Indian-held territory west of the Appalachian Mountains so that the vast, unmapped area could be divided into as many as fourteen self-governing *territories* of equal size. In the new territories, all adult white males would be eligible to vote, hold office, and write constitutions for their territorial governments. When a territory's population equaled that of the smallest existing state (Rhode Island), it would be eligible for statehood.

Before Jefferson's plan could take effect, however, the Confederation Congress revised it through the Land Ordinance of 1785, which outlined a plan of land surveys and sales for the Northwest Territory (the area that would become the states of Ohio, Michigan, Indiana, Illinois, and Wisconsin), and later on, the Great Plains. Wherever Indian lands were purchased—or taken—they were surveyed and divided into six-mile-square townships laid out along a grid of lines running east–west and north–south. Each township was in turn divided into thirty-six sections one mile square (640 acres), with each section divided into four farms. The 640-acre sections of "public lands" were to be sold at auctions, the proceeds of which went into the national treasury.

THE NORTHWEST ORDINANCE The third major land policy created by the Confederation Congress was the **Northwest Ordinance** of 1787. It set forth two key principles: the new western territories would eventually become states, and slavery was banned from the region north of the Ohio River (slaves already there would remain slaves, however). The Northwest Ordinance also included a promise, which would be repeatedly broken, that Indian lands "shall never be taken from them without their consent."

For a new territory to become a state, the Northwest Ordinance specified a three-stage process. First, Congress would appoint a territorial governor and other officials to create a legal code and administer justice. Second, when the population of adult males reached 5,000, they could elect a territorial legislature. Third, when a territory's population reached 60,000 "free inhabitants," it could draft a constitution and apply to Congress for statehood.

DIPLOMACY After the Revolutionary War, relations with Great Britain and Spain remained tense because both nations kept trading posts, forts, and soldiers on American soil, and both nations encouraged Indians to resist American efforts to settle on their tribal lands. The British refused to remove their troops south of the Canadian border in protest of the failure of Amer-

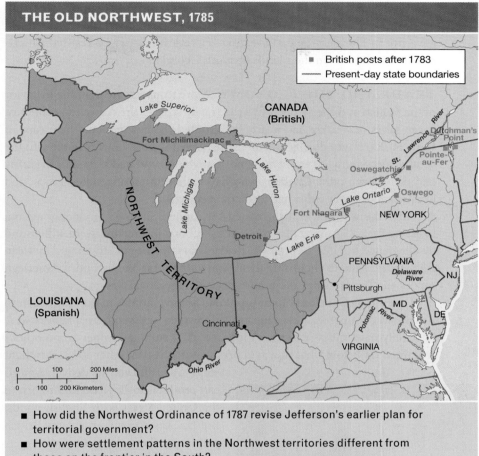

THE OLD NORTHWEST, 1785

British posts after 1783

Present-day state boundaries

Lake Superior

CANADA
(British)

Fort Michilimackinac

St. Lawrence River

Dutchman's Point

Pointe-au-Fer

Oswegatchie

NORTHWEST

Lake Michigan

Lake Huron

Lake Ontario

Oswego

Fort Niagara

NEW YORK

Detroit

Lake Erie

TERRITORY

PENNSYLVANIA

Delaware River

NJ

Pittsburgh

LOUISIANA
(Spanish)

MD

DE

Cincinnati

VIRGINIA

0   100   200 Miles

0   100   200 Kilometers

Ohio River

- How did the Northwest Ordinance of 1787 revise Jefferson's earlier plan for territorial government?
- How were settlement patterns in the Northwest territories different from those on the frontier in the South?
- How did the United States treat Native American claims to their ancestral lands in the West?

icans to pay their prewar debts to British merchants. Another major irritant in U.S.-British relations was the seizure of Loyalist property. During and after the war, Americans had confiscated Tory homes, businesses, farms, and slaves.

With Spain, the chief issues were the southern boundary of the United States and the right for Americans to send boats or barges down the Mississippi River, which Spain then controlled. After the Seven Years' War in 1763, Spain had acquired the vast Louisiana Territory, which included the valuable port of New Orleans, the Mississippi River, and all of the area west to the Rocky Mountains. After the Revolution, Spain closed the Mississippi River to American use, infuriating settlers in Kentucky and Tennessee. Spain also regained ownership of Florida, which then included southern Alabama. Thereafter, the Spanish governor in Florida provided firearms to Creek Indians, who resisted American encroachment on their lands in south Georgia.

TRADE AND THE ECONOMY More troublesome than the behavior of the British and the Spanish was the fragile state of the American economy. Seven years of warfare had nearly bankrupted the new nation. The escape of some 60,000 slaves during and after the Revolution was a terrible blow to the southern economy. At the same time, many men who had served in the army had never been paid. Civilians who had loaned money, supplies, crops, and livestock to the war effort had also not been repaid.

After the war, the British treated the United States as an enemy nation, insisting that all Americans who had been born in England were still bound by allegiance to King George III. British warships began stopping American ships in the Atlantic, boarding them, and kidnapping English-born American sailors and "impressing" them into service in the Royal Navy.

The British also closed their profitable island colonies in the Caribbean to American commerce. New England shipowners and southern planters were especially hard-hit, as exports of tobacco, rice, rum, and other commodities remained far below what they had been before the war. After 1783, merchant ships were allowed to deliver American products to England and return to the United States with English goods. But U.S. vessels could not carry British goods anywhere else in the world.

To punish Britain for banning U.S. trade with the British West Indies, many state governments imposed special taxes (called tonnage fees) on British vessels arriving in American ports and levied tariffs (taxes) on British goods brought to the United States. The British responded by sending their ships to ports in states whose tariff rates were lower.

By charging different tariffs on the same products, the states waged commercial war with each other. The result was economic chaos. By 1787, it was

Domestic industry American craftsmen, such as this cabinetmaker, favored tariffs on foreign goods that competed with their own products.

evident that the national government needed to regulate interstate trade and foreign relations, especially in regard to British and Spanish control of enormous territories bordering the United States.

SCARCE MONEY Complex financial issues also hampered economic development during the Critical Period. There was no stable national currency, and the nation had only three banks—in Philadelphia, New York City, and Boston—all created since 1782. Farmers who had profited during the war now found themselves squeezed by lower crop prices and mounting debts and taxes. The widespread shortage of "hard money" (gold and silver coins), which had gone to European merchants to buy imported goods, led people to postpone paying their bills.

By 1785, indebted citizens urged states to print new paper currency. In a drama that would be replayed many times over the next century, debtors believed that printing paper money would ease their plight by increasing the money supply (inflation). In 1785–1786, seven states began issuing their own paper money to help indebted farmers and to pay the cash bonuses promised to military veterans.

THE "GATHERING CRISIS"

The economic difficulties weakening the Confederation were compounded by growing fears among wealthy "gentlemen" leaders ("natural aristocrats") that the democratic energies unleashed by the Revolution ("all men are born equal") were undermining the authority of the traditional social and economic elite. Class distinctions were disappearing as many among the working poor and "middling classes" stopped deferring to their "betters."

The so-called better sort of people were appalled at the "leveling" behavior of the "antifederal peasants," "little folks," and "demagogues" who were challenging their leadership. A Virginia aristocrat grumbled that the "spirit of independency" that inspired the Revolution was being "converted into equality" after the war.

The political culture was also changing; more men could now vote and hold office as property-owning qualifications were reduced or eliminated in several states. The nation, said wealthy New Yorker John Jay, was headed toward "Evils and Calamities" because the masses were gaining power and often taking the laws into their own hands.

No sooner was the war over than Americans with large debts again began to protest taxes. To begin paying down their war debts, most state legislatures had sharply increased taxes. In fact, during the 1780s, most Americans paid three times as much in taxes as they had under British "tyranny." Earlier, they had objected to taxation *without* representation; now, they objected to taxation *with* representation.

Some Patriots lost farms because of their inability to pay the new taxes; other debtors were imprisoned. In New Hampshire, in what was called the Exeter Riot, hard-pressed farmers surrounded the legislative building, demanding that the representatives print paper money to ease their plight. Similar appeals occurred in other states. The economic and political elites were horrified that the "new men" were endangering the "*security of property*" by encouraging the printing of more money.

SHAYS'S REBELLION   Fears of a taxpayer "revolt from below" became all too real in western Massachusetts, when struggling farmers, many of them former soldiers, demanded that the state issue more paper money and give them more time to pay the "unjust" taxes owed on their land. Farmers also resented the new state constitution because it *raised* the property qualifications for voting and holding elected office, thus stripping poorer men of political power.

When the merchant-dominated Massachusetts legislature refused to provide relief, however, three rural counties in the western part of the state erupted in a disorganized revolt in 1786. One rebel farmer, Plough Jogger, expressed the fears of many when he charged that the "great men are going to get all we have, and I think it is time for us to rise and put a stop to it, and have no more courts, nor sheriffs, nor [tax] collectors, nor lawyers."

Shays's Rebellion Shays and his followers demanded that states issue paper currency to help ease the payment of debts and the right to postpone paying taxes until the postwar agricultural depression lifted.

Armed groups of angry farmers, called Regulators, banded together to force judges and sheriffs to stop seizing the cattle and farms of those who could not pay their taxes. "Close down the courts," they shouted. A prominent Bostonian reported that Massachusetts was "in a state of Anarchy and Confusion bordering on Civil War."

The situation worsened when a ragtag "army" of unruly farmers led by thirty-nine-year-old Daniel Shays, a war veteran, marched on the federal arsenal at Springfield in the winter of 1787. The state government responded by sending 4,400 militiamen who scattered Shays's debtor army with a single cannon blast that left four farmers dead and many wounded. Shays fled to Vermont. Several others were arrested, and two were hanged. The rebels nevertheless earned a victory of sorts, as the state legislature agreed to eliminate some of the taxes and fees on farmers.

News of **Shays's Rebellion** sent shock waves across the nation. In Massachusetts, Abigail Adams, the wife of future president John Adams, dismissed Shays and his followers as "ignorant, restless, desperadoes, without conscience or principles." In Virginia, George Washington was equally concerned. America, he exclaimed, needed a "government by which our lives, liberty, and properties will be secured." Unless an alternative could be found to the weak Confederation government, "anarchy and confusion will inevitably ensue."

CREATING THE CONSTITUTION

In the wake of Shays's Rebellion, a collective shiver passed through what wealthy New Yorker John Jay called "the better kind of people." Many among the "rich and well-born" agreed with George Washington that the nation was "tottering." The time had come to empower the national government to bring social order and economic stability.

THE "CRISIS IS ARRIVED" During the 1780s, newspapers warned that the nation's situation had grown "critical and dangerous" and that its "vices" were threatening "national ruin." The states were behaving like thirteen ungovernable nations, pursuing their own trade regulations and foreign policies (nine of them claimed to have their own navies). "Our present federal government," said Henry Knox, a Boston bookseller who was a general during the Revolutionary War, "is a name, a shadow, without power, or effect."

Such concerns led political leaders to revise their assessment of the American republic. "We have, probably," concluded Washington in 1786, "had too good an opinion of human nature in forming our confederation." Fellow Virginian James Madison agreed, declaring in 1787 that the "crisis is arrived." It was time to create a new federal constitution that would repair the "vices of the political system" and "decide forever the fate of republican government." New Yorker Alexander Hamilton urged that a national gathering of delegates from each state be given "full powers" to revise the Articles of Confederation.

THE CONSTITUTIONAL CONVENTION In 1787, the Confederation Congress responded to Hamilton and others by calling for a special "federal" convention to gather in Philadelphia's Old State House (now known as Independence Hall) for the "purpose of revising the Articles of Confederation." Only Rhode Island refused to participate.

The delegates began work on May 25, 1787, meeting five hours a day, six days a week. After four months of secret deliberations, thirty-nine delegates signed the new federal constitution on September 17. Only three delegates refused to sign.

The durability of the Constitution reflects the thoughtful men who created it. The delegates were all white; their average age was forty-two, with the youngest being twenty-six. Most were members of the political and economic elite. Twenty-six were college graduates; two were college presidents, and thirty-four were lawyers. Others were planters, merchants, bankers, and clergymen.

Yet the "Founding Fathers" were also practical men of experience, tested in the fires of the Revolutionary War. Twenty-two had fought in the war, five of whom were captured and imprisoned by the British. Seven had been state governors, and eight had helped write their state constitutions. Most had been members of the Continental or Confederation Congresses, and eight had signed the Declaration of Independence. Nearly all were considered "gentlemen," and more than half of them owned slaves.

Drafting the Constitution George Washington presides over a session of the Constitutional Convention in Philadelphia.

DRAFTING THE CONSTITUTION The widely respected—even revered—George Washington served as presiding officer at the Federal Convention (later renamed the Constitutional Convention). He participated little in the debates, however, for fear that people would take his prestigious opinions too seriously. The governor of Pennsylvania, eighty-one-year-old Benjamin Franklin, the oldest delegate, was in such poor health that he had to be carried to the meetings in a special chair, borne aloft by inmates from the Philadelphia jail. Like Washington, Franklin said little from the floor but provided a wealth of experience, wit, and common sense behind the scenes.

Most active at the Convention was James Madison of Virginia, the ablest political theorist in the group. A thirty-six-year-old attorney who owned a huge tobacco plantation called Montpelier, not far from Jefferson's Monticello, Madison had arrived in Philadelphia with trunks full of books about governments and a head full of ideas about how best to strengthen the loose confederation of "independent and sovereign states."

Madison was an unlikely giant at constitution-making. Barely five feet tall and weighing only 120 pounds (a colleague said he was "no bigger than half a piece of soap"), he was too frail to serve in the Revolutionary army and suffered from occasional epileptic seizures. "He speaks low, his person [body] is little and ordinary," and he was "too timid in his politics," remarked crusty Fisher Ames of Massachusetts.

Although painfully shy and soft-spoken, Madison had an agile mind, a huge appetite for learning, and a life-long commitment to public service. He was determined to create a constitution that would ensure the "supremacy of national authority." The logic of his arguments—and his pragmatic willingness to compromise on particular points—proved decisive in shaping the new constitution. "Every person seems to acknowledge his greatness," said a Georgia delegate.

Most delegates agreed with Madison that their young republic needed a stronger national government, weaker state legislatures, and the power to restrain the

James Madison This 1783 miniature shows Madison at thirty-two years old, just four years before he would assume a major role in drafting the Constitution.

"excessive" democratic impulses unleashed by the Revolution. "The evils we experience," said Elbridge Gerry of Massachusetts, "flow from the excess of democracy."

Two interrelated assumptions guided the Constitutional Convention: that the national government must have direct authority over the citizenry rather than governing through the state governments, and that the national government must derive its legitimacy from the people rather than from the state legislatures.

The insistence on the sovereignty of "the people," that the voters were "the legitimate source of all authority," as James Wilson of Pennsylvania stressed, was the most important political innovation since the Declaration of Independence. By declaring the Constitution to be the voice of "the people," the founders authorized the federal government to limit the powers of the state governments.

The delegates realized, too, that an effective national government needed new authority to collect taxes, borrow and issue money, regulate commerce, fund an army and navy, and make laws binding upon individual citizens. This meant that the states must be stripped of the power to print paper money, make treaties, wage war, and levy tariffs on imported goods. This concept of dividing authority between the national government and the states came to be called federalism.

THE VIRGINIA AND NEW JERSEY PLANS James Madison drafted the framework for the initial discussions at the Constitutional Convention. His proposals, called the Virginia Plan, started with a radical suggestion: that the delegates scrap their original instructions to *revise* the Articles of Confederation and instead create an entirely *new* constitution.

The Virginia Plan called for a "*national* government [with] a *supreme* legislative, executive, and judiciary." It proposed a new Congress divided into two houses (bicameral): a lower House of Representatives chosen by the voters and an upper house of senators elected by the state legislatures. The more-populous states would have more representatives in Congress than the smaller states. Madison also wanted to give Congress the power to veto state laws.

The Virginia Plan sparked furious disagreements. When asked why the small states were so suspicious of the plan, Gunning Bedford of Delaware replied: "I do not, gentlemen, trust you."

On June 15, Bedford and other delegates submitted an alternative called the New Jersey Plan, developed by William Paterson of New Jersey. It sought to keep the existing equal representation of the states in a unicameral (one-house) national legislature. It also gave Congress the power to collect taxes and regulate commerce and the authority to name a chief executive as well as a supreme court, but not the right to veto state laws.

THE THREE BRANCHES OF GOVERNMENT

The intense debate over congressional representation was finally resolved in mid-July by the so-called Great Compromise, which used elements of both plans. The more populous states won apportionment (the allocation of delegates to each state) by population in the proposed House of Representatives, while the delegates who sought to protect state power won equality of state representation in the Senate, where each state would have two members, elected by the legislatures rather than directly by the people.

THE LEGISLATURE The Great Compromise embedded the innovative concept of **separation of powers** in the new Congress. It would have two separate houses, each intended to counterbalance the other, with the House of Representatives representing the voters at large and the Senate representing the state legislatures.

The "lower" house, the House of Representatives, was designed to be, as George Mason said, "the grand repository of the democratic principle of the Government." Its members would be elected by the voters every *two* years. (Under the Articles of Confederation, none of the members of Congress had been chosen by popular vote; all of them had been elected by state legislatures.) James Madison argued that allowing individual citizens to elect one part of the new legislature was "essential to every plan of free government."

The upper house, or Senate, was intended to be a more elite group, its members elected by state legislatures for *six*-year terms. The Senate was intended to be a conservative balancing force. It could use its power to overrule the House of Representatives or the president. Madison explained that the Senate would help "protect the minority of the opulent against the majority."

THE PRESIDENCY The Constitutional Convention struggled mightily over issues related to the executive branch. Some delegates wanted a powerful president who could veto acts of Congress. Others felt the opposite: that the president should simply "execute" the laws as passed by Congress. Still others, like Benjamin Franklin, wanted a "plural executive" rather than a single man governing the nation.

The eventual decision to have a single chief executive caused many delegates "considerable pause," according to James Madison. George Mason of Virginia feared that a single president might start behaving like a king.

In the end, several compromises ensured that the president would be powerful enough to counterbalance the Congress. In some cases, the chief executive's powers actually exceeded those of the British king. The new president, to be elected for four-year terms, could veto acts of Congress, subject to being overridden by a two-thirds vote in each house; in Britain, the royal veto over parliamentary legislation had long since been abandoned. The president was to be the nation's chief diplomat and commander in chief of the armed forces, and was responsible for implementing the laws made by Congress.

Yet the powers of the president were also limited in key areas. The chief executive could neither declare war nor make peace; those powers were reserved for Congress. Unlike the British monarch, moreover, the president could be removed from office. The House of Representatives could impeach (bring to trial) the chief executive—and other civil officers—on charges of treason, bribery, or "other high crimes and misdemeanors." An impeached president could be removed from office if two-thirds of the Senate voted for conviction.

To preserve the separation of the three branches of the new national government, the president would be elected not by Congress, but by a group of highly qualified "electors" chosen by "the people" in local elections. The number of electors for each state would depend upon the combined number of

Signing the Constitution, September 17, 1787 Thomas Pritchard Rossiter's painting shows George Washington presiding over what Thomas Jefferson called "an assembly of demi-gods" in Philadelphia.

Congressional representatives and U.S. senators. This "Electoral College" was a compromise between those wanting the president elected by Congress and those preferring a direct vote of qualified citizens.

THE JUDICIARY The third proposed branch of government, the judiciary, sparked little debate. The Constitution called for a supreme national court headed by a chief justice. The Supreme Court's role was not to make laws (a power reserved to Congress) or to execute and enforce the laws (reserved to the presidency), but to *interpret* the laws and to ensure that every citizen received *equal justice* under the law.

The U.S. Supreme Court was given final authority in interpreting the Constitution and in settling constitutional disputes between states. Furthermore, Article VI of the Constitution declared that the federal Constitution, federal laws, and treaties are "the supreme Law of the Land," state laws or constitutions "to the Contrary notwithstanding."

THE LIMITS OF THE CONSTITUTION

The men who drafted the new constitution claimed to be representing all Americans. To highlight that point, the Constitution begins with the words: "We the people of the United States, in order to form a more perfect Union . . . establish this Constitution for the United States of America." In fact, however, as Senator Stephen Douglas of Illinois noted seventy years later, the Constitution was "made by white men, for the benefit of white men and their posterity [descendants] forever."

Important groups of Americans were left out of the Constitution's protections. Native Americans, for example, were not considered federal or state citizens unless they paid taxes, which very few did. The Constitution declared that Native American "tribes" were not part of the United States but instead were separate "nations."

SLAVERY Of all the issues that emerged during the Constitutional Convention of 1787, none was more explosive than slavery. When the Patriots declared independence in 1776, slavery existed in every state. By 1787, however, Massachusetts, Pennsylvania, Connecticut, and Rhode Island had abolished the practice.

Many of the framers viewed slavery as an embarrassing contradiction to the principles of liberty and equality embodied in the Declaration of Independence and the new Constitution. A New Jersey delegate declared that slavery was "utterly inconsistent with the principles of Christianity and humanity." By contrast, most delegates from the southern states stoutly defended slavery. "Religion and humanity [have] nothing to do with this [slavery] question," declared John Rutledge of South Carolina. "Interest alone is the governing principle of nations."

Most southern delegates would have walked out had there been an attempt to abolish slavery. So the framers did not consider ending the cursed system, nor did they view the enslaved as human beings whose rights should be protected. Slaves were simply viewed as a form of property with a cash value. Those with qualms about slavery salved their consciences by assuming that the practice would eventually die out naturally.

If the slaves were not to be freed or their rights to be acknowledged, however, how were they to be counted? Since the size of state delegations in the proposed House of Representatives was to be based on population, southern delegates argued that slaves should be counted to help determine how many representatives from each state would serve in the new Congress. Northerners countered that it made no sense to count slaves for purposes of congressional representation when they were treated as property rather than people.

Charles Calvert and His Slave (1761) In military regalia, the five-year-old descendant of Lord Baltimore, founder of Maryland, towers over his slave, who is dressed as a drummer boy.

The delegates finally agreed to a compromise in which three-fifths of "all other persons" (that is, the enslaved) would be included in population counts as a basis for apportioning a state's congressional representatives. In a constitution intended to "secure the blessings of liberty to ourselves and our posterity," the three-fifths clause was a glaring example of compromise being divorced from principle. The corrupt bargain over slavery would bedevil the nation for the next seventy-five years.

By design, the original Constitution never mentions the word *slavery.* Instead, it speaks of "free persons" and "all other persons," and of persons "held to service of labor." The word *slavery* would not appear in the Constitution until the Thirteenth Amendment (1865) abolished it.

The three-fifths clause gave the southern states disproportionate power in Congress by increasing the number of southern votes in the House of Representatives. This, in turn, increased southern influence in the Electoral College, since the number of each state's electors was to be the total of its senators and representatives.

It was thus no accident that in the nation's first sixteen presidential elections, between 1788 and 1848, a southern slaveholder would be elected twelve times. The pro-slavery nature of the Constitution prompted the fiery abolitionist William Lloyd Garrison to declare in the 1830s that the framers of the document had forged a "covenant with death and an agreement with hell."

THE ABSENCE OF WOMEN   The delegates at the Constitutional Convention dismissed any discussion of political rights for women. Yet not all women were willing to maintain their traditional subordinate role. Just as the experiences of the Revolutionary War led many African Americans to seize their freedom, some brave women demanded political equality for themselves.

Eliza Yonge Wilkinson, born in 1757 to a wealthy plantation family living on an island south of Charleston, South Carolina, lost her husband early in the war. In June 1780, after Wilkinson was assaulted and robbed by "inhuman" British soldiers, she became a fiery Patriot who "hated Tyranny in every shape." She assured a friend that "We may be *led*, but we never will be *driven!*"

Likewise, Wilkinson expected greater freedom for women after the war. "The men say we have no business [with politics]," she wrote to a friend. "I won't have it thought that because we are the weaker sex as to bodily strength, my dear, we are capable of nothing more than minding the dairy, visiting the poultry-house, and all such domestic concerns." Wilkinson demanded more. "They won't even allow us the liberty of thought, and that is all I want."

Judith Sargent Murray, a Massachusetts essayist, playwright, and poet, argued that the rights and liberties fought for by Patriots belonged not just to men but to women, too. In her essay "On the Equality of the Sexes," published in 1790, she challenged the prevailing view that men had greater intellectual capacities than women. She insisted that any differences resulted from prejudice and discrimination that prevented women from having access to formal education and worldly experience.

The arguments for gender equality, however, fell mostly on deaf ears. At the Constitutional Convention in Philadelphia, there was no formal discussion of women's rights, nor does the Constitution even include the word *women*. Writing from Paris, Thomas Jefferson expressed the hope that American "ladies" would be "contented to soothe and calm the minds of their husbands returning ruffled from political debate."

IMMIGRATION Although America was a nation of immigrants, the Constitution said little about immigration and naturalization (the process of gaining citizenship), and most of what it said was negative. In Article II, Section 1, it prohibits any future immigrant from becoming president, limiting the office to a "born Citizen." On defining citizenship, the Constitution gives Congress the authority "to establish a uniform Rule of Naturalization" but offers no further guidance. As a result, naturalization policy has changed repeatedly over the years in response to fluctuating social attitudes, economic needs, and political moods.

In 1790, the first Congress under the new constitution would pass a naturalization law that allowed "free white persons" who had been in the United States for as few as two years to be made naturalized citizens. This meant that persons of African descent were denied citizenship; it was left to individual states to determine whether free blacks were citizens. Because Indians were not "free white persons," they were also treated as aliens. Not until 1924 would Native Americans be granted citizenship—by an act of Congress rather than a constitutional amendment.

On September 17, 1787, the Federal Convention reported that it had completed the new constitution. "Gentlemen," announced Benjamin Franklin, "you have a republic, if you can keep it."

THE FIGHT FOR RATIFICATION

The final draft of the Constitution was submitted to thirteen special state conventions for approval (ratification) on September 28, 1787. Over the next ten months, people from all walks of life, in taverns and coffeehouses, on street corners, around dinner tables, and in the nation's ninety-two newspapers, debated the new constitution's merits. As Alexander Hamilton noted, the debate would reveal whether the people could establish good government "by reflection and choice" rather than by "accident and force."

The outcome was by no means certain, but Hamilton said that during the four-month Constitutional Convention, "there has been an astonishing revolution for the better in the minds of the people" about the new frame of government.

CHOOSING SIDES Advocates for the Constitution assumed the name *Federalists*; opponents became **anti-Federalists**. The two sides formed the seeds for America's first two-party political system.

In the prolonged debate, the Federalists, led by James Madison and Alexander Hamilton, had several advantages. First, they had a concrete proposal, the proposed constitution itself; their opponents had nothing to offer instead but criticism. Second, the Federalist leaders were, on average, ten to twelve years younger and more energetic than the anti-Federalists; many of them had been members of the Constitutional Convention and were familiar with the disputed issues in the document. Third, the Federalists were more unified and better organized.

The anti-Federalist leaders—Virginians Patrick Henry, George Mason, Richard Henry Lee, and future president James Monroe; George Clinton of New York; Samuel Adams, Elbridge Gerry, and Mercy Otis Warren of Massachusetts; Luther Martin and Samuel Chase of Maryland—were a diverse group. Some wanted to reject the Constitution and retain the Confederation. Others wanted to convene another convention and start over. Still others wanted to revise the proposed constitution.

Most anti-Federalists worried that the new national government would eventually grow corrupt and tyrannical. Mercy Otis Warren of Massachusetts, the most prominent woman then writing regular political commentary, compared the constitution to "shackles on our own necks." A Philadelphia writer denounced those who drafted the Constitution as representing "the Aristocratic Party" intent upon creating a "monarchical" national government.

The anti-Federalists especially criticized the absence of a "bill of rights" in the proposed constitution to protect individuals and states from the growing power of the national government. Other than the bill of rights, however, the anti-Federalists had no comprehensive alternative to the Constitution except the admittedly flawed Articles of Confederation.

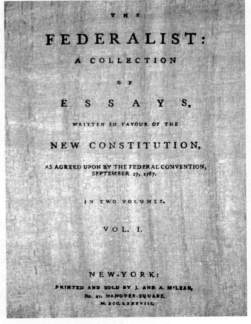

THE FEDERALIST Among the supreme legacies of the long debate over the Constitution is what came to be called *The Federalist Papers*, a collection of eighty-five essays published in New York newspapers between 1787 and 1788. Written by James Madison, Alexander Hamilton, and John Jay, the essays defended the concept of a strong national government and outlined the major principles and assumptions

The Federalist Papers Alexander Hamilton, James Madison, and John Jay published this series of essays in 1788 defending the concept of stronger central government and urging ratification of the Constitution.

embodied in the Constitution. Thomas Jefferson called *The Federalist Papers* the "best commentary on the principles of government which ever was written."

In the most famous of the *Federalist* essays, Number 10, Madison turned the conventional wisdom about republics on its head. From ancient times, it had been assumed that self-governing republics survived only if they were small and homogeneous. Patrick Henry, in fact, argued that a single national government "could not reign over so extensive a country as this is, without absolute despotism."

Madison, however, argued that small republics usually fell victim to warring factions—well-organized interest groups pursuing their self-interest at the expense of the whole. In the United States, he explained, the size and diversity of the expanding nation would make it impossible for any single faction to form a dangerous majority that could dominate the federal government—or society at large. The contending factions would, in essence, cancel each other out. In addition, he argued that it was the responsibility of the Congress to regulate "these various and interfering interests." Madison and the other framers created a legal and political system designed to protect minorities from a tyranny of the majority.

Given a new federal government in which power was checked and balanced among the three federal branches, a large republic could work better than a small one to prevent factional tyranny. "Extend the [geographic] sphere," Madison wrote, "and you take in a greater variety of parties and interests; you make it less probable that a majority of the whole will have a common motive to invade the rights of other citizens."

THE STATES DECIDE Several of the smaller states—Delaware, New Jersey, and Georgia—were among the first to ratify the Constitution. Massachusetts, still sharply divided in the aftermath of Shays's Rebellion, was the first state in which the outcome was close, approving the Constitution by 187 to 168 on February 6, 1788.

On June 21, 1788, New Hampshire became the ninth state to ratify the Constitution, thereby reaching the minimum number of states needed for approval. The Constitution, however, could hardly succeed without the approval of Virginia, the largest, wealthiest, and most populous state, or New York, which had the third-highest population and occupied a key position geographically. Both states included strong opposition groups who were eventually won over by the same pledge as had been made in Massachusetts—the addition of a bill of rights.

Upon notification that New Hampshire had become the ninth state to ratify the Constitution, the Confederation Congress chose New York City as the initial national capital and called for the new national government to assume power in 1789. The Constitution was adopted, but the spirited resistance to it

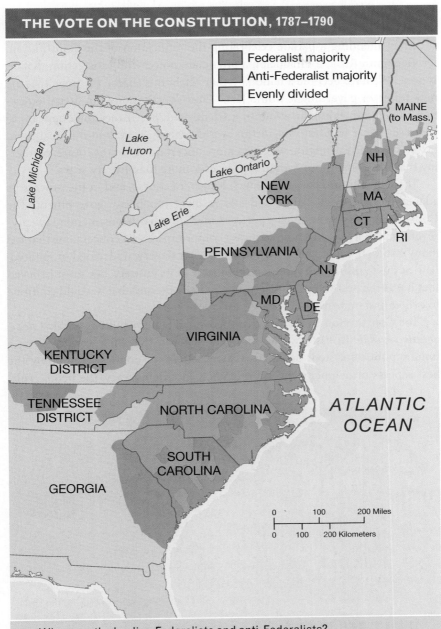

THE VOTE ON THE CONSTITUTION, 1787–1790

Legend:
- Federalist majority
- Anti-Federalist majority
- Evenly divided

Lake Michigan

Lake Huron

Lake Ontario

Lake Erie

NEW YORK

NH

MA

CT

RI

MAINE (to Mass.)

PENNSYLVANIA

NJ

MD

DE

VIRGINIA

KENTUCKY DISTRICT

TENNESSEE DISTRICT

NORTH CAROLINA

SOUTH CAROLINA

GEORGIA

ATLANTIC OCEAN

0   100   200 Miles

0   100   200 Kilometers

- Who were the leading Federalists and anti-Federalists?
- Why were the anti-Federalists opposed to the Constitution?
- How did the Federalists win the national vote ratifying the Constitution?

convinced the new Congress to propose the first ten constitutional amendments now known as the Bill of Rights.

After attending a parade celebrating the ratification of the Constitution, Dr. Benjamin Rush, a Philadelphia physician, noted with satisfaction that "It is done. We have become a nation." Other celebrants shared the hope that the new frame of government would last. "Our Constitution is in actual operation," Benjamin Franklin wrote to a friend in 1789. "Everything appears to promise that it will last; but in this world nothing is certain but death and taxes." George Washington was even more uncertain about the future, predicting that the Constitution would not "last for more than twenty years."

The Constitution has lasted much longer, of course, and in the process its adaptability has provided a model of resilient republican government. The Constitution was by no means perfect (after all, it has been amended twenty-seven times); it was a bundle of messy compromises and concessions that left many issues, the most important of which was slavery, undecided or ignored. Few of the Constitution's supporters liked it in its entirety, but most believed that it was the best frame of government obtainable and that it would continue to evolve and improve over time.

The Constitution confirmed that the United States would be the first *democratic republic* in history. The founders believed that they were creating a unique political system based on a "new science of politics" combining the best aspects of democracies and republics. In a democracy, the people rule;

Sixth pillar An engraving published in 1788 in *The Massachusetts Centinel* after Massachusetts became the sixth state to ratify the Constitution. By the end of 1788, five more states would approve, and the new Constitution would soon go into effect. The last two states to ratify were North Carolina in 1789 and Rhode Island in 1790.

RATIFICATION OF THE CONSTITUTION

ORDER OF RATIFICATION	STATE	DATE OF RATIFICATION
1	Delaware	December 7, 1787
2	Pennsylvania	December 12, 1787
3	New Jersey	December 18, 1787
4	Georgia	January 2, 1788
5	Connecticut	January 9, 1788
6	Massachusetts	February 6, 1788
7	Maryland	April 28, 1788
8	South Carolina	May 23, 1788
9	New Hampshire	June 21, 1788
10	Virginia	June 25, 1788
11	New York	July 26, 1788
12	North Carolina	November 21, 1789
13	Rhode Island	May 29, 1790

in a republic, the officials elected by the people rule. At the Constitutional Convention, the delegates combined aspects of both approaches so that they balanced and regulated each other, and ensured that personal freedoms and the public welfare were both protected in the process.

THE FEDERALIST ERA

The Constitution was ratified because it promised to create a more powerful national government better capable of managing a rapidly growing republic. Yet it was one thing to ratify a new constitution and quite another to make the new government run smoothly.

With each passing year, the United States witnessed growing debate over how to interpret and apply the provisions of the new constitution. During the 1790s, a decade called the "age of passion," the federal government would confront rebellions, states threatening to secede, international tensions, and foreign wars, as well as something left unmentioned in the Constitution: the formation of fiercely competing political parties—Federalists and Democratic Republicans, more commonly known as **Jeffersonian Republicans**, or simply as Republicans.

The two political parties came to represent very different visions for America. The Democratic Republicans were mostly southerners, like Virginians Thomas Jefferson and James Madison, who wanted the country to remain a

New beginnings An engraving from the title page of *The Universal Asylum and Columbian Magazine* (published in Philadelphia in 1790). America is represented as a woman laying down her shield to engage in education, art, commerce, and agriculture.

rural nation of small farmers dedicated to republican values. The Democratic Republicans distrusted the national government, defended states' rights, preferred a "strict" interpretation of the Constitution, and placed their trust in the masses. "The will of the majority, the natural law of every society," Jefferson insisted, "is the only sure guardian of the rights of men."

The Federalists, led by Alexander Hamilton and John Adams, were clustered in New York and New England and embraced urban culture, industrial development, and commercial growth. Federalists distrusted the "passions" of the common people and advocated a strong national government and a flexible interpretation of the Constitution. As Hamilton stressed, "the people are turbulent and changing; they seldom judge or determine right."

THE FIRST PRESIDENT On March 4, 1789, the new Congress convened in New York City. A few weeks later, the presiding officer of the Senate certified that George Washington, with 69 Electoral College votes, was the nation's first president. John Adams of Massachusetts, with 34 votes, the second-highest number, became vice president (At this time, no candidates ran specifically for the vice presidency; the presidential candidate who came in second, regardless of party affiliation, became vice president).

George Washington was a reluctant first president. He would have preferred to stay at Mount Vernon, his Virginia plantation, but agreed to serve because he had been "summoned by my country." Some complained that Washington's personality was too cold and aloof. Others thought he was unsophisticated, since he had little formal education and had never visited Europe. The acidic John Adams groused that Washington was "too illiterate, unlearned, [and] unread" to be president.

Washington had virtues that Adams lacked, however. As a French diplomat observed, President Washington had "the soul, look, and figure of a hero in action." He was a soldier who had married a wealthy young widow and become a prosperous tobacco planter and land speculator. He brought to the presidency both a detached dignity and a remarkable capacity for leadership that helped keep the young republic from disintegrating. Although capable of angry outbursts, Washington was honest, honorable, and remarkably self-disciplined; he had extraordinary stamina and patience, integrity and resolve, courage and resilience. And he exercised sound judgment. He usually asked people for their views, weighed his options, and made a decision. Most of all, he was fearless. Few doubted that he was the best person to lead the new nation.

In his inaugural address, Washington appealed for unity, pleading with the new Congress to abandon "local prejudices" and "party animosities" to create the "national" outlook necessary for the fledgling republic to thrive. Within a few months, he would see his hopes dashed. Personal rivalries, sectional tensions, and political infighting would dominate life in the 1790s.

WASHINGTON'S CABINET   America's first president took charge of a tiny national government that faced massive challenges. George Washington had a larger staff at his Mount Vernon plantation than he did as president of the United States. Unlike today, when the executive branch has hundreds of staff members, President Washington had two. And when those two secretaries went on vacation, he was forced to write all presidential letters himself. In addition, when the president's office needed new furniture, he paid for it.

During the summer of 1789, Congress created executive departments corresponding to those formed under the Confederation. To head the Department of State, President Washington named Thomas Jefferson, recently back from his diplomatic duties in France. To lead the Department of the Treasury, Washington appointed Alexander Hamilton, who was widely read in matters of government finance.

Washington selected John Jay as the first chief justice of the Supreme Court. After serving as president of the Continental Congress in 1778–1779, Jay became the American minister (ambassador) to Spain. While in Europe, he helped John Adams and Benjamin Franklin negotiate the Treaty of Paris in 1783. After the Revolution, Jay served as secretary of foreign affairs. He joined Hamilton and James Madison as co-author of *The Federalist Papers* and became one of the most effective champions of the Constitution.

President Washington routinely called his chief staff members together to discuss matters of policy. This was the origin of the president's *cabinet*, an advisory body for which the Constitution made no formal provision. The office of vice president also took on what would become its typical character. "The Vice-Presidency," John Adams wrote his wife, Abigail, is the most "insignificant office . . . ever . . . contrived."

THE BILL OF RIGHTS To address concerns raised by opponents of the new federal government, James Madison, now a congressman from Virginia, presented to Congress in May 1789 a set of constitutional amendments intended to protect individual rights from excessive government power. As Thomas Jefferson explained, such a "bill of rights is what the people are entitled to against every government on earth, general or particular, and what no just government should refuse." After considerable debate, Congress approved twelve amendments in September 1789. By the end of 1791, the necessary three-fourths of the states had approved *ten* of the twelve proposed amendments, now known as the **Bill of Rights**.

The Bill of Rights provided safeguards for individual rights of speech, assembly, and the press; the right to own firearms; the right to refuse to house soldiers; protection against unreasonable searches and seizures; the right to refuse to testify against oneself; the right to a speedy public trial, with an attorney present, before an impartial jury; and protection against "cruel and unusual" punishments. The Tenth Amendment addressed the widespread demand that powers not delegated to the national government "are reserved to the States respectively, or to the people."

The amendments were written in broad language that seemed to exclude no one. In fact, however, they technically applied only to property-owning white males. Native Americans were entirely outside the constitutional system, an "alien people" in their own land. And, like the Constitution itself, the Bill of Rights gave no protections to enslaved Americans. Instead, they were governed by state "slave codes." They had no access to the legal system; they could not go to court, make contracts, or own property. Similar restrictions applied to women, who could not vote in most state and national elections. Equally important, the Bill of Rights had a built-in flaw: it did not protect citizens from states violating their civil rights.

RELIGIOUS FREEDOM The debates over the Constitution and the Bill of Rights generated a religious revolution as well as a political revolution.

Unlike the New England Puritans whose colonial governments enforced their particular religious beliefs, the Christian men who drafted and amended the Constitution made no direct mention of God. They were determined to protect religious life from government interference and coercion.

In contrast to the monarchies of Europe, the United States would keep the institutions of church and government separate and allow people to choose their own religions ("freedom of conscience"). To that end, the First Amendment declared that "Congress shall make no law respecting an establishment of religion or prohibiting the free exercise thereof." This statement has since become one of the most important—and controversial—principles of American government.

The United States was virtually alone among nations in not designating a single "established" national religion funded by the government. France, Spain, and Italy were officially Catholic nations; Great Britain was Anglican. In addition, when the Bill of Rights was ratified, all but two states—New York and Virginia—still supported an official religion or maintained a religious requirement for holding political office. Dissenters (the members of other churches or nonbelievers) were tolerated but were prohibited from voting or holding political office.

The First Amendment was intended to create a framework within which people of all religious persuasions could flourish. It prohibited the federal government from endorsing or supporting any individual denomination or interfering with the religious choices that people make. As Thomas Jefferson later explained, the First Amendment erected a "wall of separation between church and State."

HAMILTON'S VISION OF A CAPITALIST AMERICA

In 1776, the same year that Americans were declaring their independence, Adam Smith, a Scottish philosopher, published a revolutionary book titled *An Inquiry into the Nature and Causes of the Wealth of Nations*. It provided the first full description of a modern *capitalist* economy and its social benefits.

Like the American Revolution, *The Wealth of Nations* was a declaration of independence from Great Britain's mercantilist system. Under *mercantilism*, national governments had exercised tight controls over economic life. Smith argued that instead of controlling economic activity, governments should allow individuals and businesses to compete freely for profits in the marketplace. Doing so would unleash the energies of the capitalist spirit.

Alexander Hamilton greatly admired *The Wealth of Nations*, and he eagerly took charge of managing the nation's complicated financial affairs. More than any other American, he grasped both the complex issues of government finance and envisioned what America would become: the world's most prosperous capitalist nation.

Hamilton was a self-made and self-educated aristocrat. Born out of wedlock in the West Indies, in 1755, he was deserted by his Scottish father and left an orphan at thirteen by the death of his mother. With the help of friends and relatives, he found his way, at age fifteen, to New Jersey in late 1772 before moving a year later to New York City. There he entered King's College (now Columbia University).

When the war with Britain erupted, Hamilton joined the Continental army as a captain at the ripe age of nineteen. After he distinguished himself in the battles of Trenton and Princeton, Hamilton became one of General Washington's favorite aides.

After the war, Hamilton established a thriving legal practice in New York City (a fellow lawyer said he "surpassed all of us in his abilities"), married into a prominent family, and served as a member of the Confederation Congress.

Alexander Hamilton The powerful Secretary of the Treasury from 1789 to 1795.

During the Revolutionary War, Hamilton had witnessed the near-fatal weaknesses of the Confederation Congress. Its lack of authority and money almost lost the war. Now, as Treasury secretary, he believed that the federal government should encourage the hustling, bustling, creative spirit that distinguished Americans from other peoples.

Hamilton became the foremost advocate for an "energetic government" promoting capitalist development. In contrast to Jefferson, the southern planter, Hamilton, the urban capitalist, believed that the United States was too dependent on agriculture for its economic well-being. He championed trade, banking, finance, investment, and manufacturing, as well as bustling commercial cities, as the most essential elements of America's future.

HAMILTON'S ECONOMIC REFORMS The United States was born in debt. To fight the war for independence, it had borrowed heavily from the Dutch and the French. Now, after the war, it had to find a way to pay off the debts. Yet there was no national bank, no national currency, and very few mills and factories. In essence, the American republic was bankrupt. It fell to Alexander Hamilton to determine how the debts should be repaid and how the new national government could balance its budget.

Governments have four basic ways to pay their bills: impose taxes or fees on individuals and businesses, levy tariffs (taxes on imported goods), borrow money by selling interest-paying government bonds to investors, and, last but not least, print money.

Under Hamilton's leadership, the United States did all of these things—and more. To raise funds, the new Congress, with Hamilton's support, enacted tariffs of 5 to 10 percent on the value of a wide variety of imported items. Tariffs were hotly debated for two reasons: 1) they were the source of most of the federal government's annual revenue, and, 2) tariffs also "protected" American manufacturers by taxing their foreign competitors, especially those in Britain.

By discriminating against imported goods, tariffs enabled American manufacturers to charge higher prices for their products sold in the United States. This penalized consumers, particularly those in the southern states that were most dependent upon imported goods. In essence, tariffs benefited the nation's young manufacturing sector, most of which was in New England, at the expense of the agricultural sector, since farm produce was rarely imported. Tariff policy soon became an explosive political issue.

DEALING WITH DEBTS The levying of tariffs marked but one major element in Alexander Hamilton's ambitious plan to put the new republic on a sound financial footing. In a series of brilliant reports submitted to Congress between January 1790 and December 1791, Hamilton outlined his visionary program for the economic development of the United States.

The first of two "Reports on Public Credit" dealt with how the new federal government should refinance the massive debt that the states and the Confederation government had accumulated during the war for independence. Hamilton insisted that the debts be repaid. After all, he explained, a capitalist economy depends upon its integrity and reliability: debts being paid, contracts being enforced, and private property being protected.

By selling government bonds to pay the interest due on the huge war-related debts, Hamilton argued, the U.S. government would also give investors ("the monied interest") a direct stake in the success of the new national government. A well-managed federal debt, he claimed, would become a "national blessing" by giving investors at home and abroad confidence in the national economy and the integrity of the government.

Hamilton also insisted that the federal government pay ("assume") the state debts from the Revolutionary War because they were in fact a *national* responsibility; all Americans had benefited from the war for independence. "The debt of the United States," he stressed, "was the price of liberty."

SECTIONAL DIFFERENCES Hamilton's complicated financial proposals created a storm of controversy, in part because many people, then and since, did not understand their complexities. James Madison, who had been Hamilton's close ally in the fight for the new constitution, broke with him over the federal government "assuming" the states' debts.

Madison, then the most powerful member of the new Congress, was troubled that northern states owed far more debt than southern states. Four states (Virginia, North Carolina, Georgia, and Maryland) had already paid off most of their war debts. The other states had not been as conscientious.

Madison's opposition to Hamilton's debt-assumption plan ignited a vigorous debate in Congress. In April 1790, the House of Representatives voted down Hamilton's "assumption" plan, 32–29. Hamilton did not give up, however. After failing to get a couple of members of Congress to switch their votes, he then hatched an ingenious scheme. In June 1790, Hamilton invited Jefferson and Madison to join him for dinner in New York City.

By the end of the evening, the three leaders had reached a famous compromise. First, they agreed that the national capital should move from New York City to Philadelphia for the next ten years. Then, the capital would move to a new city to be built in a "federal district" on the Potomac River between Maryland and Virginia. Hamilton agreed to find the votes in Congress to approve the move in exchange for Madison pledging to find the two votes needed to pass the debt-assumption plan.

The votes in Congress went as planned, and the federal government moved in late 1790 to Philadelphia. Ten years later, the nation's capital was moved again, this time to the new planned city of Washington, in the federal District of Columbia.

More immediately, Hamilton's debt-funding scheme proved a success. The new bonds issued by the federal government in 1790 were quickly snatched up by eager investors, thereby providing money to begin paying off the war debts while covering its operating expenses. In addition, Hamilton obtained new loans from European governments.

To raise additional government revenue, Hamilton convinced Congress to create an array of *excise* taxes—taxes on particular products, such as carriages, sugar, and salt. A 25 percent excise tax on liquor in 1791 would prove to be the most controversial of all, but the excise taxes generated much-needed revenue.

By 1794, the nation had a higher financial credit rating than all the nations of Europe. By making the new nation financially solvent, Hamilton set in motion the greatest economic success story in world history.

A NATIONAL BANK Part of the opposition to Hamilton's debt-financing scheme grew out of opposition to Hamilton himself. The brash young Treasury secretary viewed himself as President Washington's prime minister. That his Department of Treasury had *forty* staff members while Thomas Jefferson's State Department had *five* employees demonstrated the priority that President Washington gave to the nation's financial situation.

Hamilton was on a mission to develop an urban-centered economy anchored in finance and manufacturing. After securing Congressional approval of his debt-funding scheme, he called for a national bank modeled after the powerful Bank of England. Such a bank, Hamilton believed, would enable much greater "commerce among individuals" and provide a safe place for the federal government's cash.

By their nature, Hamilton explained, banks were essential to a new nation that was short on gold and silver. Banks would increase the nation's money supply by issuing currency in amounts greater than their actual "reserve"—gold and silver coins and government bonds—in their vaults. By issuing loans and thereby increasing the amount of money circulating through the economy, banks served as the engines of prosperity: "industry is increased, commodities are multiplied, agriculture and manufactures flourish, and herein consist the true wealth and prosperity" of a "genuine nation."

Hamilton's idea of a powerful national bank generated intense criticism. Once again, Madison and Jefferson led the opposition, arguing that, since the Constitution said nothing about creating a national bank, the government could not start one. Jefferson also believed that Hamilton's proposed bank would not help most Americans. Instead, a small inner circle of self-serving financiers and investors would, over time, exercise corrupt control over Congress.

Hamilton, however, had the better of the argument in Congress. Representatives from the northern states voted 33–1 in favor of the national bank; southern congressmen opposed the bank 19–6. The lopsided vote illustrated the growing political division between the North and South in the young nation.

The Bank of the United States Proposed by Alexander Hamilton, the national bank opened in Philadelphia in 1791.

Before signing the bank bill, President Washington sought the advice of his cabinet, where he found an equal division of opinion. The result was the first great debate on constitutional interpretation. Were the powers of Congress only those *explicitly* stated in the Constitution, or were other powers *implied*? The argument turned chiefly on Article I, Section 8, which authorized Congress to "make all Laws which shall be necessary and proper for carrying into Execution the foregoing Powers."

Such language left lots of room for disagreement about what was "necessary and proper" and led to a savage confrontation between Jefferson and Hamilton. The Treasury secretary had come to view Jefferson as a man of "profound ambition & violent passions" who was guided by an "unsound & dangerous" agrarian economic philosophy.

Secretary of State Jefferson, who despised banks almost as much as he hated the "monarchist" Hamilton, pointed to the Tenth Amendment of the Constitution, which reserves to the states and the people powers not explicitly delegated to Congress. Jefferson argued that a bank might be a convenient aid to Congress in collecting taxes and regulating the currency, but it was not *necessary*, as Article I, Section 8, specified.

In a lengthy 16,000 word report to the president, Hamilton countered that the power to charter corporations was an "implied" power of any government.

As he pointed out, the three banks already in existence had been chartered by states, none of whose constitutions specifically mentioned the authority to incorporate banks.

Hamilton convinced Washington to sign the bank bill. In doing so, the president had, in Jefferson's words, opened up "a boundless field of power," which in coming years would lead to a further broadening of the president's implied powers, with the approval of the Supreme Court.

The new **Bank of the United States (B.U.S.)** based in Philadelphia had three primary responsibilities: (1) to hold the government's funds and pay its bills; (2) to provide loans to the federal government and to other banks to promote economic development; and (3) to manage the nation's money supply by regulating the power of state-chartered banks to issue paper currency (called banknotes). The B.U.S. could issue national banknotes as needed to address the chronic shortage of gold and silver coins. By 1800, the B.U.S. had branches in four cities and four more were soon to be added. The American financial system was on the verge of becoming the most effective in the world.

ENCOURAGING MANUFACTURING   Hamilton's bold economic vision for the new republic was not yet complete. In the last of his celebrated recommendations to Congress, the "Report on Manufactures," distributed in December 1791, he set in place the capstone of his design for a modern capitalist economy: the active governmental promotion of new manufacturing and industrial enterprises (mills, mines, and factories). Industrialization, Hamilton believed, would bring diversification to an American economy dominated by agriculture and dangerously dependent on imported British goods; improve productivity through greater use of machinery; provide work for those not ordinarily employed outside the home, such as women and children; and encourage immigration of skilled industrial workers from other nations.

To foster industrial development, Hamilton recommended that the federal government increase tariffs on imports, three quarters of which came from Britain, while providing financial incentives (called bounties) to key industries making especially needed products such as wool, cotton cloth, and window glass. Such government support, he claimed, would enable new industries to compete "on equal terms" with longstanding European enterprises. Finally, Hamilton asked Congress to fund major transportation improvements, including the development of roads, canals, and harbors for commercial traffic.

Few of Hamilton's pro-industry ideas were enacted because of strong opposition from Jefferson, Madison, and other southerners. They did not believe the federal government should support particular industries. Hamilton's proposals, however, provided an arsenal of arguments for the advocates

Certificate of the New York Mechanick Society An illustration of the growing diversification of labor, by Abraham Godwin (ca. 1785).

of manufacturing and federally-funded transportation projects (called "internal improvements") in years to come.

HAMILTON'S VISIONARY ACHIEVEMENTS The economic impact of Hamilton's leadership was monumental. During the 1790s, as the Treasury Department began to pay off the Revolutionary War debts, foreign capitalists and banks invested heavily in the booming American economy, and European nations as well as China began a growing trade with the United States. Economic growth, so elusive in the 1780s, blossomed at the end of the century, as the number of new businesses soared. A Bostonian reported that the nation had never "had a brighter sunshine of prosperity. . . . Our agricultural interest smiles, our commerce is blessed, our manufactures flourish."

All was not well, however. By championing the values and institutions of a bustling new capitalist system and the big cities and industries that went along with it, Hamilton upset many people, especially in the agricultural South and along the western frontier. Thomas Jefferson and James Madison had grown increasingly concerned that Hamilton's urban-industrial economic program and his political deal-making were threatening American liberties. Hamilton recognized that his successes had led Jefferson and Madison to form a party "hostile to me" and one intent on making Jefferson the next president.

The political competition between Jefferson and Hamilton boiled over into a nasty personal feud. Both men were visionaries, but their visions of America's future could not have been more different. Hamilton saw Britain as the model for the kind of economy and society he wanted America to develop; Jefferson preferred France. They also had markedly different hopes for the nation's economic development.

Jefferson told President Washington that Hamilton's efforts to create a capitalist economy would "undermine and demolish the republic" and create

Thomas Jefferson A 1791 portrait by Charles Willson Peale.

"the most corrupt government on earth." Hamilton, he added, was "really a colossus [giant] to the anti-republican party." In turn, Hamilton called the agrarian Jefferson an "intriguing incendiary" who had circulated "unkind whispers" about the Treasury secretary in an effort to "stab me in the dark." He also accused Jefferson of being an agrarian romantic who failed to see that manufacturing, industry, and banking would drive the economic future of the United States.

Jefferson's spirited opposition to Hamilton's politics and policies fractured Washington's cabinet. Jefferson wrote that he and Hamilton "daily pitted in the cabinet like two cocks [roosters]." President Washington, who detested political squabbling, begged them to stop smearing each other with "wounding suspicions and irritating charges" and urged them to rise above their "dissensions." But it was too late: they had become mortal enemies—as well as the leaders of the first loosely organized political parties, the Federalists and the Democratic-Republicans.

FEDERALISTS AND DEMOCRATIC REPUBLICANS

The Federalists were centered in New York and New England. Generally, they feared the excesses of democracy, distrusted the "common people," and wanted a strong central government led by the wisest and best leaders who would be committed to economic growth, social stability, and national defense. What most worried the Federalists, as Alexander Hamilton said, was the "poison" of "DEMOCRACY." The people, he stressed, are "turbulent and changing; they seldom judge or determine right [wisely]." By contrast, the Democratic Republicans, led by Thomas Jefferson and James Madison, were most concerned about threats to individual freedoms and states' rights posed by a strong national government.

In July 1789, chaotic violence erupted in France when masses of the working poor, enraged over soaring prices for bread, their primary food, and in part inspired by the American Revolution, revolted against the absolute monarchy of Louis XVI, sending shock waves throughout Europe.

The **French Revolution** captured the imagination of many sympathetic Americans, especially Thomas Jefferson and the Republicans, as royal tyranny was displaced by a democratic republic that gave voting rights to all adult men regardless of how much property they owned. Americans formed Democratic-Republican societies that hosted rallies on behalf of the French Revolution and in support of local Republican candidates. During the 1790s, James Madison assumed leadership of Hamilton's Republican opponents in Congress.

FOREIGN AND DOMESTIC CRISES

During the fragile infancy of the new nation, George Washington was the only man able to rise above party differences and hold things together. In 1792, he was unanimously reelected to a second term. And he quickly found himself embroiled in the cascading consequences of the French Revolution, which had started in 1789. The turmoil in France threatened to draw the United States into a European war. In 1791, the monarchies of Prussia and Austria had invaded France to stop the revolutionary movement from infecting their absolutist societies. The foreign invaders, however, only inspired the French revolutionaries to greater efforts to use force to spread their ideal of democracy.

By early 1793, the most radical of the French revolutionaries, called *Jacobins*, had executed the king and queen as well as hundreds of aristocrats and priests. The Jacobins not only promoted democracy, religious toleration, and human rights, but they went well beyond the ideals of the American Revolution in supporting social, racial, and sexual equality. Then, on February 1, 1793, the French revolutionary government declared war on Great Britain, thus beginning a conflict that would last twenty-two years.

As the French republic plunged into warfare, the Revolution entered its worst phase, the so-called Reign of Terror. In 1793–1794, thousands of "counterrevolutionary" political prisoners and priests were executed, along with many revolutionary leaders. Barbarism ruled the streets of Paris and other major cities.

Secretary of State Thomas Jefferson, who loved French culture and democratic ideals, wholeheartedly endorsed the revolution as "the most sacred cause that ever man engaged in." By contrast, Alexander Hamilton and Vice President John Adams saw the French Revolution as vicious and godless. Such conflicting attitudes over events in Europe transformed the first decade of American politics into one of the most fractious periods in the nation's history—an "age of passion."

The European war against revolutionary France tested the ability of the United States to remain neutral in world affairs. Both France and Britain purchased goods from America and each sought to stop the other from trading with the United States, even if it meant attacking U.S. merchant ships.

Federalists and Jeffersonian Republicans alike agreed that a naval war with either European power would devastate the American economy. As President Washington began his second term in 1793, he faced an awkward decision. By the 1778 Treaty of Alliance, the United States was a *perpetual* ally of France. Americans, however, wanted no part of the European war. They were determined to maintain their profitable trade with both sides, although almost 90 percent of U.S. imports came from Britain.

Hamilton and Jefferson agreed that entering the European conflict would be foolish. Where they differed was in how best to stay out of the war. Hamilton had a simple answer: declare the military alliance formed with the French during the American Revolution invalid because it had been made with a monarchy that no longer existed. Jefferson preferred to delay, and to use the alliance with France as a bargaining point with the British.

In the end, President Washington took a wise middle course. On April 22, 1793, he issued a neutrality proclamation that declared the United States "friendly and impartial toward the belligerent powers" and warned U.S. citizens that they might be prosecuted for "aiding or abetting hostilities" or taking part in other un-neutral acts.

Instead of settling matters in his cabinet, however, Washington's neutrality proclamation brought to a boil the ugly feud between Jefferson and Hamilton. Jefferson dashed off an angry letter to James Madison, urging his friend to "take up your pen" and cut Hamilton "to pieces" in the newspapers.

CITIZEN GENÊT   At the same time that President Washington issued the neutrality proclamation, he accepted Secretary of State Jefferson's argument that the United States should officially recognize the new French revolutionary government (becoming the first nation to do so) and welcome its ambassador to the United States, the cocky, twenty-nine-year-old Edmond-Charles Genêt.

Early in 1793, Citizen Genêt, as he became known, landed at Charleston, South Carolina, to a hero's welcome. He then openly violated U.S. neutrality by recruiting four American privateers (privately owned warships) to capture English and Spanish merchant vessels.

After five weeks in South Carolina, Genêt sailed to Philadelphia, where his reckless efforts to draw America into the war on France's side embarrassed his friends in the Republican party. When Genêt threatened to go around President Washington and appeal directly to the American people, even Thomas Jefferson disavowed "the French monkey." In August 1793, Washington, at Hamilton's urging, demanded that the French government replace Genêt.

The growing excesses of the radicals in France were fast cooling U.S. support for the Revolution. Jefferson, however, was so disgusted by his feud with Alexander Hamilton and by Washington's refusal to support the French that he resigned as secretary of state at the end of 1793 and returned to his Virginia home, eager to be rid of the "hated occupation of politics."

Jay's Treaty A firestorm of controversy greeted Jay's Treaty in America. Opponents of the treaty rioted and burned Jay in effigy.

Vice President Adams greeted Jefferson's departure by saying "good riddance." President Washington felt the same way. He never forgave Jefferson and Madison for organizing Democratic-Republican societies to oppose his Federalist policies. After accepting Jefferson's resignation, Washington never spoke to him again.

JAY'S TREATY During 1794, tensions between the United States and Great Britain threatened to renew warfare between the old enemies. The Treaty of Paris (1783) that ended the Revolutionary War had left the western and southern boundaries of the United States in dispute. In addition, in late 1793, British warships violated international law by seizing U.S. merchant ships that carried French goods or were sailing for a French port. By early 1794, several hundred American ships had been confiscated, and their crews were given the terrible choice of joining the British navy, a process called "impressment," or being imprisoned. At the same time, British troops in the Ohio Valley gave weapons to Indians, who in turn attacked American settlers.

On April 16, 1794, President Washington sent Chief Justice John Jay to London to settle the major issues between the two nations. Jay agreed to the British demand that America not sell products to France for the construction of warships. Britain also gained trading advantages with the United States while refusing to stop intercepting American merchant ships and "impressing" their sailors. Finally, Jay conceded that the British need not compensate U.S. citizens for the enslaved African Americans who had escaped to the safety of British forces during the Revolutionary War.

In return, Jay won three important promises from the British: they would evacuate their six forts in northwest America by 1796, reimburse Americans for the seizures of ships and cargo in 1793–1794, and grant U.S. merchants the right to trade again with the island economies of British West Indies.

When the terms of **Jay's Treaty** were disclosed, however, many Americans, especially Republicans, were outraged. In Massachusetts, people shouted "Damn John Jay! Damn everyone who won't damn John Jay!" The ferocious debate over the treaty deepened the division between Federalists and Republicans. Jefferson dismissed Jay's Treaty as an "infamous act" intended to "undermine the Constitution." Another prominent Republican offered this toast to President Washington: "May he be damned if he signs Jay's Treaty."

The uproar created the most serious crisis of Washington's presidency. Some called for his impeachment. Yet the president, while admitting that the proposed agreement was imperfect, decided that it was the only way to avoid a war with Britain that the United States was bound to lose (the U.S. Army then had only 672 men, and there was no navy).

In the end, with Washington's strong support, Jay's Treaty barely won the necessary two-thirds majority in the Senate. Some 80 percent of the votes *for* the treaty came from New England or the middle Atlantic states; 74 percent of those voting *against* the treaty were southerners, most of them Jeffersonian Republicans.

FRONTIER TENSIONS Meanwhile, new conflicts erupted in the Ohio Valley between American settlers and Native Americans. In the fall of 1793, Revolutionary War hero General "Mad" Anthony Wayne led a military expedition into the Northwest Territory's "Indian Country." They marched north from Cincinnati, built Fort Greenville, in western Ohio, and soon went on the offensive in what became known as the Northwest Indian War, a conflict that

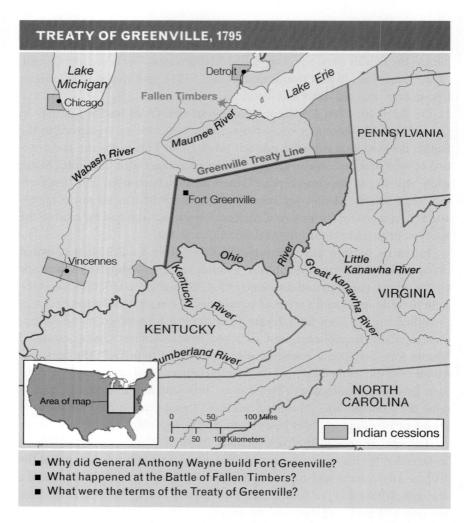

TREATY OF GREENVILLE, 1795

- Why did General Anthony Wayne build Fort Greenville?
- What happened at the Battle of Fallen Timbers?
- What were the terms of the Treaty of Greenville?

arose after the British transferred the Ohio Country to the United States. The Native Americans living in the region insisted that the British had no right to give away their ancestral lands. As pioneers moved into the Northwest Territory, the various Indian nations formed the Western Confederacy to resist American settlement.

In August 1794, the Western Confederacy of some 2,000 Shawnee, Ottawa, Chippewa, Delaware, and Potawatomi warriors, supported by the British and reinforced by Canadian militiamen, engaged General Wayne's troops and Indian allies in the Battle of Fallen Timbers, along the Michigan-Ohio border. The Americans decisively defeated the Indians, destroyed their crops and villages, and built a line of forts in northern Ohio and Indiana, one of which became the city of Fort Wayne, Indiana. The Indians finally agreed to the Treaty of Greenville, signed in

August 1795, by which the United States bought most of the territory that would form the state of Ohio and the cities of Detroit and Chicago.

THE WHISKEY REBELLION Soon after the Battle of Fallen Timbers, the Washington administration displayed another show of strength in the backcountry, this time against the so-called **Whiskey Rebellion**. Alexander Hamilton's 1791 federal tax on "distilled spirits" had ignited resentment and resistance throughout the western frontier. Liquor made from grain or fruit was the rural region's most valuable product; it even was used as a form of currency. When protesters' efforts to repeal the tax failed, many turned to violence and intimidation. Beginning in September 1791, angry groups of farmers, militiamen, and laborers attacked federal tax collectors and marshals.

In the summer of 1794, the discontent exploded into open rebellion in western Pennsylvania, home to a fourth of the nation's whiskey stills. The rebels threatened to assault nearby Pittsburgh, loot the homes of the rich, and set the town ablaze. After negotiations failed, a U.S. Supreme Court justice declared on August 4, 1794, that western Pennsylvania was in a "state of rebellion." It

Whiskey Rebellion George Washington as commander in chief reviews the troops mobilized to quell the Whiskey Rebellion in Pennsylvania in 1794.

was the first great domestic challenge to the federal government since the Constitution was ratified, and George Washington responded decisively.

At the urging of Alexander Hamilton, Washington ordered the whiskey rebels to disperse by September 1 or he would send in the militia. When the rebels failed to respond, some 12,500 militiamen from several states began marching to western Pennsylvania to suppress the rebellion. President Washington donned his military uniform and rode on horseback to greet the soldiers. It was the first and last time that a sitting president would lead troops in the field.

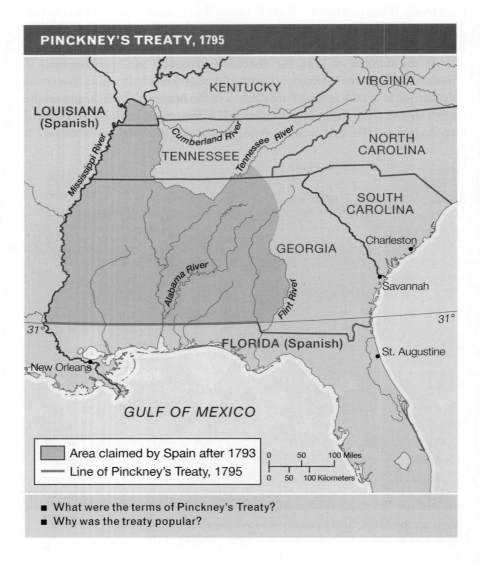

PINCKNEY'S TREATY, 1795

Legend:
- Area claimed by Spain after 1793
- Line of Pinckney's Treaty, 1795

- What were the terms of Pinckney's Treaty?
- Why was the treaty popular?

The huge army, commanded by Virginia's governor, Henry "Lighthorse Harry" Lee, quickly panicked the whiskey rebels, who vanished into the hills. Two dozen were charged with high treason; two were sentenced to hang, only to be pardoned by President Washington.

The new federal government had made its point and showed its strength. The show of force led the rebels and their sympathizers to change their tactics. Rather than openly defying federal laws, they voted for Republicans, who won heavily in the next Pennsylvania elections.

PINCKNEY'S TREATY While the turbulent events were unfolding in Pennsylvania, the Spanish began negotiations over control of the Mississippi River as well as the disputed northern boundary of their Florida colony, which they had acquired from the British at the end of the Revolutionary War. U.S. negotiator Thomas Pinckney pulled off a diplomatic triumph in 1795 when he convinced the Spanish to accept a southern American boundary at the 31st parallel in west Florida, along the northern coast of the Gulf of Mexico (the current boundary between Florida and Georgia). The Spanish also agreed to allow Americans to ship goods, grains, and livestock down the Mississippi River to Spanish-controlled New Orleans. Senate ratification of Pinckney's Treaty (also called the Treaty of San Lorenzo) came quickly, for westerners were eager to transport their crops and livestock to New Orleans.

WESTERN SETTLEMENT

The treaties signed by John Jay and Thomas Pinckney spurred a new wave of settlers into the western territories. Their lust for land aroused a raging debate in Congress over what the federal government should do with the vast areas it had acquired or taken from the British, the Spanish, and from Native Americans.

LAND POLICY Federalists and Republicans differed sharply on federal land policy. Federalists wanted the government to charge high prices for western lands to keep the East from losing both political influence and a labor force important to the growth of manufactures. They also preferred that government-owned lands be sold in large parcels to speculators, rather than in small plots to settlers. Thomas Jefferson and James Madison were reluctantly prepared to go along with such land policies for the sake of reducing the national debt, but Jefferson preferred that government-owned land be sold to farmers rather than speculators.

The prevalence of agriculture This American folk painting by Edward Hicks shows the residence of David Twining, a Pennsylvania farmer, as it appeared in 1787.

For the time being, however, the Federalists prevailed. With the Land Act of 1796, Congress doubled the price of federal land (public domain) to $2 per acre. Half the townships would be sold in 640-acre sections, making the minimum cost $1,280, a price well beyond the means of ordinary settlers. By 1800, federal land offices had sold fewer than 50,000 acres. Criticism of the land policies led to the Land Act of 1800, which reduced the minimum parcel to 320 acres and spread payments over four years. Thus, with a down payment of $160, one could buy a farm.

THE WILDERNESS ROAD The lure of western lands led thousands of settlers to follow pathfinder Daniel Boone into the territory known as Kentucky, or Kaintuck, from the Cherokee name KEN-TA-KE (Great Meadow). In the late eighteenth century, the Indian-held lands in Kentucky were a farmer's dream and a hunter's paradise. The vast area boasted fertile soil; bluegrass meadows; abundant forests; and countless buffalo, deer, and wild turkeys.

Born on a small farm in 1734 in central Pennsylvania, Boone was a dead-eye marksman by the age of twelve who became an experienced farmer and an accomplished woodsman. After hearing numerous reports about the fertile lands over the Appalachian Mountains, Boone set out in 1769 to find a trail into Kentucky. He discovered what was called the Warriors' Path, a narrow foot trail that buffalo, deer, and Native Americans had worn along the steep ridges over the centuries.

Daniel Boone Escorting Settlers through the Cumberland Gap
Painting by George Caleb Bingham.

In 1773, Boone led a group of white settlers into Kentucky. Two years later, he and thirty woodsmen used axes to widen the 208-mile-long Warriors' Path into what became known as the Wilderness Road, a rough passageway that more than 300,000 settlers would use over the next twenty-five years. At a point where a branch of the Wilderness Road intersected with the Kentucky River, near what is now Lexington, Boone built the settlement of Boonesborough. In 1780, Kentucky was divided into three counties and integrated into the state of Virginia. In 1792, it became a separate state.

In the process of settling Kentucky, Boone became one of America's first folk heroes, a larger-than-life figure known as the "Columbus of the Woods." As he admitted, however, "many heroic actions and chivalrous adventures are related of me which exist only in the regions of fancy. With me the world has taken great liberties, and yet I have been but a common man."

A steady stream of settlers, mostly Scots-Irish migrants from Pennsylvania, Virginia, and North Carolina, poured into Kentucky during the last quarter of the eighteenth century. The pioneers came on foot or horseback, often leading a mule or a cow that carried their tools and other possessions. Near a creek or spring they would buy a parcel or stake out a claim and mark its boundaries by chopping notches into "witness trees." They would then build a lean-to for temporary shelter and clear the land for planting. The larger trees—those that could not be felled with an ax—were girdled: a cut would be made around the trunk, and the tree would be left to die. Because clearing trees often took years, a farmer had to hoe and plant a field filled with stumps.

The pioneers grew melons, beans, turnips, and other vegetables, but corn was the preferred crop because it kept well and had so many uses. Ears were roasted and eaten on the cob, and kernels were ground into meal for making mush, hominy grits, and hoecakes, or johnnycakes (dry flour cakes, suitable for travelers, that were originally called *journeycakes*). Pigs provided pork, and cows supplied milk, butter, and cheese. Many frontier families also built crude stills to manufacture a potent whiskey they called *corn likker.*

TRANSFER OF POWER

In 1796, President Washington decided that two terms in office were enough. Weary of the increasingly bitter criticism directed at him, he was eager to retire to his plantation at Mount Vernon. He would leave behind a formidable record of achievement: the organization of a new national government, a prosperous economy, the recovery of territory from Britain and Spain, a stable northwestern frontier, and the admission of three new states: Vermont (1791), Kentucky (1792), and Tennessee (1796).

WASHINGTON'S FAREWELL On September 17, 1796, Washington delivered a farewell address in which he criticized the rising spirit of political partisanship and the emergence of political parties. They endangered the republic, he felt, because they pursued the narrow interests of minorities rather than the good of the nation. In foreign relations, Washington advised, the United States should stay away from Europe's quarrels by avoiding "permanent alliances with any portion of the foreign world." His warning against permanent foreign entanglements would serve as a fundamental principle in U.S. foreign policy until the early twentieth century.

THE ELECTION OF 1796 With Washington out of the race, the United States had its first contested election for president. The Federalist "caucus," a group of leading congressmen, chose Vice President John Adams as their presidential candidate. Thomas Pinckney of South Carolina, fresh from his diplomatic triumph in Spain, also ran as a Federalist presidential candidate. As expected, the Republicans chose Thomas Jefferson. Aaron Burr, a young New York attorney and senator who was distrusted by many and disliked by most, also ran as a Republican.

The campaign of 1796 was mean and nasty. The Federalists were attacked for unpopular taxes, excessive spending, and abuses of power. Republicans called the pudgy John Adams "His Rotundity" and labeled him a monarchist

Mount Vernon George Washington and the Marquis de Lafayette at Mount Vernon in 1784. Washington enlarged the estate, which overlooks the Potomac River, to nearly 8,000 acres, dividing it among five farms.

because he loved the symbols of power and despised "the people." (Adams wanted people to refer to the president as "His Highness.") Federalists countered that Jefferson was a French-loving atheist eager for another war with Great Britain and charged that the philosophical Virginian was not decisive enough to be president. Adams won the election with 71 electoral votes, but in an odd twist, Jefferson who received 68 electoral votes, became vice president. The Federalists won control of both houses of Congress.

THE ADAMS ADMINISTRATION

Vain and prickly, opinionated and stubborn, John Adams had long lusted for the presidency, but he was a much better political theorist than he was a political leader. An independent thinker with a proud, combative spirit and volcanic temper, he fought as often with his fellow Federalists, especially Alexander Hamilton, as he did with his Republican opponents. Benjamin Franklin said Adams was "always an honest man, often a wise one, but sometimes . . . absolutely out of his senses."

Adams had crafted a distinguished career as a Massachusetts lawyer, and as a leader in the Revolutionary movement. Widely recognized as the hardest-working member of the Continental Congress, he had also authored the Massa-

John Adams Political philosopher and politician, Adams was the first president to take up residence in the new White House, in the new national capital of Washington, D.C., in 1801.

chusetts state constitution. During the Revolution, Adams had served as an exceptional diplomat in France, Holland, and Great Britain, and he had been George Washington's vice president.

In contrast to the tall, lanky Jefferson, the short, stocky Adams feared democracy and despised equality, both of which, he believed, must be kept within bounds by wise leaders. He once referred to ordinary Americans as making up the "common herd of mankind." Adams also felt that he was never properly appreciated—and he may have been right. Yet on the essential issue of his presidency, war and peace, he kept his head when others about him were losing theirs—probably at the cost of his reelection.

THE WAR WITH FRANCE As America's second president, John Adams inherited a "Quasi War" with France, a by-product of the angry French reaction to Jay's Treaty between the United States and Great Britain. The navies of both nations were capturing U.S. ships headed for the other's ports. By the time of Adams's inauguration, in 1797, the French had plundered some 300 American vessels and broken diplomatic relations with the United States.

Adams sought to ease tensions by sending three prominent Americans to Paris to negotiate a settlement. When the U.S. diplomats arrived, however, they were accosted by three French officials (labeled X, Y, and Z by Adams in his report to Congress) who announced that negotiations could begin only if the United States paid a bribe of $250,000 and loaned France $12 million.

Such bribes were common in the eighteenth century, but the answer from the American side was "no, no, not a sixpence." When the so-called XYZ Affair became public, American hostility toward France soared. Many Republicans—with the exception of Vice President Thomas Jefferson—joined with Federalists in calling for war. Federalists in Congress voted to triple the size of the army and construct warships. President Adams asked George Washington to put on his military uniform and become commander of the army again.

Conflict with France A cartoon indicating the anti-French sentiment generated by the XYZ Affair. The three American negotiators (at left) reject the Paris Monster's demand for bribery money before discussions could begin.

He reluctantly agreed on the condition that Hamilton be appointed a major general. By the end of 1798, French and American ships were engaged in an undeclared naval war in the Caribbean Sea.

THE WAR AT HOME The naval conflict with France sparked an intense debate between Federalists eager for a formal declaration of war and Republicans sympathetic to France. Amid the superheated emotions, Vice President Jefferson observed that a "wall of separation" had come to divide the nation's political leaders. He told a French official that President Adams was "a vain, irritable, stubborn" man.

For his part, Adams had tried to take the high ground. Soon after his election, he had invited Jefferson to join him in creating a bipartisan administration. Jefferson refused, saying that he would not be a part of the cabinet but instead would only preside over the Senate as vice president, as the Constitution specified. Within a year, he and Adams were at each other's throats. Adams regretted losing Jefferson as a friend but "felt obliged to look upon him as a man whose mind is warped by prejudice." Jefferson, he claimed, had become "a child and the dupe" of the Republican faction in Congress led by James Madison.

Jefferson and other Republicans were convinced that the real purpose of the French crisis was to provide Federalists with an excuse to quiet their American critics. The **Alien and Sedition Acts** (1798) seemed to confirm the Republicans' suspicions. These partisan acts, passed amid a wave of patriotic war fervor, gave the president extraordinary powers to violate civil liberties in an effort to stamp out criticism of the administration. They limited freedom of speech and of the press, as well as the liberty of "aliens" (immigrants who had not yet gained citizenship).

Adams's support of the Alien and Sedition Acts ("war measures") would prove to be the greatest mistake of his presidency. Timothy Pickering, his secretary of state, claimed that Adams agreed to the acts without consulting "any member of the government and for a reason truly remarkable—because he knew we should all be opposed to the measure."

Three of the four Alien and Sedition Acts reflected hostility to French and Irish immigrants, many of whom had become militant Republicans in America. The Naturalization Act lengthened from five to fourteen years the residency requirement for U.S. citizenship. The Alien Act empowered the president to deport "dangerous" aliens, and the Alien Enemies Act authorized the president in wartime to expel or imprison enemy aliens at will. Finally, the Sedition Act outlawed writing, publishing, or speaking anything of "a false, scandalous and malicious" nature against the government or any of its officers.

Of the ten people convicted under the Sedition Act, all were Republicans, including newspaper editors. To offset the "reign of witches" unleashed by the Alien and Sedition Acts, Jefferson and Madison drafted the Kentucky and Virginia Resolutions, passed by the legislatures of those two states in late 1798. The resolutions denounced the Alien and Sedition Acts as "alarming infractions" of constitutional rights and put forth the shocking idea that state legislatures should "nullify" (reject and ignore) acts of Congress that violated the constitutional guarantee of free speech. In attacking the Alien and Sedition Acts, Jefferson was suggesting something more dangerous: disunion. George Washington told Patrick Henry in Virginia that Jefferson was threatening to "dissolve the union."

While Adams and Jefferson were waging their war of words, the president was seeking peace with France. In 1799, he dispatched another team of diplomats to negotiate with a new French government under First Consul Napoléon Bonaparte, the "general on horseback" whose army had overthrown the republic. In a treaty called the Convention of 1800, the Americans won the best terms they could from the French. They dropped their demands to be repaid for the ships taken by the French, and the French agreed to end the military alliance with the United States dating back to the Revolutionary War. The Senate quickly ratified the agreement, which became effective on December 21, 1801.

REPUBLICAN VICTORY IN 1800 The furor over the Alien and Sedition Acts influenced the pivotal presidential election of 1800. The Federalists nominated Adams, even though many of them continued to snipe at him and his policies, especially his refusal to declare war against France. Alexander Hamilton publicly questioned Adams's fitness to be president, citing his "disgusting egotism."

Thomas Jefferson and Aaron Burr, the Republican candidates, once again represented the alliance of the two most powerful states, Virginia and New York. The Federalists claimed that Jefferson's election would bring civil war and anarchy to America. Jefferson's supporters portrayed him as a passionate idealist and optimist who was a friend of farmers and a courageous champion of states' rights, a limited federal government, and personal liberty.

In the important **election of 1800**, Jefferson and Burr, the two Republicans, emerged with 73 electoral votes each. Federalist John Adams received only 65. When Burr shockingly refused to withdraw his candidacy in favor of Jefferson, the tie vote in the Electoral College sent the election into the House of Representatives (a constitutional defect corrected in 1804 by the Twelfth Amendment). Hamilton grudgingly preferred Jefferson over Burr (who would later kill Hamilton in a duel). Jefferson, Hamilton said, "is by far not so dangerous a man; he has pretensions to character." As to Burr, Hamilton added, "there is nothing in his favor."

The tie vote in the Electoral College between Thomas Jefferson and Aaron Burr created an explosive political crisis. Federalist Fisher Ames predicted that Burr "might impart vigor to the country," while Jefferson "was absurd enough to believe his own nonsense." The rumor-filled three months between the House vote for president in December 1800 and Thomas Jefferson's inauguration in March 1801 were so tense that people talked openly of civil war. "The crisis is momentous!" warned the *Washington Federalist*. There were even wild rumors of plots to assassinate Jefferson. In the end, it took thirty-six ballots for the House of Representatives to choose Jefferson over Burr as the new president.

Before the Federalists turned over power on March 4, 1801, President Adams and Congress passed the Judiciary Act of 1801. It was intended to ensure Federalist control of the judicial system by creating sixteen federal circuit courts, with a new judge for each. It also reduced the number of Supreme

Court justices from six to five in an effort to deprive the next president of appointing a new member. Before he left office, Adams appointed Federalists to all the new positions. The Federalists, quipped Jefferson, had "retired into the judiciary as a stronghold." They never again would exercise significant political power.

A NEW ERA   The election of 1800 did not resolve the fundamental political tensions that had emerged between ardent nationalists like Adams and Hamilton and those like Jefferson and Madison who clung to ideals of states' rights and an agriculture-based economy. In fact, the 1800 election further divided the young republic into warring political factions and marked a major turning point in the nation's history. It was the first time that one political party had relinquished presidential power to the opposition party, and it was the only election that pitted a sitting president (Adams) against his own vice president (Jefferson).

Jefferson's hard-fought victory signaled the emergence of a new, more democratic political culture dominated by bitterly divided parties and wider public

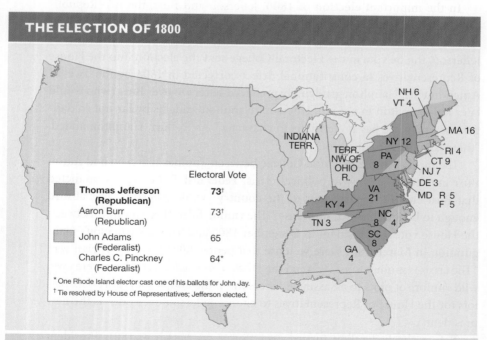

THE ELECTION OF 1800

	Electoral Vote
Thomas Jefferson (Republican)	73†
Aaron Burr (Republican)	73†
John Adams (Federalist)	65
Charles C. Pinckney (Federalist)	64*

NH 6
VT 4
MA 16
INDIANA TERR.
TERR. NW OF OHIO R.
NY 12
RI 4
PA 8   7
CT 9
NJ 7
DE 3
VA 21
MD R 5   F 5
KY 4
NC 8   4
TN 3
SC 8
GA 4

* One Rhode Island elector cast one of his ballots for John Jay.
† Tie resolved by House of Representatives; Jefferson elected.

- Why was the election of 1800 a key event in American history?
- What voting patterns emerged in the election of 1800?
- How did Congress break the tie between Thomas Jefferson and Aaron Burr?

participation. Before and immediately after independence, people took a keen interest in public affairs, but socially prominent families, the "rich, the able, and the wellborn," still dominated political life. However, the raging political battles of the late 1790s, culminating in 1800 with Jefferson's election, established the right of "common" men to play a more active role in governing the young republic. With the gradual elimination of the requirement that citizens must own property to vote, the electorate expanded enormously in the early nineteenth century.

Jefferson called his election the "Revolution of 1800," for it marked the triumph of the Republican party and the slaveholding South at the expense of the New England Federalists. Three Virginia Republican slaveholders—Jefferson, James Madison, and James Monroe—would hold the presidency for the next twenty-four years.

A bitter John Adams was so upset by his defeat (as well as by the death of his alcoholic son Charles) that he refused to participate in Jefferson's inauguration in the new federal capital in Washington, D.C. Instead, unnoticed and unappreciated, Adams boarded a stagecoach at 4 A.M. for the 500-mile trip to his home in Massachusetts. He and Jefferson would not communicate for the next twelve years. As Adams returned to work on his Massachusetts farm with his wife, Abigail, he told his eldest son, John Quincy, who would become the nation's sixth president, that anyone governing the United States "has a hard, laborious, and unhappy life." The victorious Jefferson would soon feel the same way.

SUMMARY

- **Confederation Government** Despite its many weaknesses, the national government created by the *Articles of Confederation* managed to construct important alliances during the Revolutionary War, help win the War of Independence, and negotiate the Treaty of Paris (1783). It created executive departments and established, through the *Northwest Ordinance,* the process by which new western territories would be organized and governments formed before they applied for statehood. Yet the Articles of Confederation did not allow the national government to raise taxes to fund its debts. *Shays's Rebellion* made many Americans fear that such uprisings would eventually destroy the new republic unless the United States formed a stronger national government.

- **Constitutional Convention** Delegates gathered at the convention in Philadelphia in 1787 to revise the existing government, but almost immediately they decided to scrap the Articles of Confederation and start over. An entirely new document emerged, which created a system called *federalism* in which a strong national government with clear *separation of powers* among executive, legislative, and judicial branches functioned alongside state governments with clearly designated responsibilities. Arguments about how best to ensure that the rights of individual states were protected and also that "the people" were represented in the new Congress were resolved by establishing a Senate, with equal representation for each state, and a House of Representatives, the number of whose delegates was determined by population counts.

- **Ratification of the Constitution** Ratification of the Constitution was hotly contested. *Anti-Federalists,* such as Virginia's Patrick Henry, opposed the new structure of government because the absence of a bill of rights would lead to a loss of individual and states' rights. To sway New York State toward ratification, Alexander Hamilton, James Madison, and John Jay wrote *The Federalist Papers*. Ratification became possible only when Federalists promised to add a *Bill of Rights*.

- **Federalists versus Republicans** Alexander Hamilton and the Federalists wanted to create a diverse economy in which agriculture was balanced by trade, finance, and manufacturing. Hamilton crafted a federal budget that funded the national debt through tariff and tax revenues, and he created a national bank, the first *Bank of the United States*. Thomas Jefferson and others, known as *Jeffersonian Republicans,* worried that Hamilton's plans violated the Constitution and made the federal government too powerful. They envisioned a nation dominated by farmers and planters where the rights of states would be protected against federal power.

- **Trouble Abroad** During the *French Revolution*, George Washington's policy of neutrality violated the terms of the 1778 treaty with France. At the same time, Americans sharply criticized *Jay's Treaty* with the British for giving too much away. French warships began seizing British and American ships, and an undeclared war was under way. Federalists supported Washington's approach, while Republicans were more supportive of France. During the presidency of John Adams, the United States fought an undeclared naval war with the French, which led to the controversial *Alien and Sedition Acts* of 1798.

CHRONOLOGY

1781	Articles of Confederation take effect
1783	Treaty of Paris ends the War of Independence
1786–1787	Shays's Rebellion
1787	Northwest Ordinance
	The Constitutional Convention is held in Philadelphia
1787–1788	*The Federalist Papers* are published
1789	President George Washington is inaugurated
1791	Bill of Rights is ratified
	Bank of the United States is created
1793	Washington issues a proclamation of neutrality
1794	Jay's Treaty is negotiated with England
	Whiskey Rebellion in Pennsylvania
	U.S. Army defeats Indians in the Battle of Fallen Timbers
1795	Treaty of Greenville
	Pinckney's Treaty is negotiated with Spain
1796	John Adams is elected president
1798	Alien and Sedition Acts are passed
1800	Thomas Jefferson is elected president

KEY TERMS

federalism p. 247

Articles of Confederation p. 247

Northwest Ordinance (1787) p. 250

Shays's Rebellion (1786–1787) p. 255

separation of powers p. 259

anti-Federalists p. 264

The Federalist Papers p. 265

Jeffersonian Republicans p. 269

Bill of Rights (1791) p. 272

Bank of the United States (B.U.S.) (1791) p. 279

French Revolution p. 282

Jay's Treaty (1794) p. 285

Whiskey Rebellion (1794) p. 287

Alien and Sedition Acts (1798) p. 296

election of 1800 p. 297

 INQUIZITIVE

Go to InQuizitive to see what you've learned—and learn what you've missed—with personalized feedback along the way.

7

The Early Republic

1800–1815

We Owe Allegiance to No Crown **(ca. 1814)** The War of 1812 generated a renewed
spirit of nationalism, inspiring Philadelphia sign-painter John Archibald Woodside to
create this patriotic painting.

When President Thomas Jefferson took office in early 1801, the United States and its western territories reached from the Atlantic Ocean to the Mississippi River. The nation remained primarily rural and agricultural. Nine of ten Americans lived or worked on land, with most of them growing enough food and raising enough livestock to feed their families but rarely producing enough to sell outside the community, much less overseas.

That changed during the nineteenth century. With each passing year, more and more farmers began to produce surplus crops and livestock to sell in regional and world markets. Such *commercial agriculture* was especially evident in the South, where skyrocketing European demand for cotton caused prices to soar.

The growing market economy produced the boom-and-bust cycles that have always been a regular element of capitalist economies, but overall the years from 1790 to 1830 were prosperous, with enterprising Americans experiencing unprecedented opportunities for land ownership, economic gain, geographic mobility, and political participation. The desire displayed by Americans for profits was, according to Congressman Henry Clay, "a passion as unconquerable as any with which nature has endowed us. You may attempt to regulate [it]—[but] you cannot destroy it."

Everywhere in the early Republic, it seemed, people were on the move and on the make, leading one newspaper to claim that what made the United States different from other nations was "the almost universal ambition to get forward." Americans excelled at westward expansion, economic development, rapid population growth, and intense political activity. Former president John Adams observed that "there is no people on earth so ambitious as the people of America . . . because the lowest can aspire as freely as the highest."

focus questions

1. What were the major domestic political developments that took place during Thomas Jefferson's administration?

2. How did foreign events impact the United States during the Jefferson and Madison administrations?

3. What were the primary causes of the American decision to declare war on Great Britain in 1812?

4. What were the significant outcomes of the War of 1812 on the United States?

At the end of the Revolutionary War, George Washington predicted that Americans would move westward across the mountains into the Ohio Valley "faster than any other ever did, or any one would imagine." By 1840, more than 40 percent of the population lived west of the Appalachian Mountains in eight new states. "The woods are full of new settlers," marveled a traveler in upstate New York in 1805.

Thomas Jefferson described the United States in the early nineteenth century as an "empire of liberty" spreading westward. In 1800, people eager to own their own farms bought 67,000 acres of government-owned land; the next year, they bought 498,000 acres. Native Americans fiercely resisted the invasion of their ancestral lands but ultimately succumbed to a federal government (and army) determined to relocate them.

Most whites, however, were less concerned about taking land owned by Indians and Hispanics than they were about seizing their own economic opportunities. Isaac Weld, a British visitor, remarked that the Americans at the beginning of the nineteenth century were a "restless people, always on the lookout for something better or more profitable." Restless mobility and impatient striving soon came to define the American way of life.

JEFFERSONIAN REPUBLICANISM

On March 4, 1801, the fifty-seven-year-old Thomas Jefferson was inaugurated without incident, leading some people to call his fiercely contested election "the peaceful revolution." It was the first democratic election in modern history that saw the orderly transfer of power from one political party to another.

Jefferson's installation marked the start of a long period of supremacy of the nation's political life by Republicans—and Virginians. "Virginia literally dominates" the government, one Federalist claimed. The nation's most populous state, Virginia supplied a quarter of the Republican congressmen in the House of Representatives that convened in early 1801.

Politics in the young republic was becoming increasingly sectional. Another Federalist, former secretary of state Timothy Pickering of Massachusetts, acknowledged that the northeastern states, where Federalism was centered, could no longer "reconcile their habits, views, and interests with those of the South and West," two fast-growing regions that were beginning to rule the nation with "a rod of iron."

Jefferson was the first president inaugurated in the new national capital of Washington, District of Columbia. The unfinished city of barely 3,000 people was crisscrossed with muddy avenues connecting a few buildings clustered around two centers, Capitol Hill and the "President's Palace."

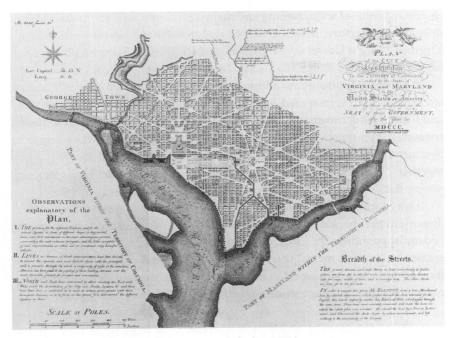

The new federal city Plan of Washington, D.C., from 1792.

THE "PEOPLE'S PRESIDENT" During his inauguration, Jefferson emphasized his connection to the "plain and simple" ways of the "common" people. Instead of wearing a ceremonial sword and riding in an elegant horse-drawn carriage, as George Washington and John Adams had done at their inaugurations, Jefferson, a widower, left his boardinghouse on New Jersey Avenue and walked to the Capitol building, escorted by members of Congress and Virginia militiamen. He read his inaugural address in a "femininely soft," high-pitched voice, then took the presidential oath administered by Chief Justice John Marshall, his Virginia cousin, with whom he shared a cordial hatred.

Jefferson's deliberate display of **republican simplicity** set the tone for his administration. He wanted Americans to notice the difference between the monarchical style of the Federalists and the down-to-earth simplicity and frugality of the Republicans. As president, he did not wear fancy clothes or host elegant parties. Jefferson often answered the door of the President's House himself, wearing a robe and slippers. A French official reported that the president "greets guests in slovenly clothes and without the least formality."

Charming and brilliant, Jefferson was trained as an attorney, read Greek and Latin, and was head of the American Philosophical Society. He was also an inventive genius of wide learning and many self-taught abilities, including "my delight," architecture. Jefferson helped design the state capitol in Richmond, Virginia, the new University of Virginia, and his thirty-three-room mountain-top mansion called *Monticello* ("Little Mountain"), near Charlottesville.

In his eloquent inaugural address, the tall, thin Jefferson, his red hair now streaked with grey, imagined America as "a rising nation, spread over a wide and fruitful land, traversing all the seas with the productions of their industry, engaged in commerce with nations" across the globe. Although determined to overturn many Federalist policies and programs, he urged Americans to work together. "We are all Republicans—we are all Federalists," Jefferson stressed, noting that "every difference of opinion is not a difference of principle."

It was a splendid message, but Jefferson's appeal for a united nation proved illusory, in part because he retained his own fierce partisanship and bitter anti-Federalist prejudices. In a letter to a British friend, Jefferson described the Federalists as "insane" men: "Their leaders are a hospital of incurables." He still feared that Federalists were determined to destroy "the liberties of the people" and convert the republic into a monarchy (he called them "monocrats").

A MORE DEMOCRATIC AMERICA The inauguration of Thomas Jefferson ushered in a more democratic political culture in which common people played a much larger role. During and after the Revolutionary War, an increasing proportion of white males, especially small farmers and wage laborers, artisans, mechanics, and apprentices, gained the right to vote or hold office as states reduced or eliminated requirements that voters and candidates own a specified amount of property.

An enlarged and more engaged citizenry of white male voters, many of them landless and illiterate, was not universally welcomed, however. "Since the war," a Massachusetts Federalist complained, "blustering ignorant men . . . have been attempting to push themselves into office." A Virginian was greatly worried by the rising evidence of the "turbulence and follies of democracy." Of all the states, South Carolina steadfastly resisted efforts to shift political power away from the slaveholding planter elite to the working poor.

Many among the founding generation of political leaders, especially Federalists but some Republicans as well, became openly anti-democratic, worried that men of humble origins, some of whom were uneducated and illiterate, were replacing the social and political elite ("natural aristocracy") in the state legislatures.

As the nineteenth century unfolded, voters were not content to be governed solely by "their betters"; they wanted to do the governing themselves. George Cabot, a Boston Federalist, called unchecked democracy "*the govern-*

ment of the worst." He was convinced that Jefferson was going to unleash "the terrible evils of democracy." When the "pot boils," another Federalist noted, the "scum will rise."

Over half of the members of the Republican-controlled Congress elected in 1800 were first-time legislators little known outside their districts. Before long, Federalist John Adams grumbled, even the poorest men "will demand an equal voice with any other." Adams so detested the democratic forces transforming politics and social life that he despaired for the nation's future: "Oh my Country," he moaned, "how I mourn over . . . thy contempt of Wisdom and Virtue and overweening admiration of fools and knaves! the never failing effects of *democracy!*"

A CONTRADICTORY GENIUS Thomas Jefferson, who owned hundreds of slaves, was a bundle of contradictions and inconsistencies. He was progressive and enlightened in some areas, self-serving and hypocritical in others. Jefferson, who had written in the Declaration of Independence that "all men are created equal," also bought, bred, flogged, and sold slaves while calling slavery "an abominable crime" and "unremitting despotism." He never freed his slaves for the simple reason that he was too dependent on their forced

The Capitol building This 1806 watercolor was painted by the building's architect, Benjamin Henry Latrobe, and inscribed to Thomas Jefferson. A prominent dome would be added later, after the building was damaged in the War of 1812.

labor. "We have the wolf by the ear," he confessed, "and we can neither hold him nor safely let him go."

Jefferson was also a man of expensive tastes who repeatedly condemned national indebtedness while deepening his own indebtedness. Although he celebrated the ideal of republican simplicity, he actually lived in an elegant mansion (Monticello) in Virginia where he indulged expensive tastes in food, wine, books, artwork, silverware, and furnishings—all of which eventually bankrupted him.

As president, Jefferson, the foremost defender of states' rights and the greatest critic of executive power, would display his peculiarly divided nature by exercising extraordinary presidential authority in negotiating the Louisiana Purchase and in enforcing a nationwide embargo shutting off all trade with warring Europe. Such inconsistencies led Federalists in the Massachusetts legislature to put Jefferson on trial for hypocrisy in 1805.

JEFFERSON IN OFFICE   The imperfect Thomas Jefferson was a consistently hardworking new president, spending ten to thirteen hours each day on his executive duties, often engaged in lobbying congressmen to support his legislation. In Jefferson's cabinet, the leading figures were Secretary of State James Madison, his best friend, Virginia neighbor, and political ally, and Secretary of the Treasury Albert Gallatin, a Pennsylvania Republican congressman whose financial skills had won him the respect of Federalists and Republicans alike.

In filling lesser offices, however, Jefferson often succumbed to pressure from the Republicans to remove Federalists, only to discover that there were few qualified candidates to replace some of them. When Gallatin asked if he might appoint able women to some posts, Jefferson revealed the limits of his liberalism: "The appointment of a woman to office is an innovation for which the public is not prepared, nor am I."

MARBURY V. MADISON   In one area—the federal judiciary—the new president decided to remove most of the offices altogether, in part because the court system was the only branch of the government still controlled by Federalists. In 1802, at Jefferson's urging, the Republican-controlled Congress repealed the Judiciary Act of 1801, which the Federalists had passed just before the transfer of power to the Jeffersonian Republicans. The Judiciary Act was intended to ensure Federalist control of the judicial system by creating sixteen federal circuit courts and appointing—for life—a new Federalist judge for each. Jefferson's controversial effort to repeal the judgeships sparked the pathbreaking case of *Marbury v. Madison* (1803).

The case went to the Supreme Court, which was presided over by Chief Justice John Marshall, a gifted Virginia Federalist. Marshall served at Valley Forge during the Revolutionary War, attended law school at the College of William and Mary, and became a respected Richmond attorney. In 1788, he helped Madison convince Virginians to ratify the U.S. Constitution. He also later served in Congress and became secretary of state under President Adams, who appointed him chief justice early in 1801. Blessed with a keen intellect and an analytical mind, Marshall was a fierce critic and lifelong enemy of his cousin Thomas Jefferson, whom he considered a war-shirking aristocrat posing as a democrat.

During the 1790s, John Jay, the first chief justice, admitted that the Supreme Court did not have "the energy, weight, and dignity" necessary to serve its role in balancing the powers of Congress and the presidency. Marshall set out to fix the problem. By the time he completed thirty-five years of service on the Supreme Court (1801–1835), spanning the terms of five presidents, he had made it the most powerful court in the world.

The Marbury case involved the appointment of the Maryland Federalist William Marbury, a prominent land speculator, as justice of the peace in the District of Columbia. Marbury's letter of appointment, called a commission, signed by President Adams two days before he left office, was still undelivered when James Madison took office as secretary of state, and Jefferson directed him to withhold it. Marbury then sued for a court order directing Madison to deliver his commission.

In the unanimous *Marbury v. Madison* ruling, Marshall and the Court held that Marbury deserved to be awarded his judgeship. Then, however, Marshall denied that the Court had jurisdiction in the case. The Federal Judiciary Act of 1789, which gave the Court authority in such proceedings, was unconstitutional, Marshall ruled, because the Constitution specified that the Court should have original jurisdiction only in cases involving foreign ambassadors or nations. The Court, therefore, could issue no order in the case.

With one bold stroke, Marshall had remarkably elevated the stature of the Court by reprimanding Jefferson while avoiding an awkward confrontation with an administration that might have defied his order. More important, the ruling subtly struck down a federal law, the Judiciary Act of 1789, on the grounds that it violated provisions of the Constitution, the "fundamental and paramount law of the nation." Marshall stressed that the Supreme Court was "emphatically" empowered "to say what the law is," even if it meant overruling both Congress and the president.

The *Marbury* decision granted to the Supreme Court a power not mentioned in the Constitution: the right of what came to be called *judicial review*, or deciding whether acts of Congress (and the presidency) are constitutional. Marshall established that the Supreme Court was the final authority in all constitutional interpretations.

President Jefferson fumed over what he called Marshall's "irregular" ruling. Giving judges "the right to decide which laws are constitutional, and what not," he wrote Abigail Adams, "would make the judiciary a despotic branch."

Jefferson, however, would lose that argument. Although the Court did not declare another federal law unconstitutional for fifty-four years, it has since struck down more than 150 acts of Congress and more than 1,100 "unconstitutional" acts of state legislatures, all in an effort to protect individual liberties and civil rights.

JEFFERSON'S ECONOMIC POLICIES   Although John Marshall got the better of Thomas Jefferson in court, the president's first term did include a series of triumphs. Surprisingly, he did not dismantle Alexander Hamilton's Federalist economic program, despite his harsh criticism of it and his ongoing feud with Hamilton. Instead, following the advice of Treasury secretary Albert Gallatin, Jefferson learned to accept the national bank as essential to economic growth.

Jefferson, however, did reject Hamilton's argument that a federal debt was a national "blessing." If the debt were not eliminated, Jefferson told Treasury secretary Gallatin, "we shall be committed to the English career of debt, corruption, and rottenness, closing with revolution."

To pay down the government debt, Jefferson slashed the federal budget. In his first message to Congress in 1801, he criticized the national government as being "too complicated, too expensive." He fired all federal tax collectors and cut the military budget in half, saying that state militias and small navy gunboats provided the nation with adequate protection against foreign enemies. Jefferson's was the first national government in history to *reduce* its own scope and power.

Jefferson also repealed the whiskey tax that Hamilton and George Washington had implemented in 1791. In doing so, he admitted that he had a peculiar affection for the "men from the Western side of the mountains"—grain farmers and backwoods distillers for whom whiskey was often the primary source of income. The prosperous economy helped the federal budget absorb the loss of the whiskey taxes. In addition, revenues from federal tariffs on imports rose with rising European trade, and the sale of government-owned western lands soared as Americans streamed westward. Ohio's admission to the Union in 1803 increased the number of states to seventeen.

***Burning of the Frigate* Philadelphia** Lieutenant William Decatur set fire to the captured *Philadelphia* during the United States' standoff with Tripoli over the enslavement of American sailors in north Africa.

ENDING THE SLAVE TRADE While shrinking the federal budget and reducing the national debt, Jefferson in 1807 signed a landmark bill that outlawed the importation of enslaved Africans into the United States, in part because southerners had come to believe that African-born slaves were more prone to revolt. The new law took effect on January 1, 1808, the earliest date possible under the Constitution. At the time, South Carolina was the only state that still permitted the purchase of enslaved Africans. For years to come, however, illegal traffic in African slaves would continue; as many as 300,000 were smuggled into the United States between 1808 and 1861.

THE BARBARY PIRATES Upon assuming the presidency, Jefferson promised "peace, commerce, and honest friendship with all nations," but some nations preferred war. On the Barbary Coast of North Africa, the Islamic rulers of Morocco, Algiers, Tunis, and Tripoli had for years engaged in piracy and extortion, preying upon unarmed European and American merchant ships. The U.S. government made numerous blackmail payments to these **Barbary pirates** in exchange for captured American ships and crews.

In 1801, however, the ruler of Tripoli upped his blackmail demands and declared war on the United States. Jefferson sent warships to blockade Tripoli. "Nothing will stop these pirates," he wrote, "but the presence of an armed force."

A sporadic naval war dragged on until 1805, punctuated in 1804 by the notable exploit of Lieutenant Stephen Decatur, who slipped into Tripoli Harbor by night and set fire to the frigate *Philadelphia,* which had been captured after it ran aground. The Tripoli ruler finally settled for a $60,000 ransom and released the *Philadelphia*'s crew. It was still blackmail (called "tribute" in the nineteenth century), but less than the $300,000 the pirates had demanded and much less than the cost of an outright war.

WESTERN EXPANSION

Thomas Jefferson often looked to the West for his inspiration, across the Appalachian Mountains and even across the Mississippi River, areas that he himself never visited. Only by expanding westward, he believed, could America avoid becoming overcrowded along the Atlantic coast. Westward expansion, however, meant invading areas long inhabited by Native Americans—and the Spanish and French.

THE LOUISIANA PURCHASE In 1801, American diplomats in Europe heard rumors that Spain had been forced to transfer its huge Louisiana province to its domineering ally, France, now led by the brilliant Napoléon Bonaparte. Short of stature but a giant on the battlefield, Napoléon was a war-loving military genius who had become the most feared ruler in the world: the conqueror of Egypt and Italy. After taking control of the French government, the ambitious Napoléon set out to restore his country's North American empire (Canada and Louisiana) that had been lost to Great Britain in 1763.

President Jefferson referred to Napoléon as both a "scoundrel" and "a gigantic force" threatening the future of the United States. A weak Spain in control of the territory west of the Mississippi River could have been tolerated, Jefferson explained, but Napoleonic France in control of the Mississippi Valley would lead to "eternal friction" and eventually war with the United States.

To prevent France from seizing control of the Mississippi River (the "greatest of evils"), Jefferson sent New Yorker Robert R. Livingston to Paris in 1801 to serve as the U.S. ambassador to France. The president told Livingston that his primary objective should be to acquire the port city of New Orleans, strategically situated at the mouth of the Mississippi, the magisterial river that begins in northern Minnesota and flows 2,552 miles south to the Gulf of Mexico. Jefferson told Livingston that purchasing New Orleans and West Florida (the territory along the Gulf coast from Pensacola, Florida, to New

Orleans) was of absolute importance, for "the day that France takes possession of New Orleans, . . . we must marry ourselves to the British fleet and nation" for protection against Napoleonic France.

Over the years, New Orleans under Spanish and then French rule had become a prosperous port city and a dynamic crossroads where people of all races and classes intermingled. For years, Americans living in Tennessee and Kentucky had begged the American government to ensure that they could send their crops and goods down the river to New Orleans.

In early 1803, Jefferson grew so concerned about the stalled negotiations in Paris over New Orleans that he sent James Monroe, his trusted friend and Virginia neighbor, to undertake "an extraordinary mission" to assist the sixty-six-year-old Livingston in Paris. "All eyes, all hopes, are now fixed on you," Jefferson told him as he prepared to depart for France.

No sooner had Monroe arrived than the French made a startling proposal: Napoléon offered to sell not just New Orleans but *all* of the immense, unmapped Louisiana Territory, from the Mississippi River west to the Rocky Mountains and from the Canadian border south to the Gulf of Mexico.

The unpredictable Napoléon had reversed himself because the large French army on the Caribbean island of Saint-Domingue (Haiti) had been decimated by epidemics of malaria and yellow fever and by a massive slave revolt led by Touissant L'Ouverture, who had proclaimed the Republic of Haiti. It was the first successful slave rebellion in history, and it panicked slaveholders in the southern states who feared that news of the Haitian revolt would spread to America.

Napoléon had tried to regain control of Saint-Domingue because it was a phenomenally profitable source of coffee and sugar. He also had hoped to connect New Orleans and Haiti as a first step in expanding France's North American trading empire. But after losing more than 50,000 soldiers to disease and warfare, Napoléon decided to cut his losses by selling the Louisiana Territory to the United States and using the proceeds to finance his "inevitable" next war with Great Britain.

By the Treaty of Cession, dated May 2, 1803, the United States agreed to pay $15 million for the entire Louisiana Territory. When Livingston and Monroe asked Charles-Maurice de Talleyrand, Napoléon's negotiator, about the precise extent of the territory they were buying, the Frenchman replied: "I can give you no direction. You have made a noble bargain for yourselves. I suppose you will make the most of it." A delighted Livingston, the U.S. negotiator, said that "from this day the United States take their place among the powers of the first rank."

The arrival of the signed treaty in Washington, D.C., presented Jefferson, who for years had harshly criticized the Federalists for stretching the meaning of the Constitution, with a frustrating political dilemma. Nowhere did the Constitution mention the purchase of territory. Was such an action even legal?

Jefferson admitted that the purchase was "not authorized by the Constitution," but in the end, his desire to double the size of the American republic trumped his concerns about an unconstitutional exercise of executive power.

Acquiring the Louisiana Territory, the president explained, would serve "the immediate interests of our Western citizens" and promote "the peace and security of the nation in general" by removing the French threat and creating a protective buffer separating the United States from the rest of the world.

Jefferson also imagined that the region might be a place to relocate Indian nations or freed slaves, since he feared a multiracial society. Besides, Jefferson and his Republican supporters argued, if the nation waited to pass a constitutional amendment to enable the acquisition, Napoléon might change his mind.

New England Federalists strongly opposed the purchase, however. Fisher Ames of Massachusetts argued that the Louisiana Territory was a waste of money, a howling "wilderness unpeopled with any beings except wolves and wandering Indians." Ames feared that adding a vast new empire in the West would weaken New England and the Federalist party, since the new western states were likely to vote Republican.

New England Federalists also worried that new territories would likely be settled by southern slaveholders who were Jeffersonian Republicans. As a newspaper editorialized, "Will [Jefferson and the] Republicans, who glory in their sacred regard to the rights of human nature, purchase an *immense wilderness* for the purpose of cultivating it with the labor of slaves?"

In a reversal of traditional stances, Federalists found themselves arguing for strict construction of the Constitution in opposing the Louisiana Purchase. "We are to give money of which we have too little for land of which we already have too much," argued a Bostonian in the *Columbian Centinel*. A Pennsylvania Federalist declared that Jefferson and the Republicans in Congress had "done more to strengthen the executive [branch] than Federalists dared think of even in [George] Washington's day."

Eager to close the deal, Jefferson called a special session of Congress on October 17, 1803, at which the Senate ratified the treaty with the French by an overwhelming vote of 26–6. On December 20, 1803, U.S. officials took formal possession of the sprawling Louisiana Territory (the Indians living there were not consulted).

The purchase included 875,000 square miles of land (529,402,880 acres). Six states in their entirety, and most or part of nine more, would eventually be carved out of the Louisiana Purchase, from Louisiana north to Minnesota and west to Montana.

The **Louisiana Purchase** was the most significant event of Jefferson's presidency and one of the most important developments in American history. It spurred western exploration and expansion, and especially enticed cotton growers to settle in the Old Southwest—Alabama, Mississippi, and Louisiana. Andrew Jackson, a slave-holding planter in Tennessee, congratulated Jefferson on acquiring the Louisiana Territory. "Every face wears a smile, and every heart leaps with joy."

LEWIS AND CLARK To learn more about the Louisiana Territory's geography, plants, and animals, as well as its prospects for trade and agriculture, Jefferson asked Congress to fund a scientific expedition. The president then appointed two army officers, Virginians Meriwether Lewis and William Clark, to lead what came to be known as the **Lewis and Clark expedition**. The twenty-nine-year-old Lewis was Jefferson's private secretary. Jefferson admired his "boldness, enterprise, and discretion." Clark was also an accomplished frontiersman. He was, it was said, "a youth of solid and promising parts, and as brave as Caesar."

On a rainy May morning in 1804, Lewis and Clark's "Corps of Discovery," numbering nearly fifty men, set out from a small village near the former French town of St. Louis in several large canoes (called *pirogues*) and one large flat-bottomed keelboat filled with food, weapons, medicine, and gifts to share with Indians. They traveled up the Missouri River through some of the most rugged wilderness in North America. Unsure of where they were going and what or whom they might encounter, they were eager to discover if the Missouri, the longest river in North America, made its way to the Pacific Ocean.

One of Lewis and Clark's maps
In their journals, Lewis and Clark sketched detailed maps of unexplored regions in the Far West.

Six months later, near the Mandan Sioux villages in what would become North Dakota, the Corps of Discovery built Fort Mandan and wintered in relative comfort, sending downriver a barge loaded with maps, soil samples, the skins and skeletons of weasels, wolves and antelope, and live specimens of prairie dogs and magpies, previously unknown in America.

In the spring of 1805, the Corps of Discovery added two guides: a French fur trader and his remarkable wife, a young Shoshone woman named Sacagawea. In appreciation for Lewis and Clark's help in delivering her baby,

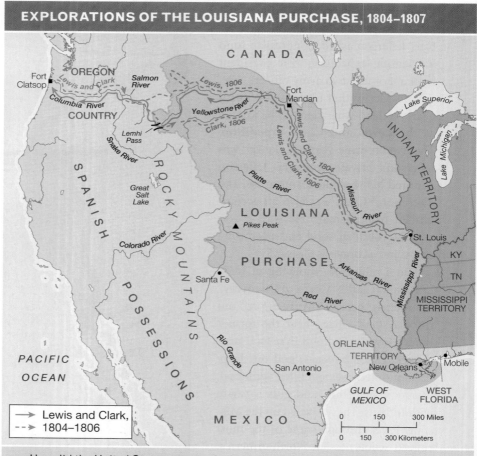

EXPLORATIONS OF THE LOUISIANA PURCHASE, 1804–1807

- How did the United States acquire the Louisiana Purchase?
- What was the mission of Lewis and Clark's expedition?
- What were the consequences of Lewis and Clark's widely circulated reports about the western territory?

Sacagawea provided crucial assistance as a guide, translator, and negotiator as they explored the Upper Missouri and encountered various Native Americans, most of whom were "hospitable, honest, and sincere people."

The Lewis and Clark expedition crossed the Rocky Mountains on foot and on horseback and used canoes to descend the Snake and Columbia Rivers to the Pacific Ocean, where they arrived in November 1805. Near the future site of Astoria, Oregon, at the mouth of the Columbia River, they built Fort Clatsop, where they spent a cold, rainy winter. The following spring they headed back, having been forced to eat their dogs and horses, and having weathered blizzards, broiling sun, fierce rapids, raging grizzly bears, numerous injuries and illnesses, and swarms of mosquitoes.

The expedition returned to St. Louis in 1806, having been gone nearly 28 months and covered some 8,000 miles. Lewis and Clark brought back extensive journals describing their experiences and observations while detailing some 180 plants and 125 animals. Their maps attracted traders and trappers to the region and led the United States to claim the Oregon Country by right of discovery and exploration.

Sacagawea Of the many memorials devoted to Sacagawea, this statue by artist Alice Cooper was unveiled at the 1905 Lewis and Clark Centennial Exposition.

POLITICAL SCHEMES The Lewis and Clark expedition and the Louisiana Purchase strengthened Jefferson's already solid support in the South and West. In New England, however, Federalists panicked because they assumed that new states carved out of the Louisiana Territory would be dominated by Jeffersonian Republicans. To protect their interests, Federalists hatched a complicated scheme to link New York politically to New England by trying to elect Vice President Aaron Burr, Jefferson's ambitious Republican rival, as governor of New York. The cunning Burr chose to drop his Republican affiliation and run for governor as an independent candidate.

Several leading Federalists opposed the scheme, however. Alexander Hamilton urged Federalists not to vote for Burr, calling him "a dangerous man, and one who ought not to be trusted with the reins of government." Burr ended up losing the election to the Republican candidate, who had been endorsed by Jefferson.

A furious Burr blamed Hamilton for his defeat and challenged him to a duel. At dawn on July 11, 1804, the two met near Weehawken, New Jersey on the Hudson River above New York City. Hamilton, whose son had been killed in a duel at the same location, fired first but intentionally missed as a demonstration of his religious and moral principles. Burr showed no such scruples. He shot Hamilton in the hip; the bullet ripped through his liver and lodged in his spine. He died the next day. Burr, who was still the vice president, was charged with murder by New Jersey authorities. He fled to South Carolina, where his daughter lived, hoping to ride out the storm.

JEFFERSON REELECTED   In the meantime, the presidential campaign of 1804 began. A congressional caucus of Republicans renominated Jefferson and chose George Clinton of New York as the vice presidential candidate. To avoid the problems associated with parties running multiple candidates for the presidency, in 1803 Congress had ratified the Twelfth Amendment to the Constitution, stipulating that the members of the Electoral College must use separate ballots to vote for the president and vice president.

Given Jefferson's first-term achievements, the Federalist candidates, South Carolinian Charles C. Pinckney and New Yorker Rufus King, never had a chance, for Jefferson had accomplished much: the Louisiana Purchase, a prosperous economy, and a reduced federal government budget and national debt. A Massachusetts Republican claimed that the United States was "never more respected abroad. The people were never more happy at home." Jefferson and Clinton won 162 of 176 electoral votes, carrying every state but Delaware and Connecticut.

DIVISIONS IN THE REPUBLICAN PARTY   Jefferson's landslide victory, however, created problems within his own party. Freed from strong opposition—Federalists made up only a quarter of the new Congress in 1805—the Republican majority began to divide into two warring factions, one calling itself the Jeffersonian or Nationalist Republicans, and the other, the anti-Jeffersonian southern Republicans, choosing the name Old Republicans.

Fiery young Virginian John Randolph was initially a loyal Jeffersonian, but over time he emerged as the most colorful of the radically conservative "Old Republicans"—a group formed mostly of southern agrarian political purists for whom protecting states' rights was more important than the need for a strong national government. Randolph, for example, detested Madison for his role in drafting and winning approval of the U.S. Constitution and broke with Jefferson over the Louisiana Purchase.

The imperious Randolph, another Jefferson cousin, stood out as the Senate's most colorful character. He often entered the chamber wearing a long, white coat and white boots with spurs, carrying a horsewhip, and trailed by a hunting hound that would sleep under his desk. He lubricated his speeches with gulps of whiskey.

Randolph quickly became the wittiest insulter in Congress, famously ordering opponents to sit down and shut up (he and Henry Clay would engage in a duel in 1826). He accurately described himself as an old-fashioned "aristocrat. I love liberty. I hate equality."

Randolph and other Old Republicans were best known for what they opposed: any compromise with the Federalists, any expansion of federal authority at the expense of states' rights, any new taxes or tariffs, and any change in the South's agrarian way of life rooted in slavery.

The Jeffersonian Republicans, on the other hand, were more moderate, pragmatic, and nationalistic. They were willing to compromise their states' rights principles to maintain national tariffs on imports, preserve a national bank, and stretch the "implied powers" of the Constitution to accommodate the Louisiana Purchase. Such compromises, said Randolph, were catastrophic. "The old republican party," he claimed, "is already ruined, past redemption."

THE BURR CONSPIRACY Meanwhile, Aaron Burr continued to plot and scheme. After the controversy over his duel with Alexander Hamilton subsided, he tried to carve out his own personal empire in the West. What came to be known as the Burr Conspiracy was hatched when Burr and General James Wilkinson, an old friend then serving as senior general of the U.S. Army and secretly being paid by the Spanish for spying, plotted to use a well-armed force of volunteers to separate part of the Louisiana Territory from the Union and declare it an independent republic, with New Orleans as its capital and Burr as its ruler. Burr claimed that "the people of the western country were ready for revolt."

Aaron Burr Burr graduated from what is now Princeton University, where he changed his course of study from theology to law.

In late 1806, Burr floated down the Ohio and Mississippi Rivers toward New Orleans with 100 volunteers, only to have Wilkinson turn on him and alert Jefferson to the scheme. The president ordered that Burr be arrested. Militiamen captured Burr in February 1807 and took him to Richmond, Virginia, where, in August, he was tried for treason before Chief Justice John Marshall.

Jefferson declared that Burr was guilty of trying to separate "the western states from us, of adding Mexico to them, and of placing himself at their head." In the end, however, Burr was acquitted because John Marshall instructed the jury that a verdict of treason required an "act of war" against the United States confirmed by at least two witnesses.

Again, Jefferson was disgusted with Marshall's ruling. "It now appears we have no law but the will of the judge," he wrote a friend. The president considered proposing a constitutional amendment to limit the power of the judiciary and even thought about asking Congress to impeach the chief justice. In the end, however, he did nothing. With further charges pending, the slippery Burr, deeply in debt, skipped bail and took refuge first in England, then in France. He returned to America in 1812 and resumed practicing law in New York.

WAR IN EUROPE

In the spring of 1803, soon after completing the sale of Louisiana to America, Napoléon Bonaparte declared war on Great Britain. The massive conflict would last eleven years and eventually involve all of Europe. Most Americans wanted to remain neutral and trade with both sides in the war, but the British and French were determined to keep that from happening.

NAVAL HARASSMENT During 1805, the spreading war in Europe reached a stalemate: The French army controlled most of Europe and the British navy dominated the seas. In May 1806, Britain issued a series of official declarations called Orders in Council which imposed a naval blockade of the entire European coast to prevent merchant ships from other nations, including the United States, from making port in France.

Soon, British warships began seizing American merchant ships bound for France. An angry Congress responded by passing the Non-Importation Act, which banned the importation of British goods. In early 1807, Napoléon announced that French warships would blockade the ports of Great Britain. The British responded that they would no longer allow any foreign ships to trade with the French-controlled islands in the Caribbean. Soon thereafter, British warships appeared along the American coast, stopping and searching U.S. merchant vessels as they headed for the Caribbean or Europe.

Preparation for War to Defend Commerce Shipbuilders, like those pictured here constructing the *Philadelphia*, played an important role in America's early wars.

The tense situation posed a terrible dilemma for American shippers. If they agreed to British demands to stop trading with the French, the French would retaliate by seizing U.S. vessels headed to and from Great Britain, and if they agreed to French demands that they stop trading with the British, the British would seize American ships headed to and from France. Lured by high profits, many American merchants decided to risk becoming victims of the Anglo-French war. Many of them paid a high price for their pursuit of overseas profits. During 1807, hundreds of American ships and their cargoes were captured by British and French warships.

IMPRESSMENT For American sailors, the danger on the high seas was heightened by the practice of *impressment*, whereby British warships stopped U.S. vessels, boarded them, and kidnapped sailors they claimed were British citizens. American merchant ships attracted British deserters because they paid seamen more than twice as much as did the Royal Navy; fully half of all sailors on American ships, about 9,000 men, had been born in Britain.

When the British stopped and searched American ships, they often did not bother to determine the citizenship of those they "impressed" into service. As a British naval captain explained, "It is my duty to keep my ship manned, & I will do so wherever I find men that speak the same language with me." Between 1803 and 1811, some 6,200 American sailors were "impressed" into the British navy.

THE *CHESAPEAKE* INCIDENT (1807) The crisis boiled over on June 22, 1807, when the powerful British warship HMS *Leopard* stopped a smaller U.S. vessel, the *Chesapeake*, only eight miles off the Virginia coast. After the *Chesapeake*'s captain refused to allow the British to search his ship for English deserters, the *Leopard* opened fire without warning, killing three Americans and wounding eighteen. A British search party then boarded the damaged *Chesapeake* and seized four men, one of whom, an English deserter, was hanged.

The attack on the *Chesapeake* was both an act of war and a national insult. The *Washington Federalist* screamed: "We have never, on any occasion, witnessed . . . such a thirst for revenge." In early July, Jefferson demanded an apology, banned all British warships from U.S. waters, and called on state governors to mobilize their militias.

Like John Adams before him, however, Jefferson resisted war fever, in part because the undersized American army and navy were not prepared to fight. His caution infuriated his critics. Federalist congressman Josiah Quincy of Massachusetts called Jefferson a "dish of skim milk curdling at the head of our nation."

THE EMBARGO President Jefferson decided on a strategy of "peaceable coercion" to force Britain and France to stop violating American rights. Late in 1807, he somehow convinced enough Republicans in Congress to cut off *all* American foreign trade. As Jefferson said, his choices were "war, embargo, or nothing."

The unprecedented **Embargo Act** (December 1807) stopped all exports of American goods—wheat, flour, pork, fish, and cattle, among other items—by prohibiting U.S. ships from sailing to foreign ports to "keep our ships and seamen out of harm's way."

Jefferson and his secretary of state, James Madison, mistakenly assumed that the embargo would quickly force the warring European nations to quit violating American rights. They were wrong. Neither Britain nor France yielded.

With each passing month, the ill-conceived embargo devastated the Republicans and the economy while reviving the political appeal of the Federalists, especially in New England, where merchants howled because the embargo cut off their primary industry: oceangoing commerce. The value of U.S. exports

Anti-Jefferson sentiment This 1807 Federalist cartoon compares George Washington (left, flanked by a British lion and American eagle) and Thomas Jefferson (right, with a snake and a lizard). Below Jefferson are volumes of French philosophy while Washington's volumes simply read: *Law, Order,* and *Religion.*

plummeted from $48 million in 1807 to $9 million a year later, and federal revenue from tariffs plunged from $18 million to $8 million. Shipbuilding declined by two-thirds, and prices for exported farm crops were cut in half. New England's once-thriving port cities became ghost towns, as thousands of ships and sailors were out of work. Meanwhile, smuggling soared, especially along the border with Canada.

Americans raged at what critics called "Jefferson's embargo." A Bostonian accused the president of being "one of the greatest tyrants in the whole world." Another letter writer told the president that he had paid four friends "to shoot you if you don't take off the embargo," while still another addressed the president as "you red-headed son of a bitch."

The embargo turned American politics upside down. To enforce it, Jefferson, the nation's leading spokesman for *reducing* the power of the federal government, now found himself *expanding* federal power into every aspect of the nation's economic life. In effect, the United States used its own warships to blockade its own ports. Jefferson even activated the New York state militia in an effort to stop smuggling across the Canadian border.

The outrage over "Jefferson's embargo" eventually demoralized the president and other Republicans and helped revive the Federalist party in New England.

At the same time, farmers and planters in the South and West also suffered; they needed to sell their surplus grain, cotton, and tobacco abroad. Yet Jefferson stubbornly refused to admit defeat. As a critic noted, the president was determined to "hug the Embargo and die in its embrace."

Congress finally rebuked the president by voting 70–0 to end the ill-conceived embargo effective March 4, 1809, the day that the "splendid misery" of Jefferson's second presidential term ended. The dejected president left the White House feeling like a freed prisoner, eager to retire "to my family, my books, and my farms" in Virginia. No one, he said, could be more relieved "on shaking off the shackles of power." His fellow Virginian and stern critic, Congressman John Randolph, declared that never had a president "left the nation in a state so deplorable and calamitous."

Jefferson learned a hard lesson that many of his successors would also confront: a second term is rarely as successful as the first. As he admitted, "No man will ever carry out of that office [the presidency] the reputation which carried him into it."

In the election of 1808, the presidency passed to another prominent Virginian, Secretary of State James Madison. The Federalists, again backing Charles C. Pinckney of South Carolina and Rufus King of New York, won only 47 electoral votes to Madison's 122.

JAMES MADISON AND THE DRIFT TO WAR   In his inaugural address, President Madison confessed that he inherited a situation "full of difficulties." He soon made a bad situation worse. Although Madison had been a talented legislator and the "Father of the Constitution," he proved to be a weak, indecisive chief executive. When members of Congress questioned several of his cabinet appointments, he backed down and ended up naming second-rate men to key positions.

Madison's sparkling wife, Dolley, was the only truly excellent member of the president's inner circle. Seventeen years younger than her husband, she was a superb First Lady who excelled at using the White House to entertain political leaders and foreign dignitaries. Journalists called her the "Queen of Washington City."

From the beginning, Madison's presidency was entangled in foreign affairs and crippled by his lack of executive experience. Like Jefferson, Madison and his advisers repeatedly overestimated the young republic's diplomatic leverage and military strength in shaping foreign policy. The result was international humiliation.

Madison insisted on upholding the principle of freedom of the seas for the United States and other neutral nations, but he was unwilling to create a navy strong enough to enforce it. He continued the policy of "peaceable coercion" against the European nations, which was as ineffective for Madison as it had been for Jefferson.

In place of the failed embargo, Congress passed the Non-Intercourse Act (1809), which reopened trade with all countries *except* France and Great Britain and their colonies. It also authorized the president to reopen trade with either France or Great Britain if it stopped violating American rights on the high seas.

In December 1810, France issued a vague promise to restore America's neutral rights, whereupon Madison gave Great Britain three months to do the same. The British refused, and the Royal Navy continued to seize American vessels and their cargoes and crews.

A reluctant Madison asked Congress to declare war against Great Britain on June 1, 1812. If the United States did not defend its rights as a neutral nation, he explained, then Americans were "not independent people, but colonists and vassals." Thomas Jefferson sent a letter of support to the president: "Heaven help you through all your difficulties."

On June 5, the House of Representatives voted for war 79–49. Two weeks later, the Senate followed suit, 19–13. Every Federalist in Congress opposed what they called "Mr. Madison's War," while 80 percent of Republicans supported it. The southern and western states wanted war; the New England states opposed it.

By declaring war, Republicans hoped to unite the nation, discredit the Federalists, and put an end to British-led Indian attacks along the Great Lakes and in the Ohio Valley by conquering British Canada. To generate popular support, Thomas Jefferson advised Madison that he needed, above all, "to stop Indian barbarities. The conquest of Canada will do this." Jefferson presumed that the French Canadians were eager to rise up against their British rulers. With their help, the Republicans predicted, American armies would easily conquer Britain's vast northern colony. It did not work out that way.

The War of 1812

The **War of 1812** marked the first time that Congress had declared war. Great Britain did not expect or want the war; it was preoccupied with defeating Napoléon in Europe. In fact, on June 16, 1812, the British government promised to quit interfering with American shipping. President Madison and the Republicans, however, were not satisfied; only war, they believed, would put an end to the British practice of impressment and stop British-inspired Indian attacks along the western frontier.

SHIPPING RIGHTS AND NATIONAL HONOR Why the United States chose to start the war remains a puzzle still debated among historians. The main cause of the war—the repeated British violations of American shipping rights and the practice of "impressing" sailors dominated President Madison's war message. Most of the votes in Congress for war came from legislators representing rural regions, from Pennsylvania southward and westward, where farmers and planters grew surpluses for export to Europe. Their economic interests were being hurt by the raids on American merchant ships.

However, the representatives from the New England states, which bore the brunt of British attacks on U.S. shipping, voted *against* the declaration of war, 20–12. As a New England minister roared, let the "southern *Heroes* fight their own battles."

Tecumseh The Shawnee leader, who tried to unite Native American peoples across the United States in defense of their lands, was later killed in 1813 at the Battle of the Thames.

One explanation for this seeming inconsistency is that many Americans in the South and West, especially Tennessee, Kentucky, and South Carolina, voted for war because they believed America's national *honor* was at stake. Andrew Jackson, a proud anti-British Tennessean who was the new state's first congressman, declared that he was eager to fight "for the re-establishment of our national character." In the popular phrase of the time, the war was needed to protect "Free Trade and Sailors' Rights!"

NATIVE AMERICAN CONFLICTS Another factor leading to war was the growing number of Indian attacks, supported by the British, in the Ohio Valley. The story took a new turn with the rise of two remarkable Shawnee leaders, Tecumseh and his brother, Tenskwatawa, who lived in a large village called Prophetstown on the Tippecanoe River in northern Indiana.

Tecumseh ("Shooting Star") knew that the fate of the native peoples depended on their being unified. He hoped to create a single Indian nation powerful enough, with British assistance, to fend off further American expansion. His half brother Tenskwatawa (the "Open Door"), a one-eyed recovering alcoholic with a fierce temper who was known as "the Prophet," gained a large following among Native Americans for his predictions that white Americans ("children of the devil") were on the verge of collapse. He demanded that the indigenous peoples abandon all things European: clothing, customs, Christianity, and especially liquor. If they did so, the Great Spirit would reward them by turning the whites' gunpowder to sand.

A "TRAIL OF BLOOD" Inspired by his brother's spiritual message, Tecumseh in 1811 made heroic efforts to form alliances with other Native American nations throughout mid-America. In Alabama, he told a gathering of 5,000 Indians that they should "let the white race perish" because "they seize your land; they corrupt your women; they trample on the ashes of your dead!" The native peoples must join together to drive out the whites on a "trail of blood." The whites "have driven us from the sea to the lakes," he declared. "We can go no further."

Tecumseh disavowed the many treaties whereby indigenous peoples had "sold" ancient Indian lands. "No tribe," he declared, "has the right to sell [land], even to each other, much less to strangers. . . . Sell a country!? Why not sell the air, the great sea, as well as the earth? Didn't the Great Spirit make them all for the use of his children?"

William Henry Harrison, governor of the Indiana Territory, learned of Tecumseh's bold plans, met with him twice, and described him as "one of those uncommon geniuses who spring up occasionally to produce revolutions and overturn the established order of things."

Yet Harrison vowed to eliminate Tecumseh. In the fall of 1811, he gathered 1,000 troops and advanced on Prophetstown while the Indian leader was away. Tenskwatawa was lured into making a foolish attack on Harrison's encampment. What became the Battle of Tippecanoe was a disastrous defeat for the Native Americans, as Harrison's troops burned the village and destroyed its supplies. **Tecumseh's Indian Confederacy** went up in smoke, and he fled to Canada.

THE LUST FOR CANADA AND FLORIDA Some Americans wanted war with Great Britain in 1812 because they wanted to seize control of Canada. That there were nearly 8 million Americans and only 300,000 Canadians led many to believe that conquering Canada would be quick and easy. Jefferson, for instance, wrote President Madison that the "acquisition of Canada" was simply a "matter of marching" north with a military force.

The British were also vulnerable far to the south. East Florida, which the British had returned to Spain's control in 1783, posed a threat to the Americans because Spain was too weak, or simply unwilling, to prevent Indian attacks across the border with Georgia. Also, in the absence of a strong Spanish presence, British agents and traders remained in East Florida, smuggling goods and conspiring with Indians against Americans. Spanish Florida had also long been a haven for runaway slaves from Georgia and South Carolina. Many Americans living along the Florida-Georgia border hoped that the war against Great Britain would enable them to oust the British and the Spanish from Florida.

WAR HAWKS   In the Congress that assembled in late 1811, new young anti-British representatives from southern and western districts shouted for war to defend "national honor" and rid the Northwest of the "Indian problem." Among the most vocal "war hawks" were Henry Clay of Kentucky and John C. Calhoun of South Carolina.

Clay, the brash young Speaker of the House of Representatives, was a tall, rawboned man who was "for resistance by the *sword*." He boasted that the Kentucky militia alone could conquer Canada. His bravado inspired others. "I don't like Henry Clay," Calhoun said. "He is a bad man, an imposter, a creator of wicked schemes. I wouldn't speak to him, but, by God, I love him" for wanting war against Britain. When Calhoun learned that President Madison had finally decided on war, he threw his arms around Clay's neck and led his war-hawk colleagues in an Indian war dance.

In New England and much of New York, however, there was little enthusiasm for war. It threatened to cripple the region's dominant industry, shipping, since Great Britain remained the region's largest trading partner. Federalists actively undermined the war effort. Both Massachusetts and Connecticut refused to send soldiers to fight in the war, and merchants openly sold supplies to British troops in Canada.

WAR PREPARATIONS   As it turned out, the United States was woefully unprepared for war, both financially and militarily, and the short, softspoken James Madison lacked the leadership ability and physical stature to inspire public confidence and military resolve. He was no George Washington.

The national economy was weak too. In 1811, Republicans had let the charter of the Bank of the United States expire. Many Republican Congressmen owned shares in state banks and wanted the B.U.S. dissolved because it both competed with and regulated their local banks. Once the B.U.S. shut down, however, the number of unregulated state banks mushroomed, all with their own forms of currency, creating commercial chaos. Treasury Secretary Albert

Gallatin was so upset by the loss of the B.U.S. that he wrote a scathing letter of resignation. President Madison begged him to reconsider, which he did, but the problems of waging a war with Britain without adequate financial resources did not go away.

Once war began, it did not go well for the Americans. The mighty British navy blockaded American ports, which caused federal tariff revenues to tumble. In March 1813, Albert Gallatin warned Madison that the U.S. Treasury had "hardly enough money to last till the end of the month." Furthermore, Republicans in Congress were so afraid of public criticism that they delayed approving tax increases needed to finance the war.

U.S. Naval victories John Bull (the personification of England as Uncle Sam was to America) "stung to agony" by *Wasp* and *Hornet*, two American warships that clinched early victories in the War of 1812.

The military situation was almost as bad. In 1812, the British had 250,000 professional soldiers and the most powerful navy in the world. By contrast, the U.S. Army numbered only 3,287 ill-trained and poorly equipped men, led by mostly incompetent officers with little combat experience. In January 1812, Congress authorized an army of 35,000 men, but a year later, just 18,500 had been recruited—many of them Irish American immigrants who hated the English—and then only by enticing them with promises of land and cash bounties.

President Madison, who refused to allow free blacks or slaves to serve in the army, was forced to plead with the state governors to provide militiamen, only to have the Federalist governors in anti-war New England decline. The British, on the other hand, had thousands of soldiers stationed in Canada and the West Indies. And, as was true during the Revolutionary War, the British, offering food, guns, and ammunition, recruited more Native American allies than did the Americans.

The U.S. Navy was in better shape than the Army, with able officers and well-trained seamen, but it had only sixteen tiny gunboats compared to Britain's 600 warships. The lopsided military strength of the British led Madison to mutter that the United States was in "an embarrassing situation."

A CONTINENTAL WAR For these reasons and more, the War of 1812 was one of the strangest wars in history. In fact, it was three wars fought on three separate fronts. One theatre of conflict was the Chesapeake Bay along the coast of Maryland and Virginia, including Washington, D.C. The second theatre was in the South—Alabama, Mississippi, and West and East Florida—where American forces led by General Andrew Jackson invaded lands owned by the Creeks and the Spanish. The third front might be more accurately called the Canadian-American War. It began in what is now northern Indiana and Ohio, southeastern Michigan, and the contested border regions around the Great Lakes. The fighting raged back and forth across the border as the United States repeatedly invaded British Canada, only to be embarrassingly repulsed.

THE WAR IN THE NORTH   Like the American Revolution, the War of 1812, often called America's second war for independence, was very much a civil war. The Canadians, thousands of whom were former American Loyalists who had fled north after the Revolutionary War, remained loyal to the British Empire, while the Americans and a few French Canadians and Irish Canadians sought to push Britain out of North America and annex Canada.

In some cases, Americans fought former Americans, including families that were divided in their allegiances. Siblings even shot each other. Once, after killing an American militiaman, a Canadian soldier began taking the clothes off the corpse, only to realize that it was his brother. He grumbled that it served him right to have died for a bad cause.

Indians armed by the British dominated the heavily wooded borderlands around the Great Lakes. Michigan's governor recognized that the British and their Indian allies were dependent on each other: "The British cannot hold Upper Canada [Ontario] without the assistance of the Indians," but the "Indians cannot conduct a war without the assistance of a civilized nation [Great Britain]." So the American assault on Canada involved attacking Indians, Canadians, and British soldiers.

INVADING CANADA   President James Madison approved a three-pronged plan for the invasion of British Canada. It called for one army to move north through upstate New York, along Lake Champlain, to take Montreal, while another was to advance into Upper Canada by crossing the Niagara River between Lakes Ontario and Erie. The third attack would come from the west, with an American force moving east into Upper Canada from Detroit, Michigan. The plan was to have all three attacks begin at the same time to force the British troops in Canada to split up.

The complicated plan of invasion, however, was a disaster. The underfunded and undermanned Americans could barely field one army, let alone three, and communications among the separated commanders was spotty at best.

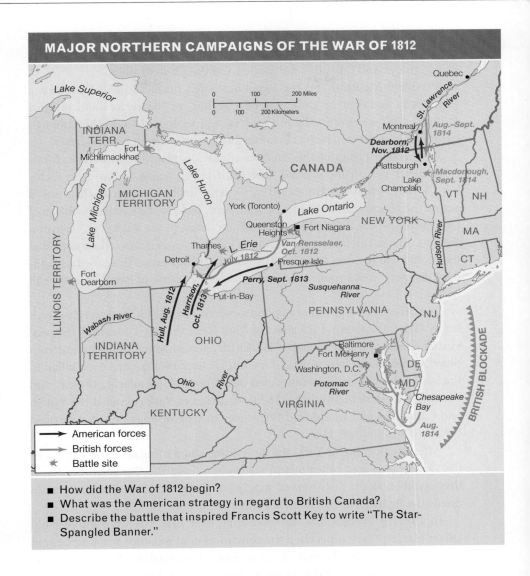

MAJOR NORTHERN CAMPAIGNS OF THE WAR OF 1812

- How did the War of 1812 begin?
- What was the American strategy in regard to British Canada?
- Describe the battle that inspired Francis Scott Key to write "The Star-Spangled Banner."

In July 1812, fifty-nine-year-old General William Hull, a Revolutionary War veteran and governor of the Michigan Territory, marched his disorganized and poorly supplied army across the Detroit River into Canada. He told the Canadians that he was there to free them from "tyranny and oppression." The Canadians, however, did not want to be liberated, and the Americans were soon pushed back to Detroit by British troops, Canadian militiamen, and their Indian allies.

Hull was tricked by the British commander's threats to unleash thousands of Indian warriors. Fearing a massacre by "savages," Hull did the unthinkable:

he surrendered his entire force of 2,500 troops without firing a shot. His capitulation shocked the nation and opened the entire western frontier to raids by British troops and Canadian militiamen and their Indian allies.

President Madison and the Republicans felt humiliated. In Kentucky, a Republican said General Hull must be a "traitor" or "nearly an idiot" or "part of both." Hull was eventually put on trial and sentenced to death. Although pardoned by Madison, he was dismissed from the army for his cowardice.

The second prong of the American invasion plan, the assault on Montreal, never got off the ground. The third prong began at dawn on October 13, 1812, when U.S. troops led by General Stephen Van Rensselaer rowed across the Niagara River from Lewiston, New York, to the Canadian village of Queenston, where they suffered a crushing defeat in the Battle of Queenston Heights. The shameful losses in Canada led many Americans to lose hope that they could win the war. In early 1813, a Kentuckian warned that any more military disasters would result in "disunion," and the "cause of Republicanism will be lost."

Then there was a glimmer of good news. In April 1813, an American force led by General Zebulon Pike attacked York (later renamed Toronto), the provincial capital of Upper Canada. The British and Canadian militiamen surrendered, and over the next several days, in part because Pike had been killed in the battle, the U.S. soldiers rampaged out of control, plundering the city and burning government buildings. The destruction of York outraged the British and Canadians and would lead them later to seek revenge on the American capital of Washington, D.C.

After the burning of York, the Americans sought to gain naval control of the Great Lakes and other inland waterways along the Canadian border. If they could break the British naval supply line and secure Lake Erie, they could divide the British from their Indian allies.

In 1813, at Presque Isle, Pennsylvania, near Erie, twenty-eight-year-old Oliver Hazard Perry supervised the construction of warships from timber cut in nearby forests. By the end of the summer, Commodore Perry's new warships set out in search of the British and some "warm fighting," finally finding them at Lake Erie's Put-in-Bay on September 10.

Two British warships used their superior weapons to pound the *Lawrence*, Perry's flagship. After four hours of intense shelling, none of the *Lawrence*'s guns was working, and most of the crew were dead or wounded. Perry refused to quit, however. He switched to another vessel, kept fighting, and, miraculously, ended up accepting the surrender of the entire British squadron. Hatless and bloodied, Perry reported that "we have met the enemy and they are ours."

American naval control of Lake Erie forced the British to evacuate Upper Canada. They gave up Detroit and were defeated at the Battle of the Thames in southern Canada on October 5, 1813. During the battle, the British fled, leaving the great chief Tecumseh and 500 warriors to face the wrath of the Americans. When Tecumseh was killed, the remaining Indians retreated.

Perry's victory and the defeat of Tecumseh enabled the Americans to recover control of most of Michigan and seize the Western District of Upper Canada. Thereafter, the war in the north lapsed into a military stalemate along the Canadian border, with neither side able to dislodge the other.

THE CREEK WAR In the South, too, the war flared up in 1813. The Creek Indians in western Georgia and Alabama had split into two factions: the Upper Creeks (called Red Sticks because of their bright-red war clubs), who opposed American expansion and sided with the British during the war, and the Lower Creeks, who wanted to remain on good terms with the Americans. On August 30, Red Sticks attacked Fort Mims on the Alabama River, thirty miles above the Gulf coast town of Mobile, and massacred 553 men, women, and children, butchering and scalping half of them.

Americans were incensed. Thirsting for revenge, Andrew Jackson, commanding general of the Army of West Tennessee, recruited about 2,500 volunteer militiamen and headed south. With him were David Crockett, a famous sharpshooter, and Sam Houston, a nineteen-year-old Virginia frontiersman who would later lead the Texas War for Independence against Mexico.

Jackson was a natural warrior and gifted commander who was both feared and respected. His soldiers nicknamed him "Old Hickory" in recognition of his toughness. From a young age, he had embraced violence, gloried in it, and prospered by it. He told all "brave Tennesseans" that their "frontier [was] threatened with invasion by the savage foe" and that the Indians were advancing "with scalping knives unsheathed, to butcher your wives, your children, and your helpless babes. Time is not to be lost."

Jackson's expedition across Alabama was not easy. It was difficult to keep his men fed and supplied so far from Tennessee and with no connecting roads. Some of the men went home once their enlistment period ended. A few deserted or rebelled. When a seventeen-year-old soldier threatened an officer, he was tried and sentenced to death. Jackson refused pleas for mercy and had the young man shot in front of the rest of the army to provide a harsh example of the general's steely determination.

Jackson's grizzled volunteers crushed the Red Sticks in a series of lopsided bloodbaths in Alabama. The decisive battle occurred on March 27, 1814, at

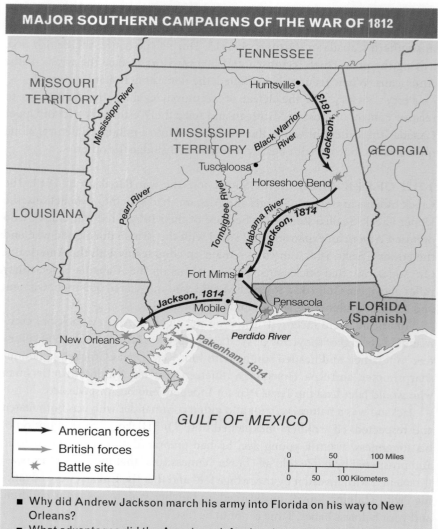

MAJOR SOUTHERN CAMPAIGNS OF THE WAR OF 1812

TENNESSEE

MISSOURI
TERRITORY

Mississippi River

Huntsville

Jackson, 1813

MISSISSIPPI
TERRITORY

Black Warrior River

GEORGIA

Tuscaloosa

Horseshoe Bend

Pearl River

Tombigbee River

Alabama River

Jackson, 1814

LOUISIANA

Fort Mims

Jackson, 1814   Mobile   Pensacola

FLORIDA
(Spanish)

New Orleans

Pakenham, 1814

Perdido River

GULF OF MEXICO

→ American forces
→ British forces
✳ Battle site

0   50   100 Miles
0   50   100 Kilometers

- Why did Andrew Jackson march his army into Florida on his way to New Orleans?
- What advantages did the American defenders have in the Battle of New Orleans?
- Why was the Battle of New Orleans important to the Treaty of Ghent?

Horseshoe Bend on the Tallapoosa River. Jackson's soldiers, with crucial help from their Cherokee and Creek allies, surrounded a Red Stick fort, set fire to it, and shot the Indians as they tried to escape. Nine hundred of them were killed, including 300 who drowned in a desperate effort to cross the river. Jackson reported to his wife that the *"carnage was dreadful."* His men had "regained all the scalps taken from Fort Mims." Fewer than fifty of Jackson's soldiers were killed.

The Battle of Horseshoe Bend was the worst defeat ever inflicted upon Native Americans, and it effectively ended the Creeks' ability to wage war. With the Treaty of Fort Jackson, signed in August 1814, the Red Stick Creeks gave up two-thirds of their land—some 23 million acres—including southwest Georgia and much of Alabama. Red Eagle, chief of the Red Sticks, told Jackson: "I am in your power. . . . My people are all gone. I can do no more but weep over the misfortunes of my nation." President Madison rewarded Jackson by naming him a major general in the regular U.S. Army.

Soon after the Battle of Horseshoe Bend, events in Europe took a dramatic turn when the British, Spanish, and Portuguese armies repelled French emperor Napoléon's effort to conquer Spain and Portugal. Now free to focus on the American war, the British sent 16,000 veteran soldiers to try yet again to invade America from Canada. The British navy off the American coast also received reinforcement, enabling it to extend its blockade to New England ports and to bombard coastal towns from Delaware to Florida. The final piece of the British plan was to seize New Orleans and thereby sever American access to the Mississippi River, lifeline of the West.

FIGHTING ALONG THE CHESAPEAKE BAY Throughout the war, the pitifully small U.S. Navy was unable to protect the nation's long coastline. In February 1813, the British had more warships in the Chesapeake Bay than were in the entire American navy, and they frequently captured and burned American merchant vessels. The British fleet also launched numerous raids along the Virginia and Maryland shore, in effect mocking the Madison administration's ability to defend the nation. One British officer dismissed the United States as "a country of *Infants in War.*"

The presence of British ships on the coast and inland rivers led many slaves to escape or revolt. As had happened during the Revolutionary War, British naval commanders promised freedom to slaves who aided or fought with them. More than 3,000 slaves in Maryland and Virginia stole boats or canoes that took them to the safety of British ships.

In September 1813, the British organized some 400 former slaves into an all-black military unit, called the Colonial Marines. The recruits were provided uniforms, meals, and $6 a month in wages. News of the all-black Colonial Marines panicked whites living along the vast Chesapeake Bay, who feared that the former slaves would "have no mercy on them." Virginia's John Randolph spoke for many southern planters when he insisted that the "question of slavery, as it is called, is to us a question of life and death." Fearing "*our worst enemy,*" the mayor of Richmond claimed that the "Slaves of this City . . . have conspired and are conspiring to burn the City."

THE BURNING OF WASHINGTON During the late summer of 1814, U.S. forces suffered their most humiliating experience of the war when British troops captured and burned Washington, D.C.

In August, 4,000 British soldiers landed at Benedict, Maryland, routed the American militia at Bladensburg, and headed for the nation's capital, only a few miles away. Thousands fled the city. President Madison frantically called out the poorly led and untrained militia, then left the White House to help rally the troops. His efforts failed, however, as the American defense disintegrated in the face of the British attack.

On August 24, British redcoats marched unopposed into the American capital. Madison and his wife, Dolley, had fled just in time ("Where I shall be tomorrow, I cannot tell!"), after first saving a portrait of George Washington and a copy of the Declaration of Independence. The vengeful British, aware that American troops had burned York, the Canadian capital, torched the White House, the Capitol, the Library of Congress, and other government buildings. A tornado the next day compounded the damage, but a violent thunderstorm dampened both the fires and the enthusiasm of the British forces, who headed north to assault Baltimore.

The destruction of Washington, D.C., shocked, embarrassed, and infuriated Americans. Even worse, people had lost confidence in the government

The Burning of the Capitol This 1817 etching of the damaged Capitol shows shackled slaves (bottom right) and angels overhead. It appeared in a book arguing that the British effort to destroy "the temple of freedom" was a sign that God disapproved of slavery.

and the military. David Campbell, a Virginia congressman, told his brother that America was "ruled by fools and the administration opposed by knaves."

John Armstrong, the secretary of war, resigned because of the embarrassing sack of the nation's capital. Madison replaced him with James Monroe, who was also serving as secretary of state. A desperate Monroe soon proposed enlisting free blacks into the army. But many worried that such changes were too few and too late. A Virginia official noted that without a miracle, "*This union is inevitably dissolved.*"

President Madison was "heartbroken" by the turn of events. He called an emergency session of Congress and appealed to Americans to "expel the invaders." A Baltimore newspaper reported that the "spirit of the nation is roused." That determination showed itself when fifty British warships sailed into Baltimore Harbor on September 13 while 4,200 British soldiers, including the all-black Colonial Marines, assaulted the city by land. About 1,000 Americans held Fort McHenry on an island in the harbor.

During the night of September 13, the British unleashed a thunderous bombardment of Fort McHenry. "The portals of hell appeared to have been thrown open," a Baltimore resident reported. Yet the Americans refused to surrender. At daybreak on the 14th, the soldiers in the battered fort stood defiant, guns at the ready. The frustrated British fleet sailed away.

Francis Scott Key, a lawyer and occasional poet, watched the bombardment of Fort McHenry from a ship, having been sent to negotiate the release of a captured American. The sight of the U.S. flag still flying over the fort at dawn meant that the city had survived the onslaught. The dramatic scene inspired Key to scribble the verses of what came to be called "The Star-Spangled Banner," which began, "Oh, say can you see, by the dawn's early light?" Later revised and set to the tune of a popular English drinking song, it eventually became America's national anthem.

THE BATTLE OF LAKE CHAMPLAIN The British failure to conquer Baltimore nixed their hopes of a quick victory in the war while giving the Americans a desperately needed morale boost. More good news soon arrived from upstate New York, where the outnumbered Americans at Plattsburgh, along Lake Champlain, were saved by the superb ability of Commodore Thomas Macdonough, commander of the U.S. naval squadron.

On September 11, 1814, just days after the burning of Washington, D.C., British soldiers attacked at Plattsburgh while their navy engaged Macdonough's warships in a battle that ended with the entire British fleet either destroyed or captured.

The Battle of Lake Champlain (also called the Battle of Plattsburgh) forced the British to abandon the northern campaign—their main military push in the war—and retreat back into Canada. When the British officers came to surrender themselves and their swords, Macdonough said, "Gentlemen, return your swords to your scabbards; you are worthy of them."

In Florida in November, an army led by Andrew Jackson seized Spanish-controlled Pensacola, on the Gulf coast, thereby preventing another British army from landing and pushing northward into the southern states. The American victories in New York and Florida convinced Congress not to abandon Washington, D.C. Instead, the members voted to rebuild the Capitol and the White House.

The Aftermath of the War

While the fighting raged, U.S. diplomats, including Henry Clay and John Quincy Adams, son of the former president, had begun meetings with British officials in Ghent, near Brussels in present-day Belgium, to discuss ending the war. The negotiations were at a standstill when news arrived of the American victory at the Battle of Lake Champlain and the failure of the British invasion of Baltimore. The news made the British more flexible, but negotiations still dragged on for weeks. Finally, on Christmas Eve, 1814, the diplomats reached an agreement to stop the fighting.

THE TREATY OF GHENT The weary British decided to end the war in part because of military setbacks but also because London merchants were eager to renew the extensive trade with America. The British government had also concluded that the war was not worth the cost.

By the **Treaty of Ghent** (1814), the two countries agreed to end the war, return each side's prisoners, and restore the previous boundaries. This was a godsend for the Americans, since British forces at the time still controlled eastern Maine, northern Michigan, a portion of western New York, and several islands off the coast of Georgia. The British also pledged to stop supporting Indian attacks along the Great Lakes.

What had begun as an American effort to protect its honor, end British impressment, and conquer Canada had turned into a second war of independence. At the end of the treaty negotiations, John Quincy Adams wrote to his wife from Ghent that he had had the honor of "redeeming our union." Although the Americans lost the war for Canada and saw their national capital destroyed, they won the southern war to defeat the Indians and take their lands. More important, the Treaty of Ghent saved the splintered republic from possible civil war and financial ruin.

THE BATTLE OF NEW ORLEANS Because it took six weeks for news of the Treaty of Ghent to reach the United States, fighting continued in America at the end of 1814. On December 1, Andrew Jackson arrived in New Orleans to prepare for a British invasion of the strategic city. He announced that he "would drive the British into the sea, or perish in the effort." Jackson declared martial law, taking control of the governance of the city, which enabled him to transform New Orleans into a large armed camp.

On December 12, a British fleet with some 8,000 seasoned soldiers took up positions on the coast of Louisiana. The British hoped to capture New Orleans and thereby gain control of the Mississippi River.

British general Sir Edward Pakenham's painfully careful preparation for an assault against the Americans gave Jackson time to organize hundreds of slaves "loaned" by planters to dig trenches, build ramparts, and stack cotton bales and barrels of sugar to protect the defenders from British fire.

The Americans built an almost-invulnerable position, but Pakenham, cocky and careless, rashly ordered a frontal assault at dawn on Sunday, January 8, 1815. His professional redcoats, including all-black units from the Caribbean islands, marched into a murderous hail of artillery shells and rifle fire. Line after line of advancing redcoats crumpled and fell, often on top of one another. When the smoke cleared, a Kentucky militiaman said that the battlefield looked first like "a sea of blood. It was not blood itself, but the red coats in which the British soldiers were dressed."

Before the devastated British withdrew, some 2,100 had been wounded or killed, including Pakenham, two other generals, and more than 80 officers.

Jackson's army defends New Orleans Andrew Jackson's defeat of the British at New Orleans, January 1815.

Only thirteen Americans had lost their lives. A British naval officer wrote that there "never was a more complete failure."

Although the **Battle of New Orleans** occurred after the Treaty of Ghent had been signed, it was still a vitally important psychological victory, as the treaty had yet to be officially ratified by either the United States or Great Britain. Had the British won at New Orleans, they might have tried to revise the treaty in their favor. Jackson's lopsided victory ensured that both governments would act quickly to approve the treaty. The unexpected American triumph at New Orleans also generated a wave of patriotic nationalism. As a Washington, D.C. newspaper crowed, "ALMOST INCREDIBLE VICTORY!"

Such pride in the Battle of New Orleans would later help transform the heroic Andrew Jackson into a dynamic presidential candidate eager to move the nation into an even more democratic era in which the "common man" would be celebrated and empowered. The rough-hewn Jackson, wrote a southerner in April 1815, "is everywhere hailed as the savior of the country. . . . He has been feasted, caressed, & I may say idolised."

THE HARTFORD CONVENTION   A few weeks before the Battle of New Orleans, many New England Federalists, frustrated by the rising expense of a war they had opposed, tried to take matters into their own hands at a meeting in Hartford, Connecticut. The **Hartford Convention** was the climax of New England's disgust with "Mr. Madison's War."

On December 15, 1814, the Hartford Convention assembled with delegates from Massachusetts, Rhode Island, Connecticut, Vermont, and New Hampshire. The convention proposed seven constitutional amendments designed to limit Republican (and southern) influence. The amendments included abolishing the counting of slaves in determining a state's representation in Congress, requiring a two-thirds supermajority rather than a simple majority vote to declare war or admit new states, prohibiting trade embargoes lasting more than sixty days, excluding immigrants from holding federal office, limiting the president to one term, and barring successive presidents from the same state (a provision clearly directed at Virginia).

Delegates at the Hartford Convention also discussed the possibility that some of the New England states might "secede" from the United States if their demands were dismissed in Washington. Yet the secessionist threat quickly evaporated. In February 1815, when messengers from the Hartford Convention reached Washington, D.C., they found the battered and burned capital celebrating the good news from New Orleans. "Their position," according to a French diplomat, was "awkward, embarrassing, and lent itself to cruel ridicule."

Ignored by Congress and the president, the Hartford delegates turned tail for home. The whole sorry episode proved fatal to the Federalist party, which never recovered from the shame of disloyalty stamped on it by the Hartford Convention. The victory at New Orleans and the arrival of the peace treaty from Europe transformed the national mood. Almost overnight, President Madison went from being denounced and possibly impeached to being hailed a national hero.

THE WAR'S LEGACIES   There was no clear military victor in the War of 1812, nor much clarification about the issues that had ignited a war that cost 7,000 killed and wounded Americans. The Treaty of Ghent ended the fighting but failed to address the reasons why President Madison had declared war in the first place: the disputes about U.S. maritime rights and the British practice of impressment.

For all the clumsiness with which the war was managed, however, in the end it generated an intense patriotism across much of the nation and reaffirmed American independence. The young republic was at last secure from British or European threats. As James Monroe said, "we have acquired a character and a rank among the other nations, which we did not enjoy before."

Forgetting their many military disasters, Americans soon decided that the war was a glorious triumph for republican values. The people, observed Treasury Secretary Albert Gallatin, "are more American; they feel and act more as a nation; and I hope that the permanency of the Union is thereby better secured."

Soon after the official copy of the Treaty of Ghent arrived in Washington, D.C., in mid-February 1815, Virginian William H. Cabell wrote his brother that the "glorious peace for America . . . has come exactly when we least expected but when we most wanted it." Another Virginian, Colonel John Taylor, recognized the happy outcome as largely resulting from "a succession of lucky accidents" that "enabled the administration to get the nation out of the war." Had the conflict dragged on, he predicted, "the Republican party and our form of government would have been blown up."

The war also propelled the United States toward economic independence, as the wartime interruption of trade with Europe forced America to expand its manufacturing sector and become more self-sufficient. The British blockade of the coast created a shortage of cotton cloth in the United States, leading to the creation of the nation's first cotton-manufacturing industry, in Waltham, Massachusetts.

By the end of the war, there were more than 100 cotton mills in New England and 64 more in Pennsylvania. Even Thomas Jefferson admitted in

1815 that his beloved agricultural republic had been transformed: "We must now place the manufacturer by the agriculturalist." After nearly forty years of independence, the new American republic was emerging as an agricultural, commercial, and industrial world power.

Perhaps the strangest result of the War of 1812 was the reversal of attitudes among Republicans and Federalists. The wartime experience taught James Madison and the Republicans some lessons in nationalism. First, the British invasion of Washington, D.C., convinced Madison of the necessity of a strong army and navy. Second, the lack of a national bank had hurt the federal government's efforts to finance the war; state banks were so unstable that it was difficult to raise the funds needed to pay military expenses. In 1816, Madison, who had opposed a national bank, changed his mind and created the Second Bank of the United States. Third, the rise of new industries during the war prompted manufacturers to call for increased tariffs on imports to protect American companies from unfair foreign competition. Madison went along, despite his criticism of tariffs in the 1790s.

While Madison reversed himself by embracing nationalism and a broader interpretation of the Constitution, the Federalists similarly pivoted by embracing Madison's and Jefferson's earlier emphasis on states' rights and strict construction of the Constitution as they tried to defend the special economic interests of their regional stronghold, New England. It was the first great reversal of partisan political roles in constitutional interpretation. It would not be the last.

The War of 1812 proved devastating to all of the eastern Indian nations, most of which had fought with the British. The war accelerated westward settlement by Americans, and Native American resistance was greatly diminished after the death of Tecumseh and his Indian Confederacy. The British essentially abandoned their Indian allies. None of their former lands were returned to them, and the British vacated the frontier forts that had long served as supply centers for Indians.

Lakota chief Little Crow expressed the betrayal felt by Native Americans after the war when he rejected the consolation gifts from the local British commander: "After we have fought for you, endured many hardships, lost some of our people, and awakened the vengeance of our powerful neighbors, you make peace for yourselves. . . . You no longer need our service; you offer us these goods to pay us for [your] having deserted us. But no, we will not take them; we hold them and yourselves in equal contempt." In the years after the war, the United States negotiated more than 200 treaties with native peoples that transferred Indian lands to the federal government and created isolated reservations for them west of the Mississippi River.

As the Indians were pushed out, tens of thousands of Americans moved west into the Great Lakes region and southwest into Georgia, Alabama, and Mississippi, occupying more territory in a single generation than had been settled in the 150 years of colonial history. The federal government hastened western migration by providing war veterans with 160 acres of land between the Illinois and Mississippi Rivers.

The trans-Appalachian population soared from 300,000 to 2 million between 1800 and 1820. By 1840, more than 40 percent of Americans lived west of the Appalachians in eight new states. At the same time, the growing dispute over slavery and its expansion into new western territories set in motion an explosive national debate that would test again the grand experiment in republican government.

CHAPTER REVIEW

SUMMARY

- **Jefferson's Administration**   The Jeffersonian Republicans did not dismantle much of Hamilton's economic program, but they did repeal the whiskey tax, cut government expenditures, and usher in a *republican simplicity* that championed the virtues of smaller government and plain living. While Republicans idealized the agricultural world that had existed prior to 1800, the first decades of the nineteenth century were a period of transformational economic and population growth in the United States. Commercial agriculture and exports to Europe flourished; Americans moved to the West in huge numbers. The *Louisiana Purchase*, which resulted from negotiations with French emperor Napoléon Bonaparte following French setbacks in Haiti, dramatically expanded the boundaries of the United States. Jefferson's *Lewis and Clark expedition* explored the new region and spurred interest in the Far West. In *Marbury v. Madison* (1803), the Federalist chief justice of the Supreme Court, John Marshall, declared a federal act unconstitutional for the first time. With that decision, the Court assumed the right of judicial review over acts of Congress and established the constitutional supremacy of the federal government over state governments.

- **War in Europe**   Thomas Jefferson sent warships to subdue the *Barbary pirates* and negotiated with the Spanish and French to ensure that the Mississippi River remained open to American commerce. Renewal of war between Britain and France in 1803 complicated matters for American commerce. Neither country wanted its enemy to purchase U.S. goods, so both declared blockades. In retaliation, Jefferson convinced Congress to pass the *Embargo Act*, which prohibited all foreign trade.

- **Aftermath of the War of 1812**   The *Treaty of Ghent (1814)* ended the war by essentially declaring it a draw. A smashing American victory in January 1815 at the *Battle of New Orleans* helped to ensure that the treaty would be ratified and enforced. The conflict established the economic independence of the United States, as many goods previously purchased from Britain were now manufactured at home. During and after the war, Federalists and Republicans seemed to exchange roles: delegates from the waning Federalist party met at the *Hartford Convention (1815)* to defend states' rights and threaten secession, while Republicans now promoted nationalism and a broad interpretation of the Constitution.

CHRONOLOGY

1800	U.S. population surpasses 5 million
1801	Thomas Jefferson inaugurated as president in Washington, D.C.
	Barbary pirates harass U.S. shipping
	The pasha of Tripoli declares war on the United States
1803	Supreme Court issues *Marbury v. Madison* decision
	Louisiana Purchase
1804–1806	Lewis and Clark expedition
1804	Jefferson overwhelmingly reelected
1807	British interference with U.S. shipping increases
1808	International slave trade ended in the United States
1811	Defeat of Tecumseh Indian Confederacy at the Battle of Tippecanoe
1812	Congress declares war on Britain
	U.S. invasion of Canada
1813–1814	"Creek War"
1814	British capture and burn Washington, D.C.
	Hartford Convention
1815	Battle of New Orleans
	News of the Treaty of Ghent reaches the United States

KEY TERMS

republican simplicity p. 305

Marbury v. Madison p. 308

Barbary pirates p. 311

Louisiana Purchase (1803) p. 314

Lewis and Clark expedition p. 315

Embargo Act (1807) p. 322

War of 1812 p. 325

Tecumseh's Indian Confederacy p. 327

Treaty of Ghent (1814) p. 338

Battle of New Orleans (1815) p. 340

Hartford Convention (1815) p. 340

INQUIZITIVE

Go to InQuizitive to see what you've learned—and learn what you've missed—with personalized feedback along the way.

part three

AN EXPANDING NATION

During the nineteenth century, the United States experienced a wrenching change from being a predominantly agrarian society to having a more diverse economy and urban society, with factories and cities emerging alongside farms and towns. The pace of life quickened with industrialization, and the possibilities for better living conditions rose. Between 1790 and 1820, the nation's boundaries expanded and its population—both white and black—soared while the number of Native Americans continued its long decline. Immigrants from Ireland, Germany,

347

Scandinavia, and China thereafter poured into the United States seeking land, jobs, and freedom. By the early 1820s, the number of enslaved Americans was more than two and a half times greater than in 1790, and the number of free blacks doubled. The white population of the United States grew just as rapidly.

Accompanying the emergence of an industrial economy in the Northeast during the first half of the nineteenth century was the relentless expansion of the United States westward. Until the nineteenth century, most of the American population was clustered near the seacoast and along rivers flowing into the Atlantic Ocean or the Gulf of Mexico. That changed dramatically after 1800. The great theme of nineteenth-century American history was the migration of millions of people across the Allegheny and Appalachian Mountains into the Ohio Valley and the Middle West. Waves of adventurous Americans then crossed the Mississippi River and spread out across the Great Plains. By the 1840s, American settlers had reached the Pacific Ocean.

These developments—the emergence of a market-based economy, the impact of industrial development, and dramatic territorial expansion—made the second quarter of the nineteenth century a time of restless optimism and rapid change. As a German visitor noted, "Ten years in America are like a century elsewhere."

Americans in the early Republic were nothing if not brash and self-assured. In 1845, an editorial in the *United States Journal* claimed that "we, the American people, are the most independent, intelligent, moral, and happy people on the face of the earth." The republic governed by highly educated "natural aristocrats" such as Thomas Jefferson, James Madison, James Monroe, and John Quincy Adams gave way to the frontier democracy promoted by Andrew Jackson and Henry Clay. Americans began to demand government of, by, and for the people.

During the first half of the nineteenth century, two very different societies—North and South—grew increasingly competitive with one another. The North, the more dynamic and faster-growing region, embraced industrial growth, large cities, foreign immigrants, and the ideal of "free labor" as opposed to the system of slavery in the southern states. The South remained rural, agricultural, and increasingly committed to enslaved labor as the backbone of its economy. Two great underlying fears worried southerners: the threat of mass slave uprisings and the possibility that a northern-controlled Congress might one day abolish slavery. The planter elite's aggressive

efforts to preserve and expand slavery stifled change and reform in the South and ignited a prolonged political controversy with the North that would eventually lead to civil war.

8

The Emergence of a Market Economy

1815–1850

Lackawanna Valley (1855) Often hailed as the father of American landscape painting, George Inness was commissioned by a railroad company to capture its trains coursing through the lush Lackawanna Valley in northeastern Pennsylvania. New inventions and industrial development would continue to invade and transform the rural landscape.

A mid the postwar celebrations in 1815, Americans set about transforming their victorious young nation. Soon after the war's end, prosperity returned as British and European markets again welcomed American ships and commerce. During the war, the loss of trade with Britain and Europe had forced the United States to develop more factories and mills of its own, spurring the development of the more diverse economy that Alexander Hamilton had envisioned in the 1790s.

Between 1815 and 1850, the United States also became a transcontinental power, expanding all the way to the Pacific coast. Hundreds of thousands of land-hungry people streamed westward toward the Mississippi River and beyond. In just six years following the end of the war in 1815, six states were added to the Union (Alabama, Illinois, Indiana, Mississippi, Missouri, and Maine).

Nineteenth-century Americans were a restless, ambitious people seeking new ways to get ahead in life by using their ingenuity, skill, faith, and tenacity. The country's energy and mobility was dizzying. A Boston newspaper commented that the whole American "population is in motion."

Everywhere, it seemed, people were moving to the next town, the next farm, the next opportunity. In many cities, half of the entire population moved every ten years. In 1826, the newspaper editor in Rochester, New York, reported that 120 people left Rochester every day while 130 moved into the growing city. Frances Trollope, an English traveler, said that Americans were "a busy, bustling, industrious population, hacking and hewing their way" westward in the pursuit of happiness.

The lure of cheap land and plentiful jobs, as well as the promise of political and religious freedom, attracted millions of hardworking immigrants in the

focus questions

1. How did changes in transportation and communication alter the economic landscape during the first half of the nineteenth century?

2. How did industrial development impact the way people worked and lived?

3. In what ways did immigration alter the nation's population and shape its politics?

4. How did the expanding "market-based economy" impact the lives of workers, professionals, and women?

first half of the nineteenth century. This great wave of humanity was not always welcomed, however. Ethnic prejudices, anti-Catholicism, and language barriers made it difficult for many new immigrants, mostly from Ireland, Germany, and China, to be assimilated into American culture.

In the Midwest, large-scale commercial agriculture emerged as big farms grew corn, wheat, pigs, and cattle to be sold in distant markets and across the Atlantic. In the South, cotton became so profitable that it increasingly dominated the region's economy, luring farmers and planters (wealthy farmers with hundreds or even thousands of acres worked by large numbers of slaves) into the new states of Alabama, Mississippi, Louisiana, and Arkansas.

In both Europe and the United States, cotton cloth was the first great consumer product of industrial capitalism; cotton from the American South provided most of the clothing for people around the world. As the cotton economy expanded, it required growing numbers of enslaved workers, many of whom were sold by professional slave traders and relocated from Virginia and the Carolinas to the Old Southwest—western Georgia and the Florida Panhandle, Alabama, Mississippi, and Louisiana, and Arkansas.

Meanwhile, the Northeast experienced a momentous surge of industrial development whose labor-saving machines and water- and steam-powered industries reshaped the region's economic and social life. Mills and factories began to dot the landscape and transform the ways people labored, dressed, ate, and lived. With the rise of the factory system, more and more economic activity in the northeastern states occurred outside the home and off the farm. "The transition from mother-daughter power [in the home] to water and steam power" in the mills and factories," said a farmer, was producing a "complete revolution in social life and domestic manners." An urban middle class began to emerge as Americans left farms and moved to towns and cities, drawn primarily by jobs in new mills, factories, stores, and banks.

By 1850, the United States had become the world's fastest growing commercial, manufacturing, agricultural, and mining nation. The industrial economy also generated changes in other areas, from politics to the legal system, from the family to social values. These developments in turn helped expand prosperity and freedom for whites and free blacks.

They also sparked vigorous political debates over economic policies, transportation improvements, and the extension of slavery into the new territories. In the process, the nation began to divide into three powerful regions—North, South, and West—whose shifting alliances and disputes would shape political life until the Civil War.

THE MARKET REVOLUTION

During the first half of the nineteenth century, a market revolution that had begun before the war of independence accelerated the transformation of the American economy into a global powerhouse. In the eighteenth century, most Americans were isolated farmers focused on a subsistence or household economy. They produced just enough food, livestock, and clothing for their own family's needs and perhaps a little more to barter (exchange) with their neighbors. Their lives revolved around a regular farmstead routine in a day-long cycle that started with the rooster crowing at dawn to the sleep of the chickens at night, punctuated by the changing seasons and unpredictable weather.

As the nineteenth century unfolded, however, more and more farm families began engaging in *commercial* rather than *subsistence* agriculture, producing surplus crops and livestock to sell for cash in distant regional and even international markets. In 1851, the president of the New York Agricultural Society noted that until the nineteenth century, "'production for consumption' was the leading purpose" of the farm economy. Now, however, "no farmer could find it profitable to do everything for himself. He now sells for money." With the cash they earned, farm families were able to buy more land, better farm equipment, and the latest manufactured household goods.

Such farming for sale rather than for consumption, often called a **market-based economy**, produced boom-and-bust cycles and was often built upon the backs of slave laborers, immigrant workers, and displaced Mexicans. Overall, however, the standard of living rose and Americans experienced unprecedented opportunities for economic gain and geographic mobility. The transition from a traditional household economy to a modern market economy involved massive changes in the way people lived, worked, traveled, and voted.

What the market economy most needed in order to flourish was what were then called "internal improvements"—deepened harbors, lighthouses, and a national network of canals, bridges, roads, and railroads—all designed to improve the flow of goods to markets by liberating people from the constraints of distance. In 1817, for example, South Carolina congressman John C. Calhoun expressed his desire to "bind the Republic together with a perfect system of roads and canals." As the world's largest republic, the United States desperately needed a national transportation system. "Let us conquer space," he told the House of Representatives.

Calhoun's proposal sparked a fierce debate over how to fund the improvements: should it be the responsibility of the federal government, the individual

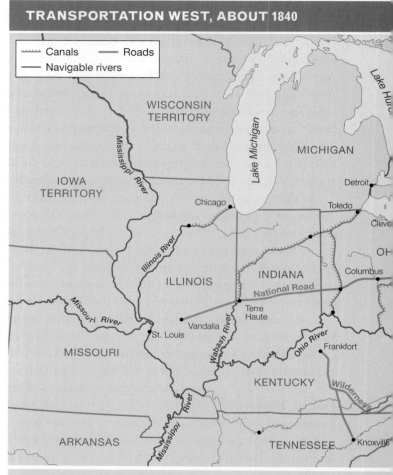

TRANSPORTATION WEST, ABOUT 1840

- Why were river towns important commercial centers?
- What was the economic impact of the steamboat and the flatboat in the West?
- How did the Erie Canal transform the economy of New York and the Great Lakes region?

states, or private corporations? Since the Constitution said nothing about the federal government's role in funding transportation improvements, many argued that such projects must be initiated by state and local governments. Others argued that the Constitution gave the federal government broad powers to promote the "general welfare," which included enhancing transportation and communication. The fierce debate over how best to fund internal improvements would continue throughout the nineteenth century.

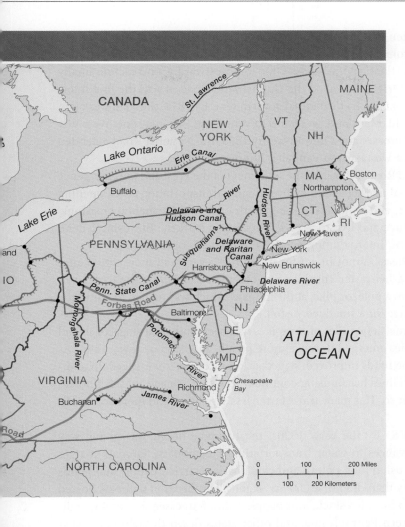

BETTER ROADS Until the nineteenth century, travel in America had been slow, tedious, uncomfortable, and expensive. It took a stagecoach, for example, four days to go from New York City to Boston. Because of long travel times, many farm products could only be sold locally before they spoiled. That soon changed, as an array of innovations—larger horse-drawn wagons (called *Conestogas*), new roads, canals, steamboats, and railroads—knit together the expanding national market for goods and services and greatly accelerated the pace of life.

As more settlers moved west, people expressed a "passion for improving roads." In 1795, the Wilderness Road, along the trail first blazed by Daniel Boone, was opened to wagon and stagecoach traffic, thereby easing the over-the-mountains route from North Carolina into Kentucky and Tennessee.

In 1803, when Ohio became a state, Congress had ordered that 5 percent of the money from land sales in the state would go toward building a National Road from the Atlantic coast across Ohio and westward. Construction finally began in 1811. Originally called the Cumberland Road, it was the first interstate roadway financed by the federal government. By 1818, the road was open from Cumberland, Maryland, westward to Wheeling, Virginia (now West Virginia), where it crossed the Ohio River. By 1838, the National Road extended 600 miles farther westward to Vandalia, Illinois.

The National Road quickened the settlement of the West and the emergence of a truly national market economy by reducing transportation costs, opening up new markets, and stimulating the growth of towns. Farmers increasingly took their produce and livestock to sell in distant markets. But using federal money to finance "internal improvements" remained controversial.

To the northeast, a movement for paved roads gathered momentum after the Philadelphia-Lancaster Turnpike was completed in 1794. (The term *turnpike* derives from a pole, or pike, at the tollgate, which was turned to admit the traffic in exchange for a small fee, or toll.)

By 1821, some 4,000 miles of turnpikes had been built, and stagecoach and freight companies emerged to move more people and cargo at lower rates. As the quality of the roads improved, stagecoaches increased their speed. In addition, stagecoach lines began using continual relays, or "stages," of fresh horses every 40 miles or so. This made travel faster, less expensive, and more accessible.

WATERWAYS By the early 1820s, the turnpike boom was giving way to dramatic advances in water transportation. Steamboats, flatboats (barges driven by men using long poles), and canal barges carried people and goods far more cheaply than did horse-drawn wagons. Hundreds of flatboats floated goods, farm produce, livestock, and people from Tennessee, Kentucky, Indiana, Ohio, western Pennsylvania, and other states down the Ohio and Mississippi Rivers. Flatboats, however, went only in one direction: downstream. Once unloaded in Natchez, Mississippi, or New Orleans, Louisiana, they were sold and dismantled to provide lumber for construction.

The difficulties of getting back upriver were solved when Robert Fulton and Robert R. Livingston sent the *Clermont*, the first commercial steamboat, up the Hudson River from New York City in 1807. Thereafter, the use of wood-fired **steamboats** spread rapidly, opening nearly half the continent to water traffic along the major rivers.

By bringing two-way travel to the Mississippi Valley, which included the areas drained by the Ohio and Missouri Rivers, steamboats created a transcontinental market and a commercial agricultural empire that produced

Traveling the western waters Steamboats at St. Paul, Minnesota, in 1859.

much of the nation's cotton, timber, wheat, corn, cattle, and hogs. By 1836, there were 750 steamboats operating on American rivers. As steamboat use increased, the price for shipping goods plunged, thus increasing profits and stimulating demand.

The use of steamboats transformed St. Louis, Missouri, from a sleepy frontier village into a booming river port. New Orleans developed even faster. By 1840, it was perhaps the wealthiest American city, having developed a thriving trade with the Caribbean islands and the new Latin American republics that had overthrown Spanish rule. A thousand steamboats a year visited New Orleans. The annual amount of trade being shipped through the river city doubled that of New York City by 1843, in large part because of the explosion in cotton production.

The wood-burning steamboats were crowded, dirty, and risky forms of transportation. Accidents, explosions, and fires were common, and sanitation was poor. Passengers crowded on board along with pigs and cattle. There were no toilets on steamboats until the 1850s, and all passengers shared the same two washbasins and towels. For all of the inconveniences, however, steamboats were the fastest and most convenient form of transportation in the first half of the nineteenth century.

Canals also sped the market revolution. The **Erie Canal** in central New York connected the Great Lakes and the Midwest to the Hudson River and New York City. New York Governor DeWitt Clinton, former mayor of New York City and vice president under James Madison, took the lead in promoting the risky engineering project, which Thomas Jefferson dismissed as "little short of madness." Clinton, however, boasted that his state of New York had the opportunity to "create a new era in history, and to erect a work more stupendous, more magnificent, and more beneficial, than has hitherto been achieved by the human race."

It was not an idle boast. After the Erie Canal opened in 1825, having taken eight years to build, it drew eastward much of the midwestern trade (furs, lumber, textiles) that earlier had been forced to go to Canada or to make the long journey down the Ohio and Mississippi Rivers to New Orleans and the Gulf of Mexico. Thanks to the Erie Canal, the backwoods village of Chicago developed into a bustling city because of its commercial connection via the Great Lakes to New York City, and eventually across the Atlantic to Europe.

The Erie Canal was a triumph of engineering audacity. Forty feet wide and four feet deep, it was the longest canal in the world, extending 363 miles across New York from Albany in the east to Buffalo and Lake Erie in the west and rising some 675 feet in elevation. Additional branches soon put most of the state within its reach.

The canal was built by tens of thousands of manual laborers, mostly German and Irish immigrants who were paid less than a dollar a day to drain

The Erie Canal *Junction of the Erie and Northern Canals* (1830–32), by John Hill.

swamps, clear forests, build stone bridges and aqueducts, and blast through solid rock. It brought a "river of gold" to New York City in the form of an unending stream of lumber, grain, flour, and other goods from western New York and the Midwest, and it unlocked the floodgates of western settlement. The canal also reduced the cost of moving a ton of freight from $100 to $5. It was so profitable that it paid off its construction costs in just seven years.

The Erie Canal had enormous economic and political consequences, as it tied together the regional economies of the Midwest and the East while further isolating the Deep South. The Genesee Valley in western New York became one of the most productive grain-growing regions in the world, and Rochester became a boom town, processing wheat and corn into flour and meal. The writer Nathaniel Hawthorne said "the town had sprung up like a mushroom." Syracuse, Albany, and Buffalo experienced similarly dramatic growth because of the Erie Canal.

The business of moving goods and people along the canal involved some 4,000 boats and over 25,000 workers. Canal boats, slender and shallow, usually eleven feet wide and seventy feet long, were pulled by teams of horses or mules walking along a towpath. The teams hauling the boats needed to be changed every ten to twelve miles.

Painted in bright colors and given colorful names, the "packet" boats carrying passengers traveled seven days a week at between two and four miles an hour. Much time was lost waiting at one of the eighty-eight locks, where boats would enter one at a time to be raised or lowered to match the changing water level of the canal. Often, the boat captains took their families with them. Most boatmen, however, were single—and rough. One traveler called them "a coarse and untaught set of vagabonds whose chief delight is to carouse and fight."

The success of the Erie and the entire New York canal system inspired other states to build some 3,000 miles of waterways by 1837, not all of which were successful. By 1834, canals connected Pittsburgh to Philadelphia, a distance of 395 miles. Canals boosted the economy by enabling speedier and less expensive transport of goods and people. They also boosted real estate prices for the lands bordering the canals and transformed sleepy rural villages like Rochester, New York, into booming cities.

RAILROADS For a brief period, canals were essential to the nation's economic growth. The canal era was short-lived, however. During the second quarter of the nineteenth century a much less expensive but much more powerful, efficient, and versatile form of transportation emerged: the railroad.

In 1825, the year the Erie Canal was completed, the world's first steam-powered railway began operating in England. Soon thereafter, a railroad-building "epidemic" infected the United States. In 1830, the nation had only 23 miles of railroad track. Over the next twenty years, railroad coverage grew to 30,626 miles.

The railroad was a truly transformational technology. It surpassed other forms of transportation because of its speed, carrying capacity, and reliability. **Railroads** could move more people and freight faster, farther, and cheaper than wagons or boats. The early trains averaged ten miles per hour, more than twice the speed of stagecoaches and four times that of boats and barges. That locomotives were able to operate year-round gave rail travel a huge advantage over canals that froze in winter and dirt roads that became rivers of mud during rainstorms.

Railroads also provided indirect benefits by encouraging new western settlement and the expansion of commercial agriculture. The power of the railroad could be seen everywhere, from rural areas to big cities. A westerner reported that the opening of a new rail line resulted in three new villages emerging along the line while "adding new life to the city." The depot or rail station became the central building in every town, a public place where people from all walks of life and places converged.

Building railroads stimulated the national economy not only by improving transportation but also by creating a huge demand for iron, wooden crossties, bridges, locomotives, freight cars, and other equipment. Railroads also became the nation's largest corporations and employers. Perhaps most important, railroads enabled towns and cities not served by canals or turnpikes to compete economically. In other words, the railroads eventually changed what had once been a cluster of mostly local markets near rivers and the coast into an interconnected national marketplace for goods and services. Railroads expanded the geography of American capitalism, making possible larger industrial and commercial enterprises and shrinking distances for passengers.

But the railroad mania had negative effects as well. Its quick and shady profits frequently led to political corruption. Railroad titans often bribed legislators. By facilitating access to the trans-Appalachian West, the railroads also accelerated the decline of Native American culture. In addition, they dramatically quickened the tempo, mobility, and noise of everyday life. Writer Nathaniel Hawthorne spoke for many when he said that the locomotive, with its startling whistle, brought "the noisy world into the midst of our slumberous space."

OCEAN TRANSPORTATION The year 1845 brought a great innovation in ocean transport with the launch of the first clipper ship, the *Rainbow*. Built for speed, the **clipper ships** were the nineteenth-century equivalent of

Building a clipper ship This 1833 oil painting captures the Messrs. Smith & Co. Ship Yard in Manhattan, where shipbuilders are busy shaping timbers to construct a clipper ship.

the supersonic jetliner. They were twice as fast as the older merchant ships. Long and lean, with taller masts and larger sails than conventional ships, they cut dashing figures during their brief but colorful career, which lasted less than two decades. The American thirst for Chinese tea prompted the clipper boom. Asian tea leaves had to reach markets quickly after harvest, and the fast clipper ships made this possible.

The discovery of gold in California in 1848 lured thousands of prospectors and entrepreneurs. When the would-be miners generated an urgent demand for goods on the West Coast, the clippers met it. In 1854, the *Flying Cloud* took eighty-nine days and eight hours to travel from New York to San Francisco, around South America, less than half as long as the trip would have taken in a conventional ship. But clippers, while fast, lacked ample space for cargo or passengers. After the Civil War, the clippers would give way to the steamship.

COMMUNICATIONS Innovations in transportation also helped spark improvements in communications, which knit the nation even closer together. At the beginning of the nineteenth century, traveling any distance was slow and difficult. It took days—often weeks—for news to travel along the Atlantic Seaboard. For example, after George Washington died in 1798 in Virginia, word of his death did not appear in New York City newspapers until a week

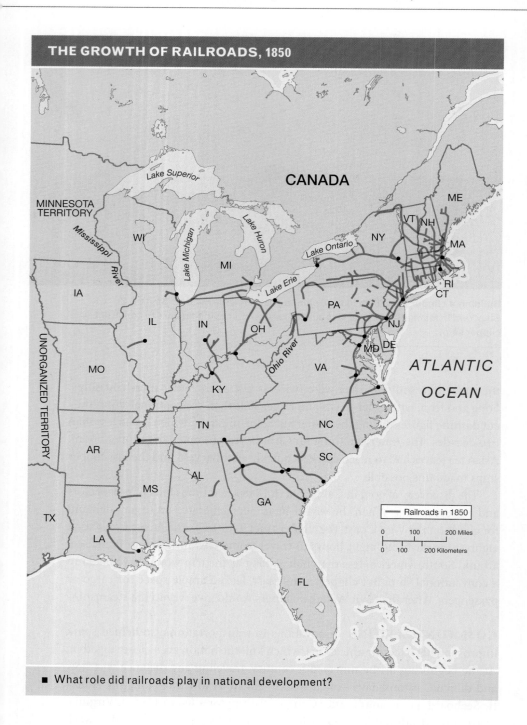

THE GROWTH OF RAILROADS, 1850

Railroads in 1850

0   100   200 Miles

0   100   200 Kilometers

■ What role did railroads play in national development?

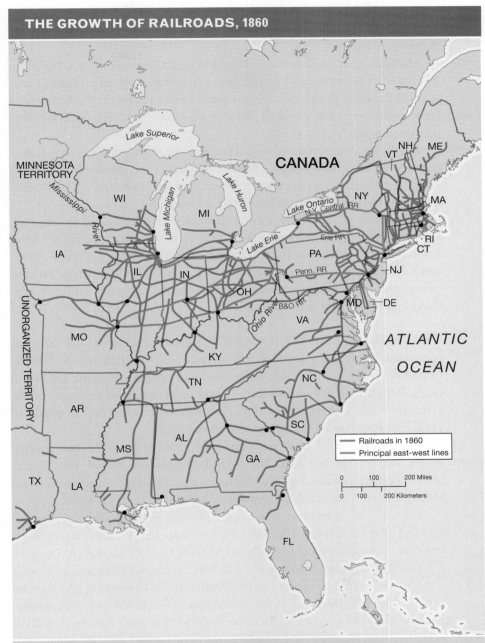

THE GROWTH OF RAILROADS, 1860

Legend:
- Railroads in 1860
- Principal east–west lines

0   100   200 Miles
0   100   200 Kilometers

■ Why did the number of railroads expand rapidly from 1850 to 1860?

■ What were the principal east–west lines?

later. By 1829, however, it was possible to deliver Andrew Jackson's inaugural address from Washington, D.C., to New York City by relay horse riders in less than twenty hours.

Mail deliveries also improved. The number of U.S. post offices soared from 75 in 1790 to 28,498 in 1860. In addition, new steam-powered printing presses enabled the mass production of newspapers by reducing their cost from six cents to a penny each, enabling virtually everyone to benefit from the news contained in the "penny press."

But the most important advance in communications was the national electromagnetic **telegraph system**, invented by Samuel F. B. Morse. In May 1844, Morse sent the first intercity telegraph message from Washington, D.C., to Baltimore, Maryland. It read: "What Hath God Wrought?"

By the end of the decade, most major cities were connected by telegraph lines that enabled people, companies, and governments to communicate faster and more reliably. The electrical telegraph system also helped railroad operators schedule trains more precisely and thus avoid collisions. A New Orleans newspaper claimed that, with the invention of the telegraph, "scarcely anything now will appear to be impossible."

THE ROLE OF GOVERNMENT Steamboats, canals, and railroads connected the western areas of the country with the East, boosted trade, helped open the Far West for settlement, and spurred dramatic growth in cities. Between 1800 and 1860, an undeveloped nation of scattered farms, primitive roads, and modest local markets was transformed into an engine of capitalist expansion, urban energy, and global reach.

The transportation improvements were financed by both state governments and private investors. The federal government helped, too, despite intense political debates over whether it was constitutional to use federal funds to finance such "internal improvements."

The national government also bought stock in turnpike and canal companies and, after the success of the Erie Canal, awarded land grants to several western states to support canal and railroad projects. In 1850, Stephen A. Douglas, a powerful Democratic senator from Illinois, convinced Congress to provide a major land grant to support a north–south rail line connecting Chicago and Mobile, Alabama. Regarded at the time as a special case, the 1850 Congressional land grant set a precedent for other bounties that totaled about 20 million acres by 1860. However, this would prove to be a small amount when compared to the land grants that Congress would award transcontinental railroads during the 1860s and after. The national government also sent federal cavalry troops to "pacify" the Indians along the route of the railroads.

INDUSTRIAL DEVELOPMENT

The concentration of huge numbers of people in commercial and factory cities, coupled with the transportation and communication revolutions, greatly increased the number of potential customers for given products. Such expanding market demand in turn gave rise to a system of *mass production*, whereby companies used new technologies (labor-saving machines) to produce greater quantities of products that could be sold at lower prices to more people, thus generating higher profits.

The introduction of steam engines, as well as the application of new technologies to make manufacturing more efficient, sparked a wave of unrelenting **industrialization** in Europe and America from the mid-eighteenth century to the late nineteenth century. Mechanized factories, mills, and mines emerged to supplement the agricultural economy. "It is an extraordinary era in which we live," reported Daniel Webster in 1847. "It is altogether new. The world has seen nothing like it before." New machines and improvements in agricultural and industrial efficiency led to a remarkable increase in productivity. By 1860, one farmer, miner, or mill worker could produce twice as much wheat, twice as much iron, and more than four times as much cotton cloth as in 1800.

AMERICAN TECHNOLOGY Such improvements in productivity were enabled by the "practical" inventiveness of Americans. Between 1790 and 1811, the U.S. Patent Office approved an annual average of 77 new patents certifying new inventions; by the 1850s, the Patent Office was approving more than 28,000 new inventions each year.

Many of the industrial inventions generated dramatic changes. In 1844, for example, Charles Goodyear patented a process for "vulcanizing" rubber, which made the product stronger, more elastic, waterproof, and winter-proof. Vulcanized rubber was soon being used for a variety of products, from shoes and boots to seals, gaskets, hoses and, eventually, tires.

In 1846, Elias Howe patented his design of the sewing machine. It was soon improved upon by Isaac Merritt Singer, who founded the Singer Sewing Machine Company, which initially produced only industrial sewing machines for use in textile mills but eventually offered machines for home use. The availability of sewing machines helped revolutionize "women's work" by dramatically reducing the time needed to make clothes at home, thus freeing up more leisure time for many women.

Technological advances improved living conditions; houses could be larger, better heated, and better illuminated. The first sewer systems helped clean up cities by ridding their streets of human and animal waste. Mechanization of factories meant that more goods could be produced faster and with less labor, and machines helped industries produce "standardized parts" that could be assembled by unskilled wage workers. Machine-made clothes using standardized forms fit better and were less expensive than those sewn by hand; machine-made newspapers and magazines were more abundant and affordable, as were clocks, watches, guns, and plows.

THE IMPACT OF THE COTTON GIN　In 1792 Eli Whitney, a recent Yale graduate from New England, visited Mulberry Grove plantation on the Georgia coast, where he "heard much said of the difficulty of ginning cotton"—

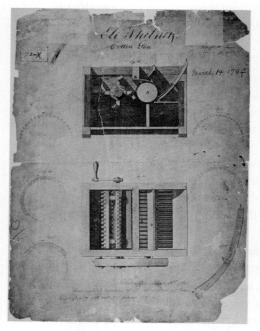

that is, separating the fibers from the seeds. Cotton had been used for clothing and bedding from ancient times, but until the nineteenth century, cotton cloth was rare and expensive because it took so long to separate the lint (fibers) from tenacious cotton seeds. One person working all day could separate barely one pound by hand.

At Mulberry Grove, Eli Whitney learned that the person who could invent a "machine" to gin cotton would become wealthy overnight. Within a few days, he had devised a simple mechanism (he called it "an absurdly simple contrivance"), using nails attached to a roller, to remove the seeds from cotton bolls. The **cotton gin** (short for *engine*) proved to be fifty times more productive than a hand laborer. Almost overnight, it made the white fiber America's most profitable cash crop. In the process, it transformed southern agriculture, northern industry, race-based slavery, national politics, and international trade.

Whitney's cotton gin Eli Whitney's drawing, which accompanied his 1794 federal patent application, shows the side and top of the machine as well as the sawteeth that separated the seeds from the fiber.

KING COTTON　During the first half of the nineteenth century, southern-grown **cotton** became the dominant force driving both the national economy and the controversial efforts to expand slavery into the western territories. Cotton was called "white gold"; it brought enormous wealth to southern planters and merchants as well as New England textile mill owners and New York shipowners.

By 1812, because of the widespread use of cotton gins, the cost of producing cotton yarn had plunged by 90 percent, and the spread of textile mills in Britain and Europe had created a rapidly growing global market for southern cotton. By the mid-nineteenth century, people worldwide were wearing more-comfortable and easier-to-clean cotton clothing. When British textile manufacturers chose the less brittle American cotton over the varieties grown in the Caribbean, Brazil, and India, the demand for southern cotton skyrocketed, as did its price.

Cotton became America's largest export and the primary driver of the nation's extraordinary economic growth during the first half of the nineteenth century. By 1860, British textile mills were processing a billion pounds of cotton a year, 92 percent of which came from the American South.

Cotton growing first engulfed the Piedmont region of the Carolinas and Georgia. After the War of 1812, it migrated into the contested Indian lands to the west—Tennessee, Alabama, Florida, Mississippi, Louisiana, Arkansas, and Texas. New Orleans became a bustling port—and active slave market—because of the cotton grown throughout the region and shipped down the Mississippi River. From the mid-1830s to 1860, cotton accounted for more than half of American exports. Planter capitalists in the South harvested raw cotton, and northern buyers and shipowners carried it to New England, Great Britain, and France, where textile mills spun the fiber into thread and fabric. Bankers in New York City and London financed the growth of global cotton capitalism.

THE EXPANSION OF SLAVERY Because cotton is a labor-intensive crop, growers were convinced that only slaves could make their farms and plantations profitable. As a result, the price of slaves soared with the price of cotton. When farmland in Maryland and Virginia lost its fertility after years of relentless tobacco planting, many whites shifted to growing corn and wheat, since the climate in Maryland and Virginia was too cold for cotton. Many Virginia and Maryland planters sold their surplus slaves to work in the new cotton-growing areas in Georgia, Alabama, Mississippi, and Louisiana. Between 1790 and 1860, some 835,000 slaves were "sold south." In 1790, planters in Virginia and Maryland had owned 56 percent of all the slaves in the United States; by 1860, they owned only 15 percent.

Cotton created boom times in the new region called the Old Southwest (southwest Georgia, Alabama, Mississippi, and the panhandle of Florida). A cotton farmer in Mississippi urged a friend in Kentucky to sell his farm and join him: "If you could reconcile it to yourself to bring your negroes to the Mississippi Territory, they would certainly make you a handsome fortune in ten years by the cultivation of Cotton." Slaves became so valuable that stealing slaves became a common problem in the southern states, especially Alabama and Mississippi.

FARMING THE MIDWEST   By 1860, more than half the nation's population lived west of the Appalachian Mountains. The flat, fertile farmlands in the Midwest—Ohio, Michigan, Indiana, Illinois, and Iowa—drew farmers from the rocky hillsides of New England and the exhausted soils of Virginia. By 1860, 30 to 40 percent of Americans born in New England had moved west, first to upstate New York and then to Ohio and the Midwest. People traveled on foot, on horseback, and in jarring wagons, all in an effort to make a fresh start on their *own* land made available by the government.

The process of settling new lands followed the old pattern of clearing underbrush and felling trees, burning the debris, grubbing out the roots by hand and using horses and oxen to dislodge stumps, removing rocks and boulders, and then plowing and planting fields.

Corn was typically the first crop grown. Women and children often planted the seeds in small mounds about three feet apart. Once the corn sprouted, pumpkin, squash, or bean seeds would be planted around the seedlings. The strong corn stalk provided a pole for the bean vines to climb, the beans and squash or pumpkins added prized nitrogen to the soil, and the squash and pumpkin plants grew and spread over the ground, smothering weeds around the corn stalks. Once the corn was harvested, the kernels could be boiled to make porridge or ground up to make flour and cornmeal that was baked into a bread called johnnycake. Corn stalks were stored to provide winter feed for the cattle and hogs.

Over time, technological advances led to greater agricultural productivity. The development of durable iron plows (replacing wooden ones) eased the backbreaking job of tilling the soil. In 1819, Jethro Wood of New York introduced an iron plow with separate parts that were easily replaced when needed. Further improvements would follow, including Vermonter John Deere's steel plow (1837), whose sharp edges could cut through the tough prairie grass in the Midwest and the Great Plains. By 1845, Massachusetts alone had seventy-three plants making more than 60,000 plows per year. Most were sold to farmers in the western states and territories, illustrating the emergence of a national marketplace for goods and services made possible by the transportation revolution.

Other technological improvements quickened the growth of commercial agriculture. By the 1840s, new mechanical seeders had replaced the process of sowing seed by hand. Even more important, in 1831 twenty-two-year-old

McCormick's Reaping Machine This illustration appeared in the catalog of the Great Exhibition, held at the Crystal Palace in London in 1851. The steel plow eased the transformation of the tough grass on the plains and prairies into fertile farmland, and the reaping machine greatly accelerated farm production.

Virginian Cyrus Hall McCormick invented a mechanical reaper to harvest wheat, a development as significant to the agricultural economy of the Midwest, Old Northwest, and Great Plains as the cotton gin was to the South.

In 1847 the **McCormick reapers** began selling so fast that he moved to Chicago and built a manufacturing plant. Within a few years McCormick had sold thousands of the giant farm machines, transforming the scale of commercial agriculture. Using a handheld sickle, a farmer could harvest a half acre of wheat a day; with a McCormick reaper, two people could work twelve acres a day.

EARLY TEXTILE MANUFACTURERS While technological breakthroughs such as the cotton gin, mechanical harvester, and railroads quickened agricultural development and created a national and international marketplace, other advances altered the economic landscape even more profoundly by giving rise to the factory system. Industrial capitalists who financed and built the first factories were the revolutionaries of the nineteenth century.

Mills and factories were initially powered by water wheels, then coal-fired steam engines. The shift from water power to coal as a source of energy is what enabled the dramatic growth of the textile industry (and industries of all types), initiating a world-wide industrial era destined to end Britain's domination of the world economy.

In the eighteenth century, Great Britain enjoyed a long head start in industrial production. The foundations of Britain's advantage were the invention of the steam engine in 1705, its improvement by James Watt in 1765, and a series of additional inventions that mechanized the production of textiles (thread, fabric, bedding, and clothing). Britain carefully guarded its hard-won industrial secrets, forbidding the export of machines or the publication of descriptions of them, even restricting the emigration of skilled mechanics.

But the secrets could not be kept forever. In 1789, Samuel Slater arrived in America from England with a detailed plan in his head of a water-powered spinning machine. He contracted with an enterprising merchant-manufacturer in Rhode Island to build a mill in Pawtucket, Rhode Island, and in that little mill, completed in 1790, nine children turned out a satisfactory cotton yarn, which was then worked up by the "putting-out system," whereby women would weave the yarn into cloth in their homes.

In 1800, the output of America's mills and factories amounted to only one-sixth of Great Britain's production, and the growth rate was slow and faltering until Thomas Jefferson's embargo in 1807 stimulated the domestic production of cloth. By 1815, hundreds of textile mills in New England, New York, and Pennsylvania were producing thread, cloth, and clothing. By 1860, the output of America's factories would be a third and by 1880 two thirds that of British industry.

After the War of 1812, however, British textile companies blunted America's industrial growth by flooding the United States with cheap cotton cloth in an effort to regain their customers who had been shut off by the war. Such postwar "dumping" nearly killed the infant American textile industry. A delegation

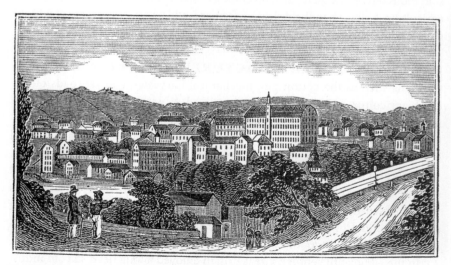

New England Factory Village (ca. 1844) Mills and factories gradually transformed the New England landscape in the early nineteenth century, as seen here in the Massachusetts villages of Salisbury and Amesbury.

of New England mill owners traveled to Washington, D.C., to demand a federal tariff (tax) on imported British cloth to make American textile mills more competitive. The efforts of the mill owners to gain political assistance created a culture of industrial lobbying for congressional tariff protection against imported products that continues to this day.

What the mill owners neglected to admit was that import tariffs hurt consumers by forcing them to pay higher prices. Over time, as Scotsman Adam Smith explained in his classic book on capitalism, *The Wealth of Nations* (1776), consumers not only pay higher prices for foreign goods as a result of tariffs, but they also pay higher prices for domestic goods, since businesses invariably seize opportunities to raise the prices charged for their products.

Tariffs helped protect American industries from foreign competition, but competition is the engine of innovation and efficiency in a capitalist economy. New England shipping companies opposed higher tariffs because they would reduce the amount of goods being carried in their vessels across the Atlantic from Britain and Europe. Many southern planters opposed tariffs because of fears that Britain and France would retaliate by imposing tariffs on American cotton and tobacco shipped to their ports.

In the end, the New England mill owners won the tariff war. Congress passed the Tariff Bill of 1816, which placed a tax of twenty-five cents on every yard of imported cloth. Such tariffs were a major factor in promoting industrialization. By impeding foreign competition, they enabled American manufacturers to dominate the national marketplace.

The Union Manufactories of Maryland in Patapsco Falls, Baltimore County (ca. 1815)
A textile mill established during the embargo of 1807. The Union Manufactories would eventually employ more than 600 people.

THE LOWELL SYSTEM The factory system centered on wage-earning workers sprang full-blown upon the American scene at Waltham, Massachusetts, in 1813, when a group known as the Boston Associates constructed the first textile mill in which the mechanized processes of spinning yarn and weaving cloth were brought together under one roof.

In 1822, the Boston Associates, led by Francis Cabot Lowell, developed another cotton mill at a village along the Merrimack River twenty-eight miles north of Boston, which they renamed Lowell. It soon became the model for textile mill towns throughout New England.

The founders of the **Lowell system** sought not just to improve industrial efficiency through the use of labor-saving machinery, but to develop model industrial communities designed to increase efficiency and profitability. They located their four- and five-story brick-built mills along rivers in the countryside.

Women were the first factory workers in the nation, as the mill owners at Waltham and Lowell hired mostly young women aged fifteen to thirty from farm families. The owners preferred women because of their skill in operating textile machines and their willingness to endure the mind-numbing boredom of operating spinning machines and looms for wages lower than those paid to men (even though their wages, $2.50 per week, were the highest in the world for women).

Moreover, by the 1820s, New England had a surplus of women because so many men had migrated westward. In the early 1820s, a steady stream of single women began flocking toward Lowell. To reassure worried parents, mill owners promised to provide the "Lowell girls" with tolerable work, prepared meals, comfortable boardinghouses (four girls to a room), moral discipline, and educational and cultural opportunities.

Initially the "Lowell idea" worked pretty much according to plan. Visitors commented on the well-designed red brick mills with their lecture halls and libraries. The Lowell girls appeared "healthy and happy" living in cramped

Mill girls Massachusetts mill workers of the mid-nineteenth century, photographed holding shuttles used in spinning thread and yarn.

dormitories staffed by housemothers who enforced church attendance and evening curfews. Despite thirteen-hour work days and five-and-a-half day workweeks (longer hours than those imposed upon prison inmates), some of the women found the time and energy to form study groups, publish a literary magazine, and attend lectures. By 1840, there were thirty-two mills and factories in Lowell.

As Lowell rapidly grew, however, the industrial village lost much of its innocence and cohesion as the mill owners accumulated "unbelievable profits." The once rural village had become a grimy industrial city. Mill owners produced too much cloth, which depressed prices. To maintain their profits, the owners cut wages and quickened the pace of work. As a worker said, "We go in at five o'clock [in the morning]; at seven we come out to breakfast; at half-past seven we return to our work, and stay until half past twelve. At one . . . we return to our work, and stay until seven at night."

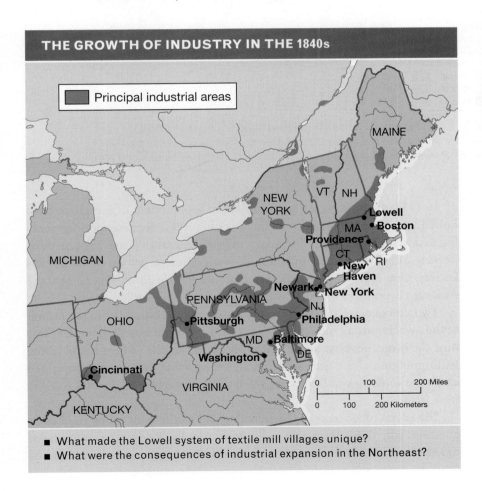

THE GROWTH OF INDUSTRY IN THE 1840s

Principal industrial areas

- What made the Lowell system of textile mill villages unique?
- What were the consequences of industrial expansion in the Northeast?

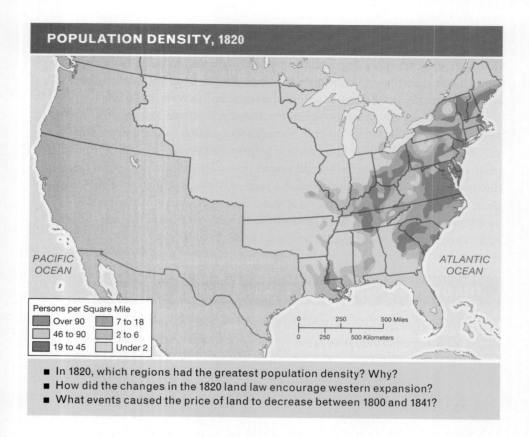

POPULATION DENSITY, 1820

Persons per Square Mile
- Over 90
- 46 to 90
- 19 to 45
- 7 to 18
- 2 to 6
- Under 2

PACIFIC OCEAN

ATLANTIC OCEAN

- In 1820, which regions had the greatest population density? Why?
- How did the changes in the 1820 land law encourage western expansion?
- What events caused the price of land to decrease between 1800 and 1841?

In 1834, the unexpected happened when about a sixth of the native-born Lowell women mill workers went on strike to protest the deteriorating working and living conditions. The angry mill owners labeled the 1,500 striking women "ungrateful" and "unfeminine"—and tried to get rid of the strike's leaders. One mill manager reported that "we have paid off several of these Amazons & presume that they will leave town on Monday."

Two years later, the Lowell workers again walked out, this time in protest of the owners raising the rents in the company-owned boarding houses. This time the owners backed down. Over time, however, the owners began hiring Irish immigrants who were so desperate for jobs that they rarely complained about the working conditions. By 1850, some 40 percent of the mill workers were Irish.

The economic success of the New England textile mills raises an obvious question: why didn't the South build its own mills close to the cotton fields to keep its profits in the region? A few mills did appear in the Carolinas and

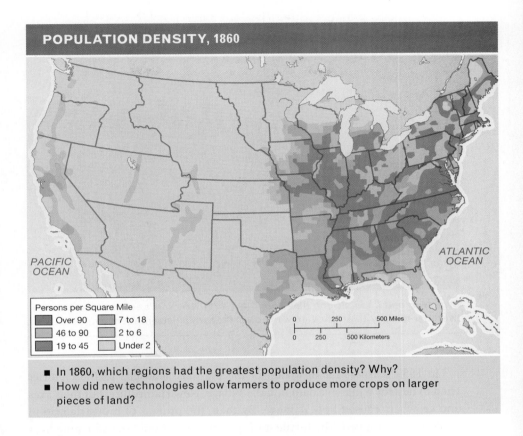

POPULATION DENSITY, 1860

PACIFIC
OCEAN

ATLANTIC
OCEAN

Persons per Square Mile

■ Over 90	■ 7 to 18		
46 to 90	2 to 6		
■ 19 to 45	Under 2		

0   250   500 Miles

0   250   500 Kilometers

- In 1860, which regions had the greatest population density? Why?
- How did new technologies allow farmers to produce more crops on larger pieces of land?

Georgia, but they struggled to find workers because whites generally resisted factory work, and planters refused to allow slaves to leave the fields. African Americans, it was assumed, could not work efficiently indoors, and cotton planters considered textile mills an inefficient use of their labor resources. Agricultural slavery had made them rich. Why should they change?

INDUSTRIALIZATION, CITIES, AND THE ENVIRONMENT

The rapid growth of commerce and industry drove the expansion of cities and mill villages. Lowell's population in 1820 was 200. By 1830, it was 6,500, and ten years later it had soared to 21,000. Other factory centers sprouted up across New England, displacing forests, farms, and villages while filling the air with smoke, noise, and stench. In addition, the profusion of dams—built to harness water to turn the mill wheels—flooded pastures and decimated fish populations, spawned rapid urban growth that polluted the rivers and aroused intense local resentment.

Broadway and Canal Street, New York City (1836) New York's economy and industry, like those of many other cities, grew rapidly in the early nineteenth century.

In 1859, farmers far upstream of the big Massachusetts textile factories tried to destroy a massive dam in Lake Village, New Hampshire, but their axes and crowbars caused little damage. By then, the process of industrialization could not be stopped. The textile mill system was not only transforming lives and property—it was reshaping nature as well.

Between 1820 and 1840, the number of Americans engaged in manufacturing increased 800 percent, and the number of city dwellers more than doubled. As Thomas Jefferson and other agrarians feared, the United States was rapidly becoming a global industrial power producing its own clothing and shoes, iron and engines.

Between 1790 and 1860, the proportion of urban to rural populations grew from 3 percent to 16 percent. Because of their strategic locations along rivers flowing into the ocean, the Atlantic seaports of New York City, Philadelphia, Baltimore, and Boston remained the largest cities. New Orleans became the nation's fifth-largest city because of its role in shipping goods that were floated down the Mississippi River for shipment to the East Coast and to Europe. New York eventually outpaced all its competitors in growth. By 1860, it was the first city to surpass a population of 1 million, largely because of its superior harbor and its unique access to commerce along the Erie Canal and the Atlantic Ocean.

POPULAR CULTURE

During the colonial era, working-class Americans had little time for play or amusement. Most adults worked from dawn to dusk six days a week. In rural areas, free time was often spent in communal activities, such as barn raisings and corn-husking parties, shooting matches and footraces, while residents of the seacoast sailed and fished. In colonial cities, people attended dances, went on sleigh rides and picnics, and played "parlor games" at home such as billiards, cards, and chess.

By the early nineteenth century, however, a more urban society enjoyed more diverse forms of recreation. As people moved to cities, they developed a distinctive urban culture, and laborers and shopkeepers sought new forms of leisure and entertainment as pleasant diversions from their long workdays.

URBAN RECREATION Social drinking was pervasive during the first half of the nineteenth century. In 1829, the secretary of war estimated that three quarters of the nation's laborers drank at least four ounces of "hard liquor" daily. Taverns and social or sporting clubs in the burgeoning cities served as the center of recreation and leisure.

So-called blood sports were also a popular form of amusement, especially among the working poor. For a time, cockfighting and dogfighting at saloons attracted excited crowds and frenzied betting, but prizefighting (boxing), eventually displaced the animal contests. Imported from Britain,

Bare Knuckles Blood sports emerged as popular urban entertainment for men of all social classes, but especially among the working poor.

boxing proved popular with all social classes. The early contestants tended to be Irish or English immigrants, often sponsored by a neighborhood fire company, fraternal association, or street gang. In the antebellum era, boxers fought with bare knuckles, and the results were brutal. A match ended only when a contestant could not continue. A bout in 1842 lasted 119 rounds and ended when a fighter died in his corner. Such deaths prompted several cities to outlaw the practice, only to see it reappear as an underground activity.

THE PERFORMING ARTS   Theaters became the most popular form of indoor entertainment. People from all walks of life flocked to opera houses, playhouses, and music halls to watch a wide spectrum of performances: Shakespeare's tragedies, "blood and thunder" melodramas, comedies, minstrel shows, operas, performances by acrobatic troupes, and local pageants. Audiences were predominantly men. "Respectable" women rarely attended; the prevailing "cult of domesticity" kept women in the home. Raucous audiences cheered the heroes and heroines and hissed at the villains. If an actor did not meet expectations, spectators hurled curses, nuts, eggs, fruit, shoes, or chairs.

The 1830s witnessed the emergence of the first uniquely American form of mass entertainment: blackface minstrel shows, featuring white performers made up as blacks. "Minstrelsy" drew upon African American folklore and reinforced prevailing racial stereotypes. It featured banjo and fiddle music, "shuffle" dances, and lowbrow humor. Between the 1830s and the 1870s, minstrel shows were immensely popular, especially among northern working-class ethnic groups and southern whites.

The most popular minstrel songs were written by a young white composer named Stephen Foster. In 1846, he composed "Oh! Susanna," which

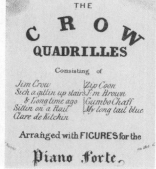

The Crow Quadrilles This sheet-music cover, printed in 1837, shows vignettes caricaturing African Americans. Minstrel shows enjoyed nationwide popularity while reinforcing racial stereotypes.

immediately became a national favorite. Its popularity catapulted Foster into the national limelight, and he responded with equally well-received tunes such as "Old Folks at Home" (popularly known as "Way Down upon the Swanee River"), "Massa's in de Cold, Cold Ground," "My Old Kentucky Home," and "Old Black Joe," all of which perpetuated the sentimental myth of contented slaves.

IMMIGRATION

More than ever before, the United States during the nineteenth century continued to be a nation of immigrants. Warfare in Europe at the start of the century restricted travel to America. After 1815, however, when Napoléon was finally defeated and forced into exile, new U.S. territories and states in the West actively recruited immigrants from Europe, often offering special incentives such as voting rights after only six-months' residency.

Why did people risk their lives and abandon their homelands to come to the United States? America offered jobs, higher wages, lower taxes, cheap and fertile land, no entrenched aristocracy, religious freedom, and voting rights.

After 1837, a worldwide financial panic and economic slump accelerated the pace of immigration to the United States. American employers aggressively recruited foreigners, in large part because they were often willing to work for lower wages than native-born Americans. The *Chicago Daily Tribune* observed that the tide of German immigrants was perfect for the "cheap and ingenious labor of the country." A German laborer was willing "to live as cheaply and work infinitely more intelligently than the negro."

The years from 1845 to 1854 marked the greatest proportional influx of immigrants in U.S. history, 2.4 million, or about 14.5 percent of the total population in 1845. By far, the largest number of immigrants between 1840 and 1860 came from Ireland and Germany.

THE IRISH No nation proportionately sent more of its people to America than Ireland. A prolonged agricultural crisis that brought immense social hardships caused many Irish to flee their homeland in the mid-nineteenth century. Irish farmers primarily grew potatoes; in fact, fully a third of them were dependent on the potato harvest for survival. The average adult male in Ireland ate five pounds of potatoes a day.

In 1845, a fungus destroyed the potato crop and triggered what came to be called the Irish Potato Famine. More than a million people died, and almost 2 million more left Ireland, a country whose total population was only 8 million. Most traveled to Canada and the United States. As one group of exiles explained, "All we want to do is get out of Ireland; we must be better anywhere but here." America, they knew, had plenty of paying jobs and "plenty to eat."

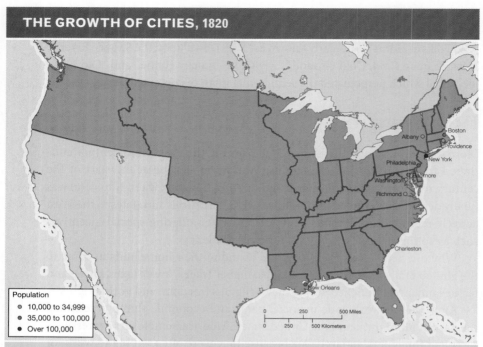

THE GROWTH OF CITIES, 1820

Population
- 10,000 to 34,999
- 35,000 to 100,000
- Over 100,000

- What were the largest cities in the United States in 1820?
- Why did those cities have the densest populations?
- Why did New Orleans grow rapidly yet eventually lag behind its northeastern counterparts?

By the 1850s, the Irish made up more than half the population of Boston and New York City and were almost as dominant in Philadelphia. Most of them were crowded into filthy, poorly ventilated tenement houses in which "the low-paid and poverty-smitten . . . crowd by the dozens." Irish neighborhoods were plagued by high crime rates, deadly diseases, prostitution, and alcoholism. The archbishop of New York described the Irish as "the poorest and most wretched population that can be found in the world."

It was the Irish who often took on the nation's hardest and most dangerous jobs. A visiting Irish journalist, commenting on the industrial transformation in America, wrote that there were "several sorts of power working at the fabric of the Republic: water-power, steam-power, horse-power, and Irish power. The last works hardest of them all." It was mostly Irish men who built the canals and railroads, and mostly Irish women who worked in the textile mills of New England and cleaned the houses of thousands of upper-middle-class Americans. One Irishman groaned that he worked like "a slave for the Americans."

THE GROWTH OF CITIES, 1860

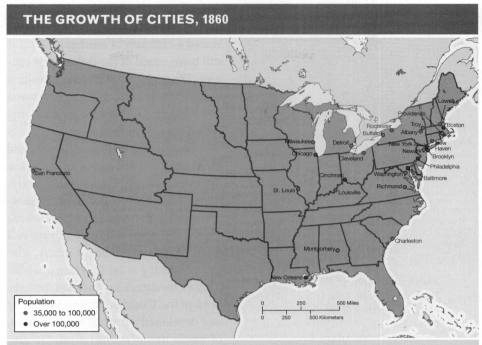

Population
- 35,000 to 100,000
- Over 100,000

- What is the connection between industrialization and urbanization?
- Why did Chicago, Pittsburgh, Cincinnati, and St. Louis become major urban centers in the mid-nineteenth century?

Irish immigrants were stereotyped as filthy, bad-tempered, and heavy drinkers. They also encountered intense anti-Catholic prejudice among native-born Protestants. Many employers posted taunting signs reading "No Irish Need Apply."

Irish Americans, however, could be equally mean-spirited toward other groups, such as free African Americans, who competed with them for low-wage, mostly unskilled jobs. In 1850, the *New York Tribune* expressed concern that the Irish, having escaped from "a galling, degrading bondage" in their homeland, opposed equal rights for blacks and frequently arrived at the polls shouting, "Down with the Nagurs! Let them go back to Africa, where they belong." Irish freedom fighter Daniel O'Connell scolded the immigrants for their racism: "It was not in Ireland you learned this cruelty."

Many African Americans viewed the Irish with equal contempt. In 1850, a slave expressed a common sentiment when he noted that his "master" was "a great tyrant, he treats me badly as if I were a common Irishman." Irish immigrants often took jobs as waiters, dockworkers, and deliverymen that had long

Irish immigration In 1847, nearly 214,000 Irish immigrated to the United States and Canada aboard the ships of the White Star Line and other companies. Despite promises of spacious, well-lit, well-ventilated, and heated accommodations on ships, 30 percent of these immigrants died on board.

been held by African Americans. A free black frustrated by the Irish insurgents voiced a criticism of immigrants that is still being made in the twenty-first century. The Irish, he said, were "crowding themselves into every place of business and labor, and driving the poor colored American citizen out."

Enterprising Irish immigrants did forge remarkable careers in America, however. Twenty years after arriving in New York, Alexander T. Stewart became the owner of the nation's largest department store and vast real estate holdings. Michael Cudahy, who began working at age fourteen in a Milwaukee meatpacking business, became head of the Cudahy Packing Company and developed a process for the curing of meats under refrigeration. Dublin-born Victor Herbert emerged as one of America's most revered composers, and Irish dancers and playwrights came to dominate the stage.

By the start of the Civil War, the Irish in America had energized trade unions, become the most important ethnic group supporting the Democratic party, and made the Roman Catholic Church the nation's largest religious denomination. Years of persecution had instilled in Irish Catholics a fierce loyalty to the church as "the supreme authority over all the affairs of the world." Such passion for Catholicism generated unity among Irish Americans and fear among American Protestants.

The Irish loved to stick together. Most of them settled in Irish neighborhoods in the nation's largest cities and formed powerful local Democratic political organizations, such as Tammany Hall in New York City, that would dominate political life during the second half of the nineteenth century.

THE GERMANS German immigrants were almost as numerous as the Irish. Unlike the Irish newcomers, however, the German arrivals included a large number of skilled craftsmen and well-educated professional people—doctors, lawyers, teachers, engineers—some of whom were refugees from the failed German revolution of 1848.

German Beer Garden, New York **(1825)** German immigrants established their own communities, where they maintained the traditions of their homeland.

In addition to an array of political opinions, the Germans brought with them a variety of religious preferences. Most were Protestants (usually Lutherans), a third were Roman Catholics, and a significant number were Jews. Among the German immigrants who prospered in the New World were Heinrich Steinweg, a piano maker who in America changed his name to Steinway and became famous for the quality of his instruments, and Levi Strauss, a Jewish tailor who followed the gold rush to California and began making work pants, later dubbed "Levi's."

Germans settled more often in rural areas than in cities. Many were independent farmers, skilled workers, and shopkeepers who were able to establish themselves immediately. More so than the Irish, they migrated in families and groups. This clannish quality helped them better sustain elements of their language and culture in the United States. More of them also tended to return to their native country. About 14 percent of the Germans eventually went back to their homeland, compared with just 9 percent of the Irish.

THE BRITISH, SCANDINAVIANS, AND CHINESE Immigrants from Great Britain and Canada continued to arrive in large numbers during the first half of the nineteenth century. They included professionals, independent farmers, and skilled workers. Two other large groups of immigrants were from Scandinavia and China. Norwegians and Swedes, mostly farmworkers, gravitated to Illinois, Wisconsin, and the Minnesota Territory, where the cold climate and dense forests reminded them of home. By the 1850s, the rapid development of California was attracting a growing number of Chinese, who, like the Irish in the East, did the heavy work of construction, especially on railroad tracks and bridges.

NATIVISM Not all Americans welcomed the flood of immigrants. A growing number of "nativists," people born in the United States who resented the newcomers, sought to restrict or stop immigration altogether. The flood of Irish and German Catholics especially aroused hostility among Protestants. A Boston minister described Catholicism as "the ally of tyranny, the opponent of material prosperity, the foe of thrift, the enemy of the railroad, the caucus, and the school."

Nativists eventually launched organized political efforts to stop the tide of immigrants. The Order of the Star-Spangled Banner, founded in New York City in 1849, grew into a powerful political group known as the American party. Members pledged never to vote for any foreign-born or Catholic candidates. When asked about the secretive organization, they were told to say, "I know nothing," a phrase which gave rise to the informal name for the party: the **Know-Nothings**.

For a while, the Know-Nothings appeared to be on the brink of major-party status, especially during the 1850s, when the number of immigrants was five times as large as it had been during the 1840s. In the state and local cam-

A Know-Nothing cartoon This cartoon shows the Catholic Church supposedly attempting to control American religious and political life through Irish immigration.

paigns of 1854, they swept the Massachusetts legislature, winning all but two seats in the lower house, and that fall they elected more than forty congressmen. Forty percent of the Pennsylvania state legislators were Know-Nothings.

The Know-Nothings demanded that immigrants and Roman Catholics be excluded from public office and that the waiting period for naturalization (earning citizenship) be extended from five to twenty-one years. The party, however, was never strong enough to enact such legislation. Nor did Congress restrict immigration during that period. For a while, the Know-Nothings threatened to control New England, New York, and Maryland, but the anti-Catholic movement subsided when slavery became the focal issue of the 1850s.

ORGANIZED LABOR AND NEW PROFESSIONS

While most Americans continued to work as farmers during the nineteenth century, a growing number found employment in new or expanding enterprises: textile mills, shoe factories, banks, railroads, publishing, retail stores, teaching, preaching, medicine, law, construction, and engineering. Technological innovations (steam power, power tools, and new modes of transportation) and their social applications (mass communication, turnpikes, the postal service, banks, and corporations) fostered an array of new industries and businesses that transformed the nature of work for many Americans, both men and women.

EARLY UNIONS In 1800, only 12 percent of Americans worked for wages; by 1860, wage earners had grown to 40 percent of the nation's workforce. Proud apprentices, journeymen, and master craftsmen, who controlled their labor and invested their work with an emphasis on quality rather than quantity, resented the spread of mills and factories populated by "half-trained" workers dependent upon an hourly wage and subject to the sharp fluctuations of the larger economy.

The rapid growth of wage workers often came at the expense of skilled self-employed artisans and craftsmen who owned their own small shops where they made or repaired carriages, shoes, hats, saddles, silverware, jewelry, glass, ropes, furniture, boats, and a broad array of other products. Other skilled craftsmen were blacksmiths, printers, or barrel makers. Throughout the first half of the nineteenth century, the number of self-employed master craftsmen steadily declined as the number of factories and mills increased.

Artisans who emphasized quality and craftsmanship in their custom-made products found it increasingly hard to compete with the low prices for similar products made in much larger numbers in the factories and mass-production workshops.

The production of shoes, for example, was transformed by the shift to mass production. Until the nineteenth century, boots and shoes were made by hand by shoemakers for local customers. Working in their own home or small shop, shoemakers might also employ one or two journeymen (assistants) as well as an apprentice, a young man learning the skilled trade.

That changed during the early nineteenth century, as the number and size of shoe shops increased in New England, largely driven by the demand for inexpensive shoes, many of which were shipped south for the rapidly growing slave population. Shoe shops were displaced by shoe factories, and the master shoemaker became a manager rather than an artisan. Instead of creating a shoe from start to finish, workers were given specific tasks such as cutting the leather or stitching the "uppers" onto the soles.

The skilled workers forced to make the transition to mass production and a strict division of labor often resented the change. A Massachusetts shoe worker complained that the factory owners were "little stuck up, self-conceited individuals" who forced workers to follow their orders or be fired. In 1850, the Board of Health in Lynn, Massachusetts, reported that the life expectancy of a shoe worker was almost twenty years shorter than a farmer.

The shoe factory When Philadelphia shoemakers went on strike in 1806, a court found them guilty of a "conspiracy to raise wages." Here, shoemakers work at a Massachusetts shoe factory.

The growing fear among artisans that they were losing status led many of them to become involved in politics and unions. Philadelphia furniture craftsmen, for example, called for a "union" to protect "their mutual independence." At first, these workers organized into interest groups representing their individual skills or trades. During the early nineteenth century, a growing fear that they were losing status led artisans in the major cities to become involved in politics and unions. Philadelphia furniture craftsmen, for example, called for their peers to form a "union" to protect "their mutual independence."

At first, these workers organized themselves into interest groups representing their individual skills or trades. Such "trade associations" were the first type of labor unions. They pressured politicians for tariffs to protect their industries from foreign imports, provided insurance benefits, and drafted regulations to improve working conditions. In addition, they sought to control the number of tradesmen in their profession so as to maintain wage levels.

Early labor unions faced major legal obstacles—in fact, they were prosecuted as unlawful conspiracies. In 1806, for instance, Philadelphia shoemakers were found guilty of conspiring "to raise their wages." The court's decision broke the union. In 1842, though, the Massachusetts Supreme Judicial Court issued a landmark ruling in *Commonwealth v. Hunt* declaring that forming a trade union was not in itself illegal, nor was a demand that employers hire only members of the union. The court also said that union workers could strike if an employer hired laborers who refused to join the union.

Until the 1820s, labor organizations took the form of local trade unions, each confined to one city and one craft or skill. From 1827 to 1837, however, organization on a larger scale began to take hold. In 1834, the **National Trades' Union** was formed to organize local trade unions into a stronger national association. At the same time, shoemakers, printers, carpenters, and weavers established national craft unions representing their particular skills.

Women also formed trade unions. Sarah Monroe, who helped organize the New York Tailoresses' Society, explained that it was intended to defend "our rights." If it was "unfashionable for men to bear [workplace] oppression in silence, why should it not also become unfashionable with the women?" In 1831, the women tailors went out on strike demanding a "just price for labor."

Skilled workers also formed political organizations to represent their interests. A New York

Symbols of organized labor
A pocket watch with an International Typographical Union insignia.

newspaper reported that people across the nation were organizing Workingmen's political parties to protect "those principles of liberty and equality unfolded in the Declaration of our Independence." Workingmen's parties called for laws to regulate banks and abolish the common practice of imprisoning people who could not pay their debts.

THE RISE OF THE PROFESSIONS

The dramatic social changes opened up an array of new **professions**. Bustling new towns required new services—retail stores, printing shops, post offices, newspapers, schools, banks, law firms, medical practices. By definition, professional workers have specialized knowledge and training. In 1849, Henry Day delivered a lecture titled "The Professions" at the Western Reserve School of Medicine. He declared that the most important social functions in modern life were the professional skills and claimed that society had become utterly dependent upon "professional services."

TEACHING Teaching was one of the fastest-growing professions in the first half of the nineteenth century. Horace Mann of Massachusetts was instrumental in promoting the idea of free public education as the best way to transform children into disciplined, judicious citizens. Many states, especially in the North, agreed, and the number of schools exploded. New schools required teachers, and Mann helped create "normal schools" around the nation to train future teachers. Public schools initially preferred men as teachers, usually hiring them at age seventeen or eighteen. The pay was so low that few stayed in the profession their entire career, but for many educated, restless young adults, teaching offered independence and social status, as well as an alternative to the rural isolation of farming. Church groups and civic leaders started private academies, or seminaries, for girls.

LAW, MEDICINE, AND ENGINEERING Teaching was a common stepping-stone for men who became lawyers. In the decades after the American Revolution, young men would teach for a year or two before joining an experienced attorney as an apprentice (what today would be called an *intern*). They would learn the practice of law in exchange for their labors. (There were no law schools yet.)

Like attorneys, physicians in the early nineteenth century often had little formal academic training. Healers of every stripe assumed the title of *doctor* and established medical practices. Most were self-taught or had learned their profession by assisting a physician for several years, occasionally supplementing their internships with a few classes at the handful of medical schools. By

1860, there were 60,000 self-styled physicians, many of whom were "quacks" or frauds. As a result, the medical profession lost the public's confidence until the emergence of formal medical schools.

The industrial expansion of the United States also spurred the profession of engineering, a field that would eventually become the nation's largest professional occupation for men. Specialized expertise was required for the building of canals and railroads, the development of machine tools and steam engines, and the construction of roads, bridges, and factories.

"WOMEN'S WORK"   Meanwhile, most women still worked primarily in the home or on a farm. The only professions readily available to them were nursing (often midwifery, the delivery of babies) and teaching. Many middle-class women spent their time outside the home doing religious and social-service work. Then as now, women were the backbone of most churches.

A few women, however, courageously pursued careers in male-dominated professions. Elizabeth Blackwell of Ohio managed to gain admission to Geneva Medical College (now Hobart and William Smith College) in western New York despite the disapproval of the faculty. When she arrived at her first class, a hush fell upon the students "as if each member had been struck with paralysis." Blackwell had the last laugh when she finished first in her class in 1849, but thereafter the medical school refused to admit more women. The first American woman to earn a medical degree, Blackwell went on to start the New York Infirmary for Women and Children and later had a long career as a professor of gynecology at the London School of Medicine for Women.

EQUAL OPPORTUNITIES

The dynamic market-based economy that emerged during the first half of the nineteenth century helped spread the idea that individuals should have an equal opportunity to better themselves through their abilities and hard work. Equality of opportunity, however, did not assume equal outcomes. Americans wanted an equal chance to earn unequal amounts of wealth. In America, observed a journalist in 1844, "one has as good a chance as another according to his talents, prudence, and personal exertions."

The same ideals that prompted so many white immigrants to come to the United States, however, were equally appealing to African Americans and women. By the 1830s, they, too, began to demand their right to "life, liberty, and the pursuit of happiness." Such desires among "common people" would quickly spill over into the political arena. The great theme of American political life in the first half of the nineteenth century would be the continuing democratization of opportunities for white men, regardless of income or background, to vote and hold office.

CHAPTER REVIEW

SUMMARY

- **Transportation and Communication Revolutions**   Canals and other improvements in transportation, such as the *steamboat*, allowed goods to reach markets more quickly and cheaply and transformed the more isolated "household economy" of the eighteenth century into a *market-based economy* in which people bought and sold goods for profit in sometimes distant markets. *Clipper ships* shortened the amount of time to transport goods across the oceans. The *railroads* (which expanded rapidly during the 1850s) and the *telegraph system* diminished the isolation of the West and united the country economically and socially. The *Erie Canal* contributed to New York City's emerging status as the nation's economic center even as it promoted the growth of Chicago and other midwestern cities. Improvements in transportation and communication linked rural communities to a worldwide marketplace.

- **Industrialization**   Inventions in machine tools and technology as well as innovations in business organization spurred a wave of *industrialization* during the nineteenth century. The *cotton gin* dramatically increased cotton production and a rapidly spreading *cotton* culture boomed in the South, with a resultant increase in slavery. Other inventions, such as John Deere's steel plow and the mechanized *McCormick reaper*, helped Americans, especially westerners, farm more efficiently and more profitably. In the North, mills and factories, powered first by water and eventually by coal-fired steam engines, spread rapidly. Mills initially produced textiles for clothing and bedding from southern cotton, as well as iron, shoes, and other products. The federal government's tariff policy encouraged the growth of domestic manufacturing, especially cotton textiles, by reducing imports of British cloth. Between 1820 and 1840, the number of Americans engaged in manufacturing increased 800 percent. Many mill workers, such as the women employed in the *Lowell system* of New England textile factory communities, worked long hours for low wages in unhealthy conditions. Industrialization, along with increased commerce, helped spur the growth of cities. By 1860, 16 percent of the population lived in an urban area.

- **Immigration**   The promise of cheap land and good wages drew millions of immigrants to America. By 1844, about 14.5 percent of the population was foreign born. The devastating potato famine led to an influx of destitute Irish Catholic families. By the 1850s, they represented a significant portion of the urban population in the United States, constituting a majority in New York and Boston; German migrants, many of them Catholics and Jews, migrated during this same time. Not all native-born Americans welcomed the immigrants. *Nativists* became a powerful political force in the 1850s, with the *Know-Nothing party* nearly achieving major-party status with its message of excluding immigrants and Catholics from the nation's political community.

- **Workers, Professionals, and Women**   Skilled workers (artisans) formed trade associations to protect their members and to lobby for their interests. As industrialization spread, some workers expanded these organizations nationally, forming the *National Trades' Union*. The growth of the market economy also expanded opportunities for those with formal education to serve in new or expanding *professions*. The number of physicians, teachers, engineers, and lawyers grew rapidly. By the mid-nineteenth century, women, African Americans, and immigrants began to agitate for equal social, economic, and political opportunities.

CHRONOLOGY

1793	Eli Whitney invents the cotton gin
1794	Philadelphia-Lancaster Turnpike is completed
1795	Wilderness Road opens
1807	Robert Fulton and Robert Livingston launch steamship transportation on the Hudson River near New York City
1825	Erie Canal opens in upstate New York
1831	Cyrus McCormick invents a mechanical reaper
1834	National Trades' Union is organized
1837	John Deere invents the steel plow
1842	Massachusetts Supreme Judicial Court issues *Commonwealth v. Hunt* decision
1845	The *Rainbow*, the first clipper ship, is launched
	Irish Potato Famine
1846	Elias Howe invents the sewing machine
1855	Know-Nothing party (American party) formed

KEY TERMS

market-based economy p. 353

steamboats p. 356

Erie Canal p. 357

railroads p. 360

clipper ships p. 360

telegraph system p. 364

industrialization p. 365

cotton gin p. 366

cotton p. 366

McCormick reapers p. 369

Lowell system p. 372

nativists p. 384

Know-Nothings p. 384

National Trades' Union p. 387

professions p. 388

 INQUIZITIVE

Go to InQuizitive to see what you've learned—and learn what you've missed—with personalized feedback along the way.

9 Nationalism and Sectionalism

1815–1828

***Parade of the Victuallers* (1821)** On a beautiful day in March 1821, Philadelphia butcher William White organized a parade celebrating America's own high-quality meats. Many townspeople watched from their windows and balconies, while the spectators below could also enjoy the foods of various street vendors, such as the African American oyster peddler (bottom left). This watercolor by John Lewis Krimmel captures the vibrant nationalism that emerged in America after the War of 1812.

After the War of 1812, the British stopped interfering with American shipping. The United States could now develop new industries and exploit new markets around the globe. It was not simply Alexander Hamilton's financial initiatives and the capitalistic energies of wealthy investors and entrepreneurs that sparked America's dramatic economic growth in the early nineteenth century. Prosperity also resulted from the efforts of ordinary men and women who were willing to take risks, uproot families, use unstable paper money issued by unregulated local banks, and tinker with new machines, tools, and inventions.

By 1828, the young agrarian republic was poised to become a sprawling commercial nation connected by networks of roads and canals as well as regional economic relationships—all enlivened by a restless spirit of enterprise, experimentation, and expansion.

For all of the energy and optimism exhibited by Americans after the war, however, the fundamental tension between *nationalism* and *sectionalism* remained: how to balance the national interest with the particular economic and social needs of the nation's three growing regions—North, South, and West?

Americans who identified themselves as nationalists promoted the interests of the country as a whole. This required each region to recognize that no single section could get all it wanted without threatening the survival of the nation. Many sectionalists, however, were single-mindedly focused on promoting their region's priorities: shipping, manufacturing, and commerce in the Northeast; slave-based agriculture in the South; low land prices and

focus questions

1. How did the new spirit of nationalism that emerged after the War of 1812 affect economic and judicial policies?

2. What were the issues and ideas that promoted sectional conflict during this era?

3. How did the "Era of Good Feelings" emerge? What factors led to its demise?

4. What were the federal government's diplomatic accomplishments during this era? What was their impact?

5. What developments enabled Andrew Jackson to become president? How did he influence national politics in the 1820s?

transportation improvements in the West. Of all the issues dividing the young republic, the passions aroused by the expansion of slavery proved to be the most difficult to resolve.

A NEW NATIONALISM

After the War of 1812, Americans experienced a wave of patriotic excitement. They had won their independence from Britain for a second time, and a postwar surge of prosperity fed a widespread sense of optimism.

POSTWAR NATIONALISM In his first message to Congress in late 1815, President James Madison revealed how much the challenges of the war, especially the weaknesses of the armed forces and federal financing, had changed his attitudes toward the role of the federal government.

Now, Madison and other leading southern Republicans, such as South Carolina's John C. Calhoun, acted like nationalists rather than states' rights sectionalists. They abandoned many of Thomas Jefferson's presidential initiatives (for example, his efforts to reduce the armed forces and his opposition to the national bank) in favor of the *economic nationalism* developed by Federalists Alexander Hamilton and George Washington. Madison now supported a larger army and navy, a new national bank, and tariffs to protect American manufacturers from foreign competition. "The Republicans have out-Federalized Federalism," one New Englander commented after Madison's speech.

THE BANK OF THE UNITED STATES After President Madison and congressional Republicans allowed the charter for the First Bank of the United States to expire in 1811, the nation's finances fell into a muddle. States began chartering new local banks with little or no regulation, and their banknotes (paper money) flooded the economy with different currencies of uncertain value. Imagine trying to do business on a national basis when each state-chartered bank had its own currency, which often was not accepted by other banks or in other states.

In response to the growing financial turmoil, Madison urged Congress to establish the **Second Bank of the United States (B.U.S.)**. The B.U.S. was intended primarily to support a stable national currency that would promote economic growth. With the help of powerful congressmen Henry Clay and John C. Calhoun, Congress created the new B.U.S. in 1816, which, like its predecessor, was based in Philadelphia and was chartered for twenty years. In return for issuing national currency and opening branches in every state, the bank had to handle all of the federal government's funds without charge, lend the government up to $5 million upon demand, and pay the government $1.5 million.

The bitter debate over the B.U.S., then and later, helped set the pattern of regional alignment for most other economic issues. Generally speaking, westerners opposed the national bank because it catered to eastern customers.

The controversy over the B.U.S. was also noteworthy because of the leading roles played by the era's greatest statesmen: John C. Calhoun of South Carolina, Henry Clay of Kentucky, and Daniel Webster of New Hampshire (and later Massachusetts). Calhoun introduced the banking bill and pushed it through, justifying its constitutionality by citing the congressional power to regulate the currency.

Clay, who had long opposed a national bank, now reversed himself, arguing that new economic circumstances had made it indispensable. Webster led the opposition to the bank among the New England Federalists, who feared the growing financial power of Philadelphia. Later, Webster would return to Congress as the champion of a much stronger national government—at the same time that unexpected events would steer Calhoun away from economic nationalism and toward a defiant embrace of states' rights, slavery, and even secession.

A PROTECTIVE TARIFF The long controversy with Great Britain over shipping rights convinced most Americans of the need to develop their own manufacturing sector to end their dependence on imported British goods. Efforts to develop iron and textile industries, begun in New York and New England during the embargo of 1807, had accelerated during the War of 1812 when America did not have access to European goods.

After the war ended, however, the more-established British companies flooded U.S. markets with their less-expensive products, which undercut their American competitors. In response, northern manufacturers lobbied Congress for federal tariffs to protect their infant industries from what they called "unfair" British competition.

Congress responded by passing the **Tariff of 1816**, which placed a 20 to 25 percent tax on a long list of imported goods. Tariffs benefited some regions (the Northeast) more than others (the South), thus intensifying sectional tensions and grievances. Debates over federal tariffs would dominate political debate throughout the nineteenth century, in part because they provided much of the annual federal revenue and in part because they benefited manufacturers rather than consumers.

The few southerners who voted for the tariff, led by John C. Calhoun, did so because they hoped that the South might also become a manufacturing center over time. Within a few years, however, New England's manufacturing

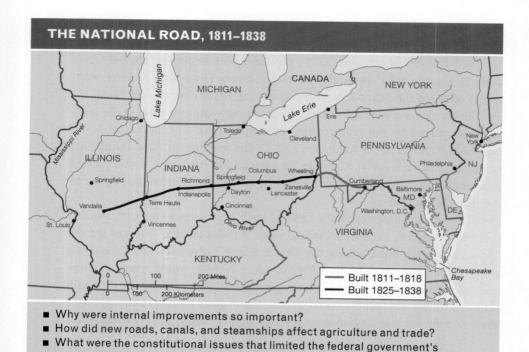

THE NATIONAL ROAD, 1811–1838

Legend:
- Built 1811–1818
- Built 1825–1838

- Why were internal improvements so important?
- How did new roads, canals, and steamships affect agriculture and trade?
- What were the constitutional issues that limited the federal government's ability to enact internal improvements?

sector would roar ahead of the South, leading Calhoun to do an about-face and begin opposing tariffs.

INTERNAL IMPROVEMENTS The third major element of economic nationalism in the first half of the nineteenth century involved federal financing of "**internal improvements**"—the construction of roads, bridges, canals, and harbors. Most American rivers flowed from north to south, so the nation needed a network of roads running east to west, including what became known as the National Road connecting the Midwest with the East coast.

In 1817, John C. Calhoun urged the House to fund internal improvements. He believed that a federally-funded network of roads and canals in the West would help his native South by opening up trading relationships between the two regions. Support for federally-financed roads and canals came largely from the West, which badly needed transportation infrastructure. Opposition was centered in New England, which expected to gain the least from projects intended to spur western development.

POSTWAR NATIONALISM AND THE SUPREME COURT The postwar emphasis on economic nationalism also surfaced in the Supreme

Court, where Chief Justice John Marshall strengthened the constitutional powers of the federal government at the expense of states' rights. In the pathbreaking case of *Marbury v. Madison* (1803), the Court had, for the first time, declared a federal law unconstitutional. In the cases of *Martin v. Hunter's Lessee* (1816) and *Cohens v. Virginia* (1821), the Court ruled that the U.S. Constitution, as well as the nation's laws and treaties, could remain the supreme law of the land only if the Court could review and at times overturn the decisions of state courts.

PROTECTING CONTRACT RIGHTS

The Supreme Court made two more major decisions in 1819 that strengthened the power of the federal government at the expense of the states: one, **Dartmouth College v. Woodward**, involved the New Hampshire legislature's effort to change Dartmouth College's charter to stop the col-

John Marshall A pillar of judicial nationalism, Marshall was appointed chief justice of the U.S. Supreme Court at the age of forty-six, ruling on *Marbury v. Madison* just two years later.

lege's trustees from electing their own successors. In 1816, the state's legislature created a new board of trustees for the college. The original group of trustees sued to block the move. They lost in the state courts but won on appeal to the Supreme Court.

The college's original charter, wrote John Marshall in drafting the Court's opinion, was a valid contract that the state legislature had impaired, an act forbidden by the Constitution. This decision implied a new and enlarged definition of *contract* that seemed to put corporations beyond the reach of the states that had chartered them. Thereafter, states commonly wrote into the charters incorporating businesses and other organizations provisions making the charters subject to modification. Such provisions were then part of the "contract."

PROTECTING A NATIONAL CURRENCY

The second major Supreme Court case of 1819 was Marshall's most significant interpretation of the constitutional system: **McCulloch v. Maryland**. James McCulloch, a B.U.S. clerk in the Baltimore office, had refused to pay state taxes on B.U.S. currency, as required by a Maryland law. The state indicted McCulloch. Acting on behalf of the national bank, he appealed to the Supreme Court, which ruled

Steamboat Travel on the Hudson River (1811) This watercolor of an early steamboat was painted by a Russian diplomat, Pavel Petrovich Svinin, who was fascinated by early technological innovations and the unique culture of America.

unanimously that Congress had the authority to charter the B.U.S. and that states had no right to tax the national bank.

Speaking for the Court, Chief Justice Marshall ruled that Congress had the right (that is, one of its "implied powers") to take any action not forbidden by the Constitution as long as the purpose of such laws was within the "scope of the Constitution." One great principle that "entirely pervades the Constitution," Marshall wrote, is "that the Constitution and the laws made in pursuance thereof are supreme: . . . They control the Constitution and laws of the respective states, and cannot be controlled by them."

REGULATING INTERSTATE COMMERCE John Marshall's last dramatic decision, *Gibbons v. Ogden* (1824), affirmed the federal government's supremacy in regulating *interstate* commerce in a ruling on an important New York case.

In 1808, the New York legislature granted Robert Fulton and Robert R. Livingston the sole right to operate steamboats on the state's rivers and lakes. Fulton and Livingston then gave Aaron Ogden the exclusive right to ferry people and goods up the Hudson River between New York and New Jersey. Thomas

Gibbons, however, operated ships under a federal license that competed with Ogden. On behalf of a unanimous Court, Marshall ruled that the monopoly granted by the state to Ogden conflicted with the federal license issued to Gibbons.

Thomas Jefferson detested John Marshall's judicial nationalism. The Court's ruling in the *Gibbons* case, said the eighty-two-year-old former president, revealed how "the Federal branch of our Government is advancing towards the usurpation of all the rights reserved to the States, and the consolidation in itself of all powers, foreign and domestic."

DEBATES OVER THE AMERICAN SYSTEM

The major economic initiatives debated by Congress after the War of 1812—the national bank, federal tariffs, and federally-financed roads, bridges, ports, and canals—were interrelated pieces of a comprehensive economic plan called the **American System**.

The term was coined by Republican Henry Clay, the powerful congressional leader from Kentucky who would serve three terms as Speaker of the House before becoming a U.S. senator. Clay wanted to free America's economy from its dependence on Great Britain while tying together the diverse regions of the nation politically. He said, "I know of no South, no North, no East, no West to which I owe my allegiance. The Union is my country."

In promoting his American System, Clay sought to give each section of the country its top economic priority. He argued that high tariffs on imports were needed to block the sale of British products in the United States and thereby protect new industries in New England and New York from unfair foreign competition.

To convince the western states to support the tariffs, Clay first called for the federal government to use tariff revenues to build much-needed infrastructure—roads, bridges, canals, and other "internal improvements"—in the frontier West to enable speedier travel and faster shipment of goods to markets.

Second, Clay's American System would raise prices for federal lands sold to the public and distribute the additional revenue from the land sales to the states to help finance more roads, bridges, and canals. Third, Clay endorsed a strong national bank to create a single national currency and to regulate the often unstable state and local banks.

Clay was the consummate deal maker and economic nationalist. In many respects, he assumed responsibility for sustaining Alexander Hamilton's vision of a strong federal government nurturing a national economy that combined agriculture, industry, and commerce.

The debates over the merits of the American System would continue throughout the first half of the nineteenth century. The success of Clay's program depended on each section's willingness to compromise. For a while, it worked.

Critics, however, argued that higher prices for federal lands would discourage western migration and that tariffs benefited the northern manufacturing sector at the expense of southern and western farmers and the "common" people, who had to pay higher prices for the goods produced by tariff-protected industries.

Many westerners and southerners also feared that the Second Bank of the United States would become so powerful and corrupt that it could dictate the nation's economic future at the expense of states' rights and the needs of particular regions. Missouri senator Thomas Hart Benton predicted that cash-strapped western towns would be at the mercy of the national bank in Philadelphia. Westerners, Benton worried, "are in the jaws of the monster! A lump of butter in the mouth of a dog! One gulp, one swallow, and all is gone!"

"AN ERA OF GOOD FEELINGS"

Near the end of his presidency, James Madison turned to James Monroe, a fellow Virginian, to be his successor. In the 1816 election, Monroe overwhelmed his Federalist opponent, Rufus King of New York, by a 183–34 margin in the Electoral College. The "Virginia dynasty" of presidents continued. Monroe's presidency started with America at peace and its economy flourishing.

Soon after his inauguration, in early 1817, Monroe embarked on a goodwill tour of New England, the stronghold of the Federalist party. In Boston, a Federalist newspaper complimented the Republican president for making the effort to "harmonize feelings, annihilate dissentions, and make us one people." Those words of praise were printed under the heading, "Era of Good Feelings," and the headline became a popular label for Monroe's administration.

JAMES MONROE Like George Washington, Thomas Jefferson, and James Madison, Monroe was a slaveholding planter from Virginia. At the outbreak of the Revolutionary War, he dropped out of the College of William and Mary to join the army. He served under George Washington, who called him a "brave, active, and sensible army officer."

After studying law under Thomas Jefferson, Monroe served as a representative in the Virginia assembly, as governor, as a representative in the Confederation Congress, as a U.S. senator, and as U.S. minister (ambassador) to Paris,

London, and Madrid. Under President Madison, he served as secretary of state and doubled as secretary of war during the War of 1812. John C. Calhoun, who would be Monroe's secretary of war, said that the new president was "among the wisest and most cautious men I have ever known." Jefferson noted that Monroe was "a man whose soul might be turned wrong side outwards without discovering a blemish to the world."

Although Monroe's presidency began peacefully enough, sectional loyalties eventually erupted at the expense of nationalist needs. Two major events signaled the end of the Era of Good Feelings and warned of stormy times ahead: the financial Panic of 1819 and the political conflict over statehood for Missouri.

James Monroe Portrayed as he began his presidency in 1817.

THE PANIC OF 1819 The young republic experienced its first major economic depression when the **Panic of 1819** led to a prolonged financial slowdown. Like so many other economic collapses, it was fundamentally the result of too many people trying to get rich too quickly.

After the War of 1812, European demand for American products, especially cotton, tobacco, and flour, soared, leading farmers and planters to increase production. To fuel the roaring postwar economy, unsound local and state banks multiplied and made it easy—too easy—for people and businesses to get loans. The Bank of the United States (B.U.S.) aggravated the problem by issuing risky loans, too.

At the same time, the federal government aggressively sold vast tracts of public land, which spurred reckless real estate speculation by people buying large parcels with the intention of reselling them. On top of all that, good weather in Europe led to a spike in crop production there, thus reducing the need to buy American commodities. Prices for American farm products plunged.

The Panic of 1819 was ignited by the sudden collapse of cotton prices after British textile mills quit buying high-priced American cotton—the nation's leading export—in favor of cheaper cotton from other parts of the world. As the price of cotton fell and the flow of commerce slowed, banks began to fail, and unemployment spiked. The collapse of cotton prices was especially devastating for southern planters, but it also reduced the world demand for other American goods. Owners of new factories and mills, most of them in New England, New York, and Pennsylvania, struggled to find markets for their goods and to fend off more-experienced foreign competitors.

The financial panic and the ensuing depression deepened tensions between northern and southern economic interests. It also spawned a widespread distrust of banks and bankers. Tennessee congressman David Crockett dismissed the "whole Banking system" as nothing more than "swindling on a large scale." Thomas Jefferson felt the same way. He wrote to John Adams that "the paper [money] bubble is then burst. This is what you and I, and every reasoning man . . . have long foreseen."

Other factors caused the financial panic to become a depression. Business owners, farmers, and land speculators had recklessly borrowed money to expand their business ventures or to purchase more land. With the collapse of crop prices and the decline of land values during and after 1819, both land speculators and settlers saw their income plummet.

The equally reckless lending practices of the numerous new state banks compounded the economic confusion. To generate more loans, the banks issued more paper money. Even the Second Bank of the United States, which was supposed to provide financial stability, was caught up in the easy-credit mania.

In 1819, newspapers revealed a case of extensive fraud and embezzlement in the Baltimore branch of the Bank of the United States. The scandal prompted the appointment of Langdon Cheves, a former South Carolina congressman, as the new president of the B.U.S. Cheves restored confidence in the national bank by forcing state banks to keep more gold coins in their vaults to back up the loans they were making. State banks in turn put pressure on their debtors, who found it harder to renew old loans or to get new ones. The economic depression lasted about three years, and many people blamed the B.U.S. After the panic subsided, many Americans, especially in the South and the West, remained critical of the national bank.

THE MISSOURI COMPROMISE As the financial panic deepened, another dark cloud appeared on the horizon: the onset of a fierce sectional controversy over expanding slavery into the western territories. The possibility of western territories becoming "slave states" created the greatest political debate of the nineteenth century. Thomas Jefferson admitted that the issue scared him "like a firebell in the night."

Jefferson realized that the United States was increasingly at risk of disintegrating over the future of slavery. By 1819, the country had an equal number of slave and free states—eleven of each. The Northwest Ordinance (1787) had banned slavery north of the Ohio River, and the Southwest Ordinance (1790) had authorized slavery south of the Ohio.

In the region west of the Mississippi River, however, slavery had existed since France and Spain first colonized the area. St. Louis became the crossroads through which southerners brought slaves into the Missouri Territory.

In 1819, residents in the Missouri Territory asked the House of Representatives to let them draft a constitution and apply for statehood, its population having passed the minimum of 60,000 white settlers (there were also some 10,000 slaves). It would be the first state west of the Mississippi River.

At that point, Representative James Tallmadge Jr., an obscure New York Republican, stunned Congress by proposing a resolution to ban the transport of any more slaves into Missouri. Tallmadge's resolution enraged southern slave owners, many of whom had developed a profitable business selling slaves

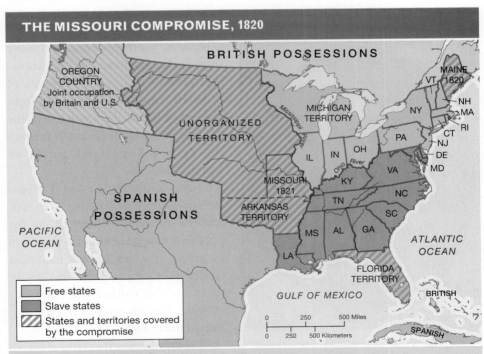

THE MISSOURI COMPROMISE, 1820

Free states
Slave states
States and territories covered by the compromise

- What caused the sectional controversy over slavery in 1819?
- What were the terms of the Missouri Compromise?
- What was Henry Clay's solution to the Missouri constitution's ban on free blacks in that state?

to traders who took them to the western territories to be sold again. Any effort to restrict slavery in the western territories, they believed, could lead to "disunion" and civil war.

In addition, southerners worried that the addition of Missouri as a free state would tip the balance of power in the Senate against the slave states. Their fears were heightened when Congressman Timothy Fuller, an anti-slavery Republican from Massachusetts, declared that it was both "the right and duty of Congress" to stop the spread "of the intolerable evil and the crying enormity of slavery." After fiery debates, the House, with its northern majority, passed the Tallmadge Amendment on an almost strictly sectional vote. The Senate, however, rejected it—also along sectional lines.

At about the same time, Maine, which had been part of Massachusetts, applied for statehood. The Senate decided to link Maine's request for statehood with Missouri's, voting in 1820 to admit Maine as a free state and Missouri as a slave state, thus maintaining the political balance between free and slave states.

Illinois senator Jesse Thomas revised the so-called **Missouri Compromise** by introducing an amendment to exclude slavery in the rest of the Louisiana Purchase north of latitude 36°30′, Missouri's southern border. Slavery thus would continue in the Arkansas Territory and in the new state of Missouri but would be excluded from the remainder of the area west of the Mississippi River. By a narrow margin, the Thomas Amendment passed on March 2, 1820.

Henry Clay of Kentucky Clay entered the Senate at twenty-eight, despite the requirement that senators be at least thirty years old. Here, Clay is pictured on a fifty-dollar bill issued in the 1860s.

Then another issue arose. The proslavery faction in Missouri's constitutional convention inserted in the proposed state constitution a provision excluding free blacks and mulattoes (mixed-race people) from residing in the state. This violated the U.S. Constitution. Free blacks were already citizens of many states.

The dispute over the status of blacks threatened to unravel the deal to admit Missouri as a state until Speaker of the House Henry Clay fashioned a "second" Missouri Compromise whereby

Missouri would be admitted as a state only if its legislature pledged never to deny free blacks their constitutional rights. The Missouri legislature approved Clay's suggestion but denied that it had any power to bind the state in the future. On August 10, 1821, Missouri became the twenty-fourth state, and the twelfth where slavery was allowed.

Nationalists praised the Missouri Compromise for deflecting the volatile issue of slavery. But the compromise settled little. In fact, it had the effect of hardening positions in both North and South.

Sectionalism erupted even within the president's cabinet. President Monroe insisted that any effort to restrict the spread of slavery violated the Constitution. His secretary of state, the future president John Quincy Adams of Massachusetts, disliked the Missouri Compromise for the opposite reason: because it sustained the Constitution's immoral "bargain between freedom and slavery."

The debate over the Missouri Compromise revealed a widening divide between North and South: the North dominated by shipping, commerce, manufacturing, and small farms, the South becoming more and more dependent on cotton and slavery.

NATIONALIST DIPLOMACY

The efforts of Henry Clay to promote economic nationalism and John Marshall to affirm judicial nationalism were reinforced by efforts to practice *diplomatic nationalism*. John Quincy Adams, secretary of state in the Monroe administration and the son of former president John Adams, aggressively exercised America's growing power to clarify and expand the nation's boundaries. He also wanted Europeans to recognize America's dominance in the Western Hemisphere.

RELATIONS WITH BRITAIN The Treaty of Ghent (1814) had ended the War of 1812, but it left unsettled several disputes between the United States and Great Britain. Adams oversaw the negotiations of two important treaties, the Rush-Bagot Treaty of 1817 (named after the diplomats who arranged it) and the Convention of 1818, both of which eased tensions.

In the Rush-Bagot Treaty, the two nations agreed to limit the number of warships on the Great Lakes. The Convention of 1818 was even more important. It settled the disputed northern boundary of the Louisiana Purchase by extending it along the 49th parallel westward, from what would become Minnesota to the Rocky Mountains. West of the Rockies, the Oregon Country would be jointly occupied by the British and the Americans.

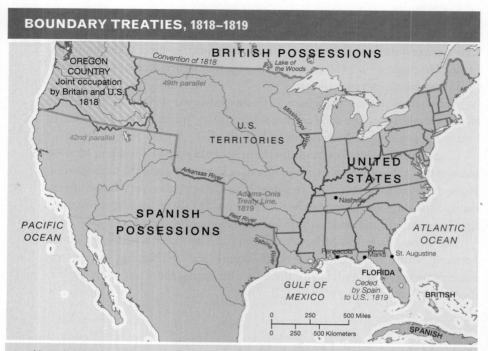

BOUNDARY TREATIES, 1818–1819

- How did the Convention of 1818 settle boundary disputes between Spain and the United States?
- How did Andrew Jackson's aggressive military actions in Florida help John Quincy Adams claim territory from Spain?

FLORIDA Still another disputed boundary involved western Florida. Spanish control over Florida during the early nineteenth century was more a technicality than an actuality. Spain was now a declining power, unable to enforce its obligations under Pinckney's Treaty of 1795 to keep Indians in the region from making raids into south Georgia.

In 1816, U.S. soldiers clashed with runaway slaves holed up in a British fort in West Florida, in the present-day Florida Panhandle. At the same time, Seminole warriors fought white settlers in the area. In 1817, Americans burned a Seminole village on the border, killing five Indians.

At that point, Secretary of War John C. Calhoun ordered General Andrew Jackson to lead an army from Tennessee into Florida, igniting what became known as the First Seminole War. Jackson was told to pursue marauding Indians into Spanish Florida but not to attack Spanish forts. Jackson, frustrated by the restrictions, wrote President Monroe that if the United States wanted Spanish Florida, he could conquer it in sixty days.

Massacre of the Whites by Indians and Blacks in Florida (1836) Published in a
southerner's account of the Seminole War, this is one of the earliest known depictions
of African Americans and Native Americans fighting as allies.

In early 1818, Jackson's force of 2,000 federal soldiers, volunteer Tennessee
militiamen, and Indian allies crossed into Spanish Florida from their encampment in south Georgia. In April, the Americans assaulted a Spanish fort at
St. Marks and destroyed several Seminole villages along the Suwannee River,
hanging two chiefs.

Jackson's soldiers also captured and court-martialed two British traders
accused of provoking Indian attacks. When told that a military trial of the
British citizens was illegal, Jackson gruffly replied that the laws of war did not
"apply to conflicts with savages."

Jackson ordered the immediate execution of the British troublemakers,
an illegal action that outraged the British government and alarmed President
Monroe's cabinet. But the Tennessee general kept moving. In May, he captured
Pensacola, the Spanish capital of West Florida, and established a provisional
American government until Florida's future was decided.

While Jackson's conquests excited expansionists, they aroused anger in
Spain and concern in Washington, D.C. Spain demanded that its territory be
returned and that Jackson be punished for violating international law. Monroe's cabinet was at first prepared to disavow Jackson's illegal acts. Privately,
Secretary of War Calhoun criticized Jackson for disobeying orders—a stand
that would later cause bad blood between them.

Jackson, however, was a hero to most Americans. He also had an important friend in the cabinet—Secretary of State John Quincy Adams, who realized that Jackson's unauthorized conquest of Florida had strengthened his
own hand in negotiating with the Spanish to purchase the territory. American
forces withdrew from Florida, but negotiations resumed with the knowledge
that the U.S. Army could retake Florida at any time.

Andrew Jackson The controversial general was painted by Anna Claypoole Peale in 1819, the year of his military exploits in Florida. She captured Jackson's confident demeanor that made him so popular.

In 1819, Adams convinced the Spanish to sign the **Transcontinental Treaty** (also called the Adams-Onís Treaty), which gave all of Florida to the United States for $5 million. In 1821, Florida became a U.S. territory; in 1845, it would become a state.

The treaty also clarified the western boundary separating the Louisiana Territory from New Spain. It would run from the Gulf of Mexico north along the Sabine River separating Louisiana from Texas and then in stair-step fashion up to the Red River, along the Red, and up to the Arkansas River. From the source of the Arkansas River, it would go north to the 42nd parallel and then west to the Pacific coast. The United States finally spanned the continent.

THE MONROE DOCTRINE The most important diplomatic policy crafted by President Monroe and Secretary of State Adams involved a determined effort to prevent any future European colonialism in the Western Hemisphere. The Spanish, British, French, Portuguese, Dutch, and Russians still controlled one or more colonies in the Americas.

One consequence of the Napoleonic Wars in Europe was the French occupation of Spain and Portugal. The turmoil in those two conquered nations helped trigger independence movements among their colonies in the Americas. Within little more than a decade after the flag of rebellion was first raised in 1809 in Ecuador, Spain had lost almost its entire empire in the Americas: La Plata (later Argentina), Bolivia, Chile, Ecuador, Peru, Colombia, Mexico, Paraguay, Uruguay, and Venezuela had all proclaimed their independence, as had Portuguese Brazil. The only areas still under Spanish control were the islands of Cuba and Puerto Rico and the colony of Santo Domingo on the island of Hispaniola.

In 1823, rumors reached America that the monarchs of Europe were planning to help Spain recover its Latin American colonies. The British foreign minister, George Canning, told the United States that the two countries should jointly oppose any new incursions by European nations in the Western Hemisphere. Monroe initially agreed—if the London government would agree to recognize the independence of the new nations of Latin America. The British refused.

Adams, however, advised Monroe to go it alone in prohibiting further European involvement in the hemisphere. Adams stressed that "it would be more candid as well as more dignified" for America to ban further European intervention than to tag along with a British statement.

Monroe agreed. In his annual message to Congress in December 1823, the president outlined the four major points of what became known as the **Monroe Doctrine**: (1) that "the American continents . . . are henceforth not to be considered as subjects for future colonization by any European powers"; (2) that the United States would consider any attempt by a European nation to intervene "in this hemisphere as dangerous to our peace and safety"; (3) that the United States would not interfere with existing European-controlled colonies in the Americas; and (4) that the United States would keep out of the internal affairs of European nations.

Reaction to the Monroe Doctrine was mixed. In France, Marquis de Lafayette, the courageous freedom-loving volunteer in the American Revolution, hailed the new policy "as the best little bit of paper that God had ever permitted any man to give to the world." Others were not as impressed by the "presumptuous" American declaration. No European nation recognized the Monroe Doctrine. In fact, the Russian ruler, Czar Alexander I, dismissed it with "profound contempt," since he knew that the tiny U.S. Navy could not protect its shores. The Russians then controlled Alaska and claimed to own the Oregon Country as well.

To this day, the Monroe Doctrine has no official standing in international law. Symbolically, however, it has been an important statement of American intentions to prevent European involvement in the Western Hemisphere and an example of the young nation's determination to take its place among the world's great powers. Since it was announced, not a single Latin American nation has lost its independence to an outside invader.

THE RISE OF ANDREW JACKSON

After the War of 1812, the United States had become a one-party political system. The refusal of the Federalists to support the war had virtually killed the party. In 1820, President Monroe was reelected without opposition; the Federalists did not even nominate a candidate.

While the Republican party was dominant for the moment, however, it was about to follow the Federalists into oblivion. If Monroe's first term was the Era of Good Feelings, his second term became an Era of Bad Feelings, as sectional controversies erupted into disputes so violent that they gave birth to a new political party, the Democrats, led by Andrew Jackson.

ANDREW JACKSON Born in 1767 along the border between the two Carolinas, Jackson grew up in a struggling single-parent household. His father was killed in a farm accident three weeks before Andrew was born, forcing his widowed mother Elizabeth to scratch out a living as a housekeeper, while raising three sons.

During the Revolution, the Jackson boys joined in the fighting against the British. One of them, sixteen-year-old Hugh, died of heat exhaustion during a battle; another, Robert, died while trudging home from a prisoner-of-war camp.

In 1781, fourteen-year-old Andrew was captured. When a British officer demanded that the boy shine his muddy boots, Andrew refused, explaining that he was a prisoner of war and expected "to be treated as such," whereupon the angry officer slashed him with his sword, leaving ugly scars on Jackson's head and hand. Soon after her son was released, Elizabeth Jackson, who had helped nurse injured American soldiers, died of cholera. The orphaned Andrew Jackson thereafter despised the British, blaming them for the deaths of his brothers and mother.

After the Revolution, the self-taught Jackson went to Charleston, South Carolina, where he quickly learned to love racehorses, gambling, and fine clothes. He returned home and tried saddle making and teaching before moving to Salisbury, North Carolina, where he earned a license to practice law. He was so combative an attorney that he challenged an opposing lawyer to a duel. He also enjoyed life. A friend recalled that young Jackson was "the most roaring, rollicking, game-cocking, card-playing, mischievous fellow that ever lived in Salisbury."

In 1788, at age twenty-one, Jackson moved to Nashville where he became a frontier attorney in backwoods Tennessee. He also fell in love with Rachel Donelson Robards, a beautiful and lively married woman with whom he lived before she was legally divorced from her first husband. The Jacksons were passionately devoted to each other, but mean-spirited gossip about the origins of their relationship dogged them until Rachel's death in December 1828.

Throughout his life, Jackson had a quick temper. He loved a good fight. "When danger rears its head," he once told his wife, "I can never shrink from it." In 1806, he challenged Charles Dickinson to a duel, claiming that Dickinson had not paid off a racing bet and had insulted his wife, Rachel. Although

Dickinson was said to be the best shot in Tennessee, Jackson let him fire first. For his gallantry, the future president received a bullet in his chest that nearly killed him. He nevertheless straightened himself, patiently took aim, and coolly killed his foe. "I should have hit him," Jackson claimed, "if he had shot me through the brain." (The bullet in his chest was never removed.)

In 1796, when Tennessee became a state, voters elected Jackson to the U.S. House and later to the Senate, where he served only a year before returning to Tennessee and becoming a judge. The ambitious Jackson made a lot of money, first as an attorney, then as a buyer and seller of horses, land, and slaves. He eventually owned 100 slaves on his large cotton plantation, called the Hermitage. He had no moral reservations about slavery and at times could be a cruel master. After one of his slaves escaped, Jackson offered a large reward for his recapture, and promised "ten dollars extra for every hundred lashes a person will give [him] to the amount of three hundred." When not farming or raising racehorses, Jackson served as the iron-willed commander of the Tennessee militia.

Many American political leaders cringed at the thought of the rough-hewn, short-tempered Jackson, who had run roughshod over international law in his war against the British and Seminoles in Florida, presiding over the nation. "His passions are terrible," said Thomas Jefferson. John Quincy Adams scorned Jackson "as a barbarian and savage who could scarcely spell his name." Jackson dismissed such criticism as an example of the "Eastern elite" trying to maintain control of American politics. He responded to Adams's criticism of his literacy by commenting that he never trusted a man who could think of only one way to spell a word.

PRESIDENTIAL POLITICS No sooner had James Monroe started his second presidential term, in 1821, than leading Republicans began positioning themselves to be the next president, including three members of the president's cabinet: Secretary of War John C. Calhoun, Secretary of the Treasury William H. Crawford, and Secretary of State John Quincy Adams. The powerful speaker of the House, Henry Clay, also hungered for the presidency. And there was Andrew Jackson, who was elected to the Senate in 1823. The emergence of so many viable candidates revealed how fractured the Republican party had become.

In 1822, the Tennessee legislature named Jackson its long-shot choice to succeed Monroe. Two years later, Pennsylvania Republicans also endorsed Jackson for president and chose Calhoun for vice president. Meanwhile, the Kentucky legislature had nominated its favorite son, Clay, in 1822. The Massachusetts legislature nominated Adams in 1824. That same year, a group of Republican congressmen nominated Crawford, a cotton planter from Georgia.

Crawford's friends emphasized his devotion to states' rights and strict construction of the Constitution. Clay continued to promote the economic nationalism of his American System. Adams, the only non-slaveholder in the race, shared Clay's belief that the national government should finance internal improvements to stimulate economic development, but he was less strongly committed to tariffs.

Jackson declared himself the champion of the common people and the foe of the entrenched social and political elite. He claimed to represent the "old republicanism" of Thomas Jefferson. But Jefferson believed that Jackson lacked the education, polish, and prudence to be president. "He is," Jefferson told a friend, "one of the most unfit men I know," a "dangerous man." In 1824, Jefferson supported Crawford.

As a self-made military hero, Jackson was an attractive candidate, especially to voters of Irish background. The son of poor Scots-Irish colonists, he was beloved for having defeated the hated English in the Battle of New Orleans. In addition, his commitment to those he called the "common men" resonated with many Irish immigrants who associated aristocracy with centuries of English rule over Ireland.

THE "CORRUPT BARGAIN" The initial results of the 1824 presidential election were inconclusive. Jackson won the popular vote and the Electoral College, where he had 99 votes, Adams 84, Crawford 41, and Clay 37. But

The presidential "race" of 1824 John Quincy Adams, William Crawford, and Andrew Jackson stride to the finish line (on the left) as Henry Clay lags behind (far right).

Jackson did not have the necessary majority of electoral votes. In such a circumstance, as in the 1800 election, the Constitution specified that the House of Representatives would make the final decision from among the top three vote-getters. By the time the House could convene, however, Crawford had suffered a stroke and was ruled out for medical reasons. So the election came down to Adams and Jackson.

Clay's influence, as Speaker of the House, would be decisive. While Adams and Jackson courted Clay's support, he scorned them both, claiming they provided only a "choice of evils." But he regarded Jackson, his fierce western rival, as a "military chieftain," a frontier Napoléon unfit for the presidency. Jackson's election, Clay predicted, would "be the greatest misfortune that could befall the country."

Although Clay and Adams disliked each other, the nationalist Adams supported most of the policies that Clay wanted, particularly high tariffs, transportation improvements, and a strong national bank. Clay also expected Adams to name him secretary of state, the office that usually led to the White House. In the end, a deal between Clay and Adams broke the deadlock. Clay endorsed Adams, and the House of Representatives elected Adams with 13 state delegation votes to Jackson's 7 and Crawford's 4.

The controversial victory proved costly for Adams, however, as it united his foes and crippled his administration before it began. Clay's scheme proved to be a colossal blunder. Jackson dismissed Clay as a "scoundrel," the "Judas of the West," who had entered into a self-serving **"corrupt bargain"** with Adams. Their "corruptions and intrigues," he charged, had "defeated the will of the People." American politics had now entered an Era of Bad Feelings.

Almost immediately after the 1824 decision, Jackson's supporters launched a campaign to undermine the Adams administration and elect the military hero president in 1828. Crawford's supporters soon moved into the Jackson camp, as did the new vice president, John C. Calhoun of South Carolina, who quickly found himself at odds with the president.

JOHN QUINCY ADAMS John Quincy Adams of Massachusetts was one of the nation's hardest working presidents, yet he was also one of the most ineffective. Like his father, the stiff, formal Adams was a great and good man of colossal learning and steely ambition, but he lacked the common touch and the politician's gift for compromise. He worried, as had his father, that republicanism was rapidly turning into democracy, and that government *of* the people was degenerating into government *by* the people, many of whom, in his view, were uneducated and incompetent.

Adams detested the democratic politicking that Andrew Jackson represented. He still wanted politics to be a "sacred" arena for the "best men," a

John Quincy Adams A brilliant man but an ineffective leader, he appears here in his study in 1843. He was the first U.S. president to be photographed.

profession limited to the "most able and worthy" leaders who were motivated by a sense of civic duty rather than a selfish quest for power and stature. The poet Walt Whitman wrote that although Adams was "a virtuous man— a learned man . . . he was not a man of the People."

Adams also suffered from bouts of depression and self-pity, qualities that did not endear him to fellow politicians or the public. In a fit of candor, he described himself as "a man of reserved, cold, austere, and forbidding manners." Yet after admitting the "defects" in his personality, Adams confessed that he could not change them.

Adams's first message to Congress, in December 1825, revealed his grand blueprint for national development. His vision of an energetic federal government funding an array of improvement projects outdid the plans of Alexander Hamilton, James Monroe, and Henry Clay.

The federal government, Adams stressed, should finance internal improvements (roads, canals, harbors, and bridges), create a great national university in Washington, D.C., support scientific explorations, build astronomical observatories, and establish a Department of the Interior to manage the vast federal lands. He challenged Congress to approve his proposals and not be paralyzed "by the will of our constituents." Adams believed that he knew what was best for the country, and he would not be stopped by the concerns of voters.

The voters thought otherwise. Reaction to Adams's speech was overwhelmingly negative. Newspapers charged that Adams was behaving like an aristocratic tyrant, and Congress quickly revealed that it would approve none of his ambitious proposals. The disastrous start shattered Adams's confidence. He wrote in his diary that he was in a "protracted agony of character and reputation."

Adams's effort to expand the powers of the federal government was so controversial and divisive that the Republican party split in two, creating a new party system. Those who agreed with the economic nationalism of Adams and Clay began calling themselves National Republicans.

The opposition—made up of those who supported Andrew Jackson and states' rights—began calling themselves Democrats. They were strongest in the South and West, as well as among the working class in large eastern cities.

The Democrats were the first party in America to recruit professional state organizers, such as Martin Van Buren of New York, who developed sophisticated strategies for mobilizing voters and orchestrating grassroots campaigns featuring massive rallies, barbecues, and parades.

Perhaps most important, the Democrats convinced voters that their primary allegiance should be to their party rather than to any particular candidate. Party loyalty became the prized virtue among Democrats; it was the most powerful weapon they could muster against the "privileged aristocracy" running the state and federal governments.

Jackson claimed that Adams was behaving like a monarch rather than a president (a charge later applied to Jackson). If the president's schemes for expanding government power were not stopped "by the voice of the people," Jackson said, "it must end in consolidation & then in despotism."

Adams's opponents sought to use the always controversial tariff issue against him. In 1828, anti-Adams congressmen introduced a new tariff bill designed to help elect Andrew Jackson. It placed duties (taxes) on various imported raw materials such as wool, hemp, and iron that were also produced in key states where Jackson needed support: Pennsylvania, New York, Ohio, Kentucky, and Missouri.

The measure passed, only to be condemned as the "Tariff of Abominations" by the cotton states of the Lower South. In South Carolina, John C. Calhoun wrote the *South Carolina Exposition and Protest* (1828), in which he ominously declared that a state could nullify an act of Congress that it found unconstitutional, such as the new tariff.

JACKSON'S ELECTION These maneuverings launched the savage **election of 1828** between John Quincy Adams and Andrew Jackson, the National Republicans versus the Jacksonian Democrats. Both sides engaged in vicious personal attacks. As a Jackson supporter observed, "The floodgates of falsehood, slander, and abuse have been hoisted" by the Adams campaign, "and the most nauseating filth is [being] poured" on Jackson's head.

Adams's supporters denounced Jackson as a hot-tempered, ignorant barbarian, a gambler and slave trader who thrived on confrontation and violence, and whose fame rested upon his reputation as a cold-blooded killer.

The most scurrilous attack on Jackson was that he had lived in adultery with his wife, Rachel. In fact, they had lived together as husband and wife for two years in the mistaken belief that the divorce from her first husband was final. As soon as the divorce was indeed official, Andrew and Rachel had remarried to end all doubts about their status. A furious Jackson blamed Henry Clay for the slurs against his wife, calling the Kentuckian "the basest, meanest scoundrel that ever disgraced the image of his god."

The Jacksonians, for their part, condemned Adams as an aristocrat and monarchist, a professional politician who had never had a real job. Newspa-

Jackson Forever!

The Hero of Two Wars and of Orleans!

The Man of the People!

HE WHO COULD NOT BARTER NOR BARGAIN FOR THE

PRESIDENCY!

Who, although "*A Military Chieftain*," valued the purity of Elections and of the Electors, **MORE** than the Office of **PRESIDENT** itself! Although the greatest in the gift of his countrymen, and the highest in point of dignity of any in the world,

BECAUSE

It should be derived from the

PEOPLE!

No Gag Laws! No Black Cockades! No Reign of Terror! No Standing Army or Navy Officers, when under the pay of Government, to browbeat, or

KNOCK DOWN

Old Revolutionary Characters, or our Representatives while in the discharge of their duty.   To the Polls then, and vote for those who will support

OLD HICKORY

AND THE ELECTORAL LAW.

"Jackson Forever" Proclaiming Andrew Jackson a "man of the people," this 1828 poster identifies him with the democratic impulse of the time.

pers claimed that the president had been corrupted by foreigners in the courts of Europe during his diplomatic career. The most outlandish charge was that Adams had allegedly delivered up an American girl to Czar Alexander I while serving as ambassador to Russia. Adams was left to gripe about the many "forgeries now swarming in the newspapers against me."

As a military hero and fabled Indian fighter, Jackson was beloved as the "people's champion" by farmers and working men. As a planter, lawyer, and slaveholder, he had the trust of the southern political elite. Jackson was for a small federal government, individual liberty, an expanded military, and white supremacy. Above all, he was a nationalist committed to preserving the Union in the face of rising sectional tensions.

Candidate Jackson benefited from a growing spirit of democracy in which many viewed Adams as an elitist. Jackson insisted that the election came down to one question: "Shall the government or the people rule?" As president, Jackson promised, he would fight against the entrenched power of the wealthy and powerful.

When Adams's supporters began referring to Jackson as a "jackass," Old Hickory embraced the name, using the animal as a symbol for his "tough" campaign. The jackass eventually became the enduring symbol of the Democratic party.

THE "COMMON MAN" IN POLITICS Jackson's campaign explicitly appealed to the common voters, many of whom were able to vote in a presidential election for the first time as a result of the ongoing democratization of the political system. New Jersey in 1807 and Maryland and South Carolina in 1810 had abolished property and taxpaying requirements for voting, and after 1815 the new states of Indiana, Illinois, Alabama, and Mississippi gave voting rights (suffrage) to all white men regardless of how much property they owned. Other states followed, and by 1824, twenty-one of the twenty-four states had dropped property-owning requirements for voting. Only Virginia and the Carolinas, still dominated by the planter elite, continued to resist the democratizing trend.

The "democratization" of politics also affected many free black males in northern states, half of which allowed blacks to vote. Rufus King, the former presidential candidate, declared that in New York, "a citizen of color was entitled to all the privileges of a citizen . . . [and] entitled to vote."

The extension of voting rights to common men led to the election of politicians sprung from "the people" rather than from the social elite. Jackson, a frontiersman of humble origin and limited education who had scrambled up the political ladder by sheer tenacity, perfectly symbolized this emerging democratic ideal.

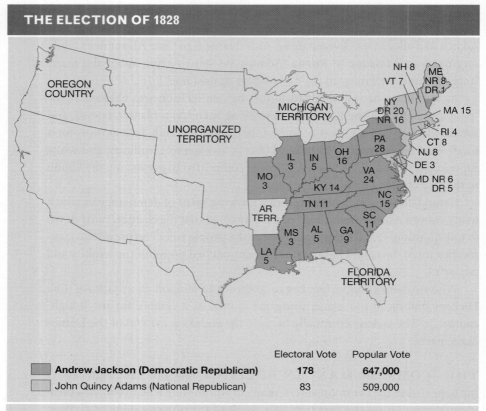

THE ELECTION OF 1828

	Electoral Vote	Popular Vote
Andrew Jackson (Democratic Republican)	**178**	**647,000**
John Quincy Adams (National Republican)	83	509,000

- How did the two presidential candidates, John Quincy Adams and Andrew Jackson, portray each other in the campaign?
- Why did Jackson seem to have the advantage in the election of 1828?
- How did the broadening of voting rights affect the presidential campaign?

LABOR POLITICS With the widespread removal of property qualifications for voting, the working class (laborers paid hourly wages) became an important political force in the form of the Working Men's parties. They were first organized in 1828 in Philadelphia, the nation's largest manufacturing center, with other parties following in New York City and Boston.

The Working Men's parties were devoted to promoting the interests of laborers, such as shorter working hours and allowing all males to vote regardless of the amount of property owned. But the overarching concern of the Working Men's parties was the widening inequality of wealth in American society.

In 1827, during a citywide carpenter's strike, the union claimed that when business owners began to "oppress" the working class, wage laborers had no choice but to organize to protect their interests against "an unequal and very excessive accumulation of wealth and power into the hands of a few."

The Working Men's parties faded quickly, however. The inexperience of labor politicians left them vulnerable to manipulation by political professionals. In addition, major national parties, especially the Jacksonian Democrats, co-opted many of their issues. Labor parties also proved vulnerable to charges of social radicalism, and the courts typically sided with management in dealing with strikes.

Yet the working-class parties succeeded in drawing attention to their demands. They promoted free public education for all children and the abolition of imprisonment for debt, causes that won widespread popular support. The labor parties and unions also called for a ten-hour workday to prevent employers from abusing workers. In large part because of Andrew Jackson's background as a "common man," union members loved him, and the new Democratic party proved adept at building a national coalition of working-class supporters.

PRESIDENT JACKSON   When the 1828 election returns came in, Jackson had won the electoral vote by 178 to 83, and his 56 percent of the popular vote would be a margin unsurpassed during the nineteenth century. Equally important was the surge in voter turnout; more than twice as many men voted as in the 1824 election. Jackson won every state west and south of Pennsylvania.

As he prepared for his inauguration, the president-elect was still boiling with resentment at the way his opponents had besmirched the reputation of his wife, who had died in mid-December 1828, just a few days after learning of the political attacks on her and her "tarnished" marriage. Jackson became obsessed with punishing her persecutors, especially his archenemy, Henry Clay.

More important, Jackson wanted to launch a new democratic era that would silence his critics, restore government to "the people," and take power away from the Eastern "elite." He trusted the people because he was one of them. Now he would be the "people's president." As he headed for Washington, D.C., he was intent on transforming the nation's political landscape—for good and for ill, as it turned out.

CHAPTER REVIEW

SUMMARY

- **Nationalism**   After the War of 1812, the federal government pursued many policies to strengthen the *national* economy. The *Tariff of 1816* protected American manufacturing, and the *Second Bank of the United States* provided a stronger currency. Led by John Marshall, the Supreme Court limited the powers of states and strengthened the power of the federal government in *Dartmouth College v. Woodward* and *McCulloch v. Maryland*. The Marshall court interpreted the Constitution as giving Congress the right to take any action not forbidden by the Constitution as long as the purpose of such laws was within the "scope of the Constitution." In *Gibbons v. Ogden*, the Court protected contract rights against state action and established the federal government's supremacy over interstate commerce, thereby promoting growth of the national economy.

- **Sectionalism**   Henry Clay's *American System* supported economic nationalism by endorsing a national bank, a protective tariff, and federally-funded *internal improvements* such as roads and canals. Many Americans, however, were more tied to the needs of their particular sections of the country. People in the different regions—North, South, and West—disagreed about which economic policies best served their interests. As settlers streamed west, the extension of slavery into the new territories became the predominant political concern, eventually requiring both sides to compromise repeatedly to avoid civil war.

- **Era of Good Feelings**   James Monroe's term in office began with peace and prosperity and was initially labeled the Era of Good Feelings. Two major events, however, ended the Era of Good Feelings: the financial *Panic of 1819* and the Missouri Compromise (1820). The explosive growth of the cotton culture transformed life in the South, in part by encouraging the expansion of slavery, which moved west with southern planters. But in 1819, the sudden collapse of world cotton prices devastated the southern economy and soon affected the national economy as well. The *Missouri Compromise*, a short-term solution to the issue of allowing slavery in the western territories, exposed the emotions and turmoil that the problem generated.

- **National Diplomacy**   The main diplomatic achievements of the period between the end of the War of 1812 and the coming Civil War concerned the extension of America's contested boundaries and the resumption of trade with its old enemy, Great Britain. The countries reached agreement on the northern U.S. borders, and to the south, the *Transcontinental Treaty (Adams-Onís Treaty)* with Spain extended the boundaries of the United States. The *Monroe Doctrine* expressed the idea that the Americas were no longer open to colonization and proclaimed American neutrality in European affairs.

- **The Election of 1828**   The demise of the Federalists left the Republicans as the only political party in the nation. The Republicans' seeming unity was shattered by the election of 1824, which Andrew Jackson lost as a result of what he believed was a *"corrupt bargain"* between John Quincy Adams and Henry Clay. Jackson won the presidency in the *election of 1828* by rallying southern and western voters with his appeal to the common man. His election opened a new era in national politics.

CHRONOLOGY

1816	Second Bank of the United States is established
	First protective tariff goes into effect
1817	Rush-Bagot Treaty between the United States and Great Britain
1818	The Convention of 1818 establishes the northern border of the Louisiana Purchase at the 49th parallel
1819	Panic of 1819
	Supreme Court issues *McCulloch v. Maryland* decision
	United States and Spain agree to the Transcontinental (Adams-Onís) Treaty
1820	Congress accepts the Missouri Compromise
1821	Maine and Missouri become states
	Florida becomes a territory
1823	President Monroe announces the Monroe Doctrine
1824	Supreme Court issues *Gibbons v. Ogden* decision
	John Quincy Adams wins the presidential election by what some claim is a "corrupt bargain" with Henry Clay
1828	Andrew Jackson wins presidency

KEY TERMS

Second Bank of the United States (B.U.S.) p. 394

Tariff of 1816 p. 395

internal improvements p. 396

Dartmouth College v. Woodward p. 397

McCulloch v. Maryland p. 397

Gibbons v. Ogden p. 398

American System p. 399

Panic of 1819 p. 401

Missouri Compromise p. 404

Transcontinental Treaty (Adams-Onís Treaty) p. 408

Monroe Doctrine p. 409

"corrupt bargain" p. 413

election of 1828 p. 415

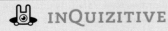 INQUIZITIVE

Go to InQuizitive to see what you've learned—and learn what you've missed—with personalized feedback along the way.

10 The Jacksonian Era

1828–1840

Hard times in the Jacksonian era Although Andrew Jackson championed the "poor and humble," his economic policies contributed to the Panic of 1837, a financial crisis that hit the working poor the hardest. This cartoon illustrates New York City during the seven-year depression: a frantic mob storms a bank, while in the foreground, a widow begs on the street with her child, surrounded by a banker or landlord and a barefoot sailor. At left, there is a drunken member of the Bowery Toughs gang and a down-on-his-luck militiaman. The cartoonist places the blame on Jackson, whose hat, glasses, and pipe overlook the scene. The white flag at left wryly states: "July 4, 1837, 61st Anniversary of Our Independence."

A ndrew Jackson was a unique personality and a transformational leader. He was the first president from a western state (Tennessee), the first to have been born in a log cabin, the first *not* to have come from a prominent colonial family, the last to have participated in the Revolutionary War, and the first to carry two bullets in his body from a duel and a barroom brawl. Most important, Jackson was the plain-spoken, polarizing emblem of a new democratic era.

Born poor, orphaned early, and largely self-educated, Jackson never discarded his backwoods personality and rural ways. He was short-tempered and thin-skinned, proud and insecure. If his prickly sense of manly honor were challenged or his authority questioned, he never hesitated to fight or get even. For Jackson, politics was personal and visceral, which helps explain why his actions and policies were at times contradictory.

Jackson believed in plain-speaking and plain pleasures. He smoked a corncob pipe and chewed—and spit—tobacco (he installed twenty spittoons in the White House). Tall and lean, Jackson was an intimidating figure with his penetrating blue eyes, long nose, jutting chin, silver-gray hair, and intense, iron-willed personality. "Old Hickory," however, was not in good health as he assumed the presidency. Scarred and bullet-ridden, he was plagued by blinding headaches and other ailments that led rival Henry Clay to describe him as "feeble in body and mind."

Despite his physical challenges, Jackson remained sharply focused and shrewdly sure of himself. More than previous presidents, he loved the

focus questions

1. What were Andrew Jackson's major beliefs regarding the common man, the presidency, and the proper role of government in the nation's economy?

2. What was Jackson's legacy regarding the status of Indians in American society?

3. How did Jackson respond to the nullification crisis?

4. What brought about the economic depression of the late 1830s and the emergence of the Whig party?

5. What were the strengths and weaknesses of Jackson's transformational presidency?

rough-and-tumble combat of the raucous new democratic political culture. "I was born for a storm," he once boasted. "A calm [life] does not suit me."

And Jackson took the nation by storm. No political figure was so widely loved or more deeply despised. As a self-made soldier, lawyer, planter, and politician, Jackson helped create and shape the Democratic party, and he helped introduce modern presidential campaigning to electoral politics. Jackson symbolized what he called the emergence of the "common man" in politics (by which he meant white men only), and he stamped his name and, more important, his ideas, personality, and values on an entire era of American history.

Jacksonian Democracy

Jackson's election marked the impact of thirty years of democratic innovations in politics. During the 1820s and 1830s, as America grew in population and people continued to move westward in ever larger numbers, most white men, whether they owned property or not, were allowed to vote and hold office. "The principle of universal suffrage," announced the U.S. Magazine and Democratic Review, "meant that white males of age constituted the political nation." Such a democratization of voting rights was unique in the world, for it gave previously excluded white men equal status as citizens regardless of wealth or background. No longer was politics the arena for only the most prominent and wealthiest Americans.

POLITICAL DEMOCRACY Campaigning was also democratized. Politics became the most popular form of mass entertainment, as people from all walks of life passionately engaged in elections and were remarkably well informed about public policy issues. Politics was "the only pleasure an American knows," observed visiting Frenchman Alexis de Tocqueville. "Even the women frequently attend public meetings and listen to political harangues as a recreation from their household labors."

Jackson was the most openly partisan and politically involved president in history to that point. Unlike previous presidents, who viewed political campaigning as unseemly, he actively sought votes among the people, lobbied congressmen, and formed "Hickory Clubs" across the nation to campaign for him. Jackson also benefited from a powerful Democratic party "machine" run by his trusted secretary of state (later his vice president), Martin Van Buren, a New York lawyer with a shrewd political sense.

Democracy, of course, is a slippery and elastic concept, and Jacksonians rarely defined what they meant by the "rule of the people." Noah Webster, the

Connecticut Federalist who produced the nation's first reliable dictionary, complained that "the men who have preached these doctrines [of democracy] have never defined what they mean by the *people*, or what they mean by *democracy*, nor how the *people* are to govern themselves." Jacksonian Democrats also showed little concern for the *undemocratic* constraints on African Americans, Native Americans, and women, all of whom were denied basic political and civil rights.

ANTI-DEMOCRATIC FORCES Many southern slaveholders worried that the surge of democratic activism would eventually threaten the slave system. Virginian Muscoe Garnett, a planter and attorney, declared that "democracy is indeed incompatible with slavery, and the whole system of Southern society." His fellow Virginian, George Fitzhugh, was more explicit in his disdain for democratic ideals. In every society, he asserted, "some were born with saddles on their backs, and others booted and spurred to ride them."

Still, in the face of such opposition, Jacksonian Democrats helped expand economic opportunity and political participation for workingmen (white factory laborers, craftsmen and mechanics, small farmers, and land-hungry frontiersmen). Andrew Jackson promised to protect "the poor and humble" from the "tyranny of wealth and power." His goal was to elevate the "laboring classes" of white men who "love liberty and desire nothing but equal rights and equal laws."

DEMOCRACY UNLEASHED The rowdy inauguration of President Jackson symbolized the democratization of political life. Dressed in a black mourning suit in honor of his recently deceased wife, the self-described people's president stepped out of the U.S. Capitol at noon on March 4, 1829. Waiting for him in the cold were 15,000 people who collectively roared and waved their hats when they saw Jackson emerge. "I never saw anything like it before," marveled Daniel Webster, the great senator from Massachusetts.

Once the wild cheering subsided, Jackson bowed before the crowd with great dignity, acknowledging their excitement and urging them to settle down. He then delivered a typically brief speech in which he promised that his administration would be committed to "the task of reform" in the federal government, taking jobs out of "unfaithful or incompetent hands" and balancing states' rights with the exercise of national power. He also pledged to pursue the will of the people in exercising his new presidential powers.

After being sworn in by Chief Justice John Marshall, President Jackson mounted his white horse and rode down a muddy Pennsylvania Avenue to the White House, where his cherished democracy lost control in a wild celebration. The huge crowd of jubilant western Democrats partying in the White House and outside on the lawn quickly turned into a drunken mob as they consumed alcohol-laced punch. Dishes, glasses, and furniture were smashed, and muddy-booted revelers broke windows, ripped down draperies, and trampled on rugs. A Washington lady marveled at the arrival of frontier democracy in the nation's capital: "What a scene we did witness! The majesty of the people had disappeared, and a rabble, a mob, of boys, negroes, women, children, scrambling, fighting, romping. What a pity, what a pity!"

Those already skeptical of Jackson's qualifications for office saw the boisterous inaugural party as a symbol of all that was wrong with the "democratic" movement. Supreme Court Justice Joseph Story said he had never seen such "a mixture" of rowdy people, from the "highest and most polished down to the most vulgar and gross in the nation." Here was Jacksonian democracy at work, he shuddered. "The reign of KING MOB seemed triumphant." Another guest reported that "no arrangements had been made" to handle such a large and misbehaving crowd at the White House. At one point, Jackson's aides became so concerned for the president's personal safety that they whisked him out a rear exit to a boardinghouse a few blocks away.

All Creation Going to the White House In this depiction of Andrew Jackson's inauguration party, satirist Robert Cruikshank draws a visual parallel to Noah's Ark, suggesting that people from all walks of life were now welcome in the White House.

JACKSON AS PRESIDENT

Jackson sought to increase the powers of the presidency at the expense of the legislative and judicial branches. One of his opponents noted that previous presidents had assumed that Congress was the primary branch of government. Jackson, however, believed that the presidency was "superior." The ruling political and economic elite must be removed, he said, for "the people" are the government, and too many government officials had grown corrupt and self-serving at the expense of the public interest.

To dislodge the "corrupt" eastern political elite, Jackson launched a policy he called "rotation in office," whereby he replaced many federal officials with his own supporters. Government jobs—district attorneys, federal marshals, customs collectors—belonged to the people, not to career bureaucrats. Democracy, he believed, was best served when the winning party's "newly elected officials" appointed new government officials. Such partisan behavior came to be called "the spoils system," since, as a prominent New York Democrat declared, "to the victor belong the spoils."

Jackson also sought to cut federal spending to help pay off the federal debt (a "national curse"); he supported internal improvements that were truly national in scope, promoted a "judicious tariff," and called for the relocation of the "ill-fated race" of Indians still living in the East to new lands across the Mississippi River so that they could be "protected" while their ancestral lands were confiscated, sold, and developed.

THE EATON AFFAIR Yet Jackson soon found himself preoccupied with squabbles within his own cabinet. From the outset, his administration was divided between supporters of Secretary of State Martin Van Buren and those allied with Vice President John C. Calhoun of South Carolina, both of whom wanted to succeed Jackson as president. Jackson turned mostly to Van Buren for advice because he did not trust Calhoun, a Yale graduate of towering intellect and fiery determination. Although earlier a nationalist, Calhoun now was focused on defending southern interests, especially the preservation of the slave-based cotton economy that had made him a wealthy planter.

In his rivalry with Calhoun, Van Buren took full advantage of a juicy social scandal known as the Peggy Eaton affair. Widower John Eaton, a former U.S. senator from Tennessee, was one of Jackson's closest friends. Eaton had also long been associated with Margaret "Peggy" O'Neale Timberlake, an outspoken Washington temptress married to John Timberlake, a naval officer frequently at sea.

The flirtatious Peggy Timberlake was devastatingly attractive to the men who kept her company while her husband was away. The ambitious daughter of an innkeeper, Peggy enjoyed "the attentions of men, young and old"; she took special delight in Senator John Eaton. In April 1828, John Timberlake died at sea. Although the official cause of death was respiratory failure, rumors swirled that he had committed suicide after learning of his wife's affair with Eaton.

Soon after the 1828 presidential election, John Eaton had written President-elect Jackson to alert him of the spiteful gossip aimed at himself and Peggy Timberlake. Jackson responded quickly and firmly: "Marry her and you will be in a position to defend her." Eaton did so on January 1, 1829.

Eaton's enemies quickly criticized the "unseemly haste" of the marriage and continued to savage Peggy Eaton as a whore. Louis McLane, a U.S. senator from Delaware who would later serve in Jackson's cabinet, gleefully sneered that Eaton, soon to be named Jackson's secretary of war, "has just married his mistress, and the mistress of eleven dozen others." Floride Calhoun, the vice president's imperious wife, especially objected to Peggy Eaton's unsavory past. At Jackson's inaugural ball, she openly ignored her, as did the other cabinet-members' wives.

The constant gossip led Jackson to explode, shouting that "I did not come here [to Washington] to make a Cabinet for the Ladies of this place, but for the Nation." In his view, women had no right to mix politics with social life; their doing so was nothing more than vicious meddling. He demanded loyalty from his administrative team—and their wives.

For his part, Calhoun acknowledged that his wife Floride had a "suspicious and fault-finding temper" that caused "much vexation in the family." Upon hearing about the spat in Washington, Louisa Adams, wife of the former president, John Quincy Adams, reported that war had been "declared between some of the ladies in the city, and ladies' wars are always fierce and hot."

Peggy Eaton's plight reminded Jackson of the mean-spirited gossip that had plagued his own wife, Rachel. Intensely loyal to John Eaton, the president defended Peggy, insisting that she was as pure "as a virgin." His cabinet members, however, were unable to cure their wives of what Martin Van Buren dubbed "the Eaton Malaria."

Nor did Peggy Eaton help her own cause. She once said that "I never had a lover who was not a gentleman." Her social enemies, she explained, were so "very jealous of me" because "none of them had beauty, accomplishments or graces in society of any kind." The rumoring and sniping continued, month after month, and became a time-consuming distraction for the president.

Jackson blamed the Eaton scandal, also known as the "Petticoat Affair," on his rivals Henry Clay and John C. Calhoun, the latter whom he called a "villain." The president assumed that Calhoun and his wife had targeted John Eaton because he did not support Calhoun's desire to be the next president. One of Calhoun's friends wrote in April 1829 that the United States was "governed by the President—the President by the Secretary of War—and the latter by his Wife." Jackson concluded that the scheming Calhoun was one of the "most dangerous men living—a man, devoid of principle" who "would sacrifice his friend, his country, and forsake his god, for selfish personal ambition."

THE MAYSVILLE ROAD VETO When Jackson was not dealing with the "Petticoat Affair," he decisively used his executive authority to limit the role of the federal government—while at the same time delivering additional blows to rivals John C. Calhoun and Henry Clay.

In 1830, Congress passed a bill pushed by Calhoun and Clay that authorized the use of federal monies to build a sixty-mile-long road across the state of Kentucky from the city of Maysville to Lexington, Clay's hometown. President

King Andrew the First Opponents considered Jackson's veto of the Maysville Road Bill an abuse of power. This cartoon shows "King Andrew" trampling on the Constitution, internal improvements, and the Bank of the United States.

Jackson vetoed the bill on the grounds that the proposed road was a "purely local matter," being solely in the state of Kentucky, and thus outside the domain of Congress because it was not an interstate project. Clay was stunned. "We are all shocked and mortified by the rejection of the Maysville road," he wrote a friend. But he had no luck convincing Congress to override the presidential veto.

THE EASTERN INDIANS

President Jackson's forcible removal of Indians from their ancestral lands was his highest priority and one of his lowest moments. Like most white frontiersmen, he saw Indians as barbarians who were to be treated as "subjects," not "nations." His National Republican opponent, Henry Clay, felt the same way, arguing that the Indians were "destined to extinction" and not "worth preserving."

After Jackson's election in 1828, he followed up on policies developed by previous presidents by urging that the Eastern Indians (east of the Mississippi River) be moved to reservations west of the Mississippi River, in what became Oklahoma. Jackson believed that moving the Indians would serve their best interests as well as the national interest, for the states in the Lower South, especially the Carolinas, Georgia, and Alabama, were aggressively restricting the rights of Indian nations and taking their land. President Jackson often told Indian leaders that he was their "Great Father" trying to protect them from the greedy state governments.

New state laws in Alabama, Georgia, and Mississippi abolished tribal units, stripped them of their civil rights, rejected ancestral Indian land claims, and denied Indians the right to vote or to testify in court. Jackson claimed that relocating the Eastern Indians was a "wise and humane policy" that would save them from "utter annihilation" if tribes tried to hold on to their lands in the face of state actions.

INDIAN REMOVAL   In 1830, Jackson submitted to Congress the **Indian Removal Act**, which authorized him to ignore treaty commitments made by previous presidents and to convince the Indians remaining in the East and South to move to federal lands west of the Mississippi River. The federal government, the new program promised, would pay for the Indian exodus and give them initial support in their new lands in Oklahoma.

Jackson's proposal provoked heated opposition, not only among the Indian peoples but also among reformers who distrusted the president's motives and doubted the promised support from the federal government. Critics flooded Congress with petitions that criticized the removal policy and warned that Jackson's plan would bring "enduring shame" on the nation. Indian leaders were skeptical from the start. As a federal agent reported, "They see that our professions are insincere, that our promises are broken, that the happiness of the Indian is a cheap sacrifice to the acquisition of new lands."

The proposal also sparked intense debate in Congress. Theodore Frelinghuysen, a New Jersey National Republican, gave a six-hour speech in the Senate during which he asked, "Do the obligations of justice change with the color of the skin? Is it one of the prerogatives of the white man, that he may disregard the dictates of moral principles, when an Indian shall be concerned?"

In the end, Congress answered yes. The House of Representatives and Senate both narrowly approved the Indian Removal Bill, with most southerners voting for it and northerners against it. Jackson eagerly signed the measure, and it became law on May 26, 1830. Federal agents thereafter bribed and bullied tribal chiefs to get their consent to relocate to the West. "Our doom is

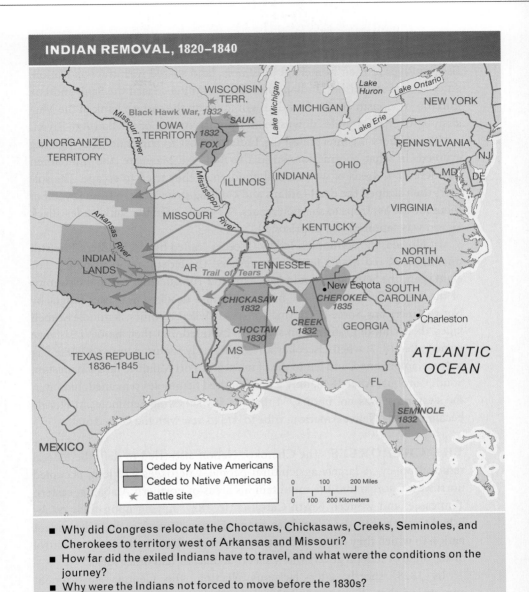

INDIAN REMOVAL, 1820–1840

- Why did Congress relocate the Choctaws, Chickasaws, Creeks, Seminoles, and Cherokees to territory west of Arkansas and Missouri?
- How far did the exiled Indians have to travel, and what were the conditions on the journey?
- Why were the Indians not forced to move before the 1830s?

sealed," lamented a Choctaw warrior. "There is no other course for us but to turn our faces to our new homes toward the setting sun."

RESISTANCE Most northern Indians gave in to federal threats and were relocated. In Illinois and the Wisconsin Territory, however, Sauk and Fox Indians fought to regain their ancestral lands. The Black Hawk War erupted in April 1832, when Chief Black Hawk led 1,000 Sauks—men, women, and children who had been relocated to the Iowa Territory—back across the Mississippi River to their homeland in Illinois, land shared with the Fox Nation. After several skirmishes, Indiana and Illinois militia chased the Sauk and Fox into the Wisconsin Territory and caught them on the eastern bank of the Mississippi River, a few miles downstream from the mouth of the Bad Axe River.

The soldiers misinterpreted the Indians' effort to surrender, and fighting erupted. In what became known as the Bad Axe Massacre, the militiamen murdered hundreds of women and children as they tried to escape. The soldiers then scalped the dead Indians and cut long strips of flesh from several of them for use as strops to sharpen razors. Six weeks later, the Sauk leader, Black Hawk, was captured and imprisoned.

In Florida, the Seminoles, led by Osceola (called by U.S. soldiers "the still unconquered red man") ferociously resisted the federal removal policy. For eight years, the Seminoles would fight a hit-and-run guerrilla war in the swamps of the Everglades—the longest, most costly, and deadliest war ever fought by Native Americans. Some 1,500 Americans were killed. At times, Seminole women killed their children rather than see them captured. But their heroic resistance waned after 1837, when Osceola was treacherously captured under a white flag of truce, imprisoned, and left to die of malaria at Fort Moultrie near Charleston, South Carolina. After 1842, only a few hundred Seminoles remained, hiding in the swamps. It was not until 1934 that the few surviving Seminoles in Florida became the last Native American tribe to end its war with the United States.

THE CHEROKEES The Cherokee Nation also tried to defy the federal removal policy. A largely agricultural people, Cherokees had long occupied northwest Georgia and the mountainous areas of northern Alabama, eastern Tennessee, and western North Carolina. In 1827, relying upon their established treaty rights, the Cherokees adopted a constitution as an independent nation in which they declared that they were not subject to the laws or control of any state or federal government. Georgia officials had other ideas.

In 1828, shortly after Jackson's election, the Georgia government announced that after June 1, 1830, the authority of state law would extend to the Cherokees. They would no longer be a "nation within a nation." The "barbarous and savage tribes" must give way to the march of white civilization. Under the new state laws, they would not be allowed to vote, own property, or testify against whites in court.

The discovery of gold in north Georgia in 1829 had increased whites' lust for Cherokee land, attracted trespassing prospectors, and led to the new state law. It prohibited the Cherokees from digging for gold on their own lands. The Cherokees sought relief in the Supreme Court, arguing that "we wish to remain on the land of our fathers. We have a perfect and original right to remain without interruption or molestation."

In *Cherokee Nation v. Georgia* (1831), Chief Justice John Marshall ruled that the Cherokees had "an unquestionable right" to maintain control of their ancestral lands, but the Court could not render a verdict because of a technicality: the Cherokees had filed suit as a "foreign nation" when in Marshall's view they were "domestic dependent nations." If it were true that "wrongs have been inflicted," Marshall explained, "this is not the tribunal which can redress the past or prevent the future."

The following year, the Supreme Court *did* rule in favor of the Cherokees in *Worcester v. Georgia* (1832). The case arose when Georgia officials arrested a group of white Christian missionaries who were living among the Cherokees in violation of a state law forbidding such interaction. Two of the missionaries, Samuel Worcester and Elihu Butler, were sentenced to four years at hard labor. They appealed to the Supreme Court.

In the *Worcester* case, John Marshall said the missionaries must be released. The anti-Cherokee laws passed by the Georgia legislature, he declared, had violated "the Constitution, laws, and treaties of the United States." He added that the Cherokee Nation was "a distinct political community" within which Georgia law had no force.

Both Supreme Court decisions favored the Cherokee argument that their ancestral lands could not be taken from them, in part because they had earlier signed treaties with the state and federal governments confirming their rights to those lands. President Jackson, however, refused to enforce the Court's "wicked" decisions, claiming that he had no constitutional authority

Cherokees divided While many Cherokee elite fought against Jackson's policies, Elias Boudinot, editor of the first Native American newspaper, *Cherokee Phoenix*, signed the Indian Removal Treaty in 1835. He was subsequently murdered.

to intervene in Georgia. A New York newspaper editor reported that Jackson said, "John Marshall has made his decision, now let him enforce it."

Thereafter, Jackson gave the Cherokees and other Indian nations a terrible choice: either abide by the discriminatory new state laws or relocate to government-owned lands west of the Mississippi River, which would be theirs "forever." Jackson told the Creeks that they and whites could not live "in harmony and peace" if they remained on their ancestral lands and told them that "a speedy removal" to the West was their only option. Soon, Georgia officials began selling Cherokee lands.

The irony of the new Georgia policy was that of all the southern tribes, the Cherokees had come closest to adopting the customs of white America. They had abandoned traditional hunting practices to develop farms, build roads, schools, and churches, and create trading posts and newspapers. Many Cherokees had married whites, adopted their clothing and food, and converted to Christianity. And the Cherokees owned some 2,000 enslaved African Americans.

THE TRAIL OF TEARS The federal officials responsible for implementing the Indian Removal Act developed a strategy of divide and conquer with the Cherokees. In 1835, for example, a minority faction of the Cherokees

Trail of Tears Thousands of Cherokees died on a nightmarish march from Georgia to Oklahoma after being forced from their native lands.

signed the fraudulent Treaty of New Echota, which was rejected by 90 percent of the Cherokee people but readily accepted by the U.S. Senate and enforced by the U.S. Army.

In 1838, after President Jackson had left office and Martin Van Buren was president, 17,000 Cherokees were evicted and moved West under military guard on the **Trail of Tears**, an 800-mile forced journey marked by the cruelty of soldiers and the neglect of irresponsible private contractors assigned to manage the process. Some 4,000 of the refugees died along the way. Van Buren's favorite niece was so upset by the treatment of the Indians that she opposed her uncle's reelection. For his part, President Van Buren told Congress in December 1838 that he took "sincere pleasure" in reporting that the entire Cherokee Nation had been relocated.

The Trail of Tears was, according to a white Georgian, "the cruelest work I ever knew." A few Cherokees held out in the mountains of North Carolina; they became known as the "Eastern Band" of Cherokees. The Creeks and Chickasaws followed the Trail of Tears a few years later, after Alabama and Mississippi used the same techniques as the Georgia government to take control of their tribal lands.

Some 100,000 Eastern Indians were relocated to the West during the 1820s and 1830s, and the government sold some 100 million acres of Indian land, most of it in the prime cotton-growing areas of Georgia, Alabama, and Mississippi, known as the Old Southwest.

The Bank War

Jackson showed the same principled stubbornness in dealing with the national bank as he did in removing the Indians. The First Bank of the United States (B.U.S.) had been renewed in 1816 as the **Second Bank of the United States**, which soon became the largest corporation in the nation and the only truly national business enterprise.

The second B.U.S. (the federal government owned only 20 percent of the bank's capital) was a private corporation with extensive public responsibilities—and powers. To benefit the government, the B.U.S. held all federal funds, including tax collections (mostly from land sales and tariff revenues) and disbursed federal payments for its obligations, all in exchange for an annual $1.5 million fee. The B.U.S., however, conducted other business throughout the country like a commercial bank, and was free to use the government deposits in its vaults as collateral for loans it made to businesses around the country. Headquartered in Philadelphia and supported by twenty-nine branches around the nation, the B.U.S. competed with state-chartered banks for local business.

The B.U.S. helped accelerate business expansion by making loans to individuals, businesses, and state banks. It also helped promote a stable money supply and deter excessive lending by requiring the 464 state banks to keep enough gold and silver coins (called specie) in their vaults to back their own paper currency, which they in turn loaned to individuals and businesses. Prior to the B.U.S. being reestablished, the number of unstable and unregulated state banks had increased dramatically. Most of them issued their own paper money, and half of those created between 1810 and 1820 had gone bankrupt by 1825. The primary benefit of the B.U.S. was its ability to monitor and regulate many of the state banks.

With federal revenues soaring from land sales during the early 1830s, the B.U.S., led by the brilliant but arrogant Nicholas Biddle, had accumulated massive amounts of money—and economic power. Even though the B.U.S. benefited the national economy, state banks, especially in the South

Rechartering the Bank Jackson's effort to defeat the recharter of the B.U.S. is likened to fighting a hydra, a many-headed serpent from Greek mythology. Just as the hydra would sprout two heads when one was severed, for each B.U.S. supporter that Jackson subdued, even more supporters would emerge to take his place.

and West, feared its growing "monopolistic" power. Critics claimed that Biddle and the B.U.S. directors, most of whom lived in the Northeast, were so focused on their own profits that they were restricting lending by state banks and impeding businesses from borrowing as much as they wanted.

Andrew Jackson had always hated banks and bankers, whom he called "vipers and thieves." His prejudice grew out of his own experiences with banks in the 1790s, when he had suffered huge financial losses. Now, as a popularly elected president, he claimed to speak for ordinary Americans who felt that banks favored the "rich and powerful" in the East. Jackson also distrusted banks because they printed too much paper money, causing prices to rise (inflation). He wanted only gold and silver coins to be used for economic transactions. "I think it right to be perfectly frank with you," Jackson told Biddle in 1829. "I do not dislike your Bank any more than [I dislike] all banks." But Jackson also disliked Biddle because he was everything that Jackson was not: an Easterner born to wealth, highly educated, financially sophisticated, and a world traveler. Ironically, Biddle had voted for Jackson.

The national bank may have become too powerful, as Jackson charged, but the **Bank War** between Jackson and Biddle revealed that the president never truly understood the national bank's role or policies, and he continued to let personal animosity drive many of his policy decisions. The B.U.S. had provided a stable monetary system for the expanding economy, as well as a mechanism for controlling the pace and integrity of economic growth by regulating the ability of branch banks and state banks to issue paper currency.

THE RECHARTER EFFORT Although the charter for the B.U.S. ran through 1836, Nicholas Biddle could not afford to wait until then for its renewal. Leaders of the National Republican party, especially Senators Henry Clay and Daniel Webster (who was a paid legal counsel to the B.U.S.), told Biddle that the charter needed to be renewed before the 1836 presidential election. They assured him that Congress would renew the charter, leading the impolitic Biddle to grow overconfident about the bank's future. Jackson, he said, "thinks because he has scalped Indians . . . he is to have his way with the Bank."

Biddle and his political allies, however, failed to appreciate Jackson's tenacity and the depth of his hatred for the B.U.S. And most voters were on Jackson's side. In the end, Biddle, Clay, and the National Republicans unintentionally handed Jackson a popular issue on the eve of the election. At their nominating convention in December 1831, the National Republicans endorsed Clay as their presidential candidate and approved the renewal of the B.U.S.

Early in the summer of 1832, both houses of Congress passed the bank recharter bill, in part because Biddle provided bribes to win votes. Upon learning of such shenanigans, Jackson's chief of staff concluded that the B.U.S. was "becoming desperate: *caught in its own net.*"

Biddle, Webster, and Clay assumed that Jackson would not veto the recharter bill because doing so might cost him reelection. "Should Jackson veto the bill," Clay boasted, "I will veto him." On July 10, 1832, however, Jackson nixed the bill, sending it back to Congress with a blistering criticism of the bank's directors for making the "rich richer and the potent more powerful" while discriminating against "the humble members of society—the farmers, mechanics, and laborers."

Daniel Webster accused Jackson of using the bank issue "to stir up the poor against the rich." To Henry Clay, Jackson's veto represented another example of the president's desire to concentrate "all power in the hands of one man." Clay and Webster, however, could not convince the Senate to override the veto, thus setting the stage for a nationwide financial debate and a dramatic presidential campaign.

The overriding issue in the election was the future of the Bank of the United States. Let the people decide, Jackson argued. "I have now done my duty to the citizens of this country," he said in explaining his veto. "If sustained by my fellow-citizens [in the upcoming election], I shall be grateful and happy; if not, I shall find in the motives which impel me ample grounds for contentment and peace."

NULLIFICATION

Andrew Jackson eventually would veto twelve congressional bills, more than all previous presidents combined. Critics claimed that his behavior was "monarchical" in its frequent defiance of the will of Congress. Jackson, however, believed that the president represented *all* of the people, unlike congressmen who were elected locally. His commitment to nationalism over sectionalism was nowhere more evident than in his handling of the nullification crisis in South Carolina. In that volatile situation he would greatly expand the scope of presidential authority by forcing the nullifiers to back down.

CALHOUN AND THE TARIFF Vice President John C. Calhoun became President Jackson's fiercest critic because of changing economic conditions in his home state of South Carolina. The financial panic of 1819 had sparked a nationwide depression. Through the 1820s, South Carolina continued to suffer from a collapse in cotton prices. The state lost almost

70,000 people during that ten-year period—the result of residents moving West in search of cheaper and more-fertile land for growing cotton. Twice as many would leave during the 1830s.

Most South Carolinians blamed their woes on the Tariff of 1828, which was labeled the **Tariff of Abominations**. By taxing British cloth coming into U.S. markets, the tariff hurt southern cotton growers by reducing British demand for raw cotton from America. It also hurt southerners by raising the prices they had to pay for imported products. The tariff debate revealed how the North and South had developed different economic interests

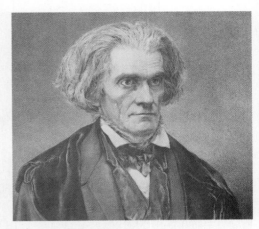

John C. Calhoun During the Civil War, the Confederate government printed, but never issued, a one-cent postage stamp bearing this likeness of Calhoun.

and different ways of protecting those interests. Massachusetts was prospering while South Carolina was struggling.

In a lengthy pamphlet called the *South Carolina Exposition and Protest* (1828), Calhoun claimed that the Tariff of 1828 favored the interests of New England textile manufacturing over southern agriculture. Under such circumstances, he argued, a state could "nullify," or veto, a federal law it deemed unconstitutional.

Nullification was the ultimate weapon for those determined to protect states' rights against federal authority. As President Jackson and others pointed out, however, allowing states to pick and choose which federal laws they would follow would create national chaos, which he would not allow.

CLASH OF TITANS—WEBSTER VERSUS HAYNE The controversy over the Tariff of 1828 simmered until 1830, when the Webster–Hayne debate in Congress sharpened the lines between states' rights and national authority. In a fiery speech, Senator Robert Y. Hayne of South Carolina argued that the anti-slavery Yankees were invading the South, "making war upon her citizens, and endeavoring to overthrow her principles and institutions." In Hayne's view, the Union was created by the states, and the states therefore had the right to nullify federal laws. The independence of the states was to him more important than the preservation of the Union.

Massachusetts senator Daniel Webster quickly challenged Hayne's arguments. Blessed with a thunderous voice and a theatrical flair, Webster was an

Webster Replying to Senator Hayne (1848) The eloquent Massachusetts senator challenges the argument for nullification in the Webster–Hayne debate.

unapologetic Unionist determined "to strengthen the ties that hold us together." He pointed out that the U.S. Constitution was created not by the states but by the American people. If states were allowed to nullify a federal law, the Union would be nothing but a "rope of sand." South Carolina's defiance of federal authority, he charged, "is nothing more than resistance by *force*—it is disunion by *force*—it is secession by *force*—it is civil war."

Webster's powerful closing statement—"Liberty and Union, now and forever, one and inseparable"—was printed in virtually every newspaper in the nation. Abraham Lincoln later called it "the very best speech ever delivered." Even Hayne was awestruck. He told Webster that "a man who can make such speeches as that ought never to die."

In the end, Webster rather than Hayne had the better argument. President Jackson did not attend the debate, but he kept abreast of it from the White House. When he asked an aide how Webster was doing, the answer was what he wanted: "He is delivering a most powerful speech . . . demolishing our friend Hayne." The president was pleased. As Jackson said, the Constitution and its laws remained "supreme."

CALHOUN VERSUS JACKSON That Jackson, like Calhoun, was a cotton-planting slaveholder led many southerners to assume that the president would support their resistance to the federal tariff. Jackson was sympathetic—

until Calhoun and others in South Carolina threatened to "nullify" federal laws they did not like. He then turned on them with the same angry force he had directed toward the advancing British army at New Orleans in 1815.

On April 13, 1830, the Democratic party hosted scores of congressmen and political leaders at the first annual Jefferson Day dinner. When it was Jackson's turn to salute Jefferson's memory, he rose to his feet, raised his glass, and, while glaring at Calhoun, growled: "Our Union—It must be preserved!"

People gasped, knowing that the vice president, as if challenged to a duel, must reply to Jackson's threat to the southern weapon of nullification. Calhoun stood and, trembling with emotion, countered with a defiant toast to "the Union, next to our liberty the most dear!" In that dramatic exchange, Jackson and Calhoun laid bare the fundamental tension between federal authority and states' rights that has remained one of the animating themes of the American republic.

Soon thereafter, another incident deepened the hatred between the two men. On May 12, 1830, the president saw for the first time a letter from 1818 in which Calhoun, then secretary of war in the Monroe administration, had wanted to discipline General Jackson for his unauthorized invasion of Spanish-held Florida. After exchanging heated letters about the incident with Calhoun, Jackson told a friend that he was finally through with the "double dealing of J.C.C."

The rift between the two proud men prompted Jackson to take a dramatic step suggested by Secretary of State Martin Van Buren, his closest and most cunning adviser. During one of their daily horseback rides together, Van Buren offered himself up as a sacrifice as a way to remove all Calhoun supporters from the cabinet and thereby end the ongoing Eaton affair that had fractured the administration.

As the first step in the planned cabinet coup, Van Buren convinced John Eaton to resign as secretary of war on April 4, 1831. Four days later, Van Buren resigned as secretary of state. "The long agony is over," crowed Samuel Ingham, the secretary of the Treasury, in a letter to Attorney General John Berrien. "Mr. V. B. and Major Eaton have resigned." What Ingham and Berrien did not realize was that a few days later, Jackson would force them—both Calhoun supporters—to resign as well. Jackson now had a clean slate on which to create another cabinet.

Never before had a president dismissed his entire cabinet. Critics saw through the secretary of state's scheme: "Mr. Van Buren may be called the 'Great Magician,'" wrote the *New York Courier*, "for he *raises his wand, and the whole Cabinet disappears*." Others claimed that the cabinet purge showed that Jackson did not have the political skill to lead the nation. One newspaper

The Rats Leaving a Falling House
During his first term, Jackson was beset by dissension within his administration. Here, "public confidence in the stability of this administration" is toppling.

announced that the ship of state "is sinking and the rats are flying! The hull is too leaky to mend, and the hero of two wars and a half has not the skill to keep it afloat." John Quincy Adams told his son that the stunning cabinet purge had put all of Washington in a state of confusion: "people stare—and laugh—and say, what next?"

The next act in the running political drama occurred when John Eaton challenged Ingham to a duel. The ousted Treasury secretary chose instead to retreat to his home in Pennsylvania. After the Eatons left Washington, D.C., a gloating Henry Clay retrieved William Shakespeare's characterization of Egyptian queen Cleopatra to mark Peggy's departure: "Age cannot wither nor time stale her infinite virginity."

NEW CABINETS By the end of August 1831, Jackson had appointed a new cabinet, all of whom agreed to treat Peggy Eaton with respect. At the same time, Jackson increasingly relied upon the advice of Martin Van Buren and others making up the president's so-called "kitchen cabinet," an informal group of close friends and supporters, many of them Democratic newspaper editors.

The kitchen cabinet soon convinced Jackson to drop his pledge to serve only one term. They explained that it would be hard for Van Buren, the president's chosen successor, to win the 1832 Democratic nomination because Calhoun would do everything in his power to stop him—and Calhoun might win the nomination himself. In early 1831, the *Washington Globe*, a Democratic newspaper, announced that Jackson would seek a second term. "The conquering Hero is again in the field, and it must now be seen who are his friends and who are his foes."

THE ANTI-MASONIC PARTY In 1832, for the first time in a presidential election, a third political party entered the field. The Anti-Masonic party grew out of popular hostility toward the Masonic fraternal order, a large, all-male social organization that originated in Great Britain early in the eighteenth century. The Masons often claimed to be the natural leaders of their communities, the "best men." By 1830, more than 2,000 Masonic "lodges" were scattered across the United States with about 100,000 members, including Andrew Jackson and Henry Clay.

The new anti-Masonic party owed its origins to a defrocked Mason, William Morgan, a fifty-two-year-old unemployed bricklayer in Batavia, New York. Morgan had been thrown out of the Masons because of his joblessness. Seeking revenge, he convinced a local printer to publish a widely circulated pamphlet revealing the secret rituals of the Masonic order. Masons then tried to burn down the print shop where the pamphlet had been published. They also had Morgan arrested on a trumped-up charge of indebtedness.

Soon thereafter, on September 12, 1826, someone paid for his release from jail and spirited Morgan away in a waiting carriage. A year later, a man's decomposed body was found in Oak Orchard Creek, near Lake Ontario. Morgan's grieving wife confirmed that it was her husband. Governor Dewitt Clinton, himself a Mason, offered a reward for anyone who would identify the kidnappers.

The Morgan mystery became a major political issue. New York launched more than twenty investigations into Morgan's disappearance (and presumed murder) and conducted a dozen trials of several Masons but never gained a conviction. Each legal effort aroused more public indignation because most of the judges, lawyers, and jurors were Masons.

People began to fear that the Masons had become a self-appointed aristocracy lacking the education and character necessary for self-denying civic leadership. John Quincy Adams said that disbanding the "Masonic institution" was the most important issue facing "us and our posterity."

Suspicions of the Masonic order as a tyrannical secret brotherhood intent on subverting democracy gave rise to the grassroots political movement known as the Anti-Masonic party whose purpose was to protect republican values from being corrupted by self-serving, power-hungry Masonic insiders. The Anti-Masons claimed that they were determined to "hand down to posterity unimpaired the republic we inherited from our forefathers."

The new party drew most of its support from New Englanders and New Yorkers alienated by both the Democratic and National Republican parties. Anti-Masonic adherents tended to be rural evangelical Protestants, many of whom also opposed slavery.

Opposition to a fraternal organization was hardly the foundation upon which to build a lasting political coalition, but the Anti-Masonic party had three important "firsts" to its credit: in addition to being the first third party

The Verdict of the People George Caleb Bingham's painting depicts a socially diverse electorate, suggesting the increasingly democratic politics of the Jacksonian Era.

with a national base of support, it was the first political party to hold a national convention to nominate a presidential candidate, and the first to announce a formal platform of specific policy goals.

THE 1832 ELECTION In preparing for the 1832 election, the Democrats and the National Republicans followed the example of the Anti-Masonic party by holding presidential nominating conventions of their own for the first time. In December 1831, the National Republicans gathered to nominate Henry Clay.

Jackson endorsed the idea of a nominating convention for the Democratic party as well, because it gave the people a greater role in choosing nominees. The Democratic convention first adopted the two-thirds rule for nomination (which prevailed until 1936, when the requirement became a simple majority), and then named New Yorker Martin Van Buren as Jackson's vice presidential running mate. The Democrats, unlike the other two parties, adopted no formal platform and relied to a substantial degree upon the popularity of the president to carry their cause.

Nicholas Biddle invested the vast resources of the B.U.S. into the campaign against Jackson and paid for thousands of pamphlets promoting Clay. By the summer of 1832, Clay declared that "the campaign is over, and I think we have won the victory." He spoke too soon. His blinding ego prevented him from seeing the sources of Jackson's popularity. Where he dismissed Jackson as a power-hungry military chief, most Americans saw the president as someone fighting for their own causes.

Clay also failed to understand Jackson's effectiveness as a new type of engaged political candidate. The *National Intelligencer*, a newspaper that supported Clay, acknowledged that Jackson's eager participation in campaign events was "certainly a new mode of electioneering. We do not recollect before to have heard of a President of the United States descending in person into the political arena." Jackson gave stump speeches, dived into crowds to shake hands, and walked in parades or ate barbecue with loving supporters who cheered and mobbed him.

In the end, Jackson earned 219 electoral votes to Clay's 49, and enjoyed a solid victory in the popular vote: 688,000 to 530,000. William Wirt, the Anti-Masonic candidate, carried only Vermont, winning 7 electoral votes. Dazzled by the president's strong showing, Wirt observed that Jackson could "be President for life if he chooses."

THE NULLIFICATION CRISIS

In the fall of 1831, Jackson tried to defuse the confrontation with South Carolina by calling on Congress to reduce tariff rates. Congress responded with the Tariff of 1832, which lowered rates on some products but kept them high on British cotton fabric and clothing.

The new tariff disappointed Calhoun and others in his home state eager for the British to buy more southern cotton. South Carolinians seethed with resentment toward the federal government. Living in the only state where enslaved Africans were a majority of the population, they feared that if the northern representatives in Congress were powerful enough to create such high tariffs that proved so harmful to the South, they might eventually vote to end slavery itself. Calhoun declared that the "peculiar domestic institutions of the southern states" (by which he meant slavery) were at stake.

SOUTH CAROLINA NULLIFIERS In November 1832, just weeks after Jackson was reelected, a special convention in South Carolina passed an Ordinance of Nullification that disavowed the "unconstitutional" federal Tariffs of 1828 and 1832 (declaring them "null, void, and no law"). If federal authorities tried to use force to collect the tariffs on foreign goods unloaded in Charleston Harbor, South Carolina would secede from the Union, they vowed. The state legislature then selected Senator Robert Hayne as governor and named Calhoun to replace him as U.S. senator. At the end of December,

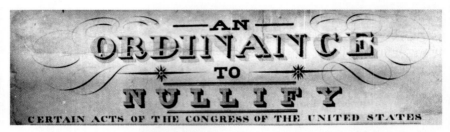

South Carolina Ordinance of Nullification The 1832 ordinance repudiated two federal tariffs designed to protect northern industries. Though armed conflict was avoided, the same tensions that led to nullification would later lead to South Carolina's secession.

Calhoun resigned as vice president so that he could openly defend his nullification theory in Congress and oppose President Jackson's "tyrannical" actions.

JACKSON SAYS NO TO NULLIFICATION President Jackson's public response was moderate. He promised to use "firmness and forbearance" with South Carolina but stressed that nullification "means insurrection and war; and the other states have a right to put it down."

In private, however, Jackson was furious. He asked the secretary of war how many soldiers it would take to go to South Carolina and "crush the monster [nullification] in its cradle." He also threatened to hang Calhoun and other "nullifiers" if there were any bloodshed. "Surely the president is exaggerating," Governor Hayne of South Carolina remarked to Senator Thomas Hart Benton of Missouri. Benton, who years before had been in a fistfight with Jackson, replied: "I have known General Jackson a great many years, and when he speaks of hanging, it is time to look for a rope."

During the fall of 1832, most northern state legislatures passed resolutions condemning the nullificationists. At the same time, the slaveholder-dominated southern states expressed sympathy for South Carolina, but none endorsed nullification. "We detest the tariff," explained a Mississippian, "but we will hold to the Union." South Carolina was left standing alone against Jackson.

On December 10, 1832, the unyielding Jackson issued his official response to the people of South Carolina. In his blistering proclamation, he dismissed nullification as "an absurdity," a "mad project of disunion" that was "*incompatible with the existence of the Union, contradicted expressly by the letter of the Constitution, unauthorized by its spirit, inconsistent with every principle on which It was founded, and destructive of the great object for which it was formed.*" He warned that nullification would lead to secession (formal withdrawal of a state from the United States), and secession meant civil war. "Be not deceived by names. Disunion by armed force is TREASON. Are you really ready to incur its guilt?"

CLAY STEPS IN President Jackson then sent federal soldiers and a warship to Charleston to protect the federal customhouse where tariffs were applied to imported products arriving on ships from Europe. Governor Hayne responded by mobilizing the state militia, and the two sides edged toward a violent confrontation. A South Carolina Unionist reported to Jackson from Charleston that many "reckless and dangerous men" were "looking for civil war and scenes of bloodshed." While taking forceful actions, Jackson still wanted "peaceably to nullify the nullifiers."

In early 1833, the president requested from Congress the authority to use the U.S. Army to "force" compliance with federal law in South Carolina. Calhoun exploded on the Senate floor, exclaiming that he and the others defending his state's constitutional rights were being threatened by what they called the **Force Bill** "to have our throats cut, and those of our wives and children." The greatest threat facing the nation, he argued, was not nullification but presidential despotism.

Calhoun and the nullifiers, however, soon backed down, and the South Carolina legislature postponed the implementation of the nullification ordinances in hopes that Congress would pass a more palatable tariff bill.

Passage of a compromise bill, however, depended upon the support of Senator Henry Clay, himself a slaveholding planter, who finally yielded to those urging him to step in and save the day for the Union. A fellow senator told Clay that these "South Carolinians are good fellows, and it would be a pity to see Jackson hang them."

Clay agreed. On February 12, 1833, he circulated a plan suggested by Jackson to reduce, gradually over several years, the federal tariff on key imported items. Clay urged Congress to treat South Carolina with respect and display "that great principle of compromise and concession which lies at the bottom of our institutions." The tariff reductions were less than South Carolina preferred, but Clay's compromise helped the nullifiers out of the dilemma they had created. Calhoun supported the compromise: "He who loves the Union must desire to see this agitating question [the tariff] brought to a termination."

On March 1, 1833, Jackson signed into law the compromise tariff and the Force Bill, the latter being a symbolic statement of the primacy of the Union. Calhoun rushed home to convince the rebels in his state to back down. The South Carolina convention then met and rescinded its nullification of the tariff acts. In a face-saving gesture, the delegates nullified the Force Bill, which Jackson no longer needed.

Both sides felt they had won. Jackson had defended the supremacy of the Union without firing a shot, and South Carolina's persistence had brought tariff reductions. Joel Poinsett, a South Carolina Unionist, was overjoyed with the resolution. "We have beat the Nullifiers and things are quiet for a time." Poinsett, however, added that the next crisis would force a choice between "union and disunion."

While the immediate crisis was defused, however, its underlying causes persisted. Southern slaveholders felt increasingly threatened by anti-slavery sentiment in the North. "There is no liberty—no security for the South," groused South Carolina radical Robert Barnwell Rhett. Others agreed. "The struggle, so far from being over," a defiant Calhoun wrote, "is not more than fairly commenced." Jackson concluded that the "tariff was only the pretext [for the nullification crisis], and disunion and southern confederacy the real object. The next pretext will be the negro, or slavery question." Two days after the nullification crisis was resolved, Jackson was sworn in for a second term as president. The triumphant Jackson, observed John Quincy Adams, "conquers every thing."

War over the B.U.S.

Jackson interpreted his lopsided reelection as a "decision of the people against the bank." Having vetoed the charter renewal of the B.U.S., Jackson ordered the Treasury Department to transfer federal monies from the national bank to twenty-three mostly western state banks—called "pet banks" by Jackson's critics because many were run by the president's friends and allies. When the Treasury secretary balked, Jackson fired him.

BIDDLE'S RESPONSE B.U.S. head Nicholas Biddle responded by ordering the bank to quit making loans and demanded that state banks exchange their paper currency for gold or silver coins as quickly as possible. Through such deflationary policies, the desperate Biddle was trying to bring the economy to a halt, create a depression, and thus reveal the importance of maintaining the national bank. An enraged Jackson said the B.U.S. under Biddle was "trying to kill me, *but I will kill it!*"

Biddle's plan to create a national financial crisis worked. Northern Democrats worried that the president's "lawless and reckless" Bank War would ruin the party. But Jackson refused to flinch. When state bankers visited the White House to plead for relief, Jackson told them to go see Nicholas Biddle. "We have no money here, gentlemen. Biddle has all the money."

In the Senate, Calhoun and Clay led the fight against Jackson. They argued that Jackson's transfer of government cash from the B.U.S. to the pet banks was illegal. On March 28, 1834, Clay convinced a majority in the Senate to *censure*

Jackson for his actions, the only time a U.S. president has been reprimanded in this way as opposed to actual impeachment. Jackson was so angry about being censured that he wanted to challenge Clay to a duel so that he could "bring the rascal to a dear account."

THE NEW WHIG PARTY The president's war on the bank led his opponents to create a new political party whose diverse members were unified by their hatred of Jackson. His critics claimed that he was ruling like a monarch; they dubbed him "King Andrew the First," and called his Democratic supporters *Tories*. The new anti-Jackson coalition called themselves **Whigs**, a name that linked them to the Patriots of the American Revolution (as well as to the parliamentary opponents of the Tories in Britain). Andrew Jackson preferred to call them Federalists.

The Whig party grew directly out of the National Republican party led by John Quincy Adams, Henry Clay, and Daniel Webster. The Whigs also found support among the Anti-Masons and even some Democrats who resented Jackson's war on the national bank. Of the forty-one Democrats in Congress who had voted against Jackson on rechartering the national bank, twenty-eight had joined the Whigs by 1836.

The Whigs, like the National Republicans they replaced, were economic nationalists who wanted the federal government to promote manufacturing, support a national bank, and finance a national road network. In the South, the Whigs tended to be bankers and merchants. In the West, the Whigs were mostly farmers who valued government-funded internal improvements. Unlike the Democrats, who attracted Catholic voters from Germany and Ireland, Whigs tended to be native-born Protestants—Congregationalists, Presbyterians, Methodists, and Baptists—who advocated social reforms such as the abolition of slavery and efforts to restrict alcoholic beverages.

For the next twenty years, the Whigs and the Democrats would be the two major political parties. In 1834, the editor of the *Richmond Whig* newspaper gave a class-based explanation of the Whig opposition to Jacksonian democracy. The Jacksonians, he wrote, have denounced "the rich and intelligent . . . as aristocrats. They have caressed, soothed, and flattered the heavy [larger] class of the poor and ignorant, because they held the power which *they* wanted." By appealing to the masses, Jacksonians had overturned the republican system created by the founding fathers: "*The Republic has degenerated into a Democracy!*" In general, the Democrats, North and South, were solidly in support of slavery, while the Whigs were increasingly divided on the issue.

KILLING THE B.U.S. In the end, the relentless Jackson won his battle with Biddle's Bank. The B.U.S. would shut down completely by 1841, and the

United States would not have a central banking system until 1914. Jackson exulted in his "glorious triumph" in killing the bank, "that mammoth of corruption and power" that could print the nation's money. (Ironically, Jackson's picture has been on the twenty-dollar bill since 1929).

Jackson's controversial efforts to destroy the B.U.S. aroused so much opposition that some of his congressional opponents talked of impeaching him. Jackson received so many death threats that he decided his political opponents *were* trying to kill him.

In January 1835, the threat became real. After attending the funeral service for a member of Congress, Jackson was leaving the Capitol when an unemployed English-born housepainter named Richard Lawrence emerged from the shadows and pointed a pistol at the president's heart—from only a few feet away.

When Lawrence pulled the trigger, however, the gun misfired. Jackson lifted his walking stick and charged at the man, who pulled out another pistol, but it, too, miraculously misfired, enabling police to arrest him. Jackson assumed that his political foes, including John C. Calhoun, had planned the attack. A jury, however, decided that Lawrence, the first person to attempt the assassination of a U.S. president, was insane and ordered him confined in an asylum.

The destruction of the B.U.S. illustrated Jackson's strengths and weaknesses. When challenged, he was a shrewd and ferocious fighter. Yet his determination to humble Biddle and destroy the B.U.S. ended up hurting the national economy. The B.U.S. had performed a needed service. Without it, there was nothing to regulate the nation's money supply or its banks. The number of banks across the nation more than doubled between 1829 and 1837. Of even greater concern, however, was that the amount of loans made by these unregulated banks quadrupled, preparing the way for a financial panic and a terrible depression.

Jackson and the Democrats grew increasingly committed to the expansion of slavery westward into the Gulf coast states, driven by an unstable banking system. "People here are run mad with [land] speculation," wrote a traveler through northern Mississippi. "They do business in a kind of frenzy." Gold was scarce but paper money was plentiful, and people rushed to buy lands freed up by the removal of Indians. In 1835, federal land offices in Mississippi sold more acres than had been sold across the entire nation just three years before. The South and West were being flooded by cotton, credit (paper money), and slaves, all of which combined to produce mountains of debt. People used paper money issued by reckless state banks to buy and sell land and slaves.

With the restraining effects of Biddle's national bank removed, scores of new state banks sprouted like mushrooms in the cotton belt, each irresponsibly printing its own paper currency that was often lent recklessly to land speculators and new businesses, especially in cotton-growing states like Mississippi and Louisiana.

The result was chaos. Too many banks emerged without adequate capital and with inadequate expertise and integrity. As Senator Thomas Hart Benton, one of Jackson's most loyal supporters, said in 1837, he had not helped his friend Jackson kill the B.U.S. to create a "wilderness of local banks. I did not join in putting down the paper currency of a national bank to put up a national paper currency of a thousand local banks." But that is what happened.

THE MONEY QUESTION During the 1830s, the federal government acquired huge amounts of money from the sale of government-owned lands. Initially, the Treasury Department used the annual surpluses from land sales to pay down the accumulated federal debt, which it eliminated completely in 1835—the first time that any nation had done so. By 1836, the federal budget was generating an annual budget surplus, which led to intense discussions about what to do with the increasingly worthless paper money flowing into the Treasury's vaults.

The surge of unstable paper money peaked in 1836, when events combined to play havoc with the economy. Two key initiatives endorsed by the Jackson administration would devastate the nation's financial system and throw the surging economy into a sudden tailspin.

First, in June 1836, Congress approved the **Distribution Act**, initially proposed by Henry Clay and Daniel Webster, that required the federal government to "distribute" to the states surplus federal revenue from land sales. The federal surplus would be "deposited" into eighty-one state banks in proportion to each state's representation in Congress. The state governments would then draw upon those deposits to fund roads, bridges, and other "internal" improvements, including the construction of new "public" schools free to everyone.

Second, a month later, in July, Jackson issued the Specie Circular (1836), which announced that the federal government would accept only specie (gold or silver coins) in payment for land purchased by speculators (farmers could still pay with paper money). Westerners were upset by the Specie Circular because most of the government land sales were occurring in their states. They helped convince Congress to pass an act overturning Jackson's policy. The president, however, vetoed it.

Once enacted, the Deposit and Distribution Act and the Specie Circular put added strains on the nation's already tight supplies of gold and silver. Eastern banks had to transfer much of their gold and silver reserves to western banks. As Eastern banks reduced their reserves of gold and silver coins, they

New Method of Assorting the Mail, As Practised by Southern-Slave Holders, Or Attack on the Post Office, Charleston S.C. (1835) On the wall of the post office a sign reads "$20,000 Reward for Tappan," referring to the bounty placed on the head of Arthur Tappan, founder and president of the American Anti-Slavery Society.

had to reduce their lending. Soon, the once-bustling economy began to slow into a recession as the money supply contracted and it proved much more difficult for individuals and businesses to get loans. Nervous depositors rushed to their local banks to withdraw their money, only to learn that there was not enough specie in their vaults to redeem their deposits.

CENSORING THE MAIL While concerns about the strength of the economy grew, slavery emerged again as a flashpoint issue. In 1835, northern organizations pushing for the immediate abolition of slavery began mailing anti-slavery pamphlets and newspapers to prominent white southerners, hoping to convince them to end the "peculiar institution." They found little support. Francis Pickens of South Carolina urged southerners to stop the abolitionists from spreading their "lies." Angry pro-slavery South Carolinians in Charleston broke into the federal post office, stole bags of the abolitionist mailings, and ceremoniously burned them. Southern state legislatures passed laws banning such "dangerous" publications. Jackson asked Congress to pass a federal censorship law that would prohibit "incendiary" materials intended to incite "the slaves to insurrection."

Congress took action in 1836, but instead of banning abolitionist materials, a bipartisan group of Democrats and Whigs reaffirmed the sanctity of the federal mail. As a practical matter, however, southern post offices began censoring the mail anyway, arguing that federal authority ended when the mail arrived at the post office door. Jackson decided not to enforce the congressional action. His failure of leadership created what would become a growing split in the Democratic party over the future of slavery. Some Democrats decided that Jackson, for all of his celebrations of democracy and equality, was no different from John C. Calhoun and other southern white racists.

The controversy over the mails proved to be a victory for the growing abolitionist movement. One anti-slavery publisher said that instead of stifling their efforts, Jackson and the southern radicals "put us and our principles up before the world—just where we wanted to be." Abolitionist groups started mailing their pamphlets and petitions to members of Congress. James Hammond, a pro-slavery South Carolinian, called for Congress to ban such anti-slavery petitions. When that failed, Congress in 1836 adopted an informal solution suggested by Martin Van Buren: whenever a petition calling for the end of slavery was introduced, someone would immediately move that it be tabled rather than discussed. The plan, Van Buren claimed, would preserve the "harmony of our happy Union."

The supporters of this "gag rule" soon encountered a formidable obstacle in John Quincy Adams, the former president who now was a congressman from Massachusetts. He devised an array of procedures to get around the rule to squelch all anti-slavery discussion. Henry Wise, a Virginia opponent, called Adams "the acutest, the astutest, the archest enemy of southern slavery that ever existed." In the 1838–1839 session of Congress, thanks to Adams, some 1,500 anti-slavery petitions were filed with 163,845 signatures. Andrew Jackson dismissed Adams, his old rival, as "the most reckless and depraved man living."

THE ELECTION OF 1836 In 1835, eighteen months before the presidential election, the Democrats nominated Jackson's handpicked successor, Vice President Martin Van Buren. The Whig coalition, united chiefly in its opposition to Jackson, adopted a strategy of multiple candidates, hoping to throw the election into the House of Representatives.

The Whigs put up three regional candidates: New Englander Daniel Webster, Hugh Lawson White of Tennessee, and William Henry Harrison of Indiana. But the multicandidate strategy failed. In the popular vote of 1836, Van Buren

Martin Van Buren Van Buren earned the nickname the "Little Magician," not only for his short stature but also his "magical" ability to exploit his political and social connections.

defeated the entire Whig field, winning 170 electoral votes while the others combined to collect only 113.

THE EIGHTH PRESIDENT

Martin Van Buren was a skillful politician whose ability to organize and manipulate legislators had earned him the nickname "Little Magician." Elected governor of New York in 1828, he had resigned to join Andrew Jackson's cabinet, first as secretary of state, and then as vice president in 1833. Now, he was the first New Yorker to be elected president.

Van Buren had been Jackson's closest political adviser and most trusted ally, but many people considered him too self-centered to do the work of the people. John Quincy Adams wrote in his diary that Van Buren was "by far the ablest" of the Jacksonians, but that he had wasted "most of his ability upon mere personal intrigues. His principles are all subordinate to his ambition." Van Buren's rival, John C. Calhoun, was even more cutting. "He is not of the race of the lion or the tiger." Rather, he "belongs to a lower order—the fox."

At his inauguration, Van Buren promised to follow "in the footsteps" of the enormously popular President Jackson. Before he could do so, however, the nation's financial sector began collapsing. On May 10, 1837, several large state banks in New York, running out of gold and silver, suddenly refused to convert customers' paper money into coins. Other banks across the nation quickly did the same, creating a panic among depositors across the nation. More than a third of the banks went under. This financial crisis, the worst yet faced by the young nation, would become known as the **Panic of 1837**. It would soon mushroom into the country's worst depression, lasting some seven years.

THE PANIC OF 1837

The causes of the financial crisis went back to the Jackson administration, but Van Buren got the blame. The problem actually started in Europe. During the mid-1830s, Great Britain, America's largest trading partner, experienced an acute financial crisis when the Bank of England, worried about a run on the gold and silver in its vaults, curtailed its loans. This forced most British companies to reduce their trade with America. As British demand for American cotton plummeted, so did the price paid for cotton. On top of everything else, in 1836 there had been a disastrous wheat crop. In the spring of 1836, *Niles' Weekly Register*, the nation's leading business journal, reported that the economy was "approaching a momentous crisis."

As creditors hastened to foreclose on businesses and farms unable to make their debt payments, government spending plunged. Many canals under construction were shut down. In many cases, state governments could not repay their debts. In the crunch, 40 percent of the hundreds of recently created state banks failed. In April 1837, some 250 businesses failed in New York City alone. By early fall, 90 percent of the nation's factories had closed down.

Not surprisingly, the economic crisis frightened people. As a newspaper editorial complained in December 1836, the economy "has been put into confusion and dismay by a well-meant, but *extremely mistaken*" pair of decisions by Congress and President Jackson: the Specie Circular and the elimination of the B.U.S. A well-managed national bank could have served as a stabilizing force amid the financial panic. Instead, weak state banks around the country flooded the economy with worthless paper money printed without adequate backing in gold or silver.

Jacksonian Treasury note A parody of the often-worthless paper money (banknotes) issued by local banks and businesses in lieu of coins. These notes proliferated during the Panic of 1837, with the emergency suspension of gold and silver payments. In the main scene, Martin Van Buren, a monster on a wagon driven by John C. Calhoun, is about to pass through an arch labeled "Wall Street" and "Safety Fund Banks."

Many desperate southerners fled their debts altogether by moving to Texas, which was then a province of Mexico. Even the federal government itself, having put most of its gold and silver in state banks, was verging on bankruptcy. The *National Intelligencer* newspaper in Washington, D.C., reported in May that the federal Treasury "has not a dollar of gold or silver in the world!"

The poor, as always, were particularly hard hit. By the fall of 1837, one third of the nation's workers were jobless, and those still fortunate enough to be employed had their wages cut by 30 to 50 percent within two years. At the same time, prices for food and clothing soared. As the winter of 1837 approached, a New York City journalist reported that 200,000 people were "in utter and hopeless distress with no means of surviving the winter but those provided by charity." The nation had a "poverty-struck feeling."

POLITICS AMID THE DEPRESSION The unprecedented economic calamity would last seven years and send shock waves through the political system. Critics among the Whigs called the president "Martin Van Ruin" because he did not believe that he nor the federal government had any responsibility to rescue hard-pressed farmers, bankers, or businessmen, or to provide relief for the jobless and homeless. Any efforts to help people in distress must come from the states, not the national government. He did call a special session of Congress in 1837, which canceled the distribution of the federal surplus to the states because there was no surplus to distribute.

How best to deal with the unprecedented depression clearly divided Democrats from Whigs. Unlike Van Buren, Whig Henry Clay insisted that suffering people were "entitled to the protecting care of a parental Government." To him, an enlarged role for the federal government was the price of a maturing, expanding republic in which elected officials had an obligation to promote the "safety, convenience, and prosperity" of the people. Van Buren and the Democrats believed that the government had no such obligations. Henry Clay, among others, savaged the president for his "cold and heartless" attitude.

AN INDEPENDENT TREASURY Van Buren believed that the federal government should stop risking its cash deposits in the insecure "pet" state banks that Jackson had selected. Instead, he wanted to establish an Independent Treasury system whereby the government would keep its funds in its own vaults and do business entirely in gold or silver, not paper currency. Van Buren wanted the federal government to regulate the nation's supply of gold and silver and let the marketplace regulate the supply of paper currency.

It took Van Buren more than three years to convince Congress to pass the **Independent Treasury Act** on July 4, 1840. Although it lasted little more than a year (the Whigs repealed it in 1841), it would be restored in 1846. Van Buren's Independent Treasury was a political disaster. Not surprisingly, the state banks that lost control of the federal funds howled in protest. Moreover, it did nothing to end the widespread suffering caused by the deepening depression.

THE 1840 CAMPAIGN By 1840, an election year, the Van Buren administration and the Democrats were in deep trouble. The continuing hot potato of Texas produced considerable damage. In 1837, Van Buren had decided *not* to annex the Republic of Texas, claiming that there was no provision in the Constitution for absorbing another nation and that doing so

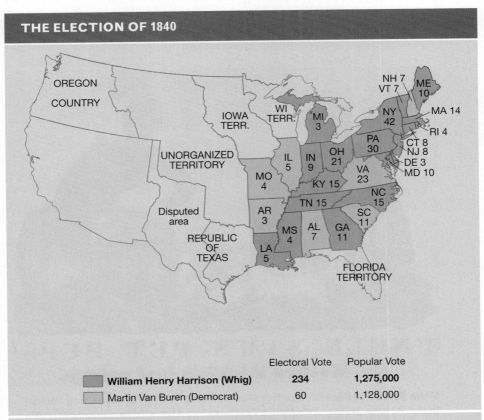

THE ELECTION OF 1840

	Electoral Vote	Popular Vote
William Henry Harrison (Whig)	**234**	**1,275,000**
Martin Van Buren (Democrat)	60	1,128,000

- Why did Van Buren carry several western states but few others?
- How did the Whigs achieve a decisive electoral victory over the Democrats?
- How was the Whig strategy in 1840 different from their campaign in 1836?

would also trigger a war with Mexico. Van Buren's decision outraged his political mentor, Andrew Jackson, and aroused strong criticism among southern Democrats.

At the same time, the depression continued to deepen and the suffering spread, leading Whigs to grow confident they could win the presidency. At their nominating convention, they passed over Henry Clay, the celebrated Kentucky legislator who had been Jackson's consistent foe, in favor of William Henry Harrison, whose credentials were impressive: victor at the Battle of Tippecanoe against Tecumseh's Shawnees in 1811, former governor of the Indiana Territory, and former congressman and senator from Ohio.

To balance the ticket geographically, the Whigs nominated John Tyler of Virginia as their vice president. Henry Clay, who yearned to be president, was bitterly disappointed, complaining that "my friends are not worth the powder and shot it would take to kill them. I am the most unfortunate man in the history of parties."

UNCLE SAM'S PET PUPS!
Or, Mother BANK'S last refuge.

Uncle Sam's Pet Pups! A woodcut showing William Henry Harrison luring "Mother Bank," Andrew Jackson, and Martin Van Buren into a barrel of hard (alcoholic) cider. While Jackson and Van Buren sought to destroy the Bank of the United States, Harrison promised to reestablish it, hence his providing "Mother Bank" a refuge in this scene.

The Whigs refused to take a stand on major issues. They did, however, seize upon a catchy campaign slogan: "Tippecanoe and Tyler Too." When a Democratic newspaper declared that General Harrison was the kind of man who would spend his retirement "in a log cabin [sipping apple cider] on the banks of the Ohio [River]," the Whigs chose the cider and log cabin symbols to depict Harrison as a simple man sprung from the people in contrast to Van Buren's aristocratic lifestyle. (Harrison was actually from one of Virginia's wealthiest families).

Harrison defeated Van Buren easily, winning 234 electoral votes to 60. The Whigs had promised a return to prosperity without explaining how it would happen. It was simply time for a change.

What was most remarkable about the election of 1840 was the turnout. More than 80 percent of white American men voted, many for the first time—the highest turnout before or since, as by this time almost every state had dropped property qualifications for voting.

JACKSON'S LEGACY

The nation that the new president-elect William Henry Harrison prepared to govern was vastly different from the one led by George Washington and Thomas Jefferson. In 1828, the United States boasted twenty-four states and nearly 13 million people, many of them recent arrivals from Germany and Ireland. The national population was growing at a phenomenal rate, doubling every twenty-three years.

During the so-called Jacksonian era, the unregulated economy witnessed booming industrialization, rapidly growing cities, rising tensions between the North and South over slavery, accelerating westward expansion, and the emergence of the **second two-party system**, this time featuring Democrats and Whigs. A surge in foreign demand for southern cotton and other American goods, along with substantial British investment in an array of new American enterprises, helped fuel an economic boom and a transportation revolution. That President-elect Jackson rode to his inauguration in a horse-drawn carriage and left Washington, D.C. eight years later on a train symbolized the dramatic changes occurring in American life.

A NEW POLITICAL LANDSCAPE A transformational figure in a transformational era, Andrew Jackson helped reshape the American political landscape. Even his ferocious opponent, Henry Clay, acknowledged that Jackson had "swept over the Government . . . like a tropical tornado."

Like all great presidents, however, Jackson left a mixed legacy. Yes, he helped accelerate the democratization of American life. In his 1837 farewell address, he stressed his crusade on behalf of "the farmer, the mechanic, and the laboring classes of society—the bone and sinew of the country—men who love liberty and desire nothing but equal rights and equal laws."

Jackson championed opportunities for the "common man" to play a greater role in the political arena at the same time that working men were forming labor unions to increase their economic power and political clout. He helped establish the modern Democratic party and attracted to it the working poor and immigrants from eastern cities, as well as farmers from the South and East. Through a nimble combination of force and compromise, he saved the Union by suppressing the nullification crisis.

And, with great fanfare on January 1, 1835, Jackson announced that the government had paid off the national debt accumulated since the Revolutionary War, which he called a "national curse." It was the first time in history that a nation had eliminated a large debt. The *Washington Globe* celebrated the momentous occasion by noting that it coincided with the twentieth anniversary of the Battle of New Orleans, writing that "New Orleans and the National Debt—the first of which paid off our scores to *our enemies*, whilst the latter paid off the last cent to *our friends*."

Jackson's concept of "the people," however, was limited to a "white men's democracy," as it had been for all earlier presidents, and the phenomenon of Andrew Jackson, the heroic symbol of the common man and the democratic ideal, continues to spark historical debate, as it did during his own lifetime.

In 1828, William P. Anderson, a former army officer who had been one of Jackson's Tennessee horse-racing friends and political supporters but had turned into an outspoken opponent, wrote an open letter to the presidential candidate that was published in several newspapers. He attacked Jackson for having killed a man in a duel, then brutally outlined Old Hickory's faults: "Your besetting sins are ambition and the love of money. . . . You are naturally and constitutionally irritable, overbearing and tyrannical. . . . When you become the enemy of any man, you will put him down if you can, no matter by what means, fair or foul. . . . You are miserably deficient in principle, and have seldom or never had power without abusing it."

Although the criticism was too harsh, it contained more than a grain of truth. Jackson was so convinced of the rightness and righteousness of his ideals that he was selectively willing to defy constitutional limits on his authority when it suited his interests and satisfied his rage. He was both the instrument of democracy and its enemy, protecting "the humble people" and the Union by expanding presidential authority in ways that the founders had never envisioned, including removing federal money from the national bank, replacing government officials with party loyalists, censoring the mails, and ending nullification in South Carolina.

Jackson often declared that the only justification for using governmental power was to ensure equal treatment for everyone, the "high and the low, the rich and the poor." Yet his own use of government force was at times contradictory and even hypocritical. While threatening to "kill" the B.U.S. and hang John Calhoun and other South Carolina nullifiers, he refused to intervene when Georgia officials violated the legal rights of Cherokees. His aggressive use of presidential authority was less principled than it was political and personal. His inconsistent approach to executive power both symbolized and aggravated the perennial tension in the American republic between a commitment to democratic ideals and the exercise of presidential authority.

CHAPTER REVIEW

SUMMARY

- **Jackson's Views and Policies** The Jacksonians sought to democratize the political process and expand economic opportunity for the "common man" (that is, "poor and humble" white men). As the representative of "the people," Andrew Jackson expanded the role of the president in economic matters, reducing federal spending and eliminating the powerful *Second Bank of the United States*. His *Bank War* painted the national bank as full of "vipers and thieves" and was hugely popular, but Jackson did not understand its long-term economic consequences. In addition, his views on limited government were not always reflected in his policies. He left the high taxes from the *Tariff of Abominations* (1828) in place until opposition in the South created a national crisis.

- **Indian Removal Act of 1830** The *Indian Removal Act* of 1830 authorized the relocation of Eastern Indians to federal lands west of the Mississippi River. The Cherokees used the federal court system to try to block this relocation. Despite the Supreme Court's decisions in their favor, President Jackson forced them to move; the event and the route they took came to be known as the *Trail of Tears*. By 1840, only a few Seminoles and Cherokees remained in remote areas of the Southeast.

- **Nullification Controversy** The concept of *nullification*, developed by South Carolina's John C. Calhoun, enabled a state to disavow a federal law. When a South Carolina convention nullified the Tariffs of 1828 and 1832, Jackson requested that Congress pass a *Force Bill* authorizing the U.S. Army to compel compliance with the tariffs. After South Carolina, under the threat of federal military force, accepted a compromise tariff put forth by Henry Clay, the state convention nullified the Force Bill. The immediate crisis was over, with both sides claiming victory.

- **Democrats and Whigs** Jackson's arrogant behavior, especially his use of the veto, led many to regard him as "King Andrew the First." Groups who opposed him coalesced into a new party, known as the *Whigs*, thus producing the country's *second two-party system*. Two acts—the *Distribution Act* and the Specie Circular—ultimately destabilized the nation's economy. Jackson's ally and vice president, Martin Van Buren, succeeded him as president, but Jacksonian bank policies led to the financial *Panic of 1837* and an economic depression. Van Buren responded by establishing an *Independent Treasury* to safeguard the nation's economy but offered no help for individuals in distress. The economic calamity ensured a Whig victory in the election of 1840.

- **The Jackson Years** Andrew Jackson's America was very different from the America of 1776. Most white men had gained the vote, but political equality did not mean economic equality. Jacksonian Democrats wanted every American to have an equal chance to compete in the marketplace and in the political arena, but they never promoted equality of results. Inequality between rich and poor widened during the Jacksonian era.

CHRONOLOGY

1828	Tariff of Abominations goes into effect
1830	Congress passes the Indian Removal Act
	Andrew Jackson vetoes the Maysville Road Bill
1831	Supreme Court issues *Cherokee Nation v. Georgia* decision
1832	Supreme Court issues *Worcester v. Georgia* decision
	South Carolina passes Ordinance of Nullification
	Andrew Jackson vetoes the Bank Recharter Bill
1833	Congress passes the Force Bill, authorizing military force in South Carolina
	Congress passes Henry Clay's compromise tariff with Jackson's support
1836	Democratic candidate Martin Van Buren is elected president
1837	Financial panic deflates the economy
1837–1838	Eastern Indians are forced west on the Trail of Tears
1840	Independent Treasury established
	Whig candidate William Henry Harrison is elected president

KEY TERMS

Indian Removal Act (1830) p. 430

Trail of Tears (1838–1839) p. 435

Second Bank of the United States p. 435

Bank War p. 437

Tariff of Abominations (1828) p. 439

nullification p. 439

Force Bill (1833) p. 447

Whigs p. 449

Distribution Act (1836) p. 451

Panic of 1837 p. 454

Independent Treasury Act (1840) p. 456

second two-party system p. 459

 INQUIZITIVE

Go to InQuizitive to see what you've learned—and learn what you've missed—with personalized feedback along the way.

11 The South, Slavery, and King Cotton

1800–1860

The Old South One of the enduring myths of the Old South is captured in this late nineteenth-century painting of a plantation on the Mississippi River: muscular slaves tending the lush cotton fields, a steamboat easing down the wide river, and the planter's family relaxing in the cool shade of their white-columned mansion. Novels and films like *Gone with the Wind* (1939) would perpetuate the notion of the Old South as a stable, paternalistic agrarian society led by white planters who were the "natural" aristocracy of virtue and talent within their communities.

Of all the regions of the United States during the first half of the nineteenth century, the pre–Civil War Old South was the most distinctive. What had once been a narrow band of settlements along the Atlantic coast dramatically expanded westward and southward to form a subcontinental empire rooted in cotton.

The southern states remained rural and agricultural long after the rest of the nation had embraced cities, immigrants, and factories. Yet the Old South was also instrumental in enabling the nation's capitalist development and its growing economic stature. After the War of 1812, southern-grown cotton became the key raw material driving industrial growth, feeding the textile mills of Great Britain and New England, where wage workers toiling over newly-invented machines fashioned it into thread, yarn, and clothing. The price of raw cotton doubled in the first year after the war, and the profits made by cotton producers flowed into the hands of northern and British bankers, merchants, and textile mill owners. Investors in Boston, New York City, and Philadelphia provided loans to southerners to buy more land and more slaves. Northerners also provided the cotton industry with other essential needs: insurance, financing, and shipping.

The story of how southern cotton clothed the world, spurred the expansion of global capitalism, and transformed history was woven with the threads of tragedy, however. The revolution spawned by the mass production of cotton was rooted in the explosive expansion of slavery across the South and into Texas, as Native Americans were pushed off their ancestral lands and relocated

focus questions

1. What factors made the South distinct from the rest of the United States during the early nineteenth century?

2. What role did cotton production and slavery play in the South's economic and social development?

3. What were the major social groups within southern white society? Why was each group committed to the continuation and expansion of slavery?

4. What was the impact of slavery on African Americans, both free and enslaved, throughout the South?

5. How did enslaved peoples respond to the inhumanity of their situation?

across the Mississippi River. A group of slaves in Virginia recognized the essential role they played in the surging national economy when they asked, "Didn't we clear the land, and raise the crops of corn, of tobacco, rice, of sugar, of everything? And then didn't the large cities in the North grow up on the cotton and the sugars and the rice that we made?"

THE DISTINCTIVENESS OF THE OLD SOUTH

People have long debated what set the Old South apart from the rest of the nation. Most arguments focus on the region's climate and geography in shaping its culture and economy. The South's warm, humid climate was ideal for cultivating profitable crops such as tobacco, cotton, rice, indigo, and sugarcane, which led to the plantation system of large commercial agriculture and its dependence upon enslaved labor.

Unlike the North, the South had few large cities, few banks, few railroads, few factories, and few schools. Most southern commerce was related to the storage, distribution, and sale of agricultural products, especially cotton. With the cotton economy booming, investors focused on buying land and slaves; there was little reason to create a robust industrial sector. "We want no manufactures; we desire no trading, no mechanical, or manufacturing classes," an Alabama politician told an English visitor.

Profitable farming thus remained the South's ideal pursuit of happiness. Education was valued by the planter elite for their own sons, but there was little interest in public schooling for the masses. The illiteracy rate in the South was three times higher than in the North.

A BIRACIAL CULTURE What made the Old South most distinctive was not its climate or soil but its expanding system of race-based slavery. The majority of southern whites did not own slaves, but they supported what John C. Calhoun called the South's **"peculiar institution"** because slavery was so central to their society's way of life. Calhoun's carefully crafted phrase allowed southerners to avoid using the charged word *slavery*, while the adjective *peculiar* implied that slavery was *unique* to the South, as it essentially was.

The profitability and convenience of owning slaves created a sense of social unity among whites that bridged class differences. Poor whites who owned no slaves and resented the planters ("cotton snobs") could still claim racial superiority over enslaved blacks ("niggers"). Because of race-based slavery, explained Georgia attorney Thomas Reade Cobb, every white "feels that he belongs to an elevated class. It matters not that he is no slaveholder; he is not of the inferior race; he is a free-born citizen."

The Old South also differed from other sections of the country in its high proportion of native-born Americans. The region attracted few European immigrants after the Revolution, in part because of geography. The main shipping routes from Britain and Europe took immigrants to northern port cities. Because most immigrants were penniless, they could not afford to travel to the South. Moreover, European immigrants, most of whom were manual laborers, could not compete with slave labor.

CONFLICTING MYTHS Southerners, a North Carolina editor wrote, are "a mythological people, created half out of dream and half out of slander, who live in a still legendary land." Myths are beliefs made up partly of truths and partly of lies, formed with accurate generalizations and willful distortions. During the nineteenth century, a powerful myth emerged among white southerners—that the South was both different from *and* better than the North. This blended notion of distinctiveness and superiority became central to the self-image of many southerners. Even today, many southerners tenaciously cultivate a defiant pride and separate identity from the rest of the nation.

In defending the South and slavery from northern critics, southerners claimed that their region was morally superior. Kind planters, according to the prevailing myth, provided happy slaves with food, clothing, shelter, and security—in contrast to a North populated with greedy bankers and heartless factory owners who treated their wage laborers worse than slaves. John C. Calhoun insisted that in the northern states the quality of life for free people of color had "become worse" since slavery there had been banned, whereas in the South the standard of living among enslaved African Americans had "improved greatly in every respect."

In this mythic version of the Old South, slavery was defended as being beneficial to both slaves and owners. In *Aunt Phillis's Cabin; or, Southern Life As It Is* (1852), novelist Mary Henderson Eastman stressed "the necessity of the existence of slavery at present in our Southern States," and claimed "that, as a general thing, the slaves are comfortable and contented, and their owners humane and kind."

The agrarian ideal and the southern passion for guns, horsemanship, hunting, and the military filled in the self-gratifying image of the Old South as a region of honest small farmers and aristocratic gentlemen, young belles and beautiful ladies who led leisurely lives of well-mannered graciousness, honor, and courage, all the while sipping mint juleps in a carefree romantic world of white-columned mansions.

The contrasting myth of the Old South was much darker. Northern abolitionists (those who wanted an immediate end to slavery) pictured the region as being built on an immoral economic system dependent on the exploitation of blacks and the displacement of Native Americans. In this version of the southern myth, the white planters were rarely "natural aristocrats," like Thomas Jefferson, who were ambivalent about slavery. More often, the planters were viewed as ambitious, self-made men who had seized opportunities to become rich by planting and selling cotton—and trading in slaves.

Northern abolitionists such as Harriet Beecher Stowe portrayed southern planters as cunning capitalists who raped enslaved women, brutalized slaves, and lorded over their communities with arrogant disdain. They treated slaves like cattle, broke up their families, and sold slaves "down the river" to toil in the Louisiana sugar mills and on rice plantations. An English woman traveling in the South in 1830 noted that what slaves in Virginia and Maryland feared most was being "sent to *the south* and sold. . . . The sugar plantations [in Louisiana] and, more than all, the rice grounds of Georgia and the Carolinas, are the terror of the American negroes."

MANY SOUTHS The contradictory elements of these conflicting myths continue to fight for supremacy in the South, each pressing its claim to legitimacy, in part because the extreme descriptions are both built upon half-truths and fierce prejudices. The South has long been defined by two souls, two hearts, two minds competing for dominance. The paradoxes associated with this southern mythmaking provided much of the region's variety, for the Old South, like the New South, was not a single culture but a diverse section with multiple interests and perspectives—and it was rapidly growing and changing.

The Old South included three distinct subsections with different patterns of economic development and diverging degrees of commitment to slavery. Throughout the first half of the nineteenth century, the seven states of the Lower South (South Carolina, Georgia, Florida, Alabama, Mississippi, Louisiana, and parts of Texas) grew increasingly dependent upon commercial cotton production supported by slave labor. A traveler in Mississippi observed in 1835 that ambitious whites wanted "to sell cotton in order to buy negroes—to make more cotton to buy negroes." By 1860, slaves represented nearly half the population of the Lower South, largely because they were the most efficient producers of cotton in the world.

The states of the Upper South (Virginia, North Carolina, Tennessee, and Arkansas) had more-varied agricultural economies—a mixture of large commercial plantations and small family farms (or "yeoman farms"), where crops were grown mostly for household use. Many southern states also had large areas without slavery, especially in the mountains of Virginia, the western Car-

Atop the Cotton Kingdom This photograph offers a glimpse of the staggering scale of cotton production. These 500-pound cotton bales are so densely packed and plentiful that men are walking upon them at this Galveston, Texas, port.

olinas, eastern Tennessee, and northern Georgia, where the soil and climate were not suited to cotton or tobacco.

In the Border South (Delaware, Maryland, Kentucky, and Missouri), slavery was slowly disappearing because cotton could not thrive there. By 1860, approximately 90 percent of Delaware's black population and half of Maryland's were already free. Slave owners in the Lower South, however, had a much larger investment in slavery. They believed that only constant supervision, intimidation, and punishment would keep the fast-growing population of enslaved workers under control, in part because the working and living conditions for the enslaved were so brutal. "I'd rather be dead," said a white overseer in Louisiana, "than a nigger in one of those big [sugarcane] plantations."

THE COTTON KINGDOM

After the Revolution, as the worn-out tobacco fields in Virginia and Maryland lost their fertility, tobacco farming spread into Kentucky and as far west as Missouri. Rice continued to be grown in the coastal areas ("low country") of the Carolinas and Georgia, where fields could easily be flooded and drained by tidal rivers flowing into the ocean. Sugarcane, like rice, was also an expensive crop to produce, requiring machinery to grind the cane to release the sugar syrup. During the early nineteenth century, only southern Louisiana focused on sugar production.

In addition to such "cash crops," the South led the nation in the production of livestock: hogs, horses, mules, and cattle. Southerners, both black and white, fed themselves largely on pork. It was the "king of the table." John S. Wilson, a Georgia doctor, called the region the "Republic of Porkdom." Southerners ate pork or bacon "morning, noon, and night." Corn was on southern plates as often as pork. During the early summer, corn was boiled on the cob; by late summer and fall it was ground into cornmeal, a coarse flour. Cornbread and hominy, as well as a "mush" or porridge made of whole-grain corn mixed with milk, were almost daily fare.

KING COTTON During the first half of the nineteenth century, cotton surpassed rice as the most profitable cash crop in the South. Southern cotton (called "white gold") drove much of the national economy and the Industrial Revolution, feeding the mechanized textile mills in New England and Great Britain.

In fact, cotton became one of the transforming forces in nineteenth-century history. It shaped the lives of the enslaved who cultivated it, the planters who grew rich by it, the mill girls who sewed it, the merchants who sold it, the people who wore it, and the politicians who warred over it. "Cotton is King," exclaimed the *Southern Cultivator* in 1859, "and wields an astonishing influence over the world's commerce." In 1832, over eighty of America's largest companies were New England textile mills converting cotton into thread and cloth.

The Cotton Kingdom resulted largely from two crucial developments. Until the late eighteenth century, cotton fabric was a rarity produced by women in India using hand looms. Then British inventors developed machinery to convert raw cotton into thread and cloth in textile mills. The mechanical production of cotton made Great Britain the world's first industrial nation, and the number of British textile mills, centered in Lancashire, grew so fast that owners could not get enough cotton fiber to meet their needs. American Eli Whitney solved the problem by constructing the first cotton gin, which mechanized the labor-intensive process of manually removing the sticky seeds from the bolls of what was called short-staple cotton.

Taken together, these two breakthroughs helped create the world's largest industry—and transformed the South in the process. By 1815, just months after Andrew Jackson's victory over British troops at New Orleans, some thirty

British ships were docked at the city's wharves because, as an American merchant reported, "Europe must, and will have, cotton for her manufacturers." During that year alone, more than 65,000 bales of cotton were shipped down the Mississippi River to New Orleans. To be sure, other nations joined the global cotton-producing revolution—India, Egypt, Brazil, and China—but the American South was the driving force of cotton capitalism.

THE OLD SOUTHWEST Because of its warm climate and plentiful rainfall, the Lower South became the global leader in cotton production. The region's cheap, fertile land and the profits to be made in growing cotton generated a frenzied mobility in which people constantly searched for more opportunities and even better land. Henry Watson, a New Englander who moved to Alabama, complained in 1836 that "nobody seems to consider himself settled [here]; they remain one, two, three or four years & must move on to some other spot."

The cotton belt moved south and west during the first half of the nineteenth century, and hundreds of thousands of land-hungry southerners moved with it. As the oldest southern states—Virginia and the Carolinas—experienced soil exhaustion from the overplanting of tobacco and cotton, restless farmers and many sons of planters moved westward to the **Old Southwest**—western Georgia, Alabama, Mississippi, Louisiana, Arkansas, and eventually, Texas.

In 1820, the coastal states of Virginia, the Carolinas, and Georgia had produced two thirds of the nation's cotton. By 1830, the Old Southwest states were producing two thirds of America's cotton. An acre of land in South Carolina produced about 300 pounds of cotton, while one acre in Alabama or in the Mississippi Delta, a 200-mile-wide strip of fertile soil between the Yazoo and Mississippi Rivers, could generate 800 pounds. It was the most profitable farmland in the world.

Such profits, however, required backbreaking labor, most of it performed by enslaved blacks. A white Virginian noted in 1807 that "there is a great aversion amongst our Negroes to be carried to distant parts, and particularly to our new countries [in the Old Southwest]." In marshy areas near the Gulf coast, slaves were put to work removing trees and stumps from the swampy muck. "None but men as hard as a Savage," said one worker, could survive such wearying conditions.

The formula for growing rich in the Lower South was simple: cheap land, cotton seed, and slaves. A North Carolinian reported that the "*Alabama Fever* . . . has *carried off* vast numbers of our citizens." Between 1810 and 1840, the combined population of Georgia, Alabama, and Mississippi increased from about 300,000 (252,000 of whom were in Georgia) to 1,657,799. Annual cotton production in the United States had grown from less than 150,000 bales (a bundle of cotton weighing 500 pounds) in 1814 to 4 *million* bales in 1860.

THE SOUTHERN FRONTIER Farm families in the Old Southwest tended to be large. "There is not a cabin but has ten or twelve children in it," reported a traveling minister. "When the boys are eighteen and the girls are fourteen, they marry—so that in many cabins you will see . . . the mother looking as young as the daughter."

Women were a minority among migrants from Virginia and the Carolinas to the Old Southwest. Many resisted moving to what they had heard was a

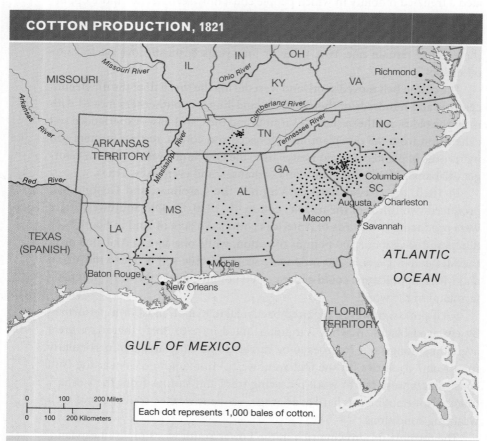

COTTON PRODUCTION, 1821

Each dot represents 1,000 bales of cotton.

- Why was cotton such a profitable crop?
- What regions produced the most cotton in 1821?
- What innovations enabled farmers to move inland and produce cotton more efficiently?

disease-ridden, male-dominated, violent, and primitive territory. As a Carolina woman prepared to depart for Alabama, she confided to a friend that "you *cannot* imagine the state of despair that I am in." Another said that "my heart bleeds within me" at the thought of the "many tender cords [of kinship] that are now severed forever."

Others feared that life on the southern frontier would produce a "dissipation" of morals. They heard wild stories of lawlessness, drunkenness, gambling, and whoring. A woman newly arrived in frontier Alabama wrote home that the farmers around her "live in a miserable manner. They think only of making money, and their houses are hardly fit to live in."

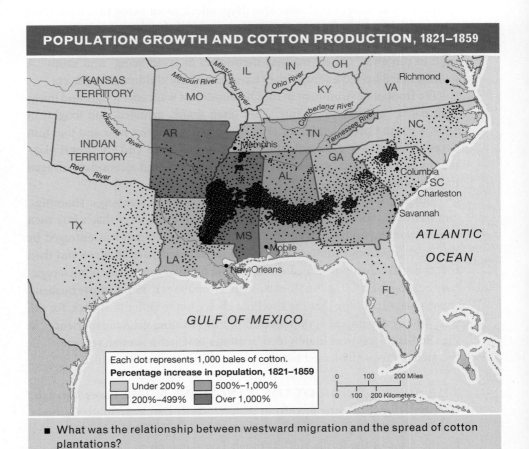

POPULATION GROWTH AND COTTON PRODUCTION, 1821–1859

Each dot represents 1,000 bales of cotton.
Percentage increase in population, 1821–1859
Under 200%   500%–1,000%
200%–499%   Over 1,000%

■ What was the relationship between westward migration and the spread of cotton plantations?
■ Why did cotton plantations cluster in certain regions of the South?
■ What were the environmental and economic consequences of the South's emphasis on cotton?

Enslaved blacks had many of the same reservations about relocating. Almost a million captive African Americans in Maryland, Virginia, and the Carolinas were forced to move to the Old Southwest during the first half of the nineteenth century. Herded onto steamboats or slave ships or forced to walk hundreds of miles manacled in iron collars and chains, they lived in "perpetual dread" of the Gulf states' harsh working conditions and broiling summer heat and humidity.

The sight of slave "coffles" being driven southward aroused a sense of shame in some observers. One described "a wretched cavalcade . . . marching half naked women, and men loaded with chains, without being charged with any crime but that of being black, from one section of the United States to another, hundreds of miles."

Slaves sent "downriver" were also despondent about being torn from their wives, children, and friends. One song expressed their anguish: "Massa sell poor negro, ho, heave, O! / Leave poor wife and children, ho, heave, O!" Some tried to run away. Others maimed themselves to avoid being "sent south." A woman killed herself because "they have carried my children off with 'em."

The frontier environment in the Old Southwest was rude, rough, and lively. Men had a "hell of a lot of fun." They often drank, gambled, and fought. In 1834, a South Carolina migrant urged his brother to move west and join him because "you can live like a fighting cock with us." Most Old Southwest plantations had their own stills to manufacture whiskey, and alcoholism ravaged many frontier families.

Violence was commonplace, and the frequency of stabbings, shootings, and murders shocked visitors. Shocking, too, were the ways that white men abused women, both black and white. An Alabama woman was outraged by the "beastly passions" of the white men who fathered slave children and then sold them like livestock. She also recorded in her diary instances of men regularly beating their wives. Another woman wrote about a friend whose husband abused her, explaining that she had little choice but to suffer in silence, for she was "wholly dependent upon his care." The contrasting gender experiences in the Old Southwest were highlighted in a letter in which a woman reported: "All the men is very well pleased but the women is not very well satisfied."

THE SPREADING COTTON KINGDOM By 1860, the center of the "**Cotton Kingdom**" stretched from eastern North Carolina, South Carolina, and Georgia through the fertile Alabama-Mississippi "black belt" (so called for the color of the fertile soil), through Louisiana, on to Texas, and up the Mississippi Valley as far as southern Illinois.

Steamboats made the Mississippi River the cotton highway by transporting millions of bales downriver from Kentucky, Tennessee, Arkansas, Mississippi, and Louisiana to New Orleans, where sailing ships took the cotton to

New York, New England, Great Britain, and France. King Cotton accounted for more than half of all U.S. exports.

By 1860, Alabama, Mississippi, and Louisiana were the three top-producing cotton states, and two thirds of the richest Americans lived in the South. More millionaires per capita lived in Natchez, Mississippi, along the great river, than anywhere in the world. The rapid expansion of the cotton belt ensured that the South became more dependent on enslaved black workers. More than half of the slaves in the South worked in cotton production.

The dynamic system of slavery was, as John Quincy Adams wrote in his diary, "the great and foul stain" upon the nation's commitment to liberty and equality. It persisted because it was such a powerful engine of economic development—and the most tangible sign of economic success. Enterprising young white men judged wealth and status by the number of slaves owned. By 1860, the dollar value of enslaved blacks outstripped the value of *all* American banks, railroads, and factories combined.

The soaring profitability of cotton fostered a false sense of security. In 1860, a Mississippi newspaper boasted that the South, "safely entrenched behind her cotton bags . . . can defy the world—for the civilized world depends on the cotton of the South." Cotton bred cockiness. In a speech to the U.S. Senate in 1858, South Carolina's former governor, James Henry Hammond, who owned a huge cotton plantation worked by more than 100 slaves, warned the critics of slavery in the North: "You dare not make war on cotton. No power on earth dares make war upon it. Cotton is King."

King Cotton Captured This engraving shows cotton being trafficked in Louisiana.

What Hammond failed to acknowledge was that the southern economy had grown dangerously dependent on European demand for raw cotton. By 1860, Great Britain was importing more than 80 percent of its cotton from the American South. Hammond and other southern leaders did not anticipate what they could least afford: a sudden collapse in world demand for southern cotton. In 1860, the expansion of the British textile industry peaked, and the price paid for southern cotton began a steady decline. By then, however, the Lower South was committed to large-scale cotton production for generations to come.

WHITES IN THE OLD SOUTH

Over time, the culture of cotton and slavery shaped the South's social structure and provided much of its political power. Unlike in the North and Midwest, southern society was dominated by an elite group of planters and merchants.

WHITE PLANTERS Although there were only a few giant plantations in each southern state, their owners exercised overwhelming influence. As a Virginian observed in the mid-1830s, "the old slaveholding families exerted a great deal of control . . . and they affected the manner and prejudices of the slaveholding part of the state."

The large planters behaved like an aristocracy, viewing their poor white neighbors with a contempt that was readily reciprocated. They often spent their time hunting and fishing, gambling and racing horses, hosting elaborate parties and importing wines and furnishings. In short, they indulged expensive habits and tastes that they often could neither afford nor control. Living the storied life of a planter was the focus of their energies, their honor, and often, their indebtedness. As a plantation slave recalled, his master on Sundays liked to "gamble, run horses, or fight game-cocks, discuss politics, and drink whisky, and brandy and water all day long."

The richest planters and merchants were determined to retain their control over southern society, in part because of self-interest and in part because they assumed they were the region's natural leaders. "Inequality is the fundamental law of the universe," declared one planter. James Henry Hammond was even more blunt, declaring that the South Carolina planters are "essentially what the nobility are in other countries. They stand at the head of society and politics." Slavery, he argued, "does indeed create an aristocracy—an aristocracy of talents, of virtue, of generosity, and courage."

In addition to its size, what distinguished a plantation from a farm was the use of a large number of slaves supervised by drivers and overseers. Planters themselves rarely engaged in manual labor. They focused on managing the overseers and handling the marketing and sale of the cotton, tobacco, rice, or sugar.

Most planters had begun their careers as land traders, investors, cotton merchants (called "factors"), and farmers. Over time, they made enough money to acquire a plantation worked by slaves. Frederick Stanton, a cotton broker near Natchez, Mississippi, became a planter with 444 slaves working 15,000 acres of cotton. Success required careful monitoring of the markets for cotton, land, and slaves as well as careful management of the workers and production.

If, as historians have agreed, one had to own at least twenty slaves to be called a **planter**, only one out of thirty whites in the South in 1860 was a planter. Eleven planters, among the wealthiest people in the nation, owned 500 slaves each; and one planter, a South Carolina rice grower, owned 1,000. The 10,000 most powerful planters, accounting for less than 3 percent of white men in the South, held more than half the slaves. The gap between the planters and the rest of southern society was wide. Two thirds of white southern families in 1830 owned no slaves.

Over time, planters and their wives (referred to as "mistresses") grew accustomed to being waited on by slaves, day and night. A Virginia planter told a British visitor that a slave girl slept in the master bedroom with him and his wife. When his British guest asked why, he replied: "Good heaven! If I wanted a glass of water during the night, what would become of me?"

From colonial times, most southern white men embraced an unwritten social code centered on a prickly sense of personal honor in which they were expected to defend their reputations with words, fists, knives, or guns. Duels to the death (called "affairs of honor") were the ultimate expression of manly honor. Many prominent southern leaders—congressmen, senators, governors, editors, and planters—engaged in duels with pistols, although dueling was technically illegal in many states. The roster of participants included President Andrew Jackson of Tennessee and Senator Henry Clay of Kentucky. But men of all classes were ready to fight at the first sign of disrespect.

THE PLANTATION MISTRESS The South, like the North, was a male-dominated society, only more so because of the slave system. A prominent Georgian, Christopher Memminger, explained that slavery heightened the need for a hierarchical social and family structure. White wives

Mary Boykin Chesnut Her diary describing life in the Confederacy during the Civil War was republished in 1981 and won the Pulitzer Prize.

and children needed to be as subservient and compliant as enslaved blacks. "Each planter," he declared, "is in fact a Patriarch—his position compels him to be a ruler in his household," and he requires "obedience and subordination."

The **plantation mistress** seldom led a life of idle leisure, nor was she a frail, helpless creature focused solely on planning parties and balls. Although she had slaves to attend to her needs, she supervised the domestic household in the same way as the planter took care of the cotton business. Overseeing the supply and preparation of food and linens, she also managed the housecleaning and care of the sick, the birthing of babies, and the operations of the dairy. A plantation slave remembered that her mistress "was with all the slave women every time a baby was born. Or, when a plague of misery hit the folks, she knew what to do and what kind of medicine to chase off the aches and pains." The son of a Tennessee slaveholder remembered that his mother and grandmother were "the busiest women I ever saw," in part because they themselves had babies every year or so, often birthing over a dozen children during their lifetimes.

Mary Boykin Chesnut, a plantation mistress in South Carolina, complained that "there is no slave, after all, like a wife." She admitted that she had few rights in the large household she managed, since her husband was the "master of the house." A wife was expected to love, honor, obey, and serve her husband. Virginian George Fitzhugh, a celebrated Virginia attorney and writer, spoke for most southern men when he said that a "man loves his children because they are weak, helpless, and dependent. He loves his wife for similar reasons."

Planters had little interest in an educated wife. When people tried to raise funds for a woman's college in Georgia, a planter angrily refused to contribute, explaining that "all that a woman needs to know is how to read the New Testament and to spin and weave clothing for her family. I would not have one of your graduates for a wife, and I will not give you a cent for any such project."

White women living in a slaveholding culture confronted a double standard in terms of moral and sexual behavior. They were expected to be examples of Christian morality and sexual purity, even as their husbands, brothers, and sons often engaged in self-indulgent hedonism, gambling, drinking, carousing, and sexually assaulting enslaved women.

"Under slavery," Mary Chesnut wrote in her famous diary, "we live surrounded by prostitutes." Yet she did not blame enslaved women for playing that role. They were usually forced to do so. In fact, many planters justified their behavior by highlighting the additional money they were creating by impregnating enslaved women. "God forgive us," Chesnut added, "but ours is a monstrous system. Like the patriarchs of old, our men live all in one house with their wives and their [enslaved] concubines [lovers]; and the mulattoes [people of mixed races] one sees in every family partly resemble the white children. Any lady is ready to tell you who is the father of all the mulatto children in everybody's household but her own. Those, she seems to think, drop from the clouds."

Such a double standard reinforced the arrogant authoritarianism of many white planters. In the secrecy of her diary, Mary Chesnut used sexual metaphors to express the limitations of most of the Carolina planters, writing that they "are nice fellows, but slow to move; impulsive but hard to keep moving. They are wonderful for a spurt, but that lets out all of their strength."

Yet for all their private complaints and daily burdens, few plantation mistresses, including Mary Chesnut, spoke out against the male-dominated social order and racist climate. They largely accepted the limited domestic role assigned them by men such as George Howe, a South Carolina religion professor. In 1850, he complimented southern women for understanding their subordinate place. "Born to lean upon others, rather than to stand independently by herself, and to confide in an arm stronger than hers," the southern woman had no desire for "power" outside the home, he said. The few women who were demanding equality were "unsexing" themselves and were "despised and detested" by their families and communities.

Most plantation mistresses agreed with Howe. With but a few exceptions, observed Julia Gardiner Tyler, the northern-born wife of President John Tyler, a Virginia slaveholder, women should limit themselves to the roles that "God designed for them"—"as wife, mother, mistress." Another prominent southern woman, Mary Howard Schoolcraft, described herself and other plantation wives in South Carolina as "old fogies" who refused to believe that "slavery is a sin." She could not imagine doing without the comforts and conveniences "afforded by slaves."

OVERSEERS AND DRIVERS On large plantations, *overseers* managed the slaves and were responsible for maintaining the buildings, fences, and grounds. They usually were white farmers or skilled workers, the sons of planters, or simply poor whites eager to rise in stature. Some were themselves slaveholders. The overseers moved often in search of better wages and cheaper land. A Mississippi planter described white overseers as "a worthless set of vagabonds." Likewise, Frederick Douglass, a mulatto who escaped from slavery in Maryland, said his overseer was "a miserable drunkard, a profane swearer, and a savage monster" always armed with a blood-stained bullwhip and a club that he used so cruelly that he even "enraged" the plantation owner. The overseer tolerated no excuses or explanations. "To be accused was to be convicted, and to be convicted was to be punished," Douglass said.

Usually, the highest managerial position a slave could hope for on a plantation was that of *driver*, a favored man whose job was to oversee a small group ("gang") of slaves, getting them up and organized each morning by sunrise, and then directing their work (and punishing them) until dark. Over the years, there were numerous examples of slaves murdering drivers for being too cruel.

There were a few black overseers. Francis Frederic, a slave in Kentucky, remembered that his grandmother's white master was a "hard one." He appointed her son, a slave, as the plantation's overseer. After the planter discovered that Frederic's grandmother had committed the crime of attending an outlawed prayer meeting, he ordered her son to give her "forty lashes with a thong of a raw cow's-hide, her master standing over her the whole time blaspheming and threatening what he would do if her son did not lay it on."

"PLAIN WHITE FOLK" About half of white southerners were small farmers, **"plain white folk"** who were usually uneducated, often illiterate, and forced to scratch out hardscrabble lives of bare self-sufficiency. These small farmers (yeomen) typically lived with their families in simple two-room cabins on fifty acres or less. They raised a few pigs and chickens and grew enough corn and cotton to live on. They traded with neighbors more than they bought from stores. Women on these small farms worked in the fields during harvest time but spent most of their days doing household chores while raising lots of children. Farm children grew up fast. By age four they could carry a water bucket from the well to the house and collect eggs from the henhouse. Young boys could plant, weed, and harvest crops, feed livestock, and milk cows.

The average slaveholder was a small farmer working alongside five or six slaves. Such "middling" farmers usually lived in a log cabin rather than a columned mansion. In the backcountry and mountainous regions of the South, where slaves and plantations were scarce, small farmers dominated the social structure.

Southern farmers tended to be fiercely independent and suspicious of government authority, and they overwhelmingly identified with the Democratic party of Andrew Jackson. Although only a minority of middle-class white farmers owned slaves, most of them supported the slave system. They feared that slaves, if freed, would compete with them for land and jobs, and, although not wealthy, the farmers enjoyed the privileged social status that race-based slavery afforded them. As a white farmer told a northern traveler, "Now suppose they [slaves] was free. You see they'd all think themselves as good as we." James Henry Hammond and other rich white planters frequently reminded their white neighbors who owned no slaves that "in a slave country, every freeman is an aristocrat" because blacks are beneath them in the social order. Such racist sentiments pervaded the Lower South—and much of the rest of the nation—throughout the nineteenth century.

"POOR WHITES" Visitors to the Old South often had trouble telling small farmers apart from the "poor whites," a category of desperately poor people who were relegated to the least desirable land and lived on the fringes of society. The "poor whites," often derided as "crackers," "hillbillies," or "trash," were usually day laborers or squatters who owned neither land nor slaves. Some 40 percent of white southerners worked as "tenants," renting land from others, or as farm laborers, toiling for others. They frequently took refuge in the pine barrens, mountain hollows, and swamps after having been pushed aside by the more enterprising and the more successful. They usually lived in log cabins or shacks and often made their own clothing, barely managing each year to keep their families clothed, dry, and fed.

BLACK SOCIETY IN THE SOUTH

Southern society was literally black and white. Whites had the power, and enslaved blacks were often treated as property rather than people. The system of slavery relied on overwhelming force and fear and was intentionally dehumanizing. "We believe the negro to belong to an inferior race," one planter declared. Southern apologists for slavery often stressed that African Americans were "inferior" beings incapable of living on their own. Thomas Reade Cobb proclaimed that they were better off "in a state of bondage."

Effective slave management therefore required teaching slaves to understand that they were supposed to be treated like animals. As Henry Garner, an escaped slave, explained, the aim of slaveholders was "to make you as much like brutes as possible." Others justified slavery as a form of benevolent paternalism. George Fitzhugh said that the enslaved black was "but a grown-up child, and must be governed as a child."

Such self-serving paternalism had one ultimate purpose: profits. Planters, explained a southerner, "care for nothing but to buy Negroes to raise cotton & raise cotton to buy Negroes." In 1818, James Steer in Louisiana predicted that enslaved blacks would be the best investment that southerners could make. Eleven years later, in 1829, the North Carolina Supreme Court declared that slavery existed to increase "the profit of the Master." The role of the slave was "to toil while another [the owners] reap the fruits."

Those in the business of buying and selling slaves reaped huge profits. One of them reported in the 1850s that "a nigger that wouldn't bring over $300, seven years ago, will fetch $1000, cash, quick, this year." Thomas Clemson of South Carolina, the son-in-law of John C. Calhoun, candidly explained that "my object is to get the most I can for the property [slaves]. . . . I care but little to whom and how they are sold, whether together [as families] or separated."

Owning, working, and selling slaves was the quickest way to wealth and social status in the South. The wife of a Louisiana planter complained in 1829 that white people talked constantly about how the profits generated by growing cotton enabled them to buy "plantations & negrows." In 1790, the United States had fewer than 700,000 enslaved African Americans. By 1830, it had more than 2 million, and by 1860, almost 4 million, virtually all of them in the South and border states.

THE SLAVE SYSTEM   As the enslaved population grew, slaveholders developed an increasingly complex *system* of rules, regulations, and restrictions. Formal **slave codes** in each state regulated the treatment of slaves in order to deter runaways or rebellions. Slaves could not leave their owner's land or household without permission or stay out after dark without an identification pass. Some codes made it a crime for slaves to learn to read and write, for fear that they might pass notes to plan a revolt. Frederick Douglass noted that slaveholders assumed that allowing slaves to learn to read and write "would spoil the best nigger in the world."

Slaves in most states could not testify in court, legally marry, own firearms, or hit a white man, even in self-defense. They could also be abused, tortured, and whipped. Despite such restrictions and brutalities, however, the enslaved managed to create their own communities and cultures within the confines of the slave system, forging bonds of care, solidarity, recreation, and religion.

"FREE PERSONS OF COLOR"   African Americans who were not enslaved were called free persons of color. They occupied an uncertain and often vulnerable social status between bondage and freedom. Many of them lived in constant fear of being kidnapped into slavery. To be sure, free blacks had more rights than slaves. They could enter into contracts, marry, own property (including slaves of their own), and pass on their property to their children. But they were not viewed or treated as equal to whites. In most states, they could not vote, own weapons, attend white church services, or testify against whites in court. In South Carolina, free people of color had to pay an annual tax and were not allowed to leave the state. After 1823, they were required to have a white "guardian" and an identity card.

Yarrow Mamout As an enslaved African Muslim, Mamout purchased his freedom, acquired property, and settled in present-day Washington, D.C. Charles Willson Peale painted this portrait in 1819, when Mamout was over 100 years old.

Some slaves were able to purchase their freedom, and others were freed ("manumitted") by their owners. By 1860, approximately 250,000 free blacks lived in the slave states, most of them in coastal cities such as Baltimore, Charleston, Savannah, Mobile, and New Orleans. Many were skilled workers. Some were tailors, shoemakers, or carpenters; others were painters, bricklayers, butchers, blacksmiths, or barbers. Still others worked on the docks or on steamships. Free black women usually worked as seamstresses, laundresses, or house servants.

Among the free black population were a large number of **mulattoes**, people of mixed racial ancestry. The census of 1860 reported 412,000 mulattoes in the United States, or about 10 percent of the black population—probably a drastic undercount. In cities such as Charleston, and especially New Orleans, "colored" society occupied a shifting status somewhere between that of blacks and that of whites.

Although most free people of color were poor, some mulattoes built substantial fortunes and even became slaveholders themselves. William Ellison was the richest freedman in the South. Liberated by his white father in 1816, he developed a thriving business in South Carolina making cotton gins while managing his own 900-acre plantation worked by more than sixty slaves. Ellison,

Free blacks This badge, issued in Charleston, South Carolina, was worn by a free black so that he would not be mistaken for someone's "property."

like other wealthy mulattoes, came to view himself as a "brown aristocrat." He yearned to be accepted as an equal in white society; during the Civil War, he supported the Confederacy. In Louisiana, a mulatto, Cyprien Ricard, paid $250,000 for an estate that had ninety-one slaves. In Natchez, Mississippi, William Johnson, son of a white father and a mulatto mother, operated three barbershops, owned 1,500 acres of land, and held several slaves.

Black or mulatto slaveholders were few in number, however. The 1830 census reported that 3,775 free blacks, about 2 percent of the total free black population, owned 12,760 slaves. Many of the African American slaveholders were men who bought or inherited their own family members.

THE TRADE IN SLAVES The rapid rise in the slave population during the early nineteenth century mainly occurred naturally, through slave births, especially after Congress and President Thomas Jefferson outlawed the African slave trade in 1808. By 1820, over 80 percent of slaves were American born.

Once the African slave trade was outlawed, the slave-trading network *within* the United States became much more important—and profitable. Between 1800 and 1860, the average price of slaves *quadrupled*, in large part because of the dramatic expansion of the cotton culture in the Old Southwest.

Breeding and selling slaves became a big business. Over a twenty year period, a Virginia plantation owned by John Tayloe III recorded 252 slave births and 142 slave deaths, thus providing Tayloe with 110 extra slaves to be deployed on the plantation, given to his sons, or sold to traders.

To manage the growing slave trade, markets and auction houses sprang up in every southern city. New Orleans alone had twenty slave-trading businesses. Each year, thousands of slaves circulated through the city's "slave pens." There they were converted from people into products with prices. They were bathed and groomed; "fattened up" with bacon, milk, and butter, like cattle; assigned categories such as Prime, No. 1, No. 2, and Second Rate; and "packaged" for sale by being dressed in identical blue suits or dresses. On auction day, they were paraded into the sale room. The tallest, strongest, and "blackest" young men brought the highest prices. As a slaver stressed, "I must have if possible the *jet black* Negroes, for they stand the climate best."

The business of slavery This advertisement for the Blount & Dawson trading company guarantees its clients "secure and good accommodations for all negroes left with us for Sale or Safe-Keeping" in its newly acquired jail, opposite the state bank.

Buyers physically inspected each slave on the "auction block" as if they were horses or cattle. They squeezed their muscles, felt their joints, worked their fingers back and forth, pried open their mouths to examine their teeth and gums. They then forced the slaves to strip and carefully inspected their naked bodies, looking for signs of disease or deformities. They particularly focused on any scars from whipping. As Solomon Northup noted, "scars on a slave's back were considered evidence of a rebellious or unruly spirit, and hurt [his chances for] sale."

During the 1830s, slave traders began advertising "fancy girls" among the slaves to be auctioned. The term referred to young African American women, distinctive for their beauty, who would fetch higher prices because of their sexual attractiveness. As a historian of the slave trade noted, "Slavery's frontier was a white man's sexual playground." Once the crude inspections ended, buyers bid on the slaves, purchased them, and then transported them to their new homes.

Almost a million captive African Americans, many of them children, were "sold South" or "downriver" and taken to the Old Southwest during the first half of the nineteenth century. Planters purchasing slaves knew what they wanted. "It is better to buy *none in families*," said a Mississippi buyer, "but to select *only choice, first rate, young hands from 16 to 25 years of age* (buying no children or aged negroes)."

The worst aspect of the domestic slave trade was the separation of children from parents and husbands from wives. Children were often taken from their parents and sold to new masters. In Missouri, one enslaved woman saw six of her seven children, ages one to eleven, sold to six different owners. Only

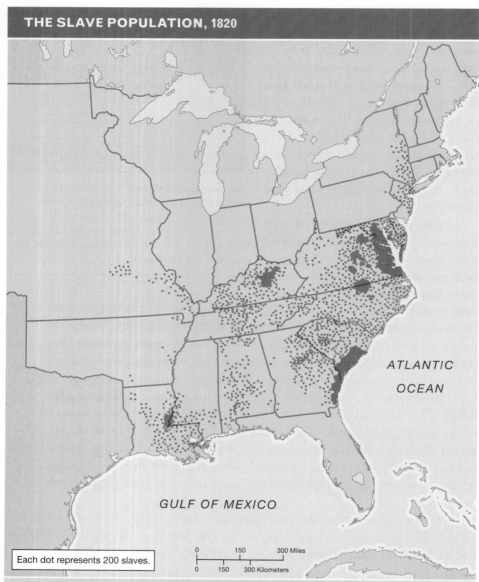

THE SLAVE POPULATION, 1820

ATLANTIC OCEAN

GULF OF MEXICO

Each dot represents 200 slaves.

0   150   300 Miles

0   150   300 Kilometers

- Consider where the largest populations of slaves were clustered in the South in 1820. Why were most slaves living in these regions and not in others?
- How was the experience of plantation slavery different for men and women?

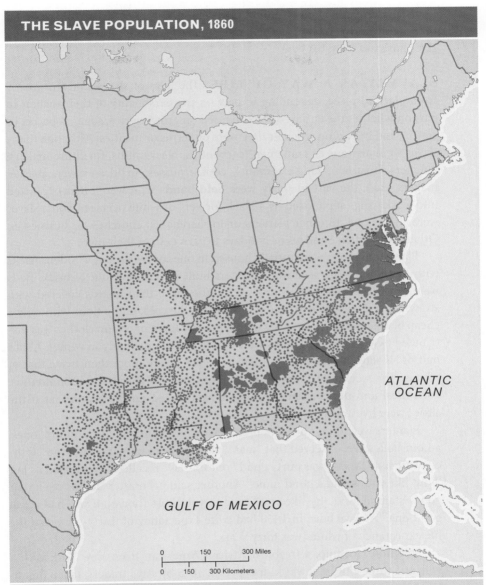

THE SLAVE POPULATION, 1860

ATLANTIC
OCEAN

GULF OF MEXICO

| 0 | | 150 | | 300 Miles |
| 0 | | 150 | 300 Kilometers | |

■ Compare this map with the map of cotton production on page 473.
What patterns do you see?
■ Why did many slaves resist migrating west?

Louisiana and Alabama (from 1852) prohibited separating a child younger than ten from his or her mother, and no state prevented the separation of a slave husband from his wife.

SLAVERY AS A WAY OF LIFE   The lives of slaves differed greatly from place to place, depending in part on the personality of their owner; in part on whether the enslaved were focused on growing rice, sugar, tobacco, or cotton; and in part on whether they were on farms or in cities. Although many slaves were artisans or craftsmen (carpenters, blacksmiths, furniture makers, butchers, boatmen, house servants, cooks, nurses, maids, weavers, basket makers, etc.), the vast majority were **field hands** who were often organized into work gangs supervised by a black "driver" or white overseer. Some slaves were "hired out" to other planters or to merchants, churches, or businesses. Others worked on Sundays or holidays to earn cash of their own.

Plantation slaves were usually housed in one- or two-room wooden shacks with dirt floors. The wealthiest planters built slave cabins out of brick. Beds were a luxury, even though they were little more than boards covered with straw. Most slaves were expected to sleep on the cold, damp floor with only a cheap blanket for warmth. A set of inexpensive linen or cotton clothes was distributed twice a year, but shoes were generally provided only in winter. About half of all slave babies died in their first year, a rate more than twice that of whites. The weekly or monthly food allotment was cheap and monotonous: corn meal and pork, often served in bowls placed on the ground, as if the slaves were livestock.

Planters were quite varied in their personalities and practices. Philip Jones, a Louisiana slave, observed that "many planters were humane and kind." Others were not. "Massa was purty good," one ex-slave recalled. "He treated us jus' 'bout like you would a good mule." Another said his master "fed us reg'lar on good, 'stantial food, jus' like you'd tend to your hoss [horse], if you had a real good one." A slave born in 1850 had a life expectancy of thirty-six years; the life expectancy of whites was forty years.

Solomon Northup, a freeborn African American from New York with a wife and three children, was kidnapped in 1845 by slave traders, taken first to Washington, D.C., and then to New Orleans, and eventually sold to a "repulsive and coarse" Louisiana cotton planter. More than a decade later, Northup was able to regain his freedom.

In *Twelve Years a Slave* (1853), Northup described his living and working conditions. His bed "was a plank twelve inches wide and ten feet long. My pillow was a stick of wood. The bedding was a coarse blanket." The log cabin where he and others slept had a dirt floor and no windows. Each day, "an hour before daylight, the horn is blown. Then the slaves arouse, prepare their breakfast . . . and hurry to the field." If found in their "quarters after daybreak," slaves were flogged. "It was rarely that a day passed by without one or more whippings. . . . The crack of the lash, and the shrieking of the slaves, can be heard from dark till bed time."

Field hands worked from sunrise to sunset, six days a week. At times they were worked at night as well, ginning cotton, milling sugarcane, grinding corn, or doing other indoor tasks. Women, remembered a slave, "had to work all day in de fields an' den come home an' do the housework at night." Sundays were precious days off. Slaves used the Sabbath to hunt, fish, dance to banjo and fiddle music, tell stories, or tend their own small gardens.

Beginning in August and lasting several months, the focus was on picking cotton. The productivity per slave increased dramatically during the first half of the nineteenth century, in large part because of the implementation of the "pushing system." During harvest season, each slave was assigned a daily quota of cotton to be picked, an amount that increased over the years.

Gangs of slaves, men and women, would sweep across a field, pull the bolls from the thorny pods, and stuff them in large sacks or baskets which they dragged behind them. All the while, they were watched and prodded by an overseer, bullwhip in hand, forcing them to keep up the pace. Solomon Northup remembered picking cotton until it was "too dark to see, and when the moon is full, they oftentimes labor till the middle of the night." Each evening, the baskets would be weighed and the number of pounds recorded on a slate board by each picker's name. Those who fell short of their quota were scolded and whipped.

THE VIOLENCE OF SLAVERY   Although some owners and slaves developed close and even affectionate relationships, slavery on the whole was a system rooted in brutal force. The difference between a good owner and a bad one, according to one slave, was the difference between one "who did not whip you too much" and one who "whipped you till he'd bloodied you and blistered you." One overseer in South Carolina whipped eight women simply for hoeing "bad corn." Others were whipped for "not picking cotton"; "for not picking as well as he can"; or for picking "very trashy cotton." Bennett Barrow, a Louisiana planter, on average had a slave whipped every four days as a means of symbolizing his absolute control.

Allen Sidney, a slave, recalled an incident on a Mississippi plantation that illustrated the ruthlessness of cotton production. A slave who fell behind while picking cotton resisted when a black driver started to "whip him up." Upon seeing the fracas, the white overseer, mounted on horseback, galloped over,

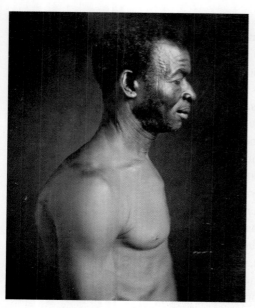

***Jack* (1850)** Daguerreotype of a slave identified only as Jack, on the plantation of B. F. Taylor in Columbia, South Carolina.

and shot the resisting slave, killing him. "None of the other slaves," Sidney noted, "said a word or turned their heads. They kept on hoeing as if nothing had happened."

At times, whites turned the punishment of slaves into grisly spectacles to strike fear into anyone considering rebellion or escape. In Louisiana, whippings often followed a horrific procedure, as a visitor reported: "Three stakes is drove into the ground in a triangular manner, about six feet apart. The culprit [slave] is told to lie down . . . flat on his belly. The arms is extended out, sideways, and each hand tied to a stake hard and fast. The feet is both tied to the third stake, all stretched tight." The overseer would then step back "seven, eight or ten feet and with a rawhide whip about 7 feet long . . . lays on with great force and address across the Buttocks," cutting strips of flesh "7 or 8 inches long at every stroke."

URBAN SLAVERY Slaves living in southern cities such as Richmond, Memphis, Atlanta, New Orleans, or Charleston had a much different experience from those on isolated farms and plantations. "A city slave is almost a freeman," claimed a Maryland slave.

Slaves in urban households tended to be better fed and clothed and had more privileges. They interacted not only with their white owners but with the extended interracial community—shopkeepers and police, neighbors and strangers. Some were hired out to others and were often allowed to keep a portion of their wages. Generally speaking, slaves in cities enjoyed greater mobility and freedom than their counterparts in rural areas.

ENSLAVED WOMEN Although enslaved men and women often performed similar chores, especially on farms, they did not experience slavery in the same way. Once slaveholders realized how profitable a fertile female slave could be by giving birth to babies that could later be sold, they "encouraged" female slaves to have as many children as possible. A South Carolina planter named William Johnson explained in 1815 that the "interest of the owner is to obtain from his slaves labor *and increase* [in their numbers]." Sometimes a woman would be locked in a cabin with a male slave whose task was to impregnate her. Pregnant slaves were given less work and more food. Some plantation owners rewarded new mothers with dresses and silver dollars.

But if motherhood provided enslaved women with greater stature and benefits, it also was exhausting. Within days after childbirth, mothers were put back to work spinning, weaving, or sewing. A few weeks thereafter, they were sent back to the fields; breast-feeding mothers were often forced to take their babies with them, strapped to their backs. Enslaved women were expected to do "man's work": cut trees, haul logs, spread fertilizer, plow fields, dig ditches, slaughter animals, hoe corn, and pick cotton. Many of them, in fact, were more productive cotton pickers than the men. As an escaped slave reported, "Women who do outdoor work are used as bad as men."

Once women passed their childbearing years, their workload increased. Slaveholders put middle-aged women to work full-time in the fields or performing

Slave family in a Georgia cotton field The invention of the cotton gin sent cotton production soaring, deepening the South's dependence on slavery in the process.

other outdoor labor. On large plantations, elderly women, called *grannies*, kept the children during the day, and slave women also worked as cooks and seamstresses, midwives and nurses, healers and folk doctors.

Enslaved girls and women also faced the constant threat of sexual abuse. James Henry Hammond, the prominent South Carolina planter and former governor, confessed that he was a powerful man of passion who nurtured a "system of roguery" among his female slaves. He had a long affair with one of his young female slaves, Sally Johnson, who bore several of his children. Later, to the horror of his long-suffering wife, Hammond began another affair with one of his and Sally's daughters, twelve-year-old Louisa, and fathered more children with her. (Hammond also had scandalous affairs with four "lovely and luscious" teen-aged nieces and two daughters of his sister-in-law).

CELIA   The tragic story of a slave girl named Celia reveals the moral complexity of slavery for African American women and the limited legal options available to the enslaved. As Celia discovered, slaves often could improve their circumstances only by making horrible choices that offered no guarantee of success.

In 1850, fourteen-year-old Celia was purchased by Robert Newsom, a Missouri farmer who told his daughters that he had bought the girl to be their servant. In fact, however, the recently widowed Newsom wanted a sexual slave. After purchasing Celia, he raped her, and for the next five years, he treated her as his mistress, even building her a brick cabin fifty yards from his house. During that time, she gave birth to two children.

On June 23, 1855, the sixty-five-year-old Newsom entered Celia's cabin, ignored her frantic appeals, and kept assaulting her until she struck and killed him with a large stick and then burned his body in the fireplace. Celia was not allowed to testify at her murder trial because she was a slave. The judge and jury, all white men, pronounced her guilty, and on December 21, 1855, she was hanged. The grim story of Celia's abusive owner and her own brief life illustrates the lopsided power structure in southern society at the time. Celia bore a double burden, that of being a slave and also of being a woman living in a male-dominated society rife with racism and sexism.

FORGING A SLAVE COMMUNITY

Despite being victims of terrible injustice and abuse, enslaved African Americans displayed endurance, resilience, and achievement. Wherever they could, they forged their own sense of community, asserted their individuality, and devised ingenious ways to resist their confinement. Many slaves, especially those on the largest plantations, would gather at secret "night meetings," usually after midnight, where they would drink stolen alcohol, dance, sing, and tell stories of resistance. Many of the stories were derived from African tales, such as that of "Brer [Brother] Rabbit," a smart little rabbit who used his wits to elude the larger animals stalking him by hiding in a patch of prickly briars. Such frequently told stories impressed upon slaves the importance of deceiving those with power over them.

Many religious **spirituals**, the predecessors to the blues, also contained double meanings, often expressing a longing to get to a "free country," what slaves called "Sweet Canaan" or the "promised land." The spiritual "Wade in the Water," for example, contained underlying instructions to runaways about how to evade capture. Avoiding dry land and running in creek beds ("wading in the water") were common ways to throw off pursuing bloodhounds. Songs such as "The Gospel Train" and "Swing Low, Sweet Chariot" included disguised references to the Underground Railroad, the secret organization that helped slaves escape to the North.

Frederick Douglass recalled that the spirituals not only helped runaways but also were a form of protest. They "breathed the prayer and complaint of souls overflowing with the bitterest anguish. . . . The songs of the slave represent the sorrows of his heart, rather than his joys. Like tears, they were a relief to aching hearts."

THE SLAVE FAMILY Although states did not recognize slave marriages, they did not prevent men and women from choosing life partners and forging families within the constraints of the slave system. Many slaveholders accepted unofficial marriages as a stabilizing influence; a black man who supported a family, they assumed, would be more reliable and obedient. Sometimes slaveholders performed "wedding" ceremonies in the slave quarters or had a minister conduct the service. Whatever the formalities, the norm for the slave community, as for the white, was the nuclear family, with the father as the head of the household.

A slave's childhood did not last long. At five or six years of age, children were put to work; they collected trash and firewood, picked cotton, scared away crows from planted fields, and ran errands. By age ten, they were full-time field hands.

Enslaved African Americans often extended the fellowship of family to those who worked with them, with older slave women being addressed as "granny," or coworkers as "sis" or "brother." Such efforts to create a sense of extended family resembled kinship practices in Africa. One white teacher visiting a slave community observed that they "all belonged to one immense family."

RELIGION IN THE OLD SOUTH

The Old South was made up of God-fearing people whose faith sustained them. Although there were pockets of Catholicism and Judaism in the large coastal cities—Baltimore, Richmond, Charleston, Savannah, and New Orleans—the vast majority of southerners, white and black, embraced evangelical Protestant denominations such as Baptists and Methodists, both of which wanted to create a Kingdom of God on earth before the millennium, when Jesus would return (the "second coming").

SLAVERY AND RELIGION   In the late eighteenth century, Baptists and Methodists had condemned slavery, welcomed blacks to their congregations, and given women important roles in their churches. Many slaveholders, led by George Washington and Thomas Jefferson, had agonized over the immorality of slavery.

By the 1830s, however, criticism of slavery in the southern states had virtually disappeared. Most preachers switched from attacking slavery to defending it as a divinely ordained, Bible-sanctioned social system that was a blessing to both master and slave. Alexander Glennie, a white minister, told slaves that their life of bondage was the "will of God." Most ministers who refused to promote slavery left the region.

***Plantation Burial* (1860)** The slaves of Mississippi governor Tilghman Tucker gather in the woods to bury and mourn for one of their own. The painter of this scene, Englishman John Antrobus, would serve in the Confederate army during the Civil War.

Frederick Douglass stressed that all of the men who owned him were Christians, but their faith never made a difference in how they treated their slaves. In 1832, Douglass's master experienced a powerful conversion to Christianity at a Methodist revival and became a religious "exhorter" himself. He prayed "morning, noon, and night," but his devotion to Christ had no effect on how he treated his slaves. In fact, he was even "more cruel and hateful," quoting a Bible verse as he whipped a lame young woman: "The servant that knoweth his master's will, and doeth it not, shall be beaten with many stripes."

AFRICAN AMERICAN RELIGION Among the most important elements of African American culture was its dynamic religion, a mixture of African, Caribbean, and Christian elements often practiced in secret because many slaveholders feared enslaved workers might use group religious services to organize rebellions. Religion provided slaves both relief for the soul and release for their emotions.

Most Africans brought with them to the Americas belief in a Creator, or Supreme God, whom they could recognize in the Christian God, and whom they might identify with Christ, the Holy Ghost, and the saints. But they also believed in spirits, magic, charms, and conjuring—the casting of spells. A conjurer, it was believed, was like a witch doctor or a voodoo priest who could suddenly make someone sick or heal the afflicted.

Whites usually tried to eliminate African religion and spirituality from the slave experience. Slaves responded by gathering secretly in what were called camp meetings, or bush meetings, to worship in their own way and share their joys, pains, and hopes.

By 1860, about 20 percent of adult slaves had joined Christian denominations. Many others practiced aspects of the Christian faith but were not considered Christians. As a white minister observed, some slaves had "heard of Jesus Christ, but who he is and what he has done for a ruined world, they cannot tell." But few whites fully understood the dynamics or mysteries of slave religion or its power.

Slaves found the Bible inspiring in its support for the poor and oppressed, and they embraced its promise of salvation through the sacrifice of Jesus. Likewise, the lyrics of religious spirituals helped slaves endure the strain of field labor and express their dreams of gaining freedom in "the promised land." Spirituals offered musical deliverance from worldly woes and strengthened solidarity among slaves. One popular spiritual, "Go Down, Moses," derived from the plight of the ancient Israelites held captive in Egypt, says: "We need not always weep and moan, / Let my people go. / And wear these slavery chains forlorn, / Let my people go." Another spiritual gave song to hope: "I do believe! / I do believe! / I will overcome some day."

Many white planters assumed that Christianized slaves would be more passive and obedient. A south Georgia planter declared that a Christian slave "is more profitable than an unfaithful one. He will do more and better work, be less troublesome, and [even] less liable to disease."

Planter James Henry Hammond despised the emotional singing, ecstatic shouting, raucous clapping, and energetic prayers that animated African American worship. He banned dancing and the beating of drums. Hammond, however, wanted his "heathen" slaves to become Christians. To do so, he hired itinerant white ministers ("plantation preachers") to conduct Christian services for them and constructed a Methodist church on his plantation. A white visitor who attended the church reported that there were no "religious excesses" or "hysteria" among the worshipping slaves. Hammond had forced them to display the religious passivity he desired.

SLAVE REBELLIONS

The greatest fear of whites in the Lower South was an organized slave revolt, as had occurred in 1791 in the French-controlled sugar colony of Saint-Domingue, which eventually became the independent Republic of Haiti. In a rebellion unprecedented in history, slaves rose up and burned plantations, destroyed cane fields, and killed white planters and their families.

The rebellion in Saint-Domingue, the world's richest colony and the leading source of sugar and coffee, was the first successful slave revolt in the Western Hemisphere. It sent shock waves across the United States. Many terrified whites who fled Haiti arrived in Charleston, where they told of the horrors they had experienced. Despite repeated attempts by both French and British armies to reconquer Haiti, the former slaves, led by Toussaint L'Ouverture, defeated them all.

The revolt in Haiti was the southern slaveholder's greatest nightmare. As a prominent Virginian explained, a slave uprising would "deluge the southern country with blood." Any sign of resistance or rebellion among the enslaved therefore risked a brutal and even gruesome response.

In 1811, for example, two of Thomas Jefferson's nephews, Lilburn and Isham Lewis, tied a seventeen-year-old slave named George to the floor of their Kentucky cabin and killed him with an axe in front of seven other slaves, all because George had run away several times. They then handed the axe to one of the slaves and forced him to dismember the body and put the pieces in the fireplace. The Lewises, who had been drinking heavily, wanted "to set an example for any other uppity slaves."

THE PROSSER CONSPIRACY The overwhelming authority and firepower of southern whites made organized resistance risky. The nineteenth-century South witnessed only four major slave insurrections. The first occurred in 1800, when a slave named Gabriel Prosser, a blacksmith on a plantation near Richmond, Virginia, hatched a revolt involving hundreds of slaves. They planned to seize key points in the city, capture the governor, James Monroe, and overthrow the white elite. Gabriel expected the "poor white people" to join their effort. But someone alerted whites to the scheme, and a ferocious rainstorm forced "Gabriel's army" to scatter. Gabriel and twenty-six of his fellow "soldiers" were captured and hanged, while ten others were deported to the West Indies. A white Virginian who observed the executions noted that the rebels on the gallows displayed a "sense of their [natural] rights, [and] a contempt for danger."

REVOLT IN LOUISIANA In early 1811, the largest slave revolt in American history occurred just north of New Orleans, where powerful sugarcane planters had acquired one of the largest populations of slaves in North America. Many of those slaves were ripe for revolt. Sugarcane was known as a "killer crop" because working conditions were so harsh that many slaves died from laboring in the intense heat and humidity.

Late on January 8, a group of slaves led by Charles Deslondes, a trusted black overseer, broke into their owner's plantation house along the east bank of the Mississippi River. The planter was able to escape, but his son was hacked to death. Deslondes and his fellow rebels seized weapons, horses, and militia uniforms. Reinforced by more slaves and emboldened by liquor, the rebels headed toward New Orleans, some fifty miles away. Along the way, they burned houses, killed whites, and gathered more recruits. Over the next two days, their ranks swelled to more than 200.

Their success was short-lived, however. The territorial governor mobilized a group of angry whites—as well as several free blacks who were later praised for their "tireless zeal and dauntless courage"—to suppress the insurrection. U.S. Army units and militia joined in. Dozens of slaves were killed or wounded, and most of those who fled were soon captured. "We made considerable slaughter," reported one white planter.

Deslondes had his hands chopped off and was then shot in both thighs and his chest. As he was slowly bleeding to death, a bale of hay was scattered over him and ignited. As many as 100 slaves were tortured, killed, and beheaded, and the severed heads were placed on poles along the Mississippi River. A month after the rebellion was put down, a white resident noted that "all the negro difficulties have subsided and gentle peace prevails."

DENMARK VESEY The Denmark Vesey plot in Charleston, South Carolina, involved a similar effort to assault the white population. Vesey was a Caribbean slave who, in 1785, was taken to Charleston, where, like many urban slaves, he was allowed to work for pay in his free time, at nights, and on Sundays. In 1799, he purchased a lottery ticket and won $1,500, which he used to buy his freedom and start his own carpentry shop. He thereafter learned to read and write and organized a Bible study class for other free blacks in the African Methodist Episcopal (AME) Church. Yet he retained a simmering hatred for whites and for the slave system they imposed on blacks.

In 1822, Vesey and several other blacks, including the colorful African-born Gullah Jack, developed a plan for a massive slave revolt. They would first capture the city's arsenal and distribute its hundreds of rifles to both free and enslaved blacks. All whites in the city would then be killed, along with any blacks who refused to join the rebellion. Vesey then planned to burn the city, seize ships, and head for the black republic of Haiti.

The Vesey plot never got off the ground, however. A slave who had been secretly recruited by Vesey told his master about the planned rebellion, and soon Vesey and 135 others were captured, arrested, and tried. The court found Vesey guilty of plotting to "trample on all laws, human and divine; to riot in blood, outrage, rapine . . . and conflagration, and to introduce anarchy and confusion in their most horrid forms." Vesey and thirty-four others were executed; three dozen more were transported to Spanish-controlled Cuba and sold into slavery. The AME church in Charleston was closed and demolished. When told that he would be hanged, Vesey replied that "the work of insurrection will go on."

Vesey's planned rebellion led South Carolina officials to place additional restrictions on the mobility of free blacks and black religious gatherings. It also influenced John C. Calhoun to abandon the nationalism of his early political career and become the South's most outspoken advocate for states' rights and slavery.

NAT TURNER'S REBELLION Vesey's thwarted slave rebellion was not the last, however. News of the Nat Turner insurrection of August 22, 1831, in Southampton County, Virginia, where blacks were the majority, panicked whites throughout the South. Turner, a trusted black overseer, was also a preacher and healer who believed God had instructed him to "proclaim liberty to the captive" slaves and lead a rebellion that would enact "the day of vengeance of our God." He interpreted a solar eclipse in February 1831 as God's signal for him to act. Turner chose August 21 as the day to launch his insurrection, in part because it was the fortieth anniversary of the Haitian slave rebellion.

The revolt began when Turner, in the middle of the night, unlocked the door of his master's house and let in a small group of slaves armed with axes. "Remember that ours is not a war for robbery, nor to satisfy our passions," he instructed them; "it is a *struggle for freedom*." They methodically murdered the owner, Joseph Travis, and his wife Sally, their twelve-year-old son, a young apprentice, and a baby, all sleeping in their beds. They then repeated the process at other farmhouses, where more slaves and some free blacks joined in. Some slaves tried to protect or hide their owners. Before the two-day revolt ended, fifty-seven whites had been killed, most of them women and children, including ten students at a school.

Federal troops, Virginia militiamen, and volunteers crushed the revolt, indiscriminately killing scores of slaves in the process. A newspaper described the behavior of the white vigilantes as comparable in "barbarity to the atrocities of the insurgents." Twenty African Americans were hanged, including three free blacks; several were decapitated, and their severed heads were placed on poles along the road. Turner, called the "blood-stained monster," avoided capture for six weeks. He then was tried, found guilty, and hanged. His dead body was dismembered, with body parts given to the victims' families.

More than any other slave uprising, **Nat Turner's Rebellion** terrified whites by making real the lurking fear that enslaved blacks might launch organized revolts. A Virginia state legislator claimed that people suspected "that a Nat Turner might be in every family, that the same bloody deed could be acted over at any time."

The Virginia legislature responded by barring slaves from learning to read and write and from gathering for religious meetings. The city of Mobile, Alabama, prohibited gatherings of three or more slaves, and white ministers were dispatched to preach obedience to enslaved workers.

In addition, states created more armed patrols to track down runaways. A former slave highlighted the "thousand obstacles thrown in the way of the flying slave. Every white man's hand is raised against him—the

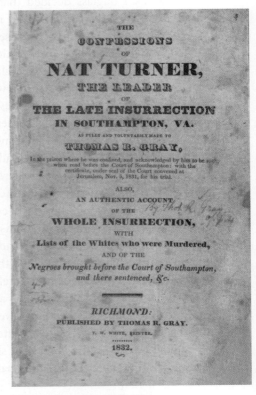

The Confessions of Nat Turner
Published account of Turner's rebellion, written by Turner's lawyer, Thomas Gray.

patrollers are watching for him—the hounds are ready to follow on his track, and the nature of the country is such as renders it impossible to pass through it with any safety." Running away meant exposing oneself to flogging—or much worse.

THE LURE OF FREEDOM　Yet stealthy and silent as fog, thousands of escaped slaves (called "fugitives") made it to freedom in spite of the obstacles facing them. The fugitive slaves were a powerful example of the enduring lure of freedom and the extraordinary courage of those who yearn for it. On average, some 50,000 enslaved people tried to escape each year. Others ran away for short periods of time, usually to avoid being beaten by flash-tempered owners or overseers. A house cook named Bertcha was so frightened that her owner was going to kill her that she "ran for the woods and hid there and stayed three weeks."

Frederick Douglass decided that risking death was better than staying in bondage: "I had as well be killed running as die standing." The odds were stacked against escape, in part because most slaves could not read, had no maps, and could not use public transportation such as stagecoaches, steamboats, and railroads. Blacks, whether free or enslaved, had to have an identity pass or official emancipation papers to go anywhere on their own. Runaways, the vast majority of whom were young males, often were forced to return when they ran out of food or lost their way. Others were tracked down by bloodhounds or bounty hunters. Only about 1,000 slaves each year safely made it to freedom.

Many slaveholders could not understand why any slave would run away. Scottish-born William Dunbar ordered that two of his runaways ("poor, ignorant devils") in Mississippi be given 500 lashes and then had logs chained to their ankles. Why would they try to escape, he asked in a letter. "They are well clothed, work easy, and have all kinds of plantation produce" for free.

Slaves who did not escape found other ways to resist. They often exasperated, enraged, and manipulated their owners. Some faked illness, stole or broke tools, destroyed crops or secretly slaughtered and ate livestock. Others slacked off when unsupervised. As a slave song confessed, "You may think I'm working / But I ain't." Yet there were constraints on such rebellious behavior, for laborers would likely eat better on a prosperous plantation than on a struggling one. And the shrewdest slaveholders knew that offering rewards was more profitable than inflicting pain.

The South—A Region Apart

The rapid settlement of the western territories during the first half of the nineteenth century set in motion a ferocious competition between North and South for political influence in the West. Would the new western territories and states be "slave" or "free"? Congressmen from the newly admitted western states would tip the delicate political balance in Washington, D.C., one way or the other, slave or free.

Because of the rapidly growing profitability of slave-grown cotton, southerners exercised immense political power, both to protect the system of slavery and expand it into new lands made available by the removal of Indians, and to embed the economy of cotton into national and world markets.

The aggressive efforts to expand slavery westward in the face of growing criticism from the North ignited a prolonged political controversy that would end in civil war. As the 1832 nullification controversy in South Carolina had revealed, southerners despised being told what to do by outsiders, and they especially resented the growing demands for the abolition of slavery.

To cement the slave system in the culture of the South, many in the 1850s imagined every white family in the region owning slaves. "Ours is a pro-slavery form of government," explained a Georgia newspaper editor. "For our part, we would like to see every white man in the South the owner of a family of negroes."

The recurring theme of southern politics and culture from the 1830s to the outbreak of civil war in 1861 was the region's determination to remain a society dominated by whites who lorded over people of color. A South Carolinian asserted that "slavery with us is no abstraction—but a great and vital fact. Without it, our every comfort would be taken from us."

Protecting their right to own, transport, and sell slaves in the new western territories became the overriding focus of southern political leaders during the 1830s and after. Race-based slavery provided the South's prosperity as well as its growing sense of separateness—and defensiveness—from the rest of the nation.

Throughout the 1830s, southern state legislatures were "one and indivisible" in their efforts to preserve race-based slavery. They shouted defiance against northern abolitionists. Virginia's General Assembly, for example, declared that only the southern states had the right to control slavery and that such control must be "maintained at all hazards." The Georgia legislature agreed, announcing that "upon this point there can be no discussion—no compromise—no doubt."

With each passing year, the leaders of the Old South equated the survival of their distinctive region with the preservation of slavery. As the governor of Mississippi insisted in 1850, slavery "is entwined with our political system and cannot be separated from it." The increasingly militant efforts of northerners to restrict or abolish slavery helped reinforce southern unity while provoking an emotional defensiveness that would result in secession and war—and the unexpected end of slavery and the Cotton Kingdom it enabled.

CHAPTER REVIEW

SUMMARY

- **Southern Distinctiveness**   The South remained rural and agricultural in the first half of the nineteenth century as the rest of the nation embraced urban industrial development. The region's climate favored the growth of cash crops such as tobacco, rice, indigo, and increasingly, cotton. These crops led to the spread of the plantation system of large commercial agriculture dependent on enslaved labor. The southern planter elite not only sought to preserve slavery but to expand it, despite growing criticism of the *"peculiar institution."*

- **A Cotton Economy**   The Old South became increasingly committed to a cotton economy. Despite efforts to diversify the economic base, the wealth and status associated with cotton, as well as soil exhaustion and falling prices from Virginia to Georgia, prompted the westward expansion of the plantation culture to the *Old Southwest*. Slaves worked in harsh conditions as they prepared the terrain for cotton cultivation and experienced the breakup of their families. By 1860, the *Cotton Kingdom* stretched from the Carolinas and Georgia through eastern Texas and up the Mississippi River to Illinois. More than half of all slaves worked on cotton plantations. As long as cotton prices rose, southern planters searched for new land and invested in slaves to increase their cotton output.

- **Southern White Culture**   White society was divided between the planter elite— those who owned twenty slaves or more—and all the rest. *Planters* represented only around 4 percent of the white population but they exercised a disproportionately powerful political and social influence. Other whites owned a few slaves, but most owned none. A majority of whites were *"plain white folk"*—simple farmers who raised corn, cotton, hogs, and chickens. Southern farmers were highly mobile and willing to move west. Southern white women spent most of their time on household chores. The *plantation mistress* supervised her home and household slaves. Most whites were fiercely loyal to the institution of slavery. Even those who owned no slaves feared the competition they believed they would face if slaves were freed, and they enjoyed the privileged status that race-based slavery gave them.

- **Southern Black Culture**   As slavery spread and the southern economy became more dependent on slave labor, the enslaved faced more regulations and restrictions on their behavior. The vast majority of southern blacks served as *field hands*. They had few rights and could be bought and sold at any time. Their movements were severely limited and they had no ability to defend themselves. Any violations could result in severe punishments. Most southern blacks were slaves, but a small percentage were free. Many of the free blacks were *mulattoes*, having mixed-race parentage. Free blacks often worked for wages in towns and cities.

- **African American Resistance and Resilience**   Originally, slaves were treated more as indentured servants and were eligible for freedom after a specified number of years. But *slave codes* eventually codified the practice of treating slaves as property rather than as people. The enslaved responded in a variety of ways. Although many attempted to escape, only a few openly rebelled because the consequences were so harsh. Organized revolts such as *Nat Turner's Rebellion* in Virginia were rare. Most slaves survived by relying on their own communities, family ties, and Christian faith, and by developing their own culture, such as the singing of *spirituals* to express frustration, sorrow, and hope for their eventual deliverance.

CHRONOLOGY

1790	The enslaved population of the United States is almost 700,000
1791	Slave revolt in Saint-Domingue (Haiti)
1800	Gabriel Prosser conspiracy in Richmond, Virginia
1808	U.S. participation in the international slave trade is outlawed
1811	Charles Deslondes revolt in Louisiana
1814	Annual cotton production in the United States is 150,000 bales
1822	Denmark Vesey conspiracy is discovered in Charleston, South Carolina
1830	U.S. slave population exceeds 2 million
1831	Nat Turner leads slave insurrection in Virginia
1840	Population in the Old Southwest tops 1.5 million
1860	Annual cotton production in the United States reaches 4 million bales
	Slave population in the United States reaches 4 million

KEY TERMS

 INQUIZITIVE

Go to InQuizitive to see what you've learned—and learn what you've missed—with personalized feedback along the way.

12 Religion, Romanticism, and Reform

1800–1860

***The Voyage of Life: Childhood* (1839–1840)** In his *Voyage of Life* series, Thomas Cole drew upon both the religious revivalism and Romantic ideals of the period to depict the four stages of a man's life: childhood (shown above), youth, manhood, and old age. In this painting, an infant drifts along the River of Life with his guardian angel into the fertile landscape from the dark cave, meant to be "emblematic of our earthly origin, and the mysterious Past."

During the first half of the nineteenth century, the United States, the world's largest republic, was a nation of contrasts. Europeans traveling in America marveled at the nation's restless energy and expansive optimism, its commitment to democratic ideals, and its remarkable capitalist spirit.

However, visitors also noticed that the dynamic young republic was experiencing growing pains as the market revolution continued to excite a lust for profits and to widen economic inequality. Sectional tensions over economic policies (such as tariffs and the regulation of banks) and increasingly heated debates over the morality and future of slavery made for a combative political scene.

Unlike the nations of Europe, which were steeped in history and romance, the United States was a young society whose founding leaders had embraced the central ideas of the Enlightenment—liberty, equality, and reason—which in turn led to the American ideals of representative government and the pursuit of happiness, most vividly set forth in Thomas Jefferson's Declaration of Independence.

During the first half of the nineteenth century, new, more-democratic ideals and expectations influenced religious life, literature, and the arts; social-reform movements grew in scope and significance as Americans sought to "perfect" their society. Politics was not the only battleground—religious and cultural life also experienced intense conflicts and radical new points of view.

After the Revolution, Americans were as interested in gaining religious salvation as they were in exercising political rights. A righteous army of Christian evangelists democratized the path to spiritual deliverance at the same time

focus questions

1. What major changes took place in the practice of religion in America in the early nineteenth century? What impact did these have on American society?

2. How did transcendentalism emerge in the early nineteenth century?

3. What were the origins of the major social-reform movements in the early nineteenth century? How did they influence American society and politics?

4. How did the emergence of the anti-slavery movement impact American society and politics?

that states were democratizing the political process. So-called freewill ministers insisted that everyone, regardless of their wealth or circumstances, could *choose* to be saved by embracing Jesus's promise of salvation just as more men who owned no property were allowed to *choose* their elected officials.

Evangelicals assumed that the American republic had a God-mandated mission to provide a shining example of representative government, much as Puritan New England had once stood as an example of an ideal Christian community. The concept of America having a special God-given *mission* to create an ideal society (often called "manifest destiny") still carried strong spiritual overtones.

The sense of America being on a God-directed mission also contained an element of perfectionism: people could become more and more perfect through a commitment to reforming themselves and society. Throughout the first half of the nineteenth century, reformers fanned out across the United States, and the combination of widespread religious energy and intense social activism brought major advances in human rights. It also at times triggered cynicism and disillusionment.

A MORE DEMOCRATIC RELIGION

The energies of the rational Enlightenment and the spiritual Great Awakening flowed from the colonial period into the nineteenth century. In different ways, these two powerful modes of thought, one scientific and rational and the other religious and optimistic, eroded the old Calvinist view that people were innately sinful and that God had chosen only a select few for heavenly salvation (a doctrine referred to as "predestination").

During the nineteenth century, many Christians embraced a more democratic religious outlook. Just as Enlightenment rationalism stressed humanity's natural goodness and encouraged a belief in progress through democratic reforms and individual improvement, Protestant churches stressed that all people were capable of perfection through the guiding light of Christ and their own activism.

RATIONAL RELIGION Enlightenment ideas, including the religious concept of *Deism*, inspired prominent leaders such as Thomas Jefferson and Benjamin Franklin. Deists believed in a rational God—creator of the rational universe—and that all people were created as equals. They prized science and reason over traditional religion and blind faith.

Interest in Deism increased after the American Revolution. Through the use of reason and scientific research, Deists believed, people might grasp the natural laws governing the universe. Deists rejected the belief that every statement in the Bible was literally true and questioned the divinity of Jesus. They also defended free speech and opposed religious coercion.

UNITARIANISM AND UNIVERSALISM The same ideals of Enlightenment rationalism that excited Deists soon began to make deep inroads into American Protestantism. The old churches in and around Boston proved especially vulnerable to the appeal of anti-Puritan religious liberalism. By the end of the eighteenth century, well-educated New Englanders, most of them Congregationalists, were embracing Unitarianism, a "liberal" faith that emphasized the oneness ("unity") and compassion of a loving God, the natural goodness of humankind, the superiority of calm reason over emotional forms of worship, the rejection of the Calvinist belief in predestination, and a general rather than literal reading of the Bible.

Unitarians abandoned the concept of the Trinity (God the Father, the Son, and the Holy Ghost) that had long been central to the Christian faith. Unitarians believed that God and Jesus are separate; Jesus was a saintly man (but not divine) who set a shining example of a good life. People are not inherently sinful, Unitarians stressed. By following the teachings of Jesus and trusting the guidance of their own consciences, *all* people are eligible for the gift of salvation from a God who is not angry and unforgiving but blessed with boundless love.

Boston became the center of the organized Unitarian movement, which initially emerged within Congregational churches. During the early nineteenth century, "liberal" churches adopted the name *Unitarian*. Many of its early supporters were among the best-educated and wealthiest New Englanders.

A parallel anti-Calvinist religious movement, Universalism, attracted a different—and much larger—social group: the working poor. In 1779, John Murray, a British clergyman, founded the first Universalist church, in Gloucester, Massachusetts. Like the Unitarians, **Universalists** proclaimed the dignity and worth of all people. They stressed that people must liberate themselves from the rule of priests and ministers and use their own capacity to reason to explore the mysteries of existence.

To Universalists and Unitarians, hell did not exist. Salvation was "universal," available to everyone through the sacrifice of Jesus. In essence, Universalists thought God was too good and caring to damn people to hell, while Unitarians thought themselves too good to be damned. (The two denominations would combine in 1961, becoming the Unitarian Universalist faith.)

THE SECOND GREAT AWAKENING The rise of Universalism and Unitarianism did not mean that traditional religious beliefs were waning. In fact, evangelism was widespread. During the first Great Awakening in the early 1700s, traveling revivalists had promoted a more intense and personal relationship with God. In addition, Anglicanism suffered from being aligned

John Wesley Wesley's gravestone reads, "Lord let me not live to be useless."

with the Church of England; it lost its status as the official religion in most states after the American Revolution. To help erase their pro-British image, Virginia Anglicans renamed themselves *Episcopalians.*

But even the new name did not prevent the Episcopal Church from losing its leadership position in the South. Newer denominations, especially Baptists and Methodists, 20 percent of whom were African American, emerged and attracted masses of excited followers. These Christian sects were organized in accord with more-democratic principles; they allowed individual congregations to exercise more power on their own than did the Anglican Church.

In 1784, Methodists met in Baltimore and announced that they were abandoning Episcopalianism and forming a distinct new denomination committed to the aggressive conversion of all people: men, women, Indians, and African Americans. The reform-minded Methodists, inspired by their founder, the English Anglican priest John Wesley, abandoned the gloomy predestination of Calvinism in favor of a life of "cheerful activism."

Around 1800, the United States experienced a huge wave of religious revivals called the **Second Great Awakening**. Without religion, revivalists warned, the American republic would give way to "unbridled appetites and lust."

While all denominations grew as a result of the Second Great Awakening, the evangelical sects—Baptists, Methodists, and Presbyterians—experienced explosive popularity. In 1780, the nation had only 50 Methodist churches; by 1860, there were 20,000, far more than any other denomination. The percentage of Americans who joined Protestant churches increased sixfold between 1800 and 1860.

The Second Great Awakening involved two different centers of activity. One developed among the elite New England colleges that were founded as religious centers of learning, then spread across western New York into Pennsylvania and Ohio, Indiana, and Illinois. The other center emerged in the backwoods of Tennessee and Kentucky and spread in every direction across rural America. Both the urban and rural phases of Protestant revivalism shared a simple message: salvation is available not just to a select few, as the Calvinist Puritans had claimed, but to *anyone* who repents and embraces Christ.

FRONTIER REVIVALS In its frontier phase, the Second Great Awakening, like the first, generated tremendous excitement and emotional excesses. It gave birth to two religious phenomena—the traveling backwoods evangelist and the frontier camp meeting—that helped keep the fires of revivalism and spiritual intensity burning.

People in the early nineteenth century found the supernatural inside as well as outside of churches; they readily believed in magic, dreams, visions, miraculous healing, and speaking in tongues (a spontaneous babbling precipitated by the workings of the Holy Spirit). Evangelists and "exhorters" (spiritual speakers who were not formal ministers) with colorful nicknames such as Jumpin' Jesus or Crazy Dow or Mad Isaac found ready audiences among lonely frontier folk hungry for spiritual intensity and a sense of community.

Mass revivals were family-oriented, community-building events; they bridged social, economic, political, and even racial divisions. Women, especially, flocked to the rural revivals and served as the backbone of religious life on the frontier.

At the end of the eighteenth century, ministers visiting the western territories reported that there were few frontier churches and few people attending them. To remedy the situation, traveling evangelists emerged.

The first large camp meeting occurred in August 1801 on a Kentucky hillside called Cane Ridge, east of Lexington. A Presbyterian minister named James McGready invited Protestants in the region to attend, and as many as 20,000 frontier folk came from miles around, camping in tents for nine days. White and black ministers, mostly Baptists and Methodists, preached day and night, often chanting their sermons in ways that prompted listeners to cry: "Amen!" "Hallelujah!" "Lord, have mercy!"

The **frontier revivals** generated intense emotions as people experienced on-the-spot conversions. One participant at Cane Ridge observed that "some of the people were singing, others praying, some crying for mercy." As news of the Cane Ridge gathering spread, Protestant evangelists, especially Methodists, organized similar revivals in other states. One participant reported that the revivals created "such a gust of the power of God" that it seemed "the very gates of hell would give way."

Not all were swept up in the religious emotionalism. Frances Trollope, a distinguished English writer who toured the United States in 1827, attended a frontier revival and thought the participants behaved like raving lunatics. She

Religious revivalism Frontier revivals and prayer meetings ignited religious fervor within both ministers and participants. In this 1830s camp meeting, the women are so intensely moved by the sermon that they shed their bonnets and fell to their knees.

fled the roiling scene in panic. Similarly, a Catholic priest in Kentucky scoffed at the absurd "mob fanaticism" of the camp meetings.

The revivals, however, were quite popular with many Americans. "Hell is trembling, and Satan's kingdom falling," reported a South Carolinian in 1802. "The sacred flame" of religious revival is "extending far and wide." In 1776, about one in six Americans belonged to a church; by 1850, it was one in three. When asked to reflect on the social changes that had occurred during his life, William Grayson, a South Carolina planter, commented that "religion had revived. The churches were filled."

DENOMINATIONAL GROWTH Among the established denominations, Presbyterianism was entrenched among those with Scots-Irish backgrounds, from Pennsylvania to Georgia. Presbyterians gained further from the Plan of Union with the Congregationalists. Since the Presbyterians and the Congregationalists agreed on theology, they were able to form unified congregations and "call" (recruit) a minister from either denomination. The result through much of the Old Northwest (Ohio, Michigan, Indiana, and Illinois) was that New Englanders became Presbyterians by way of the "Presbygational" churches.

The frontier revivals were dominated by Baptist and Methodist factions. There were Primitive Baptists, Hardshell Baptists, Freewill Baptists and Methodists, Particular Baptists, and many others.

The Baptist theology was grounded in biblical fundamentalism—a certainty that every word and story in the Bible are divinely inspired and literally true. Unlike the earlier Puritans, however, the Baptists believed that *everyone* could gain salvation by choosing (via "free will") to receive God's grace and by being baptized as adults. The Baptists also stressed the social equality of all before God, regardless of wealth, status, or education.

The Methodists, who shared with Baptists the belief in free will, developed the most effective evangelical method: the "circuit rider," a traveling evangelist ("itinerant") on horseback who sought converts in remote frontier settlements. The itinerant system began with Francis Asbury, a tireless British-born revivalist who traveled across fifteen states and preached thousands of sermons.

After Asbury, Peter Cartwright emerged as the most successful circuit rider. Cartwright grew up in one of the most violent and lawless regions of frontier Kentucky. His brother was hanged as a murderer, and his sister was said to be a prostitute. Cartwright himself had been a hellion until, at age fifteen, he decided to attend a frontier revival meeting:

> In the midst of a solemn struggle of soul, an impression was made in
> my mind, as though a voice said to me, "Thy sins are all forgiven thee."
> Divine light flashed all around me, unspeakable joy sprung up in my
> soul. I rose to my feet, opened my eyes, and it really seemed as if I
> was in heaven. . . . My mother raised the shout, my Christian friends
> crowded around me and joined me in praising God; and though I have
> been since then, in many instances, unfaithful, yet I have never for one
> moment, doubted that the Lord did, then and there, forgive my sins
> and give me religion.

The following year, Cartwright became a religious exhorter, preaching the faith even though he was not yet an ordained minister.

At age eighteen, Cartwright began roaming across Kentucky, Tennessee, Ohio, and Indiana as a Methodist circuit rider. For more than twenty years, he preached a sermon a day, three hours at a time. Crowds flocked to hear his simple message: salvation is free for all to embrace.

At one revival in Illinois, Cartwright, who was running for Congress as an anti-slavery Jacksonian Democrat, asked those who thought they were going

***Black Methodists Holding a Prayer Meeting* (1811)** This caricature of an African American Methodist meeting in Philadelphia shows a preacher in the church doorway, while his congregation engages in exuberant prayer.

to heaven to stand. He then asked those who did not desire to go to hell to do the same. The only person in the crowd who did not stand for either choice was a tall, thirty-seven-year-old Whig attorney named Abraham Lincoln—Cartwright's opponent in the election. "May I inquire of you, Mr. Lincoln," asked Cartwright, "where are you going?" Lincoln replied that he was "going to Congress." Soon thereafter, he defeated Cartwright.

REVIVALISM AND AFRICAN AMERICANS The revivals broke down conventional social barriers. Free African Americans were especially attracted to the emotional energies of the Methodist and Baptist churches, in part because many white circuit riders were opposed to slavery.

African American Richard Allen, a freed slave in Philadelphia, said in 1787 that "there was no religious sect or denomination that would suit the capacity of the colored people as well as the Methodist." He decided that the "plain and simple gospel suits best for any people; for the unlearned can understand [it]." Even more important, the Methodists actively recruited blacks. They were "the first people," Allen noted, "that brought glad tidings to the colored people." In 1816, Allen helped found the African Methodist Episcopal (AME) Church, the first black denomination in America.

CAMP MEETINGS AND WOMEN The energies of the Great Revival, as the Second Great Awakening was called, spread through the western states and into more-settled regions back East. The fastest growth was along the frontier, where camp meetings were an expression of the frontier's democratic spirit. Revivals were typically held in late summer or fall, when farmwork eased.

Baptist, Methodist, and Presbyterian ministers often worked as a team, and crowds would frequently number in the thousands. Mass excitement swept up even the most skeptical onlookers, and infusions of the spirit sparked strange behavior. Some went into trances; others contracted the "jerks," babbled in unknown tongues, or got down on all fours and barked like dogs to "tree the devil."

The camp meetings also offered a social outlet to isolated rural folk, especially women, for whom the gatherings provided a welcome alternative to the rigors and loneliness of farm life. Evangelical ministers repeatedly applauded the spiritual energies of women and affirmed their right to give public witness to their faith and to play a leading role in efforts at social reform.

At a time when women were banned from preaching, Jarena Lee, a free black who lived in the Philadelphia area, was the first African American woman to become a minister in the African Methodist Episcopal Church (AME). As she wrote, "If the man may preach, because the Saviour died for him, why not the woman? Seeing [as] he died for her also." Lee became a tireless revivalist during the 1830s; according to her own records, she "traveled 2,325 miles and preached 178 sermons."

The organizational needs of large revivals offered ample opportunities for women. Phoebe Worrall Palmer, for example, hosted prayer meetings in her New York City home and eventually traveled across the country as a camp-meeting exhorter, assuring listeners that they could gain a life without sin.

Women like Palmer found public roles within evangelical denominations because of their emphasis on individual religious experiences rather than conventional, male-dominated church structures. Palmer claimed a woman's right to preach by citing the biblical emphasis on obeying God rather than man. "It is always right to obey the Holy Spirit's command," she stressed, "and if that is laid upon a woman to preach the Gospel, then it is right for her to do so; it is a duty she cannot neglect without falling into condemnation."

Such opportunities reinforced women's self-confidence, and their religious enthusiasm often inspired them to pursue social reforms for women, including greater educational opportunities and the right to vote.

RELIGION AND REFORM Regions roiled by revival fever were compared to forests devastated by fire. Western New York, in fact, experienced such fiery levels of evangelical activity that it was labeled the *burned-over district*. One reason the area was such a hotbed of evangelical activity was the Erie Canal, which opened in 1825. Both the construction of and traffic on the canal turned many towns into rollicking scenes of lawlessness: gambling, prostitution, public drunkenness, and crime. Such widespread sinfulness made the region ripe for revivalism.

CHARLES G. FINNEY The most successful evangelist in the burned-over district was a former attorney turned Presbyterian minister named Charles Grandison Finney. In the winter of 1830–1831, he theatrically preached with "a clear, shrill voice," pouring "out fire" for six months in Rochester, then in a canal boomtown in upstate New York. In the process, he generated some 100,000 conversions, became the most celebrated minister in the country, and perfected religious revivals as well-organized and orchestrated spectacles.

While rural camp-meeting revivals attracted farm families and other working-class groups, Finney's audiences in the Northeast attracted more-prosperous seekers. "The Lord," Finney declared, "was aiming at the conversion of the highest classes of society." In 1836, he built a huge church in New York City to accommodate his rapidly growing congregation.

Finney focused on the question that had preoccupied Protestantism for centuries: what role can the individual play in earning salvation? Finney and other freewill evangelists wanted to democratize the opportunity for salvation by insisting that everyone, rich or poor, black or white, could *choose* to be "saved" simply by embracing the promise of Jesus and rejecting the lure of sinfulness.

Finney's democratic gospel combined embracing faith and doing good works. For him, revivalism led first to personal reform and then to the improvement of society. By embracing Christ, a convert could thereafter be free of sin, but Christians also had an obligation to improve society by perfecting themselves.

The evangelical revivals provided much of the energy behind the sweeping reform impulse that characterized the age of Jacksonian democracy. Catharine Beecher, a leading advocate for evangelical religion and social reform, stressed that the success of American democracy "depends upon the intellectual and moral character of the mass of people. If they are intelligent and virtuous, democracy is a blessing; but if they are ignorant and wicked, it is only a curse."

THE MORMONS

The spiritual stirrings of the Second Great Awakening also spawned new religious groups. The burned-over district in New York gave rise to several religious movements, the most important of which was Mormonism. Its founder,

Joseph Smith Jr., was the child of intensely religious Vermont farm folk who settled in the village of Palmyra, in western New York, amid the hyperemotional revivalism of the Second Great Awakening.

In 1823, the eighteen-year-old Smith reported that an angel named Moroni appeared by his bedside and announced that God needed Smith's help. Moroni had led him to a hillside near his father's farm, where he had unearthed a box containing golden plates on which was etched, in an ancient language, a lost "gospel" explaining the history of ancient America. It described a group of Israelites ("Nephites") who crossed the Atlantic on barges and settled America 2,100 years before Columbus.

Smith set about laboriously translating the "reformed Egyptian" inscriptions on the plates. Much of the language he transcribed was in fact drawn from the Bible. But that mattered not to his earnest followers. In 1830, Smith convinced a friend to mortgage his farm to pay for the publication of the first 5,000 copies of the 500-page text he called *The Book of Mormon: An Account Written by the Hand of Mormon upon Plates Taken from the Plates of Nephi*.

Young Smith began gathering thousands of converts ("saints"). Eventually, convinced that his authority came directly from God, he formed what he called the Church of Jesus Christ of Latter-day Saints, more popularly known as the **Mormons**. Smith maintained that God, angels, and people were all members of the same flesh-and-blood species.

In his self-appointed role as the Mormon Prophet, Smith criticized the sins of the rich, preached universal salvation, denied that there was a hell, urged his followers to practice a strict code of personal morality by avoiding liquor, tobacco, and caffeine, and asserted that the Second Coming of Christ was looming. He promised followers "a nation, a new Israel, a people bound as much by heritage and identity as by belief." Within a few years, Smith had gathered thousands of converts, most of them poor New England farmers who had migrated to western New York.

YEARS OF PERSECUTION From the outset, the Mormon "saints" upset both their "gentile" neighbors and the civil authorities. Mormons stood out with their secret rituals, their refusal to abide by local laws and conventions, and their clannishness. Smith denied the legitimacy of civil governments and the U.S. Constitution. As a result, no community wanted to host him and his "peculiar people," a term taken from the New Testament.

In their search for a refuge from persecution and for the "promised land," the ever-growing contingent of Mormons moved from western New York to Ohio, then to Missouri, where the governor called for them to be "exterminated or driven from the state." Forced out, Smith and the Mormons moved in 1839 to the half-built town of Commerce, Illinois, on the Mississippi River.

They renamed the town Nauvoo (a crude translation of a Hebrew word meaning "beautiful land").

Within five years, Nauvoo had become the second largest city in the state, and Joseph Smith, "the Prophet," became Nauvoo's religious dictator. He owned the hotel and general store, published the newspaper, served as mayor, chief justice, and commander of the city's 2,000-strong army, and was the trustee of the Church. Smith's lust for power and for women grew as well. He began excommunicating dissidents, and in 1844 he announced his intention to become president of the United States.

Smith's remarkable sexual energy led him to practice "plural marriage" (polygamy); he accumulated more than two dozen wives, many of them already married to other men, and he encouraged other Mormon leaders to do the same. In 1844, a crisis arose when Mormon dissenters, including Smith's first wife, Emma, denounced his polygamy. The result was not only a split in the church but also an attack on Nauvoo by non-Mormons.

When Smith ordered Mormons to destroy an opposition newspaper, he and his brother Hyrum were arrested and charged with treason. On June 27, 1844, a mob stormed the jail and killed the Smith brothers. The *New York Herald* predicted that his death would kill Mormonism.

Brigham Young Young headed the Mormons from 1847 to 1877.

BRIGHAM YOUNG In Brigham Young, however, the Mormons found a new and, in many ways, better leader. Elected in 1844 to succeed Smith, Young would not only preserve the Mormon Church but create a new theocratic empire. Strong-minded, intelligent, authoritarian, and charismatic, Young was an early convert to Mormonism. Smith, he remembered, "took heaven . . . and brought it down to earth."

Because Nauvoo continued to arouse the suspicions of non-Mormons, Young began to look for another home for his flock. Their new destination turned out to be 1,300 miles away, near the Great Salt Lake in Utah, a vast, sparsely populated area that was part of Mexico. The first to arrive at the Great Salt Lake in July 1847 found "a broad and barren plain hemmed in by the mountains . . . the paradise of the lizard, the cricket and the rattlesnake." But Young declared that "this is the place" to settle.

By the end of 1848, the Mormons had developed an efficient irrigation system for their farms, and over the next decade they brought about a spectacular greening of the desert. At first they organized their own state, named Deseret (meaning "Land of the Honeybee"), and elected Young governor.

But their independence was short-lived. In 1848, Mexico signed the Treaty of Guadalupe Hidalgo, transferring to the United States what is now California, Nevada, Utah, Texas, and parts of Arizona, New Mexico, Colorado, and Wyoming. Two years later, Congress incorporated the Utah Territory into the United States. Nevertheless, when Young was named the territorial governor, the new arrangement gave the Mormons virtual independence.

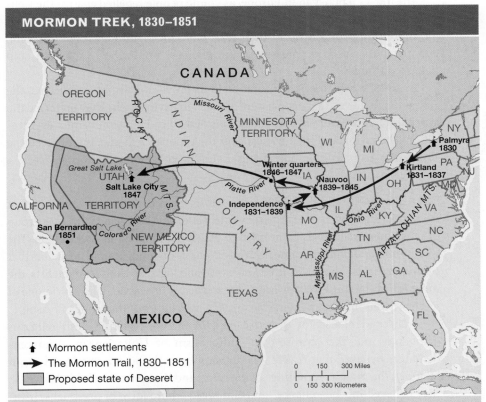

MORMON TREK, 1830–1851

- Mormon settlements
- The Mormon Trail, 1830–1851
- Proposed state of Deseret

- Where were Mormon settlements established between 1830 and 1851?
- Why did Joseph Smith initially lead his congregation west?
- Why was the Utah Territory an ideal place for the Mormons to settle, at least initially?

For more than twenty years, Young ruled with an iron hand, allowing no dissent and defying federal authority. Not until 1896, after the Mormons disavowed the practice of polygamy, was Utah admitted as a state. Out of its eerily secret beginnings and early struggles, Mormonism today is the fourth largest religious denomination in the world.

ROMANTICISM IN AMERICA

The revival of religious life during the early 1800s was one of many efforts throughout the United States and Europe to unleash the stirrings of the spirit. Another great cultural shift was the Romantic movement in thought, literature, and the arts.

The movement began in Europe, as young people rebelled against the well-ordered rational world promoted by the Enlightenment. Were there not, after all, more things in the world than reason, science, and logic could explain: spontaneous moods, impressions, and feelings; mysterious, unknown, and half-seen things?

In areas in which science could neither prove nor disprove concepts, the Romantics believed that people were justified in having faith. They preferred the stirrings of the heart over the calculations of the head, nonconformity over traditional behavior, and the mystical over the rational. Americans embraced the Romantics' emphasis on individualism and the virtues of common people.

TRANSCENDENTALISM The most intense American advocates of Romantic ideals were the transcendentalists of New England, the first group of rebellious intellectuals committed to reshaping the nation's cultural life. The word *transcendentalism* came from an emphasis on thoughts and behaviors that *transcend* (or rise above) the limits of reason and logic. To transcendentalists, the inner life of the spirit took priority over science. Transcendentalism, said one of its champions, meant an interest in areas "a little beyond" the scope of reason.

Transcendentalism at times seemed irrational, rejecting both religious orthodoxy and the "corpse-cold" rationalism of Unitarianism. Transcendentalists believed that reality was not simply what you can touch and see; it included the innate promptings of the mind and the spiritual world. Above all, they believed in "self-reliance" and embraced a pure form of personal spirituality ("intuitions of the soul") uncorrupted by theological dogma. The miracles described in the Bible were much less important to transcendentalists than the evidence of an individual's own intuitive spirituality.

Transcendentalists wanted individuals to look *within* themselves for spiritual insights. Ralph Waldo Emerson, the movement's leader, stressed that its aim was to "purify one's own soul and live with full integrity, becoming a model, rather than a nagging goad, to others."

Transcendentalists also wanted to nurture a romantic spirituality in harmony with nature. Natural beauty, they believed, had the transcendent power to startle people into self-awareness. As Henry David Thoreau described his own nature-inspired spirituality, "I believe in the forest, and in the meadow, and in the night in which the corn grows." All people, transcendentalists believed, had the capacity for self-realization, enabling them to tap the divine "spark" present in all of God's creations.

In short, transcendentalists wanted everyone to summon the courage to think their *own* thoughts and develop their *own* beliefs. Self-discovery was the essential step in fulfilling potential. By the 1830s, New England transcendentalism had become the most influential force in American culture.

RALPH WALDO EMERSON   More than anyone else, Ralph Waldo Emerson embodied the transcendentalist gospel, which rejected conventional religion in favor of individual spiritual growth and "self-culture." To Emerson, self-knowledge opened the doors to self-improvement and self-realization.

***The Indian's Vespers* (1847)**   Asher B. Durand's painting of a Native American saluting the sun captures the Romantic ideals of personal spirituality and the uncorrupted natural world that swept America during the early nineteenth century.

Ralph Waldo Emerson Emerson, a poet and philosopher, is most remembered for leading the transcendentalist movement.

Emerson became the most popular speaker in the United States during the 1840s. "We have listened too long to the courtly muses of Europe," he said. "We will walk on our own feet; we will work with our own hands; we will speak with our own minds." He exhorted the young American republic to shed its cultural inferiority complex and create its own distinctive literature, art, and thought.

The son of a Unitarian preacher, Emerson graduated from Harvard College in 1821 and became a Unitarian parson in 1829, but three years later he turned away from all organized religions because they stifled free thinking. He sought instead to cultivate a personal spirituality in communion with nature.

After traveling in Europe, where he met England's greatest Romantic writers, Emerson settled in Concord, Massachusetts, to take up the life of an essayist, poet, and lecturer ("preacher to the world"). He found God in nature and came to believe not in damnation but in human perfectibility. Impossibly optimistic, Emerson celebrated the virtues of self-reliance and the individual's unlimited potential.

In 1836, Emerson published the pathbreaking book *Nature*, which helped launch the transcendental movement. In it, he stressed that sensitive people could "transcend" the material world and discover the "spirit" animating the universe. Individuals, in other words, could exercise godlike powers.

The spirit of self-reliant individualism in Emerson's lectures and writings provided the energetic core of the transcendentalist outlook. "The American Scholar," a speech he delivered at Harvard in 1837, urged young Americans to put aside their reverence for European culture and explore the beauties and freedoms of their own world. Emerson's essay "Self-Reliance" (1841) expresses the distinctive transcendentalist outlook:

> Whoso would be a man, must be a nonconformist. . . . Nothing is at last sacred but the integrity of your own mind. . . . It is easy in the world to

live after the world's opinion; it is easy in solitude to live after our own; but the great man is he who in the midst of a crowd keeps with perfect sweetness the independence of solitude. . . . A foolish consistency is the hobgoblin of little minds, adored by little statesmen and philosophers and divines. . . . Speak what you think now in hard words and tomorrow speak what tomorrow thinks in hard words again, though it contradict everything you said today. . . . To be great is to be misunderstood.

Emerson's belief that every man and woman possessed godlike virtues inspired generations. He championed a self-reliant individualism that reinforced the democratic energies inspiring Jacksonian America.

THE TRANSCENDENTAL CLUB In 1836, an informal discussion group that came to be called the Transcendental Club began to meet in Boston and nearby Concord to discuss philosophy, literature, and religion. The transcendentalists teasingly called themselves the "club of the like-minded," quipped James Freeman Clarke, a Boston preacher and abolitionist, "because no two of us thought alike," except perhaps in their shared rejection of traditional forms of authority.

The diverse club included cultural rebels and social critics, all of whom displayed extravagant idealism and moral urgency in striving for uniqueness and originality. They were liberal clergymen, utopian reformers, militant abolitionists, innovative writers, and brilliant women such as Elizabeth Peabody, her sister Sophia (who married writer Nathaniel Hawthorne), and Margaret Fuller, the author of *Woman in the Nineteenth Century* (1845).

Fluent in six languages, the dynamic Fuller was one of America's first feminists, a brilliant conversationalist who organized a transcendentalist discussion group that met in Elizabeth Peabody's Boston bookstore. Their "Conversations" were designed to embolden the city's brightest women to think and act for themselves. Fuller helped launch and edit the *Dial* (1840–1844), a transcendentalist magazine that introduced American readers to European Romanticism.

HENRY DAVID THOREAU Emerson's young friend and neighbor, Henry David Thoreau, practiced the thoughtful self-reliance and pursuit of perfection that Emerson preached. "I like people who can do things," Emerson said, and Thoreau, fourteen years his junior, could do many things: carpentry, masonry, painting, surveying, sailing, gardening. Thoreau displayed a powerful sense of uncompromising integrity and prickly individuality. "If a man does not keep pace with his companions," he wrote, "perhaps it is because he hears a different drummer."

Henry David Thoreau Thoreau was a social rebel, environmentalist, and lifelong abolitionist.

Thoreau described himself as "a mystic, a transcendentalist, and a natural philosopher" who questioned tradition and challenged authority. Emerson said his younger friend was "stubborn and implacable; always manly and wise, but rarely sweet." A neighbor was more blunt. "I love Henry," said Elizabeth Hoar, "but I do not like him."

Born in Concord in 1817, Thoreau attended Harvard, where he exhausted the library's resources. After a brief stint as a teacher, he worked with his father, a pencil maker. Like Emerson, however, Thoreau viewed "the indescribable innocence" of nature as a living bible; the earth to him was a form of poetry, full of hidden meanings and life-giving energies. Walks in the woods inspired him more than attending church. Christianity, he believed, was a dying institution. His priorities were inward. He once described himself as a "Realometer," working his feet "downward through the mud and slush of opinion, and prejudice and tradition, and delusion, and appearances . . . to a hard bottom."

Thoreau showed little interest in friends or marriage and no interest in wealth, which he believed corrupted the pursuit of happiness by making people slaves to materialism. "The mass of men," he wrote, "lead lives of quiet desperation" because they were preoccupied with making money. Thoreau yearned to experience the "extremities" of life and not be bound by stuffy tradition, unjust laws, "good behavior," or the opinions of his elders. He committed himself to leading what Emerson called a simple life centered on "plain living and high thinking." He loved to be alone, free to think for himself.

Thoreau rented a room at the Emersons' home, where he tended the family garden, worked as a handyman, and took long walks with his host. "I delight much in my young friend," Emerson wrote, "who seems to have as free and erect a mind as any I have ever met." In 1844, when Emerson bought fourteen acres along Walden Pond, Thoreau decided to embark upon an unusual experiment in self-reliance.

On July 4, 1845, at age twenty-seven, Thoreau took to the woods to live in a tiny, one-room cabin he had built for twenty-eight dollars at Walden Pond, just over a mile outside of Concord. His goal was to demonstrate that nature was sufficient for his needs. "I went to the woods because I wished to live deliberately," he wrote in *Walden, or Life in the Woods* (1854), " . . . and not, when I came to die, discover that I had not lived."

During Thoreau's two years at Walden Pond, the United States declared war against Mexico, largely to acquire Texas, then part of Mexico. He felt it was an unjust war pushed by southern cotton planters eager to add more slave territory. His disgust for the war led him to refuse to pay taxes, for which he was put in jail (for only one night; an aunt paid the tax).

This incident inspired Thoreau to write his now-classic essay, "Civil Disobedience" (1849), which would influence Martin Luther King Jr. in shaping the civil rights movement a hundred years later. "If the law is of such a nature that it requires you to be an agent of injustice to another," Thoreau wrote, "then, I say, break the law." Until his death in 1862, Thoreau attacked slavery and applauded those who worked to undermine it. The continuing influence of Thoreau's creed of taking individual action against injustice shows the impact that a thoughtful person can have on the world.

AN AMERICAN LITERATURE Thoreau and Emerson portrayed the transcendentalist movement as an expression of moral idealism; critics dismissed it as outrageous self-centeredness. Although the transcendentalists attracted only a small following in their own time, they inspired a generation of writers that produced the first great age of American literature. The half decade of 1850 to 1855 witnessed an outpouring of extraordinary writing in the United States, a nation that had long suffered an inferiority complex about the quality of its arts. Those five years saw the writing of *Representative Men* by Emerson; *Walden, or Life in the Woods* by Thoreau; *The Scarlet Letter* and *The House of the Seven Gables* by Nathaniel Hawthorne; *Moby-Dick* by Herman Melville; *Leaves of Grass* by Walt Whitman; and hundreds of unpublished poems by Emily Dickinson.

LITERARY GIANTS

NATIONAL HAWTHORNE Nathaniel Hawthorne, the supreme writer of the New England group, never shared the sunny optimism of his neighbors or their perfectionist belief in reform. A native and longtime inhabitant of Salem, Massachusetts, he was haunted by the knowledge of evil bequeathed to him by his Puritan forebears, one of whom (John Hathorne) had been a judge at the Salem witchcraft trials. After college, Nathaniel Hawthorne worked in obscurity in Salem, gradually selling a few stories, and finally earning a degree of fame with *Twice-Told Tales* (1837). In these stories, as in most of his later

Emily Dickinson Dickinson offered the world of New England literature a fresh female voice.

work, his central themes examined sin and its consequences: pride and self-ishness, secret guilt, and the impossibility of rooting sin out of the human soul.

EMILY DICKINSON Emily Dickinson, the most strikingly original of the New England poets, never married. In fact, as she wrote, she enjoyed the habit of "shunning Men and Women." From her birth in 1830 to her death in 1886, she lived with her parents and sister in Amherst, Massachusetts. There, in a spartan corner bedroom on the second floor of the family house, the slim, red-haired poet found self-expression in poetry, ever grateful that "one is one's self & not somebody else."

Dickinson lived what her niece called a life of "exquisite self-containment." She often refused to meet visitors or even leave her room. Fired by "the light of insight and the fire of emotion," she wrote verse remarkable for its simplicity and brevity. Only a handful of her almost 1,800 poems were published before her death. As she famously wrote, "Success is counted sweetest / By those who ne'er succeed."

Whether her solitary existence was the result of severe eye trouble, aching despair generated by her love for a married minister, or fear of her possessive father, Dickinson's isolation and lifelong religious doubts led her, in the "solitude of space . . . that polar privacy," to probe the "white heat" of her heartbreak and disappointment in ways unusual for the time. Her often-abstract themes were elemental: life, death, fear, loneliness, nature, and above all, the withdrawal of God, "a distant, stately lover" who no longer could be found.

EDGAR ALLAN POE Edgar Allan Poe was even more fascinated by the deepening menace of death. Born in Boston in 1809 and orphaned as a child, he was raised by foster parents (the Allans, who gave him his middle name) in Richmond, Virginia. Poe was a misfit who led a stormy life. Although a top student and popular storyteller at the University of Virginia, he left the school after ten months, having racked up excessive gambling debts. After a two-year stint in the army, he enrolled at the U.S. Military Academy at West Point, where in 1831 he was expelled for missing classes and disobedience.

After spending time in New York City and then in Baltimore, Poe relocated in 1835 to Richmond, where he became an assistant editor of the *Southern Literary Messenger*. He secretly married Virginia Clemm, his thirteen-year-old cousin, claiming that she was twenty-one. They moved to Philadelphia in 1837, where he edited magazines and wrote scathing reviews and terrifying mystery stories. As the creator of the detective story, his influence on literature has been enormous.

In 1844, Poe moved to New York City. The following year, he published "The Raven," a poem about a man who, "once upon a midnight dreary," having lost his lover, a "sainted maiden" named Lenore, responds to a rapping at his door, only to find "darkness there and nothing more." Scanning the darkness, "dreaming dreams no mortal ever dared to dream before," he confronts a silence punctuated only by his mumbled query, "Lenore?" The man closes the door, only to hear the strange knocking again. Both angered and perplexed, he flings open the door and, "with many a flirt and flutter," in flies a raven, that "grim, ungainly, ghastly, gaunt, and ominous bird of yore." The raven utters but one haunting word: "Nevermore."

"The Raven" was so popular that Poe became a household name across America, although he received only two dollars for publishing the poem. In 1847, however, tragedy struck when Poe's young wife died of tuberculosis. Thereafter, he was seduced as much by alcohol and drug abuse as by writing. He died at age forty of mysterious causes.

Poe left behind an extraordinary collection of "unworldly" tales and haunting poems. He used horror to explore the darkest corners of human psychology and to satisfy his lifelong obsession with death. To him, fear was the most powerful emotion, so he focused on making the grotesque and the supernatural seem disturbingly real. Anyone who has read "The Tell-Tale Heart" or "The Pit and the Pendulum" can testify to his success.

HERMAN MELVILLE Herman Melville, the author of *Moby-Dick*, was a New Yorker who went to sea as a youth. After eighteen months aboard a whaler, he arrived in the Marquesas Islands, in the South Seas, and jumped ship with a companion. He spent several weeks with natives in "the valley of the Typees" before signing on with an Australian whaler. He joined a mutiny in Tahiti and finally returned home as a seaman aboard a U.S. Navy frigate. An account of his exotic adventures, *Typee* (1846), became an instant success, which he repeated in *Omoo* (1847).

In 1851, the thirty-two-year-old Melville produced *Moby-Dick*, one of the world's greatest novels. In the story of Captain Ahab's obsessive quest for an "accursed" white whale that had devoured his leg, Melville explored the darker recesses of the soul.

On one level, the book is a ripping good yarn of adventure on the high seas. On another level, however, it explores the unfathomable depths and darkness of human complexity, as the vengeful Ahab's crazed obsession with finding and killing the massive white whale turns the captain into a monster of destruction who sacrifices his ship, *The Pequod,* and his crew.

WALT WHITMAN   The most controversial writer during the nineteenth century was Walt Whitman, a New York journalist and poet. The swaggering Whitman was a self-promoting, robust personality. After meeting Whitman, Thoreau wrote that he "was not only eager to talk about himself but reluctant to have the conversation stray from the subject for long." Unlike Thoreau, Whitman did not fear "the age of steam" and wrote excitedly about industrial development, urban life, working men, sailors, and "simple humanity."

Born in 1819 on a Long Island farm, Whitman moved with his family to Brooklyn, where he worked as a carpenter, teacher, Democratic party activist, and editor of the *Brooklyn Eagle*. He frequently took the ferry across the East River to bustling Manhattan, where he was fascinated by the city's restless energy.

By the time he met Ralph Waldo Emerson, Whitman had been "simmering, simmering," but Emerson "brought him to a boil" with his emphasis on defying tradition and celebrating the commonplaces of life, including sexuality and the body. All of these themes found their way into Whitman's controversial first book of unconventional, free-verse poems, *Leaves of Grass* (1855). In its first year, it sold all of ten copies. One reviewer called it "an intensely vulgar, nay, absolutely

Walt Whitman This engraving of a thirty-seven-year-old Walt Whitman appeared in his acclaimed poetry collection *Leaves of Grass*.

beastly book." *Leaves of Grass*, however, became more influential with each passing year.

The brash Whitman introduced his book by declaring that "I celebrate myself, and sing myself." He was unapologetically "an American, one of the roughs . . . disorderly, fleshy, and sensual . . . eating, drinking, and breeding." Like Emerson, he was a self-proclaimed pioneer on behalf of "a new mightier world, a varied world," a bustling "world of labor" dignified by "common people." His poems were remarkable for their energy, exuberance, and intimacy, and were seasoned with frank sexuality and homoerotic overtones. They expressed the color and texture of American democracy, "immense in passion, pulse, and power." Thoreau, for one, viewed Whitman as a liberating force in American culture and described him as "the greatest democrat the world has seen."

Although *Leaves of Grass* was banned in Boston because of its explicit sexuality, Emerson found it "the most extraordinary piece of wit and wisdom that America has yet contributed." More conventional literary critics, however, shuddered at the shocking "grossness" of Whitman's homosexual references ("manly love"; "the love of comrades"; "for the friend I love lay sleeping by my side").

Yet Whitman could never be truly honest about such matters, for homosexuality was a felony in the nineteenth century. In the colonial period, at least five men had been executed for "sodomy," and many states retained the death penalty in the nineteenth century as the most severe punishment for "crimes against nature." (Thomas Jefferson had unsuccessfully urged that castration be substituted as the punishment in Virginia.)

NEWSPAPERS The flowering of American literature coincided with a massive expansion in newspaper readership sparked by rapid improvements in printing technology. The emerging availability of newspapers costing only a penny transformed daily reading into a form of popular entertainment. The "penny dailies," explained one editor,

***Politics in an Oyster House* (1848)**
Commissioned by social activist John H. B. Latrobe, this painting captures the public debates that were fueled by newspapers and magazines.

"are to be found in every street, lane, and alley; in every hotel, tavern, countinghouse, [and] shop."

By 1850, the United States had more newspapers than any nation in the world, and they forged a network of communications across the republic. As readership soared, the content of the papers expanded beyond political news and commentary to include society gossip, sports, and reports of sensational crimes and accidents. The proliferation of newspapers was largely a northern and western phenomenon, as literacy rates in the South lagged behind those of the rest of the country.

THE REFORM IMPULSE

In 1842, the United States was awash in reform movements led by dreamers and activists who saw social injustice or immorality and fought to correct it. Lyman Beecher, a champion of evangelical Christian revivalism (as well as the father of writer Harriet Beecher Stowe), stressed that the Second Great Awakening was not focused simply on promoting individual conversions; it was also intended to "reform human society."

While an impulse to "perfect" people and society helped excite the reform movements, social and economic changes invigorated many reformers, most of whom were women. The rise of an urban middle class enabled growing numbers of women to hire cooks and maids, thus freeing them to devote more time to societal concerns. Many women used their free time to join churches and charitable organizations, most of which were led by men.

Both women and men belonging to evangelical societies fanned out across America to organize Sunday schools, spread the gospel, and distribute Bibles to the children of the working poor. Other reformers tackled issues such as awful conditions in prisons and workplaces, care of the disabled, temperance (reducing the consumption of alcoholic beverages), women's rights, and the abolition of slavery. Transcendentalists broadened their initial emphasis on individual perfectionism to include reforms designed to improve the lot of the poor, the disenfranchised, and the enslaved.

That these earnest social reformers often met resistance, persecution, violence, and even death testified to the sincerity of their convictions and the power of their example. As Ralph Waldo Emerson said, "Never mind the ridicule, never mind the defeat, up again old heart!" For there is "victory yet for all justice."

TEMPERANCE   The **temperance** crusade was the most widespread of the reform movements, in large part because many people argued that most social problems were rooted in alcohol abuse. William Cobbett, an English reformer who traveled in the United States, noted in 1819 that one could "go into hardly any man's house without being asked to drink wine or spirits, even *in the morning.*" In 1826, a group of ministers in Boston organized the American Society for the Promotion of Temperance, which sponsored lectures, press campaigns, and the formation of local and state societies. A favorite device was to ask each person who took the pledge to put by his or her signature a letter *T* for "total abstinence." With that a new word entered the language: *teetotaler.*

In 1833, the society held a national convention in Philadelphia, where the American Temperance Union was formed. Like nearly every reform movement of the day, temperance had a wing of absolutists. They would accept no compromise with Demon Rum and passed a resolution that liquor ought to be prohibited by law. The Temperance Union, at its spring convention in 1836, called for abstinence from all alcoholic beverages—which caused moderates to abstain from the movement.

The temperance crusade A mid-nineteenth-century temperance banner depicts a young man being tempted by a woman offering him a glass of wine.

PRISONS AND ASYLUMS The Romantic impulse often included the liberal belief that people are innately good and capable of perfection. Such an optimistic view brought about major changes in the treatment of prisoners, the disabled, and dependent children. Public institutions (often called asylums) emerged for the treatment of social ills. If removed from society, the theory went, the needy and deviant could be made whole again. Unhappily, however, the underfunded and understaffed asylums often became breeding grounds for brutality and neglect.

Gradually, the idea of the penitentiary—a place where the guilty paid for their crimes but also underwent rehabilitation—developed as a new approach to reforming criminals. An early model of the system was the Auburn Penitentiary, which opened in New York in 1816.

The prisoners at Auburn had separate cells and gathered only for meals and group labor. Discipline was severe. The men marched in lockstep and were never put face-to-face or allowed to talk. But they were reasonably secure from abuse by their fellow prisoners. The system, its advocates argued, had a beneficial effect on the prisoners and saved money, since the facility's workshops supplied prison needs and produced goods for sale at a profit. By 1840, there were twelve Auburn-type penitentiaries across the nation.

The Romantic reform impulse also found an outlet in the care of the insane. Before 1800, the insane were usually confined at home, with hired keepers, or in jails or almshouses, where homeless debtors were housed. In the years after 1815, however, asylums that separated the disturbed from the criminal began to appear.

The most important figure in boosting awareness of the plight of the mentally ill was Dorothea Lynde Dix. A pious Boston schoolteacher, she was asked to instruct a Sunday-school class at the East Cambridge House of Correction in 1841. There she found a roomful of insane people who had been completely neglected.

The scene so disturbed Dix that she began a two-year investigation of jails and almshouses in Massachusetts. In a report to the state legislature in 1843, Dix revealed that insane people were confined "in *cages, closets, cellars, stalls, pens! Chained, naked, beaten with rods,* and *lashed* into obedience." She won the support of leading reformers and proceeded to carry her campaign on behalf of "the miserable, the desolate, and the outcast" throughout the country and abroad. In the process, she helped to transform social attitudes toward mental illness.

WOMEN'S RIGHTS While countless middle-class women devoted themselves to improving the quality of life in America, some argued that women should first focus on enhancing home life. In 1841, Harriet Beecher Stowe's sister, Catharine Beecher, a leader in the education movement, published *A Treatise on Domestic Economy*, which became the leading handbook promoting the **cult of domesticity**, a powerful ideology that called upon middle-class women to accept and celebrate their role as manager of the household and the children, separate from the man's sphere of work outside the home.

While Beecher upheld high standards in women's education, she and many others argued that young women should be trained not for the workplace but in the domestic arts—managing a kitchen, running a household, and nurturing the children. Women, explained a Philadelphia doctor, were crucial to the future of the Republic because they instructed their children "in the principles of liberty and government."

The official status of women during the first half of the nineteenth century remained much as it had been in the colonial era. They were barred from the ministry and most other professions. Higher education was hardly an option.

Elizabeth Cady Stanton and Susan B. Anthony Stanton (left, in 1856) was a young mother who organized the Seneca Falls Convention, while Anthony (right, in 1848) started as an anti-slavery and temperance activist in her twenties. The two would meet in 1851 and form a lifelong partnership in the fight for women's suffrage.

Women could not serve on juries, nor could they vote. A wife often had no control over her property or even her children. She could not make a will, sign a contract, or bring suit in court without her husband's permission. Her subordinate legal status was similar to that of a minor or a free black.

SENECA FALLS Gradually, however, women began to protest, and men began to listen. The organized movement for women's rights emerged in 1840, when the anti-slavery movement split over the question of women's right to participate. In 1848, two prominent advocates of women's rights, Lucretia Mott, a Philadelphia Quaker abolitionist, and Elizabeth Cady Stanton, a New York abolitionist, called a convention of men and women to gather in Stanton's hometown of Seneca Falls, New York, to discuss "the social, civil, and religious condition and rights of women."

On July 19, 1848, when the **Seneca Falls Convention** convened, revolution was in the air. In Italy, Germany, and other European states, militant nationalists, including many women, rebelled against monarchies and promoted unification. In France, the Society for the Emancipation for Women demanded that women receive equal political rights. In April, the French government abolished slavery in its Caribbean colonies, and in June, European feminists called for "the complete, radical abolition of all the privileges of sex, of birth, of race, of rank, and of fortune."

The activists at Seneca Falls did not go that far, but they did issue a clever paraphrase of the Declaration of Independence. The **Declaration of Rights and Sentiments** proclaimed that "all men and women are created equal." All laws that placed women "in a position inferior to that of men, are contrary to the great precept of nature, and therefore of no force or authority." Its most controversial demand was the right to vote.

Such ambitious goals and strong language were too radical for most of the 300 delegates, and only about a third of them signed the Declaration of Rights and Sentiments. One newspaper dismissed the convention as "the most shocking and unnatural incident ever recorded in the history of womanity." The *Philadelphia Public Ledger* sneeringly asked why women would want to climb down from their domestic pedestal and get involved with the dirty world of politics: "A woman is nothing. A wife is everything. A pretty girl is equal to ten thousand men, and a mother is, next to God, all powerful." Despite such opposition, however, the Seneca Falls gathering represented an important first step in the evolving campaign for women's rights.

From 1850 until the Civil War, leaders of the women's rights movement held annual conventions, delivered lectures, and circulated petitions. The movement struggled in the face of meager funds and widespread anti-feminist sentiment. A mother and housewife criticized the women reformers for "aping mannish manners" and wearing "absurd and barbarous attire." The typical feminist, she claimed, "struts and strides, and thinks that she proves herself superior to the rest of her sex." The women's movement was eventually successful because of the work of a few undaunted women.

SUSAN B. ANTHONY   Susan B. Anthony, already active in temperance and anti-slavery groups, joined the crusade in the 1850s. Unlike Stanton and Mott, she was unmarried and therefore able to devote most of her attention to the women's crusade. As one observer put it, Stanton "forged the thunderbolts and Miss Anthony hurled them." Both were young when the movement started, and both lived into the twentieth century, focusing after the Civil War on demands for women's suffrage (the right to vote).

Women did not gain the vote in the nineteenth century, but they did make legal gains. In 1839, Mississippi became the first state to grant married women control over their property; by the 1860s, eleven more states had done so. Still, the only jobs open to educated women in any number were nursing and teaching. Both professions brought relatively lower status and pay than "men's work," despite the skills, training, and responsibilities involved.

EARLY PUBLIC SCHOOLS   Early America, like most rural societies, offered few educational opportunities for the masses. That changed in the first half of the nineteenth century as reformers lobbied for **public schools** to serve all children, rich or poor. The working poor wanted free schools to give their children an equal chance to pursue the American dream. In 1830, the Workingmen's Party of Philadelphia called for "a system of education that shall embrace equally all the children of the state, of every rank and condition." Education, people argued, would improve manners while reducing crime and poverty.

A well-informed, well-trained citizenry was considered one of the basic premises of a republic. A Vermont newspaper editor stressed that education was "the standing army of Republics." If political power resided with the people, as the Constitution asserted, then the citizenry needed to be well educated. By 1830, however, no state had a public school system.

Horace Mann of Massachusetts, a state legislator and attorney, led the early drive for statewide, tax-supported public school systems. He proposed that these schools be free to all children regardless of class, race, or ethnicity—including immigrant children. He sponsored the creation of a state board of education, and then served as its leader. Universal access to education, Mann argued, "was the great equalizer of the conditions of men—the balance-wheel of the social machinery."

Mann went on to promote the first state-supported "normal school" for the training of teachers, a state association of teachers, and a minimum school year of six months. He saw the public school system as a way not only to ensure that everyone had a basic level of knowledge and skills but also to reinforce values such as hard work and clean living. "If we do not prepare children to become good citizens, if we do not enrich their minds with knowledge," Mann warned, "then our republic must go down to destruction."

Such a holistic education, Mann argued, would enhance social stability and equal opportunity, as well as give women opportunities for rewarding work outside the home, as teachers. Mann said they could become "mothers away from home" for the children they taught.

By the 1840s, most states in the North and Midwest, but not the South, had joined the public school movement. The initial conditions for public education, however, were seldom ideal. Funds for buildings, books, and equipment were limited; teachers were poorly paid and often poorly prepared. Most students going beyond the elementary grades attended private academies, often organized by churches. Such schools, begun in colonial days, multiplied until there were more than 6,000 of them by 1850.

In 1821, the Boston English High School opened as the nation's first free public *secondary* school, set up mainly for students not going on to college. By a law of 1827, Massachusetts required every town of 500 or more residents to have a high school; in towns of 4,000 or more, the school had to offer Latin, Greek, rhetoric, and other college-preparatory courses. Public high schools became well established only after the Civil War. In 1860 there were barely 300 in the whole nation.

By 1850, half of the white children between ages five and nineteen were enrolled in schools, the highest percentage in the world. But very few of those students were southerners. Public schools were scarce in the South until after the Civil War. In most states, enslaved children were prohibited from learning to read and write or attend school. A former slave recalled that his owner "didn't teach 'em nuthin' but work."

The South had some 500,000 illiterate whites, more than half the total in the country. In the South, North Carolina led the way in state-supported

The George Barrell Emerson School, Boston (ca. 1850) Although higher education for women initially met with some resistance, in the 1820s and 1830s, "seminaries" like this one were established to teach women mathematics, physics, and history, as well as music, art, and social graces.

education, enrolling more than two thirds of its white school-age population by 1860. But the school year was only four months long because of the rural state's need for children to do farmwork. The prolonged disparities between North and South in the number and quality of educational opportunities help explain the growing economic and cultural differences between the two regions. Then, as now, undereducated people were more likely to remain economically deprived, less healthy, and less engaged in political life.

FOOD AND SEX The widespread reform impulse in the early nineteenth century excited causes and cranks of all sorts, including an array of health reformers, the most popular of whom was Sylvester Graham, a controversial preacher-turned-lecturer who blamed most of Americans' problems on their bad eating and drinking habits.

Born in 1794 in West Suffield, Connecticut, Graham was the youngest of seventeen children. Soon after his minister father died, in 1796, his mother broke down under the strain of single-parenting and young Sylvester was farmed out to be raised by "strangers." As a young man he worked as a farmhand, clerk, and teacher before attending Amherst College in Massachusetts. He was expelled for his aggressive eccentricities, which did not prevent him from becoming a Presbyterian minister.

But religion inspired Graham less than nutrition did. He soon gave up preaching the Gospel of Christ in order to preach the gospel of bran and fiber. Although he had no medical training, Graham became the nation's leading health reformer after a cholera epidemic ravaged the nation in 1832 and led panicked people to embrace his odd explanations for the killer disease. Graham attributed cholera to people eating chicken pot pie and engaging in "excessive lewdness."

Thereafter, on the lecture circuit, in books, and in *Graham's Journal of Health and Longevity*, Graham preached convincingly against the dangers of alcohol and coffee, white flour, meat, gluttony, obesity, and body odor. Graham's "system" for a healthier America called for a diet of whole grains, fresh fruits, and nuts. The Graham diet banned all meats and spices—including pepper and salt—as well as butter, cream, and soups. Alcohol and tobacco were also prohibited.

The centerpiece of Graham's celebrated vegetarian diet was the "Graham cracker," made of coarsely ground wheat bathed in molasses and baked. Graham stressed that daily meals of his crackers needed to be precisely six hours apart, with no snacking in between. The "Graham system" also prescribed fresh air, daily bathing in cold water, drinking only when thirsty (not with meals), and singing and dancing for exercise. He discouraged "excessive" sexual activity, meaning more than once a week for married couples, because it would cause indigestion, headache, feebleness of circulation, pulmonary consumption, spinal diseases, epilepsy, and insanity. Like a cult leader, Graham urged his followers to "avoid medicine and physicians—if you value your life."

The vain and egotistical Graham (most of his siblings disowned him) became one of the most famed and hated of the professional reformers. Butchers and bakers threatened to kill him, and many people laughed at his ideas. Yet others, called Grahamites, passionately embraced his health system. There were Grahamite hotels in New York City, Boston, and Philadelphia, as well as stores, boarding houses, college dining halls, and a newspaper promoting his diet and ideas. One of Graham's followers called him an "eccentric and wayward genius."

Utopian Communities

Amid the pervasive climate of reform, the quest for utopia—communities with innovative social and economic relationships—flourished. Plans for ideal communities had long been an American passion, and more than 100 **utopian communities** sprang up between 1800 and 1900. Many of them were *communitarian* experiments that emphasized the welfare of the entire community rather than individual freedom. Some experimented with "free love," socialism, and special diets.

THE SHAKERS Communities founded by the Shakers (officially the United Society of Believers in Christ's Second Appearing) proved to be long lasting. Ann Lee (known as Mother Ann Lee) arrived in New York from England with eight followers in 1774. Believing religious fervor to be a sign of inspiration from the Holy Ghost, Mother Ann and her followers had strange fits in which they saw visions and issued prophecies (predictions about the future). These manifestations later evolved into a ritual dance—hence the name "Shakers." Shaker doctrine held God to be a dual personality. In Christ, the masculine side was revealed; in Mother Ann, the feminine element. That Mother Ann preached celibacy to prepare Shakers for the perfection that was promised them in heaven helps explain why their membership declined over time.

Mother Ann died in 1784, but the group found new leaders, and the movement spread from New York into New England, Ohio, and Kentucky. By 1830 about twenty groups were flourishing. In these Shaker communities all property was held in common. Shaker farms were among the nation's leading sources of garden seed and medicinal herbs, and many of their products, especially furniture, were prized for their simple beauty.

ONEIDA John Humphrey Noyes, founder of the Oneida Community, had a very different vision of the ideal community. The son of a Vermont congressman, Noyes attended Dartmouth College and Yale Divinity School. But in 1834 he was expelled from Yale and his license to preach was revoked after he announced that he was "perfect" and free of all sin. In 1836 Noyes gathered a group of "Perfectionists" around his home in Putney, Vermont.

Ten years later, Noyes announced a new doctrine, "complex marriage," which meant that every man in the community was married to every woman, and vice versa. "In a holy community," he claimed, "there is no more reason why sexual intercourse should be restrained by law, than why eating and drinking should be." Authorities thought otherwise, and Noyes was charged with adultery for practicing his theology of "free love" (he coined the term). He fled to New York and in 1848 established the Oneida Community, which had more than 200 members by 1851 and became famous for its production of fine silverware.

BROOK FARM Brook Farm in Massachusetts was the most celebrated utopian community because it grew out of the transcendental movement. George Ripley, a Unitarian minister and transcendentalist, conceived of Brook Farm as a kind of early-day think tank, combining high philosophy and plain living, and manual labor. In 1841, he and several dozen like-minded utopians moved to the 175-acre farm eight miles southwest of Boston.

Brook Farm became America's first secular utopian community. One of its members, novelist Nathaniel Hawthorne, called it "our beautiful scheme of a noble and unselfish life" (he later would satirize the community in his novel *The Blithedale Romance*). Its residents shared the tasks of maintaining the buildings, tending the fields, and preparing the meals. They also organized picnics, dances, lectures, and discussions. Emerson, Thoreau, and Margaret Fuller were among the visiting lecturers.

In 1846, however, Brook Farm's main building burned down, and the community spirit died in the ashes. In the end, utopian communities had little impact on the outside world, where reformers wrestled with the sins of the multitudes.

Among all the targets of the reformers' zeal, one great evil would take precedence over the others: human bondage. Transcendentalist reformer Theodore Parker declared that slavery was "the blight of this nation, the curse of the North and the curse of the South." The paradox of American freedom being coupled with American slavery, what novelist Herman Melville called "the world's fairest hope linked with man's foulest crime," would inspire the climactic crusade of the age, abolitionism, which would ultimately sweep the nation into an epic civil war.

THE ANTI-SLAVERY MOVEMENT

The men who drafted the U.S. Constitution in 1787 hoped to keep the new nation from splitting apart over the question of slavery. To that end, they negotiated compromises that avoided dealing with the issue. But most of the founders knew that there eventually would be a day of reckoning. That day approached as the nineteenth century unfolded, and growing numbers of Americans decided that the daily horrors of slavery must come to an end.

EARLY OPPOSITION TO SLAVERY   The first organized emancipation movement appeared in 1816 with the formation of the **American Colonization Society (ACS)** in Washington, D.C., whose mission was to raise funds to "repatriate" free blacks back to Africa. Its supporters included James Madison, James Monroe, Andrew Jackson, Henry Clay, John Marshall, and Daniel Webster.

Some supported the colonization movement because they opposed slavery; others saw it as a way to get rid of free blacks. "We must save the Negro," as one missionary explained, "or the Negro will ruin us." White supremacy remained a powerful assumption, even among many anti-slavery reformers.

Leaders of the free black community denounced the colonization idea from the start. The United States, they stressed, was their native land, and they had as valid a claim on U.S. citizenship as anyone else.

Nevertheless, the ACS acquired land on the Ivory Coast of West Africa, and on February 6, 1820, the *Elizabeth* sailed from New York with the first eighty-eight emigrants who formed the nucleus of a new nation, the Republic of Liberia. Thereafter, however, the African colonization movement waned. During the 1830s, only 2,638 African Americans migrated to Liberia. In all, only about 15,000 resettled in Africa.

FROM GRADUALISM TO ABOLITIONISM   The fight against slavery started in Great Britain in the late eighteenth century, and the movement's success in ending British involvement in the African slave trade helped spur the anti-slavery cause in America. British abolitionists lectured across the northern United States and often bought freedom for runaway slaves. At the same time, most of the leading American abolitionists visited Great Britain and came away inspired by the breadth and depth of anti-slavery organizations there.

The British example helped convince black and white leaders of the cause in America to adopt an aggressive new strategy in the early 1830s. Equally important was the realization that slavery in the cotton states of the South was not dying out; it was rapidly growing. This hard reality led to a change in tactics among anti-slavery organizations, many of which were energized by evangelical religions and the emerging social activism of transcendentalism. Their initial efforts to promote a *gradual* end to slavery by prohibiting it in the western territories and using moral persuasion to convince owners to free their slaves gradually gave way to demands for *immediate* **abolition** everywhere.

WILLIAM LLOYD GARRISON

A white Massachusetts activist named William Lloyd Garrison drove the movement. In 1831, free blacks helped convince Garrison to launch an anti-slavery newspaper, the *Liberator*, which became the voice of the nation's first

William Lloyd Garrison A militant abolitionist and a committed pacifist.

civil rights movement. In the Boston-based newspaper's first issue, Garrison condemned "the popular but pernicious doctrine of gradual emancipation." He dreamed of true equality in all spheres of American life, including the status of women. In pursuing that dream, he vowed to be "as harsh as truth, and as uncompromising as justice. . . . I am in earnest—I will not equivocate—I will not excuse—I will *not retreat a* single inch—and I WILL BE HEARD."

Garrison's courage in denouncing slavery forced the issue onto the national agenda and outraged slaveholders in the South, as well as some whites in the North. In 1835, a mob of angry whites dragged him through the streets of Boston. The South Carolina and Georgia legislatures promised a reward to anyone who kidnapped Garrison and brought him south for trial. A southern slaveholder warned him "to desist your infamous endeavors to instill into the minds of the negroes the idea that 'men must be free.'" The violence of the southern reaction wrecked the assumption of "Garrisonians" that moral righteousness would trump evil and that their fellow Americans would listen to reason.

The pacifist Garrison remained opposed to the use of force. "We do not preach rebellion," he stressed. The prospect "of a bloody insurrection in the South fills us with dismay," but "if any people were ever justified in throwing off the yoke of their tyrants, the slaves are the people."

During the 1830s, Garrison became the nation's most unyielding foe of slavery. Through his unflagging efforts, he helped make the impossible—abolition—seem possible to more and more people. Two wealthy New York

City evangelical silk merchants, Arthur and Lewis Tappan, provided financial support for Garrison and the *Liberator*. In 1833, they joined with Garrison and a group of Quaker reformers, free blacks, and evangelicals to organize the American Anti-Slavery Society (AASS).

That same year, Parliament freed some 800,000 enslaved colonial peoples throughout the British Empire by passing the Emancipation Act, whereby slaveholders were paid to give up their "human property." In 1835, the Tappans hired revivalist Charles G. Finney to head the anti-slavery faculty at Oberlin, a new college in northern Ohio that would be the first to admit black students.

The American Anti-Slavery Society, financed by the Tappans, created a national network of newspapers, offices, and 300 chapters, almost all of which were affiliated with a local Christian church. By 1840, some 160,000 people belonged to AASS, which stressed that "slaveholding is a heinous crime in the sight of God, and that the duty, safety, and best interests of all concerned, require its *immediate abandonment*." The AASS even argued that blacks should have full social and civil rights.

In 1835, the group began flooding the South with anti-slavery pamphlets and newspapers. The anti-slavery materials so enraged southern slaveholders that a Louisiana community offered a $50,000 reward for the capture of the "notorious abolitionist, Arthur Tappan, of New York." Post offices throughout the South began destroying what was called "anti-slavery propaganda."

DAVID WALKER   The most radical figure among the largely white Garrisonians was David Walker, a free black man who owned a used clothing store in Boston. In 1829, he published his *Appeal to the Colored Citizens of the World*, a pamphlet that denounced the hypocrisy of Christians in the South for defending slavery and urged slaves to follow the example of the Haitian rebels and revolt against the planters. "The whites want slaves, and want us for their slaves," Walker warned, "but some of them will curse the day they ever saw us."

Walker challenged African Americans, slave and free, to act like "MEN" and use the "crushing arm of power" to gain their freedom. "Woe, woe will be to you," he threatened whites, "if we have to obtain our freedom by fighting."

Copies of Walker's *Appeal* were secretly carried to the South by black sailors, but whites in major cities seized the "vile" pamphlet. In 1830, the state of Mississippi outlawed efforts to "print, write, circulate, or put forth . . . any book, paper, magazine, pamphlet, handbill or circular" intended to arouse the "colored population" by "exciting riots and rebellion."

A SPLIT IN THE MOVEMENT   As the abolitionist movement spread, debates over tactics intensified. The Garrisonians, for example, felt that slavery had corrupted virtually every aspect of American life. They therefore embraced every important reform movement of the day: abolition, temperance, pacifism, and women's rights. Garrison's unconventional religious ideas and social ideals led him to break with the established Protestant churches, which to his mind were in league with slavery; the federal government all the more so. The U.S. Constitution, he charged, was "a covenant with death and an agreement with hell."

Garrison was such a moral purist that he even refused to vote and encouraged others to do the same, arguing that the American republic could not continue to proclaim the ideal of liberty while tolerating the reality of slavery. He fiercely believed that the South could be shamed into ending slavery.

Other reformers were more practical and single-minded. They saw American society as fundamentally sound and concentrated on purging it of slavery. Garrison struck them as an unrealistic fanatic whose radicalism hurt the cause. Even Harriet Beecher Stowe, who would write *Uncle Tom's Cabin* (1852), called Garrisonians, most of whom were Unitarians, Quakers, or transcendentalists, "moral mono-maniacs." The powerful Tappan brothers broke with Garrison over religion. They argued that the anti-slavery movement should be led only by men of "evangelical piety," and they declared that the Unitarians and Universalists in New England failed to meet that standard.

THE GRIMKÉ SISTERS   A showdown between the rival anti-slavery camps erupted in 1840 over the issue of women's rights. Women had joined the abolition movement from the start, but largely in groups without men. During the early nineteenth century, women were rarely allowed to speak to organizations that included men. Then the activities of the Grimké sisters brought women's rights to center stage.

Sarah and Angelina Grimké, daughters of a wealthy South Carolina family, grew up being served by slaves. In 1821, soon after her father's death, Sarah moved from Charleston to Philadelphia, joined the Society of Friends (Quakers), and renounced slavery. Angelina soon joined her. In 1835, the sisters joined the abolitionist movement, speaking to northern women's groups in what were called "parlor meetings." After they appealed to southern Christian women to end slavery, the mayor of Charleston told their mother that they would be jailed if they ever returned home.

The Grimké sisters traveled widely, speaking first to audiences of women and eventually to groups of both sexes. Their unconventional ("promiscuous") behavior in speaking to mixed-gender audiences prompted sharp criticism from ministers in the anti-slavery movement. The chairman of the Connecticut Anti-Slavery Society declared that "no woman shall speak or vote. . . . It is enough for women to rule at home." Catharine Beecher reminded the Grimké sisters that women occupied "a subordinate relation in society to the other sex"

Sarah (left) and Angelina (right) Grimké After moving away from their South Carolina slaveholding family, the Grimké sisters devoted themselves to abolitionism and feminism.

and that they should limit their activities to the "domestic and social circle" rather than public organizations.

Angelina Grimké firmly rejected such arguments. For centuries, she noted, women had been raised to view themselves as "inferior creatures." Now, she insisted, "It is a woman's right to have a voice in all laws and regulations by which she is to be governed, whether in church or in state." Soon, she and her sister began linking their efforts to free the slaves with their desire to free women from centuries of male domination. "Men and women are CREATED EQUAL!" Sarah Grimké said. "Whatever is right for man to do is right for woman."

THE ROLE OF WOMEN The debate over the role of women in the anti-slavery movement finally exploded at the American Anti-Slavery Society's meeting in 1840, where the Garrisonians convinced a majority of delegates that women should participate equally in the organization. The Tappans and their supporters walked out and formed the American and Foreign Anti-Slavery Society.

A third faction of the American Anti-Slavery Society had grown skeptical that the nonviolent "moral suasion" promoted by Garrison would ever lead to abolition. They decided that political action was the most effective way to pursue their goal.

In 1840, activists formed the Liberty party in an effort to elect an American president who would abolish slavery. Their nominee, James Gillespie Birney, executive secretary of the American Anti-Slavery Society, was a former Alabama slaveholder turned abolitionist. His slogan was "vote as you pray, and pray as you vote." The platform called for an end to slavery in the western territories and the District of Columbia and a ban on intrastate slave trading.

Yet the Liberty party found few supporters. In the 1840 election, Birney polled only 7,000 votes. In 1844, however, he would win 60,000. From that time forward, an anti-slavery party contested every national election until the Thirteenth Amendment officially ended slavery in 1865.

BLACK ANTI-SLAVERY ACTIVITY

Although many whites worked courageously to end slavery, most of them, unlike Garrison, still insisted that blacks were socially inferior to whites. Freedom for slaves, in other words, did not mean social equality, and many white abolitionists expected free blacks to take a backseat in the movement.

WILLIAM WELLS BROWN   Yet free African Americans were active in white anti-slavery societies. Former slaves such as Henry Bibb and William Wells Brown, both runaways from Kentucky, and Frederick Douglass, who had escaped from Maryland, became the most effective critics of the South's "peculiar institution." Much of the energy and appeal of the abolitionist movement derived from the compelling testimonies provided by former slaves.

Brown was just twenty years old when he escaped from his owner, a steamboat pilot on the Ohio River. An Ohio Quaker named Wells Brown provided shelter to the runaway, and Brown adopted the man's name in the process of forging a new identity as a free man. He settled in Cleveland, Ohio, where he was a dockworker. He married, had three children, and helped runaway slaves cross the border into Canada. By 1842, he had learned to read and write, begun to publish columns in abolitionist newspapers, and was in great demand as a speaker at anti-slavery meetings. In 1847, Brown moved to Boston, where the Massachusetts Anti-Slavery Society hired him as a traveling lecturer.

That same year, the organization published Brown's autobiography, *Narrative of William W. Brown, A Former Slave, Written by Himself,* which became a best seller. Brown gave thousands of speeches in America and Europe calling for an end to slavery and equality for both blacks and women. He repeatedly stressed that African Americans were "endowed with those intellectual and amiable qualities which adorn and dignify human nature."

FREDERICK DOUGLASS Frederick Douglass was an even more effective spokesman for abolitionism. Having escaped from slavery in Baltimore, Maryland, Douglass made his way to Massachusetts, where he began speaking at anti-slavery meetings in black churches. Through his writings and dazzling presentations, he became the best-known black man in America. "I appear before the immense assembly this evening as a thief and a robber," he told a Massachusetts group in 1842. "I stole this head, these limbs, this body from my master, and ran off with them." Fearful of capture after publishing his *Narrative of the Life of Frederick Douglass, An American Slave, Written by Himself* (1845), he left for an extended lecture tour of the British Isles, returning two years later with enough money to purchase his official freedom. He then started an abolitionist newspaper for blacks, the *North Star*, in Rochester, New York. He named the newspaper after the star that runaway slaves used to guide them at night toward freedom.

SOJOURNER TRUTH The female counterpart to Frederick Douglass was Sojourner Truth. Born to enslaved parents in upstate New York in 1797, she was given the name Isabella "Bell" Hardenbergh but renamed herself in

Frederick Douglass (left) and Sojourner Truth (right) Both former slaves, Douglass and Truth were leading African American abolitionists and captivating orators.

1843 after experiencing a conversation with God, who told her "to travel up and down the land" preaching against slavery. Having been a slave until she was freed in 1827, Sojourner Truth was able to speak with conviction and knowledge about the evils of the "peculiar institution" as well as the inequality of women.

Truth traveled and spoke throughout the North during the 1840s and 1850s. As she told the Ohio Women's Rights Convention in 1851, "I have plowed, and planted, and gathered into barns, and no man could head me— and ar'n't I a woman? I have borne thirteen children, and seen 'em mos' all sold off into slavery, and when I cried out with a mother's grief, none but Jesus heard—and ar'n't I a woman?"

Through such compelling testimony, Sojourner Truth demonstrated the powerful intersection of abolitionism and feminism. In the process, she tapped the distinctive energies that women brought to reformist causes. "If the first woman God ever made was strong enough to turn the world upside down all alone," she concluded in her address to the Ohio gathering, "these women together ought to be able to turn it back, and get it right side up again!"

THE UNDERGROUND RAILROAD Between 1810 and 1850, tens of thousands of southern slaves fled north. Runaway slaves would make their way, usually at night, from one "station" or safe house to the next. The organizations and the systems of safe houses and shelters along the routes to freedom were referred to as the **Underground Railroad**. The "conductors" helping the runaways included freeborn blacks, white abolitionists, former slaves, and Native Americans. Many were motivated by religious concerns. Quakers, Presbyterians, Methodists, and Baptists participated.

In many northern cities, blacks and whites organized "vigilance committees" to thwart the slave catchers. In February 1851, Shadrach Minkins, a "stout, copper-colored man" who worked as a waiter at a Boston coffee house, was seized by U.S. marshals who claimed that he was a runaway slave from Virginia. During a court hearing, black and white members of the anti-slavery Boston Vigilance and Safety Committee active in the Underground Railroad rushed in, overcame armed guards, and snatched "the trembling prey of the slave hunters." An outraged President Millard Fillmore issued a proclamation demanding that citizens obey the law and that those responsible for "kidnapping" Minkins be prosecuted. None of the Bostonians charged in the case were convicted.

A few courageous runaway slaves returned to the South to organize more escapes. Harriet Tubman, the most celebrated member of the Underground Railroad, was born a slave in Maryland in 1820 but escaped to Philadelphia in 1849. She would return to the South nineteen times to help some 300 fugitive slaves, including her parents. She "never lost a passenger" during her legendary acts of bravery.

ELIJAH P. LOVEJOY Despite the growing efforts of anti-slavery organizations, racism remained widespread in the North, especially among the working poor. Abolitionist speakers confronted hostile white crowds who disliked blacks or found anti-slavery agitation bad for business. In 1837, a mob in Illinois killed Elijah P. Lovejoy, editor of an anti-slavery newspaper, giving the movement a martyr to the causes of both abolition and freedom of the press.

Lovejoy had begun his career as a Presbyterian minister in New England. After receiving a "sign by God" to focus his life on the "destruction of slavery," he moved to St. Louis, in slaveholding Missouri, where his newspaper denounced alcohol, Catholicism, and slavery. When a pro-slavery mob destroyed his printing office, he moved across the Mississippi River to a warehouse in Alton, Illinois, where he tried to start an anti-slavery society. There mobs twice more destroyed his printing press. When a new press arrived, Lovejoy and several supporters armed themselves and took up defensive positions.

On November 7, 1837, thugs began hurling stones and firing shots into the building. One of Lovejoy's allies fired back, killing a rioter. The mob then set fire to the warehouse, shouting, "Kill every damned abolitionist as he leaves." A shotgun blast killed Lovejoy, and his murder aroused a frenzy of indignation. At one of the hundreds of memorial services across the North, a grizzled John Brown rose, raised his right hand, and declared, "Here, before God, in the presence of these witnesses, from this time, I consecrate my life to the destruction of slavery!" Brown and other militants decided that only violence would dislodge the sin of slavery.

ABIGAIL KELLEY The powerful appeal of abolitionism and the broader reform impulse is illustrated in the colorful life of Abigail "Abbie" Kelley. A teacher born in Pelham, Massachusetts, in 1811, she initially became a Grahamite, giving up coffee, alcohol, meat, and tea in favor of vegetables and Graham crackers. Soon thereafter, she attended a lecture by William Lloyd Garrison and embraced abolitionism, joining the Female Anti-Slavery Society. In 1837, she wrote her sister that she was supporting a variety of "moral enterprises—Grahamism, Abolition, and Peace."

Kelley was a compelling speaker. In 1840, she was the first woman to be elected an officer in the American Anti-Slavery Society. Many male abolitionists were furious. One of them described Kelley as being one of those "women of masculine minds and aggressive tendencies . . . who cannot be satisfied in domestic life." The prejudice she experienced among male officers revealed to her that she and other women "were manacled [chained] *ourselves.*"

During the 1850s, Kelley, while still a passionate abolitionist, began to champion women's rights and temperance. She spoke at the fourth national woman's rights convention in Cleveland. Lucy Stone, one of the women's rights leaders, called Kelley a heroine who "stood in the thick of the fight for the slaves, and at the same time, she hewed out that path over which women are now walking toward their equal political rights."

The Defense of Slavery

The growing strength and visibility of the abolitionist movement coupled with the profitability of cotton growing prompted southerners to launch an aggressive defense of slavery. Some of them even called for the reopening of the African slave trade. During the 1830s and after, pro-slavery leaders worked out an elaborate rationale for what they considered the benefits of slavery. The Bible was frequently cited in support of slavery; had not the patriarchs of the Hebrew Bible held people in bondage? Had not Saint Paul advised servants to obey their masters and told a runaway servant to return to his master? And had not Jesus remained silent on the subject?

Soon, even bolder arguments emerged. In February 1837, South Carolina's John C. Calhoun, the most prominent southern political leader, told the Senate that slavery was "good—a great good," rooted in the Bible. He asserted that the "savage" Africans brought to America "had never existed in so comfortable, so respectable, or so civilized a condition, as that which is now enjoyed in the Southern states." If slavery were abolished, Calhoun warned, the principle of white racial supremacy would be compromised.

Calhoun and other defenders of slavery also claimed that blacks could not be expected to work under conditions of freedom. They were too shiftless, the argument went, and if freed, they would be a danger to themselves and to others. White workers, on the other hand, feared the competition for jobs if slaves were freed. Calhoun's strident defense of slavery led Henry Clay of Kentucky, himself a slaveholder, to describe Calhoun as "a rigid, fanatic, ambitious, selfishly partisan and sectional turncoat with too much genius and too little common sense, who will either die a traitor or a madman."

The increasingly heated debate over slavery drove a deep wedge between North and South. In 1831, William Lloyd Garrison predicted that an eventual "separation between the free and slave States" was "unavoidable." By midcentury, a large number of Americans had decided that southern slavery was an abomination that should not be allowed to expand into the western territories. The militant reformers who were determined to prevent slavery from expanding outside the South came to be called "free soilers." Their crusade would reach a fiery climax in the Civil War.

CHAPTER REVIEW

SUMMARY

- **Religious Developments**   Starting in the late eighteenth century, *Unitarians* and *Universalists* in New England challenged the Christian notion of predestination and advocated that all humans (not just the select few) were capable of good deeds and could receive salvation. Echoing these ideas with their conception of salvation by free will, the preachers of the *Second Great Awakening* generated widespread interest among Protestants in *frontier revivals*. The more democratic sects, such as Baptists and Methodists, gained huge numbers of converts. Religion went hand in hand with reform in the "burned-over district" in western New York, which was also the birthplace of several religious movements, including the Church of Jesus Christ of Latter-day Saints (the *Mormons*).

- **Transcendentalists**   A group of New England writers, ministers, and reformers who embraced a moral and spiritual idealism (Romanticism) in reaction to scientific rationalism and Christian orthodoxy. In their writings, they sought to "transcend" reason and the material world and encourage more-independent thought and reflection. At the same time, *transcendentalism* influenced the works of novelists, essayists, and poets, who created a uniquely "American" literature.

- **Social-Reform Movements**   The *cult of domesticity* celebrated a "woman's sphere" in the home and argued that young women should be trained not for the workplace but in the domestic arts—managing a kitchen, running a household, and nurturing the children. However, the rise of an urban middle class offered growing numbers of women more time to devote to societal concerns. Social reformers— many of them women—sought to improve society and eradicate social evils. The most widespread movement was for *temperance*—the elimination of excessive drinking. Many activists focused on reforming prisons and asylums. With the *Seneca Falls Convention* of 1848, social reformers launched the women's rights movement with the *Declaration of Rights and Sentiments*. In many parts of the country, reformers called for greater access to education through *public schools*. Amid the pervasive climate of reform, more than 100 *utopian communities* were established, including the Shakers, Brook Farm, and the Oneida Community.

- **Anti-Slavery Movement**   Northern opponents of slavery promoted several solutions, including the *American Colonization Society's* call for gradual emancipation and the deportation of African Americans to colonies in Africa. *Abolitionism* emerged in the 1830s, demanding an immediate end of slavery. Some abolitionists went even further, calling for full social and political equality among the races, although they disagreed over tactics. Abolitionist efforts in the North provoked fear and resentment among southern whites. Yet many northerners shared the belief in the racial inferiority of Africans and were hostile to the tactics and message of the abolitionists. African Americans in the North joined with abolitionists to create an *Underground Railroad*, a network of safe havens to help slaves escape bondage in the South.

CHRONOLOGY

1826	Ministers organize the American Society for the Promotion of Temperance
1830–1831	Charles G. Finney begins preaching in upstate New York
1830	Percentage of American churchgoers has doubled since 1800
	Joseph Smith publishes the *Book of Mormon*
1831	William Lloyd Garrison begins publishing the *Liberator*
1833	American Anti-Slavery Society is founded
1836	Transcendental Club holds its first meeting
1837	Abolitionist editor Elijah P. Lovejoy is murdered
1840	Abolitionists form the Liberty party
1840s	Methodists have become largest Protestant denomination in America
1845	*Narrative of the Life of Frederick Douglass* is published
1846–1847	Mormons, led by Brigham Young, make the difficult trek to Utah
1848	At the Seneca Falls Convention, feminists issue the Declaration of Rights and Sentiments
1851	Sojourner Truth delivers her famous speech "Ar'n't I a Woman?"
1854	Henry David Thoreau's *Walden, or Life in the Woods* is published

KEY TERMS

Unitarians p. 507

Universalists p. 507

Second Great Awakening p. 508

frontier revivals p. 509

Mormons p. 515

transcendentalism p. 518

temperance p. 528

cult of domesticity p. 530

Seneca Falls Convention (1848) p. 531

Declaration of Rights and Sentiments (1848) p. 532

public schools p. 533

utopian communities p. 536

American Colonization Society (ACS) p. 538

abolitionism p. 539

Underground Railroad p. 545

 INQUIZITIVE

Go to InQuizitive to see what you've learned—and learn what you've missed—with personalized feedback along the way.

part four

A HOUSE DIVIDED AND REBUILT

During the first half of the nineteenth century, Americans, restless and energetic, were optimistic about the future. The United States was the world's largest republic. Its population continued to grow rapidly, economic conditions were improving, and tensions with Great Britain had eased.

Above all, Americans continued to move westward, where vast expanses of cheap land lured farmers, ranchers, miners, and missionaries. By the end of the 1840s, the United States had again

dramatically expanded its territory, from Texas west to California and the Pacific Northwest. America had become a transcontinental nation from the Atlantic to the Pacific.

This extraordinary surge of territorial expansion was a mixed blessing, however. How to deal with slavery in the new western territories emerged as the nation's flashpoint issue as differences grew among America's three distinctive regions—North, South, and West.

A series of political compromises had glossed over the fundamental issue of slavery, but anti-slavery activists opposed efforts to extend slavery into the West, and an emerging generation of politicians proved less willing to compromise. The continuing debate over allowing slavery into new territories eventually led many Americans to decide with Abraham Lincoln that the nation could not survive half-slave and half-free. Something had to give.

In a last-ditch effort to preserve the institution of slavery, eleven southern states seceded from the Union and created a separate Confederate nation, prompting northerners such as Abraham Lincoln to risk a civil war to restore the Union.

No one realized in 1861 how costly the war would be: more than 700,000 soldiers and sailors would die in the struggle. Nor did anyone envision how sweeping the war's effects would be upon the nation's future. The northern victory in 1865 restored the Union and helped accelerate America's transformation into a modern nation-state. A national consciousness began to replace the sectional divisions of the prewar era, and a Republican-led Congress passed legislation to promote industrial and commercial development and western expansion.

Although the Civil War ended slavery, the status of the freed African Americans remained precarious. Former slaves found themselves legally free, but few had property, homes, education, or training. Although the Fourteenth Amendment (1868) guaranteed the civil rights of African Americans and the

Fifteenth Amendment (1870) declared that black men could vote, southern officials often ignored the new laws (as did some in northern states as well).

The restoration of the former Confederate states to the Union did not come easily. Bitterness and resistance grew among the defeated southerners. Although Confederate leaders were stripped of voting rights, they continued to exercise considerable authority. In 1877, when the last federal troops were removed from the occupied South, former Confederates declared themselves "redeemed" from the stain of northern military occupation. By the end of the nineteenth century, most states of the former Confederacy had developed a system of legal discrimination against blacks that re-created many aspects of slavery.

13 Western Expansion

1830–1848

***Emigrants Crossing the Plains, or the Oregon Trail* (1869)** German American painter Albert Bierstadt captures the majestic sights of the frontier, though the transcontinental trek was also often grueling and bleak.

I n the American experience, the westward march of settlement was always a source of energy, hope, and yearning. Henry David Thoreau exclaimed that Americans "go westward as into the future, with a spirit of enterprise and adventure"—and the hope of freedom.

The West—whether imagined as the enticing lands over the Allegheny Mountains that became Ohio and Kentucky or, later, the "black belt" farmlands of the Old Southwest, the fertile prairies watered by the Mississippi River, or the spectacular area along the Pacific coast that became the states of California, Oregon, and Washington—served as a powerful magnet for adventurous people dreaming of freedom, self-fulfillment, and economic gain. The Pacific Northwest teemed with fish, forests, and fur-bearing animals. Acquiring the ports along the Pacific coast would also allow the United States to expand its trade with Asia.

During the 1840s and after, waves of people moved westward, seeking a better chance and more space in the West. "If hell lay to the west," one pioneer declared, "Americans would cross heaven to get there." Millions of people endured unrelenting hardships to fulfill their "providential destiny" to subdue the entire continent, even if it meant displacing the Indians in the process. By 1860, some 4.3 million people had settled in the trans-Mississippi West.

Emigrants moved west largely for economic reasons. "To make money was their chief object," said a pioneer woman in Texas, "all things else were subsidiary to it." Waves of enterprising trappers and farmers, miners, merchants, and clerks, hunters, ranchers, teachers, household servants, and prostitutes, among others, headed west to seek their fortunes. Others sought religious freedom or new converts to Christianity. Whatever the reason, the pioneers formed an unceasing migratory stream flowing across the Great Plains and the Rocky Mountains.

focus questions

1. Why did Americans move west of the Mississippi River during the 1830s and 1840s? How did they accomplish this, and where did they move to?

2. How did Texas become part of the United States? Why was the process so complicated, and how did it impact national politics?

3. What were the similarities and differences in the process for how California and Texas were settled and how they became part of the United States?

4. How did the Mexican-American War impact national politics?

Of course, the West was not empty land waiting to be developed. Others had been there long before the American migration. But the Indian and Hispanic inhabitants of the region soon found themselves swept aside by American settlers, all facilitated by U.S. presidents and congressmen who encouraged the nation's continental expansion.

Westward expansion was especially important to southerners, many of whom wanted cheap new lands to plant using slave labor. In addition, southerners had long enjoyed disproportionate political power because of the provision in the U.S. Constitution that counted slaves as part of the population in determining the number of congressional seats for each state. Thirteen of the first sixteen presidents were from the South, and most congressional leadership positions were held by southerners.

But southern political influence began dwindling as the industrializing Midwest and Northeast grew and increased their representation in Congress. Southerners wanted new western states to boost pro-southern representation and ensure that slavery was never threatened. As a Mississippi senator said, "I would spread the blessings of slavery . . . to the uttermost ends of the earth." Such motives made the addition of new western territory especially controversial. Would the territory be slave or free?

Moving West

During the mid–nineteenth century, America remained a nation in motion. In 1845, New York newspaper editor and Democratic-party propagandist John L. O'Sullivan gave a catchy name to the nation's aggressive expansion. "Our **manifest destiny**," he wrote, "is to overspread and to possess the whole of the continent which Providence has given us for the free development of our yearly multiplying millions . . . [and for the] great experiment of liberty." O'Sullivan spoke for many Americans who saw no reason not to take control of all of North America: "Yes, more, more, more! . . . until our national destiny is fulfilled."

The concept of "manifest destiny" assumed that the United States had a God-given mission to extend its Christian republic and capitalist civilization from the Atlantic to the Pacific—and beyond. It also took for granted the superiority of American ideals and institutions, including the opportunity to bring liberty and prosperity to native peoples. This widely embraced notion of manifest ("self-evident") destiny offered a moral justification for territorial expansion and the expansion of slavery. But God was not driving American expansion; Americans were. However idealized, manifest destiny for many Americans was in essence a cluster of flimsy rationalizations and racist attitudes justifying the conquest of weaker peoples.

THE WESTERN FRONTIER Most western pioneers during the second quarter of the nineteenth century were American-born whites from the Upper South and the Midwest. Only a few free African Americans joined in the migration. What spurred the massive migration westward was the continuing population explosion in the United States and the desire for land and wealth.

Although some people traveled by sea to the Pacific coast, most went overland. Between 1841 and 1867, some 350,000 men, women, and children made the difficult trek to California or Oregon, while hundreds of thousands of others settled in such areas as Colorado, Texas, and Arkansas.

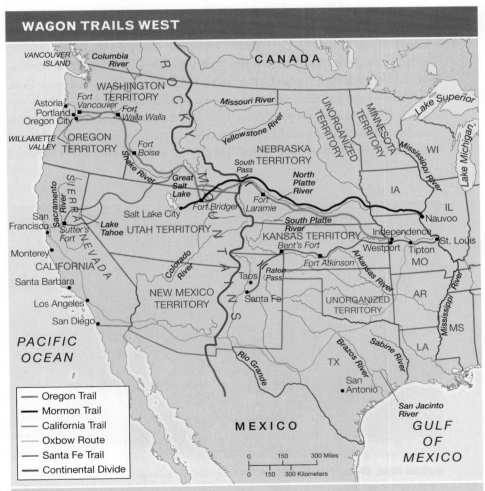

WAGON TRAILS WEST

Legend:
— Oregon Trail
— Mormon Trail
— California Trail
— Oxbow Route
— Santa Fe Trail
— Continental Divide

- What did settlers migrating west of the Mississippi River hope to find?
- What were the perils of the Overland Trails?
- Describe the experience of a typical settler traveling on the Overland Trails.

Most of the pioneers who made their way west on the **Overland Trails** traveled in family groups. By 1845, some 5,000 people were making the six-month journey annually. The discovery of gold in California in 1848 brought some 30,000 pioneers along the Oregon Trail in 1849. By 1850, the peak year of travel along the trail, the annual count had risen to 55,000.

PLAINS INDIANS More than 325,000 Indians inhabited the Southwest, the Great Plains, California, and the Pacific Northwest in 1840, when the great migration of white settlers into the region began. The Native Americans were divided into more than 200 nations, each with its own language, religion, cultural practices, and system of governance. Plains Indians included the Arapaho, Blackfoot, Cheyenne, Kiowa, and Sioux. Some were primarily farmers; others were nomadic, following buffalo herds across the prairie grasslands.

In the arid Southwest region that today includes Arizona, New Mexico, and southern Utah, the peaceful Pueblo nations—Acoma, Hopi, Laguna, Taos, Zia, Zuni—were sophisticated farmers who lived in adobe villages along rivers that irrigated their crops of corn, beans, and squash. Their rivals were the Apache and the Navajo, warlike hunters who roamed the countryside in small bands and preyed upon the Pueblos. They, in turn, were periodically harassed

Buffalo Hunt, Chasing Back (1860s) This painting by George Catlin shows a hunter outrunning a buffalo.

by their powerful enemies, the Comanche. Many Indian nations were hostile to each other, resulting in frequent wars and raids.

To the north in the Great Basin, Paiutes and Gosiutes struggled to survive in the harsh, arid region of what is today Nevada, Utah, and eastern California. They traveled in family groups and subsisted on berries, pine nuts, insects, and rodents. Along the California coast, Indians lived in small villages. They gathered wild plants and acorns and were experts at fishing.

The Native Americans in the Pacific Northwest—the Nisqually, Spokane, Yakama, Chinook, Klamath, and Nez Perce (Pierced Nose)—enjoyed the most abundant natural resources and the most temperate climate. The ocean and rivers provided whales, seals, salmon, and crabs, and lush inland forests harbored game, berries, and nuts. Majestic forests of fir, redwood, and cedar offered wood for cooking and shelter.

All these Indian societies eventually felt the unrelenting pressure of white expansion and conquest, and the influx of white settlers and hunters posed a direct threat to the Indians' cultural survival. When federal officials could not coerce, cajole, or confuse Indian leaders into selling the title to their tribal lands, fighting ensued. And, after the discovery of gold in California in early 1848, the tidal wave of white expansion flowed all the way to the west coast, violently engulfing Native Americans and Mexicans in its wake.

MEXICO AND THE SPANISH WEST As American settlers trespassed across Indian lands, they also encountered Spanish-speaking peoples. Many whites were as prejudiced toward Hispanics as they were toward Indians. Senator Lewis Cass from Michigan, who would be the Democratic candidate for president in 1848, expressed the common bias among white expansionists: "We do not want the people of Mexico, either as citizens or as subjects. All we want is their . . . territory."

The centuries-old Spanish efforts at colonization in the northernmost provinces of Mexico had been less successful in Arizona and Texas than in New Mexico and Florida. The Yuma and Apaches in Arizona and the Comanches and Apaches in Texas thwarted Spanish efforts to establish Catholic missions. By 1790, the Hispanic population in Texas numbered only 2,510, while in New Mexico it exceeded 20,000.

In 1807, French forces led by Napoléon had occupied Spain and imprisoned the king, creating confusion throughout Spain's colonial possessions in the Western Hemisphere, including Mexico. Miguel Hidalgo y Costilla, a creole priest (born in Mexico of European ancestry), took advantage of the fluid situation to convince Indians and Hispanics to revolt against Spanish rule in Mexico. But the poorly organized uprising failed miserably.

"¡Viva El Cura Hidalgo!" This patriotic image celebrating Mexican independence shows Father Miguel Hidalgo in an oval medallion.

In 1820, Mexican creoles again tried to liberate themselves from Spanish authority. Facing a growing revolt, the last Spanish officials withdrew in 1821, and Mexico became an independent nation. However, the infant republic struggled to develop a stable government and an effective economy. Americans eagerly took advantage of Mexico's instability, especially in its sparsely populated northern provinces—areas that included present-day Texas, New Mexico, Arizona, Nevada, California, and portions of Colorado, Oklahoma, Kansas, and Wyoming.

American fur traders streamed into New Mexico and Arizona, developing a profitable trade in beaver pelts along the Santa Fe Trail to St. Louis. During the 1830s and 1840s, thousands of Americans made the arduous journey in wagons on the Santa Fe Trail from Missouri to New Mexico. The trek was not for the fainthearted. In 1847 alone, marauding Indians killed forty-seven Americans, destroyed 330 wagons, and stole 6,500 horses, cattle, and oxen along the trail.

THE OVERLAND TRAILS During the early nineteenth century, the Far Northwest consisted of the Nebraska, Washington, and Oregon Territories. The Oregon Country included what became the states of Oregon, Idaho, and Washington, parts of Montana and Wyoming, and the Canadian province of British Columbia. It was an unsettled region claimed by both Great Britain and the United States. By the Convention of 1818, the two nations agreed to "joint occupation" of the Oregon Country, each drawn there initially by the profitable trade in fur pelts.

During the 1820s and 1830s, the fur trade inspired a reckless breed of "mountain men" to abandon civilization and embrace a primitive existence in the wilderness. The rugged trappers were the first whites to find their way around the Rocky Mountains, and they pioneered the trails that settlers would

***Fur Traders Descending the Missouri* (1845)** Originally titled "French-Trader, Half-Breed Son," this oil painting depicts a white settler sailing down the river with his half–Native American son—not an uncommon sight in western America.

travel as they flooded the Oregon Country and headed across the border into California.

THE GREAT MIGRATION Word of Oregon's fertile soil, plentiful rainfall, and magnificent forests gradually spread eastward. By 1840, a trickle of emigrants—farmers, missionaries, teachers, fur traders, and shopkeepers—was flowing along the Oregon Trail, a 2,000-mile footpath that formed the great highway west connecting the Missouri River near St. Louis with Oregon.

Soon, "**Oregon fever**" swept the nation. To an Ohio woman, "going to the Far West seemed like the entrance to a new world, one of freedom, happiness, and prosperity." Some pioneers desperately sought to escape debts, or dull lives, or bad marriages. "We had nothing to lose," wrote one woman, "and we might gain a fortune." For whatever reason, tens of thousands of Americans began pulling up stakes and moving their families west.

In 1841 and 1842, the first sizable wagon trains made the long trip across half the continent, and in 1843 the movement became a mass migration. One pioneer said that the wagon trains, sometimes six miles long, were like mobile communities. "Everybody was supposed to rise at daylight, and while the women were preparing breakfast, the men rounded up the cattle, took down the tents, yoked the oxen to the wagons, and made everything ready to start."

The Oregon-bound wagon trains followed the trail west from Independence, Missouri, then along the winding North Platte River into what is now

Wyoming, through South Pass down to Fort Bridger (abode of the celebrated mountain man Jim Bridger), then down the meandering Snake River through what is now Idaho to the salmon-filled Columbia River. From there, they moved through the Cascade Mountains to their goal: Oregon's fertile Willamette Valley.

LIFE ON THE TRAIL Traveling in "prairie schooners," sturdy canvas-covered wagons pulled by teams of tramping oxen, sunburned settlers bumped and jostled their way across the rugged trails, mountains, and plains blackened by vast herds of buffaloes.

Indians rarely attacked the wagon trains; they allowed most settlers to pass through their tribal lands unmolested. Many wagon trains received generous aid from Indians who served as guides, advisers, or traders. The Indians, one female pioneer noted, "proved better than represented." To be sure, as the number of pioneers increased dramatically during the 1850s, disputes with Indians over land and water increased, but never to the degree portrayed in novels, films, and television shows.

Still, the long journey west, usually five to six months, was extraordinarily difficult, an exodus of grinding hardship during broiling summers, fierce thunderstorms, and bitterly cold winters reliable for their heavy snows. Wagons broke down, oxen died, and diseases like cholera and dysentery took their toll on pioneers. "The cowards never started," a popular saying went, "and the weak died on the way."

WOMEN PIONEERS The diary of Amelia Knight, who set out for Oregon in 1853 with her husband and seven children, reveals the mortal threats along the trail: "Chatfield quite sick with scarlet fever. A calf took sick and died before breakfast. Lost one of our oxen; he dropped dead in the yoke. I could hardly help shedding tears. Yesterday my eighth child was born."

Cholera claimed many lives because of tainted water and contaminated food. On average, there was one grave every eighty yards along the trail. Each step "of the slow, plodding cattle," wrote a woman emigrant, "carried us farther and farther from civilization into a desolate, barbarous country."

Initially, the western pioneers adopted the same division of labor used back East. Women cooked, washed, sewed, and monitored the children, while men drove the wagons, tended the horses and cattle, and did the heavy labor. But the unique demands of the western trails soon dissolved such neat distinctions. Women found themselves gathering buffalo dung for fuel, driving wagons, working to dislodge wagons mired in mud, helping to construct makeshift bridges, pitching tents, or participating in a variety of other "unladylike" tasks. Elizabeth Smith described a typical daily routine along the trail when she wrote in her diary: "Men making rafts. Women cooking and washing. Chil-

Gathering buffalo chips Women on the Overland Trails not only cooked and washed and took care of their children but also gathered dried buffalo dung to use as fuel as their wagons crossed the treeless plains.

dren crying." Another noted that "we have no time for sociability. From the time we get up in the morning, until we are on the road, it's hurry scurry."

Southerner Lavinia Porter said that the trip along the California Trail was so difficult that it was still "a source of wonder to me how we [women] were able to endure it." Men on the plains, she observed, were not willing "to wait upon women as they were in more civilized communities." Through her hardships, she became convinced that the American woman was "endowed with the courage of her brave pioneer ancestors, and no matter what the environment she can adapt herself to all situations, even the perilous trip across the western half of this great continent."

The hard labor of the trail understandably provoked tensions within families and powerful yearnings for home. Divorces soared in the West. Many a tired pioneer could identify with the following comment in a girl's journal: "Poor Ma said only this morning, 'Oh, I wish we had never started.' She looks so sorrowful and dejected." Another woman wondered "what had possessed my husband, anyway, that he should have thought of bringing us away out through this God forsaken country."

Some of the emigrants turned back, but most continued on. "Oh dear," an Iowa woman confided in her journal, "I do so want to get there. It is now almost four months since we have slept in a house." Once in Oregon or California, the emigrants set about establishing stable communities. Noted one settler: "Friday, October 27. Arrived at Oregon City at the falls of the Willamette River. Saturday, October 28. Went to work."

Pioneers in Oregon found themselves initially living in a "primitive state" requiring backbreaking work to create self-sustaining homesteads. Mirroring their duties on the Overland trails, women who settled in Oregon did much of the same hard physical labor as men, day and night. "I am a very old woman," reported twenty-nine-year-old Sarah Everett. "My face is thin, sunken, and wrinkled, my hands bony, withered, and hard." Another Oregon pioneer warned that a "woman that cannot endure almost as much as a horse has no business here."

Many pioneer families were devastated by the struggle of scratching out new lives in the West. The Malick family, for example, left Illinois in 1848 and started a farm in the Oregon Territory. George Malick, the father, died soon thereafter, as did three of the older children. "We are all well," widow Abigail Malick wrote in 1855 to relatives back in Illinois. "All that are left of us."

THE SETTLEMENT OF CALIFORNIA   California was also a powerful magnet for settlers and adventurers. It had first felt the influence of European culture in 1769, when Spain grew concerned about Russian seal traders moving south along the Pacific coast from Alaska. To thwart Russian intentions, Spain sent a naval expedition to settle the region. The Spanish discovered San Francisco Bay and constructed *presidios* (military garrisons) at San Diego and Monterey. Even more important, Franciscan friars, led by Junípero Serra, established a Catholic mission at San Diego.

Over the next fifty years, Franciscans built twenty more missions, spaced a day's journey apart along the coast from San Diego northward to San Francisco. The mission-centered culture created by the Hispanic settlers who migrated to California from Mexico was quite different from those in Texas and New Mexico, where the original missions were converted into secular communities, and the property was divided among the Indians. In California, however, the missions were much larger, more influential, and longer lasting.

By the nineteenth century, Spanish Catholic missionaries, aided by Spanish soldiers, controlled most of the Indians living along the California coast. The friars (priests) enticed the Indians into "missions" by offering gifts or impressing them with their "magical" religious rituals. Once inside the missions, the Indians were baptized as Catholics, taught Spanish, and stripped of their cultural heritage.

CATHOLIC MISSIONS The California Catholic missions served as churches, villages, fortresses, homes, schools, shops, farms, and outposts of Spanish rule. The missions also quickly became agricultural enterprises, producing crops, livestock, clothing, and household goods, both for profit and to supply the neighboring presidios. Indians provided most of the labor. The Franciscans viewed forced Indian labor as both a practical necessity and a morally enriching responsibility essential to transforming unproductive Indians into industrious Christians.

A mission's daily routine began at dawn with the ringing of a bell, which summoned the community to prayer. Work began an hour later and did not end until an hour before sunset. Most Indian men worked in the fields. Some were trained in special skills, such as masonry, carpentry, or leatherwork. Women handled domestic chores, but during harvest season, everyone was expected to help in the fields. Instead of wages, the Indians received clothing, food, housing, and religious instruction.

The Franciscans used force to control their captive laborers. Rebellious Indians were whipped or imprisoned, and mission Indians died at an alarming rate. One Franciscan friar reported that "of every four Indian children born, three die in their first or second year, while those who survive do not reach the age of twenty-five." Infectious disease was the primary threat, but the grueling labor regimen took a high toll as well. The Native American population along the California coast declined from 72,000 in 1769 to 18,000 by 1821. Saving souls cost many lives.

With Mexican independence in 1821, the Spanish missions slowly disintegrated and fell into disuse. By the time the first Americans began to trickle into California, they found a vast, beautiful province with only a small, scattered population of 6,000 Mexicans ruled by a few dominant *caballeros* or *rancheros*—"gentlemen" who owned the largest ranches in the province, much like the planters who lorded over the Lower South.

Hispanic Californians, called *Californios*, took comfort that Mexico City, the capital, was too far away to exercise effective control over them. Between 1821, when Mexico gained its independence, and 1841, Spanish-speaking Californians, as well as many recent American arrivals, staged ten revolts against Mexican governors.

Among the white immigrants in California in the mid–nineteenth century was John A. Sutter, a Swiss settler who had founded a colony of European emigrants. At the junction of the Sacramento and American Rivers (later the site of the city of Sacramento), Sutter built an enormous fort with walls eighteen feet tall to protect the settlers and their shops.

New Helvetia (Americans called it Sutter's Fort), completed in 1843, stood at the end of what became the California Trail, which forked southward off the Oregon Trail and crossed the Sierra Nevada, a soaring mountain range running north/south along eastern California. By the start of 1846 there were perhaps 800 Americans in California, along with approximately 10,000 Californios. The Americans learned to speak Spanish, often embraced Catholicism, won Mexican citizenship and spouses, and participated in local politics.

THE DONNER PARTY The most tragic story of the efforts to get to California using the Overland Trails involved the party headed by George Donner, a prosperous sixty-two-year-old farmer from Illinois who in some respects epitomized the restless mobility of nineteenth-century Americans. Born in North Carolina, he had moved first to Kentucky, then Indiana, and eventually Illinois. Now, he was determined to relocate to California.

In mid-April 1846, Donner led his family and a train of seventy-four other settlers and twenty-three wagons to the Oregon Trail. Early on, Donner's wife reported that the Indians were friendly and the prairie "beautiful beyond description." Her outlook was optimistic: "Indeed, if I do not experience something far worse than I have yet done, I shall say that the trouble all is in getting started."

But "the trouble" soon appeared, for the Donner Party made several fatal mistakes: starting too late in the year, overloading their wagons, and taking a foolish shortcut to California across the Wasatch Mountains in the Utah Territory. They had inadequate food, water, clothing, and experience for the journey ahead.

In the Wasatch Range, the Donner Party got lost taking a supposed "short-cut" and was forced to backtrack, losing three precious weeks in the process. An early September snow further slowed their progress. They eventually found their way across the Wasatch Mountains and into the desert leading to the Great Salt Lake, but crossing the parched desert exacted a terrible toll. They lost more than 100 oxen and were forced to abandon several wagons and their precious supplies. Most important, they had lost valuable time as winter weather began to set in.

When the Donner Party reached Truckee Pass in eastern California, the last mountain barrier before the Sacramento Valley, a two-week-long blizzard trapped them in two separate camps. By December, the pioneers, half of them children, were marooned with only enough food to last through the end of the month. Seventeen of the strongest members, calling themselves the "Forlorn Hope," decided to cross the pass on their own, but they were trapped by more snow. Two of them turned back; eight more died of exposure and starvation.

Just before he died, Billy Graves urged his daughters to eat his body. The daughters were appalled at first, but soon saw no other choice. When two more died, they, too, were eaten. Only seven lived to reach the Sacramento Valley.

Back at the main camps, the survivors had slaughtered and eaten the last of the livestock, then boiled hides and bones. They had also killed two Indian guides and eaten them. When a rescue party finally reached them two months later, they discovered a grisly scene. Thirteen people had died, and cannibalism had become commonplace; one pioneer had noted casually in his diary, "Mrs. Murphy said here yesterday that she thought she would commence on Milt and eat him." As the rescuers led the forty-seven survivors over the pass, George Donner, so weakened and distressed that he was unable to walk, stayed behind to die. His wife chose to remain with him.

THE PATHFINDER: JOHN FRÉMONT   Despite the hardships and dangers of the overland crossing, the Far West proved an irresistible attraction for hundreds of thousands of pioneers. The most enthusiastic champion of American settlement in Mexican California and the Far West was John Charles Frémont, an impetuous junior army officer who during the 1840s became America's most famous celebrity and a notorious troublemaker.

Born out of wedlock in Savannah, Georgia, and raised in the South, Frémont developed a robust love of the outdoors. In 1838, after attending the College of Charleston, he was commissioned a second lieutenant in the U.S. Topographical Corps, an organization whose mission was to explore and map new western territories. Frémont soon excelled at surveying, mapmaking, and woodcraft while becoming versed in geology, botany, ornithology, and zoology.

In 1841, Frémont courted and married seventeen-year-old Jessie Benton, the feisty daughter of Thomas Hart Benton, the powerful Missouri senator. Once Benton's anger at his daughter subsided, he became Frémont's foremost booster and helped arrange the explorations that would bring Frémont fame as the nation's leading scientific explorer-adventurer.

"The Pathfinder" John Charles Frémont became a national hero as a result of his explorations in the Far West.

In 1842, the fearless Frémont, who believed he was a man of destiny, set out from present-day Kansas City with two dozen soldiers to map the eastern half of the Oregon Trail. They spent five months collecting plant and animal specimens and drawing maps in uncharted territory.

With his wife's considerable help, Frémont published in newspapers across the nation excerpts from a rip-roaring account of his explorations titled *A Report on an Exploration of the Country Lying between the Missouri River and the Rocky Mountains on the Line of the Kansas and Great Platte Rivers*. In describing the Great Plains, the Frémonts wrote that the "Indians and buffalo were the poetry and life of the prairie, and our camp was full of exhilaration."

The popular stories of Frémont's adventures made him an instant national celebrity and earned him the nickname, "the Pathfinder." After reading about the expedition, Henry Wadsworth Longfellow, the nation's most popular poet, announced that "Frémont has touched my imagination. What a wild life, and what a fresh kind of existence! But ah, the discomforts!"

The success of Frémont's first western explorations quickly led to another expedition, this time intended to map the second and more difficult half of the Oregon Trail from the South Pass, a 20-mile gap in the Rocky Mountains in present-day Wyoming. The expedition would then go down the Snake River to the Columbia River and into Oregon, eventually making its way south through the Sierra Nevada to Sutter's Fort near what would become Sacramento, California, before heading back.

Frémont's group was the first to cross the snow- and ice-covered Sierra Nevada in the winter, a spectacular feat. His report of his expedition and the maps it generated spurred massive migrations to Utah, Oregon, and California throughout the 1840s, including the trek of the Mormons from Illinois to Salt Lake City, Utah.

Rarely one to follow orders, keep promises, or admit mistakes, the impulsive, iron-willed Frémont surprised his superior officers when he launched a "military" expedition on his own. In August 1845, Frémont, now a captain, and sixty-two heavily armed soldiers, sailors, scientists, hunters, and frontiersmen, headed west from St. Louis on another mysterious expedition.

In December, Frémont's adventurers swept down the western slopes of the Sierra Nevada and headed southward through the Central Valley of Mexican-controlled California. Frémont told Mexican authorities that his mission was strictly scientific and that his men were civilians. In Monterey, in January 1846, Frémont received secret instructions from President James K. Polk indicating that the United States intended to take control of California from Mexico. Frémont was ordered to encourage a "spontaneous" uprising among the Americans living there.

Suspicious Mexican officials ordered Frémont to leave the province. He did so, leading his explorers into Oregon, attacking Indian villages along the way. But the Americans soon returned. To cover his efforts to spark a revolution among the English-speaking Californians, most of whom were Americans, Frémont officially submitted his resignation from the army so that he thereafter would be acting as a private citizen rather than as a member of the U.S. government.

Then Frémont and his band of soldiers and "rough, leather-jacketed frontiersmen" began stirring unrest. On June 14, 1846, American settlers captured Sonoma in northern California and proclaimed the Republic of California. They hoisted a linen flag featuring a grizzly bear and star, a version of which would later become the California state flag. On June 25, Frémont and his band marched into Sonoma. All of California was in American control when news arrived there of the outbreak of the Mexican-American War.

AMERICAN SETTLEMENTS IN TEXAS The American passion for new western land focused largely on Texas, the closest of all the northern

American pioneers This 1850 photograph captures some of the many pioneers who headed west for brighter futures.

Mexican borderlands, and an area of rich soil, lush prairie grass, plentiful timber, abundant wildlife, and numerous creeks and rivers. During the 1820s, the United States had twice offered to buy Texas, but the Mexican government refused to sell. Mexicans were frightened and infuriated by the idea of Yankees acquiring their "sacred soil"—but that is what happened.

The leading promoter of American settlement in the coastal plain of Texas was Stephen Fuller Austin, a visionary land developer (*empresario*) who convinced the Mexican government that he could recruit 300 American families to settle between the Colorado and Brazos Rivers along the Gulf coast of Texas and create a "buffer" on the northern frontier between the feared Comanche Indians and the Mexican settlements to the south.

Americans eagerly settled in Austin's Anglo "colony" in east Texas. They each received 177 free acres and had access to thousands of acres of common pasture for ranching (Austin received 65,000 acres for his efforts). Most of the Anglos were ranchers or farmers drawn to the fertile, inexpensive lands in the river valleys. A few of the settlers were wealthy planters who brought large numbers of slaves with them at a time when Mexico was prohibiting the importation of slaves. An American reported that eastern Texas was "literally alive with all kinds of game. We have only to go out a few miles into a swamp . . . to find as many wild cattle as one could wish." There were as many buffalo in the area as cattle.

By 1830, coastal Texas had far more Americans living there than Hispanics (Tejanos) or Indians—about 20,000 white settlers (called Anglos, or *Texians*), and 1,000 enslaved blacks, brought to grow and harvest cotton. By 1835, there were 35,000 Texians, 3,000 African American slaves, and a booming cotton economy. So many people in the Carolinas, Georgia, Alabama, Tennessee, and Missouri had migrated to Texas that the phrase "Gone to Texas"—or its initials, "GTT," were often carved into the doors of cabins left behind.

The flood of Americans into Texas led to numerous clashes with Indians as well as Mexican officials, who began having second thoughts about their "tolerated guests." A Mexican congressman issued an accurate warning in 1830: "Mexicans! Watch closely, for you know all too well the Anglo-Saxon greed for territory. We have generously granted land to these Nordics; they have made their homes with us, but their hearts are with their native land. We are continually in civil wars and revolutions; we are weak, and know it—and they know it also. They may conspire with the United States to take Texas from us. From this time, be on your guard!"

THE TEXAS WAR FOR INDEPENDENCE   Mexican officials were so worried about the behavior and intentions of Americans living in Texas that in April 1830 they suddenly outlawed further immigration from the United States. But Americans, who viewed the Mexicans, their army, and their fractured and incompetent government with contempt, kept coming. By 1835, the Texians and their enslaved blacks outnumbered the Tejanos (Spanish-speaking Texans) ten to one. In a letter to his cousin in 1835, Stephen Austin left no doubt about his plans: "It is very evident that Texas should be effectually, and fully, *Americanized*—that is—settled by a population that will harmonize with their neighbors on the *East*, in language, political principles, common origin, sympathy, and even interest. *Texas must be a slave country. It is no longer a matter of doubt.*"

A changing political situation in Mexico aggravated the growing tensions. In 1834, General Antonio López de Santa Anna, the Mexican president, suspended the national congress and became a dictator, calling himself the "Napoleon of the West." Texans feared that Santa Anna planned to free "our slaves and to make slaves of us."

When Santa Anna imprisoned Austin in 1834, Texans decided that the Mexican ruler had to go. Upon his release from jail eighteen months later, Austin called for Texans to revolt: "War is our only resource. There is no other remedy. We must defend our rights, ourselves, and our country by force of arms." He urged that Texas become fully American, promote slavery, and join the United States.

In the fall of 1835, Texans followed Austin's lead and rebelled against Santa Anna's "despotism." An infuriated Santa Anna ordered all Americans expelled, all Texans disarmed, and all rebels arrested and executed as "pirates." As sporadic fighting erupted, hundreds of armed volunteers from southern states rushed to assist the 30,000 Texians and Tejanos fighting for their independence against a Mexican nation of 7 million people. "The sword is drawn!" Austin proclaimed.

THE ALAMO   At San Antonio, the provincial capital in southern Texas, General Santa Anna's 3,000-man army assaulted a group of fewer than 200 Texians, Tejanos, and members of the Texas volunteer army holed up in an abandoned Catholic mission called the Alamo.

The outnumbered and outgunned Texas rebels were led by three colorful adventurers with checkered pasts: James "Jim" Bowie, William Barret Travis, and David Crockett. They symbolized the role of Texas as a haven for people wanting second chances.

The sandy-haired Bowie, born in Kentucky but raised in Louisiana, had become a ruthless slave trader and deceitful land speculator. However, he was most famous for the "bowie knife" he used to wound and kill men in numerous fights. Bowie claimed he had never started a fight nor lost one. And he was hard to bring down. In his most famous brawl, he was shot twice, stabbed, and impaled by a sword before he killed his opponent with his knife.

Bowie wore out his welcome in Louisiana and migrated to Texas in 1828, settled near San Antonio, and came to own about a million acres of Texas land. He married a prominent Mexican woman, became a Mexican citizen, and learned Spanish, but a cholera epidemic killed his wife and two children, as well as his in-laws.

Upon learning of the Texas Revolution, Bowie joined the volunteer army and fought in several battles before arriving in San Antonio in January 1836. Bowie, often "roaring drunk," commanded the Texas volunteers in the Alamo while William Travis, a hot-tempered, twenty-six-year-old lawyer and teacher, led the Texian "regular army" soldiers. Travis had come to Texas by way of Alabama, where he had left behind a failed marriage, a pregnant wife, a two-year-old son, considerable debts, and, rumors claimed, a man he had killed. Travis pledged that he would redeem his life by doing something great and honorable in Texas—or die trying. His determination to face an honorable death led him to refuse orders to retreat from the Alamo.

The most famous American at the Alamo was David Crockett, the Tennessee frontiersman, sharpshooter, bear hunter, and storyteller who had fought under Andrew Jackson and served in Congress as an anti-Jackson Whig. In his last speech before Congress after being defeated for reelection, Crockett, who was not called "Davy" until long after his death, told his colleagues that he "was done with politics for the present, and that they might go to hell, and I would go to Texas." He told his son and daughter that he planned to make "a fortune for myself and family" in Texas.

Soon after arriving in Texas with his trusty rifle "Old Betsy," Crockett, the "Lion of the West," was told he would receive 4,000 acres of land for his service as a fighter. He then was assigned to join the garrison at the Alamo. Full of bounce and brag, the forty-nine-year-old Crockett was thoroughly expert at killing. As he once told his men, "Pierce the heart of the enemy as you would a feller that spit in your face, knocked down your wife, burnt up your houses, and called your dog a skunk!"

What Crockett, Travis, and Bowie shared with the other defenders of the Alamo was a commitment to liberty in the face of Santa Anna's growing despotism. In late February 1836, Santa Anna demanded that the Alamo's defenders surrender. By then, Bowie had fallen seriously ill, was bedridden, and had turned over his command to Travis, who answered the Mexican ultimatum with cannon fire. He then sent urgent appeals to Texian towns for supplies and more men, while promising that "*I shall never surrender or retreat . . .* VICTORY OR DEATH!"

The Alamo David Crockett, pictured fighting with his rifle over his head, joined the legendary effort to defend the Alamo against the Mexican army's repeated assaults.

Help did not come, however, and Santa Anna launched a series of assaults against the outnumbered defenders. For twelve days, the Mexicans were thrown back and suffered heavy losses.

The ferocious fighting at the Alamo turned the rebellion into a war for Texan independence. On March 2, 1836, delegates from all fifty-nine Texas towns, most of them American immigrants, met at the tiny village of Washington-on-the-Brazos, some 150 miles northeast of San Antonio. There they signed a declaration of independence and drafted a constitution for the new Republic of Texas. The delegates then named Sam Houston as the commander of their disorganized but growing "army."

Four days later, the defenders of the Alamo were awakened at four o'clock in the morning by the sound of Mexican bugles playing the dreaded "Degüello" ("No Mercy to the Defenders"). Colonel Travis shouted: "The Mexicans are upon us—give 'em Hell!"

The climactic Battle of the Alamo was fought in the predawn dark. Wave after wave of Santa Anna's men attacked. They were twice forced back, but on the third try they broke through the battered north wall. Travis was killed by a bullet between the eyes. Some of the Texans took the fight outside the Alamo with tomahawks, knives, rifle butts, and fists, but in the end, virtually all of them were killed or wounded.

Seven Alamo defenders, perhaps including Crockett, survived and were captured. Santa Anna ordered them hacked to death with swords. A Mexican officer wrote that the captives "died without complaining and without humiliating themselves before their torturers."

By dawn, the battle was over. The only survivors were a handful of women and children, and Joe, Travis's slave. It was a costly victory, however, as more than 600 Mexicans died. The Battle of the Alamo also provided a rallying cry for vengeful Texians. While Santa Anna proclaimed a "glorious victory" and ordered the bodies of the revolutionaries burned, his aide wrote ominously in his diary, "One more such 'glorious victory' and we are finished."

GOLIAD Two weeks later, at the Battle of Coleto, a Mexican force again defeated a smaller Texian army, many of them recently arrived volunteers from southern states. The Mexicans marched the 465 captured Texians to a fort in the nearby town of Goliad. Despite pleas from his own men to show mercy, Santa Anna ordered the captives killed as "pirates and outlaws." On Palm Sunday, March 27, 1836, more than 300 Texians were marched out of Goliad and murdered. The massacres at the Alamo and Goliad fueled a burning desire for revenge among the Texians.

SAM HOUSTON The fate of the **Texas Revolution** was now in the hands of the already legendary Sam Houston, a hulking, rowdy, larger-than-life frontier statesman born in Virginia to Scots-Irish immigrants. At age fourteen, after his father died, Houston had moved with his mother and siblings to eastern Tennessee. Two years later, he ran away from home and lived among the Cherokees, earning the nickname "The Raven." Like David Crockett, Houston had served under General Andrew Jackson during the War of 1812, where he was grievously wounded at the Battle of Horseshoe Bend. Thereafter, he returned to Tennessee and soon became a federal Indian agent, an attorney, a U.S. congressman, commanding general of the Tennessee militia, and, at the ripe age of thirty, governor.

Unlike his friend David Crockett, however, Houston adored Andrew Jackson and became his devoted disciple and surrogate son, leading many people to speculate that he might become the next president. Like Jackson, however, Houston was at heart an oddball ruffian: he had an untamed yet gallant personality and violent temper cloaked in a charming brashness. A friend called him a "magnificent barbarian." He drank. He gambled. He chased women. And he brawled.

After learning that William Stanbery, an anti-Jackson Ohio congressman, had questioned his integrity, Congressman Houston assaulted him with a hickory cane on a Washington, D.C., street. Stanbery pulled a pistol, pushed it into Houston's stomach, and pulled the trigger, only to have it misfire. Houston then beat him about the head before ending the fight with a swift kick between Stanbery's thighs. Stanbery filed charges, and the Speaker of the House ordered Houston arrested and put on trial in Congress. Found guilty of assault, he was reprimanded and fined.

Controversy dogged Houston thereafter. In 1829, he suddenly resigned the governorship of Tennessee because Eliza Allen, his beautiful, aristocratic, and much younger wife, had left him soon after their wedding and returned to her father's plantation near Nashville.

Houston never revealed the cause of the dispute ("sudden calamities"), but Eliza's family did its best to destroy his reputation, accusing him of "dishonoring" her. He, in turn, kept silent because, he explained to President Jackson, doing so reinforced his "notion of honor." If his character could not stand the "shock" of mean-spirited gossip, he said, then "let me lose it."

For years, wild rumors circulated about what had happened on Houston's wedding night. Some claimed that Eliza had discovered to her horror that Houston had sustained a "dreadful injury" (true, a wound in the groin from an Indian arrowhead) in the Creek War that had left him scarred and impotent (a falsehood). Others reported that his bride had confessed she was in love with someone else and had only married him to please her family.

Whatever the cause, Houston later wrote that his ugly public divorce threw him into an "agony of despair" over his "private afflictions" that ruined his political career and exiled him from Nashville society. Jackson wrote Houston a consoling letter: "Oh, what a reverse of fortune" his friend had experienced. "Oh, how unstable are human affairs."

Having shouldered the blame for the mysterious scandal, the disconsolate Houston was now an outcast. He decided that suicide was his only option. As he was preparing to kill himself, however, an eagle suddenly swooped down and then soared upward into the sunset. Then and there, Houston later wrote, "I knew that a great destiny waited for me in the West."

In 1829, Houston boarded a steamboat and headed west to Cairo, Illinois. He then traveled on a flatboat down the Mississippi, then up the Arkansas River to Little Rock, where he bought a horse and made his way several hundred miles to the Arkansas Territory along the Oklahoma border. There he rejoined the Cherokee, adopted their clothing, customs, and language, changed his name, married a Cherokee woman, and was formally "adopted"

Sam Houston Houston was commander in chief of the forces fighting for Texas's independence.

by the Cherokee Nation. As he recalled, he "felt like a weary wanderer returned at last to his father's house."

Houston proved adept at helping rival Indian tribes—Cherokee, Creek, Osage, and Choctaws—negotiate differences among themselves and with the federal government. He also grew addicted to alcohol; the Cherokees called him "Big Drunk." In December 1832, Houston moved to Texas at Jackson's behest. Two months later, he sent a secret report to the president, indicating that Texas was ripe for revolt from unstable Mexico, which was then embroiled in a civil war. Houston joined the rebellion against Mexico, and his fearlessness was a quality sorely needed by the Texians.

THE BATTLE OF SAN JACINTO After learning of the massacre at the Alamo, Houston led his outnumbered troops on a long strategic retreat to buy time while hoping that Santa Anna's pursuing army would make a mistake. On April 21, 1836, the cocky Mexican general walked into Houston's trap, when his army of 900 whooping fighters caught the 1,600 Mexicans napping near the San Jacinto River, about twenty-five miles southeast of the modern city of Houston. The Texians and Tejanos charged, yelling "Remember the Alamo." They overwhelmed the panic-stricken Mexicans, most of whom were sleeping. General Santa Anna left his army leaderless that afternoon while he retreated to his tent, accompanied, some said, by a mistress.

The battle lasted only eighteen minutes, but Houston's troops spent the next two hours slaughtering fleeing Mexican soldiers. It was, said a Texian, a "frightful sight to behold." Some 630 Mexicans were killed and 700 captured. The Texians lost only nine men. Santa Anna escaped but was captured the next day. He bought his freedom by signing a treaty recognizing the independence of the Republic of Texas, with the Rio Grande as its southern boundary with Mexico. The Texas Revolution had been accomplished in seven weeks.

THE LONE STAR REPUBLIC In 1836, the Lone Star Republic, as Texians called their new nation, legalized slavery, banned free blacks, elected Sam Houston as its first president, and voted overwhelmingly for annexation to the United States. No one expected the Republic of Texas, with only 40,000 people, to remain independent for long. But statehood for Texas soon became embroiled in the explosive sectional dispute over slavery.

John C. Calhoun told the Senate in 1836 that "there were powerful reasons why Texas should be part of this Union. The southern states, owning a slave population, were deeply interested in preventing that country from having the power to annoy them." Anti-slavery northerners disagreed. In 1837, the Vermont state legislature "solemnly protested" against the admission "of any state whose constitution tolerates domestic slavery."

The American president at the time was Houston's old friend and former commander, Andrew Jackson, who eagerly wanted Texas to join the Union. "Old Hickory," however, decided it was better to wait a few years. He knew that adding Texas as a slave state would ignite an explosive quarrel between North and South that would fracture the Democratic party and endanger the election of New Yorker Martin Van Buren, his handpicked successor. Worse, any effort to add Texas to the Union would likely mean a war with Mexico, which refused to recognize Texan independence.

So Jackson delayed official recognition of the Republic of Texas until his last day in office, early in 1837. Van Buren, Jackson's successor, did as predicted: he avoided all talk of Texas annexation during his single term as president.

WHIGS AND DEMOCRATS When William Henry Harrison succeeded Martin Van Buren as president in 1841, he was the oldest man (68) and the first Whig to win the office. The Whigs, who now controlled both houses of Congress, had first emerged in opposition to Andrew Jackson and continued to promote strong federal government support for industrial development and economic growth: high tariffs to deter imports and federal funding for roads, bridges, and canals.

Yet Harrison was elected primarily on his prominence as a military hero. He had avoided taking public stances on controversial issues. In the end, it mattered little, as Harrison served the shortest term of any president. On April 4, 1841, exactly one month after his inauguration, he died of pneumonia, and Vice President John Tyler became president.

The surprising turn of events pleased former president Andrew Jackson. "A kind and overruling providence had interfered," he wrote a friend, "to prolong our glorious Union and happy republican system which General Harrison and his cabinet was [sic] preparing to destroy under the dictation of that profligate demagogue, Henry Clay." Another former president, John Quincy Adams, had the opposite reaction. He dismissed Tyler, the new president, as "a political sectarian, of the slave-driving, Virginian, Jeffersonian school" of politics, whose talents were barely "above mediocrity."

Henry Clay hoped to dominate the mild-mannered new president. Tyler "dares not resist," the imperious Clay threatened, or "I will drive him before me." Tyler, however, was not willing to be dominated. After an argument in the White House over a proposed new national bank, he told Clay go back down Pennsylvania Avenue to the Capitol and perform his duties in Congress. "So help me God, I shall do mine at this end of it as I shall think proper."

JOHN TYLER The tall, thin, slave-owning Virginian was a political maverick and the youngest president to date—fifty-one, but he had lots of political experience, having served as a state legislator, governor, congressman, and senator. He also fathered fifteen children, the most of any president. Perhaps most important, he was a man of stubborn independence and considerable charm. A political acquaintance said Tyler was "approachable, courteous, always willing to do a kindly action, or to speak a kindly word."

Originally a Democrat who had endorsed the Jeffersonian commitment to states' rights, strict construction of the Constitution, and opposition to national banks, Tyler had broken with the party and joined the Whigs over President Jackson's "condemnation" of South Carolina's attempt to nullify federal laws. Tyler believed that South Carolina had a constitutional right to secede from the nation. Yet he never truly embraced the Whigs. As president, Tyler opposed everything associated with Henry Clay's much-celebrated program of economic nationalism (the American System) that called for high tariffs, a national bank, and internal improvements.

When Congress met in a special session in 1841, Clay introduced a series of controversial resolutions. He called for the repeal of the Independent Treasury Act and the creation of another Bank of the United States, proposed to revive the distribution program whereby the money generated by federal land sales was given to the states, and urged that tariffs be raised on imported goods to hamper foreign competitors.

Clay might have avoided a nasty dispute with Tyler over financial issues had he been more tactful. But for once, driven by his compulsive quest to be president, Clay, the Great Compromiser, lost his instinct for compromise. Although Tyler agreed to the repeal of the Independent Treasury Act and signed a higher tariff bill, he vetoed Clay's pet project: the new national bank.

An incensed Clay responded by calling Tyler a traitor who had disgraced his party. He claimed that the president was left "solitary and alone, shivering by the pitiless storm" against his veto. The dispute was so heated that scuffles and fistfights between Whigs and Democrats broke out in Congress. Clay then convinced Tyler's entire cabinet to resign, with the exception of Secretary of State Daniel Webster. A three-year-long war between Clay and Tyler had begun.

Tyler replaced the defectors in his cabinet with anti-Jackson Democrats who, like him, had become Whigs. The Whigs then expelled Tyler from the party, calling him "His Accidency," and the "Executive Ass." Sixty Whig members of Congress signed a statement denouncing Tyler and declaring him no longer their representative. Some even talked of impeachment. An exasperated Tyler confided to a friend his frustration: "Did you ever expect to see your old friend under trial for 'high crimes and misdemeanors'?" By 1842, Tyler had become a president without a party, shunned by both Whigs and Democrats.

The political turmoil coincided with the ongoing economic depression that had begun in the late 1830s. Bank failures mounted, businesses shut down, and unemployment soared. Yet Tyler refused to let either the sputtering economy or an international crisis with Great Britain deter him from annexing more territory into the United States.

TENSIONS WITH BRITAIN   In late 1841, slaves being transported from Virginia to Louisiana on the American ship *Creole* revolted and took charge of the ship. They sailed into Nassau, in the Bahamas, where British authorities set 128 of them free. (Great Britain had abolished slavery throughout its empire in 1834.)

It was the most successful slave revolt in American history. Southerners were infuriated, and the incident mushroomed into an international crisis. Secretary of State Daniel Webster demanded that the slaves be returned as American property, but the British refused.

Rather than risk a war that the United States might lose, Tyler and Webster acquiesced to the British refusal to return the slaves. This only made southern slaveholders more furious. James Henry Hammond, the South Carolina planter, lashed out at the Tyler administration: "With such a stupid imbecile as Tyler at the head of affairs and such an unprincipled and cowardly Sec. of State as Webster, we should fare badly for a time. They are bent on peace."

At this point, the British government decided to send Alexander Baring, Lord Ashburton, head of a major bank, to meet with Secretary of State Webster, who viewed good relations with Britain as essential for the America economy. The meetings concluded with the signing of the Webster-Ashburton Treaty (1842), which provided for joint naval patrols off Africa to police the outlawed slave trade. The treaty also resolved a long-standing dispute over the northeastern U.S. boundary with British Canada. But it did nothing about returning the freed slaves. The dispute was not settled until 1853, when England paid $110,000 to the owners of the freed slaves.

THE "EXTENSION OF OUR EMPIRE": TEXAS   From the moment he became president, John Tyler had his eyes fixed on annexing the

Austin, Texas, in 1840 A view of the capital of the newly formed Republic of Texas—the city's population at the time numbered less than a thousand.

Republic of Texas into the United States. His wife Julia later said that Texas was "the great object of his ambition" to secure his place in history. In Tyler's first address to Congress, he pledged to do so, explaining that there was nothing to fear from "the extension of our Empire."

Tyler's efforts to recruit senators to approve an annexation treaty exhilarated Texas leaders who had long been frustrated that their Lone Star Republic had not yet been welcomed into the United States. Sam Houston threatened to expand the Republic of Texas to the Pacific. But with little money, a rising government debt, and continuing tensions with Mexico, this was mostly talk.

The Lone Star Republic had no infrastructure—no banks, no schools, no industries. It remained largely a frontier community. Houston decided that the rickety Republic of Texas had only two choices: annexation to the United States or closer economic ties to Great Britain, which extended formal diplomatic recognition to the republic and began buying cotton from Texas planters.

Meanwhile, thousands more Americans poured into Texas, enticed by the republic's offer of 1,280 acres of land to each white family. The population more than tripled between 1836 and 1845, from 40,000 to 150,000, and the enslaved black population grew even faster than the white population.

A TRAGIC CRUISE On February 28, 1844, President Tyler and a group of 300 dignitaries boarded the U.S.S. *Princeton*, a new propeller-driven steam warship, for an excursion on the Potomac River. As sailors fired the ship's huge fifteen-foot-long cannons, one of them, "the Peacemaker," exploded, killing eight people, including the secretary of state, the secretary of the navy, and a New York state legislator. More than a dozen others were seriously wounded. President Tyler, who was below deck at the time of the accident, rushed to see what had happened: "A more heart-rending scene scarcely ever occurred," he wrote. "What a loss I have sustained. . . ."

After the funerals for the accident victims, Tyler seized the opportunity created by the tragic accident to reorganize his entire cabinet by naming southern Democrats to key positions. He appointed John C. Calhoun secretary of state, primarily because he wanted the prominent South Carolinian to complete the annexation of Texas. On April 12, 1844, Calhoun signed a treaty of annexation with the Republic of Texas, and Tyler submitted it to the Senate for approval. Texas would become an American territory in exchange for the United States assuming all of its debts. Tyler explained that the addition of Texas would "add to national greatness and wealth" and would "strengthen rather than weaken the Union."

Calhoun, however, unwittingly undermined the annexation treaty by writing the British ambassador what he thought was a confidential letter in which he declared that blacks were inferior to whites and better off enslaved than free. Slavery, Calhoun insisted, was "essential to the peace, safety, and prosperity" of the South. Adding Texas, he concluded, was necessary to keep the South in the Union. On June 8, 1844, outraged northerners in the Senate voted down Calhoun's annexation treaty 35 to 16.

THE ELECTION OF 1844   Thereafter, leaders in both political parties hoped to keep the divisive Texas issue out of the 1844 presidential campaign. Whig Henry Clay and Democrat Martin Van Buren, the leading candidates for each party's nomination, agreed that adding Texas to the Union would be a mistake.

For his part, Tyler, having alienated both parties, initially announced that he would run for reelection as an independent, using the campaign slogan, "Tyler and Texas." Within a few weeks, however, he realized he had little support and dropped out of the race, giving his endorsement to Polk.

Van Buren's southern supporters, including former president Andrew Jackson, abandoned him because he opposed the annexation of Texas. They instead nominated James Knox Polk, former Speaker of the House and former governor of Tennessee. Like Tyler, Polk was an enthusiastic expansionist who wanted to make the United States a transcontinental global power. Unlike Tyler, Polk was a loyal Democrat who hated Whigs. On the ninth ballot, he became the first "dark horse" (unexpected) candidate to win a major-party

THE ELECTION OF 1844

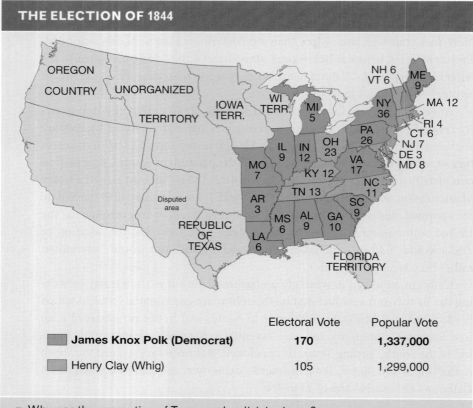

	Electoral Vote	Popular Vote
James Knox Polk (Democrat)	170	1,337,000
Henry Clay (Whig)	105	1,299,000

- Why was the annexation of Texas such a divisive issue?
- Why was Polk's platform especially appealing to southerners and westerners?
- How did Polk carry New York, and why was winning that state so decisive?

nomination. The Democrats' platform called for the annexation of Texas and declared that the United States had a "clear and unquestionable claim" to all of the Oregon Country.

The 1844 presidential election proved to be one of the most significant in history. By promoting southern and western expansionism, the Democrats offered a winning strategy, one so popular it forced Clay, the Whig candidate, to alter his position on Texas at the last minute; he now claimed that he had "no personal objection to the annexation" if it could be achieved "without dishonor, without war, with the common consent of the Union, and upon just and fair terms."

Clay's waffling on Texas shifted more anti-slavery votes to the new Liberty party (the anti-slavery party formed in 1840), which increased its count in the presidential election from about 7,000 in 1840 to more than 62,000 in 1844. In the western counties of New York, the Liberty party drew enough votes away from Clay and the Whigs to give the crucial state to Polk.

Had Clay carried New York, he would have won the election by 7 electoral votes. Instead, Polk won a narrow national plurality of 38,000 popular votes (the first president since John Quincy Adams to win without a majority) but a clear majority of the electoral college, 170 to 105. Julia Tyler, the president's wife, was overjoyed with the outcome: "Hurrah for Polk! What will become of Henry Clay and of the downfall of our Whig friends?" A devastated Clay had lost his third and last presidential election. He could not understand how he lost to Polk, whom he considered a "third-rate" politician lacking leadership abilities.

JAMES K. POLK Yet James K. Polk had been surprising people his whole career. Born near Charlotte, North Carolina, the oldest of ten children, he graduated first in his class at the University of North Carolina, then moved to Tennessee, where he became a successful lawyer and planter, entered politics, and served fourteen years in Congress (four as Speaker of the House) and two years as governor.

At age forty-nine, Polk was America's youngest president up to that time. Short, thin, and humorless, he was called "Young Hickory" because of his admiration for Andrew Jackson. And like Jackson, he believed that any efforts by the federal government to promote economic growth necessarily helped some people and regions and hurt others. He was thus opposed to tariffs, a national bank, and federally funded roads.

Polk's greatest virtue was his relentless work ethic. "I am the hardest working man in this country," he declared. True to his word, he often worked from dawn to midnight and rarely took a vacation. Such unrelenting intensity eventually wore him out, however. Polk would die in 1849, at fifty-three years old, just three months after leaving office.

THE STATE OF TEXAS Texas, the hottest political potato, had been added as a new state just *before* Polk was sworn in as president. In his final months in office, President John Tyler had taken an unusual step by asking Congress to annex Texas by joint resolution, which required only a simple majority in each house rather than the two-thirds Senate vote needed to ratify a *treaty* of annexation.

The resolution narrowly passed, with most Whigs opposed. On March 1, 1845, in his final presidential action, Tyler signed the resolution admitting Texas to the Union as the twenty-eighth state, and fifteenth slave state, on December 29, 1845. Six weeks later, on February 16, 1846, the Lone Star flag of the Republic of Texas was lowered, and the flag of the United States was raised over the largest state in the nation.

At the time, Texas had a population of 100,000 whites and 38,000 enslaved blacks. By 1850, the population—both white and black—had soared by almost 50 percent. (The census then did not include Native Americans.) By 1860, Texas had 600,000 people, most of them from southern states focused on growing cotton.

POLK'S GOALS Perhaps because he pledged to serve only one term, Polk was a president in a hurry. He focused on four major objectives, all of which he accomplished. He managed to (1) reduce tariffs on imports; (2) reestablish the Independent Treasury ("We need no national banks!"); (3) settle the Oregon boundary dispute with Britain; and (4) acquire California from Mexico. His top priority was territorial expansion. He wanted to add Oregon, California, and New Mexico to the Union to fill out the continent.

In keeping with long-standing Democratic beliefs, Polk wanted lower tariffs to allow more foreign goods to compete in the American marketplace, and thereby help drive consumer prices down. Congress agreed by approving the Walker Tariff of 1846, named after Robert J. Walker, the secretary of the Treasury.

In the same year, Polk persuaded Congress to restore the Independent Treasury Act that Martin Van Buren had signed into law in 1840 and the

Tariff of 1846 This political cartoon illustrates the public outcry—represented by a Quaker woman ready to whip Polk—against the Tariff of 1846, one of the lowest in the nation's history.

Whig-dominated Congress had repealed the next year. The act established Independent Treasury deposit offices to receive all federal government funds. The system was intended to replace the Second Bank of the United States, which Jackson had "killed," so as to offset the chaotic growth of unregulated state banks whose reckless lending practices had helped cause the depression of the late 1830s.

The new Independent Treasury entrusted the federal government, rather than state banks, with the exclusive management of government funds and required that all disbursements be made in gold or silver, or paper currency backed by gold or silver.

Polk also twice vetoed Whig-passed bills for federally funded infrastructure projects. His efforts to reverse Whig economic policies satisfied the slaveholding South but angered northerners, who wanted higher tariffs to protect their industries from British competition, and westerners, who wanted federally financed roads and harbors.

OREGON Meanwhile, the dispute with Great Britain over the Oregon Country boundary heated up as expansionists insisted that Polk take the whole region rather than split it with the British. Polk was willing to go to the brink of war to achieve his goals. "If we do have war," the president blustered, "it will not be our fault."

Fortunately, neither Polk nor the British were willing to risk war. On June 15, 1846, James Buchanan, Polk's secretary of state, signed what was called the Buchanan-Pakenham Treaty, which extended the border between the United States and British Canada westward to the Pacific coast along the 49th parallel. Once the treaty was approved by both nations, the *New York Herald* announced that "Now, we can thrash Mexico into decency at our leisure."

THE MEXICAN-AMERICAN WAR

The settlement of the Oregon Country boundary dispute allowed the United States to turn its attention southward. On March 6, 1845, two days after James Polk took office, the Mexican government broke off relations with the United States to protest the annexation of Texas. Polk was willing to wage war against Mexico to acquire California and New Mexico, but he did not want Americans to fire the first shot.

Nor did Polk want a war that might produce a military hero who would become a Whig candidate for the presidency. Senator Thomas Hart Benton of Missouri, a powerful Democrat, disclosed that Polk "wanted a small war, just large enough to require a treaty for peace, and not large enough to create military reputations" that might pose a political challenge after the war.

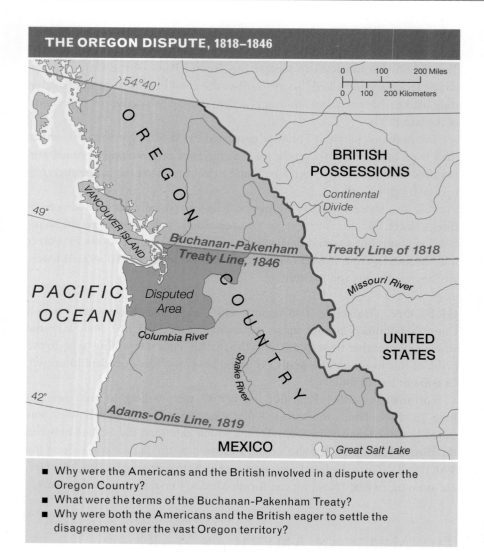

THE OREGON DISPUTE, 1818–1846

- Why were the Americans and the British involved in a dispute over the Oregon Country?
- What were the terms of the Buchanan-Pakenham Treaty?
- Why were both the Americans and the British eager to settle the disagreement over the vast Oregon territory?

So Polk ordered several thousand U.S. troops under General Zachary Taylor to take up positions around Corpus Christi, near the Rio Grande. The U.S. troops were knowingly in disputed territory, and Mexico viewed the arrival of U.S. troops along the Rio Grande as an act of war.

On the evening of May 9, 1845, Polk learned that Mexican troops had attacked U.S. soldiers north of the Rio Grande. Eleven Americans were killed, five wounded, and the remainder taken prisoner. "Hostilities may now be considered as commenced," Taylor reported.

Polk's scheme to provoke an attack had worked. To avoid the risk that Congress would vote down a declaration of war, Polk simply declared that the Mexicans had started a war that now needed to be funded. Mexico, he reported, "has invaded our territory, and shed American blood upon the American soil." Congress quickly authorized the recruitment of 50,000 soldiers.

Some congressmen, however, were skeptical of Polk's explanation. Whig Garret Davis of Kentucky asserted that the Rio Grande was a part of Mexico, not Texas: "It is our own President who began this war." Even Democrats were concerned about the president's account of what had happened. A New York senator, John Dix, said he would not be "surprised if the next accounts should show that there is no Mexican invasion of our soil." The war, he later added, "was begun in fraud . . . and I think will end in disgrace."

President Polk steadfastly denied that the war against Mexico had anything to do with the expansion of slavery. He argued instead that his efforts to extend America's boundaries to the Pacific were intended to replace sectional tensions with national unity. For Polk, the notion of manifest destiny was a means of promoting national unity. After all, he stressed, slavery could not flourish in places like New Mexico and California because cotton could not be grown there because of the climate.

With the outbreak of fighting, most Americans accepted the president's account of what happened along the Mexico-Texas border and rushed to support the military. "LET US GO TO WAR," screamed a New York newspaper. Another headline blared: "MEXICO OR DEATH!"

The New York journalist-poet Walt Whitman got caught up in the war fever, urging those enlisting in the army to show the world that "America knows how to crush, as well as how to expand!" The South was especially excited over the war because of the possibility of acquiring more territory. So many southerners ("wild, reckless young fellows") rushed to volunteer that thousands had to be turned away.

Eventually, 112,000 whites served in the war (blacks were banned). In Tennessee, there were so many volunteers that it became "difficult even to purchase a place in the ranks." Among the warriors were young army officers who would later distinguish themselves as opposing leaders in the Civil War: Pierre Beauregard, Braxton Bragg, Ulysses S. Grant, Joseph Hooker, Thomas Jackson, James Longstreet, Robert E. Lee, George McClellan, George Meade, William T. Sherman, and George Thomas.

OPPOSITION TO THE WAR   In New England and among northern abolitionists, there was much less enthusiasm for "Mr. Polk's War." Congressman John Quincy Adams called it "a most unrighteous war" designed to extend slavery into new territories. Many other New Englanders involved with the growing

Zachary Taylor Like Andrew Jackson, Taylor was a popular war hero whose military exploits paved the way to the presidency.

abolitionist movement denounced the war as an unjustified act of aggression designed to satisfy pro-slavery southerners eager for more cotton territory.

William Lloyd Garrison, the fiery Boston abolitionist, charged that the war was one of "aggression, of invasion, of conquest." A few miles away, in Concord, Henry David Thoreau spent a night in jail rather than pay taxes that might help fund the war. Thoreau's mentor, Ralph Waldo Emerson, predicted that the "United States will conquer Mexico, but it will be as the man who swallows arsenic, which brings him down in turn. Mexico will poison us."

Most northern Whigs, including a young Illinois congressman named Abraham Lincoln, opposed the Mexican-American War, arguing that Polk had maneuvered the Mexicans into attacking. The United States, they insisted, had no reason to place its army in the disputed border region between Texas and Mexico. In what came to be called "Spot Resolutions," Lincoln repeatedly asked the president to locate the precise "spot" where the American troops were fired upon, implying that they may have illegally crossed into Mexican territory. Whig leader Henry Clay called the war "unnatural" and "lamentable," expressing concern that the nation was "becoming a warlike and conquering power," while Daniel Webster charged that the war's disputed origins were "unconstitutional." (Both Clay and Webster would lose sons in the war).

PREPARING FOR BATTLE The United States was again ill prepared for a major war. At the outset, the regular army numbered barely more than 7,000, in contrast to the Mexican force of 32,000. Before the war ended, the U.S. military had grown to almost 79,000 troops, many of whom were frontier toughs who lacked uniforms, equipment, and discipline. Repeatedly, these soldiers engaged in plunder, rape, and murder. Yet they outfought the larger Mexican forces, which had their own problems with training, discipline, morale, supplies, and munitions.

The Mexican-American War would last two years, from March 1846 to April 1848, and would be fought on four fronts: southern Texas/northern Mexico, central Mexico, New Mexico, and California. Early in the fighting, the U.S. Army scored two victories north of the Rio Grande, at Palo Alto (May 8) and Resaca de la Palma (May 9).

On May 18, Taylor's army crossed the Rio Grande and occupied Matamoros. These quick victories brought Taylor, a Whig, instant popularity, and Polk agreed to public demand that Taylor be made overall commander. It was an excellent choice, since Taylor, "Old Rough and Ready," had spent thirty-eight years in the army and had earned the respect and affection of his men.

THE ANNEXATION OF CALIFORNIA   President Polk's foremost objective through the war was not the defeat of Mexico but the acquisition of California. Not only did the Mexican province along the Pacific have wonderful harbors (San Francisco, Monterey, and San Diego), but the president also feared that Great Britain or France would take control of California if the United States did not.

Polk had sent secret instructions to Commodore John D. Sloat, commander of the Pacific naval squadron, telling him that if war erupted with Mexico, he was to use his warships to gain control "of the port of San Francisco, and blockade or occupy such other ports as your force may permit."

In May 1846, Sloat, having heard of the outbreak of hostilities along the Rio Grande, set sail for California. In early July, U.S. sailors and troops went ashore in San Francisco, took down the flag of the Republic of California, raised the American flag, and claimed California as part of the United States.

Soon thereafter, Sloat turned his command over to Commodore Robert F. Stockton, who sailed south to capture San Diego and Los Angeles. By mid-August, Mexican resistance had evaporated.

At the same time, another American military expedition headed for California. On August 18, General Stephen Kearny's army captured Santa Fe, the capital of New Mexico, then moved on to join Stockton's forces. They took control of Los Angeles on January 10, 1847, and the remaining Mexican forces surrendered three days later. Stockton and Kearny then quarreled over who was in command, since each had similar orders to conquer and govern California.

In the meantime, the unpredictable John C. Frémont arrived from Sonoma with 400 newly recruited troops and claimed that Stockton was in charge. Stockton responded by naming Frémont governor of California, and the power-hungry Frémont immediately set about giving orders, making proclamations, and appointing officials. This left Kearny in a bind; President Polk had ordered *him* to be the governor, but Frémont defied his orders.

Two months later, in June, 1847, General Kearny had seen enough. He had Governor Frémont arrested, charged him with insubordination and mutiny, and transported him across the country for a court-martial. In Washington, D.C., Kearny was hailed as a hero while the jailed Frémont awaited the military trial.

In the most celebrated trial since that of Vice President Aaron Burr in 1807, Frémont was found guilty of mutiny and insubordination and dismissed from the army. President Polk, however, quickly reversed the sentence in light of Frémont's "meritorious and valuable services." He urged Frémont to remain in the army and "resume the sword," but "the Pathfinder" was so enraged at the court ruling that he resigned his commission and settled in California, where he would become the state's first U.S. senator.

WAR IN NORTHERN MEXICO   Both California and New Mexico had been taken from Mexican control before General Zachary Taylor fought his first major battle in northern Mexico. In September 1846, Taylor's army assaulted the fortified city of Monterrey, which surrendered after a five-day siege. Then, General Antonio López de Santa Anna, who had been forced out of power in 1845, sent word to Polk from his exile in Cuba that he would end the war if he were allowed to return. Polk assured the exiled Mexican leader that the U.S. government would pay well for any territory taken from Mexico. In August 1846, on Polk's orders, Santa Anna was permitted to return to Mexico.

But the crafty Santa Anna had lied. Soon he was again president of Mexico and in command of the Mexican army. As it turned out, however, he was much more talented at raising armies than leading them in battle.

In October 1846, Santa Anna invited the outnumbered Americans to surrender. Taylor responded, "Tell him to go to hell." That launched the hard-fought Battle of Buena Vista (February 22–23, 1847), in northern Mexico. Both sides claimed victory, but the Mexicans suffered five times as many casualties as the Americans. Thereafter, the Mexicans continued to lose battles, but they refused to accept Polk's terms for surrender. "The United States may triumph," said a Mexican newspaper, "but its prize, like that of the vulture, will lie in a lake of blood."

Frustrated by Taylor's inability to win a decisive victory, Polk authorized an assault on Mexico City, the nation's capital. On March 9, 1847, a large American force led by Winfield Scott, the general-in-chief of the U.S. Army, landed on the beaches south of Veracruz. It was considered to be the strongest fortress in North America, with three forts guarding the approaches to the port city. The American assault on Veracruz was the largest amphibious operation ever attempted by U.S. military forces and was carried out without loss. The news of the American victory made General Scott a national hero. Veracruz surrendered on March 29. The American troops then rested, accumulating

MAJOR CAMPAIGNS OF THE MEXICAN-AMERICAN WAR

- Why did John C. Frémont and his troops initially settle in the Salinas Valley before marching north, only to turn around and march south to San Francisco?
- How did Polk's fear of Zachary Taylor's popularity undermine the Americans' military strategy?

supplies and awaiting reinforcements to replace the many volunteers whose enlistments had run out and were eager to go home.

In August, General Scott's formidable invasion force set out on the route taken by Cortés and his Spanish troops in their assault on the Aztec Empire more than 300 years earlier, marching toward the heavily defended Mexican capital, 200 miles away. In England, the Duke of Wellington, who had defeated

Fall of Mexico City General Winfield Scott formally enters Mexico City upon its capture by American soldiers on September 14, 1847.

Napoléon at the Battle of Waterloo more than thirty years before, predicted that "Scott is lost—he cannot capture the city, and he cannot fall back upon his base."

Yet the English hero could not have been more wrong. After four brilliantly orchestrated battles in which they overwhelmed the Mexican defenders, U.S. forces arrived at the gates of Mexico City in early September 1847. The Duke of Wellington now changed his tune, calling General Scott the world's "greatest living soldier." Ulysses S. Grant also applauded his commander, pointing out that with only half as many troops as the Mexicans, Scott had "won every battle, he captured the capital, and conquered the government."

THE SAINT PATRICK'S BATTALION General Scott's triumphant assault on Mexico City was not without problems, however. Since the start of the war, some 7,000 soldiers had deserted, the highest of any foreign war. Several hundred of them, mostly poor Catholic Irish and German immigrants who had recently arrived in New York City, crossed over to form the Saint Patrick's Battalion in the Mexican army, which included many foreign fighters.

Why the American soldiers, called *San Patricios* in Spanish, chose to switch sides remains in dispute, but several factors were at work: many of the Catholic defectors resented the abuse ("harsh and cruel handling") they received from native U.S. Protestant officers and the atrocities they saw committed against Catholic Americans. Some were also attracted by the higher wages, land grants, and promises of citizenship provided by the Mexican government, which claimed that it was the victim of America's "barbarous aggression." The Mexican army circulated leaflets to American soldiers which urged the foreign-born to switch sides and fight for their shared "sacred imperiled religion. If you are Catholic, the same as we, if you follow the doctrines of Our Savior, why are you murdering your brethren? Why are you antagonistic to those who defend their country and your own God?"

Whatever their motives, the *San Patricios* fought tenaciously against the Americans. During one of the battles for Mexico City, the Americans captured seventy-two defectors fighting in the St. Patrick's Battalion. They were quickly tried, and most of them were sentenced to death. Although military law at the time called for traitors to be shot by a firing squad, General Scott ordered that about fifty of the deserters be hanged. The others were whipped and branded with a "D" on each cheek.

At dawn on September 13, 1847, twenty-nine of the captured *San Patricios*, their hands and feet bound, were taken in wooden carts to stand in the hot sun under a gallows in sight of Chapultepec, the last Mexican fortress protecting Mexico City. There they were forced to watch the battle unfold over four hours. When the American troops finally scaled the walls of the fortress and raised the U.S. flag, the *San Patricios* were all hanged simultaneously.

St. Patrick's Battalion The men of St. Patrick's Battalion continue to be celebrated in Mexico as martyrs, with numerous cities, schools, and streets bearing the name *San Patricio.*

Just before the mass executions, the army surgeon reported to Colonel William Harney, an officer infamous for his brutality, that one of the *San Patricios*, Francis O'Connor, had lost both legs in the fighting. The doctor asked what should be done with the man. Harney yelled: "Bring the damned son of a bitch out! My order was to hang 30, and by God I'll do it." The Mexican government, which erected a monument in honor of the *San Patricios*, described the executions as "improper in a civilized age, and [ironic] for a people who aspire to the title of illustrious and humane."

THE TREATY OF GUADALUPE HIDALGO After the fall of Mexico City, Santa Anna resigned from office and fled the country. The Mexican government was left in turmoil. Peace talks began on January 2, 1848, at the village of Guadalupe Hidalgo, just outside the capital, but dragged on for weeks, in part because different people claimed to be in charge of the Mexican government.

When the **Treaty of Guadalupe Hidalgo** was signed on February 2, a humiliated Mexican government was forced to agree that the border with Texas would be the Rio Grande and to transfer control of all or parts of the future states of California, New Mexico, Nevada, Utah, Arizona, Wyoming, and Colorado. This represented over half of the entire nation of Mexico.

With the addition of territory in southern Arizona and New Mexico through the Gadsden Purchase of 1853, these annexations rounded out the continental United States, doubled its size, and provided routes for eventual transcontinental rail lines. In return for what Polk called "an immense empire" that encompassed more than half a million square miles, the United States agreed to pay $15 million. The Senate ratified the treaty on March 10, 1848. By the end of July, the last remaining U.S. soldiers had left Mexico.

THE WAR'S LEGACIES The Mexican-American War was America's first major military intervention outside the United States and the first time that U.S. military forces had conquered and occupied another country. More than 13,000 Americans died, 11,550 of them from disease, especially measles and dysentery. The war remains the deadliest in American history in terms of the percentage of soldiers lost. Out of every 1,000 soldiers in Mexico, some 110 died. The next highest death rate would be in the Civil War, with 65 dead out of every 1,000 participants.

The victory also helped end America's prolonged economic depression. As the years passed, however, the Mexican-American War was increasingly seen as a shameful war of conquest directed by a president bent on territorial expansion for the sake of slavery. Ulysses S. Grant later called it "one of the most unjust wars ever waged by a stronger against a weaker nation." He wrote his wife that she would not believe how many Mexican civilians had been "murdered" by American soldiers. The "number would startle you." Even General Zachary Taylor called it an "unnecessary and senseless" war.

News of the victory over Mexico, however, thrilled American expansionists. The editor John O'Sullivan, who had coined the term *manifest destiny*, shouted, "More, More, More! Why not take all of Mexico?" Treasury secretary Robert Walker was equally giddy about the addition of California and the Oregon Country. "Asia has suddenly become our neighbor, . . . inviting our steamships upon the trade of a commerce greater than all of Europe combined."

The acquisition of the northern Mexican provinces made the United States a transcontinental nation and required a dramatic expansion of the federal government. In 1849, Congress created the Department of the Interior to supervise the distribution of land, the creation of new territories and states, and the "protection" of the Indians and their reservations. Americans now had their long coveted western empire. But what were they to do with it?

President Polk had naively assumed that the expansion of American territory to the Pacific would strengthen "the bonds of Union." He was wrong. No sooner was Texas annexed and gold was discovered in California than a violent debate erupted over the extension of slavery into the territories acquired from Mexico. That debate would enflame sectional rivalries that would nearly destroy the Union.

CHAPTER REVIEW

SUMMARY

- **Westward Migration**   In the 1830s Americans came to believe in *"manifest destiny"*—that the West was divinely ordained to be part of the United States. Although populated by Indians and Hispanics, the West was portrayed as an empty land. But a population explosion and the lure of cheap, fertile land prompted Americans to move along the *Overland Trails*, enduring great physical hardships, toward Oregon (*Oregon fever*) and California. Traders and trappers were the first Americans to move into California during the 1830s. The discovery of gold there in 1848 brought a flood of people from all over the world. Many southerners also moved to the Mexican province of Texas to grow cotton, taking their slaves with them. The Mexican government opposed slavery, however, and in 1830 forbade further immigration. Texians rebelled, winning their independence from Mexico in the *Texas Revolution*, but statehood would not come for another decade because political leaders were determined to avoid war with Mexico over the territory and the issue of adding another slave state to the Union.

- **Mexican-American War**   When the United States finally annexed Texas in 1845, Mexico was furious. The newly elected U.S. president, James K. Polk, sought to acquire California and New Mexico as well, but negotiations soon failed. When Mexican troops crossed the Rio Grande, Polk urged Congress to declare war. American forces eventually won, despite high casualties. In 1848, in the *Treaty of Guadalupe Hidalgo*, Mexico ceded California and New Mexico to the United States and gave up claims to land north of the Rio Grande. The vast acquisition did not strengthen the Union, however. Instead it ignited a fierce dispute over the role of slavery in the new territories.

CHRONOLOGY

1821	Mexico gains independence from Spain
1836	Americans are defeated at the Alamo
1841	John Tyler becomes president
1842	Americans and British agree to the Webster-Ashburton Treaty
1845	United States annexes Texas
1846	Mexican-American War begins
1848	Treaty of Guadalupe Hidalgo ends the Mexican-American War
1853	With the Gadsden Purchase, the United States acquires an additional 30,000 square miles from Mexico

KEY TERMS

 INQUIZITIVE

Go to InQuizitive to see what you've learned—and learn what you've missed—with personalized feedback along the way.

14 The Gathering Storm

1848–1860

"Bleeding Kansas" (1856) This engraving depicts the sack of Lawrence, Kansas, in May 1856 by pro-slavery "border ruffians." The violence sparked by these slave-holding Missourians proved to be a foreboding sign of the destruction that would engulf the nation in the coming decade.

At midcentury, political storm clouds were forming over the fate of slavery. The United States was a powerful nation, but, as Henry Clay said, it was an "unhappy country" torn by the "uproar, confusion, and menace" caused by the deepening agony over slavery. Without intending to, the United States had developed two quite different societies, one in the North and the other in the South, and the two sections increasingly disagreed over the nation's future. In 1833, Andrew Jackson had predicted that southerners "intend to blow up a storm on the slave question." He added that pro-slavery firebrands like John C. Calhoun "would do any act to destroy this union and form a southern confederacy bounded, north, by the Potomac River." By 1848, Jackson's prediction seemed close to reality.

At midcentury the sectional tensions over slavery generated constant political conflict. The Compromise of 1850 provided a short-term resolution of some of the issues dividing North and South, but new controversies such as the fate of slavery in the Kansas Territory, the creation of the anti-slavery Republican party, and the growing militancy of abolitionists led more and more people to decide that the United States could not continue to be a nation "half slave and half free," as Abraham Lincoln insisted. The result was first the secession of eleven southern states and then a bloody civil war to force them back into the Union. In the process, the volatile issue of slavery was resolved by ending the "peculiar institution."

SLAVERY IN THE TERRITORIES

THE WILMOT PROVISO On August 8, 1846, soon after the Mexican-American War erupted, David Wilmot, an obscure Democratic congressman from Pennsylvania, delivered a speech to the House of Representatives in which he endorsed the annexation of Texas as a slave state. But if any *new* territory should be acquired as a result of the war with Mexico, he declared, "God

focus questions

1. How did the federal government try to resolve the issue of slavery in the western territories during the 1850s?

2. What appealed to northern voters about the Republican party? How did this lead to Abraham Lincoln's victory in the 1860 presidential contest?

3. Why did seven southern states secede from the Union shortly after Lincoln's election in 1860?

SECTION OF THE PANORAMA OF THE MISSISSIPPI

Taylor

For sale at White & Fellers 15 State St   Mississippi River

The Wilmot Proviso Taylor would refuse to veto the proviso as president, even though he was a slave owner. This political cartoon, "Old Zack at Home," highlights his seeming hypocrisy.

forbid" that slavery would be allowed there. He proposed a bill ("proviso") doing just that. In part, his opposition to slavery in Mexican territories reflected his desire to keep southern political power in Congress from expanding.

The **Wilmot Proviso** reignited debate over the westward extension of slavery. The Missouri Compromise (1820) had provided a temporary solution by protecting slavery in states where it already existed but not allowing it in newly acquired territories. Now, with the possible addition of territories taken from Mexico, the stage was set for an even more explosive debate.

The House of Representatives approved the Wilmot Proviso, but the Senate balked at the insistence of southerners. When Congress reconvened in December 1846, President Polk dismissed the proviso as "mischievous and foolish." He convinced Wilmot to withhold his amendment from any bill dealing with the annexation of Mexican territory. By then, however, others were ready to take up the cause. In one form or another, Wilmot's idea would continue to frame the debate in Congress over the expansion of slavery for the next fifteen years. During his one term as a congressman, in 1847–1849, Abraham Lincoln voted for it "as good as forty times."

POPULAR SOVEREIGNTY Senator Lewis Cass of Michigan, a Democrat, tried to remove the explosive controversy over slavery from national politics by giving the voters in each *territory* the right to "regulate their own internal concerns in their own way," like the citizens of a state.

Popular sovereignty, as Cass's idea was called, appealed to many because it seemed to be the most democratic solution to the question of allowing slavery or not. The moral defects of popular sovereignty, however, were obvious: it did not allow African Americans to vote on their fate, and it allowed a majority of whites to take away the most basic human right: freedom.

When Polk followed through on his promise to serve only one term and refused to run again in 1848, Cass won the Democrats' presidential nomination. But the party refused to endorse his "popular sovereignty" plan. Instead, it simply denied the power of Congress to interfere with slavery in the states and criticized all efforts by anti-slavery activists to bring the question of restricting or abolishing slavery before Congress.

The Whigs, as in 1840, again passed over their leader, Henry Clay, a three-time presidential loser. This time they nominated General Zachary Taylor, whose fame had grown during the Mexican-American War. Taylor, born in Virginia and raised in Kentucky, now owned a Louisiana plantation with more than 100 slaves. But he was also an ardent nationalist who vigorously opposed the extension of slavery into new western territories.

THE FREE-SOIL MOVEMENT As it had done in 1840, the Whig party offered no platform during the 1844 campaign in an effort to avoid the divisive issue of slavery. The anti-slavery crusade was not easily silenced, however. Americans who worried about the morality of slavery but could not endorse abolition could support banning slavery from the western territories. As a result, "free soil" in the new territories became the rallying cry for a new political organization: the Free-Soil party.

The **Free-Soil party** attracted three groups: northern Democrats opposed to slavery, anti-slavery northern Whigs, and members of the abolitionist Liberty party. In 1848, the Free Soil party nominated former president Martin Van Buren as their candidate. The party's platform stressed that slavery would not be allowed in the western territories. As their campaign slogan shouted, "Free soil, Free Speech, Free Labor, and Free Men." The new party infuriated John C. Calhoun and other southern Democrats. Calhoun called Van Buren a "bold, unscrupulous, and vindictive demagogue."

In the 1848 election, punctuated by parades, rallies, barbecues, banners, and bands, the Free-Soilers were spoilers: they split the Democratic vote enough to throw New York to the Whigs' Zachary Taylor, and they split the

Whig vote enough to give Ohio to the Democrat Lewis Cass. But nationwide, Van Buren's 291,000 votes lagged well behind the totals of 1,361,000 for Taylor and 1,222,000 for Cass. Taylor won with 163 to 127 electoral votes.

THE CALIFORNIA GOLD RUSH Meanwhile, a new issue had emerged to complicate the growing debate over territorial expansion and slavery. On January 24, 1848, gold nuggets were discovered in a stream on the property of John A. Sutter along the south fork of the American River in the Mexican province of California, which nine days later would be transferred to the United States through the treaty ending the Mexican-American War.

News of the gold strike spread like wildfire, especially after President Polk announced to Congress that there was an "extraordinary abundance of gold" in California and other territories acquired from Mexico. Suddenly, a gold mania infected the nation. "We are on the brink of the Age of Gold," gushed Horace Greeley, editor of the *New York Tribune*.

In 1849, nearly 100,000 Americans, mostly men, set off for California, eager to find riches. Sailors jumped ship, soldiers deserted, and husbands abandoned their families to join the **California gold rush**. "Men are here nearly crazed with the riches forced suddenly into their pockets," a Tennessean wrote. By 1854, the number of newcomers would top 300,000, and the surge of interest in California's golden news added to the urgency of bringing the profitable new western territory into the Union.

Among the "forty-niners" (also called argonauts) who rushed to California were several family members of former President John Tyler. His wife, Julia, wrote her mother that "the president" was not much taken with "this California fever. . . . He thinks a good farm on the James River [in Virginia] with plenty of slaves is gold mine enough."

Others, however, raced to California as fast as they could get there. The gold rush was the greatest mass migration in American history—and one of the most significant events in the first half of the nineteenth century. Between 1851 and 1855, California produced almost half the world's output of gold.

The infusion of California gold into the U.S. economy led to a prolonged national prosperity that eventually helped finance the Union military effort in the Civil War. In addition, it spurred the construction of railroads and telegraph lines, hastened the demise of the Indians, and excited dreams of an American economic empire based in the Pacific.

The gold rush also transformed San Francisco into the nation's largest city west of Chicago. In just two years, it grew from a small coastal village of 800 to a bustling city of 20,000. New business enterprises—saloons, taverns, restaurants, stores—emerged to serve the burgeoning population of miners, including one dedicated to the production of sturdy denim trousers made of sailcloth,

California News (1850) by William Sidney Mount During the California gold rush, San Francisco quickly became a bustling city as the population increased almost fiftyfold in a few months.

with their pockets reinforced by copper rivets. The blue jeans, known to this day as Levi's, were developed by the German-Jewish immigrant Levi Strauss.

The forty-niners included people from every social class and every state and territory, as well as local Indians and slaves brought by their owners. "Never was there such a gold-thirsty race of men brought together," a Californian said of the waves of prospectors flowing into the newest American territory.

On one December day in 1848, a New York City newspaper announced that sixty-two different ships were leaving for California. When one steamship arrived in San Francisco harbor, its entire crew deserted and headed for the gold diggings. The influx of gold seekers quickly reduced the 14,000 Mexican natives in California to a minority, and sporadic conflicts with the Indians of the Sierra Nevada foothills decimated California's Native American population.

MINING LIFE The miners were mostly unmarried young men of varied ethnic and cultural backgrounds. Few were interested in staying in California; they wanted to strike it rich and return home. Mining camps thus sprang up like mushrooms and disappeared almost as rapidly. As soon as rumors of a new strike made the rounds, miners converged on the area; when no more gold could be found, they picked up and moved on.

Gold miners Chinese immigrants and white settlers mine for gold in the Auburn Ravine of California in 1856.

The wild mining camps and shantytowns may have had colorful names—Whiskey Flat, Lousy Ravine, Petticoat Slide, Piety Hill—but they were dirty, lawless, and dangerous places. In Calaveras County, there were fourteen murders in a single week. Vigilante justice prevailed; one newcomer reported that "in the short space of twenty-four days, we have had murders, fearful accidents, bloody deaths, a mob, whippings, a hanging, an attempt at suicide, and a fatal duel." Within six months of arriving in California in 1849, one gold seeker in every five was dead. The goldfields and mining towns were so dangerous that insurance companies refused to provide coverage. Suicides were common and disease was rampant.

Women were as rare in the mining camps as liquor and guns were abundant. In 1850, less than 8 percent of California's population was female. The few women who dared to live in the camps could demand a premium for their work as cooks, laundresses, entertainers, and prostitutes. In the mining camps, white miners often looked with disdain upon the Hispanics and Chinese, who were most often employed as wage laborers to help in the panning process, separating gold from sand and gravel. But the whites focused their contempt on the Indians: it was not considered a crime to kill Indians or work them to death.

THE COMPROMISE OF 1850 By late 1849, as confrontations over slavery mounted, each national political party was dividing into factions along North–South lines. Irate southern Whigs abandoned their party and joined the pro-slavery Democrats. Some threatened that their states would leave the Union if President Taylor followed through on his proposal to bring California and New Mexico directly into the Union as free states, skipping the territorial phase.

Jefferson Davis, Taylor's son-in-law, dismissed the president's plan as being anti-southern. Taylor responded by criticizing "intolerant and revolutionary southerners." Southerners—ministers, planters, and politicians—rushed to attack the president. "I avow before this House and country, and in the presence of the living God," shouted Robert Toombs, a Georgia congressman, "that if by your legislation you seek to drive us [slaveholders] from the territories of California and New Mexico . . . and to abolish slavery in this District [of Columbia] . . . *I am for disunion.*"

As the controversy unfolded, the spotlight fell on the Senate, where an all-star cast of outsized personalities with swollen egos resolved to find a way to preserve the Union. The "lions" of the Senate—Henry Clay, John C. Calhoun, and Daniel Webster (all of whom would die within two years)—took center stage, with William H. Seward, Stephen A. Douglas, and Jefferson Davis in supporting roles. Together, they staged one of the great dramas of American politics: the **Compromise of 1850**, a ten-month-long debate over a series of resolutions intended to reduce the crisis between North and South that had "unhinged" both political parties.

IN SEARCH OF COMPROMISE With southern extremists threatening secession, congressional leaders again turned to an aging Henry Clay, now seventy-two years old and struggling with tuberculosis. As Abraham Lincoln acknowledged, Clay was "regarded by all, as *the* man for the crisis." No man had amassed a more distinguished political career. Clay had gained every position he had sought except the presidency: senator, congressman, Speaker of the House, secretary of state.

Now, as his career was winding down, Clay hoped to save the Union by presenting his own plan to end another sectional crisis. On December 3, 1849, as the Thirty-First Congress assembled for what would become the longest session in its history, Clay strode into the Senate to waves of applause. He asked to be relieved of all committee responsibilities so that he could focus on the national crisis. Unless some compromise could be found, the slaveholding Clay warned, a "furious" civil war would fracture the Union.

The next day, in his annual message to Congress, President Taylor urged immediate statehood for California and the same as soon as possible for New Mexico. He then pleaded with Congress to avoid injecting slavery into the issue. It was too late, however. Admitting California as a free state would tip the political balance against slavery, with sixteen free states to fifteen slave states. The slaveholding states would become a permanent minority. As Jefferson Davis argued, the South could not allow that to happen.

Taylor hoped that his proposals would "create confidence and kind feeling" among the contending sections. But his speech only aggravated the seething tensions. It took weeks of combative debate before a Speaker of the House, Georgia slaveholder Howell Cobb, could be elected on the sixty-third ballot. "Madness rules the hour," wrote Philip Hone, a New York Whig, in his diary. For the first time in history, he noted, members of Congress were openly threatening to dissolve the Union.

Clay then stepped into the breach. On January 29, 1850, having gained the wholehearted support of Daniel Webster, the senior senator from Massachusetts whom he had known for thirty-six years, Clay presented to Congress his "amicable" plan for "compromise and harmony." Eager to see the Great Compromiser, people filled the Senate.

Using all of his charm and passion, Clay pleaded with the Senate to pass eight resolutions, six of which were paired as compromises between North and South, and all of which were designed to settle the "controversy between the free and slave states, growing out of the subject of slavery." He proposed (1) to admit California as a free state; (2) to organize the territories of New Mexico and Utah without restrictions on slavery, allowing the residents to decide the issue for themselves; (3) to deny Texas its extreme claim to much of New Mexico; (4) to compensate Texas by having the federal government pay the pre-annexation Texas debts; (5) to retain slavery in the District of Columbia, but (6) to abolish the sale of slaves in the nation's capital; (7) to adopt a more effective federal fugitive slave law ("the recapture of fugitives was not just a legal duty, but a *moral* one"); and (8) to deny congressional authority to interfere with the interstate slave trade.

Clay's cluster of proposals became in substance the Compromise of 1850, but only after seven months of negotiations punctuated by the greatest debates in congressional history. Clay's eloquence had won over the moderates but not those at the extremes: northern abolitionists or southern secessionists.

THE GREAT DEBATE On March 4, a feeble John C. Calhoun, desperately ill with tuberculosis, arrived in the Senate chamber. The uncompromising defender of slavery was so sick and shriveled that a colleague had to read his defiant speech. Calhoun urged that Clay's compromise be rejected. The "great questions" dividing the nation must be settled on southern terms. The South, he explained, needed Congress to protect the rights of slave owners to take their "property" into the new territories. Otherwise, Calhoun warned, the "cords which bind" the Union would be severed. If California were admitted as a free state, the South could no longer "remain honorably and safely in the Union." The southern states would leave the Union (secede) and form their own national government.

Three days later, Calhoun, who would die in three weeks, hobbled into the Senate to hear Daniel Webster speak. Webster was so famous for his theatrical

Clay's compromise (1850) Warning against an impending sectional conflict, Henry Clay outlines his plan for "compromise and harmony" on the Senate floor.

speeches that they were major public events. The visitors' galleries were packed as he rose to address the Senate.

"I wish to speak today," Webster began, "not as a Massachusetts man, not as a Northern man, but as an American. . . . I speak today for the preservation of the Union." He blamed both northerners and southerners for the crisis but acknowledged that both regions had legitimate grievances: the South understandably objected to the excesses of "infernal fanatics and abolitionists" in the North, and the North resented aggressive southern efforts to expand slavery into the new western territories. With respect to escaped slaves, Webster shocked his fellow New Englanders by declaring that "the South, in my judgment, is right, and the North is wrong." Fugitive slaves must be returned to their owners.

Webster had no patience, however, with the notion of secession. Leaving the Union would bring civil war. "Secession! Peaceable secession! Sir, your eyes and mine are never destined to see that miracle." Instead of looking into such "caverns of darkness," let "men enjoy the fresh air of liberty and union.

Let them look to a more hopeful future." For almost four hours, he pleaded with his colleagues not to be uncompromising "pigmies" but compromising statesmen.

Webster's evenhanded speech angered both sides. No sooner had he finished than Calhoun stood to assert that the Union could indeed "be broken. Great moral causes will break it." At the same time, northern abolitionists savaged Webster for calling them fanatics.

On March 11, William Seward, a first-year Whig senator from New York, gave an intentionally provocative speech in which he opposed Clay's compromise, declaring that *any* compromise with slavery was "radically wrong and essentially vicious." There was, he said, "a *higher law* than the Constitution," and it demanded the abolition of slavery through acts of civil disobedience. He encouraged his fellow New Yorkers to defy the federal fugitive slave law by extending a "cordial welcome" to escaped slaves and defending them from all efforts to return them south. The southern supporters of slavery, he concluded, must give way to the inevitable "progress of emancipation."

Seward's inflammatory speech outraged southerners, who repudiated his "fanatical and wild notion" of there being a "higher law" than the Constitution and the implication that the godly abolitionists were somehow above the law. Clay felt compelled to dismiss Seward's "wild, reckless, and abominable theories." Seward, however, was unapologetic. He had sought to speak for the enslaved as well as all of humankind.

COMPROMISE EFFORTS For his part, Henry Clay was "angry at everybody." The extremists had taken control of the debate and were postponing a vote on his compromise proposal. He got little help from President Taylor, who continued to focus solely on the admission of California as a new state. In a letter to his son, Clay reported that the "Administration, the Abolitionists, the Ultra Southern men, and the timid Whigs of the North are all combined against" his compromise plan.

On July 4, 1850, Congress took a break and celebrated Independence Day by gathering beneath a broiling summer sun at the base of the unfinished Washington Monument. President Taylor suffered a mild heatstroke while listening to three hours of patriotic speeches. He tried to recover by gorging himself on iced milk, cherries, and raw vegetables. That night, he suddenly developed a violent stomach disorder. He died five days later, the second president to die in office.

Taylor's shocking death actually bolstered the chances of a compromise in Congress, for his successor, Vice President Millard Fillmore, supported Clay's proposals. It was a striking reversal: Taylor, the Louisiana slaveholder, had been ready to make war on his native South to save the Union; Fillmore, whom southerners thought opposed slavery, was ready to make peace. The new president asserted his control by asking his entire cabinet to resign. He then appointed Webster as secretary of state, signaling that he also joined Webster in supporting compromise.

Fillmore was aided by Illinois senator Stephen A. Douglas, a rising young star in the Democratic party, who was friendly to the South. Douglas dramatically stepped up to rescue Clay's struggling plan. Brash and brilliant, short and stocky—he stood just five feet four—Douglas, the "Little Giant" who modeled himself after Andrew Jackson, cleverly suggested that the best way to salvage Clay's "comprehensive

Millard Fillmore Fillmore's support of the Compromise of 1850 helped sustain the Union through the crisis.

scheme" was to break it up into separate proposals and vote on them one at a time. Fillmore endorsed the idea.

The plan worked, in part because John C. Calhoun had died and was no longer in the Senate to obstruct efforts at conciliation. Each component of Clay's compromise plan passed in the Senate and the House, several of them by the narrowest of margins. (Only five senators voted for all of the items making up the compromise.)

In its final version, the Compromise of 1850 included the following elements: (1) California entered the Union as a free state, ending forever the old balance of free and slave states; (2) the Texas–New Mexico Act made New Mexico a territory and set the Texas boundary at its present location. In return for giving up its claims, Texas was paid $10 million, which secured payment of the state's debt; (3) the Utah Act set up the Utah Territory and gave the territorial legislature authority over "all rightful subjects of legislation" (slavery); (4) a Fugitive Slave Act required the federal government and northern states to help capture and return runaway slaves; and (5) as a gesture to anti-slavery groups, the public sale of slaves, but not slavery itself, was abolished in the District of Columbia.

By September 20, President Fillmore had signed the last of the measures into law, claiming that they represented a "final settlement" to the sectional

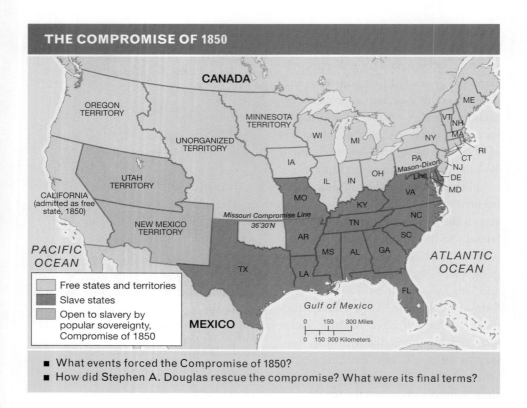

THE COMPROMISE OF 1850

Free states and territories

Slave states

Open to slavery by popular sovereignty, Compromise of 1850

- What events forced the Compromise of 1850?
- How did Stephen A. Douglas rescue the compromise? What were its final terms?

tensions over slavery. "Let us cease agitating," Douglas urged, "stop the debate, and drop the subject" of slavery.

The nation celebrated the compromise. "Harmony is secured. Patriots rejoice!" blared one newspaper. Henry Clay predicted that his solution would "pacify, tranquilize, and harmonize the country." At the least, Daniel Webster sighed, he could "now sleep nights."

The so-called Compromise of 1850 defused an explosive situation and settled each of the major points at issue, but it was not so much an example of warring people making concessions as it was a temporary and imperfect truce. As Salmon P. Chase, an Ohio Free-Soiler, stressed, "the question of slavery in the territories has been avoided. It has not been settled." The Compromise of 1850 only postponed secession and civil war for ten years. It was a brilliant form of evading the fundamental issue dividing the nation. Soon, aspects of the compromise would reignite sectional tensions.

THE FUGITIVE SLAVE ACT People were naive to think that the Compromise of 1850 would eliminate discussions about the legitimacy of slavery. Within two months of the bill's passage, the squabbling between North and South resumed.

The **Fugitive Slave Act** was the most controversial element of the Compromise of 1850. It did more than strengthen the hand of slave catchers; it sought to recover slaves who had already escaped. The law also unwittingly enabled slave traders to kidnap free blacks in northern "free" states, claiming that they were runaway slaves. The law denied fugitives a jury trial. In addition, citizens under the new law were forced to help locate and capture runaways.

Abolitionists fumed. "This filthy enactment was made in the nineteenth century, by people who could read and write," Ralph Waldo Emerson marveled in his diary. He urged people to break the new law "on the earliest occasion."

In late October 1850, two slave catchers from Georgia arrived in Boston, determined to use the new federal Fugitive Slave Act to recapture William and Ellen Craft, husband-and-wife cabinet-makers. Abolitionists mobilized to prevent the Crafts from being seized by the "man stealers." After five days, the slave catchers gave up and returned to Georgia.

Upon learning of the incident, President Fillmore assured the South that he would use federal troops, if necessary, to return the Crafts to Georgia. But he was too late. Abolitionists had spirited the Crafts to safety in Great Britain. Theodore Parker, a prominent white Boston minister who was a leading abolitionist, wrote a letter to President Fillmore explaining the willingness of his congregation to engage in civil disobedience in order to protect the Crafts, who were church members: "You cannot think that I am to stand by and see my own church carried off to slavery and do nothing to hinder such a wrong."

The occasion soon arose in Detroit, Michigan, where only military force stopped the rescue of a fugitive slave by an outraged mob in October 1850.

CAUTION!!
COLORED PEOPLE
OF BOSTON, ONE & ALL,
You are hereby respectfully CAUTIONED and advised, to avoid conversing with the
Watchmen and Police Officers of Boston,
For since the recent ORDER OF THE MAYOR & ALDERMEN, they are empowered to act as
KIDNAPPERS
AND
Slave Catchers,
And they have already been actually employed in KIDNAPPING, CATCHING, AND KEEPING SLAVES. Therefore, if you value your LIBERTY, and the *Welfare of the Fugitives* among you, *Shun* them in every possible manner, as so many *HOUNDS* on the track of the most unfortunate of your race.

Keep a Sharp Look Out for KIDNAPPERS, and have TOP EYE open.
APRIL 24, 1851.

Threats to free blacks This 1851 notice warned free blacks about police and others who could easily kidnap and sell them back into slavery under the new Fugitive Slave Act.

There were relatively few such incidents, however. The efforts to protect the Crafts was one of several similar episodes of public resistance to slave catchers in the North. In the eleven years of the Fugitive Slave Act, barely more than 300 escaped slaves were returned to bondage.

The mere existence of the Fugitive Slave Act, however, was intolerable to many northern abolitionists; several of them advocated violence. "The only way to make the Fugitive Slave Law a dead letter," Frederick Douglass threatened, "is to make half-a-dozen or more dead kidnappers." In Springfield, Massachusetts, a fiery abolitionist named John Brown formed an armed band of African Americans, called the League of Gileadites, to attack slave catchers. Such efforts led Horace Greeley, the prominent New York newspaper editor, to write that the Fugitive Slave Act was proving to be "a very bad investment for slaveholders" because it was creating such a backlash against slavery itself throughout the northern states.

UNCLE TOM'S CABIN   During the 1850s, anti-slavery advocates gained a powerful new weapon in the form of Harriet Beecher Stowe's best-selling novel, *Uncle Tom's Cabin; or Life among the Lowly* (1852). The pious Stowe epitomized the powerful religious underpinnings of the abolitionist movement. While raising six children in Cincinnati, Ohio, during the 1830s and 1840s, she helped runaway slaves who had crossed the Ohio River from Kentucky. Like many anti-slavery activists, Stowe was disgusted by the Fugitive Slave Act. In the spring of 1850, having moved to Maine, she began writing *Uncle Tom's Cabin*. "The time has come," she wrote, "when even a woman or a child who can speak a word for freedom and humanity is bound to speak."

Uncle Tom's Cabin was a smashing success. Within two days, the first printing had sold out, and by the end of its first year, it had sold 300,000 copies in the United States and more than a million in Great Britain. Soon there was a children's version and a traveling theater production. By 1855, it was called "the most popular novel of our day."

Uncle Tom's Cabin depicted a combination of improbable saints and sinners, crude stereotypes, impossibly virtuous black victims, and melodramatic escapades involving fugitive slaves. The persecuted Uncle Tom, whose gentleness and generosity grow even as he is sold as a slave and taken south; the villainous white planter Simon Legree, who torments and tortures Tom before ordering his death; the angelic Little Eva, a white girl who dies after befriending Tom; the beautiful but desperate Eliza, who escapes from slave catchers by carrying her child to freedom across the icy Ohio River—all became stock characters in American folklore.

The novel revealed how the brutal realities of slavery harmed everyone associated with it. Abolitionist leader Frederick Douglass, a former slave himself, said that *Uncle Tom's Cabin* was like "a flash" that lit "a million camp fires in front of the embattled host of slavery." Slaveholders were incensed by the book, calling Stowe that "wretch in petticoats." One of them mailed her a parcel containing the severed ear of a disobedient slave.

THE ELECTION OF 1852 In 1852, it took the Democrats forty-nine ballots before they chose Franklin Pierce of New Hampshire as their presidential candidate. When Pierce heard the results, he was stunned: "You are looking at the most surprised man who ever lived!" When his wife Jane learned of the nomination, she fainted. Their concerns were well-founded.

135,000 SETS, 270,000 VOLUMES SOLD.

UNCLE TOM'S CABIN

FOR SALE HERE.

AN EDITION FOR THE MILLION, COMPLETE IN 1 Vol., PRICE 37 1-2 CENTS.
"   "   IN GERMAN, IN 1 Vol., PRICE 50 CENTS.
"   "   IN 2 Vols., CLOTH, 6 PLATES, PRICE $1.50.
SUPERB ILLUSTRATED EDITION, IN 1 Vol., WITH 153 ENGRAVINGS,
PRICES FROM $2.50 TO $5.00.

The Greatest Book of the Age.

"The Greatest Book of the Age"
Uncle Tom's Cabin, as this advertisement indicated, was an influential best seller.

The Democrats' platform endorsed the Compromise of 1850, including enforcement of the Fugitive Slave Act. For their part, the Whigs repudiated the lackluster Millard Fillmore, who had faithfully supported the Compromise of 1850, and chose General Winfield Scott, a hero of the Mexican-American War.

Scott, however, proved to be an inept campaigner. He carried only Tennessee, Kentucky, Massachusetts, and Vermont. The Whigs, now without their greatest leaders, Henry Clay and Daniel Webster, had lost virtually all of their support in the Lower South. Pierce overwhelmed Scott in the electoral college, 254 to 42, although the popular vote was close: 1.6 million to 1.4 million. The third-party Free-Soilers mustered only 156,000 votes.

The forty-eight-year-old Pierce, an undistinguished congressman and senator who had fought in the Mexican-American War, was, like James K. Polk, touted as another Andrew Jackson. Pierce eagerly promoted western expansion and the conversion of more territories into states, even if it meant adding more slave states to the Union, but he also acknowledged that the Compromise of 1850 had defused a "perilous crisis." He urged both North and South to avoid aggravating the other. As a Georgia editor noted, however, the feud between the two regions might be "smothered, but never overcome."

Pierce was burdened by the death of his eleven-year-old son, Benjamin, killed in a train accident just days before his father was sworn in as president. Benjamin was the third son that the Pierces had lost. Still in mourning, Jane

Pierce refused to attend her husband's inauguration and thereafter lived in seclusion, writing letters to her dead children, cursing politics, and blaming Franklin for her troubles. Writer Nathaniel Hawthorne, Pierce's close friend, confided in a letter that he wished the new president "had a better wife, or none at all."

President Pierce, an intelligent man capable of eloquent speechmaking, had tragic flaws and private demons: blinded by a desire to be liked and cursed with raging ambition, he was a timid, indecisive leader who was often drunk. (He would die in 1869 of alcoholism.) Commissioned as a general in the Mexican-American War, he had fainted during his first battle.

As president, Pierce proved unable to unite the warring factions of his own party. By the end of his first year in office, Democratic leaders had decided that he was a failure. James W. Forney, a political friend, confessed that the presidency "overshadows him. He is crushed by its great duties and seeks refuge in [alcohol]." By trying to be all things to all people, Pierce was labeled a "doughface": a "Northern man with Southern principles." His closest friend in the cabinet was Secretary of War Jefferson Davis, the future president of the Confederacy. Such friendships led Harriet Beecher Stowe to call Pierce an "arch-traitor."

THE KANSAS-NEBRASKA CRISIS During the mid–nineteenth century, Americans discovered the vast markets of Asia. As trade with China and Japan grew, merchants and manufacturers called for a transcontinental railroad connecting the Eastern Seaboard with the Pacific coast to facilitate both the flow of commerce with Asia and the settlement of the western territories. Those promoting the railroad did not realize that the issue would renew sectional rivalries and reignite the debate over the westward extension of slavery.

In 1852 and 1853, Congress considered several proposals for a transcontinental rail line. Secretary of War Jefferson Davis of Mississippi favored a southern route across the territories acquired from Mexico. Senator Stephen A. Douglas of Illinois insisted that Chicago be the Midwest hub for the new rail line and urged Congress to pass the **Kansas-Nebraska Act** so that the vast territory west of Missouri and Iowa could be settled.

To win the support of southern legislators, Douglas championed "popular sovereignty," whereby voters in each new territory would decide whether to allow slavery. It was a clever way to get around the 1820 Missouri Compromise, which excluded slaves north of the 36th parallel, where Kansas and Nebraska were located.

Southerners demanded more, however, and Douglas reluctantly complied. Although he knew it would "raise a hell of a storm" in the North, Douglas supported the South in recommending the formal repeal of the Missouri Compromise and the creation of *two* new territorial governments rather than one: Kansas, west of Missouri, and Nebraska, west of Iowa and Minnesota. This meant that millions of fertile acres would be opened to slaveholders. What came to be called the Kansas-Nebraska Act "took us by surprise—astounded us," recalled Abraham Lincoln.

In May 1854, Douglas masterfully assembled the votes for his Kansas-Nebraska Act, recruiting both Democrats and southern Whigs. The measure passed by a vote of 37 to 14 in the Senate and 113 to 100 in the House. The anti-slavery faction in Congress, mostly Whigs, had been crushed, and the national Whig party essentially died with them. Out of its ashes would arise a new party: the Republicans.

Stephen A. Douglas, ca. 1852 The Illinois Democratic senator authored the Kansas-Nebraska Act.

THE EMERGENCE OF THE REPUBLICAN PARTY

The dispute over the Kansas-Nebraska Act led northern anti-slavery Whigs and some northern anti-slavery Democrats to gravitate toward two new parties. One was the American ("Know-Nothing") party, which had emerged in response to the surge of mostly Catholic immigrants from Ireland and Germany, nearly 3 million of whom arrived in the United States between 1845 and 1854. Many of the immigrants were poor and Catholic, which made them especially unwanted. The "Know-Nothings" embraced nativism (opposition to foreign immigrants) by denying citizenship to newcomers. Many also were opposed to the territorial expansion of slavery and the "fanaticism" of abolitionists.

The other new party, the Republicans, attracted even more northern Whigs. It was formed in February 1854 in Ripon, Wisconsin, when the so-called "conscience Whigs" (those opposed to slavery) split from the southern pro-slavery "cotton Whigs." The conscience Whigs joined with anti-slavery

Democrats and Free-Soilers to form a new party dedicated to the exclusion of slavery from the western territories.

"BLEEDING KANSAS" The passage of the Kansas-Nebraska Act soon placed Kansas at the center of the increasingly violent debate over slavery. While Nebraska would become a free state, Kansas was up for grabs. According to the Kansas-Nebraska Act, the residents of the Kansas Territory were "perfectly free to form and regulate their domestic institutions [slavery] in their own way." The law, however, said nothing about *when* Kansans could decide about slavery, so each side tried to gain political control of the vast territory. "Come on then, Gentlemen of the Slave States," New York senator William Seward taunted. "We will engage in competition for the virgin soil of Kansas, and God give the victory to the side which is stronger in numbers as it is in the right."

Groups for and against slavery recruited armed emigrants to move to Kansas. "Every slaveholding state," said an observer, "is furnishing men and money to fasten slavery upon this glorious land, by means no matter how foul." When Kansas's first federal governor arrived in 1854, he sent an urgent message to President Pierce, reporting that southerners were arriving with a "dogged determination to force slavery into this Territory" in advance of an election of a territorial legislature in March 1855.

On Election Day, thousands of heavily armed "border ruffians" from Missouri traveled to Kansas, illegally elected pro-slavery legislators, and vowed to kill every "God-damned abolitionist in the Territory." As soon as it convened, the territorial legislature expelled its few anti-slavery members and declared that the territory would be open to slavery. The governor then rushed to Washington, D.C., to plead with Pierce to intervene with federal troops. Pierce acknowledged that he was concerned about the situation, but his spineless solution was to replace the territorial governor with a man who would support the pro-slavery faction.

Outraged free-state advocates in Kansas, now a majority, spurned this "bogus" government and elected their own delegates to a constitutional convention which met in Topeka in 1855. They drafted a state constitution excluding slavery and applied for statehood. By 1856, a free-state "governor" and "legislature" were operating in Topeka. There were now two illegal governments claiming to rule the Kansas Territory. And soon there was a territorial civil war, which journalists called "**Bleeding Kansas.**"

In May 1856, a pro-slavery force of more than 500 Missourians, Alabamans, and South Carolinians invaded the free-state town of Lawrence, Kansas, just twenty-five miles from the Missouri border. David Atchison, a

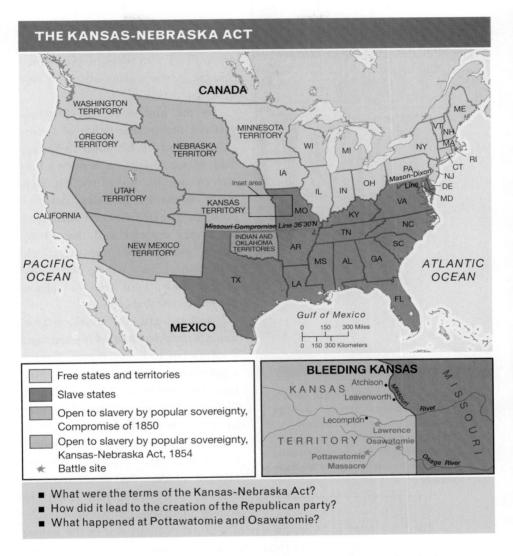

THE KANSAS-NEBRASKA ACT

CANADA

WASHINGTON TERRITORY

OREGON TERRITORY

NEBRASKA TERRITORY

MINNESOTA TERRITORY

UTAH TERRITORY

KANSAS TERRITORY

CALIFORNIA

NEW MEXICO TERRITORY

INDIAN AND OKLAHOMA TERRITORIES

Inset area

Missouri Compromise Line 36°30'N

WI   MI

IA

IL   IN   OH

MO   KY

TN

AR

MS   AL   GA

TX   LA

FL

NY

PA   Mason-Dixon Line

VA   MD

NC

SC

ME

VT   NH   MA

CT   RI

NJ

DE

PACIFIC OCEAN

ATLANTIC OCEAN

Gulf of Mexico

MEXICO

0   150   300 Miles

0   150   300 Kilometers

- ☐ Free states and territories
- ■ Slave states
- ☐ Open to slavery by popular sovereignty, Compromise of 1850
- ☐ Open to slavery by popular sovereignty, Kansas-Nebraska Act, 1854
- ✴ Battle site

BLEEDING KANSAS

KANSAS

Atchison

Leavenworth

Lecompton

Lawrence

TERRITORY   Osawatomie

Pottawatomie Massacre

Missouri River

Osage River

- What were the terms of the Kansas-Nebraska Act?
- How did it lead to the creation of the Republican party?
- What happened at Pottawatomie and Osawatomie?

former U.S. senator from Missouri, urged the southern raiders not "to slacken or stop until every spark of free-state, free-speech, free-niggers, or *free* in any shape is quenched out of Kansas." The mob rampaged through the town, destroying the newspaper printing presses, burning homes, and ransacking shops.

The "Sack of Lawrence" ignited the passions of abolitionist John Brown. The son of fervent Ohio Calvinists who taught their children that life was a crusade against sin, the grim, humorless Brown believed that Christians must "break the jaws of the wicked," and that the wickedest Americans were those

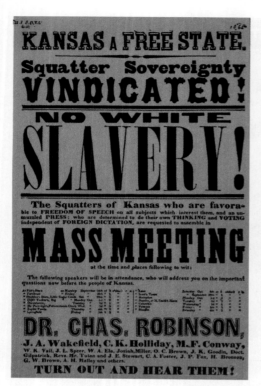

KANSAS A FREE STATE.

Squatter Sovereignty

VINDICATED!

NO WHITE

SLAVERY!

The Squatters of Kansas who are favorable to FREEDOM OF SPEECH on all subjects which interest them, and an unmuzzled PRESS; who are determined to do their own THINKING and VOTING independent of FOREIGN DICTATION, are requested to assemble in

MASS MEETING

at the time and places following to wit:

The following speakers will be in attendance, who will address you on the important questions now before the people of Kansas.

DR. CHAS. ROBINSON,
J. A. Wakefield, C. K. Holliday, M.F. Conway,
W. K. Vail, J. L. Speer, W. A. Ela, Josiah Miller, O. C. Brown, J. K. Goodin, Doct. Gilpatrick, Revs. Mr. Tuton and J. E. Stewart, C. A. Foster, J. P. Fox, H. Bronson, G. W. Brown, A. H. Malley and others.

TURN OUT AND HEAR THEM!

Kansas a Free State This broadside advertises a series of mass meetings in Kansas in support of the free-state cause, based on the principle of "squatter" or popular sovereignty, letting the residents decide the issue of slavery.

who owned and traded slaves. Upon meeting Brown, many declared him crazy; those who supported his efforts thought he was a saint. He was a little of both.

By the mid-1850s, the fifty-five-year-old Brown, the father of twenty children, had left his home in Springfield, Massachusetts, to become a holy warrior against slavery. In his view, blacks in the United States deserved both liberty and full social equality. A newspaper reporter said that Brown was a "strange" and "iron-willed" old man with a "fiery nature and a cold temper, and a cool head—a volcano beneath a covering of snow."

Two days after the attack on Lawrence, Brown led four of his sons and a son-in-law to Pottawatomie, Kansas, a pro-slavery settlement near the Missouri border. On the night of May 24, Brown and his group dragged five men from their houses and hacked them to death with swords. "God is my judge," Brown told one of his sons. "We were justified under the circumstances." Without "the shedding of blood," he added, "there is no remission of sins."

The Pottawatomie Massacre started a brutal guerrilla war in the Kansas Territory. On August 30, pro-slavery Missouri ruffians raided a free-state settlement at Osawatomie. They looted and burned houses and shot Frederick Brown, John's son, through the heart. By the end of 1856, about 200 settlers had been killed in "Bleeding Kansas."

SENATE BLOODSHED On May 22, 1856, two days before the Pottawatomie Massacre, an ugly incident in the U.S. Senate astounded the nation. Two days before, Republican senator Charles Sumner of Massachusetts, a passionate abolitionist, had delivered a fiery speech ("The Crime Against Kansas") in which he showered slave owners with insults and charged them with unleashing thugs and assassins in Kansas. His most savage attack was directed at Andrew Pickens Butler, an elderly senator from South Carolina, a state that Sumner said displayed a "shameful imbecility" resulting from its passion for slavery. Butler, Sumner charged, was a fumbling old man who had "chosen a mistress . . . who . . . though polluted in the sight of the world, is chaste [pure] in his sight—I mean the harlot [prostitute], Slavery."

Sumner's speech enraged Butler's cousin Preston S. Brooks, a South Carolina congressman with a hair-trigger temper. On May 22, Brooks confronted Sumner as he sat at his Senate desk. Brooks shouted that Sumner had slandered Butler and the state of South Carolina, then began beating him about the head with a gold-knobbed walking stick until the cane splintered. Sumner, his head gushing blood, nearly died; he would not return to the Senate for almost four years.

In the South, Butler was celebrated as a hero. The *Richmond Enquirer* described his attack as "good in conception, better in execution, and best of all in consequences." Dozens of southerners sent Butler new canes. In satisfying his rage, though, Brooks had created a martyr—"Bloodied Sumner"—for the anti-slavery cause. Sumner's empty Senate seat would serve as a solemn reminder of the violence done to him. His brutal beating also had an unintended political effect: it drove more northerners into the new Republican party.

"Bully" Brooks attacks Charles Sumner This violent incident in Congress worsened the strains on the Union.

SECTIONAL SQUABBLES The violence of "Bleeding Kansas" and "Bloodied Sumner" spilled over into the tone of the 1856 presidential election—one in which the major parties could no longer evade the slavery issue. At its first national convention, the Republicans fastened on the eccentric John C. Frémont, "the Pathfinder," who had led the conquest of Mexican California.

The Republican platform borrowed heavily from the former Whigs. It endorsed federal funding for a transcontinental railroad and other transportation improvements. It denounced the repeal of the Missouri Compromise, the Democratic party's policy of territorial expansion, and the "barbarism" of slavery. For the first time, a major-party platform had taken a stand against slavery.

The southern-dominated Democrats dumped President Franklin Pierce, who remains the only elected president to be denied renomination by his party. Instead, they chose sixty-five-year-old James Buchanan of Pennsylvania, a former senator and secretary of state who had long sought the nomination. The Democratic platform endorsed the Kansas-Nebraska Act, called for vigorous enforcement of the Fugitive Slave Act, and stressed that Congress should not interfere with slavery in states or territories.

In the campaign of 1856, the Republicans had very few southern supporters and only a handful in the border slave states of Delaware, Maryland, Kentucky, and Missouri. Frémont swept the northernmost states with 114 electoral votes, but Buchanan added five free states—Pennsylvania, New Jersey, Illinois, Indiana, and California—to his southern majority for a total of 174. The Democrats now would control the White House, the Congress, and the Supreme Court.

PRESIDENT BUCHANAN As Franklin Pierce prepared to leave the White House in March 1857, a friend asked what he was going to do. Pierce replied: "There's nothing left to do but get drunk."

James Buchanan also loved to drink, but he had different priorities. The president-elect had built his political career on his commitment to states' rights and his aggressive promotion of territorial expansion. Saving the Union, he believed, depended upon making concessions to the South. Republicans charged that he lacked the backbone to stand up to the southern slaveholders who dominated the Democratic majorities in Congress. His choice of four slave-state men and only three free-state men for his cabinet seemed another bad sign. It was.

Although Buchanan had vast experience, he had limited ability—and bad luck. During his first six months in office, two major events caused his undoing: (1) the Supreme Court decision in the *Dred Scott* case, and (2) new troubles in strife-torn Kansas.

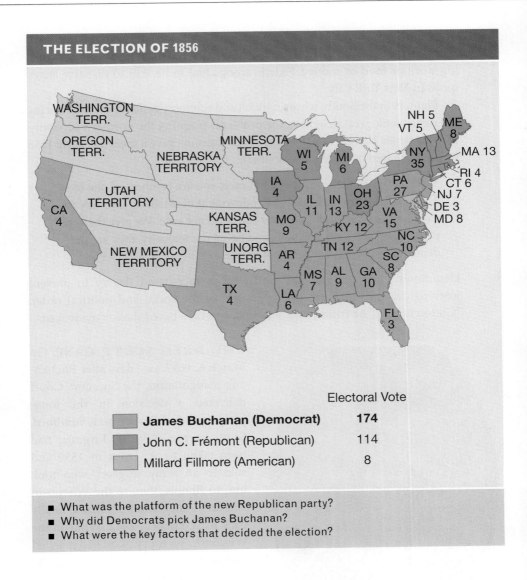

THE ELECTION OF 1856

WASHINGTON TERR.
OREGON TERR.
MINNESOTA TERR.
NEBRASKA TERRITORY
UTAH TERRITORY
CA 4
KANSAS TERR.
NEW MEXICO TERRITORY
UNORG. TERR.
TX 4
WI 5
IA 4
MO 9
AR 4
LA 6
MS 7
MI 6
IL 11
IN 13
KY 12
TN 12
AL 9
GA 10
OH 23
VA 15
NC 10
SC 8
FL 3
NH 5
VT 5
ME 8
NY 35
PA 27
MA 13
RI 4
CT 6
NJ 7
DE 3
MD 8

Electoral Vote

James Buchanan (Democrat)	**174**	
John C. Frémont (Republican)	114	
Millard Fillmore (American)	8	

- What was the platform of the new Republican party?
- Why did Democrats pick James Buchanan?
- What were the key factors that decided the election?

The financial Panic of 1857 only made a bad situation worse, for the new president and for the nation. By the summer of 1857, the economy was growing too fast. Too many railroads and factories were being built, and European demand for American corn and wheat was declining. The result was a financial panic triggered by the failure of the Ohio Life Insurance and Trust Company on August 24, 1857.

Upon hearing the news, worried customers began withdrawing their money from banks, which forced the banks to call in loans, causing many businesses to go bankrupt. By the fall, newspapers across the North highlighted the "hard times" that had befallen the nation. Jobless men roamed city streets demanding work or food or money. Federal troops had to be sent to disperse angry mobs in New York City.

Planters in the South, whose agricultural economy suffered the least during the panic, took great delight in the problems plaguing the northern economy. Senator James Henry Hammond of South Carolina gave a speech in early 1858 in which he told northern businessmen

> Your slaves are white, of your own race; you are brothers of one blood. They are your equals in natural endowment of intellect, and they feel galled by your degradation. Our slaves do not vote. We give them no political power. Yours do vote, and being the majority, they are the depositories of all your political power.

Hammond suggested that the North adopt race-based slavery to prevent working-class whites from taking control of the social and political order. "Cotton is king," he triumphantly roared, and race-based slavery made it so.

Dred Scott The Supreme Court's refusal to give Scott and his family their freedom fanned the flames of the intense debate over slavery.

THE *DRED SCOTT* CASE On March 6, 1857, two days after Buchanan's inauguration, the Supreme Court delivered a decision in the long-pending case of ***Dred Scott v. Sandford***. Scott, born a slave in Virginia, had been taken to St. Louis in 1830 and sold to an army surgeon, who took him to Illinois, then to the Wisconsin Territory (later Minnesota), and finally back to St. Louis in 1842. While in the Wisconsin Territory, Scott had married Harriet Robinson, and they eventually had two daughters.

In 1846, Scott filed suit in Missouri, claiming that his residence in Illinois and the Wisconsin Territory had made him free because slavery was outlawed in those areas. A jury decided in his favor, but the state supreme court ruled against him. When the case was appealed to the U.S. Supreme Court, the nation anxiously awaited its opinion on whether freedom once granted could be lost by returning to a slave state.

Seven of the nine justices were Democrats, and five were southerners. The vote was 7 to 2 against Scott. Seventy-nine-year-old Chief Justice Roger B. Taney of Maryland, a supporter of the South and of slavery, wrote the majority opinion. The chief justice ruled that Scott lacked legal standing because, like all former slaves, he was not a U.S. citizen. At the time the Constitution was adopted, Taney claimed, blacks "had for more than a century been regarded as . . . so far inferior, that they had no rights which the white man was bound to respect." On the issue of Scott's residency, Taney argued that the now-defunct Missouri Compromise of 1820 had deprived citizens of property by prohibiting slavery in selected states, an action "not warranted by the Constitution."

In the *Dred Scott* decision, the Supreme Court had declared an act of Congress (the Missouri Compromise) unconstitutional for the first time since *Marbury v. Madison* (1803). Even more important, the decision now challenged the concept of popular sovereignty. If Congress itself could not exclude slavery from a territory, as Taney argued, then neither could a territorial government created by an act of Congress.

Yet instead of settling the issue of slavery in the territories, Taney's ruling fanned the flames. Pro-slavery advocates loved the Court's decision. Even President Buchanan approved. Republicans, on the other hand, protested the *Dred Scott* decision because it nullified their anti-slavery program.

THE LECOMPTON CONSTITUTION Meanwhile, in the Kansas Territory, the furious fight over slavery continued, with both sides resorting to voting trickery and violence. Just before James Buchanan's inauguration, in early 1857, the pro-slavery territorial legislature scheduled a constitutional convention. The governor vetoed the measure, but the legislature overrode his veto. The governor resigned in protest, and Buchanan replaced him with Robert J. Walker.

With Buchanan's approval, Governor Walker pledged to free-state Kansans (who made up an overwhelming majority of the residents) that the new constitution would be submitted to a fair vote. But when the pro-slavery constitutional convention, meeting at Lecompton, drafted a constitution under which Kansas would become a slave state, opponents of slavery boycotted the vote on the new constitution.

At that point, Buchanan took a critical step. Influenced by southern advisers and politically dependent upon southern congressmen, he endorsed the pro-slavery Lecompton convention. A new wave of outrage swept across the northern states. Stephen A. Douglas, the most prominent Midwestern Democrat, sided with anti-slavery Republicans because the majority of Kansas voters had been denied the right to decide the issue. Douglas told a newspaper reporter that "I made Mr. James Buchanan, and by God, sir, I will unmake him."

The rigged election in Kansas went as predicted: 6,226 for the constitution with slavery, 569 for the constitution without slavery. Meanwhile, a new acting governor had organized the anti-slavery legislature, which scheduled another election to decide the fate of the Lecompton Constitution. Most of the pro-slavery settlers boycotted this election.

The result, on January 4, 1858, was decisive: 10,226 voted against the Lecompton Constitution, while only 138 voted for it. In April 1858, Congress ordered that Kansans vote again. On August 2, 1858, they rejected the constitution, 11,300 to 1,788. With that vote, Kansas cleared the way for its eventual admission as a free state.

DOUGLAS VERSUS LINCOLN The controversy over slavery in Kansas fractured the Democratic party. Stephen A. Douglas, one of the few remaining Democrats with support in both the North and the South, struggled to keep the party together. But first he had to secure his home base in Illinois, where in 1858 he faced reelection to the Senate.

To challenge Douglas, Illinois Republicans selected a respected lawyer from Springfield, Abraham Lincoln. Lincoln had served in the Illinois legislature and in 1846 had won a seat in the U.S. Congress. After a single unremarkable term, he returned to Springfield. In 1854, however, the Kansas-Nebraska Act drew Lincoln back into the political arena. Lincoln hated slavery but was no abolitionist. He did not believe that the nation should force the South to end "the monstrous injustice" but did insist that slavery not be expanded into new western territories.

In 1856, Lincoln joined the Republican party, and two years later he emerged as the obvious choice to oppose Douglas. Lincoln sought to raise his profile by challenging Douglas to a series of debates across the state. The seven **Lincoln-Douglas debates** took place from August 21 to October 15, 1858. They attracted tens of thousands of spectators and transformed the Illinois Senate race into a battle for the very future of the republic.

The two men differed as much physically as they did politically. Lincoln was six feet four, sinewy and craggy-featured, with a long neck, big ears, and deep-set, brooding gray eyes. Unassuming in manner and attire, he lightened his demeanor with a refreshing sense of humor. To sympathetic observers, he conveyed an air of simplicity, sincerity, and common sense.

Abraham Lincoln and Stephen A. Douglas—Debate at Charleston, Illinois,
September 18, 1858 This mural by Midwestern impressionist Robert Marshall Root,
painted to commemorate the sixtieth anniversary of the debates, can still be seen
hanging in the Governor's Office in Springfield, Illinois.

The short, stocky Douglas, on the other hand, was quite the dandy and
wore only the finest custom-tailored suits. A man of considerable abilities and
even greater ambition, he strutted with the pugnacious air of a predestined
champion. Douglas traveled to the debate sites in a private railroad car; Lincoln rode alone on his horse.

The basic dispute between the two candidates, Lincoln insisted, lay in Douglas's indifference to the immorality of slavery. Douglas, he said, was preoccupied only with process ("popular sovereignty"); in contrast, Lincoln claimed to
be focused on principle. "I have always hated slavery as much as any abolitionist," he stressed. The American government, he predicted, could not "endure,
permanently half *slave* and half *free*. . . . It will become *all* one thing, or *all* the
other." Douglas disagreed, asking what was to keep the United States from tolerating both slavery for blacks and freedom for whites? Douglas won the close
election, but Lincoln's energetic underdog campaign made him a national figure. And across the northern states, the Republicans won so many congressional seats in 1858 that they seized control of the House of Representatives.

AN OUTNUMBERED SOUTH By the late 1850s, national politics
was undergoing profound changes. In May 1858, the free state of Minnesota entered the Union; in February 1859, another non-slave territory, Oregon, gained statehood. The slave states of the South were quickly becoming a
besieged minority, and their insecurity, even paranoia, deepened.

At the same time, political tensions over slavery were becoming more violent. In 1858, members of Congress engaged in the largest brawl ever staged on the floor of the House of Representatives. Harsh words about slavery incited the free-for-all, which involved more than fifty legislators shoving, punching, and wrestling one another. The fracas ended when John "Bowie Knife" Potter of Wisconsin yanked off the wig of a Mississippi congressman and claimed, "I've scalped him."

Like the scuffling congressmen, more and more Americans began to feel that compromise was impossible: slavery could be ended or defended only with violence. The editor of a pro-slavery Kansas newspaper wanted to kill abolitionists: "If I can't kill a man, I'll kill a woman; and if I can't kill a woman, I'll kill a child." Some southerners were already talking of secession again. In 1858, former Alabama congressman William L. Yancey, the leader of a group of hot-tempered southern secessionists called "fire-eaters," said that it would be easy "to precipitate the Cotton States into a revolution."

JOHN BROWN'S RAID The gradual return of prosperity in 1859 offered hope that the sectional storms of the 1850s might pass, but the slavery issue continued to simmer. In October 1859, the militant abolitionist John Brown surfaced again, this time in the East. Since the Pottawatomie Massacre in Kansas in 1856, he had kept a low profile while acquiring money and weapons from New England sympathizers. His heartfelt commitment to abolishing slavery and promoting racial equality had intensified because he saw slavery becoming more deeply entrenched, cemented by law, economics, and religious sanction.

Brown was convinced that he was carrying out a divine mission on behalf of a vengeful God. He struck fear into supporters and opponents alike, for he was a moral absolutist who disdained compromise. As one of the few whites willing to live among black people and die for them, he was a brilliant propagandist for the abolitionist cause.

In 1859, Brown hatched a plan to steal federal weapons and give them to rebellious slaves in western Virginia and Maryland, in the hope of triggering mass uprisings across the South. "I want to free all the negroes in this state," Brown said. "If the citizens interfere with me, I must burn the town and have blood."

When Brown asked Frederick Douglass to join the effort, the nation's leading black abolitionist declined, saying the suicidal plan "would array the whole country against us." He warned Brown that he was "going into a perfect steel trap" and would never get out alive. Brown, the fiery crusader, replied that something "startling" must be done to awaken the nation to the evil of slavery. He decided to proceed without Douglass.

On the cool, rainy night of October 16, 1859, Brown left a Maryland farm and crossed the Potomac River with about twenty men, including three of his sons and five African Americans. Under cover of darkness, they walked five miles to the federal rifle arsenal in Harpers Ferry, Virginia (now West Virginia). Brown and his righteous soldiers took the sleeping town by surprise, cut the telegraph lines, and occupied the arsenal with its 100,000 rifles. He then dispatched several men to kidnap prominent slave owners and sound the alarm for local slaves to rise up and join the rebellion.

Only a few slaves heeded the call, however, and by dawn, armed townsmen had surrounded the raiders. Brown and a dozen of his men, along with eleven white hostages (including George Washington's great-grandnephew) and two of their slaves, holed up for thirty-two hours in a firehouse. Meanwhile, hundreds of armed whites poured into Harpers Ferry. Lieutenant Colonel Robert E. Lee also arrived with a force of U.S. Marines.

On the morning of October 18, a marine officer ordered the abolitionists to surrender. Brown replied that he preferred to die fighting, warning that he "would sell his life as dearly as possible." Twelve marines then broke open the barricaded doors and rushed in. Lieutenant Israel Green reported that he found himself face to face with "an old man kneeling with a carbine in his hand, with a long gray beard falling away from his face." Green would have killed Brown had his sword not bent back double when he plunged it into the abolitionist's chest. He then beat Brown until he passed out.

Brown's men had killed four townspeople and one marine while wounding another dozen. Of their own force, ten were killed (including two of Brown's sons) and five were captured; another five escaped.

A week later, Brown and his accomplices were tried and convicted of treason, murder, and "conspiring with Negroes to produce insurrection." At his sentencing, Brown delivered an eloquent speech in which he expressed pride in his effort to "mingle my blood further with the blood of my children

John Brown On his way to the gallows, Brown predicted that slavery would end only "after much bloodshed."

and with the blood of millions in this slave country whose rights are disregarded by wicked, cruel, and unjust enactments."

For four weeks, as Brown waited to be hanged, he met with newspaper reporters and wrote a host of letters, many of which were printed in antislavery newspapers. Henry Wise, governor of Virginia, visited Brown in jail and reported that he was a man "of courage, fortitude, and simple ingeniousness. He is cool, collected, and indomitable."

On December 2, 1859, some 1,500 Virginia militiamen, including a young actor named John Wilkes Booth, who would later assassinate Abraham Lincoln, assembled for Brown's execution. Just before being placed atop his coffin in a wagon to take him to the scaffold, Brown wrote a final message, predicting that the "crimes of this *guilty* land will never be purged away, but with Blood." Although John Brown's Raid on Harpers Ferry failed to ignite a massive slave rebellion, it achieved two things: he became a martyr for the abolitionist cause, and he set off a hysterical panic throughout the slaveholding South.

The pacifist abolitionist William Lloyd Garrison called Brown, the man with the burning eyes, "misguided, wild, and apparently insane." Others were not so sure. "John Brown may be a lunatic," said a Boston newspaper, but if so, "one-fourth of the people of Massachusetts are madmen." The transcendentalist leader Ralph Waldo Emerson called Brown a "saint" who had made "the gallows glorious like a cross." Frederick Douglass proclaimed Brown "our noblest American hero" whose commitment to ending slavery "was far greater than mine."

Caught up in a frenzy of fear, southerners circulated wild rumors about slave rebellions. They "have declared war on us," warned a Mississippi legislator. Southern congressmen brought weapons to the Capitol. One of them reported that the only ones "who do not have a revolver and a knife are those who have two revolvers."

John Brown's raid convinced southern states to strengthen their militia units and pass new restrictions on the movements of slaves. "We regard every man in our midst an enemy to the institutions of the South," said the *Atlanta Confederacy*, "who does not boldly declare that he believes African slavery to be a social, moral, and political blessing." Other newspapers claimed that Brown's raid had dramatically increased support for secession in the South. The *Richmond Whig* reported that thousands of Virginians had decided that the Union's "days are numbered, its glory perished" as a result of John Brown's actions.

THE DEMOCRATS DIVIDE President Buchanan had chosen not to seek a second term, leaving Stephen A. Douglas as the frontrunner for the nomination. His northern supporters tried to straddle the slavery issue by promising to defend the institution in the South while assuring northerners that slavery would not spread to new states. Southern firebrands, however, demanded federal protection for slavery in the territories as well as the states. When the pro-slavery advocates lost, delegates from eight southern states walked out of the convention in Charleston, South Carolina.

The delegates then decided to leave Charleston. Douglas's supporters reassembled in Baltimore on June 18 and nominated him for president. Southern Democrats met first in Richmond and then in Baltimore, where they adopted the pro-slavery platform defeated in Charleston and named John C. Breckinridge, vice president under Buchanan, as their candidate because he promised to ensure that Congress would protect the right of emigrants to take their slaves to

Abraham Lincoln A lanky and rawboned small-town lawyer, Lincoln won the presidential election in 1860.

the western territories. Thus another cord of union had snapped: the last remaining national party had split into northern and southern factions. The fracturing of the Democratic party made a Republican victory in 1860 almost certain.

LINCOLN'S ELECTION The Republican convention was held in May in the fast-growing city of Chicago, where everything came together for Abraham Lincoln. The uncommon common man won the nomination over New York senator William H. Seward, and the resulting cheer, wrote one journalist, was "like the rush of a great wind." The convention reaffirmed the party's opposition to the extension of slavery and, to gain broader support, endorsed a series of traditional Whig policies promoting national economic expansion: a higher protective tariff, free farms on federal lands out west, and federally financed internal improvements, including a transcontinental railroad.

The presidential nominating conventions revealed that opinions tended to be more radical in the Northeast and the Lower South. Attitude followed latitude. In the border states of Maryland, Delaware, Kentucky, and Missouri, a sense of moderation aroused former Whigs to make one more try at reconciliation. Meeting in Baltimore a week before the Republicans met in

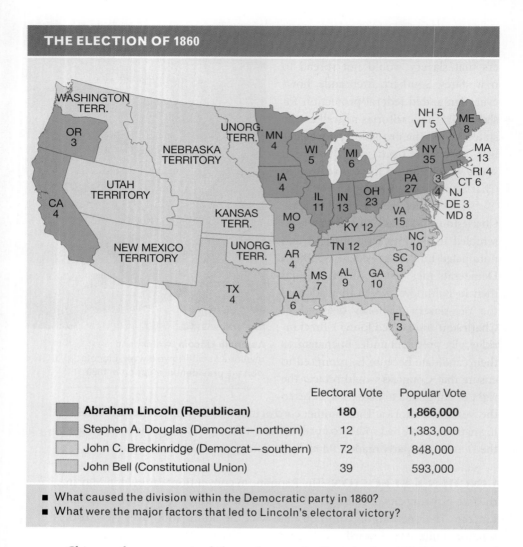

THE ELECTION OF 1860

	Electoral Vote	Popular Vote
Abraham Lincoln (Republican)	180	1,866,000
Stephen A. Douglas (Democrat—northern)	12	1,383,000
John C. Breckinridge (Democrat—southern)	72	848,000
John Bell (Constitutional Union)	39	593,000

■ What caused the division within the Democratic party in 1860?
■ What were the major factors that led to Lincoln's electoral victory?

Chicago, they reorganized themselves as the Constitutional Union party and nominated John Bell of Tennessee for president. Their platform centered on a vague statement promoting "the Constitution of the Country, the Union of the States, and the Enforcement of the Laws."

The bitterly contested campaign became a choice between Lincoln and Douglas in the North (Lincoln was not even on the ballot in the South), and Breckinridge and Bell in the South. Douglas, the only candidate to mount a nationwide campaign, promised that he would "make war boldly against Northern abolitionists and Southern disunionists." But his heroic effort did no good.

By midnight on November 6, Lincoln's victory was announced. He had won 39 percent of the popular vote, the smallest plurality ever, but garnered a clear majority (180 votes) in the electoral college. He carried all eighteen free states but none of the slave states.

Lincoln, a man of remarkable humility and empathy, agreed with the many journalists and politicians who said his election was a fluke. His political experience was meager, his learning limited, and his popular support shallow. "Never did a President enter upon office with less means at his command," the poet and Harvard professor James Russell Lowell remarked. Yet the unassuming prairie lawyer from Springfield, Illinois would emerge the acknowledged leader of his distinguished cabinet, earning the respect of colleagues and opponents who had originally scorned him, and becoming in the process, as the poet Walt Whitman wrote, "the grandest figure yet, on all the crowded canvas of the Nineteenth Century."

THE RESPONSE IN THE SOUTH

Between November 8, 1860, when Lincoln was officially named president-elect, and March 4, 1861, when he was inaugurated, the United States of America disintegrated. The election of Lincoln, an anti-slavery Midwesterner, panicked southerners who believed that the Republican party, as a Richmond, Virginia, newspaper asserted, was founded for one reason: "hatred of African slavery." Former president John Tyler wrote that with Lincoln's election the nation "had fallen on evil times" and that the "day of doom for the great model Republic is at hand."

False rumors that Lincoln planned to free the slaves raced across the South. One newspaper editorial called the president-elect a "bigoted, unscrupulous, and cold-blooded enemy of peace and equality of the slaveholding states." Lincoln responded that southern fears were misguided. He stressed in a letter to a Georgia congressman that he was not a radical abolitionist and his administration would not interfere with slavery, either "*directly or indirectly*." Lincoln, however, refused to provide such assurances in public, in part because he misread the depth of southern anger and concern over his election.

SOUTH CAROLINA SECEDES Pro-slavery fire-eaters in South Carolina viewed Lincoln's election as the final signal to abandon the Union. After Lincoln's victory, the state's entire congressional delegation resigned and left Washington, D.C. The state legislature then appointed a convention to decide whether it should remain in the Union.

South Carolina had a higher percentage of slaves in its population (60 percent) than any other state, and its political leadership was dominated by slave-owning hotheads. It had been a one-party state (Democratic) for decades,

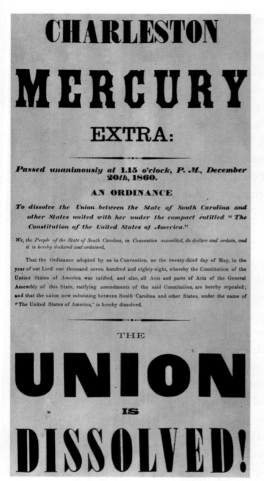

CHARLESTON

MERCURY

EXTRA:

Passed unanimously at 1.15 o'clock, P. M., December 20th, 1860.

AN ORDINANCE

To dissolve the Union between the State of South Carolina and other States united with her under the compact entitled " The Constitution of the United States of America."

We, the People of the State of South Carolina, in Convention assembled, do declare and ordain, and it is hereby declared and ordained,

That the Ordinance adopted by us in Convention, on the twenty-third day of May, in the year of our Lord one thousand seven hundred and eighty-eight, whereby the Constitution of the United States of America was ratified, and also, all Acts and parts of Acts of the General Assembly of this State, ratifying amendments of the said Constitution, are hereby repealed; and that the union now subsisting between South Carolina and other States, under the name of "The United States of America," is hereby dissolved.

THE

UNION

IS

DISSOLVED!

"The Union Is Dissolved!" An 1860 newspaper headline announcing South Carolina's secession from the Union.

and it was the only state that did not allow its citizens to vote in presidential elections; the legislature, controlled by white planters, did the balloting.

Meeting in Charleston on December 20, 1860, the special convention unanimously voted to secede from the Union. David Jamison Rutledge, who presided over the convention, announced that "the Ordinance of Secession has been signed and ratified, and I proclaim the State of South Carolina an Independent Commonwealth." (Rutledge would have four sons killed in the Civil War and see his house burned to the ground.) James L. Petigru, one of the few Unionists in Charleston, quipped that his newly independent state was "too small to be a Republic and too large to be an insane asylum."

As the news of South Carolina's secession spread through Charleston, church bells rang, and shops closed. Cadets at the Citadel, the state military college, fired artillery salutes, new flags were unfurled, and volunteers donned militia uniforms. "THE UNION IS DISSOLVED!" screamed the *Charleston Mercury*. One Unionist in Charleston kept a copy of the newspaper, scribbling on the bottom of it: "You'll regret the day you ever done this. I preserve this to see how it ends."

PRESIDENT BUCHANAN BALKS The nation needed a decisive president, but James Buchanan was not up to the task. The president blamed the crisis on fanatical northern abolitionists, then declared that secession was illegal, only to claim that he lacked the constitutional authority to force a state to rejoin the Union. In the face of Buchanan's inaction, all the southerners in his cabinet resigned, and secessionists seized federal property, arsenals, and forts in the southern states.

Among those federal facilities was Fort Sumter, nestled on a tiny island at the mouth of Charleston Harbor. When South Carolina secessionists demanded that Major Robert Anderson, a Kentucky Unionist, surrender the under-manned fort, he refused, vowing to hold on at all costs. On January 5, 1861, Buchanan sent an unarmed ship, the *Star of the West*, to resupply Fort Sumter.

As the ship approached Charleston Harbor on January 9, Confederate cannons opened fire and drove it away. It was an act of war, but Buchanan chose to ignore the challenge and try to ride out the remaining weeks of his term, hoping against hope that a compromise would be reached to avoid war. Many southerners, however, were not in a compromising mood. The crisis, said a southern senator, could only be defused when "northern people" agreed "to review and reverse their whole policy upon the subject of slavery."

SECESSION OF THE LOWER SOUTH By February 1, 1861, the states of the Lower South—South Carolina, Mississippi, Florida, Alabama, Georgia, Louisiana, and Texas—had seceded. Although the states' secession ordinances mentioned various grievances against the federal government, including tariffs on imports, they made clear that the primary reason for leaving the Union was the preservation of slavery.

Texas's ordinance, stoutly opposed by Governor Sam Houston, explained that the purpose of secession and the formation of the Confederacy was to "*secure the rights of the slave-holding States in their domestic institutions.*" The Texas convention displayed the paternalistic racism at work in secession, calling Africans "an inferior and dependent race" for whom slavery was actually "beneficial." An Alabama secessionist explained that the people in his state "are calmly and fully determined never to submit to Lincoln's administration, or to any Compromise with the Northern States."

On February 4, 1861, fifty representatives of the seceding states, all but one of whom were slave owners, twenty-one of them wealthy planters, met in Montgomery, Alabama, where they adopted a constitution for the Confederate States of America. The Confederate Constitution mandated that "the institution of negro slavery, as it now exists in the Confederate States, shall be recognized and protected."

Mississippi's Jefferson Davis, a Kentucky-born West Point graduate who had served in the House of Representatives and the Senate, was elected president, with Alexander H. Stephens of Georgia as vice president. The tiny, sickly Stephens, weighing no more than ninety pounds, left no doubt about why the Confederacy was formed. "Our new government," he declared, "is founded upon . . . the great truth that the negro is not equal to the white man; that slavery, subordination to the superior [white] race, is his natural and normal condition."

In mid-February, Davis traveled from Mississippi to Montgomery, Alabama, the Confederate capital, for his installation. On February 18, William Yancey, an Alabama fire-eater, introduced Davis to the crowd by announcing that the "man and the hour have met." In his remarks, Davis ominously claimed that "the time for compromise is now passed."

FINAL EFFORTS AT COMPROMISE Members of Congress, however, desperately sought a compromise to avoid a civil war. On December 18, 1860, John J. Crittenden of Kentucky offered a series of resolutions that would allow the extension of slavery into the new western territories *south* of the Missouri Compromise line (36°30′ parallel) and guaranteed the preservation of slavery where it already existed. Lincoln, however, opposed any plan that would expand slavery westward, and the Senate defeated the Crittenden Compromise, 25 to 23.

Several weeks later, in February 1861, twenty-one states sent delegates to a peace conference in Washington, D.C. Former president John Tyler presided, but the peace convention's proposal, substantially the same as the Crittenden Compromise, had little support in either house of Congress. (Tyler himself voted against it and urged Virginia to secede at once.) The only proposal that generated much interest was a constitutional amendment guaranteeing slavery where it existed. Many Republicans, including Lincoln, were prepared to go that far to save the Union, but no further.

As it happened, after passing the House, the slavery amendment passed the Senate 24 to 12 on the morning of March 4, 1861, Lincoln's inauguration day. It would have become the Thirteenth Amendment, and would have been the first time the word *slavery* had appeared in the Constitution, but the states never ratified it. When a Thirteenth Amendment was eventually ratified, in 1865, it did not protect slavery—it ended it.

LINCOLN'S INAUGURATION In mid-February 1861, Abraham Lincoln boarded a train in Springfield, Illinois, headed to Washington, D.C., for his inauguration. Along the way, he told the New Jersey legislature that he was "devoted to peace" but warned that "it may be necessary to put the foot down."

In his inaugural address on March 4, the fifty-two-year-old Lincoln repeated his pledge not "to interfere with the institution of slavery in the states where it exists." But the immediate question facing the nation had shifted from slavery to secession. Lincoln insisted that "the Union of these States is perpetual." No state, he stressed, "can lawfully get out of the Union." He pledged to defend "federal forts in the South," but beyond that "there will be no invasion, no using of force against or among the people anywhere." In closing, he appealed for the Union:

> We are not enemies, but friends. We must not be enemies. Though passion may have strained, it must not break our bonds of affection. The mystic chords of memory, stretching from every battlefield and patriot grave to every living heart and hearthstone all over this broad land, will yet swell the chorus of the Union, when again touched, as surely they will be, by the better angels of our nature.

Southerners were not impressed. A North Carolina newspaper warned that Lincoln's speech made civil war "inevitable." On both sides, however, people assumed that any warfare would be over quickly and that their lives would then go on as usual.

THE END OF THE WAITING GAME On March 5, 1861, his first day in office, President Lincoln found on his desk a letter from Major Anderson at Fort Sumter. Time was running out for the Union soldiers. Anderson reported that his men had enough food for only a few weeks, and that the Confederates were encircling the fort with a "ring of fire." It would take thousands of federal soldiers to rescue them.

On April 4, 1861, Lincoln ordered that unarmed ships take food and supplies to the sixty-nine soldiers at Fort Sumter. Jefferson Davis was equally determined to stop any effort to supply the fort, even if it meant using military force. The secretary of state for the new Confederacy, Richard Lathers, warned Davis that if the South fired first, it would unify northern opinion against the secessionists: "There will be no compromise with Secession if war is forced upon the north." Davis ignored the warning.

On April 11, Confederate general Pierre G. T. Beauregard, who had studied under Robert Anderson at West Point, urged his former professor to surrender Fort Sumter and sent him cases of whiskey and boxes of cigars to help convince him. Anderson refused the gifts and the request. At 4:30 A.M. on April 12, Confederate cannons began firing on Fort Sumter. The bright flashes and thundering boom of guns awakened the entire city; thousands rushed to the Battery to watch the incessant shelling. Finally, the outgunned Major Anderson, his ammunition and food gone, lowered the "stars and stripes." A civil war of unimagined horrors had begun.

CHAPTER REVIEW

SUMMARY

- **Slavery in the Territories**   Representative David *Wilmot's Proviso*, although it never became law, declared that since Mexican territories acquired by the United States had been free, they should remain so. Like the Wilmot Proviso, the new *Free-Soil party* demanded that slavery not be expanded in the territories. But it was the discovery of gold in California and the ensuing *California gold rush* of 1849 that escalated tensions. Californians wanted to enter the Union as a free state. Southerners feared that they would lose federal protection of their "peculiar institution" if there were more free states than slave states. It had been agreed that *popular sovereignty* would settle the status of the territories, but when the territories applied for statehood, the debate over slavery was renewed. Through the wildly celebrated *Compromise of 1850*, California entered the Union as a free state; the territories of Texas, New Mexico, and Utah were established without direct reference to slavery; the slave trade (but not slavery) was banned in Washington, D.C.; and a new *Fugitive Slave Act* was passed. Tensions turned violent with the passage of the *Kansas-Nebraska Act*, which overturned the Missouri Compromise by allowing slavery in the territories where the institution had been banned by Congress in 1821.

- **The Republican Party's Appeal**   The efforts of pro-slavery advocates in Kansas to force slavery on the territory enraged northern opinion, even though anti-slavery settlers such as John Brown were equally violent in the events known as *Bleeding Kansas*. The Supreme Court's *Dred Scott v. Sandford* decision, which ruled that Congress could not interfere with slavery in the territories, further fueled sectional conflict. Northern voters gravitated toward the Republican party as events unfolded. Republicans also advocated raising protective tariffs and funding the development of the nation's infrastructure, which appealed to northern manufacturers and commercial farmers. Abraham Lincoln's narrow failure to unseat Democrat Stephen A. Douglas in the 1858 Illinois Senate election, which included the famous *Lincoln-Douglas debates*, revealed the Republican party's growing appeal. In 1860, Lincoln carried every free state and won a clear electoral college victory.

- **The Secession of the Lower South and Civil War**   Following Lincoln's election, South Carolina seceded. Six other Lower South states quickly followed. Together they formed the Confederate States of America, citing their belief that secession was necessary for the preservation of slavery. In his inaugural address, Lincoln made it clear that secession was unconstitutional but that the North would not invade the South. However, the Confederate states stood by their declarations of secession, and war came when South Carolinians fired on the "stars and stripes" at Fort Sumter.

CHRONOLOGY

1848	Free-Soil party is organized
1849	California gold rush begins
1854	Congress passes the Kansas-Nebraska Act
	The Republican party is founded
1856	A pro-slavery mob sacks Lawrence, Kansas; John Brown stages the Pottawatomie Massacre in retaliation
	Charles Sumner of Massachusetts is caned and seriously injured by a pro-slavery congressman in the U.S. Senate
1857	U.S. Supreme Court issues the *Dred Scott* decision
	Lecompton Constitution declares that slavery will be allowed in Kansas
1858	Abraham Lincoln debates Stephen A. Douglas during the 1858 Illinois Senate race
1859	John Brown and his followers stage a failed raid at Harpers Ferry, Virginia, in an attempt to incite a slave insurrection
1860–1861	South Carolina and six other southern states secede from the Union
	Crittenden Compromise is proposed but fails
March 4, 1861	Abraham Lincoln is inaugurated president
April 1861	Fort Sumter falls to Confederate forces, triggers Civil War

KEY TERMS

Wilmot Proviso (1846) p. 600

popular sovereignty p. 601

Free-Soil party p. 601

California gold rush (1849) p. 602

Compromise of 1850 p. 605

Fugitive Slave Act (1850) p. 611

Kansas-Nebraska Act (1854) p. 614

Bleeding Kansas (1856) p. 616

Dred Scott v. Sandford (1857) p. 622

Lincoln-Douglas debates (1858) p. 624

 **InQUIZITIVE**

Go to InQuizitive to see what you've learned—and learn what you've missed—with personalized feedback along the way.

15 The War of the Union

1861–1865

***Lincoln's Drive through Richmond* (1866)** Shortly after the Confederate capital of Richmond, Virginia, fell to Union forces in April 1865, President Abraham Lincoln visited the war-torn city. His carriage was swarmed by enslaved blacks who were freed by the war, as well as whites whose loyalties were with the Union.

The fall of Fort Sumter started the war of the Union and triggered a wave of patriotic bluster on both sides. A southern woman prayed that God would "give us strength to conquer them, to exterminate *them*, to lay waste every Northern city, town and village, to destroy them utterly." By contrast, the writer Nathaniel Hawthorne reported from Massachusetts that his transcendentalist friend Ralph Waldo Emerson was "breathing slaughter" as the Union army prepared for its first battle. The pacifist Emerson now said that "sometimes gunpowder smells good."

Many southerners, then and since, argued that the Civil War was not about slavery but about the South's effort to defend states' rights. Confederate president Jefferson Davis, for example, owner of a huge Mississippi plantation with 113 slaves, claimed that the war was fought on behalf of the South's right to secede from the Union and its need to defend itself against a "tyrannical majority," meaning those who had elected President Abraham Lincoln, the anti-slavery Republican.

For his part, Lincoln stressed repeatedly that the "paramount object in this struggle *is* to save the Union, and is *not* either to save or to destroy slavery. If I could save the Union without freeing *any* slave I would do it, and if I could save it by freeing *all* the slaves I would do it; and if I could save it by freeing some and leaving others alone I would also do that." If the southern states returned to the Union, he promised, they could retain their slaves. None of the Confederate states accepted Lincoln's offer, in large part because most white southerners were convinced that the new president was lying. The "Black Republican," as they called the president, was determined to end slavery, no matter what he said.

focus questions

1. What were the respective advantages of the North and South as the Civil War began? How did those advantages affect the military strategies of the Union and the Confederacy?

2. Why did Lincoln decide to issue the Emancipation Proclamation? How did it impact the war?

3. In what ways did the war affect social and economic life in the North and South?

4. What were the military turning points in 1863 and 1864 that ultimately led to the Confederacy's defeat?

5. How did the Civil War change the nation?

However much Jefferson Davis and other southerners argued that secession and the war were about states' rights, the states of the Lower South seceded in 1860–1861 to protect slavery. The evidence is overwhelming. The South Carolina Declaration on the Immediate Causes of Secession, for example, was quite clear on the reasons for secession, highlighting the "increasing hostility on the part of the non-slaveholding states to the institution of slavery." Mississippi only mentioned one reason for seceding: preserving slavery. Georgian Alexander Stephens, the vice president of the Confederate States of America, was equally emphatic, saying that slavery was the "immediate cause" of secession and war. And, as Lincoln noted in his second inaugural address, everyone knew that slavery "was somehow the cause of the war."

Certainly that was true for Nathan Bedford Forrest, a Tennessee slave trader and wealthy planter who would become one of the Confederacy's most valued and controversial cavalry generals. Years after the war, he exploded while listening to Confederate veterans giving flowery orations in which they claimed that the South had fought the Civil War to defend states' rights. The plain-speaking Forrest stood and shouted that he fought for one reason: "to keep his niggers, and other folks' niggers."

On April 15, three days after the Confederate attack on Fort Sumter, Lincoln called upon the "loyal" states to supply 75,000 soldiers to suppress the rebellion. Senator Stephen Douglas insisted that "there are only two sides to the question [of civil war]. Every man must be for the United States or against it. There can be no neutrals in this war, only patriots—or traitors."

The Civil War would force everyone—men and women, white and black, immigrants and Native Americans, free and enslaved—to choose sides. Thousands of southerners fought for the Union; thousands of northerners fought for the Confederacy. Thousands of European volunteers fought on each side.

Choosing Sides

The first seven states to secede were all from the Lower South—South Carolina, Mississippi, Florida, Alabama, Georgia, Louisiana, and Texas—where the cotton economy was strongest and slaves the most numerous. All the states in the Upper South, especially Tennessee and Virginia, had areas (mainly in the mountains) where whites were poor, slaves were scarce, and Union support was strong. Nevertheless, the outbreak of actual fighting led four more southern slave states to join the Confederacy: Virginia, Arkansas, Tennessee, and North Carolina.

In east Tennessee, however, the mountain counties would provide more Union soldiers than Confederate fighters. Thirty-nine counties in mountainous western Virginia were so loyal to the Union that they split off and formed the new state of West Virginia in October 1861.

Of the slaveholding states along the border between North and South, Delaware remained firmly in the Union, but Maryland, Kentucky, and Missouri went through bitter struggles to decide which side to support. "I think to lose Kentucky is nearly the same as to lose the whole game," Lincoln said to a friend, explaining the situation in the state where he was born. If Kentucky were to join the Confederacy, "we cannot hold Missouri, nor, as I think, Maryland." Lincoln hoped "to have God on my side, but I must have Kentucky." The president was so determined to keep slaveholding Kentucky on the Union side that he muffled all talk of abolition.

If Maryland had seceded, Confederates would have surrounded Washington, D.C. To keep Maryland in the Union, Lincoln had pro-Confederate

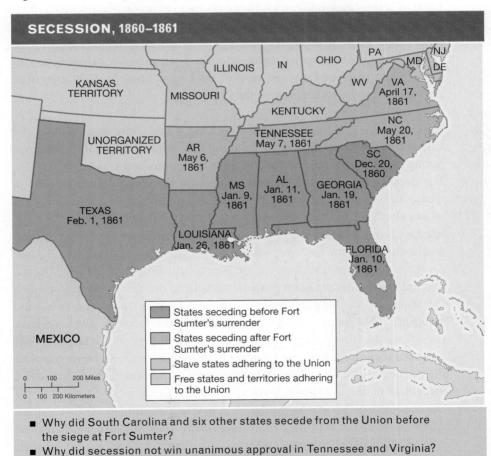

SECESSION, 1860–1861

PA
NJ
ILLINOIS   IN   OHIO   MD   DE
KANSAS
TERRITORY   MISSOURI   WV   VA April 17, 1861
KENTUCKY
NC May 20, 1861
UNORGANIZED
TERRITORY   AR May 6, 1861   TENNESSEE May 7, 1861   SC Dec. 20, 1860
MS Jan. 9, 1861   AL Jan. 11, 1861   GEORGIA Jan. 19, 1861
TEXAS
Feb. 1, 1861
LOUISIANA Jan. 26, 1861
FLORIDA Jan. 10, 1861
MEXICO

☐ States seceding before Fort Sumter's surrender
☐ States seceding after Fort Sumter's surrender
☐ Slave states adhering to the Union
☐ Free states and territories adhering to the Union

0   100   200 Miles
0   100   200 Kilometers

■ Why did South Carolina and six other states secede from the Union before the siege at Fort Sumter?
■ Why did secession not win unanimous approval in Tennessee and Virginia?
■ How did Lincoln keep Maryland in the Union?

leaders arrested, including Baltimore's mayor and chief of police. The fragile neutrality of Kentucky lasted until September 3, when Confederate and Union armies moved into the divided state. Kentucky voters elected a secessionist governor and a Unionist majority in the state legislature, as did Missouri, a state with many European immigrants, especially Germans.

When a pro-Confederate militia gathered in St. Louis, hoping to take control of the federal arsenal, it was surprised and disarmed by German immigrants "eager to teach the German-haters a never-to-be-forgotten lesson." The German militiamen then chased the pro-Confederate governor across the border to Arkansas. When news of the Civil War reached Missouri, 4,200 men volunteered to join the Union army; all but 100 of them were German Americans.

On the eve of the Civil War, the U.S. Army had only 16,400 men, about 1,000 of whom were officers. Of them, about 25 percent, like future Confederate general Robert E. Lee, resigned to join the Confederate army. On the other hand, many southerners made great sacrifices to remain loyal to the Union. Some left their native region once the fighting began; others remained in the South but found ways to support the Union. Some 100,000 men from the southern states fought *against* the Confederacy.

REGIONAL ADVANTAGES   Once battle lines were finally drawn, the Union held twenty-three states, including four border slave states, Missouri, Kentucky, Maryland, and Delaware, while the Confederacy had eleven states. The population count was about 22 million in the Union (some 400,000 of whom were enslaved African Americans) to 9 million in the Confederacy (of whom about 3.5 million were enslaved). To help balance the odds, the Confederacy mobilized 80 percent of its military-age white men, a third of whom would die during the four-year war.

An even greater advantage for the North was its superior industrial development. As southerner Rhett Butler complains in the classic movie *Gone with the Wind* (1939), "Why, all we have [in the South] is cotton and slaves and arrogance." The hated Yankees, he adds, have "the factories, the foundries, the shipyards, the iron and coal mines—all the things we haven't got." The southern states produced just 7 percent of the nation's manufactured goods on the eve of the war. The Union states produced 97 percent of the firearms and 96 percent of the railroad equipment.

The North also had a huge advantage in transportation, particularly ships. At the start of the war, the Union had ninety warships; the South had no navy at all. Federal gunboats and transports played a direct role in securing the Union's control of the Mississippi River and its larger tributaries, which provided easy invasion routes into the center of the Confederacy. Early on,

The U.S. Watervliet Arsenal in Watervliet, New York The North had a huge advantage in industrial development, and its foundries turned out most of the firearms used by Union forces.

the Union navy's blockade of the major southern ports sharply reduced the amount of cotton that could be exported to Britain and France as well as the flow of goods (including military weapons) imported from Europe. In addition, the Union had more wagons and horses than the Confederacy, and an even more impressive edge in the number of railroad locomotives.

The Confederates, however, had major geographic and emotional advantages: they could fight a war on their own territory in defense of their homeland. In warfare, it is usually easier to defend than to attack, since defending troops have the opportunity to dig protective trenches and fortifications. In the Civil War, 90 percent of the time, armies that assaulted well-defended positions were mauled. Many Confederate leaders thought that if they could hold out long enough, disgruntled northern voters might convince Lincoln and Congress to end the war.

As the two sides mobilized, the Confederacy had more-experienced military leaders and better horsemen. Many Confederates also displayed a brash sense of confidence. After all, had not the Revolutionaries of 1776 defeated a much stronger British army? "Britain could not conquer three million [Americans]," a Louisianan declared, and "the world cannot conquer the South."

THE WAR'S EARLY STRATEGIES

The two sides initially had quite different goals. The Confederacy sought to convince the Union and the world to recognize its independence. The United

States, on the other hand, fought to restore the Union. The future of slavery was not yet an issue.

After the fall of Fort Sumter, neither side was ready to wage war, but excited newspaper editors and politicians on both sides pressured the generals to strike quickly. "Forward to Richmond!" screamed a New York newspaper headline. In the summer of 1861, Jefferson Davis told General Pierre G. T. Beauregard to rush the main Confederate army to Manassas Junction, a railroad crossing in northern Virginia, about twenty-five miles southwest of Washington. President Lincoln hoped that the Union army (often called *Federals*) would overrun the outnumbered Confederates (often called *Rebels*) and quickly push on to Richmond, only 107 miles to the south. "What a picnic," predicted a New York soldier, "to go down South for three months and clean up the whole business."

FIRST BULL RUN When word reached Washington, D.C., that the two armies were converging for battle, hundreds of civilians packed picnic lunches and went to watch the spectacle, assuming that the first clash of arms would be short, glorious, and bloodless. It was a hot, dry day on July 21, 1861, when 37,000 untested Union recruits breezily marched to battle, some of them breaking ranks to eat blackberries or drink water from streams along the way.

Many of them died with the berry juice still staining their lips as they engaged the Confederates dug in behind a branch of the Potomac River called

First Bull Run Moments before battle, a spectator in a top hat chats with Union soldiers (bottom right), while an artist sketches the passing troops breezily heading to war (at left).

Bull Run near the Manassas Junction railroad station. For most of the soldiers, the battle at Bull Run was their first taste of the chaos and confusion of combat. Many were disoriented by the smoke from gunpowder and saltpeter, the deafening roar of cannon fire, the screaming of fallen comrades, and the distinctive sound of bullets whizzing past. Because neither side yet wore standard-colored uniforms, the soldiers had trouble deciding friend from foe.

The Union troops almost won the battle early in the afternoon. "We fired a volley," wrote a Massachusetts private, "and saw the Rebels running. . . . The boys were saying constantly, in great glee, 'We've whipped them.' 'We'll hang Jeff Davis from a sour apple tree.' 'They're running.' 'The war is over.'"

But Confederate reinforcements poured in to tip the balance. Amid the furious fighting, a South Carolina officer rallied his troops by pointing to the courageous example of Thomas Jackson's men: "Look! There is General Jackson with his Virginians, standing like a stone wall!" Jackson ordered his men to charge the faltering Union ranks, urging them to "yell like furies!" From that day forward, "Stonewall" became Jackson's popular nickname, and he would be the most celebrated—and feared—Confederate commander.

The Union army's retreat from Bull Run turned into a panicked rout (the "great skedaddle") as fleeing soldiers and terrified civilians clogged the road to Washington, D.C. The victorious Confederates, however, were so disorganized and exhausted that they failed to give chase. As the armies moved on, they left behind a battlefield strewn with the dead and the dying—mangled men and bloated horses and mules, all scattered among discarded knapsacks, canteens, blankets, rifles, wagons, and cannons. Stonewall Jackson sent his wife a letter reporting that "we fought a great battle and gained a great victory, for which all the glory is due to God alone." His Union counterpart, General William T. Sherman, admitted that the Federals had suffered a "terrible defeat" during which many inexperienced soldiers "degenerated into an armed mob."

The news of the Confederate victory triggered sharp criticism of President Lincoln. Michigan senator Zachariah Chandler, a Republican, dismissed the president as "timid, vacillating & inefficient." An Ohio Republican was even more critical, denouncing Lincoln as "an admitted failure" who "has no will, no courage, no executive capacity."

Lincoln, however, learned from defeat. The hallmark of his presidency was his ability to acknowledge his mistakes and move forward. With each passing year, he would grow more sure of himself as a wartime leader.

The First Battle of Bull Run (or First Manassas)* was a sobering experience for both sides, each of which miscalculated the other's strength and tenacity.

---

*The Federals most often named battles for natural features; the Confederates, for nearby towns—thus Bull Run (Manassas), Antietam (Sharpsburg), Stones River (Murfreesboro), and the like.

Much of the romance of war—the colorful uniforms, bright flags, marching bands, and rousing songs—gave way to the agonizing realization that this would be a long, costly, grim struggle. *Harper's Weekly* bluntly warned: "From the fearful day at Bull Run dates war. Not polite war, not incredulous war, but war that breaks hearts and blights homes."

THE UNION'S "ANACONDA" PLAN   The Battle of Bull Run demonstrated that the war would not be decided with one sudden stroke. General Winfield Scott, the seventy-five-year-old commander of the Union war effort, devised a three-pronged strategy that called first for the Army of the Potomac, the main Union army, to defend Washington, D.C., and exert constant pressure on the Confederate capital at Richmond.

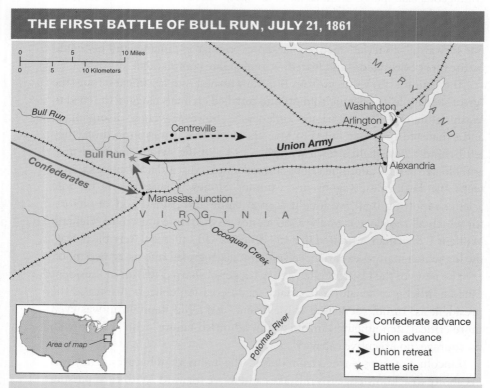

THE FIRST BATTLE OF BULL RUN, JULY 21, 1861

- Why did the Confederate and Union armies rush to battle before they were ready?
- How did General Beauregard win the First Battle of Bull Run?
- Why did the Confederates not pursue the retreating Union army?

At the same time, the Federal navy's blockade of southern ports would cut off the Confederacy's access to foreign goods and weapons. The final component of the plan called for other Union armies to divide the Confederacy by pushing south along the crucial inland water routes: the Mississippi, Tennessee, and Cumberland Rivers. This so-called **Anaconda Plan** was intended to slowly trap and crush the southern resistance, like an anaconda snake strangling its prey.

CONFEDERATE STRATEGY Confederate president Jefferson Davis was better prepared than Lincoln at the start of the war to guide military strategy. A graduate of the U.S. Military Academy at West Point, he had served with distinction both as an officer during the Mexican-American War and as U.S. secretary of war from 1853 to 1857. If the war could be prolonged, Davis and others hoped, then the British or French, desperate for southern cotton, might be persuaded to join their cause. Or, perhaps a long war would influence public sentiment in the North and force Lincoln to seek a negotiated settlement. So while armies were forming in the South, Confederate diplomats were seeking military and financial assistance in London and Paris, and Confederate sympathizers in the North were urging an end to the Union's war effort.

The Confederate representatives in Paris won a promise from France to recognize the Confederacy as a new nation *if* Great Britain would do the same. But the British refused, partly in response to pressure from President Lincoln and partly out of Britain's desire to maintain its trade with the United States. Confederate leaders had assumed that Britain would support the South in order to get its cotton. "The cards are in our hands!" crowed the *Mercury*, a Charleston newspaper. "And we intend to play them out to the bankruptcy of every cotton factory in Great Britain and France for the acknowledgement of our independence." As it turned out, however, the British were able to import enough cotton from India to maintain production. In the end, Confederate diplomacy in Europe was more successful in getting military supplies than in gaining official recognition of the Confederacy as an independent nation.

FORMING ARMIES Once fighting began, President Lincoln called for 500,000 more men, a staggering number at the time and one that the Confederacy struggled to match. "War! And volunteers are the only topics of conversation or thought," wrote a student at Ohio's Oberlin College. "I cannot study. I cannot sleep, and I don't know as I can write." In Illinois, Ulysses S. Grant, a mediocre graduate of the U.S. Military Academy at West Point who had displayed courage and a knack for leadership in the Mexican-American War, as well as a fondness for horses, liquor, and cigars, rejoined the army in 1861, explaining that there "are but two parties now—traitors and patriots—and I want hereafter to be ranked with the latter."

Confederates were equally committed to their cause. Charleston, wrote Mary Chesnut, the literary wife of a prominent planter, was "crowded with soldiers" who feared "the war will be over before they get a sight of the fun." Tennessee's twenty-one-year-old Sam Watkins reported that everyone in his town "was eager for the war."

The basic unit of the nineteenth-century U.S. Army was the regiment, about 1,000 soldiers, and during the Civil War most regiments were made up of friends, neighbors, and relatives from the same local community. Ethnic groups also formed their own regiments. A quarter of the Union troops were foreign-born. The Union army, for example, included a Scandinavian regiment (the 15th Wisconsin Infantry), a French regiment (the 55th New York Infantry), a Polish Legion (the 58th New York Infantry), and a mixed regiment of Poles, Hungarians, Germans, Spaniards, and Italians (the 39th New York Infantry). Many immigrant soldiers did not speak English.

Immigrants were attracted to serve for many reasons: a strong belief in the Union cause, cash bonuses, regular pay, or the need for a steady job. Whatever the reason, the high proportion of immigrants in the Union army gave it an ethnic diversity absent in the Confederate ranks. Many of the first Confederate army units chose flamboyant names: the Frontier Guards, Rough-and-Ready Grays, Game Cocks, Tigers, Cherokee Lincoln Killers, Tallapoosa Thrashers, and Raccoon Roughs.

Because the Confederacy had a smaller male population than the North, Jefferson Davis was forced to enact a conscription law (mandatory military draft). On April 16, 1862, all white males between eighteen and thirty-five were required to serve in the army for three years. "From this time until the end of the war," a Tennessee soldier wrote, "a soldier was simply a machine, a conscript. . . . All our pride and valor had gone, and we were sick of war and cursed the Southern Confederacy."

The Confederate conscription law included controversial loopholes. A draftee might avoid service either by paying a "substitute" who was not of draft age or by paying $500 to the government. Elected officials and key civilian workers, as well as planters with twenty or more slaves, were exempted from military service. Many among the planter elite argued that if they left to fight, their slaves would escape or riot. Equally galling to many Confederate soldiers was the behavior of wealthy officers who brought their enslaved servants with them to army camps.

The U.S. Army recruiting office in City Hall Park, New York City The sign advertises the money offered to those willing to serve: $677 to new recruits, $777 to veteran soldiers, and $15 to anyone who brought in a recruit.

The Union waited nearly a year to force men into service. In 1863, with the war going badly for the Federal armies, the government began to draft men. As in the South, northerners found ways to avoid military service. Exemptions were granted to selected federal and state officeholders and to others on medical or compassionate grounds; or a draftee might pay $300 to avoid service. Such exemptions led to bitter complaints on both sides about the conflict being "a rich man's war and a poor man's fight."

The Civil War also divided families. Lincoln's wife had four brothers who fought for the Rebel side. The son of Lincoln's attorney general, Edward Bates, fought for the Confederacy. In June 1862, two brothers, Alexander and James Campbell, fought against each other at the Battle of Secessionville on James Island, South Carolina. Alexander joined Union forces in assaulting a Confederate fort, one of whose defenders was his brother. Afterward, James wrote his brother, expressing astonishment that Alexander had been among the Union attackers. "I was . . . doing my best to Beat you, but I hope that you and I will never again meet face to face." But if they should, he urged his brother to "do your duty to your cause, for I can assure you I will strive to discharge my duty to my country & my cause."

THE LIFE OF A SOLDIER The average Civil War soldier or sailor was twenty-five years old, stood five feet eight inches, and weighed 143 pounds.

A third of the southern soldiers could neither read nor write. One in nine would be killed or wounded. Half of the Union soldiers and two-thirds of the Confederates were farmers.

Army camps featured their own libraries, theatrical stages, churches, and numerous "mascot" pets—and monotonous routine. Because most of the fighting was seasonal, in the spring and summer, soldiers spent far more time preparing for war than actually fighting. A Pennsylvania private wrote home that "the first thing in the morning is drill. Then drill, then drill again. Then drill, drill, a little more drill, then drill, lastly drill."

Life in army camps was difficult at best. When not training, soldiers spent time outdoors, in makeshift shelters or in small tents—talking, reading books, newspapers, or letters; playing cards or checkers; singing songs, smoking pipes; washing and mending clothes; and fighting swarms of lice, ticks, chiggers, and mosquitoes. Their diet was plain and dull: baked bread crackers (called hardtack), salted meat (pork or beef), and coffee.

A favorite camp song included the following lyrics:

Let us close our game of poker,
Take our tin cups in our hand,
While we gather round the cook's tent door,
Where dry mummies of hard crackers
Are given to each man;
O hard crackers, come again no more!

Some soldiers could not stand the rigors and strains of combat and camp life. Desertions soared with each passing year, as did incidents of drunkenness, thievery, and insubordination. Punishments varied. Some deserters were executed, either shot or hanged. Others were tied to a ball and chain, forced to bury dead horses or tend to animals, or drummed out of the service. Most of those who served on either side, however, came to view their military experience as beneficial. Charles Biddlecom, for example, concluded that the army was "a very good school for hot heads such as I was." Military service helped him mature into a man.

MIXED MOTIVES Several million mostly young and inexperienced Americans fought in the Civil War. As in all great wars, their motives for doing so varied dramatically. Sullivan Ballou, a thirty-two-year-old Rhode Island lawyer and legislator who enlisted in the Union army, wrote his wife that he would have loved nothing more than to have stayed with his family and seen their sons grow to "honorable manhood," but his ultimate priority was serving his country. He felt a great debt to "those who went before us through the

Union soldiers Smoking their pipes, these soldiers share a moment of rest and a bottle of whiskey.

blood and sufferings of the Revolution." A week later, Ballou was killed in the first Battle of Bull Run. In his last letter to his wife, he had expressed a premonition of death: "do not mourn me dead . . . wait for me, for we shall meet again."

Southerners felt the same sense of patriotism and manly honor. An Alabama planter explained to his anxious wife why he had to fight. "My honor, my duty, your reputation & that of my darling little boy," he stressed, forced him to don a uniform "when our bleeding country needs the services of every man."

As the months passed and the suffering grew, however, many combatants on both sides saw their initial enthusiasm fade. Charles Biddlecom, a farmer from upstate New York, volunteered in May 1861 as an enlisted man in the Union army. He was eager to get the "fuss" with the South over and whip the "Southern whelps."

By 1863, however, Biddlecom had had enough of war. Sick with dysentery, overrun with lice, and miserably lonesome, he and three comrades were forced to live in a "little dog kennel" just four feet high. Although he still hated slaveholders, he now felt it might have been "better in the end to have let the South go out peaceably and tried her hand at making a nation."

Like many other soldiers and sailors on both sides, Biddlecom's moods and motives for fighting fluctuated wildly depending upon the course of the war. In 1864, he confessed that the Union army was "worn out, discouraged, [and] demoralized." He stuck it out to preserve his sense of manly honor, but "as for men fighting from pure love of country, I think them as few as white blackbirds." He declared that he was neither a "Union saver" nor a "freedom shrieker." At one point, he had heard enough about a war to free the slaves: "to hell with the devilish twaddle about freedom."

By the time the war ended, however, Biddlecom's emotions had again reversed themselves with the Union victory. He celebrated the defeat of the Confederacy for affirming that "freedom shall extend over the whole nation." The "greatest nation of Earth" showed that it would not surrender to "traitors in arms."

BLACKS IN THE SOUTH   As had happened during the Revolutionary War and the War of 1812, enslaved African Americans took advantage of the confusion created by the war to run away, engage in sabotage, join the Union war effort, or pursue their own interests. A plantation owner in Tennessee was disgusted by the war's effect on his slaves, as he confessed in his diary: "My Negroes all at home, but working only as they see fit, doing little." Some slaves had reported that they would "serve the federals rather than work on the farm." Later, he revealed that when Union armies arrived in the area, his slaves had "stampeded" to join the Yankees: "Many of my servants have run away and most of those left had [just] as well be gone, they being totally demoralized and ungovernable." Some enslaved blacks escaped and served as spies or guides for Union forces; others joined the Union army or navy.

FIGHTING IN THE WEST

KANSAS   The most intense fighting west of the Mississippi occurred along the Kansas-Missouri border, where the disputes that had developed between the pro-slavery and anti-slavery settlers in the 1850s turned into brutal guerrilla warfare. The most prominent pro-Confederate leader in the area was William Quantrill. He and his followers, mostly teenagers, fought under a black flag, meaning that they would kill anyone who surrendered. In destroying Lawrence, Kansas, in 1863, Quantrill ordered his men to "kill every male and burn every house." By the end of the day, 182 boys and men had been massacred. Their opponents, the Jayhawkers, responded in kind. They tortured and hanged pro-Confederate prisoners, burned houses, and destroyed livestock.

Many Indian nations got caught up in the war on both sides, and in Oklahoma they fought against each other. Indians among the "Five Civilized Tribes" held African American slaves and felt a bond with southern whites. Oklahoma's proximity to Texas influenced the Choctaws and Chickasaws to support the Confederacy. The Cherokees, Creeks, and Seminoles were more divided in their loyalties. The Cherokees, for example, split in two, some supporting the Union and others the South.

KENTUCKY AND TENNESSEE Little happened of military significance east of the Appalachian Mountains before May 1862. On the other hand, important battles occurred in the West (from the Appalachians to the Mississippi River). In western Kentucky, Confederate general Albert Sidney Johnston had perhaps 40,000 men stretched over some 150 miles. Early in 1862, General Ulysses S. Grant made the first Union thrust against the weak center of Johnston's overextended lines. Moving on boats out of Cairo, Illinois, and Paducah, Kentucky, the Union army steamed up the Tennessee River and captured Fort Henry in northern Tennessee on February 6. The relentless Grant then moved quickly overland to attack nearby Fort Donelson, on the Cumberland River, where, on February 16, some 12,000 Confederates surrendered.

This first major Union victory touched off wild celebrations throughout the North. President Lincoln's delight, however, was tempered by the death of his eleven-year-old son Willie, who succumbed to typhoid fever. The tragedy "overwhelmed" the president. A White House staff member said she had never seen "a man so bowed down in grief."

SHILOH After defeats in Kentucky and Tennessee, the Confederate forces in the West fled southward before regrouping under General Johnston at Corinth in northern Mississippi near the Tennessee border. Their goal was to protect the Memphis and Charleston Railroad linking the lower Mississippi Valley and the Atlantic coast.

While planning his attack on Corinth, Grant made a costly mistake when he exposed his 42,000 troops on a rolling plateau between Lick and Snake Creeks flowing into the Tennessee River. Johnston recognized Grant's blunder, and at dawn on Sunday, April 6, he launched a surprise attack, urging his men to be "worthy of your race and lineage; worthy of the women of the South."

The 44,000 Confederates struck at Shiloh, a whitewashed Methodist chapel in the center of the Union camp in southwestern Tennessee. Most of Grant's troops were still sleeping or eating breakfast; many died in their bedrolls.

After a day of confused fighting and terrible losses on both sides, including Confederate general Johnston, the fleeing Union soldiers were pinned against the river. One of them wrote that "this is going to be a great battle, such as I have been anxious to see for a long time, and I think I have seen *enough* of it." The new Confederate commander, Pierre G. T. Beauregard, telegraphed President Jefferson Davis that his army had scored "a complete victory, driving the enemy from every position." But his celebration was premature.

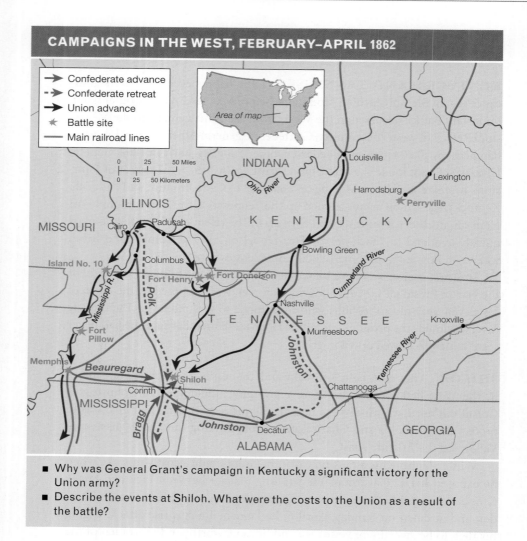

CAMPAIGNS IN THE WEST, FEBRUARY–APRIL 1862

→ Confederate advance
-→ Confederate retreat
→ Union advance
✶ Battle site
— Main railroad lines

Area of map

0   25   50 Miles
0   25   50 Kilometers

INDIANA

Louisville
Lexington
Harrodsburg
✶ Perryville

ILLINOIS

Ohio River

MISSOURI   Cairo   Paducah

K   E   N   T   U   C   K   Y

Island No. 10   Columbus

Bowling Green

Cumberland River

Fort Henry   ✶   Fort Donelson

Mississippi R.   Polk

Nashville

Fort Pillow

T   E   N   N   E   S   S   E   E   Knoxville

Murfreesboro

Johnston

Memphis

Beauregard   ✶ Shiloh

Tennessee River

Corinth   Chattanooga

MISSISSIPPI

Bragg

Johnston   Decatur   GEORGIA

ALABAMA

■ Why was General Grant's campaign in Kentucky a significant victory for the Union army?
■ Describe the events at Shiloh. What were the costs to the Union as a result of the battle?

Union General William T. Sherman, who had been wounded twice and had three horses shot from under him, visited Grant as rain fell. "Well, Grant," he said, "we've had the devil's own day, haven't we?" "Yes," Grant answered. But we will "lick 'em tomorrow." And they did.

Reinforced by 25,000 fresh Union troops, Grant's army took the offensive at dawn the next day, and the Confederates glumly withdrew twenty miles to Corinth. The Union troops were too battered and weary to pursue. Confederate private Sam Watkins observed that "those Yankees were whipped, fairly whipped, and according to all the rules of war they ought to have retreated. But they didn't." Another Rebel soldier wrote home to his family that his first battle had shaken him: "Oh God, forever keep me out of such another fight. I was not scared. I was just in danger."

Shiloh, a Hebrew word meaning "Place of Peace," was the largest and costliest battle in which Americans had ever engaged to that point. Viewing the battle, said General Sherman, "would have cured anybody of war." Of the 100,000 men who participated, a quarter of them were killed or wounded, seven times the casualties at the Battle of Bull Run. Grant remembered that the battlefield was so littered with corpses that he could not walk in any direction without "stepping on dead bodies." He now realized that the only way the war would end would be through "complete conquest."

Like Bull Run earlier and so many battles to come, Shiloh was a story of missed opportunities and lucky accidents. Throughout the Civil War, winning armies would fail to pursue their retreating foes, thus allowing the wounded opponent to slip away and fight again.

After Shiloh, Union general Henry Halleck, already jealous of Grant's success, spread a false rumor that Grant had been drinking during the battle. Some urged Lincoln to fire Grant, but the president refused: "I can't spare this man; he fights." Halleck, however, took Grant's place as field commander, and as a result the Union thrust in the Mississippi Valley southward ground to a halt.

NEW ORLEANS Just three weeks after the Battle of Shiloh, however, the Union won a great naval victory at New Orleans, as sixty-year-old David G. Farragut's warships blasted their way past Confederate forts under cover of darkness to take control of the largest city in the Confederacy. Union general Benjamin F. Butler, a cross-eyed Massachusetts Democrat, thereafter served as the military governor of captured New Orleans. When a Confederate sympathizer ripped down a Union flag, Butler had him hanged. After a Rebel woman leaned out her window and emptied her chamber pot on the head of newly promoted Admiral Farragut, General Butler decreed that any woman who was disrespectful of Union soldiers would be treated as a "woman of the town plying her avocation" (that is, as a prostitute). Residents of the captured towns thereafter referred to General Butler as "the Beast," but they also quit harassing Union soldiers and sailors.

The loss of New Orleans was a devastating blow to the Confederate economy. The Union army gained control of 1,500 cotton plantations and liberated 50,000 slaves in the Mississippi Valley. As a result, the slave system in Louisiana was "forever destroyed and worthless," reported a northern journalist.

PERRYVILLE In the late summer of 1862, General Braxton Bragg's Army of Mississippi, 30,000 strong, used railroads to link up with General Edmund

Kirby Smith's Army of East Tennessee. Their goal was to invade the North by taking control of the border state of Kentucky. They hoped to recruit volunteers for the Confederacy as well as push the Union army out of the state across the Ohio River. The Confederates met the Union Army of Ohio, led by General Don Carlos Buell, at the central Kentucky village of Perryville in October 1862. The outnumbered Confederates attacked the Union lines, pushing them back more than a mile. When Bragg learned that Union reinforcements were approaching, however, he ordered the Army of Mississippi to withdraw south toward Tennessee. After the Battle of Perryville, the Union retained control of Kentucky for the rest of the war.

FIGHTING IN THE EAST

The fighting in the East remained fairly quiet for nine months after the Battle of Bull Run. In the wake of the Union defeat, Lincoln had appointed glamorous General George B. McClellan, Stonewall Jackson's classmate at West Point and a former railroad president, as head of the Army of the Potomac. The thirty-four-year-old McClellan, who encouraged journalists to call him "Little Napoleon," set about building the Union's most powerful, best-trained army.

Yet for all of his boundless self-confidence ("I can do it all") and demonstrated organizational ability, McClellan's paralyzing cautiousness would prove crippling. Months passed while he remained in a state of perpetual preparation, building and training his massive army to meet the superior numbers of Confederates he mistakenly believed were facing him. "Tardy George" McClellan always found a reason to do something other than engage the Confederates in battle. Lincoln finally lost his patience and ordered McClellan to attack.

MCCLELLAN'S PENINSULAR CAMPAIGN   In mid-March 1862, McClellan moved his huge army of 122,000 men on 400 ships and barges down the Potomac River and the Chesapeake Bay to the mouth of the James River at the tip of the Yorktown peninsula, within sixty miles of the Confederate capital of Richmond, Virginia. Thousands of residents fled the city in panic, but McClellan overestimated the number of Confederate defenders and waited too long to strike. A frustrated Lincoln told McClellan that the war could be won only by *engaging* the Rebel army. "Once more," Lincoln told his commanding general, "let me tell you, it is indispensable to *you* that you strike a blow."

On May 31, 1862, Confederate general Joseph E. Johnston struck first at McClellan's army along the Chickahominy River, six miles east of Richmond. In the Battle of Seven Pines (Fair Oaks), only the arrival of Federal

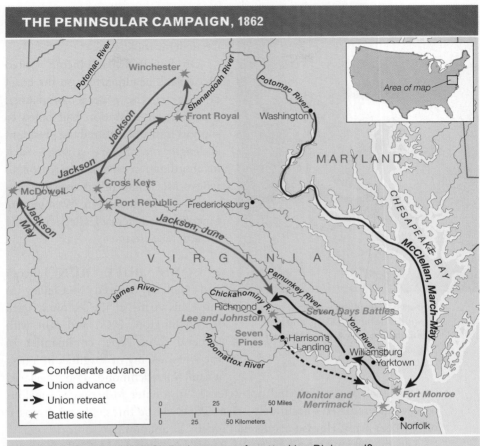

THE PENINSULAR CAMPAIGN, 1862

Legend:
→ Confederate advance
→ Union advance
--→ Union retreat
★ Battle site

0   25   50 Miles
0   25   50 Kilometers

Area of map

- What was General McClellan's strategy for attacking Richmond?
- How did General Jackson divert the attention of the Union army?
- Why did President Lincoln demote McClellan after the Peninsular campaign?

reinforcements, who somehow crossed the swollen river, prevented a disastrous Union defeat. Both sides took heavy casualties, and Johnston was severely wounded.

At this point, Robert E. Lee assumed command of the Confederates' main army, the Army of Northern Virginia, a development that changed the course of the war. The brilliant, dignified Lee had graduated second in his class at West Point, and during the Mexican-American War, he had impressed General Winfield Scott as the "very best soldier I ever saw in the field." In 1857, Scott predicted that Lee would become America's greatest military leader. Lee would prove to be a daring, even reckless, strategist who was as aggressive

Robert E. Lee Military adviser to President Jefferson Davis and later commander of the Army of Northern Virginia.

as McClellan was timid. "He is silent, inscrutable, strong, like a God," said a Confederate officer.

On July 9, when Lincoln visited McClellan's headquarters on the coast of Virginia, the general complained that the administration had failed to support him and lectured the president at length on military strategy. Such insubordination was ample reason to relieve McClellan of his overall command. After returning to Washington, Lincoln called Henry Halleck from the West to take charge.

SECOND BULL RUN Lincoln and Halleck ordered McClellan to move his Army of the Potomac back to Washington, D.C., and join with General John Pope, commander of the Union Army of Virginia, in a new assault on Richmond. Pope declared that his goal "was attack and not defense." In a letter to his wife, a jealous McClellan predicted—accurately—that "Pope will be thrashed and disposed of" by Lee's army. He also dismissed Lincoln "as an idiot."

Lee moved northward to strike Pope's army before McClellan's troops could arrive. Lee knew that his only chance was to drive a wedge between the two larger Union armies so that he could deal with them one at a time.

Violating a basic rule of military strategy, Lee boldly divided his forces, sending Stonewall Jackson's "foot cavalry" around Pope's flank to attack his supply lines in the rear. At the Second Battle of Bull Run (or Manassas), fought on almost the same site as the earlier battle, a confused Pope assumed that he faced only Jackson, but Lee's main army by that time had joined in.

On August 30, 1862, a crushing Confederate attack drove the larger Union army from the field, giving the Confederates a sensational victory and leading one disheartened Union officer to confess from his deathbed that "General Pope had been outwitted. . . . Our generals have defeated us." In contrast, a Rebel soldier wrote home that "General Lee stands now above all generals in modern history. Our men will follow him to the end."

EMANCIPATION

The Confederate victories in 1862 devastated morale in the North and convinced Lincoln that he had to take bolder steps to win the war. Now the North had to assault slavery itself. When fighting began in 1861, the need to keep the border slave states (Delaware, Kentucky, Maryland, and Missouri) in the Union dictated caution on the volatile issue of emancipation. Beyond that, Lincoln had to contend with a deep-seated racial prejudice among most northerners, who were willing to allow slavery to continue in the South as long as it was not allowed to expand into the West. Lincoln himself harbored doubts about his constitutional authority to end slavery, and he did not believe that blacks, if freed, could coexist with whites.

SLAVES IN THE WAR The expanding war forced the issue. As Federal forces pushed into the Confederacy, fugitive slaves began to turn up in Union army camps, and the commanders did not know whether to declare them free. One general designated them as being "contraband of war," and thereafter the slaves who sought protection and freedom with Union forces were known as **contrabands**. Some Union officers put the refugee slaves to work digging trenches, building fortifications, and burying the dead; others simply set them free.

Lincoln, meanwhile, began to edge toward ending slavery. On April 16, 1862, he signed an act that abolished slavery in the District of Columbia; on June 19, he signed another bill that excluded slavery from the western territories. Still, he insisted that the war was about restoring the Union and ending secession, not ending slavery.

But the course of the war changed Lincoln's outlook. In the summer of 1862, he decided that emancipation of slaves in the Confederate states was necessary to win the war. Many of the more than 3 million enslaved laborers in the Confederacy were being forced to aid the Rebel war effort—digging trenches, hauling supplies or cooking meals for the armies, repairing railroads, and working as servants for Confederate officers.

In July 1862, Lincoln confided to his cabinet that "decisive and extreme measures [to win the war] must be adopted." Emancipation, he said, had become "a military necessity, absolutely necessary to the preservation of the Union. We must free the slaves or be ourselves subdued." Secretary of State William H. Seward agreed, but advised Lincoln to delay the announcement until after a Union battlefield victory, to avoid being viewed as desperate.

Contrabands Former slaves on a farm in Cumberland Landing, Virginia, 1862.

ANTIETAM: A TURNING POINT Robert E. Lee made his own momentous decision in the summer of 1862: he would invade Maryland and thereby force the "much weakened and demoralized" Army of the Potomac and its "timid" commander McClellan to leave northern Virginia and relieve the pressure on Richmond, the Confederate capital. Lee also hoped to influence the upcoming elections in the North; he wanted to gain official British and French recognition of the Confederacy, which would bring his troops desperately needed military supplies. In addition, Lee and Jefferson Davis planned to capture Maryland, with its many Confederate supporters, separate it from the Union, and gain control of its farms and foodstuffs needed for the war effort. For those reasons and others, in September 1862, Lee and his 40,000 troops, many of them ragged, barefoot, and underfed, pushed north into western Maryland.

On September 17, 1862, the Union and Confederate armies clashed in the furious **Battle of Antietam** (Sharpsburg). Had not Union soldiers discovered Lee's detailed battle plans wrapped around three cigars that a Rebel soldier had carelessly dropped on the ground, the Confederates might have won.

McClellan, had he moved his 100,000 men more quickly, could have destroyed Lee's Army of Northern Virginia while it was scattered and on the move. As always, however, McClellan moved slowly, enabling Lee and his troops to regroup at Sharpsburg, between Antietam Creek and the Potomac River.

There, over the course of fourteen hours, the poorly coordinated Union army launched repeated attacks. The fighting was savage; a Union officer counted "hundreds of dead bodies lying in rows and in piles." The scene after "five hours of continuous slaughter" was "sickening, harrowing, horrible. O what a terrible sight!"

Lincoln's search for a "fighting general" Abraham Lincoln and George C. McClellan confer at Antietam, in Maryland, October 4, 1862.

The next day, Lee braced for another Union attack, but it never came. That night, cloaked by fog and drizzling rain, the battered Confederates slipped south back across the Potomac River to the safety of Virginia. "The 'barefoot boys' have done some terrible fighting," a Georgian wrote his parents. "We are a dirty, ragged set [of soldiers], mother, but courage & heroism find many a true disciple among us."

Although the battle was technically a draw, Lee's northern invasion had failed. Both sides displayed heroic courage and reckless bravery in what one Rebel general called the "hardest fought battle of the war." McClellan, never known for his modesty, claimed that he "had fought the battle splendidly" against great odds. To him, the Battle of Antietam was "the most terrible battle of the age." Indeed, it was the bloodiest single day in American military history. Some 6,400 soldiers on both sides were killed, twice as many as at Shiloh, and another 17,000 were wounded or listed as missing. The Confederate people, said a soldier, wanted "an active [military] campaign, and General Lee has certainly given it to us."

President Lincoln was pleased that Lee's army had been forced to retreat, but he was disgusted by McClellan's failure to attack the retreating Confederates and win the war. The president sent a sarcastic message to the general: "I have just read your dispatch about sore-tongued and fatigued horses. Will you pardon me for asking what the horses of your army have done . . . that fatigues anything?" Failing to receive a satisfactory answer, Lincoln sacked McClellan as commander of the Army of the Potomac and assigned him to recruiting duty in New Jersey. Never again would McClellan command troops, but he would challenge Lincoln for the presidency in 1864 as a Democrat.

The Battle of Antietam had several important results. It revived sagging northern morale, dashed the Confederacy's hopes of forging alliances with Great Britain and France, and convinced Lincoln to transform the war from an effort to restore the Union to a crusade to end slavery.

EMANCIPATION PROCLAMATION   On September 22, 1862, five days after the battle, he issued the preliminary **Emancipation Proclamation**, which warned the Confederacy that if it did not stop fighting, all slaves still under Rebel control were to be made "forever free" in exactly 100 days, on January 1, 1863.

The Emancipation Proclamation was not based on ideas of racial equality or on abstract ideals of human dignity. It was, according to Lincoln, a "military necessity." The proclamation freed only those slaves in areas still controlled by the Confederacy; it had no bearing on slaves in the four border states, because they remained in the Union. Lincoln believed that the Constitution allowed each state to decide the fate of slavery, so his only legal avenue was to act as commander in chief of the armed forces rather than as president. He would declare the end of slavery as a "fit and necessary war measure" to save the Union.

Union view of the Emancipation Proclamation A thoughtful Lincoln composes the proclamation with the Constitution and the Bible in his lap. The Scales of Justice hangs on the wall behind him.

When Lincoln officially signed the Emancipation Proclamation in January, however, he amended his original message, adding that the proclamation was "an act of justice" as well as a military necessity. Lincoln's constitutional concerns about abolishing slavery would lead him to promote the Thirteenth Amendment ending slavery across the nation. As Lincoln signed the Emancipation Proclamation, he said, "I never, in my life, felt more certain that I was doing the right thing than I do in signing this paper." Simply restoring the Union was no longer the purpose of the war; the transformation of the South and the slave system was now the goal.

REACTIONS TO EMANCIPATION Lincoln's threat to free slaves under Confederate control triggered emotional reactions. The *Illinois State Register* savaged the president for violating the Constitution and causing "the permanent disruption of the republic." Democrats exploded with rage, calling the president's decision dictatorial, unconstitutional, and catastrophic. "We Won't Fight to Free the Nigger," proclaimed one popular banner. Many voters felt likewise.

Lincoln forcefully responded to his critics. "You say you will not fight to free negroes," he wrote. "Some of them seem willing to fight for you; but, no

Confederate view of the Emancipation Proclamation Surrounded by demonic faces hidden in his furnishings, Lincoln pens the proclamation with a foot trampling the Constitution. The devil holds the inkwell before him.

matter. Fight you, then, exclusively to save the Union. I issued the [emancipation] proclamation on purpose to aid you in saving the Union."

In the November 1862 congressional elections, Republicans lost almost two dozen seats. Illinois, Indiana, Pennsylvania, New York, and Ohio went Democratic, largely because of opposition to the Emancipation Proclamation. Even Lincoln's home district in Illinois elected a Democrat.

Although Lincoln's proclamation technically would free only the slaves where Confederates remained in control, many slaves in the northern border states and the South claimed their freedom anyway. As Lincoln had hoped, word spread rapidly among the slave community in the Confederacy, arousing hopes of freedom, creating general confusion in the cities, and encouraging hundreds of thousands to escape. A Union general said that emancipation "was like an earthquake. It shook and shattered the whole previously existing social system."

George Washington Albright, an enslaved teen in Mississippi, recalled that white planters tried to prevent slaves from learning about the proclamation but word of it slipped through the "grapevine." His father was inspired to escape and join the Union army, and the younger Albright served as a "runner" for the 4Ls ("Lincoln's Legal Loyal League"), a secret group created to spread the news about the proclamation to slaves throughout the region.

Confederate leaders were incensed by Lincoln's action, predicting it would ignite a race war in the South. By contrast, Frederick Douglass, the African American abolitionist leader, was overjoyed at the "righteous decree"; he knew that, despite its limitations, it would inspire abolitionists in the North and set in motion the eventual end of slavery.

As Lincoln had hoped, the Emancipation Proclamation did aid the Union war effort by undermining support for the Confederacy in Europe. The decision to end slavery in the Confederacy gave the Federal war effort greater moral legitimacy in the eyes of Europeans—and many Americans.

As the war continued and Union armies advanced into the southern states, they became an army of liberation, freeing slaves in their path and circulating thousands of copies of the Emancipation Proclamation as they went. At Camp Saxton, a former plantation on the coast of South Carolina, the First South Carolina Volunteers, a new Union regiment made up of former slaves, gathered on January 1, 1863, to celebrate Lincoln's official signing of the Emancipation Proclamation.

After the proclamation was read aloud, it was "cheered to the skies." As Colonel Thomas W. Higginson, the new unit's commander, unfurled an American flag, the black troops spontaneously began singing "My Country 'Tis of Thee / Sweet land of liberty / Of thee I sing!" Higginson reported his emotional reaction: "I never saw anything so electric; it made all other words cheap; it seemed the choked voice of a race at last unloosed."

FREDERICKSBURG In selecting a new commanding general, Lincoln made his poorest choice of all in the fall of 1862, when he turned to Ambrose E. Burnside, a tall, imposing man whose massive facial hair gave rise to the term "sideburns." Twice before, Burnside had turned down the job, saying he was not worthy of such responsibility. Now he accepted, although he still neither sought the command nor wanted it. He was right to be hesitant. Burnside was an eager fighter but a poor strategist who, according to Fanny Seward, the secretary of state's daughter, had "ten times as much heart as he has head." The Union army soon paid for his mistakes.

On December 13, 1862, Burnside foolishly sent the 122,000 men in the Army of the Potomac west across the icy Rappahannock River to assault Lee's outnumbered forces, who were well entrenched on a line of ridges and behind stone walls at the base of Marye's Heights, west of Fredericksburg, Virginia, midway between Richmond and Washington, D.C. Confederate cannons and muskets chewed up the advancing Federal soldiers as they crossed half a mile of open land.

A Rebel artillery officer boasted that "a chicken could not live on that field when we open fire on it." One of the Federal survivors said it felt like "the ground were bursting underfoot and the very sky was crashing down upon us—the bullets hissed like a seething sea." Still, they charged over dead men and fragments of arms and legs, only to be "mown down in heaps." The assault across the plain in front of the heights was, a Union general regretted, "a great slaughter-pen," more like murder than warfare.

Wave after wave of blue-clad troops surged toward the well-protected Confederates. None of the Union soldiers made it to the Rebel lines. The awful scene of dead and dying Federals, some stacked three deep on the battlefield, led Lee to remark: "It is well that war is so terrible—we should grow too fond of it." After 12,600 Federals were killed or wounded, compared with fewer than 5,300 for the Confederates, a weeping Burnside told his men to withdraw back across the river as darkness fell. As Burnside rode past his retreating men, his aide called for three cheers for their commander. All he got was sullen silence.

That night, however, there was no silence as thousands of wounded and dying soldiers left on the battlefield moaned and shrieked in agony amid the corpses of their friends. A soldier said death was preferable to the experience of the "fearfully and mortally wounded." Abraham Lincoln was devastated by the news of the Union catastrophe. "We are now on the brink of destruction," he wrote. "It appears to me the Almighty is against us, and I can hardly see a ray of hope."

The year 1862 ended with a stalemate in the East and the Union thrust in the West mired down. Northern morale plummeted, and northern Democrats' victories in the fall congressional elections sharply reduced the Republican majorities in the House and the Senate. Many Democrats were calling for a negotiated peace, and Republicans—even Lincoln's own cabinet members—grew increasingly critical of the president's leadership. "If there is a worse place than hell," Lincoln sighed, "I am in it."

Newspapers circulated rumors that the president was going to resign. General Burnside, too, was under fire, with some of his own officers eager to testify publicly to his shortcomings. One of them claimed that the general was "fast losing his mind."

NEW YORK CITY DRAFT RIOTS Lincoln's proclamation freeing slaves in the Confederacy created anxiety and anger among many laborers in the North who feared that freed slaves would eventually migrate north and take their jobs. In New York City, such fears erupted into violence. In July 1863, a group of 500 wage workers, led by volunteer firemen, assaulted the army draft office, shattering its windows, then burning it down. When the city police superintendent arrived at the scene, he was beaten unconscious, and the outnumbered policemen were forced to retreat.

The rioters, now swollen by thousands of working-class whites, mostly Irish, were angry over the unfair military draft, ruthlessly taking out their frustrations on blacks. Mobs rampaged through the streets of Manhattan, randomly assaulting African Americans, beating them, dragging them through the streets, and lynching a disabled black man while chanting "Hurrah for Jeff Davis." Thugs also burned down more than fifty buildings, including the mayor's home, police stations, two Protestant churches, and the Colored Orphan Asylum, forcing 233 children to flee.

The raging violence went on for three days, killing 105 people and injuring thousands. Only the arrival of Federal soldiers put an end to the rioting. Thousands of terrified blacks thereafter moved out of the city for fear of continuing racial violence. Similar riots occurred in other northern cities, including Boston.

BLACK SOLDIERS AND SAILORS In July 1862, in an effort to strengthen the Union war effort, the U.S. Congress had passed the **Militia Act**, which authorized the army to use freed slaves as laborers or soldiers (They were already eligible to serve in the navy). Lincoln, however, did not encourage the use of freed slaves as soldiers because he feared the reaction in the border states where slavery remained in place. It was only after the formal signing of the Emancipation Proclamation in January 1863 that the Union army recruited blacks in large numbers.

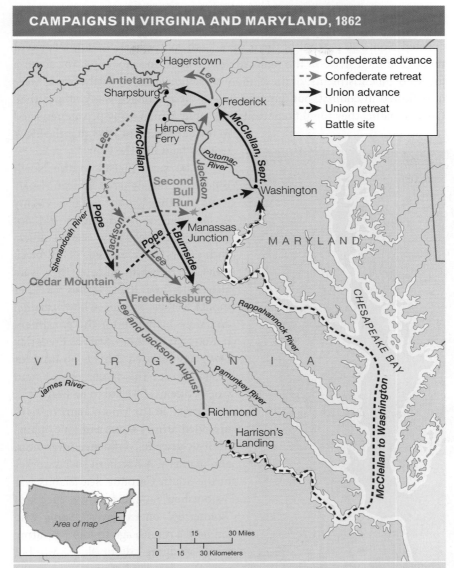

CAMPAIGNS IN VIRGINIA AND MARYLAND, 1862

Legend:
- → Confederate advance
- --→ Confederate retreat
- → Union advance
- --→ Union retreat
- ✳ Battle site

Hagerstown

Antietam
Sharpsburg

Frederick

Lee

Harpers Ferry

McClellan

McClellan, Sept.

Potomac River

Jackson

Second Bull Run

Washington

Shenandoah River

Pope

Jackson

Manassas Junction

MARYLAND

Cedar Mountain

Pope

Lee

Burnside

Fredericksburg

Rappahannock River

Lee and Jackson, August

CHESAPEAKE BAY

McClellan to Washington

VIRGINIA

Pamunkey River

James River

Richmond

Harrison's Landing

Area of map

0   15   30 Miles
0   15   30 Kilometers

■ How did the Confederate army defeat General Pope at the Second Battle of Bull Run?

■ Why was General Burnside's decision to attack at Fredericksburg a mistake?

On May 22, 1863, the U.S. War Department created the Bureau of Colored Troops to recruit free blacks and freed slaves. More than 180,000 blacks enlisted. Some 80 percent of them were from southern states, and 38,000 of them gave their lives. In the navy, African Americans accounted for about a fourth of all enlistments; of these, more than 2,800 died. Initially, blacks were not allowed in combat, but the need to win the prolonged war changed that. Once in battle, they fought tenaciously. A white Union army private reported in the late spring of 1863 that the black troops "fight like the Devil."

Black Union army sergeant Wearing his uniform and sword, he poses with a copy of J. T. Headley's *The Great Rebellion* in his hand.

To be sure, racism in the North influenced the status of African Americans in the Union military. Many people who opposed slavery did not support racial equality. Black soldiers and sailors were placed in all-black units led by white officers. They were also paid less than whites ($7 per month versus $16 for white recruits) and were ineligible for the enlistment bonus paid to whites. Still, as Frederick Douglass declared, "this is no time for hesitation. . . . This is our chance, and woe betide us if we fail to embrace it."

Service in the Union army or navy provided former slaves a unique opportunity to grow in confidence, awareness, and maturity. A northern social worker in the South Carolina Sea Islands was "astonished" at the positive effects of "soldiering" on ex-slaves: "Some who left here a month ago to join [the army were] cringing, dumpish, slow," but now they "are ready to look you in the eye—are wide awake and active." Commenting on Union victories at Port Hudson and Milliken's Bend, Louisiana, Lincoln reported that "some of our commanders . . . believe   that . . . the use of colored troops constitutes the heaviest blow yet dealt to the rebels."

THE WAR BEHIND THE LINES

Feeding, clothing, and supplying the vast armies required tremendous sacrifices on both home fronts. Farms and villages were transformed into battlefields, churches became makeshift hospitals, civilian life was disrupted, and families grieved for soldiers who would not be coming home.

WOMEN AND THE WAR While breaking the bonds of slavery, the Civil War also loosened traditional restraints on female activity. "No conflict in history," a journalist wrote, "was such a woman's war as the Civil War." Women on both sides played prominent roles. They worked in mills and factories, sewed uniforms, composed patriotic poems and songs, and raised money and supplies. In Greenville, South Carolina, when T. G. Gower went off to fight, his wife Elizabeth took over the family business, converting production in their carriage factory to military wagons and ambulances. Three thousand northern women worked as nurses with the U.S. Sanitary Commission, a civilian agency that provided medical relief and other services for soldiers. Other women, black and white, supported the freedmen's aid movement to help impoverished freed slaves.

In the North alone, some 20,000 women served as nurses and health-related volunteers. The most famous nurses were Clara Barton and Dorothea Lynde Dix. Barton explained that her place was "anywhere between the bullet and the battlefield." Dix declared that nurses should be "plain looking" women between the ages of thirty-five and fifty who could "bear the presence of suffering and exercise entire self-control." Barton, who later founded the American Red Cross, claimed that the war advanced by fifty years the progress of women in gaining social and economic equality.

In many southern towns and counties, the home front became a world of white women and children and African American slaves. A resident of Lexington, Virginia, reported that

Clara Barton She oversaw the distribution of medicines to Union troops and would later help found the American Red Cross.

there were "no men left" in town by mid-1862. Women suddenly found themselves full-time farmers or plantation managers, clerks, and schoolteachers. A few women disguised themselves as men and fought in the war, while dozens served as spies. Others traveled with the armies, cooking meals, writing letters, and assisting with amputations.

New Yorker Mary Edwards Walker, a Union battlefield surgeon, was captured and imprisoned by the Confederates for spying. She was the only woman in the war (and since) to be awarded the Congressional Medal of Honor, the nation's highest military award. In 1864, President Lincoln told a soldier that all the praise of women over the centuries did not do justice "for their conduct during the war."

WARTIME GOVERNMENT   Whi-le freeing the slaves in the Confederacy was a transformational development, a political revolution began as a result of the shift in congressional power from the South to the North after secession.

In 1862, the Republican-dominated Congress sought to promote the "prosperity and happiness of the whole people" by passing a more comprehensive

Susie King Taylor Born into slavery, she served as a nurse in Union-occupied Georgia and operated a school for freed slaves.

tariff bill (called the Morrill Tariff in honor of its sponsor, Vermont Republican congressman Justin Smith Morrill) to raise government revenue and "protect" America's manufactures, agriculture, mining, and fishing industries from foreign competition. For the rest of the nineteenth century, U.S. manufacturers were the most protected in the world in terms of high federal tariffs discouraging foreign imports.

The Republicans in Congress, with Lincoln's support, enacted legislation reflecting their belief (and that of the old Whig party) that the federal government could benefit the nation by actively promoting economic development. To that end, Congress approved the Pacific Railway Act (1862), which provided federal funding and grants of land for construction of a 1,900 mile-long transcontinental railroad line from Omaha, Nebraska, to Sacramento, California. In addition, a **Homestead Act** (1862) granted 160 acres of public land to each settler who agreed to work the land for five years. To help farmers become more productive, Congress created a new federal agency, the Department of Agriculture.

Two other key pieces of Republican legislation were the **Morrill Land Grant Act** (1862), which provided states with 30,000 acres of federal land to establish public universities that would teach "agriculture and mechanic arts," and the National Banking Act (1863), which created national banks that could issue paper money that would be accepted across the country. These wartime measures had long-term significance for the growth of the national economy—and the expansion of the federal government.

UNION FINANCES   In December 1860, as southern states announced their plans to secede, the federal treasury was virtually empty. To meet the war's huge expenses, Congress needed money fast—and lots of it. It focused on three options: raising taxes, printing paper money, and selling government bonds to investors. The taxes came chiefly in the form of the Morrill Tariff on imports and a 3 percent tax on manufactures and most professions.

In 1862, Congress created the Internal Revenue Service within the Treasury department to collect the first income tax on citizens and corporations. The tax rate was 3 percent on those with annual incomes more than $800. The tax rate went up to 5 percent on incomes more than $10,000. Yet very few people paid the taxes. Only 250,000 people out of a population of 39 million had income high enough to pay taxes.

Congressman Justin S. Morrill, who had authored the Land Grant Act and the Tariff Act of 1862, endorsed the concept of "progressive" taxation, in which tax *rates* rose with designated income levels. Taxation, he argued, "must be distributed equally, not upon each man an equal amount, but a tax [rate] proportionate to his ability to pay."

The new federal tax revenues, however, fell short of what was needed—in the end they would meet only 21 percent of wartime expenditures. In 1862, Congress approved the printing of paper money. With the Legal Tender Act of 1862, the Treasury issued $450 million in new paper currency, called *greenbacks* because of the color of the ink used to print the bills.

The federal government also relied upon the sale of bonds. A Philadelphia banker named Jay Cooke (the "Financier of the Civil War") mobilized a nationwide campaign to sell $2 billion in government bonds to private investors.

CONFEDERATE FINANCES   In comparison to the Union, the Confederate efforts to finance the war were a disaster. Jefferson Davis had to create

State currency Banknotes were paper currency. Generally, the better the art on the note, the more it was trusted.

a treasury and a revenue-collecting system from scratch. Moreover, the South's agrarian economy was land-rich but cash-poor. While the Confederacy owned 30 percent of America's assets (businesses, land, slaves) in 1861, its currency in circulation was only 12 percent of that in the North.

In its first year, the Confederacy created a property tax, which should have yielded a hefty amount of revenue. But collecting taxes was left to the states, and the result was chaos. In 1863, the desperate Confederate Congress began taxing nearly everything, but enforcement was poor and evasion easy. Altogether, taxes covered no more than 5 percent of Confederate war costs, and bond issues accounted for less than 33 percent.

During the course of the war, the Confederacy issued more than $1 billion in paper money, which, along with a shortage of consumer goods, caused prices to soar. By 1864, a turkey sold in the Richmond market for $100, flour brought $425 a barrel, and bacon was $10 a pound. Such rampant inflation (price increases) caused great distress, and frustrations over the burdens of war increasingly erupted into rioting, looting, and mass protests.

By 1865, some 100,000 Confederate soldiers had deserted the army for various reasons, including the defense of slavery. A poor farmer in Alabama refused to serve in the Confederate army because the war was being fought to preserve the "infernal negroes" owned by wealthy planters. Another Confederate said he and his comrades were "tired of fighting for this negro-owning aristockracy [sic]." David Harris, a farmer, deserted from the army because the cause was lost: "I am now going to work instead of to the war," he wrote home.

UNION POLITICS The North had its share of dissension and factionalism. President Lincoln was forced to use all of his substantial political genius to fend off uprisings against him in Congress and conspiracies against him among cabinet members. He loved the jockeying of backroom politics, and he excelled at it. Throughout the war, the president faced a radical wing of Republicans composed mainly of militant abolitionists who criticized his leadership of the war effort.

Led by Thaddeus Stevens in the House and Charles Sumner in the Senate, the so-called Radical Republicans in Congress wanted more than defeat of the Confederacy; they wanted to "reconstruct" it by allowing Union armies to seize southern plantations and give the land to the former slaves. The majority of Republicans, however, continued to back Lincoln's more cautious approach.

The Democratic party was devastated by the departure of its long-dominant southern wing and the death of its nationalist spokesman, Stephen A. Douglas, in June 1861. What were called Peace Democrats favored restoring the Union "as it was [before 1860] and the Constitution as it is." They reluctantly supported Lincoln's war policies but opposed Republican economic legislation. So-called War Democrats, such as Tennessee senator Andrew Johnson and Secretary of War Edwin M. Stanton, backed Lincoln's policies.

A few Peace Democrats verged on disloyalty to the Union cause. The **Copperhead Democrats** (poisonous snakes) were strongest in states such as Ohio, Indiana, and Illinois, that had substantial numbers of former southerners. The Copperheads openly sympathized with the Confederacy, savagely criticized Lincoln, and called for an end to the war.

CIVIL LIBERTIES Such support for the enemy led Lincoln to crack down hard. Like all wartime leaders, he faced the challenge of balancing the urgent needs of winning a war with the protection of civil liberties. Using his authority as commander in chief in wartime, Lincoln exercised emergency powers, including suspending the writ of *habeas corpus*, which guarantees arrested citizens a speedy hearing before a judge. The Constitution states that habeas corpus may be suspended only in cases of invasion, but Supreme Court justice Roger Taney and several congressional leaders argued that Congress alone had the authority to take such action.

By the Habeas Corpus Act of 1863, Congress allowed the president to order people arrested on the suspicion of treason. Thereafter, Union soldiers and local sheriffs arrested thousands of Confederate sympathizers in the northern states without using a writ of habeas corpus. Union general Henry Halleck jailed one Missourian for saying, "[I] wouldn't wipe my ass with the stars and stripes."

CONFEDERATE POLITICS AND STATES' RIGHTS Unlike Lincoln, Jefferson Davis never had to worry about reelection. He and his vice president, Alexander Stephens, were elected in 1861 for six-year terms. But discontent with their leadership grew as the war dragged on. Poor white southerners expressed bitter resentment of the planter elite while food grew scarce and prices skyrocketed.

A food riot erupted in Richmond on April 2, 1863, when an angry mob, mostly women armed with pistols or knives, marched to the governor's mansion to demand that bread in Confederate warehouses be shared with civilians. When the governor announced that nothing could be done, the protesters shouted "Bread or blood!" They broke into stores, stealing shoes and clothing, as well as food. The riot ended only when President Davis arrived and threatened to shoot the protesters. Police then arrested forty-four women and twenty-nine men.

Davis's greatest challenge came from the southern politicians who criticized the "tyrannical" powers of the Confederate government in Richmond. As a general reported, "The state of feeling between the President [Davis] and Congress is bad—could not be worse." Critics asserted states' rights against the authority of the Confederate government, just as they had against the Union. Georgia's governor Joseph Brown hated Jefferson Davis, explaining that he joined the Confederacy to "sustain the rights of the states and prevent the consolidation of the Government, and I am still a *rebel* . . . no matter who may be in power."

Jefferson Davis President of the Confederacy.

The Confederacy also suffered from Davis's difficult personality and constant political squabbling. Where Lincoln was a pragmatist, Davis was a brittle ideologue with a stinging temper. Once he made a decision, nothing could change his mind, and he could never admit a mistake. One southern politician said that Davis was "as stubborn as a mule."

Such a dogmatic personality was ill suited to the chief executive of an infant—and fractious—nation. Cabinet members resigned almost as soon as they were appointed. During the four years of the Confederacy, there were three secretaries of state and six secretaries of war, and Vice President Stephens constantly warred against Davis's "military despotism." Stephens's brother described President Davis as a "little, conceited, hypocritical, sniveling, canting, malicious, ambitious, dogged knave and fool."

THE FALTERING CONFEDERACY

The Confederate strategy of fighting largely a defensive war worked well at first. As the armies maneuvered for battle in the spring of 1863, however, President Lincoln found a commanding general in the West as capable as Robert E. Lee was in the East. Humble, unassuming, plain-spoken Ulysses S. Grant, five feet eight inches tall and weighing only 135 pounds, calm and steady under fire, was blessed with an uncommonly ruthless determination to win on the battlefield—at all cost.

CHANCELLORSVILLE After the Union disaster at Fredericksburg at the end of 1862, President Lincoln turned to General Joseph Hooker, a hard-fighting, hard-drinking leader who had earned the nickname "Fighting Joe," to lead the Army of the Potomac. With a force of 130,000 men, the largest Union army yet gathered, an overconfident Hooker failed his leadership test at Chancellorsville, in eastern Virginia, during the first week of May, 1863. "My plans are perfect. . . . May God have mercy on General Lee," Hooker boasted, "for I will have none."

Hooker spoke too soon. Robert E. Lee, with perhaps half as many troops, split his army in thirds and gave Hooker a lesson in the art of elusive mobility when Stonewall Jackson's 28,000 Confederates surprised the Union army by smashing into its exposed right flank. The attack sparked days of confusing and desperate fighting, ultimately forcing Hooker's army to retreat. "My God, my God," moaned

Thomas "Stonewall" Jackson The celebrated Confederate commander, Jackson would later die of friendly fire in the Battle of Chancellorsville.

Lincoln when he heard the news. "What will the country say?" Chancellorsville was the peak of Lee's military career, but it would also be his last significant victory.

VICKSBURG   While Lee frustrated the Federals in the East, General Grant had been inching his army down the Mississippi River toward the Confederate stronghold of Vicksburg, Mississippi, a busy commercial town situated on high bluffs overlooking a sharp, sweeping horseshoe bend in the river. Capturing the Rebel stronghold, Grant stressed, "was of the first importance," because Vicksburg was the only rail and river junction between Memphis, Tennessee,

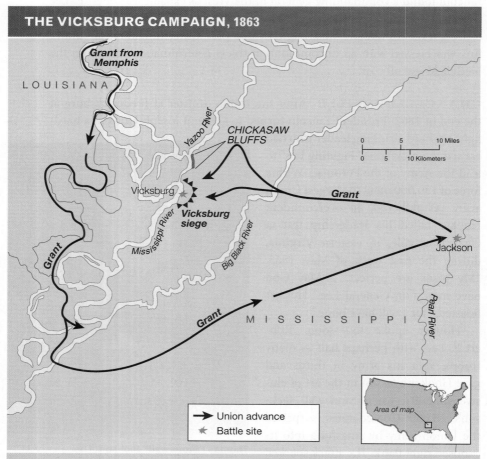

THE VICKSBURG CAMPAIGN, 1863

- Why was the capture of Vicksburg a strategic victory?
- Why was Vicksburg difficult to seize from the Confederacy?
- How did General Lee hope to save Vicksburg from the Union siege?

and New Orleans. President Lincoln said that Vicksburg held the "key" to a Union victory in the war, and Jefferson Davis agreed, saying that holding the Mississippi River open was "vital" to the Confederacy. "Vicksburg must not be lost!" If Union forces could gain control of the river, they could split the Confederacy in two and prevent western food and livestock from reaching Confederate armies.

While Union warships sneaked past the Confederate cannons overlooking the river, Grant moved his army eastward on a campaign across Mississippi that Lincoln later called "one of the most brilliant in the world." Grant captured Jackson, Mississippi, before pinning the 31,000 Confederates inside Vicksburg so tightly that "not a cat could have crept out . . . without being discovered." The Union forces dug twelve miles of interconnected trenches encircling the besieged city.

In the **Battle of Vicksburg**, Grant decided to use constant bombardment and gradual starvation to wear down the Confederates holed up in the town. Many people were forced to live in cellars or caves dug to protect them from the unending shelling. The Rebel soldiers and the city's residents were hopelessly trapped; they could neither escape nor be reinforced nor resupplied with food and ammunition. As the weeks passed, desperate Confederates and civilians ate their horses and mules, then dogs and cats, and, finally, rats, which sold for a dollar each. One starving girl ate her pet bird.

General John C. Pemberton, the Confederate commander at Vicksburg, wrote Jefferson Davis that the situation in the beleaguered city was "hopeless." A group of ragged soldiers pleaded with their commander: "If you can't feed us, you had better surrender us, horrible as that idea is."

GETTYSBURG Vicksburg's dilemma led Jefferson Davis to ask Robert E. Lee to send troops to break the siege. Lee, however, thought he had a better plan. He would make another daring strike into the North in hopes of forcing the Union army surrounding Vicksburg to retreat. He also wagered that a bold northern offensive would persuade peace-seeking northern Copperhead Democrats to end the war on terms favorable to the Confederacy. The stakes were high. A Confederate general said the invasion into Maryland and Pennsylvania would "either destroy the Yankees or bring them to terms." Or be a disaster for Lee.

In June 1863, the fabled Army of Northern Virginia, which Lee said was made up of "invincible troops" who would "go anywhere and do anything if properly led," again moved northward, taking thousands of animals and wagons as well as throngs of slaves for support.

The Confederates moved quickly. As a Rebel soldier said, he had enjoyed "breakfast in Virginia, whiskey in Maryland, and supper in Pennsylvania." A Maryland woman reported that the Confederate soldiers were "the dirtiest I ever saw, a most ragged, lean, and hungry set of wolves." One reason Lee moved into the North was the need for food. His soldiers and slaves gathered thousands of horses, cattle, and hogs, as well as tons of wheat and corn. They also captured free blacks in Maryland and Pennsylvania and sent them back to slavery in Virginia.

Once the Union commander, General George Meade, realized the Confederates were again moving north, he gave chase, knowing that the next battle would "decide the fate of our country and our cause." As he moved into Pennsylvania, Lee lost track of the Federals because of the unexplained absence of General J. E. B. Stuart's 5,000 horse soldiers, who were Lee's "eyes and ears." Stuart, it turned out, had decided to create a panic in the Union capital by threatening an attack on Washington, D.C. On June 28, Lee uttered in exasperation: "I cannot think what has become of Stuart. I ought to have heard from him long before now."

Neither side expected Gettysburg, a hilly crossroads farming town of 2,400 people in southeastern Pennsylvania, to be the site of the largest battle ever fought in North America. Both armies were caught by surprise when Confederate troops entered the town at dawn on June 30 and collided with Union cavalry units that had been tracking their movements.

The main forces of both sides—65,000 Confederates and 85,000 Federals—then raced to the scene, and on July 1, the armies clashed in what came to be called the **Battle of Gettysburg**, the most dramatic contest of the war. While preparing to fight, a Union cavalryman who sensed the importance of the coming battle, yelled at the soldiers from New York and Pennsylvania: "You stand alone, between the Rebel army and your homes. Fight like hell!"

Initially, the Confederates forced the Federals to retreat, but the Union troops regrouped to stronger positions on high ridges overlooking the town. Meade rushed reinforcements to his new lines along the heights. That night he wrote his wife that both sides had been "shattered" by the first day's combat.

On July 2, wave after wave of screaming Confederates assaulted Meade's army, pushing the Federal lines back across blood-soaked wheat fields and through peach orchards, but never breaking through. A wounded Confederate officer scrawled a note before he died: "Tell my father I died with my face to the enemy." Some 16,000 were killed or wounded on both sides during the inconclusive second day of fighting. Worse was to come.

The next day, July 3, against the advice of his senior general, Georgian James Longstreet, Robert E. Lee risked all on a climactic assault against the well-defended Union lines along Cemetery Ridge. For two hours, both sides

"A Harvest of Death" Timothy H. O'Sullivan's grim photograph of the dead at Gettysburg.

bombarded the other, leading a Union soldier to write that it felt "as if the heavens and earth were crashing together." Deafening sounds "more terrible never greeted human ears."

Then, the cannons stopped firing. At about two o'clock on the broiling summer afternoon, three Confederate infantry divisions—about 12,500 men in all—emerged from the woods and prepared to attack in the 90-degree heat. General George Pickett, commander of the lead division, told them to "Charge the enemy and remember Old Virginia!"

With drums pounding and bugles blaring, a gray wave of sweating Rebels began a desperate, mile-long dash up a grassy slope of newly mown hay criss-crossed with fences. Awaiting them behind a low stone wall at the top of the ridge were 120 Union cannons and thousands of rifles. It was as hopeless a situation as the Union charge at Fredericksburg. A Union soldier remembered that the attacking Confederates displayed a desperate courage: they "came on in magnificent order with the step of men who believed themselves invincible."

When the Federals opened fire, the Confederates were "enveloped in a dense cloud of dust. Arms, heads, blankets, guns, and knapsacks were tossed into the clear air." Only a few Rebels made it to the top of the ridge, where they fought bravely in hand-to-hand combat. A general leading the assault climbed atop the stone wall and shouted: "Come on, boys! Give them the cold steel!

Who will follow me?" Two minutes later, he was dead—as was the Confederate attack—when Union soldiers held in reserve rushed to close the gap in their lines.

With stunning suddenness, the carnage was over. The surviving Confederates retreated in a jostling mob to where they had started. The once roaring battlefield was now a deathly quiet field of horror punctuated by the "moanings and groanings" of thousands of wounded soldiers and horses.

What General Lee had called the "grand charge" was, in the end, a grand failure. As he watched the survivors straggling back across the bloody field, he muttered, "All this has been my fault. It is I who have lost this fight." He then ordered General Pickett to prepare his battered division for another attack,

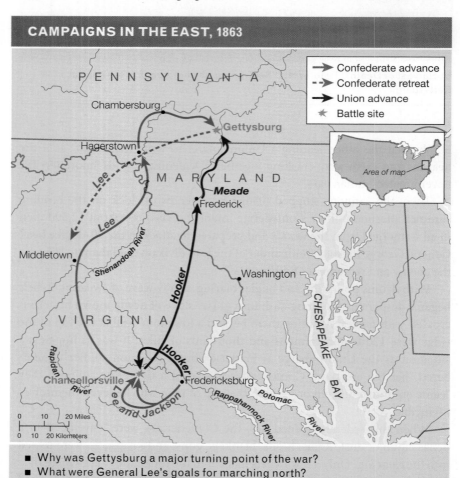

CAMPAIGNS IN THE EAST, 1863

- Why was Gettysburg a major turning point of the war?
- What were General Lee's goals for marching north?
- Why did his assault at Cemetery Ridge fail?

only to have Pickett tartly reply: "General Lee, I have no division now." Every one of his regimental commanders had fallen, and fully half of his men lay dead or wounded.

Some 42,000 on both sides were killed, wounded, or missing during three days at Gettysburg, and thousands of horses were also killed and left rotting in the summer heat. A Union soldier who witnessed the slaughter on the final day wrote home: "Great God! When will this horrid war stop?" Others asked the same question. John Futch, a Confederate private from North Carolina, saw his brother Charley shot in the head, suffer, and die at Gettysburg on July 3. He wrote his wife that the slaughter had left him "half crazy." A few weeks after the battle, he deserted, was captured, tried, and executed.

LEE'S RETREAT Again, as after Antietam, Lee's mangled army was forced to retreat back to Virginia, this time in a driving rain—and again, the Federals failed to give chase. Had General Meade pursued Lee's army, he might have ended the war. President Lincoln was outraged: "We had them within our grasp!" Lee had escaped to fight again—and the war would grind on for another twenty-one months.

But Lee's desperate gamble had failed in every way, not the least being its inability to save the besieged Confederate army at Vicksburg, Mississippi. On July 4, as Lee's defeated army left Pennsylvania, the Confederate commander at Vicksburg surrendered his entire 30,000-man army, ending the forty-seven-day siege. Union vessels now controlled the Mississippi River, and the Confederacy was effectively split in two, with Louisiana, Texas, and Arkansas cut off from the other Rebel states. Jefferson Davis said in late July that it was the Confederacy's "period of disaster."

After Gettysburg, a group of northern states funded a military cemetery in commemoration of the thousands of soldiers killed in the battle. On November 19, 1863, President Lincoln spoke at the ceremony dedicating the new national cemetery. In his brief remarks, known now as the Gettysburg Address, he expressed the pain and sorrow of the uncivil war. The prolonged conflict was testing whether a nation "dedicated to the proposition that all men are created equal . . . can long endure." In stirring words, Lincoln predicted that "this nation, under God, shall have a new birth of freedom—and that government of the people, by the people, and for the people, shall not perish from the earth."

CHATTANOOGA The third Union triumph of 1863 occurred in southern Tennessee around Chattanooga, the river port that served as a gateway to northern Georgia. In the late summer, a Union army led by General William

Rosecrans took Chattanooga on September 9 and then chased General Braxton Bragg's Rebel forces into Georgia, where they clashed at Chickamauga (a Cherokee word meaning "river of death").

The Confederates, for once, had a numerical advantage, and the battered Union forces fell back into Chattanooga while the Confederates surrounded the city. Rosecrans reported that "we have met a serious disaster. Enemy overwhelmed us, drove our right, pierced our center, and scattered troops there." Lincoln urged him to persevere: "If we can hold Chattanooga, and East Tennessee, I think [the] rebellion must dwindle and die."

The Union command rushed in reinforcements, and on November 24 and 25, the Federal troops dislodged the Confederates from Lookout Mountain and Missionary Ridge, thereby gaining effective control of Tennessee. The South had lost the war in the West.

THE CONFEDERACY AT RISK The dramatic Union victories at Vicksburg, Gettysburg, and Chattanooga turned the tide against the Confederacy. During the summer and fall of 1863, however, Lincoln's generals in the East lost the momentum that Gettysburg had provided, thereby allowing the Army of Northern Virginia to nurse its wounds and continue fighting.

By 1864, Robert E. Lee was ready to renew the war. His men were "in fine spirits and anxious for a fight." Still, the tone had changed. Earlier, Confederate leaders assumed they could actually win the war. Now, they began to worry about defeat. A Confederate officer in Richmond, writing in his diary after the defeats at Gettysburg and Vicksburg, noted that "today absolute ruin seems to be our fortune. The Confederacy totters to its destruction." Mary Chesnut confessed in her diary that the war was not going well for her beloved Confederacy. On January 1, 1864, she wrote: "God help my country!"

A WARTIME ELECTION War or no war, 1864 was still a presidential election year, and by autumn the contest would become a referendum on the war itself. No president since Andrew Jackson had won reelection, and Lincoln became convinced that he would lose without a dramatic change in the course of the war. Radical Republicans, frustrated that the war had not been won, tried to prevent Lincoln's nomination for a second term, but he consistently outmaneuvered them. Once Lincoln was assured of the nomination, he selected Andrew Johnson, a War Democrat from Tennessee, as his running mate on the "National Union" ticket.

The War Democrats had indiscreetly asked General Grant to be their candidate against Lincoln. He firmly declined, explaining that "I am not a politician, never was, and hope never to be." Becoming president "is the last thing in the world I desire."

Spurned by Grant, the Democrats at their national convention in Chicago stressed that people were tired of the costly war and called for an immediate end to the fighting. They nominated General George B. McClellan, the former Union commander who had clashed with Lincoln, his commander in chief. McClellan pledged that if elected he would stop the war and, if the Rebels refused to return to the Union, he would allow the Confederacy to "go in peace."

Lincoln knew that the election would be decided on the battlefields. To save the Union before a new Democratic administration could stop the war and recognize the independence of the Confederacy, the president had brought his best commander, Ulysses S. Grant, to Washington, D.C., in March 1864, promoted him to lieutenant general, the rank held by George Washington, and given him overall command of the war effort, promising him all the troops and supplies he needed. "Grant is my man," Lincoln exclaimed, "and I am his the rest of the war!" A New York newspaper reported that Lincoln's presidency was now "in the hands of General Grant, and the failure of the General will be the overthrow of the president."

GRANT'S STRATEGY   The cigar-chewing Grant was a hard-nosed warrior with unflagging energy and tenacity. One soldier said that Grant always looked like he was "determined to drive his head through a brick wall and was about to do it." The Union commander had a simple concept of war: "Find out where your enemy is, get to him as soon as you can, and strike him as hard as you can, and keep moving on"— regardless of the number of dead and wounded.

Grant dramatically changed the Union military strategy. He would focus on crippling Rebel armies rather than attacking particular cities, like Richmond. He planned for the three largest Union armies, one in Virginia, one in Tennessee, and one in Louisiana, to launch offensives in the spring of 1864. No more short battles followed by long pauses. The Union armies would force the outnumbered Confederates to keep fighting, day after day, week after week, until they were worn out. "Grant is like a bulldog," Lincoln said. "Let him get his teeth in, and nothing can shake him loose."

Ulysses S. Grant At his headquarters in City Point (now Hopewell), Virginia.

Grant assigned his trusted friend, General William Tecumseh Sherman, a rail-thin, red-haired Ohioan, to lead the Union army in Tennessee southward and apply Grant's strategy of "complete conquest" to the heart of the Confederacy. Sherman, cool under pressure and obsessed with winning at all costs, owed much of his success to Grant's support. "He stood by me when I was crazy, and I stood by him when he was drunk," Sherman said.

Grant and Sherman would now wage total war, confiscating or destroying civilian property that might be of use to the military. It was a ruthless and costly plan, but in the end it would prove effective. The full-bearded Confederate general James Longstreet, an old friend of Grant, told Lee that the Union commander "will fight us every day and every hour until the end of the war."

CHASING LEE In May 1864, General Grant's massive Army of the Potomac, numbering about 115,000 to General Lee's 65,000, moved south across the Rappahannock and Rapidan Rivers in eastern Virginia. In the nightmarish Battle of the Wilderness (May 5–6), the armies clashed in an impenetrable tangle of dense forest and thickety undergrowth. Explosions set off brushfires in which many wounded soldiers were burned to death. "What a medley of sounds," wrote a soldier: "the incessant roar of the rifle; the screaming bullets; the forest on fire; men cheering, groaning, yelling, swearing, and praying!"

At one point in the intense battle, the Union forces threatened to overrun General Lee's headquarters. Lee himself helped organize a counterattack, lining up soldiers from Texas to lead the effort. Spurred by a rush of adrenaline, he stood high in his stirrups, waved his hat, and yelled: "Texans always move them!" The Rebel commander then turned his horse toward the enemy to lead the men in a charge. The worried soldiers shouted, "Go back, General Lee, go back!" But he kept moving forward. "Lee to the rear!" they chanted. Yet he still kept going. Finally, an officer pulled ahead of Lee, grabbed the reins of his horse, and prevented him from moving. "Can't I, too, die for my country," the general muttered. His mood brightened as the Confederates swept the Federals from the field and broke the Union advance.

Grant's men suffered more casualties than the Confederates in the awful slugging match, but the Rebels struggled to find replacements. Always before, when bloodied by Lee's troops, Union armies had quit fighting to rest and nurse their wounds, but now Grant refused to halt. Instead, he continued to push southward, forcing the Rebels to keep fighting.

The Union army engaged Lee's men again near Spotsylvania Court House, eleven miles southwest of Fredericksburg, on the road to Richmond. For twelve days in May, the two armies engaged in some of the fiercest combat of the war. Grant's troops kept the pressure on, pushing relentlessly toward Richmond.

In the first days of June, just as Republican party leaders were gathering to renominate Lincoln as their presidential candidate, Grant foolishly ordered a poorly coordinated frontal attack on Lee's army. The Confederates were well entrenched at Cold Harbor near the Chickahominy River, just ten miles east of Richmond. In twenty minutes, almost 4,000 Federals, caught in a blistering cross fire, were killed or wounded. It was, according to a Union general, "one of the most disastrous days the Army of the Potomac has ever seen." A Confederate commander from Alabama reported that "it was not war; it was murder."

The frightful losses nearly unhinged Grant, who later admitted that the botched attack was his greatest mistake as a commander. Critics, including Lincoln's wife Mary, called him "the Butcher" after Cold Harbor. In just two months, Grant's massive offensive across Virginia, labeled the Overland Campaign, had cost some 60,000 killed and wounded Union soldiers and 33,000 Rebel casualties. Criticism of the war in the North skyrocketed. Even Horace Greeley, the powerful Unionist publisher of the *New York Tribune*, urged Lincoln to negotiate with Confederate leaders to save the "bleeding, bankrupt, almost dying country." During the summer of 1864, the Union war effort came close to ending.

Yet Grant, for all of his mistakes, knew that his army could more easily replace its dead and wounded than could the Rebels. While the Confederates were winning battles, they were losing the war. In June 1864, Grant brilliantly maneuvered his battered forces around Lee's army and headed for Petersburg, a major supply center and transportation hub twenty-five miles south of Richmond. There the opposing armies dug in along long lines of trenches above and below Petersburg. Grant would now lay siege to the Confederate army, tightening the noose around Lee and the Rebels as he had done at Vicksburg.

For nine months, the two sides held each other in check around Petersburg. Grant's troops, twice as numerous as Lee's, were generously supplied by Union vessels moving up the James River, while the Confederates, hungry and cold, wasted away. The number of deserters grew so large that Lee asked permission to shoot them when caught. Petersburg had become Lee's prison while disasters piled up for the Confederacy elsewhere. Lee admitted that it was "a mere question of time" before he would have to retreat or surrender. On June 15, 1864, a Rebel soldier noted in his diary that "our affairs do look gloomy." Grant, he added later, "will no doubt capture the place."

SHERMAN PUSHES SOUTH Meanwhile, General Grant ordered William T. Sherman to drive through the heart of Dixie and "break it up," inflicting "all the damage you can." As General Sherman moved his large army south from Chattanooga through the Georgia mountains toward the crucial

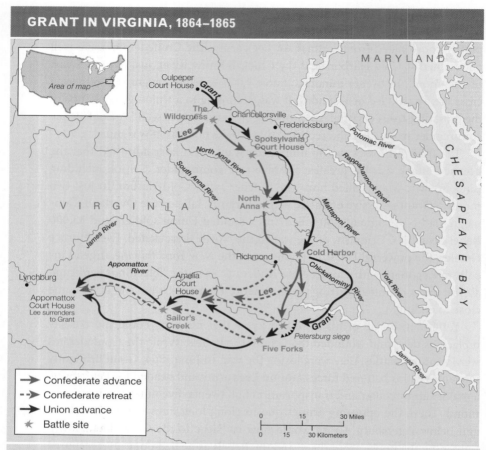

GRANT IN VIRGINIA, 1864–1865

Area of map

MARYLAND

Culpeper Court House

Grant

The Wilderness

Chancellorsville

Fredericksburg

Potomac River

Lee

Spotsylvania Court House

North Anna River

South Anna River

Rappahannock River

VIRGINIA

North Anna

Mattaponi River

CHESAPEAKE BAY

James River

Richmond

Cold Harbor

Chickahominy River

York River

Appomattox River

Lynchburg

Amelia Court House

Lee

Appomattox Court House
Lee surrenders to Grant

Sailor's Creek

Grant

Petersburg siege

Five Forks

James River

→ Confederate advance
--→ Confederate retreat
→ Union advance
✳ Battle site

| 0 | 15 | 30 Miles |
| 0 | 15 | 30 Kilometers |

- How were General Grant's tactics in the Battle of the Wilderness different from the Union's previous encounters with General Lee's army?
- Why did Grant have the advantage at Petersburg?

railroad hub of Atlanta, he sent a warning to the city's residents intended to frighten them: "prepare for my coming."

By the middle of July, Sherman's troops had reached the outskirts of heavily-fortified Atlanta, trapping the 40,000 Confederate soldiers there. Jefferson Davis was so concerned about the situation that he made the hugely controversial decision to replace the Confederate commander, General Joseph Johnston, with General John Bell Hood, who had been Lee's most aggressive general after the death of Stonewall Jackson.

Hood, a Texan, was a reckless fighter. A Confederate senator's wife said that "a braver man, a purer patriot, a more gallant soldier never breathed than

The tattered colors of the 56th and 36th Massachusetts Regiments Union soldiers march through Virginia in 1864.

General Hood." His arm had been shattered at Gettysburg, and he had lost a leg at Chickamauga. Strapped to his saddle, he refused simply to "defend" Atlanta; instead, he attacked Sherman's army, which is exactly what Sherman, the Union commander, wanted him to do. Three times in eight days, the Confederates lashed out at the Union lines encircling the city. Each time they were turned back, suffering *seven* times as many casualties as the Federals. The Battle of Atlanta left Hood's army shattered, surrounded, and outnumbered.

Finally, on September 1, the Confederates, desperately low on food and supplies, evacuated the city. Sherman then moved his troops into Atlanta. In Richmond, Mary Chesnut took the news hard. "We are going to be wiped off the earth," she wrote. "Since Atlanta," she added, "I have felt as if all were dead within me, forever."

Sherman's soldiers stayed in Atlanta until November, resting and resupplying themselves in the heart of the Confederacy. The 20,000 residents were told to leave. When city officials protested, the Union commander replied: "War is cruelty." His men then set fire to the city's railroads, iron foundries, shops, mills, hotels, and businesses.

LINCOLN REELECTED William Tecumseh Sherman's conquest of Atlanta turned the tide of the **election of 1864**. As a Republican senator said, the Union victory in Georgia "created the most extraordinary change in public opinion here [in the North] that ever was known." The capture of Mobile,

Alabama, by Union naval forces in August, and Confederate defeats in Virginia's Shenandoah Valley in October also spurred the dramatic revival of Abraham Lincoln's political support in the North. The South's hope that northern discontent would lead to a negotiated peace vanished.

In the 1864 election, the Democratic candidate, McClellan, carried only New Jersey, Delaware, and Kentucky, with just 21 electoral votes to Lincoln's 212, and won only 1.8 million popular votes (45 percent) to Lincoln's 2.2 million (55 percent). Union soldiers and sailors voted in large numbers, and their choice was Lincoln. The president's victory sealed the fate of the Confederacy, for it ensured that the Union armies would keep the pressure on the Rebels.

SHERMAN'S "MARCH TO THE SEA" In November 1864, General Sherman led 60,000 soldiers out of burning Atlanta on their famous **"March to the Sea,"** advancing rapidly through Georgia toward the coast.

Lincoln's second inauguration As Lincoln delivered his second inaugural address on the Capitol portico, John Wilkes Booth was among those standing on the porch, overhead.

Sherman planned to wage a modern war against soldiers and civilians. He pledged to "whip the rebels, to humble their pride, to follow them into their inmost recesses, and make them fear and dread us."

John Bell Hood's Confederate Army of Tennessee, meanwhile, tried a desperate gamble by heading in the opposite direction from the Union forces, pushing northward into Alabama and then Tennessee. Hood hoped to trick Sherman into chasing him. Sherman refused to take the bait, however. He was determined to keep his main army moving southward to the Georgia coast and then into South Carolina, the seedbed of secession. But he did send General George Thomas and 30,000 soldiers north to shadow Hood's Confederates.

The two forces clashed in Tennessee. Hood was a ferocious fighter but a foolish commander. In the Battle of

William Tecumseh Sherman Sherman's campaign through Georgia developed into a war of maneuver as they raced to the coast, without the pitched battles of Grant's campaign in Virginia.

Franklin (November 30, 1864), near Nashville, he sent his 18,000 soldiers in a hopeless frontal assault against dug-in Union troops backed by cannons. In a few hours, Hood lost six generals and saw 6,252 of his men killed or wounded, a casualty figure higher than "Pickett's Charge" at Gettysburg. Two weeks later, in the Battle of Nashville, the Federals led by General Thomas scattered what was left of Hood's bloodied army. A few days later, a grieving Hood was relieved of his command.

Meanwhile, Sherman's army pushed southward across Georgia, living off the land while destroying plantations, barns, crops, warehouses, bridges, and rail lines. "We are not only fighting hostile armies," Sherman explained, "but a hostile people" who must "feel the hard hand of war." An Ohio sergeant confirmed their intent: "Every house, barn, fence, and cotton gin gets an application of the torch. That prospect is revolting, but war is an uncivil game, and can't be civilized."

After the war, a Confederate officer acknowledged that Sherman's march through Georgia was well conceived and well managed. "I don't think there was ever an army in the world that would have behaved better, in a similar expedition, in an enemy country. Our army certainly wouldn't have."

On December 24, 1864, Sherman sent a whimsical telegram to President Lincoln offering him the coastal city of Savannah as a Christmas present. By the time Sherman's army arrived in Savannah, it had freed more than 40,000 slaves, burned scores of plantations, and destroyed all of the railroads. "God bless you, Yanks!" shouted a freed slave in Georgia. "Come at last! God knows how long I been waitin'."

SOUTH CAROLINA On February 1, 1865, Sherman's army headed north across the Savannah River into South Carolina, the "hell-hole of secession" in

Destroying southern railroads Sherman's troops cut a swath of destruction across Georgia in his "March to the Sea." Here, Union troops rip up railroad tracks in Atlanta.

the eyes of Union troops. Sherman reported that his "whole army is burning with an insatiable desire to wreak vengeance upon South Carolina. I almost tremble at her fate, but feel she deserves all that seems in store for her." General Joseph Johnston, who had been called out of retirement to take charge of the scattered remnants of the Rebel forces, knew that the war was all but over. All he could hope to do, he said, was "annoy" the advancing Federals.

South Carolina paid a high price for having led the South out of the Union. Sherman's men burned more than a dozen towns, including Barnwell, which they called "Burnwell." On February 17, 1865, Sherman's men captured the state capital of Columbia. Soon thereafter, Charleston itself surrendered after Confederate soldiers set fires to buildings containing material that would valuable to the Yankees. It was no accident that Sherman ordered two all-black regiments to lead the Union advance into the city that launched secession and war. On April 14, Major Robert Anderson was given the honor of raising the Union flag once again over Fort Sumter.

A LOSING CAUSE During the late winter and early spring of 1865, the Confederacy found itself besieged on all sides. Defeat was in the air. Some Rebel leaders wanted to negotiate a peace settlement. Confederate secretary of war John C. Breckinridge, the Kentuckian who had served as vice president under James Buchanan and had run for president in 1860, urged Robert E. Lee to negotiate an honorable end to the war. "This has been a magnificent epic," he said. "In God's name, let it not terminate in a farce."

Jefferson Davis rejected any talk of surrender, however. If his armies should be defeated, he wanted the soldiers to scatter and fight an unending guerrilla war. "The war came and now it must go on," he stubbornly insisted, "till the last man of this generation falls in his tracks, and his children seize his musket and fight our battle." Davis, Lee, and others finally became so desperate that they did the unthinkable: on March 13, 1865, Davis signed a Virginia bill calling for the immediate recruitment of blacks into the army. Before they could be enlisted and trained, however, the war came to an end.

A SECOND TERM While Confederate forces made their last stands, Abraham Lincoln prepared for his second term as president. The weary commander in chief had weathered constant criticism during his first term, but with the war nearing its end, Lincoln now garnered deserved praise. The *Chicago Tribune* observed that the president "has slowly and steadily risen in the respect, confidence, and admiration of the people."

On March 4, 1865, amid rumors of a Confederate attempt to abduct or assassinate the president, the six-foot-four-inch Lincoln, dressed in a black

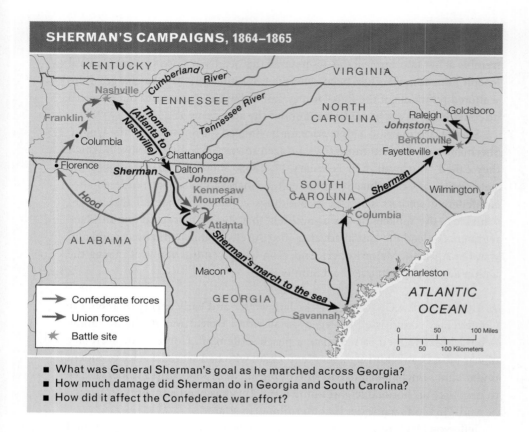

SHERMAN'S CAMPAIGNS, 1864–1865

- What was General Sherman's goal as he marched across Georgia?
- How much damage did Sherman do in Georgia and South Carolina?
- How did it affect the Confederate war effort?

suit and stovepipe hat, his face weathered by prairie wind and political worry, delivered his second inaugural address on the East Portico of the Capitol. Not a hundred feet away, looking down on Lincoln from the Capitol porch, was a twenty-six-year-old actor named John Wilkes Booth, who five weeks later would kill the president in a desperate attempt to do something "heroic" for his beloved South.

Lincoln's second inaugural address was more a sermon than a speech. Slavery, he said, had "somehow" caused the war, and everyone bore some guilt for the national shame of racial injustice and the awful war to end it. Both sides had known before the fighting began that war was to be avoided at all costs, but "one of them would *make* war rather than let the nation survive; and the other would *accept* war rather than let it perish."

Lincoln longed for peace and reunion. "Fondly do we hope—fervently do we pray—that this mighty scourge of war may speedily pass away." He noted the paradoxical irony of both sides in the civil war reading the same Bible, praying to the same God, and appealing for divine support in its fight against the other. Now the president urged the Union forces "to finish the work we are in," bolstered with "firmness in the right insofar as God gives us to see the right."

As Lincoln looked ahead to the end of the fighting and a "just and lasting peace," he stressed that vengeance must be avoided at all costs. Reconciliation must be pursued "with malice toward none; with charity for all." Those eight words captured Lincoln's hopes for a restored Union. Redemption and reunion were his goals, not vengeance. With a loving tolerance of human complexity and sinfulness, Lincoln revealed how the rigors of war had helped him see the need for humility in victory. The abolitionist leader Frederick Douglass proclaimed Lincoln's second inaugural address "a sacred effort."

APPOMATTOX   During the spring of 1865, General Grant's army kept pounding the Rebels defending Petersburg, Virginia. Lee was on the horns of a dilemma, and he knew it. He had no way to replace the men he was losing, and his dwindling army couldn't kill enough Yankees to make Grant quit. On April 2, 1865, the badly outnumbered Confederates tried to break out of Petersburg, but the Union army was in hot pursuit. Five days later, on April 7, Grant sent a note urging Lee to surrender. With his army virtually surrounded, Lee told General James Longstreet that "there is nothing left for me to do but go and see General Grant, and I would rather die a thousand deaths."

On April 9 (Palm Sunday), four years to the day since the Confederate attack on Fort Sumter, the dignified Lee, stiff and formal in his dress uniform, met the short, mud-spattered Grant in the village of **Appomattox Court House**. After discussing their service in the Mexican-American War, Lee asked what the terms of surrender would be. In keeping with Lincoln's desire for a gracious peace, Grant let the Confederates keep their pistols, horses, and mules, and he ensured that none of them would be tried for treason. Lee then confessed that his men were starving, and Grant ordered that they be provided food. After signing the surrender documents in the parlor of a farmhouse, Lee mounted his horse and returned to his army.

The next day, as the gaunt Confederates formed ranks for the last time, Joshua Chamberlain, the Union general in charge of the surrender ceremony, ordered his men to salute the Rebel soldiers as they paraded past to give up their weapons. His Confederate counterpart signaled his men to do likewise. Chamberlain remembered that there was not a sound—no trumpets or drums, no cheers or jeers, simply an "awed stillness . . . as if it were the passing of the dead." The remaining Confederate forces surrendered in May. Jefferson Davis fled Richmond ahead of the advancing Federal troops, only to be captured in Georgia on May 10. He was eventually imprisoned in Virginia for two years.

The brutal war was at last over. Upon learning of the Union victory, John Wilkes Booth, a popular young actor in Washington, D.C., who hated Lincoln and the Union, wrote in his diary that "something *decisive* and great must be done" to avenge the Confederate defeat. He began plotting to kill President Lincoln and members of his cabinet.

Two days after Lee surrendered, President Lincoln gave a speech on the White House lawn in which he looked forward to "reconstructing" the Confederate states. He also hoped that literate freed blacks and those who had served in the Union military would be able to vote. Booth, who was in the audience, noted that Lincoln's pledge "meant nigger citizenship. Now, by God, I'll put him through [kill him]. That is the last speech he will ever make."

A TRANSFORMING WAR

The Civil War was the most traumatic event in American history. "We have shared the incommunicable experience of war," reflected Oliver Wendell Holmes Jr., the twice-wounded Union officer who would one day become the nation's leading jurist. "We have felt, we still feel, the passion of life to its top. . . . In our youth, our hearts were touched by fire." In Virginia, elderly Edmund Ruffin, the arch secessionist planter who had been given the honor of firing the first shots at Fort Sumter, was so distraught by the Confederate surrender that he put his rifle barrel in his mouth and blew off the top of his head.

The long war changed the nation in profound ways. A *New York Times* editorial said that the war left "nothing as it found it. . . . It leaves us a different people in everything." The war destroyed the South's economy, many of its railroads and factories, much of its livestock, and several of its cities. In 1860, the northern and southern economies were essentially equal in size. By 1865, the southern economy's productivity had been cut in half. Many southern economic and political leaders had been killed during the war or had seen their plantations and businesses destroyed.

THE UNION PRESERVED The war ended the Confederacy and preserved the Union; shifted the political balance of power in Congress, the U.S. Supreme Court, and the presidency from South to North; and boosted the northern economy's industrial development, commercial agriculture, and western settlement. The Homestead Act (1862) made more than a billion acres in the West available to the landless. The power and scope of the federal government were expanded at the expense of states' rights. In 1860, the annual federal budget was $63 million; by 1865, it was more than $1 billion. In winning the war, the federal government had become the nation's largest employer.

By the end of the war, the Union was spending $2.5 million per day on the military effort, and whole new industries had been established to meet its needs for weapons, uniforms, food, equipment, and supplies. The massive amounts of preserved food required by the Union armies, for example, helped create the canning industry and transformed Chicago into the meatpacking capital of the world.

Federal contracts also provided the money needed to accelerate the growth of new industries such as the production of iron, steel, and petroleum, thus laying the groundwork for a postwar economic boom. Ohio senator John Sherman, in a letter to his brother, General William T. Sherman, said the war had dramatically expanded the vision "of leading capitalists" who now talk of earning "millions as confidently as formerly of thousands."

THE FIRST "MODERN" WAR   In many respects, the Civil War was the first modern war. Its scope and scale were unprecedented, as it was fought across the entire continent. And armies for the first time used railroads and steamboats to move around. One of every twelve men on both sides served in the war, and few families were unaffected. More than 750,000 soldiers and sailors (37,000 of whom were blacks fighting for the Union) died, 50 percent more than the number who would die in the Second World War. The comparable number of deaths relative to today's population would be almost 7.5 million. Of the surviving combatants, 50,000 returned home with one or more limbs amputated. Disease, however, was the greatest threat to soldiers, killing twice as many as were lost in battle. Some 50,000 civilians were also killed during the war, and virtually every community hosted uncounted widows and orphans.

Unlike previous conflicts, much of the fighting in the Civil War was distant and impersonal, in part because of improvements in the effectiveness of muskets, rifles, and cannons. Men were killed at long distance, without knowing who had fired the shots that felled them. The opposing forces used an array of new weapons and instruments of war, such as cannons with "rifled," or grooved, barrels for greater accuracy; repeating rifles; ironclad ships; railroad artillery; the first military telegraph; observation balloons;

and wire entanglements. The war was also modern because civilians could follow its activities by reading the newspapers that sent reporters to the front lines, or by visiting exhibitions of photographs taken at the battlefields and camps.

THIRTEENTH AMENDMENT   The most important result of the war was the liberation of almost 4 million slaves. The Emancipation Proclamation had technically freed only those slaves in areas still controlled by the Confederacy. As the war entered its final months, however, freedom for all slaves emerged more fully as a legal reality as President Lincoln moved from viewing emancipation as a military weapon to seeing it as the mainspring of the conflict itself.

Three major steps occurred in January 1865: Missouri and then Tennessee abolished slavery, and, at Lincoln's insistence, the U.S. House of Representatives passed an amendment to the Constitution that banned slavery everywhere. Upon ratification by three-fourths of the reunited states, the **Thirteenth Amendment** became law eight months after the war ended, on December 18, 1865. It removed any lingering doubts about the legality of emancipation. By then, slavery remained only in the border states of Kentucky and Delaware.

THE DEBATE CONTINUES   Historians have provided conflicting assessments of the Union victory. Some have focused on the inherent weaknesses of the Confederacy: its lack of industry and railroads, the tensions between the states and the central government in Richmond, poor political leadership, faulty coordination and communication, the expense of preventing slave rebellions and runaways, and the advantages in population and resources enjoyed by the North. Still others have highlighted the erosion of Confederate morale in the face of terrible food shortages and unimaginable human losses.

The debate about why the North won and the South lost will probably never end, but as in other modern wars, disparities in resources were key factors. Robert E. Lee's own explanation remains accurate: "After four years of arduous service marked by unsurpassed courage and fortitude, the Army of Northern Virginia has been compelled to yield to overwhelming numbers and resources."

Whatever the reasons, the North's victory resolved a key issue: no state could divorce itself from the Union. The Union, as Lincoln had always maintained, was indissoluble. At the same time, the war led to the Constitution being permanently amended to eliminate slavery. The terrible war thus served to clarify the meaning of the ideals ("All men are created equal") on which the United States had been established. The largest slaveholding nation in the world had at last chosen liberty—for all. In his first message to Congress in December 1861, Lincoln recognized early on what was at stake amid the onrush of civil war: "The struggle of today is not altogether for today; it is for a vast future also." So it was. The "fiery ordeal" of a war both "fundamental and astounding" produced, as Lincoln said, not just a preserved Union but "a new birth of freedom."

CHAPTER REVIEW

SUMMARY

- **Civil War Strategies** When the war began, the Confederacy had a geographic advantage of fighting a defensive war on their own territory. The Union, however, held strong advantages in population and industrial development, particularly in the production of weapons, ships, and railroad equipment. After suffering a defeat at the First Battle of Bull Run, the Union military leaders adopted the "*Anaconda Plan*," imposing a naval blockade on southern ports and slowly crushing resistance on all fronts. The Union's industrial might was a deciding factor in the long war of attrition.

- **Emancipation Proclamation** Initially, President Lincoln declared that the war's aim was to restore the Union and that slavery would be maintained where it existed. Gradually, Lincoln came to see that winning the war required ending slavery. He justified the *Emancipation Proclamation (1862)* as a military necessity because it would deprive the South of its captive labor force. After the *Battle of Antietam* in September 1862, he announced plans to free the slaves. He hoped that southern states would return to the Union before his deadline of January 1, 1863, when all slaves living in areas under Confederate control were declared free.

- **Wartime Home Fronts** The federal government proved much more capable with finances than did the Confederacy. Through a series of tariffs, income taxes, bond issues, and banking reforms, the Union was better able to absorb the war's soaring costs. In the absence of the southern delegation in Congress, the Republican Congress approved a higher tariff, a transcontinental railroad, and a *Homestead Act*, all of which accelerated Union settlement of the West and the growth of a national economy. The *Morrill Land Grant Act* provided large land grants for the creation of state universities intended to promote economic development by turning out engineers and entrepreneurs. Both sides experienced pockets of opposition to the war efforts. In the North, *Copperhead Democrats* opposed the war and Lincoln's decision to end slavery.

- **The Winning Union Strategy** The Union victories at the *Battles of Vicksburg and Gettysburg* in July 1863 turned the war in the Union's favor. With the capture of Vicksburg, the last Confederate-controlled city along the Mississippi River, Union forces cut the Confederacy in two, depriving armies in the East of supplies and manpower. In 1864, Lincoln placed General Ulysses S. Grant in charge of the Union's war efforts. For the next year, his forces constantly attacked Robert E. Lee's in Virginia while, farther south, General William T. Sherman's *"March to the Sea"* destroyed plantations, railroads, and morale in Georgia and South Carolina. His successes helped propel Lincoln to victory in the *election of 1864*. After that, southern resistance wilted. Lee surrendered his army to Grant at *Appomattox Court House* in April 1865.

- **The Significance of the Civil War** The Civil War involved the largest number of casualties of any American war, and the Union's victory changed the course of the nation's development. Most important, the war ended slavery, embodied in the adoption of the *Thirteenth Amendment* to the U.S. Constitution in 1865. Not only did the power of the federal government increase, but the center of political and economic power shifted away from the South and the planter class. The Republican-controlled Congress enacted legislation during the war to raise tariffs, fund the first transcontinental railroad, and introduce many financial reforms that would drive the nation's economic development for the rest of the century.

CHRONOLOGY

April 1861	Virginia, North Carolina, Tennessee, and Arkansas join Confederacy; West Virginia splits from Virginia to stay with Union
July 1861	First Battle of Bull Run (Manassas)
April–September 1862	Battles of Shiloh, Second Bull Run, and Antietam
September 1862	Lincoln issues Emancipation Proclamation
May–July 1863	New York City draft riots; siege of Vicksburg; Battle of Gettysburg
March 1864	Lincoln places General Ulysses S. Grant in charge of Union military operations
September 1864	General William T. Sherman seizes and burns Atlanta
November 1864	Lincoln is reelected
April 9, 1865	General Robert E. Lee surrenders at Appomattox Court House
1865	Thirteenth Amendment is ratified

KEY TERMS

Anaconda Plan p. 647

contrabands p. 659

Battle of Antietam (1862) p. 660

Emancipation Proclamation (1862) p. 662

Militia Act (1862) p. 666

Homestead Act (1862) p. 671

Morrill Land Grant Act (1862) p. 671

Copperhead Democrats p. 673

Battle of Vicksburg (1863) p. 677

Battle of Gettysburg (1863) p. 678

election of 1864 p. 687

"March to the Sea" p. 688

Appomattox Court House p. 693

Thirteenth Amendment (1865) p. 696

 INQUIZITIVE

Go to InQuizitive to see what you've learned—and learn what you've missed—with personalized feedback along the way.

16 The Era of Reconstruction

1865–1877

A Visit from the Old Mistress **(1876)** This powerful painting by Winslow Homer depicts a plantation mistress visiting her former slaves in the postwar South. Although their living conditions are humble, these freedwomen stand firmly and eye-to-eye with the woman who had kept them in bondage.

I n the spring of 1865, the terrible conflict was finally over. The war to restore the Union ended up transforming American life. The United States was a "new nation," said an Illinois congressman, because it was now "wholly free." At a cost of some 750,000 lives and the destruction of the southern economy, the Union had won the costly war, and almost 4 million enslaved Americans had won their freedom. This was the most dramatic social change in the history of the nation. But the end of slavery did not bring the end of racism.

The defeated Confederates had seen their world turned upside down. The abolition of slavery, the war-related disruptions to the southern economy, and the horrifying human losses had destroyed the plantation system and upended racial relations in the South. "Change, change, indelibly stamped upon everything I meet, even upon the faces of the people!" marveled Alexander Stephens, the vice president of the Confederacy. His native region now had to come to terms with a new era and a new order as the United States government set about "reconstructing" the South and policing defiant ex-Confederates. Diarist Mary Chesnut expressed the angry frustration felt by the defeated southern white elite when she wished that "they were *all* dead—all Yankees!"

Freed slaves felt just the opposite. Yankees were their saviors. No longer would enslaved workers be sold and separated from their families or prevented from learning to read and write or attending church. "I felt like a bird out of a cage," said former slave Houston Holloway of Georgia who had been sold to three different owners during his first twenty years. "Amen. Amen. Amen. I could hardly ask to feel any better than I did that day." Eda Harper from Mississippi was even more ecstatic. Upon learning of the end of the war, she and her fellow slaves "danced all night long."

focus questions

1. What major challenges faced the federal government in reconstructing the South after the Civil War during the period from 1865 to 1877?

2. How and why did Reconstruction policies change over time?

3. In what ways did white and black southerners react to Reconstruction?

4. What were the political and economic factors that helped lead to the end of Reconstruction in 1877?

5. What was the significance of Reconstruction for the nation's future?

Few owners, however, willingly freed their slaves until forced to by the arrival of Union soldiers. A North Carolina planter pledged that he and other whites "will never get along with the free negroes" because they were an "inferior race." Similarly, a Mississippi planter predicted that "these niggers will all be slaves again in twelve months."

At war's end in the spring of 1865, Henry Adams left the Louisiana plantation where he had been enslaved "to see whether I am free by going without a pass." A group of whites confronted him on the road, asked his owner's name, and beat him when he declared that "I now belong to no one." Some newly freed slaves rushed to give themselves new names to symbolize their changed status. Others left plantations and farms for towns and cities, where, as one of them said, "freedom was free-er."

The ratification of the Thirteenth Amendment to the U.S. Constitution in December 1865 was intended to end all doubt about the status of former slaves by abolishing slavery everywhere. Now the nation faced the huge task of "reconstructing" and reuniting a war-ravaged South while transforming ex-slaves into free workers and equal citizens.

It would not be easy. Freedom did not bring independence or self-reliance for millions of former slaves. At the same time, many white southerners resented and resisted efforts to "reconstruct" their region. As a South Carolina planter told a federal official in the fall of 1865, "The war is not over."

During the Reconstruction era, from 1865 to 1877, political leaders wrestled with how best to bring the Confederate states back into the Union and how best to help former slaves make the transition from bondage to citizenship. Those turbulent years witnessed a complex debate about the role of the federal government in ensuring civil rights.

Some northerners wanted the former Confederate states returned to the Union with little or no changes in their social, political, and economic life. Others called for former Confederate political and military leaders to be imprisoned or executed and the South rebuilt in the image of the rest of the nation. The editors of the nation's most popular magazine, *Harper's Weekly*, expressed this vengeful attitude when they declared that "the forgive-and-forget policy . . . is mere political insanity and suicide."

Although the Reconstruction era lasted only twelve years, it was one of the most significant periods in U.S. history. At the center of the debate over how best to restore the Union were questions of continuing significance: Who is deserving of citizenship and what does it entail? What rights should all Americans enjoy? What role should the federal government play in ensuring freedom and equality? Those questions are still shaping American life nearly 150 years later.

THE WAR'S AFTERMATH IN THE SOUTH

The postwar South presented a sharp contrast to the victorious North, where the economy had been strengthened by the war efforts. Between 1860 and 1870, northern wealth grew by 50 percent while southern wealth dropped 60 percent. Along the path that General William Tecumseh Sherman's Union army had blazed across Georgia and the Carolinas, one observer reported in 1866, the countryside "looked for many miles like a broad black streak of ruin and desolation." Burned-out Columbia, South Carolina, said another witness, was "a wilderness of ruins"; Charleston, the birthplace of secession, had become a place of "vacant houses, of widowed women, of rotting wharves, of deserted warehouses, of weed-wild gardens, of miles of grass-grown streets, of acres of pitiful and voiceless barrenness."

Throughout the South, property values had collapsed. In the year after the war ended, eighty-one plantations in Mississippi were sold for less than a tenth of what they had been worth in 1860. Confederate government bonds and

Richmond after the Civil War Before evacuating the capital of the Confederacy, Richmond, Virginia, Rebels set fire to warehouses and factories to prevent their falling into Union hands. Pictured here is one of Richmond's burnt districts in April 1865. Women in mourning attire walk among the shambles.

paper money were worthless; personal savings had vanished. Amanda Worthington, a planter's wife from Mississippi, saw her whole world destroyed. In the fall of 1865, she assessed the damage: "None of us can realize that we are no longer wealthy—yet thanks to the Yankees, the cause of all unhappiness, such is the case."

Union soldiers who fanned out across the defeated South to impose order were cursed and spat upon. A Virginia woman expressed a spirited defiance common among her circle of Confederate friends: "Every day, every hour, that I live increases my hatred and detestation, and loathing of that race. They [Yankees] disgrace our common humanity. As a people I consider them vastly inferior to the better classes of our slaves." Fervent southern nationalists, both men and women, implanted in their children a similar hatred of Yankees and a defiance of northern rule. One mother said that she trained her children to "fear God, love the South, and live to avenge her."

Many of the largest southern cities—Richmond, Atlanta, Charleston—were in ruins; most southern railroads were damaged or destroyed. Cotton that had not been destroyed by invading Union armies was now seized by federal troops. Emancipation had eliminated $4 billion invested in slaves and left the agricultural economy in confusion. It would take decades before farm production regained its pre-war levels. In 1860, just before the war began, the South generated 30 percent of the nation's wealth; in 1870, only ten years later, it produced but 12 percent.

Many southerners were homeless and hungry, emotionally exhausted and physically disabled. Lives had been shattered—literally. Countless families had lost sons and husbands, and many surviving war veterans returned home with one or more limbs missing. In 1866, the state of Mississippi spent a fifth of its annual budget on artificial limbs for Confederate soldiers. Confederate general Braxton Bragg returned to his "once prosperous" Alabama home to find "all, all was lost, except my debts."

Rebuilding the former Confederacy would not be easy, and the issues related to reconstruction were often complicated and controversial. For example, the process of forming new state governments required first determining the official status of the states that had seceded: Were they now conquered territories? If so, then the Constitution assigned Congress authority to re-create their state governments. But what if, as Abraham Lincoln had argued, the Confederate states had never officially left the Union because the act of secession was itself illegal? In that circumstance, the president would be responsible for re-forming state governments.

Whichever branch of government—Congress or the presidency—directed the reconstruction of the South, it would have to address the most difficult issue: What would be the political, social, and economic status of the freed slaves? Were they citizens? If not, what was their status as Americans? What the freed slaves wanted most was to become self-reliant as soon as possible. That meant being able to control their labor, reunite with their family members, gain education for their children, enjoy full participation in political life, and create their own community organizations and social life. Many whites were just as determined to prevent that from happening.

DEBATES OVER POLITICAL RECONSTRUCTION

The reconstruction of former Confederate states actually began during the war and went through several phases, the first of which was Presidential Reconstruction. In 1862, with Union forces advancing into the South, President Lincoln had named army generals to serve as temporary military governors for conquered Confederate areas. By the end of 1863, he had formulated a plan to reestablish governments in states liberated from Confederate rule.

LINCOLN'S PLAN In late 1863, President Lincoln issued a Proclamation of Amnesty and Reconstruction, under which any Confederate state could recreate a Union government once a number equal to 10 percent of those who had voted in 1860 swore allegiance to the Constitution. They also received a presidential pardon acquitting them of treason. Certain groups, however, were denied pardons: Confederate government officials; senior officers of the Confederate army and navy; judges, congressmen, and military officers of the United States who had left their posts to aid the rebellion; and those who had abused captured African American soldiers.

CONGRESSIONAL PLANS A few conservative and most moderate Republicans supported Lincoln's program that immediately restored pro-Union southern governments. However, the Radical Republicans argued that Congress, not the president, should supervise Reconstruction.

The **Radical Republicans** favored a drastic transformation of southern society that would grant ex-slaves full citizenship rights. Many Radicals, motivated primarily by religious values and moral ideals, believed that all people, regardless of race, were equal in God's eyes. They wanted no compromise with the "sin" of racism.

The Radicals also hoped to replace the white, Democratic planter elite with a new generation of small farmers, along with wage-earning and middle-class

Republicans. "The middling classes who own the soil, and work it with their own hands," explained Radical leader Thaddeus Stevens, "are the main support of every free government."

THE WADE-DAVIS BILL In 1864, with the war still raging, the Radical Republicans tried to take charge of Reconstruction by passing the Wade-Davis Bill, sponsored by Senator Benjamin Franklin Wade of Ohio and Representative Henry Winter Davis of Maryland. Unlike Lincoln's 10-percent plan, the Wade-Davis Bill required that a *majority* of white males swear their allegiance to the Union before a Confederate state could be readmitted.

But the Wade-Davis Bill never became law: Lincoln vetoed it as being too harsh. In retaliation, Republicans issued the Wade-Davis Manifesto, which accused Lincoln of exceeding his constitutional authority. Unfazed, Lincoln moved ahead with his efforts to restore the Confederate states to the Union. He also acted boldly to provide assistance to the freed slaves in the South.

THE FREEDMEN'S BUREAU In early 1865, Congress approved the Thirteenth Amendment to the Constitution, officially abolishing slavery in the United States. The amendment, and the war that enabled it, liberated 4 million slaves. Yet what did freedom mean for the former slaves, most of whom had no land, no home, no food, no jobs, and no education? Throughout the major northern cities, people had formed Freedmen's Aid Societies to raise funds and recruit volunteers to help the African Americans in the South. Many churches did the same. But the needs far exceeded such grassroots efforts.

It soon fell to the federal government to address the desperate plight of the former slaves. On March 3, 1865, Congress created the **Freedmen's Bureau** (within the War Department) to assist the "freedmen and their wives and children." It was the first federal experiment in providing assistance directly to people rather than to states.

In May 1865, General Oliver O. Howard, commissioner of the Freedmen's Bureau, declared that freed slaves "must be free to choose their own employers, and be paid for their labor." He sent agents to the South to negotiate labor contracts between blacks and white landowners, many of whom resisted. The Bureau also provided the former slaves with medical care and food and clothing, and also helped set up schools.

By 1870, the Bureau was supervising nearly 4,000 new schools serving almost 250,000 students, many of whose teachers were initially women volunteers from the North. The Freedmen's Bureau also helped former slaves reconnect with family members. Marriages that had been prohibited during slavery were now made legal.

Freedmen's school in Virginia Throughout the former Confederate states, the Freedmen's Bureau set up schools for former slaves, such as this one.

FREED SLAVES AND LAND A few northerners argued that what the ex-slaves needed most was their own land. A New Englander traveling in the postwar South noted that the "sole ambition of the freedman" was ". . . to become the owner of a little piece of land, there to erect a humble home, and to dwell in peace and security at his own free will and pleasure." In coastal South Carolina and in Mississippi, former slaves had been "given" land by Union armies that had taken control of Confederate areas during the war.

Even northern abolitionists balked at Radical proposals to confiscate white-owned land and distribute it to the freed slaves, however. Citizenship and legal rights were one thing, wholesale confiscation of property and land redistribution quite another. Nonetheless, the discussions fueled false rumors that freed slaves everywhere would get "forty acres and a mule," a slogan that swept across the South. Ulysses S. Grant, still general-in-chief of the U.S. Army, reported that the mistaken belief among the freed slaves that they would receive their own farmland was "seriously interfering" with their willingness to sign labor contracts agreeing to work as farmhands for pay.

In July 1865, hundreds of freed slaves gathered near an old church on St. Helena Island off the South Carolina coast. There, Virginia-born freeman

Major Martin Delaney Delaney urged former slaves to achieve economic self-sufficiency by accepting paying jobs from whites.

Martin Delaney, the highest-ranking officer in the U.S. Colored Troops, addressed them. Before the Civil War, he had been a prominent abolitionist in the North. Now, Major Delaney assured the gathering that slavery had indeed been "absolutely abolished." But abolition, he stressed, was less the result of Abraham Lincoln's leadership than it was the outcome of former slaves and free blacks like him deciding to resist and undermine the Confederacy. Slavery was dead, and freedom was now in their hands. "Yes, yes, yes," his listeners shouted.

Delaney then noted that many of the white planters in the area claimed that the former slaves were lazy and "have not the intelligence to get on for yourselves without being guided and driven to the work by [white] overseers." Delaney dismissed such assumptions as lies intended to restore a system of forced labor for blacks. He then told the freed slaves that their best hope was to become self-sustaining farmers: "Get a community and get all the lands you can—if you cannot get any singly." Then "grow as much vegetables etc., as you want for your families; on the other part of land, you cultivate rice and cotton." They must find ways to become economically self-reliant, he stressed. Otherwise, they would find themselves slaves again.

Several white planters attended Delaney's talk, and an army officer at the scene reported that they "listened with horror depicted in their faces" when Delaney urged the former slaves to become independent farmers. The planters predicted that such speeches would incite "open rebellion" among southern blacks.

WAGE SLAVERY The intensity of racial prejudice in the South often thwarted the efforts of Freedmen's Bureau agents—as well as federal troops—to protect and assist the former slaves. In late June 1865, for example, a white planter in the Lowcountry of South Carolina, near Charleston, signed a contract with sixty-five of his former slaves calling for them to "attend & cultivate" his fields "according to the usual system of planting rice & provision lands, and to conform to all reasonable rules & regulations as may be prescribed" by the white owner. In exchange, the workers would receive "half of the crop raised after having deducted the seed of rice, corn, peas & potatoes." Any workers who violated the terms of the contract could be evicted from the plantation, leaving them jobless and homeless.

A federal army officer who witnessed the contract reported that he expected "more trouble on this place than any other on the river." Another officer objected to the contract's provision that the owner could require workers to cut wood or dig ditches without compensation. But most worrisome was that the contract essentially enslaved the workers because no matter "how much they are abused, they cannot leave without permission of the owner." If they chose to leave, they would forfeit any right to a portion of the crop. Across the former Confederacy, it was evident that the former white economic elite was determined to continue to control and constrain African Americans.

DEATH OF A PRESIDENT The possibility of a lenient federal reconstruction of the Confederacy would die with Abraham Lincoln. The president offered his last view of Reconstruction in the final speech of his life. On April 11, 1865, he rejected calls by Radicals for a vengeful peace. He wanted "no persecution, no bloody work," no hangings of Confederate leaders, and no extreme efforts to restructure southern social and economic life. Three days later, on April 14, Abraham Lincoln and his wife Mary went to see a play at Ford's Theatre in Washington, D.C.

With his trusted bodyguard called away to Richmond, Lincoln was defenseless as John Wilkes Booth, a popular actor and a rabid Confederate, slipped into the unguarded presidential box and shot the president in the head. Lincoln, Booth claimed, was the cause of all the nation's "troubles," and God had directed him to kill the president. As the mortally wounded Lincoln slumped forward, Booth stabbed a military aide and jumped from the box to the stage, breaking his leg in the process. Booth limped out a stage door, mounted a waiting horse, and fled the city. Lincoln died nine hours later.

At the same time that Booth was shooting the president, other Confederate assassins were hunting Vice President Andrew Johnson and Secretary of State William H. Seward. Johnson escaped injury because his would-be assassin got drunk in the bar of the vice president's hotel. Seward and four others, including his son, however, suffered severe knife wounds when attacked at home.

The nation extracted a full measure of vengeance from the conspirators. After a desperate eleven-day manhunt, soldiers and deputies pursued Booth into Virginia. He was starving and "despairing," he wrote in his diary, nursing a broken leg while being "hunted like a dog." Booth's pursuers finally found and killed him at sunrise in a burning barn. Three of his collaborators were convicted by a military court and hanged, as was Mary Surratt, who owned the Washington boardinghouse where the assassinations had been planned.

Some people celebrated Lincoln's death. "They've shot Abe Lincoln," a Massachusetts Democrat shouted. "He's dead and I'm glad he's dead." A Republican congressman from Indiana reported that the president's "death is a god-send" to the Radicals.

Most felt otherwise, however. The outpouring of grief after Lincoln's death was overwhelming. Planned events celebrating victory were canceled. Even a Richmond, Virginia, newspaper called the assassination the "heaviest blow which has fallen on the people of the South." Confederate president Jefferson Davis, fleeing Federal troops, learned about Lincoln's murder in Charlotte, North Carolina. He too worried that the assassination would be "disastrous for our people." General Ulysses S. Grant observed that the fallen president "was incontestably the greatest man I ever knew."

Lincoln's body lay in state for several days in Washington, D.C., before being transported 1,600 miles by train on April 21 for burial in Springfield, Illinois. In Philadelphia, 300,000 mourners paid their last respects; in New York City, 500,000 people viewed Lincoln's body. On May 4, Lincoln was laid to rest for eternity.

Paying respect The only photograph of Lincoln in his coffin, displayed here in New York's City Hall rotunda.

JOHNSON'S PLAN Lincoln's shocking death propelled into the White House Andrew Johnson of Tennessee, a pro-Union Democrat who was the only senator from a seceding state to remain in Washington. He had been added to Lincoln's National Union ticket in 1864 solely to help the president win reelection. Humorless and insecure, combative and obstinate, Johnson nursed fierce prejudices (he hated both the white southern elite and the idea of racial equality). He also had a weakness for liquor. At the inaugural ceremonies in early 1865, he had delivered his vice-presidential address in a state of slurring drunkenness.

Like Lincoln and his hero Andrew Jackson, Johnson was a self-made man.

Born in poverty in Raleigh, North Carolina, he never attended school. At age thirteen he relocated to Greeneville, in the mountains of east Tennessee, where he was apprenticed to a tailor who helped him learn to read. Eventually, as the self-proclaimed friend of the "common man," he served as the mayor, a state legislator, governor, congressional representative, and U.S. senator.

Johnson's supporters were primarily small farmers and the working poor. He called himself a Jacksonian Democrat "in the strictest meaning of the term. I am for putting down the [Confederate] rebellion, because it is a war [of wealthy plantation owners] against democracy." He had long disliked the planter elite, whom he damned as "a pampered, bloated, corrupted aristocracy."

Johnson, however, hated African Americans, too. He shared the racist attitudes of most southern whites, rich and poor. "Damn the negroes," he exclaimed to a friend during the war. "I am fighting those traitorous aristocrats, their masters." Johnson maintained that "white men alone must manage the South." As a states' rights Democrat, he also strongly opposed Republican economic policies designed to spur industrial development. And he also insisted that the federal government should be as small and inactive as possible.

With Congress in recess, Johnson was temporarily in control of what he called the "restoration" of the Union. He needed to put his plan in place over the next seven months before the new Congress convened and the Radical Republicans would take charge.

In May 1865, Johnson issued a new Proclamation of Amnesty that excluded not only those ex-Confederates whom Lincoln had barred from a presidential pardon but also anyone with property worth more than $20,000. Johnson also wanted to prosecute Robert E. Lee and other high-ranking Confederate officers for treason. He finally backed down when Ulysses S. Grant threatened to resign if the president persisted in his efforts to put Lee and others on trial.

Johnson was determined to keep the wealthiest southerners from regaining political power. Surprisingly, however, he eventually pardoned most of the white "aristocrats" he claimed to despise. What brought about this

Andrew Johnson A pro-Union Democrat from Tennessee.

change of heart? Johnson had decided that he could buy the political support of prominent southerners by pardoning them, improving his chances of reelection.

Johnson's Restoration Plan included the appointment of a Unionist as provisional governor in each southern state, a position with the authority to call a convention of men elected by "loyal" (that is, not Confederate) voters. His plan required that each state convention ratify the Thirteenth Amendment ending slavery before the state could be readmitted to the Union. Johnson also encouraged the conventions to give a few blacks voting rights, especially those with some education or with military service, so as to "disarm" the Republican "radicals who are wild upon" giving *all* African Americans the right to vote. Except for Mississippi, each state of the former Confederacy held a convention that met Johnson's requirements but ignored his suggestion about voting rights for blacks.

THE RADICALS REBEL Johnson's initial assault on the southern planter elite won him the support of the Radical Republicans, but not for long. Many Radicals who wanted "Reconstruction" to provide social and political equality for blacks were infuriated by Johnson's efforts to bring the South back into the Union as quickly as possible.

The iron-willed Thaddeus Stevens viewed the Confederate states as "conquered provinces" to be readmitted to the Union by the U.S. Congress, not the president. President Johnson, however, balked at such an expansion of federal authority. He was committed to the states' rights to control their affairs. "White men alone must manage the South," Johnson told a visitor.

By the end of 1865, the Radical Republicans had gained a majority in Congress and were warring with Andrew Johnson over the control of Reconstruction. On December 4, 1865, the president announced that the South had been restored to the Union. The final step in reconstruction, he added, would be for Congress to admit the newly elected southern representatives to the House and Senate.

Republicans, however, were not about to welcome back former Confederate leaders who had been elected to Congress. Georgia, for example, had elected Alexander Stephens, former vice president of the Confederacy. Across the South, four Confederate generals, eight colonels, six Confederate cabinet members, and several Confederate legislators were also elected to Congress. Outraged Republicans denied seats to all such "Rebel" officials and appointed a congressional committee to develop a new plan to "reconstruct" the South.

JOHNSON VERSUS THE RADICALS President Johnson started a war with Congress over reconstruction when he vetoed a bill that renewed funding for the Freedmen's Bureau and allowed the federal agency to begin providing homesteads and schools to former slaves in the South as well as the border states. Thaddeus Stevens and other Radicals realized that Johnson and the Democrats were trying to redefine the Civil War as a conflict between states' rights and federal power, not a struggle over slavery.

In mid-March 1866, the Radical-led Congress passed the pathbreaking Civil Rights Act, which announced that "all persons born in the United States" (except Indians) were citizens entitled to "full and equal benefit of all laws."

The new legislation enraged Johnson. Congress, he fumed, had no authority to grant citizenship to lazy former slaves who did not deserve it, and he argued that the Civil Rights Act discriminated against the "white race." So he vetoed both bills.

Now it was the Republicans' turn to be infuriated. In April 1866, Congress overrode Johnson's vetoes. From that point on, Johnson, a stubborn, uncompromising loner, steadily lost both public and political support.

Soon thereafter, in the spring and summer of 1866, rampaging white vigilantes and policemen in the South, many of them former Confederate soldiers, murdered and wounded hundreds of African Americans during riots in Memphis and New Orleans. "We are going to shoot down all these God-damned niggers," a white policeman threatened. A Memphis newspaper glorified the killing of African Americans: "The negroes now know, to their sorrow, that it is best not to arouse the fury of the white man."

Northerners were incensed. The massacres, Radical Republicans argued, resulted from Andrew Johnson's lenient policy toward white supremacists. "Witness Memphis, witness New Orleans," Massachusetts senator Charles Sumner cried. "Who can doubt that the President is the author of these tragedies?" The mob attacks helped motivate Congress to pass the Fourteenth Amendment that year, extending federal civil rights protections to blacks.

"(?) Slavery Is Dead (?)" (1867)
Thomas Nast's cartoon argues that southern blacks were still being treated as slaves despite the passage of the Fourteenth Amendment. This detail illustrates a case in Raleigh, North Carolina: a black man was whipped for a crime despite federal orders specifically prohibiting such forms of punishment.

BLACK CODES The violence directed against southern blacks was partly triggered by African American protests over restrictive laws being passed by the new all-white southern state legislatures in 1865 and 1866. These "**black codes**," as a white southerner explained, were intended to make sure "the ex-slave was not a free man; he was a free Negro." A northerner visiting the South said the black codes in each state were designed to enforce a widespread insistence that "the blacks at large belong to the whites at large."

The black codes differed from state to state, but their shared purpose was clear: to restore white supremacy. While black marriages were recognized for the first time, African Americans could not vote, serve on juries or in the militia, testify against whites, or attend public schools. They could not own farmland in Mississippi or city property in South Carolina. In Alabama, they could not own guns. In Mississippi, every black male over the age of eighteen had to be apprenticed to a white, preferably a former slave owner. The Texas black code prohibited blacks from marrying whites and from holding elected office. Virtually all of the state black codes required that adult freed slaves sign annual labor contracts. Otherwise, they would be jailed as "vagrants."

If they could not pay the vagrancy fine—and most of them could not—they were forced to work for whites as convict laborers in "chain gangs." In part, states employed this "convict lease" system as a means of increasing government revenue and cutting the expenses of holding prisoners. But convict leasing at its worst was one of the most exploitative labor systems in history, as people convicted of crimes, mostly African Americans who were often falsely accused, were hired out by county and state governments to work for individuals and businesses—coal mines, lumber camps, brickyards, railroads, quarries, mills, and plantations. Convict leasing was a thinly disguised form of neo-slavery.

The black codes angered Republicans. "We [Republicans] must see to it," Senator William Stewart of Nevada resolved, "that the man made free by the Constitution of the United States is a freeman indeed." And that is what they set out to do. A former slave who had served in the Union army shared the disbelief felt by most African Americans at the black codes: "If you call this Freedom, what do you call Slavery?"

FOURTEENTH AMENDMENT To ensure the legality of the new federal Civil Rights Act, the Congressional Joint Committee on Reconstruction proposed in April 1866 a pathbreaking **Fourteenth Amendment** to the U.S. Constitution. It guaranteed citizenship to anyone born or naturalized in the United States, except Native Americans. It also prohibited any efforts to violate the civil rights of "citizens," black or white; to deprive any person "of life, liberty, or property, without due process of law"; or to "deny any person . . . the equal protection of the laws."

With the Fourteenth Amendment, Congress gave the federal government responsibility for protecting (and enforcing) the civil rights of virtually all Americans. The amendment was approved by Congress on June 16, 1866. Not a single Democrat in the House or the Senate voted for it. All states in the former Confederacy were required to ratify the amendment before they could be readmitted to the Union and to Congress.

Again, President Johnson seethed. "This is a country for white men," he insisted, "and, by God, as long as I am President, it shall be a government by white men." Johnson urged the southern states to refuse to ratify the amendment. He predicted that the Democrats would win the congressional elections in November and then nix the new amendment. But Johnson was steadily losing support in the North. New York newspaper editor Horace Greeley called Johnson "an aching tooth in the national jaw, a screeching infant in a crowded lecture room."

JOHNSON VERSUS RADICALS To win votes for Democratic candidates, Johnson went on a speaking tour of the Midwest during which he denounced Radical Republicans as traitors who should be hanged. Several of his speeches backfired, however. In Cleveland, Ohio, Johnson exchanged hot-tempered insults with a heckler. At another stop, while the president was speaking from the back of a railway car, the engineer mistakenly pulled the train out of the station, making the president appear quite the fool. Republicans charged that such unseemly incidents confirmed Johnson's image as a "ludicrous boor" and a "drunken imbecile."

In the end, the 1866 congressional elections were a devastating defeat for Johnson and the Democrats; in each house, Radical Republican candidates won more than a two-thirds majority, the margin required to override presidential vetoes. Congressional Republicans would now take over from the president the process of reconstructing the former Confederacy.

CONGRESS TAKES CHARGE On March 2, 1867, the new Congress passed, over Johnson's vetoes, three crucial new laws creating what came to be called **Congressional Reconstruction**: the Military Reconstruction Act, the Command of the Army Act, and the Tenure of Office Act.

The Military Reconstruction Act was the capstone of the Congressional Reconstruction plan. It abolished all new governments "in the rebel States" established under President Johnson's lenient reconstruction policies. In their place, Congress established military control over ten of the eleven former Confederate states. Tennessee was exempted because it had already ratified the Fourteenth Amendment. The other ten ex-Confederate states were divided into five military districts, each commanded by a general who acted as governor.

The Military Reconstruction Act required each state to create a new constitution that guaranteed the right to vote for all adult males—black or white, rich or poor, landless or property owners. Women—black or white—did not yet have the vote and were not included in the discussions.

The Military Reconstruction Act also stipulated that the new state constitutions in each of the former Confederate states were to be drafted by conventions elected by male citizens "of whatever race, color, or previous condition." Each state constitution had to guarantee the right of African American males to vote. Once a constitution was ratified by a majority of voters and accepted by Congress, other criteria had to be met. The new state legislature had to ratify the Fourteenth Amendment, and once the amendment became part of the Constitution, any given state would be entitled to representation in Congress. Several hundred African American delegates participated in the statewide constitutional conventions.

The Command of the Army Act required that the president issue all army orders through General-in-Chief Ulysses S. Grant. The Radical Republicans feared that President Johnson would appoint generals to head up the military districts who would be too lenient. So they bypassed the president and entrusted Grant to enforce Congressional Reconstruction in the South.

The Tenure of Office Act required Senate permission for the president to remove any federal official whose appointment the Senate had confirmed. This act was intended to prevent Johnson from firing Secretary of War Edwin Stanton, the president's most outspoken critic in the cabinet.

Congressional Reconstruction embodied the most sweeping peacetime legislation in American history to that point. Its various measures sought to ensure that freed slaves could participate in the creation of new state governments in the former Confederacy. As Thaddeus Stevens explained, the Congressional Reconstruction plan was designed to create a "perfect republic" based on the principle of *equal rights* for all citizens. "This is the promise of America," he insisted. "No More. No Less."

IMPEACHING THE PRESIDENT The first two years of Congressional Reconstruction produced dramatic changes in the South, as new state legislatures rewrote their constitutions and ratified the Fourteenth Amendment. Radical Republicans now seemed fully in control of Reconstruction, but one person still stood in their way—Andrew Johnson. During 1867 and early 1868, more and more Radicals decided that the defiant Democratic president must be removed from office if their reconstruction program were to succeed.

Johnson himself opened the door to impeachment (the formal process by which Congress charges the president with "high crimes and misdemeanors") when, in violation of the Tenure of Office Act, he fired Secretary of War Edwin Stanton, who had refused to resign from the cabinet despite his harsh criticism of the president's Reconstruction policy. Johnson, who considered the Tenure of Office Act an illegal restriction of presidential power, fired Stanton on August 12, 1867, and replaced him with Ulysses S. Grant. To the Republicans, this was a declaration of war. John F. Farnsworth, an Illinois congressman, denounced the president as an "ungrateful, despicable, besotted, traitorous man."

The Radicals now saw their chance. By removing Stanton without congressional approval, Johnson had violated the law. On February 24, 1868, the Republican-dominated House passed eleven articles of impeachment (that is, specific charges against the president), most of which dealt with Stanton's

Trial of Andrew Johnson In this *Harper's Weekly* illustration, Johnson is seated at the center of the foreground among his defense committee. The galleries of the Senate are packed with men and women watching the trial.

firing, and all of which were flimsy. In reality, the essential grievance against the president was that he had opposed the policies of the Radical Republicans. According to Secretary of the Navy Gideon Welles, Radicals were so angry at Johnson that they "would have tried to remove him had he been accused of stepping on a dog's tail."

The first Senate trial of a sitting president began on March 5, 1868, with Chief Justice Salmon P. Chase presiding. It was a dramatic spectacle before a packed gallery of journalists, foreign dignitaries, corporate executives, and political officials. As the trial began, Thaddeus Stevens, the Radical leader, warned the president: "Unfortunate, unhappy man, behold your doom!"

The five-week trial ended in stunning fashion, but not as the Radicals had hoped. The Senate voted 35 to 19 for conviction, only *one* vote short of the two-thirds needed for removal from office. Senator Edmund G. Ross, a young Radical from Kansas, cast the deciding vote in favor of acquittal, knowing that his vote would ruin his political career. "I almost literally looked down into my open grave," Ross explained afterward. "Friendships, position, fortune, every-thing that makes life desirable . . . were about to be swept away by the breath of my mouth." Ross was thereafter shunned by the Republicans. He lost his reelection campaign and died in near poverty.

The effort to remove Johnson was in the end a grave political mistake, for it weakened public support for Congressional Reconstruction. Nevertheless, the Radical cause did gain something: to avoid being convicted, Johnson had privately agreed to stop obstructing Congressional Reconstruction.

REPUBLICAN RULE IN THE SOUTH In June 1868, congressional Republicans announced that eight southern states were allowed again to send delegates to Congress. The remaining former Confederate states—Virginia, Mississippi, and Texas—were readmitted in 1870, with the added require-ment that they ratify the **Fifteenth Amendment**, which gave voting rights to African American men. As black leader Frederick Douglass, himself a former slave, had declared in 1865, "slavery is not abolished until the black man has the ballot."

The Fifteenth Amendment prohibited states from denying any man the vote on grounds of "race, color, or previous condition of servitude." But Susan B. Anthony and Elizabeth Cady Stanton, seasoned leaders of the move-ment to secure an "honorable independence" and voting rights for women, demanded that the amendment be revised to include women. As Anthony stressed in a famous speech, the U.S. Constitution said: "We, the people; not we, the white male citizens; nor yet we, the male citizens; but we, the whole people, who formed the Union—women as well as men." Most men, however, remained unreconstructed when it came to voting rights for women. Radical Republicans tried to deflect the issue by declaring that it was the "Negro's hour." Women would have to wait—another fifty years, as it turned out.

BLACKS UNDER RECONSTRUCTION

When a federal official asked Garrison Frazier, a former slave in Georgia, if he and others wanted to live among whites, he said that they preferred "to live by ourselves, for there is a prejudice against us in the South that will take years to get over." In forging new lives, Frazier and many other former slaves set about creating their own social institutions.

FREED BUT NOT EQUAL African Americans in the postwar South were active agents in affecting the course of Reconstruction. It was not an easy process, however, because whites, both northern and southern, still practiced racism. A northern journalist traveling in the South after the war reported that the "whites seem wholly unable to comprehend that freedom for the negro means the same thing as freedom for them."

Once the excitement of freedom wore off, most southern blacks realized that their best chance to make a living was by doing farmwork for their former owners. In fact, the Freedmen's Bureau and the federal soldiers urged and even ordered them to sign labor contracts with local whites. Many planters, however, conspired to control the wages paid to freedmen. "It seems humiliating to be compelled to bargain and haggle with our own servants about wages," complained a white planter's daughter.

White southerners also used terror, intimidation, and violence to suppress black efforts to gain social and economic equality. In many respects, the war had not ended, as armed men organized to thwart federal efforts to reconstruct the South. In July 1866, a black woman in Clinch County, Georgia, was arrested and given sixty-five lashes for "using abusive language" during an encounter with a white woman. The Civil War had brought freedom to enslaved African Americans, but it did not bring them protection against exploitation or abuse.

After emancipation, Union soldiers and northern observers in the South often commented that freed slaves did not go far away from where they had been enslaved. But why would they leave what they knew so well? As a group of African Americans explained, they did not want to abandon "land they had laid their fathers' bones upon." A Union officer noted that southern blacks seemed "more attached to familiar places" than any other group in the nation.

Participation in the Union army or navy had provided many freedmen with training in leadership. Black military veterans would form the core of the first generation of African American political leaders in the postwar South. Military service gave many former slaves their first opportunities to learn to read and write, and army life also alerted them to new opportunities for economic advancement, social respectability, and civic leadership. Fighting for the Union cause also instilled a fervent sense of nationalism. A Virginia freedman explained that the United States was "now *our* country—made emphatically so by the blood of our brethren."

BLACK CHURCHES AND SCHOOLS African American religious life in the South was transformed during and after the war. Many former slaves identified with the biblical Hebrews, who were led out of slavery into the "promised land." Emancipation demonstrated that God was on *their* side. Before the war, slaves who were allowed to attend white churches were forced to sit in the back. After the war, with the help of many northern Christian

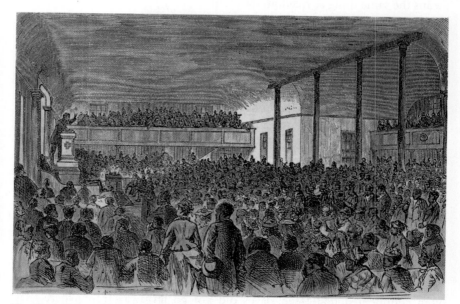

The First African Church On the eve of its move to a new building, the First African Church of Richmond, Virginia, was featured in a short article, including illustrations such as this one, in *Harper's Weekly*, in June 1874.

missionaries, both black and white, ex-slaves eagerly established their own African American churches.

The black churches were the first social institution the former slaves could control and quickly became the crossroads for black community life. Black ministers emerged as social and political leaders as well as preachers. One could not be a real minister, one of them claimed, without looking "out for the political interests of his people." Many African Americans became Baptists or Methodists, in part because these were already the largest denominations in the South, and in part because they reached out to the working poor. In 1866 alone, the African Methodist Episcopal (AME) Church gained 50,000 members. By 1890, more than 1.3 million African Americans in the South had become Baptists, nearly three times as many as had joined any other denomination.

African American communities also rushed to establish schools. Education, said a freed slave in Mississippi, was "the next best thing to liberty." Starting schools, said another former slave, was the "first proof" of freedom. Most plantation owners had denied education to blacks in part because they feared that literate slaves would read abolitionist literature and organize uprisings. After the war, the white elite worried that formal education would distract poor whites and blacks from their work in the fields or encourage them to leave the South in search of better social and economic opportunities. "They didn't want us to learn nothin'," claimed one former slave.

White opposition made education all the more important to African Americans. South Carolina's Mary McLeod Bethune rejoiced in the opportunity: "The whole world opened to me when I learned to read." She walked five miles to school as a child, then earned a scholarship to college, and went on to become the first black woman to found a school that became a four-year college: what is today known as Bethune-Cookman University, in Daytona Beach, Florida.

POLITICS AND AFRICAN AMERICANS Participation in the Union army or navy had given many former slaves their first opportunity to express their loyalty to the American nation. A Virginia freedman explained that the United States was "now *our* country," paid for "by the blood of our brethren" who died while serving in the Union military during the Civil War. Serving in the military enabled many former slaves to learn to read and write— and develop leadership qualities suitable for political roles after the war.

Groups encouraging freed slaves to embrace the Republican party were organized throughout the South. They were chiefly sponsored by the Union League, founded in Philadelphia in 1862. League recruiters in the South enrolled African Americans and loyal whites, initiated them into the secrets and rituals of the order, and instructed them "in their rights and duties." The Union League was so successful in its recruiting efforts among African Americans that in 1867, it had eighty-eight chapters in South Carolina alone. The League claimed to have enrolled almost every adult black male in the state.

Of course, *any* African American participation in southern political life was a first. Some 600 blacks—most of them former slaves—served as state legislators under Congressional Reconstruction. In Louisiana, Pinckney Pinchback, a northern free black and former Union soldier, was elected lieutenant governor. Several other African Americans were elected lieutenant governor, state treasurer, or secretary of state. There were two black senators in Congress, Hiram Revels and Blanche K. Bruce, both Mississippi natives who had been educated in the North, as well as fourteen black members of the U.S. House of Representatives.

White southerners were appalled at the election of black politicians. Democrat extremists claimed that Radicals were trying to "organize a hell in the South" by putting "the Caucasian race" under the rule of "their own negroes." Southern whites complained that freed slaves were illiterate and had no civic

African American political figures of Reconstruction Blanche K. Bruce (left) and Hiram Revels (right) served in the U.S. Senate. Frederick Douglass (center) was a major figure in the abolitionist movement.

experience or appreciation of political issues and processes. In this regard, blacks were no different from millions of poor or immigrant white males who had been allowed to vote in many jurisdictions for years.

Some freedmen frankly confessed their disadvantages. Beverly Nash, an African American delegate to the South Carolina convention of 1868, told his colleagues: "I believe, my friends and fellow-citizens, we are not prepared for this suffrage [the vote]. But we can learn. Give a man tools and let him commence to use them, and in time he will learn a trade. So it is with voting."

LAND, LABOR, AND DISAPPOINTMENT A few northerners argued that what the former slaves needed most was their own land, where they could gain economic self-sufficiency. "What is freedom," Ohio congressman James A. Garfield, a former general and future president, asked in 1865. "Is it the bare privilege of not being chained? If this is all, then freedom is a bitter mockery, a cruel delusion." Freed slaves felt the same way. Freedom, explained a black minister from Georgia, meant the freedom for blacks to "reap the fruit of our own labor, and take care of ourselves."

In several southern states, former slaves had been "given" land by Union armies after they had taken control of Confederate areas during the war. But

Freedmen voting in New Orleans The Fifteenth Amendment, ratified in 1870, guaranteed at the federal level the right of citizens to vote regardless of "race, color, or previous condition of servitude." But former slaves had been registering to vote—and voting in large numbers—in some state elections since 1867, as in this scene.

transfers of white-owned property to former slaves were reversed during 1865 by President Andrew Johnson. In South Carolina, the Union general responsible for evicting former slaves urged them to "lay aside their bitter feelings, and become reconciled to their old masters." But the assembled freedmen shouted "No, never!" and "Can't do it!" They knew that ownership of land was the foundation of their freedom. Yes, they had no deeds or titles for the land they now worked, but it had been "earned by the sweat of *our* brows," said a group of Alabama freedmen.

President Johnson, however, insisted that the federal government had no right to take land from former Confederates. Tens of thousands of former slaves were forced to return their farms to the white owners. In addition, it was virtually impossible for former slaves to get loans to buy farmland because so few banks were willing to lend to blacks. Their sense of betrayal was profound. Reconstruction of the South would not include the redistribution of southern property. An ex-slave in Mississippi whose farm was returned to its white owner said the former slaves were left with nothing: "no *land*, no *house*, not so much as a place to lay our head."

Most former slaves were farm workers. After the war, their lack of cash and land led to the system of **sharecropping**—where the landowner provided land, seed, and tools to a poor farmer in exchange for a *share* of the crop—which essentially re-enslaved the workers because, as a federal army officer objected, no matter "how much they are abused, they cannot leave without permission of the owner." If they chose to leave, they would forfeit any right to a portion of the crop, and any workers who violated the terms of the contract could be evicted from the plantation, leaving them jobless and homeless. Across the former Confederacy, most white plantation owners and small farmers were determined to continue to control African Americans.

Sharecroppers A family is shown outside their Virginia home in this 1899 photograph, taken by Frances Benjamin Johnston, one of the earliest American female photojournalists.

Many freed blacks preferred sharecropping over working for wages, since it freed them from day-to-day supervision by white landowners. But over time, most sharecroppers, black and white, found themselves deep in debt to the landowner, with little choice but to remain tied to the same discouraging system of dependence that, over the years, felt much like slavery. As a former slave acknowledged, he and others had discovered that "freedom could make folks proud but it didn't make 'em rich."

TENSIONS AMONG SOUTHERN BLACKS African Americans in the postwar South were by no means a uniform community. They had their own differences and disputes, especially between the few who owned property and the many who did not. In North Carolina, for example, less than 7 percent of blacks owned land by 1870, and most of them owned only a few acres; half of black property owners had fewer than twenty acres.

Affluent northern blacks and the southern free black elite, most of whom were city dwellers and mulattos (people of mixed parentage), often opposed efforts to redistribute land to the freedmen, and many insisted that political equality did not mean social equality. As an African American leader in Alabama stressed, "We do not ask that the ignorant and degraded shall be put on a social equality with the refined and intelligent." In general, however, unity rather than dissension prevailed, and African Americans focused on common concerns such as full equality under the law. "All we ask," said a black member of the state constitutional convention in Mississippi, "is justice, and to be treated like human beings."

With little or no training or political experience, many African Americans served in state governments with distinction. Nonetheless, the scornful label "black Reconstruction," used by critics then and since, distorts African American political influence. Such criticism also overlooks the political clout of the large number of white Republicans, especially in the mountain areas of the Upper South, who also favored the Radical plan for Reconstruction.

Only South Carolina's Republican state convention had a black majority. Louisiana's was evenly divided racially, and in only two other state conventions were more than 20 percent of the members black: Florida and Virginia. The Texas convention was only 10 percent black, and North Carolina's was 11 percent—but that did not stop a white newspaper from calling it a group of "baboons, monkeys, mules . . . and other jackasses."

"CARPETBAGGERS" AND "SCALAWAGS" Most of the offices in the new southern state governments went to white Republicans, who were dismissed as "carpetbaggers" or "scalawags." Carpetbaggers, critics argued, were scheming northerners who rushed South with all their belongings in cheap suitcases made of carpeting ("carpetbags") to grab political power.

Some northerners in the postwar South were indeed corrupt opportunists. However, most were Union military veterans drawn to the South by the

Carpetbagger The cartoonist's caption to this critique of carpetbaggers reads: "The bag in front of him, filled with others' faults, he always sees. The one behind him, filled with his own faults, he never sees."

desire to rebuild the region's devastated economy. New Yorker George Spencer, for example, arrived in Alabama with the Union army during the war and decided to pursue his "chances of making a fortune" in selling cotton and building railroads. He eventually was elected to the U.S. Senate (and later found guilty of political corruption).

Many other so-called carpetbaggers were well-educated, middle-class teachers, social workers, attorneys, physicians, editors, and ministers motivated by a genuine desire to help the free blacks and poor whites improve the quality of their lives. Union general Adelbert Ames, a native of Maine who won the Medal of Honor, stayed in the South after the war because he felt a "sense of Mission with a large M" to help the former slaves develop healthy communities. He served as the military governor of Mississippi before being elected a Republican U.S. senator in 1870. From 1874 to 1876, Ames was Mississippi's governor before resigning in the face of a resurgent white Democratic party. As Ames witnessed, the "war still exists in a very important phase here."

The scalawags, or white southern Republicans, were especially hated by southern Democrats, who considered them traitors. A Nashville newspaper editor called them the "merest trash." Most scalawags had been Unionists opposed to secession. They were especially prominent in mountain counties as far south as Georgia and Alabama and especially in the hills of eastern Tennessee. Among the scalawags were several distinguished figures, including the former Confederate general James Longstreet, who decided after Appomattox that the Old South must change its ways. He became a successful cotton broker in New Orleans, joined the Republican party, and supported the Radical Reconstruction program. Other scalawags were former Whigs attracted by the Republican party's activist economic program of industrial and commercial expansion.

Another unlikely scalawag was Joseph E. Brown, the Confederate governor of Georgia, who urged southerners to support Republicans because they were the only source of economic investment in the devastated region. What the diverse "scalawags" had in common was a willingness to work with Republicans to rebuild the southern economy.

SOUTHERN RESISTANCE AND WHITE "REDEMPTION"

Most southern whites viewed secession not as a mistake but as a noble "lost cause." They used all means possible—legal and illegal—to "redeem" their beloved South from northern control, Republican rule, and black assertiveness. An Alabama planter admitted that southern whites simply "can't learn to treat the freedmen like human beings."

White southern ministers, for example, assured their congregations that God endorsed white supremacy. In an attempt to reunite the Protestant

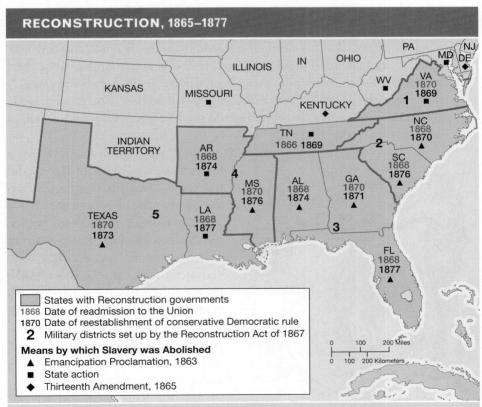

RECONSTRUCTION, 1865–1877

Legend:
- States with Reconstruction governments
- 1868 Date of readmission to the Union
- 1870 Date of reestablishment of conservative Democratic rule
- **2** Military districts set up by the Reconstruction Act of 1867

Means by which Slavery was Abolished
- ▲ Emancipation Proclamation, 1863
- ■ State action
- ◆ Thirteenth Amendment, 1865

- How did the Military Reconstruction Act reorganize governments in the South in the late 1860s and 1870s?
- What did the former Confederate states have to do to be readmitted to the Union?
- Why did "Conservative" white parties gradually regain control of the South from the Republicans in the 1870s?

denominations of the North and South, many northern religionists became "apostles of forgiveness" for their southern white brethren. Even abolitionists such as the Reverend Henry Ward Beecher, whose sister Harriet Beecher Stowe had written *Uncle Tom's Cabin* (1857), called for southern whites—rather than federal officials or African Americans themselves—to govern the South after the war.

The Civil War had brought freedom to enslaved African Americans, but it did not bring them protection against exploitation or abuse. The "black codes" created in 1865 and 1866 were the first of many continuing efforts to deny equality to African Americans. With each passing year, resistance to Congressional Reconstruction and Radical Republican ("Radical") rule became more and more violent. Hundreds were killed and many more injured in systematic efforts to "keep blacks in their place."

In Texas a white farmer, D. B. Whitesides, told a former slave named Charles Brown that his newfound freedom would do him "damned little good . . . as I intend to shoot you"—and he did, shooting Brown in the chest as he tried to flee. Whitesides then rode his horse beside Brown and asked, "I got you, did I Brown?" "Yes," a bleeding Brown replied. "You got me good." Whitesides yelled that the wound would teach "niggers [like you] to put on airs because you are free."

"Worse Than Slavery" This Thomas Nast cartoon condemns the Ku Klux Klan for promoting conditions "worse than slavery" for southern blacks after the Civil War.

Such ugly incidents revealed a harsh truth: the death of slavery did not mean the birth of true freedom for many African Americans. For a growing number of southern whites, resistance to Radical Reconstruction became more and more violent. Several secret terrorist groups, including the Ku Klux Klan, the Knights of the White Camelia, the White Line, and the White League, as well as local militia units, emerged to harass, intimidate, and even kill scalawags, carpetbaggers, and African Americans.

The **Ku Klux Klan (KKK)** was formed in 1866 in Pulaski, Tennessee. The name *Ku Klux* was derived from the Greek word *kuklos*, meaning "circle" or "band" and *Klan* came from the English word *clan*, or family. The Klan, and other groups like it, began initially as a social club, with costumes and secret rituals. But its members, most of them former Confederate soldiers, soon began harassing blacks and white Republicans. Federal general Philip Sheridan called them "terrorists" intent on suppressing black political participation.

Their motives were varied—anger over the Confederate defeat, resentment against federal soldiers occupying the South, complaints about having to pay black workers, and an almost paranoid fear that former slaves might seek violent revenge against whites. Klansmen rode about at night spreading rumors, issuing threats, and burning schools and churches. "We are going to kill all the Negroes," a white supremacist declared during one massacre.

THE LEGACY OF REPUBLICAN RULE One by one, the Republican state governments were gradually overturned. Yet they left behind an important accomplishment: the new constitutions they created remained in effect for years, and later constitutions incorporated many of their most progressive features.

Among the most significant innovations brought about by the Republican state governments were protecting black voting rights, restructuring legislatures to reflect shifting populations, and making more state offices elective to weaken the "good old boy" tradition of rewarding political supporters with state government jobs. In South Carolina, former Confederate leaders opposed the Republican state legislature not simply because of its black members but because poor whites were also enjoying political clout for the first time, thereby threatening the traditional power of wealthy white plantation owners and merchants.

Given the hostile circumstances under which Republican state governments operated in the South, their achievements were remarkable. They constructed an extensive railroad network and established public, though racially segregated, school systems—schools funded by state governments and open to all children. Some 600,000 black pupils were enrolled in southern schools by 1877.

The Radicals also gave more attention to the poor and to orphanages, asylums, and institutions for the deaf and blind of both races. Public roads, bridges, and buildings were repaired or rebuilt. African Americans achieved rights and opportunities that would repeatedly be violated in coming decades but would never completely be taken away, at least in principle: equality before the law and the rights to own property, attend schools, learn to read and write, enter professions, and carry on business.

Yet several Republican state governments also engaged in corrupt practices. Bribes and kickbacks, whereby companies received government contracts in return for giving government officials cash or stock, were commonplace. In Louisiana, a twenty-six-year-old carpetbagger, Henry Clay Warmoth, a Union war veteran and an attorney, somehow turned an annual salary of $8,000 into a million-dollar fortune over four years as governor. (He was eventually impeached and removed from office.) "I don't pretend to be honest," he admitted. "I only pretend to be as honest as anybody in politics."

As was true in the North and the Midwest at the time, southern state governments awarded money to corporations, notably railroads, under conditions that invited shady dealings and outright corruption. In fact, some railroad officials received state funds but never built any railroads. Such corruption was not invented by the Radical Republican regimes, nor did it die with them. Governor Warmoth recognized as much: "Corruption is the fashion" in Louisiana, he explained.

THE GRANT ADMINISTRATION

Andrew Johnson's crippled presidency created an opportunity for Republicans to elect one of their own in 1868. Both parties wooed Ulysses S. Grant, the "Lion of Vicksburg" credited by most Americans with the Union victory in the Civil War. His falling-out with President Johnson, however, had pushed him toward the Republicans, who unanimously nominated him as their presidential candidate.

THE ELECTION OF 1868 The Republican party platform endorsed Congressional Reconstruction. More important, however, were the public expectations driving the candidacy of Ulysses S. Grant, whose campaign slogan was "Let us have peace." Grant promised that, if elected, he would enforce the laws and promote prosperity for all.

The Democrats charged that the Radical Republicans were subjecting the South "to military despotism and Negro supremacy." They nominated Horatio Seymour, the wartime governor of New York and a passionate critic of Congressional Reconstruction. His running mate, Francis P. Blair Jr., a former Union general from Missouri who had served in Congress, appealed directly to white bigotry when he denounced Republicans for promoting equality for "a semi-barbarous race" of black men who sought to "subject the white women to their unbridled lust."

A Democrat later said that Blair's "stupid and indefensible" remarks cost Seymour a close election. Grant swept the electoral college, 214 to 80, but his popular majority was only 307,000 out of almost 6 million votes. More than 500,000 African American voters, mostly in the South, accounted for Grant's margin of victory. The efforts of Radical Republicans to ensure that voting rights for southern blacks had paid off. As Frederick Douglass, the revered black leader, explained, "the Republican party is the ship and all else is the sea" as far as black voters were concerned.

Grant, the youngest president ever (forty-six years old at the time of his inauguration), had proved himself a great military leader, but he was not a strong politician. He passively followed the lead of Congress and was often blind to the political forces and self-serving influence peddlers around him. Members of his own party would become his greatest disappointments and worst enemies. A failure as a storekeeper and farmer before the Civil War, Grant was awestruck by men of wealth who lavished gifts on him. He also showed poor judgment in his selection of cabinet members, often favoring friendship and loyalty over integrity and ability.

"The Working-Man's Banner" This campaign banner makes reference to the working-class origins of Ulysses S. Grant and his vice-presidential candidate, Henry Wilson, by depicting Grant as a tanner of hides and Wilson as a shoemaker.

During Grant's two terms in office, his seven cabinet positions changed twenty-four times. Some of the men betrayed his trust and engaged in criminal behavior. His former comrade in arms, General William T. Sherman, said he felt sorry for Grant because so many supposedly "loyal" Republicans used the president for their own selfish gains. Carl Schurz, a Union war hero who became a Republican senator from Missouri, expressed frustration that Grant was misled by cunning advisers who "prostituted" his administration.

SCANDALS President Grant's administration was quickly mired in scandal. In the summer of 1869, two unprincipled financial schemers, Jay Gould and the colorful James Fisk Jr. (known as "Diamond Jim"), both infamous for bribing politicians and judges, plotted with Abel Corbin, the president's brother-in-law, to corner the gold market. They intended to create a public craze for gold by purchasing massive quantities of the precious metal to drive up its value. The only danger to the complicated scheme lay in the possibility that the federal Treasury would burst the bubble by selling large amounts of its gold supply, which would deflate the value of gold by putting more in circulation. When Grant was seen in public with Gould and Fisk, people assumed that he supported their scheme. As the false rumor spread in New York City's financial district that the president endorsed the run-up in gold, its value soared.

On September 24, 1869—soon to be remembered as "Black Friday"—the scheme to drive up the price of gold worked, at least at first. Starting at $150 an ounce, the bidding for gold started to rise, first to $160, then $165, leading more and more investors across the nation and around the world to join the stampede. Then, around noon, President Grant and his Treasury secretary realized what was happening and began selling huge amounts of government gold. Within fifteen minutes, the bubble created by Fisk and Gould burst, and the price of gold plummeted to $138. People who had bought gold in large amounts lost fortunes. Their agony, said a New Yorker, "made one feel as if the Battle of Gettysburg had been lost and the Rebels were marching down Broadway."

Soon, the turmoil spread to the entire stock market, claiming thousands of victims. As Fisk noted, "It was each man drag out his own corpse." For weeks after the gold bubble collapsed, financial markets were paralyzed and business confidence was shaken. Congressman James Garfield wrote privately to a friend that President Grant had compromised his office by his "indiscreet acceptance" of gifts from Fisk and Gould and that any investigation of "Black Friday" would lead "into the parlor of the President."

The plot to corner the gold market was only the first of several scandals that rocked the Grant administration. The secretary of war, it was revealed, had accepted bribes from merchants who traded with Indians at army posts in the West. In St. Louis, whiskey distillers—dubbed the "whiskey ring" in the press—bribed federal agents in an effort to avoid taxes, bilking the government out of millions of dollars in revenue. Grant's personal secretary was embroiled in the scheme, caught taking secret payments for confidential information he shared.

Various congressional committees investigated most of the scandals, but uncovered no evidence that Grant was involved; his poor choice of associates, however, earned him widespread criticism. Democrats scolded Republicans for their "monstrous corruption and extravagance" and reinforced the public suspicion that elected officials were less servants of the people than they were self-serving bandits.

THE MONEY SUPPLY Complex financial issues—especially monetary policy—dominated Grant's presidency. Prior to the Civil War, the economy operated on a gold standard; state banks issued paper money that could be exchanged for an equal value of gold coins. So both gold coins and state bank notes circulated as currency. **Greenbacks** (so called because of the dye color used on the printed dollars) were issued during the Civil War to help pay for the war.

When a nation's supply of money grows faster than the economy itself, prices for goods and services increase (inflation). This happened when the greenbacks were issued. After the war, the U.S. Treasury assumed that the greenbacks would be recalled from circulation so that consumer prices would decline and the nation could return to a "hard-money" currency—gold, silver, and copper coins—which had always been viewed as more reliable in value than paper currency.

The most vocal supporters of a return to "hard money" were eastern creditors (mostly bankers and merchants) who did not want their debtors to pay them in paper currency. Critics of the gold standard tended to be farmers and other debtors. These so-called soft-money advocates opposed taking greenbacks out of circulation because shrinking the supply of money would bring lower prices (deflation) for their crops and livestock, thereby reducing their income and making it harder for them to pay their long-term debts. In 1868 congressional supporters of such a "soft-money" policy—mostly Democrats— forced the Treasury to stop withdrawing greenbacks.

President Grant sided with the "hard-money" camp. On March 18, 1869, he signed the Public Credit Act, which said that the investors who purchased government bonds to help finance the war effort must be paid back in gold. The Public Credit Act led to a decline in consumer prices that hurt debtors and helped creditors. It also ignited a ferocious political debate over the merits of "hard" and "soft" money that would last throughout the nineteenth century— and beyond.

FINANCIAL PANIC President Grant's effort to withdraw the greenbacks from circulation unintentionally helped cause a major economic collapse. During 1873, two dozen overextended railroads stopped paying their bills, forcing Jay Cooke and Company, the nation's leading business lender, to go bankrupt and close its headquarters' doors in Philadelphia on September 18, 1873. The shocking news created a snowballing effect as hard-pressed banks began shutting down. A Republican senator sent President Grant an urgent telegram from New York City: "Results of today indicate imminent danger of general national bank panic."

The resulting **Panic of 1873** triggered a deep depression. Tens of thousands of businesses closed, millions of workers lost their jobs, and those with jobs saw their wages slashed. In the major cities, the unemployed and homeless roamed the streets and formed long lines at charity soup kitchens.

The depression led the U.S. Treasury to reverse course and begin printing more greenbacks. For a time, the supporters of paper money celebrated, but in 1874, Grant, after a period of agonized reflection, overruled his cabinet and vetoed a bill to issue even more greenbacks. His decision pleased the financial community but also ignited a barrage of criticism. A prominent Republican, Edwards Pierrepont, telegraphed Grant that his veto represented "the bravest battle and biggest victory of your life." A Tennessee Republican congressman, however, called the veto of the currency bill "cold-blooded murder." In the end, Grant's decision only prolonged what was then the worst depression in the nation's history.

LIBERAL REPUBLICANS   The sudden collapse of the economy in 1873 helped further distract northerners from the controversy over reconstructing the South and divided Republicans into two warring factions: the Liberals (or Conscience Republicans) and the Capitalists (or Stalwart Republicans). The Liberal Republicans, led by senators Charles Sumner and Carl Schurz, called for the "best elements" in both national parties to join together.

Their goal was to oust the "tyrannical" Grant from the presidency, end federal Reconstruction efforts in the South, lower the tariffs intended to line the pockets of big corporations, and promote "civil service reforms" to end the "partisan tyranny" of the "patronage system" whereby new presidents rewarded the "selfish greed" of political supporters with federal government jobs. The Liberal Republicans charged that Grant and his cronies were pursuing policies and making decisions solely to benefit themselves, putting profits above principles.

In 1872, the breakaway Liberal Republicans, many of whom were newspaper editors suspicious of the "working classes," held their own national convention in Cincinnati, at which they accused the Grant administration of corruption, incompetence, and "despotism." They then committed political suicide by nominating an unlikely and ill-suited presidential candidate: Horace Greeley, the editor of the *New York Tribune* and a longtime champion of a variety of causes: abolitionism, socialism, vegetarianism, and spiritualism. His image as an eccentric who repeatedly reversed his political positions was complemented by his record of hostility to the Democrats, whose support the Liberal Republicans needed if they were going to win the election.

The Democrats nevertheless gave their nomination to Greeley. Southern Democrats liked his criticism of federal reconstruction policies in the South.

His *New York Tribune*, for example, claimed that "ignorant, superstitious, semi-barbarian" former slaves were "extremely indolent, and will make no exertion beyond what is necessary to obtain food enough to satisfy their hunger." Moreover, Radical Republicans had given the vote to "ignorant" former slaves whose "Nigger Government" exercised "absolute political supremacy" in several states and was transferring the wealth from the "most intelligent" and "influential" southern whites to themselves. Georgia Democrat Robert Toombs, a former Confederate official, agreed with Greeley and his newspaper, arguing that the "dangerous, irresponsible element" among the lower classes was threatening to "attack the interests of the landed proprietors."

Most northerners, however, were appalled at Greeley's candidacy. By nominating Greeley, said the *New York Times*, the Liberal Republicans and Democrats had killed any chance of electoral victory. In the 1872 balloting, Greeley carried only six southern states and none in the North. Grant won thirty-one states and carried the national election by 3,598,235 votes to Greeley's 2,834,761. An exhausted Greeley confessed that he was "the worst beaten man who ever ran for high office." He died three weeks later. Grant was delighted that the "soreheads and thieves who had deserted the Republican party" were defeated, and he promised to be a better president by avoiding the "mistakes" he had made in his first term as a novice statesman.

WHITE TERROR   President Grant initially fought hard to enforce federal efforts to reconstruct the postwar South. But southern resistance to "Radical rule" increased and turned brutally violent. In Grayson County, Texas, a white man and two friends murdered three former slaves because they wanted to "thin the niggers out and drive them to their holes."

Klansmen focused their program of murder, violence, and intimidation on prominent Republicans, black and white—elected officials, teachers in black schools, state militias. They intentionally avoided clashes with federal troops. In Mississippi, they killed a black Republican leader in front of his family. Three white "scalawag" Republicans were murdered in Georgia in 1870. That same year an armed mob of whites assaulted a Republican political rally in Alabama, killing four blacks and wounding fifty-four. An Alabama Republican pleaded with President Grant to intervene against the Klansmen. "Give us poor people some guarantee of our lives," G. T. F. Boulding wrote. "We are hunted and shot down as if we were wild beasts."

In South Carolina, white supremacists were especially active—and violent. In 1871, some 500 masked men laid siege to South Carolina's Union County jail and eventually lynched eight black prisoners. In March 1871, the Klan killed thirty African Americans in Meridian, Mississippi. General William T. Sherman reported that the violence across the South was commonplace and went unpunished: "Any Southern citizen may kill or abuse a Negro or Union man [Republican] with as much safety as one of our frontiersmen may kill an Indian."

At the urging of President Grant, Republicans in Congress responded with three Enforcement Acts (1870–1871). The first of these measures imposed penalties on anyone who interfered with any citizen's right to vote. The second dispatched federal supervisors and marshals to monitor elections in southern districts where political terrorism flourished. The third, called the Ku Klux Klan Act, outlawed the main activities of the KKK—forming conspiracies, wearing disguises, resisting officers, and intimidating officials.

In general, however, the Enforcement Acts were not consistently enforced. As a result, the efforts of southern whites to use violence to thwart Reconstruction escalated. On Easter Sunday in 1873 in Colfax, Louisiana, a mob of white vigilantes, most of them ex-Confederate soldiers disappointed by local election results, used a cannon, rifles, and pistols to attack a group of black Republicans in the courthouse, slaughtering eighty-one and burning down the building. It was the bloodiest racial incident during the Reconstruction period.

A Visit from the Ku Klux Klan African Americans in the South lived in constant fear of racial violence, as this 1872 engraving from *Harper's Weekly*, published to elicit Northern sympathy, illustrates.

SOUTHERN "REDEEMERS" The Ku Klux Klan's impact on southern politics varied from state to state. In the Upper South, it played only a modest role in helping Democrats win local elections. In the Lower South, however, Klan violence and intimidation had more serious effects. In overwhelmingly black Yazoo County, Mississippi, vengeful whites used terrorism to reverse the political balance of power. In the 1873 elections, for example, the Republicans cast 2,449 votes and the Democrats 638; two years later the Democrats polled 4,049 votes, the Republicans 7.

Throughout the South, the activities of white supremacists disheartened black and white Republicans alike. "We are helpless and unable to organize," wrote a Mississippi scalawag. We "dare not attempt to canvass [campaign for candidates], or make public speeches." At the same time, northerners displayed a growing weariness with using federal troops to reconstruct the South. "The plain truth is," noted the *New York Herald*, "the North has got tired of the Negro."

President Grant, however, desperately wanted to use more federal force to preserve peace and asked Congress to pass new legislation that would "leave my duties perfectly clear." Congress responded with the Civil Rights Act of 1875, the most comprehensive guarantee of civil rights to that point. It said that people of all races must be granted equal access to hotels and restaurants, railroads and stagecoaches, theaters, and other places of public entertainment. Unfortunately for Grant, however, the new law provided little authority to enforce its provisions. Those who felt their rights were being violated had to file suit in court, and the penalties for violators were modest.

Public interest in protecting civil rights in the South continued to wane as other issues emerged to distract northerners. Western expansion, Indian wars, and economic issues surged to the forefront of voter concerns.

Republican political control in the South gradually loosened as all-white "Conservative" parties mobilized the anti-Reconstruction vote. White Democrats—the so-called **redeemers** who supposedly "saved" the South from Republican control and "black rule"—used the race issue to excite the white electorate and intimidate black voters. Where persuasion failed to work, Democrats used trickery. As one enthusiastic Democrat boasted, "The white and black Republicans may outvote us, but we can outcount them."

Republican political control ended in Virginia and Tennessee as early as 1869; in Georgia and North Carolina, it collapsed in 1870, although North Carolina had a Republican governor until 1876. Reconstruction lasted longest in the Lower South, where whites abandoned Klan robes for barefaced intimidation in paramilitary groups such as the Mississippi Rifle Club and the South

Carolina Red Shirts. The last Radical Republican regimes collapsed, however, after the elections of 1876, and the return to power of the old white political elite in the South further undermined the country's commitment to Congressional Reconstruction.

THE CONTESTED ELECTION OF 1877 President Grant wanted to run for an unprecedented third term in 1876, but many Republicans had lost confidence in his leadership. In the summer of 1875, Grant acknowledged the inevitable, announced that he would retire, and admitted that he had entered the White House with "no political training" and had made "errors in judgment." James Gillespie Blaine of Maine, former Speaker of the House, was the likeliest Republican to succeed Grant, but his candidacy crumbled when it was revealed that he had promised political favors to railroad executives in exchange for shares of stock in the company.

The scandal led the Republican convention to pass over Blaine in favor of Ohio's favorite son, Rutherford B. Hayes. Elected governor of Ohio three times, most recently as a "hard money" gold advocate, Hayes also was a civil service reformer eager to reduce the number of federal jobs subject to political appointment. But his chief virtue was that he offended neither Radicals nor reformers. As a journalist put it, he was "obnoxious to no one."

The Democratic convention was uncharacteristically harmonious from the start. On the second ballot, the nomination went to Samuel J. Tilden, a wealthy corporate lawyer and reform governor of New York.

The 1876 campaign avoided controversial issues. Both candidates favored relaxing federal military authority in the South. In the absence of strong ideological differences, Democrats highlighted the scandals embroiling the Republicans. In response, Republicans avoided discussion of the depression and repeatedly waved "the bloody shirt," linking the Democrats to secession, civil war, and the violence committed against Republicans in the South. As Robert G. Ingersoll, the most celebrated Republican public speaker of the time, insisted: "The man that assassinated Abraham Lincoln was a Democrat. . . . Soldiers, every scar you have on your heroic bodies was given you by a Democrat!"

Despite the lack of major issues, the 1876 election generated the most votes of any national election in U.S. history to that point. Early returns pointed to a victory for Tilden. Nationwide, he outpolled Hayes by almost 300,000 votes; by midnight following Election Day, Tilden had won 184 electoral votes, just one short of the total needed for victory. Overnight, however, Republican activists realized that the election hinged on 19 disputed electoral votes from Florida, Louisiana, and South Carolina.

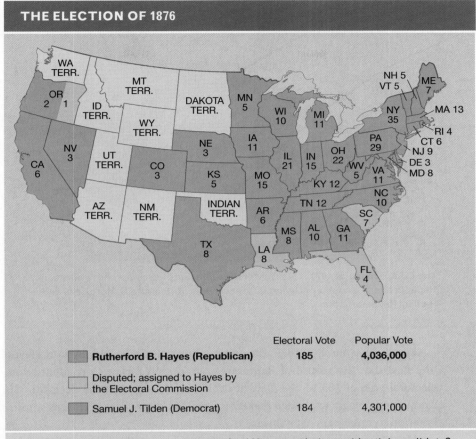

THE ELECTION OF 1876

	Electoral Vote	Popular Vote
Rutherford B. Hayes (Republican)	**185**	**4,036,000**
Disputed; assigned to Hayes by the Electoral Commission		
Samuel J. Tilden (Democrat)	184	4,301,000

- Why did the Republicans pick Rutherford Hayes as their presidential candidate?
- Why were the electoral votes of several states disputed?
- What was the Compromise of 1877?

The Democrats needed only one of the challenged votes to claim victory; the Republicans needed all nineteen. Republicans in those key states had engaged in election fraud, while Democrats had used physical intimidation to keep black voters at home. But all three states were governed by a Republican who appointed the election boards, each of which reported narrow victories for Hayes. The Democrats immediately challenged the results.

In all three states, rival election boards submitted conflicting vote counts. The nation watched and wondered as days, then weeks, passed with no solution. On January 29, 1877, Congress set up an electoral commission to settle the dispute. It met daily for weeks trying to verify the disputed vote counts.

The Compromise of 1877 This illustration represents the compromise between Republicans and southern Democrats that elected Rutherford B. Hayes and ended Radical Reconstruction.

Finally, on March 1, 1877, the commission voted 8 to 7 in favor of Hayes. The next day, the House of Representatives declared Hayes president by an electoral vote of 185 to 184. Tilden decided not to protest the decision. His campaign manager explained that they preferred "four years of Hayes's administration to four years of civil war."

Hayes's victory hinged on the defection of key southern Democrats, who, it turned out, had made a number of secret deals with the Republicans. On February 26, 1877, prominent Ohio Republicans and powerful southern Democrats struck a private bargain—the **Compromise of 1877**—at Wormley's Hotel in Washington, D.C. The Republicans promised that if Hayes were named president, he would remove the last federal troops from the South.

THE END OF RECONSTRUCTION In 1877, newly inaugurated President Hayes withdrew federal troops from Louisiana and South Carolina, whose Republican governments collapsed soon thereafter. Hayes insisted that it was not his fault: "The practical destruction of the Republican organization in the South was accomplished before my southern policy was announced."

Over the next thirty years, the protection of black civil rights in the South crumbled. As Henry Adams, a former Louisiana slave, observed in 1877, "The whole South—every state in the South—has got [back] into the hands of the very men that held us as slaves." New white state governments rewrote their constitutions, rid their administrations of "carpetbaggers, scalawags, and blacks," and cut spending. "The Yankees helped free us, so they say," a former North Carolina slave named Thomas Hall remembered, "but [in 1877] they let us be put back in slavery again."

RECONSTRUCTION'S SIGNIFICANCE

Congressional Reconstruction gave African Americans an opportunity to experience freedom—but not security or equality. As Thomas Hall noted in acknowledging the end of Reconstruction, African Americans were still dependent "on the southern white man for work, food, and clothing," and most southern whites remained hostile to the notion of civil rights and social equality. The collapse of Congressional Reconstruction in 1877 had tragic consequences, as the South aggressively renewed traditional patterns of discrimination against African Americans. Black activist W. E. B. DuBois called the effort to make slaves into citizens a "splendid failure."

Yet for all of the unfulfilled promises of Congressional Reconstruction, it left an enduring legacy—the Thirteenth, Fourteenth, and Fifteenth Amendments. If Reconstruction's experiment in interracial democracy did not provide true social equality or substantial economic opportunities for African Americans, it did create the essential constitutional foundation for future advances in the quest for equality and civil rights—and not just for African Americans, but for women and other minority groups. Until the pivotal Reconstruction era, the states were responsible for protecting citizens' rights. Thereafter, thanks to the Fourteenth and Fifteenth Amendments, blacks had gained equal rights (in theory), and the federal government had assumed responsibility for ensuring that states treated blacks equally. A hundred years later, the cause of civil rights would be embraced again by the federal government—this time permanently.

CHAPTER REVIEW

SUMMARY

- **Reconstruction Challenges**   With the defeat of the Confederacy and the passage of the Thirteenth Amendment, the federal government had to develop policies and procedures to address a number of vexing questions: What was the status of the defeated states and how would they be reintegrated into the nation's political life? What would be the political status of the former slaves and what would the federal government do to integrate them into the nation's social and economic fabric?

- **Reconstruction over Time**   Abraham Lincoln and his successor, southerner Andrew Johnson, wanted a lenient plan for Reconstruction. The *Freedmen's Bureau* helped to educate and aid freed slaves, negotiate labor contracts, and reunite families. Lincoln's assassination led many northerners to favor the *Radical Republicans*, who wanted to end the grasp of the old plantation elite on the South's society and economy. Whites resisted and established *black codes* to restrict the freedom of former slaves. *Congressional Reconstruction* responded by stipulating that former Confederate states had to ratify the *Fourteenth* and *Fifteenth Amendments* to the U.S. Constitution to protect the rights of African Americans. Congress also passed the Military Reconstruction Act, which used federal troops to enforce the voting and civil rights of African Americans.

- **Views of Reconstruction**   Many former slaves found comfort in their families and in the churches they established, but land ownership reverted to the old white elite, reducing newly freed blacks to *sharecropping*. African Americans enthusiastically participated in politics, with many serving as elected officials. Along with white southern Republicans (scalawags) and northern carpetbaggers, they worked to rebuild the southern economy. Many white southerners, however, supported the *Ku Klux Klan's* violent intimidation of the supporters of Reconstruction and pursued "redemption," or white Democratic control of southern state governments.

- **Political and Economic Developments and the End of Reconstruction**
  Scandals during the Grant administration involved an attempt to corner the gold market, and the "whiskey ring's" plan to steal millions of dollars in tax revenue. In the face of these troubles and the economic downturn caused by both the *Panic of 1873* and disagreement over whether to continue the use of *greenbacks* or return to the gold standard, northern support for the status quo in government eroded and weakened Reconstruction. Southern white "*redeemers*" were elected in 1874, successfully reversing the political progress of Republicans and blacks. In the *Compromise of 1877*, Democrats agreed to the election of Republican Rutherford B. Hayes, who put an end to the Radical Republican administrations in the southern states.

- **The Significance of Reconstruction**   Southern state governments quickly renewed long-standing patterns of discrimination against African Americans, but the Fourteenth and Fifteenth Amendments remained enshrined in the Constitution, creating the essential constitutional foundation for future advances in civil rights.

CHRONOLOGY

1865	Congress sets up the Freedmen's Bureau
April 14, 1865	Lincoln assassinated
1865	Johnson issues Proclamation of Amnesty
	All-white southern state legislatures pass various "black codes"
1866	Ku Klux Klan organized
	Congress passes the Civil Rights Act
1867	Congress passes the Military Reconstruction Act
1868	Fourteenth Amendment is ratified
	The U.S. House of Representatives impeaches President Andrew Johnson; the Senate fails to convict him
	Grant elected president
	Eight former Confederate states readmitted to the Union
1869	Reestablishment of white conservative rule ("redeemers") in some former Confederate states
1870	Fifteenth Amendment ratified
	First Enforcement Acts passed in response to white terror in the South
1872	Grant wins reelection
1873	Panic of 1873 triggers depression
1877	Compromise of 1877 ends Reconstruction; Hayes becomes president

KEY TERMS

Radical Republicans p. 705

Freedmen's Bureau p. 706

Johnson's Restoration Plan p. 712

black codes p. 714

Fourteenth Amendment (1866) p. 714

Congressional Reconstruction p. 715

Fifteenth Amendment (1870) p. 718

sharecropping p. 724

Ku Klux Klan (KKK) p. 728

greenbacks p. 733

Panic of 1873 p. 734

redeemers p. 737

Compromise of 1877 p. 740

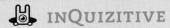 INQUIZITIVE

Go to InQuizitive to see what you've learned—and learn what you've missed—with personalized feedback along the way.

part five

GROWING PAINS

The defeat of the Confederacy in 1865 restored the Union and, in the process, helped accelerate America's transform-ation into an agricultural empire and an industrial powerhouse. A stronger sense of nationalism began to replace the regional conflicts of the prewar era. During and after the Civil War, the Republican-led Congress pushed through legislation to promote industrial and commercial development and western expansion at the same time that it was "reconstructing" the former Confederate states. The United States forged a dynamic new industrial economy serving an increasingly national and international market for

745

American goods. Yet, that progress, and the process of settling the rest of the continent, was tarnished by the relentless and ruthless relocation of Native Americans onto reservations and the exploitation of the continent's natural resources.

Fueled by innovations in mass production and mass marketing, and by advances in transportation and communications such as transcontinental railroads and transatlantic telegraph systems, huge corporations began to dominate the economy by the end of the nineteenth century. As the prominent social theorist William Graham Sumner remarked, the process of industrial development "controls us all because we are all in it. It creates the conditions of our own existence, sets the limits of our social activity, and regulates the bonds of our social relations."

Late-nineteenth-century American life drew much of its energy from the mushrooming industrial cities. "This is the age of cities," declared Midwestern writer Hamlin Garland. "We are now predominantly urban." But the transition from an economy made up of mostly small local and regional businesses to one dominated by large-scale national and international corporations affected rural life as well.

As early as 1869, novelist Harriet Beecher Stowe reported that the "simple, pastoral" America "is a thing forever gone. The hurry of railroads, and the rush and roar of business" had displaced the Jeffersonian ideal of America as a nation of small farms. She exaggerated, of course. Small farms and small towns survived the impact of the Industrial Revolution, but farm folk, as one New Englander stressed, must now "understand farming as a business; if they do not it will go hard with them." The friction between the new forces of the national marketplace and the traditional folkways of small-scale family farming generated social unrest and political revolts (what one writer called "a seismic shock, a cyclonic violence") during the last quarter of the nineteenth century.

The clash between tradition and modernity, sleepy farms and bustling cities, peaked during the 1890s, one of the most strife-ridden decades in American history. A deep economic depression, political activism by farmers, and violent conflicts between industrial workers and employers transformed the presidential campaign of 1896 into a clash between rival visions of America's future.

The Republican candidate, William McKinley, campaigned on modern urban and industrial values. By contrast, William Jennings Bryan, the nominee of both the Democratic and the Populist parties, was an eloquent defender of America's rural past. McKinley's victory proved to be a turning point in American political and social history. By 1900, the United States had emerged as one of the world's greatest industrial powers, and it would thereafter assume a new leadership role in world affairs—for good and for ill.

17 Business and Labor in the Industrial Era

1860–1900

Carnegie Steel Company Steelworkers operate the massive and dangerous Bessemer converters at Andrew Carnegie's huge steel mill in Pittsburgh, Pennsylvania.

The Civil War devastated the economy of the South. In the North, however, the need to supply the massive Union armies with shoes, boots, uniforms, weapons, supplies, food, wagons, and railroads ushered in an era of unprecedented industrial development. The scope of the war favored large-scale business enterprises and hastened the maturation of a truly national economy. An Indiana congressman told business leaders in 1864 that the war effort had sparked the development of "resources and capabilities such as you never before dreamed you possessed."

During the war years, the number of manufacturing companies in the United States almost doubled. In 1865, Ohio's John Sherman, a powerful U.S. senator, wrote a letter to his brother, William T. Sherman, the celebrated Union general, in which he observed that the northern states had emerged from the war "unimpaired." The process of mass-producing mountains of goods for the war effort had given a widened "scope to the ideas of leading capitalists, far higher than anything undertaken in this country. They talk of millions as confidently as before [they talked] of thousands."

Between the end of the war and 1900, America experienced explosive growth. The nation's population tripled, agricultural production more than doubled, and manufacturing output grew *six* times over. When the Civil War ended there was not a single industrial corporation listed on the New York Stock Exchange. By 1900, there were dozens of them employing hundreds of thousands of managers, clerks, and workers. In the thirty-five years after the Civil War, the United States achieved the highest rate of economic growth in

focus questions

1. What primary factors stimulated the unprecedented industrial and agricultural growth in the late nineteenth century?

2. Who were the leading entrepreneurs who pioneered the growth of Big Business? What were their goals and what strategies did they use to dominate their respective industries?

3. What role did the federal government play in the nation's economic development during this period?

4. In what ways did the social class structure and lives of women change in the late nineteenth century?

5. How effective were the efforts of workers to organize unions to promote their interests during this era?

the world, more than double that of its closest rival, Great Britain. By 1900, American industries and corporate farms dominated global markets in steel and oil, wheat and cotton.

Such phenomenal growth caused profound social changes, the most visible of which was the sudden prospering of large industrial cities such as Pittsburgh, Chicago, and Cleveland. Millions of young adults left farms and villages to work in factories, mines, and mills and to revel in the energies of city life. In growing numbers, women left the "cult of domesticity" at home and entered the urban-industrial workplace as clerks, typists, secretaries, teachers, nurses, and seamstresses.

While a few people made enormous fortunes, however, most laborers remained in unskilled, low-wage jobs. Big Business, a term commonly used to refer to the giant corporations that emerged after the Civil War, was as untamed and reckless as the cow towns and mining camps of the West. New technologies and business practices outpaced the ability of the outdated legal system to craft new laws and fashion rules of ethics to govern the rapidly changing economy. Business owners took advantage of this lawless environment to build fortunes, destroy reputations, exploit both workers and the environment, and gouge consumers. Yet out of the scramble for profits emerged an undreamed-of prosperity and a rising standard of living that became the envy of the world.

In the process of generating wealth, capitalism fosters inequality. People with different talents, opportunities, and resources receive unequal rewards from their labors and innovations. In a capitalist democracy like America, the tensions between equal political rights and unequal economic status produce inherent social instability. The overwhelming influence exercised by the business tycoons led to tensions that spurred the formation of labor unions and farm associations. Increasingly, those tensions erupted into violent clashes that demanded government intervention and produced class conflict.

INDUSTRIAL AND AGRICULTURAL GROWTH

Several factors converged during the second half of the nineteenth century to accelerate the nation's industrial development. Perhaps the most important was the creation of new transportation systems—canals, steamboats, railroads—along with instantaneous communication networks (telegraph and, later, telephone), which combined to create a truly national marketplace for the sale and distribution of goods and services.

In addition, Americans enjoyed the benefits of vast and valuable natural resources—land, forests, minerals, oil, coal, water, and iron ore. At the same time, a rising tide of immigrants created an army of low-wage, high-energy workers while expanding the pool of consumers eager to buy new products. Between 1865 and 1900, more than 15 million newcomers arrived in the United States.

A new generation of business leaders drove the transition to an urban-industrial society. Investment banker Jay Cooke marveled at the new breed of cold-blooded capitalists who emerged during and after the Civil War, most of them northerners and all of them driven by the "same all-pervading, all-engrossing anxiety to grow rich."

The uncommon men who spearheaded the postwar economic boom elicited both praise and scorn. Admirers called them "captains of industry," while critics called them "robber barons" because they controlled the flow of money and commerce. Whatever the label, the post–Civil War business tycoons were shrewd men determined to create large enterprises never before imagined. They were proponents of free enterprise and self-reliance who were convinced that what was good for their businesses was good for the country as a whole. Hated, feared, envied, or admired, the titans of the industrial era were the catalysts for a new America of cities and factories, prosperity amid poverty, and growing social strife and political corruption.

Bigness was the driving goal of industrial capitalism. Mass, scale, and size were the watchwords of the day. Daring entrepreneurs took advantage of new money-making opportunities, technologies, and political lobbying (including bribery) to build gigantic corporations (called *trusts*) that dominated industries such as oil refining, steel, sugar, and meatpacking.

The promoters of Big Business scrambled for wealth by ruthlessly improving efficiency and productivity, cutting costs, buying politicians, and suppressing competition. These predatory men—Cornelius Vanderbilt, John D. Rockefeller, Andrew Carnegie, and J. P. Morgan, among others—wanted to *dominate* their industries. When Vanderbilt, a commodore first of steamboats and then railroads, learned that some rivals had tried to steal one of his properties while he was away, he penned a brief message: "Gentlemen: You have undertaken to cheat me. I will not sue you, for law takes too long. I will ruin you." And he did.

CORPORATE AGRICULTURE

At the same time that the manufacturing sector was experiencing rapid growth, the agricultural sector was also shifting to a large-scale industrial model of operation. Giant corporate-owned "bonanza" farms spread across the West. They were run like factories by professional, college-educated managers, who during harvest season would hire hundreds of migrant workers to bring in the crops, usually wheat or corn destined for eastern or foreign markets.

The farm sector stimulated the industrial sector—and vice versa. In the West, bonanza farms using the latest machinery and scientific techniques became internationally famous for their productivity. By 1870, the United States had become the world's leading agricultural producer. And, with the growth of the commercial cattle industry, the process of slaughtering, packing, and shipping cattle, hogs, and sheep evolved into a major industry itself, especially in Chicago, the nation's fastest growing city and the largest slaughterhouse in the world.

TECHNOLOGICAL INNOVATIONS

America has always nurtured a culture of invention and innovation. Abraham Lincoln had often praised the nation's peculiar talent for "discoveries and inventions," which was especially evident in the decades after the Civil War. Inventors, scientists, research laboratories, and business owners developed labor-saving machinery and mass-production techniques (such as the use of interchangeable parts) that spurred dramatic advances in efficiency, productivity, and the size of industrial enterprises.

New technologies Business executives watch Alexander Graham Bell at the New York end of the first long-distance telephone call to Chicago, 1892.

Such innovations helped businesses turn out more products more cheaply while enabling more people to buy more of them. Technological advances created *economies of scale*, whereby larger business enterprises, including huge commercial farms, could afford expensive new machinery and large workforces that boosted their productivity.

After the Civil War, technological improvements spurred phenomenal increases in industrial productivity. The U.S. Patent Office, which had recorded only 276 inventions during the 1790s, registered almost 235,000 new patents in the 1890s. The list of innovations was lengthy: barbed wire; mechanical harvesters, reapers, and combines; refrigerated railcars; air brakes for trains; steam turbines; typewriters; sewing machines; vacuum cleaners; electric motors; and countless others.

BELL'S TELEPHONE Few, if any, inventions could rival the importance of the telephone. In 1875, twenty-eight-year-old Alexander Graham Bell began experimenting with the concept of a "speaking telegraph," or talking through wires. The following year, he developed a primitive "electric speaking telephone" that enabled him to send a famous message to his assistant in another room: "Mr. Watson, come here, I want to see you." Bell then patented his device and started a company, the American Telephone and Telegraph Company (AT&T), to begin manufacturing telephones. Five years later, he perfected the long-distance telephone lines that revolutionized communication. By 1895, there were more than 300,000 telephones in use. Bell's patent became the most valuable one ever issued.

TYPEWRITERS AND SEWING MACHINES Other inventions changed the nature of work. Typewriters, for example, transformed the operations of business offices. Because women showed greater dexterity in their fingers, business owners hired them to operate typewriters, in part because they could be paid much less than men. Clerical positions soon became the fastest-growing job category for women.

Likewise, the introduction of sewing machines for the mass production of clothing and linens opened new doors to women—if not usually pleasant

Office typists In new roles enabled by typewriters, women served as clerks or secretaries at many offices, such as the Remington Typewriter Company, pictured here.

ones to walk through. So-called sweatshops emerged in the major cities, where large numbers of mostly young women, often immigrants, worked long hours in cramped, stifling conditions.

THOMAS EDISON No American inventor was more influential or prolific than Thomas Alva Edison. As a boy in Michigan, he could not sit still; he loved to "make things" and "do things." His mother home-schooled him and allowed him to explore the outdoors and perform chemical "experiments," except when he "mussed things up."

Edison later said his mother "was the making of me. She understood me; she let me follow my bent." His "bent" was toward telegraphy and electricity. He built his own telegraph set and dreamed of being a telegraph operator sending messages in Morse code.

When Edison was twelve, he began working for the local railroad, selling newspapers, food, and candy to passengers. "Being poor," he explained, "I already knew that money is a valuable thing." One day he was late for the train and ran after it. A conductor reached down and lifted him into the train by his ears. Edison felt something snap in his head, and soon he was deaf. Despite losing his hearing, however, he said that his work as a trainboy "was the happiest time of my life." It was in 1862, early in the Civil War, that the deaf, solitary Edison fastened on his real passion: being a telegraph operator first in Cincinnati, then in Louisville, then in Boston, since the clicking key enabled him to listen to others and tinker with the equipment.

Despite having no formal scientific education, the self-taught Edison developed an insatiable curiosity and mechanical genius. In January 1869, at the age of twenty-one, he announced that he would "hereafter devote his full time to bringing out his inventions." He moved to New York City to be closer to the center of America's financial district. He developed dozens of new machines, including a "stock market ticker" that would report the transactions on Wall Street in real time. Soon, job offers and "real money" flooded his way. Edison, however, had a different goal: he wanted to become a full-time inventor, an electrical engineer devoted to creating new products.

In 1876, he moved into his "science village" in Menlo Park, New Jersey, twenty-five miles southwest of New York City. There, Edison became a mass-production inventor, promising to produce "a minor invention every ten days and a big thing every six months or so."

In the nation's first industrial research laboratory, Edison and his assistants created the first phonograph in 1877 and a long-lasting electric lightbulb in 1879. He also improved upon the telephone. By the ripe age of thirty, Edison was the nation's foremost inventor. Altogether, he created or perfected hundreds of new devices and processes, including the storage battery, Dictaphone, mimeograph copier, electric motor, and motion picture camera and projector.

Edison soon became world famous. A magazine saluted him as the "Wizard of Menlo Park" and called him one of the "wonders of the world." President Rutherford B. Hayes invited him to the White House, and Congress honored him.

GEORGE WESTINGHOUSE AND ELECTRIC POWER Until the 1880s, buildings and streets were lit mostly by kerosene or gas lamps. In 1882, the Edison Electric Illuminating Company, later renamed General Electric, supplied electrical current to eighty-five customers in New York City, launching the electric utility industry. Several companies that made lightbulbs merged into the Edison General Electric Company in 1888.

The use of direct electrical current, however, limited Edison's lighting system to a radius of about two miles. To cover greater distances required an alternating current, which could be transmitted at high voltage and then stepped down by transformers. George Westinghouse, inventor of the railway air brake, developed the first alternating-current electric system in 1886, and set up the Westinghouse Electric Company to manufacture the equipment.

Edison resisted the new method as too risky, but the Westinghouse system of transmitting electricity over long distances won the "battle of the currents," and the Edison companies had to switch over to AC (alternating current) from DC (direct current). After the invention in 1887 of the alternating-current motor by a Croatian immigrant named Nikola Tesla, Westinghouse improved upon it, and the company began selling dynamos.

The invention of dynamos, or electric motors, dramatically increased the power, speed, and efficiency of machinery. Electricity enabled factories to be located wherever the owners wished: factories and mills no longer had to cluster around waterfalls and coal deposits to have a ready supply of energy. Electricity also spurred urban growth by improving lighting, facilitating the development of trolley and subway systems, and stimulating the creation of elevators that enabled the construction of taller buildings.

THE RAILROAD REVOLUTION

More than any other industry, the railroads symbolized the impact of innovative technologies on industrial development and the maturation of a truly national economy. No other form of transportation played so large a role in the development of the interconnected national marketplace.

TRAINS AND TIME Railroads compressed time and distance. They moved masses of people and goods faster and farther than any other form of transportation. The railroad network prompted the creation of uniform national and international time zones and spurred the use of wristwatches, for the trains were scheduled to run on time. Towns that had rail stations thrived; those that did not died. A town's connection to a railroad, observed Anthony Trollope, a celebrated British writer touring the United States, was "the first necessity of life, and gives the only hope of wealth."

Although the first great wave of railroad building occurred in the 1850s, the most spectacular growth took place during the quarter century after the Civil War. From about 35,000 miles of track in 1865, the national rail network grew to nearly 200,000 miles by 1897. Such a sprawling railroad system was expensive, and the long-term debt required to finance it would become a major cause of the financial panic of 1893 and the ensuing depression.

TRAINS AND THE INDUSTRIAL ERA Railroads were America's first truly *big business*, the first beneficiary of the great financial market known

Chinese railroad workers Using horse-drawn carts, picks, shovels, and dynamite, Chinese laborers played a large role in constructing the transcontinental Central Pacific Railroad track.

as Wall Street in New York City, the first industry to have operations in several states, and the first to develop a large-scale management bureaucracy.

The railroad boom was the essential catalyst for America's transition to an urban-industrial economy. For a century, from the 1860s to the 1960s, most people entered or left a city through its railroad stations. Trains opened the West to economic development, enabled federal troops to suppress Indian resistance, ferried millions of European and Asian immigrants across the country, helped transform commercial agriculture into a major international industry, and transported raw materials to factories and finished goods to retailers.

Railroads were expensive enterprises, however. Locomotives, railcars (called "rolling stock"), and the construction of track, trestles, and bridges required enormous investments. Railroads became the first industry to contract with "investment banks" to raise capital by selling shares of stock to investors around the world. They also stimulated other industries through their mammoth purchases of iron and steel, coal, timber, leather (for seats), and glass. In addition, railroad companies were the nation's largest employers. By the 1870s, the Pennsylvania Railroad alone had 55,000 employees, as many as the entire federal government.

THE DOWNSIDE OF THE RAILROAD BOOM Many developers, however, cared more about making money than building safe railroads. Companies often overlooked dangerous working conditions that caused thousands of laborers to be killed or injured. Too many unneeded railroads were built; by the 1880s, there were twice as many railroad companies as the economy could support.

Some railroads were poorly or even criminally managed and went bankrupt. Those that succeeded often broke the rules. Railroad lobbyists helped to corrupt state and federal legislators by "buying" the votes of politicians with cash or shares of stock in the new railroad companies. Admitted Charles Francis Adams Jr., head of the Union Pacific Railroad, "Our method of doing business is founded upon lying, cheating, and stealing—all bad things."

BUILDING THE TRANSCONTINENTALS

For decades, visionaries had dreamed of the United States being the first nation in the world to build a railroad spanning a continent. In the 1860s, the dream became reality as construction began on the first of four rail lines that would bridge the nation—and, as one promoter boasted, establish "our empire on the Pacific."

THE "WORK OF GIANTS" The transcontinental railroads were, in the words of General William T. Sherman, the "work of giants." Their construction required heroic feats by the surveyors, engineers, and laborers who laid the rails, built the bridges, and gouged out the tunnels through rugged mountains.

The first transcontinental railroads were much more expensive to build than were the shorter "trunk" lines in the East. Because the western routes passed through vast stretches of unpopulated plains and deserts, construction materials as well as workers and their food and water had to be hauled long distances. Locomotives, railcars, rails, ties, spikes, and much more were often shipped from the East Coast to San Francisco and then moved by train to the remote construction sites.

The construction process was like managing a moving army. Herds of cattle, horses, mules, and oxen had to be fed and tended. Huge mobile camps, called "Hell on Wheels," had to be built to house the crews and then picked up and transported as the tracks progressed. The camps even included tents for dance halls, saloons, gambling, and prostitution. Nightlife in the construction camps was raucous. As a British reporter wrote, "Soldiers, herdsmen, teamsters, women, railroad men, are dancing, singing, or gambling. There are men here who would murder a fellow-creature for five dollars. Nay, there are men who have already done it. Not a day passes but a dead body is found somewhere in the vicinity with pockets rifled of their contents."

THE PACIFIC RAILWAY ACT (1862) Before the Civil War, construction of a transcontinental line had been delayed because northern and southern congressmen clashed over the choice of routes. Secession and the departure of southern congressmen for the Confederacy in 1861 finally permitted Republicans in Congress to pass the Pacific Railway Act in 1862. It authorized construction along a north-central route by two competing companies: the Union Pacific Railroad (UP) westward from Omaha, Nebraska, across the prairie, and the Central Pacific Railroad (CP) eastward from Sacramento, California, through the Sierra Nevada. Both companies began construction during the war, but most of the work was done after 1865.

The risks were enormous. There was no guarantee that the CP could cross the Sierra Nevada, east of Sacramento. Collis Huntington, one of the CP owners, was so nervous about the undertaking that he refused to attend a ceremony celebrating the laying of the first rail. "If you want to jubilate over driving the first spike," he wrote one of his partners, "go ahead and do it. I don't. Those mountains over there look too ugly. We may fail, and if we do, I want as few people to know it as I can."

Constructing a railroad across the continent entailed feats of daring, engineering, and construction, often punctuated by heartbreak and heroism. Laying rail around and through the mountains required extensive use of gunpowder, dynamite, and costly tunnels and bridges; harsh weather caused frequent work disruptions. Many workers were killed or injured in the process. At times, some 15,000 people, mostly men, worked for each of the companies as they literally raced against each other to complete their tasks. The company that laid the most track in the shortest time would be awarded more money by Congress.

The competition led both companies to cut corners. Collis Huntington, one of the CP owners, confessed that his goal was to build "the cheapest road that I could . . . so that it moves ahead fast." If bridges or trestles collapsed under the weight of freight trains, they could be fixed later. Mark Hopkins, one of Huntington's partners, agreed, noting that his goal was to build as "poor a road as we can."

RAILROAD WORKERS The UP crews were composed largely of young, unmarried former Civil War soldiers, both Union and Confederate, along with ex-slaves and Irish and German immigrants. The CP crews were mainly young Chinese workers lured to America by the California gold rush or by the railroad jobs. Most of these "coolie" laborers were single men eager to make money to take back to China, where they could then afford to marry and buy a parcel of land. Their temporary status and dreams of a good life made them more willing than American laborers to endure the low pay, dangerous working conditions, and intense racial prejudice.

What distinguished the Chinese from other laborers was their disciplined ability to work together in accomplishing daunting tasks. Mark Twain described the Chinese as "quiet, peaceable, tractable, free from drunkenness, and they are as industrious as the day is long. A disorderly Chinaman is rare, and a lazy one does not exist. . . . He is a great convenience to everybody—even to the worst class of white men, for he bears the most of their sins, suffering fines for their petty thefts, imprisonment for their robberies, and death for their murders."

LAYING TRACK The process of building the rail lines involved a series of sequential tasks. First came the surveyors, who selected and mapped the routes and measured the grade changes. Engineers then designed the bridges, trestles, tunnels, and snowsheds. Tree cutters and graders followed by preparing the rail beds. Wooden cross ties were then placed in the ground and leveled before thirty-foot-long iron rails weighing 560 pounds were laid atop them. Next came spikers, who used special hammers to wallop two-pound spikes attaching the rails to the ties. Finally, workers shoveled gravel between the ties to stabilize them against the weight of rolling trains. A journalist reported that "all this work is executed with great rapidity and mechanical regularity."

Yet for all of its precision and efficiency, the process of building the lines faced constant interruptions: terrible weather, late deliveries of key items, accidents, epidemics, or Indian attacks. Arthur Ferguson, a supervisor who kept a daily journal, frequently noted the hazards of constructing the first transcontinental in 1868:

> May 17—Two more men drowned in the river yesterday.
> June 4—At about sunrise, were attacked by Indians and succeeded in shooting one.
> June 21—Indians killed two men. Both had been horribly mutilated about the face by cuts made by a knife or a tomahawk.
> June 30—Four men were killed and scalped today about two miles above camp.

But it was not only Indians doing the killing. Workers often fought and killed each other. On June 7, Ferguson recorded that "two men were shot this evening in a drunken row—one was instantly killed, and the other is not expected to live."

THE RACE TO THE FINISH The drama of constructing the first transcontinental railroad seized the nation's imagination. Every major news-

The Union Pacific meets the Central Pacific On May 10, 1869, the celebration of the first transcontinental railroad's completion took place in Promontory, Utah.

paper carried stories about the progress of the two competing companies. Finally, on May 10, 1869, former California governor Leland Stanford, one of the owners of the Central Pacific, drove a gold spike to complete the line at Promontory Summit in the Utah Territory north of the Great Salt Lake. The Union Pacific had built 1,086 miles of track compared with the Central Pacific's 689. The railroad builders had changed the landscape and widened the horizons of American ambition.

The golden spike used to connect the final rails symbolized the uniting of East and West just as Robert E. Lee's surrender four years earlier had come to represent the reunion of North and South. Soon, the entire process would be repeated, as other companies constructed more lines across the continent.

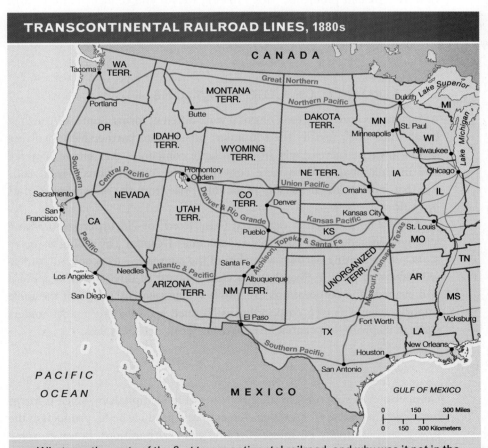

TRANSCONTINENTAL RAILROAD LINES, 1880s

- What was the route of the first transcontinental railroad, and why was it not in the South?
- Who built the railroads? How were they financed?

THE RISE OF BIG BUSINESS

The transcontinental railroads were the first of many investor-owned, publicly traded corporations during the industrial era. The emergence of Big Business was one of the most significant developments in American history. Corporations grew much larger and more powerful, transacting business across the nation and abroad. They were also much more influential politically as they worked to influence governors, legislators, Congress, and presidents.

Before the Civil War, most businesses had been small, local enterprises. After 1865, much of America suddenly got bigger—towns and cities, ships, locomotives, factories, machines, mines, and mills—and business organizations followed the same path. The rapid expansion in businesses, however, created problems. "The growing wealth and influence of our large corporations," warned the *New York Times*, "is one of the most alarming phenomena of our time. Our public companies already wield gigantic power, and they use it like unscrupulous giants."

THE GROWTH OF CORPORATIONS

As businesses grew, they took one of several different forms. Some were owned by an individual, usually their founder; others were partnerships involving several owners. Increasingly, however, large companies that served national and international markets were converted into "corporations"—legal entities that separate the *ownership* of an enterprise from the *management* of its operations.

Once a corporation is registered ("chartered" or "incorporated") with a state government, it can raise money to operate ("capital") by selling shares of stock—representing partial ownership of the company—to people not otherwise involved with it. Shareholders elect a board of directors who appoint and evaluate the corporation's executives ("management"). One of the most important benefits of a corporation is "limited legal liability": stockholders share in its profits but cannot be held liable for its debts if it fails.

FIGHTING COMPETITION

Competition is supposed to be the great virtue of capitalism, since it forces businesses to place a premium on efficiency and produce better products at the lowest cost. As many businesses became giant corporations, however, some business titans came to view competition as a burden rather than a blessing. Competition, many owners argued, created a chaotic and wasteful economic environment. Financier J. P. Morgan, for example, claimed that "bitter, destructive competition" always led to "destruction and ruin."

To eliminate cutthroat competition and thereby stabilize production, wages, and prices, rival companies selling similar products often formed "pools" whereby they secretly agreed to keep production and prices at specified levels. Such pools rarely lasted long, however, because they were unenforceable. One or more participants usually violated the agreement by cutting prices or increasing production—or both. The more effective strategy for the most aggressive companies was to get rid of weaker competitors by driving them out of business or buying them out.

Strategies like these, as well as the methods used to carry them out, led critics to call the corporate titans "robber barons." In the process of forming huge companies and eliminating competition, many business leaders cut corners, bribed politicians, double-crossed partners, exploited workers, hired strikebreakers, and broke laws. When asked how people might react to the shady methods he used to build his network of railroads, William Henry Vanderbilt famously replied: "The public be damned!"

THE BARONS OF BUSINESS

Most of the men (few women had such opportunities) who created big businesses in the late nineteenth century were driven by a compulsive desire to become rich and influential. Moreover, during and after the Civil War, becoming rich emerged as a national ideal sanctified by many religious leaders. "To secure wealth is an honorable ambition," stressed Russell Conwell, a prominent Baptist minister who crisscrossed the nation preaching a sermon called "Acres of Diamonds," in which he celebrated the benefits of hard work and its just rewards. "Money is power," he explained, and "every good man and woman ought to strive for power, to do good with it when obtained. I say, get rich! get rich!"

The industrial and financial giants personified the values that Conwell celebrated. They were men of grit and genius who found innovative—and at times unethical—ways to increase production, create efficiencies, and eliminate competition. The captains of industry were also mercilessly adept at cutting costs and lowering prices.

Several of the post–Civil War business barons stood out for their extraordinary accomplishments: John D. Rockefeller and Andrew Carnegie for their innovations in organization, J. Pierpont Morgan for his development of investment banking, and Richard Sears and Alvah Roebuck for their creation of mail-order retailing. In their different ways, each dealt a mortal blow to the small-scale economy of the early republic, fostering vast enterprises that

John D. Rockefeller Co-founder of the Standard Oil Company.

forever altered the size and scope of business and industry.

JOHN D. ROCKEFELLER Born in New York in 1839, John D. Rockefeller moved as a child to Cleveland, Ohio, nestled beside Lake Erie. Soon thereafter, his con-man father abandoned the family. Raised by his mother, a devout Baptist, Rockefeller developed a single-minded passion for systematic organization. As a young man in the 1860s, he decided to bring order and rationality to the new boom-and-bust oil industry. He was ambitious, disciplined, and obsessed with precision, efficiency, tidiness—and money. (A childhood friend recalled that he was "mad about money, though sane about everything else.") Rockefeller said little, rarely smiled, and hardly ever laughed.

The railroad and shipping connections around Cleveland made it a strategic location for serving the booming oil fields of nearby western Pennsylvania. The first oil well in the United States began producing in 1859 in Titusville, Pennsylvania, and led to the Pennsylvania oil rush of the 1860s. Because oil could be refined into kerosene, which was widely used for lighting, heating, and cooking, the economic importance of the oil rush soon outstripped that of the California gold rush ten years earlier. Well before the end of the Civil War, oil refineries sprang up in Pittsburgh and Cleveland. Of the two cities, Cleveland had better rail service, so Rockefeller focused his energies there.

In 1870, Rockefeller teamed with his brother William and two other businessmen, Henry M. Flagler and Samuel Andrews (inventor of an inexpensive means of refining crude oil) to establish the **Standard Oil Company** of Ohio. Although the company quickly became the largest oil refiner in the nation, John Rockefeller wanted to eliminate his competitors and take control of the entire industry, in large part because he believed his competitors were inefficient and distracting.

During the 1870s, Rockefeller used various schemes to eliminate his competitors. Early on, he pursued a strategy that came to be called **horizontal**

integration, in which a dominant corporation buys or forces out most of its competitors. Rockefeller viewed competition as a form of warfare. In a few cases, he hired former competitors as executives, but only "the big ones," he said, "those who have already proved they can do a *big business*. As for the others, unfortunately they will have to *die*."

By 1879, Standard Oil controlled more than 90 percent of the nation's oil refining business. Still, Rockefeller intended "to secure the entire refining business of the world." His goal was a **monopoly**, a business so large that it effectively controls an entire industry.

Rockefeller was an innovative genius with the fierce focus of a shark and the pinched priorities of a bookkeeper obsessed with the smallest details. He methodically reduced expenses, incorporated the latest technologies, and eliminated any hint of waste while paying "nobody a profit." Because he shipped so much oil by rail, he forced railroads to pay him secret "rebates" on the shipments, enabling him to pay less for shipping than his competitors paid.

Most important, instead of depending upon the products or services of other firms, known as middlemen, Standard Oil eventually owned everything it needed to produce, refine, and deliver oil—from wells to the finished product. The company had its own pipelines, built factories to make its own wagons and storage barrels, did its own hauling, owned its own storage tanks

The rise of oil Crowding this Pennsylvania farm are wooden derricks that extracted crude oil.

and tanker ships. In economic terms, this business strategy is called **vertical integration**. Rockefeller's Standard Oil Company was both horizontally and vertically integrated.

During the 1870s, Standard Oil bought so many of its competitors that it developed a virtual monopoly over the industry. Many state legislatures responded by outlawing the practice of one corporation owning stock in competing ones. In 1882, Rockefeller tried to get around such laws by organizing the Standard Oil Trust.

A **trust** gives a person or corporation (the "trustee") the legal power to manage another person's money or another company. Instead of owning other companies outright, the Standard Oil Trust controlled more than thirty companies by having their stockholders transfer their shares "in trust" to Rockefeller and eight other trustees. In return, the stockholders received "trust certificates," which paid them annual dividends from the trust's earnings. The Standard Oil Trust was Rockefeller's attempt to hide his virtual monopoly over the American oil industry.

Soon, however, the formation of huge corporate trusts, a practice widely copied by other industries, generated intense criticism. In 1890, Congress responded by passing the Sherman Anti-Trust Act with only one dissenting vote. It declared that corporate efforts to monopolize industries and thereby "restrain" competition were illegal. But the bill's language was so vague that it proved to be virtually toothless.

State laws against monopolies were initially more effective than the Sherman Act. In 1892, Ohio's Supreme Court ordered the Standard Oil Trust dissolved. A furious Rockefeller then developed another way to maintain control of his numerous companies: a **holding company**, which is a huge corporation that controls other companies by "holding" most or all of their stock certificates. A holding company produces nothing itself; it simply owns a majority of the stock in other companies.

Rockefeller was convinced that ending competition among companies was a good thing for the nation. Monopolies, he insisted, were the natural result of capitalism at work. "It is too late," he declared in 1899, "to argue about the advantages of [huge] industrial combinations. They are a necessity. The day of individualism is gone. Never to return." That year, Rockefeller brought his empire under the direction of the Standard Oil Company of New Jersey, a gigantic holding company. A Wall Street investor spoke for many business observers when he asked "How can you beat the Standard Oil party?" After all, "they have control of all the industries, are getting all the railroads and the street railways, and will in a few years own the whole country. I can see no stopping them."

ANDREW CARNEGIE Like Rockefeller, Andrew Carnegie, who created the largest steel company in the world, rose to wealth from boyhood poverty. Born in Scotland, the son of weavers, he migrated with his family in 1848 to western Pennsylvania. At age thirteen, he went to work in a textile mill. In 1853, he became personal secretary to Thomas Scott, then district superintendent of the Pennsylvania Railroad and later its president. When Scott moved up, the shrewd and charming Carnegie became superintendent in a region "teeming with treasure." During the Civil War, when Scott became assistant secretary of war in charge of transportation, Carnegie went with him to Washington, D.C., and helped develop a military telegraph system.

Andrew Carnegie Established the Carnegie Steel Company and became the wealthiest man in the world.

The ambitious Carnegie worked his way up—from telegraphy to railroading to bridge building, and then to steelmaking and investments. In the early 1870s, he decided "to concentrate on the manufacture of iron and steel and be master in that." A tiny man (barely five feet tall), Carnegie wanted to tower over the steel industry, just as John D. Rockefeller was doing with oil. Like Rockefeller, Carnegie accumulated vast wealth, and he often treated his workers ruthlessly.

Until the mid–nineteenth century, steel, which is stronger and more flexible than iron, could be made only from wrought iron—itself expensive since it had to be imported from Sweden—and could only be manufactured in small quantities. Bars of wrought iron were heated with charcoal over several days to add carbon and produce steel. It took three tons of coke, a high-burning fuel derived from coal, to produce one ton of steel. As a result, steel was too costly to make in large quantities.

That changed in the 1850s, when England's Sir Henry Bessemer invented the **Bessemer converter**, a process by which high-quality steel could be produced more quickly by blasting oxygen through the molten iron in a furnace. In the early 1870s, Carnegie decided to concentrate on steel, because

Bessemer's process had made it so inexpensive to produce and the railroad industry required massive amounts of it.

As more steel was produced, its price dropped and its industrial uses soared. In 1860, the United States produced only 13,000 tons of steel. By 1880, production had reached 1.4 million tons annually. Between 1880 and 1900, Carnegie dominated the steel industry, acquiring competitors or driving them out of business by cutting prices and taking their customers. By 1900, the United States was producing more steel than Great Britain and Germany combined.

Carnegie was a resilient promoter, salesman, and organizer. He insisted upon up-to-date machinery and equipment, expanded production quickly and cheaply by purchasing struggling companies, and preached a philosophy of continuous innovation to reduce operating costs.

He also sought to expand his industry by vertical integration—gaining control of every phase of the steelmaking business. He owned coal mines in West Virginia, bought huge deposits of iron ore in Michigan and Wisconsin, and transported the ore in his own ships across the Great Lakes and then by rail to his steel mills in Pittsburgh.

The result was phenomenal. By 1900, the **Carnegie Steel Company**, with 20,000 employees, was the largest industrial company in the world. And Carnegie worked his people hard. His mills operated nonstop, with two 12-hour shifts every day and night.

Carnegie insisted that what he, Rockefeller, and other titans of industry were doing in forging dominant corporations was simply the wave of the future. Rockefeller agreed, saying that the formation of huge trusts was simply "the working out of a law of nature and a law of God."

J. PIERPONT MORGAN Unlike Rockefeller and Carnegie, J. Pierpont Morgan was born to wealth in Connecticut. His father was a partner in a large English bank. After attending school in Switzerland and college in Germany, Morgan was sent in 1857

J. Pierpont Morgan Despite his privileged upbringing and financial success, he was self-conscious about his deformed nose, caused by chronic skin diseases.

to work in New York City for a new enterprise, **J. Pierpont Morgan and Company**. The firm, under various names, invested European money into American businesses. It grew into a financial power by helping competing corporations merge and by purchasing massive amounts of stock in American companies and selling them at a profit.

Morgan took over poorly run companies, appointed new executives, and supervised operations. Like Rockefeller and Carnegie, he believed in capitalism but hated the chaos of competition. In his view, high profits required order and stability, and stability required consolidating competitors into trusts that he would own and manipulate.

Morgan recognized early on the importance of railroads, and by the 1890s, he controlled a sixth of the nation's railway system. But his crowning triumph was the consolidation of the steel industry. After a rapid series of mergers, he bought out Andrew Carnegie's huge steel and iron holdings in 1901. Morgan added scores of related companies to form the United States Steel Corporation, the world's first billion-dollar corporation, employing 168,000 people. It was the climactic event in the efforts of the great financial capitalists to reduce competition and form ever-larger corporations capable of dominating their industries.

SEARS AND ROEBUCK   After the Civil War, American inventors helped manufacturers produce a vast number of new products. But the most important economic challenge was extending commerce to the millions who lived on isolated farms and in small towns. A traveling salesman from Chicago named Aaron Montgomery Ward decided that he could reach more people by mail than on foot and thus eliminate the middlemen whose services increased the retail price of goods. Beginning in the early 1870s, Montgomery Ward and Company began selling goods at a 40 percent discount through mail-order catalogs.

By the end of the century, a new retailer had come to dominate the mail-order industry: Sears, Roebuck and Company, founded by two midwestern entrepreneurs, Richard Sears and Alvah Roebuck. The Sears, Roebuck catalog in 1897 was 786 pages long. It featured groceries, drugs, tools, furniture, household products, musical instruments, farm implements, shoes, clothes, books, and sporting goods. The company's ability to buy goods in high volume from wholesalers enabled it to sell items at prices below those offered in rural general stores. By 1907, Sears, Roebuck and Company, headquartered in Chicago, had become one of the largest businesses in the nation.

The Sears catalog helped create a national market and transformed the lives of millions of people. With the advent of free rural mail delivery in 1898 and the widespread distribution of the catalogs, families on farms and in small

Cover of the 1897 Sears, Roebuck and Company catalog Sears, Roebuck's extensive mail-order business and discounted prices allowed its many products to reach customers in cities and in the backcountry.

towns and villages could purchase by mail the products that heretofore were either prohibitively expensive or available only to city dwellers. By the turn of the century, 6 million Sears catalogs were being distributed each year, and the catalog had become the most widely read book in the nation after the Bible.

THE GOSPEL OF WEALTH

However harsh the methods employed by the captains of industry, the men were convinced that they benefited the public by accelerating America's transformation into an industrial colossus. In their eyes, it was a law of societal evolution that those most talented at producing wealth should accumulate enormous personal fortunes.

Some of them, however, insisted that great wealth brought great responsibilities. In his essay "The Gospel of Wealth" (1889), Andrew Carnegie argued that "not evil, but good, has come to the [Anglo-Saxon] race from the accumulation of wealth by those who have the ability and energy that produces it." But he also felt the need to justify his wealth and denounced the "worship of money." He and John D. Rockefeller gave much of their money back to society.

By 1900, Rockefeller had become the world's leading philanthropist. "I have always regarded it as a religious duty," he said late in life, "to get all I could honorably and to give all I could." He donated more than $500 million during his lifetime, including tens of millions to Baptist causes and $35 million to found the University of Chicago. His philanthropic influence continues today through the Rockefeller Foundation.

As for Carnegie, after retiring from business at age sixty-five, he declared that the "man who dies rich dies disgraced" and devoted himself to dispensing his $400 million fortune. Calling himself a "distributor" of wealth (he disliked the term *philanthropy*), he gave huge sums to numerous universities; built

Celebrating Big Business A lavish dinner celebrated the merger of the Carnegie and Morgan interests in 1901. The shape of the banquet table is meant to symbolize a rail.

2,500 public libraries; and helped fund churches, hospitals, parks, and halls for meetings and concerts, including New York City's Carnegie Hall.

THE ALLIANCE OF BUSINESS AND POLITICS

The building of big businesses depended on more than just entrepreneurial energy. Most of the corporate titans developed cozy relationships with local, state, and federal officials, a process of buying influence ("lobbying") that continues to this day. Big Business has legitimate political interests, but, because of its size and resources, it also at times exercises a corrupt influence on government. Nowhere was this conflicting role more evident than during the decades after the Civil War. The *New York Times* noted that the largest corporations "control the Legislatures."

REPUBLICANS AND BIG BUSINESS During and after the Civil War, the Republican party and state and federal governments grew increasingly allied with Big Business. A key element of this alliance was tariff policy. Since 1789, the federal government had imposed **tariffs**—taxes on imported goods—to raise revenue and to benefit American manufacturers by penalizing their foreign competitors. In 1861, as the Civil War was starting, the Republican-dominated Congress enacted the Morrill Tariff, which doubled tax rates on hundreds of imported items as a means of raising money for the war and rewarding the businesses that supported the Republican party.

After the war, President Ulysses S. Grant, and later, Republican presidents and Congresses, continued the party's commitment to high tariffs despite complaints that the tariffs increased consumer prices at home by restricting foreign imports and thereby relieving American manufacturers of the need to keep their prices down. Farmers in the South and Midwest resented tariffs because, while they had to sell their crops in an open world market, they had to buy manufactured goods whose prices were artificially high because of tariffs.

During the Civil War, Congress passed other key pieces of legislation related to the economy. The Legal Tender Act of 1862 authorized the federal government to issue paper money ("greenbacks") to help pay for the war. Having a uniform paper currency was essential to a modern national economy. To that end, the National Banking Act (1863) created national banks authorized to issue greenbacks, which discouraged state banks from continuing to issue their own paper money.

Congress also took steps to tie the new states and territories of the West into the national economy. In the Homestead Act of 1862, Congress provided free 160-acre (or even larger) homesteads to settlers in the West. By encouraging western settlement, the Homestead Act created new markets for goods and services and spurred railroad construction to connect frontier communities with major cities.

The Morrill Land Grant Act of the same year transferred to each state 30,000 acres of federal land for each member of Congress the state had. The sale of those lands provided funds for states to create colleges of "agriculture and mechanic arts," such as Iowa State University and Kansas State University. The "land grant" universities were created specifically to support economic growth by providing technical training needed by farmers and rapidly growing industries such as mining, steel, petroleum, transportation, forestry, and construction (engineering).

LAISSEZ-FAIRE Equally important in propelling the postwar economic boom was what government did *not* do. In 1870, historian Henry Adams expressed concern that there "was no authority" capable of restraining the leaders of the nation's largest corporations. At the time, the federal government did not regulate the activities of big businesses, impose high corporate taxes, or provide any meaningful oversight of business operations or working conditions.

Homesteaders An African American family poses outside their log and sod cabin in 1889.

In general, both Congress and the presidents opposed government inter-ference in the economy and accepted the economic doctrine of *laissez-faire*, a French phrase meaning "let them do as they will." Business leaders spent time—and money—ensuring that government officials stayed out of their businesses. For their part, the politicians were usually eager to help the titans of industry in exchange for campaign contributions—or bribes for looking the other way.

AN INDUSTRIAL SOCIETY

Industrialization transformed not only the economy and the workplace, but also the nation's social life. Class divisions became more visible. The growing gap between rich and poor was like "social dynamite," said the Reverend Josiah Strong in 1885. Massachusetts reformer Lydia Maria Child reported that the rich "do not intermarry with the middle classes; the middle classes do not intermarry with the laboring class," nor did different classes "mix socially."

The Nouveaux Riches Upper-class members of New York City society pose for a photograph at the James Hazen Hyde Ball on January 31, 1905.

The Ways of the Wealthy

The financiers and industrialists who dominated social, economic, and political life in post–Civil War America amassed so much fabulous wealth and showed it off so publicly that the period is still called the "Gilded Age."

The name derived from a popular novel by Mark Twain and Charles Dudley Warner, *The Gilded Age: A Tale of Today*, which mocked the crooked dealings of political leaders and the business elite. In 1861, there were only a few dozen millionaires in the United States. By 1900, there were more than 4,000. Most of them were white Protestants who voted Republican, except for a small number of wealthy southern Democrats.

Many of the *nouveaux riches* (French for "newly rich") indulged in what came to be called "conspicuous consumption," competing to host the fanciest parties and live in the most extravagantly furnished houses. One tycoon gave a lavish dinner honoring his dog and presented it with a $15,000 diamond necklace. At a party at New York's Delmonico's restaurant, the guests smoked cigarettes wrapped in $100 bills. Mrs. Bradley Martin received such a torrent of criticism after spending $368,000 on a banquet that she and her husband fled to England.

When they were not attending parties, the rich were relaxing in monumental mansions overlooking the cliffs at Newport, Rhode Island, atop Nob Hill in San Francisco, along Chicago's Lake Shore Drive and New York City's Fifth Avenue, and down the "Main Line" in suburban Philadelphia. "Who knows how to be rich in America?" asked E. L. Godkin, a magazine editor. "Plenty of people know how to get money, but . . . to be rich properly is, indeed, a fine art. It requires culture, imagination, and character."

A GROWING MIDDLE CLASS

It was left to the fast-growing middle class to display good "character" by practicing such traditional virtues as self-discipline and restraint, simplicity and frugality. The term *middle class* had first appeared in the 1830s and had become commonplace by the 1870s, as more and more Americans came to view themselves as members of a distinct social class between the ragged and the rich. The middle class, explained the Chicago writer George Ade in an 1895 essay, "The Advantage of Being 'Middle Class,'" meant those people who "work either with hand or brain, who are neither poverty-stricken nor offensively rich."

Accompanying the spread of huge corporations after the Civil War was a rapidly growing middle class enjoying a rising standard of living. While the rich were getting richer, many other people were also becoming better off in terms of their income and quality of life. Most middle-class Americans working outside the home were salaried employees of large businesses who made up a new class of "white-collar" professionals: editors, engineers, accountants, supervisors, managers, marketers, and realtors. Others, mostly unmarried women, were a growing share of the total: clerks, secretaries, salespeople, and government employees, including teachers and librarians. During the 1870s, the number of office clerks quadrupled, and the number of accountants and bookkeepers doubled. At the same time, the number of attorneys, physicians, professors, journalists, nurses, and social workers rose dramatically.

MIDDLE-CLASS WOMEN The growing presence of middle-class women in the workforce partly reflected the increasing number of women who were gaining access to higher education. Dozens of women's colleges were founded after the Civil War, and many formerly all-male colleges began admitting women. By 1900, a third of college students were women. "After a struggle of many years," a New York woman boasted, "it is now pretty generally admitted that women possess the capacity to swallow intellectual food that was formerly considered the diet of men exclusively."

To be sure, college women were often steered into home economics classes and "finishing" courses intended to perfect their housekeeping or social skills. Still, the doors of the professions—law, medicine, science, and the arts—were at least partially opened.

In this context, then, the "woman question" that created so much public discussion and controversy in the second half of the nineteenth century involved far more than the issue of voting rights; it also concerned the liberation of at least some women from the home and from longstanding limits on their social roles and even character traits.

Middle-class women also took advantage of other public venues for interaction: charitable associations, women's clubs, literary societies, and church work. "If there is one thing that pervades and characterizes what is called the 'woman's movement,'" E. L. Youmans, a prominent science writer, remarked, "it is the spirit of revolt against the home, and the determination to escape from it into the outer spheres of activity."

NEURASTHENIA Women who tried to escape the "cult of domesticity" and pursue careers outside the home often paid a high price. Many contracted

College women By the end of the century, women made up more than a third of college students. Here, an astronomy class at New York's Vassar College is underway in 1880.

a peculiar affliction, which male physicians called *neurasthenia*, a draining psychological and physical disorder whose symptoms usually included insomnia, hysteria, headaches, depression, and a general state of fatigue. Although neurasthenia plagued both sexes, it most often affected college-educated middle-class women.

Some prominent doctors sought to use the prevalence of neurasthenia to force women back into the "cult of domesticity." George M. Beard, a neurologist who popularized the term *neurasthenia*, concluded—incorrectly—that women were "more nervous, immeasurably, than men," and that female neurasthenics tended to be "overly active" outside the home. This explanation led one doctor to insist that the malady provided the best "argument against higher education of women."

Many women objected to such self-serving male arguments. Charlotte Perkins Gilman, for instance, wrote her short story "The Yellow Wallpaper" to expose the horrors of the "rest cure" she was subjected to at age twenty-seven. A doctor had ordered her to "live as domestic a life as possible; have your child with you all the time; lie down an hour after each meal; have but two hours intellectual life a day; and *never touch pencil, brush, or pen as long as you live*." This regimen, Gilman explained, took her "as near lunacy as one can, and come back."

JANE ADDAMS Social worker Jane Addams also struggled with neurasthenia and the dominant male notions of women's roles. After graduating in 1881 from Rockford College in Illinois, she found few opportunities to use her degree and lapsed into a state of depression during which she developed an intense "desire to live in a really *living* world." Middle-class women, she charged, were "so besotted with our [sentimental] novel reading that we have lost the power of seeing certain aspects of life with any sense of reality because we are continually looking for the possible romance."

Addams's desire to engage "real life" eventually led her to found Hull House

Jane Addams She believed that social service requires a "scientific" observation of one's community in order to "see the needs" and provide data for legislative reform.

in Chicago. There, she and other social workers helped immigrants adapt to American life and mentored young women to "learn of life from life itself." Addams and others helped convince many middle-class women to enter the "real" world. By 1890, a magazine called the *Arena* would urge progressive-minded people to recognize the traditional view of "women as homebodies" for what it was: "hollow, false, and unreal."

THE *LADIES' HOME JOURNAL* Not all middle-class women, however, wanted to venture out into the world. Many of them identified more with the domestic life that was the focus of numerous mass-circulation magazines, the most popular of which was the *Ladies' Home Journal*. By 1910, it had almost 2 million subscribers, the largest circulation of any magazine in the world.

Mennen's Toilet Powder This advertisement appeared in the Independence Day edition of *Ladies' Home Journal* in 1908, suggesting that a homemaker's ability to protect her family from skin discomforts was her own declaration of independence.

Edward Bok, a Dutch immigrant raised in Brooklyn, New York, became editor of *Ladies' Home Journal* in 1889 at the age of twenty-six. Under his direction for the next thirty years, the magazine provided a "great clearing house of information" to the large and rapidly growing urban middle class. The *Journal* included sections on sewing, cooking, religion, politics, and fiction.

Bok was no feminist; "my idea," he stressed, "is to keep women in the home." There, he believed, they would maintain a high moral tone for society, for women were "better, purer, conscientious, and morally stronger than men." Bok saw the middle-class woman as the crucial "steadying influence" between the "unrest among the lower classes and [the] rottenness among the upper classes."

Bok's view of the ideal life for a woman included "a healthful diet, simple, serviceable clothing, a clean, healthy dwelling-place, open-air exercise, and good reading." He preached contentment rather than conspicuous consumption, a message directed not just to his middle-class readers but also to the working poor. In a Christmas editorial, though, Bok recognized that "it is a hard thing for those who have little to believe that the greatest happiness of life is with them: that it is not with those who have abundance."

THE WORKING CLASS

The continuing demand for unskilled workers by railroads, factories, mills, mines, slaughterhouses, and sweatshops attracted new groups to the work-force: immigrants above all, but also growing numbers of women and children. In addition, millions of rural folk, especially young people, formed a migratory stream from the agricultural regions of the South and Midwest to cities and factories across the country.

Although wage levels rose overall during the Gilded Age, there was a great disparity in pay for skilled and unskilled workers. During the recessions and depressions that occurred about every six years, unskilled workers were the first to be laid off or to have their wages slashed. In addition, working conditions were difficult and often dangerous for those at the bottom of the occupational scale.

The average workweek was fifty-nine hours, or nearly six 10-hour days. American industry had the highest rate of workplace accidents and deaths in the world, and there were virtually no safety regulations or government inspections. Few machines had safety devices; few factories or mills had fire escapes. Respiratory diseases were common in mines and unventilated buildings, especially textile mills. Between 1888 and 1894, there were 16,000 railroad workers killed and 170,000 maimed in on-the-job accidents. The United States was also the only industrial nation with no insurance program to cover medical expenses for on-the-job injuries.

WORKING WOMEN Industrial development after the Civil War transformed the nature of the workplace. Mills, mines, factories, and large businesses needed far more unskilled workers than skilled ones. Employers often recruited women and children for the unskilled jobs because they were willing to work for lower wages than men received. In addition to operating sewing machines or tending to textile machines spinning yarn or thread, millions of women worked as maids, cooks, or nannies. In the manufacturing sector, women's wages averaged $7 a week, compared to $10 for unskilled men.

A social worker reported that it was widely assumed in many factories that a married woman would accept lower wages because she "has a man to support her," which was not always the case. The number of women working outside the home tripled between 1870 and 1900, when 5 million women (17 percent of all women) held full-time jobs.

In a letter to the editor of the *Nation* in 1867, a "working woman" described the changing nature of gender roles in American life. Most middle-class women, she acknowledged, still lived in a "world of love, of a sweet and guarded domesticity, of drawing-rooms and boudoirs, of dainty coquetries, of quiet graces, where they flourish like fair flowers in a south window." But each year "thousands of women" were entering a different world "of mud, carts, ledgers, packing-boxes, counting-houses, paste, oils, leather, iron, boards, committees, big boots, and men who . . . meet women on a cool, business level of dollars and cents."

CHILD LABOR   Most young people had always worked in America; farms required everyone to pitch in. In the late nineteenth century, however, millions of children took up work outside the home, sorting coal, stitching clothes, shucking oysters, peeling shrimp, canning food, blowing glass, tending looms,

Children in industry These four young boys performed the dangerous work of mine helpers in West Virginia around 1900.

and operating other kinds of machinery. **Child labor** increased as parents desperate for income felt forced to put their children to work. By 1880, one of every six children under age fourteen was working full-time; by 1900, the United States had almost 2 million child laborers.

In Pennsylvania, West Virginia, and eastern Kentucky, soot-smeared boys worked in the coal mines. In New England and the South, children labored in dusty textile mills where, during the night shift, they had water thrown in their faces to keep them awake. In the southern mills, a fourth of the employees were below the age of fifteen, and children as young as eight worked alongside adults twelve hours a day, six days a week. As a result, they received little or no education.

Factories, mills, mines, and canneries were especially dangerous places for children, who suffered three times as many accidents as adult workers and suffered higher rates of respiratory diseases. A child working in a southern textile mill was only half as likely to reach the age of twenty as a child who did not work in a mill.

THE "DREADFUL CHILL OF CHANGE"

When novelist Henry James returned to the United States in the early twentieth century after a long stay in England, he was shocked by the "dreadful chill of change." Urban-industrial development and western expansion had generated unparalleled prosperity, but the United States, he feared, had lost much of its social stability and cohesion. In 1885, another writer said that the working poor were unleashing "a seismic shock, a cyclonic violence" that threatened to tear society apart.

ORGANIZED LABOR The efforts of the working poor to form unions to improve their pay and working conditions faced formidable obstacles during the Gilded Age. Many executives fought against unions. They "blacklisted" union organizers by circulating their names to keep them from being hired, fired labor leaders, and often hired "scabs" (nonunion workers) to replace workers who went on strike. Another factor impeding the growth of unions was that much of the workforce was made up of immigrants who spoke different languages and often distrusted people from other ethnic groups. Nonetheless, with or without unions, workers began to stage strikes that often led to violence. Perhaps at no time before or since have class tensions—both social and cultural—been so bitter.

THE MOLLY MAGUIRES During the early 1870s, violence erupted in the eastern Pennsylvania coalfields, when a secret Irish American group called the Molly Maguires took economic justice into their own hands. The Mollies took their name from an Irish patriot who had led the resistance against the British. Outraged by dangerous working conditions in the mines and the owners' brutal efforts to suppress union activity, the Mollies used intimidation, beatings, and killings to avenge the wrongs done to Irish workers.

Their terrorism reached its peak in 1874–1875, prompting mine owners to hire men from the Pinkerton Detective Agency (commonly referred to as "Pinkertons") to stop the movement. One of the agents who infiltrated the Mollies uncovered enough evidence to have the leaders indicted for the coalfield murders. In 1876, twenty-four Molly Maguires were convicted by a non-Irish jury; ten were hanged.

THE GREAT RAILROAD STRIKE (1877) After the financial panic of 1873, the major rail lines, fearful of a recession, had slashed workers' wages. In 1877, the companies announced another 10 percent wage cut, which led most of the railroad workers at Martinsburg, West Virginia, to walk off the job and block the tracks to shut down all rail traffic.

The strike spread to hundreds of other cities and towns. Tens of thousands of workers walked off the job, and the resulting violence left more than 100 people dead and millions of dollars in damaged property. In Pittsburgh, thousands of striking workers burned thirty-nine buildings and destroyed more than 1,000 railcars and locomotives. The violence was not directed solely at employers, either. Workers who refused to join the strike or participate in the riots were harassed and beaten.

The **Great Railroad Strike** became one of the most spectacular incidents of widespread violence in American history and revealed how polarized the working poor and business elites had become. Local and state officials interpreted the growing insurgency as evidence of Communist ideology born in Europe. Governors mobilized state militia units to suppress the rioters.

In Philadelphia, the militia dispersed a crowd at the cost of twenty-six lives, but looting and burning continued until President Rutherford B. Hayes dispatched federal troops finally to end it. A reporter described the scene as "the most horrible ever witnessed, except in the carnage of war. There were fifty miles of hot rails, ten tracks side by side, with as many miles of ties turned into glowing coals and tons on tons of iron car skeletons and wheels almost at white heat." Eventually the disgruntled workers, lacking organized bargaining power, had little choice but to return to work. The strike had failed.

For many Americans, the railroad strike raised the possibility of what a Pittsburgh newspaper saw as "a great civil war in this country between labor and capital." Many workers felt that violence was their only option. "The working people everywhere are with us," a unionist told a reporter. "They know what it is to bring up a family on ninety cents a day, to live on beans and corn meal week in and week out, to run in debt at the [company] stores until you cannot get trusted any longer, to see the wife breaking down . . . and the children growing sharp and fierce like wolves day after day because they don't get enough to eat."

Equally disturbing to those in positions of corporate and political power was the presence of many women among the protesters. A Baltimore journalist noted that the "singular part of the disturbances is the very active part taken by the women, who are the wives and mothers of the [railroad] firemen."

President Hayes knew that the army had suppressed the strikers but had not solved the underlying problems. "The strikes have been put down by *force*," he wrote in his diary. "But now for the *real* remedy. Can't something be done by education of the strikers, by judicious control of the capitalists, by wise general policy, to end or diminish the evil?" It was a fair question that largely went unanswered.

THE SAND-LOT INCIDENT In California, the national railroad strike indirectly gave rise to a working-class political movement. In 1877, a

"The Chinese Must Go" In this advertisement for the Missouri Steam Washer, the American-made washing machine drives a Chinese laundryman back to China, playing on the growing anti-Chinese sentiments in the 1880s.

meeting held in a sandy San Francisco vacant lot to express sympathy for the railroad strikers ended with attacks on passing Chinese workers. In the aftermath of the so-called Sand-Lot Incident, white mobs attacked Chinatown. The Chinese were handy scapegoats for frustrated white laborers who believed the Asians had taken their jobs.

Soon an Irish immigrant, Denis Kearney, had organized the Workingmen's Party of California, whose platform called for the United States to stop Chinese immigration. Kearney lectured the "sand-lotters" about the "foreign peril" and blasted the railroad barons for exploiting the poor. The Workingmen's movement peaked in 1879, when it elected a number of state legislators and the mayor of San Francisco. Although Kearney failed to build a lasting movement, his anti-Chinese theme became a national issue. In 1882, Congress voted to prohibit Chinese immigration for ten years.

THE NATIONAL LABOR UNION As the size and power of corporations increased, efforts to build a national labor union movement gained momentum. During the Civil War, because of the increased demand for skilled labor, so-called "craft unions" made up of workers expert at a particular handicraft grew in strength and number. Yet there was no overall connection among such groups until 1866, when the **National Labor Union (NLU)** convened in Baltimore.

The NLU was more interested in advocating for improved workplace conditions than in bargaining with employers about wages and hours. The group promoted an eight-hour workday, workers' cooperatives (in which workers, collectively, would create and own their own large-scale manufacturing and mining operations), "greenbackism" (the printing of paper money to inflate the currency and thereby relieve debtors), and equal voting rights for women and African Americans.

Like most such organizations in the nineteenth century, however, the NLU did not allow women as members. As one official explained the attitude of male unionists, "Woman was created to be man's companion," not his competitor in the workplace who would cause his wages to fall. The NLU also discriminated against African American workers. They were forced to organize black-only unions of their own. W. E. B. DuBois, an outspoken black civil rights activist, charged that the "white worker did not want the Negro in his unions, did not believe in him as a man."

After the NLU's head, William Sylvis, died suddenly in 1869, its support declined, and by 1872 the union had disbanded. The NLU was not a total failure, however. It was influential in persuading Congress to enact an eight-hour workday for federal employees and to repeal the 1864 Contract Labor Act, which had been passed to encourage the importation of laborers by allowing employers to pay for the passage of foreign workers to America. In exchange, the workers were committed to labor for a specified number of years. Employers had taken advantage of the Contract Labor Act to recruit foreign laborers willing to work for lower wages than their American counterparts.

THE KNIGHTS OF LABOR In 1869, another national labor group had emerged: the Noble Order of the **Knights of Labor**. The union grew slowly at first, but even as other unions collapsed during the depression of the 1870s, it spread more rapidly.

The Knights of Labor endorsed most of the reforms advanced by previous workingmen's groups, including the creation of bureaus of labor statistics and mechanics' lien laws (to ensure payment of wages), the elimination of convict-labor competition, the establishment of the eight-hour day and worker cooperatives, and the use of paper currency. One reform the group advocated was far ahead of the times: equal pay for equal work by men and women.

The Knights of Labor allowed as members all who had ever worked for wages, except lawyers, doctors, bankers, and those who sold liquor. Such inclusiveness was both a strength and a weakness. By recruiting all types of workers, the Knights grew very large, but they also struggled with internal tensions between skilled and unskilled workers.

Knights of Labor This national union was the most egalitarian union during the Gilded Age.

In 1879, Terence V. Powderly, the thirty-year-old mayor of Scranton, Pennsylvania, became head of the Knights of Labor. Born of Irish immigrant parents, Powderly had started working for a railroad at age sixteen. Frail, sensitive to criticism, and indecisive, he was in many ways unsuited to the job. He was opposed to strikes, and when they did occur, he did not always support the groups involved. Yet the Knights owed their greatest growth to strikes that occurred under his leadership. In the early 1880s, the Knights increased their membership from about 100,000 to more than 700,000.

MOTHER JONES   One of the most colorful and beloved labor agitators at the end of the nineteenth century was a remarkable woman known simply as Mother Jones. White haired, pink cheeked, and dressed in matronly black dresses and hats, she was a tireless champion of the working poor who used fiery rhetoric to excite crowds and attract media attention. She led marches, dodged bullets, served jail terms, and confronted business titans and police with disarming courage. In 1913, a district attorney called her the "most dangerous woman in America."

Born in Cork, Ireland, in 1837, Mary Harris was the second of five children in a poor Catholic family that fled the Irish potato famine at midcentury and settled in Toronto. In 1861, she moved to Memphis, Tennessee, and began teaching. There, as the Civil War was erupting, she met and married George Jones, an iron molder and staunch union member. They had four children, and then disaster struck. In 1867 a yellow fever epidemic devastated Memphis, killing Mary Jones's husband and four children.

The grief-stricken thirty-seven-year-old widow moved to Chicago and took up dressmaking, only to see her shop, home, and belongings destroyed in the great fire of 1871. Having lost her family and her finances, and angry at the social inequality and injustices she saw around her, Mary Jones drifted into the labor movement and soon emerged as its most passionate advocate. Chicago was then the seedbed of labor radicalism, and the union culture nurtured in Mary Jones a lifelong dedication to the cause of wage workers and their families.

The gritty woman who had lost her family now declared herself the "mother" of the fledgling labor movement. She joined the Knights of Labor as an organizer and public speaker. In the late 1880s she became an ardent speaker for the United Mine Workers (UMW), various other unions, and the Socialist party. For the next thirty years, she crisscrossed the nation, recruiting union members, supporting strikers (her "boys"), raising funds, walking picket lines, defying court injunctions, berating politicians, and spending time in prison.

Wherever Mother Jones went, she promoted higher wages, shorter hours, safer workplaces, and restrictions on child labor. Coal miners, said the UMW president, "have had no more staunch supporter, no more able defender than the one we all love to call Mother." During a miners' strike in West Virginia, Jones was arrested, convicted of "conspiracy that resulted in murder," and sentenced to twenty years in prison. The outcry over her plight helped spur a Senate committee to investigate conditions in the coal mines; the governor set her free.

Mother Jones was especially determined to end the exploitation of children in the workplace. In 1903, she organized a highly publicized weeklong march of child workers from Pennsylvania to the New York home of President Theodore Roosevelt. The children were physically stunted and mutilated, most of them missing fingers or hands from machinery accidents. President Roosevelt refused to see the ragtag children, but as Mother Jones explained, "Our march had done its work. We had drawn the attention of the nation to the crime of child labor." Soon the Pennsylvania state legislature increased the legal working age to fourteen.

Mother Jones lost most of the strikes she participated in, but over the course of her long life she saw average wages increase, working conditions improve, and child labor diminish. Her commitment to the cause of social justice never wavered. At age eighty-three, she was arrested after joining a miners' strike in Colorado and jailed in solitary confinement. At her funeral, in 1930, one speaker urged people to remember her famous rallying cry: "Pray for the dead and fight like hell for the living."

ANARCHISM One of the many challenges facing the labor union movement during the Gilded Age was growing hostility from middle-class Americans who came to view unionized workers, especially those involved in clashes with police, as "radicals" or "anarchists." Anarchists believed that government—any government—was a device used by powerful capitalists to oppress and exploit the working poor. They dreamed of the elimination of government altogether, and some were willing to use bombs and bullets to achieve their revolutionary goal.

Many European anarchists immigrated to the United States during the last quarter of the nineteenth century. Although most of them disavowed violence, the terrorists among them ensured that the label "anarchist" provoked frightening images in the minds of many Americans.

Labor-related violence increased during the 1880s as the gap between the rich and working poor widened. Between 1880 and 1900, some 6.6 million hourly workers participated in more than 23,000 strikes nationwide. Chicago was a hotbed of labor unrest and a magnet for immigrants, especially German and Irish laborers, some of whom were socialists or anarchists who endorsed violence. The Chicago labor movement's foremost demand was for an eight-hour workday, and what came to be called the **Haymarket riot** grew indirectly out of prolonged agitation for this goal.

THE HAYMARKET RIOT (1886) In 1886, some 40,000 Chicago workers went on strike in support of an eight-hour workday. On May 3, violent clashes between strikers and nonunion "scabs" hired to replace striking workers erupted outside the McCormick Harvesting Machine Company plant. The police arrived, shots rang out, and two strikers were killed. The killings infuriated the leaders of the tiny but outspoken anarchist movement in Chicago. August Spies, a German-born anarchist leader, printed leaflets in English and German demanding "Revenge!" and calling "Workingmen, to Arms!" A mass protest was planned for the following night at Haymarket Square.

On the evening of May 4, after listening to speeches complaining about low wages and long working hours, the crowd of angry laborers was beginning to break up when police arrived and ordered them to disperse. At that point, someone threw a bomb that left dozens of maimed and dying policemen scattered in the street. The police then fired into the fleeing crowd, resulting in more casualties. Seven policemen were killed and sixty more wounded in what journalists called America's first terrorist bombing.

The next day, Chicago's mayor banned all labor meetings in the city, and newspapers printed sensational headlines about anarchists terrorizing Chicago. One New York newspaper demanded stern punishment for "the few long-haired, wild-eyed, bad-smelling, atheistic, reckless foreign wretches" who promoted such unrest.

During the summer of 1886, seven anarchist leaders, all but one of them German speakers, were sentenced to death despite the lack of evidence linking them to the bomb thrower, whose identity was never determined. After being sentenced to be hanged, Louis Lingg declared that he was innocent but was "in favor of using force" to end the abuses of the capitalist system. Lawyers for the anarchists appealed the convictions to the Illinois Supreme Court.

Meanwhile, petitioners from around the world appealed for clemency. One of the petitioners was Samuel Gompers, the founding president of the American Federation of Labor (AFL). "I abhor anarchy," Gompers stressed, "but I also abhor injustice when meted out even to the most despicable being on earth."

On November 10, 1887, Louis Lingg committed suicide in his cell. That same day, the governor commuted the sentences of two of the convicted conspirators to life imprisonment. The next day, as armed police and soldiers surrounded the Cook County Jail, the four remaining condemned men were hanged. Some 200,000 people lined the streets of Chicago as the caskets of those executed were taken for burial. To labor militants around the world, the executed anarchists were working-class martyrs; to the police and the economic elite in Chicago, they were demonic assassins.

A BACKLASH AGAINST UNIONS After the Haymarket riot, tensions between workers and management reached a fever pitch. In 1886 alone, there were 1,400 strikes across the country involving 700,000 workers. But the violence in Chicago had also triggered widespread hostility to the Knights of Labor and labor groups in general. Despite his best efforts, union leader Terence Powderly could never separate in the public mind the Knights from the anarchists, since one of those convicted of conspiracy in the bombing was a member of the union.

Powderly clung to leadership until 1893, but after that the union evaporated. Yet the Knights did attain some lasting achievements, among them an 1880 federal law providing for the arbitration of labor disputes, and the creation of the federal Bureau of Labor Statistics in 1884. Another of their successes was the Foran Act of 1885, which, though poorly enforced, penalized employers who imported immigrant workers. By their example, the Knights also spread the idea of unionism and initiated a new type of organization: the industrial union, which included all skilled and unskilled workers within a particular industry, such as railroad workers or miners.

Samuel Gompers The head of the American Federation of Labor strikes an assertive pose.

GOMPERS AND THE AFL
The craft unions, representing skilled workers, generally opposed efforts to unite with industrial unionism.

Leaders of the craft unions feared that joining with unskilled laborers would mean a loss of their identity and bargaining power. Thus, in 1886, delegates from twenty-five craft unions organized the **American Federation of Labor (AFL)**. Its structure differed from that of the Knights of Labor in that it was a federation of many separate national unions, each of which was largely free to act on its own in dealing with business owners.

Samuel Gompers served as president of the AFL from its founding until his death, in 1924, with only one year's interruption. Born in England, Gompers came to the United States as a teenager, joined the Cigar Makers' Union in 1864, and became president of his New York City local union in 1877. Unlike Terence Powderly and the Knights of Labor, Gompers focused on concrete economic gains—higher wages, shorter hours, and better working conditions.

The AFL at first grew slowly, but by the turn of the century, it claimed 500,000 members in affiliated unions. In 1914, on the eve of World War I, it had 2 million, and in 1920, it reached a peak of 4 million. But even then, the AFL embraced less than 15 percent of the nation's nonagricultural workers. In fact, all unions, including the so-called railroad brotherhoods unaffiliated with the AFL, accounted for little more than 18 percent of those workers.

Organized labor's strongholds were in transportation and the building trades. Most of the larger manufacturing industries—including steel, textiles, tobacco, and meatpacking—remained almost untouched. Gompers never opposed industrial unions, and several became important affiliates of the AFL: the United Mine Workers, the International Ladies Garment Workers, and the Amalgamated Clothing Workers. But the AFL had its greatest success in organizing skilled workers.

Two incidents in the 1890s stalled the emerging industrial-union movement: the **Homestead Steel strike** of 1892 and the **Pullman strike** of 1894. These violent labor conflicts were the climactic economic events of the Gilded Age and represented a test of strength for the organized labor movement. They also served to reshape the political landscape.

THE HOMESTEAD STEEL STRIKE The Amalgamated Association of Iron and Steel Workers, founded in 1876, was the nation's largest craft union. At the massive steel mill at Homestead, Pennsylvania, along the Monongahela River near Pittsburgh, the union had enjoyed friendly relations with Andrew Carnegie's company until Henry Clay Frick became chief executive in 1889.

A showdown was delayed until 1892, however, when the union contract came up for renewal. Carnegie, who had previously expressed sympathy for the unions, went on a lengthy hunting trip in his native Scotland, intentionally leaving the rigid Frick to handle the difficult negotiations.

Carnegie knew what was in the works: a cost-cutting reduction in the number of highly paid skilled workers through the use of labor-saving machinery, even though the corporation was enjoying high profits. It was a deliberate attempt to smash the union. "Am with you to the end," Carnegie wrote to Frick after leaving for Scotland. William Jones, the mill manager, disagreed with his bosses. He opposed cutting wages because "our men are working hard and faithfully. . . . Now, mark what I tell you. Our labor is the cheapest in the country."

Jones's protests did little good. As negotiations dragged on, the company announced on June 25 that it would stop negotiating with the 3,800 workers on June 29 unless an agreement was reached. A strike—or, more properly, a lockout in which management closed down the mill to try to force the union to make concessions—would begin on that date. Frick told journalists that he was determined to have "absolute control of our plant and business."

Frick ordered construction of a twelve-foot-high fence around the plant and equipped it with watchtowers, searchlights, barbed wire, and high-pressure water cannons. He also hired a private army of 316 Pinkerton agents to protect what was soon dubbed Fort Frick. Before dawn on July 6, 1892, the "Pinkertons" floated up the Monongahela River on two barges pulled by a tugboat.

Thousands of unionists and their supporters, many of them armed, were waiting on shore. A fourteen-hour battle broke out in which seven workers and three Pinkertons were killed, and dozens wounded. Hundreds of women on shore shouted, "Kill the Pinkertons!"

In the end, the Pinkertons surrendered, having agreed to be tried for murder, and were marched away to taunts from crowds lining the streets. A week later, the Pennsylvania governor dispatched 4,000 state militiamen to Homestead, where they surrounded the steel mill and dispersed the picketing workers. Frick then hired strikebreakers to operate the mill. He refused to resume negotiations: "I will never recognize the union, never, never!"

The strike dragged on until November, but by then the union was dead and its leaders had been charged with murder and treason. The union cause was not helped when Alexander Berkman, a Lithuanian anarchist, tried to assassinate Frick on July 23, shooting him twice in the neck and stabbing him three times. Despite his wounds, Frick fought back fiercely and, with the help of staff members, subdued the would-be assassin.

Much of the local sympathy for the strikers evaporated. As a union leader explained, Berkman's bullets "went straight through the heart of the Homestead strike." Penniless and demoralized, the defeated workers ended their walkout on November 20 and accepted the company's harsh wage cuts. Only a fifth of the strikers were hired back; the rest were "blacklisted" to prevent other steel mills from hiring them. Carnegie and Frick, with the support of local, state, and national government officials, had eliminated the union. After the Homestead strike, none of Carnegie's steel plants employed unionized workers. Within a few years, Carnegie could confide to a friend that he was "ashamed to tell you" how large his profits were from the Homestead plant.

With each passing year, Carnegie nursed regrets about how Frick handled the Homestead strike. In the end, an embittered Frick split with Carnegie after he learned that his boss had been telling lies about him and making "insults" about his character. Frick told Carnegie that he had grown "tired of your business methods, your absurd newspaper interviews and personal remarks and unwarranted interference in matters you know nothing about." When Carnegie sought to reconcile with his former lieutenant, Frick told the messenger: "You can say to Andrew Carnegie that I will meet him in hell where we are both going."

THE PULLMAN STRIKE The Pullman strike of 1894 was even more notable, as it paralyzed the economies of the twenty-seven states and territories in the western half of the nation. It involved a dispute at Pullman, Illinois, a "model" industrial suburb of Chicago owned by the Pullman Palace Car Company, which made passenger train cars (called "Pullmans" or "sleeping cars").

Employees were required to live in the town's 1,400 cottages, which had been built to high standards, with gas heat and indoor plumbing. With 12,000 residents, the town also boasted a library, a theater, a school, parks and playgrounds, and a glass-roofed shopping mall owned by the company. There were no saloons, social clubs, newspapers, or private property not owned by the company. No political activities were allowed.

As a "company town," Pullman was of much higher quality than the villages in the South owned by textile mills, and the death rate was less than half of that in neighboring communities. Yet over time, many workers complained that they did not like living under the thumb of the company's owner, George Pullman.

During the depression of 1893, Pullman laid off 3,000 of his 5,800 employees and cut wages 25 to 40 percent for the rest, but did not lower rents for housing or the price of food in the company store. In the spring of 1894, desperate workers joined the American Railway Union, founded the previous year by Eugene V. Debs.

Eugene V. Debs Founder of the American Railway Union, and later the presidential candidate for the Socialist Party of America.

The charismatic Debs was a child of working-class immigrants who had quit school at age fourteen to work for an Indiana railroad. By the early 1890s, he had become a tireless spokesman for labor radicalism, and he worked to organize all railway workers—skilled or unskilled—into the American Railway Union, which soon became a powerful organization. He quickly turned his attention to the Pullman controversy, urging the workers to obey the laws and avoid violence. After George Pullman fired three members of a workers' grievance committee, the workers went on strike on May 11, 1894.

In June, after Pullman refused Debs's plea for a negotiated settlement, the Railway Union workers stopped handling trains containing Pullman railcars. By the end of July, they had shut down most of the railroads in the Midwest and cut off all traffic through Chicago. To keep the trains running, railroad executives hired strikebreakers, and the U.S. attorney general, a former attorney for railroad companies, swore in 3,400 special deputies to protect them. Angry workers assaulted strikebreakers and destroyed property.

Finally, on July 3, President Grover Cleveland sent 2,000 federal troops into the Chicago area, claiming it was his duty to ensure delivery of the mail. Meanwhile, the attorney general convinced a federal judge to sign an *injunction* (an official court decree) prohibiting the labor union from interfering.

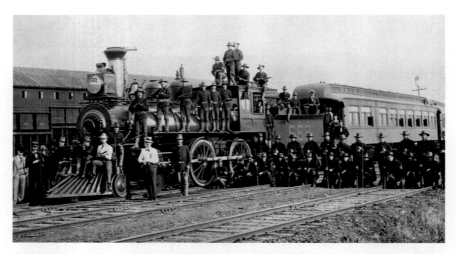

The Pullman Strike Federal troops guarding the railroads, 1894.

On July 13, the union called off the strike. A few days later, a court cited Debs for violating the injunction; he served six months in jail. The Supreme Court upheld the decree in the case of *In re Debs* (1895) on broad grounds of national sovereignty: "The strong arm of the national government may be put forth to brush away all obstructions to the freedom of interstate commerce or the transportation of the mails."

Debs emerged from jail a socialist who would later run for president. In 1897, George Pullman died of a heart attack, and the following year, the city of Chicago annexed the town of Pullman. A reporter for the *Nation* noted that despite the town's attractive features, what the workers wanted most was the chance to own a house of their own. "Mr. Pullman," he explained, "overlooked this peculiar American characteristic."

Economic Success and Excess

For all of the stress and strain caused by swift industrialization, American productivity soared in the late nineteenth century. By 1900, the United States was producing a third of the world's goods, and millions of immigrants from around the world continued to risk all in hopes of chasing the American Dream. Corporate empires generated enormous fortunes for a few and real improvements in the quality of life for many. The majority of workers now labored in factories and mines rather than on farms. "One can hardly believe," observed philosopher John Dewey, "there has been a revolution in history so rapid, so extensive, so complete."

The urban-industrial revolution and the gigantic new corporations it created transformed the size, scope, and power of the American economy, for good and for ill. As the twentieth century dawned, an unregulated capitalist economy had grown corrupt and recklessly out of balance—and only government intervention could restore economic fairness and social stability.

CHAPTER REVIEW

SUMMARY

- **The Causes of Industrial Growth** During the late nineteenth century, agricultural and industrial production increased sharply. The national railroad network grew to nearly 200,000 miles, the most extensive in the world. The surge of industrialization expanded use of electrical power and the application of scientific research to industrial processes. The *Bessemer converter* allowed for the mass production of steel, which was used to construct railroads, ships, bridges, and buildings.

- **The Rise of Big Business** Many businesses grew to enormous size and power, often ignoring ethics and the law in doing so. Entrepreneurs like John D. Rockefeller, Andrew Carnegie, and J. Pierpont Morgan were extraordinarily skilled at gaining control of particular industries. Companies such as *Standard Oil* and *Carnegie Steel* practiced both *vertical integration*, through which they controlled all the enterprises needed to produce and distribute their products, and *horizontal integration*, in which they absorbed or eliminated their competitors. To consolidate their holdings and sidestep laws prohibiting *monopolies*, they created *trusts* and eventually *holding companies*. *J. Pierpont Morgan and Company*, an investment bank, pioneered methods for consolidating corporations and eliminating competition, all in an effort to bring "order and stability" to the marketplace.

- **The Alliance of Business and Politics** The federal government encouraged economic growth after the Civil War by imposing high *tariffs* on imported products, granting public land to railroad companies and settlers in the West, establishing a stable currency, and encouraging the creation of universities to spur technical innovation and research. Equally important, local, state, and federal governments made little effort to regulate the activities of businesses. This *laissez-faire* policy allowed entrepreneurs to experiment with new methods of organization, but also created conditions for rampant corruption and abuse.

- **A Changed Social Order** While the business and financial elite showed off their new wealth with extravagant homes and parties, the urban and industrial workforce was largely composed of unskilled workers, including recent immigrants, former farmers, and growing numbers of women and children. *Child labor* sometimes involved children as young as eight working twelve-hour days. Business owners and managers showed little concern for workplace safety, and accidents and work-related diseases were common. With industrialization and the rise of Big Business also came an increase in the number of people who considered themselves middle class. Growing numbers of women went to college, took business and professional jobs, and participated in other public activities.

- **Organized Labor** It was difficult for unskilled workers to organize effectively into unions, in part because of racial and ethnic tensions among laborers, language barriers, and the efforts of owners and supervisors to undermine unionizing efforts. Business owners often hired "strikebreakers," usually desperate immigrant workers who were willing to take jobs at the prevailing wage. Nevertheless, several unions did advocate for workers' rights at a national level. The *National Labor Union* and the *Knights of Labor* organized strikes and lobbied for workers in the 1870s and 1880s, but both groups eventually fell apart. After the violence associated with the *Haymarket riot*, the *Homestead Steel strike*, and the *Pullman strike*, many Americans grew fearful of unions and viewed them as politically radical. Craft unions made up solely of skilled workers became more successful at organizing, as the *American Federation of Labor* focused on better working conditions and avoided involvement in politics.

CHRONOLOGY

1859	First oil well is struck in Titusville, Pennsylvania
1861	Congress creates the Morrill Tariff
1869	First transcontinental railroad is completed at Promontory Summit, Utah
1876	Alexander Graham Bell patents his telephone
1877	Great Railroad Strike
1879	Thomas A. Edison makes the first durable incandescent lightbulb
1882	John D. Rockefeller organizes the Standard Oil Trust
1886	Haymarket riot
	American Federation of Labor is organized
1892	Homestead Steel strike
1894	Pullman strike
1901	J. Pierpont Morgan creates the U.S. Steel Corporation

KEY TERMS

Standard Oil Company p. 764

horizontal integration p. 764

monopoly p. 764

vertical integration p. 766

trust p. 766

holding company p. 766

Bessemer converter p. 767

Carnegie Steel Company p. 768

J. Pierpont Morgan and Company p. 769

tariff p. 771

laissez-faire p. 773

child labor p. 781

Great Railroad Strike of 1877 p. 782

National Labor Union (NLU) p. 784

Knights of Labor p. 785

Haymarket riot p. 788

American Federation of Labor (AFL) p. 790

Homestead Steel strike p. 790

Pullman strike p. 790

 INQUIZITIVE

Go to InQuizitive to see what you've learned—and learn what you've missed—with personalized feedback along the way.

18

The New South and the New West

1865–1900

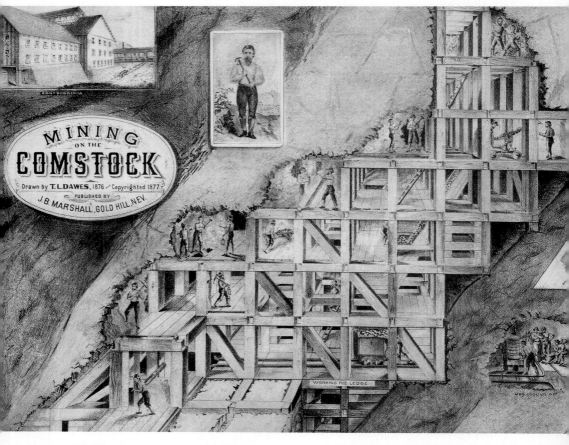

***Mining on the Comstock* (1877)** The Comstock Lode was one of the largest gold and silver mines in America, yielding more than $300 million over two decades. This illustration shows a cutaway of the Comstock Lode, revealing the complex network of shafts and supports, as well as the various tasks performed by miners within its tunnels.

After the Civil War, the devastated South and the untamed West provided enticing frontiers for economic enterprise. The South had to be rebuilt, while the sparsely settled territories and states west of the Mississippi River were ripe for the development of farms, businesses, railroads, and towns. Bankers and financiers in America and in Europe took advantage of these conditions to invest heavily in both regions, but especially in the far western region between the Mississippi River and California.

The Great Plains had long been viewed as a barren landscape suitable only for Indians and animals. Half of Texas, for instance, was still not settled at the end of the Civil War. After 1865, however, the federal government encouraged western settlement and economic development in what was then called "Indian Country." Two thirds of Native Americans in 1865 lived on the Great Plains, often warring with one another over rival "hunting rights" to the vast buffalo herds.

The construction of transcontinental railroads, the military conquest of the Indians, and the policy of distributing government-owned lands at low cost to settlers, ranchers, miners, and railroads combined to lure millions of pioneers and enterprising capitalists westward. Charles Goodnight, a Texas cattle rancher, recalled that "we were adventurers in a great land . . . fresh and

focus questions

1. In what ways did a "New South" emerge economically in the late nineteenth century?

2. What was the crop-lien system that emerged in the South and how did it shape the region after the Civil War?

3. How and why did white southerners take away African Americans' right to vote and adopt "Jim Crow" segregation laws at the end of the nineteenth century?

4. Who were the various groups of migrants to the West after the Civil War? Why did they move there?

5. What were the experiences of miners, farmers, ranchers, and women in the West in the late nineteenth century?

6. How did the federal government's post–Civil War policies in the West affect Native Americans?

7. How did the South and West change by 1900?

full of the zest of darers." By 1900, a New West and a New South had emerged, and eleven new states had been created out of the western territories.

The Myth of the New South

After the war between the states, the South fought an inner civil war over the region's future. Many white southerners embraced the "Lost Cause," a romanticized interpretation of the war that painted the Confederates as noble defenders of their distinctive way of life against a tyrannical federal government headed by Abraham Lincoln. Southerners were haunted by a lingering nostalgia for the mythic Old South of white-columned plantations, white supremacy, and cotton-generated wealth produced by armies of enslaved blacks. As one southerner said, his native region remained "old-fashioned, medieval, [and] provincial, worshipping the dead."

At the same time, no region has inspired a more tenacious pride of place, a localism anchored in family life enlivened by visions of a mythic past. Mississippi writer Eudora Welty once explained that in the South, "feelings are bound up with place." *Home* and *history* are two of the most revered words in southern life. Nineteenth-century southerners did not simply live in the present and dream of the future. They were forever glancing backward in the process of moving forward. As William Faulkner recognized in his novel *Intruder in the Dust*, "The past isn't dead. It's not even past."

Other prominent southerners, however, looked more to the future. They called for a New South where the region's predominantly agricultural economy would be diversified by an expanded industrial sector. The tireless champion of the New South ideal was Henry Woodfin Grady (1850–1889), the powerful managing editor of the *Atlanta Constitution*.

In 1886, Grady told a New York City audience that there had been an Old South "of slavery and secession—that South is dead. There is now a New South of union and freedom—that South, thank God, is living, breathing, and growing every hour." The Old South, he added, "rested everything on slavery and agriculture, unconscious that these could neither give nor maintain healthy growth."

Grady saw the New South becoming "a perfect democracy" of small farms complemented by mills, mines, factories, and cities. The postwar South, Grady claimed, would become a real democracy, no longer run by the planter aristocracy or dependent upon slave labor.

Many southerners shared Grady's vision. The Confederacy, they concluded, had lost the war because it had relied too much upon King Cotton—

and slavery. In the future, the New South must follow the North's example ("out-Yankee the Yankees") and develop a strong industrial sector to go with its agricultural foundation. New South advocates also stressed that more-efficient farming, using the latest machinery and technical expertise, was essential; that widespread vocational training was urgently needed; and that racial harmony built upon the acceptance by blacks of white supremacy (a peculiar form of a "perfect democracy") would provide a stable social environment for economic growth.

TEXTILE MILLS The chief accomplishment of the New South's effort to industrialize was a dramatic expansion of the region's **textile industry**, which produced thread and cotton bedding and clothing. From 1880 to 1900, the number of cotton mills in the South grew from 161 to 400, the number of mill workers (most of whom were white, with women and children outnumbering men) increased fivefold, and the demand for cotton products went up eightfold.

Thousands of dirt-poor farm folk—many of them children—rushed to take jobs in the mill villages that arose after the war. Seventy percent of mill workers were under the age of twenty-one, and many were under the age of fourteen. A dawn-to-dusk job in a mill paying fifty cents a day "was much more interesting than one-horse farming," noted one worker, "because you can meet your bills." Those bills were usually paid to the mill owner, who provided housing and supplies to the workers in his village—for a fee. By 1900, the South had surpassed New England as the largest producer of cotton fabric in the nation.

THE TOBACCO INDUSTRY Tobacco growing and cigarette production also soared in the New South. Essential to the rise of the tobacco industry was the Duke family of Durham, North Carolina. At the end of the Civil War, Washington Duke took his barn load of tobacco, dried it, and, with the help of his two sons, hitched two mules to his wagon, and traveled across the state, selling tobacco in small pouches as he went. By 1872, the Dukes had a cigarette factory producing 125,000 pounds of tobacco annually.

Washington's son, James Buchanan Duke, wanted even greater success, however. He spent millions on advertising schemes and perfected the mechanized mass production of cigarettes. Duke also undersold competitors and cornered the supply of ingredients needed to make cigarettes. Eventually his primary competitors agreed to join forces with him, and in 1890 Duke brought most of them into the **American Tobacco Company**, which controlled 90 percent of the nation's cigarette production. A ferociously hard worker, Duke was

Southern smokes Allen & Ginter was a major tobacco manufacturer that was acquired by the American Tobacco Company. This advertisement, featuring black laborers in the tobacco fields, plays to the southern nostalgia for the "Old Dominion" before the Civil War.

well on his way to becoming one of the wealthiest and most powerful men in the nation. "I needed no vacation or time off," Duke explained. "There ain't a thrill in the world to compare with building a business and watching it grow before your eyes."

OTHER NEW SOUTH INDUSTRIES Effective use of other natural resources helped revitalize the South along the Appalachian chain from West Virginia to Alabama. Coal production in the South grew from 5 million tons in 1875 to 49 million tons by 1900. At the southern end of the mountains, Birmingham, Alabama, sprang up during the 1870s in large part because of the massive deposits of iron ore in the surrounding ridges, leading boosters to label the steelmaking city the "Pittsburgh of the South."

Urban and industrial expansion as well as rapid population growth created a need for housing, and after 1870 lumbering became the fastest growing industry in the South. Northern investors bought up vast forests of yellow pine and set about clear-cutting them and hauling the logs to new sawmills, where they were milled into lumber for the construction of homes and businesses. By 1900, lumber had surpassed textiles in annual economic value. Still, for all of its advances, the South continued to lag behind the rest of the nation in industrial development.

THE REDEEMERS Henry Grady's vision of a New South celebrated the **Redeemers**, the conservative, pro-business, white politicians in the Democratic party who had embraced the idea of industrial progress grounded in white supremacy. Their supporters referred to them as Redeemers because they supposedly saved ("redeemed") the South from Yankee domination and "black rule" during Reconstruction.

The Redeemers included a rising class of lawyers, merchants, railroad executives, and entrepreneurs who wanted a more diversified economy. They also sought cuts in state taxes and expenditures, including those for the public-school systems started after the war. "Schools are not a necessity," claimed a Virginia governor. Louisiana cut school funding so much that the percentage of its residents unable to read and write actually increased between 1880 and 1900. Black children in particular suffered from such cutbacks. But the Redeemers did not want educated African Americans. "What I want here is Negroes who can make cotton," explained a white planter, "and they don't need education to help them make cotton."

THE FAILINGS OF THE NEW SOUTH

Despite the development of mills and factories, the South in 1900 remained the least industrial, least urban, least educated, and least prosperous region in the nation. Per capita income in the South in 1900 was only 60 percent of the national average. The typical southerner was less likely to be tending a textile loom or a steel furnace than, as the saying went, facing the eastern end of a westbound mule. The South was still dependent on the North for investment capital and manufactured goods.

Cotton remained king after the Civil War, although it never regained the huge profitability it had generated in the 1850s. By the 1880s, southern farmers were producing as much cotton as they had before the war, but were earning far less money because the world price for cotton had declined.

SOUTHERN POVERTY Henry Grady also hoped that growing numbers of southern farmers would own their own land by the end of the nineteenth century. But the opposite occurred. Many southern farmers actually *lost* ownership of the land that they worked each year. A prolonged decline in crop prices during the last third of the nineteenth century made it more difficult than ever to buy and own land. By 1900, an estimated 70 percent of farmers did not own the land they worked, and in no southern state were more than half of farmers landowners.

THE CROP-LIEN SYSTEM Because most southern communities had no banks after the Civil War, people had to find ways to operate with little or no cash. Many rural areas adopted a barter economy in which a "crossroads"

"Free slaves" Sharecroppers painstakingly pick cotton while their white overseer watches them from atop his horse.

or "furnishing" merchant would provide food, clothing, seed, fertilizer, and other items to poor farmers "on credit" in exchange for a share (or "lien") of their crops when harvested.

Southern farmers, white and black, who participated in the **crop-lien system** fell into three distinct categories: small farm owners, sharecroppers, and tenants. The farms owned by most southerners were small and did not generate much cash income. As a result, even those who owned their own farms had to pledge a portion of their future crop to the local merchant in return for supplies purchased "on credit."

Sharecroppers, mostly blacks who had nothing to offer but their labor, worked an owner's land in return for shelter, seed, fertilizer, mules, supplies, food—and a share of the crop, generally about half. **Share tenants**, mostly white farmers who were barely better off, might have their own mule or horse, a plow and tools, and a line of credit with the country store, but they still needed to rent land to farm. A few paid their rent in cash, but most, like sharecroppers, pledged a share of the harvested crops to the landowner.

Usually, the tenant farmers were able to keep a larger share of the crop (about 60 percent) than allowed to the sharecroppers, which meant that landowners often preferred to rent to "croppers" rather than tenants. And many African American sharecroppers worked for the same planter who had owned them as slaves. "The colored folks," said a black Alabama sharecropper, "stayed with the old boss man and farmed and worked on the plantations. They were still slaves, but they were free slaves." Eighty percent of southern blacks lived on farms in the late nineteenth century.

The crop-lien system was self-destructive. The overwhelming focus on planting cotton or tobacco year after year stripped the soil of its fertility and stability. This led to disastrous erosion of farmland during rainstorms as soil washed into nearby creeks, collapsing riverbanks and creating ever-deepening gullies. In addition, landowners required croppers and tenants to grow only a "cash crop," usually cotton or tobacco. This meant that the landless farmers could not grow their own vegetable gardens; they had to get their food from the local merchant in exchange for promised cotton.

Because most farmers did not own the land they worked, the cabins they lived in, or the tools they used, they had little incentive to enrich the soil or maintain buildings and equipment. "The tenant," explained a study of southern agriculture in 1897 written by Matthew B. Hammond, a South Carolina–born economist, "is interested only in the crop he is raising, and makes no effort to keep up the fertility of the land." The tenant system of farming, Hammond concluded, had been "more wasteful and destructive than slavery was anywhere."

The crop-lien system was a post–Civil War version of economic slavery for poor whites as well as for blacks. The landowner or merchant (often the same person) decided what crop would be planted and how it would be cultivated, harvested, and sold. In good times, croppers and tenants barely broke even; in bad times, they struggled to survive. Sharecroppers and share tenants were among the poorest people in the nation. Most of them had little or no education, rarely enough healthy food, and little hope for a better future.

Those who worked the farms developed an intense suspicion of their landlords, who often swindled workers by not giving them their fair share of the crops. Landlords kept the books, handled the sale of the crops, and gave the cropper or tenant his share of the proceeds after deducting for all the items supplied during the year, plus interest that ranged, according to one newspaper, "from 24 percent to grand larceny." Often, the cropper or tenant received nothing at the end of a harvest but a larger debt to be rolled over to the next year's crop. Over time, the high interest charged on the credit offered by the local store or landowner, coupled with sagging prices for cotton and other crops, created a hopeless cycle of debt among small farmers, sharecroppers, and share tenants.

FALLING COTTON PRICES As cotton production soared during the last quarter of the nineteenth century, largely because of dramatic growth in

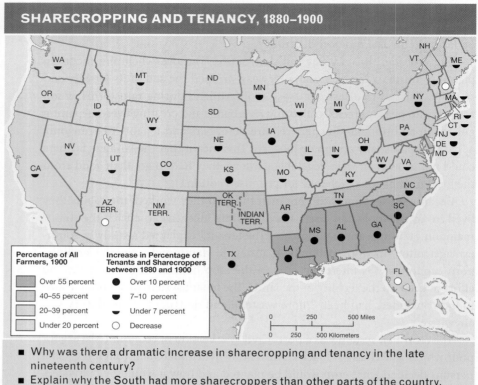

SHARECROPPING AND TENANCY, 1880–1900

Percentage of All Farmers, 1900	Increase in Percentage of Tenants and Sharecroppers between 1880 and 1900
Over 55 percent	● Over 10 percent
40–55 percent	◗ 7–10 percent
20–39 percent	◗ Under 7 percent
Under 20 percent	○ Decrease

0   250   500 Miles

0   250   500 Kilometers

■ Why was there a dramatic increase in sharecropping and tenancy in the late nineteenth century?

■ Explain why the South had more sharecroppers than other parts of the country.

Texas cultivation, the price paid for raw cotton fell steadily. "Have you all felt the effects of the low price of cotton," Mary Parham of Amite, Louisiana, wrote to her father in 1892. "It nearly ruined us. I did not get my house built. The farmers are very blue here. But [they are] getting ready to plant cotton again." As the price paid for cotton dropped, desperate farmers planted even more cotton, which only accelerated the decline in price.

In the 1870s, annual production of cotton was about 2.6 billion pounds, which brought an average price of 11.77 cents per pound. In the 1880s, the average annual production was 3 billion pounds at 10.44 cents per pound. By 1896, the average price of cotton was down to 7.72 cents.

The average annual income of white southerners in 1900 was about half that of Americans outside the South. Eleven percent of whites in the South were illiterate, twice the national average. The region's poorest people were the 9 million former slaves and their children. Per capita black income in 1900 was a third of that of southern whites, and the black illiteracy rate in the South was nearly 50 percent, almost five times higher than that of whites.

RACE RELATIONS DURING THE 1890S

The desperate plight of southern farmers in the 1880s and 1890s affected race relations—for the worse. During the 1890s, white farmers and politicians demanded that blacks be stripped of their voting rights and other civil rights. A violent "Negrophobia" swept across the South and much of the nation. In part, the new wave of racism was spurred by the revival of the old idea that the Anglo-Saxon "race" was intellectually and genetically superior to blacks. Another reason was that many whites had come to resent any signs of African American financial success and political influence. An Alabama newspaper editor declared that "our blood boils when the educated Negro asserts himself politically."

DISFRANCHISING AFRICAN AMERICANS By the 1890s, a new generation of African Americans born and educated since the end of the Civil War was determined to gain true equality. They were more assertive and less patient than their parents. "We are not the Negro from whom the chains of slavery fell a quarter century ago, most assuredly not," a black editor announced. A growing number of young white adults, however, were equally determined to keep "Negroes in their place."

Mississippi took the lead in stripping blacks of their voting rights. The so-called **Mississippi Plan**, a series of state constitutional amendments in 1890, set the pattern of disfranchisement that nine more states would follow. The disfranchisement plan first instituted a residence requirement for voting—two years in the state, one year in a local election district. This was aimed at African American tenant farmers who were in the habit of moving yearly in search of better economic opportunities. Second, Mississippi disqualified blacks from voting if they had committed certain crimes. Third, in order to vote, people had to have paid all of their taxes on time, including a so-called poll tax specifically for voting—a restriction that hurt both poor blacks and poor whites. Finally, all voters had to be able to read or at least "understand" the U.S. Constitution. White registrars decided who satisfied this requirement, and they usually discriminated against blacks.

Other states added variations on the Mississippi Plan. In 1898, Louisiana inserted into its state constitution the "grandfather clause," which allowed illiterate whites to vote if their fathers or grandfathers had been eligible to vote on January 1, 1867, when African Americans were still disfranchised. By 1910, Georgia, North Carolina, Virginia, Alabama, and Oklahoma had incorporated the grandfather clause. Also in the Democratic "Solid South," every southern state created a Democratic primary process to select candidates, and most of these primaries excluded African American voters.

When such "legal" means were not enough to ensure their political dominance, white candidates used fraud and violence. Benjamin Tillman, the white supremacist who served as South Carolina's governor from 1890 to 1894, maintained that his state's problems were caused by white farmers renting their land to "ignorant lazy negroes." His effective use of such racist explanations gained him the support of poor whites in his crusade to oust the ruling Redeemers. Tillman claimed that "I organized the majority [of voters] and put the old families out of business, and we became and are the rulers of the state."

To ensure his election, Tillman and his followers effectively eliminated the black vote. He admitted that "we have done our level best [to prevent blacks from voting]. . . . We stuffed ballot boxes. We shot them. We are not ashamed of it." The whites had regained control of the state government, he concluded, and they were determined to maintain their supremacy.

By the end of the nineteenth century, widespread racial discrimination—segregation of public facilities, political disfranchisement, and vigilante justice—had elevated government-sanctioned bigotry to an official way of life in the South. Tillman bluntly declared in 1892 that blacks "must remain subordinate or be exterminated."

The efforts to suppress the black vote succeeded throughout the South. In 1896, Louisiana had 130,000 registered black voters; by 1900, it had only 5,320. In Alabama in 1900, the census reported that 121,159 black men were literate; only 3,742, however, were registered to vote. By that year, black voting across the South had declined by 62 percent, the white vote by 26 percent.

THE SPREAD OF SEGREGATION At the same time that southern blacks were being shoved out of the political arena, they were also being segregated socially. The symbolic first target was the railroad passenger car. In 1885, novelist George Washington Cable noted that in South Carolina, blacks "ride in first-class [rail] cars as a right" and "their presence excites no comment." From 1875 to 1883, in fact, any local or state law requiring racial segregation violated the federal Civil Rights Act (1875).

By 1883, however, many northern whites endorsed the resegregation of southern life. In that year, the U.S. Supreme Court ruled that the Civil Rights Act of 1875 was unconstitutional. The judges explained that private individuals and organizations could engage in acts of racial discrimination because the Fourteenth Amendment specified only that "no State" could deny citizens equal protection of the law.

The Court's interpretation in what came to be called the Civil Rights Cases (1883) left as an open question the validity of state laws requiring racially segregated public facilities under the principle of "separate but equal," a slogan popular in the South in the late nineteenth century. In the 1880s, Tennessee and Mississippi required railroad passengers to ride in segregated cars.

When Louisiana followed suit in 1890 with a similar law, blacks challenged it in the case of *Plessy v. Ferguson* (1896). The case originated in New Orleans when Homer Plessy, an octoroon (a person having one-eighth African ancestry), refused to leave a whites-only railroad car and was convicted of violating the law. In 1896, the Supreme Court ruled that states had a right to create laws segregating public places such as schools, hotels, and restaurants. Justice John Marshall Harlan, a Kentuckian who had once owned slaves, was the only member of the Court to dissent. He stressed that the Constitution is "color-blind, and neither knows nor tolerates classes among citizens. In respect of civil rights, all citizens are equal before the law." He feared that the Court's ruling would plant the "seeds of race hate" under "the sanction of law."

That is precisely what happened. The Court's ruling in the *Plessy* case legitimized the widespread practice of racially **"separate but equal"** facilities in virtually every area of southern life. In 1900, the editor of the *Richmond Times* insisted that racial segregation "be applied in every relation of Southern life. God Almighty drew the color line, and it cannot be obliterated. The negro must stay on his side of the line, and the white man must stay on his side, and the sooner both races recognize this fact and accept it, the better it will be for both."

The new regulations came to be called "Jim Crow" laws. The name derived from "Jump Jim Crow," an old song-and-dance caricature of African Americans. During the 1890s, the term *Jim Crow* became a derisive expression meaning "Negro." Signs reading "white only" or "colored only" above restrooms and water fountains emerged as hallmarks of the Jim Crow system. Old racist customs dating back before the Civil War were revived. If whites walked along a sidewalk, blacks were expected to step aside and let them pass. There were even racially separate funeral homes, cemeteries, and churches. When a white deacon in a Mississippi Baptist church saw a black man in the sanctuary, he asked: "Boy, what you doin' in there? Don't you know this is a white church?" The black man replied: "Boss, I'm here to mop the floor." The white man paused and said, "Well, that's all right then, but don't let me catch you prayin'."

Widespread racist violence accompanied the Jim Crow laws. From 1890 to 1899, the United States averaged 188 racial lynchings per year, 82 percent of which occurred in the South. Lynchings usually involved a black man (or men) accused of a crime, often rape. White mobs would seize, torture, and kill the accused, always in ghastly ways. Participating whites viewed lynchings as forms of outdoor recreation. Large crowds, including women and children, would watch amid a carnival-like atmosphere. The governor of Mississippi

The lynching of Henry Smith Despite lack of evidence, Smith was convicted of murdering a white girl in Paris, Texas. A large crowd assembled to watch her family torture Smith on a platform labeled "Justice." After Smith was burned alive, the townspeople kept his charred teeth and bones as souvenirs.

declared that "if it is necessary that every Negro in the state will be lynched, it will be done to maintain white supremacy."

MOB RULE IN NORTH CAROLINA White supremacy was violently imposed in the thriving coastal port of Wilmington, North Carolina, then the largest city in the state, with about 20,000 residents. In 1894 and 1896, black voters, by then a majority in the city, elected African Americans to various municipal offices, infuriating the white elite. "We will never surrender to a ragged raffle of Negroes," warned Alfred Waddell, a former congressman and Confederate colonel, "even if we have to choke the Cape Fear River with [black] carcasses." It was not an idle threat.

On the morning of November 10, 1898, some 2,000 white men and teens rampaged through the streets of Wilmington. They first destroyed the offices of the *Daily Record*, the black-owned newspaper, then moved into black neighborhoods, shooting African Americans and destroying homes and businesses. Almost 100 blacks were killed.

The mob then stormed the city hall, declared that Colonel Waddell was the new mayor, and forced the African American business leaders and elected officials to board northbound trains. The new, self-appointed city government issued a "Declaration of White Independence" that stripped blacks of their jobs and voting rights. Desperate black residents appealed for help to the governor as well as President William McKinley, but received none.

The Wilmington insurrection marked the first time that a lawfully elected municipal government had been overthrown in the United States. Two years later, in the 1900 statewide elections, white supremacist Democrats vowed to cement their control of the political process. The night before the election, Colonel Waddell urged supporters to use any means necessary to suppress black voting: "You are Anglo-Saxons. You are armed and prepared and you will do your duty. . . . Go to the polls tomorrow, and if you find the negro out voting, tell him to leave the polls, and if he refuses, kill him, shoot him down in his tracks. We shall win tomorrow if we have to do it with guns." The Democratic party won by a landslide.

THE BLACK RESPONSE

By the end of the nineteenth century, white supremacy had triumphed across the South. Some African Americans chose to leave in search of equality and opportunity. Those who stayed and resisted white supremacy—even in self-defense—were ruthlessly suppressed. When a white woman, Mrs. Pines, struck her black maid, Sarah Barnett, with a stick, Barnett retaliated, hitting the woman. Infuriated that a black woman would hit his wife, Pines's husband Richard grabbed his pistol and shot Barnett through the shoulder. She survived, only to be convicted of assault and jailed. Another black house servant,

Wilmington insurrection A mob of white supremacists pose with their rifles before the demolished printing press of the *Daily Record*, an African American newspaper.

Ann Beston, stabbed and killed her abusive mistress in Rome, Georgia. A mob then lynched her.

In the face of such overwhelming discrimination and abuse, most African Americans had no choice but to accommodate themselves to the realities of white supremacy and segregation. "Had to walk a quiet life," explained James Plunkett, a Virginian. "The least little thing you would do, they [whites] would kill ya." Survival in the Jim Crow South required blacks to wear a mask of deference and discretion. They readily behaved in a "servile way" when shopping at white-owned stores. News of lynchings, burnings, and beatings sent chilling reminders of the dangers they constantly faced.

Black novelist Richard Wright remembered how in his native Mississippi the "sustained expectation of violence" at the hands of whites induced a "paralysis of will and impulse" in him and others. It unconsciously affected his speech, movements, and manners around whites. "The penalty of death awaited me if I made a false move."

Yet accommodation did not mean surrender, as African Americans constructed their own lively culture. A young white visitor to Mississippi in 1910 noticed that nearly every black person he met had "two distinct social selves, the one he reveals to his own people, the other he assumes among the whites."

African churches continued to provide an anchor and hub for black communities. In fact, they were often the only public buildings blacks could use for large group gatherings, such as club meetings, political rallies, and social events. For men especially, churches offered leadership roles and political status. Being elected or appointed a deacon was one of the most prestigious roles a black man could achieve. As was the case in many white churches, men preached and governed church affairs; the women often did everything else. Religious life provided great comfort to people worn down by the daily hardships and abuses associated with segregation. As the Reverend Benjamin Mays explained, he and his black neighbors in South Carolina "believed that the trials and tribulations of the world would be all over when one got to heaven. Beaten down at every turn by the white man, as they were, Negroes could perhaps not have survived without this kind of religion."

One irony of Jim Crow segregation is that it opened up new economic opportunities for African Americans. Black entrepreneurs emerged to provide essential services to the black community—insurance, banking, barbering, funerals, hair salons. At the same time, blacks formed their own social and fraternal clubs and organizations, all of which provided fellowship, mutual support, and opportunities for service.

Middle-class African American women formed a network of thousands of social clubs that served as engines of social service across the South and the nation. They cared for the aged, infirm, orphaned, and abandoned. They provided homes for single mothers and nurseries for working mothers, and they sponsored health clinics and classes in home economics. In 1896, the leaders of women's clubs formed the National Association of Colored Women. The organization's first president, Mary Church Terrell, told the members that they had an obligation to serve the "lowly, the illiterate, and even the vicious to whom we are bound by the ties of race and sex, and put forth every effort to uplift and reclaim them." Courageous African American women declared that black men were not providing sufficient leadership. An editorial in the *Woman's Era* called for "timid men and ignorant men" to step aside and let the women show the way.

IDA B. WELLS One of the most outspoken African American activists of the time was Ida B. Wells. Born into slavery in 1862 in Mississippi, she attended a school staffed by white missionaries. She moved in 1880 to Memphis, where she taught in segregated schools and gained entrance to the social life of the city's African American middle class.

In 1883, after being denied a seat on a railroad car because she was black, Wells became the first African American to file suit against such discrimination. The circuit court decided in her favor and fined the railroad, but the Tennessee Supreme Court overturned the ruling. Wells thereafter discovered "[my] first and [it] might be said, my only love"—journalism—and, through it, a weapon with which to wage her crusade for justice. She became editor of *Memphis Free Speech*, a newspaper that focused on African American issues.

In 1892, when three of her friends were lynched by a white mob, Wells launched a crusade against lynching. Angry whites responded by destroying her office and threatening to lynch her. She moved to New York, where she continued to criticize Jim Crow laws and demand that blacks have their voting rights restored. She helped found the National Association for

Ida B. Wells While raising four children, Wells sustained her commitment to ending racial and gender discrimination and lynching.

Booker T. Washington Founder of the Tuskegee Institute, a historically black vocational training school. He went on to become the nation's most prominent African American leader.

the Advancement of Colored People (NAACP) in 1909 and worked for women's suffrage. In promoting racial equality, Wells often found herself in direct opposition to Booker T. Washington, the most influential African American leader of the time.

BOOKER T. WASHINGTON

Born a slave in Virginia, in 1856, the son of a black mother and a white father, Booker T. Washington at sixteen had enrolled at Hampton Normal and Agricultural Institute, one of several colleges for ex-slaves created during Reconstruction. There he met the school's founder, Samuel Chapman Armstrong, who preached moderation and urged the students: "Be thrifty and industrious," "Command the respect of your neighbors by a good record and a good character," "Make the best of your difficulties," and "Live down prejudice." Washington listened and learned well.

Nine years later, Armstrong received a request from a group in northern Alabama starting a black college called Tuskegee Institute. The new college needed a president, and Armstrong urged them to hire Washington. Although only twenty-five years old, Washington was, according to Armstrong, "a very capable mulatto, clear headed, modest, sensible, polite, and a thorough teacher and superior man."

Young Washington quickly went to work. He became a skilled fundraiser, gathering substantial gifts from wealthy whites, most of them northerners. The complicated racial dynamics of the late nineteenth century required him to walk a tightrope between being candid and being an effective college president. He learned that he needed to be like a fox rather than a lion if he hoped to maintain the support of the white community. As the years passed, Tuskegee Institute became celebrated for its dedication to discipline and vocational training, and Booker T. Washington became a source of inspiration and hope to millions.

Washington's recurring message to black students focused on the importance of gaining "practical knowledge." In part to please his white donors, he argued that

African Americans should not focus on fighting racial segregation. They should instead work hard and remain silent; their priority should be self-improvement rather than social change. Washington told young African Americans to begin "at the bottom" as well-educated, hardworking farmers, not as social activists.

In a famous speech at the Cotton States and International Exposition in Atlanta in 1895, Washington urged the African American community to "Cast down your bucket where you are—cast it down in making friends . . . of the people of all races by whom we are surrounded. Cast it down in agriculture, mechanics, in commerce, in domestic service, and in the professions." Fighting for "social equality" and directly challenging white rule would be a huge mistake ("the extremest folly"). Any effort at "agitation" in the white-dominant South would, he warned, backfire. African Americans first needed to become self-sufficient economically. Civil rights would have to wait.

W. E. B. DU BOIS Other African American leaders disagreed with Booker T. Washington's "accommodationist" strategy. W. E. B. Du Bois emerged at the turn of the century as Washington's foremost rival. A native of Massachusetts, Du Bois first experienced racial prejudice as a student at Fisk University in Nashville, Tennessee.

Later he became the first African American to earn a doctoral degree from Harvard (in history and sociology). In addition to promoting civil rights, he left a distinguished record as a scholar, authoring more than twenty books.

Du Bois had a flamboyant personality and a combative spirit. Not long after he began teaching at Atlanta University in 1897, he launched a public assault on Washington's strategy for improving the quality of life for African Americans.

Du Bois called Washington's celebrated 1895 speech "the **Atlanta Compromise**" and said that he would not "surrender the leadership of this race to cowards." Washington, Du Bois argued, "accepted the alleged inferiority of the Negro" so blacks could "concentrate all their energies on industrial education,

W. E. B. Du Bois A fierce advocate for black education and civil rights.

the accumulation of wealth, and the conciliation of the South." Du Bois stressed that African American leaders should adopt a strategy of "ceaseless agitation" directed at ensuring the right to vote and winning civil equality. The education of blacks, Du Bois maintained, should not be merely vocational but comparable to that enjoyed by the white elite. Black education should help develop bold leaders willing to challenge Jim Crow segregation and discrimination.

The dispute between Washington and Du Bois came to define the tensions that would divide the twentieth-century civil rights movement: militancy versus conciliation, separatism versus assimilation, social justice versus economic opportunities. What Du Bois and others did not know was that Washington secretly worked to finance lawsuits challenging segregation and disfranchisement, to stop the brutal culture of race lynching, and to increase funding for public schools. He acted privately because he feared that public activism would trigger violence against Tuskegee and himself.

THE SETTLING OF THE NEW WEST

Like the South, the West has always been a region wrapped in myths and stereotypes. The vast land west of the Mississippi River contains remarkable geographic extremes: majestic mountains, roaring rivers, deep-sculpted canyons, searing deserts, grassy plains, and dense forests. For most western Americans, the Civil War and Reconstruction were remote events that hardly touched the lives of the Indians, Mexicans, Asians, farmers, ranchers, trappers, miners, and Mormons scattered through the plains, valleys, and mountains. In the West, the relentless march of white conquest, settlement, and exploitation continued, propelled by a special sense of "manifest destiny," a lust for land, a hope for quick fortunes, and a restless desire to improve one's lot in life.

Between 1870 and 1900, Americans settled more land in the West than they had in the centuries before 1870. By 1900, a third of the nation lived west of the Mississippi River. The post–Civil War West came to symbolize economic opportunity and personal freedom. On another level, however, the economic exploitation of the West was a story of irresponsible behavior and reckless abuse of nature that scarred the land, decimated its wildlife, and nearly exterminated much of Native American culture.

THE WESTERN LANDSCAPE After midcentury, farmers and their families began spreading west to the Great Plains—western Kansas, Nebraska, Oklahoma, northern Texas, the Dakotas, eastern Colorado, Wyoming, and Montana. From California, miners moved eastward through the mountains to Utah and Nevada, drawn by one new strike after another. From Texas, nomadic cowboys annually migrated with herds of cattle northward onto the plains and even across the Rocky Mountains, into the Great Basin of Utah and Nevada.

The settlers in the West encountered challenges markedly different from those they had left behind. The Great Plains had little rainfall and few rivers. The scarcity of water and timber rendered useless the familiar trappings of the pioneer—the ax, the log cabin, the rail fence—as well as traditional methods of tilling the soil.

For a long time, the region had been called the Great American Desert, unfit for human habitation and therefore, in the minds of most Americans, the perfect refuge for Indians who refused to embrace the white way of life. But that view changed in the last half of the nineteenth century. The discovery of gold, silver, copper, iron, and coal; the completion of the transcontinental railroads; the collapse of Indian resistance; and the rise of the buffalo hide and range-cattle industries convinced many Americans, as well as the federal government, that economic development of the West held the key to national prosperity. Capitalists made huge profits investing in western mines, cattle, railroads, and commercial farms. With the use of what water was available, new techniques of dry farming and irrigation could make the vast western lands fruitful after all.

THE MIGRATORY STREAM During the second half of the nineteenth century, an unrelenting stream of migrants flowed into what had been the largely Indian and Hispanic West. As millions of Anglo-Americans, Native Americans, African Americans, Mexicans, South Americans, and European and Chinese immigrants intermingled, they transformed western life and culture. Most of the settlers were white, native-born farm folk. Three quarters of the post–Civil War western migrants were men, but they often traveled with wives and children.

The largest number of foreign immigrants to the West came from northern Europe and Canada. In the northern plains, Germans, Scandinavians, and Irish were especially numerous. In Nebraska in 1870, a quarter of the 123,000 residents were foreign-born. In North Dakota in 1890, immigrants composed 45 percent of the residents.

Compared with European immigrants, those from China and Mexico were much less numerous but nonetheless significant. More than 200,000 Chinese arrived in California between 1876 and 1890, joining some 70,000 others who had come earlier to build railroads and work in mining communities. The Chinese were frequently discriminated against and denied citizenship rights, and they became scapegoats whenever there was an economic downturn. In 1882, Congress passed the Chinese Exclusion Act, effectively banning further immigration from China.

THE AFRICAN AMERICAN MIGRATION In the aftermath of the collapse of Radical Republican rule in the South, some blacks decided to

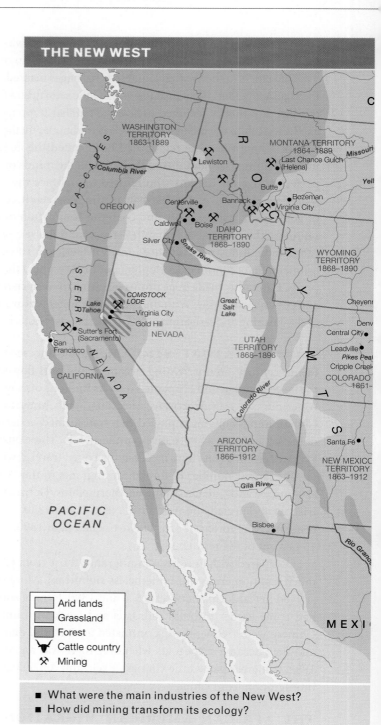

THE NEW WEST

What were the main industries of the New West?
How did mining transform its ecology?

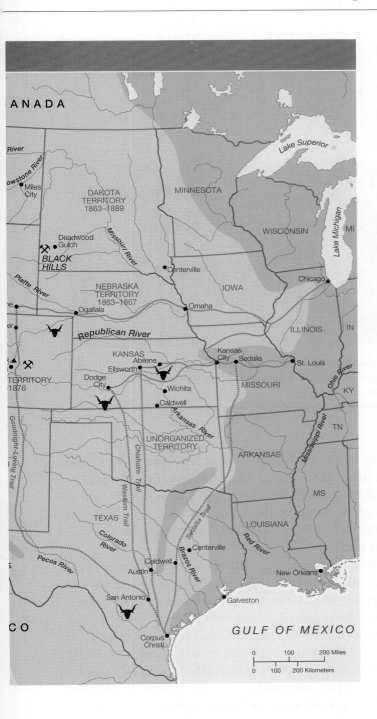

Nicodemus, Kansas By the 1880s, this African American colony had become a thriving town of Exodusters. Here, its residents are photographed in front of the First Baptist Church and general store.

found their own towns in Kansas, Oklahoma, and Mississippi. Others had larger communities in mind. Thousands of African Americans began migrating westward; some 6,000 southern blacks arrived in Kansas in 1879, and as many as 20,000 followed the next year. These migrants came to be known as **Exodusters** because they were making their exodus from the South in search of a haven from racism and poverty.

The foremost promoter of black migration to the West was Benjamin "Pap" Singleton. Born a slave in Tennessee in 1809, he escaped and made his way to Michigan. After the Civil War, he returned to Tennessee and decided that African Americans could never gain equal treatment if they stayed in the former Confederacy. When he learned that land in Kansas could be had for $1.25 an acre, he led a party of 200 colonists to the state in 1878, bought 7,500 acres that had been an Indian reservation, and established the Dunlop community.

Over the next several years, thousands of African Americans followed Singleton to Kansas, leading many southern leaders to worry about the loss of black laborers. In 1879, white southerners closed access to the Mississippi River and threatened to sink all boats carrying blacks to the West. An army officer reported to President Rutherford B. Hayes that "every river landing is blockaded by white enemies of the colored exodus; some of whom are mounted and armed, as if we are at war."

By the early 1880s, however, the exodus of black southerners to the West had petered out. Many African American settlers were unprepared for the harsh living conditions on the plains. Their Kansas homesteads were often not large enough to be self-sustaining, and most of the black farmers were forced to supplement their income by hiring themselves out to white ranchers. Drought, grasshoppers, prairie fires, and dust storms led to frequent crop failures and bankruptcy.

The sudden influx of so many southern blacks also taxed resources and patience. There were not enough houses, stores, or construction materials; few government services; and rarely enough water. Disappointed and frustrated, many African American pioneers in Kansas soon abandoned their land and moved to the few cities in the state. The frontier was not the "promised land" that they had been led to expect, but it was better than what they had experienced in the South. As an Exoduster minister stressed, "We had rather suffer and be free."

By 1890, some 520,000 African Americans lived west of the Mississippi River. As many as 25 percent of the cowboys who participated in the Texas cattle drives were African Americans, and many federal horse soldiers in the West were black.

WESTERN MINING After the Civil War, the dream of striking it rich by finding gold or silver continued to be the most powerful lure to the West. The nature of mining, however, had changed drastically. Like much of western agriculture, mining had become a mass-production industry as individual prospectors gave way to large mining companies.

The first wave of miners who rushed to California in 1849 had sifted gold dust and nuggets out of riverbeds by means of "placer" mining, or "panning." But once the placer deposits were exhausted, efficient mining required large-scale operations, massive machinery, and substantial capital investment. Companies shifted from surface digging to hydraulic mining, dredging, or deep-shaft "hard-rock" mining.

Industrial miners used huge hydraulic cannons to strip canyon walls of rock and topsoil in a search for veins of gold or silver. The tons of dirt and debris unearthed by the water cannons covered rich farmland downstream and created sandbars that clogged rivers and killed fish. All told, some 12 billion tons of earth were blasted out of the Sierra Nevada and washed into local rivers.

Irate California farmers in the fertile Central Valley bitterly protested the damage done downstream by the industrial mining operations. In 1878, they formed the Anti-Debris Association to challenge the powerful mining companies. Efforts to pass state legislation restricting hydraulic mining repeatedly

Deadwood, Dakota Territory A gold-rush town in 1876, before the Dakotas became states.

failed because mining companies controlled the votes. The Anti-Debris Association then turned to the courts. On January 7, 1884, the farmers won their case when federal judge Lorenzo Sawyer, a former miner, outlawed the dumping of mining debris where it could reach farmland or navigable rivers. Thus *Woodruff v. North Bloom-field Gravel Mining Company* became the first major environmental legal victory in the nation. As a result of the ruling, hydraulic mining dried up, leaving a legacy of abandoned equipment, ugly ravines, ditches, gullies, and mountains of discarded rock and gravel.

MINING BOOMTOWNS Tombstone, Arizona, only thirty miles from the Mexican border, was a major silver mining site in the 1870s. By only its fourth year of existence, it was the fastest-growing **boomtown** in the Southwest. It boasted a bowling alley, four churches, a school, two banks, three newspapers, and an ice cream parlor alongside 110 saloons, fourteen gambling halls, and numerous dance halls and brothels.

Some of the other largest and most famous mining boomtowns included Virginia City in Nevada, Cripple Creek and Leadville in Colorado, and Deadwood in the Dakota Territory. They were male-dominated communities with a substantial population of immigrants: Chinese, Chileans, Peruvians, Mexicans, French, Germans, Scots, Welsh, Irish, and English.

Ethnic prejudice was as common as violence in mining towns. The Chinese, for example, were usually prohibited from laboring in the mines but were allowed to operate laundries and work in boardinghouses. Mexicans were often treated the worst. "Mexicans have no business in this country," a Californian insisted. "The men were made to be shot at, and the women were made for our purposes."

Most of the boomtowns lasted only a few years. Once the mines played out, the people moved on, leaving ghost towns behind. In 1870, Virginia City, then called the richest city in America, had a population of 20,000. Today, it has fewer than 1,000 residents.

New discoveries of gold and silver kept occurring throughout the late nineteenth century. The **Comstock Lode** was found near Gold Hill, Nevada, on the eastern slope of the Sierra Nevadas near the California border. Henry Comstock, a Canadian-born fur trapper, gave the new discovery (actually made by other prospectors in 1859) his name. The Comstock Lode, a seam of gold and silver more than fifty feet wide and thousands of feet deep, was the most profitable mine in history to that point.

The rapid growth of mining spurred the creation of territorial governments and cries for statehood. But after Colorado's admission in 1876, there was a long pause in admitting new states because of party divisions in Congress; Democrats refused to create states out of territories that were dominated by Republicans. After the sweeping Republican victory in the 1888 legislative races, however, Congress admitted North and South Dakota, Montana, and Washington as states in 1889, and Idaho and Wyoming in 1890. Utah entered the Union in 1896 (after the Mormons agreed to abandon the practice of polygamy), Oklahoma in 1907; and in 1912 Arizona and New Mexico became the forty-seventh and forty-eighth contiguous states. (The final two states, Alaska and Hawaii, were added fifty years later.)

LIFE IN THE NEW WEST

In the 1880s, James H. Kyner, a railroad builder in Oregon, witnessed "an almost unbroken stream of emigrants from horizon to horizon." These "hardy, optimistic folk" traveled west in wagons, on horses, and on foot, "going west to seek their fortunes and to settle an empire." Most of them thought little about forcing out the Native Americans, Chinese workers, and Hispanic cowboys who were there first. Americans claimed a special "destiny" to settle, develop, and dominate the entire continent.

To encourage new settlers in the West, the federal government generously helped finance the construction of four transcontinental railroads, dispatched federal troops to conquer and relocate Indians to designated reservations, and sold government-owned land at low prices—or gave it to railroad companies as a means of rapidly populating areas served by trains. The transcontinental railroads received some 200 million acres of government land. Over time, the railroads sold much of the land to create towns and ranches along the rail lines. The New West of ranchers and farmers was in fact largely the product of the railroads; the arrival of trains was the lifeblood of the western economy.

The surge of western migration had many of the romantic qualities so often depicted in novels, films, and television shows. Those who braved harsh conditions and uncertain circumstances were indeed courageous and tenacious. Cowboys and Indians; outlaws and vigilantes; farmers, ranchers, and herders populated the plains, while miners and trappers led more nomadic lives in the hills and backwoods.

These familiar images of western life tell only part of the story, however. Drudgery and tragedy were as commonplace as adventure and success. In contrast to the Hollywood versions of the West, the people who settled the trans-Mississippi frontier were a diverse lot: they included women as well as men, African Americans, Hispanics, Asians, and European immigrants. The feverish quest for quick profits also helped fuel a boom/bust economic cycle that injected chronic instability into the society and politics of the region.

While the West was being taken from the Indians, cattle were herded into the grasslands where the buffalo had roamed. For many years, wild cattle first brought to America by the Spanish had competed with buffalo in the borderlands of Texas and Arizona. Breeding them with Anglo-American domesticated cattle produced the hybrid Texas longhorns: tough, lean and rangy, they were noted more for speed and endurance than for yielding lots of choice steak. By the time the Confederacy surrendered, millions of longhorns in Texas were wandering freely across the state. They had marginal value, moreover, because the largest urban markets for beef were so far away—until the railroads arrived.

THE CATTLE BOOM   At the end of the Civil War, the Kansas Pacific Railroad crews were beginning to lay rails in the buffalo country of the southern plains, between St. Louis and Kansas City. As buffalo hunters roamed the prairies, a few entrepreneurs began to imagine how the extension of the railroad might "establish a market whereat the Southern [cattle] drover and Northern buyer would meet upon an equal footing."

That junction was Abilene, Kansas, a "very small, dead place, consisting of about one dozen log huts." Once the rail lines reached Kansas from Missouri, Joseph G. McCoy, an Illinois livestock dealer, recognized the possibilities of driving vast herds of cattle raised in Texas northward to Kansas, where they would be loaded onto freight cars and sent to the rest of the nation. In 1867, in tiny Abilene in eastern Kansas, McCoy bought 250 acres and built a stockyard, barn, an office building, livestock scales, a hotel, and a bank. He then sent an agent to Texas to convince the owners of herds bound north on the Chisholm Trail to go through Abilene. Once the bellowing mass of Texas longhorns reached Abilene in August, 1867, cattle by the thousands were loaded onto rail cars and shipped to Chicago stockyards where they were slaughtered and then sent (as sides of beef) to the cities around the nation.

Herding cattle Cowboys on horseback herd cattle into a corral beside the Cimarron River in 1905.

Abilene flourished as the first successful cow town. By 1871, there were 700,000 steers passing through it every year. The ability to ship huge numbers of cattle by rail transformed ranching into a huge national industry and turned Kansas into a major economic crossroads. Other cattle towns sprouted along the rail line: Ellsworth, Wichita, Caldwell, Dodge City. None of them lasted more than a few years. Once people bought farms nearby, they lobbied successfully to stop the stampeding Texas herds from coming through their area. The cattlemen simply developed new routes north, to new cow towns and rail hubs in Colorado, Wyoming, and Montana. Soon, those states had their own cattle ranches. By 1883, there were half a million cattle in eastern Montana alone, as the disappearing buffalo herds gave way to steers and sheep.

Like miners, cattle ranchers were forced to meet together and develop their own code of laws and ways of enforcing them. As cattle often wandered onto other ranchers' land, cowboys would "ride the line" to keep the animals off the adjoining ranches. In the spring they would "round up" the herds, which invariably got mixed up, and sort out ownership by identifying the distinctive ranch symbols "branded," or burned, into the cattle.

All that changed in 1873, when Joseph Glidden, an Illinois farmer, developed the first effective and inexpensive form of barbed-wire fencing. Soon the **open range**—owned by all, where a small rancher could graze his cattle anywhere—was no more. Barbed-wire fences triggered "range wars," where small ranchers, called fence cutters, fought to retain the open range.

Fencing converted prairie into pastures put a lot of ranchers out of business, and many of them became cowboys working for wages. Cattle raising, like mining, evolved from a romantic adventure into a business dominated by "cattle barons" and large corporations. As one cowboy lamented, "times have changed."

CHICAGO The rise of the cattle industry helped make Chicago the fastest growing city in the nation in the decades after the Civil War. No city had more influence on the development of post–Civil War America than Chicago. Located on Lake Michigan and served by several rivers and nine railroads in 1865, it was the gateway to the western economy, a crossroads where city and frontier intersected for mutual benefit. Its lumber yards, grain elevators, stockyards, and slaughterhouses became magnets for immigrants seeking jobs.

Chicago, so large, so powerful, so rapidly growing, was the catalyst for much of the West's development; the bridge between city and country, urban and rural. "The Great Grey City, brooking no rival," wrote Frank Norris in his novel *The Pit* (1903), "imposed its dominion upon a reach of country larger than many a kingdom of the Old World. For thousands of miles beyond its confines its influence was felt. . . . Here, mid-most in the land, beat the Heart of the Nation, whence inevitably must come its immeasurable power, its infinite, infinite, inexhaustible vitality."

The meatpacking industry in places like Cincinnati and Chicago had started not with cattle but with hogs, in part because pork could be preserved longer with salt and smoking than beef. Since colonial days, pork packing had been one of the earliest and most important frontier industries. Hogs reproduce much faster than cattle, and they thrive on corn. As a nineteenth-century economist explained, "what is a hog, but fifteen or twenty bushels of corn on four legs?"

In 1850, Chicago slaughterhouses butchered and packed 20,000 hogs. By contrast, Cincinnati (called "Porkopolis") processed 334,000 each year. That changed after the Civil War as the federal government ordered vast quantities of pork for its armies. By 1862, Chicago had displaced Cincinnati as the world's largest pork-packing center. By the 1870s, thanks to the railroad connections, the city was processing over 2 million hogs per year. The use of ice cut from frozen Lake Michigan and placed in freight trains enabled Chicago pork to be shipped all the way to the East Coast.

But there was no ice in the summer months. This challenge led Gustavus F. Swift, a New Englander who arrived in Chicago in 1875, to begin experimenting with ways to "refrigerate" railcars year round. Within a few years, Swift, and his main competitor Philip Armour, had engineered refrigerated freight cars that enabled them to ship processed meat rather than live hogs and cattle long distances.

It was this key innovation that enabled Chicago to add beef packing to its already huge hog-processing operations. "The refrigerator car," announced Swift and Company, "is one of the vehicles on which the packing industry has ridden to greatness." By the end of the nineteenth century, the economies of scale enjoyed by the four dominant Chicago meatpacking corporations drove most local butchers across the nation out of business. A New York City butcher in 1888 confessed that, up and down the East Coast, "the slaughtering of cattle by butchers is a thing of the past."

Gustavus Swift and Philip Armour became two of the richest men in the world. They soon branched out beyond pork and beef processing by becoming traders in grain—wheat and corn. They also built packing plants across the West, in cattle towns such as Kansas City and Omaha, which soon were processing almost half as much meat as Chicago.

FARMING ON THE PLAINS Farming on the Great Plains was made harder by the region's unforgiving environment, bitterly cold winters, and scorching summers. A New York newspaper publisher traveling to California described the Great Plains as "a treeless desert" that baked during daylight and was "chill and piercing" cold at night. Still, people made the dangerous trek, lured by inexpensive federal land and misleading advertisements celebrating life on the plains. Between 1870 and 1900, homesteaders, ranchers, miners, railroad operators, and commercial farmers took control of 430 million acres of land west of the Mississippi River.

HOMESTEADERS The first homesteaders in the Great Plains were mostly landless folk eager to try their hand at farming. Many of them had never used a hoe or planted a seed. "I was raised in Chicago without so much as a back yard to play in," said a Montana homesteader, "and I worked 48 hours a week for $1.25. When I heard you could get 320 acres just by living on it, I felt that I had been offered a kingdom."

Yet the farmers faced a grim struggle. Although land was essentially free as a result of the Homestead Act (1862), horses, livestock, wagons, wells, lumber, fencing, seed, machinery, and fertilizer were not. Freight rates and interest rates were criminally high. Declining crop prices produced chronic indebtedness, leading strapped farmers to embrace virtually any plan to increase the money supply and thus pay off their debts with inflated currency. The virgin land itself, although fertile, resisted planting; the heavy sod woven with tough

Innovative farming Powered by over a dozen horses and driven by two men, this early nineteenth-century "combine" machine could cut, thresh, bag, and weigh wheat all at the same time.

grass roots broke many a plow. Since wood and coal were rare on the prairie, pioneer families initially had to use buffalo chips (dried dung from buffaloes and cattle) for fuel.

Farm families also fought a constant battle with the elements: tornadoes, hailstorms, droughts, prairie fires, blizzards, and pests. Swarms of locusts often clouded the horizon; a Wichita newspaper reported in 1878 that they devoured "everything green . . . destroying every plant that is good for food or pleasant to the eyes." In the late 1880s, a prolonged drought forced many homesteaders to give up. In the end, two-thirds of the people who gained land under the Homestead Act failed to become self-sustaining farmers.

COMMERCIAL FARMING Eventually, as the railroads brought piles of lumber from the East, farmers could upgrade their houses built of sod ("Kansas brick") into more comfortable wood-framed dwellings. New machinery and equipment, for those who could afford them, improved productivity. In 1868, James Oliver, a Scottish immigrant living in Indiana, made a sturdy chilled-iron "sodbuster" plow that greatly eased the task of preparing land for planting. At the same time, new threshing machines, hay mowers, planters, manure spreaders, and other equipment lightened the burden of farm labor but often deepened the debts that farmers owed.

In Minnesota, the Dakotas, and central California, wealthy capitalists created gigantic "bonanza farms" that became the marvels of the age. On one bonanza farm in North Dakota, a single field of wheat encompassed 13,000 acres. Wheat became for farmers in the High Plains what cotton had been for southern planters: a perennial cash crop. American-grown wheat was exported around the world. Another bonanza farm in South Dakota employed more than 1,000 migrant workers to tend 34,000 acres. Such agribusinesses were the wave of the future. Thomas Jefferson's dream of an America primarily made up of small farmers continued to give way to industrial agriculture and bonanza farms.

While the overall value of farmland and farm products increased in the late nineteenth century, small farmers did not keep up. Their numbers grew in size but decreased in proportion to the population at large. Wheat in the Western states, like cotton in the antebellum South, was the great export crop that spurred economic growth. For a variety of reasons, however, including an inability to afford new machinery, few small farmers prospered. By the 1890s they were in open revolt against the "system" of corrupt processors (middlemen) and "greedy" bankers who they believed conspired against them.

WOMEN IN THE WEST The West remained a largely male society throughout the nineteenth century. Women in mining towns, most of whom worked as house cleaners, were as valued as gold. Many mining towns had a male-to-female ratio as high as nine to one. When four "respectable" women arrived in Nevada City, one of them reported that the men stood and gazed "at us with mouth and eyes wide open, every time we go out" in the streets.

In both mining and farming communities, women were prized as spouses, in part because farming required help. In 1900, an estimated 98 percent of the women in Nebraska were married. But the women pioneers continued to face many of the same legal barriers and social prejudices prevalent in the East. A wife could not sell property without her husband's approval, for example. Texas women could not sue except for divorce, nor could they serve on juries, act as lawyers, or witness a will.

The constant fight for survival west of the Mississippi, however, made men and women more-equal partners than in the East. Many women who lost their mates to the deadly toil of "sod busting" assumed complete responsibility for their farms. In general, women on the prairie became more independent than

Women of the frontier A woman and her family in front of their sod house. The difficult life on the prairie led to more egalitarian marriages than were found in other regions of the country because women had to play so many roles.

women leading domestic lives back East. A Kansas woman explained "that the environment was such as to bring out and develop the dominant qualities of individual character. Kansas women of that day learned at an early age to depend on themselves—to do whatever work there was to be done, and to face danger when it must be faced, as calmly as they were able."

It was not coincidental, then, that the new western territories and states were among the first to allow women to vote and hold office—in the hopes that by allowing women to vote they would attract more women settlers. In 1890, Wyoming was admitted to the Union as the first state that allowed women to vote in all elections. Utah, Colorado, and Idaho followed soon thereafter.

THE FATE OF WESTERN INDIANS

As settlers spread across the continent, some 250,000 Native Americans, many of them originally from east of the Mississippi, were forced into what was supposed to be their last refuge, the Great Plains and mountain regions of the Far West. The 1851 Fort Laramie Treaty, in which the chiefs of the Plains Indians agreed to accept definite tribal borders and allow white emigrants to travel across their lands, worked for a while. Fighting resumed, however, as Indians continued their ancient practice of following the buffalo herds and as white (and black) emigrants began to settle on Indian lands rather than pass through them.

INDIAN RELATIONS IN THE WEST From the early 1860s until the late 1870s, the trans-Mississippi West, often called "Indian Country," raged with the so-called **Indian wars**. Although the U.S. government had signed numerous treaties with Indian nations giving them ownership of reservation lands for "as long as waters run and the grass shall grow," those commitments were repeatedly violated by buffalo hunters, miners, ranchers, farmers, railroad surveyors—and horse soldiers.

In the 1860s, the federal government ousted numerous tribes from lands they had been promised "forever." A Sioux chieftain named Spotted Tail expressed the grieving anger felt by many Indians when he asked "Why does not the Great Father [U.S. president] put his red children on wheels so that he can move them as he will?"

In the two decades before the Civil War, the U.S. Army's central mission in the West was to protect pioneers traveling on the major Overland Trails. During and after the war, the mission changed to ensuring that Native Americans stayed on the reservations they had been assigned and that Americans did not trespass on Indian lands.

Americans, however, repeatedly violated treaties with Native American peoples. The result was simmering frustration punctuated by outbreaks of tragic violence. In the summer of 1862, an uprising of Sioux warriors killed 644 white traders, settlers, government officials, and soldiers in the Minnesota Valley. It was the first of many clashes between the growing number of American settlers and miners and the Indians living on reservations in the Great Plains.

THE SAND CREEK MASSACRE Two years later, a horrible incident occurred in Colorado as a result of the influx of white miners into the territory. After Indians murdered a white family near Denver, John Evans, the territorial governor, called on whites to "kill and destroy" the "hostile Indians on the plains." At the same time, Evans persuaded "friendly Indians" (mostly Cheyenne and Arapaho) to gather at "places of safety" such as Fort Lyon, in southeastern Colorado near the Kansas border, where they were promised protection.

Despite that promise, at dawn on November 29, 1864, Colonel John M. Chivington's 700 untrained militiamen attacked a camp of Cheyennes and Arapahoes along Sand Creek, about forty miles from Fort Lyon. Black Kettle, the chief, frantically waved first an American flag and then a white flag, but the attacking soldiers paid no heed. Over seven hours, the Colorado militiamen slaughtered, scalped, and mutilated 165 peaceful Indians—men, women, children, and the elderly. Chivington, a former abolitionist and Methodist minister (the "Fighting Parson") who had preached against the brutalities of slavery, had told his men to "kill and scalp all [Indians], big and little, you come across."

In his report on the lopsided bloodbath to army officials, Chivington lied, claiming a great victory against 1,000 entrenched Cheyenne warriors. The bloodthirsty colonel was greeted as a hero back in Denver. "Colorado soldiers have again covered themselves in glory," the *Rocky Mountain News* in Denver initially proclaimed.

Then the truth about Sand Creek began to come out. Captain Silas Soule, an abolitionist from Kansas who had joined the Union army at the start of the Civil War, witnessed the massacre but, along with his company of soldiers, had disobeyed orders to join the attack. "I refused to fire and swore [to my men] that none but a coward" would shoot unarmed women and children.

Three weeks after the massacre, Soule wrote a letter to a superior officer revealing in graphic detail what had actually happened at Sand Creek: "Hundreds of women and children were coming toward us, and getting on their knees for mercy," he noted, only to be murdered and "have their brains beat out by men professing to be civilized." Far from being a hero, Soule added, Chivington encouraged the one-sided slaughter through his *lack* of leadership: "There was no organization among our troops, they were a perfect mob—every man on his own hook." Soule's company "was the only one that did not fire a shot." He predicted that "we will have a hell of a time with Indians this winter" because of what had happened at Sand Creek.

Congress and the army launched lengthy investigations into the tragedy at Sand Creek, and Captain Soule was among those called to testify in January 1865. The eventual congressional report concluded that Chivington had "deliberately planned and executed a foul and dastardly massacre," murdering "in cold blood" Indians who "had every reason to believe they were under [U.S.] protection." An army general described the Sand Creek Massacre as the "foulest and most unjustifiable crime in the annals of America."

Chivington resigned from the militia in disgrace in order to escape a military trial. He soon became the Denver sheriff. On April 23, 1865, Soule, the whistle-blower, was shot and killed in Denver. One of his murderers—never prosecuted—was identified as one of Chivington's soldiers.

Instead of pacifying the Indians, the **Sand Creek Massacre** ignited warfare that raged across the central plains for the next three years. Arapaho, Cheyenne, and Sioux war parties attacked scores of ranches and stagecoach stations, killing hundreds of white men and kidnapping many white women and children. More massacres were to come, on both sides. The federal government responded by authorizing the recruitment of soldiers from among Confederate military prisoners (called "white-washed Rebels") and the creation of African American cavalry regiments.

In 1866, Congress passed legislation establishing two "colored" cavalry units and dispatched them to the western frontier. The Cheyenne nicknamed them "buffalo soldiers" because they "fought like a cornered buffalo; who, like a buffalo, had suffered wound after wound, yet had not died; and who, like a buffalo, had a thick and shaggy mane of hair."

The buffalo soldiers were mostly Civil War veterans from Louisiana and Kentucky. They built and maintained forts, mapped vast areas of the Southwest, strung hundreds of miles of telegraph lines, protected railroad construction crews, subdued hostile Indians, and captured outlaws and rustlers. Eighteen of the buffalo soldiers won Congressional Medals of Honor for their service.

INDIAN RELOCATION With other scattered battles erupting, a congressional committee in 1865 gathered evidence on the grisly Indian wars and massacres. Its 1867 "Report on the Condition of the Indian Tribes" led to the creation of an Indian Peace Commission charged with removing the causes of the Indian wars. Congress decided that this would be best accomplished by persuading nomadic Indians yet again to move to out-of-the-way federal reservations where they would take up farming that would "civilize" them. They were to give up their ancestral lands in return for peace so that the whites could move in. In 1870, Indians outnumbered whites in the Dakota Territory by two to one; by 1880, whites, mostly gold prospectors, would outnumber Indians by more than six to one. The U.S. government had decided it had no choice but to gain control of the region—by purchase if possible, by force if necessary.

In 1867, a conference at Medicine Lodge, Kansas, ended with the Kiowas, Comanches, Arapahoes, and Cheyennes reluctantly agreeing to move to land in western Oklahoma. The following spring, the western Sioux, the Lakotas, signed the Treaty of Fort Laramie (1868), in which they agreed to settle within the huge Black Hills Reservation in southwestern Dakota Territory, in part because they viewed the Black Hills as holy ground.

GRANT'S INDIAN POLICY In his inaugural address in 1869, President Ulysses S. Grant urged Congress to adopt more-progressive policies toward Native Americans: "The proper treatment of *the original inhabitants of* *this land"* should enable the Native Americans to become *citizens* with all the rights enjoyed by every other American."

Grant's noble intentions, however, ran afoul of longstanding prejudices against Native Americans and the unrelenting efforts of miners, farmers, railroaders, and ranchers to trespass on Indian lands and reservations. The president recognized the challenges he faced. Indians, he admitted, "would be harmless and peaceable if they were not put upon by whites." Yet he also stressed that protecting the new transcontinental railroad across the plains was his top priority. In the end, however, Grant told army officers that "it is much better to support a peace commission than a [military] campaign against Indians."

Periodic clashes brought vengeful demands for military action. William T. Sherman, commanding general of the U.S. Army, directed General Philip Sheridan, who was in charge of the military effort in the West, to "kill and punish the hostiles [Indian war parties], capture and destroy the ponies" of the "Cheyennes, Arapahoes, and Kiowas." Sherman then declared that "the more we kill this year, the less we will have to kill next year."

Neither Sherman nor Sheridan agreed with Grant's "peace policy." In their view, the president's naive outlook was shaped by the distance between the Great Plains and Washington, D.C. Fairness and understanding were not the correct weapons against Indian warriors. Sherman ordered Sheridan to force all "nonhostile" Indians onto federal reservations, where they would be provided land for farming, immediate rations of food, and supplies and equipment (a promise that was rarely kept).

Some Native Americans refused to be moved again. In the southern plains of New Mexico, north Texas, Colorado, Kansas, and Oklahoma, the Native Americans, dominated by the Comanches, the greatest horse-borne warriors in America, focused on hunting buffalo. Armed clashes occurred with increasing frequency until the Red River War of 1874–1875, when Sheridan's soldiers won a series of battles in the Texas Panhandle. He boasted that it was "the most successful of any Indian Campaign in this country since its settlement by the whites." The defeated Comanches, Cheyennes, Kiowas, and Arapahoes were forced onto reservations.

CUSTER AND THE SIOUX Meanwhile, trouble was brewing again in the northern plains. White prospectors searching for gold were soon trespassing on Sioux hunting grounds in the Dakotas despite promises that the army would keep them out. Ohio senator John Sherman warned that nothing would stop the mass migration of Americans across the Mississippi River: "If the whole Army of the United States stood in the way, the wave of emigration would pass over it to seek the valley where gold was found."

The massive gold rush in the Black Hills convinced some Indians to make a last stand. As Red Cloud, a Sioux chief, said, "The white men have crowded the Indians back year by year, and now our last hunting ground, the home of my people, is to be taken from us. Our women and children will starve, but for my part I prefer to die fighting rather than by starvation." Another prominent Sioux war chief, Sitting Bull, told Indians living on the Black Hills reservation that "the whites may get me at last, but I will have good times till then."

George A. Custer The reckless and glory-seeking lieutenant colonel of the U.S. Army.

In 1875, Lieutenant Colonel George Armstrong Custer, a veteran Indian fighter driven by reckless ambition and courage, led 1,000 soldiers in the Seventh Cavalry regiment into the Black Hills, where he announced the discovery of gold on French Creek near present-day Custer, South Dakota. The news set off a massive gold rush, and within two years, the mining town of Deadwood overflowed with 10,000 miners. The undermanned army units in the area could not keep the miners from violating the rights guaranteed the Sioux by federal treaties. President Grant and federal authorities tried to convince the Sioux to sell the Black Hills to the government. Sitting Bull told the American negotiator to tell "the Great Father [Grant] that I do not want to sell any land to the government."

With that news, Custer was sent back to the Black Hills, this time to find roving bands of Sioux and Cheyenne warriors and force them back onto reservations. If they resisted, he was to kill them.

The colorful Custer, strikingly handsome with golden curly hair, stood out among his 600 horse soldiers. Having graduated last in his class at West Point, he was first in his class at gambling and socializing. Free-spirited and fun-loving, he studied and behaved just enough to graduate. He later urged cadets not to follow his own example. Custer loved war and the thrill of combat. An army officer said Custer was one of the few soldiers who fought for the fun of it; to him, war was "glorious." Like Crazy Horse, Custer was a natural warrior whose goal was "not to be wealthy, not to be learned, but to be great."

For all of Custer's flamboyant rebelliousness and lust for adventure, he was a bold, talented cavalry officer with remarkable endurance. During the Civil

War, he had been promoted to general at the age of twenty-three (reporters dubbed him the "Boy General") and had played an important role in the Union victory at Gettysburg, leading a gallant cavalry charge. Now he was in charge of an expedition to attack the wandering bands of Sioux hunting parties, even though he recognized that intruding American miners had caused the renewal of warfare. As Custer told newspaper reporters, "We are goading the Indians to madness by invading their hallowed [hunting] grounds."

What became the **Great Sioux War** was the largest military campaign since the end of the Civil War. The war against the northern Indians lasted fifteen months and entailed fifteen battles in present-day Wyoming, Montana, South Dakota, and Nebraska. In June 1876, after several indecisive encounters, Custer found a large encampment of Sioux and their Northern Cheyenne and Arapaho allies on the Little Bighorn River in the southeast corner of the Montana Territory.

On June 25, Custer ordered his exhausted men to attack the Indian camp. "Hurrah boys, we've got them," he shouted, not realizing how vastly outnumbered they were. Within minutes, they were surrounded by as many as 2,500 warriors led by the fierce Crazy Horse ("A good day to fight, a good day to die!").

After a half hour of desperate fighting, Custer's 210 men, their ammunition exhausted, were all dead. Custer was said to laugh as he fired his last bullet, for

Battle of Little Bighorn, 1876 Amos Bad Heart Bull, an Oglala Sioux artist and historian, painted this scene from the Battle of Little Bighorn.

he knew his fate. Among the dead were two of Custer's brothers, a brother-in-law, and a nephew. Afterwards, Cheyenne women pierced Custer's eardrums with sewing needles because he had failed to listen to their warnings to stay out of their ancestral lands. Custer's brave death echoed a line from his favorite Shakespeare play, *Julius Caesar*: "I shall have glory by this losing day."

The Sioux had won their greatest battle, but in doing so they helped ensure that they would lose the war. Upon learning of the Battle of Little Bighorn ("Custer's Last Stand"), President Grant and Congress abandoned the "peace policy" and dispatched more supplies and troops ("Custer's Avengers") to the plains. General Sheridan now planned for "total war" against the Sioux.

Under Sheridan's aggressive leadership, the army quickly regained the offensive and relentlessly pursued the Sioux and Cheyenne across Montana. Warriors were slain, villages destroyed, and food supplies burned. Iron Teeth, a Cheyenne woman, recalled an attack by "white soldiers" in November 1876. "They killed our men, women, and children." She ran away with her three daughters. Her husband and two sons remained to fight. "My husband," she remembered, "was walking, leading his horse, and stopping at times to shoot. Suddenly, I saw him fall. I started to go back to him, but my sons made me go on." The last time she saw her husband he was dead in the snow. "From the hilltops, we Cheyennes saw our lodges and everything in them burning."

Forced back onto reservations, the remaining Native Americans soon found themselves struggling to survive. Many of them died of starvation or disease. By the end of 1876, the chiefs living on the Dakota reservation agreed to sell the Black Hills to the U.S. government. In the spring of 1877, Crazy Horse and his people surrendered. The Great Sioux War was over. By 1880, most of the western Indians were confined on reservations.

THE DEMISE OF THE BUFFALO   Over the long run, the collapse of Indian resistance in the face of white settlement on the Great Plains resulted as much from the decimation of the buffalo herds as from the actions of federal troops. In 1750, there were an estimated 30 million buffalo on the plains; the herds were so vast that one traveler said they changed the color of the landscape, "blackening the whole surface of the country." By 1850, there were fewer than 10 million; by 1900, only a few hundred were left. What happened to them?

The conventional story focuses on intensive harvesting of buffalo by white commercial hunters after the Civil War. The construction of railroads through buffalo country brought hundreds of commercial hunters who shipped huge numbers of hides each year to cities in the East, where consumers developed a voracious demand for buffalo robes, buffalo leather, and trophy heads. The average commercial hunter killed 100 of the shaggy beasts a day. "The buffalo," reported an army officer, "melted away like snow before a summer's sun."

The story is more complicated, however. The buffalo disappeared for a variety of health and environmental reasons, notably a prolonged drought during the late 1880s into the 1890s that severely reduced the grasslands upon which the animals depended. At the same time, the buffalo had to compete for food with other grazing animals; by the 1880s, more than 2 million horses were roaming buffalo lands.

The Plains Indians themselves, empowered by horses and rifles and spurred by the profits reaped from selling hides and meat to white traders, accounted for much of the devastation of the buffalo herds after 1840. If there had been no white hunters, the buffalo would probably have lasted only another thirty years because their numbers had been so greatly reduced by other factors. Whatever the reasons, the disappearance of the buffalo gave the Plains Indians little choice but to settle on the government reservations.

Chief Joseph Leader of the Nez Perce, he was widely recognized as a strong, eloquent voice against the injustices suffered by the Native Americans.

THE LAST RESISTANCE In the Rocky Mountains and west to the Pacific Ocean, the same story of courageous yet hopeless resistance to masses of white intruders was repeated again and again. Indians were the last obstacle to white western expansion, and they suffered as a result.

The Blackfeet and Crows had to leave their homes in Montana. In a war along the California-Oregon boundary, the Modocs held out for six months in 1871–1872 before they were overwhelmed. In 1879 the Utes were forced to give up their vast territories in western Colorado. In Idaho the peaceful Nez Perce bands refused to surrender land along the Salmon River, and prolonged fighting erupted there and in eastern Oregon.

In 1877, Joseph, a Nez Perce chief, led some 650 of his people on a 1,300-mile journey through Montana in hopes of reaching safety in Canada. Just before reaching the border, they were caught by U.S. soldiers. As he surrendered, Joseph delivered an eloquent speech that served as an epitaph to the Indians' efforts to withstand the march of the American empire: "I am tired of fighting. Our chiefs are killed. . . . The old men are all dead. . . . I want to have time to look for my children, and see how many of them I can find. . . . Hear me, my chiefs! I am tired. My heart is sick and sad. From where the sun now stands I will fight no more forever." The Nez Perce requested that they be allowed to return to their ancestral lands in western Idaho, but they were forced to settle in the Indian Territory (Oklahoma), where many died of malaria.

A generation of Indian wars virtually ended in 1886 with the capture of Geronimo, a powerful chief of the Chiricahua Apaches, who had outridden, outwitted, and outfought American forces in the Southwest for fifteen years. Once, the Apaches captured a group of settlers, tied them to their wagon wheels, and roasted them alive. U.S. Army units routinely lynched captured Apaches and treated women and children as combatants. General Nelson A. Miles, the commander of the soldiers who captured Geronimo, called him "one of the brightest, most resolute, determined-looking men that I have ever encountered."

THE GHOST DANCE The last major clash between Indians and American soldiers occurred near the end of the nineteenth century. Late in 1888, Wovoka (or Jack Wilson), a Paiute in western Nevada, fell ill. In a delirium, he imagined being in the spirit world, where he learned of a deliverer coming to rescue the Indians and restore their lands. To hasten their deliverance, he said, the Indians must perform a ceremonial dance that would make them bulletproof against white soldiers. The Ghost Dance craze fed upon old legends of the dead reuniting with the living and bringing prosperity and peace.

The **Ghost Dance movement** spread rapidly. In 1890, the western Sioux adopted it with such passion that it alarmed white authorities. They banned the Ghost Dance on Lakota reservations, but the Indians defied the order and a crisis erupted.

On December 29, 1890, a bloodbath occurred at Wounded Knee, South Dakota, after nervous soldiers fired into a group of Indians who had surrendered. Nearly 200 Indians, men, women, and children, and 25 soldiers died in the Battle of Wounded Knee. The Indian wars had ended with characteristic brutality and misunderstanding. General Philip Sheridan, commander of U.S. troops in these conflicts, was acidly candid in summarizing how whites had treated the Indians: "We took away their country and their means of support, broke up their mode of living, their habits of life, introduced disease and

INDIAN WARS

- What was the Great Sioux War?
- What happened at the Little Bighorn battle, and what were the consequences?
- Why were hundreds of Native Americans killed at Wounded Knee?

decay among them, and it was for this and against this that they made war. Could anyone expect less?"

Many politicians and religious leaders condemned the persistent mistreatment of Indians. In his annual message of 1877, President Rutherford B. Hayes joined the protest: "Many, if not most, of our Indian wars have had their origin in broken promises and acts of injustice on our part." Helen Hunt Jackson, a novelist and poet, focused attention on the Indian cause in *A Century of Dishonor* (1881), a book that powerfully detailed the sad history of America's exploitation of Native Americans over the centuries.

In part as a reaction to Jackson's book, U.S. policies regarding Native Americans gradually improved, but they did little to enhance the Indians' difficult living conditions and actually helped destroy remnants of their culture. The reservation policy inaugurated by the Peace Commission in 1867 did little more than extend a practice that dated from colonial Virginia. Partly humanitarian in motive, it also saved money: housing and feeding Indians on reservations cost less than fighting them.

Well-intentioned but biased white reformers sought to "Americanize" Indians by forcing them to become self-reliant farmers owning their own plots of land rather than allowing them to be members of nomadic bands or tribes holding property in common. Such reform efforts produced the **Dawes Severalty Act** of 1887 (also called the General Allotment Act), the most sweeping policy directed at Native Americans in U.S. history. Sponsored by Senator Henry L. Dawes of Massachusetts, the act divided tribal lands and "allotted" them to individuals, granting 160 acres to each head of a family and lesser amounts to others.

White Bear, a Kiowa chief, expressed a common complaint when he said that his people did "not want to settle down in houses you [the federal government] would build for us. I love to roam over the wild prairie. There I am free and happy." But his preferences were not heeded. Between 1887 and 1934, Indians lost an estimated 86 million of their 130 million acres. As New York-born Henry Teller, a Congressman from Colorado, pointed out, the allotment policy was designed solely to strip the "Indians of their lands and to make them vagabonds on the face of the earth."

THE END OF THE FRONTIER

The end of Native American resistance was one of several developments at the close of the nineteenth century that suggested that the New West was indeed different from the Old West. Other indicators of the region's transformation led some scholars to conclude that American society itself had reached a turning point as the century came to a close.

FREDERICK JACKSON TURNER The 1890 national census reported that the frontier era was over; Americans by then had spread across the entire continent. This news led Frederick Jackson Turner, a young historian at the University of Wisconsin, to announce his "frontier thesis" in 1893, in which he argued that more than slavery or any other single factor, "the existence of an area of free land, its continuous recession, and the advance of American settlement westward, explain American development." The experience of taming and settling the frontier, he added, had shaped the national character in fundamental ways. It was

> to the frontier [that] the American intellect owes its striking characteristics. That coarseness and strength combined with acuteness and acquisitiveness; that practical, inventive turn of mind, quick to find expedients; that masterful grasp of material things, lacking in the artistic but powerful to effect great ends; that restless, nervous energy; that dominant individualism, working for good and for evil, and withal that buoyancy and exuberance which comes with freedom—these are traits of the frontier, or traits called out elsewhere because of the existence of the frontier.

Now, however, Turner stressed, "the frontier has gone and with its going has closed the first period of American history."

Turner's view of the frontier—as the westward-moving source of the nation's democratic politics, open society, unfettered economy, and rugged individualism—gripped the popular imagination. But his frontier thesis left out much of the story of American development. The frontier experience that Turner described was in many respects a self-serving myth involving only Christian white men and devoid of towns and cities, which in fact grew along with the frontier, not after it had been tamed. He virtually ignored the role of women, African Americans, Native Americans, Hispanics, and Asians in shaping the human geography of the western United States. Moreover, Turner's frontier was always the site of heroism, triumph, and progress. He downplayed the evidence of greed, exploitation, and failure in the settling of the West.

Turner also implied that America would be fundamentally different after 1890 because the frontier experience was essentially over. In many respects, however, the West has retained the qualities associated with the rush for land, gold, timber, and water rights. The mining frontier, as one historian has recently written, "set a mood that has never disappeared from the West: the attitude of every extractive industry—get in, get rich, get out."

DISCONTENTED FARMERS By 1900, both the South and West were quite different socially and culturally from what they had been in 1865. In both cases, dramatically changed economic conditions spurred the emergence of a New South and a New West. In the West, the widespread use of mechanized commercial agriculture changed the dynamics of farming. By the end of the nineteenth century, many homesteaders had been forced to abandon their own farms and become wage-earning laborers, "migrant workers" moving with the seasons to different states to harvest different crops produced on large commercial farms or ranches. Migrant workers were often treated as poorly as the white and black sharecroppers in the South. One western worker complained that the landowner "looked at me, his hired hand, as if I was just another workhorse."

As discontent rose among farmers and farmworkers in the South and the West, many of them joined the People's party, whose followers were known as Populists, a grassroots social and political movement that was sweeping the poorest rural regions of the nation. In 1892, a Minnesota farm leader named Ignatius Donnelly told Populists at their national convention that "We meet in the midst of a nation brought to the verge of moral, political, and material ruin." He affirmed that Populism sought "to restore the Government of the Republic to the hands of the 'plain people' with whom it originated."

The Populist movement would tie the South and West together in an effort to wrest control of the political system from Republicans in the Northeast and Midwest. That struggle would come to define the 1890s and determine the shape of the twentieth century.

CHAPTER REVIEW

SUMMARY

- **The New South** Many southerners embraced the vision of the *New South* promoted by Henry Grady and others, who called for a more diverse economy with greater industrialization, more vocational training, and a widespread acceptance of white supremacy in social relations. The cotton *textile industry* grew to surpass that of New England, iron manufacturing increased, and the *American Tobacco Company* became the world's largest manufacturer of cigarettes. But agriculture—and especially the growing of cotton—still dominated the southern economy, much as it had before the Civil War. Under the *crop-lien system*, large landowners rented land to cash-poor tenant farmers or *sharecroppers* (the latter usually African Americans) in return for a "share" of the cotton they grew each year. The crop-lien system kept millions in long-term debt and limited where they could live and how they could make a living.

- **Jim Crow Policies in the South** During the 1890s, southern states disfranchised the vast majority of African American voters and instituted a series of policies known as Jim Crow laws segregating blacks and whites in public facilities. Starting with the *Mississippi Plan*, state governments passed a series of comprehensive measures that included poll taxes, grandfather clauses, literacy tests, and residency requirements, making voting nearly impossible for most African Americans and some poor whites. Disfranchisement was followed by legalized segregation, ruled constitutional by the Supreme Court in the 1896 *Plessy v. Ferguson* decision. African Americans who resisted were often the target of violence at the hands of whites, the worst form being organized lynching.

- **Western Migrants** Life in the West was often harsh and violent, but the promise of cheap land or wealth from mining drew settlers from the East. Although most westerners were white Protestant Americans or immigrants from Germany and Scandinavia, Mexicans, African Americans (the *Exodusters*), and Chinese, as well as many other nationalities, contributed to the West's diversity. About three-fourths of those who moved to the West were men.

- **Miners, Farmers, Ranchers, and Women** Many migrants to the West were attracted to opportunities to mine, ranch, farm, or work on the railroads. Miners were drawn to the discovery of precious minerals such as silver at the *Comstock Lode* in Nevada in 1861. But most miners and cattle ranchers did not become wealthy, because mining and raising cattle, particularly after the development of barbed wire and the end of the *open range*, became large-scale enterprises. Farmers on the Great Plains were able to produce wheat for export, but declining grain prices and the need for expensive machinery and transportation meant that only large-scale farms owned by a wealthy few could sustain real profits.

- **Indian Wars and Policies** By 1900, Native Americans were no longer free to roam the plains, as the influx of miners, ranchers, farmers, and soldiers had curtailed their traditional way of life. Instances of armed resistance, such as the *Great Sioux*

War, were crushed. Beginning in 1887, with the *Dawes Severalty Act*, the American government's Indian policy shifted. It now forced Indians to relinquish their traditional culture and adopt the "American way" of individual landownership.

- **The South and West in 1900**   By 1900, the West resembled the South where agricultural resources were concentrated in the hands of a few. In the 1890s, poor farmers in the West joined with tenant farmers in the South to support the People's party or the Populist movement, which sought to wrest control of the political and economic system from the powerful East and return it to the "plain" folk. This contest would dominate the nation's politics in the 1890s and set its course for the twentieth century.

CHRONOLOGY

1862	Congress passes the Homestead Act
1864	Sand Creek Massacre
1873	Joseph Glidden invents barbed wire
1876	Battle of Little Bighorn
1880s	Henry Grady spreads the New South idea
1886	Surrender of Geronimo marks the end of the Indian wars
1887	Congress passes the Dawes Severalty Act
1890	Battle of Wounded Knee
	James Duke forms the American Tobacco Company
1893	Frederick J. Turner outlines his "frontier thesis"
1896	*Plessy v. Ferguson* mandates "separate but equal" racial facilities

KEY TERMS

textile industry p. 801

American Tobacco Company p. 801

Redeemers p. 802

crop-lien system p. 804

sharecroppers p. 804

share tenants p. 804

Mississippi Plan (1890) p. 807

"separate but equal" p. 809

Atlanta Compromise (1895) p. 815

Exodusters p. 820

boomtown p. 822

Comstock Lode p. 823

open range p. 826

Indian wars p. 831

Sand Creek Massacre (1864) p. 832

Great Sioux War p. 836

Ghost Dance movement p. 839

Dawes Severalty Act (1887) p. 841

 INQUIZITIVE

Go to InQuizitive to see what you've learned—and learn what you've missed—with personalized feedback along the way.

19 Political Stalemate and Rural Revolt

1865–1900

Wet Night on the Bowery (1911) This scene of early twentieth-century life in New York City by John Sloan captures people of all walks of life converging on a rainy night: a smartly dressed society woman (left), a prostitute (center), and drunks stumbling about farther down the block. Running overhead is the elevated train, while an electric trolley gleams from the wet street.

W ithin three decades after the Civil War, American life had experienced a stunning transformation. An agricultural society long rooted in the soil and little involved in global issues had become an urban and industrialized nation deeply entwined in world markets and international politics.

The period from the end of the Civil War to the beginning of the twentieth century was an era noted for the widening social, economic, and political gap between the powerful and the powerless, the haves and have-nots. It was sardonically labeled the **Gilded Age** for its greed and vulgarity, and was a time marked by conspicuous consumption by the newly rich as they flaunted their enormous personal wealth—the same wealth that financed extensive political and corporate corruption. While the Gilded Age brought dramatic changes across all socioeconomic classes, the resulting transformations to social and cultural life could hardly be considered "gilded" to average Americans or recent immigrants.

Urban America

During the late nineteenth century, the United States became a nation dominated by rapidly growing cities. Between 1865 and 1900, the urban population skyrocketed from 8 million to 30 million. In 1865, fewer than twenty cities had populations of more than 50,000; by 1900, there were four times that many.

focus questions

1. What were the effects of urban growth during the Gilded Age? What problems did it create?

2. Who were the "new immigrants" of the late nineteenth century? How were they viewed by American society?

3. How did urban growth and the increasingly important role of science influence leisure activities, cultural life, and social policy in the Gilded Age?

4. How did the nature of politics during the Gilded Age contribute to political corruption and stalemate?

5. How effective were politicians in developing responses to the major economic and social problems of the Gilded Age?

6. Why did the money supply become a major political issue, especially for farmers, during the Gilded Age? How did it impact American politics?

Millions of European and Asian immigrants, as well as migrants from America's rural areas, streamed into cities, attracted by the plentiful jobs and excitements they offered. "We cannot all live in cities," cautioned Horace Greeley, the New York newspaper editor and Democratic presidential candidate in 1872, "yet nearly all seem determined to do so."

The growth of cities brought an array of problems, among them widespread poverty, unsanitary living conditions, and new forms of political corruption. How to feed, shelter, and educate the new city dwellers taxed the imaginations and resources of government officials. Even more challenging was the development of neighborhoods divided by racial and ethnic background as well as social class. At the same time, researchers were making discoveries that improved public health, economic productivity, and communications. Advances in modern science stimulated public support for higher education, but also opened up doubts about many long-accepted "truths" and religious beliefs. More and more people began to question the literal truth of the Bible.

POLITICAL CULTURE Political life during the Gilded Age was shaped by three main factors: the balance of power between Democrats and Republicans, the high level of public participation in everyday politics, and the often corrupt alliance between business and political leaders at all levels of government. In 1873, Job Stevenson, an Ohio congressman, claimed that members of the House of Representatives were so often selling their votes to Big Business lobbyists that it should have been renamed an "auction room."

The most important political issue of the Gilded Age, however, was the growing conflicts between city and country, industry and agriculture. Millions of financially distressed farmers felt ignored or betrayed by the political process. While industrialists and large commercial farmers prospered, small farmers struggled with falling crop prices, growing indebtedness to banks and railroads, and what they considered big-city greed and exploitation.

By the 1890s, discontented farmers would channel their frustrations into political action and enliven a growing movement to expand ("inflate") the nation's money supply as a way to relieve economic distress. The election of 1896 symbolized the central conflict of the Gilded Age: the clashing cultural and economic values of two Americas, one older, small-scale, and rural, the other newer, large-scale, and urban.

AMERICA'S MOVE TO TOWN Americans moved to towns and cities after the Civil War, many of which evolved into major metropolitan areas. People from rural areas were attracted by the jobs and excitements of city life. Many had been pushed off the land by new agricultural machinery that sharply reduced the need for farmworkers. Four farmworkers or ranchers could now perform the labor that earlier had required fourteen. Immigrants especially congregated in the cities along the Atlantic and Pacific coast where they arrived on ships from Europe or Asia. "The greater part of our population must live in cities," announced Josiah Strong, a prominent Congregationalist minister, in 1898. "There was no resisting the trend."

While the Far West had the greatest proportion of urban dwellers, concentrated in cities such as San Francisco and Denver, the Northeast and Midwest held far more people in huge cities—New York, Boston, Philadelphia, Pittsburgh, Chicago, Cincinnati, St. Louis, and others. More and more of these city dwellers had little or no money and nothing but their labor to sell. By 1900, more than 90 percent of the people in New York City's most densely populated borough, Manhattan, lived in rented houses or in congested, low-cost buildings called **tenements**, where residents, many of them immigrants, were packed like sardines in poorly ventilated and poorly lit apartments.

GROWTH IN ALL DIRECTIONS Several advances in technology helped city buildings handle the surging populations. In the 1870s, heating innovations, such as steam radiators, enabled the construction of much larger apartment buildings, since coal-burning fireplaces and chimneys, expensive to build, were no longer needed in each apartment. In 1889, the Otis Elevator Company installed the first electric elevator, which made it possible to construct much taller buildings; before the 1860s, few structures had been more than five or six stories. During the 1880s, engineers also developed cast-iron and steel-frame construction techniques that allowed for taller structures—"skyscrapers."

Cities grew out as well as up, as horse-drawn streetcars and commuter railways let people live farther away from their downtown workplaces. In 1873, San Francisco became the first city to use cable cars that clamped onto a moving underground cable driven by a central power source. Some cities ran steam-powered trains on elevated tracks, but by the 1890s, electric trolleys were preferred. Mass transit received an added boost from underground subway trains built in Boston, New York City, and Philadelphia.

The commuter trains and trolleys allowed a growing middle class of business executives and professionals (accountants, doctors, engineers, sales clerks, teachers, store managers, and attorneys) to retreat from crowded downtowns to quieter, tree-lined "streetcar suburbs." But the working poor, many of them immigrants or African Americans, could rarely afford to leave the inner cities. As their populations grew, cities became dangerously congested and plagued with fires, violent crimes, and diseases.

CROWDS, DIRT, AND DISEASE The wonders of big cities—electric lights, streetcars, telephones, department stores, theaters, and many other

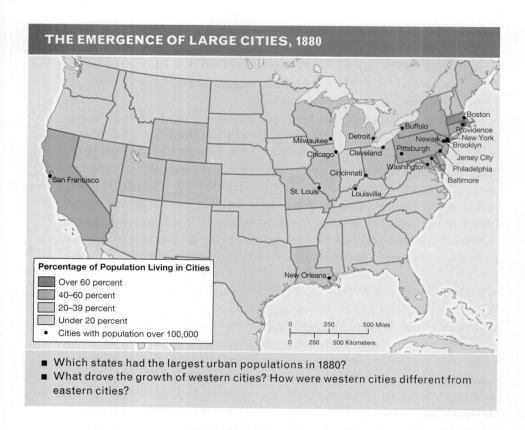

THE EMERGENCE OF LARGE CITIES, 1880

Percentage of Population Living in Cities
- Over 60 percent
- 40–60 percent
- 20–39 percent
- Under 20 percent
- • Cities with population over 100,000

- Which states had the largest urban populations in 1880?
- What drove the growth of western cities? How were western cities different from eastern cities?

attractions—were magnetic lures for rural youth bored by the routines of iso-lated farm life. Thousands moved to the cities in search of economic opportu-nity and personal freedom.

Yet in doing so they often traded one set of problems for another. In New York City in 1900, some 2.3 million people—two-thirds of the city's population—were living in overcrowded, often filthy tenement housing. Such urban growth frequently occurred with little planning or regulations. Rapidly expanding cities often suffered from poor housing, unhealthy living conditions, and frequent infectious diseases and fires. "The only trouble with New York City," said writer Mark Twain, "is that it is too large. You cannot accomplish anything in the way of business . . . without devoting a whole day to it. The distances are too great."

Tenement buildings were usually six to eight stories tall, lacked elevators, and were jammed so tightly together that most of the apartments had little or no natural light or fresh air. They typically housed twenty-four to thirty-two families,

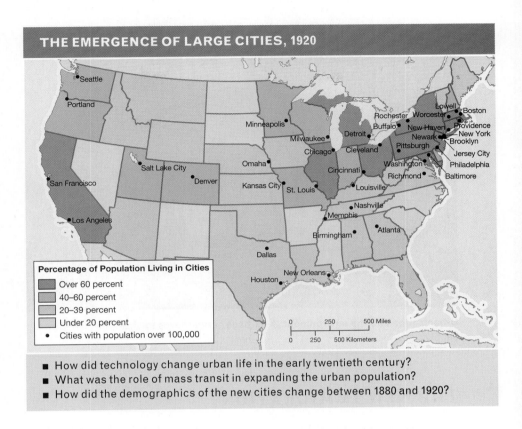

THE EMERGENCE OF LARGE CITIES, 1920

Percentage of Population Living in Cities
- Over 60 percent
- 40–60 percent
- 20–39 percent
- Under 20 percent
- Cities with population over 100,000

- How did technology change urban life in the early twentieth century?
- What was the role of mass transit in expanding the urban population?
- How did the demographics of the new cities change between 1880 and 1920?

usually with lots of children who had few places to play except in the streets. On average, there was only one toilet (called a *privy*) for every twenty people.

Late nineteenth-century cities were dirty, smelly, and disease ridden. The child-mortality rate in many tenements was as high as 40 percent. Streets were filled with contaminated water, horse urine and manure, and roaming pigs. Garbage and raw sewage were carelessly dumped into streets and waterways, causing epidemics of infectious diseases such as cholera, typhoid fever, and yellow fever. In one poor Chicago district at the end of the century, three of every five babies died before their first birthday.

So-called sanitary reformers—public health officials and engineers—eventually created regulations requiring more space per resident as well as more windows and plumbing facilities. Reformers also pushed successfully for new water and sewage systems and for regular trash collection. They lobbied to ban slaughterhouses and the raising of hogs and cattle within city limits, and to replace horse-drawn trolleys with electric-powered streetcars or trolleys.

Urbanization and the environment A garbage cart retrieves trash in New York City, ca. 1890.

THE NEW IMMIGRATION

America's roaring prosperity and promise of political and religious freedom attracted waves of immigrants from every part of the globe after the Civil War. By 1900, nearly 30 percent of the residents of major cities were foreign-born. These newcomers provided much-needed labor for the growing economy, but their arrival also sparked racial and ethnic tensions.

A SURGE OF NEWCOMERS FROM EUROPE Immigration has always been one of the most powerful forces shaping American history. This was especially true between 1860 and 1900, as more and more immigrants, most of them poor, arrived from eastern and southern Europe. The number of immigrants rose from just under 3 million annually in the 1870s to more than 5 million per year in the 1880s, and reached nearly 9 million annually in the first decade of the twentieth century. In 1890, four out of five New Yorkers were foreign-born, a higher proportion than in any other city in the world. Chicago was not far behind.

Rapidly growing industries seeking low-wage workers—including mines, railroads, mills, and factories—sent recruiting agents abroad to stir up interest

Ellis Island To accommodate the soaring numbers of immigrants passing through New York City, Congress built a reception center on Ellis Island, near the Statue of Liberty. Pictured here is its registry room, where immigrants awaited close questioning by officials.

in migration to the United States. Under the Contract Labor Act of 1864, the federal government helped pay for immigrants' travel expenses to America. The law was repealed in 1868, but not until 1885 did the government stop companies from importing foreign laborers, a practice that put immigrant workers under the control of their employers.

The so-called "old immigrants" who came before 1880 were mainly Protestants and Roman Catholics from northern and western Europe. This pattern began to change, however, as the proportion of immigrants from southern and eastern Europe, especially Russia, Poland, Greece, and Italy, rose sharply. After 1890, these **"new immigrants"** made up a majority of the newcomers, and by the first decade of the new century, they formed 70 percent. Their languages and cultural backgrounds were markedly different from those of most old immigrants or of most native-born Americans. The dominant religions of the new immigrants, for example, were Judaism, Eastern Orthodox, and Roman Catholicism, whereas Protestants still formed a large majority of the total U.S. population.

In 1907, Congress appointed the bipartisan Dillingham Commission to examine the changes in immigration patterns. In its forty-one-volume report, released in 1911, the Commission concluded that the "new" immigrants were

> far less intelligent than the old, approximately one-third of all those over 14 years of age when admitted being illiterate. Racially, they are for the most part essentially unlike the British, German and other peoples who came during the prior period to 1880, and generally speaking they are actuated in coming by different ideals, for the old immigration came to be a part of the country, while the new in a large measure, comes with the intention of profiting, in a pecuniary way, by the superior advantages of the new world and then returning to the old country.

Immigrants were usually desperately poor and needed to find jobs—quickly. Many were greeted at the docks by family and friends, others were met by representatives of immigrant-aid societies or by company agents offering low-paying and often dangerous jobs in mines, mills, sweatshops, and on railroads.

Since most immigrants knew little if any English and nothing about American employment practices, they were easy targets for exploitation. Many unwittingly lost a healthy percentage of their wages to unscrupulous hiring agents in exchange for a bit of whiskey and a job. Companies eager for workers gave immigrants train tickets to inland cities such as Buffalo, Pittsburgh, Cleveland, Chicago, Milwaukee, Cincinnati, and St. Louis.

As strangers in America, most immigrants naturally wanted to live in neighborhoods populated by people from their homeland. The largest cities had vibrant immigrant districts with names such as Little Italy, Little Hungary, and Chinatown, where immigrants practiced their native religions and customs, and spoke and read newspapers in their native languages. But they paid a price for such community solidarity. When new immigrants moved into an area, the previous residents often moved out, taking with them whatever social prestige and political influence they had achieved. Living conditions often quickly deteriorated as housing and sanitation codes went unenforced.

THE NATIVIST RESPONSE Then, as now, many native-born Americans saw the newest immigrants as a threat to their jobs and way of life. Many "**nativists**" were racists who believed that "Anglo-Saxon" Americans—people of British or Germanic background—were superior to the Slavic, Italian, Greek, and Jewish newcomers. A Stanford University professor called immigrants from southern and eastern Europe "illiterate, docile, lacking in self-reliance and initiative, and not possessing the Anglo-Teutonic conceptions of

Mulberry Street, 1900 This photograph captures the many Italian immigrants who made Mulberry Street in downtown New York City their home at the turn of the century. Horse-drawn carts weave through people shopping, socializing, and people-gazing.

law, order, and government." Many were illiterate, but others only appeared so because they could not speak or read English. Some resorted to crime to survive, fueling suspicions that European nations were sending their criminals to America.

Throughout American history, Congress has passed laws regulating immigration; largely, these statutes have been inconsistent in their goals and frequently motivated by racial and ethnic prejudice. During the late nineteenth century, such prejudice took an especially ugly turn against the Chinese.

By 1880, some 75,000 Chinese formed about a ninth of the population of California. They were the first non-European and non-African group to migrate in large numbers to America. Chinese immigrants were easy targets for discrimination; they were not white, they were not Christian, and many could not read or write. Whites resented them for supposedly taking their jobs, although in many instances the Chinese were willing to do menial work that whites refused to do.

John Jeong, a young Chinese immigrant, arrived in San Francisco and quickly encountered ethnic persecution. As he and others made their way to the Chinatown neighborhood in an open carriage, "some white boys came up and started throwing rocks at us." Another Chinese newcomer experienced

Chinese Exclusion Act The Chinese caricature "John Chinaman" is escorted out of America by Lady Liberty with his ironing board and opium pipe, while other accepted minorities look on.

similar treatment. Whenever he and his friends strayed outside their own neighborhood, the "whites would attack you with stones."

In 1882, anti-Chinese sentiment in Congress prompted passage of the **Chinese Exclusion Act**, the first federal law to restrict the immigration of free people on the basis of race and class. The act, which barred unskilled Chinese laborers from entering the country for ten years, was periodically renewed before being extended indefinitely in 1902. With the Chinese Exclusion Act, the golden door welcoming foreigners to the United States began to close. Not until 1943 were barriers to Chinese immigration finally removed.

The Chinese were not the only group targeted. In 1887, Protestant activists in Iowa formed the American Protective Association (APA), a secret organization whose members pledged never to employ or vote for a Roman Catholic. Working often within local Republican party organizations, the APA quickly enlisted 2.5 million members and helped shape the 1894 election results in Ohio, Wisconsin, Indiana, Missouri, and Colorado.

In 1891, nativists in New England formed the Immigration Restriction League to save the Anglo-Saxon "race" from being "contaminated" by "alien" immigrants, especially Roman Catholics and Jews. The League sought to convince Congress to ban immigrants who were illiterate. Three presidents vetoed bills banning illiterate immigrants: Grover Cleveland in 1897, William H. Taft in 1913, and Woodrow Wilson in 1915 and 1917. The last time, however, Congress overrode the veto, and the restriction of illiterate immigrants became law.

CULTURAL LIFE

The flood of people into cities brought changes in recreation and leisure. Middle- and upper-class families, especially those in streetcar suburbs, often spent free time together at home, singing around a piano, reading novels, or playing games. In congested urban areas, politics as a form of public entertainment attracted large crowds, and saloons became even more popular social centers for working-class men. New forms of mass entertainment—movie theaters, music halls, vaudeville shows featuring singers, dancers, and comedians; art museums, symphony orchestras, sporting events, and circuses—drew a broad cross-section of residents. In large cities, new streetcar transit systems allowed people to travel easily to sporting events, and rooting for the home team helped unify a city's ethnic and racial groups and social classes. By the end of the century, sports of all kinds had become a major part of popular culture.

Urbanization and technological progress also contributed to the prestige of modern science. By encouraging what one writer called a "mania for facts," scientists generated changes throughout social, intellectual, and cultural life. Scientific research led to transformational technologies such as electric power and lights, telephones, phonographs, motion pictures, bicycles, and automobiles.

Although only men could vote in most states, both men and women flocked to hear candidates speak at political meetings. In the largest cities, membership in a political party offered many social benefits. As labor unions became increasingly common, they too took on social roles for working-class men.

Vaudeville For as little as 1¢ for admission, vaudeville shows aimed to please the tastes of their wildly diverse audience with a great range of entertainment.

SALOONS Still, the most popular leisure destinations for the urban working class were **saloons**, beer gardens, and dance halls. By 1900, the United States had more saloons (over 325,000) than grocery stores and meat markets. New York City alone had 10,000 saloons, 1 for every 500 residents.

Saloons were the workingman's social club and were especially popular among male immigrants seeking companionship in a strange land. In cities such as New York, Boston, Philadelphia, and Chicago, the customers were disproportionately Irish, German, and Italian Catholics. Politics was often the topic of intense discussions in saloons; in fact, in New York City in the 1880s, saloons doubled as polling places, where patrons could cast their votes in elections. One journalist called the saloon "the social and intellectual center of the neighborhood."

Men also went to saloons to check job postings, engage in labor union activities, cash paychecks, mail letters, read newspapers, and gossip. Because saloons were heated and offered public restrooms, they served as refuges for the homeless, especially in the winter. Patrons could play chess, billiards, darts, cards, dice, or even handball, since many saloons included gymnasiums.

Although the main barroom was for men only, women and children were allowed to enter a side door to buy a pail of beer to carry home (a task called "rushing the growler"). Some saloons also provided "snugs," separate rooms for women customers. "Stall saloons" included "wine rooms" where prostitutes worked.

LEISURE FOR WOMEN Married working-class women had even less leisure time than working-class men. Many were working for pay themselves, and even those who were not were frequently overwhelmed by housework and child-rearing responsibilities. As a social worker noted, "The men have the saloons, political clubs, trade-unions or [fraternal] lodges for their recreation . . . while the mothers have almost no recreation, only a dreary round of work, day after day, with occasionally doorstep gossip to vary the monotony of their lives." Married working-class women often used the streets as their public space. Washing clothes, supervising children at play, or shopping at the local market provided opportunities for socializing.

Single women, many of whom worked as domestic servants ("maids") and had more leisure time than working mothers, flocked to dance halls, theaters, amusement parks, and picnic grounds. With the advent of movie theaters, the cinema became the most popular form of entertainment for working women. As an advertisement promised, "If you are tired of life, go to the movies. If you are sick of troubles rife, go to the picture show. You will forget your unpaid bills, rheumatism and other ills, if you stow your pills and go to the picture show."

Steeplechase Park, Coney Island, Brooklyn, New York Members of the working class could afford the inexpensive rides at this popular amusement park.

THE IMPACT OF DARWINISM

Virtually every field of thought felt the impact of natural scientist Charles Darwin's controversial *On the Origin of Species* (1859), one of the most influential books ever written. Basing his conclusions on extensive yet "imperfect" field research, Darwin showed how the chance processes of evolution give energy and unity to life. At the center of his concept was what Darwin called "natural selection." He demonstrated that most organisms produce many more offspring than can survive. Those offspring with certain favorable characteristics adapt and live, while others die from starvation, disease, or predators.

This "struggle for existence" in a crowded world drove the process of natural selection, Darwin said. Over many millions of years, modern species "evolved" from less complex forms of life; individuals and species that had characteristics advantageous for survival reproduced, while others fell by the wayside. As Darwin wrote, "the vigorous, the healthy, and the happy survive and multiply."

Darwin's theory of biological evolution was shocking because most people still embraced a literal interpretation of the biblical creation story, which claimed that all species were created at the same moment by God and remained the same thereafter. Although Darwin had trained for the ministry and was

Charles Darwin Darwin's scientific theories influenced more than a century of political and social debate.

reluctant to be drawn into religious controversy, his biological findings suggested to many, then and since, that there was no providential God controlling the universe. People were no different from plants and animals; they too evolved by trial and error rather than by God's purposeful hand. What came to be called *Darwinism* spelled the end of a God-given world.

Many Christians charged that Darwin's ideas led to atheism, a denial of the existence of God, while others found their faith severely shaken not only by evolutionary theory but also by new scientific standards of scholarly analysis that were being applied to the Bible. Most of the faithful, however, came to reconcile science and religion. They decided that the process of evolutionary change in nature must be God's doing.

SOCIAL DARWINISM Although Darwin's theory of evolution applied only to biological phenomena, many applied it to human society. Englishman Herbert Spencer, a leading social philosopher, was the first major prophet of what came to be called **social Darwinism**.

Spencer argued that human society and its institutions, like the organisms studied by Darwin, evolved through the same process of natural selection. The "survival of the fittest," in Spencer's chilling phrase, was the engine of social progress. By encouraging people, ideas, and nations to compete with one another for dominance, society would generate "the greatest perfection and the most complete happiness."

Darwin dismissed Spencer's social theories as "unconvincing." He did not believe that the evolutionary process in the natural world had any relevance to human social institutions. Others, however, eagerly endorsed social Darwinism. E. L. Youmans, founding editor of *Popular Science Monthly*, became the foremost champion of Spencer's ideas in America. He claimed that in the United States, Darwinism really meant Spencerism, the "anti-philanthropic, anti-meddling side" of Spencer's philosophy. If, as Spencer believed, society naturally evolved for the better through "survival of the fittest," then interference with human competition in the marketplace was a serious mistake because it would help "unfit" people survive, and thereby hinder progress.

Social Darwinism implied the need for hands-off, laissez-faire government policies; it argued against the regulation of business or of required minimum standards for sanitation and housing. To Spencer, the only acceptable charity was voluntary, and even that was of dubious value. Spencer warned that "fostering the good-for-nothing [people] at the expense of the good, is an extreme cruelty" to the health of civilization.

For Spencer and his many American supporters, successful businessmen and corporations provided proof of the concept of "survival of the fittest." If the unregulated process of capitalist development led to small businesses being destroyed or acquired by huge corporate monopolies, it was simply a necessary phase of the evolutionary process. Oil tycoon John D. Rockefeller revealed his own embrace of social Darwinism when he told his Baptist Sunday-school class that the "growth of a large business is merely a survival of the fittest. . . . This is not an evil tendency in business. It is merely the working-out of a law of nature and a law of God."

Popular Science Monthly, founded in 1872, became the chief magazine for promoting social Darwinism in the United States. That year, Spencer's chief academic disciple, William Graham Sumner, began teaching at Yale University, where he preached the gospel of natural selection. Sumner's most lasting contribution, made in his book *Folkways* (1907), was to argue that it would be a mistake for government to try to promote equality, since doing so would interfere with the "survival of the fittest."

REFORM DARWINISM Sumner's efforts to use Darwinism to promote "rugged individualism" and oppose government regulation of business prompted an alternative use of Darwinism in the context of human society. What came to be called **reform Darwinism** found its major advocate in Lester Frank Ward, a government employee who fought his way up from poverty and never lost his empathy for the underdog. Ward's *Dynamic Sociology* (1883) singled out one aspect of evolution that both Darwin and Spencer had neglected: the human brain. True, as Sumner claimed, people, like animals, compete. But, as Ward explained, people also collaborate. Unlike animals, people can plan for a distant future; they have minds capable of shaping and directing social change. Far from being the helpless object of irresistible evolutionary forces, Ward argued, humanity could actively control social evolution through long-range planning.

Ward's reform Darwinism held that *cooperation*, not *competition*, would better promote social progress. Government, in Ward's view, should pursue two main goals: alleviating poverty, which impeded the development of the mind, and promoting the education of the masses. Intellect, informed by science, could foster social improvement. Reform Darwinism would prove to be one of the pillars of the "progressive" movement during the late nineteenth century and after.

REALISM IN LITERATURE AND ART

Before the Civil War, Romanticism had dominated American literature and painting. Romantics such as the transcendentalists in New England believed that fundamental truths rested in the unseen world of ideas and spirit. The most prominent writers and artists were more concerned with romantic or biblical themes than with depicting everyday life.

During the second half of the nineteenth century, however, a new generation calling themselves "realists" began to challenge the Romantic tradition. A writer in *Putnam's Monthly* noted in 1854 a growing emphasis on "the real and the practical." This emphasis on "realism" matured into a full-fledged cultural force, as more and more writers and artists focused on depicting the actual aspects of urban-industrial America: scientific research and technology, factories and railroads, cities and immigrants, labor unions and social tensions.

For many Americans, the horrors of the Civil War had led to a less romanticized and more realistic view of life. An editor attending an art exhibition in 1865 sensed "the greater reality of feeling developed by the war. We have grown more sober, perhaps, and less patient of romantic idealism."

Another factor contributing to the rise of realism was the impact of modern science. "This is a world of reality," admitted a Romantic writer, "and romance breaks against the many hard facts." The "stupendous power of Science," announced one editor, will rid American thought of "every old-time idea, every trace of old romance and art, poetry and romantic or sentimental feeling" and wash away the "ideal . . . and visionary."

Realism, as writer Fanny Bates stressed, appealed especially to people living in busy, swarming cities, people "whose lives are crowded with a variety of interests." The worship of money was the most common theme in realistic novels and short stories during the Gilded Age. In William Dean Howells's *The Rise of Silas Lapham* (1885), Bromfield Corey announces that money "is the romance, the poetry of our age." Lily Bart, the heroine of Edith Wharton's *The House of Mirth* (1905), declares that she "must have a great deal of money" to be happy.

City streets, sidewalks, and parks provided countless scenes of *real* life to depict on canvas and in words. Novelist Henry James said that the daily urban scene unleashed a "flood of the real" to study and portray. John Sloan, a

Stag at Sharkey's (1909) New York painter George Bellows witnessed such fierce boxing matches across the street from his studio, at the saloon of retired heavyweight boxer "Sailor" Sharkey. Bellows is one of the most famous artists from the Ashcan School, which was committed to capturing the gritty reality of the urban scene.

New York City painter, chose his subjects by spying on people from his Manhattan studio. He confided in his diary that he was addicted to "watching every bit of human life" through his windows and along the sidewalks.

Others shared Sloan's "spectatorial" sensibility. "My favorite pastime," writer Theodore Dreiser remembered, "was to walk the city streets and view the lives and activities of others." In his influential novel *Sister Carrie* (1900), Carrie Meeber uses her "gift of observation" to view strangers through the open windows of shops, offices, and factories, imagining what "they deal with, how they labored, to what end it all came."

The realists' emphasis on closely observing everyday life grew out of the scientific spirit. Just as scientists observed visible and verifiable facts and transformed them into knowledge, cultural realists studied the world around them and expressed it in art and literature. Like a gust of fresh air, they made Americans aware of the significance of their everyday surroundings, in all their beauty and ugliness.

GILDED AGE POLITICS

The Gilded Age was an era of more political corruption than political innovation. In 1879, Woodrow Wilson, then a young college graduate, described the political system as having "no leaders, no principles."

The real movers and shakers of the Gilded Age were not the men in the White House or Congress but the owners of giant corporations. These "captains of industry" regularly used their wealth to "buy" elections and favors at all levels of government. Jay Gould, one of the most aggressive railroad tycoons, admitted that he elected "the [New York] legislature with my own money."

"Special interests," businesses that bought favors from government officials, dominated Gilded Age politics. By the end of the nineteenth century, however, new movements and parties were pushing to reform the excesses and injustices created by a political system that had grown corrupt in its efforts to support the "special interests" promoted by Big Business.

LOCAL POLITICS AND PARTY LOYALTIES Perhaps the most important feature of Gilded Age politics was its local focus. Most political activity occurred at the state and local levels. Unlike today, the federal government was an insignificant force in the daily lives of most citizens, in part because it was so small. In 1871, the entire federal civilian workforce totaled 51,000 (most of them postal workers), of whom only 6,000 actually worked in Washington, D.C. Not until the twentieth century did the importance of the federal government begin to surpass that of local and state governments.

Americans during the Gilded Age were intensely loyal to their political party, which they joined as much for the fellowship and networking connections as for its positions on issues. Unlike today, party members paid dues to join, and party leaders regularly demanded large campaign contributions from the captains of industry and finance. Collis Huntington, a California railroad tycoon, admitted that bribery in the form of campaign contributions was expected: "If you have to pay money to have the right thing done, then it is only just and fair to do it." Roscoe Conkling, a powerful Republican senator from New York, was equally candid: "Of course, we do rotten things in New York. . . . Politics is a rotten business." Democrat Horatio Seymour, a presidential candidate in 1868, explained that "our people want men in office who will not steal, but who will not interfere with those who do."

In cities crowded with new immigrant voters, politics was usually controlled by "rings"—small groups who shaped policy and managed the nomination and election of candidates. Each ring typically had a powerful "boss" who used his "machine"—a network of neighborhood activists and officials—to govern.

Colorful, larger-than-life figures such as New York City's William "Boss" Tweed shamelessly ruled, plundered, and occasionally improved municipal government, often through dishonest means and frequent bribes. Until his arrest in 1871 and his conviction in 1873, Tweed used the Tammany Hall ring to dominate the nation's largest city. The Tammany Hall machine doled out contracts to business allies and jobs to political supporters. In the late 1870s one of every twelve New York men worked for the city government. The various city rings and bosses were often corrupt, but they did bring structure, stability, and services to rapidly growing inner-city communities, many of them composed of immigrants newly arrived from Ireland, Germany, and, increasingly, from southern and eastern Europe.

William "Boss" Tweed A larger-than-life political boss was New York City's William "Boss" Tweed, whose powerful connections made "no prison big enough to hold the Boss."

The party in power expected the government employees it appointed to become campaign workers and to do the bidding of **party bosses**. Those bosses in "smoke-filled back rooms" often decided who the candidates would be and commanded loyalty and obedience by rewarding and punishing their party members. They helped settle local disputes, provided aid for the poor, and distributed government jobs and contracts to loyal followers and corporate donors through the **patronage** system. President Ulysses S. Grant's secretary told a Republican party boss that he hoped "you will distribute the patronage in such a manner as will help the Administration."

Throughout the Gilded Age, almost every government job—local, state, and federal—was subject to the latest election results. As a Democratic party official in New York City admitted, "You can't keep a [political] organization together without patronage. Men ain't in politics for nothin'. They want to get somethin' out of it."

The jobs given to party loyalists covered a wide range, from cabinet posts to courthouse clerk positions. The largest single source of political jobs was the postal service, which accounted for half of all federal civilian employees. Those who were awarded government jobs were expected to contribute a percentage of their salary to the political party.

The corruption associated with the patronage system eventually drew criticism from "civil service reformers," who pushed through legislation designed to limit such patronage and introduced a "merit system" for government employment based on ability and experience.

NATIONAL POLITICS   Several factors gave national politics during the Gilded Age its distinctive texture. First in importance was the close division between Republicans and Democrats in Congress. Because neither party was dominant after the revival of the national Democratic party in 1876, they both avoided controversial issues or bold initiatives for fear of losing a close election. Yet, paradoxically, voter intensity at all levels peaked during the Gilded Age at the same time that many divisive issues were suppressed or ignored. Voter turnout was commonly about 70 to 80 percent. (By contrast, the turnout for the 2012 U.S. presidential election was 58 percent.)

During the Gilded Age, most voters cast their ballots for the same party year after year. Party loyalty was often an emotional choice. In the 1870s and 1880s, for example, people continued to fight the Civil War during political campaigns. Republican candidates regularly "waved the bloody shirt," accusing Democrats of having caused "secession and civil war," while Republicans took credit for abolishing slavery and saving the Union.

Democrats, especially in the South, where they monopolized political power after 1877, responded by reminding voters that they stood for limited government, states' rights, and white supremacy. Republicans tended to favor high tariffs on imports, but many Democrats also supported tariffs if they benefited the dominant businesses in their districts or states. Third parties, such as the Greenbackers, Populists, and Prohibitionists, appealed to specific interests and issues, such as currency inflation, railroad regulations, or legislation to restrict alcohol consumption.

Party loyalties reflected religious, ethnic, and geographic divisions. After the Civil War, the Republican party remained strongest in New England, upstate New York, Pennsylvania, Ohio, and the Midwest. Republicans tended to be Protestants of English or Scandinavian descent. As the party of Abraham Lincoln (the "Great Emancipator") and Ulysses S. Grant, Republicans could also rely upon the votes of African Americans in the South (until their right to vote was taken away) and the support of a large bloc of Union veterans of the Civil War, who were organized into a powerful national interest group called the Grand Army of the Republic.

The Democrats were a more diverse coalition of conservative southern whites, northern Catholics of German or Irish Catholic backgrounds, and others repelled by the Republicans' claim to be the "party of morality." As one

Chicago Democrat explained, "A Republican is a man who wants you t' go t' church every Sunday. A Democrat says if a man wants to have a glass of beer on Sunday he can have it."

During the 1880s, Protestant Republicans infuriated many immigrants and Catholics of Irish, Italian, or German background by promoting efforts to limit or prohibit the consumption of alcoholic beverages. They also pushed for nativist policies designed to restrict immigration and the employment of foreigners.

Among the immigrants crowded into the growing cities were many Irish, Germans, and Italians, all of whom had brought their robust drinking traditions with them into their new country. The mostly rural Protestant Republicans considered saloons the central social evil around which all others revolved, and they associated these evils with the ethnic groups that frequented saloons.

Carrie Nation, the most colorful member of the Women's Christian Temperance Union (WCTU), became nationally known for attacking saloons with a hatchet. Saloons, she argued, stripped a married woman of everything by

"COMING OUT" FOR HARRISON.
Protected Monopolist.—Chuck in your votes there, and don't forget that you're "working for—Kaze!"

"'Coming Out' – For Harrison" This 1888 cartoon depicts efforts by employers to force the working class to vote for the Republican party ticket, including presidential nominee Benjamin Harrison.

turning working men into alcoholics, as had happened with Nation's first husband: "Her husband is torn from her, she is robbed of her sons, her home, her food, and her virtue."

Between 1869 and 1913, from the first term of Ulysses S. Grant through the election of William Howard Taft, Republicans monopolized the White House except for two nonconsecutive terms of New York Democrat Grover Cleveland. Otherwise, national politics was remarkably balanced. Between 1872 and 1896, *no* president won a majority of the popular vote. In each of those presidential elections, sixteen states invariably voted Republican and fourteen, including every southern state, voted Democratic, leaving six "swing" states to determine the outcome. Two of those states, New York and Ohio, decided the election of eight presidents from 1872 to 1908.

Presidents during the Gilded Age, both Republican and Democrat, deferred to their party leaders in the Senate and House of Representatives. They believed that Congress, not the White House, should formulate major policies that the president would implement. As Senator John Sherman of Ohio stressed, "the President should merely obey and enforce the law" as laid out by Congress.

HAYES TO HARRISON

Both Republicans and Democrats had their share of officials willing to buy and sell government jobs or legislative votes. Yet as early as the 1870s, in response to the corruption uncovered in the Grant administration, each party developed factions promoting honesty in government. The struggle for "clean" government became one of the foremost issues of the Gilded Age.

HAYES AND CIVIL SERVICE REFORM

President Rutherford B. Hayes brought to the White House in 1877 both a lingering controversy over the disputed election results (critics called him "His Fraudulency" or "His Accidency") and an uprightness that was in sharp contrast to the barely concealed graft of the Grant era. Hayes appointed a Democrat as postmaster general in an effort to clean up an office infamous for trading jobs for political favors.

The son of an Ohio farmer, Hayes was wounded four times in the Civil War. He went on to serve in Congress and as governor of Ohio. Honest and conservative, he was, said a Republican journalist, a "third-rate nonentity" whose only virtue was that he was "obnoxious to no one."

Hayes had been the compromise presidential nominee of two factions fighting for control of the Republican party, the so-called Stalwarts and

"The Bosses of the Senate" This 1889 cartoon bitingly portrays the period's corrupt alliance between big business and legislators.

Half-Breeds, led, respectively, by Senators Roscoe Conkling of New York and James G. Blaine of Maine. The Stalwarts had been "stalwart" in their support of President Grant during the furor over the misdeeds of his cabinet members. Further, they had mastered the patronage system (spoils system) of distributing political jobs to party loyalists. The Half-Breeds supposedly were only half loyal to Grant and half committed to reform of the spoils system. But in the end, the two factions existed primarily to advance the careers of Conkling and Blaine, who detested each other.

To his credit, President Hayes tried to stay above the petty bickering. He joined the growing public outrage over corruption, admitting that his party "must mend its ways" by focusing on Republican principles rather than fighting over the spoils of office. "He serves his party best who serves his country best," Hayes declared. It was time "for **civil service** [government jobs] **reform**." He appointed a committee to consider a "merit system" for hiring government employees, as used in some European countries. In a dramatic gesture, Hayes also fired Chester A. Arthur, a Stalwart Republican who ran the New York Customs House, because Arthur had abused the patronage system in ways, according to Hayes, that promoted "ignorance, inefficiency, and corruption."

Hayes's commitment to cleaning up politics enraged Republican leaders. In 1879, Ohio congressman James Garfield warned Hayes that "if he wishes to hold any influence" with fellow Republicans, he "must abandon some of his notions of Civil Service reform." For his part, Hayes confessed that he had little hope of success because he was "opposed by . . . the most powerful men in my party."

On economic issues, Hayes held to a conservative line that would guide his successors—from both parties—for the rest of the century. His answer to demands for expansion of the nation's money supply (which would become one of the leading issues of the late nineteenth century) was a resounding no: he vetoed the Bland-Allison Act (1878), a bipartisan effort to increase the supply of silver coins. (More money in circulation was generally believed to raise farm prices and help those trying to pay off debts.) Hayes believed only in "hard money"—gold coins.

When the Democrat-controlled Congress convinced many Republicans to help overturn Hayes's veto, the president confided in his diary that he had become a president without a party. In 1879, with a year still left in his term, Hayes was ready to leave the White House. "I am now in my last year of the Presidency," he wrote a friend, "and look forward to its close as a schoolboy longs for the coming vacation."

GARFIELD, ARTHUR, AND THE PENDLETON ACT

With Hayes choosing not to pursue a second term, the Republican presidential nomination in 1880 was up for grabs. Former president Grant wanted the nomination but was unwilling to campaign for it. In the end, the Stalwarts and Half-Breeds were forced to select a compromise candidate, Congressman James A. Garfield.

Garfield had been a minister, a lawyer, and a college president before serving in the Civil War as a Union army general. In an effort to please the Stalwarts and also win the crucial swing state of New York, the Republicans named Chester A. Arthur, whom Hayes had fired as head of the New York Customs House as their candidate for vice president.

The Democrats, even more divided than the Republicans, selected Winfield Scott Hancock, a retired Union general who had distinguished himself at the Battle of Gettysburg but had done little since. In large part, Hancock was chosen to help deflect the Republicans' "bloody-shirt" attacks on Democrats as the party of the Confederacy. Yet Hancock undermined that effort by supporting southern efforts to strip blacks of voting rights. In an election marked by widespread bribery, Garfield eked out a popular-vote plurality of only 39,000, or 48.5 percent. He won a more comfortable margin of 214 to 155 in the electoral college. Republicans took control of Congress as well.

Embedded in the voting, however, was a worrisome pattern: the Democrats won all the southern states, and the Republicans won all the northern states. Politically, the Civil War was not over. Moreover, in future presidential elections, if the Republicans lost New York State, they would lose the White House. Securing the nation's most-populous state thus became central to Republican strategy.

A PRESIDENCY CUT SHORT In his inaugural address, President Garfield gave an impassioned defense of civil rights, arguing that the "elevation of the negro race from slavery to the full rights of citizenship is the most important political change we have known since the adoption of the Constitution of 1787." The end of slavery, he said, "has added immensely to the moral and industrial forces of our people. It has liberated the master as well as the slave from a relation which wronged and enfeebled both." But he also confirmed that the Republicans had ended efforts to reconstruct the former Confederacy. Southern blacks were on their own now; they had been "surrendered to their own guardianship."

In the continuing feud between the Half-Breed and Stalwart factions of the Republican party, Garfield chose the Half-Breeds. He appointed James G. Blaine as secretary of state over the objection of Ulysses S. Grant, leading the former president to tell reporters that Garfield "is a man without backbone. A man of fine ability but lacking stamina. He wants to please everybody."

Garfield would have no time to prove himself as president, however. On July 2, 1881, after only four months in office, he was walking through the Washington, D.C., railroad station, headed to a vacation in Vermont, when he was shot in the arm and back by Charles Guiteau, a former Republican who had been turned down for a federal job. As a policeman wrestled the assassin to the ground, Guiteau shouted: "Yes! I have killed Garfield! [Chester] Arthur is President of the United States. I am a Stalwart!"—a declaration that would eventually destroy the Stalwart wing of the Republican party.

On September 19, after seventy-nine days, Garfield died of complications resulting from inept medical care. During a sensational ten-week trial, Guiteau said that God had ordered him to kill the president. The jury refused to believe that he was insane and pronounced him guilty of murder. On June 30, 1882, Guiteau was hanged; an autopsy revealed that his brain was diseased.

THE CIVIL SERVICE COMMISSION In their grief over Garfield's death, Americans blamed Roscoe Conkling and the Stalwart Republicans for inciting Guiteau. One New York newspaper headline read: "murdered by the spoils system!"

People saw little potential in the new president, Chester A. Arthur, who had been Roscoe Conkling's trusted lieutenant. Grant wrote an associate that he did not "expect much from this administration." Yet Arthur surprised most political observers by distancing himself from Conkling and the Stalwarts and becoming a civil service reformer. Throughout his presidency, he kept a promise not to remove any federal office holder purely for political reasons. He also made cabinet appointments based on merit rather than partisanship. One of Arthur's former New York associates, a Stalwart, grumbled that "he has done less for us than Garfield, or even Hayes."

Very little is known about President Arthur. Just before he died, he had all of his official papers and correspondence burned. Why he did so remains a mystery. Unlike most presidents, there is no library or museum dedicated to Arthur's career. He wanted obscurity and he got it.

In 1883, momentum against the spoils system generated by Garfield's assassination enabled George H. Pendleton, a Democratic senator from Ohio, to convince Congress to establish a Civil Service Commission, the first federal regulatory agency. Because of the Pendleton Civil Service Reform Act, at least 15 percent of federal jobs would now be filled on the basis of competitive tests (the "merit system") rather than political favoritism. In addition, federal employees running for office were prohibited from receiving political contributions from other government workers.

The Pendleton Act was a limited first step in cleaning up the patronage process. It was sorely needed, in part because the federal government was expanding rapidly. By 1901, there would be 256,000 federal employees, five times the number in 1871. A growing number of these federal workers were women, who by 1890 held a third of the government's clerical jobs.

The Campaign of 1884

Chester Arthur's efforts to clean up the spoils system might have attracted voters, but they did not please Republican leaders. So in 1884 the Republicans dumped the ailing Arthur (he had contracted a kidney disease) and chose as their nominee James Gillespie Blaine of Maine, the handsome, colorful secretary of state, former senator, and longtime leader of the Half-Breeds.

Blaine inspired the party faithful with his electrifying speeches, and he knew how to wheel and deal in the backrooms. One critic charged that Blaine "wallowed in spoils like a rhinoceros in an African pool." Newspapers soon uncovered evidence of his corruption in the so-called Mulligan letters, which revealed that, as Speaker of the House, Blaine had secretly sold his votes on measures favorable to a railroad corporation. Nobody proved that he had committed any crimes, but the circumstantial evidence was powerful: his senatorial salary alone could not have built either his mansion in Washington, D.C., nor his palatial home in Augusta, Maine.

During the presidential campaign, more embarrassing letters surfaced linking Blaine to shady deal making. In one of them, Blaine told the recipient: "Burn this letter!" For the reform element of the Republican party, this was too much, and many independent-minded Republicans refused to endorse Blaine's candidacy. "We are Republicans but we are not slaves," said one of the independents. He insisted that the party of Lincoln must recommit itself to "retrenchment, purity and reform." Party regulars scorned such critics as "goo-goos"—the "good-government" crowd who were outraged

Senator James Gillespie Blaine of Maine The Republican presidential candidate in 1884.

by the corrupting influence of money in politics. The editor of a New York newspaper jokingly called the anti-Blaine Republicans **Mugwumps**, after an Algonquian Indian word meaning "big chief."

The Mugwumps, a self-appointed group of reformers dedicated to promoting honest government, saw the election as a "moral rather than political" contest. Centered in the large cities and major universities of the northeast, the Mugwumps were mostly professors, editors, and writers who included in their number the most famous American of the time, writer and humorist Mark Twain. Like the Liberal Republicans before them, the Mugwumps sought to reform the patronage system by declaring that *all* federal jobs would be filled solely on the basis of merit. Their break with the Republican party over patronage testified to the depth of their convictions.

The rise of the Mugwumps, as well as growing national concerns about political corruption, prompted the Democrats to nominate New Yorker Grover Cleveland. Cleveland had first attracted national attention in 1881, when he was elected mayor of Buffalo on an anti-corruption platform. He was elected governor of New York in 1882, and he continued to build a reform record by fighting New York City's corrupt Tammany Hall ring. As mayor and as governor, he repeatedly vetoed bills that he felt served private interests at the expense of the public good. He supported civil service reform, opposed expanding the money supply, and preferred free trade to high tariffs.

Although Cleveland was known for his honesty and integrity, he was hurt by two personal issues: the discovery that he had paid for a substitute to take his place in the Union army during the Civil War, and a juicy sex scandal that erupted when a Buffalo newspaper revealed that Cleveland, a bachelor, had befriended an attractive widow named Maria Halpin, who named him the father of her baby born in 1874. Cleveland had discreetly provided financial support for the child.

The escapades of Blaine and Cleveland inspired some of the most colorful battle cries in political history: "Blaine, Blaine, James G. Blaine, the continental liar from the state of Maine," Democrats chanted. Republicans countered with "Ma, ma, where's my pa?" Democrats also paraded through the streets chanting, "Burn this letter!"

Near the end of the nasty campaign, Blaine and his supporters committed two fateful blunders in the crucial state of New York. The first occurred at New York City's fashionable Delmonico's restaurant, where Blaine went to a private dinner with 200 of the nation's wealthiest business leaders to ask them to help finance his campaign. Accounts of the unseemly event appeared in the newspapers for days afterward. One headline blared: "Blaine Hobnobbing with the Mighty Money Kings!" The article explained that the banquet was intended to collect contributions for a "Republican corruption fund."

Blaine's second blunder occurred when a Protestant minister visiting Republican headquarters in New York referred to the Democrats as the party

Grover Cleveland As president, Cleveland made the issue of tariff reform central to the politics of the late 1880s.

of "rum, Romanism, and rebellion [the Confederacy]." Blaine, who was present, let pass the implied insult to Catholics—a fatal oversight, since he had cultivated Irish American support with his anti-English talk and repeated references to his mother being a Catholic. Democrats claimed that Blaine was, at heart, anti-Irish and anti-Catholic.

The two incidents may have tipped the 1884 presidential election. The electoral vote was 219 to 182 in Cleveland's favor, but the popular vote ran far closer: Cleveland's plurality was fewer than 30,000 votes out of 10 million cast. Cleveland won New York by only 1,149 votes out of 1,167,169 cast. At long last, a Democrat was back in the White House.

Cleveland's Reform Efforts

During his first few months in office, President Cleveland struggled to keep Democratic leaders from reviving the self-serving patronage system. In a letter to a friend, the new president reported that he was living in a "nightmare," that "dreadful, damnable, office-seeking hangs over me and surrounds me" and that it made him "feel like resigning." Democratic newspapers heaped scorn on him for refusing to award federal jobs to his supporters. One accused Cleveland of "ingratitude" toward those who had "delivered the vote." Despite the president's best efforts, about two-thirds of the 120,000 federal jobs went to Democrats as patronage during his administration.

Cleveland was an old-style Democrat who believed in minimal government activity. During his first term, he vetoed over 400 acts of Congress, more than twice as many as all previous presidents combined. In 1887, he illustrated his "do as little as possible" philosophy by vetoing a congressional effort to provide desperate Texas farmers with seeds in the aftermath of a terrible drought. "Though the people support the government, the government should not support the people," Cleveland asserted.

RAILROAD REGULATION For all of his commitment to limited government intervention, President Cleveland urged Congress to adopt an important new policy: federal regulation of the rates charged by interstate railroads (those whose tracks crossed state lines) to ship goods, crops, or livestock. He believed that railroads were charging unfairly high freight rates. States had adopted laws regulating railroads since the late 1860s, but in 1886 the Supreme Court declared in *Wabash, St. Louis, and Pacific Railroad Company v. Illinois* that no state could regulate the rates charged by railroads engaged in interstate traffic. Because most railroads crossed state lines, Cleveland urged Congress to close the loophole.

Congress followed through, and in 1887, Cleveland signed an act creating the **Interstate Commerce Commission (ICC)**, the first federal regulatory agency. The law empowered the ICC's five members to ensure that railroad freight rates were "reasonable and just." But one senator called the new agency "a delusion and a sham" because its members tended to be former railroad executives. Moreover, the commission's actual powers proved to be weak when challenged in the courts by railroads. Over time, the ICC came to be ignored, and the railroads continued to charge high rates while making secret pricing deals with large shippers.

TARIFF REFORM AND THE ELECTION OF 1888 President Cleveland's most dramatic challenge to Big Business focused on **tariff reform**.

During the late nineteenth century, the government's high-tariff policies, shaped largely by the Republican party, had favored American manufacturers by effectively shutting out foreign imports, thereby enabling U.S. corporations to dominate the marketplace and charge higher prices for their products. Tariffs on some 4,000 imported items had also brought in more revenue from foreign manufacturers than the federal government spent. As a result, the tariff revenues were producing an annual government surplus, which proved to Cleveland and the Democrats that the rates were too high.

In 1887, Cleveland argued that Congress should reduce both the tariff rates ("the vicious, inequitable and illogical source of unnecessary taxation . . . [and] a burden upon the poor") and the number of imported goods subject to tariffs to enable European companies to compete in the American marketplace. His outspoken stance set the stage for his reelection campaign in 1888.

To oppose Cleveland, the Republicans, now calling themselves the GOP (Grand Old Party) to emphasize their longevity, turned to the obscure Benjamin Harrison, a Civil War veteran whose greatest attributes were his availability and the fact that he was from Indiana, a pivotal state in presidential elections. The grandson of President William Henry Harrison, he had a modest political record; he had lost a race for governor and had served one term in the U.S. Senate (1881–1887). In the eyes of the party leadership, however, Harrison had the most important attribute: he would do as he was told.

The Republicans accepted Cleveland's challenge to make tariffs the chief issue in the campaign. They enjoyed a huge advantage in campaign funding, as business executives contributed generously to their campaign.

Still, the outcome was incredibly close. Cleveland won the popular vote by the thinnest of margins—5,540,329 to 5,439,853—but Harrison carried crucial New York State and the electoral college by 233 to 168. "Providence," said the new president, "has given us the victory." Matthew Quay, the powerful Republican boss of Pennsylvania who managed Harrison's campaign, knew better. Harrison, he muttered, "ought to know that Providence hadn't a damned thing to do with it! [A] number of men were compelled to approach the penitentiary to make him President."

Quay's decision to distribute campaign money in key states and to promise federal jobs to loyalists also helped Republicans gain control of the House and the Senate. As the Republicans prepared for the inauguration, *Frank Leslie's Illustrated Newspaper*, co-edited by Harrison's son Russell, made clear the new president's priorities: "This is to be a businessman's Administration," and "businessmen will be thoroughly well content with it."

Republican Activism Under Harrison

Harrison owed a heavy debt to Civil War veterans, whose votes had been critical to his election, and he paid it by signing the Dependent Pension Act. As a result, the number of Union war veterans (and their family members) receiving federal pensions almost doubled between 1889 and 1893.

The Republicans also took advantage of their control of Congress to pass a cluster of significant legislation in 1890: the Sherman Anti-Trust Act, the Sherman Silver Purchase Act, the McKinley Tariff Act, and the admission of Idaho and Wyoming as new states, which followed the admission of North and South Dakota, Montana, and Washington in 1889.

The Sherman Anti-Trust Act, named for Ohio senator John Sherman, prohibited powerful corporations from "conspiring" to establish monopolies or "restrain trade" in their industries. It made the United States the first nation in the world to outlaw monopolistic business practices.

Though badly needed, the Sherman Anti-Trust Act was a toothless hoax intended to make it appear that Congress was clamping down on the gigantic corporations dominating more and more industries. That it passed without any opposition suggested that the bill was mostly for show. Critics called it the "Swiss Cheese Act" because it had so many holes in its language. As the *New York Times* recognized in 1890, the "so-called Anti-Trust law" was passed "to deceive the people" and prepare the way for a much higher tariff bill. Senator Sherman, the article added, supported this "humbug" of a law so that party spokesmen "might say 'Behold! We have attacked the trusts. The Republican Party is the enemy of all such rings.'"

The Sherman Anti-Trust Act was rarely enforced, in large part because of its vague definitions of "trusts" and "monopolies." From 1890 to 1901, only eighteen lawsuits were instituted, four of which were filed against labor unions rather than corporations, claiming that striking workers were "conspiring" to "restrain trade."

BILLION- DOLLARISM ? HOLE

A billion-dollar hole In an attack on Benjamin Harrison's spending policies, Harrison is shown pouring Cleveland's huge surplus down a hole.

"King of the World" Reformers targeted the growing power of monopolies, such as that of John D. Rockefeller's Standard Oil.

The Sherman Silver Purchase Act (1890), which required the Treasury to purchase 4.5 million ounces of silver each month to convert into dollar coins, was an effort by the Republicans to please the new western states with numerous silver mines. The bill's sponsor, Senator John Sherman, admitted that he proposed the bill only to defuse cries for the "unlimited coinage" of silver. "I voted for it," he confessed, "but the day it became law I was ready to repeal it." The Sherman act helped set the stage for the currency issue to eclipse all others during the financial panic that would sweep the country in 1893.

As for tariff policy, Republicans viewed their victory as a mandate to reward the support of large corporations by raising tariff rates even higher. Piloted through Congress by Ohio representative William McKinley, the McKinley Tariff Act of 1890 raised duties (taxes) on imported manufactured goods to their highest level ever and added many agricultural products to the tariff list to appease farmers. Its passage encouraged many businesses to raise prices, because their European competitors were now effectively shut out of the U.S. market. The *New York Times* expressed the indignation of many voters when it charged in a huge headline: "MCKINLEY'S PICKPOCKETS [WERE] PAYING A PARTY DEBT" to large corporate donors by passing the new tariff bill.

The Republican efforts to reward Big Business backfired, however. In the November 1890 congressional elections, Democrats won big, regaining control of the House by a three to one margin. William McKinley, who had sponsored the tariff bill, lost his seat (although the following year he would be elected Ohio's governor). In the Senate, the Republican majority was reduced to four. Republicans were "astounded and dazed" by the shellacking in the election. Even more worrisome was the emergence of the Populists, a new political party representing disgruntled farmers and wage laborers. Revolution was in the air.

FARMERS AND THE "MONEY PROBLEM"

More than tariffs, trusts, and efforts to clean up political corruption, national politics during the Gilded Age was preoccupied with monetary issues. The nation's money supply had not grown along with the expanding economy. From 1865 to 1890, the amount of money in circulation (both coins and paper currency) actually *decreased* about 10 percent.

Such currency deflation raised the cost of borrowing money as the shrinking money supply enabled lenders to hike interest rates on loans. Creditors—bankers and others who loaned money—supported a "sound money" policy limiting the currency supply as a means of increasing their profits. By contrast, farmers, ranchers, miners, and others who had to borrow money to make ends meet claimed that the "sound money" policy lowered prices for their crops and herds and drove them deeper into debt. Farmers in the Midwest, Great Plains, and South, and miners in the West, demanded more paper money and the increased coinage of silver, which would inflate the currency supply, raise commodity prices, and provide them with more income.

In 1876, several farm organizations across the nation had organized the independent "Greenback" party to promote the benefits of paper money over gold and silver coins; "Greenbackers" won fifteen seats in Congress in 1878, illustrating the significance of currency issues to voters. Although the Greenback party died out, the demands for increasing the money supply survived. All six western states admitted to the Union in 1889 and 1890 had substantial silver mines, and their new congressional delegations—largely Republican—wanted the federal government to buy more silver for minting as coins.

AGRICULTURAL UNREST The 1890 congressional elections revealed a deep-seated unrest in the farming communities of the South, on the plains of Kansas and Nebraska, and in the mining towns of the Rocky Mountain region. Over the previous twenty years, corn prices had fallen by a third, wheat by more than half, cotton by two-thirds. The drastic decline in prices was caused by overproduction and growing international competition in world food markets. The vast new lands brought under cultivation in the plains as a result of the extension of rail lines and the use of new farm machinery poured an ever-increasing supply of grains into world markets, driving prices down.

Meanwhile, farmers in the South and West had become increasingly indebted to local banks or merchants who loaned them money at high interest rates to buy seed, fertilizer, tools, and other supplies. As prices for their crops dropped, however, so did the income the farmers received, thus preventing them from paying their debts on time.

In response, most farmers had no choice but to grow even more wheat, cotton, or corn, but the increased supply pushed down prices and incomes even further. High tariffs on imported goods also hurt farmers because they allowed U.S. companies to raise the prices of manufactured goods needed by farm families.

Besides bankers, merchants, and high tariffs, struggling farmers blamed the railroads, warehouse owners, and food processors—the so-called middlemen—who helped get crops and livestock to market. Farmers especially resented that railroads, most of which had a monopoly over the shipping of grains and animals, charged such high rates to ship agricultural products.

At the same time that farm income was dropping, successive years of parched summers and bitterly cold winters had destroyed harvests in many states. "This season is without parallel in this part of the country," reported the editor of a Nebraska agricultural journal in 1891. "The hot winds burned up the entire crop, leaving thousands of families wholly destitute" and vulnerable to the "money loaners and sharks" charging criminal rates of interest. In a slap at the cutthroat capitalism justified by the heartless logic of social Darwinism, the editor dismissed the popular slogan "survival of the fittest" as a "satanic creed" that means "slavery to millions."

In drought-devastated Kansas in 1890, Populists won five congressional seats from Republicans. In early 1891, the newly elected Populists and Democrats took control of Congress just as an acute economic crisis appeared on the horizon: farmers' debts were mounting as crop prices continued to fall.

THE GRANGER MOVEMENT When the Department of Agriculture sent Oliver H. Kelley on a tour of the South in 1866, he was struck by the social isolation of people living on small farms. To address the problem, Kelley helped found the National Grange of the Patrons of Husbandry, better known as the Grange (an old word for places where crops were stored).

The Grange grew quickly, reaching a membership of 858,000 men and women by 1875. It started out offering social events and educational programs for farmers and their families, but as it grew, it began to promote "cooperatives" where farmers could join together to store and sell their crops to avoid the high fees charged by brokers and other middlemen.

In five Midwest states, Grange chapters persuaded legislatures to pass "Granger laws" to regulate the prices charged by railroads and grain warehouses (called "elevators"). Railroad and warehouse owners challenged the laws, but in *Munn v. Illinois* (1877), the Supreme Court ruled that states had the right to regulate property that operated in the public interest. Nine years later, however, the Court threw out the *Munn* ruling, finding in

"I Feed You All!" (1875) The farmer is the cornerstone of American society, according to this Granger-inspired poster. Without the food he produces, no man in any occupation can do his job—including the railroad magnate (left) and warehouse owners who try to exploit him.

Wabash v. Illinois that only Congress could regulate industries involved in interstate commerce.

FARMERS' ALLIANCES The Granger movement failed to address the foremost concerns of struggling farmers: declining crop prices and the inadequate amount of money in circulation. As a result, people shifted their allegiance to a new organization called the Farmers' Alliance. Like the Grange, the Farmers' Alliances organized social and recreational activities for small farmers and their families while also emphasizing political action and economic cooperation to address the hardships caused by chronic indebtedness, declining crop prices, and droughts.

Emerging first in Texas, the Alliance movement swept across the South, Kansas, Nebraska, and the Dakotas. In 1886, a white minister in Texas responded to the appeals of African American farmers by organizing the Colored Farmers' National Alliance. By 1890, the white Alliance movement had about 1.5 million members, and the Colored Farmers' National Alliance claimed more than 1 million members. Most white Alliance members refused to integrate their efforts with blacks, not only because of racism but also because most black farmers were tenants and sharecroppers rather than landowners. Although many landless farmers supported the Alliances, the majority of members were landowners who sold their crops in the marketplace.

In the states west of the Mississippi River, political activism intensified after record blizzards in 1887, which killed most of the cattle and hogs across the northern plains, and a prolonged drought two years later that destroyed millions of acres of corn, wheat, and oats. Distressed farmers lashed out against what they considered to be a powerful conspiracy of eastern financial and industrial interests, which they variously called "monopolies," "the money power," or "Wall Street." As William Jennings Bryan, a Democratic congressman from Nebraska, explained: "We simply say to the East: take your hands out of our pockets and keep them out."

The Alliances called for the federal government to take ownership of the railroads and create an income tax on wealthy Americans. They also organized economic "cooperatives" to bind together their collective strength. In 1887, Charles W. Macune, the Southern Alliance president, explained that "the Alliance is the people and the people are together." He exhorted Texas farmers to create their own Alliance Exchange to free themselves from dependence on commercial warehouses, grain elevators, food processors, and banks. Members of the Alliance Exchange would act collectively, pooling their resources to borrow money from banks and purchase their goods and supplies from a new corporation created by the Alliance in Dallas. The exchange would also build warehouses to store and market members' crops. With these crops as collateral, members would receive cash loans to buy household goods and agricultural supplies. Once the farmers sold their crops, they would pay back the loans provided by the Alliance warehouse.

This *cooperative* scheme collapsed when Texas banks refused to accept paper money. Undaunted, Alliance members then focused on what Macune called a "subtreasury plan," whereby farmers would store their crops in *government*-run warehouses and obtain cash loans for up to 80 percent of the crops' value. This would free them from their traditional dependence on banks that charged high interest rates. Besides providing immediate credit, the subtreasury plan would allow farmers the option of storing a crop in hopes of getting a better price later. The plan would also promote inflation of the money supply because the loans to farmers would be made in new paper money. Monetary inflation was popular with farmers because it allowed them to repay their debts with cheaper money.

Despite the strong support from farmers, however, Congress nixed the subtreasury plan in 1890. Its defeat, as well as setbacks to other Alliance proposals, convinced many farm leaders that they needed more political power to secure the reforms necessary to save the agricultural sector: railroad regulation, currency inflation, state departments of agriculture, anti-trust laws, and more accessible farm-based credit (loans).

About one-fourth of Alliance members were women. The Alliance welcomed rural women and men over sixteen years of age who displayed a "good moral character," believed in God, and demonstrated "industrious habits." The slogan of the Southern Alliance was "equal rights to all, special privileges to none." A North Carolina woman relished the "grand opportunities" the Alliance provided women, allowing them to emerge from household drudgeries. "Drudgery, fashion, and gossip," she declared, "are no longer the bounds of woman's sphere." One Alliance publication made the point explicitly: "The Alliance has come to redeem woman from her enslaved condition, and place her in her proper sphere." The number of women in the movement grew rapidly, and many assumed key leadership roles in the "grand army of reform."

NEW THIRD PARTIES The Alliances called for third-party political action to address their concerns. In 1890, farm activists in Colorado joined with miners and railroad workers to form the Independent party, and Nebraska farmers formed the People's Independent party. Leonidas Polk, a former Confederate general who was the head of the North Carolina Alliance, traveled to Kansas and was so impressed by the size of the open-air farm rallies that he declared that farmers across the nation "have risen up and inaugurated a movement such as the world has never seen."

In the South, the Alliance movement forced Democrats to nominate candidates who supported its farm program and succeeded in electing four of them as governors, forty-four as congressmen, and several as U.S. senators, as well as seven pro-Alliance state legislatures. Among the most respected of the southern Alliance leaders was Thomas E. Watson, a lawyer from Georgia. The son of prosperous slaveholders who had lost everything after the Civil War, Watson took the lead in urging black and white tenant farmers to join forces. "You are [racially] kept apart," he told blacks and whites, "that you may be separately fleeced of your earnings." He insisted on cooperation by black and white farmers to resist the power of the wealthy political elite in the South.

In Kansas, Mary Elizabeth Lease emerged as a fiery speaker for the farm protest movement. Born in Pennsylvania to Irish immigrants, Lease migrated to Kansas, taught school, raised a family, and failed at farming in the mid-1880s. She then studied law and became one of the state's first female attorneys.

Mary Elizabeth Lease A charismatic leader in the farm protest movement.

A proud, tall, and imposing woman with a magical voice, Lease began giving fiery speeches during the 1890s on behalf of struggling farmers. "The people are at bay," she warned; "let the bloodhounds of money beware." She urged angry farmers to take control "with the ballot if possible, but if not that way then with the bayonet."

Like so many Alliance supporters, Lease viewed Eastern financiers as the enemy. "Wall Street owns the country. It is no longer a government of the people, by the people, and for the people, but a government of Wall Street, by Wall Street, and for Wall Street. The great common people of this country are slaves, and monopoly is the master." The two political parties "lie to us" in blaming farmers for overproduction, "when 10,000 little children starve to death every year in the United States." She declared that the Alliances wanted to abolish "loan-shark" banks and replace them with subtreasury warehouses that would make loans to farmers backed up by their stored crops.

THE ELECTION OF 1892 In 1892, Alliance leaders organized a convention in Omaha, Nebraska, at which they formed the **People's party (Populists)**. The delegates approved a platform that called for unlimited coinage of silver, a "progressive" income tax whose rates would rise with income levels, and federal ownership of the railroads. The Populists also endorsed the eight-hour workday and new laws restricting immigration, for fear that foreigners were taking Americans' jobs. "We meet in the midst of a nation brought to the verge of moral, political, and material ruin," the Populists announced. "The fruits of toil of millions are boldly stolen to build up colossal fortunes for a few. . . ."

The Populist party's platform turned out to be more exciting than its presidential candidate: Iowa's James B. Weaver, a former Union army officer who had headed the Greenback party ticket twelve years earlier. The major parties renominated the same candidates who had run in 1888: Democrat Grover Cleveland and Republican president Benjamin Harrison. Each major candidate received more than 5 million votes, but Cleveland won a majority

The Populist party A Populist gathering in Callaway, Nebraska, 1892.

of the electoral college. Weaver received more than 1 million votes and carried Colorado, Kansas, Nevada, and Idaho. Alabama was the banner Populist state of the South, with 37 percent of its vote going to Weaver.

THE DEPRESSION OF 1893 AND THE "FREE SILVER" CRUSADE

While farmers were funneling their discontent into politics, a fundamental weakness in the economy was about to cause a major collapse and a social rebellion. Just ten days before Grover Cleveland was inaugurated in the winter of 1893, the Philadelphia and Reading Railroad declared bankruptcy, setting off a national financial crisis, now called the **Panic of 1893**. It grew into the worst depression the nation had ever experienced.

Other overextended railroads collapsed, taking many banks with them. European investors withdrew their funds from America. A quarter of unskilled urban workers lost their jobs, many others had their wages cut, and by the fall of 1893, more than 600 banks had closed and 15,000 businesses had failed. Farm foreclosures soared in the South and West, and by 1900, a third of all American farmers rented their land rather than owned it.

By 1894, the nation's economy had reached bottom. But the depression lasted another four years, with unemployment hovering at 20 percent. In New York City, the rate was close to 35 percent.

National panic The New York Stock Exchange on the morning of Friday, May 5, 1893.

President Cleveland's response was recklessly conservative: he convinced Congress to return the nation's money supply to a gold standard by repealing the Sherman Silver Purchase Act of 1890, a move that made the depression worse. The weak economy needed *more* money in circulation, not *less*. Investors rushed to exchange their silver dollars for gold, further constricting the money supply.

Hard times triggered a wave of labor unrest. In 1894, some 750,000 workers went on strike. Railroad construction workers, laid off in the West, began tramping east and talked of marching on Washington, D.C.

One protest group, called Coxey's Army, was led by "General" Jacob S. Coxey, a wealthy Ohio quarry owner turned Populist who demanded that the federal government provide the unemployed with meaningful work. Coxey, his wife, and their son, Legal Tender Coxey, rode in a carriage ahead of some 400 protesters who marched hundreds of miles to Washington, D.C., where police arrested Coxey for walking on the grass. Although his ragtag army dispersed peacefully, the march, as well as the growing strength of Populism, struck fear into the hearts of many conservatives.

Republicans portrayed Populists as "tramps" and "hayseed socialists" whose election would endanger the capitalist system. The Populists responded by charging that Americans were divided into "tramps and millionaires."

In this climate of class warfare and social anxiety, the 1894 congressional elections devastated President Cleveland and the Democrats, who were blamed for the economic crisis. The Republicans gained 118 seats in the House, the largest increase ever. Only in the solid Democratic South did the party retain its advantage. The Populists emerged with six senators and seven representatives, and they expected the festering discontent in rural areas to carry them to national power in 1896. Their hopes would be dashed, however.

SILVERITES VERSUS GOLDBUGS Cleveland's decision to repeal the Sherman Silver Purchase Act created an irreparable division in his party. One pro-silver Democrat labeled the president a traitor. Politicians from western states with large silver mines increased their demands for the "unlimited" coinage of silver, presenting a strategic dilemma for Populists: should the party promote the long list of reforms it had originally advocated, or should it try to ride the silver issue into power?

Although flooding the economy with silver currency would probably not have provided the benefits its advocates claimed, the "free silver" crusade had taken on powerful symbolic overtones. Over the protests of more-radical members, Populist leaders decided to hold their 1896 nominating convention *after* the two major-party conventions, confident that the Republicans and Democrats would at best straddle the silver issue and enable the Populists to lure away pro-silver advocates from both.

The major parties, however, took opposite positions on the currency issue. The Republicans, as expected, nominated William McKinley, a former congressman and governor of Ohio, on a platform committed to gold coins as the only form of currency. A small but vocal group of "Silver Republicans" from western states, led by Senator Henry Teller of Colorado, were so upset that they stormed out of the convention. After the convention, a friend told McKinley that the **"money question"** would determine the election. He was right.

The Democratic convention, held in Chicago, was one of the great turning points in political history. The pro-silver, largely rural delegates surprised the party leadership and the "Gold Democrats," or "goldbugs," by capturing control of the convention.

WILLIAM JENNINGS BRYAN Thirty-six-year-old William Jennings Bryan of Nebraska gave the final speech before the balloting began. A fiery evangelical moralist, Bryan was a two-term congressman who had lost a race for the Senate in 1894, when Democrats by the dozens were swept out of office. In the months before the convention, he had traveled throughout the South and West, speaking passionately for the unlimited coinage of silver, attacking Cleveland's "do-nothing" response to the depression, and endorsing both Democrats and Populists who embraced the cause of "free silver."

Bryan was a compelling speaker, a crusading preacher in the role of a Populist politician. In his carefully crafted and well-rehearsed speech, he claimed that two ideas about the role of government were competing for the American voter. The Republicans, he said, believed "that if you just legislate to make the well-to-do prosperous, that their prosperity will leak through on those below."

The Democrats, by contrast, believed "that if you legislate to make the masses prosperous their prosperity will find its way up and through every class that rests upon it." For his part, Bryan spoke for the "producing masses of this nation" against the eastern "financial magnates" who had "enslaved" them by manipulating the money supply to ensure high interest rates.

As Bryan brought his electrifying twenty-minute speech to a climax, he fused Christian imagery with Populist anger:

> I come to speak to you in defense of a cause as holy as the cause of liberty—the cause of humanity. . . . We have petitioned, and our petitions have been scorned. . . . We have begged, and they have mocked when our calamity came. We beg no longer; we entreat no more; we petition no more. We defy them!

Bryan then identified himself with Jesus Christ. Sweeping his fingers across his forehead, he shouted: "You shall not press down upon the brow of labor this crown of thorns. You shall not crucify mankind upon a cross of gold!"—

William Jennings Bryan His "cross of gold" speech at the 1896 Democratic Convention roused the delegates and secured him the party's presidential nomination.

at which point he extended his arms straight out from his sides, as if he were being crucified. His riveting performance worked better than even he could have imagined. As he strode triumphantly off the stage, the delegates erupted in wild applause. "Everybody seemed to go mad at once," reported the *New York World*.

For their part, the Republicans were not all amused by Bryan's antics. A Republican newspaper observed that no political movement had "ever before spawned such hideous and repulsive vipers." Theodore Roosevelt claimed that Bryan was a demagogue with an "unsound mind" who was promoting mob rule by "the shiftless and the disorderly and the criminal and the semi-criminal" elements of society.

The next day, Bryan won the presidential nomination on the fifth ballot, but in the process the Democratic party was fractured. Disappointed Democrats who had supported Grover Cleveland dismissed Bryan as a fanatic and a socialist. They were so alienated by his positions and his rhetoric that they walked out of the convention and nominated their own candidate, Senator John M. Palmer of Illinois. "Fellow Democrats," Palmer announced, "I will not consider it any great fault if you decide to cast your vote for William McKinley."

When the Populists gathered in St. Louis for their nominating convention two weeks later, they faced an impossible choice. They could name their own candidate and divide the pro-silver vote with the Democrats, or they could endorse Bryan and probably lose their identity. In the end, they backed Bryan but chose their own vice-presidential candidate, Thomas E. Watson, and invited the Democrats to drop their vice-presidential nominee. Bryan refused the offer.

THE ELECTION OF 1896 The election of 1896 was one of the most dramatic in history, in part because of the striking contrast between the candidates and in part because the terrible depression made the stakes so high. One observer said that the campaign "took the form of religious frenzy." Indeed, Bryan campaigned like the evangelist he was. He was the first major candidate since Andrew Jackson to champion the poor, the discontented, and the oppressed. He excited struggling farmers, miners, and union members. And he was the first leader of a major party to call for the expansion of the federal government to help the working class.

No one loved campaigning more than Bryan. He traveled some 18,000 miles by train, visiting 26 states and 250 cities and towns, delivering impassioned speeches. His populist crusade was for whites only, however. Like so many otherwise progressive Democratic leaders, Bryan never challenged

Presidential campaign badges On the left wings of the "goldbug" and "silverite" badges are McKinley (top) and Bryan (bottom), with their running mates on the right.

the practices of racial segregation and violence against blacks in the solidly Democratic South. And he alienated many working-class Catholics in northern states by supporting prohibition of alcoholic beverages.

McKinley, meanwhile, stayed at home and kept his mouth shut, letting other Republicans speak for him. He knew he could not compete with Bryan as a speaker, so he conducted a "front-porch campaign," welcoming supporters at his home in Canton, Ohio, and giving only prepared statements to the press which warned middle-class voters of the dangers of Bryan's ideas. McKinley's brilliant campaign manager, Marcus "Mark" Hanna, shrewdly portrayed Bryan as a "Popocrat," a radical whose "communistic spirit" would ruin the capitalist system and stir up a class war. Hanna convinced the Republican party to declare that it was "unreservedly for sound money"—meaning gold coins.

By appealing to such fears, the Republicans raised vast sums of money from corporations and wealthy donors to finance an army of 1,400 speakers who

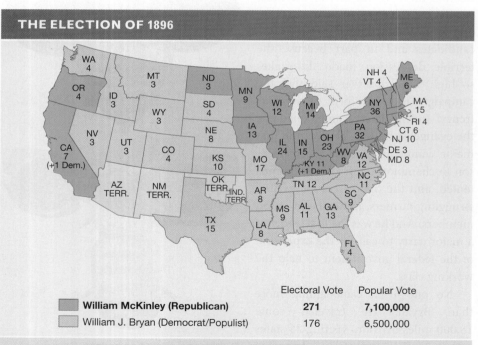

THE ELECTION OF 1896

	Electoral Vote	Popular Vote
William McKinley (Republican)	271	7,100,000
William J. Bryan (Democrat/Populist)	176	6,500,000

- How did Bryan's "cross of gold" speech divide the Democratic party?
- How did McKinley's campaign strategy differ from Bryan's?
- Why was Bryan able to carry the West and the South but unable to win in cities and the Northeast?

traveled the country promoting McKinley. It was the most sophisticated—and expensive—presidential campaign in history to that point.

In the end, Bryan won the most votes of any candidate in history—6.5 million—but McKinley won even more: 7.1 million. The better-organized and better-financed Republicans won the electoral college vote by 271 to 176.

Bryan carried most of the West and all of the South but found little support in the North and East. In the critical Midwest, from Minnesota and Iowa eastward to Ohio, he did not win a state. His evangelical Protestantism repelled many Roman Catholic voters, who were normally drawn to the Democrats. Farmers in the Northeast, moreover, were less attracted to radical reform than were farmers in the West and South. Workers in the cities found it easier to identify with McKinley's focus on reviving the industrial economy than with Bryan's farm-based, free-silver evangelism. Of the nation's twenty largest cities, Bryan carried only New Orleans.

Although Bryan lost, he launched the Democratic party's shift from pro-business conservatism to its eventual twentieth-century role as a party of liberal reform. The Populist party, however, virtually disintegrated. Having won a million votes in 1896, it collected only 50,000 in 1900. Conversely, McKinley's victory climaxed a generation-long struggle for political control of an industrialized urban America. The Republicans would be dominant for sixteen years.

By 1897, when McKinley was inaugurated, economic prosperity was returning. Part of the reason was inflation of the currency, which bore out the arguments of the Greenbackers and silverites that the nation's money supply had been inadequate during the Gilded Age. But inflation came, in one of history's many ironies, not from more greenbacks or silver dollars but from a flood of gold discovered in South Africa, northwest Canada, and Alaska. In 1900, Congress passed, and McKinley signed, a bill affirming that the nation's money supply would be based only on gold.

Even though the Populist movement faded after William Jennings Bryan's defeat, most of the ideas promoted by Bryan Democrats and Populists, dismissed as too radical in 1896, would be implemented over the next two decades by a more diverse coalition of Democrats and Republicans who would call themselves "progressives."

CHAPTER REVIEW

SUMMARY

- **America's Move to Town**   America's cities grew in all directions during the *Gilded Age*. Electric elevators and steel-frame construction allowed architects to extend buildings upward, and mass transit enabled the middle class to retreat to suburbs. Crowded *tenements* bred disease and crime and created an opportunity for urban *party bosses* to accrue power, in part by distributing to the poor various forms of assistance.

- **The New Immigration**   By 1900, an estimated 30 percent of Americans living in major cities were foreign-born, with the majority of "*new immigrants*" coming from eastern and southern Europe rather than western and northern Europe, like most immigrants of generations past. Their languages, culture, and religion were quite different from those of native-born Americans. Beginning in the 1880s, *nativists* advocated restrictive immigration laws and won passage of the *Chinese Exclusion Act*.

- **Changes in Culture and Thought**   Many areas of American life underwent profound changes during the Gilded Age. The growth of large cities led to the popularity of vaudeville and Wild West shows and to the emergence of spectator sports. *Saloons* served as local social and political clubs for men, despite the disapproval of anti-liquor groups. Charles Darwin's *On the Origin of Species* shocked people who believed in a literal interpretation of the Bible's account of creation. Proponents of *social Darwinism* applied Darwin's theory of evolution to human society by equating economic and social success with "survival of the fittest" and arguing that government should not try to promote equality or protect the less successful. *Reform Darwinism* held that collective efforts and social reform could guide human progress.

- **Gilded Age Politics**   Huge corporations corrupted politics and used their money to buy political influence. Political activity was still concentrated at the state and local levels. Americans were intensely loyal to the two major parties, whose local "bosses" and "machines" won votes by distributing *patronage* jobs and contracts to members, as well as charitable relief. Party loyalties reflected regional, ethnic, and religious differences. Although Republicans almost always held the presidency, the overall strength of the major parties was so balanced that neither wanted to risk alienating voters by taking bold stands.

- **Corruption and Reform**   National politics during the Gilded Age focused on tariffs, the regulation of corporations, and *civil service reform*. The passage of the Pendleton Civil Service Reform Act in 1883 began the professionalization of federal workers. In the 1884 presidential election, Republicans favoring reform, the *Mugwumps*, helped elect Democrat Grover Cleveland. Cleveland signed the 1887 act creating the *Interstate Commerce Commission (ICC)* to regulate railroads. In 1890, under President Benjamin Harrison, Republicans passed the Sherman Anti-Trust Act, the Sherman Silver Purchase Act, and the McKinley Tariff Act. The first proved ineffective; the third, which raised tariff rates, proved unpopular and led to Cleveland's return to the White House in the 1892 election.

- **Inadequate Currency Supply and Unhappy Farmers**   Over the course of the late nineteenth century, the *"money question"* had become a central political issue. The supply of money had not increased as the economy had grown. Many farmers believed that the coinage of silver, rather than a gold standard system, would result in inflation, which in turn would increase the value of their crops and reduce their debts. Farmers and others unsatisfied with the Republican and Democratic parties formed a series of political parties and alliances, one of which, the *People's party*, briefly operated as a national third party. In the election of 1896, the Democratic party nominated William Jennings Bryan, who adopted the coinage of silver as his crusade. He was opposed by Republican William McKinley, who supported the gold standard. McKinley, better organized and better financed, won the election in part by appealing to the growing number of city dwellers and industrial workers.

CHRONOLOGY

1859	Charles Darwin's *On the Origin of Species* is published
1881	President James A. Garfield is assassinated
1882	Congress passes the Chinese Exclusion Act
1883	Congress passes the Pendleton Civil Service Reform Act
1886	Supreme Court issues *Wabash, St. Louis, and Pacific Railroad Company v. Illinois* decision
1887	Interstate Commerce Commission is created
1890	Congress passes the Sherman Anti-Trust Act, the Sherman Silver Purchase Act, and the McKinley Tariff

KEY TERMS

Gilded Age p. 847

tenements p. 849

"new immigrants" p. 853

nativists p. 854

Chinese Exclusion Act (1882) p. 856

saloons p. 858

social Darwinism p. 860

reform Darwinism p. 861

party bosses p. 865

patronage p. 865

civil service reform p. 869

Mugwumps p. 873

Interstate Commerce Commission (ICC) p. 875

tariff reform p. 875

People's party (or **Populists**) p. 884

Panic of 1893 p. 885

"money question" p. 887

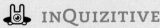 INQUIZITIVE

Go to InQuizitive to see what you've learned—and learn what you've missed—with personalized feedback along the way.

part six

MODERN AMERICA

The United States entered the twentieth century on a wave of unrelenting change, not all of it beneficial. The nation was on the threshold of modernity, which both excited and scared Americans. Old truths and beliefs clashed with unsettling scientific discoveries and social practices. People debated the legitimacy of Darwinism, the existence of God, the dangers of jazz, and the federal effort to prohibit the sale of alcoholic beverages. The advent of automobiles and airplanes helped shrink distance, and such

895

communications innovations as radio and film helped strengthen the sense that America now had a *national* culture.

Spurred by its growing industrial power, the United States began to emerge from its isolationist shell. Previously, presidents and statesmen had sought to isolate America from the intrigues and conflicts of European powers. As early as 1780, John Adams had warned against U.S. involvement in Europe's affairs. "Our business with them, and theirs with us," he wrote, "is commerce, not politics, much less war."

With only a few exceptions, statesmen during the nineteenth century followed such advice. Noninvolvement in foreign wars and nonintervention in the internal affairs of foreign governments formed the pillars of U. S. foreign policy. During the 1890s, however, expanding commercial interests led Americans to broaden their concerns.

Imperialism was the focus of the major European powers, and a growing number of expansionists demanded that the United States join in the hunt for new territories and markets. Others believed the United States should support democratic ideals abroad. Such mixed motives helped spark the Spanish-American War (the War of 1898) and helped justify the resulting acquisition of colonies outside the continental United States. Entangling alliances with European powers soon followed.

The outbreak of the Great War in Europe in 1914 posed an even greater challenge to America's tradition of nonintervention. The prospect of a German victory over the French and British threatened the European balance of power, which had long ensured the security of the United States. By 1917, it appeared that Germany might emerge triumphant and begin to menace the Western Hemisphere. As German submarines began sinking American merchant ships, President Woodrow Wilson's patience finally ran out, and in April 1917, the United States entered the war.

Wilson's crusade to transform international affairs in accordance with his idealistic principles dislodged American foreign policy from its isolationist moorings. It also spawned a prolonged debate about the nation's role in world affairs—a debate that World War II would resolve (for a time) on the side of internationalism.

While the United States was becoming a formidable military power, it was also settling in as a great industrial nation. Cities and factories sprouted across the landscape, and an abundance of new jobs and affordable farmland attracted millions of foreign immigrants. They were not always welcomed, nor were they readily assimilated. Ethnic and racial strife grew, as did labor agitation.

In the midst of such social turmoil and unparalleled economic development, reformers made their first sustained attempt to adapt political and social institutions to the realities of the industrial age. The worst excesses and injustices of urban-industrial development—corporate monopolies, child labor, political corruption, hazardous working conditions, urban ghettos—were finally  addressed in a comprehensive way. During the Progressive Era (1890–1917), local, state, and federal governments sought to rein in the excesses of industrial capitalism and develop a more rational and efficient public policy.

A conservative Republican resurgence challenged the notion of the new regulatory state during the 1920s, and free enterprise and corporate capitalism witnessed a dramatic revival. But the stock market crash of 1929 helped propel the United States and the world into the worst economic downturn in history. The unprecedented severity of the Great Depression renewed demands for federal programs to protect the general welfare. The many New Deal initiatives and agencies instituted by President Franklin Delano Roosevelt and his Democratic administration created the framework for a welfare state that has since served as the basis for public policy.

The New Deal revived public confidence and put people back to work, but it took a second world war to end the Great Depression and restore full employment. The necessity of mobilizing the nation to support the Second World War also accelerated the growth of the federal government, and the unparalleled scope of the war helped catapult the United States into a leadership role in world politics. The use of atomic bombs ushered in a new era of nuclear diplomacy that held the fate of the world in the balance. For all the new creature comforts associated with modern life, Americans in 1945 found themselves living amid an array of new anxieties.

20 Seizing an American Empire

1865–1913

The Charge of the Rough Riders of San Juan Hill **(1898)** Before Frederic Remington pursued art professionally, he had unsuccessful forays into hunting, ranching, and even the saloon business in the West. His intimacy with the Western way of life, along with his technical skill and keen sense of observation, were not lost on Theodore Roosevelt, who invited Remington to travel with the Rough Riders during the Spanish-American War.

After the Civil War, a mood of isolationism—a desire to stay out of conflicts elsewhere in the world—dominated American public opinion. The nation's geographic advantages encouraged this isolationist attitude: oceans to the east and west, and militarily weak neighbors in the Western Hemisphere. That the powerful British navy protected the shipping lanes between the United States and the British Isles gave Americans a heightened sense of security.

By the end of the nineteenth century, however, a dramatic transformation occurred in America's outlook. People grew increasingly aware that the country was a world power with global responsibilities and imperial ambitions. As a Kentucky newspaper editor proclaimed in 1893, the United States was "the most advanced and powerful" nation in the world, an "imperial Republic" destined to shape the "future of the world." The *Washington Post* agreed, revealing that "the Taste of Empire is in the mouth of the people."

While still wanting to stay out of European conflicts, a growing number of Americans urged officials to acquire additional territory outside North America. The old idea of "manifest destiny"—that the United States had been blessed by God ("destined") to expand its territory westward across the continent—was enlarged to include extending American control into other regions of the Western Hemisphere, and even to the Pacific and Asia. Americans embraced a new form of expansionism that sought distant territories as "colonies," with no intention of admitting them to the nation as equal states. The new manifest destiny, in other words, became a justification for imperialism.

focus questions

1. What factors motivated America's new imperialism after the Civil War?

2. How and why did America expand its influence in the Pacific before the Spanish-American War (War of 1898)?

3. What were the causes of the Spanish-American War (War of 1898)? What were its major events?

4. What were the consequences of the Spanish-American War (War of 1898) for American foreign policy?

5. What reasons were behind Theodore Roosevelt's rapid rise to the presidency? What were the main elements of his foreign policies?

In *The Law of Civilization and Decay* (1895), historian Brooks Adams argued that for the United States to survive and prosper, it had to keep pushing beyond its borders. As historian Frederick Jackson Turner had proclaimed in 1893, the continental "frontier" was gone, so Americans needed new frontiers in which to exercise their "expansive character" and to spread their democratic ideals, capitalist investments, and Christian beliefs.

Manifest destiny also took on racial meaning; many Americans agreed with future president Theodore Roosevelt that the United States needed to expand "on behalf of the *destiny* of the [Anglo-Saxon] race." Roosevelt and others believed that the Americans and British were at the top of the racial pyramid, superior to all others in intellect, ambition, and creativity.

Political and business leaders argued that America's rapid industrial development required the nation to acquire foreign territories—by conquest if necessary—to gain easier access to vital raw materials such as rubber, tin, copper, palm oil, and various dyes. At the same time, manufacturers and commercial farmers had become increasingly dependent on international trade, which required an expanded force of warships to protect the merchant vessels. And a modern, steam-powered navy needed ocean bases in the Caribbean and Pacific, where its ships could replenish their supplies of coal and water.

For these and other reasons, America expanded its military presence and territorial possessions both within and beyond the Western Hemisphere. During just a few months in 1898, as the result of a one-sided war against Spain, the United States, born in a revolution against British colonial rule, would itself become an imperial ruler of colonies around the world. Motivated by a mixture of moral and religious idealism, assumptions of "Anglo-Saxon" racial superiority, and naked greed, the expansionist push also met with strong opposition. But most Americans sided with future president Theodore Roosevelt, who in his 1896 book *The Winning of the West* declared that the conquest of the "backward peoples" of the world, like the defeat of the Indians in the American West, benefited "civilization and the interests of mankind."

Toward the New Imperialism

The United States was a latecomer to **imperialism**. By the 1880s, the British, French, Belgians, Italians, Dutch, Spanish, and Germans had conquered most of Africa and Asia. Often competing with one another for territories, they had established colonial governments to rule over the native populations and exploited the colonies economically. Each imperial nation dispatched missionaries to convert conquered peoples to Christianity. By 1900, some 18,000 Protestant and Catholic missionaries were scattered around the world. Writing in 1902, the British economist J. A. Hobson declared that imperialism was "the most powerful factor in the current politics of the Western world."

A small yet influential group of public officials aggressively encouraged the idea of expansion beyond North America. In addition to Theodore Roosevelt, they included naval captain Alfred Thayer Mahan, president of the U.S. Naval War College, and Senators Albert J. Beveridge of Indiana and Henry Cabot Lodge of Massachusetts. Referring to European imperialism, Lodge said, "We must not be left behind."

In 1890, Mahan published *The Influence of Sea Power upon History, 1660–1783*, in which he argued that national greatness flowed from naval power. Mahan insisted that industrial development required a powerful navy centered on huge battleships, a strong merchant marine, foreign commerce, colonies to provide raw materials and new markets for American products, and global naval bases.

Mahan urged leaders to "look outward" beyond the continental United States. He championed America's "destiny" to control the Caribbean Sea, build a canal across Central America to connect the Atlantic and Pacific Oceans, acquire Hawaii and the Philippine Islands, and spread American values and investments across the Pacific. His ideas were widely circulated, and by 1896 the United States had built eleven new battleships, making its navy the third most powerful in the world, behind Great Britain and Germany.

Claims of racial superiority reinforced the new imperialist spirit. Many Americans and Europeans readily assumed that some races were dominant (Anglo-Saxons) and some inferior (Indians, Africans). Such racist notions were given "scientific" authority by researchers at universities throughout Europe and America.

Prominent Americans used the arguments of social Darwinism to justify economic exploitation and territorial conquest abroad and racial segregation at home. Among nations as among individuals, they claimed, only the strongest survived. John Fiske, a Harvard historian, proclaimed the superior character of "Anglo-Saxon" institutions and peoples. The English-speaking "race," he argued, was destined to dominate the globe and transform the institutions, traditions, language, and even the blood of the world's "backward" races. Such theories of racial superiority were often used to justify armed conquest. Theodore Roosevelt, for example, insisted that "all the great masterful races have been fighting races. . . . No triumph of peace is so great as the triumphs of war."

EXPANSION IN THE PACIFIC

For John Fiske and other imperialists, Asia offered an especially attractive target. In 1866, Secretary of State William H. Seward had predicted that the United States must inevitably impose its economic domination "on the Pacific Ocean, and its islands and continents." Eager for American manufacturers to take advantage of the huge Asian markets, Seward believed that the nation first had to remove all foreign powers from its northern Pacific coast and gain access to the region's valuable ports. To that end, he tried to acquire the English colony of British Columbia, sandwiched between Russian-owned Alaska and the Washington Territory.

Late in 1866, while encouraging business leaders and civil authorities in British Columbia to consider becoming a U.S. territory, Seward learned of Russia's desire to sell Alaska. He leaped at the opportunity, thinking the purchase might influence British Columbia to join the union. In 1867, the United States bought Alaska for $7.2 million, thus removing the threat of Russian imperialism in North America. Critics scoffed at "Seward's folly," but the purchase of Alaska proved to be the biggest bargain since the Louisiana Purchase, in part because of its vast deposits of gold and oil.

Seward's successors at the State Department sustained his expansionist vision. Acquiring key ports in the Pacific Ocean was the major focus of overseas activity throughout the rest of the nineteenth century. Two island groups occupied especially strategic positions: Samoa and Hawaii (the Sandwich Islands). Both had major harbors, Pago Pago and Pearl Harbor, respectively. In the years after the Civil War, American interest in those islands deepened.

SAMOA In 1878, the Samoans signed a treaty with the United States that granted a naval base at Pago Pago and extraterritoriality for Americans (meaning that in Samoa, Americans remained subject only to U.S. law), exchanged trade concessions, and called for the United States to help resolve any disputes with other nations. The Senate ratified this accord, and in the following year the German and British governments worked out similar arrangements with other islands in the Samoan group. There matters rested until civil war broke out in Samoa in 1887. A peace conference in Berlin in 1889 established a protectorate over Samoa, with Germany, Great Britain, and the United States in an uneasy partnership.

HAWAII Seward and other Americans also wanted the Hawaiian Islands. The islands, a unified kingdom since 1795, had a sizable population of American missionaries and a profitable crop, sugarcane. In 1875, Hawaii had signed

"Our New Senators" Mocking the Alaska Purchase, this political cartoon shows President Andrew Johnson and Secretary of State Seward welcoming two new senators from Alaska: an Eskimo and a Penguin.

a reciprocal trade agreement with the United States through which Hawaiian sugar would enter the country duty free in exchange for Hawaii's promise that none of its territory would be leased or granted to a third power.

This agreement led to a boom in sugar production based on cheap immigrant labor, mainly Chinese and Japanese, and white American sugar planters soon formed an economic elite. By the 1890s, the native Hawaiian population had been reduced to a minority by smallpox and other foreign diseases, and Asians became the largest ethnic group.

Beginning in 1891, Queen Liliuokalani, the Hawaiian ruler, tried to restrict the growing political power exercised by American planters in the islands.

Queen Liliuokalani The Hawaiian queen sought to preserve her nation's independence.

Two years later, however, Hawaii's white population (called *haoles*) overthrew the monarchy with the help of U.S. Marines brought in by John L. Stevens, the U.S. ambassador. Within a month, a committee representing the *haoles* came to Washington, D.C., to ask the United States to annex the islands. President Benjamin Harrison sent an annexation treaty to the Senate just as he was leaving the presidency.

To investigate the situation, the new president, Grover Cleveland, sent a special commissioner to Hawaii, who reported that the Americans there had acted improperly and that most native Hawaiians opposed annexation. Cleveland tried to restore the queen to power but met resistance from the *haoles*. On July 4, 1894, the government they controlled created the Republic of Hawaii, which included in its constitution a provision for American annexation.

In 1897, when William McKinley became president, he was looking for an excuse to annex the islands. "We need Hawaii," he claimed. "It is [America's] manifest destiny." The United States annexed Hawaii in the summer of 1898 over the protests of native Hawaiians.

The Spanish-American War (The War of 1898)

The annexation of Hawaii set in motion a series of efforts to create an American presence in Asia. Ironically, this imperialist push originated in Cuba, a Spanish colony ninety miles south of Florida. Even more ironically, the chief motive for American intervention in Cuba was outrage at Spain's brutal imperialism.

"FREE CUBA" Throughout the second half of the nineteenth century, Cubans had repeatedly revolted against Spanish rule, only to be ruthlessly suppressed. As one of Spain's oldest colonies, Cuba was a major market for

Spanish goods. Yet powerful American sugar and mining companies had also invested heavily in Cuba. In fact, the United States traded more with Cuba than Spain did, and American owners of sugar plantations in Cuba had grown increasingly concerned about the security of their investments.

On February 24, 1895, Cubans began another guerrilla war against Spanish troops. During what became the Cuban War for Independence (1895–1898), tens of thousands of Cuban peasants died of combat wounds as well as disease and starvation in Spanish detention camps.

Americans followed the conflict through the newspapers. Two newspapers locked in a fierce competition for readers, William Randolph Hearst's *New York Journal* and Joseph Pulitzer's *New York World*. Both worked to outdo the other with sensational headlines about Spanish atrocities in Cuba, real or invented. Hearst explained that the role of newspapers was to shape public opinion and legislation. Newspapers, he claimed, had the power to "declare wars." Hearst's efforts to manipulate public opinion came to be called **yellow journalism**. Editors sent their best reporters to Cuba and encouraged them to distort, exaggerate, or even make up stories to attract more readers.

In addition to boosting the *Journal's* circulation, Hearst wanted a war against Spain to propel the United States to world-power status. Once war was declared, he took credit for it; one of his headlines blared, "How Do You Like the *Journal's* War?" Many Protestant ministers and publications also campaigned for war, in part because of antagonism toward Catholic Spain.

THE POLITICAL PATH TO WAR At the outset of the Cuban War for Independence, President Grover Cleveland tried to protect U.S. business interests while avoiding military involvement. Mounting public sympathy for the rebel cause prompted concern in Congress, however. By concurrent resolutions on April 6, 1896, the House and Senate endorsed granting official recognition to the Cuban rebels. After his inauguration in March 1897, President William McKinley continued the official policy of neutrality while taking a sympathetic stance toward the rebels. McKinley, a Civil War veteran, did not want war. "I have been through one war," he said. "I have seen the dead piled up, and I do not want to see another." Later that year, Spain offered Cubans autonomy (self-government without formal independence) in return for ending the rebellion, but the Cubans rejected the offer.

Early in 1898, events pushed Spain and the United States into a war that neither wanted. On January 25, the **U.S. battleship *Maine*** docked in Havana, the Cuban capital, supposedly on a courtesy call. On February 9, the *New York Journal* released the text of a letter from Dupuy de Lôme, Spanish ambassador

"$50,000 Reward!" As if the news of the *Maine* sinking were not disturbing enough, the *New York Journal* sought to sensationalize the incident by offering a $50,000 reward for the perpetrator—the equivalent of $1.3 million today.

to the United States, to a friend in Havana, summarizing McKinley's annual message to Congress. In the **de Lôme letter**, the Spaniard called McKinley "weak and a bidder for the admiration of the crowd, besides being a would-be politician who tries to leave a door open behind himself while keeping on good terms with the jingoes [warmongers] of his party."

Six days later, at 9:40 on the night of February 15, the *Maine* mysteriously exploded. Within minutes, its ruptured hull filled with water. Sailors, most of whom were asleep, struggled frantically in the dark, only to drown as the ship sank. Of the 350 sailors on board, 260 died. Years later, the sinking was ruled an accident resulting from a coal explosion, but in 1898 those eager for war with Spain saw no need to delay judgment. Theodore Roosevelt, the thirty-nine-year-old assistant secretary of the navy, called the sinking "an act of dirty treachery" and told a friend that he "would give anything if President McKinley would order the fleet to Havana tomorrow." The United States, he claimed, "needs a war," and he hoped it would "come soon."

Congress authorized $50 million to prepare for combat with Spain, but McKinley, who assumed that the sinking was an accident, did his best to resist demands for war while negotiating with the Spanish and gauging the public mood. He also avoided interacting with Roosevelt, who he said was "too pugnacious." As the days passed, Roosevelt told his war-hungry friends that the president had "no more backbone than a chocolate éclair." With Roosevelt's encouragement, the public's antagonism toward Spain grew behind the popular saying "Remember the *Maine*, to Hell with Spain!"

In the weeks following the sinking, the Spanish government grudgingly agreed to virtually every American demand regarding Cuba, but the weight of public opinion, the cry of revenge from Democratic leaders, and the influence of Republican jingoists eroded McKinley's neutrality. As a senator explained, "the current was too strong, the demagogues too numerous, the fall elections too near" for McKinley to hold out against war.

On April 11, McKinley asked Congress for authority to use the armed forces to end the fighting in Cuba. On April 20, Congress declared Cuba independent from Spain and demanded the withdrawal of Spanish forces. The Spanish government quickly broke diplomatic ties with the United States and, after U.S. ships began blockading Cuban ports, declared war on April 24. The next day, Congress passed its own declaration of war. The **Teller Amendment** to the war resolution denied any U.S. intention to annex Cuba.

President McKinley called for 125,000 volunteers to supplement the 28,000 men already serving in the U.S. Army. Among the first to enlist was Theodore Roosevelt, who resigned from his government post and told his tailor to make him a dashing army uniform.

Never has an American war generated such unexpected and far-reaching consequences. Although McKinley had gone to war reluctantly, he soon saw it as an opportunity to acquire overseas territories. "While we are conducting war and until its conclusion," he wrote privately, "we must keep all we get; when the war is over we must keep what we want." A war to free Cuba became a way to gain an empire. (What had long been called the Spanish-American War has been renamed the War of 1898 because it involved not just Spanish and American combatants, but Cubans, Filipinos, and Puerto Ricans.)

"A SPLENDID LITTLE WAR"

The war with Spain lasted only 114 days, but it set the United States on a course toward overseas imperialism that would transform America's role in the world. The conflict was barely under way before the U.S. Navy produced a spectacular victory 7,000 miles away from Cuba, in the Pacific, at Manila Bay in the Philippine Islands, a colony controlled by the Spanish for more than 300 years. Just before war was declared, Roosevelt, who was still assistant secretary of the navy, had taken advantage of his boss being away from the office one afternoon to order Commodore George Dewey, commander of the U.S. Asiatic Squadron, to engage Spanish forces in the Philippines in case of war in Cuba.

Dewey arrived in Manila Bay on April 30 with six modern warships, which quickly destroyed or captured the outdated Spanish vessels there. Almost 400 Spaniards were killed or wounded. One overweight American sailor died—of

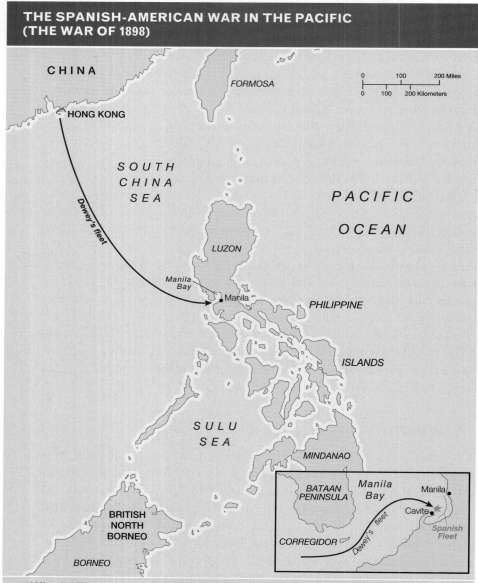

THE SPANISH-AMERICAN WAR IN THE PACIFIC (THE WAR OF 1898)

- Why did Theodore Roosevelt order Commodore Dewey to take Manila?
- What role did Filipino nationalist leader Emilio Aguinaldo play?
- Why were many Americans opposed to the acquisition of the Philippines?

heatstroke. An English reporter called it "a military execution rather than a real contest." News of the battle set off wild celebrations in America.

Dewey was now in possession of Manila Bay but had no soldiers to go onshore. He and his warships stayed for several months waiting for reinforcements while German and British warships cruised offshore like watchful vultures, ready to seize the Philippines if the United States did not.

In the meantime, Emilio Aguinaldo, the leader of the Filipino nationalist movement, declared the Philippines independent on June 12, 1898. With Aguinaldo's help, Dewey's forces entered Manila on August 13 and accepted the surrender of the Spanish troops, who had feared revenge if they surrendered to the Filipinos.

News of the American victory sent President McKinley in search of a map of Asia to locate the islands now occupied by U.S. soldiers and sailors. Senator Lodge was delighted with the news from the Philippines: "We hold the other side of the Pacific," he announced. "We must on no account let the [Philippine] Islands go."

THE CUBAN CAMPAIGN At the start of the war, the Spanish army in Cuba was five times as large as the entire U.S. Army. But McKinley's call for volunteers inspired nearly a million men to enlist. The new recruits, including some 10,000 African American soldiers (mostly northerners eager to "show our loyalty to our land") had to be equipped and trained before they would be ready for battle. In the "Jim Crow" South, however, blacks were less eager to enlist because, as a Richmond newspaper editor observed, they suffered "a system of oppression as barbarous as that which is alleged to exist in Cuba."

In the meantime, the U.S. Navy blockaded the Spanish fleet inside Santiago Harbor while some 17,000 American troops hastily assembled at Tampa,

African American troops in Cuba
Soldiers stand in formation wearing old wool uniforms unsuited to Cuba's tropical heat.

Florida. One prominent unit was the First Volunteer Cavalry, better known as the Rough Riders, a special regiment made up of former Ivy League athletes, ex-convicts, western cowboys, Texas Rangers, and Cherokee, Choctaw, Chickasaw, Pawnee, and Creek Indians. All were "young, good shots, and good riders." The Rough Riders are best remembered because Theodore Roosevelt was second in command. One of the Rough Riders said that Roosevelt was "nervous, energetic, virile [manly]. He may wear out some day, but he will never rust out."

When the 578 Rough Riders, accompanied by a gaggle of reporters and photographers, landed on June 22, 1898, at the undefended southeastern tip of Cuba, chaos followed. Except for Roosevelt's horse, Little Texas, almost all of the other horses and mules had been mistakenly sent elsewhere, leaving the Rough Riders to become the "Weary Walkers." Nevertheless, land and sea battles on the southern coast around Santiago quickly broke Spanish resistance.

On July 1, about 7,000 U.S. soldiers took the fortified village of El Caney. While a much larger force attacked San Juan Hill, a smaller unit, led by Roosevelt on horseback and including the Rough Riders on foot, seized nearby Kettle Hill. Thanks to widespread newspaper coverage, much of it exaggerated, Roosevelt became a home-front legend for his headlong gallop toward the Spanish defenders. The *New York Times* reported that he had led the charge with "bulldog ferociousness," acting in a "grand drama for the world to watch and admire."

Roosevelt loved being in the headlines. Being a military hero was his lifelong dream. According to the *New York World,* the young lieutenant colonel had become "more talked about than any man in the country." A friend reported to Roosevelt's wife that her husband was "reveling in victory and gore." Unburdened by humility, Roosevelt requested a Congressional Medal of Honor for his much-publicized charge in Cuba. It did not come. (President Bill Clinton finally awarded the medal posthumously in 2001.)

While Colonel Roosevelt was basking in the glory of battle, other U.S. soldiers in Cuba were less enthusiastic about the terrors of modern warfare. Walter Bartholomew, a private from New York, reported that the war "in all its awfulness" was so "much more hideous than my wildest imagination that I have not yet recovered from the shock." A soldier standing beside him had "the front of his throat torn completely off" by a Spanish bullet. As his unit was charging up San Juan Hill, they "became totally disorganized and thrown into utter confusion" amid the intense shooting. He discarded all he carried except for his rifle "in the mad scramble to get out of the valley of death." While stopping to shoot, he saw the 24th Regiment of Colored Infantry racing up the hill and he decided to follow their lead, "so excited that I forgot to fire my gun, and I actually charged clean up to the top of the hill without shooting, in as great panic as if I had been retreating."

Colonel Roosevelt With one hand on his hip, Roosevelt rides with the Rough Riders in Cuba. Most of his regiment was culled from Arizona, New Mexico, and Texas because the Southwestern climate resembled that of Cuba.

SPANISH DEFEAT AND CONCESSIONS On July 3, the Spanish navy trapped at Santiago made a gallant run to evade the American fleet blockading the harbor. "The Spanish ships," reported Captain John Philip, commander of the U.S. warship *Texas*, "came out as gaily as brides to the altar." But they were quickly destroyed. The casualties were as one-sided as those at Manila: 474 Spaniards were killed or wounded, while only 1 American was killed and 1 wounded. Spanish officials in Santiago surrendered on July 17. On July 25, an American force moved into Spanish-held Puerto Rico ("wealthy port" in English), meeting only minor resistance.

The next day, July 26, the Spanish government sued for peace. A cease-fire agreement was signed on August 12. In Cuba, the Spanish forces formally surrendered to the U.S. commander and then sailed for home; excluded from the ceremony were the Cubans, for whom the war had supposedly been fought. On December 10, 1898, the United States and Spain signed the Treaty of Paris.

Under its terms, Cuba was to become independent, and the United States was to annex Puerto Rico and continue to occupy Manila, pending a transfer of power in the Philippines. Thus the Spanish Empire in the Americas, initiated by the voyages of Christopher Columbus some four centuries earlier, came to a humiliating end. Now the United States was ready to create its own empire.

During the four-month War of 1898, more than 60,000 Spanish soldiers and sailors died of wounds or disease—mostly malaria, typhoid, dysentery,

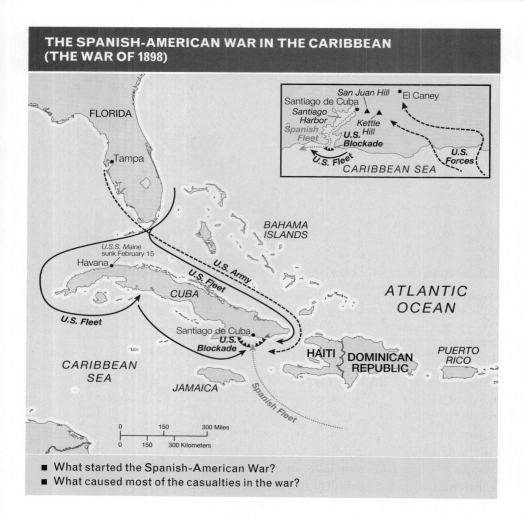

THE SPANISH-AMERICAN WAR IN THE CARIBBEAN (THE WAR OF 1898)

- What started the Spanish-American War?
- What caused most of the casualties in the war?

or yellow fever. Some 10,500 Cubans died. Among the Americans who served in the war, 5,462 died, but only 379 in battle; most died from disease. At such a cost, the United States was launched onto the world scene as a great power, with all the benefits—and burdens—that come with being an imperial nation.

Halfway through the conflict in Cuba, John Hay, the U.S. ambassador to Great Britain, who would soon become secretary of state, wrote a letter to Roosevelt, calling the conflict "a splendid little war, begun with the highest motives, carried on with magnificent intelligence and spirit, favored by that fortune which loves the brave." The U.S. ambassador to France concluded that "no war in history has accomplished so much in so short a time with so little loss." The Spanish reaction was quite different, for the war destroyed the remnants of the Spanish Empire. Spaniards called the catastrophic war "The Disaster," a humiliating defeat that called into question Spain's status as a major world power. "Everything is broken in this unhappy country," a Spanish newspaper reported.

CONSEQUENCES OF VICTORY

Victory in the War of 1898 boosted American self-confidence and reinforced the self-serving belief, influenced by racism and social Darwinism, that the United States had a "manifest destiny" to reshape the world in its own image.

In 1885, the Reverend Josiah Strong wrote a best-selling book titled *Our Country* in which he used a Darwinian argument to strengthen the appeal of manifest destiny. The "wonderful progress of the United States," he boasted, was an illustration of Charles Darwin's concept of "natural selection," since Americans had demonstrated that they were the world's "superior" civilization, "a race of unequaled energy" who represented "the largest liberty, the purest Christianity, the highest civilization" in the world, a race of superior people destined to "spread itself over the earth." Strong asserted that the United States had a Christian duty and economic opportunity to expand "Anglo-Saxon" influence. A growing international trade, he noted, would emerge from America's missionary evangelism and racial superiority. "Can anyone doubt," he asked, "that this race . . . is destined to dispossess many weaker races, assimilate others, and mold the remainder until . . . it has Anglo-Saxonized mankind?"

Europeans agreed that the United States had now made a forceful entrance onto the world stage. The *Times* of London announced that the American victory over Spain must "effect a profound change in the whole attitude and policy of the United States. In the future America will play a part in the general affairs of the world such as she has never played before."

ANNEXING THE PHILIPPINES

The United States had liberated most of Spain's remaining colonies, yet it soon substituted its own imperialism for Spain's. If war with Spain had saved many lives by ending the insurrection in Cuba, it had also led the United States to take many lives in suppressing another anti-colonial insurrection, in the Philippines. The acquisition of America's first imperial colonies created a host of long-lasting moral and practical problems, from the difficulties of imposing U.S. rule on native peoples to those of defending far-flung territories.

McKINLEY'S MOTIVES The Treaty of Paris had left the political status of the Philippines unresolved. American business leaders wanted the United States to keep the islands so that they could more easily penetrate the vast markets of nearby China. As Mark Hanna, McKinley's top adviser, stressed, controlling the Philippines would enable the United States to "take a large slice of the commerce of Asia." American missionary organizations, mostly Protestant, also favored annexation; they viewed the Philippines as a base from which to bring Christianity to "the little brown brother." Not long after the United States took control, American authorities ended the Roman Catholic Church's status as the Philippines' official religion and made English the official language, thus opening the door for Protestant missionaries in the region.

These factors helped convince President McKinley of the need to annex "those darned islands" making up the Philippines. He explained that

> one night late it came to me this way—I don't know how it was, but it came: (1) that we could not give them back to Spain—that would be cowardly and dishonorable; (2) that we could not turn them over to France or Germany—our commercial rivals in the Orient—that would be bad business and discreditable; (3) that we could not leave them to themselves—they were unfit for self-government—and they would soon have anarchy and misrule over there worse than Spain's was; and (4) that there was nothing left for us to do but to take them all, and to educate the Filipinos, and uplift and civilize and Christianize them, and by God's grace do the very best we could by them, as our fellow-men for whom Christ also died. And then I went to bed, and went to sleep and slept soundly.

In this brief statement, McKinley had summarized the motivating ideas of American imperialism: (1) national glory, (2) commerce, (3) racial superiority, and (4) evangelism. American negotiators in Paris finally offered Spain $20 million for the Philippines, Puerto Rico, and Guam, a Spanish-controlled island between Hawaii and the Philippines that would serve as a coaling station for ships headed across the Pacific.

Meanwhile, the nation took other expansive steps. In addition to annexing Hawaii in 1898, the United States also claimed Wake Island, between Guam and Hawaii, which would become a vital link in a future transpacific telegraph cable. Then, in 1899, Germany and the United States agreed to divide the Samoa Islands.

DEBATING THE TREATY By early 1899, the Treaty of Paris had yet to be ratified in the Senate because of growing opposition to the idea of a global

American empire. Anti-expansionists argued that taking control of former Spanish colonies would violate the longstanding American principle embodied in the Constitution that people should be self-governing.

The opposition might have killed the treaty had not the most prominent Democratic leader, William Jennings Bryan, argued that ending the war would open the way for the future independence of the Philippines. His position convinced enough Senate Democrats to support the treaty on February 6, 1899, by the narrowest of margins: only one vote more than the necessary two thirds.

President McKinley, however, had no intention of granting independence to the Philippines. Although he privately told a friend that "if old Dewey had just sailed away when he smashed that Spanish fleet, what a lot of trouble he would have saved us," he publicly insisted that the United States take control of the islands as an act of "benevolent assimilation" of the native population. A California newspaper gave a more candid explanation, however. "Let us be frank," the editor exclaimed. "WE DO NOT WANT THE FILIPINOS. WE WANT THE PHILIPPINES."

Many Filipinos had a different vision. In January 1899, they declared again their independence and named twenty-nine-year-old Emilio Aguinaldo president. The following month, an American soldier outside Manila fired on soldiers in Aguinaldo's nationalist forces, called *insurrectos*, killing two. The next day, the U.S. Army commander, without investigating the cause of the

Turmoil in the Philippines Emilio Aguinaldo (seated third from right) and other leaders of the Filipino insurgence.

shooting, ordered his troops to assault the *insurrectos*, beginning a full-scale armed conflict that continued for weeks. General Elwell S. Otis rejected Aguinaldo's proposals for a truce, saying that "fighting, having begun, must go on to the grim end." He would accept only the unconditional surrender of the Filipino forces.

On June 2, 1899, the Philippine Republic declared war against the United States. Since the *insurrectos* more or less controlled the Philippines outside Manila, what followed was largely an American war of conquest at odds with the founding principle of the United States: that people have the right to govern themselves. The war would rob the Filipinos of the chance to be their own masters.

THE PHILIPPINE-AMERICAN WAR (1898–1902) The effort to crush Filipino nationalism lasted three years and involved some 126,000 U.S. troops, four times as many as had been sent to liberate Cuba. It cost the American government $600 million and took the lives of 200,000 Filipinos (most of them civilians) and 4,234 American soldiers.

It was an especially brutal conflict fought in tropical heat and humidity, with massacres committed by both sides and racism contributing to numerous atrocities by the Americans, many of whom referred to the Filipinos as "niggers." U.S. troops burned villages, tortured and executed prisoners, and imprisoned civilians in overcrowded concentration camps. A reporter for the *Philadelphia Ledger* noted that U.S. soldiers had "killed to exterminate men, women, children, prisoners and captives, active insurgents and suspected people from lads of ten up, the idea prevailing that the Filipino as such was little better than a dog." One U.S. soldier from Indiana celebrated the slaughter of an entire village in retaliation for the murder of an American: "I am in my glory when I can sight my gun on some dark skin and pull the trigger."

Both sides in the war used torture to gain information. A favorite method employed by Americans was the "water cure," a technique to simulate drowning developed in the Spanish Inquisition during the sixteenth century. (Today it is called waterboarding.) A captured insurgent would be placed on his back on the ground. While soldiers stood on his outstretched arms and feet, they pried his mouth open and held it in place with a bamboo stick. They then poured salt water into the captive's mouth and nose until his stomach was bloated, whereupon the soldiers would stomp on his abdomen, forcing the water, now mixed with gastric juices, out of his mouth. This process would be repeated until the captive told the soldiers what they wanted to know—or died. Theodore Roosevelt was convinced that "nobody was seriously damaged" by the "water cure," whereas "Filipinos had inflicted terrible tortures upon our own people."

Thus did the United States destroy a revolutionary movement modeled after America's own struggle for independence. Organized Filipino resistance had collapsed by the end of 1899. On April 1, 1901, Aguinaldo swore an oath accepting the authority of the United States over the Philippines and pledging his allegiance to the U.S. government.

Against the backdrop of this nasty guerrilla war, the great debate over imperialism continued in the United States. In 1899, several anti-imperialist groups combined to form the **American Anti-Imperialist League**. Andrew Carnegie footed the bills for the League and even offered $20 million to buy independence for the Filipinos. Other prominent anti-imperialists included union leader Samuel Gompers, who feared the competition of cheap Filipino labor, college presidents Charles Eliot of Harvard and David Starr Jordan of Stanford, and social reformer Jane Addams. Even former presidents Grover Cleveland and Benjamin Harrison urged President McKinley to withdraw U.S. forces from the Philippines.

The drive for imperialism in Asia, said Harvard philosopher William James, had caused the United States to "puke up its ancient soul." Of the Philippine-American War, James asked, "Could there be any more damning indictment of that whole bloated ideal termed 'modern civilization'?" Senator George Frisbie Hoar led the opposition to annexation of the Philippines.

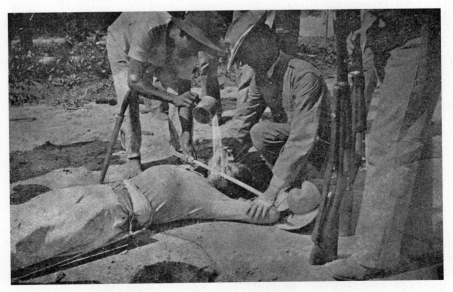

"The water cure" American soldiers torture a Filipino prisoner during the Philippine-American War.

Under the Constitution, he pointed out, "no power is given the Federal government to acquire territory to be held and governed permanently as colonies" or "to conquer alien people and hold them in subjugation."

ORGANIZING THE NEW COLONIES

In the end, the imperialists won the debate over the status of the territories acquired from Spain. Senator Albert J. Beveridge boasted in 1900: "The Philippines are ours forever. And just beyond the Philippines are China's illimitable

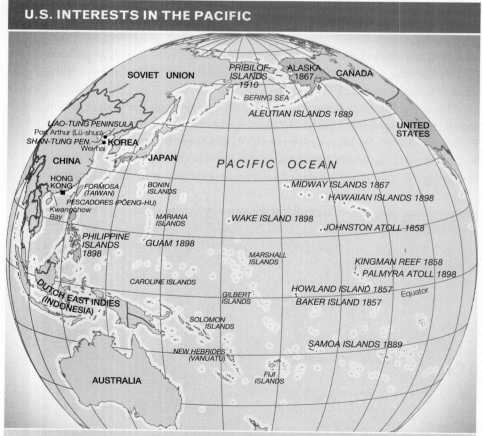

U.S. INTERESTS IN THE PACIFIC

Dates indicate year of acquisition or occupation by the United States.

- Why was President McKinley eager to acquire territory in the Pacific and the Caribbean?
- What kind of political system did the U.S. government create in Hawaii and in the Philippines?
- How did Filipinos and Hawaiians resist the Americans?

markets. We will not retreat from either. . . . The power that rules the Pacific is the power that rules the world." He added that the U.S. economy was producing "more than we can consume, making more than we can use. Therefore we must find new markets for our produce." American-controlled colonies would make the best new markets. Without acknowledging it, Beveridge and others were using many of the same arguments that England had used in founding the American colonies in the seventeenth century.

On July 4, 1901, the U.S. military government in the Philippines came to an end, and William Howard Taft became the civil governor. In 1902, Congress passed the Philippine Government Act, which declared the islands an "unorganized territory." In 1917, the Jones Act affirmed America's intention to grant the Philippines independence, but that would not happen until 1946.

Closer to home, Puerto Rico had been acquired in part to serve as a U.S. outpost guarding the Caribbean Sea. On April 12, 1900, the Foraker Act established a government on the island, and its residents were declared citizens of Puerto Rico; they were not made citizens of the United States until 1917.

"Well, I hardly know which to take first!" With a growing appetite for foreign territory, Uncle Sam browses his options: Cuba Steak, Puerto Rico Pig, Philippine Floating Islands, and others. An expectant President McKinley waits to take his order.

In Cuba, the United States finally fulfilled the promise of independence after restoring order, organizing schools, and improving sanitary conditions. The problem of widespread disease prompted the work of Dr. Walter Reed, who made an outstanding contribution to health in tropical regions around the world. Named head of the Army Yellow Fever Commission in 1900, he proved that mosquitoes carry yellow fever. The commission's experiments led the way to effective control of the disease worldwide.

In 1900, on McKinley's order, Cubans drafted a constitution modeled on that of the United States. The Platt Amendment, added to an army appropriations bill in 1901, sharply restricted the Cuban government's independence, however. The amendment required that Cuba never impair its independence by signing a treaty with a third power, that it keep its debt within the government's power to repay it out of ordinary revenues, and that it acknowledge the right of the United States to intervene whenever it saw fit. Finally, Cuba had to sell or lease to the United States lands to be used for coaling or naval stations, a stipulation that led to a U.S. naval base at Guantánamo Bay that still exists today.

IMPERIAL RIVALRIES IN EAST ASIA

While the United States was conquering the Philippines, other nations were threatening to carve up China. After Japan defeated China in the First Sino-Japanese War (1894–1895), European nations set out to exploit the weakness of the huge, virtually defenseless nation. By the end of the century, Russia, Germany, France, and Great Britain had each established spheres of influence in China—territories that they (rather than the Chinese government) controlled but did not formally annex.

In 1898 and again in 1899, the British asked the American government to join them in preserving the territorial integrity of China against further imperialist actions. Both times, however, the Senate rejected the request because the United States as yet had no strategic investment in the region. The American outlook changed with the defeat of Spain and the acquisition of the Philippines. Instead of acting jointly with Great Britain, though, the U.S. government decided to act alone.

What came to be known as the **Open Door policy** was outlined in Secretary of State John Hay's Open Door Note, dispatched in 1899 to his European counterparts. Without consulting the Chinese, Hay announced that China should remain an "Open Door" to European and American trade and that other nations should not try to take control of Chinese ports or territory. None of the European powers except Britain accepted Hay's principles, but none rejected them, either. So Hay announced that all major powers involved in China had accepted the policy.

Intervention in China After quelling the Boxer Rebellion, U.S. troops march in the Forbidden Palace, the imperial palace in the Chinese capital of Beijing.

The Open Door policy was rooted in the desire of American businesses to exploit and ultimately dominate Chinese markets. However, it also appealed to those who opposed imperialism because it pledged to keep China from being carved up by powerful European nations.

The policy had little legal standing, however. When the Japanese became concerned about growing Russian influence in the disputed region of Manchuria in northeast China and asked how the United States intended to enforce the policy, Hay replied that America was "not prepared . . . to enforce these views." So the situation would remain for forty years, until continued Japanese military expansion in China would bring about a diplomatic dispute with America that would lead to war.

THE BOXERS A new Asian crisis arose in 1900 when a group of Chinese nationalists known to the Western world as Boxers—they called themselves the "Fists of Righteous Harmony"—rebelled against foreign involvement in China, especially Christian missionary efforts, and laid siege to foreign embassies in Peking (now known as Beijing). An expedition of British, German, Russian, Japanese, and American soldiers was organized to rescue the international diplomats and their staffs. Hay, fearful that the intervention might become an excuse for other nations to dismember China, took the opportunity to refine the Open Door policy. The United States, he said, sought a solution that would "preserve Chinese territorial and administrative integrity" as well as "equal and impartial trade with all parts of the Chinese Empire." Six weeks later, the foreign military expedition reached Peking and ended the Boxer Rebellion.

ROOSEVELT'S "BIG-STICK" DIPLOMACY

On September 6, 1901, President McKinley was shaking hands at the Pan-American Exposition in Buffalo, New York, when a twenty-eight-year-old unemployed laborer named Leon Czolgosz (pronounced chol-GOTS), an anarchist who did not believe in governments or rulers, approached him with a concealed gun and fired twice at point-blank range. One bullet was deflected by the president's coat button and breastbone, but the other tore through his stomach and lodged in his back. For several days, the attending doctors issued optimistic reports about the president's condition, but after a week, McKinley knew he was dying. "It is useless, gentlemen," he told the doctors and nurses. "I think we ought to have a prayer." Theodore Roosevelt, his vice president, became the new president and soon launched a new era in national development.

More than any other American of his time, Roosevelt transformed the role of the United States in world affairs. The nation had emerged from the War of 1898 a world power with major international responsibilities. To ensure that Americans accepted their new global role, Roosevelt stretched both the Constitution and executive power to the limit. In the process, he pushed a reluctant nation onto the center stage of world affairs.

A "ROCKET" RISE TO PROMINENCE

Born in 1858, "Teedie" Roosevelt had grown up in New York City in an upper-class family. He visited Europe as a child, studied with a personal tutor, spoke German fluently, and graduated from Harvard with honors in 1880. A frail and sickly boy, nearly blind in one eye, he followed his father's advice to "make your own body." He compulsively lifted weights, wrestled, hiked, rowed, swam, boxed, and climbed mountains, all in an effort to build himself into a physical and intellectual athlete. The results were startling. Roosevelt transformed himself into a man of almost superhuman energy who fiercely championed the "strenuous life." He told his children that he would rather see them dead than have them grow up to be "weaklings" and "sissies."

Roosevelt was a fearless "he-man" who also displayed extraordinary intellectual curiosity. He became a voracious reader and talented writer, a natural scientist, a dedicated bird-watcher, a renowned historian and essayist, and a zealous moralist who divided the world into two camps: good and evil. Roosevelt's zest for life and his combative spirit were contagious, and he was ever eager to express an opinion on any subject. After young Roosevelt participated in a buffalo hunt in the Dakotas, one of the cowboys said: "There goes the most remarkable man I ever met. Unless I am badly mistaken, the world is due to hear from him one of these days."

Within two years after graduating from Harvard, Roosevelt, a reform-minded Republican, won election as the youngest member of the New York legislature. Fearlessly independent, he could not be bought. Nor did he tolerate the excesses of the spoils system. "Though I am a strong party man," he warned, "if I find a corrupt public official, I would take off his head."

With the world seemingly at Roosevelt's feet, however, disaster struck. In 1884, his mother, Mittie, only forty-eight years old, died of typhoid fever. Eleven hours later, his "bewitchingly pretty," twenty-two-year-old wife, Alice, died in his arms of kidney failure, having given birth to their only child just two days earlier. The "light has gone out of my life," Roosevelt noted in his diary. The double funeral service for his wife and mother was so emotional that the officiating minister wept throughout his prayer.

To recover from this "strange and terrible fate," Roosevelt turned his newborn daughter over to his sister, quit his political career, sold the family house, and moved to a cattle ranch in the Dakota Territory, where he threw himself into roping and branding steers, shooting buffalo and bears, capturing outlaws, fighting Indians (whom he called a "lesser race"), and reading novels by the campfire. He was, by his own admission, a poor shot, a bad roper, and an average horseman, but he loved every minute of his western life. Although his time in the West lasted only two years, he never got over being a cowboy. "I owe more than I can express to the West," he wrote in his memoirs.

Back in New York City, Roosevelt remarried and ran unsuccessfully for mayor in 1886. He later served six years as a U.S. Civil Service commissioner and two years as the city's police commissioner. In 1896, he campaigned energetically for William McKinley, and the new president was asked to reward him with the position of assistant secretary of the navy. McKinley resisted at first, saying that Roosevelt was too "hotheaded," but eventually gave in.

Roosevelt took full advantage of the celebrity he had gained with the Rough Riders in Cuba to win the governorship of New York in 1898. By then, he had become the most visible young Republican in the nation. "I have played it in bull luck this summer," he wrote a friend about his recent streak of successes.

"First, to get into the war; then to get out of it; then to get elected." Two years later, Republican leaders were urging him to become the vice presidential running mate for McKinley, who was hoping for a second term.

FROM VICE PRESIDENT TO PRESIDENT

In the 1900 presidential contest, the Democrats turned again to William Jennings Bryan, who wanted to make American imperialism the "paramount issue" of the campaign. The Democratic platform condemned the Philippine conflict as "an unnecessary war" that had placed the United States "in the false and un-American position of crushing with military force the efforts of our former allies to achieve liberty and self-government."

The Republicans renominated McKinley and named Roosevelt, now known as "Mr. Imperialism," their candidate for vice president. Roosevelt, who despised Bryan, crisscrossed the nation condemning Bryan's "communistic and socialistic doctrines" promoting higher taxes and the unlimited coinage of silver. In the end, McKinley and Roosevelt won by 7.2 million to 6.4 million popular votes and 292 to 155 electoral votes. Bryan even lost Nebraska, his home state.

On September 14, 1901, McKinley died, and Theodore Roosevelt was elevated to the White House. "Now look," exclaimed Marcus "Mark" Hanna, the Ohio senator who had been McKinley's political manager, "that damned cowboy is President of the United States!" McKinley's assassination marked the end of one political era and the beginning of another.

Six weeks short of his forty-third birthday, Roosevelt was the youngest man ever to become president. But he had more experience in public affairs than most new presidents, and perhaps more vitality than any. One observer compared his boundless personality and energy to Niagara Falls—"both great wonders of nature." Roosevelt's glittering spectacles, glistening teeth, and overflowing enthusiasm were like divine gifts to political cartoonists, as was his famous motto, an old African proverb: "Speak softly, and carry a big stick."

Roosevelt's unshakable self-righteousness led him to cast nearly every issue in moral and patriotic terms. He was the first truly activist president. The presidency was, as he put it, a "bully pulpit"—a wonderful platform for delivering fist-pumping speeches on the virtues of honesty, courage, and civic duty.

Nowhere was Roosevelt's forceful will more evident than in his handling of foreign affairs. Like many of his political friends and associates, he was convinced that the "civilized" and "barbarian" people of the world faced inevitable

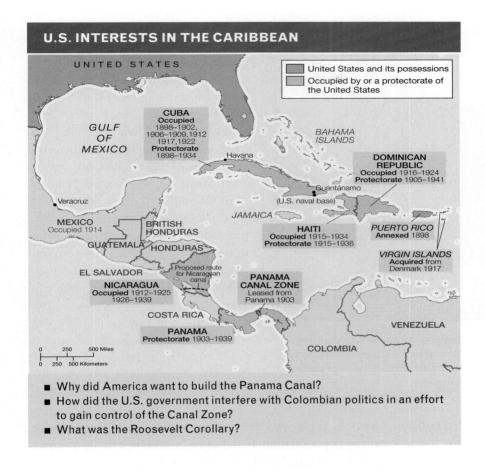

U.S. INTERESTS IN THE CARIBBEAN

UNITED STATES

- United States and its possessions
- Occupied by or a protectorate of the United States

GULF OF MEXICO

BAHAMA ISLANDS

CUBA
Occupied 1898–1902, 1906–1909, 1912 1917, 1922
Protectorate 1898–1934

Havana

DOMINICAN REPUBLIC
Occupied 1916–1924
Protectorate 1905–1941

Guantánamo
(U.S. naval base)

Veracruz

JAMAICA

MEXICO
Occupied 1914

BRITISH HONDURAS

HAITI
Occupied 1915–1934
Protectorate 1915–1936

PUERTO RICO
Annexed 1898

GUATEMALA   HONDURAS

VIRGIN ISLANDS
Acquired from Denmark 1917

EL SALVADOR

Proposed route for Nicaraguan canal

PANAMA CANAL ZONE
Leased from Panama 1903

NICARAGUA
Occupied 1912–1925 1926–1939

COSTA RICA

VENEZUELA

PANAMA
Protectorate 1903–1939

COLOMBIA

0   250   500 Miles
0   250   500 Kilometers

- Why did America want to build the Panama Canal?
- How did the U.S. government interfere with Colombian politics in an effort to gain control of the Canal Zone?
- What was the Roosevelt Corollary?

conflict, not unlike the fate of the Native Americans pushed off their ancestral lands by Americans. In 1899, Roosevelt argued that the United States, as a "great civilized power," needed to take control of other regions of the world to bring "law, order, and righteousness" to "backward peoples." He believed that American imperialists would be missionaries of civic virtue rather than colonial masters, spreading the merits of their superior "race."

THE PANAMA CANAL After the Spanish-American War (the War of 1898), as the United States became more deeply involved in the Caribbean, one issue overshadowed every other: the proposed Panama Canal. By enabling ships to travel from the Pacific Ocean to the Gulf of Mexico, such a canal would cut the travel distance between San Francisco and New York City by almost 8,000 miles.

Digging the canal President Theodore Roosevelt operating a steam shovel during his 1906 visit to the Panama Canal.

The narrow nation of Panama had first become a major concern of Americans in the late 1840s, when it became an important overland link in the sea route from the East Coast to the California goldfields. Two treaties dating from that period loomed as obstacles to the construction of a canal, however. The Bidlack Treaty (1846) with Colombia (then called New Granada) guaranteed Colombia's control over Panama. In the Clayton-Bulwer Treaty (1850), the British had agreed to acquire no more Central American territory, and the United States joined them in agreeing to build or fortify a canal only by mutual consent.

Secretary of State John Hay asked the British ambassador for consent to build a canal, and the outcome was the Hay-Pauncefote Treaty of 1901. Other obstacles remained, however. From 1881 to 1887, a French company led by Ferdinand de Lesseps, who had engineered the Suez Canal in Egypt, had already spent nearly $300 million and some 20,000 lives to dig a canal a third of the way across Panama, which was still under Colombian control. The company asked that the United States purchase the partially completed canal, which it did.

Meanwhile, Secretary Hay had opened negotiations with Ambassador Tomás Herrán of Colombia. In return for acquiring a canal zone six miles wide, the United States agreed to pay $10 million. The U.S. Senate ratified the Hay-Herrán Treaty in 1903, but the Colombian Senate held out for $25 million. As President Roosevelt raged against the "foolish and homicidal corruptionists in Bogotá," the Panamanians revolted against Colombian rule. Philippe Bunau-Varilla, an employee of the French canal company, assisted them and reported, after visiting Roosevelt and Hay in Washington, D.C., that U.S. warships would arrive at Colón, Panama, on November 2.

Colombian troops, who could not penetrate the overland jungle separating them from the Canal Zone, found the U.S. ships blocking the sea-lanes to the area. On November 13, the Roosevelt administration received its first ambassador from the newly independent Panama: Bunau-Varilla, who eagerly signed a treaty that extended the Canal Zone from six to ten miles wide.

For a $10 million down payment and $250,000 a year, the United States received "in perpetuity the use, occupation and control" of the fifty-mile-long Canal Zone. Not everyone applauded the president's actions. A Chicago newspaper attacked Roosevelt for his "rough-riding assault upon another republic over the shattered wreckage of international law." The U.S. attorney general, asked to supply a legal opinion upholding Roosevelt's actions, responded wryly, "No, Mr. President, if I were you I would not have any taint of legality about it." He then added, "You were accused of seduction and you have conclusively proved that you were guilty of rape." Roosevelt later explained, "I took the Canal Zone and let Congress debate; and while the debate goes on the [construction of the] Canal does also."

THE BIG STICK IN THE CARIBBEAN SEA

Big Stick diplomacy President Theodore Roosevelt wields "the big stick," symbolizing his aggressive diplomacy. As he stomps through the Caribbean, he drags a string of American warships behind him.

Building the Panama Canal was one of the greatest engineering feats in history. Over ten years, some 60,000 mostly unskilled workers from Europe, Asia, and the Caribbean used dynamite and steam shovels to gouge out the canal from dense jungle. Almost a third of the workers died. "People get killed and injured almost every day," a worker reported in his journal. "And all the bosses want is to get the canal built." With great fanfare, the canal opened on August 15, 1914, two weeks after the outbreak of the Great War in Europe.

ROOSEVELT AND LATIN AMERICA Theodore Roosevelt's "theft" of the Panama Canal Zone created ill will throughout Latin America that would last for generations. Latin Americans were also upset by constant interference from both the United States and European countries in their internal affairs. A frequent excuse for intervention was to promote a safe and stable environment for American businesses, including the collection of debts owed by Latin American governments. The Latin Americans responded with the Drago Doctrine (1902), named after Argentinian foreign minister Luis María Drago, which prohibited armed intervention by other countries to collect debts.

In December 1902, however, German and British warships blockaded Venezuela to force repayment of debts in defiance not only of the Drago Doctrine but also of the Monroe Doctrine, the U.S. policy dating to 1823 that prohibited European intervention in the Western Hemisphere. Roosevelt decided that if the United States were to keep European nations from intervening militarily in Latin America, "then sooner or later we must keep order [there] ourselves."

In 1904, a crisis over the debts of the Dominican Republic prompted Roosevelt to send two warships to the island nation and issue what came to be known as the **Roosevelt Corollary** to the Monroe Doctrine: the principle, in short, that in certain circumstances, the United States was justified in intervening in Latin American nations to prevent Europeans from doing so. Thereafter, U.S. presidents would repeatedly use military force to ensure that Latin American nations paid their debts to U.S. and European banks.

RELATIONS WITH JAPAN

While wielding a "big stick" in Latin America, Roosevelt was playing the role of peacemaker in East Asia. The principle of equal trading rights represented by the Open Door policy was tested in 1904 when the long-standing rivalry between Russia and Japan flared into the Russo-Japanese War over Japan's attempts to expand its influence in China and Korea.

On February 8, Japanese warships devastated the Russian fleet. The Japanese then occupied the Korean peninsula and drove the Russians back into Manchuria. When the Japanese signaled that they would welcome a negotiated settlement, Roosevelt sponsored a peace conference in Portsmouth, New Hampshire. In the Treaty of Portsmouth, signed on September 5, 1905, Russia acknowledged Japan's "predominant political, military, and economic interests in Korea." (Japan would annex the kingdom in 1910.) Both powers agreed to leave Manchuria.

Japan's show of strength against Russia raised concerns among U.S. leaders about the security of the Philippines. During the Portsmouth talks, Roosevelt sent William Howard Taft to meet with the Japanese foreign minister in Tokyo. They negotiated the Taft-Katsura Agreement of July 29, 1905, in which the United States accepted Japanese control of Korea in exchange for Japan acknowledging U.S. control of the Philippines. Three years later, the Root-Takahira Agreement, negotiated by Secretary of State Elihu Root and the Japanese ambassador to the United States, reinforced the Open Door policy by supporting "the independence and integrity of China" and "the principle of equal opportunity for commerce and industry in China."

Behind the outward appearances of goodwill, however, lay mutual distrust. For many Americans, the Russian threat in East Asia now gave way to concerns about the "yellow peril" (a term apparently coined by Kaiser Wilhelm II of Germany). Racial conflict on the West Coast, especially in California, helped sour relations with Japan. In 1906, San Francisco's school board ordered students of Asian descent to attend a separate public school. When

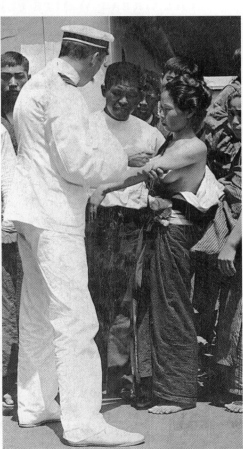

Japanese immigration Japanese immigrants are vaccinated aboard a steamship on their way to Hawaii. By 1900, about 40 percent of Hawaii's population was Japanese.

the Japanese government protested, President Roosevelt persuaded the school board to change its policy, but only after making sure that Japanese authorities would stop encouraging unemployed Japanese "laborers" to go to America. This "Gentlemen's Agreement" of 1907, the precise terms of which have never been revealed, halted the influx of Japanese immigrants to California and relieved some of the racial tension.

THE GREAT WHITE FLEET

After Roosevelt's election to a full term as president in 1904, he celebrated America's rise as a world power. Since his youth, he had retained a boyish enthusiasm for ships and sea power. In 1907, he sent the entire U.S. Navy, by then second in strength only to Britain's Royal Navy, on a grand fourteen-month tour around the world as a demonstration of America's power.

At every port of call—down the Atlantic coast of South America, then up the Pacific coast, out to Hawaii, and down to New Zealand and Australia—the "Great White Fleet" of sixteen gleaming battleships received a rousing welcome. The triumphal procession continued to Japan, China, the Philippines, then Egypt through the Suez Canal, and across the Mediterranean Sea before steaming back to Virginia in early 1909, just in time to close Roosevelt's presidency on a note of triumph.

Roosevelt's success in expanding U.S. power abroad would have mixed consequences, however, because underlying his imperialism was a militantly racist view of the world. Roosevelt and others believed that the world was made up of "civilized" societies, such as the United States, Japan, and the nations of Europe, and those they described as "barbarous," "backward," or "impotent." It was the responsibility of the "civilized" nations to exercise control of the "barbarous" peoples, by force if necessary. Roosevelt called warfare the best way to promote "the clear instinct for race selfishness" and insisted that "the most ultimately righteous of all wars is a war with savages." Such belligerent, self-righteous bigotry defied American ideals of equality and would come back to haunt the United States.

TAFT'S "DOLLAR DIPLOMACY" Republican William Howard Taft, who succeeded Roosevelt as president in 1909, continued to promote America's economic interests abroad, practicing what Roosevelt called **"dollar diplomacy."** Taft used the State Department to help American companies and banks invest in foreign countries, especially East Asia and the less developed nations of Latin America and the Caribbean. To ensure the stability of those investments, Taft did not hesitate to intervene in nations experiencing political and economic turmoil. In 1909, he dispatched U.S. Marines to support a revolution in Nicaragua. Once the new government was formed, Secretary of State Philander C. Knox helped U.S. banks negotiate loans to prop it up. Two years later, Taft again sent American troops to restore political stability. This time they stayed for more than a decade.

WILSON'S INTERVENTIONISM In 1913, the new Democratic president, Woodrow Wilson, attacked dollar diplomacy as a form of economic imperialism. He promised to treat Latin American nations "on terms of equality and honor." Yet Wilson, along with William Jennings Bryan, his secretary of state, dispatched American military forces to Latin America more often than Taft and Roosevelt combined.

Wilson argued that the United States must intervene to stabilize weak governments in the Western Hemisphere to keep European nations from doing so. During his two presidential terms, Wilson sent U.S. troops into Cuba once, Panama twice, and Honduras five times.

In 1915, when the Dominican Republic refused to sign a treaty that would have given the United States a "special" role in governing the island nation, Wilson sent U.S. Marines, who established a military government and fought a nasty guerrilla war against anti-American rebels. That same year, Wilson intervened in Haiti, next door to the Dominican Republic. He admitted that his actions were "high-handed" but argued that they were justified because the "necessity for exercising control there is immediate, urgent, imperative." Others disagreed. As the *New York Times* charged, Wilson's frequent interventions made Taft's dollar diplomacy look like "ten cent diplomacy."

THE UNITED STATES IN MEXICO Mexico was a much thornier problem. In 1910, long-suffering Mexicans had revolted against the dictatorship of Porfirio Díaz, who had given foreign corporations a free rein in developing the nation's economy. After revolutionary armies occupied Mexico City in 1911, the victorious rebels began squabbling among themselves. The leader of the rebellion, Francisco Madero, was overthrown by his chief of staff, General Victoriano Huerta, who assumed power in early 1913 and then had Madero and thirty other political opponents murdered.

A shocked President Wilson refused to recognize "a government of butchers." Huerta ignored Wilson's criticism and established a dictatorship. Wilson decided that Huerta must be removed and ordered U.S. warships to halt shipments of foreign weapons to the new government. Meanwhile, several rival revolutionary Mexican armies, the largest of which was led by Francisco Pancho Villa, began trying to unseat Huerta.

Intervention in Mexico U.S. Marines enter Veracruz, Mexico, in 1914.

On April 9, 1914, nine American sailors were arrested in Tampico, Mexico, while trying to buy supplies. Mexican officials quickly released them and apologized to the U.S. naval commander. There the incident might have ended, but the imperious U.S. admiral demanded that the Mexicans fire a twenty-one-gun salute to the American flag. After they refused, Wilson sent U.S. troops ashore at Veracruz on April 21, 1914. They occupied the city at a cost of 19 American lives; at least 300 Mexicans were killed or wounded.

The use of military force in Mexico played out like many previous American interventions in the Caribbean and Central America. Congress readily supported the decision because American honor was supposedly at stake, and Wilson was sure that most Mexicans would welcome U.S. intervention since his intentions were so "unselfish." But his strategy backfired. Instead of welcoming the Americans as liberators, Mexicans viewed them as invaders. For seven months, the Americans governed Veracruz. They left in late 1914 after Huerta was overthrown by Venustiano Carranza.

Still, the troubles south of the border continued. In 1916, rebel leader Pancho Villa launched raids into Texas and New Mexico in a deliberate attempt to trigger U.S. intervention. On March 9, he and his men attacked Columbus, New Mexico, just three miles across the border. Villa shouted "Kill all the Gringos!" as his army of 500 peasant revolutionaries burned the town and killed seventeen Americans. A furious Wilson sent General John J. Pershing to Mexico with 6,000 U.S. soldiers. For nearly a year, Pershing's troops chased Villa's army through the rugged mountains of northern Mexico. As Pershing muttered, "It's like trying to chase a rat in a cornfield." In 1917, the American troops were ordered home. The elusive Villa, meanwhile, named his mule "President Wilson." By then, however, Wilson paid little notice, for he was distracted by a much greater threat: massive war in Europe.

CHAPTER REVIEW

SUMMARY

- **Toward the New Imperialism**   Near the end of the nineteenth century, the popular idea that America had a "manifest destiny" to expand its territory abroad, combined with industrialists' desire for new markets for their goods, helped to fuel America's "new *imperialism*." White Americans believed that their advanced industrial development proved their racial superiority, and by conquering "backward peoples," the United States was simply enacting the theory of the survival of the fittest. American evangelical Protestants also thought they had a duty to Christianize and "uplift" people throughout the world.

- **Expansion in the Pacific**   Business leaders hoped to extend America's commercial reach across the Pacific to exploit vast Asian markets. American planters in the Kingdom of Hawaii developed a thriving sugar industry, which increased Hawaii's commercial connections to the United States. In 1894, Hawaii's minority white population ousted the native Hawaiian queen, declared a republic, and requested that Hawaii be annexed by the United States. In 1898, President William McKinley agreed to annex the Hawaiian Islands.

- **The Spanish-American War (The War of 1898)**   When Cubans revolted against Spanish colonial rule in 1895, many Americans supported their demand for independence. *Yellow journalism* publicizing the harsh Spanish suppression of the revolt further aroused Americans' sympathy. Early in 1898, the publication of the *de Lôme letter*, followed by the sinking the *U.S. battleship* Maine in Havana Harbor, helped propel America into war with Spain. The war lasted only 114 days. Under the Treaty of Paris ending the war, Cuba became independent and the United States annexed Spain's other Caribbean possession, Puerto Rico, which it had occupied. In the Spanish colony of the Philippine Islands, America's Pacific naval fleet under Commodore George Dewey defeated the Spanish fleet in the Battle of Manila Bay.

- **Consequences of Victory**   A vicious guerrilla war followed in the Philippines when Filipinos rebelled against American control. The rebellion was suppressed, and President McKinley announced that the United States would annex the Philippines. The *Anti-Imperialist League* and others argued that acquiring overseas territories violated American principles of self-determination and independence. But the imperialists won the debate, and Congress set up a government in the Philippines and in Puerto Rico. In the Pacific region, the United States also annexed Hawaii, Guam, Wake Island, and some of the Samoa Islands during or shortly after the Spanish-American War (the War of 1898). In East Asia, Secretary of State John Hay promoted the *Open Door policy* of preserving China's territorial integrity and equal access by all nations to trade with China.

- **Theodore Roosevelt and Big-Stick Diplomacy**   Theodore Roosevelt pursued an imperialist foreign policy that confirmed the United States' new role as a world power.

He helped negotiate the treaty that ended the Russo-Japanese War, seized control of the Panama Canal, and sent the navy's fleet of new battleships around the world as a symbol of American might. He also proclaimed the *Roosevelt Corollary* to the Monroe Doctrine, asserting that the United States would intervene in Latin America as necessary in order to prevent European intervention.

- **Taft and Wilson's Interventionism Abroad** William H. Taft and Woodrow Wilson continued Roosevelt's pattern of intervening in the internal affairs of other nations, especially in Latin America and the Caribbean. What Taft called "*dollar diplomacy*" involved the U.S. government fostering American investments in less-developed nations and then using U.S. military force to protect those investments. Wilson's frustrations at the instability of the Mexican government led him to intervene with American troops twice. In both cases, the presence of U.S. soldiers only deepened the resentment of "Yankee imperialism" throughout Latin America.

CHRONOLOGY

1894	Republic of Hawaii is proclaimed
1898	U.S. battleship *Maine* explodes in Havana Harbor
	The Spanish-American War (War of 1898)
	United States annexes Hawaii
1899	U.S. Senate ratifies the Treaty of Paris, ending the War of 1898
1899–1902	Insurgents resist U.S. conquest of the Philippines
1914	Panama Canal opens
1909–1917	U.S. military interventions in Mexico and Latin America

KEY TERMS

imperialism p. 900

yellow journalism p. 905

U.S. battleship *Maine* p. 905

de Lôme letter p. 906

Teller Amendment p. 907

American Anti-Imperialist League p. 917

Open Door policy p. 920

Roosevelt Corollary p. 928

"dollar diplomacy" p. 930

 INQUIZITIVE

Go to InQuizitive to see what you've learned—and learn what you've missed—with personalized feedback along the way.

21 The Progressive Era

1890–1920

"Votes For <u>Us</u> When <u>We</u> Are Women!" Parades organized by women's suffrage groups attracted women of all ages and social classes. Here, from a patriotically outfitted automobile, some young suffragists ask their many spectators for "votes for <u>us</u> when <u>we</u> are women."

T heodore Roosevelt's emergence as a national political leader coincided with the onset of what historians have labeled the Progressive Era (1890–1920), an extraordinary period of social activism and political innovation during which compelling public issues forced profound changes in the role of government and presidential leadership. Millions of "progressives" believed that America was experiencing a "crisis of democracy" because of the urban-industrial revolution. Widespread inner-city poverty; countless children working in unregulated mines and factories; tainted food; and miserable, unsafe working conditions required bold action by churches, charitable organizations, experts, and individuals—and an expanded role for governments.

"Our country is going through a terrific period of unrest," said Amos Pinchot, a progressive attorney and reformer from New York City. Corruption was "destroying our respect for government, uprooting faith in political parties, and causing every precedent and convention of the old order to strain at its moorings."

Progressives argued that the United States had been changing so rapidly since the end of the Civil War that the nation was at risk of imploding, and the widening gap between rich and poor during the Gilded Age had become a major concern. Walter Weyl, a progressive economist, insisted that "we shall not advance far in working out our American ideals without striking hard at . . . inequality." Political equality, he added, "is a farce and a peril unless there

focus questions

1. What were the various motives of progressive reformers?

2. Which various sources of thought and activism contributed to the progressive movement?

3. What were the specific goals of progressive reformers? In what ways did they pursue these public goals?

4. What contributions did Presidents Theodore Roosevelt and William Howard Taft make to the progressive movement? How and why did these two men come to disagree about how best to advance progressive ideals?

5. Which policies of President Woodrow Wilson were influenced by the progressive movement? How and why did these differ from the policies of Presidents Roosevelt and Taft?

is at least some measure of economic equality." The growth of new industries like railroading, steel, coal, and oil had attracted waves of poor farm folk and foreign immigrants to cities whose basic social services—food, water, housing, education, sanitation, transportation, and medical care—could not keep pace with the rate of urban growth.

Between 1890 and 1920, armies of progressive reformers attacked the problems created by unregulated industrialization and unplanned urbanization. Most of all, they insisted that something must be done to control the large, powerful corporations that dominated America's economy and corrupted its political life.

By the beginning of the twentieth century, progressivism had become the most dynamic social and political force in the nation. In 1910, Woodrow Wilson, then president of Princeton University, told a gathering of clergymen that progressivism had generated "an extraordinary awakening in civic consciousness."

THE PROGRESSIVE IMPULSE

Progressives were liberals, not revolutionaries. They wanted to reform and regulate capitalist society, not destroy it. Most were Christian moralists who felt that politics had become a contest between good and evil, honesty and corruption. What they all shared was the assumption that governments—local, state, and national—must take a more active role in addressing the problems created by rapid urban and industrial growth.

Progressivism was more a widespread impulse supported by elements of both major political parties than it was a single movement with a common agenda. Republican Theodore Roosevelt called it the "forward movement" because it emphasized modernizing "old-fashioned" ways of doing things. He and other reformers stood "for the cause of progress, for the cause of the uplift of humanity and the betterment of mankind."

To make governments more responsive and "efficient" and businesses more honest and safe, progressives drew upon the new "social sciences"—sociology, political science, psychology, public health, and economics—being developed at research universities. The progressive approach was to enable "experts" to "investigate, educate, and legislate." Florence Kelley, a tireless activist, voiced the era's widespread belief that once people knew "the truth" about social ills, "they would act upon it."

Unlike populism, whose grassroots appeal was largely confined to poor rural regions in the South and Midwest, progressivism was a national movement, centered in large cities but also popular in rural areas among what came to be called Populist progressives. Progressive activists came in all stripes: men and women; Democrats, Republicans, Populists, and Socialists; labor unionists and business executives; teachers, engineers, editors, and professors; social workers, doctors, ministers, and journalists; farmers and homemakers; whites and blacks; clergymen, atheists, and agnostics. Whatever their motives and methods, their combined efforts led to significant improvements.

Yet progressivism also displayed inconsistencies and hypocrisies. Progressives often armed themselves with Christian moralism, but their "do-good" perspective was often limited by the racial and ethnic prejudices of the day, as well as by social and intellectual snobbery. The goals of upper-class white progressives rarely included racial equality. Many otherwise "progressive" people, including Theodore Roosevelt and Woodrow Wilson, believed in the supremacy of the "Anglo-Saxon race" and their own superiority to the working poor. They assumed that the workings of modern society were too complicated for the uninformed masses to understand, much less improve, without direction by those who knew better.

THE VARIED SOURCES OF PROGRESSIVISM

During the last quarter of the nineteenth century, political progressives at the local and state levels began to attack corrupt political bosses and irresponsible corporate barons. They sought more honest and more efficient government, more effective regulation of big businesses ("the trusts"), and better lives for the working poor. Only by expanding the scope of local, state, and federal governments, they believed, could these goals be attained.

ECONOMIC DEPRESSION AND DISCONTENT More than any other factor, the devastating depression of the 1890s ignited the progressive spirit of reform. The nation's worst economic calamity to that point brought massive layoffs; nearly a quarter of the adults in the workforce lost their jobs. Although the United States boasted the highest per capita income in the world, it also had some of the highest concentrations of poverty. In 1900, the U.S. population numbered 82 million; at the turn of the new century, an estimated 10 million Americans were living in poverty with annual incomes barely adequate to provide the minimum necessities of life. The devastating effects of the depression prompted many upper-middle-class urban people—lawyers, doctors, executives, social workers, teachers, professors, journalists, and college-educated women—to organize efforts to reform society, both to help those in need and to keep them from becoming revolutionaries.

POPULISM Populism, with its roots in the rural South and West, was another thread in the fabric of progressivism. The Populist party platforms of 1892 and 1896 included reforms intended to give more power to "the people," such as the direct election of U.S. senators by voters rather than by state legislatures. Although William Jennings Bryan's loss in the 1896 presidential campaign ended the Populist party as a serious political force, many reforms pushed by the Populists were implemented by progressives.

"HONEST GOVERNMENT" The Mugwumps—"gentlemen" reformers who had fought the patronage system and insisted that government jobs be awarded on the basis of merit—supplied progressivism with another key goal: the "honest government" ideal. Over the years, the good-government movement expanded beyond ending political corruption to addressing persistent urban issues such as crime, access to electricity, clean water and municipal sewers, mass transit, and garbage collection.

SOCIALISM Another significant "progressive" force was the growing influence of socialist ideas. The Socialist Party of America, supported mostly by militant farmers and immigrant Germans and Jews, served as the radical wing of progressivism. Unlike European socialists, most American socialists did not call for the government to take ownership of large corporations. They focused instead on improving working conditions and closing the widening income gap between rich and poor through "progressive" taxation. Most progressives were capitalist reformers, not socialist radicals. They rejected the extremes of both socialism and laissez-faire individualism, preferring a new, regulated capitalism "softened" by humanitarianism.

MUCKRAKING JOURNALISM Progressivism depended upon newspapers and magazines to inform the public about political corruption and social problems. The so-called **muckrakers** were America's first investigative journalists. Their aggressive reporting played a crucial role in educating the upper and middle classes about political and corporate wrongdoing and revealing "how the other half lives"—the title of Danish immigrant Jacob Riis's pioneering 1890 work of photojournalism about life in the sordid slums of New York City, where some 1.2 million people, mostly immigrants, lived in poverty amid killing diseases.

The muckrakers got their nickname from Theodore Roosevelt, who said that crusading journalists were "often indispensable to . . . society, but only if they know when to stop raking the muck." By uncovering political corruption and writing about social ills in newspapers and popular monthly magazines such as *McClure's*, *Munsey's*, and *Cosmopolitan*, the muckrakers changed the face of journalism and gave it a new political role. Roosevelt, both as governor of New York and as president, frequently used muckrakers to drum up support for his policies; he corresponded with them, invited them to the White House, and used their popularity to help shape public opinion.

The golden age of muckraking is sometimes dated from 1902, when Samuel S. McClure, the owner of *McClure's*, recruited idealistic journalists to root out the corruption in politics and corporations. McClure was determined to make his magazine a "power for good"; the "vitality of democracy," he insisted, depended upon educating the public about "complex questions."

McClure's and other muckraking magazines investigated corporate monopolies and crooked political machines while revealing the miserable conditions in which poor Americans lived and worked.

Cover of *McClure's* magazine, 1902
This issue features Ida Tarbell's muckraking series investigating the Standard Oil Company.

Ida Tarbell, one of the most dedicated muckrakers, spent years doggedly investigating the illegal means by which John D. Rockefeller had built his gigantic Standard Oil trust. At the end of her series of nineteen *McClure's* articles on the topic, she asked readers: "And what are we going to do about it?" She stressed that it was "the people of the United States, and nobody else, [who] must cure whatever is wrong in the industrial situation."

Without the muckrakers, progressivism would never have achieved widespread popular support. During the early twentieth century, investigative journalism became such a powerful force for change that one editor said that Americans now had "Government by Magazine."

Religious Activism

Social justice progressives believed that society had an ethical obligation to help its poorest and most vulnerable members. Others were inspired by the **social gospel**, a newer, specifically Protestant belief that Christians should help the poor to bring about the "Kingdom of God" on earth.

In many respects, the progressive movement as a whole represented a new, energetic form of public outreach that incorporated religious (and nonreligious) groups and focused not so much on saving souls as on social action. More and more Christians adopted the mission of social reform. "We believe," a social gospel organization said, "that the age of sheer individualism is past, and the age of social responsibility has arrived."

THE SOCIAL GOSPEL During the last quarter of the nineteenth century, a growing number of churches and synagogues began emphasizing community service and the care of the unfortunate. New organizations made key contributions to the movement. The Young Men's Christian Association (YMCA) and a similar group for women, the YWCA, both entered the United States from England in the 1850s and grew rapidly after 1870. The Salvation Army, founded in London in 1878, came to the United States a year later.

The YMCA and YWCA combined nondenominational religious evangelism with social services and fitness training in community centers (segregated by race and gender) across the country. Intended to provide low-cost housing and healthful exercise in a "safe Christian environment" for young men and women from rural areas or foreign countries, the YMCA/YWCA centers often included libraries, classrooms, and kitchens. "Hebrew" counterparts—YMHAs and YWHAs—provided many of the same facilities in cities with large Jewish populations. Salvation Army centers offered "soup kitchens" to feed the poor and day nurseries for the children of working mothers.

The major forces behind the social gospel movement were Protestants and Catholics who feared that Christianity had become too closely associated with the upper and middle classes and was losing its appeal to the working poor. In 1875, Washington Gladden, a prominent pastor in Springfield, Massachusetts, invited striking shoe-factory workers to his church, but they refused because the factory owners and managers were members of the congregation. Gladden, heartbroken that Christianity was dividing along class lines, responded by writing *Working People and Their Employers* (1876), which argued that true Christianity was based on the principle that "thou shalt love thy neighbor as thyself." Gladden rejected the view of social Darwinists that the poor deserved their fate and should not be helped. He became the first prominent religious leader to support the rights of workers to form unions. He also spoke out against racial segregation and efforts to discriminate against immigrants.

Gladden's efforts helped launch a new era in religious life in which churches engaged with the urgent problems created by a rapidly urbanizing and industrializing society. He and other "social gospelers" reached out to the working poor who labored long hours for low wages, lived in miserable slum housing, had no insurance for on-the-job accidents, and lacked the legal right to form unions.

Walter Rauschenbusch, a German American Baptist minister serving immigrant tenement dwellers in the Hell's Kitchen neighborhood of New York City, became the greatest champion of the social gospel. In 1907, he published a pathbreaking book, *Christianity and the Social Crisis*, in which he argued emphatically that "whoever uncouples the religious and social life has not understood Jesus." The Christian emphasis on personal salvation, he added, must be linked with an equally passionate commitment to social justice. Churches must embrace "the social aims of Jesus," he stressed, for Christianity was intended to be a "revolutionary" faith.

In Rauschenbusch's view, religious life needed the social gospel to revitalize it and make it socially relevant: "We shall never have a perfect social life, yet we must seek it with faith." Like the muckrakers, Rauschenbusch sought to expose the realities of poverty in America and convince statesmen to deal with the crisis. His message resonated with Theodore Roosevelt, Woodrow Wilson, and many other progressives in both political parties. Years later, Rev. Martin Luther King Jr. spoke for three generations of radicals and reformers when he said that *Christianity and the Social Crisis* "left an indelible imprint on my thinking."

Rauschenbusch, Gladden, and other social gospelers sought to expand the "Kingdom of God" by following Christ's example by serving the poor and powerless. Rugged individualism may have been the path to wealth, they argued, but "Christian socialism" offered hope for unity among all classes. "Every religious and political question," said George Herron, a religion professor at Grinnell College, "is fundamentally economic." And the solution to economic tensions was social solidarity. As progressive economist Richard Ely put it, America could only truly thrive when it recognized that "our true welfare is not an individual matter purely, but likewise a social affair."

SETTLEMENT HOUSES Among the most visible soldiers in the social gospel movement were those who volunteered in innovative community

Jane Addams By the end of the century, thanks to the efforts of Jane Addams and others, religious groups were joining the settlement house movement.

centers called settlement houses. At the Hull House settlement on Halsted Street in a working-class Chicago neighborhood, two women from privileged backgrounds, Jane Addams and Ellen Gates Starr, addressed the everyday needs of the working poor, especially newly arrived European immigrants.

Addams and Starr were driven by an "impulse to share the lives of the poor" and to make social service "express the spirit of Christ." Their staff of two dozen women served thousands of people each week. Besides a nursery for the infant children of working mothers, Hull House also sponsored health clinics, lectures, music lessons and art studios, men's clubs, an employment bureau, job training, a gymnasium, a coffeehouse, and a savings bank. By the early twentieth century, there were hundreds of settlement houses in cities across the United States, most of them in the Northeast and Midwest.

To Addams, the social gospel driving progressive reformers reflected their "yearning sense of justice and compassion." She and other settlement house leaders soon realized, however, that their work in the rapidly spreading immigrant slums was like bailing out the ocean with a teaspoon. They thus added political reform to their already lengthy agenda and began lobbying for new laws and regulations to improve the living conditions in poor neighborhoods.

As her influence in Chicago grew, Addams was appointed to prominent governmental and community boards, where she focused on improving public health and food safety. She pushed for better street lighting and police protection in poor neighborhoods, and sought to reduce the misuse of narcotics. An ardent pacifist and outspoken advocate for suffrage (voting rights) for women, Addams would become the first American woman to win the Nobel Peace Prize.

THE WOMAN SUFFRAGE MOVEMENT

From 1880 to 1910, the number of employed women tripled from 2.6 million to 7.8 million. As women, especially college-educated women, became more involved in the public world of work and wages, the women's rights movement grew. Immediately after the Civil War, women in the movement had hoped that the Fifteenth Amendment, which guaranteed voting rights for African American men, would aid their own efforts to gain the vote. The majority of men, however, still insisted that women stay out of politics because it would corrupt their moral purity.

In 1869 the Wyoming Territory became the first place in the United States to extend equal voting rights to women. In that year, the women's rights movement split over the issue of whether to concentrate solely on gaining the vote or to adopt a broader agenda. Susan B. Anthony and Elizabeth Cady

East meets West San Francisco suffragists marched across the country in 1915 to deliver a petition calling for a constitutional amendment with more than 500,000 signatures to Congress in Washington, D.C. Along the way, they were warmly received by other suffragists, like those of New Jersey, pictured here.

Stanton founded the National Woman Suffrage Association (NWSA) to promote a **woman suffrage** amendment to the Constitution, but they considered it only one among many feminist causes to be championed. For example, they also campaigned for new laws requiring higher pay for women workers and making it easier for abused wives to get divorces. Other suffrage activists insisted that pursuing multiple issues hurt their cause. In 1869, they formed the American Woman Suffrage Association (AWSA), which focused single-mindedly on voting rights.

In 1890, the rival groups united as the National American Woman Suffrage Association (NAWSA). That same year, Wyoming was admitted as a state, the first with full voting rights for women. It was in the territories and states west of the Mississippi River that the suffrage movement had its earliest successes. In those areas, women were more engaged in grassroots political activities than they were in the East.

Between 1890 and 1896, the suffrage cause won three more victories in western states—Utah, Colorado, and Idaho. The movement then stalled for a time until proposals for voting rights at the state level easily won a Washington State referendum in 1910 and carried California by a close majority in 1911. The following year three more western states—Arizona, Kansas, and Oregon—joined in to make a total of nine western states with full suffrage. In 1913, Illinois granted women voting rights in presidential and municipal elections. Yet not until New York acted in 1917 did a state east of the Mississippi River allow women to vote in all elections.

Many advocates for women's suffrage argued that the right to vote and hold office was a matter of simple justice: women were just as capable as men of exercising the rights and responsibilities of citizenship. Others insisted that women were morally superior to men and therefore would improve the quality of the political process.

Women voters and politicians, advocates argued, would promote the welfare of society as a whole, creating a powerful engine for progressive social change. One activist explicitly linked women's suffrage with the social gospel, declaring that women followed the teachings of Christ more faithfully than men. If they were elected to public office, they would "far more effectively guard the morals of society and the sanitary conditions of cities."

Yet the women's suffrage movement was not free from social, ethnic, and racial prejudices. Carrie Chapman Catt, who became president of the National American Woman Suffrage Association in 1900, warned of the danger that "lies in the votes possessed by the males in the slums of the cities, and the ignorant foreign [immigrant] vote." She added that the nation, with "ill-advised haste," had given "the foreigner, the Negro and the Indian" the vote but still

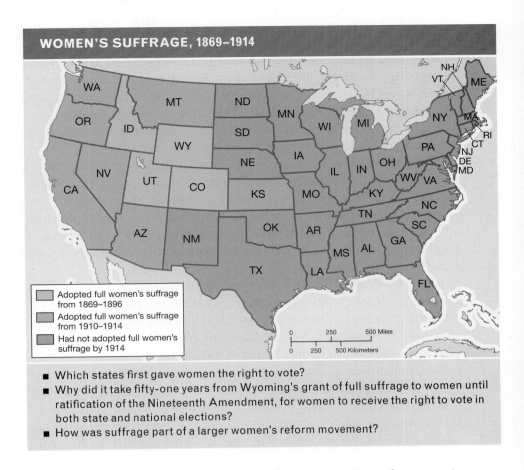

WOMEN'S SUFFRAGE, 1869–1914

Adopted full women's suffrage from 1869–1896

Adopted full women's suffrage from 1910–1914

Had not adopted full women's suffrage by 1914

- Which states first gave women the right to vote?
- Why did it take fifty-one years from Wyoming's grant of full suffrage to women until ratification of the Nineteenth Amendment, for women to receive the right to vote in both state and national elections?
- How was suffrage part of a larger women's reform movement?

withheld it from white women. Throughout the country, most suffrage organizations excluded African American women.

PROGRESSIVES' AIMS AND ACHIEVEMENTS

The impulses and groups comprising the progressive movement grew out of what Theodore Roosevelt called the "fierce discontent with evil" that many Americans felt at the turn of the nineteenth century. Progressives focused on many different goals and used many different methods. They assaulted a wide array of what they saw as social and political evils, from corrupt politicians to too-powerful corporations, from economic distress on small farms and in big cities to the general feeling that "the people" had lost control of the nation to "the special interests"—businesses and their leaders who were solely interested in "money-getting" at the expense of public welfare.

POLITICAL REFORMS

Progressivism set in motion the two most important political developments of the twentieth century: the rise of direct democracy and the expansion of federal power. In his monthly articles in *McClure's* magazine, Lincoln Steffens, a leading muckraker, regularly asked: "Will the people rule? Is democracy possible?" Steffens and other progressives often answered that the way to improve America's democracy was to make it even more democratic.

To empower citizens to clean up the corrupt political system, progressives pushed to make the political process more open and transparent. One process was the *direct primary*, which would allow all members of a political party to vote on the party's nominees, rather than the traditional practice in which an inner circle of party leaders chose the candidates. In 1896, South Carolina became the first state to adopt a statewide primary, and within twenty years nearly every state had done so.

Progressives also developed other ways to increase public participation in the political process ("direct democracy") so as to curb the power of corporate giants over state legislatures. In 1898, South Dakota became the first state to adopt the *initiative* and *referendum*, procedures that allowed voters to create laws directly rather than having to wait for legislative action. Citizens could sign petitions to have a proposal put on the ballot (the initiative) and then vote it up or down (the referendum). Still another progressive innovation was the recall, whereby corrupt or incompetent elected officials could be removed by a public petition and vote. By 1920, nearly twenty states had adopted the initiative and referendum, and nearly a dozen had sanctioned the recall procedure.

Progressives also fought to change the way that U.S. senators were elected. Under the Constitution, state legislatures elected senators, a process frequently corrupted by lobbyists and vote buying. In 1900, for example, Senate investigators revealed that a Montana senator had given more than $100,000 in secret bribes to members of the legislature that chose him. In 1913, thanks to the efforts of progressives, the **Seventeenth Amendment**, providing for the direct election of senators, was ratified by enough states to become law.

THE EFFICIENCY MOVEMENT

A second major theme of progressivism was the "gospel of efficiency." Louis D. Brandeis, a Kentucky attorney who became Woodrow Wilson's progressive adviser and later a justice of the Supreme Court, believed that "efficiency is the hope of democracy."

The champion of progressive efficiency was Frederick Winslow Taylor, a Philadelphia-born industrial engineer who during the 1890s became a celebrated business consultant, helping mills and factories implement "scientific management." The nation's first "efficiency expert," Taylor showed employers how to cut waste and improve productivity. By breaking down work activities (filling a wheelbarrow, driving a nail, shoveling coal) into a sequence of mechanical steps and using stopwatches to measure the time it took each worker to perform each step, Taylor established detailed performance standards (and cash rewards) for each job classification, specifying how fast people should work and when they should rest. His celebrated book, *The Principles of Scientific Management* (1911), influenced business organizations for decades.

The goal of what came to be called **Taylorism** was to usher in a "mental revolution" in business management that would improve productivity and profits, raise pay for the most efficient workers, and reduce the likelihood of worker strikes. As Taylor wrote, "Men will not do an extraordinary day's work for an ordinary day's pay."

Many workers, however, resented Taylor's innovations, seeing them as just a tool to make people work faster. Yet his approach to industrial management became one of the most important contributions to capitalist economies in the twentieth century and brought concrete improvements in productivity.

Political progressives applied Taylorism to the operations of government by calling for the reorganization of state and federal agencies to eliminate duplication, the establishment of clear lines of authority, and the replacement of political appointees with trained specialists. By the early twentieth century, many complex functions of government had come to require specialists with technical expertise. As Woodrow Wilson wrote, progressive ideals could be achieved only if government at all levels was "informed and administered by experts." Many cities set up "efficiency bureaus" to identify government waste and apply more cost-effective "best practices."

MUNICIPAL REFORM Two Taylorist ideas for reform of city and county governments emerged in the first decade of the new century. One, the commission system, was first adopted in 1901 by the city of Galveston, Texas, after the local government collapsed following a devastating hurricane and tidal wave that killed more than 8,000—the greatest natural disaster in American history. The commission system placed ultimate authority in a board composed of commissioners who combined both legislative and executive powers in heading up city departments (sanitation, police, utilities, and so on).

Houston, Texas, created a commission system in 1906. Dallas and Des Moines, Iowa, followed in 1907, as did Memphis in 1909.

Even more popular than the commission system was the city-manager plan, under which an appointed professional administrator ran a city or county government in accordance with policies set by the elected council and mayor. Staunton, Virginia, adopted the first city-manager plan in 1908. Five years later, the inadequate response of municipal officials to a flood led Dayton, Ohio, to become the first large city to adopt the plan.

Yet the efforts to make local governments more "business-like" and professional had a downside. Shifting control from elected officials representing individual neighborhoods to at-large commissioners and nonpartisan specialists separated local government from party politics, which for many working-class voters had been the main way they could have a voice in how they were governed locally. In addition, running a city like a business led commissioners and managers to focus on reducing expenses rather than expanding services, even when such expansion was clearly needed.

THE WISCONSIN IDEA   At the state level, the ideal of efficient government run by nonpartisan experts was pursued most notably by progressive Republican governor Robert M. La Follette of Wisconsin. "Fighting Bob" La Follette declared war on "vast corporate combinations" and political corruption by creating a nonpartisan state government that would become a "laboratory for democracy." He established a Legislative Reference Bureau, which provided elected officials with nonpartisan research, advice, and help in drafting legislation. La Follette used the bureau's reports to enact such reforms as the direct primary, stronger railroad regulation, the conservation of natural resources, and workmen's compensation programs to support people injured on the job.

The "Wisconsin idea" was widely publicized and copied by other progressive governors. La Follette explained that the Wisconsin idea was a commitment to use government power to make "a happier and better state to live in, that its institutions are more democratic, that the opportunities of all its people are more equal, that social justice more nearly prevails."

REGULATION OF BUSINESS   Of all the problems facing American society at the turn of the century, one towered above all: the regulation of giant corporations. The threat of corporate monopolies increased during the depression of the 1890s as struggling companies were gobbled up by larger ones. Between 1895 and 1904, some 157 new holding companies gained control of 1,800 different businesses. Almost fifty of these giant holding companies controlled more than 70 percent of the market in their respective industries. In

Friends of the working class (Left to right) American labor leader Andrew Furuseth, Governor Robert M. La Follette, and muckraker Lincoln Steffens, ca. 1915.

1896, fewer than a dozen companies other than railroads were worth $10 million or more. By 1903, that number had soared to 300.

Concerns over the concentration of economic power in trusts and other forms of monopolies had led Congress to pass the Sherman Anti-Trust Act in 1890, but it proved ineffective. In addition, government agencies responsible for regulating businesses often came under the influence of those they were supposed to regulate. Retired railroad executives, for instance, were appointed to the Interstate Commerce Commission (ICC), which had been created to regulate railroads. The issue of regulating the regulators has never been fully resolved.

SOCIAL JUSTICE

Another important focus of the progressive movement was greater social justice for the working poor, the jobless, and the homeless. In addition to their work in settlement houses and other areas, many progressives formed advocacy organizations such as the National Consumers' League, which educated consumers about harsh working conditions in factories and mills and the widespread use of child workers.

Other organizations, such as the General Federation of Women's Clubs, insisted that civic life needed the humanizing effect of female leadership.

Women's clubs across the country sought to clean up filthy slums by educating residents about personal and household hygiene ("municipal housekeeping"), urging construction of sewer systems, and launching public-awareness campaigns about the connection between unsanitary conditions and disease. Women's clubs also campaigned for child-care centers; kindergartens; government inspection of food processing plants; stricter housing codes; laws protecting women in the workplace; and more social services for the poor, sick, disabled, and abused. Still others addressed prostitution and alcohol abuse.

THE CAMPAIGN AGAINST DRINKING Middle-class women reformers, most of them motivated by strong religious convictions, were the driving force behind the social justice movement. Among the most powerful campaigns was that of the Women's Christian Temperance Union (WCTU). Founded in 1874 in Cleveland, Ohio, by 1900 the WCTU had grown into the largest women's group in the nation, boasting 300,000 members. While some of them were motivated by Protestant beliefs that consuming any alcohol was a sin, most saw excessive drinking, especially in saloons, as a threat to social progress and family stability.

Frances Willard Founder of the WCTU who lobbied for women's suffrage.

By attacking drunkenness and closing saloons, reformers hoped to (1) improve family life by preventing domestic violence by husbands and fathers, (2) reduce crime in the streets, and (3) remove one of the worst tools of corruption—free beer on Election Day—in an effort to "buy" votes among the working class. As a Boston sociologist concluded, the saloon had become "the enemy of society because of the evil results produced upon the individual."

Initially, WCTU members met in churches to pray and then marched to nearby saloons to try to convince their owners to close. As its name suggests, the Women's Christian Temperance Union advocated *temperance*—the reduction of alcohol consumption. But the WCTU also urged individuals to embrace *abstinence* and refuse to drink any alcoholic beverages.

Under the leadership of Frances Willard, president of the WCTU between 1879 and 1898, the organization moved beyond moral persuasion of saloon-keepers and drinkers and began promoting legislation to ban alcohol ("prohibition"). Willard also pushed the WCTU to lobby for other progressive reforms important to women, including an eight-hour workday, the regulation of child labor, government-funded kindergartens, the right to vote, and federal inspections of the food industry. More than anything else, however, the WCTU continued to campaign against drinking.

The battle against alcoholic beverages took on new strength in 1893 with the formation of the Anti-Saloon League, an organization based in local churches that pioneered the strategy of the single-issue political pressure group. Describing itself as "the Protestant church in action against the saloon," the bipartisan League, like the WCTU, initially focused on closing down saloons rather than abolishing alcohol. Eventually, however, it decided to force the prohibition issue into the forefront of state and local elections. At its "Jubilee Convention" in 1913, the League endorsed an amendment to the Constitution prohibiting the manufacture, sale, and consumption of alcoholic beverages, which Congress approved in 1917.

LABOR LEGISLATION In 1890, almost half of the nation's wage workers toiled up to twelve hours a day—sometimes seven days a week—in unsafe, unsanitary, and unregulated conditions for extremely low wages. Legislation to ensure better working conditions and limit child labor was perhaps the most significant reform to emerge from the drive for progressive social justice.

At the end of the nineteenth century, fewer than half of working families lived solely on the husband's earnings. Many married women engaged in "homework"—making clothes, selling flower arrangements, preparing food for others, and taking in boarders. Parents in poor families also frequently took their children out of school and put them to work in factories, shops, mines, mills, and canneries, and on farms. In 1900, some 1.75 million children between the ages of ten and fifteen were working outside the home.

Many progressives argued that children, too, had rights in a democracy. The National Child Labor Committee campaigned for laws prohibiting the employment of children. Within ten years, most states had passed such laws, although some were lax in enforcing them.

Progressives who focused on children's issues also demanded that cities build more parks and playgrounds. Further, reformers made a concerted effort to regulate the length of the workday for women, in part because some of them were pregnant and others had children at home with inadequate supervision.

Child labor Child workers shuck oysters in 1913 at the Varn & Platt Canning Company in Bluffton, South Carolina.

Spearheaded by Florence Kelley, the first president of the National Consumers' League, progressives convinced many state governments to ban the hiring of children below a certain age, and to limit the hours that both women and children could work.

It took a tragic disaster, however, to spur meaningful government regulation of dangerous workplaces. On March 25, 1911, a fire broke out at the Triangle Shirtwaist factory (called a "sweatshop" because of its cramped and unventilated work areas) in New York City. Escape routes were limited because the owner kept the stairway door locked to prevent theft, and 146 workers trapped on the upper floors of the ten-story building died or leaped to their deaths. The victims were mostly young, foreign-born women in their teens, almost all of them Jewish, Italian, or Russian immigrants. In the fire's aftermath, dozens of new city and state regulations dealing with fire hazards, dangerous working conditions, and child labor were enacted across the nation.

The Supreme Court was inconsistent in its rulings on state labor laws. In *Lochner v. New York* (1905), the Court ruled that a state law limiting bakers to a sixty-hour workweek was unconstitutional because it violated workers' right to accept any jobs they wanted, no matter how bad the working conditions or how low the pay. Three years later, however, in *Muller v. Oregon* (1908), the Court changed its mind. Based on evidence that long working hours increased the chances of health problems, the Court approved an Oregon law restricting the workday to no more than ten hours for women.

THE "PROGRESSIVE" INCOME TAX Progressives also addressed America's growing economic inequality. One way to redistribute wealth was through a "progressive" federal income tax—so called because the tax rates "progress," or rise, as income levels rise, thus forcing the rich to pay more. Such a "graduated" or "progressive" tax system was the climax of the progressive movement's commitment to a more equitable distribution of wealth.

The progressive income tax was an old idea. In 1894, William Jennings Bryan had persuaded Congress to approve a 2 percent tax on annual incomes of more than $4,000. When millionaires responded by threatening to leave America, Bryan exclaimed, "If some of our 'best people' prefer to leave the country rather than pay the tax . . . let them depart." Soon after the tax became law, however, the Supreme Court declared it unconstitutional on a technicality.

Progressives continued to believe, however, that a "graduated" tax would help slow the concentration of wealth in the hands of the richest Americans. In 1907, President Theodore Roosevelt announced his support. Two years later, his successor, William Howard Taft, endorsed a constitutional amendment allowing such a tax, and Congress agreed. Finally, in 1913, the **Sixteenth Amendment** was ratified by enough states to become law.

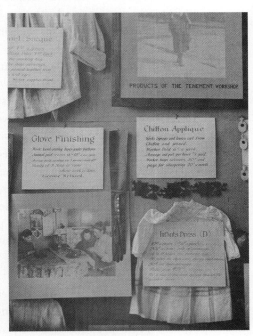

National Consumers' League exhibit
To raise awareness about labor reform, everyday objects are displayed alongside descriptions of the poor working conditions and exploitation that went into their manufacture.

Progressivism under Roosevelt and Taft

Most progressive legislation originated at the state and local levels. Federal reform efforts began in earnest only when Theodore Roosevelt became president in 1901. During his rapid rise to national fame and leadership, Roosevelt had grown more progressive with each passing year. "A great democracy," he said, "has got to be *progressive* or it will soon cease to be great or a democracy."

Unlike his predecessor, William McKinley, who was unwilling to confront business leaders, "T.R." thrived on confrontation. One journalist described him as "impetuous, impatient, and wholly lacking in tact." He could not stand indecision or inaction and did everything emphatically, at full speed. For him, a life of public service was both an exciting dream and a sobering responsibility.

Roosevelt was a boundless force of nature, an American original, a "steam engine in trousers" with an oversized intellect and ego. His exuberance, charm, and humor, however, made him an irresistible personality. Even his political opponent, Woodrow Wilson, was smitten after meeting Roosevelt in person: "You can't resist the man."

In the White House, Roosevelt jumped into his duties with what he called "strenuosity." He invited guests to wrestle or box with him, or to fight with wooden swords or climb trees. His outsized personality, said a friend, "so crowds the room that the walls are worn thin and threaten to burst outward."

Roosevelt transformed the presidency and the role of the federal government by breaking with the Gilded Age tradition in which presidents had deferred to Congress. In his view, the problems caused by explosive industrial growth required powerful responses, and he was unwilling to wait for Congress to act. Only an activist president armed with new regulatory agencies and laws could counterbalance the power of the corporations and trusts. "I believe in a strong executive," Roosevelt asserted. "I believe in power." During his administration, the White House became the focus of policy-making.

Like Lincoln, his hero, Roosevelt believed that great presidents must take "noble risks" to address national needs, even if it meant stretching the limits of the Constitution. People quickly noticed his expansive view of presidential powers. Joseph "Joe" Cannon, the powerful Republican Speaker of the House, complained that Roosevelt had "no more use for the Constitution than a tomcat has for a marriage license."

TAMING BIG BUSINESS Roosevelt was the first president to use executive power to rein in Big Business. As governor of New York, he had pushed for legislation regulating sweatshops, instituting state inspections of factories and slaughterhouses, and limiting the workday to eight hours. Roosevelt believed in capitalism and the accumulation of wealth, but he was willing to adopt radical methods to ensure that the social unrest caused by the insensitivity of business owners to the rights of workers and the needs of the poor did not mushroom into a revolution.

Roosevelt applauded the growth of American industrial capitalism but declared war on corruption and on cronyism—the awarding of political appointments, government contracts, and other favors to politicians' personal friends. He endorsed a **Square Deal** for "every man, great or small, rich or poor." His Square Deal program featured what was called the "Three Cs": greater government *control* of corpo-

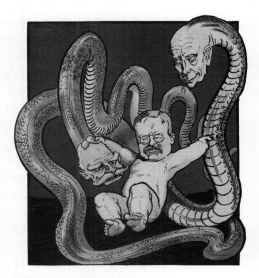

Square Deal This 1906 cartoon likens Roosevelt to the Greek legend Hercules, who as a baby strangled snakes sent from hell to kill him. Here, the serpents are pro-corporation senator Nelson Aldrich and Standard Oil's John D. Rockefeller.

rations, enhanced *conservation* of natural resources, and new regulations to protect *consumers* against contaminated food and medications.

CURBING THE TRUSTS In December 1901, just a few months after entering the White House, Roosevelt declared that it was time to deal with the "grave evils" resulting from huge corporations exercising dominance over their industries and the nation's economic life. In his view, the federal government had the right and the obligation to curb the excesses of Big Business on behalf of the public good.

Roosevelt's version of progressivism centered on the belief that governments must ensure fairness. He would wage war against the robber barons who displayed "swinish indifference" to the public good and the "unscrupulous politicians" whose votes were regularly bought and sold by corporate lobbyists.

Early in 1902, just five months into his presidency, Roosevelt shocked the business community when he ordered the U.S. attorney general to break up the Northern Securities Company, a vast network of railroads and steamships in the Pacific Northwest organized by J. Pierpont Morgan.

Morgan could not believe the news. The world's most powerful capitalist and wealthiest man rushed from New York City to the White House and told the president: "If I have done anything wrong, send your man to my man and they can fix it up." But the attorney general, who was also at the meeting, told Morgan: "We don't want to 'fix it up.' We want to stop it." Turning to Roosevelt, Morgan then asked if the president planned to attack his other trusts, such as U.S. Steel and General Electric. "Certainly not," Roosevelt replied, "unless we find out that . . . they have done something wrong."

After Morgan left, the president told the attorney general to file the anti-trust paperwork. In 1904, the Supreme Court would rule in a 5–4 decision that the Northern Securities Company was indeed a monopoly and must be dismantled, thereby opening the way for more aggressive enforcement of the Sherman Anti-Trust Act. Roosevelt fully recognized the benefits of large-scale capitalism, and he thought that the rise of Big Business was the inevitable result of the industrial era. He did not want to destroy the titans of industry and finance, but he did insist that they be regulated for the public good.

Altogether, Roosevelt approved about twenty-five anti-trust suits against oversized corporations. He also sought stronger regulation of the railroads. By their very nature, railroads often exercised a monopoly over the communities they served, enabling them to charge customers whatever they wanted. In 1903, Congress passed the Elkins Act, making it illegal for railroads to give secret rebates (cash refunds) on freight charges to high-volume business customers. That same year, Congress approved Roosevelt's request that a federal Department of Commerce and Labor be formed, within which a Bureau of Corporations would monitor the activities of big businesses.

THE 1902 COAL STRIKE In everything he did, Roosevelt acted forcefully. On May 12, 1902, for example, some 150,000 members of the United Mine Workers (UMW) labor union walked off the job at coal mines in Pennsylvania and West Virginia. The miners were seeking a wage increase, a shorter work day, and official recognition of the union by the mine owners, who refused to negotiate. Instead, the owners shut down the mines. The miners, many of whom were immigrants from eastern Europe, were in a bind. One owner expressed the ethnic prejudices shared by many of his colleagues when he proclaimed, "The miners don't suffer—why, they can't even speak English."

By October, the lengthy shutdown had caused the price of coal to soar, and hospitals and schools reported empty coal bins as winter approached. In many northern cities, the poor had run out of coal for heating. "The country is on the verge of a vast public calamity," warned Walter Rauschenbusch. The

Reverend Washington Gladden led a petition drive urging Roosevelt to step in to mediate the strike.

The president decided upon a bold move: he invited leaders of both sides to a conference in Washington, D.C., where he appealed to their "patriotism, to the spirit that sinks personal considerations and makes individual sacrifices for the public good." The mine owners in attendance, however, refused even to speak to the UMW leaders.

Roosevelt was so infuriated by what he called the "extraordinary stupidity and temper" of the "wooden-headed" and "arrogant" owners that he wanted to grab their spokesman "by the seat of his breeches" and "chuck him out" a window. Instead, he threatened to declare a national emergency so that he could take control of the mines and use soldiers to run them. When a congressman questioned the constitutionality of such a move, Roosevelt roared, "To hell with the Constitution when the people want coal!"

The threat worked: the strike ended on October 23. The miners won a nine-hour workday and a 10 percent wage increase. Roosevelt was the first president to use his authority to referee a dispute between management and labor.

ROOSEVELT'S REELECTION

Roosevelt's forceful leadership won him friends and enemies. As he prepared to run for reelection in 1904, he acknowledged that the "whole Wall Street crowd" would do all they could to defeat him. Nevertheless, he won the Republican nomination.

The Democrats, having lost twice with William Jennings Bryan, essentially gave the election to Roosevelt and the Republicans by nominating the virtually unknown Alton B. Parker, chief justice of the New York Supreme Court. Parker was the dullest—and most forgettable—presidential candidate in history. One journalist dubbed him "the enigma from New York." The most interesting item in his official campaign biography was that he had trained pigs to come when called by name.

The Democrats suffered their worst election defeat in thirty-two years. After winning the popular vote by 7.6 million to 5.1 million and the electoral vote 336 to 140, Roosevelt told his son it was his "greatest triumph." Having succeeded to the presidency after William McKinley's assassination, he had now won election on his own and, in his view, had a popular mandate to do great things. On the eve of his inauguration in March 1905, he announced: "Tomorrow I shall come into office in my own right. Then watch out for me!"

Roosevelt's duality Theodore Roosevelt as an "apostle of prosperity" (top) and as a Roman tyrant (bottom). Roosevelt's energy, self-righteousness, and impulsiveness elicited conflicting reactions.

PROGRESSIVE REGULATION Now elected in his own right, Roosevelt launched his second term with an even stronger commitment to regulating corporations and their corrupt owners (the "criminal rich") who exploited their workers and tried to eliminate competition. His comments irked many of his corporate contributors and congressional Republican leaders. Said the Pittsburgh steel baron Henry Frick, "We bought the son of a bitch and then he did not stay bought."

To promote the "moral regeneration of business," Roosevelt first took aim at the railroads. In 1906, he persuaded Congress to pass the Hepburn Act, which for the first time gave the federal Interstate Commerce Commission the power to set maximum freight rates for the railroad industry.

Under Roosevelt's Square Deal programs, the federal government also assumed oversight of key industries affecting public health: meat packers, food processors, and makers of drugs and patent medicines. Muckraking journalists had revealed all sorts of unsanitary and dangerous activities in the preparation of food and drug products by many companies. Perhaps the most

Bad meat Government inspectors closely examine tainted sides of beef at a meatpacking plant.

powerful blow against these abuses was struck by Upton Sinclair's novel *The Jungle* (1906), which told the story of a Lithuanian immigrant working in a filthy Chicago meatpacking plant:

> It was too dark in these storage places to see well, but a man could run his hand over these piles of meat and sweep off handfuls of the dried dung of rats. These rats were nuisances, and the packers would put poisoned bread out for them, they would die, and then rats, bread, and meat would go into the hoppers [to be ground up] together.

After reading *The Jungle*, Roosevelt urged Congress to pass the Meat Inspection Act of 1906. It required the Department of Agriculture to inspect every hog and steer whose carcass crossed state lines—both before and after slaughter. The Pure Food and Drug Act (1906), enacted the same day, required the makers of prepared food and medicines to host government inspectors, too.

ENVIRONMENTAL CONSERVATION Theodore Roosevelt was the first president passionately committed to environmental conservation. An avid outdoorsman and naturalist, he feared that unregulated logging and mining companies were destroying the nation's landscape "by their reckless extermination of all useful and beautiful wild things." Roosevelt championed efforts to protect wilderness areas and manage and preserve the nation's natural resources for the benefit of future generations. He created fifty federal wildlife refuges, approved five new national parks and fifty-one federal bird sanctuaries, and designated eighteen national monuments, including the Grand Canyon.

Yosemite Valley A couple playfully poses atop Glacier Point Rock in Yosemite National Park in 1902; adventurous tourists flocked to national parks and monuments in the early twentieth century, and still do today.

In 1898, Roosevelt had endorsed the appointment of his friend Gifford Pinchot, the nation's first professionally trained forest manager, as head of the U.S. Department of Agriculture's Division of Forestry. Pinchot, like Roosevelt, believed in economic growth as well as environmental preservation.

Pinchot said that the conservation movement promoted the "greatest good for the greatest number for the longest time."

Roosevelt and Pinchot used the Forest Reserve Act (1891) to protect 172 million acres of federally owned forests from being logged. Lumber companies were furious, but the president held firm, declaring, "I hate a man who skins the land." Overall, Roosevelt set aside more than 234 million acres of federal land for conservation purposes and created forty-five national forests in eleven western states. As Pinchot recalled, "Launching the conservation movement was the most significant achievement of the T.R. Administration, as he himself believed."

ROOSEVELT AND RACE Roosevelt's most significant failure as a progressive, as it was for so many of his successors, was his refusal to confront the movement's major blind spot: racism. Like Populists, progressives worked to empower "the people." For many of them, however, "the people" did not include African Americans, Native Americans, or some immigrant groups. Most white progressives shared the prevailing racist attitudes of the time. They ignored or even endorsed the passage of Jim Crow laws in the South that prevented blacks from voting and subjected them to rigid racial separation.

By 1901, nearly every southern state had prevented almost all African Americans from voting or holding political office by disqualifying or terrorizing them. Hundreds of African Americans were being lynched each year across the South, where virtually no blacks were allowed to serve on juries or work as sheriffs or policemen. A white candidate for governor in Mississippi in 1903 announced that he believed "in the divine right of the white man to rule, to do all the voting, and to hold all the offices, both state and federal." The South, wrote W. E. B. Du Bois, then a young black sociologist at Atlanta University, "is simply an armed camp for intimidating black folk."

At the same time, few progressives raised objections to the many informal and private patterns of segregation and prejudice in the North and West. "The plain fact is," muckraking journalist Ray Stannard Baker admitted in 1909, "most of us in the North do not believe in any real democracy between white and colored men." Roosevelt confided to a friend in 1906 his belief that "as a race and in the mass," African Americans "are altogether inferior to whites."

Yet the president made a few exceptions. On October 16, 1901, Roosevelt invited Booker T. Washington, the nation's most prominent black leader, to the White House to discuss presidential appointments in the South. Upon learning of the meeting, white southerners exploded with fury. The *Memphis Scimitar* screamed that inviting a "nigger" to dine in the White House was

Theodore Roosevelt and Booker T. Washington Roosevelt addresses the National Negro Business League in 1900 with Washington seated to his left.

"the most damnable outrage that has ever been perpetrated by a citizen of the United States." South Carolina senator Benjamin R. Tillman threatened that "a thousand niggers in the South will have to be killed to teach them 'their place' again."

A stunned Roosevelt insisted that he had done nothing wrong. In the end, however, he gave in to the criticism. Never again would he host a black leader. During a tour of the South in 1905, he pandered to whites by highlighting his own southern ancestry (his mother was from Georgia) and expressing his admiration for the Confederacy and Robert E. Lee. His behavior, said a black leader, was "national treachery to the Negro."

THE BROWNSVILLE RIOT The following year, 1906, brought a violent racial incident in Brownsville, Texas, where a dozen or so members of an African American army regiment from a nearby fort got into a shootout with whites who had been harassing them outside a saloon. One white bartender was killed, and a police officer was seriously wounded. Both sides claimed the other started the shooting. An investigation concluded that the soldiers were at fault, but no one could identify any of the shooters and none of the soldiers was willing to talk.

Roosevelt responded by dishonorably discharging the entire regiment of 167 soldiers, several of whom had been awarded the Congressional Medal of Honor for their service in Cuba during the War of 1898. Critics flooded the White House with angry telegrams. Secretary of War William H. Taft urged the president to reconsider his decision, but Roosevelt refused to show any mercy to "murderers, assassins, cowards, and comrades of murderers." (Sixty years later, the U.S. Army "cleared the records" of all the black soldiers.) Disheartened black leaders predicted that Roosevelt's harsh language would ignite "race hatred and violence" against innocent African Americans.

TAFT AND RETRENCHMENT

After his 1904 election victory, Roosevelt had decided he would not run for president again, in part because he did not want to be the first president to serve the equivalent of three terms. It was a noble gesture but a blunder that would have momentous political consequences. For now, however, he urged Republicans to nominate his long-time friend, Secretary of War William Howard Taft, whom the Republican Convention endorsed on its first ballot in 1908.

The Democrats again chose William Jennings Bryan, who still retained a faithful following, especially in the South. Taft promised to continue Roosevelt's policies, and the Republican platform endorsed the president's progressive program. The Democratic platform echoed the Republican emphasis on regulation of business but called for a lower tariff. Bryan struggled to attract national support and was defeated for a third time, as Taft swept the electoral college, 321 to 162.

A LIFE OF PUBLIC SERVICE William Howard Taft was superbly qualified to be president. Born in Cincinnati in 1857, he was the son of a prominent attorney who had served in President Grant's cabinet. He had graduated second in his class at Yale and gone on to become a leading legal scholar, serving on the Ohio Supreme Court. In 1900, President McKinley had appointed him the first American governor-general of the Philippines, and three years later Roosevelt named him secretary of war. Until becoming president, Taft had never held an elected office.

Taft was a cautious, conservative progressive who embraced a "strict construction" of the Constitution, which meant that he believed the Founding Fathers had intentionally limited the powers of each of the three government branches—executive, legislative, and judicial. Unlike Roosevelt, who believed that the president, to serve the public interest, could take any action

William Howard Taft Speaking at Manassas, Virginia, in 1911.

not explicitly prohibited by the Constitution, Taft insisted that the president's authority should be limited to what the Constitution specified. Taft went so far as to insist that the president had no role in the development of legislation. That was solely the responsibility of Congress.

Once elected, Taft explained that his focus was to "complete" the programs and policies that Roosevelt had initiated. He vowed to preserve capitalism by protecting "the right of private property" and the "right of liberty." In practice, this meant that he was even more determined than Roosevelt to support "the spirit of commercial freedom" against monopolistic trusts, but he was not interested in pushing for additional reforms or exercising extraordinary presidential power. Taft viewed himself as a judge-like administrator, not an innovator, and was reluctant to exercise presidential authority. (After leaving the White House, he got the job he had always wanted: chief justice of the U.S. Supreme Court.) Taft proved neither as energetic nor as wide-ranging as Roosevelt in his role as a reformer president—a difference that would lead to a fateful break between the two men.

TAFT AND THE TARIFF President Taft displayed his credentials as a progressive Republican by supporting *lower* tariffs on imports; he even called a special session of Congress to address the matter. But he proved less skillful than Roosevelt in dealing with Congress. Taft also discontinued Roosevelt's practice of using interviews with journalists to influence congressmen by using his "big stick through the press."

In the end, Taft's failure of leadership enabled Congress to pass the flawed Payne-Aldrich Tariff (1909), which did little to change federal policies. Tariff policies continued to favor the industrial Northeast. Taft's failure to gain real reform and his lack of a "crusading spirit" angered progressive, pro-Roosevelt Republicans, whom Taft called "assistant Democrats." Spurned by the progressive members of his party, Taft gravitated to the "Old Guard" Republican conservatives. Roosevelt was not happy.

THE BALLINGER–PINCHOT CONTROVERSY In 1910, the split between the conservative and progressive Republican factions was widened by what came to be called the Ballinger-Pinchot controversy. Taft's new secretary of the interior, Richard A. Ballinger, opened to commercial development millions of acres of federal lands that Roosevelt had ordered protected. As chief of forestry, Gifford Pinchot complained about the "giveaway," but Taft refused to intervene. When Pinchot made his opposition public early in 1910, Taft fired him, labeling him a "fanatic." In doing so, Taft set in motion a feud with Roosevelt that would eventually end their friendship—and cost him his reelection.

THE TAFT–ROOSEVELT FEUD In 1909, soon after Taft became president, Roosevelt and his son Kermit sailed to Africa, where they would spend nearly a year hunting big-game animals. (When he heard about the extended safari, business tycoon J. Pierpont Morgan expressed the hope that "every lion would do its duty.") Roosevelt had left the White House assuming that Taft would continue to pursue a progressive agenda. But by filling the cabinet with corporate lawyers and firing Gifford Pinchot, Taft had, in Roosevelt's view, failed to "carry out my work unbroken."

Roosevelt's rebuke of Taft was in some ways undeserved. Taft had at least attempted tariff reform, which Roosevelt had never dared. Although Taft had fired Pinchot, he had replaced him with another conservationist. Taft's administration actually preserved more federal land in four years than Roosevelt's had in nearly eight, and it filed twice as many anti-trust suits, including the one that led to the breakup of the Standard Oil Company in 1911. Taft also supported giving women the right to vote and workers the right to join unions.

None of that satisfied Roosevelt, however. On August 31, 1910, the angry former president, eager to return to the political spotlight, gave a speech at Osawatomie, Kansas, in which he announced his latest progressive principles and proposals—his "New Nationalism." Roosevelt explained that he wanted to go beyond ensuring a "Square Deal" in which corporations were forced to "play by the rules"; he now promised to "change the rules" to force large corporations to promote social welfare and to serve the needs of working people.

Political giants A cartoon showing Roosevelt charging through the air at Taft, who is seated on a mountaintop.

To save capitalism from the threat of a working-class revolution, Roosevelt called for tighter federal regulation of "arrogant" corporations that too often tried to "control and corrupt" politics; for a federal income tax (the Sixteenth Amendment had still not become law); and for federal laws regulating child labor. It was a sweeping agenda that would greatly expand the power of the federal government over economic and political life. "What I have advocated," he explained, "is not wild radicalism. It is the highest and wisest kind of conservatism."

Then, on February 24, 1912, Roosevelt abandoned his earlier pledge and announced his entry into the race for the 1912 Republican presidential nomination. He dismissed the "second-rate" Taft as a "hopeless fathead" who had "sold the Square Deal down the river." Taft responded by calling Roosevelt a "dangerous egotist" and a "demagogue." They began a bitter war in which Roosevelt had the better weapons, not the least of which was his love of a good fight. Elihu Root, a Republican leader, described his friend Roosevelt as "essentially a fighter, and when he gets into a fight he is completely dominated by the desire to destroy" his opponent.

By 1912, a dozen or so "progressive" states were letting citizens vote for presidential candidates in party primaries instead of following the traditional practice in which a state's party leaders chose the nominee. Roosevelt decided that if he won big in the Republican primaries, he could claim to be "the people's choice." But even though he won all but two primaries, including the one in Taft's home state of Ohio, his personal popularity was no match for Taft's authority as party leader. In the thirty-six states that still chose candidates by conventions dominated by party bosses, the Taft Republicans prevailed. At the Republican National Convention, Taft was easily nominated for reelection.

Roosevelt was furious. He denounced Taft and his supporters as thieves and stormed out of the convention along with his delegates—mostly social workers, teachers, professors, journalists, and urban reformers, along with a few wealthy business executives.

THE PROGRESSIVE PARTY Six weeks later, Roosevelt urged the breakaway faction of Republicans to reconvene in Chicago to create the **Progressive party**. They enthusiastically nominated him as their candidate. He assured the delegates that he felt "fit as a bull moose," leading journalists to nickname the Progressives the "Bull Moose party."

When Roosevelt closed his acceptance speech by saying, "We stand at Armageddon [the climactic encounter between Christ and Satan], and we battle for the Lord," the delegates stood and burst into the hymn "Onward, Christian Soldiers." One reporter wrote that the "Bull Moose" movement was not so much a party as it was a political religion, and Roosevelt was its leading evangelist. Progressives loved him because he showed what a government dedicated to the public good might achieve. And he loved to campaign because it enabled him to engage the people in the democratic process. "The first duty of the American citizen," he stressed, "is that he shall work in politics." No man loved being president as much as Roosevelt, and in 1912 no man worked harder to be president.

The Progressive party platform, audacious for its time, revealed Roosevelt's

Sideshow Ted This 1912 cartoon criticizes the Bull Moose Party for being just a sideshow (with suffragists selling lemonade outside) and points out the menacing ego of Roosevelt himself.

growing liberalism. It supported a minimum "living wage" for hourly workers, women's suffrage, campaign finance reform, and a system of "social security" insurance to protect people against sickness, unemployment, and disabilities. It also pledged to end the "boss system" governing politics and destroy the "unholy alliance between corrupt business and corrupt politics." Conservative critics called Roosevelt "a socialist," a "revolutionist," "a virtual traitor to American institutions," and a "monumental egotist."

Once nominated, Roosevelt repeatedly declared that Taft was not a progressive because he had tried to "undo" efforts at environmental conservation and had failed to fight either for social justice or against the "special interests." Instead, the former president charged, Taft had aligned himself with the "privileged" political and business leaders who steadfastly opposed "the cause of justice for the helpless and the wronged."

WOODROW WILSON: A PROGRESSIVE SOUTHERNER

The fight between William Howard Taft and Theodore Roosevelt gave hope to the Democrats, whose presidential nominee, New Jersey governor Woodrow Wilson, had enjoyed remarkable success in his brief political career. Until his nomination and election as governor in 1910, Wilson had been a college professor and then president of Princeton University; he had never run for political office or worked in business. He was a man of ideas who had a keen intellect, an analytical temperament, a tireless work ethic, an inspiring speaking style, and a strong conviction that he knew what was best for the nation.

TO SERVE HUMANITY Born in Staunton, Virginia, in 1856, the son, grandson, nephew and son-in-law of Presbyterian ministers, Thomas Woodrow Wilson had grown up in Georgia and the Carolinas during the Civil War and Reconstruction. The South, he once said, was the only part of the nation where nothing had to be explained to him. Tall and slender, with a long, chiseled face, he developed an unquestioning religious faith. Driven by a consuming sense that God had destined him to "serve" humanity, he often displayed an unbending self-righteousness and a fiery temper, qualities that would prove to be his undoing as president.

Wilson graduated from Princeton in 1879. After law school at the University of Virginia, he briefly practiced law in Atlanta, but he found legal work "dreadful drudgery" and soon enrolled at Johns Hopkins University to study history and political science, earning one of the nation's first doctoral degrees. He became an expert in constitutional government and taught at several colleges before being named president of Princeton in 1902.

Eight years later, Wilson accepted the support of New Jersey Democrats for the 1910 gubernatorial nomination. And he already harbored higher ambitions. If he could become governor, he reflected, "I stand a very good chance of being the next President of the United States." Like Roosevelt, Wilson was an intensely ambitious and idealistic man who felt destined to preside over America's emergence as the greatest world power.

Woodrow Wilson The only president to hold a PhD degree.

Wilson proved a surprisingly effective campaigner and won a landslide victory. The professor-turned-governor then persuaded the state legislature to adopt an array of progressive reforms to curb the power of political party bosses and corporate lobbyists. "After dealing with college politicians," Wilson joked, "I find that the men who I am dealing with now seem like amateurs."

Governor Wilson soon attracted the attention of national Democratic leaders. At the 1912 Democratic convention, he faced stiff competition from several veteran party leaders for the presidential nomination. But with the support of William Jennings Bryan, he won on the forty-sixth ballot. It was, Wilson said, a "political miracle."

THE 1912 ELECTION The 1912 presidential campaign was one of the most exciting in history. It involved four distinguished candidates: Democrat Woodrow Wilson, Republican William Howard Taft, Socialist Eugene V. Debs, and Progressive Theodore Roosevelt. For all of their differences in personality and temperament, the candidates shared a basic progressive assumption that modern social problems could be resolved only through active governmental intervention.

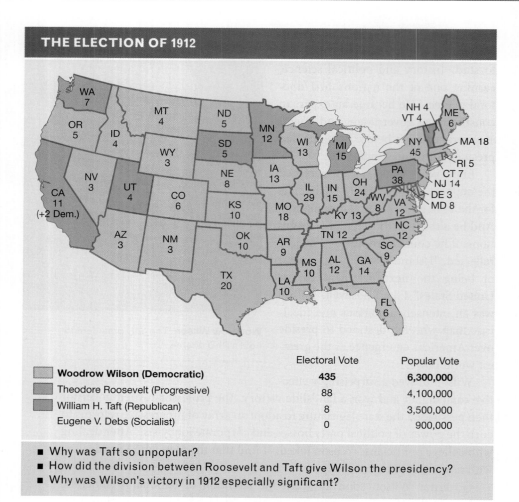

THE ELECTION OF 1912

	Electoral Vote	Popular Vote
Woodrow Wilson (Democratic)	**435**	**6,300,000**
Theodore Roosevelt (Progressive)	88	4,100,000
William H. Taft (Republican)	8	3,500,000
Eugene V. Debs (Socialist)	0	900,000

- Why was Taft so unpopular?
- How did the division between Roosevelt and Taft give Wilson the presidency?
- Why was Wilson's victory in 1912 especially significant?

No sooner did the formal campaign open than Roosevelt's candidacy almost ended. While on his way to deliver a speech in Milwaukee, Wisconsin, he was shot by John Schrank, a lunatic who believed that any president seeking a third term should be shot. The bullet went through Roosevelt's thick overcoat, a steel eyeglass case, and fifty-page speech, then fractured a rib before nestling just below his right lung, an inch from his heart. "Stand back, don't hurt the man," Roosevelt yelled at the crowd as they mobbed Schrank. Refusing medical attention, Roosevelt demanded that he be driven to the auditorium to deliver an eighty-minute speech to 10,000 supporters. In a dramatic gesture, he showed the audience his bloodstained shirt and punctured text and vowed, "It takes more than this to kill a bull moose."

As the campaign developed, Taft quickly lost ground. "There are so many people in the country who don't like me," he lamented. The contest settled into a debate over the competing programs touted by the two front-runners: Roosevelt's New Nationalism and Wilson's **New Freedom**. The New Freedom, designed by Louis Brandeis, aimed to restore economic competition by eliminating all trusts rather than simply regulating them. Where Roosevelt admired the power and efficiency of law-abiding corporations, no matter how large, Brandeis and Wilson were convinced that huge, "heartless" industries needed to be broken up.

On Election Day, Wilson won handily, collecting 435 electoral votes to 88 for Roosevelt and only 8 for Taft. After learning of his election, the self-righteous Wilson told the chairman of his campaign committee that "I owe you nothing. God ordained that I should be the next president of the United States. Neither you nor any other mortal could have prevented that."

Had the Republicans not divided their votes between Taft and Roosevelt, however, Wilson would have lost. His was the victory of a minority candidate over a divided opposition. Since all four candidates called themselves progressives, however, the president-elect expressed his hope "that the thoughtful progressive forces of the nation may now at last unite."

The election of 1912 profoundly altered the character of the Republican party. The defection of the Bull Moose Progressives had weakened its progressive wing. As a result, when Republicans returned to power in the 1920s, they would be more conservative in tone and temperament.

EUGENE DEBS The real surprise of the 1912 election was the strong showing of the Socialist party candidate, Eugene V. Debs, running for the fourth time. The tall, blue-eyed idealist had devoted his adult life to fighting against the "monstrous system of capitalism" on behalf of the working class, first as a labor union official, then as a socialist promoting government ownership of railroads and the sharing of profits with workers.

Although fierce in his commitment to improving the lives of the poor, Debs was kind and gentle in his interactions with people. He voiced a brand of socialism that was flexible rather than rigid, Christian rather than Marxist, democratic rather than totalitarian. He believed in political transformation, not violent revolution. As one of his supporters said, "That old man with the burning eyes actually believes that there can be such a thing as the brotherhood of man. And that's not the funniest part of it. As long as he's around I believe it myself."

Debs became the unifying symbol of a diverse movement that united West Virginia coal miners, Oklahoma sharecroppers, Pacific Northwest lumberjacks, and immigrant workers in New York City sweatshops. One newspaper described "The Rising Tide of Socialism" in 1912, as some 1,150 Socialists won election to local and state offices across the nation, including eighteen mayoral seats.

To many voters, the Socialists, whose 118,000 dues-paying members in 1912 were double the number from the year before, offered the only real alternative to a stalemated political system in which the two major parties had few real differences. A business executive in New York City explained that he had become a Socialist "because the old parties [Democrats and Republicans] were flimflamming us all the time."

But fear of socialism was also widespread. Theodore Roosevelt warned that the rapid growth of the Socialist party was "far more ominous than any Populist or similar movement in the past."

In 1912, with few campaign funds, Debs crisscrossed the nation giving fiery speeches. He dismissed Roosevelt as "a charlatan, mountebank [swindler], and fraud" whose progressive promises were nothing more than "the mouthings of a low and utterly unprincipled self-seeker and demagogue." Debs's untiring efforts brought him more than 900,000 votes, more than twice as many as he had received four years earlier.

A BURST OF REFORM BILLS

On March 4, 1913, a huge crowd surrounded the Capitol in Washington, D.C., to watch Wilson's inauguration. The new president with the long nose and spectacles declared that it was not "a day of triumph" but "a day of dedication." He promised to lower "the stiff and stupid" Republican tariff, create a new national banking system, strengthen anti-trust laws, and establish an administration "more concerned about human rights than about property rights."

Wilson worried about people comparing him to the colorful, hyperactive Roosevelt: "He appeals to their imagination; I do not. He is a real, vivid person. . . . I am a vague, conjectural [philosophical] personality, more made up of opinions and academic prepossessions than of human traits and red corpuscles." Roosevelt had been a strong president by force of personality; Wilson became a strong president by force of conviction.

Like Roosevelt, Wilson was an activist president; he was the first to speak to the nation over the radio and to host weekly press conferences. A brilliant, intense man, the first president with a PhD degree, Wilson was a spellbinding speaker with a fervent sense of destiny. He frequently spoke to Congress and visited legislators in their offices in the Capitol. As a political scientist, Wilson was an expert at the processes of government. During his first two years, he pushed through Congress more new bills than any previous president. Like "most reformers," however, Wilson "had a fierce and unlovely side," according to the president of Harvard University. The new president found it hard to understand—much less work with—people who disagreed with him.

Wilson's victory, coupled with Democratic majorities in the House and Senate, gave his party effective national power for the first time since the Civil War. It also gave southerners a significant role in national politics for the first time since the war. Five of Wilson's ten cabinet members were born in the South.

COLONEL HOUSE Wilson's closest adviser was "Colonel" Edward M. House of Texas, who held no official government position but was Wilson's constant companion, a "small, frail, courteous bright-eyed man with a gentle voice and winning manners." House was one of the most skilled political operators in history, working mostly behind the scenes to excite and mobilize others, and he and Wilson developed the most famous political partnership of the twentieth century. The president described House as "my second personality. He is my independent self." Wilson told House that he thanked "God every day that I have so generous" a friend and adviser.

House told Wilson that the theme of his presidency should be a form of Christian democracy: the "strong should help the weak, that the fortunate should aid the unfortunate, and that business should be conducted upon a higher and more humane plane." He helped steer Wilson's proposals through a Congress in which southerners, by virtue of their seniority, held the lion's share of committee chairmanships. As a result, much of the progressive legislation of the Wilson era would bear the names of southern Democrats.

THE TARIFF AND THE INCOME TAX Like Taft, Wilson pursued tariff reform, but with much greater success. By 1913, the federal tariff included hundreds of taxes on different imported goods, from oil to nails. The president believed that U.S. corporations were misusing the tariff to keep out foreign competitors and create American monopolies that kept consumer prices artificially high.

To attack high tariff rates, Wilson took a bold step: he summoned Congress to a special session that lasted eighteen months, the longest in history, and he addressed its members in person—the first president to do so since John

Adams. The new tariff bill passed the House easily. The crunch came in the Senate, the traditional graveyard of tariff reform, where swarms of industry lobbyists grew so thick, Wilson said, that "a brick couldn't be thrown without hitting one of them." The president finally won approval there by publicly criticizing the "industrious and insidious" tariff lobby.

The Underwood-Simmons Tariff Act (1913) lowered tariff rates on almost 1,000 imported products. To compensate for the reduced tariff revenue, the bill created the first income tax allowed under the newly ratified Sixteenth Amendment: the initial tax rates were 1 percent on income more than $3,000 ($4,000 for married couples) up to a top rate of 7 percent on annual income of $50,000 or more. Most Americans (99 percent) paid no income tax because they earned less than $3,000 a year.

THE FEDERAL RESERVE ACT   No sooner had the new tariff passed the Senate than the administration proposed the first major banking reform since the Civil War. Ever since Andrew Jackson had killed the Second Bank of the United States in the 1830s, the nation had been without a central bank. Instead, the money supply was chaotically "managed" by thousands of local and state banks.

Such a decentralized system was unstable and inefficient because, during financial panics, fearful depositors who were eager to withdraw their money would create "runs" that often led to the failure of smaller banks. The primary reason for a new central bank was to prevent more such panics, which had occurred five times since 1873. Wilson believed that the banking system needed a central reserve agency that, in a crisis, could distribute emergency cash to banks threatened by runs. But he insisted that any new banking system must be overseen by the government rather than by bankers themselves (the "money power"). He wanted a central bank that would benefit the entire economy, not just the large banks headquartered on Wall Street in New York City.

After much dickering, Congress passed the **Federal Reserve Act** on December 23, 1913. It created a national banking system with twelve regional districts, each of which had its own Federal Reserve Bank owned by member banks in the district. Nationally chartered banks, which agreed to regulation by a Federal Reserve Bank in exchange for the right to issue money, had to be members of the Federal Reserve System. State-chartered banks—essentially unregulated—did not (and, indeed, two-thirds of the nation's banks chose not to become members of the Federal Reserve System). The twelve regional Federal Reserve banks were supervised by a central board of directors in Washington, D.C.

The overarching purpose of the Federal Reserve System was to adjust the nation's currency supply to promote economic growth and ensure the stability and integrity of member banks. When banks were short of cash, they could borrow from the Federal Reserve ("the Fed"), using their loans as collateral. Each of the new regional banks issued Federal Reserve notes (currency) to member banks in exchange for their loans. By doing so, "the Fed," as the system came to be called, promoted economic growth and helped preserve the stability of banks during panics. The Federal Reserve board required member banks to have a certain percentage of their total deposits in cash on hand ("reserve") at all times.

A conservative Republican called the Federal Reserve Act "populistic, socialistic, half-baked, destructive, and unworkable." The new system soon proved its worth, however, and the criticism eased. The Federal Reserve Act was the most significant new program of Wilson's presidency.

ANTI-TRUST ACTIONS Wilson made "trust-busting" the central focus of his New Freedom program. Giant corporations had continued to grow despite the Sherman Anti-Trust Act and the Bureau of Corporations, the federal watchdog agency created by Theodore Roosevelt.

Wilson decided to make a strong **Federal Trade Commission (FTC)** the cornerstone of his anti-trust program. Created in 1914, the five-member FTC replaced the Bureau of Corporations and assumed new powers to define "unfair trade practices" and issue "cease and desist" orders when it found evidence of such practices.

Like Roosevelt, Wilson also supported efforts to strengthen and clarify the Sherman Anti-Trust Act. Henry D. Clayton, a Democrat from Alabama, drafted an anti-trust bill in 1914. The **Clayton Anti-Trust Act** declared that labor unions were not to be viewed as "monopolies in restraint of trade," as courts had maintained since 1890. It also prohibited corporate directors from serving on the boards of competing companies and further clarified the meaning of various "monopolistic" activities.

WILSON DECLARES VICTORY

In November 1914, just two years after his election, President Wilson announced that he had accomplished the major goals of progressivism. He had fulfilled his promises to lower the tariff, create a national banking system, and strengthen the anti-trust laws. The New Freedom was now complete, he wrote.

Wilson's victory declaration, however, bewildered many progressives, especially those who had long advocated additional federal social-justice legislation that Wilson had earlier supported. Herbert Croly, the influential editor of the *New Republic* magazine, wondered how the president could assert "that the fundamental wrongs of a modern society can be easily and quickly righted as a consequence of [passing] a few laws." Wilson's about-face, he concluded, "casts suspicion upon his own sincerity [as a progressive] or upon his grasp of the realities of modern social and industrial life."

PROGRESSIVISM FOR WHITES ONLY African Americans continued to resent the racial conservatism displayed by most progressives. Carter Glass, the Virginia senator who was largely responsible for developing the Federal Reserve Act in 1913, was an enthusiastic supporter of his state's efforts to disfranchise black voters. When questioned by a reporter about being a racist progressive, Glass embraced the label: "Discrimination! Why that is exactly what we propose. To remove every Negro voter who can be gotten rid of."

Similarly, Woodrow Wilson showed little concern about the discrimination and violence that African Americans faced. In fact, he shared many of

New freedom, old rules Woodrow Wilson and the First Lady ride in a carriage with African American drivers.

the racist attitudes common at the time. As a student at Princeton, he had expressed his disgust at the Fifteenth Amendment, which had guaranteed voting rights for black men after the Civil War, arguing that whites must resist domination by "an ignorant and inferior race." As a politician, Wilson did court African American voters, but he rarely consulted black leaders and largely avoided associating with them.

Josephus Daniels, a North Carolina newspaper editor who became Wilson's secretary of the navy, was a white supremacist who stressed that "the subjection of the negro, politically, and the separation of the negro, socially, are paramount to all other considerations in the South." For Daniels and other southern progressives, "progress" was possible only if blacks were "kept in their place."

Daniels and other cabinet members racially segregated the employees in their agencies. Wilson endorsed the policy, claiming that racial segregation "is not humiliating but a benefit." To him, "separate but equal" was the best way to resolve racial tensions. He was the first president since the Civil War who openly endorsed discrimination against African Americans.

In November 1914, a delegation of African American leaders met with Wilson to ask how a "progressive" president could adopt such "regressive" racial policies. Wilson responded that both races benefited from the policies because they eliminated "the possibility of friction." William Monroe Trotter, a Harvard-educated African American newspaper editor who had helped found the National Association for the Advancement of Colored People (NAACP), scolded the president: "Have you a 'new freedom' for white Americans, and a new slavery for 'your Afro-American fellow citizens' [a phrase Wilson had used in a speech]? God forbid." A furious Wilson told Trotter and the other visitors to leave, saying that their unchristian "tone offends me."

THE VOTE FOR WOMEN Activists for women's suffrage were also disappointed in President Wilson. Despite having two daughters who were suffragists, he insisted that the issue of women's voting rights should be left to the states rather than embodied in a constitutional amendment.

Wilson's lack of support led some leaders of the suffrage movement to revise their tactics. In 1910, Alice Paul, a New Jersey–born Quaker and social worker, returned from working with the militant suffragists of England, where she had participated in various forms of civil disobedience to generate attention and support. After Paul joined the National American Woman Suffrage Association (NAWSA), she urged activists to use more aggressive tactics: picket

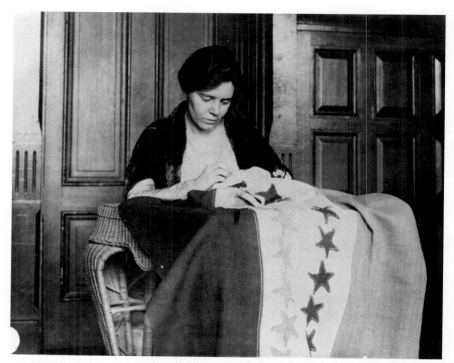

Alice Paul Sewing a suffrage flag—orange and purple, with stars—that she and other suffragists often waved at strikes and protests.

state legislatures, target and "punish" politicians who failed to endorse suffrage, chain themselves to public buildings, incite police to arrest them, and undertake hunger strikes.

In March 1913, Paul organized 5,000 suffragists to protest at Wilson's inauguration. Four years later, having broken with the NAWSA and formed the National Woman's Party, Paul decided that suffragists must do something even more dramatic: picket the White House. Beginning on January 11, 1917, Paul and her followers took turns carrying signs all day, five days a week, for months, until the president ordered their arrest. Some sixty suffragists were jailed.

Paul was sentenced to seven months in prison. She then went on a hunger strike, leading prison officials to force-feed her raw eggs through a tube inserted in her nose. She later recalled that "it was shocking that a government of men could look with such extreme contempt on a movement that was asking nothing except such a simple little thing as the right to vote." Under an avalanche of negative press coverage and public criticism, Wilson finally pardoned Paul and the other activists.

PROGRESSIVISM RENEWED By 1916, Wilson's determination to win reelection revived his commitment to progressive activism. The president nominated Bostonian Louis D. Brandeis, the "people's attorney," to the Supreme Court. Brandeis was not just a famed defender of unions against big businesses; he would also be the first Jewish member of the Supreme Court. Progressives viewed the nomination as a "landmark in the history of American democracy." Others disagreed. Former president Taft dismissed Brandeis as "a muckraker, an emotionalist for his own purposes, a socialist . . . who is utterly unscrupulous." The Senate, however, confirmed Brandeis's appointment. Justice Oliver Wendell Holmes Jr., the leading figure on the court, sent Brandeis a one-word telegram: "WELCOME."

FARM LEGISLATION President Wilson also urged Congress to pass the first federal legislation directed at assisting farmers. He first supported a proposal to set up rural banks to provide long-term farm loans. The Federal Farm Loan Act became law in 1916. Under the control of the Federal Farm Loan Board, twelve Federal Land banks offered loans to farmers for five to forty years at low interest rates. Farmers could borrow up to 50 percent of the value of their land. At about the same time, a dream long advocated by Populists—federal loans to farmers on the security of their crops stored in warehouses—finally came to fruition when Congress passed the Warehouse Act of 1916. These crop-security loans were available to sharecroppers, tenant farmers, and to farmers who owned the land that they worked.

Farmers also benefited from the Smith-Lever Act of 1914, which provided federal programs to educate farmers about new machinery and new ideas related to agricultural efficiency, and the Smith-Hughes Act (1917), which funded agricultural and mechanical education in high schools. Farmers with the newfangled automobiles had more than a passing interest as well in the Federal Highways Act of 1916, which helped finance new highways, especially in rural areas.

LABOR LEGISLATION One of the long-standing goals of many progressive Democrats was a *federal* child-labor law. When Congress passed the Keating-Owen Act in 1916, banning products made by child workers under fourteen from being shipped across state lines, Wilson expressed doubts about its constitutionality but eventually signed it.

Another landmark law was the eight-hour workday for railroad workers. The Adamson Act of 1916 resulted from a threatened strike by railroad unions demanding an eight-hour day and other concessions. Wilson, who objected to some of the unions' demands, nevertheless asked Congress to approve the Adamson Act. It required time-and-a-half pay for overtime work beyond eight hours and appointed a commission to study working conditions in the railroad industry.

ASSESSING PROGRESSIVISM

Progressivism reached its peak during Woodrow Wilson's two terms as president. After decades of political upheaval and social reform, progressivism had shattered the traditional "laissez-faire" notion that government had no role in protecting the public welfare by regulating the economy. The courage and compassion displayed by progressives demonstrated that people of good will could make a difference in improving the quality of life for all.

Progressivism awoke people to the evils and possibilities of modern urban-industrial life. Most important, progressives established the principle that governments—local, state, and federal—had a responsibility to ensure that Americans were protected from abuse by powerful businesses and corrupt politicians. Yet on several fronts, progressivism fell short of its supporters' hopes and ideals. It would take the Great Depression during the 1930s to lead to the passage of a national minimum wage and the creation of a government-administered pension program for retirees and disabled workers (Social Security).

Like all great historic movements, progressivism produced unexpected consequences. For all of its efforts to give more power to "the people," voter participation actually fell off during the Progressive Era. Probably the main reason for the decline of party loyalty and voter turnout was that, by the twentieth century, people had more activities to distract them. New forms of recreation like movies, cycling, automobiles, and spectator sports competed with politics for time and attention. Also, people showed less interest in political parties and public issues in part because of the progressive emphasis on government by appointed specialists and experts rather than elected politicians.

Ultimately, progressivism faded as an organized political movement because international issues pushed aside domestic concerns. By 1916, the optimism of a few years earlier was challenged by the distressing slaughter occurring in Europe in the Great War. The twentieth century, which had dawned with such bright hopes for social progress, held in store episodes of unprecedented brutality that led people to question whether "progress" was even possible anymore.

CHAPTER REVIEW

SUMMARY

- **The Progressive Impulse**   Progressives were mostly middle-class idealists in both political parties who promoted reform and government regulation to ensure social justice. Many progressives wished to restrict the powers of local political machines and establish honest and efficient government. They also called for legislation to end child labor, promote workplace safety, ban the sale of alcoholic beverages, regulate or eliminate trusts and other monopolies, and grant *woman suffrage*.

- **The Varied Sources of Progressivism**   Many religious reformers, such as those involved in the *social gospel* movement, urged their fellow Protestants to reject social Darwinism and do more to promote a better life for the urban poor. The settlement house movement sprang from this idea and spread through urban America as educated middle-class women formed community centers in poverty-stricken neighborhoods. Progressives drew inspiration from the women's suffrage movement, as more women became involved in social reform efforts and in the workplace. Many progressive ideas arose from the ongoing efforts of reformers to end political corruption. Progressives, while not radicals, also responded to the growing socialist movement and its calls for economic justice for the working class. *Muckrakers*—investigative journalists who exposed political and corporate corruption—further fueled the desire of progressive reformers to address abuses of power in American society.

- **Progressives' Aims and Achievements**   Progressives focused on stopping corruption in politics. They advanced political reforms such as the direct primary; the initiative, referendum, and recall at the state level; and the direct election of U.S. senators through the passage of the *Seventeenth Amendment*. Other progressives focused on incorporating new modes of efficiency and scientific management in business, known as *Taylorism*, into government. Their efforts inspired many cities and counties to adopt the commission system and the city-manager plan. Still other progressives, who saw regulation of Big Business as the overriding issue facing the nation, focused on legislation and bureaucratic oversight to control or eliminate trusts and other forms of monopolies.

- **Progressivism under Roosevelt and Taft**   The administrations of Theodore Roosevelt and William H. Taft increased the power of the presidency and the federal government to regulate corporate power and improve the lives of many Americans. Roosevelt promoted his progressive *Square Deal* program, which included regulating trusts through the creation of the Bureau of Corporations, arbitrating the 1902 coal strike, persuading Congress to regulate the railroads through the Elkins and Hepburn Acts, and to clean up the meat and drug industries with the Meat Inspection and Pure Food and Drug Acts. Roosevelt also initiated an environmental conservation campaign to manage and preserve the nation's natural resources.

- **Woodrow Wilson's Progressivism** Wilson's *New Freedom* program included a low tariff and anti-trust regulation. He also established a central banking system with the *Federal Reserve Act*, and launched a rigorous anti-trust program with the passage of the *Clayton Anti-Trust Act* and the creation of the *Federal Trade Commission*. But he opposed a constitutional amendment guaranteeing women's suffrage. A southerner, he believed blacks were inferior and he supported increased segregation in the federal workforce.

CHRONOLOGY

1901	William McKinley is assassinated; Theodore Roosevelt becomes president
	Galveston, Texas, adopts the commission system of city government
1902	Justice Department breaks up Northern Securities Company
1903	Congress passes the Elkins Act and creates the Bureau of Corporations
1906	Upton Sinclair's *The Jungle* is published
	Congress passes the Meat Inspection Act and the Pure Food and Drug Act
1909	William Howard Taft inaugurated
1911	Triangle Shirtwaist fire
	Frederick Taylor's *The Principles of Scientific Management* is published
1912	Woodrow Wilson wins four-way presidential election
1913	Alice Paul and 5,000 suffragists protest Wilson's inauguration
	Sixteenth and Seventeenth Amendments ratified
	Underwood-Simmons Tariff and Federal Reserve Act passed
1914	Congress passes the Clayton Anti-Trust Act

KEY TERMS

muckrakers p. 940

social gospel p. 942

woman suffrage p. 946

Seventeenth
Amendment (1913) p. 948

Taylorism p. 949

Sixteenth Amendment
(1913) p. 955

Square Deal p. 957

Progressive party p. 969

New Freedom p. 973

Federal Reserve Act (1913) p. 976

Federal Trade
Commission (FTC) (1914) p. 977

Clayton Anti-Trust
Act (1914) p. 977

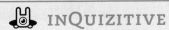 INQUIZITIVE

Go to InQuizitive to see what you've learned—and learn what you've missed—with personalized feedback along the way.

22 America and the Great War

1914–1920

Make American History In this U.S. Navy recruiting poster in New York City, a sailor encourages a young man to play an active role in the Great War.

Throughout the nineteenth century, the Atlantic Ocean had protected America from the major land wars on the continent of Europe. During the early twentieth century, however, the nation's century-long isolation from European conflicts ended. Ever-expanding world trade meant that U.S. interests were becoming deeply entwined with the global economy. In addition, the development of steam-powered ships and submarines meant that foreign navies could directly threaten American security.

At the same time, the election of Woodrow Wilson in 1912 brought to the White House a self-righteous moralist determined to impose his standards on what he saw as renegade nations. This combination of circumstances made the outbreak of the "Great War" in Europe in 1914 a profound crisis for the United States. The war would become the defining event of the early twentieth century.

For almost three years, President Wilson maintained America's stance of "neutrality" in the war while providing increasing amounts of food and supplies to Great Britain and France. In 1917, however, German submarine attacks on U.S. ships forced Congress into declaring war. The decision would turn the tide in the fighting and reshape America's international role as a dominant world power.

focus questions

1. What caused the outbreak of the Great War, and why was the United States drawn into it? What was distinctive about the fighting on the Western Front?

2. How did the Wilson administration mobilize the home front? How did these mobilization efforts affect American society?

3. What were the major events of the war after the United States entered the conflict? How did the American war effort contribute to the defeat of the Central Powers?

4. How did Wilson promote his plans for a peaceful world order as outlined in his Fourteen Points?

5. What were the consequences of the war at home and abroad?

AN UNEASY NEUTRALITY

Woodrow Wilson once declared that he had "a first-class mind," and he was indeed highly intelligent, thoughtful, principled, and courageous. Upon learning of death threats against him, for example, he refused to change his schedule of public appearances. "The country," he explained, "cannot afford to have a coward for President."

For all of his accomplishments and abilities, however, Wilson had no experience or expertise in international relations before he was elected president. He confessed that "it would be an irony of fate if my administration had to deal chiefly with foreign affairs"—a topic he did not even mention in his 1913 inaugural address. But from the summer of 1914, when war erupted in Europe, Wilson was forced to shift his attention from the New Freedom's progressive reforms to foreign affairs.

Wilson did have strong beliefs and principles about global issues. "Sometimes people call me an idealist," he once said. "Well, that is the way I know I'm an American." He saw himself as being directed by God to help create a new world order governed by morality and ideals rather than by selfish national interests. Both Wilson and William Jennings Bryan, his secretary of state, believed that America had a duty to promote democracy and Christianity around the world. "Every nation of the world," Wilson declared, "needs to be drawn into the tutelage [guidance] of America."

THE GREAT WAR

Woodrow Wilson faced his greatest challenge beginning in the summer of 1914, when a war that few wanted yet no one could stop broke out in Europe. The "dreadful conflict" erupted suddenly, like "lightning out of a clear sky," a North Carolina congressman said. Wilson admitted that he was shocked by "this incredible European eruption." Unfortunately, it coincided with a sharp decline in the health of his wife Ellen, who died on August 6. "God has stricken me," the president wrote a friend, "almost beyond what I can bear."

Wilson would also have trouble bearing the accelerating horrors of the war in Europe. Its scope and destruction shocked everyone. Lasting for more than four years, from 1914 to 1918, it would become known as the Great War because it would involve more nations and cause greater destruction than any previous war: 20 million military and civilian deaths, and 21 million more wounded. The Great War would topple monarchs, destroy empires, create new nations, and set in motion a series of events that would lead to an even greater war in 1939.

CAUSES The Great War resulted from complex and long-simmering national rivalries and ethnic conflicts in central Europe. At the core of the tensions was the Austro-Hungarian Empire, an unstable collection of eleven nationalities that was determined to stop the expansionism of its neighbor and longstanding enemy, Serbia, in the Balkan Peninsula. Serbia had long hoped to create "Yugoslavia," a nation encompassing all Serbs from throughout the Austro-Hungarian Empire.

At the same time, a recklessly militaristic Germany, led by Kaiser (Emperor) Wilhelm II, sought to assert its dominance against its old enemies, the Russian Empire and France, while expanding its navy to challenge the British Empire's supremacy on the seas.

FIGHTING ERUPTS War erupted after Gavrilo Princip, a nineteen-year-old Serbian nationalist in Sarajevo (the capital of Austrian Bosnia), shot and killed the heir to the Austro-Hungarian throne, 50-year-old Archduke Franz Ferdinand, and his pregnant wife Sophie, on June 28, 1914. The killings in Sarajevo set Europe on fire.

To avenge the murders, Austria-Hungary, with Germany's unconditional approval, sought to bully and humiliate Serbia by demanding a say in its internal affairs. Serbia gave in to virtually all of the demands, but Austria-Hungary declared war anyway. In turn, Russia mobilized its army to defend Serbia, which triggered reactions by a complex set of European military alliances: the Triple Alliance, or **Central Powers** (Germany, Austria-Hungary, and Italy), and the Triple Entente, or **Allied Powers** (France, Great Britain, and Russia).

Germany, expecting a limited war and quick victory, declared war on Russia on August 1, 1914, and on France two days later. Germany then invaded neutral Belgium, murdering hundreds of civilians. Events spiraled out of control. The "rape of Belgium" brought Great Britain into the war against Germany on August 4 on the **Western Front**, the line of fighting in northern France and Belgium. Despite the Triple Alliance, Italy at first declared its neutrality before joining the Allies in return for a promise of territory taken from Austria-Hungary.

On the evening of August 4, as five global empires—Austria-Hungary, France, Germany, Great Britain, and Russia—mobilized for war, the British foreign minister, Sir Edward Grey, expressed the fears of many when he observed that "the lamps are going out all over Europe; we shall not see them lit again in our time."

On the Eastern Front, Russian armies began clashing with German and Austro-Hungarian forces as well as those of the Turkish (Ottoman) Empire. Within five weeks of the assassination in Sarajevo, a "great war" had consumed

THE GREAT WAR IN EUROPE, 1914

Central Powers (Triple Alliance)
Allied Powers (Triple Entente)
Neutral countries

- How did the European system of military alliances spread conflict across all of Europe?
- How was the Great War different from previous wars?
- How did the war in Europe lead to ethnic tensions in the United States?

all of Europe. (It would not be called the First World War until the second one came along in 1939.)

AN INDUSTRIAL WAR

No one envisioned that a local conflict in the Balkans would develop into a catastrophic war that would reshape the twentieth-century world. But by its end, in November 1918, more than forty nations had joined the fighting.

The Great War was the first industrial war, involving the total mobilization of the economy and civilians as well as warriors. Of the approximately

70 million soldiers and sailors who fought on both sides, more than half were killed, wounded, imprisoned, or unaccounted for. New weapons dramatically changed the nature of warfare. Machine guns, submarines, aerial bombing, poison gas, flame throwers, land mines, mortars, long-range artillery, and armored tanks produced appalling casualties and widespread destruction, a slaughter on a scale unimaginable to this day. An average of 900 Frenchmen and 1,300 Germans died *every* day on the Western Front.

The early weeks of the war involved fast-moving assaults as German armies swept across Belgium and northeastern France. The casualties were appalling. On a single day, August 22, 1914, the French army lost 27,000 men.

TRENCH WARFARE   But the war on the Western Front soon bogged down into hellish **trench warfare**, in which often inept generals sent masses of brave soldiers (German generals referred to the British army as "lions led by donkeys") out of waterlogged, zigzagging trenches—some of them 40 feet deep and swarming with rats—that had been dug along the Western Front from the coast of Belgium across northeastern France to the border of Switzerland.

On either side, the attackers were usually at a disadvantage as they slogged across muddy acres of devastated "no-man's-land" between the opposing

Trench warfare American troops eat amid the reek of death and threat of enemy fire in a frontline trench in France.

entrenchments, where they encountered corpse-filled shell holes, webs of barbed wire, and constant gunfire and artillery shelling that left the barren landscape pockmarked with craters and whole forests shattered into nothingness. Along the Western Front, not a blade of grass was left, only ruin and rubble, flooded trenches and thickets of barbed wire.

From 1914 to 1918, the opposing armies in northeastern France attacked and counterattacked but gained hardly any ground, while casualties rose into the millions. By the end of 1914, the Germans had captured 19,500 square miles of territory in France and Belgium; by the end of 1915, the Allies had recaptured only 8 of those miles.

Words cannot convey the titanic scale of the fighting and its impact on the home front as telegrams arrived telling families that their son would not be returning. By 1918, the Allies (France, Great Britain, Italy, Russia, and the United States, among others), had suffered 5.4 million killed and 7 million wounded. "The War is everything," a British diarist wrote. "It is noble, filthy, great, petty, degrading, inspiring, ridiculous, glorious, mad, bad, hopeless yet full of hope."

Heroism was entangled with futility as battles were now determined not so much by skillful maneuvers or courageous leadership but by overwhelming firepower, the huge cannons and weighty shells that turned the ritual of close combat into a long-distance contest of killing machines. Bayonets gave way to bombardments. Two-thirds of the casualties in the Great War resulted from long-distance artillery barrages.

Thousands of soldiers on both sides fell victim to "shell shock," now known as post-traumatic stress disorder, as they were bombarded into numbness. Trenches shook, trees tumbled, and the ground trembled under the feet of panicked combatants. The unprecedented firepower ravaged the landscape, obliterated whole villages, and turned farmland and forests into cratered wastelands. The scars of war are still visible 100 years later.

Trench warfare gave the Great War its lasting character. Soldiers often ate, slept, lived, and died without leaving their crowded underground homes. A French soldier described life in the trenches as a "physical, almost animal" existence in which "the primitive instincts of the race have full sway: eating, drinking, sleeping, fighting—everything but loving."

The object in such a war of attrition was not so much to gain ground as to keep inflicting death and destruction on the enemy until its manpower and resources were exhausted. In one assault against the Germans at Ypres in Belgium, the British lost 13,000 men in three hours of fighting—during which time they gained 100 meaningless yards. As the war ground on, nations on

Total ruin German soldiers stand before the French Fort Souville between the Battles of Verdun in September 1916. The constant artillery fire gouged out huge craters and destroyed forests.

both sides found themselves using up their available men, resources, courage, and cash.

Amid the senseless killing in the mucky trenches, the innocence about the true nature of warfare died, too. "Never such innocence again," wrote the English poet Philip Larkin. An American journalist covering the war in Europe reported that the massive casualties changed the way men looked at war. In earlier conflicts, soldiers were eager to fight and confident they would return unscathed. Now, the new recruits seemed to have "left hope behind" and were confident that they were "going to their death." By 1915, the great powers were engaged in a global war with no end in sight.

In 1917, George Barnes, a British official whose son had been killed in the war, went to speak at a military hospital in London where injured soldiers were being fitted with artificial limbs. At the appointed hour, the men, in wheelchairs and on crutches, all with empty sleeves or pants legs, arrived to hear the speaker. Yet when Barnes was introduced and rose to talk, he found himself speechless—literally. As the minutes passed in awkward silence, tears rolled down his cheeks. Finally, without having said a word, he simply sat down. What the mutilated soldiers heard was not a war-glorifying speech but the muted sound of grief. The war's mindless horrors had come home.

INITIAL AMERICAN REACTIONS

Disbelief in the United States over the bloodbath in Europe mingled with relief that a wide ocean stood between America and the killing fields. President Wilson, an avowed pacifist, maintained that the United States "was too proud to fight" in Europe's war, "with which we have nothing to do, whose causes cannot touch us." He repeatedly urged Americans to remain "neutral in thought as well as in action." Privately, however, Wilson sought to ensure that the United States could provide Great Britain and France as much financial assistance and supplies as possible.

That most Americans wanted the nation to stay out of the fighting did not keep them from choosing sides. More than a third of the nation's citizens were first- or second-generation immigrants still loyal to their homelands. Eight million German-born Americans lived in the United States in 1914, and most of the 4 million Irish-born Americans detested England, which had ruled the Irish for centuries. For the most part, these groups supported the Central Powers, while other Americans, largely of British origin, supported the Allied Powers.

SUPPORTING THE ALLIES   By the spring of 1915, the Allied Powers' need for food and supplies had generated an economic windfall for American businesses, bankers, and farmers. Exports to France and Great Britain quadrupled from 1914 to 1916. To finance their record-breaking purchases of American supplies, the Allies, especially Britain and France, needed loans from U.S. banks and "credits" from the U.S. government that would allow them to pay for their purchases later.

Early in the war, Secretary of State William Jennings Bryan, a strict pacifist, took advantage of Wilson's absence from Washington after the death of his wife to tell J. Pierpont Morgan, the world's richest banker, that loans to any nations at war were "inconsistent with the true spirit of neutrality." Upon his return, an angry Wilson reversed Bryan's policy by removing all restrictions on loans to the warring nations ("belligerents"). American banks and other investors would eventually send more than $2 billion to the Allies before the United States entered the fighting, and only $27 million to Germany. What Bryan feared, and what Wilson did not fully realize, was that as Britain and France borrowed and purchased more from the United States, it became harder for America to remain neutral.

Despite the disproportionate financial assistance provided to the Allies, the Wilson administration maintained its official neutrality for thirty months. In particular, Wilson tried valiantly to defend the age-old principle of "freedom of the seas." As a neutral nation, the United States, according to international law, should have been able to continue to trade with all the nations at war.

On August 6, 1914, Bryan urged the warring nations to respect the rights of neutral nations to ship goods across the Atlantic. The Central Powers agreed, but the British refused. In November 1914, the British ordered the ships of neutral nations to submit to searches to discover if cargoes were bound for Germany. A few months later, the British announced that they would seize any ships carrying goods to Germany.

"The Sandwich Man" To illustrate America's biased brand of neutrality, this political cartoon shows Uncle Sam wearing a sandwich board that advertises the nation's conflicting desires.

NEUTRAL RIGHTS AND SUBMARINE ATTACKS With its warships bottled up by a British blockade, the German government announced a "war zone" around the British Isles. All ships in those waters would be attacked by submarines, the Germans warned, and "it may not always be possible to save crews and passengers." The Germans' use of submarines, or **U-boats** (*Unterseeboot* in German), violated the long-established wartime custom of stopping an enemy vessel and allowing the passengers and crew to board lifeboats before sinking it. During 1915, German U-boats sank 227 British ships in the Atlantic Ocean and the North Sea.

The United States called the submarine attacks "an indefensible violation of neutral rights," and Wilson warned that he would hold Germany to "strict accountability" for the loss of American lives and property. Then, on May 7, 1915, a German submarine sank the *Lusitania*, an unarmed British luxury liner. Of the 1,198 persons on board who died, 128 were Americans.

The sinking of the *Lusitania*, asserted former president Theodore Roosevelt, was mass murder that called for a declaration of war. Wilson at first urged patience: "There is such a thing as a man being too proud to fight. There is such a thing as a nation being so right that it does not need to convince others by force that it is right."

Critics scolded Wilson for his bloodless response. Roosevelt dismissed it as "unmanly," called the president a "jackass," and threatened to "skin him alive if he doesn't go to war." Wilson privately admitted that he had misspoken. The timid language, he said, had "occurred to me while I was speaking, and I let it out. I should have kept it in."

Wilson's earlier threat of "strict accountability" now required a tough response. On May 13, Secretary of State Bryan demanded that the Germans stop unrestricted submarine warfare, apologize, and pay the families of those killed on the *Lusitania*. The Germans countered that the ship was armed (which was false) and secretly carried rifles and ammunition (which was true). On June 9, Wilson dismissed the German claims and reiterated that the United States was "contending for nothing less high and sacred than the rights of humanity."

Bryan resigned as secretary of state in protest of Wilson's pro-British stance. Upon learning of Bryan's departure, Edith Bolling Galt, soon to be Wilson's second wife, shouted: "Hurrah! Old Bryan is out!" She called the former secretary of state an "awful Deserter." The president confided that he, too, viewed Bryan as a "traitor." He complimented Edith on her vindictiveness: "What a dear partisan you are . . . and how you can hate, too!" Bryan's successor, Robert Lansing, signed the second "*Lusitania* Note."

Stunned by the global outcry over the *Lusitania*, the German government told its U-boat captains to quit attacking passenger vessels. Despite the order, however, a German submarine sank the British liner *Arabic*, and two Americans on board were killed. The Germans paid a cash penalty to their families and issued what came to be called the *Arabic* Pledge on September 1, 1915: "Liners will not be sunk by our submarines without warning and without safety of the lives of non-combatants, provided that the liners do not try to escape or offer resistance."

In early 1916, Wilson sent his closest adviser, Colonel Edward M. House, to London, Paris, and Berlin in hopes of stimulating peace talks, but the mission failed. On March 24, 1916, a U-boat sank the French passenger ferry *Sussex*, killing eighty passengers and injuring two Americans. After Wilson threatened to end relations with Germany, its leaders renewed their promise not to sink merchant and passenger ships. The *Sussex* Pledge implied the virtual abandonment of submarine warfare. Colonel House noted in his diary that Americans were "now beginning to realize that we are on the brink of war and what war means."

PREPARING FOR WAR The sinking of U.S. passenger vessels led to efforts to strengthen the army and navy in case the nation was forced into war. On December 1, 1914, a "preparedness" movement, led by Theodore Roosevelt and Henry Cabot Lodge, created the National Security League to convince Congress and the president to begin preparing for war.

Wilson, too, believed in preparedness. After the *Lusitania* sinking, he directed the War and Navy Departments to develop plans for a $1 billion military expansion. His efforts were controversial, however. Many Americans—pacifists, progressives, and non-interventionists—opposed the "preparedness" effort, seeing it as simply a propaganda campaign to benefit defense industries ("war traffickers") that made weapons and other military equipment.

Despite such opposition, Congress in 1916 passed the National Defense Act, which provided for the expansion of the U.S. Army from 90,000 to 223,000 men over the next five years. While Bryan and others complained that Wilson wanted to "drag this nation into war," the reverse was actually true. Wilson told an aide that he was determined not to "be rushed into war, no matter if every damned congressman and senator stands up on his hind legs and proclaims me a coward."

Opponents of "preparedness" insisted that the expense of military expansion should rest upon the wealthy munitions makers who they believed were promoting it in order to profit from trade with the Allies. The income tax became their weapon. The Revenue Act of 1916 doubled the income tax rate from 1 to 2 percent, created a 12.5 percent tax on munitions makers, and added a new tax on "excessive" corporate profits. The new taxes were the culmination of the progressive legislation that Wilson approved to strengthen his chances in the upcoming presidential election. Fearing that Theodore Roosevelt would be the Republican presidential candidate challenging Wilson, Colonel House believed that the "Democratic Party must change its historic character and become the progressive party in the future."

THE 1916 ELECTION

As the 1916 election approached, Theodore Roosevelt hoped to become the Republican nominee. But his decision in 1912 to run as a third-party candidate had alienated many powerful Republicans, and his eagerness to enter the European war scared many voters. So instead, the Republicans nominated Supreme Court Justice Charles Evans Hughes, a progressive who had served as governor of New York from 1907 to 1910.

The Democrats, staying with Wilson, adopted a platform centered on social-welfare legislation and prudent military preparedness. The peace theme, refined in the slogan "He kept us out of war," became the campaign's rallying cry, although the president now acknowledged that the United States could no longer refuse to play the "great part in the world which was providentially cut out for her. . . . We have got to serve the world." Colonel House was more blunt. He told Secretary of State Robert Lansing that they "could not permit the Allies to go down in defeat, for if they did, we would follow."

Peace with honor Woodrow Wilson's neutrality policies proved popular in the 1916 campaign.

Both Wilson and Hughes were sons of preachers; both were attorneys and former professors; both had been progressive governors; both were known for their integrity. Hughes called for higher tariffs, attacked Wilson for being hostile to Big Business, and implied that Wilson was not neutral enough in responding to the war. Theodore Roosevelt, who was devastated that his party did not nominate him, called the bearded Hughes a "whiskered Wilson." Wilson, however, proved to be the better campaigner—barely.

By midnight on election night, Wilson went to bed assuming that he had lost. Roosevelt was so sure Hughes had won that he sent him a congratulatory telegram. At 4 A.M., however, the results from California were tallied. Wilson had eked out a victory in that state by only 4,000 votes, and thus had become the first Democrat to win a second consecutive term since Andrew Jackson in 1832. His pledge of "peace, prosperity, and progressivism" won him the western states, Ohio, and the Solid South.

AMERICA GOES TO WAR

After his reelection, Wilson again urged the warring nations to negotiate a peace settlement, but to no avail. On January 31, 1917, desperate German military leaders renewed unrestricted submarine warfare in the Atlantic. All vessels from the United States headed for Britain, France, or Italy would be sunk without warning. "This was practically ordering the United States off the Atlantic," said an angry William McAdoo, Wilson's secretary of the Treasury.

The German decision, Colonel House wrote in his journal, left Wilson "sad and depressed," for the president knew it meant war. For their part, the Germans greatly underestimated the American reaction. The United States, the German military newspaper proclaimed, "not only has no army, it has no artillery, no means of transportation, no airplanes, and lacks all other instruments of modern warfare." When his advisers warned that German submarines might cause the United States to enter the war, Kaiser Wilhelm scoffed, "I don't care."

THE ZIMMERMANN TELEGRAM On February 3, President Wilson informed Congress that the United States had formally ended diplomatic relations with the German government. Three weeks later, on February 25, Wilson learned that the British had intercepted a message from a German official, Arthur Zimmermann, to the Mexican government, urging the Mexicans to invade the United States. In exchange, Germany would give Mexico "lost territory in Texas, New Mexico, and Arizona." On March 1, newspapers broke the news of the so-called **Zimmermann telegram**. Infuriated Americans called for war against the Germans, whose attacks on American vessels increased.

AMERICA ENTERS THE WAR In March 1917, German submarines torpedoed five U.S. ships in the North Atlantic. For Wilson, this was the last straw. On April 2, he called on Congress to declare war against Germany.

In one of his greatest speeches, Wilson insisted that "the world must be made safe for democracy." He warned that waging war in Europe would require mobilizing "all the material resources of the country" and he called for 500,000 men to bolster the armed forces. The United States, he asserted, was entering the war to lead a "great crusade" not simply to defeat Germany but to end wars forever. Congress greeted Wilson's message with thunderous applause. On April 4, the Senate passed the war resolution by a vote of 82 to 6. The House followed, 373 to 50, and Wilson signed the measure on April 6.

Jeanette Rankin of Montana, the first woman elected to the House, was one of the few members who voted against war. "You can no more win a war than you can win an earthquake," she explained. "I want to stand by my country, but I cannot vote for war." Wilson had doubts of his own. The president feared—accurately, as it turned out—that mobilizing the nation for war and stamping out dissent would destroy the ideals and momentum of progressivism: "Every reform we have made will be lost if we go into this war." Yet he saw no choice.

America's long embrace of isolationism was over. The nation had reached a turning point in its relations with the world that would test all of President Wilson's political and diplomatic skills—and his stamina.

MOBILIZING A NATION

In April 1917, the U.S. Army remained small, untested, and poorly armed. With only 107,000 men, it was only the seventeenth largest army in the world. Now the Wilson administration needed to recruit, equip, and train an army of millions and transport them across an ocean infested with German submarines.

Mobilizing the nation for war led to an unprecedented expansion of federal authority. The government drafted millions of men between the ages of twenty-one and thirty into the armed services, forced the conversion of industries and farms to wartime needs, took over the railroads, and in many other respects assumed control of national life.

Soon after the U.S. declaration of war, President Wilson called for complete economic mobilization and created new federal agencies to coordinate the effort. The War Industries Board (WIB), established in 1917, soon became the most important of all the federal mobilization agencies. Bernard Baruch, a savvy financier, headed the WIB, which had the authority to ration raw materials, construct new factories, and set prices.

Wilson appointed Republican Herbert Hoover to head the new Food Administration, whose slogan was "Food will win the war." Its purpose was to increase agricultural production while reducing civilian food consumption, since Great Britain and France needed massive amounts of American corn and wheat. Hoover organized a huge group of volunteers who fanned out across the country to urge house-

FOOD WILL WIN THE WAR
You came here seeking Freedom
You must now help to preserve it
WHEAT is needed for the allies
Waste nothing

UNITED STATES FOOD ADMINISTRATION

The immigrant effort This Food Administration poster emphasizes that "wheat is . . . for the allies," an important message to immigrants who hailed from Central Powers nations such as Germany and Austria.

wives and restaurants to participate in "Wheatless" Mondays, "Meatless" Tuesdays, and "Porkless" Thursdays and Saturdays.

Fighting in the Great War would cost the U.S. government $30 billion, which was more than thirty times the entire federal budget in 1917. In addition to raising taxes to finance the war effort, the Wilson administration launched a campaign across the nation to sell "liberty bonds," government securities in the form of paper certificates that guaranteed the purchaser a fixed rate of return. The government recruited dozens of celebrities to promote bond purchases, arguing that a liberty bond was both a patriotic investment in the nation and a smart investment in one's own financial future. Even the Boy Scouts and Girl Scouts sold bonds, using advertising posters that said "Every Scout to Save a Soldier." By war's end, the government had sold over $20 billion in bonds, most of which were purchased by banks and investment houses rather than by individuals.

A NEW LABOR FORCE   Removing 4 million men from the workforce to serve in the armed forces created an acute labor shortage. To meet it, women were encouraged to take jobs previously held mostly by men. One government poster shouted: "Women! Help America's Sons Win the War: Learn to Make Munitions." Another said, "For Every Fighter, a Woman Worker."

Initially, women had supported the war effort mostly in traditional ways. They helped organize fund-raising drives, donated canned food and war-related materials, volunteered for the Red Cross, and joined the army nurse corps. As the scope of the war widened, however, women were recruited to work on farms, loading docks, and railway crews, as well as in the armaments industry, machine shops, steel and lumber mills, and chemical plants. "At last, after centuries of disabilities and discrimination," said a speaker at a Women's Trade Union League meeting in 1917, "women are coming into the labor [force] and festival of life on equal terms with men."

But the changes in female employment were limited and brief. About 1 million women participated in "war work," but most were young and single and already working outside the home, and most returned to their previous jobs once the war ended. In fact, after the war, male-dominated unions encouraged women to go back to domestic roles. The Central Federated Union of New York insisted that "the same patriotism which induced women to enter industry during the war should induce them to vacate their positions after the war."

The Great War also generated dramatic changes for many members of minority groups. Hundreds of thousands of African American men enlisted or were drafted into the military, where they were required to serve in racially segregated units commanded by white officers, as in the Civil War half a century earlier.

At the munitions factory Women on both sides played crucial roles in the war effort, from building airplanes to cooking for soldiers overseas. Here, American women use welding torches to build bombs.

On the home front, northern businesses sent recruiting agents into the southern states, which were still largely rural and agricultural, to find workers for their factories and mills. For the first time, such efforts were directed at African Americans as well as whites. More than 400,000 southern blacks, mostly farmers, joined what came to be known as the **Great Migration**, a mass movement that would continue through the 1920s and change the political and social chemistry of northern cities such as St. Louis, Chicago, Detroit, New York, and Philadelphia. By 1930 the number of African Americans living in the North was triple that of 1910.

Recruiting agents and newspaper editors, both black and white, portrayed the North as the "land of promise" for southern blacks. Northern factory jobs were plentiful and high paying by southern standards, and racism was less obvious and violent—at least at first. A black migrant from Mississippi wrote home from Chicago in 1917 that he wished he had moved north twenty years earlier. "I just begin to feel like a man [here]," he explained. "It's a great deal of pleasure in knowing that you have some privilege. My children are going to the same school with the whites, and I don't have to be humble to no one."

Many Mexican Americans found similar opportunities to improve their status during the war and after. Some joined the military. David Barkley Hernandez had to drop his last name when he enlisted in San Antonio, Texas, because the local draft board was not accepting Mexicans. In 1918, just two days before the war ended, he died in France while returning from a dangerous mission behind German lines. Hernandez became the first person of Mexican descent in the U.S. Army to win the Congressional Medal of Honor. Even more Latinos pursued economic opportunities created by the war effort. Between 1917 and 1920, some 100,000 Mexicans crossed the border into the United States. The economic expansion caused by the war enabled migrant farmworkers already living in states such as Texas, New Mexico, Arizona, and California to take better jobs in factories and mills in rapidly growing cities such as Phoenix, Los Angeles, and Houston, where they moved into Spanish-speaking neighborhoods called *barrios*.

Segregation in the military Most African American enlistees served in support units because whites believed them unfit for combat, despite evidence of black military contributions since the Revolution. Here, soldiers in the 92nd Infantry Division (one of the few "colored" units sent overseas) march in Verdun, France.

But the newcomers, whether Latinos or blacks, were often resented rather than welcomed. J. Luz Saenz, a Mexican American from Texas, noted in his diary that it took only three days after he was discharged from the army to have whites "throw us out from restaurants and deny us service as human beings." In 1917 more than forty African Americans and nine whites were killed during a riot in a weapons plant in East St. Louis, Illinois. Two years later, a Chicago race riot left twenty-three African Americans and fifteen whites dead.

A LOSS OF CIVIL LIBERTIES   Once war was declared, Americans often equated anything German with disloyalty. German Americans were publicly harassed and discriminated against. Many Americans quit drinking beer because most breweries were owned by German Americans. Symphonies refused to perform music by Bach and Beethoven, schools canceled German language classes, and grocers renamed *sauerkraut* "liberty cabbage." President Wilson had predicted as much. "Once [we] lead this people into war," he said, "they'll forget there ever was such a thing as tolerance." What Wilson did not say was that he himself would lead the effort to suppress civil liberties, for, as he claimed, subversive forces in a nation at war must be "crushed out."

Keep out of it   In this 1918 war poster, the Kaiser—with his famous moustache and spiked German helmet—is depicted as a spider, spinning an invisible web to catch the stray words of Allied civilians.

Under the Espionage and Sedition Acts, Congress prohibited any criticism of government leaders and war policies. The Espionage Act of 1917 called for twenty years in prison for anyone who helped the enemy; encouraged insubordination, disloyalty, or refusal of duty in the armed services; or interfered with the war effort in other ways.

During the war, 1,055 people were convicted under the Espionage Act. Most were simply critics of the war. Socialist leader Eugene V. Debs, a militant pacifist, was convicted simply for opposing the war and was sentenced to ten years in prison. He told the court he would always criticize wars imposed by the "master" class: "While there is a lower class, I am in it. While there is a criminal element, I am of it. While there is a soul in prison, I am not free."

The Sedition Act of 1918 broadened the Espionage Act to those who tried to impede the sale of war bonds or promoted cutbacks in production; it even outlawed saying, writing, or printing anything "disloyal, profane, scurrilous, or abusive" about the American form of government, the Constitution, or the army and navy.

The Supreme Court endorsed the Espionage and Sedition Acts in two rulings issued just after the war ended. *Schenck v. United States* (1919) reaffirmed the conviction of Charles T. Schenck, head of the Socialist party, for circulating leaflets opposing the war among members of the armed forces. Justice Oliver Wendell Holmes wrote the unanimous court opinion that freedom of speech did not apply to words that represented "a clear and present danger to the safety of the country." In *Abrams v. United States* (1919), the Court upheld the conviction of a man who had distributed pamphlets opposing military intervention in Russia to remove the Bolsheviks, who had seized power in 1917.

THE AMERICAN ROLE IN THE WAR

In 1917, America's war strategy focused on helping the struggling French and British armies on the Western Front. The Allied leaders stressed that they needed at least a million American troops (called "doughboys") to defeat the Germans, but it would take months to recruit, equip, and train that many new soldiers. On December 21, 1917, French premier Georges Clemenceau urged the Americans to rush their army, called the American Expeditionary Force, to France. "A terrible blow is imminent," he told an American journalist about to leave Paris. "Tell your Americans to come quickly." Clemenceau was referring to the likelihood of a massive German attack, made more probable by the end of the fighting on the Eastern Front following the Bolshevik Revolution in Russia in November 1917.

THE BOLSHEVIK REVOLUTION   Among the many casualties of the Great War, none was greater in scale than the destruction of the backward Russian Empire and its monarchy. It was the first nation to crack under the stress and strain of the Great War. On March 15, 1917, bumbling Tsar Nicholas II, having presided over a war that had ruined the Russian economy and the nation's transportation system, abdicated his throne and turned the nation over to the "provisional government" of a new Russian republic committed to continuing the war.

Vladimir Lenin Communist revolutionary who led the Bolsheviks in overthrowing the Russian monarchy and ultimately establishing the Soviet Union.

The fall of the tsar gave Americans the illusion that all the major Allied powers were now fighting for the ideals of constitutional democracy—an illusion that was shattered after the Germans in April helped exiled radical Vladimir Ilyich Lenin return to Russia from Switzerland. The Germans hoped that he would cause turmoil in his homeland. He did much more than that.

As Lenin observed, power in war-weary Russia was lying in the streets, waiting to be picked up. To do so, he mobilized the Bolsheviks, a group of ruthless Communist revolutionaries who were convinced that they were in the vanguard of the irresistible force of history. During the night of November 6, the Bolsheviks seized power from the provisional government, established a dictatorship, and called for a quick end to the war.

Lenin banned political parties and all organized religions (atheism became the official belief), eliminated civil liberties and the free press, and killed or imprisoned opposition leaders, including the tsar and his family. In short, he imposed his totalitarian blueprint of the perfect society on the Russian people. In 1918, Lenin instructed Bolshevik leaders to crack down on peasants who resisted the revolution: "Comrades! Hang (hang without fail, so that people will see) no fewer than one hundred kulaks, rich men, bloodsuckers. Yours, Lenin."

The Bolshevik Revolution triggered a prolonged civil war throughout Russia. President Wilson sent 20,000 American soldiers to Siberia to support the anti-Communist Russian forces, but they were unsuccessful.

FOURTEEN POINTS Woodrow Wilson was determined to ensure that the Great War would be the last world war. In September 1917, he asked Colonel Edward House to organize a group of 150 experts in politics, history, geography, and foreign policy, called the Inquiry, to draft a peace plan, since America, according to Wilson, had no selfish goals; it was simply "one of the champions of the rights of mankind." Drawing upon their advice, Wilson developed what would come to be called the **Fourteen Points**, which he presented to Congress on January 8, 1918, calling it "the only possible program" for peace.

The first five of the fourteen points endorsed the open conduct of diplomacy rather than secret treaties, the recognition of neutral nations' right to continue maritime commerce in time of war ("freedom of the seas"), the removal of international trade barriers, the reduction of armaments, and the transformation of colonial empires.

Most of the other points dealt with territorial claims. In redrawing the map of Europe, Wilson demanded that the victors follow the difficult principle of "self-determination," allowing overlapping nationalities and ethnic groups to develop their own independent nations. Point thirteen called for a new nation for Poland, long dominated by the Russians on the east and the Germans on the west. Point fourteen, the capstone of Wilson's postwar scheme, called for the creation of a "league" of nations to preserve global peace. When the Fourteen Points were made public, African American leaders asked the president to add a fifteenth point: an end to racial discrimination. Wilson did not respond. Overall, the reaction to the speech was positive. The headline for the *New York Times* editorial proclaimed: "The President's Triumph."

As the war ground on, the battling nations grew weary of the costs and shortages of food, clothing, and gasoline. But no diplomatic solution was in sight. In Germany, food and fuel shortages led to growing discontent. Workers went on strike, and servicemen mutinied and deserted. "The Monarchy," said a German official, "is lurching toward the edge of the abyss."

RUSSIA SURRENDERS Conditions were even worse in Russia. After taking power, Lenin declared that the world would be freed from war only by a global revolution in which capitalism was replaced by communism. To that end, he wanted Russia out of the Great War as soon as possible. On March 3, 1918, Lenin signed a humiliating peace agreement with Germany, the Treaty of Brest-Litovsk. The treaty forced Russia to transfer vast territories to Germany and Turkey and to recognize the independence of the Ukraine region, thereby depriving Russia of much of its population, coal and wheat production, and heavy industry. In addition, Russia had to pay $46 million to Germany. Lenin was willing to accept such a harsh peace because he needed to concentrate on his internal enemies in the ongoing Russian civil war.

With Russia out of the war, the Germans could focus on the Western Front. Erich Ludendorff, the German army commander, said that the ability to move hundreds of thousands of soldiers from the Russian front to France would give him numerical superiority for the first time and enable him to "deal an annihilating blow to the British before American aid can become effective."

Meuse-Argonne Offensive American soldiers of the 23rd Infantry, 2nd Division, fire machine guns at the Germans from what was left of the Argonne Forest in France.

AMERICANS ON THE WESTERN FRONT   On March 21, the Germans began the first of several offensives in France and Belgium designed to win the war before the American soldiers arrived in force. By May, the German armies had advanced within fifty miles of Paris, and the British Fifth Army was destroyed.

The massive German offensive nearly defeated the Allies. In early April, however, the Germans suddenly lost their momentum. On April 5, the German commander called a halt because so many soldiers were exhausted and demoralized, convinced, as one officer admitted, that their "hope [for victory] had been dashed" by their inability to sustain the supply lines needed for such a widespread advance.

In May, French and British leaders pressed Wilson to hurry American troops into the fighting. By the end of the month, some 650,000 American soldiers were in Europe. In June, they were ready to fight. At the month-long Battle of Belleau Wood, which began on June 2, U.S. forces commanded by General John J. Pershing joined the French in driving the Germans back. A French officer watching the high-spirited, if untrained, American soldiers remarked that they were providing "a wonderful transfusion of blood" for the Allied cause.

Pershing was determined to use U.S. troops to break the stalemate on the Western Front. During the ferocious fighting, a French officer urged an American unit to retreat. In a famous exchange, U.S. Marine Captain Lloyd W. Williams refused the order, saying: "Retreat? Hell, we just got here."

In a massive Allied offensive, begun on September 26, 1918, American troops joined British and French armies in a drive toward Sedan, France, and its strategic railroad, which supplied the German army occupying northern France. With 1.2 million U.S. soldiers involved, including some 200,000 African Americans, it was the largest American action of the war, and it resulted in 117,000 American casualties, including 26,000 dead. But along

American casualties A Salvation Army worker writing a letter home for a wounded soldier.

the entire French-Belgian front, the outnumbered Germans were in retreat during the early fall of 1918. "America," wrote German General Erich Ludendorff, "became the decisive power in the war."

On October 6, the German government asked Wilson for peace negotiations based on his Fourteen Points. British and French leaders accepted the Fourteen Points as a basis of negotiations, but with two significant reservations: the British insisted on the right to discuss limiting freedom of the seas to preserve their naval dominance, and the French demanded massive reparations (payments) from Germany and Austria for war damages.

THE GERMAN COLLAPSE By the end of October 1918, Germany was on the verge of collapse. Revolutionaries rampaged through the streets. Sailors mutinied. Germany's allies (Bulgaria, Turkey, and Austria-Hungary) dropped out of the war, and panicked military leaders demanded that the civilian government ask for an armistice (cease-fire agreement). On November 9, the German Kaiser resigned, and a republic was proclaimed. Early on the morning of November 11, an armistice was signed in which the Germans were assured that Wilson's Fourteen Points would be the basis for the peace conference.

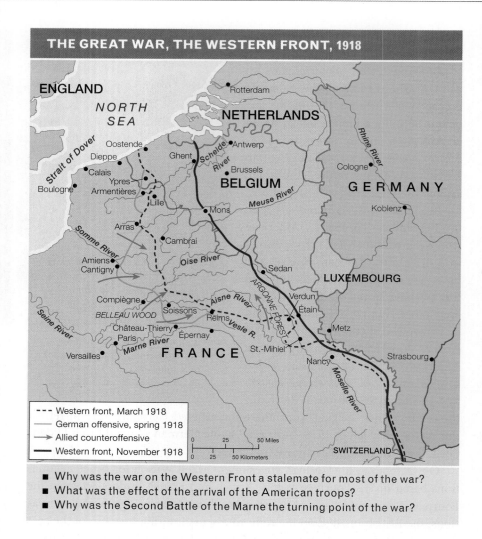

THE GREAT WAR, THE WESTERN FRONT, 1918

Legend:
- - - Western front, March 1918
—— German offensive, spring 1918
→ Allied counteroffensive
━━ Western front, November 1918

0   25   50 Miles
0   25   50 Kilometers

- Why was the war on the Western Front a stalemate for most of the war?
- What was the effect of the arrival of the American troops?
- Why was the Second Battle of the Marne the turning point of the war?

Six hours later, at the eleventh hour of the eleventh day of the eleventh month, and after 1,563 days of terrible warfare, the killing ended. From Europe, Colonel House sent Wilson a telegram: "Autocracy [government by an individual with unlimited power] is dead; long live democracy and its immortal leader."

The end of fighting led to wild celebrations throughout the world. "The nightmare is over," wrote African American activist W. E. B. Du Bois. "The world awakes. The long, horrible years of dreadful night are passed. Behold the sun!" Wilson was not as joyful. The Great War, he said, had dealt a grievous injury to civilization "which can never be atoned for or repaired."

During its nineteen months in the Great War, the United States had lost 53,000 servicemen in combat. Another 63,000 died of diseases, largely casu-

Armistice Night in New York **(1918)** George Luks, known for his vivid paintings of urban life, captured the unbridled outpouring of patriotism and joy that extended into the night of Germany's surrender.

alties of the influenza epidemic that swept through the world in 1918. Germany's war dead totaled more than 2 million, including civilians; France lost nearly 1.4 million combatants, Great Britain 703,000, and Russia 1.7 million. The war also ruined the economies of Europe while decimating a whole generation of young men. The new Europe would be very different from the prewar version: much poorer, more violent, more polarized, more cynical, less sure of itself, and less capable of decisive action. The United States, for good or ill, emerged from the war as the world's dominant power.

THE POLITICS OF PEACE

On June 25, 1918, Colonel Edward House wrote President Wilson from France, urging him to take charge of the peacemaking process. "It is one of the things with which your name should be linked during the ages." House was right. Woodrow Wilson and the peace agreement ending the Great War would be forever linked, but not in a positive light.

In the making of the peace agreement, Wilson showed himself both at his best and worst. His Fourteen Points embodied his vision of a better world governed by fairer principles. He felt guided "by the hand of God." His vision of a peacekeeping "League of Nations" was, in his view, the key element to a "secure and lasting peace" and was the "most essential part of the peace settlement." If the diplomats gathering to draft the peace treaty failed to follow his ambitious plans to reshape the world in America's image, he warned, "there will be another world war" within a generation.

WILSON'S KEY ERRORS

Whatever the merits of President Wilson's peace plan, his efforts to implement it proved clumsy. He made several key decisions that would come back to haunt him. First, against the advice of his staff and of European leaders, he decided to attend the peace conference in Paris that opened on January 18, 1919. Never before had an American president left the nation for such a prolonged period (six months). During his months abroad, Wilson lost touch with political developments at home.

Wilson's second error of judgment involved politics. In the congressional elections of November 1918, Wilson defied his advisers and political tradition by urging voters to elect a Democratic Congress as a sign of approval of his policies in handling the war—and the peace. He "begged" the public not to "repudiate" his leadership. Prior to that time, presidents had remained neutral during congressional elections and abstained from campaigning.

Republicans, who for the most part had backed Wilson's war measures, were not pleased. Theodore Roosevelt, whose son Kermit, a pilot, had been killed in the war, called Wilson's self-serving appeal for votes "a cruel insult to every Republican father or mother whose sons have entered the Army or Navy." Voters were not impressed, either. In the elections, the Democrats lost control of both houses of Congress, which was a bad omen for Wilson's peace-making efforts, since any treaty to end the war would have to be approved by at least two-thirds of the Senate, now controlled by Republicans.

Meanwhile, Wilson had dispatched Colonel House and several aides to Europe to begin convincing Allied leaders to embrace the Fourteen Points. The lopsided defeat of Wilson and the Democrats in the elections, said House, "made his difficulties enormously greater." Gordon Auchincloss, House's son-in-law who was serving as one of his lieutenants in Europe, displayed the brash confidence symptomatic of many American diplomats when he boasted from London that "before we get through with these fellows over here, we will teach them how to do things and to do them quickly." It would not be so easy.

Wilson further weakened support for his peacemaking efforts when, in a deliberate slight, he refused to appoint a prominent Republican to the American delegation headed to the peace conference. Although House had urged him to appoint Theodore Roosevelt or Senator Henry Cabot Lodge, the president's archenemy and the leading Republican in Congress, Wilson refused. In the end, he appointed Harry White, an obscure Republican. Former president William Howard Taft groused that Wilson's real intention in going to Paris was "to hog the whole show." He almost did.

Wilson's participation in the Paris Peace Conference would be the climactic event of his career, an opportunity for him to convince Europe to follow his impassioned idealism in creating a very different postwar world. As Wilson prepared to board the *George Washington* with 113 staff members bound for Europe over a ten-day voyage, Ray Stannard Baker, a muckraking journalist, wrote that the president "has yet to prove his greatness. The fate of a drama lies in its last act, and Wilson is now coming to that."

Wilson's last act would indeed be dramatic—tragically so. Initially, however, his entrance on the European stage was triumphant in December 1918. The cheering crowds in London, Paris, and Rome verged on hysteria. Millions of grateful Europeans greeted him as an almost mystical hero, even a savior. An Italian mayor described Wilson's visit as the "second coming of Christ." The ecstatic welcome led Wilson to think he truly was being directed by God to save the world. In a sign of his growing egotism, he claimed that he was now "at the apex of my glory in the hearts of these people." He was determined to shape a peace treaty and postwar world based on principles of justice, fairness, and self-determination.

Fit for a messiah Wilson rode down the Champs Élysées as the crowds showered him with flower petals and cheered, *"Vive Wilson! Vive l'Amérique! Vive la liberté!"*

From such a height, there could only be a fall. Although popular with the European people, Wilson had to negotiate with tough-minded, wily European statesmen who shared neither his lofty goals nor his ideals. In fact, they resented his efforts to forge a peace settlement modeled on American values. That Wilson had not bothered to consult them about his Fourteen Points peace proposal before announcing it to the world did not help. In the end, the European leaders would force him to abandon many of his ideals.

THE PARIS PEACE CONFERENCE

The Paris Peace Conference lasted from January to June 1919. The participants had no time to waste. The German, Austro-Hungarian, and Ottoman thrones and empires were in ruins. Across much of Europe, food was scarce and lawlessness rampant. The threat of revolution hung over central Europe as Communists in the defeated nations threatened to take control.

The peace conference dealt with immensely complex and controversial issues (including creating new nations and redrawing the maps of Europe and the Middle East) that required both political statesmanship and technical expertise. The British delegation alone included almost 400 members, many of them specialists in political geography or economics. The peacemakers met daily, debating, arguing, and compromising.

THE BIG FOUR   From the start, the Paris Peace Conference was controlled by the Big Four: the prime ministers of Britain, France, and Italy, and the president of the United States. Georges Clemenceau, the seventy-seven-year-old French premier known as "The Tiger," had little patience with President Wilson's preaching. In response to Wilson's declaration that "America is the only idealistic nation in the world," Clemenceau grumbled that talking with Wilson was like talking to Jesus Christ. "God gave us the Ten Commandments and we broke them," the French leader sneered. "Wilson gave us the Fourteen Points—we shall see."

The Big Four fought in private and in public. The French and the British, led by Prime Minister David Lloyd George, insisted that Wilson agree to their harsh provisions to weaken Germany, while Vittorio Orlando, prime minister of Italy, focused on gaining territories from defeated Austria.

THE LEAGUE OF NATIONS   Although suffering from chronic health issues, including hypertension and blinding headaches, Wilson lectured the other statesmen about the need to embrace his beloved **League of Nations**, which he insisted must be the "keystone" of any peace settlement. He believed that a world peace organization would abolish war by settling international disputes and mobilizing united action against aggressors. Article X of the charter, which Wilson called "the heart of the League," allowed member nations to impose military and economic sanctions, or penalties, against military aggressors. The League, Wilson predicted, would have such moral influence that it would make military action to preserve peace unnecessary. These unrealistic expectations became, for Wilson, a self-defeating crusade.

On February 14, 1919, Wilson presented the final draft of the League covenant to the Allies and left Paris for a ten-day visit home, where he faced growing opposition among Republicans. The League of Nations, Theodore Roosevelt complained, would revive German militarism and undermine American morale. "To substitute internationalism for nationalism," Roosevelt argued, "means to do away with patriotism." Henry Cabot Lodge, chairman of the Senate Foreign Relations Committee, also scorned Wilson and his idealism. Lodge told Roosevelt, "I never expected to hate anyone in politics with the hatred I feel toward Wilson." He dismissed the League of Nations because he feared it would involve the U.S. military in foreign conflicts without Senate approval.

THE TREATY OF VERSAILLES

When Wilson returned to Paris in the spring of 1919, he had lost his leverage with the British and French because it was increasingly uncertain that the U.S. Senate would approve any treaty he endorsed. Although a skilled debater, Wilson was forced to concede many controversial issues to ensure that the Europeans would approve his League of Nations.

Wilson yielded to French demands that Germany transfer vast territories to France on its west and to Poland on its east and north. In other territorial matters, Wilson had to abandon his principle of national self-determination, whereby every ethnic group would be allowed to form its own nation. As Secretary of State Robert Lansing correctly predicted, allowing each ethnic group to determine its own fate "will raise hopes which can never be realized." (Wilson himself later told the Senate that he wished he had never said that "all nations have a right to self-determination.")

In their efforts to allow for at least some degree of ethnic self-determination in multiethnic regions, the statesmen at Versailles created the independent countries of Austria, Hungary, Poland, Yugoslavia, and Czechoslovakia in central Europe and four new nations along the Baltic Sea: Finland, Estonia, Lithuania, and Latvia. The victorious Allies, however, did not create independent nations out of the colonies of the defeated and now defunct European empires. Instead, they assigned the former German colonies in Africa and the Turkish colonies in the Middle East to France and Great Britain to govern while they prepared themselves for independence at some undesignated point in the future. At the same time, Japan took control of the former German colonies in east Asia.

The issue of reparations—payments by the vanquished to the victors—triggered especially bitter arguments. The British and the French (on whose soil much of the war was fought) wanted Germany to pay the entire financial cost of the war, including their veterans' pensions. On this point, Wilson made perhaps his most fateful concessions. Although initially opposed to reparations, he eventually agreed to a crucial clause in the peace treaty by which Germany was forced to accept responsibility for the war and its entire expense. The "war guilt" clause, written by American John Foster Dulles, a future secretary of state, so offended Germans that it became a major factor in the rise of the Nazi party during the 1920s. Wilson himself privately admitted that if he were a German, he would refuse to sign the flawed treaty.

Colonel House, the president's closest confidante, privately blamed Wilson for many problems associated with the treaty. He found the president "so contradictory that it is hard to pass judgment on him." He "speaks constantly of teamwork but seldom practices it." Wilson was "becoming stubborn and angry, and he never was a good negotiator." House worried that Wilson was too "unreasonable" about the League of Nations, "which does not make for solutions." It was an eerily accurate prediction of what was in store.

On May 7, 1919, the victorious powers presented the treaty to the German delegates, who returned three weeks later with 443 pages of criticism. Among other things, they noted that Germany would lose 13 percent of its territory, 10 percent of its population, and all of its colonies in Asia and Africa.

A few minor changes were made, but when the Germans still balked, the French threatened to launch a new military attack. Finally, on June 28, the Germans gave up and signed the treaty in the glittering Hall of Mirrors at Versailles, the magnificent palace built by King Louis XIV in the late seventeenth century. Thereafter, the agreement was called the **Treaty of Versailles**.

None of the peacemakers was fully satisfied. As France's Clemenceau observed, "it was not perfect," but it was, after all, the "result of human beings. We did all we could to work fast and well." A British official reversed Wilson's claim that it had been a "war to end all wars" by saying it was a "peace to end peace"—as turned out to be the case.

When Adolf Hitler, a young German soldier who had been wounded in the war, learned of the treaty's provisions, he vowed revenge. "It cannot be that two million Germans have fallen in vain," he screamed during a speech in Munich in 1922. "We demand vengeance!"

THE TREATY DEBATE   On July 8, 1919, Wilson arrived back in Washington, D.C., to begin working for approval of the treaty by the Senate, where the Republicans outnumbered the Democrats. Before leaving Paris, he had assured a French diplomat that he would not allow any changes to the treaty.

EUROPE AFTER THE TREATY OF VERSAILLES, 1918

Legend:
- 1914 boundaries
- New nations
- Plebiscite areas
- Occupied area

0   250   500 Miles

0   250   500 Kilometers

■ Why was self-determination so difficult to apply in Central Europe?
■ How did territorial concessions weaken Germany?

"I shall consent to nothing," he vowed. "The Senate must take its medicine." Thus began one of the most brutally partisan and bitterly personal disputes in American history.

On July 10, Wilson became the first president to enter the Senate and deliver a treaty to be voted on. He called upon senators to accept their "great duty" and ratify the treaty, which had been guided "by the hand of God." Wilson then grew needlessly confrontational. He dismissed critics of the League of Nations as "blind and little provincial people." The world, he claimed, was relying on the United States to sign the treaty: "Dare we reject it and break the heart of the world?"

Yes, answered Senate Republicans, who had decided that Wilson's commitment to the League was a reckless threat to America's independence. Henry Cabot Lodge denounced the treaty's "scheme of making mankind suddenly virtuous by a statute or a written constitution." Lodge's strategy was to stall approval of the treaty in hopes that public opposition would grow. He took six weeks simply reading aloud the lengthy text to his Foreign Relations committee. He then organized a parade of expert witnesses, most of them opposed to the treaty, to appear at the hearings on ratification.

In the Senate, a group of "irreconcilables," fourteen Republicans and two Democrats, refused to support American membership in the League. They were mainly western and midwestern progressives, isolationists who feared that such sweeping foreign commitments would threaten domestic reforms.

Lodge himself belonged to a larger group called the "reservationists," who insisted upon limiting American participation in the League in exchange for approving the treaty. The only way to get Senate approval was for Wilson to meet with Lodge and others and agree to revisions, the most important of which was the requirement that Congress authorize any American participation in a League-approved war. Colonel House urged the president to "meet the Senate in a conciliatory spirit." Wilson replied that he had long ago decided that you "can never get anything in this life that is worthwhile without fighting for it." House courageously disagreed, reminding the president that American civilization was "built on compromise." It was the last time the two men would speak to or see each other.

As Republican senator Frank B. Kellogg of Minnesota noted, the proposed changes were crafted not by enemies of the treaty but by friends who wanted to save it. Republican senator James Watson of Indiana told Wilson that he had no choice but to accept some revisions: "Mr. President, you are licked. There is only one way you can take the United States into the League of Nations."

But the self-righteous president was temperamentally incapable of compromising. He refused to negotiate, declaring that "if the Treaty is not ratified by the Senate, the War will have been fought in vain."

LET THE PEOPLE DECIDE In September 1919, after a summer of fruitless debate, an exhausted Wilson decided to bypass his Senate opponents by speaking directly to voters. On September 2, against his doctor's orders and his wife's advice, he left Washington for a grueling railroad tour through the Midwest to the West Coast, intending to visit twenty-nine cities and deliver forty speeches on behalf of the treaty.

No president had ever made such a strenuous effort to win public support. In St. Louis, Wilson said that he had returned from Paris "bringing one of the greatest documents of human history," which was now in danger of being rejected by the Senate. He pledged to "fight for a cause . . . greater than the Senate. It is greater than the government. It is as great as the cause of mankind. . . ."

Wilson traveled and spoke, sometimes as many as four times a day, despite suffering from pounding headaches. It did not help his morale to learn that his secretary of state, Robert Lansing, had said that the League of Nations was "entirely useless." By the time Wilson's train reached Spokane, Washington, the president was visibly fatigued. But he kept going through Oregon and California. Some 200,000 people greeted him in Los Angeles. In all, he had covered 10,000 miles in twenty-two days and given thirty-two major speeches.

Then disaster struck. After delivering an emotional speech on September 25, 1919, in Pueblo, Colorado, Wilson collapsed from headaches so severe that he had to cancel the trip. On the train heading back, as he looked out the window with tears rolling down his cheeks, he told his doctor that he had suffered the "greatest disappointment of [his] life."

A STRICKEN PRESIDENT   Back in Washington, D.C., a week later, the president suffered a crushing stroke (cerebral hemorrhage) that left him paralyzed on his left side; he could barely speak or see. Only his secretary, his doctor, and his wife, Edith, knew his true condition. For five months at the end of 1919 and in early 1920, Wilson lay flat on his back while his doctor issued reassuring medical bulletins. If a document needed Wilson's signature, his wife guided his trembling hand. Lansing urged the president's aides to declare him disabled and appoint Vice President Thomas Marshall in his place; they angrily refused. Soon thereafter, Lansing was replaced.

The stroke made Wilson even more arrogant and stubborn and paralyzed his administration as well. He became emotionally unstable, at times crying uncontrollably and displaying signs of paranoia. For the remaining seventeen months of his term, his protective wife, along with aides and trusted cabinet members, kept him isolated from all but the most essential business. When a group of Republican senators visited the White House, one of them said: "Well, Mr. President, we have all been praying for you." Wilson replied, "Which way, Senator?"

THE TREATY UNDER ATTACK   Such presidential humor was rare, however. Wilson's hardened arteries seemed to have hardened his political judgment as well. For his part, Lodge pushed through the Senate fourteen changes (the number was not coincidental) in the draft of the Treaty of Versailles. The exiled Colonel House became so concerned that he wrote Edith Wilson a letter in which he said how "vital" it was for some form of the treaty to be approved: The president's "place in history is in the balance." He pleaded for Wilson to negotiate a compromise. The First Lady refused to share his concerns with her husband.

In the end, Wilson rejected any proposed changes to the treaty. As a result, his supporters in the Senate were thrown into an unlikely alliance with the irreconcilables, who opposed the treaty under any circumstances. The final Senate vote in 1920 on Lodge's revised treaty was 39 in favor and 55 against. On the question of approving the original treaty without changes, the irreconcilables and the reservationists, led by Lodge, combined to defeat ratification, with 38 for and 53 against.

Woodrow Wilson's grand effort at global peacemaking had failed miserably. (Although, he did receive the Nobel Peace Prize for his efforts.) When told of the final Senate vote, he said it "would have been better if I had died last fall."

After refusing to ratify the treaty, Congress tried to declare an official end to American involvement in the war by a joint resolution on May 20, 1920, which Wilson vetoed in a fit of spite. It was not until July 2, 1921, four months after he had left office and almost eighteen months after the fighting had stopped, that another joint resolution officially ended the state of war with Germany and Austria-Hungary. Separate peace treaties with Germany, Austria, and Hungary were ratified on October 18, 1921, but by then Warren G. Harding was president.

The U.S. failure to ratify the Versailles Treaty or to exercise strong world leadership would prove to have long-range consequences. With Great Britain and France too exhausted and too timid to keep Germany weak and isolated, a dangerous power vacuum would emerge in Europe, one which Adolf Hitler and the Nazis would fill.

Stumbling from War to Peace

After the war, most Americans were far more concerned with domestic issues than with the Treaty of Versailles, as celebration over the war's end soon gave way to widespread inflation, unemployment, labor unrest, socialist and Communist radicalism, race riots, terrorist bombings, and government tyranny. With millions of servicemen returning to civilian life, war-related industries shutting down, and wartime price controls ending, unemployment and prices for consumer goods spiked.

Bedridden by his stroke, the president became increasingly distant, depressed, and peevish. Wilson, observed David Lloyd George, the British prime minister, was "as much a victim of the war as any soldier who died in the trenches." His administration was in disarray, he had never been so unpopular, and the Democratic party was floundering along with him.

THE SPANISH FLU Beginning in 1918, many Americans confronted an infectious enemy that produced far more casualties than the war. It became known as the Spanish flu (although its origins continue to be debated), and its contagion spread around the globe.

The disease appeared suddenly in the spring of 1918. Its initial outbreak lasted a year and killed as many as 100 million people worldwide, twice as many as died

Influenza epidemic Office workers wearing gauze masks during the Spanish flu epidemic of 1918.

in the war. In the United States alone, it accounted for 675,000 deaths, more than ten times the number of U.S. combat deaths in France. A fifth of the nation's population caught the flu, and the public health system was strained to the breaking point. Hospitals ran out of beds, and funeral homes ran out of coffins.

By the spring of 1919, the pandemic had run its course, ending as suddenly—and as inexplicably—as it had begun. Although another outbreak occurred in the winter of 1920, people had grown more resistant to it. No disease in human history had killed so many people, and no war, famine, or natural catastrophe had killed so many in such a short time.

SUFFRAGE AT LAST   As the first outbreak of the Spanish flu was ending, American women finally gained a Constitutional guarantee of their right to vote. After six months of delay, debate, and failed votes, Congress passed the **Nineteenth Amendment** in the spring of 1919 and sent it to the states for ratification.

Tennessee's legislature was the last of thirty-six state assemblies to approve the amendment, and it did so in dramatic fashion. The initial vote was 48–48. Then a twenty-four-year-old Republican legislator named Harry T. Burn changed his vote to yes at the insistence of his mother.

The Nineteenth Amendment became official on August 18, 1920, making the United States the twenty-second nation to allow women's suffrage. It was a climactic achievement of the Progressive Era. Suddenly, 9.5 million women were eligible to vote in national elections; in the 1920 presidential election, they would make up 40 percent of the electorate.

Their first votes Women of New York City's East Side vote for the first time in the presidential election of 1920.

ECONOMIC TURBULENCE As consumer prices rose, discontented workers, released from wartime controls on wages, grew more willing to go out on strike. In 1919, more than 4 million hourly wage workers, 20 percent of the U.S. workforce, participated in 3,600 strikes. Most of them wanted nothing more than higher wages and shorter workweeks, but their critics linked them with the worldwide Communist movement. Charges of a Communist conspiracy were greatly exaggerated, however. In 1919, fewer than 70,000 Americans nationwide belonged to the Communist party.

The most controversial labor dispute was in Boston, where most of the police went on strike on September 9, 1919. Massachusetts governor Calvin Coolidge mobilized the National Guard to maintain order. After four days, the striking policemen offered to return, but instead Coolidge ordered that they all be fired. When labor leaders appealed for their reinstatement, Coolidge responded in words that made him an instant national hero: "There is no right to strike against the public safety by anybody, anywhere, any time."

RACE RIOTS The summer of 1919 also brought a wave of deadly race riots. As more and more African Americans, including many of the 367,000 who were war veterans, moved out of the South to different parts of the country,

Safe, briefly Escorted by a police officer, an African American family moves its belongings from their home, likely destroyed by white rioters, and into a protected area of Chicago.

developed successful careers, and asserted their civil rights, resentful whites reacted with an almost hysterical racism. In 1919 alone, seventy-six African Americans, including nine military veterans, were killed by southern whites. Among the victims was Sergeant Major Joe Green in Birmingham, Alabama, because he "had the insolence" to ask for his change on a streetcar, and Private William Little in Blakely, Georgia, because he had walked around town wearing his army uniform.

What African American leader James Weldon Johnson called the Red Summer (*red* signifying blood) began in July, when a mob of whites invaded the black neighborhood in Longview, Texas, angry over rumors of interracial dating. They burned shops and houses and ran several African Americans out of town. A week later, in Washington, D.C., exaggerated and false reports of black assaults on white women stirred up white mobs, and gangs of white and black rioters waged a race war in the streets until soldiers and driving rains ended the fighting.

The worst was yet to come. In late July, 38 people were killed and 537 injured in five days of race rioting in Chicago, where some 50,000 blacks, mostly from the rural South, had moved during the war, leading to tensions with local whites over jobs and housing. White unionized workers especially resented blacks who were hired as strikebreakers. Altogether, twenty-five race riots erupted in 1919, and eighty African Americans were lynched, including eleven war veterans.

The race riots of 1919 were a turning point for many African Americans. "We made the supreme sacrifice," a black veteran told poet-journalist Carl Sandburg. "Now we want to see our country live up to the Constitution and the Declaration of Independence." Another ex-soldier noted how much the war experience had changed the outlook of blacks: "We were determined not to take it anymore."

THE RED SCARE With so many people convinced that the strikes and riots were inspired by Communists and anarchists (two very different groups who shared a hatred for capitalism), a New York journalist reported that Americans were "shivering in their boots over Bolshevism, and they are far more scared of Lenin than they ever were of the [German] Kaiser. We seem to be the most frightened victors the world ever saw."

Fears of revolution were fueled by the violent actions of a few militants. In early 1919, the Secret Service discovered a plot by Spanish anarchists to kill President Wilson and other government officials. In April 1919, postal workers intercepted nearly forty homemade mail bombs addressed to government officials. One mail bomb, however, blew off the hands of a Georgia senator's maid. In June, another bomb damaged U.S. Attorney General A. Mitchell Palmer's house. Palmer, who had ambitions to succeed Wilson as president, concluded that a "Red Menace," a Communist "blaze of revolution," was "sweeping over every American institution of law and order."

That August, Palmer appointed a twenty-four-year-old attorney named J. Edgar Hoover to lead a new government division created to collect information on radicals. Hoover and others in the Justice Department worked with a network of 250,000 informers in 600 cities, all of them members of the American Protective League, which had been founded during the war to root out "traitors" and labor radicals.

On November 7, 1919, federal agents rounded up 450 alien "radicals," most of whom were law-abiding Russian immigrants. All were deported to Russia without a court hearing. On January 2, 1920, police in dozens of cities arrested 5,000 more suspects.

What came to be called the **First Red Scare** (another would occur in the 1950s) represented one of the largest violations of civil liberties in American history. In 1919, novelist Katharine Fullerton Gerould announced in *Harper's Magazine* that, as a result of the government crackdown, America "is no longer a free country in the old sense." Panic about possible foreign terrorists erupted across the nation as vigilantes took matters into their own hands. At a patriotic pageant in Washington, D.C., a sailor shot a spectator who refused to rise for "The Star-Spangled Banner"; the crowd cheered. In Hammond, Indiana, a jury took only two minutes to acquit a man who had murdered an immigrant for yelling "To hell with the U.S." In Waterbury, Connecticut, a salesman was sentenced to six months in jail for saying that Vladimir Lenin was "one of the brainiest" of the world's leaders.

By the summer of 1920, the Red Scare had begun to subside. Although Attorney General Palmer kept predicting more foreign-inspired terrorism, it never came. But the Red Scare left a lasting mark by strengthening the conservative crusade for "100 percent Americanism" and new restrictions on immigration.

J. Edgar Hoover Fresh out of law school, Hoover joined the Justice Department and rose the ranks to become the first director of the FBI.

EFFECTS OF THE GREAT WAR

The extraordinary turbulence in 1919 and 1920 was an unmistakable indication of how the Great War had changed the shape of modern history: it was a turning point after which little was the same. It had destroyed old Europe—not only many of its cities, people, economies, and four grand empires, but also its self-image as the center of civilized Western culture. Winston Churchill, the future British prime minister, called postwar Europe "a crippled, broken world."

Peace did not bring stability. Most Germans and Austrians believed they were the victims of a harsh peace, and many wanted revenge. At the same time, the war had hastened the already simmering Bolshevik Revolution that caused Russia to exit the war, abandon its western European allies, and, in 1922, reemerge as the Union of Soviet Socialist Republics (USSR). Thereafter, Soviet communism would be one of the most powerful forces shaping the twentieth century.

Postwar America was a much different story. For the first time, the United States had decisively intervened in a major European war. The American economy had emerged from the war largely unscathed, and bankers and business executives were eager to fill the vacuum created by the destruction of the major European economies. The United States was now the world's dominant power. What came to be called the "American Century" was at hand.

CHAPTER REVIEW

SUMMARY

- **An Uneasy Neutrality**   The Wilson administration declared the nation neutral but allowed businesses to extend loans to the warring nations, principally the Allies (Britain, France, and Russia), to purchase food and military supplies. Americans were outraged by the Germans' use of submarine (*U-boat*) warfare, especially after the sinking of the *Lusitania*. In 1917, submarine attacks and the publication of the *Zimmermann telegram*, which revealed that Germany had tried to encourage Mexico to wage war against the United States, led America to enter the Great War.

- **Mobilizing a Nation**   The Wilson administration drafted young men into the army and created new agencies such as the War Industries Board and the Food Administration to coordinate industrial production and agricultural consumption. As white workers left their factory jobs to join the army, hundreds of thousands of African Americans migrated from the rural South to the urban North as part of the *Great Migration*. Many southern whites and Mexican Americans also migrated to industrial centers. One million women participated in war work but were encouraged to leave these jobs as soon as the war ended. The federal government severely curtailed civil liberties, and the Espionage and Sedition Acts of 1917 and 1918 criminalized virtually any public opposition to the war.

- **The American Role in Fighting the War**   Communists seized power in November 1917 in Russia and negotiated a separate peace treaty with Germany, thus freeing the Germans to focus on the Western Front. By 1918, however, the arrival of millions of American troops turned the tide of the war. German leaders sued for peace, and an armistice was signed on November 11, 1918. Woodrow Wilson insisted that the United States wanted a new, democratic Europe. His *Fourteen Points (1918)* speech outlined his ideas for a *League of Nations* to promote peaceful resolutions to future conflicts.

- **The Fight for the Peace**   At the Paris Peace Conference, President Wilson was only partially successful. The *Treaty of Versailles (1919)* did create a *League of Nations* but included a "war guilt clause" that forced Germany to pay reparations for war damages to France and Britain. In the end, Wilson's illness following a stroke, his refusal to compromise on the terms of the treaty, and his alienation of Republican senators resulted in the Senate voting against ratification.

- **Lurching from War to Peace**   The United States struggled to come to terms with its new status as the leading world power and with changes at home. As wartime industries shifted to peacetime production, wage and price controls ended. As former soldiers reentered the workforce, unemployment rose, and consumer prices increased, provoking labor unrest in cities across the nation. Many Americans believed these problems were part of a Bolshevik plot. Several incidents of domestic terrorism provoked what would be known as the *First Red Scare (1919–1920)*, during which the Justice Department illegally arrested and deported many suspected radicals, most of whom were immigrants. At the same time, race riots broke out as resentful white mobs tried to stop African Americans from exercising their civil rights. The summer of 1919 also brought the ratification of the *Nineteenth Amendment (1919)* to the Constitution, which gave women the right to vote.

CHRONOLOGY

1914	The Great War (World War I) begins in Europe
1915	The *Lusitania* is torpedoed by a German U-boat
March 1917	Germany announces unrestricted submarine warfare in the Atlantic
April 1917	United States enters the Great War
January 1918	Woodrow Wilson delivers Fourteen Points speech
November 11, 1918	Representatives of warring nations sign armistice
1919	Paris Peace Conference convenes
	Race riots break out during the Red Summer
	First Red Scare leads to arrests and deportations of suspected radicals
	Woodrow Wilson suffers stroke
1920	The Senate rejects the Treaty of Versailles
	The Nineteenth Amendment is ratified

KEY TERMS

Central Powers p. 989

Allied Powers p. 989

Western Front p. 989

trench warfare p. 991

U-boats p. 995

Lusitania p. 995

Zimmermann telegram p. 999

Great Migration p. 1002

Fourteen Points (1918) p. 1007

League of Nations p. 1014

Treaty of Versailles (1919) p. 1016

Nineteenth Amendment (1920) p. 1021

First Red Scare (1919–1920) p. 1024

 INQUIZITIVE

Go to InQuizitive to see what you've learned—and learn what you've missed—with personalized feedback along the way.

23 A Clash of Cultures
1920–1929

***Nightclub* (1933)** With all its striking sights and sounds, the roar of the twenties subsided for some at the heart of it all. In this painting by American artist Guy Pène du Bois, flappers and their dates crowd into a fashionable nightclub, yet their loneliness amid the excitement is deafening.

The decade between the end of the Great War and the onset of the Great Depression at the end of 1929 was perhaps the most dynamic in American history, a period of rapid urbanization, technological innovation, widespread prosperity, social rebelliousness, cultural upheaval, and political conservatism. Women were at last allowed to vote in all states (although most African American women—and men—in the South were prevented from doing so) and to experience many freedoms previously limited to men. At the same time, the Eighteenth Amendment outlawed alcoholic beverages in 1920 ("Prohibition"), setting off an epidemic of lawbreaking—by citizens, police, and public officials.

Cultural conflicts resulted largely from explosive tensions between rural and urban ways of life. For the first time in the nation's history, more people lived in cities than in rural areas. While the urban middle class prospered, farmers suffered as the wartime boom in exports of grains and livestock to Europe ground to a halt. Four million people moved from farms to cities during the twenties, in part because of the better quality of life and in part because of the prolonged agricultural recession. Amid this massive rural/urban population shift, bitter fights erupted between traditionalists and modernists, as old and new values fought a cultural civil war that continues today.

The postwar wave of strikes, bombings, anti-Communist hysteria, and race riots created a widespread sense of alarm that led many to cling to traditional religious beliefs and moral values and "native" ways of life. America during the twenties, said one social commentator, was the most "volcanic of any area on earth." It was a period of "deep domestic strife" as new and old ways of life fought for influence. All of the changes punctuating the twenties created what one historian called a "nervous generation" of Americans "groping for what certainty they could find."

focus questions

1. Assess the consumer culture that emerged in America in the 1920s. What are the factors that contributed to its growth?

2. What were the other major new social and cultural trends and movements that became prominent during the twenties? How did they challenge traditional standards and customs?

3. What does "modernism" mean in intellectual and artistic terms? How did the modernist movements influence American culture in the early twentieth century?

During the twenties, the new and unusual clashed openly with the conventional and the commonplace. Modernists and traditionalists waged cultural warfare with one another, one group looking to the future for inspiration and the other looking to the past for guidance. Terrorist attacks increased, as did labor and racial violence.

In 1920, a horse-drawn wagon loaded with dynamite exploded at the corner of Wall and Broad streets in New York City, killing thirty-eight people and wounding hundreds. That the bombers were never found fueled public concern that the United States was on the brink of chaos and revolution.

The scope and pace of societal changes were bewildering, as the emergence of national radio networks, talking motion pictures, mass ownership of automobiles, and national chain stores, combined with the soaring popularity of spectator sports and the rise of mass marketing and advertising, transformed America into the world's leading consumer society. The culture of mass consumption fueled the explosive growth of middle-class urban life while assaulting traditional virtues such as frugality, prudence, and religiosity.

In the political arena, reactionaries and rebels battled for control. The brutal fight between Woodrow Wilson and the Republican-led Senate over the Treaty of Versailles, coupled with the administration's crackdown on dissenters and socialists, had weakened an already fragmented and disillusioned progressivism. As reformer Amos Pinchot bitterly observed, President Wilson had "put his enemies in office and his friends in jail." By 1920, many progressives had grown skeptical of any politician claiming to be a reformer or an idealist. Social reformer Jane Addams sighed that the 1920s were "a period of political and social sag."

The desire to restore traditional values and social stability led voters to elect Republican Warren G. Harding president in 1920. He promised to return America to "normalcy." Both major parties still included progressive wings, but they were shrinking. The demand for honest, efficient government and public services remained strong; the impulse for social reform, however, shifted into a drive for moral righteousness and social conformity. By 1920, many veteran progressives had withdrawn from public life.

Mainstream Americans were also shocked by new, "modernist" forms of artistic expression and sexual liberation. Mabel Dodge Luhan, a leading promoter of modern art and literature, said that the generation of young literary and artistic rebels that emerged during and after the war was determined to overthrow "the old order of things."

In sum, postwar life in America and Europe was fraught with turbulent changes, contradictory impulses, superficial frivolity, and seething tensions. As the French painter Paul Gauguin acknowledged, the upheavals of cultural modernism and the chaotic aftermath of the war produced "an epoch of confusion," a riotous clash of irreverent new ideas with traditional manners and morals.

The Nation in 1920

The 1920 census reported that 106 million people lived in the United States, a third of the number today. America's population was remarkably young. Over half the people were under the age of twenty-five. The average life expectancy was just fifty-six years for men and fifty-eight for women.

American society remained overwhelmingly white—90 percent (persons of Hispanic origin were considered to be white). African Americans were 9 percent, and Native Americans and Asian Americans made up most of the rest. Almost half of the white population were either immigrants or the children of immigrants, the highest percentage since the late eighteenth century.

For the first time in American history, over half of the population lived in "cities," meaning towns and cities with more than 2,500 residents. Towns with less than 3,000 residents could hardly be called urban. But some 16 million Americans lived in the ten largest cities. American society was relentlessly becoming more urban and less rural.

The South remained the most rural and poorest region of the nation. Only about half of the farmers in the former Confederate states owned their land. Three-quarters of farmers in the rest of the nation owned their lands. The others were either tenants who rented lands or sharecroppers who gave the landowner a share of the crop in exchange for access to land. Most sharecroppers, especially black sharecroppers, were grimly poor, in large part because the entire agricultural sector struggled with low crop prices during the twenties. And most tenants and sharecroppers were in the South.

A "New Era" of Consumption

America experienced so many dramatic changes during the twenties that people referred to it as a "New Era." The robust U.S. economy became the envy of the world. Following the brief postwar recession in 1920–1921, economic growth soared to record levels. Jobs were plentiful, and average income rose throughout the decade. The nation's total wealth almost doubled between 1920 and 1930, while wage workers enjoyed record-breaking increases in average income. By 1929, the United States enjoyed the highest standard of living in the world.

Construction led the way. The war had caused people to postpone building offices, plants, homes, and apartments. By 1921, however, a building boom was underway that would last the rest of the decade. At the same time, the remarkable growth of the automotive industry created an immediate need for roads and highways. New construction and new cars stimulated other industries such as lumber, steel, concrete, rubber, gasoline, and furniture.

Technology also played a key role in the prosperity of the twenties. Manufacturing grew more mechanized and efficient. Powerful new machines (electric motors, steam turbines, dump trucks, tractors, bulldozers, steam shovels) and more-efficient ways of operating farms, factories, plants, mines, and mills generated dramatic increases in production. In 1920, the nation's factories produced 5,000 electric refrigerators; in 1929, almost a million.

A GROWING CONSUMER CULTURE

In the late nineteenth century, the U.S. economy had been driven by commercial agriculture and large-scale industrial production—the building of railroads and bridges, the manufacturing of steel, and the construction of housing and businesses in cities. During the twenties, the dominant aspect of the economy involved an explosion of new consumer goods.

The success of mass production made mass consumption more important than ever. A 1920 newspaper editorial insisted that, with the war over, the American's "first importance to his country is no longer that of citizen but that of *consumer*." To keep factory production humming required converting once-frugal people into enthusiastic shoppers. "People may ruin themselves by saving instead of spending," warned one economist.

During the Great War, the government had urged Americans to work long hours, conserve resources, and do without. After the war, a new **consumer culture** encouraged carefree spending. "During the war," a journalist noted in 1920, "we accustomed ourselves to doing without, to buying carefully, to using economically. But with the close of the war came reaction. A veritable orgy of extravagant buying is going on. Reckless spending takes the place of saving, waste replaces conservation."

To keep people buying, businesses developed new ways for consumers to finance purchases over time ("layaway") rather than have to pay cash up front ("Buy Now, Pay Later"). As paying with cash and staying out of debt came to be seen as needlessly "old-fashioned" practices, consumer debt almost tripled during the twenties. By 1929, almost 60 percent of American purchases were made on the installment plan.

During the New Era, advertising, first developed in the late nineteenth century, grew into a huge enterprise. President Calvin Coolidge declared that advertising had become "the most potent influence in adopting and changing the habits and modes of life, affecting what we eat, what we wear, and the work and play of the whole nation."

Does the Home You Love Love You?

For the loving care you have lavished on this home—for your effort to make it attractive and beautiful—does it do anything for you in return?

Does it make your days easier and your evenings brighter? It both *can* and *does*, if it is an electrified home.

Pressing a button—or pushing a plug into a handy convenience outlet—will boil your coffee on the table, make your toast or broil your bacon, cook your meals without a cook, keep your iron hot, turn on the breezy fan, sweep your floors, heat your bath room, warm baby's milk, and heat your curling iron.

Thus should a modern home—with *Westinghouse Electrical Appliances*—serve its mistress.

Westinghouse Appliances are obtainable in the better electrical shops and stores everywhere. Right now, while you are considering house furnishings, is a good time to buy them.

WESTINGHOUSE ELECTRIC & MANUFACTURING COMPANY
Offices in all Principal Cities   Representatives Everywhere
Tune in with KDKA — KYW — WBZ — KFKX

Westinghouse
Tumbler Heater

Cozy Glow, Jr.

Turnover Toaster

Sol-Lux
Luminaire

Westinghouse Grecian Urn
Percolator Set

Westinghouse
Bell-Ringer

Westinghouse Waffle Iron

Westinghouse
Warming Pad

Westinghouse Junior Cabinet
Electric Range

Westinghouse
Electric Iron

Westinghouse Rectigon
(Battery Charger)

© 1925, W. E. & M. Co

Westinghouse

A modern home This 1925 Westinghouse advertisement urges homemakers to buy its "Cozy Glow, Jr." heater and "Sol-Luk Luminaire" lamp, among other new electrical appliances that would "do anything for you in return."

The visibility of ads helped shape how people behaved and how they defined the pursuit of happiness. Zelda Sayre Fitzgerald, the writer and wife of the wildly popular novelist F. Scott Fitzgerald, recalled that "we grew up founding our dreams on the infinite promises of American advertising."

New weekday radio programs popular with middle-class housewives, for example, were often sponsored by national companies advertising laundry detergent and hand soap—hence the term "soap operas." Because women purchased two-thirds of consumer goods, advertisers targeted them. An ad in *Photoplay* magazine appealed to the "woman of the house" because "she buys most of the things which go to make the home happy, healthful, and beautiful. Through her slim, safe fingers goes most of the family money."

The consumer culture generated bewildering changes in everyday life. The huge jump in the use of electricity was a revolutionary new force. In 1920, only 35 percent of homes had electricity; by 1930, the number was 68 percent. Similar increases occurred in the number of households with indoor plumbing, washing machines, and automobiles. Moderately priced creature comforts and conveniences such as flush toilets, electric irons and fans, handheld cameras, wristwatches, cigarette lighters, vacuum cleaners, and linoleum floors, became more widely available, especially among the urban middle class. As always, the poor, with little discretionary income, remained on the margins of the consumer culture.

THE RISE OF MASS CULTURE

The powerful consumer culture helped create a marketplace of retail stores and national brands (Kellogg's Corn Flakes, General Electric toasters, etc.) in which local and regional businesses were increasingly squeezed out by giant department stores and national "chain" stores. By the 1920s, Woolworth's, for example, had 1,500 stores scattered across the country; Walgreen's had 525. Such national retailers bought goods in such large quantities that they were able to get discounted prices that they passed on to consumers.

Mass advertising and marketing campaigns promoting national products increasingly led to a *mass culture*: more and more Americans now saw the same advertisements and bought the same products at the same stores. They also read the same magazines, listened to the same radio programs, drove the same cars, adored the same sports stars and celebrities, and watched the same movies.

MOVIE-MADE AMERICA In 1896, a New York audience viewed the first moving-picture show. By 1924, there were 20,000 theaters showing 700 new "silent" films a year, and the movie business had become the nation's chief form of mass entertainment. Hollywood, California, became the international center of movie production, grinding out cowboy Westerns, crime dramas, murder mysteries, and the timeless comedies of Mack Sennett's Keystone Company, where a raft of slapstick comedians, most notably London-born Charlie Chaplin, a comic genius, perfected their art, transforming it into a form of social criticism.

Movie attendance during the 1920s averaged 80 million people a week, more than half the national population, and attendance surged even more after 1927 with the appearance of "talkies," movies with sound. In 1930, some 115 million people attended weekly movies out of a total population of 123 million (many people went more than once). Americans spent ten times as much on movies as they did on tickets to baseball and football games.

Charlie Chaplin An English-born actor who rose to international fame as the "Tramp," pictured above in the 1921 silent film *The Kid*.

But movies did much more than entertain. They helped expand the consumer culture by feeding the desires of moviegoers, setting standards and tastes in fashion, music, dancing, and hairstyles. They also helped stimulate the sexual revolution. One boy admitted that it was the movies that taught him how "to kiss a girl on her ears, neck, and cheeks, as well as on the mouth." A social researcher concluded that movies made young Americans in the twenties more "sex-wise, sex-excited, and sex-absorbed" than previous generations.

RADIO Radio broadcasting enjoyed even more spectacular growth. In 1920, station WWJ in Detroit began transmitting news bulletins, and KDKA in Pittsburgh began broadcasting regularly scheduled programs. The first radio commercial aired in New York in 1922. By the end of that year, there were 508 stations. In 1926, the National Broadcasting Company (NBC), a subsidiary of the Radio Corporation of America (RCA), began linking its stations into a national network; the Columbia Broadcasting System (CBS) entered the field the next year.

In 1920, some 41 million radios were manufactured in the United States. The widespread ownership of radios changed the patterns of everyday life. At night after dinner, families gathered around the radio to listen to live music, political speeches, news broadcasts, weather forecasts, baseball and football games, boxing matches, comedy shows, and worship services. One ad claimed that the radio "is your theater, your college, your newspaper, your library." Calvin Coolidge was the first president to address the nation by radio, and his monthly talks paved the way for Franklin Delano Roosevelt's influential "fireside chats" during the thirties.

Radio transformed jazz music into a national craze. Big band leaders Paul Whiteman, Guy Lombardo, Duke Ellington, Glenn Miller, and Tommy and Jimmy Dorsey regularly performed live over the radio. Country western music also developed a national following as a result of radio broadcasts. In 1925 a Nashville, Tennessee station, WSM, began offering a weekly variety show, The Grand Ole Opry, which featured an array of country music stars.

FLYING MACHINES Advances in transportation were as significant as the impact of commercial radio and movies on popular culture. In 1903, Wilbur and Orville Wright, owners of a bicycle shop in Dayton, Ohio, had built and flown the first "flying machine" over the beach at Kitty Hawk, North Carolina.

The development of airplanes advanced slowly until the outbreak of war in 1914, when Europeans began using the airplane as a military weapon. When the United States entered the war, it had no combat planes; American pilots flew British or French warplanes. An American aircraft industry arose during the war but collapsed in the postwar demobilization. Under the Kelly Act of 1925, however, the federal government began to subsidize the industry through airmail contracts. The Air Commerce Act of 1926 provided federal funds for the advancement of air transportation and navigation, including the construction of airports.

The aviation industry received a huge psychological boost in 1927 when twenty-six-year-old Charles A. Lindbergh Jr., a St. Louis–based mail pilot, made the first *solo* transatlantic flight, traveling from New York City to Paris in thirty-three and a half hours through severe storms and dense fog. When Lindbergh, known as the "Lone Eagle," landed in France, 100,000 people greeted him with thunderous cheers. The New York City parade celebrating his accomplishment surpassed the celebration of the end of the Great War. (When Lindbergh met Britain's King George V soon after his long flight, the monarch asked him, "How did you pee?" "In paper cups," the pilot answered.) Five years after Lindbergh's famous flight, New York City celebrated another

Amelia Earhart The pioneering aviator would tragically disappear in her 1937 attempt to fly around the world.

pioneering aviator—Amelia Earhart, a former stunt pilot at air shows who became the first woman to fly solo across the Atlantic.

THE CAR CULTURE By far the most significant economic and social development of the early twentieth century was the widespread ownership of automobiles. In 1924, when asked about the changes transforming American life, a resident of Muncie, Indiana replied: "I can tell you what's happening in just four letters: A-U-T-O." A neighbor in Muncie said he would "go without food before I'll see us give up the car."

The first motorcar ("horseless carriage") had been manufactured for sale in 1895, but the founding of the Ford Motor Company in 1903 had revolutionized the infant industry. The first cars were handmade, expensive, and designed for the wealthy. Henry Ford changed all that by building "a car for the multitude." During the twenties, he became the godfather of mass production. He vowed "to democratize the automobile. When I'm through, everybody will be able to afford one, and about everyone will have one." Ford's Model T, the celebrated "Tin Lizzie," cheap and rugged, "built to last forever," came out in 1908 at a price of $850 (about $22,000 today). By 1924, as a result of Ford's ever-more efficient production techniques, the same car sold for $290 (less than $4,000

Ford Motor Company's Highland Park plant, 1913 Gravity slides and chain conveyors contributed to the mass production of automobiles.

today). The Model T changed little from year to year, and it came in only one color: black.

Other automakers followed Ford's mass production/low-priced model. In 1920, there were more than 8 million registered vehicles; in 1929, there were more than 23 million. The automobile revolution was in part propelled by the discovery of vast oil fields in Texas, Oklahoma, Wyoming, and California. By 1920, the United States produced two-thirds of the world's oil and gasoline.

The automobile industry also became the leading example of modern mass-production techniques. Ford's Highland Park plant outside Detroit used a moving conveyor system that pulled the chassis down an assembly line of sequential work stations. Each worker performed a single task, such as installing a fender or a wheel, as the car-in-process moved down the line. Through this technique, a new car could be pieced together in ninety-three minutes.

Such efficiency enabled Ford to lower the price of his cars, thereby increasing the number of people who could afford them. His high profits helped him pay his workers the highest wages in the industry. Although Ford was a notorious taskmaster—he prohibited his workers from talking, sitting, smoking, or singing while on the job—his methods worked. During the twenties, the United States built ten times more automobiles than all of Europe combined.

Just as the railroad helped transform the pace and scale of life in the second half of the nineteenth century, the automobile changed social life during the twentieth century. Americans literally developed a love affair with cars. In the words of one male driver, young people viewed the car as "an incredible engine of escape" from parental control and a safe place to "take a girl and hold hands, neck, pet, or . . . go the limit."

Cars and networks of new roads enabled people to live farther away from their workplaces, thus encouraging suburban sprawl. Cars also helped fuel the economic boom of the 1920s by creating tens of thousands of new jobs and a huge demand for steel, glass, rubber, leather, oil, and gasoline. The car culture stimulated road construction, sparked a real estate boom in Florida and California, and dotted the landscape with gasoline stations, traffic lights, billboards, and motor hotels ("motels"). By 1929, the federal government was constructing 10,000 miles of paved highways each year.

SPECTATOR SPORTS During the 1920s, automobile ownership and rising incomes changed the way people spent their leisure time. Americans fell in love with spectator sports; people in cities could drive into the countryside, visit friends and relatives, and go to ballparks, stadiums, or boxing rinks to see baseball or football games and prizefights.

Baseball, created in the 1870s, had become the "national pastime" by the 1920s. Its popularity fed on superstars. With larger-than-life heroes such as New York Yankee legends George Herman "Babe" Ruth Jr. and Henry Louis "Lou" Gehrig, baseball teams attracted intense loyalties and huge crowds. Ruth may well have been the most famous athlete of all time. In 1920, more than a million spectators attended Ruth's games.

Two years later, the Yankees built a new stadium, dubbing it the "House That Ruth Built," and went on to win World Series championships in 1923, 1927, and 1928. More than 20 million people attended professional games in 1927, the year that Ruth, the "Sultan of Swat," set a record by hitting sixty home runs. Because baseball remained a segregated sport in the 1920s, so-called Negro Leagues were organized for African Americans.

Football, especially at the college level, also attracted huge crowds. It, too, benefited from outsized heroes such as running back Harold Edward "Red" Grange of the University of Illinois, the first athlete to appear on the cover of *Time* magazine. In a game against the University of Michigan, the "Galloping Ghost" scored a touchdown the first four times he carried the ball. After Illinois won, students carried Grange on their shoulders for two miles across the campus. When he signed a contract with the Chicago Bears in 1926, he single-handedly made professional football competitive with baseball as a spectator sport.

What Ruth and Grange were to their sports, William Harrison "Jack" Dempsey was to boxing. In 1919, he won the world heavyweight title from Jess Willard, a giant of a man weighing three hundred pounds and standing

Babe Ruth This star pitcher and outfielder won the hearts of Americans, first with the Boston Red Sox, then the New York Yankees, and, finally, the Boston Braves. Here, he autographs bats and balls for soldiers at training camp.

six and a half feet tall. Dempsey knocked him down seven times in the first round. Willard, his face bruised and bloodied, gave up in the fourth round, and Dempsey thereafter became a dominant force in boxing. Like Babe Ruth, the brawling Dempsey was especially popular with working-class men, for he too had been born poor. In 1927, when James Joseph "Gene" Tunney defeated Dempsey, more than 100,000 people attended, including a thousand reporters, ten state governors, and numerous Hollywood celebrities. Some 60 million people listened to the fight over the radio.

THE "JAZZ AGE"

While the masses of Americans devoted their free time to spectator sports, radio programs, and movies, many young people, especially college students, focused their energies on social and cultural rebellion. F. Scott Fitzgerald, a boyishly handsome Princeton University dropout, was labeled "the voice of his generation" after his first novel, *This Side of Paradise* (1920), became a best seller with its colorful account of rowdy student life at Princeton. Fitzgerald fastened upon the **"Jazz Age"** as a label for the spirit of rebelliousness and spontaneity he observed among many young Americans.

THE BIRTH OF JAZZ

Fitzgerald's Jazz Age label referred to the popularity of jazz music, a dynamic blend of several musical traditions. It had first emerged as piano-based "ragtime" at the end of the nineteenth century. Thereafter, African American musicians such as Jelly Roll Morton, Duke Ellington, Louis Armstrong, and Bessie Smith (the "Empress of the Blues") combined the energies of ragtime with the emotions of the blues to create *jazz*, originally an African American slang term meaning sexual intercourse. With its improvisations, variations, and sensual spontaneity, jazz appealed to people of all ethnicities and ages because it was all about pleasure and immediacy, letting go and enjoying the freedom of the moment.

Louis Armstrong, an inspired trumpeter with a uniquely froggy voice, was the Pied Piper of jazz, an inventive and freewheeling performer who reshaped the American music scene. Born in a New Orleans shack in 1900, the grandson of slaves, he was abandoned by his father and raised by his prostitute mother, who was fifteen when he was born. As a youth, he saw the mean and ugly side of America. "I seen everythin' from a child comin' up," he said once. "Nothin' happen I ain't never seen before." Then he found music, using his natural genius to explore the fertile possibilities of jazz.

As a teen, he sneaked into music halls to watch Joe "King" Oliver and other early jazz innovators. In 1922, Armstrong moved to Chicago, where he delighted audiences with his passionate trumpet performances and open-hearted personality. Throughout the twenties, Armstrong and his band crisscrossed the United States, spreading the gospel of jazz.

The culture of jazz quickly spread from its origins in New Orleans, Kansas City, Memphis, and St. Louis to the African American neighborhoods of Harlem in New York City and Chicago's South Side. Large dance halls accommodated the demand for jazz music and the new dances it inspired, like the Charleston and the Black Bottom. Affluent whites flocked to the dance halls as well as to "black" nightclubs and "jazz joints." During the 1920s, people commonly spoke of *jazzing* something up" (invigorating it) or "jazzing around" (acting youthfully and energetically).

Many Americans, however, were not fans of jazz or the sexually suggestive dances it inspired. Dr. Francis E. Clark, a Christian moralist, denounced "indecent dance" as "an offense against womanly purity." Princeton professor

Henry van Dyke dismissed jazz as "merely an irritation of the nerves of hearing, a sensual teasing of the strings of physical passion." Such criticism, however, failed to stem the popularity of jazz, which swept across Europe as well as America. Europeans, including modernist painters Henri Matisse and Pablo Picasso, grew infatuated with the inventive energies of jazz music.

A SEXUAL REVOLUTION?

What most shocked old-timers during the Jazz Age was a defiant sexual revolution among young people, especially those on college campuses. "None of the Victorian mothers—and most of the mothers were Victorian—had any idea how casually their daughters were accustomed to being kissed," wrote F. Scott Fitzgerald in *This Side of Paradise* (1920).

During the twenties, Americans learned about the hidden world of "flaming youth" (the title of a popular novel): wild "petting parties," free love, speakeasies, "joyriding," and skinny-dipping. A promotional poster for the 1923 silent film *Flaming Youth* asked: "How Far Can a Girl Go?" Other ads

Duke Ellington and his band Jazz emerged in the 1920s as a uniquely American expression of the modernist spirit. African American artists bent musical conventions to give freer rein to improvisation and sensuality.

claimed the movie appealed especially to "neckers, petters, white kisses, red kisses, pleasure-mad daughters, [and] sensation-craving mothers."

THE IMPACT OF SIGMUND FREUD The increasingly frank treatment of sex resulted in part from the influence of Sigmund Freud, the Austrian founder of modern psychoanalysis. Freud, trained as a physician, insisted that the human mind was mysteriously "conflicted" by often unconscious efforts to repress powerful irrational impulses and sexual desires ("libido").

In 1899, Freud had published *The Interpretation of Dreams*, a pathbreaking book that stressed the crucial role of the subconscious in shaping behavior and moods. He also highlighted the significance of dreams as providing the "royal road to the unconscious," for dreams revealed "repressed" sexual

Sigmund Freud Founder of modern psychoanalysis, in 1926.

yearnings, many of which resulted from early childhood experiences. Women and men, Freud argued, are endowed with equal sexual energy, and human behavior is driven by a variety of intense sexual desires and efforts to release pent-up aggression. These natural human conflicts cause unhappiness because people desire more pleasures than they can attain.

It did not take long for Freud's ideas to penetrate society at large. Books, movies, and plays included frequent references to Freud's ideas, and some of the decade's most popular magazines—*True Confessions, Telling Tales,* and *True Story*—focused on romance and sex. Likewise, the most popular female movie stars—Madge Bellamy, Clara Bow, and Joan Crawford—projected images of sensual freedom, energy, and independence.

Advertisements for new movies reinforced the self-indulgent images of the Jazz Age: "brilliant men, beautiful jazz babies, champagne baths, midnight revels, petting parties in the purple dawn, all ending in one terrific climax that makes you gasp." Traditionalists were shocked by the behavior of rebellious young women. "One hears it said," lamented a Baptist magazine, "that the girls are actually tempting the boys more than the boys do the girls, by their dress and conversation."

Psychoanalysis, whose purpose is to explain activities in the mind, soon became the world's most celebrated—and controversial—technique for helping troubled people come to grips with the demons haunting them by using "talk therapy," getting patients to tell the story of their lives and inner frustrations and repressed fears and urges. By 1916, there were some 500 psychoanalysts in New York City alone.

Freud's emphasis on unruly sexual desires swirling about in the subconscious fascinated some people and scared others. For many young Americans, Freud seemed to provide scientific justification for rebelling against social conventions and indulging in sex. Some oversimplified his theories by claiming that sexual pleasure was essential for emotional health, that all forms of sexual activity were good, and that all inhibitions about sex were bad.

MARGARET SANGER AND BIRTH CONTROL   Perhaps the most controversial women's issue of the Jazz Age was birth control. Christians— both Protestants and Catholics—opposed it as a violation of God's law. Other crusaders saw it differently. Margaret Sanger, a New York nurse and midwife in the working-class tenements of Manhattan, saw many young mothers struggling to provide for their growing families. Born in 1883, one of eleven children born to Irish immigrants, she herself had experienced the poverty often faced by large immigrant families. "Our childhood," she remembered, "was one of longing for things that were always denied."

As a nurse and midwife, Sanger witnessed at firsthand the consequences of unwanted pregnancies, tragic miscarriages, and amateur abortions. To her, the problems had an obvious solution: *birth control*, a term she and friends coined in 1914. In 1912, Sanger began to distribute birth-control information to working-class women and resolved to spend the rest of her life helping women gain control of their bodies. To do so, she began publishing a magazine called *Woman Rebel* in which she promoted woman's suffrage, workers' rights, and contraception to frighten the "capitalist class." In 1916, she was arrested and charged with disseminating obscenity through the mail, but months later the case was dropped. She then opened the nation's first birth-control clinic, in Brooklyn.

In 1921, Sanger organized the American Birth Control League, which in 1942 changed its name to Planned Parenthood. The Birth Control League distributed information to doctors, social workers, women's clubs, and the scientific community, as well as to thousands of women. In the 1920s, however, Sanger alienated supporters of birth control by endorsing sterilization for the mentally incompetent and for people with certain hereditary conditions. Birth control, she stressed, was "the most constructive and necessary of the means to racial health."

Although Sanger did not succeed in legalizing the distribution of contraceptives and contraceptive information through the mail, she had laid the foundation for such efforts. In 1936 a federal court ruled that physicians could prescribe contraceptives—a vital step in Sanger's efforts to realize her slogan, "Every child a wanted child."

THE "NEW WOMEN" New clothing fashions reflected the rebellion against traditional female roles in an especially powerful way. The emancipated "new women" of the twenties seized the right to vote while eagerly discarding the confining wardrobe of their mothers' generation—pinched-in

The "new woman" of the 1920s Two risk-taking flappers dance atop the Hotel Sherman in Chicago, 1926.

corsets, layers of petticoats, and floor-length dresses. In 1919, skirts were typically six inches above the ground; by 1927, they were at the knee. The Utah legislature in 1921 debated a bill that would have jailed women wearing "skirts higher than three inches above the ankle."

The shortest skirts were worn by the so-called **flappers**, pleasure-seeking young women who—in defiance of proper prewar standards—drove automobiles, "bobbed" their hair (cut it short, requiring the invention of the "bobby pin"), and wore minimal underclothing, gauzy fabrics, sheer stockings, dangling necklaces, and plenty of makeup, especially rouge and lipstick. They often joined young men in smoking cigarettes, drinking, gambling, and dancing to jazz music.

Flappers attracted so much attention in part because they were both defiantly independent and desperately seductive. After interacting with flappers in New York City, British novelist Elinor Glynn asked: "Has the American girl no innate modesty—no sub-conscious self-respect, no reserve, no dignity?"

The flappers wanted more out of life than marriage and motherhood. Their carefree version of feminism was fun-loving, defiant, self-indulgent, and often

The beautiful and the damned In an outfit typical of flappers, Zelda Fitzgerald poses with her husband, author F. Scott Fitzgerald, on the Riviera in 1926.

self-destructive. F. Scott Fitzgerald claimed that his rebellious wife, Zelda, was the "First American Flapper." The wayward daughter of a strict Alabama judge, Zelda was wild to the point of exhaustion. Stimulated by alcohol, she loved doing "crazy things": dancing in New York City fountains and stripping off her clothes in the middle of Grand Central Station. The craziness of such flappers shocked and scared observers. A Catholic priest in Brooklyn complained that the feminism of the 1920s had provoked a "pandemonium of powder, a riot of rouge, and a moral anarchy of dress."

NOT SO NEW WOMEN Most women in the 1920s were not flappers, however. Lillian Symes, a longtime activist, stressed that her "generation of feminists" had little in common with the "spike-heeled, over-rouged flapper of today. We grew up before the postwar disillusionment engulfed the youth of the land." Although more middle-class women attended college in the 1920s than ever before, a higher percentage of them married soon after graduation than had been the case in the nineteenth century.

The conservative political mood helped to steer women who had worked for the war effort back into their traditional roles as homemakers, and college curricula began to shift accordingly. At Vassar College, an all-women's school outside of New York City, students took courses such as "Husband and Wife," "Motherhood," and "The Family as an Economic Unit." At the same time, fewer college-educated women pursued careers: the proportion of physicians who were women fell during the twenties from 6 to 4 percent, and similar reductions occurred among dentists, architects, and chemists. A student at all-female Smith College in Massachusetts expressed frustration "that a woman must choose between a home and her work, when a man may have both. There must be a way out, and it is the problem of our generation to find the way."

As before, most women who worked outside the home labored in unskilled, low-paying jobs. Only 4 percent of working women in the 1920s were salaried professionals. Some women moved into new vocations created by the growing consumer culture, such as accounting assistants and department-store clerks. The number of beauty shops soared from 5,000 in 1920 to 40,000 in 1930, creating jobs for hair stylists, manicurists, and cosmeticians.

But the majority of women were still either full-time wives and mothers or household servants. Fortunately, the growing availability of electricity and electrical appliances—vacuum cleaners, toasters, stoves, refrigerators, washing machines, irons—made housework easier. Likewise, "supermarkets" offered year-round access to fruits, vegetables, and meats, which greatly reduced the traditional tasks of food preparation—canning, baking bread, and plucking chickens. African American and Latino women faced the greatest challenges. As a New York City newspaper observed, they were forced to do "work which white women will not do." Women of color usually worked as maids, laundresses, or seamstresses, or on farms.

THE COLOR LINE In addition to sexism, racism also continued to limit the freedom of women during the twenties. For example, in 1919, an interracial couple from Ayer, Massachusetts, Mabel Puffer, a wealthy college graduate, and Arthur Hazzard, a handyman and leader within the local black community, decided to get married in Concord, New Hampshire. They checked into separate rooms in a hotel, then met in the lobby and walked three blocks to the courthouse to apply for a marriage license, only to be told that there was a five-day waiting period. So they waited and made preparations for the wedding. The mayor of Concord agreed to perform the service, and Hazzard's siblings and mother made plans to attend.

When news of the interracial couple strolling the streets of Concord reached the Boston newspapers, the first story's headline, in the *Boston Traveller,* read: "Will Marry Negro in 'Perfect Union': Rich Ayer Society Woman Determined to Wed Servant Although Hometown Is Aflame with Protest." The news had outraged many residents of Ayer. The next day, the *Boston Evening Globe* ran the now provocative story on its front page. The headline was sensational: "Hope to Prevent White Woman Wedding Negro: Two Friends of Mabel E. Puffer Have Gone to Concord, N.H."

Suddenly, the mayor of Concord reversed himself and announced he could not perform the wedding. The betrothed couple, after being turned down several times, finally found a minister willing to marry them. The night before the wedding was to occur, the Ayer police chief arrived, arrested Hazzard on a charge of "enticement," and took Puffer into custody because she had been deemed "insane." In reporting the story, the Concord newspaper concluded that the community "gazed after their departing dust with no regrets." The nation that Woodrow Wilson had led into World War I to "make the world safe for democracy" remained an unsafe place for those bold enough to cross the color line.

AFRICAN AMERICAN LIFE

The most significant development in African American life during the early twentieth century was the **Great Migration** northward from the South. The mass movement of blacks began at the start of the twentieth century but accelerated in 1915–1916, when rapidly expanding war industries in the northern states needed new workers. It continued throughout the twenties, as poor blacks boarded trains with one-way tickets, bound for the "promised land" up North.

Between 1920 and 1930, almost a million African Americans, mostly sharecroppers, joined the exodus from the South. Many landed in New York City, Chicago, Detroit, Cleveland, Washington, D.C., Philadelphia, and other large cities. The Great Migration continued in fits and starts throughout the twentieth century, producing dramatic social, economic, and political changes. In 1900, only 740,000 African Americans lived outside the South, just 8 percent of the nation's black population. By 1970, more than 10.6 million African Americans lived outside the South, 47 percent of the nation's total.

The African Americans making up the Great Migration were lured by what writer Richard Wright called the "warmth of other suns"—better living conditions and better-paying jobs. In the North, for the most part, they were able to speak more freely and were treated more equally than in the South, and educational opportunities for children were much better. Collectively, blacks gained more political leverage by settling in populous states like New York, Pennsylvania, Ohio, and Illinois, with many electoral votes. The political effects of the Great Migration were evident in 1928 when a Chicago Republican, Oscar De Priest, became the first black elected to Congress since Reconstruction and the first ever from a northern district.

The Great Migration was fraught with challenges, however. For the black migrants, the difficult decision to leave their native South ended one set of troubles only to begin another. "Never in history," said Richard Wright, "has a more utterly unprepared folk wanted to go to the city." The refugees arriving in northern cities from the Jim Crow South were strangers in a strange land, where they were not always welcomed. In densely populated northern cities, black newcomers sometimes clashed with local ethnic groups, especially Irish and Italians who feared that the newcomers would take their jobs. Many

The Migration of the Negro, Panel no. 1 In Jacob Lawrence's series of paintings, African Americans leave the South behind for the northern industries of cities like New York, Chicago, and St. Louis.

southern blacks, ignorant of city ways, were taken advantage of by white landlords, realtors, and bankers, forced into substandard and segregated housing, and paid lower wages than whites.

But northern discrimination still paled beside the ferocious injustices faced by African Americans in the segregated South. "If all of their dream does not come true," a black newspaper in Chicago stressed, "enough will come to pass to justify their actions." The Missouri-born black poet Langston Hughes spoke for many when he wrote that he was "fed up With Jim Crow laws, / People who are cruel And afraid, /Who lynch and run, / Who are scared of me And me of them." Over time, the transplanted African Americans forged new lives in a strange new land, building new churches, new communities, new families, even new cultures while reconstructing new identities.

THE NAACP The mass migration of southern blacks northward helped spur the creation of the **National Association for the Advancement of Colored People (NAACP)**, founded in 1910 by black activists and white progressives. Black NAACP members came mainly from the Niagara movement, a group formed in 1905 to fight racial discrimination nationwide. W. E. B. Du Bois became the organization's director of publicity and research and the editor of its journal, *Crisis*.

Politically, the NAACP focused on legal action to bring the Fourteenth and Fifteenth Amendments back to life. One early victory came with *Guinn v. United States* (1915), in which the Supreme Court struck down Oklahoma's efforts to deprive African Americans of the vote. In *Buchanan v. Worley* (1917), the Court invalidated a residential segregation ordinance in Louisville, Kentucky. In 1919, the NAACP launched a national campaign against lynching, then a still-common form of vigilante racist violence. An anti-lynching bill to make mob murder a federal crime passed the House in 1922 but was defeated by southerners in the Senate.

THE HARLEM RENAISSANCE So many blacks converged in New York City during the twenties that they inspired the **Harlem Renaissance**, the nation's first black literary and artistic movement. It started in the fast-growing African American community of Harlem in northern Manhattan. In 1890, one in seventy people in Manhattan had been African American; by 1930, it was one in nine.

The "great, dark city" of Harlem, in poet Langston Hughes's phrase, con-tained more blacks per square mile than any other urban neighborhood in the nation. Such rapid population growth generated a sense of common identity, growing power, and distinctive self-expression that transformed Harlem into the cultural capital of African American life. Writer James Weldon Johnson described a "Black Manhattan" as a "typically Negro" community of 175,000 in that it featured "movement, color, gaiety, singing, dancing, boisterous laughter, and loud talk."

Dotted with lively taverns, lounges, supper clubs, dance halls, and saloons ("speakeasies") that hosted writers and painters talking about literature and art while listening to jazz and drinking illegal booze, Harlem became what journalists called the "Nightclub Capital of the World." Alain Locke, the first black Rhodes Scholar, announced that the Harlem Renaissance was led by a self-confident "new Negro" who no longer felt subservient to white culture. Hughes explained that the Harlem writers and artists were at last ready "to express our individual dark-skinned selves without fear or shame. If white people are pleased, we are glad. If they are not, it doesn't matter. We know we are beautiful. And ugly too."

In poetry and prose, Harlem Renaissance writers celebrated African Amer-ican culture, including jazz and the blues. As Hughes wrote, "I am a Negro— and beautiful. . . . The night is beautiful. So [are] the faces of my people." But while Hughes loved Africa and its cultural heritage, his outlook emphatically "was not Africa. I was [shaped by] Chicago and Kansas City and Broadway and Harlem."

Women, both black and white, were active in the Harlem Renaissance. In January 1925, a thirty-four-year-old African American woman named Zora Neale Hurston arrived in Harlem from Eatonville, an all-black community in rural central Florida. Born in Alabama in 1891, she was an aspiring writer and inventive storyteller in search of the "New Negro Movement." With only $1.50 in her purse, "no job, no friends and a lot of hope," she became the first African American to enroll at Barnard College, the woman's college of Columbia University on the edge of Harlem, where she majored in cultural anthropology.

Into Bondage This painting by Aaron Douglas exemplifies how black artists in the Harlem Renaissance used their African roots and collective history as artistic inspiration.

A brassy, flamboyant woman, Hurston had mastered the art of survival by learning to reinvent herself as the need arose. Motherless at nine, a runaway at fourteen, she became a calculating opportunist blessed with remarkable willpower. The spirited Hurston said she came to Harlem to immerse herself in the "clang and clamor" of city life, in a continuing effort to "jump at the sun," to stretch her ambitions well beyond her resources.

Within a few months, Hurston was behaving, in her words, as the queen of the Harlem Renaissance, writing short stories and plays about the "Negro furthest down" on the social scale while positioning herself at the center of the community's raucous social life. ("How can any deny themselves the pleasure of my company! It's beyond me.") She reveled in the black pride and cultural confidence enlivening Harlem. Her outspokenness invited controversy, as when she claimed that she "did not belong to the sobbing school of Negrohood who hold that nature somehow has given them a lowdown dirty deal and whose feelings are all hurt about it." Hurston went on to become a leading anthropologist, folklorist, and novelist, expert at describing the ways in which African Americans in the Lower South forged cohesive communities in the face of white bigotry and violence.

The Harlem Renaissance also celebrated the distinctive contributions of poor African Americans to American culture. Hurston spoke out on behalf of those who "having nothing, still refused to be humble." So did many other members of the Harlem Renaissance. Writer James Weldon Johnson coined

Augusta Savage The sculptor, shown with her statue *Realization* (1938), found success in America and abroad, despite experiencing racial prejudice along the way.

the term "Aframerican" to designate Americans with African ancestry and to emphasize that blacks were no longer divided by their heritage; they were proud to be Americans who happened to have an African ancestry. Aframericans, he insisted, were "conscious collaborators" in the creation of American society and culture. The black sculptor Augusta Savage agreed. She explained that African Americans for three centuries had shared the "same cultural background, the same system, the same standard of beauty as white Americans. . . . It is impossible to go back to primitive [African] art for our models."

By 1930, Harlem Renaissance writers had produced dozens of novels and volumes of poetry; several Broadway plays; and a flood of short stories, essays, and films. A people capable of producing such great art and literature, Johnson declared, should never again be "looked upon as inferior."

GARVEYISM The celebration of black culture found much different expression in what came to be called **Negro nationalism**, which promoted black separatism from mainstream American life. Its leading spokesman was Marcus Garvey, who claimed to speak for all 400 million blacks worldwide. In 1916, Garvey brought to Harlem the headquarters of the Universal Negro Improvement Association (UNIA), which he had started in his native Jamaica two years before.

Garvey insisted that blacks had *nothing* in common with whites. In passionate speeches and in editorials in the UNIA's popular newspaper, the *Negro World*, Garvey urged African Americans to remove themselves from the surrounding white culture and to cultivate black solidarity and "black power."

The UNIA quickly became the largest black political organization in the nation. By 1923, Garvey, who often wore gaudy military uniforms and feather-plumed hats, claimed the UNIA had as many as 4 million members served by

800 offices. His goal was to build an all-black empire in Africa. To that end, he began calling himself the "Provisional President of Africa," raising funds to send Americans to Africa, and expelling any UNIA member who married a white.

Garvey's message of black nationalism and racial solidarity appealed especially to poor blacks in northern cities, but he also had supporters across the rural South. Garveyism, however, appalled some black leaders, especially those leading the NAACP. W. E. B. Du Bois labeled Garvey "the most dangerous enemy of the Negro race. . . . He is either a lunatic or a traitor." An African American newspaper pledged to help "drive Garvey and Garveyism in all its sinister viciousness from the American soil."

Marcus Garvey The Jamaican-born founder of the Universal Negro Improvement Association and leading spokesman for "Negro nationalism" in the 1920s.

Garvey's eccentric crusade collapsed in 1923 when he was convicted of fraud for overselling shares of stock in a steamship corporation, the Black Star Line, which he founded to transport American blacks to Africa. Sentenced to a five-year prison term, he was pardoned in 1927 by President Calvin Coolidge on the condition that he be deported to Jamaica, where he received a hero's welcome. Garvey died in obscurity in 1940, but the memory of his movement kept alive an undercurrent that would reemerge in the 1960s under the slogan "black power."

THE MODERNIST REVOLT

The dramatic changes in society and the economy during the twenties were spurred by transformations in science and the arts during the previous two decades. Since the eighteenth-century Enlightenment, conventional wisdom had held that the universe was governed by basic underlying laws of time and energy, light and motion. This rational world of order and certainty disintegrated in the early twentieth century, thanks to the discoveries of European physicists.

ALBERT EINSTEIN

During a century remarkable for its scientific discoveries and technological advances, one genius stands out: Albert Einstein, a scientific rebel with an unrivaled imagination. Many of his greatest discoveries emerged not from research but from his remarkable ability to *picture* in his mind the strange effects of natural forces, from the infinitesimally small to the infinitely large.

In 1905, Einstein, a twenty-six-year-old German-born physicist working in Switzerland, published several research papers that changed science forever while at times defying common sense. The first paper, which would earn him the Nobel Prize in 1921, revealed that light was not simply a wave of continuous energy but a stream of tiny particles, called *quanta* (now called *photons*). This breakthrough would provide the theoretical basis for quantum physics and new electronic technologies such as television, laser beams, and semiconductors used to make computers.

In his second research paper, Einstein confirmed the existence of molecules and atoms by showing how their random collisions explained the jerky motions of tiny particles in water.

Einstein's third paper introduced the special theory of relativity, which argues that no matter how fast one is moving toward or away from a source of light, the speed of that light beam will appear the same, a constant 186,000 miles per second. But space and time will appear relative to the speed of light. So if a train were traveling at the speed of light, time would slow down from the perspective of an observer, and the train itself would get shorter and heavier.

In 1916, Einstein unveiled his *general theory of relativity*, which maintained that the fundamental concepts of space, time,

Albert Einstein One of the most influential scientists of the twentieth century, Einstein was awarded a Nobel Prize in 1921.

matter, and energy are not distinct, independent things with stable dimensions, as Sir Isaac Newton had assumed in the eighteenth century, but that they are interacting elements constantly changing one another. As a beam of light travels through space-time, gravity causes it to curve. Likewise, the hands of a clock traveling at high speeds move more slowly than those of a stationary clock.

Nothing is fixed or absolute in Einstein's bewildering universe; everything is *relative* to the location and motion of the observer and the distorting effects of gravity, which warp space and time. Things are big or little, long or short, slow or fast, light or heavy only by comparison to something else. Einstein also explained that all matter is a special form of energy, and that a very small amount of material could yield enormous energy if its atomic structure were disrupted.

By showing that much more was going on in the universe than had long been assumed, Einstein's discoveries revolutionized the way scientists perceived the natural world. A British newspaper said the general theory of relativity was "one of the most momentous . . . pronouncements of human thought." In 1919, after astronomers had spent three years testing Einstein's theories, the *New York Times* announced: "Einstein's Theory Triumphs."

Einstein was so influential in deciphering the forces of the cosmos that his ideas became impossible to ignore—and almost as difficult to explain. Many of his complex discoveries entered popular culture as people oversimplified his theory of relativity by claiming that there were no absolute standards; all was "relative." During the twenties, the idea of "relativity" emerged in popular discussions of topics such as sexuality, the arts, and politics; there was less faith in absolutes. Notions of relativity shaped many of the intellectual, cultural, and social currents of the twentieth century.

MODERNIST ART AND LITERATURE

The scientific breakthroughs associated with Sigmund Freud, Albert Einstein, and other scientists helped to inspire a "modernist" cultural revolution. **Modernism** as a recognizable movement appeared first in the capitals of Europe (London, Paris, Berlin, and Vienna) in the 1890s. By the second decade of the twentieth century, it had spread to the United States, especially New York City and Chicago. Put most simply, modernism was the widespread awareness that new ideas and ways of doing things were making a sharp break with tradition. The modernist point of view arose out of recognition that new technologies, modes of transportation and communication, and scientific discoveries were transforming the nature of everyday life as well as the way people "saw" the world.

The horrors of the Great War served to accelerate and expand the appeal of modernism—and helped explain why modernists cared little for established standards of good taste or for history. To be "modern" was to break free of tradition, take chances, violate artistic rules and moral restrictions, and behave in deliberately shocking ways. "Art," said a modernist painter, "is meant to disturb."

As an experimental cultural movement, modernism was loosely based on three unsettling assumptions: (1) God did not exist; (2) "reality" was not rational, orderly, or obvious; and, in the aftermath of the Great War, (3) social progress could no longer be taken for granted. In the arts, these modernist premises challenged writers, artists, musicians, and architects to risk poverty and humiliation by rudely rebelling against good taste, old-fashioned morals, and old-time religion.

Modernists were artistic revolutionaries who delighted in the madness of the unexpected and refused to be conventional. In its simplest sense, modernism was a disrespectful war of new values against old ones. Experimental poet Ezra Pound provided the slogan for the modernist movement: "Make It New!"

Much about modernism provoked, perplexed, and upset people. Until the twentieth century, most writers and artists had taken for granted an accessible "real" world that could be readily observed, scientifically explained, and accurately represented in words or paint or even music. The modernists, however, applied Einstein's ideas about relativity to a world in which "reality" no longer had an objective or recognizable basis. They agreed wholeheartedly with Freud that reality, in fact, was an intensely inward and subjective experience—something deeply personal and even unrecognizable by others, something to be imagined and expressed by one's innermost being rather than observed and reproduced. Walter Pach, an early American champion of modern art, explained that modernism resulted from the discovery of "the role played by the unconscious in our lives."

THE ARMORY SHOW The crusade to bring European-inspired modernism to the United States reached a climax in the **Armory Show** of 1913, the most scandalous event in the history of American art. Mabel Dodge, one of the organizers, wrote to Gertrude Stein that the exhibition would cause "a riot and revolution and things will never be the same afterwards." To house the 1,200 modernist works collected from more than 300 painters and sculptors in America and Europe, the two dozen young painters who organized the show leased the vast 69th Regiment Armory in New York City.

The Armory Show, officially known as the International Exhibition of Modern Art, opened on February 17, 1913. It created an immediate sensation. For many, modern art became the thing that they loved to hate. Modernism, grumbled a prominent critic, "is nothing else than the total destruction of the

Russian Ballet **(1916)** Jewish American artist Max Weber's painting is a modernist take on a traditional subject. Splicing the scene of the performance into overlapping planes of jarring colors, this painting exemplifies the impact of psychoanalysis and the theory of relativity on the arts.

art of painting." The *New York Times* warned visitors that they would enter "a stark region of abstractions" at the "lunatic asylum" show that was "hideous to our unaccustomed eyes."

The experimentalist ("*avant-garde*") artists whose works were on display (including paintings by Vincent Van Gogh, Paul Gauguin, and Henri Matisse, as well as Cezanne and Picasso) were "in love with science but not with objective reality," the *Times* critic complained, and had produced paintings "revolting in their inhumanity." Former president Theodore Roosevelt dismissed the show as "repellent from every standpoint."

Yet the show also generated excited praise. "A new world has arisen before our eyes," announced an American art magazine. "To miss modern art," an art critic stressed, "is to miss one of the few thrills that life holds." From New York, the show went on to Chicago and Boston, where it aroused similarly strong responses and attracted more huge crowds.

After the Armory Show, modern art became one of the nation's favorite topics of debate. Many found a new faith in the disturbing powers of art. "America in its newness," predicted Walt Kuhn, a painter who helped organize the exhibition, "is destined to become the coming center" of modernism. Indeed, the Museum of Modern Art, founded in New York City in 1929, came to house the world's most celebrated collection of avant-garde paintings and sculpture.

POUND, ELIOT, AND STEIN The leading American champions of modern art and literature lived not in Chicago or in New York but in England and Europe: Idaho-born Ezra Pound and St. Louis–born T. S. Eliot in London, and Californian Gertrude Stein in Paris. Working separately but spreading their influence together, they were self-conscious revolutionaries deeply concerned with creating strange, new, and often beautifully difficult forms of modernist expression. They found more inspiration and more receptive audiences in Europe than in the United States.

As the foreign editor of the Chicago-based *Poetry* magazine, Pound became the cultural impresario of modernism, the conduit through which many experimental American poets gained publication and exposure. In bitter poems and earnest essays denouncing war and commercialism, he displayed an incessant, uncompromising urgency to transform the literary landscape. An English poet called him a "solitary volcano." T. S. Eliot claimed that Pound was single-handedly responsible for the modernist movement in poetry.

Pound recruited, edited, published, and reviewed the best among the new generation of modernist writers, improving their writing, bolstering their courage, and propelling their careers. In his own poetry, he expressed the feeling of many that the war had wasted a whole generation of young men who died in defense of a "botched civilization."

One of the young American writers Pound took under his wing was Eliot, who had recently graduated from Harvard. Within a few years, Eliot surpassed Pound to become the leading American modernist. Eliot declared that traditional poetry "was stagnant to a degree difficult for any young poet to imagine."

Eliot's epic 433-line poem *The Waste Land* (1922), which Pound edited, became a monument of modernism. It expressed a sense of postwar disillusionment and melancholy that had a powerful effect on other writers. As a poet and critic for the *Criterion,* which he founded in 1922, Eliot became the arbiter of modernist taste in Anglo-American literature.

Gertrude Stein was the self-appointed champion of the American modernists who chose to live in Paris. Long regarded as simply the literary eccentric who wrote, "Rose is a rose is a rose is a rose," Stein was in fact one of the chief promoters of the triumphant subjectivity undergirding modernist expression.

She sought to capture in words the equivalent of abstract painting and its self-conscious revolt against portraying recognizable scenes from "real" life. Stein, who declared that literature that "tells about what happens [in life] is of no interest to anybody," became famous for hosting a cultural salon in Paris that became a gathering place for American and European modernists.

THE "LOST GENERATION" Along with the shock of modernism, the arts and literature of the twenties were also greatly influenced by the horrors of the Great War. F. Scott Fitzgerald wrote in *This Side of Paradise* that the "sad young men" who had fought in Europe to "make the world safe for democracy" had "grown up to find all Gods dead, all wars fought, all faiths in man shaken."

Cynicism had displaced idealism in the wake of the war's horrific senselessness. As Fitzgerald asserted, "There's only one lesson to be learned from life anyway. . . . That there's no lesson to be learned from life." Frederic Henry, a character in Ernest Hemingway's novel *A Farewell to Arms* (1929), declares that "abstract words such as *glory, honor, courage* . . . were obscene" in the context of the war's colossal casualties.

Fitzgerald, Hemingway, and other young modernists were labeled the **Lost Generation**—those who had lost faith in the values and institutions of Western civilization and were frantically looking for new gods to worship. It was Gertrude Stein who in 1921 told Hemingway that he and his friends who had served in the war "are a lost generation." When Hemingway objected, she held her ground. "You are [lost]. You have no respect for anything. You drink yourselves to death."

In his first novel, *The Sun Also Rises* (1926), Hemingway used the phrase "lost generation" in the book's opening quotation. The novel centers on Jake Barnes, a young American journalist castrated by a war injury. His despairing impotence leads him to wander the cafes and nightclubs of postwar Europe with his unhappy friends, who acknowledge that they are all wounded and sterile in their own way: they have lost their innocence, their illusions, and their motivation to do anything with their lives.

Fitzgerald, the earliest chronicler of the "lost generation," blazed up brilliantly and then quickly flickered out, like many of the characters in his novels. His works centered on self-indulgent and self-destructive people who drank and partied too much. A friend and fellow writer called Fitzgerald "our darling, our genius, our fool." What gave depth to the best of his work was what a character in *The Great Gatsby* (1925), his finest novel, called "a sense of the fundamental decencies" amid all the surface gaiety—and a sense of impending doom in a world that had lost its meaning through the disorienting discoveries of modern science and the horrors of world war.

CHAPTER REVIEW

SUMMARY

- **A "New Era" of Consumption**   The American economy grew at its fastest rate in history during the 1920s, led by an explosion in mass production and sales of new consumer goods. Innovations in production, advertising, and financing, and a jump in the use of electricity, enabled and encouraged millions of Americans to purchase automobiles, radios, and other electrical appliances. The automobile industry was at the center of these changes, as Ford Motor Company pioneered mass production using moving assembly lines, a highly efficient method that helped make its cars affordable for a majority of Americans. The new *consumer culture* valued leisure, self-expression, and self-indulgence. During the twenties, consumer debt tripled. Innovations in communications (especially the growth in radio ownership), transportation, finance, and advertising also brought about a mass culture, as more and more Americans purchased national brand-name items from retail chain stores, listened to the same radio shows, watched the same movies, and followed the lives and careers of national celebrities and superstars.

- **The "Jazz Age"**   Other new social and cultural trends and movements rapidly challenged the traditional order. The carefree fads and attitudes of the 1920s, perhaps best represented by the frantic rhythms of jazz music, led writer F. Scott Fitzgerald to call the decade the *Jazz Age*. A "new woman" appeared, best represented by *flappers*—young women who challenged prewar restrictions with their short hemlines, drinking, smoking, and open discussions of sex. The majority of women, however, remained full-time housewives and mothers or domestic servants, and fewer young women pursued professional careers. With the *Great Migration* continuing, African Americans in northern cities felt freer to speak out against racial injustice and express pride in their race. The *Harlem Renaissance* movement gave voice to African American literature and music. Racial separatism and black nationalism grew popular under the leadership of Marcus Garvey, while other African Americans joined white supporters in the *National Association for the Advancement of Colored People (NAACP)* and supported its efforts to undo racism through education, legislation, and court challenges.

- **The Modernist Revolt**   Many American artists and intellectuals were attracted to *modernism*, a movement that had begun in Europe before the Great War and reflected new developments in science, particularly Albert Einstein's theory of relativity and Sigmund Freud's exploration of how the subconscious mind shapes human behavior. To be "modern" meant to break free of tradition, to violate restrictions, to shock the public, and to make one's works difficult to explain or interpret. Americans were first exposed to modern art in a substantial way with the *Armory Show* of 1913.

CHRONOLOGY

1903	Wright Brothers fly first motorized airplane
	Ford Motor Company is founded
1910	National Association for the Advancement of Colored People (NAACP) is founded
1913	Armory Show introduces Americans to modern art
1916	Marcus Garvey brings Universal Negro Improvement Association to New York
1920	Prohibition begins
	F. Scott Fitzgerald's *This Side of Paradise* is published
	Warren G. Harding is elected president
1921	Albert Einstein receives Nobel Prize in physics
1922	First radio commercial is aired
1927	Charles A. Lindbergh Jr. makes first solo transatlantic airplane flight

KEY TERMS

consumer culture p. 1032

"Jazz Age" p. 1041

flappers p. 1045

Great Migration p. 1048

National Association for the Advancement of Colored People (NAACP) p. 1049

Harlem Renaissance p. 1050

Negro nationalism p. 1052

modernism p. 1055

Armory Show p. 1056

Lost Generation p. 1059

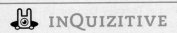 INQUIZITIVE

Go to InQuizitive to see what you've learned—and learn what you've missed—with personalized feedback along the way.

24 The Reactionary Twenties

Black Tuesday In this photograph, panic-stricken crowds take to Wall Street as news of the plummeting stock market spread on the morning of Tuesday, October 29, 1929. An account of the crash in the *New York Times* wrote that "the streets were crammed with a mixed crowd—agonized little speculators, ... sold-out traders, ... inquisitive individuals and tourists seeking ... a closer view of the national catastrophe.... Where was it going to end?"

T he self-indulgent excesses of the "lost generation" and the frivolities of the Jazz Age made little sense to the vast majority of Americans during the twenties. Most people still led traditional lives; they aggressively defended established values, old certainties, and the comfort of past routines, and they were shocked by the decade's social turmoil and cultural rebelliousness. They traced the germs of dangerous radicalism to the multiethnic cities teeming with immigrants and foreign ideas such as socialism, communism, and anarchism. The reactionary conservatism of the 1920s fed on the popularity of **nativism**, the fear of and prejudice against immigrants from countries outside of western Europe, and a militant Protestantism that sought to restore the primacy of traditional Christian morality.

REACTIONARY CONSERVATISM AND IMMIGRATION RESTRICTION

The United States has opened its borders and ports to more people from more countries than any other nation. But newcomers have never been universally welcomed or embraced. After the end of the Great War, masses of people emigrated from Europe to the United States. Between 1919 and 1924, more than 600,000 people from southern and eastern Europe, most of them Italians, entered the United States, along with 150,000 Poles and 50,000 Russians. At the same time, some 150,000 Mexicans crossed the border; most of them landed in the Southwest and California. In the early 1920s, more than half of the white men and a third of the white women working in mines, mills, and factories

focus questions

1. How did the reactionary conservatism during the 1920s manifest itself in social life and governmental policies?

2. To what extent did the policies of the Republican party dominate the federal government during the twenties? In what ways were these policies a rejection of progressivism?

3. How did Herbert Hoover emerge as the most popular political figure during the twenties?

4. What were the major causes of the Great Depression?

5. How did the Great Depression impact the American people?

were immigrants, some of whom had a passion for socialism or anarchism—as well as a willingness to use violence to achieve their political goals.

Fears of an invasion of foreign radicals led Congress to pass the Emergency Immigration Act of 1921, which limited total immigration to 150,000 a year and restricted newcomers from each European country to 3 percent of the total number of that nationality represented in the 1910 census. Three years later, after people complained that too many eastern and southern Europeans were still being admitted, Congress passed the **Immigration Act of 1924**. It reduced the number of admitted Europeans to 2 percent of the 1890 census, so as to include fewer "new" immigrants from southern and eastern Europe: Jews, Italians, Poles, and Russians.

The purpose of the new quotas was to shrink the total number of immigrants, to favor immigrants from northern and western Europe, and to reduce those from southern and eastern Europe. A Kansas congressman expressed the prejudices against German and Italian Catholics felt by many rural American Protestants: "On the one side is beer, bolshevism, unassimilating settlements and perhaps many flags—on the other side is constitutional government; one flag, stars and stripes."

The immigration laws targeted particular groups. For example, they banned immigrants from Japan or China. The Immigration Act of 1924, however, allowed newcomers from countries in the Western Hemisphere. An unintended result was that people of Latin American descent (chiefly Mexicans, Puerto Ricans, and Cubans) became the fastest-growing ethnic minority during the twenties.

The number of Mexicans living in Texas increased tenfold between 1900 and 1930 in response to the needs of Texas farmers for "stoop" laborers. "Cotton picking suits the Mexican," was the common assertion among Texas growers. Because Mexican migrant workers were mostly homeless nomads willing to move with the seasons, farm owners came to prefer them over black and white tenants and farm laborers.

SACCO AND VANZETTI The nativism embedded in the new immigration laws reinforced the connection between European immigrants and political radicalism. That connection erupted in the most widely publicized criminal case of the twenties.

On May 5, 1920, two Italian immigrants who described themselves as revolutionary anarchists eager to topple the American government, shoemaker Nicola Sacco and fish peddler Bartolomeo Vanzetti, were arrested outside Boston, Massachusetts, for stealing $16,000 from a shoe factory and killing the paymaster and a guard. Both men were armed with loaded pistols when

Sacco and Vanzetti The trial and conviction of these working-class Italian immigrants became a public spectacle amid the growing mood of nativism.

arrested, both lied to police, and both were identified by eyewitnesses. The stolen money, however, was never found, and several people claimed that they were with Sacco and Vanzetti far from the scene of the crime when it occurred.

The **Sacco and Vanzetti case** occurred at the height of Italian immigration to the United States and against the backdrop of numerous terror attacks by anarchists, some of which Sacco and Vanzetti had participated in. The charged atmosphere, called "the Red hysteria" by one journalist, ensured that the men's trial would be a public spectacle.

In July 1921, Sacco and Vanzetti were convicted and sentenced to death. Their legal appeals lasted six years before they were electrocuted on August 23, 1927, still claiming their innocence. To millions of workers and liberals around the world, Sacco and Vanzetti became martyrs, victims of capitalist injustice. People still debate their guilt or innocence.

THE NEW KLAN The most violent of the reactionary movements during the twenties was a revived Ku Klux Klan, the infamous post–Civil War group of anti-black racists that had re-created itself in 1915. The old Klan had died out in the 1870s once white Democrats regained control of the former Confederate states after Reconstruction. The new Klan—the Invisible Empire of the Knights of the Ku Klux Klan—was, by 1920, a *nationwide* organization devoted to "the maintenance of White Supremacy" and "100 percent Americanism"; only "natives"—white Protestants born in the United States—could be members. At its peak, the new Klan numbered over 4 million members, making it the largest far-right movement in history.

Shrouded in secret signs and codes, practicing weird rituals, and costumed in white sheets and spooky hats, the Klan called for militant patriotism, restrictions on immigration and voting, and strict personal morality. It opposed bootleg liquor and labor unions, and it preached hatred against not only African Americans but Roman Catholics, Jews, immigrants, Communists, atheists, prostitutes, and adulterers. The United States was no melting pot, shouted Imperial Wizard William J. Simmons: "It is a garbage can! . . . When the hordes of aliens walk to the ballot box and their votes outnumber yours, then that alien horde has got you by the throat."

Bigotry became big business. The new Klan was mobilized by shrewd marketers eager to make money on racism. Each member of a local "klavern" paid a $10 initiation fee and $5 in annual dues, and was required to buy an official Klan robe, a pointed hood, and other accessories. Whole families attended Klan gatherings, "klasping" hands while listening to violent speeches, watching fireworks, and burning crosses. A Colorado judge said that his neighbors had "paid ten dollars to hate somebody [by joining the Klan], and they were determined to get their money's worth."

In Texas, the Klan focused on imposing its severe view of righteous Protestant morality on others. Members used the instruments of terrorism— harassment, intimidation (often in the form of burning crosses), beatings, and "tar and feathers"—to discipline alcoholics, gamblers, adulterers, and other sinners. In the spring of 1922 alone, the Dallas Klan flogged sixty-eight men.

The reborn Klan, headquartered in Atlanta, grew rapidly across the nation, and especially in the rural Midwest. During the twenties, 40 percent of its "Anglo-Saxon" members were in three midwestern states: Illinois, Indiana, and Ohio. Recruiters, called Kleagles, were told to "play upon whatever prejudices were most acute in a particular area." In Texas, the Klan fed on prejudice against Mexicans; in California, hatred focused on Japanese Americans; in New York, the enemy was primarily Jews and Catholics.

Most Klan members were small farmers, sharecroppers, or wage workers, but the organization also attracted clergymen, engineers, doctors, lawyers, accountants, business leaders, and teachers. As a prominent southern journalist observed, the new Klan was "anti-Negro, anti-alien, anti-red, anti-Catholic, anti-Jew, anti-Darwin, anti-Modern, anti-Liberal; Fundamentalist, vastly Moral, militantly Protestant." African Americans grew increasingly concerned. The Chicago *Defender*, the black newspaper with the widest circulation in the nation, urged its readers to fight back against Klansmen trying to "win what their fathers [in the Civil War] lost by fire and sword."

By 1923, the Klan's membership had surpassed 4 million, including judges, mayors, sheriffs, state legislators, six governors, and three U.S. senators. The Grand Dragon, an Indiana con man named David C. Stephenson, grew so influential in electing local and state officials (the "kluxing" of America, as he called it) that he boasted, "I am the law in Indiana!" Klan-endorsed candidates won the Indiana governorship and controlled the state legislature. At the 1924 Republican State Convention, Stephenson patrolled the aisles with a pistol. He later confessed that he "purchased the county and state officials." Stephenson, who had grown wealthy by skimming from the dues he collected from Klan members as well as selling robes and hoods, planned to run for president of the United States.

The Klan's influence, both in Indiana and nationwide, suddenly crumbled, however, after Stephenson was arrested and sentenced to life in prison in 1925 for kidnapping and raping a twenty-eight-year-old woman who then

Ku Klux Klan rally In 1925, the KKK marched down Pennsylvania Avenue in Washington, D.C.

committed suicide. Membership tumbled, and Klan organizations splintered or shut down altogether. Several states passed anti-Klan laws, and others banned the wearing of masks and burning of crosses. By 1930, nationwide membership had dwindled to 100,000, mostly southerners. Yet the impulse underlying the Klan lived on, fed by deep-seated fears and hatreds that have yet to disappear.

FUNDAMENTALISM

While fighting "growing immorality" and the "alien menace," the Klan also defended "old-time religion" against dangerous ideas circulating in "progressive" or "liberal" Protestant churches. The most threatening ideas were that the Bible was not literally the word of God and that Charles Darwin's theories of biological evolution were true. Conservative Protestants embraced a militant fundamentalism, distinctive for its hostility toward new "liberal" beliefs and its insistence on the literal truth of the Bible.

The result was a religious civil war, often called the modernist–fundamentalist conflict. It divided congregations and whole denominations. A burst of Protestant fundamentalism swept the country, largely as a reaction to the spread of modernism in mainline Protestantism, which sought to accommodate Christian teaching with modern science.

In a famous 1922 sermon titled "Shall the Fundamentalists Win?" Harry Emerson Fosdick, the progressive pastor at New York City's First Presbyterian Church, dismissed biblical fundamentalism as "immeasurable folly." The Bible, he explained, was not literally the "word of God," but instead was a representation of God's wonders. Christianity had nothing to fear from Darwinian evolution or modern science, he argued, for liberal Christianity "saves us from the necessity of apologizing for immature states in the development of the biblical revelation." Fosdick's liberalism—he was an outspoken critic of racism and social injustice—outraged fundamentalists who launched an effort to "try" him for heresy. Fosdick decided to resign instead.

Among national leaders, however, only the "Great Commoner," William Jennings Bryan, the former Democratic congressman, secretary of state, and three-time presidential candidate, had the support, prestige, and eloquence to transform fundamentalism into a popular crusade. Bryan was a strange bird, a liberal progressive and pacifist populist in politics and a right-wing religious crusader. He remained a firm believer in the literal truth of the Bible.

Bryan backed new state laws banning the teaching of evolution in public schools. He condemned Darwin's theory of evolution, which suggested that human beings over millions of years had evolved from monkeys and apes, with the same passion he had once directed against Republican presidential candidates.

THE SCOPES TRIAL During the 1920s, anti-evolution bills were introduced in numerous state legislatures, but the only victories came in the South—and there were few of those. Miriam "Ma" Ferguson, the first woman governor of Texas (her husband "Pa" Ferguson had earlier been impeached as governor), outlawed school textbooks that included sections on Darwinism. "I am a Christian mother who believes that Jesus Christ died to save humanity," she declared, "and I am not going to let that kind of rot go into Texas schoolbooks."

The dramatic highpoint of the fundamentalist war on Darwinism came not in Texas but in Tennessee, where in 1925 the legislature outlawed the teaching of evolution in public schools and colleges.

In the mining town of Dayton, in eastern Tennessee, civic leaders eager to create publicity for their depressed economy persuaded John T. Scopes, a twenty-four-year-old substitute high-school science teacher, to become a test case against the new law. He was arrested for "teaching" Darwin's theory of evolution. The **Scopes Trial** did indeed bring worldwide publicity to Dayton, but not the kind town leaders had hoped for.

Before the start of the twelve-day trial on July 10, 1925, the sweltering streets of Dayton overflowed with evangelists, atheists, hot-dog and soda-pop peddlers, and some 200 newspaper and radio reporters. Main Street merchants festooned their shop windows with pictures of apes and monkeys lampooning Darwinian evolution. One store urged visitors, "Don't monkey around when you come to Dayton—come to us." A man tattooed with Bible verses preached on a street corner while a live monkey was paraded about town.

The two warriors pitting science against fundamentalism were both national celebrities: Bryan, who had offered his services to the prosecution, and Chicagoan Clarence Darrow, the nation's most famous defense attorney, a tireless defender of the rights of the working class, who had volunteered to defend Scopes and evolution.

Bryan insisted that the trial was about a state's right to determine what was taught in the public schools. It was a "contest between evolution and Christianity, a duel to the death." Darrow, who viewed the law as a blood sport, countered: "Scopes is not on trial. Civilization is on trial." His goal was to prevent "bigots and ignoramuses from controlling the education of the United States" by proving that America was "founded on liberty and not on narrow, mean, intolerable and brainless prejudice of soulless religio-maniacs."

On July 20, the seventh day of the trial, the defense called Bryan as an "expert" witness on biblical interpretation. Darrow began by asking him about

Monkey trial In this snapshot of the courtroom, Scopes (far left) clasps his face in his hands and listens to one of his attorneys (second from right). Darrow (far right), too, listens on, visibly affected by the sweltering weather.

biblical stories. Did he believe that Jonah was swallowed by a whale and that Joshua made the sun stand still? Yes, Bryan replied. All things were possible with God. Darrow pressed on relentlessly, even cruelly. What about the great flood and Noah's ark? Was Eve really created from Adam's rib? Bryan hesitated and fumbled to reply.

The crowd grew uneasy as the hero of fundamentalism crumpled in the heat. Bryan appealed to the judge for relief, claiming that the Bible was not on trial, only to have Darrow yell: "I am examining you on your fool ideas that no intelligent Christian on earth believes." A humiliated Bryan claimed that Darrow was insulting Christians. Darrow, his thumbs clasping his colorful suspenders, shot back: "You insult every man of science and learning in the world because he does not believe in your fool religion." At one point, Darrow and Bryan, their patience exhausted, lunged at each other, prompting the judge to adjourn court.

As the trial ended, the judge said that the only question for the jury was whether John T. Scopes had taught evolution, and no one had denied that he had done so. The jurors did not even sit down before deciding, in nine minutes, that Scopes was guilty. But the Tennessee Supreme Court, while upholding the anti-evolution law, waived Scopes's $100 fine on a technicality. Both sides claimed victory.

Five days after the trial ended, Bryan, still in Dayton, died in his sleep at age sixty-five. Scopes left Dayton to study geology at the University of Chicago; he became a petroleum engineer.

For all of its comic aspects, the Scopes Trial symbolized the waning of an old order in America and the rise of a *modern* outlook—more pluralistic, diverse, and skeptical, more tolerant of controversial ideas, and less obsessed with intellectual control. Still, the debate between fundamentalism and modernism continues today.

PROHIBITION

William Jennings Bryan died knowing that one of his crusades had succeeded: the distribution of alcoholic beverages had been outlawed nationwide. The movement to prohibit the sale of beer, wine, and liquor forged an unusual alliance between rural and small-town Protestants and urban political progressives—between believers in "old-time religion," who opposed drinking as sinful, and progressive social reformers, mostly women, who were convinced that **Prohibition** would reduce prostitution and alcohol-related violence.

What connected the two groups were the ethnic and social prejudices that many members shared. The head of the Anti-Saloon League, for example, declared that German Americans "eat like gluttons and drink like swine." For many anti-alcohol crusaders, in fact, the primary goal of Prohibition seemed to be policing the behavior of the foreign-born, the working class, and the poor, just as fundamentalists sought to enforce their religious beliefs on others.

During the Great War, the need to use grain for food rather than for making booze, combined with a grassroots backlash against beer brewers because of their German background, also transformed the cause of Prohibition into a virtual test of American patriotism. On December 18, 1917, Congress sent to the states the Eighteenth Amendment. Ratified on January 16, 1919, it banned "the manufacture, sale, and transportation of intoxicating liquors," effective one year later. The popular Christian evangelist Billy Sunday, who described himself as a "temperance Republican down to my toes," told the 10,000 people gathered at his tabernacle to celebrate the outlawing of booze, that the age of righteousness was at hand: "Men will walk upright now; women will smile and the children will laugh."

As the most ambitious social reform ever attempted in the United States, however, Prohibition proved to be a colossal and costly failure. It did not suddenly persuade people to quit drinking. Instead, it compelled millions to break—or stretch—the law. In 1923, a federal agent said it would take a visitor in any city less than thirty minutes to find a drink. In New Orleans, he added, it would only take thirty-five seconds.

The National Prohibition Act of 1919 (commonly called the Volstead Act) outlined the rules and regulations needed to enforce the Eighteenth Amendment. It had so many loopholes that it virtually guaranteed failure, however. Technically, it never said that *drinking* alcohol was illegal, only the manufacture, distribution, and sale of alcoholic beverages.

In addition, individuals and organizations were allowed to keep and drink any liquor owned on January 16, 1919. Not surprisingly, people stocked up before the law took effect. Farmers were allowed to "preserve" their fruits through the process of fermenting them, which resulted in barns stockpiled with "hard cider" and homemade wine. So-called medicinal liquor was also still allowed, which meant that physicians (and even veterinarians) wrote numerous prescriptions for "medicinal" brands such as Old Grand-Dad and Jim Beam whiskies.

Thousands of people set up home breweries to make their own beer, producing 700 million gallons in 1929 alone. Wine was made just as easily, and "bathtub gin" was the easiest of all, requiring little more than a one-gallon still and some fruit, grain, or potatoes. Liquor crossed the nation's 18,700-mile-long borders more easily than people did. Two-thirds of the illegal liquor came from Canada, most of the rest from Mexico or overseas.

The new law was too sweeping to enforce and too inconveniencing for most Americans to respect. It also had unexpected consequences. The loss of liquor taxes cost the federal government 10 percent of its annual revenue, and the closing of breweries, distilleries, and saloons eliminated thousands of jobs.

An even greater weakness of Prohibition was that Congress never supplied adequate funding to enforce it. Given the public thirst for alcohol and the profits to be made in making and selling it illegally ("bootlegging") it would have taken armies of agents to police the nation, and jail cells would have overflowed with violators. New York's mayor said it would take 250,000 policemen to enforce Prohibition in his city alone. In working-class and ethnic-rich Detroit, the bootleg industry was second in size only to the auto industry.

Moreover, a huge number of prominent Americans regularly broke the law. President Warren G. Harding drank and served bootleg liquor in the White House, explaining that he was "unable to see this as a great moral issue," and the largest bootlegger in Washington, D.C., reported that "a majority of both houses" of Congress were regular customers.

The efforts to defy Prohibition generated widespread police corruption and boosted organized crime. Many of the activities and images associated with the Roaring Twenties were fueled by bootleg liquor supplied by crime syndicates and sold in speakeasies, which local policemen often ignored in exchange for bribes. Well-organized crime syndicates behaved like giant corporations; they controlled the entire stream of liquor's production, pricing, distribution, and sales. As a result, the Prohibition Era was a fourteen-year orgy of unparalleled criminal activity. By 1930, more than one-third of Americans in federal prison were Prohibition violators.

All fair in drink and war Torpedoes filled with malt whiskey were discovered in the New York harbor in 1926, an elaborate attempt by bootleggers to smuggle alcohol during Prohibition. Each "torpedo" had an air compartment so it could be floated to shore.

Although total national alcohol consumption did decrease during the twenties, as did the number of deaths from alcohol abuse, in many cities drinking actually *increased* during Prohibition. New York City's police commissioner estimated that there were 32,000 speakeasies in the city in 1929. There had been only 15,000 saloons when Prohibition started. As the popular humorist Will Rogers quipped, "Prohibition is better than no liquor at all."

Prohibition supplied organized crime with a source of enormous new income. The most famous Prohibition-era gangster was Alphonse "Scarface" Capone. In 1927, his Chicago-based bootlegging, prostitution, and gambling empire brought him an annual income of $60 million and involved an army of 700 gangsters involved in 300 murders (none solved). Capone was a larger-than-life hero to many. He gave huge tips to waiters and hatcheck girls and provided a soup kitchen for Chicago's poorest residents. When criticized, he claimed to be providing the public with the goods and services it demanded: "Some call it bootlegging. Some call it racketeering. I call it business. They say I violate the prohibition law. Who doesn't?"

Capone neglected to add that he had also beaten to death several police officers; ordered the execution of dozens of rivals; and bribed mayors, judges, and policemen. Law-enforcement officials led by FBI agent Eliot Ness began to smash Capone's bootlegging operations in 1929. In the end, he was tried and convicted on charges of tax evasion and sentenced to eleven years in prison.

A REPUBLICAN RESURGENCE

In national politics, the small-town backlash against the immorality of modern city life—whether represented by fears of immigrant radicals plotting revolution, liberal churches not taking the Bible literally, or jazzed-up flappers swilling cocktails—was mirrored by a Republican resurgence determined to reverse the progressivism of Theodore Roosevelt and Woodrow Wilson.

Progressivism lost its energies for several reasons. For one thing, its leaders were no more. Roosevelt died in 1919 at the age of sixty, just as he was beginning to campaign for the 1920 Republican presidential nomination. Wilson, too, had envisioned an unprecedented third term, but a stroke forced him to finish out his second term broken physically and mentally.

Many Americans preferred other candidates anyway. Organized labor resented the Wilson administration's crackdown on striking workers in 1919–1920. Farmers in the Great Plains and the West thought that wartime price controls on commodities had discriminated against them. Liberal intellectuals became disillusioned with grassroots democracy because of popular support for Prohibition, the Ku Klux Klan, and religious fundamentalism.

By 1920, middle-class voters had become preoccupied with restoring a "new era" of prosperity based on mass production and mass consumption. Finally, the public turned away from progressivism in part because it had accomplished its major goals: the Eighteenth Amendment (1919), which outlawed alcoholic beverages, and the Nineteenth Amendment (1920), which allowed women nationwide to vote.

Progressivism did not disappear in the 1920s, however. Progressive Republicans and Democrats dominated key leadership positions in Congress during much of the decade even while conservative Republicans occupied the White House. The progressive impulse for honest, efficient government and regulation of business remained strong, especially at the state and local levels, where efforts to improve public education, public health, and social-welfare programs gained momentum during the decade. At the national level, however, conservative Republicans returned to power.

HARDING AND "NORMALCY"   After the Great War and the furious debate over the League of Nations, most Americans were weary of Woodrow Wilson's crusading idealism. Wilson himself recognized the shifting public mood. "It is only once in a generation," he remarked, "that a people can be lifted above material things. That is why conservative government is in the saddle two-thirds of the time."

In 1920, Republican leaders turned to a likeable mediocrity as their presidential candidate: Warren G. Harding, a dapper, silver-haired U.S. senator from Ohio. Harding was selected not for his abilities or experience (which were minimal) but because he was from a key state and looked presidential.

Harding set the conservative tone of his campaign when he told a Boston audience that it was time to end Wilson's progressivism and internationalism: America did not need "heroics, but healing; not nostrums, but normalcy; not revolution, but restoration; not agitation, but adjustment; not surgery, but serenity; not the dramatic, but the dispassionate." Harding pledged to "safeguard America first . . . to exalt America first, to live for and revere America first."

The Democrats were initially encouraged by the Republicans' decision to nominate Harding, but they also had to find a candidate of their own. At their convention, the divided delegates finally chose another Ohioan, James Cox, a former newspaper publisher and three-term governor of the state. For vice president, the convention chose New Yorker Franklin Delano Roosevelt, only thirty-eight years old, who as assistant secretary of the navy occupied the same position his Republican cousin Theodore Roosevelt had once held. Handsome, vigorous, and a stirring speaker, he would deliver more than 1,000 speeches during the campaign.

But Cox's campaign was disorganized and underfunded, and the Democrats struggled against the conservative postwar mood. In the words of progressive journalist William Allen White, Americans were "tired of issues, sick at heart of ideals, and weary of being noble." The Republicans took the offensive, blaming Wilson and the Democrats for the nation's troubles.

Harding won big, getting 16 million votes to 9 million for Cox, who carried no state outside the Solid South. "It wasn't a landslide," a Democratic organizer contended. "It was an earthquake." The lopsided victory increased the Republican majority in both houses of Congress. Franklin Roosevelt predicted that his party could not hope to return to power until the Republicans led the nation "into a serious period of depression and unemployment." He was right.

"JUST A PLAIN FELLOW" Harding's vanilla promise of a **"return to normalcy"** reflected his unexceptional background and limited abilities. One of his own speechwriters admitted that his boss was both "indolent" and "ignorant of most of the big questions that would confront him." A farmer's

The Ohio gang President Warren G. Harding (third from right) surrounded himself with a network of friends, often appointing them to public office despite inferior qualifications.

son and newspaper editor, Harding described himself as "just a plain fellow" who was "old-fashioned and even reactionary in matters of faith and morals" and had pledged "total abstinence" from alcohol.

In fact, however, Harding was a hell-raiser. He drank outlawed liquor in the White House, smoked and chewed tobacco, hosted twice-weekly poker games, and had numerous extramarital affairs and even fathered children with women other than his domineering wife, Florence Harding, whom he called "the Duchess." His dalliances brought him much grief. One of the women blackmailed him, demanding money for her silence—which she received.

The public was virtually unaware of Harding's escapades. Voters saw him as a handsome, charming politician who looked the part of a leader. Yet Harding privately worried about his own limitations. "I am not fit for this office and should never have been here," he once admitted. "I cannot hope to be one of the great presidents, but perhaps I may be remembered as one of the best loved." Tart-tongued Alice Roosevelt Longworth, daughter of Theodore Roosevelt, said Harding "was not a bad man. He was just a slob."

Harding in office had much in common with Ulysses S. Grant. His cabinet, like Grant's, mixed some of the "best minds" in the party, whom he had promised to seek out, with a few of the worst. Charles Evans Hughes, like Grant's Hamilton Fish, became a distinguished secretary of state. Herbert Hoover in the Commerce Department, Andrew W. Mellon in the Treasury Department, and Henry C. Wallace in the Agriculture Department functioned efficiently and made policy on their own. Other cabinet members and administrative appointees, however, were not so conscientious. The secretary of the interior landed in prison, and the attorney general narrowly escaped serving time. Many lesser offices went to members of the "Ohio gang," a group of Harding's drinking buddies who met in a house on K Street near the White House to help the president relieve the pressures of his high office.

Harding and his lieutenants set about dismantling or neutralizing many progressive regulatory laws and agencies. The president's four Supreme Court appointments were all conservatives, including Chief Justice William Howard Taft, who announced that he had been "appointed to reverse a few decisions." During the 1920s, the Taft-led court struck down a federal child-labor law and a minimum-wage law for women, issued numerous injunctions against striking unions, and passed rulings limiting the powers of federal agencies that regulated big businesses.

ANDREW MELLON AND THE ECONOMY The Harding administration inherited a slumping economy burdened by high wartime taxes and a national debt that had ballooned from $1 billion in 1914 to $27 billion in 1920 because of the expenses associated with the war. Unemployment was at nearly 12 percent.

To generate economic growth, Secretary of the Treasury Andrew Mellon, at the time the third-richest man in the world behind John D. Rockefeller and Henry Ford, developed what came to be called the Mellon plan, which called for reducing federal spending and lowering tax rates. Mellon persuaded Congress to pass the landmark Budget and Accounting Act of 1921, which created a Bureau of the Budget to streamline the process of preparing an annual federal budget to be approved by Congress. The bill also created a General Accounting Office to audit spending by federal agencies. This act fulfilled a long-held progressive desire to bring greater efficiency and nonpartisanship to the budget preparation process.

The brilliant but cold Mellon (his son described him as a "thin-voiced, thin-bodied, shy and uncommunicative man") also proposed a series of tax reductions. By 1918, the tax rate on the highest income bracket had risen to 73 percent. Mellon believed that such high rates were pushing wealthy Americans to avoid paying taxes by investing their money in foreign countries or in tax-free government bonds. His policies systematically reduced tax rates while increasing tax revenues. The top tax rate was cut from 73 percent in 1921 to 24 percent in 1929. Rates for individuals with the lowest annual incomes were also cut substantially, helping the working poor.

By 1926, those with incomes of $300,000 or more were the source of 65 percent of federal income tax revenue. In 1921, less than 20 percent had come from this group. During this same period, the overall tax burden on those with incomes of less than $10,000 dropped from $155 million to $32.5 million. By 1929, barely 2 percent of American workers had to pay any income tax at all.

At the same time, Mellon helped Harding reduce the federal budget from its wartime highs. Government expenditures fell, as did the national debt, and the economy soared. Unemployment plummeted to 2.4 percent in 1923. Mellon's supporters labeled him the greatest secretary of the Treasury since Alexander Hamilton in the late eighteenth century.

In addition to tax cuts, Mellon, who had earlier built huge empires in the steel, oil, shipbuilding, coal, banking, and aluminum industries, promoted the long-standing Republican policy of high tariffs on imported goods. The Fordney-McCumber Tariff of 1922 increased rates on imported chemical and metal products to help prevent the revival of German corporations that had dominated those industries before the Great War. To please commercial farmers, the new act included tariffs on agricultural imports as well.

REDUCED REGULATION The Republican economic program also sought to dismantle or neutralize many progressive regulatory laws and agencies. Harding appointed commissioners to these federal agencies who would promote "regulatory capitalism" and policies "friendly" to business interests. The prominent Republican senator Henry Cabot Lodge, who helped guide Harding's choice of men to lead the regulatory agencies, boasted that "we have torn up Wilsonism by the roots."

RACIAL PROGRESSIVISM In one area, however, Warren G. Harding proved to be more progressive than Woodrow Wilson. He reversed the Wilson administration's segregationist policy of excluding African Americans from federal government jobs. He also spoke out against the vigilante racism that had flared up across the country during and after the war. In his first speech to a joint session of Congress in 1921, Harding insisted that the nation must deal with the festering "race question." The horrific racial incidents were a stain on America's democratic ideals. The new president, unlike his Democratic predecessor, attacked the Ku Klux Klan for fomenting "hatred and prejudice and violence," and he urged Congress "to wipe the stain of barbaric lynching from the banners of a free and orderly, representative democracy." The Senate, however, failed to pass the bill Harding promoted.

SETBACKS FOR UNIONS Urban workers shared in the affluence of the 1920s. "A workman is far better paid in America than anywhere else in the world," a French visitor wrote in 1927, "and his standard of living is enormously higher." Nonfarm workers gained about 30 percent in real wages between 1921 and 1928, while farm income rose only 10 percent. Yet organized labor suffered in the 1920s. Although President Harding endorsed collective bargaining and tried to reduce the twelve-hour workday and the six-day workweek to give the working class "time for leisure and family life," he ran into stiff opposition in Congress. The widespread strikes of 1919 had created fears that unions promoted radical socialism.

Between January 1920 and August 1921, the unemployment rate jumped from 2 percent to 14 percent, and industrial production fell by 23 percent as

The Gastonia strike These textile workers pit their strength against that of a National Guardsman during a strike at the Loray Mill in Gastonia, North Carolina, in 1929.

the economy made the transition from war to peace. The brief postwar depression so weakened the unions that in 1921 business groups in Chicago designated the **open shop** to be the "American plan" of employment. Unlike the closed shop, which forced businesses to hire only union members, the open shop gave an employer the right to hire anyone. A labor organizer identified another reason for the weakness of unions in the New Era: "The Ford car has done an awful lot of harm to the unions. . . . As long as men have enough money to buy a second-hand Ford and tires and gasoline, they'll be out on the road and paying no attention to union meetings."

Employers often required workers to sign "yellow-dog" contracts, which forced them to agree not to join a union. Owners also used labor spies, blacklists, and intimidation to block unions. Some employers, such as Henry Ford, tried to kill the unions with kindness by introducing programs of "industrial democracy," guided by company-sponsored unions, or various schemes of "welfare capitalism," such as profit sharing, bonuses, pensions, health programs, and recreational activities.

The result was that union membership dropped from about 5 million in 1920 to 3.5 million in 1929 as industrial production soared and joblessness fell to 3 percent. But the anti-union effort, led by businesses that wanted to keep wages low and unions weak, helped to create a "purchasing-power crisis" whereby the working poor were not earning enough income to buy the abundance of goods being churned out by ever more-productive industries. Productivity increased by 43 percent in the Roaring Twenties, but wages barely rose. In fact, large groups of hourly workers, such as miners and textile mill hands, saw their income *drop*. Executives used company profits to pay dividends to stockholders, invest in new equipment, and increase their own salaries, while doing little to help wage earners. In 1929, an estimated 5 percent of the nation's workforce (executives) received one-third of the nation's income.

In other words, the much-trumpeted "new economy" was not benefiting enough working-class Americans to be sustainable. The gap between income levels and purchasing power would be a major cause of the Great Depression, as the Republican formula of high tariffs, low wages, low taxes, little regulation, and anti-unionism would eventually implode.

Isolationism in Foreign Affairs

In addition to the Senate's rejection of American membership in the League of Nations, the postwar spirit of isolation found other expressions. George Jean Nathan, a drama critic, expressed the sentiments of many Americans when he announced that the "great problems of the world—social, political, economic and theological—do not concern me in the slightest. . . . What concerns me alone is myself, and the interests of a few close friends."

Yet the desire to stay out of foreign wars did not mean that the United States could ignore its expanding global interests. As a result of the Great War, the United States had become the world's chief banker, and American investments and loans enabled foreigners to purchase U.S. exports.

WAR DEBTS AND REPARATIONS Probably nothing did more to heighten America's isolationism from foreign affairs—and anti-American feelings among Europeans—than the complex issue of paying off huge war debts during the 1920s. In 1917, when France and Great Britain ran out of money to pay for military supplies during the First World War, the U.S. government had advanced them massive loans, first for the war effort and then for postwar reconstruction projects.

Most Americans, including Andrew W. Mellon, expected the war-related debts to be paid back, but Europeans had a different perception. The European Allies had held off the German army at great cost while the United States was raising an army in 1917. The British also noted that after the American Revolution, the newly independent United States had repudiated old debts to British investors; the French likewise pointed out that they had never been repaid for helping the Americans win the Revolution and gain their independence.

But the most difficult challenges in the 1920s were the practical problems of repayment. To get U.S. dollars to use to pay their war-related debts, European nations had to sell their goods to the United States. However, soaring American tariff rates during the 1920s made imported European goods more expensive and the war-related debts incurred by Britain and France harder to pay. The French and the British insisted that they could repay their debts to the United States only if they could collect the $33 billion in reparations owed them by defeated Germany. That was an unrealistic assumption because the German economy was in a shambles during the 1920s, ravaged by runaway inflation.

Twice during the 1920s the financial strain on Germany brought the structure of international payments to the verge of collapse, and both times the international Reparations Commission called in private American bankers to work out rescue plans. Loans provided by U.S. banks thus propped up the German economy so that Germany could pay its reparations to Britain and France, thereby enabling them to pay their debts to the United States.

ATTEMPTS AT DISARMAMENT After the Great War, many Americans decided that the best way to keep the peace was to limit the size of armies and navies. The United States had no intention of maintaining a large army after 1920, but under the shipbuilding program begun in 1916, it had constructed a powerful navy second only to that of Great Britain. Although neither the British nor the Americans wanted a naval armaments race, both were worried about the growth of Japanese power.

To address the problem, President Harding in 1921 invited diplomats from eight nations to a peace conference in Washington, D.C., at which Secretary of State Charles Evans Hughes made a blockbuster proposal. The only way out of an expensive naval arms race, he declared, "is to end it now" by eliminating scores of existing warships. He pledged that America would junk 30 battleships and cruisers and then named 36 British and Japanese warships that would also be destroyed. It was one of the most dramatic moments in diplomatic history. The stunned audience of diplomats, ambassadors, admirals, and senators stood and roared its approval. In less than fifteen minutes, one journalist reported, Hughes had destroyed more warships "than all the admirals of the world have sunk in a cycle of centuries."

Following Hughes's lead, delegates from the United States, Britain, Japan, France, and Italy signed the Five-Power Treaty (1922), which limited the size of their navies. It was the first disarmament treaty in history. The agreement also, in effect, divided the world into regions: U.S. naval power became supreme in the Western Hemisphere, Japanese power in the western Pacific, and British power from the North Sea to Singapore.

THE KELLOGG-BRIAND PACT During and after the Great War, many Americans embraced the fanciful ideal of simply abolishing war with a stroke of a pen. In 1921, a wealthy Chicagoan founded the American Committee for the Outlawry of War. "We can outlaw this war system just as we outlawed slavery and the saloon," said one of the more enthusiastic converts.

The seductive notion of simply abolishing war culminated in the signing of the Kellogg-Briand Pact. This unique treaty started with an initiative by the French foreign minister Aristide Briand, who in 1927 proposed to Secretary of State Frank B. Kellogg that the two countries agree never to go to war against each other. This innocent-seeming proposal was actually a clever ploy to draw the United States into the French security system by the back door. In any future war, for instance, such a pact would inhibit the United States from seeking reprisals in response to any French intrusions on neutral rights. Kellogg was outraged to discover that Briand had urged leaders of the American peace movement to put pressure on the government to sign the accord.

Kellogg then turned the tables on Briand. He countered with a plan to have all nations sign the pact. Caught in a trap of his own making, the French foreign minister finally agreed. The Pact of Paris (its official name), signed on August 27, 1928, declared that the signatories "renounce it [war] as an instrument of national policy." Eventually sixty-two nations signed the pact, but all reserved the right of "self-defense" as an escape hatch. The U.S. Senate ratified the agreement by a vote of 85 to 1. One senator who voted for "this worthless, but perfectly harmless peace treaty" wrote a friend later that he feared it would "confuse the minds of many good people who think that peace may be secured by polite professions of neighborly and brotherly love."

THE WORLD COURT The isolationist mood in the United States was no better illustrated than in the repeated refusal by the Senate during the 1920s to approve American membership in the World Court, formally called the Permanent Court of International Justice, at The Hague in the Netherlands. Created in 1921 by the League of Nations, the World Court, composed of fifteen international judges, was intended to arbitrate disputes between nations. Presidents Harding, Coolidge, and Hoover all asked the Senate during the 1920s to approve American membership in the World Court, but the legislative body refused, for the same reasons that the Senate had refused to sign the Versailles Treaty: they did not want the United States to be bound in any way by an international organization.

IMPROVING RELATIONS IN LATIN AMERICA The isolationist attitude during the 1920s led the decade's Republican presidents—Harding, Calvin Coolidge, and Herbert Hoover—to soothe tensions with America's neighbors to the south, most of which harbored long-festering resentments against "Yankee imperialism." The Harding administration agreed in 1921 to pay the republic of Colombia the $25 million it had demanded for America's rights to the Panama Canal. In 1924, American troops left the Dominican Republic after eight years of intervention. U.S. Marines left Nicaragua in 1925 but returned a year later at the outbreak of disorder and civil war. There, in 1927, the Coolidge administration brought both parties into an agreement for U.S.-supervised elections, but one rebel leader, César Augusto Sandino, held out, and the marines stayed until 1933.

The troubles in Nicaragua increased strains between the United States and Mexico. Relations had already been soured by repeated Mexican threats to expropriate American oil properties in Mexico. In 1928, however, the U.S. ambassador negotiated an agreement protecting American rights acquired before 1917. Expropriation did in fact occur in 1938, but the Mexican government agreed to reimburse American owners.

Teapot Dome scandal In this 1924 political cartoon, Republican officials try to outrun the Teapot Dome scandal, represented by a giant steamrolling teapot, on an oil-slicked highway.

THE HARDING SCANDALS

As time passed, President Harding found himself increasingly distracted by scandals in his administration. Early in 1923, the head of the Veterans Bureau resigned when faced with an investigation for stealing medical and hospital supplies intended for former servicemen. A few weeks later, the legal adviser to the bureau killed himself. Soon thereafter, Jesse Smith, a colleague of Attorney General Harry M. Daugherty who was illegally selling federal paroles, pardons, and judgeships from his Justice Department office, was found shot dead in a hotel room after he had threatened to "quit the racket." Then, Daugherty himself was accused of selling for personal gain German assets seized after the war. When asked to testify about the matter, he refused on the grounds that doing so might incriminate him.

The most serious of the scandals was called the "**Teapot Dome Affair.**" The Teapot Dome was a government-owned oil field in Wyoming that provided reserve fuel for warships. After Harding moved administrative control of the oil field from the Department of the Navy to the Department of the Interior, Secretary of the Interior Albert B. Fall, deeply in debt and eight years overdue in paying his taxes, began signing overly generous federal contracts with close friends who were executives of petroleum companies that wanted access to the oil. In doing so, Fall took bribes of about $400,000 from an oil tycoon. Fall was convicted of conspiracy and bribery and sentenced to a year in prison, the first former cabinet official to serve time because of misconduct in office.

How much Harding knew of the scandals remains unclear, but he knew enough to be troubled. "My God, this is a hell of a job!" he confided to a journalist. "I have no trouble with my enemies; I can take care of my enemies all right. But my damn friends, my God-damn friends. . . . They're the ones that keep me walking the floor nights!"

In 1923, Harding left on what would be his last journey, a speaking tour to the West Coast and a trip to the Alaska Territory. Along the way, he discussed with Herbert Hoover, the secretary of commerce, what he should do about the scandal involving Albert Fall. Hoover gave the correct response: "Publish it, and at least get credit for integrity on your side." Before Harding had time to act on such advice, he suffered an attack of food poisoning in Seattle, then seemed to be recovering, only to die in San Francisco. He was fifty-seven years old.

Largely as a result of Harding's corrupt associates, his administration came to be viewed as one of the worst in history. Even Hoover admitted that Harding was not "a man with either the experience or the intellectual quality that the position needed" and that he was unable to admit or resolve the "terrible corruption by his playmates."

More recent assessments, however, suggest that the scandals obscured Harding's accomplishments. He led the nation out of the turmoil of the postwar years and helped create the economic boom of the 1920s. He endorsed diversity and civil rights and was a forceful proponent of women's rights. Still, even Harding's foremost scholarly defender admits that he lacked good judgment and "probably should never have been president."

COOLIDGE CONSERVATISM

The news of Harding's death reached Vice President Calvin Coolidge when he was visiting his father in the isolated village of Plymouth Notch, Vermont, his birthplace. There, at 2:47 A.M. on August 3, 1923, Colonel John Coolidge, a farmer and merchant, issued the presidential oath of office to his son.

Calvin Coolidge, born on the fourth of July in 1872, was a throwback to an earlier era. A puritan in his personal life, he was horrified by the jazzed-up

Roaring Twenties. He sincerely believed in the ideals of personal integrity and devotion to public service, and, like Harding, he was an evangelist for capitalism and minimal government regulation of business.

AN INACTIVE PRESIDENT Although Coolidge had won every political race he had entered, beginning in 1898, he had never loved the limelight. Shy and awkward, he was a man of famously few words—hence, his nickname, "Silent Cal." Voters liked his uprightness, his straight-talking style, and his personal humility. He was a simple, direct man of strong principles and intense patriotism who championed self-discipline and hard work. Alice Roosevelt Longworth said the atmosphere in the Coolidge White House compared to that of Harding was "as different as a New England front parlor is from the back room in a speak easy." Coolidge, she quipped, looked like he had been "weaned on a pickle."

As a state senator in Massachusetts, Coolidge had often aligned himself with Republican progressives. He voted for women's suffrage, a state income tax, a minimum wage for female workers, and salary increases for public school teachers. By the time he entered the White House, however, he had abandoned most of those causes.

Calvin Coolidge "Silent Cal" was so inactive as president that when he died in 1933, American humorist Dorothy Parker remarked, "How could they tell?"

Coolidge was determined *not* to be an activist president. Walter Lippmann, the foremost political journalist of the twenties, wryly observed that "it is a grim, determined, alert inactivity, which keeps Mr. Coolidge occupied constantly." To Coolidge, activist presidents created more problems than solutions. Unlike Theodore Roosevelt and Woodrow Wilson, he knew he was "not a great man." Nor did he have an ambitious program to push through Congress. "Four-fifths of our troubles," Coolidge believed, "would disappear if we would sit down and keep still." Following his own logic, he insisted on twelve hours of sleep *and* a lengthy afternoon nap. The irreverent journalist H. L. Mencken claimed that Coolidge "slept more than any other president."

EVANGELIST FOR CAPITALISM Americans embraced the unflappability and unstained integrity of Silent Cal. He was refreshingly simple and direct, a man of strong principles, intense patriotism, pinched frugality, and few words. He promoted his regressive conservatism with a ruthless consistency. Even more than Harding, Coolidge linked the nation's welfare with the success of big business. "The chief business of the American people is business," he preached. "The man who builds a factory builds a temple. The man who works there worships there." Coolidge famously declared that "wealth is the *chief* end of man."

With the help of Treasury Secretary Mellon and Republican-controlled Congresses, Coolidge continued Harding's efforts to lower income tax rates. Where Harding had sought to balance the interests of labor, agriculture, and industry, he focused on promoting industrial development by limiting federal regulation of business and industry and reducing taxes.

The nation had too many laws, Coolidge insisted, and "we would be better off if we did not have any more." True to his word, he vetoed fifty acts of Congress. As a journalist said, "In a great day of yes-men, Calvin Coolidge was a no-man." After having dinner with the president at the White House, Colonel House, the prominent Democrat, decided that "he has more ability than I had given him credit for, but he has little imagination and no initiative. He will make a safe President," but would not do "anything brilliant or spectacular."

Coolidge was also "obsessed" with reducing federal spending, even to the point of issuing government workers only one pencil at a time—and only after they turned in the stub of the old pencil. His fiscal frugality and pro-business stance led the *Wall Street Journal* to rejoice: "Never before, here or anywhere else, has a government been so completely fused with business."

In filling out Harding's unexpired term, Calvin Coolidge distanced himself from the scandals of the administration by putting in charge of the prosecutions two lawyers of undoubted integrity. A man of honesty and ability, he was a good administrator who delegated well and managed Republican factions adroitly.

THE ELECTION OF 1924 Coolidge restored the dignity of the presidency while capably managing the warring Republican factions. He easily gained the party's 1924 presidential nomination.

Meanwhile, the Democrats again fell to fighting among themselves, prompting humorist Will Rogers's classic statement that "I am a member of no organized political party. I am a Democrat." The party's fractiousness reflected the ongoing divisions between urban and rural America, North and South. The nominating convention split down the middle on a proposal to express disapproval of Ku Klux Klan bigotry. It then took 103 ballots to decide on a presidential candidate: former ambassador John W. Davis, a prominent Wall Street lawyer from West Virginia who could nearly outdo Coolidge in his limited-government conservatism.

While the Democrats bickered, rural populists and urban progressives decided to abandon both major parties, as they had done in 1912. Reorganizing the old Progressive party, they nominated Robert M. "Fighting Bob" La Follette for president. As a Republican senator, La Follette had voted against the 1917 declaration of war against Germany. Now, in addition to the Progressives, he won the support of the Socialist party and the American Federation of Labor.

In the 1924 election, Coolidge swept both the popular and the electoral votes by decisive majorities. Davis and the Democrats took only the solidly Democratic South, and La Follette carried only Wisconsin, his home state. The popular vote went 15.7 million for Coolidge, 8.4 million for Davis, and 4.8 million for La Follette—the largest popular vote ever polled by a third-party candidate up to that time.

Coolidge's big victory represented the height of postwar political conservatism. Business executives interpreted the Republican victory as an endorsement of their influence on government, and Coolidge saw the economy's surging prosperity as confirmation of his aggressive support of the interests of business.

THE RISE OF HERBERT HOOVER

During the twenties, the drive for industrial efficiency, which had been a prominent theme among progressives, powered the wheels of mass production and consumption and became a cardinal belief of Republican leaders. Herbert Hoover, secretary of commerce in the Harding and Coolidge cabinets, was himself a remarkable success story.

Born into an Iowa farm family in 1874, orphaned at age eight, and raised by Quaker uncles in Iowa and Oregon, he was a shy but industrious "loner" who graduated from Stanford University and became a world-renowned mining engineer, oil tycoon, financial wizard, and multimillionaire before the age of forty. His meteoric success and genius for managing difficult tasks bred in him a self-confidence that bordered on conceit. Short-tempered and quick to take offense, Hoover had to have complete control of any project he managed. In his twenties, he was already planning to be president of the United States.

A PROGRESSIVE CONSERVATIVE After applying his managerial skills to the Food Administration during the Great War, Hoover served with the U.S. delegation at the Versailles peace conference. He idolized Woodrow Wilson and supported American membership in the League of Nations. A young Franklin Roosevelt, then assistant secretary of the navy, was dazzled by Hoover, the man he would eventually defeat in the presidential election of 1932. In 1920, Roosevelt said that Hoover was "certainly a wonder [boy], and I wish we could make him President of the United States."

Hoover, however, soon disappointed Roosevelt by declaring himself a Republican "progressive conservative." In a book titled *American Individualism* (1922), Hoover wrote of an "ideal of *service*" that went beyond "rugged individualism" to promote the greater good. He wanted government officials to encourage business leaders to forgo "cutthroat competition" and engage in "voluntary cooperation" by forming trade associations that would share information and promote standardization and efficiency.

As secretary of commerce during the 1920s, Hoover transformed the small Commerce Department into the government's most dynamic agency. He looked for new markets for business, created a Bureau of Aviation to promote the new airline industry, and established the Federal Radio Commission.

THE BUSINESS OF FARMING During the 1920s, agriculture remained the weakest sector in the economy. The wartime boom fed by agricultural exports lasted into 1920 before commodity prices collapsed as European agricultural production returned to prewar levels. Overproduction brought

Farming technology Mechanization became increasingly important in early twentieth-century agriculture. Here, farmers pose alongside their new equipment, ca. 1920.

lower prices for crops that persisted into 1923, and after that, improvement was spotty. A bumper cotton crop in 1926 resulted only in a price collapse and an early taste of depression in much of the South, where foreclosures and bankruptcies spread.

Yet the most successful farms, like the most successful corporations, were getting larger, more efficient, and more mechanized. By 1930, about 13 percent of all farmers had tractors; the proportion was even higher on the western plains. Better plows, harvesters, combines, and other machines accompanied improved crop yields, fertilizers, and methods of animal breeding.

Most farmers, however, were still struggling to survive. They asked for political help, and in 1924, Senator Charles L. McNary of Oregon and Representative Gilbert N. Haugen of Iowa introduced the first McNary-Haugen bill, which sought to secure "equality for agriculture in the benefits of the protective tariff." The proposed bill called for surplus American crops to be sold on the world market to raise prices in the home market. The goal was to achieve "parity"—that is, to raise domestic prices so that farmers would have the same purchasing power relative to the prices they had enjoyed between 1909 and 1914, a time viewed as a golden age of American agriculture.

The McNary-Haugen bill passed both houses of Congress in 1927 but was vetoed by President Coolidge, who dismissed it as unsound and unconstitutional. The process was repeated in 1928. In a broader sense, however, McNary-Haugenism did not fail. The debates over the bill made the "farm problem" a national policy issue and defined it as a matter of surpluses. Moreover, the evolution of the McNary-Haugen plan revived the idea of a political alliance between the rural South and the West, a coalition that in the next decade would have a dominant influence on national farm policy.

THE 1928 ELECTION: HOOVER VERSUS SMITH On August 2, 1927, while on vacation in the Black Hills of South Dakota, President Coolidge suddenly announced, "I do not choose to run for President in 1928." His decision surprised the nation and cleared the way for Hoover to win the Republican nomination. The party's platform took credit for the nation's longest period of sustained prosperity, the government's cost cutting, debt and tax reduction, and the high tariffs ("as vital to American agriculture as . . . to manufacturing") designed to "protect" American businesses from foreign competition.

The Democratic nomination went to four-term New York governor Alfred E. Smith, called the "Happy Warrior" by Franklin D. Roosevelt in his nominating speech. The candidates presented sharply different images: Hoover, the successful businessman and bureaucratic manager from an Iowa farm, and Smith, a professional Irish American politician from New York City's Lower East

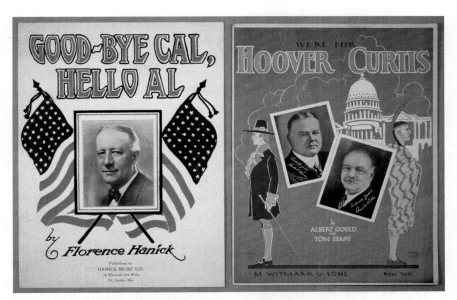

Campaign sheet music The sheet music for the Democratic nominee, Alfred E. Smith (left), and the Republican nominee, Herbert Hoover (right), drew on popular tunes and motifs of the time.

Side. To working-class Democrats in northern cities, Smith was a hero, the poor grandson of Irish Catholic immigrants who had worked himself up to governor of the most populous state. His outspoken criticism of Prohibition also endeared him to the Irish, Italians, and others who wanted to have a drink at a saloon.

On the other hand, as the first Roman Catholic nominated for president by a major party, a product of New York's machine-run politics, and a "wet" on Prohibition (in direct opposition to his party's platform), Smith represented all that was opposed by southern and western rural Democrats—as well as most rural and small-town Republicans. A Kansas newspaper editor declared that the "whole puritan civilization, which has built a sturdy, orderly nation, is threatened by Smith." The Ku Klux Klan issued a "Klarion Kall for a Krusade" against him, mailing thousands of postcards proclaiming that "Alcohol" Smith, the Catholic New Yorker, was the Antichrist.

While Hoover stayed above the fray, reminding Americans of their unparalleled prosperity and promising a "job for every man," Smith was forced to deal with constant criticism. He denounced his opponents for injecting "bigotry, hatred, intolerance and un-American sectarian division" into the campaign.

Herbert Hoover "I have no fears for the future of our country," Hoover told the nation at his inauguration in 1929.

But no Democrat could have beaten Hoover in 1928. The nation was prosperous and at peace, and Hoover seemed the best person to sustain the good times. He was perhaps the best-trained economic mind ever to run for president, and he was widely viewed as the brilliant engineer "who never failed."

On Election Day, Hoover, the first Quaker to be president, won in a landslide, with 21 million popular votes to Smith's 15 million and an electoral college majority of 444 to 87. He even penetrated the Democrats' Solid South, winning Virginia, North Carolina, Tennessee, Florida, and Texas, leaving Smith only six Deep South states plus Massachusetts and Rhode Island. Republicans also kept control of both houses of Congress.

Hidden in the results, however, was a glimpse of hope for Democrats. Overall, Smith's vote total, especially strong in the largest cities, doubled that of John Davis four years earlier. In 1932, Franklin D. Roosevelt would build upon that momentum to win back the presidency for the Democrats.

But for now, Hoover was in command. Coolidge, however, was skeptical that Hoover could sustain the good times. He quipped that the "Wonder Boy" had offered him "unsolicited advice for six years, all of it bad." Coolidge's doubts about Hoover's political abilities would prove all too accurate, as the new president would soon be struck by an economic earthquake that would test all of his skills—and expose his weaknesses as a leader.

THE CAUSES OF THE GREAT DEPRESSION

Herbert Hoover's election in 1928 boosted the hopes of investors in what had come to be called "the Great Bull Market." Since 1924, the prices of stock shares invested in U.S. companies had steadily risen. Beginning in 1927, prices soared further on wings of reckless speculation driven by a mass mania unmatched in history. In 1919, some 317 million shares of stock changed hands; in 1929, the number was more than a billion. Much of the nation's total capital was sucked into the stock market. Treasury Secretary Andrew W. Mellon's tax reductions had given people more money to spend or invest, and much of it went into the stock market. In some respects, the stock market had become the economy. In April 1929, Hoover voiced concern about the "orgy of mad speculation" in the stock market and urged investors to be more cautious—while privately telling his own broker to sell many of his stock holdings.

THE STOCK MARKET What made it so easy for hundreds of thousands of people to invest in stocks was the common practice of buying "on margin"—that is, an investor could make a small cash down payment (the "margin") on shares of stock and borrow the rest from a stockbroker, who held the stock certificates as security in case the price plummeted. If stock prices rose, as they did in 1927, 1928, and most of 1929, the investor made enough profits to pay for the "margin loan" and reinvest the rest.

But if the stock price declined and the buyer failed to meet a "margin call" for cash to pay off the broker's loan, the broker could sell the stock at a much lower price to cover the loan. By August 1929, stockbrokers were lending investors more than two-thirds of the face value of the stocks they were buying. Yet few people seemed concerned, and stock prices kept rising.

Despite the soaring stock market, there were signs that the economy was weakening. By 1927, steel production, residential construction, and automobile sales were slowing, as was the rate of consumer spending. By mid-1929, industrial production, employment, and other measures of economic activity were also declining. Still, the stock market rose.

Then, in early September 1929, the speculative bubble burst when the stock market fell sharply. By the middle of October, world markets had gone into a steep decline. Still, most investors remained upbeat. The nation's foremost economist, Irving Fisher of Yale University, told investors on October 17 that "stock prices have reached what looks like a permanently high plateau." Five days later, a leading bank president assured reporters that there was "nothing fundamentally wrong with the stock market or with the underlying business and credit structure."

THE CRASH The next week, however, stock market values wobbled, then tumbled again, triggering a wild scramble among terrified investors. As they rushed to sell their shares, the decline in stock prices accelerated. On Black Tuesday, October 29—the worst day in the stock market's history to that point—widespread panic set in. Stock prices went into free fall, and brokers found themselves flooded with stocks they could not sell. On that day, investors lost $15 billion. By the end of the month, they had lost $50 billion.

An atmosphere of gloom settled over the financial community. "Life would no longer be, ever again, all fun and games," comedian Harpo Marx sighed as he anticipated the onset of the worst depression in history. Even the zany Marx Brothers movies during the thirties could not "laugh the big bad wolf of the Depression out of the public mind."

The carefree pleasure-seeking of the Jazz Age ended not with a whimper but with the booming crash on Wall Street. Fear and uncertainty spread like a virus across the nation and the world.

Wild rumors circulated of fortunes lost and careers ruined. Investors who had borrowed heavily to buy stocks were now forced to sell their holdings at huge losses so they could pay their debts. Some stockbrokers and investors committed suicide. In New York, the president of a bankrupt cigar company jumped off the ledge of a hotel, and two business partners joined hands and leaped to their deaths from the Ritz Hotel. Room clerks in Manhattan hotels began asking guests at registration if they wanted a room for jumping or sleeping.

The national economy began to sputter and stumble. In 1930, at least 26,355 businesses shut down; even more failed the following year. The resulting slowdown in economic growth, called a *recession*, became so severe and long-lasting that it came to be known as the Great Depression. But the collapse of the stock market did not *cause* the **Great Depression**. Rather, it revealed that the prosperity of the 1920s had been built on weak foundations.

The stock market crash had the added effect of creating a psychological panic that accelerated the economic decline. Frightened of losing everything, people rushed to take their money out of banks and out of the stock market. Such behavior only made things worse. By 1932, more than 9,000 banks had closed as the nation's formerly robust economy experienced a shocking collapse.

WHY THE ECONOMY COLLAPSED

What were the underlying *causes* of the Great Depression? Most scholars emphasize a combination of interrelated elements.

The economy had actually begun to fall into a recession months *before* the stock market crash. Put most simply, the once roaring economy fell victim to *overproduction* and *underconsumption*. During the twenties, manufacturing production increased 43 percent, but the purchasing power of consumers did not grow nearly as fast. In essence, the economy was producing more and more products that consumers could not afford to buy, and too many people had been borrowing too much money for unproductive purposes, such as speculating in the stock market.

Bank run As news of the Great Crash spread across the world, people rushed to banks to withdraw their deposits. The line for this Millbury, Massachusetts, savings bank wraps around the building.

Too many business owners had taken large profits while denying wage increases to employees. By plowing profits into business expansion, executive salaries, and stock dividends rather than wage increases, employers created a growing imbalance between production and consumption, supply and demand. Because union membership plummeted during the twenties, organized labor no longer exerted as much leverage with management over wage increases. Two-thirds of families in 1929 earned less than $2,000 annually, an amount said by economists to provide "only basic necessities."

At the same time that the stock market was crashing, factories were reducing production or shutting down altogether. From 1929 to 1933, U.S. economic output (called *gross domestic product*, or GDP) dropped almost 27 percent. By 1932, one-quarter of the workforce was out of work. As the financial and industrial sectors collapsed, the farm sector stagnated. Farm incomes had soared during the Great War because the European nations needed American grains, beef, and pork. Eager to sustain their prosperity, farmers took out mortgages to buy more acreage or equipment to boost output. Increasing production during the twenties, however, led to lower prices for grains and livestock. To make matters worse, record harvests in the summer and fall of 1929 caused prices for corn, wheat, and cotton to fall precipitously, pinching the income of farmers with mounting debts.

GOVERNMENT'S ROLE Government policies also contributed to the Depression. High tariffs hurt the economy by reducing foreign trade. Like most Republican presidents, Herbert Hoover supported congressional efforts to raise tariffs on imported goods to keep out foreign competition. The Smoot-Hawley Tariff of 1930, authored by Republicans Reed Owen Smoot and Willis C. Hawley, was intended to help the farm sector by raising tariff barriers on farm products imported into the United States. But a swarm of corporate lobbyists convinced Congress to add hundreds of new imported manufactured items to the tariff bill.

More than 1,000 economists urged Hoover to veto the tariff bill because its logic was flawed: by trying to "protect" American farmers from foreign competition, the bill would actually raise prices on most raw materials and consumer products. And by reducing European imports into the United States, the bill would make it much harder for France and Great Britain to repay their war debts. Hoover signed the bill anyway, causing another steep drop in the stock market. The Smoot-Hawley Tariff also prompted other countries to retaliate by passing tariffs of their own, thereby making it more difficult for American farms and businesses to sell their products abroad. U.S. exports plummeted, worsening the Depression.

Another factor contributing to the Great Depression was the stance of the Federal Reserve Board ("the Fed"), the government agency that served as a "central bank" by managing the nation's money supply and interest rates. Instead of expanding the money supply to generate growth, the Federal Reserve did the reverse, reducing the money supply out of concern for possible inflation in consumer prices. Between 1929 and 1932, the money supply shrank by a third, leading almost 10,000 small banks to close—and take millions of their depositors with them into bankruptcy.

THE IMPACT OF EUROPE A final cause of the Depression was the chaotic state of the European economy, which had never fully recovered from the Great War. During the late 1920s, nations such as Great Britain, France, Spain, and Italy slowed their purchases of American goods as their economies began slowly recovering. Meanwhile, the German economy continued to flounder.

A related factor was the inability of European nations to pay their war debts to each other—and to the United States. The American government insisted that the $11 billion it had loaned the Allies be repaid, but Great Britain and France had no money. They were forced to borrow huge sums ($5 billion) from U.S. banks, which only increased their overall indebtedness. After the stock market crash in October 1929, American banks could no longer prop up the European economies.

The Federal Reserve's tighter monetary policy also drastically slowed the amount of American capital (money) going abroad. The German economy, which had grown dependent on loans from American banks, was devastated as American money dried up. Then the Smoot-Hawley Tariff made it even more difficult for European nations to sell their products in the United States. So as the European economy sputtered, it dragged the American economy deeper into depression.

The Human Toll of the Depression

The Depression came to be called "Great" because its effects were so severe and long lasting. By 1932, perhaps a quarter of the U.S. population could not afford housing or adequate food. The carefree optimism of the twenties disappeared; grassroots protests erupted as the Depression worsened. Hungry people looted grocery stores, angry mobs stopped local sheriffs from foreclosing on farms, and judges were threatened at bankruptcy hearings.

Some talked of revolution and radical change. "Folks are restless," Mississippi governor Theodore Bilbo told reporters in 1931. "Communism is gaining a foothold. . . . In fact, I'm getting a little pink myself." Yet for all the radical talk, few Americans embraced communism. "There was anger and rebellion among a few," recounted an Iowa farmer, but most people lived in "helpless despair and submission."

UNEMPLOYMENT AND "RELIEF" As the economy spiraled downward between 1930 and 1933, growing numbers of workers were fired or had their wages cut. Unemployment soared to 4 million in 1930, then 8 million in 1931, and to 12 million by 1932.

Desperate unemployed city dwellers became street-corner merchants. Some 6,000 jobless New Yorkers sold apples on street corners to survive. They could buy a crate of apples grown in the Pacific Northwest for $1.75. If they sold a crate of sixty apples at a nickel apiece, they could pocket $1.25. The motto of the apple sellers was, "Buy an apple a day and eat the Depression away."

Many struggling business executives and professionals—lawyers, doctors, dentists, accountants, stockbrokers, teachers, nurses, and engineers—went without food and medical care to save money and avoid the humiliation of "going on relief." The sense of shame cut across class lines. In *The Grapes of Wrath* (1939), John Steinbeck's best-selling novel about the victims of the Depression, a poor but proud woman is disgraced by accepting "charity" from the Salvation Army: "We was hungry. They made us crawl for our dinner. They took our dignity."

HUNGER Hard-pressed families went without fruit and most vegetables. Surveys of children in the nation's public schools in 1932 showed that one-quarter suffered from malnutrition. The U.S. Public Health Service revealed that the families of unemployed workers had 66 percent more illnesses than the families of employed workers. In 1931, New York City hospitals reported about 100 cases of death by starvation.

Hungry people by the millions lined up at "soup kitchens," where churches and charities distributed minimal amounts of food and water. Others rummaged through trash cans or garbage dumps. In Detroit, "we saw the city at its worst," wrote Louise V. Armstrong. "One vivid, gruesome moment of those dark days we shall never forget. We saw a crowd of some fifty men fighting over a barrel of garbage which had been set outside the back door of a restaurant. American citizens fighting over scraps of food like animals!"

HOMELESSNESS The contraction of the economy especially squeezed debtors who had monthly mortgages to pay. A thousand Americans per day lost

The morning news in a Chicago shantytown In response to the economic devastation of the Great Depression, numerous shantytowns emerged in cities across the country to house the recently-homeless; here, a man reads a newspaper outside his makeshift dwelling in Chicago.

their homes to foreclosure, and millions were forced to move in with relatives or friends. At first, the poor made homeless by the Depression were usually placed in almshouses, also called *poorhouses* or *workhouses*. By 1933, however, the homeless overwhelmed the small number of public facilities; more than 40 percent of home mortgages were in default. People were forced to live in culverts, under bridges, on park benches, and in doorways and police stations. To make matters worse, the poor were subject to frequent abuse and arrest. The constitutions of fourteen states even banned paupers from voting.

Millions of homeless people, mostly men, took to living on the road or the rails. These hobos, or *tramps*, walked, hitchhiked in cars, or sneaked onto empty railway cars and rode from town to town. One railroad, the Missouri Pacific, counted 200,000 vagrants living in its empty boxcars in 1931. The following year, the Southern Pacific Railroad reported that it had evicted 683,457 people from its freight trains. A black military veteran recalled life as a hobo: "Black and white, it didn't make any difference who you were, 'cause everybody was poor. . . . They didn't have no mothers or sisters, they didn't have no home; they were dirty, they had overalls on, they didn't have no food, they didn't have anything."

DESPERATE RESPONSES As always, those hardest hit were the most disadvantaged groups—immigrants, women, farmers, the urban unemployed, Native Americans, and African Americans. Desperate conditions led desperate people to do desperate things. Crime soared, as did street-corner begging, homelessness, and prostitution.

Although the divorce rate dropped during the decade, in part because couples could not afford to live separately or pay the legal fees to obtain a divorce, many jobless husbands simply deserted their wives and children. "You don't know what it's like when your husband's out of work," a woman told a reporter. "He's gloomy and unhappy all the time. Life is terrible. You must try all the time to keep him from going crazy." With their future so uncertain, married couples often decided not to have children, and birthrates plummeted. Many struggling parents sent their children to live with relatives or friends. Some 900,000 children simply left home and joined the growing army of homeless "tramps." During the Great Depression, for the first time ever, more people left the United States than arrived as immigrants.

PLIGHT OF WORKING WOMEN The Depression put women in a peculiar position. By 1932, an estimated 20 percent of working women were unemployed, a slightly lower percentage than men. Because women held a disproportionate number of the lowest-paying jobs, they were often able to keep them. Even so, many women also had the added burden of keeping their families together emotionally with their husbands out of work. Magazines

Just dropping off a résumé In October 1938, the federal government opened six custodian positions and 15,000 African American women lined up overnight to turn in their applications. Pictured here is a policeman leaping over a hedge to keep the crowd under control.

published numerous articles about the challenge of maintaining households when the husband had been "unmanned" by losing his job.

As the Depression deepened, however, married women in the workforce became the primary targets of layoffs. Some twenty-six states passed laws prohibiting their employment. The reasoning was that a married woman—who presumably had a husband to take care of her—should not "steal" a job from a man supporting a family. It was acceptable for single women to find jobs because these were usually considered "women's work": salesgirls, beauticians, schoolteachers, secretaries, and nurses. The job market for African American women was even more restricted, with most of them working as maids, cooks, or laundresses. In a desperate attempt to create jobs for unemployed men, many employers and even whole states adopted policies barring married women from employment. For example, three-fourths of the public school systems across the nation during the Great Depression fired women teachers who got married. As a legislator commented, the working woman in Depression-era America was "the first orphan in the storm."

MINORITIES Most African Americans still lived in the eleven southern states of the former Confederacy, where the farm-dominated economy was depressed before 1929 and worsened during the Great Depression. African Americans in the South earned their meager livelihoods from farming, as tenants and sharecroppers. Pervasive racial discrimination kept blacks out of the few labor unions in the South and consigned them to the most menial, lowest-paying jobs.

They also continued to be the victims of violence and intimidation. Most blacks were still excluded from voting and were segregated in public places like hotels and trains. Already living in poverty, they were among the hardest hit by the Depression. As a blues song called "Hard Times Ain't Gone Nowhere" revealed, "Hard times don't worry me; I was broke when it first started out." Some 3 million rural blacks in the South lived in cramped cabins without electricity, running water, or bathrooms.

In many mills, factories, mines, and businesses, the philosophy of "last hired, first fired" meant that the people who could least afford to be jobless were fired first. Blacks who had left the South to take factory jobs in the North were among the first to be laid off. Blacks had the highest rate of joblessness in the early years of the Great Depression. "At no time in the history of the Negro since slavery," reported the Urban League, "has his economic and social outlook seemed so discouraging." Churches and other charity organizations gave aid, but some refused to provide support for blacks, Mexicans, and Asians.

Impoverished whites found themselves competing with local Hispanics and Asians for seasonal farmwork in the cotton fields or orchards of large corporate farms. Many Chinese, Japanese, and Filipino farm laborers moved to cities. Mexicans, who had come to the United States during the 1920s, were also mostly migrant farmworkers, traveling from farm to farm to work during harvest and planting seasons of different crops. They settled in California, New Mexico, Arizona, Colorado, Texas, and the midwestern states. As economic conditions worsened, government officials called for the deportation of Mexican-born Americans to avoid the cost of providing them with public services. By 1935, more than 500,000 Mexican Americans (250,000 from Texas alone) and their American-born children were deported to Mexico.

Everywhere one looked in the early 1930s, people were suffering. City, county, and state governments quickly proved incapable of managing the spreading misery. As Americans turned to the federal government for ideas and answers, Herbert Hoover, the "Great Engineer," struggled to provide adequate responses to the unprecedented crisis of the Great Depression.

CHAPTER REVIEW

SUMMARY

- **The Reactionary Twenties** With the end of the Great War, a renewed surge of immigration led to a wave of *nativism*. To Americans who feared that many immigrants were political radicals, the *Sacco and Vanzetti case* confirmed their suspicions. Nativists persuaded Congress to restrict future immigration, particularly from eastern and southern Europe, in the *Immigration Act of 1924*. Other reactionary movements reflected the feeling of many white Protestants that their religion and way of life were under attack. A revived Ku Klux Klan promoted hatred of Catholics, Jews, immigrants, Communists, and liberals, as well as African Americans. Fundamentalist Protestants campaigned against teaching evolution in public schools. Their efforts culminated in the 1925 *Scopes Trial* in Dayton, Tennessee, where a high school teacher was convicted of violating a state law prohibiting the teaching of evolution. Along with progressive reformers, conservative Protestants also supported the nationwide *Prohibition* of alcoholic beverages that had gone into effect in 1920, despite widespread disregard for the law and the increased criminal activity and violence associated with it. Union membership declined in the 1920s as businesses adopted new techniques (such as the so-called *open shop*) to resist unions, a conservative Supreme Court rolled back workers' rights, and workers themselves lost interest in organizing amid the general prosperity of the decade.

- **Republican Resurgence** Although the Eighteenth Amendment (paving the way for Prohibition) and the Nineteenth Amendment (guaranteeing women's right to vote) marked the culmination of progressivism at the national level, the movement lost much of its appeal as disillusionment with the Great War and its results created a public preference for disarmament and isolationism, stances reflected in the Five-Power Treaty of 1922. Warren G. Harding's landslide presidential victory in 1920 was based on his call for a *"return to normalcy."* Harding and his fellow Republicans, including his vice president and successor, Calvin Coolidge, followed policies advocated by Secretary of the Treasury Andrew Mellon that emphasized lowering taxes and government spending as well as raising tariffs to protect domestic industries. The plan succeeded spectacularly in reviving the economy. Harding died suddenly in 1923, soon after news broke about the *Teapot Dome Affair* involving a government-owned oil field in Wyoming, one of many incidents of corruption growing out of Harding's appointments. Coolidge, an austere, frugal man who identified with the interests of business, restored trust in the presidency and won reelection in a landslide in 1924. In the 1928 presidential election, Herbert Hoover, secretary of commerce under Harding and Coolidge, won a third straight decisive victory for the Republicans.

- **The Great Depression** The 1929 stock market crash revealed the structural flaws in the economy, but it was not the only cause of the *Great Depression (1929–1941)*. During the twenties, business owners did not provide adequate wage increases for workers, thus preventing consumers' "purchasing power" from keeping up with increases in production. The nation's agricultural sector also suffered from overproduction throughout the decade. Government policies—such as high tariffs that helped to reduce international trade and the reduction of the nation's money supply as a means of dealing with the financial panic—exacerbated the emerging economic depression.

- **The Human Toll of the Depression**   Thousands of banks and businesses closed, and millions of homes and jobs were lost. By the early 1930s, many people were homeless and hopeless, begging on street corners and sleeping in doorways. Many state laws and business practices discouraged the employment of married women, and discrimination against African Americans, Native Americans, Hispanics, and Asian Americans in hiring was widespread.

CHRONOLOGY

1920	Prohibition begins
	Sacco and Vanzetti trial
	Warren G. Harding is elected president
1921	Washington Naval Conference and Five-Power Treaty
	Congress passes Emergency Immigration Act
1923	Teapot Dome scandal becomes public
	President Harding dies in office and is succeeded by Calvin Coolidge
1924	Congress passes Immigration Act
	Coolidge is reelected president
1925	Scopes "monkey trial"
1927	Sacco and Vanzetti are executed
1928	Herbert Hoover is elected president
1929	Stock market crashes in late October

KEY TERMS

nativism p. 1063

Immigration Act of 1924 p. 1064

Sacco and Vanzetti case p. 1065

Scopes Trial p. 1069

Prohibition p. 1071

"return to normalcy" p. 1075

open shop p. 1080

Teapot Dome Affair p. 1084

Great Depression (1929–1941) p. 1094

 INQUIZITIVE

Go to InQuizitive to see what you've learned—and learn what you've missed—with personalized feedback along the way.

25 The Great Depression

1929–1939

Construction of a Dam **(1939)** One of the most famous and controversial of the artists commissioned by the New Deal's Works Progress Administration was William Gropper, who painted this mural displayed in the Department of the Interior building in Washington, D.C. Based on his observations of dam construction on the Columbia and Colorado Rivers, Gropper illustrates the triumph and brotherhood that emerged from the New Deal's massive public projects during the Great Depression.

The year 1929 dawned with high hopes. Rarely had a new president entered office with greater expectations. In fact, Herbert Hoover, a man of boundless self-confidence, was worried that people viewed him as "a superman; that no problem is beyond my capacity." He was right to be concerned. People did consider him a superman—"the man who had never failed"—a dedicated public servant whose engineering genius and business savvy would ensure continued prosperity. In 1929, more Americans were working than ever before and earning record levels of income. But that was about to change.

The **Great Depression**, which began at the end of 1929, brought the worst of times. No business slump had been so deep, so long, or so painful. By 1932, one of every four Americans was unemployed; in many large cities, nearly *half* of the adults were out of work. Millions of others saw their working hours and wages reduced. Some 500,000 people had lost homes or farms because they could not pay their mortgages. Over 4,000 banks failed in the first two months of 1933, with more than $3.6 billion in lost deposits. Record numbers of people were out of work, out of money, and out of hope. One California woman wrote that she was the "mother of seven children, and utterly heart broken, in that they are hungry, have only 65¢ in money. The father is in Los Angeles trying to find something to do."

What made the Great Depression so severe and so lasting was its global nature. In 1929, Europe was still reeling from the Great War. Once the American economy tumbled, it sent shock waves throughout the world. Economic distress fed the rise of totalitarian regimes—fascism and Nazism in Italy and Germany, communism in the Soviet Union. "Capitalism is dying," theologian Reinhold Niebuhr proclaimed. "Let no one delude himself by hoping for reform from within."

focus questions

1. How did the Hoover administration respond to the Great Depression?

2. What were the goals and accomplishments of the First New Deal?

3. What were the major criticisms of the First New Deal?

4. How did the New Deal evolve? How did it transform the role of the federal government in American life?

Yet that is exactly what Franklin Delano Roosevelt sought to do in 1932 as he assumed the presidency. He would save capitalism by transforming it. Like his hero, his cousin Theodore Roosevelt, he believed that the basic problem of twentieth-century life was the excessive power of large corporations. Only the federal government could regulate corporate capitalism for the public benefit.

Few leaders have taken office in more dire circumstances. Yet within days of becoming president, Roosevelt took dramatic steps that forever changed the scope and role of the federal government. He believed that America's democratic form of government had the ultimate responsibility to help people who were in distress, not out of a sense of charity but out of a sense of obligation. Along with a supportive Congress, he set about enacting dozens of bold measures to relieve human suffering and promote economic recovery.

Roosevelt was an inspiring personality, overflowing with cheerful strength, strong convictions, and an unshakeable confidence in himself and in the resilience of the American people. He was also a pragmatist willing to try different approaches. His program for recovery, the New Deal, was therefore a series of trial-and-error actions rather than a comprehensive scheme. None of the well-intentioned but often poorly planned initiatives worked perfectly, and some failed miserably. Yet their combined effect was to restore hope and energy to the nation.

From Hooverism to the New Deal

The Great Depression revealed Herbert Hoover to be a brilliant mediocrity. His initial response to the economic disaster was denial: there was no crisis, he insisted. All that was needed, he and others in his administration argued, was to let the economy cure itself. The best policy, Treasury Secretary Andrew Mellon advised, would be to "liquidate labor, liquidate stocks, liquidate the farmers, liquidate real estate." Letting events run their course, he claimed, would "purge the rottenness out of the [capitalist] system." But Mellon's do-nothing approach did not work. Falling wages and declining land and home values made it even harder for struggling farmers, businesses, and households to pay their bills. With so many people losing jobs and income, consumers and businesses simply could not buy enough goods and services to reenergize the economy.

Hoover's Efforts at Recovery

As the months passed, President Hoover proved less willing than Andrew Mellon to sit by and let events take their course. As the "Great Engineer," he in fact did more than any previous president in addressing such calamitous economic circumstances. He invited business, labor, government, and agricultural leaders to a series of White House conferences in which he urged companies to maintain employment and wage levels, asked union leaders to end strikes, and pleaded with state governors to accelerate planned construction projects so as to keep people working. He also formed committees and commissions to study various aspects of the economic calamity, and he cut the income tax. Yet nothing worked. Unemployment continued to rise, and wage levels continued to fall.

UPBEAT MESSAGES   In speech after speech, Hoover became an ineffective cheerleader for American capitalism. In early May 1930, the president told the U.S. Chamber of Commerce that he was "convinced we have passed the worst and with continued effort we shall rapidly recover." A few weeks later, Hoover assured a group of bankers that the "depression is over." The Hoover administration also circulated upbeat slogans such as "Business IS Better" and "Keep Smiling."

But uplifting words were not enough. More and more people kept losing their jobs and homes. Hoover never felt comfortable giving comfort to a desperate

Hooverville Of the many Hoovervilles set up in Seattle, Washington, alone, this particular shantytown near the shipyards was the largest. It lasted nine years.

nation. His recurring statement—"No one has yet starved"—was hardly reassuring, or, as it turned out, accurate.

SHORT-SIGHTED TAX INCREASES The Great Depression was the greatest national emergency since the Civil War, and the nation was woefully unprepared to deal with it. As personal income plummeted, so did government tax revenues. Despite the Depression, President Hoover insisted on trying to balance the federal budget by raising taxes and cutting budgets—precisely the wrong prescription for a sick economy. He pushed through Congress the Revenue Act of 1932, the largest—and most poorly timed—peacetime tax increase in American history. By taking money out of consumers' pockets, the higher taxes accelerated the economic slowdown. People had less money to spend when what the struggling economy most needed was increased consumer spending.

HOOVER'S REACTION TO THE SOCIAL CRISIS By the fall of 1930, many cities were buckling under the strain of lost revenue and human distress. The federal government had no programs to deal with homelessness and joblessness. State and local governments cut spending, worsening the economic situation. All across the country, shantytowns sprouted in vacant lots. People erected shacks out of cardboard and scrap wood and metal. They called their makeshift villages *Hoovervilles* to mock the president. To keep warm, they wrapped themselves in newspapers, calling them *Hoover blankets*. As their numbers rose, more and more homeless and jobless people called for government to step in. Frustrated by his critics, Hoover dismissed the concerns of "calamity mongers and weeping men."

Hoover feared that the nation would be "plunged into socialism" if the government provided direct support to the poor. His governing philosophy, rooted in America's mythic

Young and hungry A toddler begs for change in one of the homeless camps.

commitment to rugged individualism and free enterprise, set firm limits on emergency government action. The president still trumpeted the virtues of "self-reliance" and individual initiative, claiming that government assistance would rob people of the desire to help themselves.

Hoover hoped that the "natural generosity" of the American people and charitable organizations would be sufficient, and he believed that volunteers (the backbone of local charity organizations) would relieve the social distress caused by the Depression. But his faith in traditional "voluntarism" was misplaced. Local and state relief agencies were overwhelmed by the magnitude of the social crisis, as were churches and charitable organizations like the Salvation Army and the Red Cross.

RISING CRITICISM OF HOOVER

That the economic collapse was so unexpected made people all the more insecure and anxious, and President Hoover increasingly became the target of their frustration. The Democrats shrewdly exploited his predicament. In November 1930, they gained their first national election victory since 1916, winning a majority in the House and a near majority in the Senate.

Hoover refused to see the elections as a warning. Instead, he grew more resistant to calls for federal intervention in the struggling economy. By 1932, 15 million people were unemployed. The *New York Times* concluded that Hoover had "failed as a party leader. He has failed as an economist. . . . He has failed as a business leader. . . . He has failed as a personality because of [his] awkwardness of manner and speech and lack of mass magnetism." When Hoover asked Treasury Secretary Andrew Mellon for a nickel to phone a friend, the secretary replied: "Here are two nickels—call all of them."

CONGRESSIONAL INITIATIVES With a new Congress in session in 1932, demands for federal action forced Hoover to do more. That year, Congress set up the **Reconstruction Finance Corporation (RFC)** to make emergency loans to banks, life-insurance companies, and railroads. But if the federal government could help huge banks and railroads, asked New York Democratic senator Robert F. Wagner, why not "extend a helping hand to that forlorn American, in every village and every city of the United States, who has been without wages since 1929?" Hoover, however, held back and signed only the Emergency Relief Act (1932), which authorized the RFC to make loans to the states for construction projects. Critics called the RFC a "breadline" for businesses while the unemployed went hungry.

Anger and frustration Unemployed military veterans, members of the Bonus Expeditionary Force that served during the Great War, clash with Washington, D.C., police at Anacostia Flats in July 1932.

FARMERS AND VETERANS IN PROTEST Meanwhile, the average *annual* income of families working the land during the early 1930s was $240. Prices for agricultural products fell so low that farmers lost money if they took them to market. Thousands of midwestern farmers protested the low prices by dumping milk, vegetables, and fruits on the highways.

Fears of organized revolt arose when thousands of unemployed military veterans converged on the nation's capital in the spring of 1932. The "**Bonus Expeditionary Force**," made up of veterans of the American Expeditionary Force (AEF) that fought in Europe in the Great War, pressed Congress to pay the cash bonuses owed to nearly 4 million veterans. The House passed a bonus bill, but the Senate voted it down because it would have forced a tax increase. Most of the disappointed veterans went home. The rest, along with their wives and children, having no place to go, camped in vacant federal buildings and in a shantytown within sight of the Capitol.

Eager to remove the homeless veterans, Hoover persuaded Congress to pay for their train tickets home. More left, but others stayed even after Congress adjourned, hoping to meet with the president. Late in July, Hoover ordered the government buildings cleared. In doing so, a policeman panicked, fired into the crowd, and killed two veterans. The secretary of war then dispatched 700 soldiers to remove the "Bonus Army." The soldiers, commanded by army chief of staff General Douglas MacArthur, used horses and tanks to disperse the unarmed veterans and their families. Then, exceeding orders, the soldiers burned the makeshift camp. Fifty-five veterans were injured and 135 arrested.

Widespread news coverage of the assault on the unemployed veterans led even more people to view Hoover and the Republicans as heartless. The Democratic governor of New York was horrified as he read newspaper accounts of the army's violent assault on the Bonus Army. "Well," Franklin Roosevelt told an aide, "this elects me" as the next president. (The veterans were finally paid their "bonus" in 1936.)

The disheartened, angry mood of the Bonus Army matched that of the country and of President Hoover himself. He worked hard, but the stress sapped his health and morale. "I am so tired," he said, "that every bone in my body aches." When aides urged him to be more of a public leader, he replied, "I have no Wilsonian qualities." He hated giving speeches, and when he did his tone came across as cold and uncaring. He also got along badly with journalists, who often highlighted his sour demeanor and dull, monotone voice. A sculptor claimed that "if you put a rose in Hoover's hand, it would wilt."

The man who, in 1928, had promised Americans "permanent prosperity" was now a laughingstock. In the end, Hoover failed because he never understood or acknowledged the seriousness of the nation's economic problems.

THE 1932 ELECTION In June 1932, glum Republicans gathered in Chicago to nominate President Hoover for a second term. By contrast, the Democrats arrived in Chicago for their convention a few weeks later confident that they would nominate the next president. Fifty-year-old New York governor Franklin Delano Roosevelt won on the fourth ballot.

Roosevelt broke precedent by traveling to Chicago to accept the nomination in person. The stakes were high, he said, because Hoover and the Republicans had failed to address the economic disaster. "I pledge you, I pledge myself to a *new deal* for the American people" that would "break foolish traditions" and create a new, enlightened administration "of competence and courage."

Roosevelt first had to defeat Hoover, however. The race, he said, would be "more than a political campaign; it is a call to arms." It was a vague but uplifting message of hope at a time when many people were slipping into despair. Roosevelt exuded energy and confidence. His campaign song was "Happy Days Are Here Again."

Throughout the campaign, Roosevelt attacked Hoover for his "extravagant government spending" and repeatedly promised a "New Deal" for the American people, stressing that a revitalized economy required new ideas and aggressive action. "The country needs, and, unless I mistake its temper, the country demands bold, persistent experimentation," he said. "Above all, try something."

In contrast to Roosevelt, Hoover lacked vitality and vision. Roosevelt's proposals for unprecedented government action, he warned, "would destroy the very foundations of our American system." The election was more than a contest between two men and two political parties; it was a battle "between two philosophies of government" that would decide "the direction our nation will take over a century to come."

Hoover lost decisively. Americans swept Roosevelt into office with 23 million votes to Hoover's 16 million. In 1928, Hoover had carried 40 states; four years later, he won but six.

THE ELECTION OF 1932

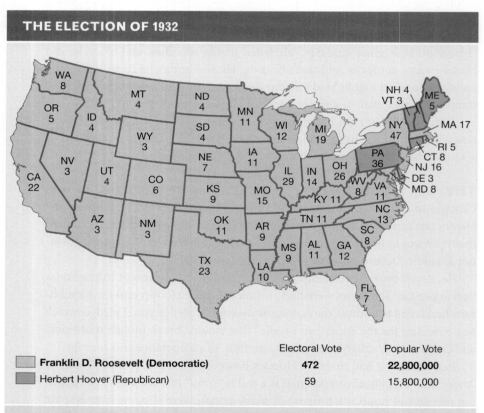

	Electoral Vote	Popular Vote
Franklin D. Roosevelt (Democratic)	472	22,800,000
Herbert Hoover (Republican)	59	15,800,000

- Why did Franklin Roosevelt win over so many voters struggling during the Depression?
- What were Herbert Hoover's criticisms of Roosevelt's New Deal?
- During the 1932 presidential campaign, what did Roosevelt pledge to fight the Depression?

ROOSEVELT'S NEW DEAL

Franklin Roosevelt promised voters a "New Deal," and within hours of being inaugurated, he and his aides set about creating a "new order of competence and courage." For better or worse, the federal government assumed responsibility for national economic planning and for restoring prosperity and ensuring social security—for all. What Roosevelt called the "forgotten man" would no longer be forgotten.

ROOSEVELT'S RISE   Born in 1882, the adored only child of wealthy, aristocratic parents, young Franklin Roosevelt had enjoyed a pampered life that freed him from worrying about a job or a paycheck. He was educated by tutors at Springwood, his father's Hudson River estate near Hyde Park, north of New York City. He attended Harvard College and Columbia University Law School. (He did not graduate.) While a law student in 1905, he married Anna Eleanor Roosevelt, the favorite niece of Theodore Roosevelt, then president of the United States, who was also Franklin's distant cousin.

In 1910, Franklin Roosevelt won a Democratic seat in the New York State Senate. Tall, handsome, athletic, and blessed with a sparkling personality and infectious smile, he seemed destined for greatness. In 1913, Woodrow Wilson appointed him assistant secretary of the navy. In 1920, Roosevelt became James Cox's vice presidential running mate on the Democratic ticket.

"TRIAL BY FIRE"   Then a tragedy occurred. In 1921, at age thirty-nine, Roosevelt, who loved to swim and sail, play tennis and golf, contracted polio, an infectious neuromuscular disease that left him permanently disabled and forced him to use cumbersome leg braces to stand or walk. But Roosevelt fought back. For seven years, aided by his remarkable wife, Eleanor, he strengthened his body to compensate for his disability. The exhausting daily regimen of physical therapy transformed Roosevelt. Polio crippled his legs but expanded his sympathies. He became less pompous, more considerate, more focused, and more able to identify with the problems of people facing hard times.

Roosevelt had a remarkable ability to make people feel at ease and express concern about their troubles. The aristocrat had developed the common touch as well as a great talent for public relations, but he also was vain and calculating and a clever manipulator. In other words, he was a consummate politician.

A PEOPLE'S PRESIDENT   Roosevelt was neither a masterful administrator nor a deep thinker. One of his closest aides said the president never "read a serious book." But Roosevelt had many virtues: courage, good instincts, unrelenting optimism, and a charming personality. He loved talking to people, and he was determined to help those who could not help themselves. Colonel Edward House, the veteran Democratic counselor, explained that his former boss, Woodrow Wilson, "liked humanity as a whole and disliked people individually." Roosevelt, by contrast, was "genuinely fond of people and shows it."

What truly set Roosevelt apart was his willingness to experiment with different ways of using government power and resources to address pressing problems. He embraced the orthodoxy of a balanced budget and complained about a "bloated bureaucracy," for example, only to incur more budget deficits than all his predecessors combined as he dramatically expanded the scope of federal government. His inconsistencies reflected his distinctive personality as he launched his presidency and the New Deal.

THE 1933 INAUGURATION Inaugurated in March 1933, Franklin Delano Roosevelt assumed leadership during a crisis that threatened the very fabric of American capitalism. "The situation is critical, Franklin," the prominent journalist Walter Lippmann warned. "You may have to assume dictatorial powers"—as had already happened in Germany, Italy, and the Soviet Union.

Roosevelt did not become a dictator, but he did take extraordinary steps while assuring Americans "that the only thing we have to fear is fear itself." He confessed in his inaugural address that he did not have all the answers, but he did know that "this nation asks for action, and action now." He asked Congress for "a broad Executive power to wage a war against the emergency" just as "if we were in fact invaded by a foreign foe." Roosevelt's uplifting speech won rave reviews. Nearly 500,000 Americans wrote letters to the new president, and even the pro-Republican *Chicago Tribune* praised his "courageous confidence."

THE FIRST HUNDRED DAYS In March 1933, President Roosevelt confronted four major challenges: reviving the industrial economy, relieving the widespread human misery, rescuing the ravaged farm sector, and reforming those aspects of the capitalist system that had helped cause the Depression. He quickly addressed all of those challenges—and more.

The new president admitted that he would try several different "experiments." Some would succeed, and others would fail, but the important thing was to do something bold—and fast. It was no time for timid leadership or paralyzing doubts. The defining characteristic of Roosevelt's approach to presidential leadership was *action*. He had a genius for leading others—even when he did not know for sure where he was taking them. To advise him, Roosevelt assembled a "brain trust" of brilliant specialists who feverishly developed fresh ideas to address the nation's urgent problems.

Roosevelt and his advisers initially settled on a three-pronged strategy to revive the economy. First, they addressed the immediate banking crisis and provided short-term emergency relief for the jobless. Second, the New Dealers—men and women (professors, journalists, economists, social workers, and political appointees) who swarmed to Washington during the winter of 1933—encouraged agreements between management and unions. Third, they attempted to raise depressed commodity prices (corn, cotton, wheat, beef, pork, etc.) by paying farmers "subsidies" to *reduce* the sizes of their crops and herds so that prices would *rise* and thereby increase farm income.

Franklin Delano Roosevelt Preparing to deliver the first of his popular "fireside chats" to a national radio audience. This message focused on measures to reform the American banking system.

The new Congress was as ready to take action as was the new president. From March 9 to June 16, the so-called First Hundred Days, Congress approved fifteen major pieces of legislation proposed by Roosevelt. Several of these programs comprised what came to be called the **First New Deal** (1933–1935).

SHORING UP THE FINANCIAL SYSTEM

Money is the lubricant of capitalism, and money was fast disappearing from circulation by 1933. Ever since the stock market crash of 1929, panicky depositors had been withdrawing their money from banks and the stock market. Taking so much money out of circulation worsened the Depression and brought the banking system to the brink of collapse. Throughout the twenties, an average of almost 700 banks a year failed. After 1929, that number doubled and then tripled.

BANKING REGULATION On his second day in office, March 9, 1933, Roosevelt called Congress into special session to pass the Emergency Banking Relief Act, which declared a four-day bank holiday to allow the financial panic to subside. (Herbert Hoover criticized the move as a step toward "gigantic socialism.") For the first time in history, all U.S. banks closed their doors.

Roosevelt's financial experts worked all night drafting a bill to restore confidence in the banks. On March 12, in the first of his radio-broadcast "fireside chats" to the nation, the president assured the 60 million listeners that it was safer to "keep your money in a reopened bank than under the mattress." The following day, people took their money back to the banks. "Capitalism was saved in eight days," said one of Roosevelt's advisers.

A few weeks later, on June 16, Roosevelt signed the Glass-Steagall Banking Act of 1933, part of which created the **Federal Deposit Insurance Corporation (FDIC)**, which guaranteed customer accounts in banks up to $2,500,

The galloping snail A vigorous Roosevelt drives Congress to action in this *Detroit News* cartoon from March 1933.

thus reducing the likelihood of future panics. In addition to insuring savings accounts, the Glass-Steagall Act called for the separation of commercial banking from investment banking to prevent conventional banks from investing the savings of depositors in the risky stock market; only banks that specialized in investment could trade shares in the stock market after 1933. In addition, the Federal Reserve Board was given more authority to intervene in future financial emergencies. The banking crisis had ended, and the administration was ready to pursue a broader program of economic recovery.

REGULATING WALL STREET Before the Great Crash in 1929, there was little government oversight of the securities (stocks and bonds) industry. In 1933, the Roosevelt administration developed two important pieces of legislation intended to regulate the operations of the stock market and eliminate fraud and abuses. The first, the Securities Exchange Act of 1933, was the first major federal legislation to regulate the sale of stocks and bonds. It required corporations that issued stock for public sale to "disclose" all relevant information about the operations and management of the company so that purchasers could know what they were buying. The second bill, the Securities Exchange Act of 1934, established the **Securities and Exchange Commission**, a federal agency to enforce the new laws and regulations governing the issuance and trading of stocks and bonds.

THE FEDERAL BUDGET Roosevelt next convinced Congress to pass an Economy Act (1933) allowing him to cut government workers' salaries, reduce payments to military veterans for non-service-connected disabilities, and reorganize federal agencies to help reduce government expenses. He then took the dramatic step of ending Prohibition, in part because it was being so widely violated, in part because most Democrats wanted it ended, and in part because he wanted to regain the federal tax revenues from the sale of alcoholic beverages. The Twenty-First Amendment, ratified on December 5, 1933, ended the "noble experiment" of Prohibition.

HELPING THE UNEMPLOYED AND HOMELESS

Another urgent priority in 1933 was relieving the widespread human distress. Herbert Hoover had stubbornly refused to help the unemployed and homeless, since he assumed that individual self-reliance, acts of charity, and the efforts of local organizations (the Red Cross, churches, and "city missions") would be sufficient.

The Roosevelt administration, however, knew that the numbers of people in need far exceeded the capacity of charitable organizations and local agencies. As Harry L. Hopkins, an aide to Roosevelt, said, "Hunger is not debatable."

The new president pushed through a series of programs that created what came to be called the "welfare state." He did not believe that the government should give people cash (called a "dole"), but he insisted that the federal government help the unemployed and homeless by getting them jobs. For the first time, the federal government took primary responsibility for assisting the most desperate Americans.

PUTTING PEOPLE TO WORK   The Federal Emergency Relief Administration (FERA), headed by Harry L. Hopkins, was Roosevelt's first major effort to deal with unemployment. It sent grants to the states to spend on the unemployed and homeless. After the state-sponsored programs funded by the FERA proved inadequate, Congress created the Civil Works Administration (CWA) in November 1933. It marked the first large-scale *federal* experiment with work relief by putting people directly on the government payroll at competitive wages: 40¢ an hour for unskilled workers, $1 for skilled.

The CWA provided 4 million federal jobs during the winter of 1933–1934 and organized a variety of useful projects: repairing 500,000 miles of roads, laying sewer lines, constructing or improving more than 1,000 airports and 40,000 public schools, and providing 50,000 teaching jobs that helped keep small rural public schools open. As the number of people employed by the CWA soared, however, the program's costs skyrocketed to more than $1 billion. Roosevelt balked at such high costs and worried that the people hired would become dependent upon federal jobs. So in the spring of 1934, he ordered the CWA dissolved. By April, some 4 million workers were again unemployed.

THE CCC   The most successful of the New Deal jobs programs was the Civilian Conservation Corps (CCC), managed by the War Department. It built 2,500 camps to house up to half a million unemployed, unmarried young men ages seventeen to twenty-seven. They worked as "soil soldiers" in national forests, parks, and recreational areas, and on soil-conservation projects. The CCC also recruited 150,000 unemployed military veterans and 85,000 Native Americans, housing them in separate camps.

CCC workers had to be between 60 and 78 inches tall, weigh more than 107 pounds, and have at least six teeth. They were to be paid $1 a day for no more than nine months so as to make room for others. Critics charged that the CCC would undermine wage gains made by the labor union movement, but Roosevelt responded that the young men selected for the program would be those who "have no chance to get a job." Congress passed the bill only after Oscar De Priest, an African American legislator from Illinois, introduced an amendment requiring that the agency not discriminate on account of race, color, or creed.

Federal relief programs Civilian Conservation Corps enrollees in 1933, on a break from work. Directed by army officers and foresters, the CCC camps were operated like military bases.

CCC workers cleared brush; built trails, roads, bridges, campgrounds, fire towers, fish hatcheries, and 800 parks; planted 3 *billion* trees; taught farmers how to control soil erosion; and fought fires. The enrollees, supervised by soldiers, were given shelter, clothing, and food, and took classes to learn to read and earn high-school diplomas. Women were excluded from the CCC, and African Americans and Native Americans were housed in segregated facilities.

Roosevelt loved to visit the CCC camps. After sharing a meal with one group, he said: "I wish I could spend a couple of months here myself." By 1942, when the CCC was dismantled, some 3 million young men had passed through the program.

SAVING HOMES During 1933, a thousand homes or farms were being foreclosed upon each day because people could not afford to pay their mortgages. To address the problem, Roosevelt convinced Congress to create the Home Owners' Loan Corporation, which helped people refinance their mortgages at lower interest rates so as to avoid bankruptcy. In 1934, Roosevelt created the Federal Housing Administration (FHA), which offered Americans much longer home mortgages (twenty years) in order to reduce their monthly payments. Up to that point, most mortgages were for less than ten years duration and covered only a portion of the purchase price.

REVIVING THE INDUSTRIAL SECTOR The centerpiece of the New Deal's efforts to revive the industrial economy was the National Industrial Recovery Act (NIRA) of 1933. One of its two major sections created massive public-works construction projects funded by the federal government as a means of creating jobs. The NIRA started the Public Works Administration (PWA), granting $3.3 billion for the construction of government buildings, highways, bridges, dams, port facilities, and sewage plants.

·The second, and more controversial, part of the NIRA created the **National Recovery Administration (NRA)**, headed by Hugh S. Johnson, a hard-drinking retired army general known for his administrative expertise, a "blustering, dictatorial, and appealing" bureaucrat. The NRA represented a radical shift in the federal government's role in the economy. Never before in peacetime had Washington bureaucrats taken charge of setting prices, wages, and standards for working conditions.

The primary purpose of the NRA was to promote economic growth by ignoring anti-trust laws and allowing executives of competing businesses to negotiate among themselves and with labor unions to create "codes of fair competition" that would set prices, production levels, minimum wages, and maximum hours within each industry, no matter how small. In New York City, for example, women who made their living as burlesque show strippers agreed to an NRA code limiting the number of performers on stage and the number of performances they could provide each night.

In exchange for allowing companies to "cooperate" rather than compete, the NRA codes included "fair labor" policies long sought by unions and social progressives: a national forty-hour work week, minimum weekly wages of $13 ($12 in the South, where living costs were lower), and a ban on the employment of children under the age of sixteen. The NRA also included a provision that guaranteed the right of workers to organize unions.

These were landmark changes, and, for a time, the downward spiral of wages and prices subsided. But as soon as economic recovery began, small business owners complained that the larger corporations dominated the NRA, whose price-fixing robbed small producers of the chance to compete. And because the NRA wage codes excluded agricultural and domestic workers (at the insistence of southern Democrats), most African Americans derived no direct benefit from the program. When the Supreme Court declared the NRA unconstitutional in May 1935, few regretted its demise.

The NRA experiment did, however, have lasting effects. It set new workplace standards, such as the forty-hour work week, created a national minimum wage, and helped end the abuse of child labor. Its endorsement of collective bargaining between workers and owners spurred the growth of unions. Yet, as 1934 ended, industrial recovery was still nowhere in sight.

AGRICULTURAL ASSISTANCE In addition to rescuing the banks and providing jobs to the unemployed, Roosevelt created the Farm Credit Administration to help farmers deal with their crushing debts and lower their mortgage payments to avoid bankruptcy.

The **Agricultural Adjustment Act** of 1933 created a new federal agency, the Agricultural Adjustment Administration (AAA), which sought to raise prices for crops and herds by paying farmers to cut back production. The money for such payments came from a tax levied on the "processors" of certain basic commodities—cotton gins, flour mills, and slaughterhouses. By the time the AAA was created, however, the spring growing season was already under way.

The prospect of another bumper cotton crop forced the AAA to organize a "plow-under" program in which farmers were paid to kill the sprouting seeds in their fields. To destroy a growing crop was a "shocking commentary on our civilization," Agriculture Secretary Henry A. Wallace admitted. "I could tolerate it only as a cleaning up of the wreckage from the old days of unbalanced production." Moreover, in an effort to raise pork prices, some 6 million baby pigs were slaughtered and buried. By the end of 1934, the AAA efforts had worked: wheat, cotton, and corn production had declined and prices for those commodities had risen. Farm income increased by 58 percent between 1932 and 1935.

At the end of the First Hundred Days of Roosevelt's presidency, the principle of an activist federal government had been established. While journalists characterized the AAA, NRA, CCC, CWA, and other new programs as "alphabet soup," and conservative critics warned that Roosevelt was leading America toward fascism or communism, the president had become the most popular man in the nation.

DUST BOWL MIGRANTS At the same time that the agricultural economy was struggling, a terrible drought created an ecological catastrophe known as the **Dust Bowl**. Colorado, New Mexico, Kansas, Nebraska, Texas, Arkansas, and Oklahoma were hardest hit. Crops withered, and income plummeted. Strong winds swept across the treeless plains, scooping up tons of parched topsoil into billowing dark clouds, called black blizzards, which engulfed farms and towns. By 1938, topsoil had disappeared from more than 25 million acres of prairie land.

Okies on the run A sharecropping family reaches its destination of Bakersfield, California, in 1935, after "we got blowed out in Oklahoma."

Parched farmers could not pay their debts, and banks foreclosed on family farms. Suicides soared, and millions of people abandoned their farms. Many uprooted farmers and their families from the South and the Midwest headed toward California, where jobs were said to be plentiful. Frequently lumped together as "Okies" or "Arkies," most of the Dust Bowl refugees were from cotton belt communities in Arkansas, Texas, Missouri, and Oklahoma. During the 1930s and 1940s, some 800,000 people, mostly whites, headed to the Far West.

Without money to pay rent or a mortgage, homeless migrants set up squatter camps, often called "Little Oklahomas" alongside highways or close to towns where they could get food and supplies. When one crop was harvested, the migrants moved on to the next, carrying their belongings with them.

Most people uprooted by the Dust Bowl went to California's urban areas—Los Angeles, San Diego, or San Francisco. Others moved into the San Joaquin Valley, the state's agricultural heartland. There they discovered that California was no paradise. Only a few could afford to buy land. Most had to work as farm laborers. Living in tents or crude cabins, migrant workers suffered from exposure to the elements, poor sanitation, and social abuse. As an Okie reported, when the big farmers "need us they call us *migrants*, and when we've picked their crop, we're *bums* and we got to get out."

THE TENNESSEE VALLEY AUTHORITY Early in his presidency, Franklin Roosevelt declared that the "South is the nation's No. 1 economic problem." Indeed, since the end of the Civil War, the economy and quality of life in the southern states had lagged far behind the rest of the nation. That gap only widened during the Depression.

To help the blighted South, Roosevelt created one of the most innovative programs of the First New Deal: the Tennessee Valley Authority (TVA), which would bring electrical power, flood control efforts, and jobs to Appalachia, the desperately poor mountainous region that stretched from West

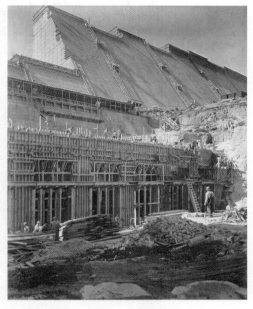

Norris Dam The massive dam in Tennessee, completed in 1936, was essential in creating jobs and expanding electricity under the TVA.

Virginia through western Virginia and North Carolina, Kentucky, eastern Tennessee, and northern Georgia and Alabama.

By 1940, the TVA, a multipurpose public corporation, had constructed twenty-one hydroelectric dams which created the "Great Lakes of the South" and produced enough electricity to power the entire region, at about half the average national rate. The TVA also dredged rivers to allow for boat and barge traffic, promoted soil conservation and forestry management, drew new industries to the region, encouraged the formation of labor unions, and improved schools and libraries. It gave 1.5 million farms access to electricity and indoor plumbing for the first time.

Progress is rarely without its burdens or inconsistencies. Many New Deal programs helped some people and hurt others. Tough choices had to be made. Building all of those huge dams in Appalachia and the resulting lakes meant displacing thousands of hardscrabble people from homes and villages that were destroyed to make way for progress. "I don't want to move," said an elderly east Tennessee woman. "I want to sit here and look out over these hills where I was born. My folks are buried down the road a piece, and our babies are over there on the hill under the cedars."

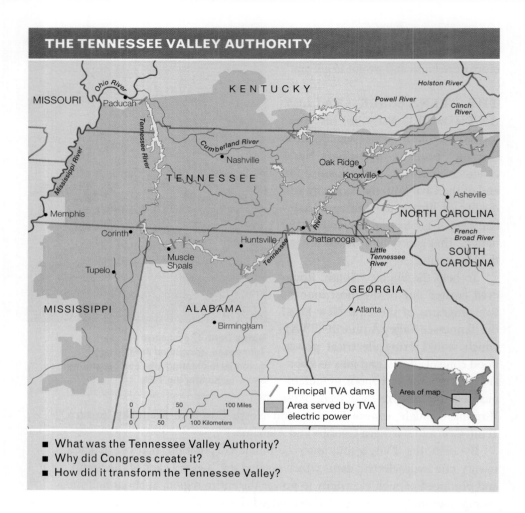

THE TENNESSEE VALLEY AUTHORITY

- What was the Tennessee Valley Authority?
- Why did Congress create it?
- How did it transform the Tennessee Valley?

During Roosevelt's first year in office, his programs and his personal charm generated widespread support. The First New Deal programs—as well as Roosevelt's leadership—had given Americans a sense of renewed faith in the future. In the congressional elections of 1934, the Democrats increased their dominance in Congress with an almost unprecedented midterm victory for a party in power.

ELEANOR ROOSEVELT One of the reasons for Franklin Roosevelt's popularity was his energetic wife, Eleanor Roosevelt, who would prove to be one of the most influential leaders of the time. She ceaselessly prodded her husband about social justice issues and sometimes scolded him, yet she always supported his ambitions and decisions.

Born in 1884 in New York City, Eleanor married her distant cousin Franklin in 1905. All too quickly, she learned that Franklin's domineering mother, Sara Delano Roosevelt, would always be the most important woman in his life. "He might have been happier with a wife who was completely uncritical," like his mother, Eleanor wrote later. "That I was never able to be, and he had to find it in other people."

During the 1920s, Eleanor, shy and insecure, revealed that at heart she was a creature of conscience. She began a lifelong crusade on behalf of women, blacks, and youth, giving voice to the voiceless. Her tireless compassion resulted in large part from the self-doubt and loneliness she had experienced as the child of an alcoholic father and an aloof mother.

Equally influential in shaping Eleanor's outlook was the sense of betrayal she felt upon discovering in 1918 that her husband had fallen recklessly in love with Lucy Mercer, her friend and secretary. "The bottom dropped out of my own particular world," she recalled.

Eleanor and Franklin decided to maintain their marriage, but as their son James said, it became an "armed truce." Eleanor later observed that she could "forgive, but never forget," but she never truly forgave or forgot. Tart-tongued Alice Roosevelt Longworth—the daughter of Theodore Roosevelt, and a cousin of Eleanor's—actually nurtured the affair, hosting Mercer and Franklin for dinner several times. She later explained that Roosevelt "deserved a good time . . . he was married to Eleanor." Franklin and Eleanor were both strong-willed people who were concerned for each other's happiness while acknowledging their inability to provide it. In the White House, they lived entirely apart, rarely seeing each other except for formal occasions and public events.

Eleanor Roosevelt redefined the role of the First Lady. She was not content just to host social events in the White House. Instead, she became an outspoken and relentless activist: the first woman to address a national political convention, to write a nationally syndicated newspaper column, and to hold regular press conferences. The tireless "Eleanor Everywhere" crisscrossed the

Eleanor Roosevelt Intelligent, principled, and a political figure in her own right, she is pictured here addressing the Red Cross Convention in 1934.

nation, speaking in support of the New Deal, meeting with African American leaders, supporting women's causes and labor unions, and urging Americans to live up to their humanitarian ideals. In 1933, she convened a White House conference on the emergency needs of women which urged the Federal Emergency Relief Administration (FERA) to ensure that it "pay particular attention to see that women are employed wherever possible." Within six months, some 300,000 women were at work on various federal government projects.

A popular joke in Washington claimed that President Roosevelt's nightly prayer was: "Dear God, please make Eleanor a little tired." But he was in fact deeply dependent on his industrious wife. She was the impatient agitator dedicated to what *should* be done; he was the calculating politician concerned with what *could* be done.

The New Deal under Fire

By 1934, Franklin Roosevelt had become the best loved and most hated president of the twentieth century. He was loved because he believed in and fought for the common people, for the "forgotten man" (and woman). And he was loved for what one French leader called his "glittering personality." Roosevelt radiated energy and hope, joy in his work, courage in a crisis, optimism for the future, and a monumental self-assurance bordering on arrogance. His famously arched eyebrows, upturned chin, and twinkling eyes, along with his cigarette holder, itself tilted upward, symbolized his jaunty determination to triumph over the nation's massive problems. "Meeting him," said British prime minister Winston Churchill, "was like uncorking a bottle of champagne." Roosevelt, he added, was "the greatest man I have ever known."

Roosevelt was perhaps the most visible and accessible president who had occupied the White House. Twice a week he held press conferences, explaining new legislation, addressing questions and criticisms, and, in the process, winning over most journalists. Roosevelt also mastered the art of using carefully timed radio addresses ("fireside chats") to speak to the nation.

But he was hated, too, especially by business leaders and political conservatives who believed that the New Deal and the higher taxes it required were moving America toward socialism. Some called Roosevelt a "traitor to his class." Even his cousin Alice, Theodore's daughter, accused him of being a dictator. Others, on the left, hated him for not doing enough to end the Depression. By the mid-1930s, the early New Deal programs had slowed the economy's downward slide, but prosperity remained elusive. "We have been patient and long suffering," said a farm leader. "We were promised a New Deal. . . . Instead, we have the same old stacked deck."

In many respects, the conflicting opinions of Roosevelt reflected his own divided personality and erratic management style. He was at the same time a man of idealistic principles and a practical politician prone to snap judgments, capable of both compromise and contradictory actions. He once admitted to an aide that to implement the New Deal he had to "deceive, misrepresent, leave false impressions . . . and trust to charm, loyalty, and the result to make up for it. . . . A great man cannot be a good man."

CONTINUING HARDSHIPS

Although the programs making up the First New Deal helped ease the devastation caused by the Depression, they did not restore prosperity or end the widespread suffering. As late as 1939, some 9.5 million workers (17 percent of the labor force) remained unemployed. Critics stressed that the economy, while stabilized, remained mired in the Depression.

"There's no way like the American way" Margaret Bourke-White's famous 1937 photograph of desperate people waiting in a Louisville, Kentucky, disaster-relief line captures the continuing racial divide of the era and the elusiveness of the "American Dream" for many minorities.

AFRICAN AMERICANS AND THE NEW DEAL However progressive Franklin Delano Roosevelt was on social issues, he showed little interest in the plight of African Americans, even as black voters were shifting from the Republicans (the "party of Lincoln") to the Democrats. Roosevelt, like Woodrow Wilson before him, failed to address long-standing patterns of racism and segregation in the South for fear of angering conservative southern Democrats in Congress.

As a result, many New Deal programs discriminated against blacks. As Mary White Ovington, the treasurer of the National Association for the Advancement of Colored People (NAACP), stressed, the racism in any agency "varies according to the white people chosen to administer it, but always there is discrimination." For example, the payments from the AAA to farm owners to take land *out* of production in an effort to raise the prices for farm products forced hundreds of thousands of tenant farmers and sharecroppers, both blacks and whites, off the land.

The FHA refused to guarantee mortgages on houses purchased by blacks in white neighborhoods, and both the CCC and the TVA practiced racial segregation. The NAACP waged an energetic legal campaign against racial prejudice throughout the 1930s, but a major setback occurred in the Supreme Court ruling on *Grovey v. Townsend* (1935), which upheld the Texas Democrats' whites-only election primary.

Thanks to relentless pressure from Eleanor Roosevelt, the president did appoint more African Americans to government positions than ever before. One of the most visible was Mary McLeod Bethune, the child of former slaves from South Carolina, who had founded Bethune-Cookman College in Florida and served as head of the NAACP in the 1920s. In 1935, Roosevelt approved her appointment as the director of the Division of Negro Affairs within the National Youth Administration, an agency that provided jobs to unemployed young Americans. Bethune worked with other blacks in New Deal agencies to form an informal "Black Cabinet" to ensure that African Americans had equal access to federal programs.

COURT CASES AND CIVIL LIBERTIES The continuing prejudice against blacks in the South was vividly revealed in a controversial case in Alabama. In 1931, an all-white jury, on flimsy, conflicting testimony, convicted nine black youths, ranging in age from thirteen to twenty-one, of raping two young white women while riding a freight train. Eight of the "Scottsboro Boys" were sentenced to death before cheering whites who packed the courtroom, while 10,000 spectators outside celebrated with a brass band. In his award-winning novel *Native Son* (1940), African American writer Richard Wright

Scottsboro case Haywood Patterson (center), one of the defendants in the case, with his attorney, Samuel Liebowitz (left) in Decatur, Alabama, in 1933.

recalled the "mob who surrounded the Scottsboro jail with rope and kerosene" after the initial conviction.

The injustice of the Scottsboro case sparked protests throughout the nation and the world. The two white girls, it turned out, had been selling sex to white and black boys on the train. One of the girls eventually recanted the rape charges and began appearing at rallies on behalf of the defendants.

No case in legal history had produced as many trials, appeals, reversals, and retrials as the Scottsboro case. Further, it prompted two important legal interpretations. In *Powell v. Alabama* (1932), the U.S. Supreme Court overturned the original convictions because the judge had not ensured that the accused were provided adequate defense attorneys. The Court ordered new trials. In another case, *Norris v. Alabama* (1935), the Court ruled that the systematic exclusion of African Americans from Alabama juries had denied the Scottsboro defendants equal protection under the law—a principle that had widespread impact on state courts by opening up juries to blacks. Although the state of Alabama eventually dropped the charges against the four youngest of the Scottsboro defendants and granted paroles to the others, their lives were ruined. The last defendant was released from prison in 1950.

NATIVE AMERICANS AND THE DEPRESSION The Great Depression also ravaged Native Americans. They were initially encouraged by Roosevelt's appointment of John Collier as commissioner of the Bureau of Indian Affairs (BIA). Collier steadily increased the number of Native Americans employed by the BIA and ensured that Native Americans gained access to the various relief programs. Collier's primary objective, however, was passage of the Indian Reorganization Act. Designed to reinvigorate Native American cultural traditions by restoring land to tribes, the proposed law would have granted them the right to start businesses, establish self-governing constitutions, and receive federal funds for vocational training and economic development. The act that Congress passed, however, was a much-diluted version of Collier's original proposal, and the "Indian New Deal" brought only partial improvement to the lives of Native Americans. But it did spur the various tribes to revise their constitutions so as to give women the right to vote and hold office.

CULTURAL LIFE DURING THE DEPRESSION

In view of the celebrated—if exaggerated—alienation felt by the "lost generation" of writers, artists, and intellectuals during the 1920s, one might have expected the onset of the Great Depression to have deepened their despair. Instead, it brought a renewed sense of militancy and affirmation, as if society could no longer afford the art-for-art's-sake outlook of the 1920s. Said one writer early in 1932: "I enjoy the period thoroughly. The breakdown of our cult of business success and optimism, the miraculous disappearance of our famous American complacency, all this is having a tonic effect."

In the early 1930s, the "tonic effect" of commitment sometimes sparked revolutionary political activities. By the summer of 1932, even the "golden boy" of the "lost generation," the writer F. Scott Fitzgerald, had declared that "to bring on the revolution, it may be necessary to work within the Communist party." But few Americans remained Communists for long. Being a notoriously independent lot, most writers rebelled at demands to hew to a shifting party line. And many abandoned communism upon learning that the Soviet leader Josef Stalin practiced a tyranny more horrible than anything under the Russian czars.

LITERATURE AND THE DEPRESSION Among the writers who addressed themes of social significance during the 1930s, two deserve special notice: John Steinbeck and Richard Wright. The novel that best captured the ordeal of the Depression, Steinbeck's *The Grapes of Wrath* (1939), treats workers as people rather than variables in a political formula. Steinbeck had traveled with displaced "Okies" driven from the Oklahoma Dust Bowl to pursue the illusion of good jobs in the fields of California's Central Valley. This firsthand experience allowed him to create a vivid tale of the Joad family's painful journey west.

Among the most talented novelists to emerge in the 1930s was Richard Wright. The grandson of former slaves and the son of a Mississippi sharecropper who deserted his family, Wright ended his formal schooling with the ninth grade (as valedictorian of his class). He then worked in Memphis and devoured books he borrowed on a white friend's library card, all the while saving to go north to escape the racism of the South. In Chicago, the Federal Writers' Project gave him a chance to develop his talent. His period as a Communist, from 1934 to 1944, gave him an intellectual framework that did not overpower his fierce independence. *Native Son* (1940), Wright's masterpiece, is the story of Bigger Thomas, a product of the ghetto who is hemmed in by forces beyond his control, and finally impelled to commit murder.

POPULAR CULTURE While many writers and artists dealt with the suffering and social tensions aroused by the Great Depression, the more popular cultural outlets, such as radio programs and movies, provided a welcome escape from the decade's grim realities. In 1930, more than 10 million families owned a radio; by the end of the decade, the number had tripled. Franklin Roosevelt was the first president to take full advantage of the popularity of radio broadcasting. He hosted sixteen "fireside chats" to generate support for his New Deal initiatives.

In the late 1920s, movies were transformed by the introduction of sound. The "talkies" made movies by far the most popular form of entertainment during the 1930s—much more popular than they are today. The introduction of double features in 1931 and the construction of outdoor drive-in theaters in 1933 boosted interest and attendance. More than 60 percent of the population—70 million people—paid a quarter to see at least one movie each week.

The movies of the 1930s rarely dealt directly with hard times. People wanted to be cheered up when they entered movie houses. In *Stand Up and Cheer!* (1934), featuring child star Shirley Temple, President Roosevelt appoints a Broadway producer to his cabinet as the Secretary of Amusement. His goal is to use entertainment to distract people from the ravages of the Depression.

Most feature films transported viewers into the escapist realm of adventure, spectacle, and fantasy. *Gone with the Wind* (1939), based on Margaret Mitchell's Pulitzer Prize-winning novel, was a good example of such escapism, as were *The Wizard of Oz* (1939) and Walt Disney's feature cartoons. Moviegoers also relished shoot-'em-up gangster films, spectacular musicals (especially those starring dancers Fred Astaire and Ginger Rogers), "screwball" romantic comedies featuring wacky situations, zany characters, and witty dialogue like *It Happened One Night* (1934), *My Man Godfrey* (1936), and *Mister Deeds Goes to Town* (1936), and horror films such as *Dracula* (1931), *Frankenstein* (1931), *The Mummy* (1932), *King Kong* (1933), *The Invisible Man* (1933), and *Werewolf of London* (1935).

***A Paramount Picture* (1934)** The glamor of actress Claudette Colbert's Cleopatra is sharply contrasted with the exhaustion of the average theatergoer in this painting by Reginald Marsh. The growing popularity of movies offered Americans escape from the daily challenges of the Great Depression, though Marsh's work suggests that this was fleeting at best.

Perhaps the best way to escape the daily troubles of the Depression was to watch one of the zany comedies of the Marx Brothers, former vaudeville performers turned movie stars. As one Hollywood official explained, the movies of the 1930s were intended to "laugh the big bad wolf of the depression out of the public mind." *The Cocoanuts* (1929), *Animal Crackers* (1930), *Monkey Business* (1931), *Horse Feathers* (1932), and *Duck Soup* (1933) introduced moviegoers to the anarchic antics of Chico, Groucho, Harpo, and Zeppo Marx, who combined slapstick humor with verbal wit to create plotless masterpieces of irreverent satire.

CRITICS ASSAULT THE NEW DEAL

For all of their criticisms of the inadequacy of New Deal programs, Native Americans and African Americans still voted in large majorities for Franklin Roosevelt. Other New Deal critics, however, hated Roosevelt the man, as much as they despised his policies. Many Republican business executives were so angered by the president's promotion of a welfare state and the goals of labor unions that they refused to use the president's name, calling him instead "that man in the White House."

HUEY LONG Others criticized Roosevelt for not doing enough to help the common people. The most potent of the president's "populist" opponents was Huey Pierce Long Jr., a Democratic senator from Louisiana. A short, colorful man with wild, curly hair, Long, known as "Kingfish," was a theatrical politician (a demagogue) who appealed to the raw emotions of the masses. The swaggering son of a backwoods farmer, he sported pink suits and pastel shirts, red ties, and two-toned shoes. He claimed to serve the poor, arguing that his Louisiana would be a place where "every man [is] a king, but no one wears a crown."

Huey Long As the powerful governor of Louisiana, Long was a shrewd lawyer and consummate "wheeler-dealer" politician.

First as Louisiana's governor, then as its most powerful U.S. senator, Long viewed the state as his personal empire. Reporters called him the "dictator of Louisiana." True, he reduced state taxes, improved roads and schools, built charity hospitals, and provided better public services, but in the process, he used bribery, intimidation, and blackmail to get his way.

In 1933, Long arrived in Washington as a supporter of Roosevelt and the New Deal, but he quickly grew suspicious of the NRA's efforts to cooperate with big business. Having developed presidential aspirations, he had also grown jealous of "Prince Franklin" Roosevelt's popularity.

To launch his own presidential candidacy, Long devised a simplistic plan for dealing with the Great Depression that he called the Share-the-Wealth Society. Long wanted to raise taxes on the wealthiest Americans and redistribute the money to "the people"—giving every poor family $5,000 and every worker an annual income of $2,500, providing pensions to retirees, reducing working hours, paying bonuses to military veterans, and enabling every qualified student to attend college. It did not matter that his plan would have spent far more money than would have been raised by his proposed taxes. As he told a group of Iowa farmers, "Maybe somebody says I don't understand it [government finance]. Well, you don't have to. Just shut your damn eyes and believe it. That's all."

By early 1935, Long claimed to have enough support to unseat Roosevelt. "I can take him," he bragged. "He's a phony. . . . He's scared of me. I can out-promise him, and he knows it. People will believe me, and they won't believe him." Long's antics led the president to declare that the Louisiana senator was "one of the two most dangerous men in the country." (The other was General Douglas MacArthur.)

THE TOWNSEND PLAN Another popular critic of Roosevelt was a retired California doctor, Francis E. Townsend. Shocked by the sight of three elderly women digging through garbage cans for food scraps, he began promoting the Townsend Recovery Plan in 1934. Townsend wanted the federal government to pay $200 a month to every American over sixty who agreed to quit working. The recipients would have to spend the money each month.

Townsend claimed that his plan would create jobs for young people by giving older people the means to retire, and it would energize the economy by enabling retirees to buy more products. But like Huey Long's Share-the-Wealth scheme, the numbers in Townsend's plan did not add up; although it would have served only 9 percent of the population, it would have paid those retirees more than half the total national income.

Townsend, like Long, didn't care about the plan's cost. Not surprisingly, it attracted great support among Americans sixty years of age and older. Thousands of Townsend Clubs sprang up across the nation, and advocates flooded the White House with letters urging Roosevelt to enact it.

FATHER COUGHLIN A third outspoken critic was Father Charles E. Coughlin, a Roman Catholic "radio priest" in Detroit, Michigan. In fiery weekly broadcasts that attracted as many as 40 million listeners, he assailed Roosevelt as "anti-God" and claimed that the New Deal was a Communist conspiracy. During the 1930s, Coughlin became increasingly anti-Semitic, claiming that Roosevelt was a tool of "international Jewish bankers" and relabeling the New Deal the "Jew Deal." He praised Adolf Hitler and the Nazis for killing Jews because he believed that all Jews were Communists who must be hunted down. During the 1940 presidential campaign, the thuggish Coughlin gave a Nazi salute and bragged, "When we get through with the Jews in America they'll think the treatment they received in Germany was nothing."

Of Long, Townsend, and Coughlin, Long had the largest political following. A 1935 poll showed that he could draw more than 5 million votes as a third-party candidate for president, perhaps enough to prevent Roosevelt's reelection. Roosevelt decided to "steal the thunder" from his most vocal critics by instituting an array of new programs. "I'm fighting Communism, Huey Longism, Coughlinism, Townsendism," Roosevelt told a reporter in early 1935. He needed "to save our system, the capitalist system" from such "crackpot ideas."

Promoters of welfare capitalism Dr. Francis E. Townsend, Rev. Gerald L. K. Smith, and Rev. Charles E. Coughlin (left to right) attend the Townsend Recovery Plan convention in Cleveland, Ohio.

OPPOSITION FROM THE COURT

The opposition to the New Deal came from all directions. Among the most powerful opponents was the U.S. Supreme Court. By the mid-1930s, businesses were filing lawsuits against various elements of the New Deal, and some of them made their way to the Supreme Court.

On May 27, 1935, the U.S. Supreme Court killed the National Industrial Recovery Act (NIRA) by a unanimous vote. In *Schechter Poultry Corporation v. United States*, the justices ruled that Congress had given too much of its authority to the president when the NIRA created the National Recovery Administration (NRA), giving it the power to bring business and labor leaders together to create "codes of fair competition" for their industries—an activity that violated federal anti-trust laws. In a press conference soon after the Court announced its decision, Roosevelt fumed: "We have been relegated to the horse-and-buggy definition of interstate commerce."

Then, on January 6, 1936, in *United States v. Butler*, the Supreme Court declared the Agricultural Adjustment Act's tax on "middle men," the companies that processed food crops and commodities like cotton, unconstitutional. In response to the Court's decision, the Roosevelt administration passed the Agricultural Adjustment Act of 1938, which reestablished the earlier crop-reduction payment programs but left out the tax on processors. Although the AAA helped boost the overall farm economy, conservatives criticized its sweeping powers. By the end of its 1936 term, the Supreme Court had ruled against New Deal programs in seven of nine major cases. The same line of conservative judicial reasoning, Roosevelt warned, might endanger other New Deal programs—if he did not act swiftly to prevent it.

THE SECOND NEW DEAL

To rescue his legislative program from judicial and political challenges, Roosevelt in January 1935 launched the second, more radical phase of the New Deal, explaining that "social justice, no longer a distant ideal, has become a definite goal" of his administration. In his effort "to steal Huey Long's thunder," the president called on Congress to pass a cluster of what he designated as "must" legislation that included a federal construction program to employ the jobless; banking reforms; increased taxes on the wealthy; and "social security" programs to protect people during unemployment, old age, and illness. Roosevelt's closest aide, Harry L. Hopkins, told the cabinet: "Boys—this is our hour. We've got to get everything we want—a [public] works program, social security, wages and hours, everything—now or never."

THE WPA In the first three months of 1935, dubbed the Second Hundred Days, Roosevelt convinced Congress to pass most of the **Second New Deal**'s "must" legislation. The results changed the face of American life. The first major initiative was the $4.8 billion Emergency Relief Appropriation Act. The largest peacetime spending bill in history to that point, it included an array of federal job programs managed by a new agency, the **Works Progress Administration (WPA)**.

The WPA quickly became the nation's largest employer, hiring an average of 2 million people annually over four years. WPA workers built New York's LaGuardia Airport, restored the St. Louis riverfront, and managed the bankrupt city of Key West, Florida. The WPA also employed a wide range of writers, artists, actors, and musicians in new cultural programs: the Federal Theatre Project, the Federal Art Project, the Federal Music Project, and the Federal Writers' Project.

The National Youth Administration (NYA), also under the WPA, provided part-time employment to students and aided jobless youths. Two future presidents were among the beneficiaries; twenty-seven-year-old Lyndon B. Johnson

Federal art project A group of WPA artists at work on *Building the Transcontinental Railroad*, a mural celebrating the contributions of foreign newcomers that appears in the immigrants' dining hall on Ellis Island, outside of New York City.

directed an NYA program in Texas, and Richard M. Nixon, a struggling Duke University law student, found work through the NYA at 35¢ an hour. Although the WPA took care of only 3 million of some 10 million jobless at any one time, it helped some 9 million people before it expired in 1943.

THE WAGNER ACT Another major element of the Second New Deal was the National Labor Relations Act, often called the **Wagner Act** in honor of the New York senator, Robert Wagner, who drafted it and convinced Roosevelt to support it. The Wagner Act was one of the most important pieces of labor legislation in history, guaranteeing workers the right to organize unions and bargain directly with management about wages and other issues. It also created a National Labor Relations Board to oversee union activities.

SOCIAL SECURITY As Francis Townsend had stressed, the Great Depression hit the oldest Americans and those with disabilities especially hard. To address the problems faced by the elderly and disabled, Roosevelt proposed the **Social Security Act** of 1935. Social Security was, he announced, the "cornerstone" and "supreme achievement" of the New Deal.

The basic concept of government assistance to the elderly was not new. Progressives during the early 1900s had proposed a federal system of social security for the aged, poor, disabled, and unemployed. Other nations had already enacted such programs, but not the United States. The hardships caused by the Great Depression revived the idea, however, and Roosevelt masterfully guided the legislation through Congress.

The Social Security Act was designed largely by Secretary of Labor Frances Perkins, the first woman cabinet member in history. Its centerpiece was a self-financed federal retirement fund for people over sixty-five. Beginning in 1937, workers and employers contributed payroll taxes to establish the fund. Most of the collected taxes were spent on pension payments to retirees; whatever was left over went into a trust fund for the future. Roosevelt stressed that Social Security was not intended to guarantee everyone a comfortable retirement. Rather, it was meant to supplement other sources of income and protect the elderly. Only during the 1950s did voters and politicians come to view Social Security as the *primary* source of retirement income for working-class Americans.

The Social Security Act also set up a shared federal–state unemployment-insurance program, financed by a payroll tax on employers. In addition, it committed the national government to a broad range of social-welfare activities based upon the assumption that "unemployables"—people who were unable to work—would remain a state responsibility while the national government would provide work relief for the able-bodied. To that end, the Social Security Act provided federal funding for three state-administered public-assistance programs—old-age assistance, aid to dependent children, and aid for the blind—and further aid for maternal, child-welfare, and public health services.

When compared with similar programs in Europe, the U.S. Social Security system was conservative. It was the only government-managed retirement program in the world financed by taxes on the earnings of workers; most other countries funded such programs out of general government revenues.

The Social Security payroll tax was also a regressive tax because it used a single withholding tax *rate* for everyone, regardless of income level. It thus pinched the poor more than the rich, and it hurt efforts to revive the economy because it removed from circulation a significant amount of money. In addition, the Social Security system, at the insistence of southern Democrats

Social Security A poster distributed by the government to educate the public about the new Social Security Act.

determined to maintain white supremacy, excluded 9.5 million workers who most needed the new program: farm laborers, domestic workers (maids and cooks), and the self-employed, a disproportionate percentage of whom were African Americans.

Roosevelt regretted the act's limitations, but he knew that they were necessary compromises to gain congressional approval and to withstand court challenges. As he told an aide who criticized funding the program out of employee contributions:

> I guess you're right on the economics, but those taxes were never a problem of economics. They are politics all the way through. We put those payroll contributions there so as to give the contributors a moral, legal, and political right to collect their pensions and their unemployment benefits. With those taxes in there, no damn politician can ever scrap my Social Security program.

Roosevelt also preferred that workers fund their own Social Security pensions because he wanted Americans to view their retirement checks as an *entitlement*—as something that they had paid for and deserved. Conservatives condemned the Social Security Act as tyrannical and "socialistic." Former president Herbert Hoover refused to apply for a Social Security card because of his opposition to the "radical" program. He received a Social Security number anyway.

TAXING THE RICH Another major bill in the second phase of the New Deal was the Revenue Act of 1935, sometimes called the "Wealth-Tax Act" but popularly known as the "soak-the-rich" tax. It raised tax rates on annual income above $50,000, in part because of stories that many wealthy Americans were not paying taxes. The powerful banker J.P. Morgan confessed to a Senate committee that he had created fictitious sales of stock to his wife that enabled him to pay no taxes.

Labor union violence This 1935 photograph captures unionized strikers fighting "scabs," or nonunion replacement employees, as the scabs try to pass the picket line and enter the factory.

Morgan and other business leaders fumed over Roosevelt's tax and spending policies. Newspaper tycoon William Randolph Hearst growled that the wealth tax was "essentially communism." Roosevelt countered by stressing that "I am fighting communism. . . . I want to save our system, the capitalistic system." Yet he added that saving capitalism and "rebalancing" its essential elements required a more equal "distribution of wealth."

A NEW DIRECTION FOR UNIONS The New Deal reinvigorated the labor union movement. When the National Industrial Recovery Act (NIRA) demanded that every industry code affirm workers' rights to organize, unionists quickly translated it to mean "the president wants you to join the union." John L. Lewis, head of the United Mine Workers (UMW), was among the first to capitalize on the pro-union spirit of the NIRA. He rebuilt the UMW from 150,000 members to 500,000 within a year.

Encouraged by Lewis's success, Sidney Hillman of the Amalgamated Clothing Workers and David Dubinsky of the International Ladies Garment Workers organized workers in the clothing industry. As leaders of industrial unions (composed of all types of workers in a particular industry, skilled or unskilled), which were in the minority by far, they found the smaller, more restrictive craft unions (composed of skilled male workers only, with each union serving just one trade) to be obstacles to organizing workers in the country's basic industries.

In 1935, with the passage of the Wagner Act, industrial unionists formed a Committee for Industrial Organization (CIO). Craft unionists began to fear submergence by the mass unions made up mainly of unskilled workers. Jurisdictional disputes divided them, and in 1936 the American Federation of Labor (AFL) expelled the CIO unions, which then formed a permanent structure, called after 1938 the Congress of Industrial Organizations (also known by the initials CIO). The rivalry spurred both groups to greater efforts.

The CIO focused on organizing the automobile and steel industries. Until the Supreme Court upheld the Wagner Act in 1937, however, companies failed to cooperate with its pro-union provisions. Employers instead used various forms of intimidation to fight the infant unions. Early in 1937, automobile workers spontaneously tried a new tactic, the "sit-down strike," in which they refused to leave a workplace until employers had granted them collective-bargaining rights.

Led by the fiery Walter Reuther, thousands of employees at the General Motors assembly plants in Flint, Michigan, occupied the factories and stopped all production. Company officials called in police to harass the strikers, sent spies to union meetings, and threatened to fire the workers. They also pleaded with President Roosevelt to dispatch federal troops. He refused, while expressing his displeasure with the sit-down strike, which the courts later declared illegal. The standoff lasted more than a month. Then, on February 11, 1937, the company relented and signed a contract recognizing the United Automobile Workers (UAW) as a legitimate union.

ROOSEVELT'S SECOND TERM

On June 27, 1936, Franklin Delano Roosevelt accepted the Democratic party's nomination for a second term. The Republicans chose Governor Alfred M. Landon of Kansas, a progressive Republican who had endorsed many New Deal programs. "We cannot go back to the days before the depression," he scolded conservative Republicans. "We must go forward, facing our new problems." The Republicans hoped that the followers of Huey Long, Charles E. Coughlin, Francis E. Townsend, and other Roosevelt critics would combine to draw enough Democratic votes away from the president to give Landon a winning margin.

But that possibility faded when an assassin, the son-in-law of a Louisiana judge whom Long had sought to remove, shot and killed the forty-two-year-old senator in 1935. In the 1936 election, Roosevelt carried every state except

Campaigning for a second term Roosevelt campaigning with labor leader John L. Lewis (to the right of Roosevelt) in Wilkes-Barre, Pennsylvania.

Maine and Vermont, with a popular vote of 27.7 million to Landon's 16.7 million, the largest margin of victory to that point. Democrats would also dominate the new Congress, by 77 to 19 in the Senate and 328 to 107 in the House.

In winning another landslide election, Roosevelt forged a new electoral coalition that would affect national politics for years to come. While holding the support of most traditional Democrats, North and South, he made strong gains in the West among beneficiaries of New Deal agricultural programs. In the northern cities, he held on to the ethnic groups helped by New Deal welfare policies. Many middle-class voters whose property had been saved by New Deal measures flocked to support Roosevelt, as did intellectuals stirred by the ferment of new ideas coming from the government. The revived labor union movement also threw its support to Roosevelt, and in the most meaningful shift of all, a majority of African Americans voted for a Democratic president. "My friends, go home and turn Lincoln's picture to the wall," a Pittsburgh journalist told black voters. "That debt has been paid in full."

THE COURT-PACKING PLAN Roosevelt's landslide victory convinced him that he could do almost anything and the voters would support him. He believed his reelection demonstrated that the nation wanted even more government action to revive the economy. The three-to-one Democratic majorities in Congress ensured that he could pass new legislation. But one major roadblock stood in the way: the conservative Supreme Court, made up of "nine old men."

Lawsuits challenging the constitutionality of the Social Security and Wagner Acts were pending before the Court. Given the Court's conservative bent and its earlier anti–New Deal rulings, Roosevelt feared that the Second New Deal was in danger of being nullified.

For that reason, he hatched a clumsy plan to "reform" the Court by enlarging it. Congress, not the Constitution, determines the size of the Supreme Court, which over the years had numbered between six and ten justices. In 1937, the number was nine. On February 5, 1937, Roosevelt, without consulting congressional leaders or even his own advisers, asked Congress to name up to six new Supreme Court justices, one for each of the current justices over seventy years old, explaining that the aging members of the Court were falling behind in their work and needed help.

But the **"Court-packing" scheme**, as opponents labeled the plan, backfired. It was too manipulative and far too political, and quickly became the most controversial proposal of Roosevelt's presidency. The plan ignited a firestorm of opposition among conservative Republicans and even aroused fears among Democrats that the president was seeking dangerous new powers.

As it turned out, several Court decisions during the spring of 1937 surprisingly upheld disputed provisions of the Wagner and Social Security Acts. In addition, a conservative justice resigned, and Roosevelt replaced him with a New Dealer, Senator Hugo Black of Alabama.

Despite criticism from both parties, Roosevelt insisted on forcing his Court-packing bill through Congress. On July 22, 1937, the Senate overwhelmingly voted it down. It was the biggest political blunder and greatest humiliation of Roosevelt's career. The episode fractured the Democratic party and damaged the president's prestige. The momentum of his 1936 landslide victory was lost. As Secretary of Agriculture Henry A. Wallace later remarked, "The whole New Deal really went up in smoke as a result of the Supreme Court fight."

A SLUMPING ECONOMY During 1935 and 1936, the economy finally began showing signs of revival. By the spring of 1937, industrial output had risen above the 1929 level. In 1937, however, Roosevelt, worried about federal budget deficits and rising inflation, ordered sharp cuts in government spending. The economy stalled, then slid into a slump deeper than that of 1929. In only three months, unemployment rose by 2 million people. When the spring of 1938 failed to bring economic recovery, Roosevelt reversed himself and asked Congress to adopt a new federal spending program, and Congress voted $3.3 billion in new expenditures. The increase in government spending reversed the economy's decline, but only during World War II would employment again reach pre-1929 levels.

The Court-packing fight, the sit-down strikes, and the 1937 recession all undercut Roosevelt's prestige and power. When the 1937 congressional session ended, the only major New Deal initiatives were the Wagner-Steagall National Housing Act and the Bankhead-Jones Farm Tenant Act. The Housing Act, developed by Senator Robert F. Wagner, set up the federal Housing Authority, which extended long-term loans to cities to build public housing projects in blighted neighborhoods and provide subsidized rents for poor people. Later, during World War II, it financed housing for workers in new defense plants.

The Farm Tenant Act created a new agency, the Farm Security Administration (FSA), which provided loans to keep farm owners from losing their land to bankruptcy. It also made loans to tenant farmers to enable them to purchase farms. In the end, however, the FSA proved to be little more than another relief operation that tided a few farmers over during difficult times. A more effective answer to the problem eventually arrived in the form of national mobilization for war, which landed many struggling tenant farmers in military service or the defense industry, broadened their horizons, and taught them new skills.

In 1938, the Democratic Congress also enacted the Fair Labor Standards Act. It replaced many of the provisions that had been in the NIRA, which had been declared unconstitutional. The federal government established a minimum wage of 40¢ an hour and a maximum workweek of forty hours. The act, which applied only to businesses engaged in *interstate* commerce, also prohibited the employment of children under the age of sixteen.

SETBACKS FOR THE PRESIDENT During the late 1930s, the Democrats in Congress increasingly split into two factions, with conservative southerners on one side and liberal northerners on the other. Many white southern Democrats balked at the party's growing dependence on the votes of northern labor unions and African Americans. Senator Ellison "Cotton Ed" Smith of South Carolina and several other southern delegates walked out of the 1936 Democratic party convention, with Smith declaring that he would not support any party that views "the Negro as a political and social equal." Other critics believed that Roosevelt was exercising too much power and spending too much money. Some southern Democrats began to work with conservative Republicans to veto any additional New Deal programs.

Roosevelt now headed a divided party, and the congressional elections of November 1938 handed the administration another setback when the Democrats lost 7 seats in the Senate and 80 in the House. In his State of the Union message in 1939, Roosevelt for the first time presented no new reform programs but instead spoke of the need "to *preserve* our reforms." The conservative coalition of Republicans and southern Democrats had stalemated the president. As one observer noted, the New Deal "has been reduced to a movement with no program, with no effective political organization, with no vast popular party strength behind it."

A HALFWAY REVOLUTION The New Deal's political momentum petered out in 1939 just as a new world war was erupting in Europe and Asia. Many New Deal programs had failed or were poorly conceived and implemented, but others were changing American life for the better: Social Security, federal regulation of stock markets and banks, minimum wage levels for workers, federally insured bank accounts, the right to join labor unions. Never before had the federal government intervened so directly in the economy or spent so much on social welfare programs. Franklin Roosevelt had also transformed the nation's political dynamics, luring black voters in large numbers to the Democratic party, and he had raised the nation's spirits through his relentless optimism.

Roosevelt had led the nation out of the Depression and changed the role of the federal government. By the end of the 1930s, its power and scope were vastly larger than in 1932. Landmark laws expanded the powers of the national

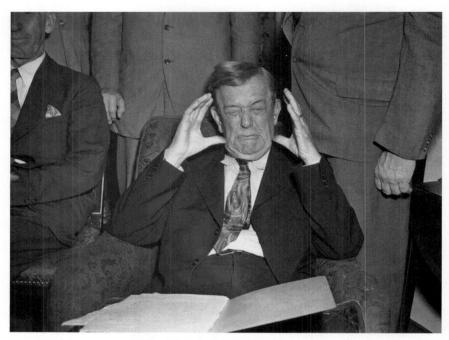

Meeting of the anti–New Dealers Democratic senator Ellison D. "Cotton Ed" Smith of South Carolina cringes at the thought of a fourth term for Roosevelt, while meeting with fellow anti–New Dealers at the Mayflower Hotel in Washington, D.C.

government by establishing new regulatory agencies and laying the foundation of a social welfare system.

Most important of all, the New Deal brought faith and hope to the discouraged and desperate. As a CCC worker recalled late in life, Roosevelt "restored a sense of confidence and morale and hope—hope being the greatest of all." New Deal programs provided stability for tens of millions of people. "We aren't on relief anymore," one woman noted with pride. "My husband is working for the government."

The enduring reforms of the New Deal also constituted a significant change from the progressivism of Theodore Roosevelt and Woodrow Wilson. They had assumed that the function of government was to use aggressive *regulation* of industry and business to ensure that people had an equal opportunity to pursue the American Dream. But Franklin Roosevelt and the New Dealers insisted that the government should provide at least a minimal quality of life for all Americans. The enduring protections afforded by bank-deposit insurance, unemployment benefits, a minimum hourly wage, the Wagner Act, and Social Security pensions gave people a sense of security and protected the nation against future economic crises. (There has not been a similar "depression" since the 1930s.)

The greatest failure of the New Deal was its inability to restore prosperity and end record levels of unemployment. In 1939, 10 million Americans—nearly 17 percent of the workforce—remained jobless. Only the Second World War would finally produce full employment—in the armed forces as well as in factories supporting the military.

Roosevelt's energetic pragmatism was his greatest strength—and weakness. He was flexible in developing new policies and programs; he kept what worked and discarded what failed. He sharply increased the regulatory powers of the federal government and laid the foundation for what would become an expanding system of social welfare programs. Despite what his critics charged, however, Roosevelt was no socialist; he sought to preserve the basic capitalist economic structure while providing protection to the nation's most vulnerable people. In this sense, the New Deal represented a "halfway revolution" that permanently altered the nation's social and political landscape. In a time of peril, Roosevelt created for Americans a more secure future.

CHAPTER REVIEW

SUMMARY

- **Hoover's Failure**   The first phase of the federal response to the *Great Depression* included President Hoover's attempts at increasing public works and exhorting unions, businesses, and farmers to cooperate to revive economic growth. His belief in voluntary self-reliance prevented him from using federal intervention to relieve the human suffering and contributed to his underestimation of the financial collapse. Such programs as the *Reconstruction Finance Corporation* were too few and too late. By March 1933, the economy was shattered. Millions of Americans were without jobs, without the basic necessities, and without hope.

- **The First New Deal**   In 1933, newly inaugurated president Franklin Delano Roosevelt and his "brain trust" set out to restore the economy and public confidence. During his early months in office, Congress and Roosevelt enacted the *First New Deal*, which propped up the banking industry with the *Federal Deposit Insurance Corporation*, provided short-term emergency work relief in the form of jobs for the unemployed, promoted industrial recovery with the *National Recovery Administration*, and passed the *Agricultural Adjustment Act* intended to raise agricultural prices by encouraging farmers to cut production. Most of the early New Deal programs eased hardships but did not restore prosperity; they helped to end the economy's downward spiral but still left millions unemployed and mired in poverty.

- **New Deal Under Fire**   The Supreme Court ruled that many of the First New Deal programs were unconstitutional violations of private property and states' rights. Many conservatives criticized the New Deal for expanding the scope and reach of the federal government so much that it was steering the nation toward socialism. The "radio priest," Father Charles E. Coughlin, charged that the New Deal was a Jewish-atheist-Communist conspiracy. Other critics did not think the New Deal reforms went far enough. Senator Huey Long of Louisiana and Dr. Francis Townsend of California proposed radical plans to reshape the distribution of wealth from the rich to the poor. African Americans criticized the widespread racial discrimination in New Deal policies and agencies.

- **The Second New Deal and the New Deal's Legacy**   Roosevelt responded to the criticism and the continuing economic hardship with a *Second New Deal*, which sought to reshape the nation's social structure by expanding the role of the federal government. Many of the programs making up the Second New Deal, such as the *Works Progress Administration*, *Social Security*, and the *Wagner Act*, aimed to achieve greater social justice by establishing new regulatory agencies and laying the foundation of a federal social welfare system. Frustrated by the Supreme Court's opposition to the First New Deal, Roosevelt proposed his *"Court-packing" scheme*, but it was rejected by the Senate. Support for the New Deal began to lose steam amid the lingering effects of the Great Depression. However, the New Deal established the idea that the federal government should provide at least a minimal quality of life for all Americans, and it provided people with some security against a future crisis, reaffirming for millions a faith in American capitalism.

CHRONOLOGY

November 1932	Franklin D. Roosevelt is elected president
March 1933	Congress passes the Emergency Banking Relief Act ("Bank Holiday")
	Congress establishes the Civilian Conservation Corps
May 1933	Congress creates the Tennessee Valley Authority and the Agricultural Adjustment Act
June 1933	Congress establishes the Federal Deposit Insurance Corporation (Banking Act) and passes National Industrial Recovery Act
December 1933	Prohibition repealed with the passage of the Twenty-First Amendment to the Constitution
May 1935	Supreme Court finds National Industrial Recovery Act unconstitutional
1935	President Roosevelt creates the Works Progress Administration
1936	President Roosevelt is reelected in a landslide
1937	Social Security payments begin

KEY TERMS

Great Depression (1929–1941) p. 1105

Reconstruction Finance Corporation (RFC) (1933) p. 1109

Bonus Expeditionary Force p. 1110

First New Deal (1933–1935) p. 1115

Federal Deposit Insurance Corporation (FDIC) (1933) p. 1116

Securities and Exchange Commission (1934) p. 1117

National Recovery Administration (NRA) (1933) p. 1120

Agricultural Adjustment Act (1933) p. 1121

Dust Bowl p. 1121

Second New Deal (1935–1938) p. 1137

Works Progress Administration (WPA) (1935) p. 1137

Wagner Act (1935) p. 1138

Social Security Act (1935) p. 1138

"Court-packing" scheme (1937) p. 1143

 INQUIZITIVE

Go to InQuizitive to see what you've learned—and learn what you've missed—with personalized feedback along the way.

26 The Second World War

1933–1945

***Raising the Flag on Iwo Jima* (February 23, 1945)** Five members of the United States Marine Corps raise the U.S. flag on Mount Suribachi, during the Battle of Iwo Jima. Three of these Marines would die within days after this photograph was taken. The image earned photographer Joe Rosenthal the Pulitzer Prize. A bronze statue of this scene is the centerpiece of the Marine Corps War Memorial in Virginia.

W hen Franklin Roosevelt became president in 1933, he shared with most Americans a determination to stay out of international disputes. His focus was on combating the Great Depression at home. While the United States had become deeply involved in global trade during the twenties, it had remained aloof from global conflicts. So-called isolationists insisted that there was no justification for America to become embroiled in international affairs, much less another major war. With each passing year during the thirties, however, Germany, Italy, and Japan threatened the peace and stability of Europe and Asia.

Roosevelt strove mightily to keep the United States out of what he called the "spreading epidemic of world lawlessness," as fascist dictatorships in Germany and Italy and ultranationalist militarists in Japan violated international law by invading neighboring countries. By the end of the decade, Roosevelt had decided that the only way for the United States to avoid fighting in another war was to offer all possible assistance to its allies, Great Britain, France, and China.

Roosevelt's efforts to stop "aggressor nations" ignited a fierce debate between isolationists and interventionists which ended with shocking suddenness on December 7, 1941, when Japan staged a surprise attack against U.S. military bases at Pearl Harbor in Hawaii. The second world war that Americans had struggled to avoid had arrived at last. It would become the most significant event of the twentieth century, engulfing five continents and leaving few people untouched.

The Japanese attack unified Americans as never before. Men and women rushed to join the armed forces. Eventually, 16.4 million people would serve

focus questions

1. How did German and Japanese actions lead to the outbreak of war in Europe and Asia?

2. How did President Roosevelt and Congress respond to the outbreak of wars in Europe and Asia between 1933 and 1941?

3. What were the effects of the Second World War on American society?

4. What were the major factors that enabled the United States and its allies to win the war in Europe?

5. How were the Japanese defeated in the war in the Pacific?

6. How did President Roosevelt and the Allies work to shape the postwar world?

in the military during the war, including 350,000 women. To defeat Japanese imperialism and German and Italian fascism, the United States mobilized all of its economic resources. The massive government spending required to wage total war boosted industrial production and wrenched the economy out of the Great Depression.

Four years after the attack on Pearl Harbor, the United States and its allies emerged victorious in the costliest and most destructive war in history. Cities were destroyed, nations dismembered, and societies transformed. More than 50 million people were killed in the war between 1939 and 1945—perhaps 60 percent of them civilians, including millions of Jews and other ethnic minorities in Nazi death camps and Soviet concentration camps.

The global scope and scale of the Second World War ended America's tradition of isolationism. By 1945, the United States was the world's most powerful nation, with new international interests and global responsibilities. The war left power vacuums in Europe and Asia that the Soviet Union and the United States sought to fill to protect their military, economic, and political interests. Instead of bringing peace, the end of the war led to a "cold war" between the two former allies. As the *New Yorker* magazine asked, "If you do not know that your country is now entangled beyond recall with the rest of the world, what do you know?"

THE RISE OF FASCISM IN EUROPE

In 1917, Woodrow Wilson had led the United States into the First World War to make the world "safe for democracy." In fact, though, democracy was in retreat after 1919, while Soviet communism was on the march. So, too, was **fascism**, a radical form of totalitarian government in which a dictator uses propaganda and brute force to seize control of all aspects of national life—the economy, the armed forces, the legal and educational systems, and the press. Fascism in Germany and Italy thrived on a violent ultranationalist patriotism and almost hysterical emotionalism built upon claims of racial superiority and the simmering resentments that grew out of defeat in the First World War.

At the same time, halfway around the world, the Japanese government fell under the control of expansionists eager to conquer China and most of Asia. Japanese leaders were convinced that they were a "master race" with a "mission" to lead a resurgent Asia, just as Adolf Hitler claimed that Germany's "mission," as home of the supposedly superior "Aryan" race, was to dominate Europe. By 1941, there would be only a dozen or so democratic nations left on earth.

ITALY AND GERMANY In 1922, former journalist Benito Mussolini and 40,000 of his black-shirted supporters seized control of Italy, taking advantage of a paralyzed political system incapable of dealing with widespread unemployment, runaway inflation, mass strikes, and fears of communism. By 1925, Mussolini was wielding dictatorial power as "Il Duce" (the Leader). He called his version of antisocialist totalitarian nationalism *fascism*. All political parties except the Fascists were eliminated, and several political opponents were murdered. There was something darkly comical about the strutting, chest-thumping Mussolini, who claimed that "my animal instincts are always right."

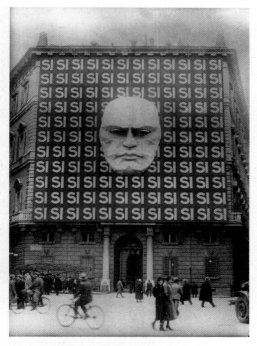

Fascist propaganda Benito Mussolini's headquarters in Rome's Palazzo Braschi, which bore an oversized reproduction of his head.

There was nothing amusing, however, about Mussolini's German counterpart, the Austrian-born Adolf Hitler. Hitler's remarkable transformation during the 1920s from social misfit to head of the National Socialist German Workers' (Nazi) party startled the world. Hitler and the Nazis claimed that they represented a German ("Aryan") master race whose "purity and strength" were threatened by liberals, Jews, socialists, Communists, homosexuals, Gypsies, and other "inferior" peoples. Hitler promised to make Germany strong again by renouncing the Versailles Treaty, defying the limits on its armed forces, and uniting the German-speaking people of Europe into a Greater German Empire that would give the nation "living space" to expand, dominate "lesser" races, and rid the continent of Jews.

Hitler portrayed himself as Germany's savior from the humiliation of having lost the Great War and the widespread suffering caused by the Great Depression. Appointed chancellor on January 30, 1933, five weeks before Franklin Roosevelt was first inaugurated, Hitler, like Mussolini, was idolized by the masses of voters. He declared himself absolute leader, or *Führer*, became president in 1934 and supreme commander of the armed forces, banned all

Adolf Hitler Hitler performs the Nazi salute at a rally. The giant banners, triumphant music, powerful oratory, and expansive military parades were all designed to stir excitement and allegiance among Nazis.

political parties except the Nazis, created a secret police force known as the *Gestapo*, and stripped people of voting rights. There would be no more elections, labor unions, or strikes.

During the mid-1930s, Hitler's brutal Nazi police state cranked up the engines of tyranny and terrorism, propaganda and censorship. Two million brown-shirted, brawling thugs, called "storm troopers," fanned out across the nation, burning books and persecuting, imprisoning, and murdering Communists, Jews, Gypsies—and their sympathizers.

THE EXPANDING AXIS As the 1930s unfolded, a catastrophic series of events in Asia and Europe sent the world hurtling toward disaster. In 1931–1932, some 10,000 Japanese troops had occupied Manchuria in northeast China, a territory rich in raw materials and deposits of iron ore and coal. At the time, China was fragmented by civil war between Communists led by Mao Zedong and Nationalists led by Chiang Kai-shek. The Japanese took advantage of China's weakness to proclaim Manchuria's independence, renaming it the "Republic of Manchukuo." In 1934, Japan began an aggressive military buildup in anticipation of conquering all of east Asia.

The next year, Mussolini launched Italy's reconquest of Ethiopia, a weak nation in eastern Africa that Italy had controlled until 1896. When the League of Nations branded Mussolini an aggressor and imposed economic sanctions on Italy, the racist Italian leader expressed surprise that European leaders would prefer a "horde of barbarian Negroes" in Ethiopia over Italy, the "mother of civilization."

In 1935, Hitler, in flagrant violation of the Versailles Treaty, began rebuilding Germany's armed forces. The next year, he sent 35,000 soldiers into the Rhineland, the demilitarized buffer zone between France and Germany. In a staged vote, 99 percent of the Germans living in the Rhineland approved Hitler's action. The failure of France and Great Britain to enforce the Versailles Treaty convinced Hitler that the western democracies were cowards and would not try to stop him from achieving his goal of German dominance.

The year 1936 also witnessed the outbreak of the Spanish Civil War, which began when Spanish troops loyal to General Francisco Franco, with the support of the Roman Catholic Church, revolted against the fragile new republican government. Hitler and Mussolini rushed troops ("volunteers"), warplanes, and military and financial aid to support Franco's fascist insurgency.

While peace in Europe was unraveling, the Japanese government fell under the control of aggressive militarists. In 1937, a government official announced that the "tide has turned against the liberalism and democracy that once swept over the nation." On July 7, 1937, Japanese and Chinese soldiers clashed at China's Marco Polo Bridge, near Beijing. The incident quickly escalated into a full-scale conflict, the Sino-Japanese War.

By December, the Japanese had captured the Nationalist Chinese capital of Nanjing, whereupon the undisciplined soldiers ran amok, looting the city and mercilessly murdering and raping civilians. As many as 300,000 Chinese were murdered in what came to be called the Rape of Nanjing. Thereafter, the Sino-Japanese War bogged down into a stalemate.

From Isolationism to Intervention

Most Americans responded to the mounting crises abroad by deepening their commitment to isolationism. In his 1933 inaugural address, President Roosevelt announced that he would continue to promote what he called "the good neighbor policy" in the Western Hemisphere, declaring that no nation "has the right to intervene in the internal or external affairs of another." True to his word, Roosevelt withdrew U.S. troops from Nicaragua and Haiti.

The nation's deeply rooted isolationist mood was reinforced by a prominent Senate inquiry into the role of bankers and businesses in the

Neutrality A 1938 cartoon shows U.S. foreign policy entangled by the serpent of isolationism.

American decision to enter World War I. Chaired by Senator Gerald P. Nye of North Dakota, the "Nye Committee" began hearings in 1934 that lasted until early 1936. The committee concluded that weapons makers and bankers (the "merchants of death") had spurred U.S. intervention in the European conflict in 1917 and were continuing to "help frighten nations into military activity."

U.S. NEUTRALITY In 1935, *Christian Century* magazine declared that "ninety-nine Americans out of a hundred would today regard as an imbecile anyone who might suggest that, in the event of another European war, the United States should again participate in it." Such widespread isolationism led President Roosevelt to sign the first of several **"neutrality laws"** passed by Congress to help avoid the supposed mistakes that had led the nation into the First World War. The Neutrality Act of 1935 prohibited Americans from selling weapons or traveling on ships owned by nations at war. In 1936, Congress revised the Neutrality Act by banning loans to warring nations.

Roosevelt, however, was not so sure that the United States could or should remain neutral. In October 1937, he delivered a speech in Chicago, the heartland of isolationism, in which he called for international cooperation to "quarantine the aggressors" who were responsible for disturbing world peace. But his appeal fell flat.

The Neutrality Act of 1937 allowed Roosevelt to require that nonmilitary American goods bought by warring nations be sold on a cash-and-carry basis—that is, a nation would have to pay cash and then carry the American-made goods away in its own ships. This was intended to preserve America's profitable trade with warring nations without running the risk of being drawn into the fighting.

THE AXIS ALLIANCE In 1937, Japan joined Germany and Italy in establishing the Rome-Berlin-Tokyo **"Axis" alliance**. Hitler and Mussolini vowed to create a "new order in Europe," while the Japanese imperialists pursued their "divine right" to control all of east Asia by creating what they called the Greater East Asia Co-Prosperity Sphere.

ANSCHLUSS In March 1938, Hitler forced the *Anschluss* (union) of Austria with Germany. Hitler's triumphant return to his native country was greeted by pro-German crowds waving Nazi flags and tossing flowers. Soon, "Jews not Wanted" signs appeared in Austrian cities.

A month later, after arresting more than 70,000 opponents of the Nazis, German leaders announced that a remarkable 99.75 percent of Austrian voters had "approved" the forced annexation. (In fact, some 400,000 Austrians, mostly liberals and Jews, were prevented from voting.) Again, no nation stepped up to oppose Hitler, and soon the Nazi government in Austria began arresting or murdering opponents and imprisoning or exiling Jews, including the famed psychiatrist Sigmund Freud.

THE MUNICH PACT (1938) Hitler then threatened to annex the Sudeten territory (Sudetenland), a mountainous region in western Czechoslovakia along the German border where more than 3 million ethnic Germans lived. British and French leaders repeatedly tried to "appease" Hitler, hoping that if they agreed to his demands for the Sudeten territory he would stop his aggressions.

On September 30, 1938, the British prime minister, Neville Chamberlain, and the French prime minister, Édouard Daladier, joined Mussolini and Hitler in signing the notorious Munich Pact, which transferred the Sudetenland to Germany. In Prague, the capital, the Czechs listened to the official announcement of the Munich Pact with the excruciating sadness of people too weak to preserve their own independence. As pawns in the chess game of European politics, the

Czech people now faced a grim future. A disgusted President Roosevelt privately grumbled that Britain and France had left Czechoslovakia "to paddle its own canoe" and predicted that they would "wash the blood from their Judas Iscariot hands." Hitler, he had decided, was a "wild man," a "nut" with an insatiable desire for a new German empire.

Chamberlain claimed that the Munich treaty had provided "peace for our time. Peace with honor." Winston Churchill, a member of the British Parliament who would become prime minister in May 1940, strongly disagreed. In a speech to the House of Commons, he claimed that "England has been offered a choice between war and shame. She has chosen shame, and will get war." The Munich Pact, he predicted, would not end Hitler's assaults. "This is only the beginning of the reckoning."

Churchill was right. Hitler had already confided to aides that he had no intention of abiding by the Munich Pact. Although Hitler had promised that the Sudetenland would be his last territorial demand, he scrapped his pledge in March 1939, when he sent German tanks and soldiers to conquer the remainder of the Czech Republic. The European democracies, having shrunk their armies after the Great War, continued to cower in the face of his ruthless behavior and seemingly unstoppable military.

After German troops seized Czechoslovakia on March 15, 1939, Hitler announced it was "the greatest day of my life." Jews were immediately lumped together with "thieves, criminals, swindlers, insane people, and alcoholics." By the end of May, the Nazis were filling prisons with Czechs who resisted or resented the German occupation.

The rape of Czechoslovakia convinced Roosevelt that Hitler and Mussolini were "madmen" who "respect force and force alone." Throughout late 1938 and 1939, Roosevelt tried to convince Americans, as well as British and French leaders, that the fascists would respond only to force, not words. He also persuaded Congress to increase military spending in anticipation of a possible war.

THE CONQUEST OF POLAND Later in 1939, the insatiable Hitler, having decided that he had "the world in my pocket," turned to Poland, Germany's eastern neighbor. Conquering Poland would give the German army a clear path to invade the Soviet Union, especially the fertile Ukraine region.

To ensure that the Soviets did not interfere with his plans, Hitler camouflaged his virulent anticommunism on August 23, 1939, when he signed the Nazi-Soviet Non-Aggression Pact with Josef Stalin, the antifascist Soviet premier. The announcement of the treaty stunned a world that had understood fascism and communism to be enemies. The two tyrants agreed to divide northern and eastern Europe between them; the Germans took most of Poland, and the Soviet Union claimed a "sphere of interest" in Estonia, Latvia, Finland,

and a portion of Lithuania. Just nine days later, at dawn on September 1, an estimated 1.5 million German troops invaded Poland from the north, south, and west. Hitler ordered them "to kill without mercy men, women, and children of the Polish race or language." He also ordered all terminally ill patients in German hospitals killed to make room for soldiers wounded in Poland.

This was the final straw for the western democracies. Having allowed Austria and Czechoslovakia to be seized by Hitler's war machine, Great Britain and France now did an about-face. On September 3, they honored their commitment to defend Poland. Europe, the world's smallest continent, was again embroiled in what would soon become another world war. The nations making up the British Empire and Commonwealth—Canada, India, Australia, New Zealand—joined the war. Americans watched in horror as

Josef Stalin Brutal leader of the Soviet Union who rose to power in the mid-1920s after the death of Vladimir Lenin.

another world war erupted. "This nation," declared Franklin Roosevelt, "will remain a neutral nation, but I cannot ask that every American remain neutral in thought as well. Even a neutral cannot be asked to close his mind or conscience."

Sixteen days after German troops stormed across the Polish border, the Soviet Union invaded Poland from the east. Pressed from all sides, 700,000 poorly equipped Polish soldiers surrendered after a few weeks, having suffered 70,000 deaths and many more wounded. On October 6, 1939, the Nazis and Soviets divided Poland between them. Hitler's goal was to obliterate Polish civilization, especially the Jews, and Germanize the country. For his part, Stalin wanted to recapture Polish territory lost during the First World War. Over the next five years, millions of Poles were arrested, deported, enslaved, or murdered. In April and May 1940, the Russians executed some 22,000 Polish military officers to ensure that its conquered neighbor would never mount a rebellion.

In late November 1939, the Soviets invaded neighboring Finland, leading President Roosevelt to condemn their "wanton disregard for law." Outnumbered five to one, Finnish troops held off the invaders for three months before being forced to negotiate a treaty that gave the Soviet Union a tenth of Finland.

REVISING THE NEUTRALITY ACT In September 1939, President Roosevelt decided that the United States must do more to stop "aggressor" nations. He summoned Congress into special session to revise the Neutrality Act. "I regret that Congress passed the Act," the president said. "I regret equally that I signed the Act."

After six weeks of heated debate, Congress passed the Neutrality Act of 1939, which allowed Britain and France to send their ships to the United States to bring back American military supplies. Public opinion supported such measures as long as other nations did the actual fighting.

WAR IN EUROPE The war in Europe settled into a three-month stalemate during early 1940, as Hitler's generals waited out the winter. Then, in the early spring, Germany attacked again. At dawn on April 9, Nazi armies occupied Denmark and landed along the Norwegian coast. German paratroopers, the first ever used in warfare, seized Norway's airports. Denmark fell in a day, Norway within a few weeks. On May 10, German forces invaded the Low Countries—Belgium, Luxembourg, and the Netherlands (Holland). Luxembourg fell the first day, the Netherlands three days later. Belgium lasted until May 28.

A few days later, German tanks roared into northern France. "The fight beginning today," Hitler declared, "decides the fate of the German nation for the next thousand years!" His brilliant *Blitzkrieg* ("lightning war") strategy centered on speed. Fast-moving columns of tanks, motorized artillery, and truck-borne infantry, all supported by warplanes and paratroopers, moved so fast that they paralyzed their stunned opponents.

British and French troops sent to help the Belgians were forced to make a frantic retreat to the English Channel coast, with the Germans in hot pursuit. On May 26, while German *Panzer* divisions (made up of tanks and other armored vehicles) followed Hitler's surprising order to rest and refuel, Great Britain was able to organize a weeklong evacuation of British and French soldiers from the beaches at Dunkirk, on the northern French coast near the border with Belgium. Despite attacks from German warplanes, some 338,000 defeated and demoralized soldiers escaped to England, leaving behind vast stockpiles of vehicles, weaponry, and ammunition. "Wars are not won by evacuations," observed Prime Minister Churchill, "but there was a victory inside this deliverance."

While the evacuation was unfolding, German forces decimated the remaining French armies. Tens of thousands of panicked French refugees clogged the roads to Paris. The crumbling French war effort prompted Italy's dictator, Mussolini, to declare war on France and Great Britain, which he dismissed as "the reactionary democracies of the West." On June 14, 1940, German soldiers marched unopposed into Paris. Eight days later, French leaders surrendered, whereupon the Germans established a puppet fascist government in the city of Vichy.

The rapid fall of France stunned the world. In the United States, complacency about the Nazis turned to fear and even panic as people realized the Germans could eventually assault America. The Second World War was but ten months old, yet Germany ruled most of western Europe. Only the "neutral" nations of Spain, Sweden, and Switzerland had avoided the Nazi onslaught. Great Britain now stood alone against Hitler's relentless military power. "The war is won," an ecstatic Hitler bragged to Mussolini. "The rest is only a matter of time."

AGGRESSION IN EUROPE, 1935–1939

- Keeping in mind the terms of the Treaty of Versailles ending the First World War, explain why Hitler began his campaign of expansion by invading the Rhineland and the Sudetenland.
- Why did the German attack on Poland begin the Second World War, whereas Hitler's previous invasions of Austria and Czechoslovakia did not?

PREPARING AMERICA FOR WAR As Hitler's armies conquered Europe, the United States found itself in no condition to wage war. After the First World War, the U.S. Army was reduced to a small force; by 1939, it numbered only 175,000. By contrast, Germany had almost 5 million soldiers. In promoting "military preparedness," President Roosevelt in May 1940 called for increasing the size of the army and producing 50,000 combat planes in 1942, a seemingly outlandish goal, since Germany was producing only 15,000 warplanes that year.

Roosevelt also responded to Winston Churchill's repeated requests for assistance by increasing military shipments to Great Britain and promising to provide all possible "aid to the Allies short of war." Churchill was focused on one strategic objective: to convince, coax, bluff, charm, seduce, or frighten the United States into entering the war.

THE MANHATTAN PROJECT Adding to Roosevelt's concerns was the possibility that Germany might have a secret weapon. The famous physicist Albert Einstein, a Jewish Austrian refugee from Nazism, had alerted Roosevelt

Winston Churchill Prime Minister of Great Britain who led the nation during the Second World War.

in the fall of 1939 that the Germans were trying to create atomic bombs. In June 1940, Roosevelt set up the National Defense Research Committee to coordinate military research, including a top-secret effort to develop an atomic bomb—the Manhattan Project—before the Germans did. Almost 200,000 people worked on the Manhattan Project, including Dr. J. Robert Oppenheimer, who led the team of distinguished scientists scattered among thirty-seven secret facilities in thirteen states.

THE BATTLE OF BRITAIN Having conquered western Europe, Hitler began planning the invasion of Great Britain ("Operation Sea Lion"), scheduled for September 1940. The late summer brought the Battle of Britain, as the Germans first sought to destroy Britain's Royal Air Force (RAF). The Nazis deployed some 2,500 warplanes, outnumbering the RAF two to one. "Never has a nation been so naked before its foes," Churchill admitted.

Churchill became the symbol of Britain's determination to stop Hitler. With his bulldog face, ever-present cigar, and "V for Victory" gesture, he urged the British citizenry to make the war "their finest hour." He breathed defiance while preparing for a German invasion, building fortifications, laying mines, digging trenches and fashioning tank traps, and mobilizing the population. The British, he pledged, would confront Hitler's invaders with "blood, toil, tears, and sweat." They would "never surrender."

In July and August, 1940, the German air force (*Luftwaffe*) launched day and night bombing raids against military targets across southeast England. The pilots in the Royal Air Force (their average age was twenty-three), with the benefit of radar, a secret new technology, fended off the German assault, ultimately destroying 1,700 German warplanes. Hitler then ordered his bombers to target civilians and cities (especially London) in night raids designed to terrorize British civilians. In what came to be called "the Blitz" during September and October of 1940, the Germans caused massive damage in Britain's major cities, destroying a million homes and killing 40,000 civilians. "The last three

The London "Blitz" An aerial photograph of London set aflame by German bombing raids in 1940. Winston Churchill responded, "We shall never surrender."

nights in London," reported the U.S. ambassador to Great Britain on September 10, "have been simply hell."

The Blitz, however, enraged rather than demoralized the British people. A London newspaper headline summarized the nation's courage and defiant mood: "Is That the Best You Can Do, Adolf?" The British success in the air proved decisive, for in October 1940, Hitler gave up his invasion plans. It was the first battle he had lost, and it was Britain's finest hour.

"ALL AID SHORT OF WAR" During 1940, Franklin Roosevelt began a crucial campaign to convince Americans that isolationism was impractical and even dangerous. His phrase, all "aid short of war," became the label for his efforts to help Great Britain. The president was especially concerned about a likely German invasion of the British Isles. "It is now most urgent," Prime Minister Churchill cabled Roosevelt, "that you let us have the destroyers" needed to stop such an invasion. "This is a thing to do now!"

To address the challenge, Roosevelt and Churchill, whose mother was an American, negotiated a trade on September 2, 1940, called the Destroyers for Bases Agreement, by which fifty old U.S. warships went to the British Royal Navy in return for allowing the United States to build military bases on British island colonies in the Caribbean.

Two weeks later, on September 16, 1940, Roosevelt pushed through a reluctant Congress the first peacetime conscription (military draft) in American history. The Selective Training and Service Act required all 16 million men ages twenty-one to thirty-five to register for the draft at one of 6,500 local draft boards. (The minimum age was later reduced to eighteen.)

A SAVAGE DEBATE The world crisis transformed Roosevelt. Having been stalemated for much of his second term by congressional opposition to the New Deal, he was revitalized by the need to stop Nazism. Yet his efforts to aid Great Britain and prepare America for war outraged isolationists. A prominent Democrat remembered that the dispute between isolationists and so-called interventionists was "the most savage political debate during my lifetime."

Isolationists, mostly midwestern and western Republicans, formed the America First Committee to oppose "military preparedness." Charles Lindbergh, the first man to fly solo across the Atlantic ocean, led the isolationist effort. To Lindbergh, Roosevelt's efforts to help Britain were driven primarily by Jews who owned "our motion pictures, our press, our radio, and our government." Lindbergh assured Americans that Britain was doomed; they should join hands with Hitler.

ROOSEVELT'S THIRD TERM The isolationists sought to make the 1940 presidential campaign a debate about the war. In June, just as France was falling to Germany, the Republicans nominated Wendell L. Willkie of Indiana, a plainspoken corporate lawyer and former Democrat who had voted for Roosevelt in 1932.

Once the campaign started, Willkie warned that Roosevelt was a "warmonger" and predicted that "if you re-elect him you may expect war in April, 1941." Roosevelt responded that he had "said this before, but I shall say it again and again and again: Your boys are not going to be sent into any foreign wars." In November 1940, Roosevelt won an unprecedented third term by 27 million votes to Willkie's 22 million and by an even more decisive margin, 449 to 82, in the electoral college. Winston Churchill wrote Roosevelt that he had "prayed for your success and I am truly thankful for it."

THE LEND-LEASE ACT Once reelected, Roosevelt found an ingenious way to provide more military aid to Britain, whose cash was running out. The

Lend-lease Members of the isolationist "Mother's Crusade," urging defeat of the lend-lease program, kneel in prayer in front of the Capitol in Washington, D.C. They feared the program aiding America's allies would bring the United States into the wars in Europe and Asia.

Lend-Lease Act, introduced in Congress on January 10, 1941, allowed the president to lend or lease military equipment to "any country whose defense the President deems vital to the defense of the United States." It was a bold challenge to the isolationists. As Senator Hiram Johnson of California claimed, "This bill is war."

Roosevelt responded to critics by arguing that "no nation can appease the Nazis. No man can turn a tiger into a kitten by stroking it." The United States, he added, would provide everything the British needed while doing the same for China in its war against Japan, all in an effort to keep Americans from going to war themselves. "We must again be the great arsenal of democracy," Roosevelt explained. Churchill shored up the president's efforts by announcing that Britain did not need American troops to defeat Hitler: "Give us the tools and we will finish the job." In early March, 1941, Congress approved the Lend-Lease Act. "Let not the dictators of Europe or Asia doubt our unanimity now," Roosevelt declared.

Between 1941 and 1945, the Lend-Lease program would ship $50 billion worth of supplies to Great Britain, the Soviet Union, France, China, and other Allied nations. The Lend-Lease Act was Roosevelt's most emphatic effort to move America from isolationism to interventionism and it gave a huge boost to British morale. Churchill called it the most generous "act in the history of any nation."

GERMANY INVADES THE SOVIET UNION While Americans continued to debate Roosevelt's efforts to help Great Britain, the European war expanded. In the spring of 1941, German troops joined Italian soldiers in Libya, forcing the British army in North Africa to withdraw to Egypt. In April 1941, Nazi forces overwhelmed Yugoslavia and Greece. With Hungary, Romania, and Bulgaria also part of the Axis, Hitler controlled nearly all of Europe. But his ambition was unbounded.

On June 22, 1941, without warning, Hitler launched "Operation Barbarossa," a shocking invasion of the Soviet Union, his supposed ally. Hitler's objective in turning on Stalin was his long-standing obsession to destroy communism, enslave the vast population of the Soviet Union, open up new lands for German settlement, and exploit Russia's considerable natural resources.

Hitler's foolhardy decision was the defining moment of the European war. The 3 million German soldiers sent to the Soviet Union would eventually be worn down and thrown back. At first, however, the invasion seemed a great success, as the German armies raced across the vast plains of Ukraine and western Russia. Entire Soviet armies and cities were surrounded and destroyed. During the second half of 1941, an estimated 3 million Soviet soldiers, 50 percent of the Soviet army, were captured. For four months, the Soviets retreated in the face of the German blitzkrieg.

During the summer of 1941, German forces surrounded Leningrad, now called St. Petersburg, and began a siege of the city. As weeks passed, food and supplies became scarce. Hunger alone would kill 800,000 people. Desperate people ate cats, dogs, rats, and even sawdust. As the bitterly cold winter set in, corpses were left to freeze in the snow. Still, the soldiers and civilians held out. Leningrad became known as the city that refused to die. By December, 1941, other German armies had reached the suburbs of Moscow, a thousand miles east of Berlin.

To American isolationists, Germany's invasion of Russia confirmed that America should stay out of the war and let two dreadful dictatorships bleed each other to death. Roosevelt, however, insisted on including the Soviet Union in the Lend-Lease agreement; he and Churchill were determined to keep the Russians fighting Hitler so that Hitler could not concentrate on Great Britain.

Gradually, Stalin slowed the Nazi advance by forcing the Russian people to fight—or be killed by their own troops. During the Battle of Moscow, Soviet defenders showed their pitiless resolve by executing 8,000 civilians charged with "cowardice."

Slowly, the tide started to turn against the Germans. By the winter of 1941–1942, Hitler's generals were learning the same bitter lesson that the Russians had taught Napoléon and the French in 1812. Invading armies must contend not only with Russia's ferocious fighters and enormous population but also vast distances, deep snow, and subzero temperatures.

THE ATLANTIC CHARTER By the late summer of 1941, the United States was no longer a "neutral" nation. In August, Roosevelt and Churchill drew up a joint statement of "common principles" known as the **Atlantic Charter**. The agreement pledged that after the "final destruction of the Nazi tyranny," the victors would promote certain common values: the self-determination of all peoples, economic cooperation, freedom of the seas, and a new system of international security to be called the United Nations. Within weeks, eleven anti-Axis nations, including the Soviet Union, had endorsed the Atlantic Charter.

WAR IN THE ATLANTIC No sooner had Roosevelt signed the Atlantic Charter than U.S. warships came under fire. On September 4, 1941, the *Greer* was tracking a German submarine ("U-boat") off the coast of Iceland and sharing the information with British warplanes when it was attacked. Roosevelt seized the opportunity to tell Americans that the ship was the victim of an unprovoked attack. In response, he essentially began an undeclared war in the Atlantic by ordering naval warships to provide protection for convoys all the way to Iceland, allowing them to "shoot on sight" any German submarines.

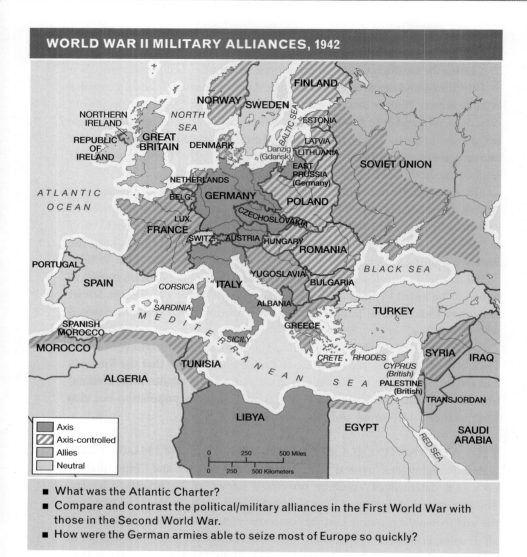

WORLD WAR II MILITARY ALLIANCES, 1942

- What was the Atlantic Charter?
- Compare and contrast the political/military alliances in the First World War with those in the Second World War.
- How were the German armies able to seize most of Europe so quickly?

Six weeks later, on October 17, 1941, a German U-boat sank the American warship *Kearny*. Eleven sailors were killed. "The shooting has started," Roosevelt reported, "and history has recorded who fired the first shot." Two weeks later, the destroyer *Reuben James* was torpedoed and sunk while escorting a convoy near Iceland, with a loss of 115 seamen.

The sinkings spurred Congress to change the 1939 Neutrality Act by allowing merchant vessels to be armed and to enter combat zones and the ports of nations at war ("belligerents"). Step by step, the United States had begun to engage in naval warfare against Nazi Germany. Still, Americans hoped to avoid all-out war.

THE STORM IN THE PACIFIC

In 1940, Japan and the United States had begun a series of moves that pushed them closer to war. Convinced that they were Asia's "leading race," the Japanese had forced the helpless Vichy French government, under German control, to permit the construction of Japanese airfields in French-controlled Indochina (now Cambodia, Laos, and Vietnam). The United States responded with the Export Control Act of July 2, 1940, which authorized President Roosevelt to restrict the export of military supplies and other strategic materials crucial to Japan. Three weeks later, on July 26, Roosevelt ordered that all Japanese assets in the United States be frozen and that oil shipments be stopped.

THE TRIPARTITE PACT On September 27, 1940, the Imperial Japanese government signed a Tripartite Pact with Nazi Germany and Fascist Italy, by which each pledged to declare war on any nation that attacked any of them. Roosevelt called the pact an "unholy alliance" designed to "dominate and enslave the entire human race." Several weeks later, the United States expanded its trade embargo against Japan to include iron ore, copper, and brass, deliberately leaving oil as the remaining bargaining chip.

Without access to American products, Japan's expansionist plans stalled; more than half of its imports came from the United States. In July 1941, Japan announced that it was taking complete control of French Indochina in its effort to expand the "Empire of the Rising Sun" and gain access to the raw materials denied it by the United States. Roosevelt responded by restricting oil exports to Japan. He also closed the Panama Canal to Japanese shipping and merged the Filipino army with the U.S. Army. *Time* magazine claimed that Roosevelt was "waging the first great undeclared war in U.S. history."

THE ATTACK ON PEARL HARBOR On October 16, 1941, Hideki Tōjō became the Japanese prime minister. Viewing war with the United States as inevitable, he ordered

Hideki Tōjō Prime minister and war minister of Japan simultaneously until 1944, one year before Japan's unconditional surrender.

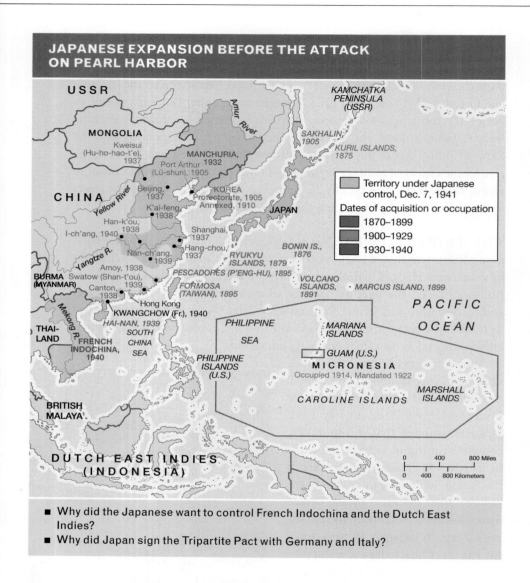

JAPANESE EXPANSION BEFORE THE ATTACK ON PEARL HARBOR

USSR

MONGOLIA

Kweisui (Hu-ho-hao-t'e), 1937

MANCHURIA, 1932

Port Arthur (Lü-shun), 1905

KAMCHATKA PENINSULA (USSR)

SAKHALIN, 1905

KURIL ISLANDS, 1875

Beijing, 1937

KOREA Protectorate, 1905 Annexed, 1910

K'ai-feng, 1938

CHINA

Yellow R.

Han-k'ou, 1938

I-ch'ang, 1940

JAPAN

Shanghai, 1937

Hang-chou, 1937

Yangtze R.

Nan-ch'ang, 1939

BONIN IS., 1876

RYUKYU ISLANDS, 1879

Amoy, 1938

PESCADORES (P'ENG-HU), 1895

BURMA (MYANMAR)

Swatow (Shan-t'ou), 1939

FORMOSA (TAIWAN), 1895

VOLCANO ISLANDS, 1891

MARCUS ISLAND, 1899

Canton, 1938

Hong Kong

KWANGCHOW (Fr.), 1940

PACIFIC OCEAN

HAI-NAN, 1939

THAI-LAND

Mekong R.

FRENCH INDOCHINA, 1940

SOUTH CHINA SEA

PHILIPPINE SEA

MARIANA ISLANDS

GUAM (U.S.)

PHILIPPINE ISLANDS (U.S.)

MICRONESIA Occupied 1914, Mandated 1922

MARSHALL ISLANDS

CAROLINE ISLANDS

BRITISH MALAYA

	Territory under Japanese control, Dec. 7, 1941

Dates of acquisition or occupation

	1870–1899
	1900–1929
	1930–1940

DUTCH EAST INDIES (INDONESIA)

0   400   800 Miles
0   400   800 Kilometers

- Why did the Japanese want to control French Indochina and the Dutch East Indies?
- Why did Japan sign the Tripartite Pact with Germany and Italy?

a powerful fleet of Japanese warships to prepare for a secret attack on the U.S. bases in Hawaii. The Japanese naval commander, Admiral Isoroku Yamamoto, knew that his country could not defeat the United States in a long war; its only hope was "to decide the fate of the war on the very first day" by launching a "fatal attack" on the U.S. Navy.

On November 5, 1941, the Japanese asked the Roosevelt administration to end its embargo or "face conflict." The American secretary of state, Cordell Hull, responded on November 26 that Japan must remove its troops from China

Explosion of the USS *Shaw* The destroyer exploded after being hit by Japanese warplanes at Pearl Harbor. The *Shaw* was repaired shortly thereafter and went on to earn eleven battle stars in the Pacific campaign.

before the United States would lift its embargo. The Japanese then ordered a fleet of warships to begin steaming toward Hawaii. By this time, political and military leaders on both sides considered war inevitable. Yet Hull continued to meet with Japanese diplomats in Washington, privately dismissing them as being as "crooked as a barrel of fish hooks."

In late November, Roosevelt told his "war cabinet" that the United States or Great Britain was "likely to be attacked, perhaps next Monday." He and others expected the Japanese to attack Singapore or the Philippines. The U.S. Navy Department sent an urgent message to its commanders in the Pacific: "Negotiations with Japan . . . have ceased, and an aggressive move by Japan is expected within the next few days."

Roosevelt staked his desperate hope for a peaceful solution on a last-minute message to Japan's Emperor Hirohito. "Both of us," Roosevelt said, "have a sacred duty to restore traditional amity [cooperation] and prevent further death and destruction in the world."

By the time Roosevelt's message arrived, Japanese warplanes were already headed for U.S. bases in Hawaii. In the early morning of Sunday, December 7, 1941, Japanese planes began bombing the unsuspecting U.S. fleet at **Pearl Harbor**. Of the eight American battleships, all were sunk or disabled, along with eleven other ships. Japanese bombers also destroyed 180 American warplanes. The raid, which lasted less than two hours, killed more than 2,400 American servicemen (mostly sailors) and civilians, and wounded nearly 1,200 more. At the same time that the Japanese were attacking Pearl Harbor, they were assaulting U.S. military facilities in the Philippines and on Guam and Wake islands in the Pacific, as well as British bases in Singapore, Hong Kong, and Malaya.

The surprise attack actually fell short of military success in two important ways. First, the bombers ignored the maintenance facilities and oil storage tanks that supported the U.S. fleet, without which the surviving ships might have been forced back to the West Coast. Second, the Japanese missed the U.S. aircraft carriers that had left port a few days earlier. In the naval war to come, aircraft carriers, not battleships, would prove to be decisive.

In a larger sense, the attack on Pearl Harbor was a spectacular miscalculation, for it brought the American isolationist movement to an abrupt end. Even the Japanese admiral who planned the attack had misgivings amid his officers' celebrations: "I fear that we have only succeeded in awakening a sleeping tiger."

At half past noon on December 8, President Roosevelt delivered his war message to Congress: "Yesterday, December 7, 1941—a date which will live in infamy—the United States of America was suddenly and deliberately attacked by naval and air forces of the Empire of Japan." He asked Congress to declare a "state of war." The Senate approved the resolution twenty-five minutes after Roosevelt finished speaking; the House followed immediately thereafter.

Three days later, on December 11, Germany and Italy declared war on what Hitler called the "half Judaized and the other half Negrified" United States. After learning of the attack on Pearl Harbor, Hitler shouted that "it is impossible for us to lose the war." The separate wars in Asia, Europe, and Africa had now become one global conflict. Roosevelt told the American people in a radio address that "it will not only be a long war. It will be a hard war." Yet he assured everyone that "we are going to win, and we are going to win the peace that follows."

ARSENAL OF DEMOCRACY

Waging war against Germany and Japan required all of America's immense industrial capacity. On December 18, 1941, Congress passed the War Powers Act, which gave the president far-reaching authority to reorganize government agencies and create new ones, regulate business and industry, and even censor mail and other forms of communication. With the declaration of war, men between the ages of eighteen and forty-five were drafted.

Some 16 million men and several hundred thousand women served in the military during the war. The average American soldier or sailor in the Second World War was twenty-six years old, stood five feet eight, and weighed 144 pounds, an inch taller and eight pounds heavier than the typical recruit in the First World War. Only one in ten had attended college and only one in four had graduated from high school.

In 1940, Adolf Hitler had scoffed at the idea that the United States could produce 50,000 warplanes a year, claiming that America was nothing but "beauty queens, millionaires, and Hollywood." His ignorance of America's industrial potential proved fatal. By the end of 1942, U.S. war production had already exceeded the *combined* output of Germany, Japan, and Italy. At an Allied planning conference in Iran in 1943, Josef Stalin raised a glass to toast "American production, without which this war would have been lost."

The **War Production Board**, created by Roosevelt in 1942, directed the conversion of industries to war production. In 1941, more than 3 million automobiles were manufactured in the United States; only 139 were built during the next four years, as automobile plants began making huge numbers of tanks, jeeps, trucks, and warplanes. "Something is happening that Hitler doesn't understand," announced *Time* magazine in 1942. "It is the Miracle of production."

In making the United States the "great arsenal of democracy," the Roosevelt administration transformed the nation's economy into the world's most efficient military machine. By 1945, the year the war ended, the United States would be manufacturing half of the goods produced in the world. American factories, many running twenty-four hours a day, seven

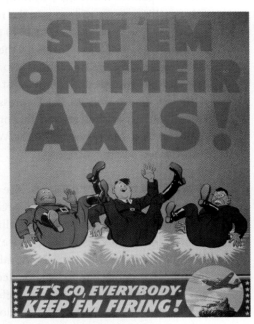

War Production Board This 1942 poster features caricatures of Mussolini, Hitler, and Tōjō, who—according to the poster—will fall on their "axis" if Americans continued their relentless production of military equipment.

days a week, produced 300,000 warplanes, 89,000 tanks, 3 million machine guns, and 7 million rifles.

FINANCING THE WAR To cover the war's huge cost (more than $3 trillion in today's values), Congress passed the Revenue Act of 1942 (also called the Victory Tax). Whereas in 1939 only about 4 million people (about 5 percent of the workforce) filed tax returns, the new act made most workers taxpayers. By the end of the war, 90 percent of workers were paying income tax. Tax revenues covered about 45 percent of military costs from 1939 to 1946; the government borrowed the rest, mostly through a massive promotional campaign that sold $185 billion worth of government war bonds, which paid interest to purchasers. By the end of the war, the national debt was six times what it had been at the start.

The size of the federal government soared during the war. More than a dozen new federal agencies were created, and the number of civilian federal workers quadrupled from 1 million to 4 million. Jobs were suddenly plentiful as millions quit work to join the military. The nation's unemployment rate plummeted from 14 percent in 1940 to 2 percent in 1943.

People who had long lived on the margins of the economic system, especially women, were now brought into the labor force. Stubborn pockets of poverty did not disappear, but for most civilians, especially those who had lost their jobs and homes in the Depression, the war spelled a better life. Some 24 million Americans moved during the war to take advantage of new job opportunities. Many headed to the West Coast, where shipyards and airplane factories were hiring nonstop.

ECONOMIC CONTROLS The need for the United States not only to equip and feed its own military forces but also provide massive amounts of food, clothing, and weapons to its allies created shortages of virtually all consumer goods that caused sharp price increases. In 1942, Congress responded by authorizing the Office of Price Administration to set price ceilings. With prices frozen, basic goods had to be allocated through rationing, with coupons doled out for limited amounts of sugar, coffee, gasoline, automobile tires, and meat.

The government promoted patriotic conservation by urging every family to become a "fighting unit on the home front." Posters featured slogans such as "Save Your Stuff to Make Us Tough," "Use it up, wear it out, make it do, or do without," and "Save Your Scraps to Beat the Japs." People collected scrap metal and tin foil, rubber, and cardboard for military use. Households were even encouraged to save cooking fat, from which glycerin could be extracted to make explosives.

Businesses and workers often grumbled about the wage and price controls, and on occasion the government seized industries threatened by strikes. Despite these problems, the effort to stabilize wages and prices succeeded. By the end of the war, consumer prices had risen about 31 percent, far better than the rise of 62 percent during the First World War.

A CONSERVATIVE BACKLASH For all of the patriotism inspired by the war effort, criticism of government actions such as rationing increased with each passing year. In the 1942 congressional elections, Republicans gained forty-six seats in the House and nine in the Senate. During the 1940s, a coalition of conservatives from both parties dismantled "nonessential" New Deal agencies such as the Work Projects Administration (originally the Works Progress Administration), the National Youth Administration, and the Civilian Conservation Corps.

Organized labor, despite substantial gains in membership and power during the war, felt the impact of the conservative trend. In the spring of 1943, when 400,000 coal miners went on strike demanding a $2-a-day wage increase, conservatives in Congress passed, over Roosevelt's veto, the Smith-Connally War Labor Disputes Act, which authorized the government to seize plants and mines and keep them operating if workers went on strike.

THE WAR AT HOME

The Second World War transformed life at home as it was being fought abroad. Housewives went to work as welders and riveters, and farmers joined industrial unions. Some 3.5 million rural folk from the South left farms for cities. The federal government paid for a national day-care program for young children to enable their mothers to work full-time. The dramatic changes required by the war also caused unexpected changes in many areas of social life, the impact of which would last long after the war's end.

WOMEN IN THE WAR The war marked a watershed in the status of women. During the war, nearly 350,000 women served in the **Women's Army Corps (WAC)**, the navy's equivalent, Women Accepted for Volunteer Emergency Service (WAVES), the Marine Corps, the Coast Guard, and the Army Air Force.

With millions of men going into military service, the demand for civilian workers shook up old prejudices about gender roles. Sidney Hillman, appointed by Roosevelt to find workers for defense plants, announced that "war is calling on the women of America for production skills." More than 8 million women entered the civilian workforce. To help recruit women for

Women of the workforce, 1942 At the Douglas Aircraft Company in Long Beach, California, three women assemble the tail section of a Boeing B-17 Flying Fortress bomber.

traditionally male jobs, the government launched a promotional campaign featuring the story of "Rosie the Riveter," a woman named Rosina Bonavita, who excelled as a riveter at an airplane factory.

Many men opposed the surge of women taking traditionally male jobs. A disgruntled male legislator asked who would handle traditional household tasks if women flocked to factories: "Who will do the cooking, the washing, the mending, the humble homey tasks to which every woman has devoted herself; who will rear and nurture the children?" Many women, however, were eager to escape the grinding routines of domestic life and earn good wages. A female welder remembered that her wartime job "was the first time I had a chance to get out of the kitchen and work in industry and make a few bucks. This was something I had never dreamed would happen."

AFRICAN AMERICANS While President Roosevelt focused on military strategy, his wife Eleanor focused on organizing the home front. She insisted that the government's wartime partnership with business not neglect the needs of workers, argued that America could not fight racism abroad while tolerating it at home, and championed the mass influx of women into the once-male work force during the war.

More than a half million African Americans left the South for better opportunities during the war years, and more than a million blacks nationwide joined the industrial workforce for the first time. Lured by jobs and higher wages in military-related plants and factories, African Americans from Texas, Oklahoma, Arkansas, and Louisiana headed west, where the dramatic expansion of defense-related jobs had significant effects on the region's population. During the war years, the number of African Americans rose sharply in western cities such as Seattle, Portland, and Los Angeles.

At the same time, the war provided a boon to southern textile mills by requiring millions of military uniforms. Manufacturing jobs led thousands of

Bigotry at home During the Detroit Riots of 1943, police officers do nothing when a white thug hits a black man.

Tuskegee Airmen The Tuskegee Airmen were the first African American military pilots. Here, the first graduates are reviewed at Tuskegee, Alabama, in 1941.

"dirt poor" sharecroppers and tenant farmers, many of them African Americans, to leave the land for steady work in new mills and factories. Sixty of the 100 army camps created during the war were in southern states, further transforming local economies. During the war, the U.S. rural population decreased by 20 percent.

RACIAL TENSION AT HOME The most volatile social issue ignited by the war was African American participation in the military. Although the armed forces were still racially segregated in 1941, African Americans rushed to enlist after the attack on Pearl Harbor. As African American Joe Louis, the world heavyweight boxing champion, put it, "Lots of things [are] wrong with America, but Hitler ain't going to fix them." Altogether, about a million African Americans—men and women—served in the armed forces during the war.

Black soldiers and sailors, assigned to racially segregated units, were initially excluded from combat units. They loaded ships, drove trucks, dug latrines, and handled supplies and mail. Black officers could not command white soldiers or sailors. Henry L. Stimson, the secretary of war, claimed that "leadership is not embedded in the negro race." Military bases had segregated facilities—and experienced frequent racial "incidents."

In late 1944, however, the need for more troops led the government to revisit its racial policies. Under pressure from the African American community as well as Eleanor Roosevelt, General Dwight Eisenhower, commander of the U.S. forces in Europe, agreed to let black volunteers fight in fifty-two all-black fifty-man platoons commanded by white officers. A black officer said the decision was "the greatest" for African Americans "since enactment of the constitutional amendments following the Civil War."

The black soldiers earned the reputation of being fierce fighters. The same was true of some 600 African American pilots trained in Tuskegee, Alabama. The so-called **Tuskegee Airmen** flew more than 15,000 missions, and their unquestionable excellence spurred military and civilian leaders to desegregate the armed forces after the war. At war's end, however, the U.S. Army reimposed segregation. It would be several more years before the military was truly integrated.

MEXICAN AMERICANS As rural dwellers moved west, many farm counties experienced a labor shortage. In an ironic about-face, local and federal authorities who before the war had forced migrant laborers back across the Mexican border now recruited them to harvest crops on American farms. The Mexican government would not consent to provide the laborers, however, until the United States promised to ensure them decent working and living conditions. The result was the creation of the **bracero program** in 1942, whereby Mexico agreed to provide seasonal farmworkers on year-long contracts. Under the bracero program, some 200,000 Mexican farmworkers entered the western United States, mostly packed in cattle cars on trains. At least that many more crossed the border as undocumented workers.

The rising tide of Mexican Americans in Los Angeles prompted a stream of anti-Mexican editorials and ugly racial incidents. Even though some 300,000 Mexican Americans served in the war and earned a higher percentage of Congressional Medals of Honor than any other minority group, racial prejudices still prevailed. In southern California, there was constant conflict between white servicemen and Mexican American gang members and teenage "zoot-suiters." (Zoot suits were flamboyant clothing worn by some young Mexican American men.) In 1943, several thousand off-duty sailors and soldiers, joined

Off to court Latinos dressed in zoot suits are loaded onto a Los Angeles County Sheriff's bus for a court appearance in June 1943.

by hundreds of local whites, rampaged through Los Angeles, assaulting Hispanics, African Americans, and Filipinos. The weeklong violence came to be called the "Zoot Suit Riots."

NATIVE AMERICANS IN THE MILITARY Indians supported the war effort more fully than any other group in American society. Almost a third of eligible Native American men served in the armed forces. Many others worked in defense-related industries, and thousands of Indian women volunteered as nurses or joined the WAVES. As was the case with African Americans, Indians benefited from the experiences afforded by the war by gaining vocational skills and a greater awareness of how to succeed within mainstream society.

Why did so many Native Americans fight for a nation that had stripped them of their land and ravaged their heritage? Some felt that they had no choice. Mobilization for the war effort ended many New Deal programs that had provided Indians with jobs. At the same time, many viewed the Nazis and Japanese warlords as threats to their own homeland. Whatever their motivations, Indians distinguished themselves in the military. Unlike their African American counterparts, Indian servicemen were integrated into regular units with whites. Perhaps their most distinctive role was serving as "code talkers": every military branch used Indians, especially Navajos, to encode and decipher messages using Indian languages unknown to the Germans and Japanese.

Navajo code talkers The complex Navajo language made it impossible for the Germans and Japanese to decode American messages. Here, a code talker relays messages for U.S. marines in the Battle of Bougainville in the South Pacific in 1943.

DISCRIMINATION AGAINST JAPANESE AMERICANS The attack on Pearl Harbor ignited a hunger for vengeance against the nisei—people of Japanese descent living in the United States. Many Americans saw no difference between the Japanese who attacked Pearl Harbor and Japanese Americans. As Idaho's governor declared, "A good solution to the Jap problem would be to send them all back to Japan, then sink the island."

Such hysteria helps explain why the U.S. government sponsored one of the worst violations of civil liberties during the twentieth century, when more than 120,000 nisei were forcibly removed from their homes and transported to ten **"war relocation camps."** Forced to sell their farms and businesses at great loss within forty-eight hours, ordered to bring with them only what they could carry, the internees were sent by train and bus to ten barbed-wire enclosed internment camps scattered across remote areas in the western states. They lost not only their property but also their liberty.

President Roosevelt initiated the relocation when he issued Executive Order 9066 on February 19, 1942, authorizing the forcible removal of all ethnic Japanese living on the Pacific coast. It was perhaps his worst decision as president. Roosevelt called his action a "military necessity" although not a single incident of espionage involving Japanese Americans was proved. As it turned out, more than 70 percent of those affected were U.S. citizens.

On Evacuation Day, Burt Wilson, a white schoolboy in Sacramento, California, was baffled as soldiers ushered the nisei children out of his school:

> We wondered what had happened. They took somebody out of eighth grade, a boy named Sammy, who drew wonderful cartoons. He was my friend, and one day he was there and the next day he was gone. And that was very difficult for us to understand because we didn't see Sammy or any Japanese American—at least I didn't—as the enemy.

Few if any nisei were disloyal. In fact, 39,000 Japanese Americans served in the armed forces during the war, and others worked as interpreters and translators. But all were victims of fear and racial prejudice. Not until 1983 did the government acknowledge the injustice of the internment policy. Five years later,

A farewell to civil rights American troops escorted Japanese Americans by gunpoint to remote internment camps, some of which were horse-racing tracks, whose stables served as housing.

it granted those nisei still living $20,000 each in compensation, a tiny amount relative to what they had lost during four years of confinement.

THE ALLIED DRIVE TOWARD BERLIN

By mid-1942, the "home front" was hearing good news from Europe. U.S. naval forces had been increasingly successful at destroying German U-boats off the Atlantic coast. Up to that point, German submarines had sunk hundreds of Allied cargo vessels, killing 2,500 sailors. Stopping the submarine attacks was important because the Grand Alliance—Great Britain, the United States, and the Soviet Union—called for the defeat of Germany first. Defeating the Japanese could wait.

WAR AIMS AND STRATEGY

A major consideration for Allied military strategy was the fighting on the vast Eastern Front in the Soviet Union. During 1941–1942, the Nazis and Soviets waged colossal battles. The Soviet population—by far—bore the brunt of the war against the Nazis, leading Josef Stalin to insist that the Americans and British relieve the pressure on his troops by attacking the Germans in western Europe, thereby forcing Hitler to pull units away from the Russian Front.

Meanwhile, with most of the German army deployed on the Russian Front, the British and American air forces, flying from bases in England, would bomb military and industrial targets in German-occupied western Europe, and especially in Germany itself, while American and British generals prepared plans to attack Nazi troops in North Africa, Italy, and France.

Franklin Roosevelt and Winston Churchill agreed that they needed to create a second front in western Europe, but they could not agree on the timing or location of an invasion. U.S. military planners wanted to attack the Germans in France before the end of 1942. The British, however, were wary of moving too fast. An Allied defeat on the French coast, Churchill warned, was "the only way in which we could possibly lose this war." Finally, Roosevelt decided to accept Churchill's compromise proposal for a joint Anglo-American invasion of North Africa, which was occupied by German and Italian armies not nearly as strong as those in Europe.

THE NORTH AFRICA CAMPAIGN On November 8, 1942, British and American forces landed in Morocco and Algeria on the North African coast ("Operation Torch"). They were led by an untested, little-known U.S. general, Dwight D. Eisenhower. Farther east, British armies were pushing the Germans and Italians back across Libya.

The Americans lost badly in early battles. In early 1943, however, Eisenhower, soon known by his nickname, "Ike," found an audacious field commander in General George Patton, who said he loved war "more than my life." Armed with ivory-handled pistols and brimming with bravado, Patton showed American troops how to fight a war of speed and daring. Corporal Morris Zimmerman, a soldier fighting under Patton, wrote his mother from North Africa, "This is your son reporting from the land of Arabs and wine, sticky flies and red sand. I have always wanted to cross an ocean to see what was on the other side and darned if I didn't."

Hammered from all sides and unable to retreat, some 250,000 Germans and Italians surrendered on May 12, 1943, leaving all of North Africa in Allied control. The "continent had been redeemed," said Winston Churchill. Ernie Pyle, a war correspondent embedded with the American army, reported that

Major General George S. Patton Patton commanded the U.S. invasion of Sicily, the largest amphibious action in the war up to that point. He believed that war "brings out all that is best in men."

the U.S. troops "fought like veterans. They were well handled. We had enough of what we needed. Everything meshed perfectly, and the end was inevitable. . . . Tunisia has been a good warm-up field for our armies." But, he added, "the worst was yet to come."

THE CASABLANCA CONFERENCE Five months earlier, in January 1943, Roosevelt, Churchill, and the Anglo-American military chiefs met at a seaside resort near Casablanca, the largest city in French Morocco. It was a historic occasion. No U.S. president had ever flown abroad while in office, and none had ever visited Africa. Stalin chose to stay in the Soviet Union, but he sent a message which again urged the Allies to invade Nazi-controlled western Europe to relieve the pressure on the Russians.

At the Casablanca conference, the British convinced the Americans that they should follow up the anticipated victory in North Africa with an assault on the Italian island of Sicily before attacking Italy itself. Roosevelt and Churchill also decided to step up the bombing of Germany and to increase shipments of military supplies to the Soviet Union and the Nationalist Chinese forces fighting the Japanese.

Before leaving the Casablanca conference, Roosevelt announced, with Churchill's blessing, that the war would end only with the "unconditional surrender" of all enemy nations. This decision was designed to quiet Soviet suspicions that the Americans and British might negotiate separately with Hitler to end the war in western Europe. The announcement also reflected Roosevelt's determination that "every person in Germany should realize that this time Germany is a defeated nation." Whatever its impact on Soviet morale or enemy resistance, however, the decision to require unconditional surrender ensured the destruction of Germany and Japan that would create power vacuums along the western and eastern borders of the Soviet Union.

THE BATTLE OF THE ATLANTIC While fighting raged in North Africa, the Battle of the Atlantic reached its climax. Great Britain desperately needed more food and military supplies from the United States, but German submarines operating in groups called "wolfpacks" were sinking the British vessels transporting American goods faster than British shipyards could replace them. There could be no invasion of German-occupied France until the U-boat menace was defeated. By July 1942, some 230 Allied ships and almost 5 million tons of war supplies had been lost. "The only thing that ever frightened me during the war," recalled Churchill, "was the U-boat peril."

By the end of 1942, however, the British and Americans had discovered ways to defeat the U-boats. British experts cracked the German naval radio codes, enabling Allied convoys to steer clear of U-boats or to hunt them down with long-range warplanes (called "subchasers") and anti-submarine weapons deployed on warships. New technology also helped, as sonar and radar allowed Allied ships to track submarines. Yet the best tactic against U-boats was to group cargo vessels into tightly bunched convoys so that warships could protect them more effectively. In May 1943, the Allies destroyed forty-one U-boats. Thereafter, the U-boats were on the defensive, and Allied shipping losses fell significantly.

SICILY AND ITALY On July 10, 1943, following the Allied victory in North Africa, about 250,000 British and American troops landed on the coast of Sicily. General Eisenhower called it the "first page of the liberation of the European continent." The island was in Allied hands by August 17, bringing to an end Benito Mussolini's twenty years of fascist rule in Italy.

On July 25, 1943, the Italian king had dismissed Mussolini as prime minister and had him arrested. The new Italian government startled the Allies when it offered not only to surrender but also to switch sides. To prevent them from doing so, Hitler sent German armies into Italy.

The Italian campaign thereafter became a series of stalemated battles that left people wondering if it had been worth the cost. Winter came early to southern Italy, making life even more miserable for the soldiers. The Germans positioned themselves behind formidable defenses and rugged terrain that enabled them to slow the Allied advance to a crawl. "Italy was one hill after another," said a U.S. soldier, "and when it was wet, you were either going up too slow or down too fast, but always the mud. And every hill had a German [machine] gun on it." Allied casualties soared as the stalemate continued.

By February 1944, the two sides were, in the words of U.S. commander Mark W. Clark, like "two boxers in the ring, both about to collapse." Mussolini, plucked from prison by a daring German airborne commando raid, became head of a puppet fascist government in northern Italy as Allied forces finally took control of the rest of the country. On June 4, 1944, the U.S. Fifth Army entered Rome, just two days before D-day on the coast of France. "We were woken by trucks moving through the street," one overjoyed Italian remembered. "At first I thought it was the Germans, but then I heard American accents. . . . By dawn people were lining the streets. I cried."

THE TEHRAN CONFERENCE Late in the fall of 1943, in Tehran, Iran, Churchill and Roosevelt had their first joint meeting with Josef Stalin. Their discussions focused on the planned invasion of Nazi-controlled France and a simultaneous Russian offensive westward across eastern Europe. The three

leaders agreed to create an international organization—the United Nations—
to maintain peace after the war. Upon arriving back in the United States, Roosevelt confided to Churchill his distrust of Stalin, saying that it was a "ticklish"
business keeping the "Russians cozy with us" because of the tension between
communism and capitalism. As General Eisenhower stressed, however, the
fate of Britain and the United States depended on the Soviets' survival as an ally.
"The prize we seek," he said in 1942, "is to keep 8 million Russians [soldiers] in
the war."

THE STRATEGIC BOMBING OF EUROPE   Months of preparation
went into the long-anticipated Allied invasion of German-occupied France.
While waiting for D-day (the day the invasion would begin), the U.S. Army
Air Force tried to pound Germany into submission with an air campaign
that dropped thousands of bombs and killed some 350,000 civilians. Yet the
air offensive failed to shatter either German morale or war-related production. Many bombs missed their targets because of thick clouds, high winds,
and inaccurate navigational systems, and many Allied planes were shot down.
The bombing campaign, however, did force the Germans to commit precious
resources to air-raid defense and eventually wore down their air force. With
Allied air supremacy assured by 1944, the much-anticipated invasion of Hitler's "Fortress Europe" could move forward.

PLANNING AN INVASION   In early 1944, Dwight D. Eisenhower
arrived in London with a new title: Supreme Commander of the Allied Expeditionary Force (AEF) that would invade Nazi-controlled western Europe.
Eisenhower faced enormous challenges, ranging from creating an effective
command structure to handling disagreements between President Roosevelt
and Prime Minister Churchill.

Eisenhower also faced the daunting task of planning **Operation Overlord**,
the daring assault on Hitler's "Atlantic Wall," a formidable array of fortifications, mines, machine guns, barbed wire, and jagged beach obstacles along the
French coastline. An attack by sea against heavily fortified defenders was the
toughest of military operations. The planned invasion gave Churchill night-
mares: "When I think of the beaches . . . choked with the flower of American
and British youth . . . I see the tides running red with their blood. I have my
doubts. I have my doubts."

For months, Eisenhower, neither an experienced strategist nor a combat
commander, dedicated himself to planning the risky invasion and managing the complex political and military rivalries among the Allied leaders. Well-
organized and efficient, he was a high-energy perfectionist, impatient and

General Dwight D. Eisenhower Eisenhower visiting with U.S. paratroopers before they began the D-day assault in Operation Overlord.

often short-tempered with his staff. He attended to every detail, including the amassing of 5 million tons of military equipment and munitions and thousands of warplanes and ships.

As D-day approached, Eisenhower's chief of staff predicted only a fifty-fifty chance of success. The seaborne invasion was the greatest gamble and most complex military operation in history. "I am very uneasy about the whole operation," admitted Sir Alan Brooke, head of British forces. "It may well be the most ghastly disaster of the whole war." Eisenhower was so concerned that he carried in his wallet a note to be circulated if the Allies failed. It read: "If any blame or fault attaches to the attempt, it is mine alone."

D-DAY AND AFTER Operation Overlord succeeded in part because it surprised the Germans. The Allies made elaborate efforts—including the positioning of British decoy troops and making misleading public statements—to fool the Nazis into believing that the invasion would come at Pas-de-Calais, on the French-Belgian border, where the English Channel was narrowest. Instead, the landings would occur along fifty miles of shoreline in northern Normandy, a French coastal region almost 200 miles south.

On the blustery evening of June 5, 1944, Eisenhower visited some of the 16,000 American paratroopers preparing to drop behind the German lines in France. The soldiers, their faces blackened by burnt cork and heads shaved to resemble Indian warriors, noticed Eisenhower's concern and tried to lift his spirits. "Now quit worrying, General," one of them said, "we'll take care of this thing for you." A sergeant said, "We ain't worried. It's Hitler's turn to worry." After the planes took off, Eisenhower returned to his car with tears in his eyes. He later confided to an aide: "I hope to God I know what I'm doing." As he got into bed that night, Winston Churchill, with tears running down his cheeks, asked his wife: "Do you know that by the time you wake up in the morning, 20,000 men may have been killed?"

As the planes carrying the paratroopers arrived over France, thick clouds and German anti-aircraft fire disrupted the formations. Some soldiers were dropped miles from their landing sites, some were dropped far out at sea, and some were dropped so low that their parachutes never opened. Yet the U.S. 82nd and 101st Airborne Divisions outfought three German divisions during the chaotic night and prepared the way for the main invasion by destroying bridges and capturing artillery positions and key road junctions.

Donald Burgett, a nineteen-year-old paratrooper in the 101st Airborne Division, recalled dropping into France in the dark of night and being alone: "My throat went dry and I swallowed, but nothing went down. My heart pounded, sending blood throbbing through my temples and causing a weak-feeling in the pit of my stomach." But he had no time for fear. As he stumbled upon others who had survived the landing, they soon found themselves embroiled in combat.

THE NORMANDY LANDINGS As the gray, misty light of dawn broke on D-day, June 6, 1944, the biggest invasion fleet in history—some 5,300 Allied ships carrying 370,000 soldiers and sailors—filled the horizon off the Normandy coast. Sleepy German soldiers guarding the beaches awoke to see the breathtaking array of ships. "I saw an armada like a plague of locusts," said a German officer. "The number of ships was uncountable."

Major battles often depend on luck. (When asked what kind of generals he preferred, Napoléon said "lucky ones.") Eisenhower was lucky on D-day, for the Germans misinterpreted the Normandy landings as a diversion for the "real" attack at Pas-de-Calais. It helped that the German commander, Field Marshal Erwin Rommel, assuming that the weather was too rough for an invasion, had gone home to Germany to celebrate his wife's June 6 birthday. "How stupid of me," Rommel said when he heard the news. "How stupid of me!" By one in the afternoon, he was racing back to France.

The landing at Normandy D-Day, June 6, 1944. Before they could huddle under a seawall and begin to dislodge the Nazi defenders, U.S. soldiers on Omaha Beach had to cross a fifty-yard stretch that exposed them to machine guns housed in concrete bunkers.

When Hitler learned of the Allied landings, he boasted that "the news couldn't be better. As long as they [the Allied armies] were in Britain, we couldn't get at them. Now we have them where we can destroy them." In the United States, word that the long-anticipated liberation of Nazi Europe had begun captured the nation's attention. Businesses closed, church bells tolled, and traffic was stopped so that people could pray in the streets. Stalin cabled to Churchill and Roosevelt that the news brought "joy to us all."

Resilience and creativity are crucial virtues amid the confusion of great battles (the "fog of war"), which rarely go according to plan. Despite Eisenhower's meticulous preparations, the huge operation almost failed. During the first day, foul weather and rough seas caused injuries and nausea and capsized dozens of landing craft. More than 1,000 men, weighed down by seventy pounds of equipment, drowned as they stepped off landing craft into water up to their necks.

Some of the boxy, flat-bottomed landing craft delivered their often seasick troops to the wrong locations. "We have landed in the wrong place," shouted fifty-six-year-old Brigadier General Theodore Roosevelt Jr. (son of the former president), who would receive the Medal of Honor for his courage that day. "But we will start the war from here."

The noise was deafening as shells exploded across the beach and in the surf. The bodies of the killed, wounded, and drowned piled up amid wrenching cries for help. "As our boat touched sand and the ramp went down," Private Harry Parley remembered, "I became a visitor to Hell" as German gunners fired on the attacking soldiers.

The first U.S. units ashore at Omaha Beach, beneath 130-foot-tall cliffs defended by German machine guns and mortars, lost more than 90 percent of their men. In one company, 197 of the 205 men were killed or wounded within ten minutes. Officers struggled to rally the exhausted, bewildered troops pinned down on the beach. "Two kinds of men are staying on this beach," shouted cigar-smoking Colonel George Taylor on Omaha Beach. "The dead and those who are going to die. Get up! Move in! Goddammit! Move in and die! Get the hell out of here!" He then began to run forward and his men followed, stumbling across the deadly beach into the dunes.

Inch by inch, backed by waves of reinforcements, the U.S. soldiers pushed across the beach and up the cliffs. By nightfall, 170,000 Allied soldiers—57,000 of them Americans—were scattered across fifty miles of windswept Normandy coastline. So too were the bodies of some 10,724 dead or wounded Allied soldiers.

On June 13, a week after the Normandy landings, Erwin Rommel, the German commander, told his wife that the "battle is not going at all well for us." Within three weeks, the Allies had landed more than 1 million troops, 566,000 tons of supplies, and 171,000 vehicles. "Whether the enemy can still be stopped at this point is questionable," German headquarters near Paris warned Hitler. "The enemy air superiority is terrific and smothers almost every one of our movements. . . . Losses in men and equipment are extraordinary."

Operation Overlord was the greatest seaborne invasion in the annals of warfare, but it was small when compared with the offensive launched by the Soviet army in Russia a few weeks later. Between June and August 1944, the Soviets killed, wounded, or captured more German soldiers (350,000) than were stationed in all of western Europe.

Still, the Normandy invasion was a turning point in the war. With the beachhead secured, the Allied leaders knew that victory was just a matter of time, as Hitler's armies were caught between the Soviets advancing from the east and the Allied forces from the west. "What a plan!" Churchill exclaimed to the British Parliament. Even Stalin applauded the invasion's "vast conception and masterly execution."

For all of the Allied success, however, Eisenhower privately struggled with the daily casualty reports. "How I wish this cruel business of war could be completed quickly," he wrote his wife. "War demands real toughness of fiber— not only in the soldiers [who] must endure, but in the homes that must sacrifice their best."

THE LIBERATION OF PARIS It would take seven more weeks and 37,000 more lives for the Allied troops to gain control of Normandy; the Germans lost more than twice that many, and some 19,000 French civilians were killed. Then, on July 25, 1944, American armies broke out from Normandy and headed east toward Paris. On August 15, a joint American-French invasion force landed on the Mediterranean coast and raced up the Rhone Valley in eastern France.

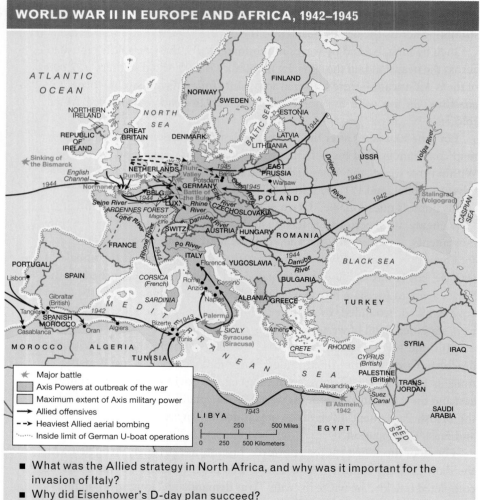

WORLD WAR II IN EUROPE AND AFRICA, 1942–1945

Legend:
- ★ Major battle
- Axis Powers at outbreak of the war
- Maximum extent of Axis military power
- → Allied offensives
- -→ Heaviest Allied aerial bombing
- ⋯ Inside limit of German U-boat operations

- What was the Allied strategy in North Africa, and why was it important for the invasion of Italy?
- Why did Eisenhower's D-day plan succeed?
- What was the role of strategic bombing in the war? Was it effective?

German resistance collapsed after only ten weeks of ferocious fighting. On D-day, one German unit, the 21st Panzer Division, boasted 12,000 men and 127 tanks; ten weeks later, having retreated across France, it had 300 men and just 10 tanks. A division of the Free French Resistance, aided by American units, had the honor of liberating Paris on August 25. As U.S. soldiers marched through the cheering crowds, a reporter said that he had never "seen in any place such joy as radiated from the people of Paris this morning."

By mid-September, most of France and Belgium had been cleared of German troops. Meanwhile, the Soviet army moved relentlessly westward along a 1,200-mile front, pushing the Germans out of Russia. Between D-day and the end of the war in Europe a year later, 1.2 million Germans were killed and wounded.

ROOSEVELT'S FOURTH TERM In 1944, amid the largest war in history, the calendar required another presidential election. The Republicans nominated New York governor Thomas E. Dewey, who argued that it was time for a younger man to replace the "tired" Democratic leader. Voters, however, preferred the seasoned Franklin Roosevelt. On November 7, 1944, the president was elected for a fourth term, this time by a popular vote of 25.6 million to 22 million and an electoral vote of 432 to 99.

THE RACE TO BERLIN By the time Franklin Roosevelt was reelected, Allied armies were approaching the German border from the east and west. Churchill, worried that if the Soviets arrived first in Berlin, the German capital, Stalin would control the postwar map of Europe, urged Eisenhower to beat the Soviets to Berlin. Eisenhower, however, decided it was not worth the estimated 100,000 Americans who would be killed or wounded in such an operation.

THE YALTA CONFERENCE As the Allied armies converged on Berlin, Stalin hosted Roosevelt and Churchill at the **Yalta Conference** (February 4–11, 1945) in Crimea, on the Black Sea. The leaders agreed that, once Germany surrendered, the Soviets would occupy eastern Germany, and the Americans and British would control western Germany. Berlin, the German capital within the Soviet zone, would be subject to joint occupation. The Americans and British later created a fourth occupation zone in Germany for the French to administer.

Stalin's goals at Yalta were to retrieve former Russian territory transferred to Poland after the First World War and to impose Soviet control over the countries of eastern and central Europe. Roosevelt, exhausted and in failing health, agreed to Stalin's proposals because he needed the Soviets to support the creation of a new international peacekeeping organization, the United

Nations, and to help defeat Japan. Military analysts estimated that Japan could hold out for eighteen months after the defeat of Germany unless the Soviets joined the war in the Pacific. Stalin agreed to do so but the price was high: he demanded territories from Japan and China.

Roosevelt and Churchill got Stalin to sign the Yalta Declaration of Liberated Europe, which called for free and open elections in the liberated nations of eastern Europe. Nevertheless, the wily Stalin would fail to live up to his promises. When the Red Army "liberated" Hungary, Romania, Bulgaria, Czechoslovakia, Poland, and eastern Germany, it plundered and sent back to Russia anything of economic value, dismantling thousands of factories and mills and rebuilding them in the Soviet Union. To ensure control over eastern Europe, the Soviets shipped off to prison anyone who questioned the new Communist governments they created.

Roosevelt viewed the Yalta meeting as a test of whether the wartime alliance between the United States and the Soviet Union would survive once the conflict ended. He staked his hopes for postwar cooperation on the creation of the United Nations (UN).

The Yalta Conference Churchill, Roosevelt, and Stalin (with their respective foreign ministers behind them) confer on plans for the postwar world in February 1945.

At Yalta, the "Big Three" agreed to hold organizational meetings for the UN beginning on April 25, 1945. Like Woodrow Wilson, Roosevelt was determined to replace America's "outdated" isolationism with an engaged internationalism. But to get Stalin's approval of the UN, Roosevelt gave in to his demands for territory held by Japan in northeast Asia.

Republicans later savagely attacked Roosevelt for "giving" eastern Europe over to Soviet domination. Some blamed his behavior on his declining health. (He would die in a few weeks.) But even a robust Roosevelt could not have dislodged the Soviet army from its control of eastern Europe. The course of the war shaped the outcome at Yalta, not Roosevelt's failed diplomacy. The United States had no real leverage. As a U.S. diplomat admitted, "Stalin held all the cards." "I didn't say the result was good," Roosevelt said after returning from the Yalta Conference. "I said it was the best I could do."

DEATH OF A PRESIDENT By early 1945, Nazi Germany was on the verge of defeat, but sixty-three-year-old Franklin Roosevelt would not live to join the victory celebrations. In the spring of 1945, he went to the "Little White House" in Warm Springs, Georgia, to rest up for the conference that would create the United Nations. On the morning of April 12, 1945, he complained of a headache but seemed to be in good spirits. It was nearly lunchtime when he said to an artist painting his portrait, "Now we've got just about 15 minutes more to work." Then, as she watched him reading some documents, he groaned, saying that he had "terrific pain" in the back of his head. Suddenly he slumped over and fell into a coma. He died two hours later.

On hand to witness the president's death was Lucy Mercer Rutherford, the woman with whom Roosevelt had an affair thirty years before. Eleanor Roosevelt was in Washington, D.C., when Franklin died, unaware of the president's guest. Although Franklin had promised in 1918 to end all communications with Mercer, he had in fact secretly stayed in touch, even enabling her to attend his presidential inauguration in 1933.

Roosevelt's death shocked and saddened the world, in part because few people were aware that he was sick. Even his sharpest critics were devastated. Ohio senator Robert Taft, known as "Mr. Republican," called Roosevelt's death one of the worst tragedies in the nation's history. "The President's death removes the greatest figure of our time at the very climax of his career. . . . He dies a hero of the war, for he literally worked himself to death in the service of the American people." By contrast, Hitler viewed Roosevelt's death as a "great miracle." "The war is not lost," he told an aide. "Read it. Roosevelt is dead!"

A U.S. soldier was on a warship in the Pacific when he heard the news of Roosevelt's death. "I felt a great sense of loss," he said, for Roosevelt had been president almost all his life. "He was our leader, but he was also, in some way, our friend." In the short term, he worried about the military implications of Roosevelt's death. "How will we go on fighting the war when our Commander in Chief is dead?"

THE COLLAPSE OF NAZISM Adolf Hitler's shrinking Nazi empire collapsed less than a month later. In Berlin on April 28, as Soviet troops prepared to enter the city, Hitler married his mistress, Eva Braun, in an underground bunker. That same day, Italian freedom fighters captured Mussolini and his mistress. Despite his plea to "Let me live, and I will give you an empire,"

May 8, 1945 The celebration in New York City's Times Square on V-E day.

Mussolini and his mistress were shot and hung by their heels from a girder above a Milan gas station. On April 30, Hitler and his wife retired to their underground bedroom, where she poisoned herself and he put a bullet in his head. Their bodies were taken outside, doused with gasoline, and burned.

On May 2, Berlin fell. Axis forces in Italy surrendered the same day. Five days later, on May 7, the chief of staff of the German armed forces agreed to unconditional surrender. So ended Nazi domination of Europe, little more than twelve years after Hitler had come to power proclaiming his "Thousand-Year Reich."

On May 8, V-E day ("Victory in Europe") generated massive celebrations. In Paris, an American bomber pilot flew his plane through the Eiffel Tower. In New York City, 500,000 people celebrated in the streets. But the elation was tempered by the ongoing war against Japan and the immense challenges of helping Europe rebuild. The German economy had to be revived, a new democratic government had to be formed, and millions of displaced Europeans had to be clothed, housed, and fed.

THE HOLOCAUST The end of the war in Europe revealed the horrific extent of the **Holocaust**, Hitler's systematic effort to destroy the Jews and other racial, political, sexual, and religious "undesirables," including Communists and prostitutes. Reports of the Nazis' methodical slaughter of Jews had appeared as early as 1942, but the gruesome stories seemed beyond belief until the Allied armies liberated the hundred or so "death camps" where the Germans had imposed their shocking "Final Solution": the wholesale extermination of some 6 million Jews, along with more than 1 million other captured peoples. At the Auschwitz-Birkenau camp in Poland, 865,000 were killed as soon as they arrived, and up to 6,000 were gassed in a single day.

The Allied troops were appalled by what they discovered in the huge extermination camps. Bodies were piled as high as buildings; survivors were living skeletons. General Eisenhower reported to his wife that the evidence of "starvation, cruelty, and bestiality were so overpowering as to leave me a bit sick."

American officials, even some Jewish leaders, had dragged their feet in acknowledging the Holocaust during the war for fear that relief efforts for Jewish refugees might stir up anti-Semitism at home. Under pressure, President Roosevelt had set up a War Refugee Board early in 1944. It managed to rescue about 200,000 European Jews and some 20,000 others. But the president refused appeals to bomb the concentration camp at Auschwitz, arguing that the Nazis would simply build another one. Overall, the Allied response to the

Holocaust survivors American troops liberate survivors of the Mauthausen concentration camp in May 1945. The Nazis tattooed the prisoners with identification numbers on their wrists or chests, as seen on the man at left.

Nazi atrocities was inept at best and disgraceful at worst. In 1944, Churchill called the Holocaust the "most horrible crime ever committed in the history of the world." He did not know at the time that Stalin's death camps killed more people than Hitler's.

THE PACIFIC WAR

For months after the attack on Pearl Harbor at the end of 1941, the news from the Pacific was "all bad," as President Roosevelt acknowledged. With stunning speed, the Japanese captured numerous territories in Asia, including the British colonies of Hong Kong, Burma, Malaya, and Singapore, and the French colony of Indochina. "Everywhere in the Pacific," said Winston Churchill, "we were weak and naked."

THE PHILIPPINES In the Philippines, U.S. forces and their Filipino allies were overwhelmed by Japanese invaders. On April 10, 1942, the Japanese gathered some 12,000 captured American troops along with 66,000 Filipinos and forced them to march sixty-five miles in six days up the Bataan peninsula. Already underfed, ravaged by tropical diseases, and provided with little food and water, the prisoners were brutalized in what came to be known as the Bataan Death March. Those who fell out of line were bayoneted or shot. Others were beaten, stabbed, or shot for no reason. More than 10,000 died along the way. News of the Bataan Death March outraged Americans and contributed to the Pacific war's ferocious emotional intensity and mutual atrocities.

By the summer of 1942, Japan had seized control of a vast Asian empire and was on the verge of assaulting Australia when its naval leaders succumbed to what one admiral called "victory disease." Intoxicated with easy victories and lusting for more, they pushed into the South Pacific, intending to isolate Australia and strike again at Hawaii.

CORAL SEA AND MIDWAY During the spring of 1942, U.S. forces in the Pacific finally had some success. In the Battle of the Coral Sea (May 2–6, 1942), U.S. naval warplanes forced a Japanese fleet headed toward the island of New Guinea to turn back after sinking an aircraft carrier and destroying seventy planes.

A few weeks later, Admiral Yamamoto steered his main Japanese battle fleet of eighty-six warships toward Midway, the westernmost of Hawaii's inhabited islands, from which he hoped to strike Pearl Harbor again. This time, however, the Japanese were taken by surprise. Americans had broken the

General Douglas MacArthur MacArthur theatrically coming ashore at the island of Leyte in the Philippines, October 1944.

Japanese military radio code, allowing Admiral Chester Nimitz, commander of the U.S. central Pacific fleet, to learn where Yamamoto's fleet was heading.

The first Japanese attack hit Midway hard on June 4, 1942, but at the cost of about a third of their warplanes. American planes from the *Yorktown* and *Enterprise* then struck back, crippling the Japanese fleet. The **Battle of Midway** was the first major defeat for the Japanese navy in 350 years and the turning point of the Pacific war. The American victory blunted Japan's military momentum, eliminated the threat to Hawaii, and bought time for the United States to organize its massive industrial productivity for a wider war.

MACARTHUR'S PACIFIC STRATEGY American and Australian forces were jointly under the command of the imperious General Douglas MacArthur, a military genius with tremendous willpower and courage who constantly irritated his superiors in Washington with his "unpleasant personality" and his repeated efforts to embellish his image. MacArthur had retired in 1937 but was called back into service in mid-1941, in part because he was such a brilliant strategist. In 1942, he assumed command of the Allied forces in the southwest Pacific.

On August 7, 1942, after first pushing the Japanese back in New Guinea, MacArthur landed 16,000 U.S. Marines on Guadalcanal Island, one of the so-called Solomon Islands, where the Japanese had built an air base. The U.S. commander was optimistic that his undersupplied troops could defeat the entrenched Japanese, even though, he said, there were "a hundred reasons why this operation should fail." But it did not fail. The savage fighting on Guadalcanal lasted through February 1943 but resulted in the Japanese army's first defeat and a loss of 20,000 men, compared to 1,752 Americans. "I had never heard or read of this kind of fighting," said a U.S. Marine. "These people refuse to surrender."

The Japanese were skilled defensive fighters who rarely surrendered, and they controlled most of the largest islands in the Pacific. Their suicidal intensity led General MacArthur and Admiral Nimitz to adopt a shrewd "leapfrogging" strategy whereby they focused on the most important islands and used airpower and sea power to bypass the others, leaving the isolated Japanese bases to "wither on the vine," as Nimitz put it. For example, when U.S. warplanes destroyed the Japanese airfield at Rabaul in eastern New Guinea, 135,000 Japanese troops were left stranded on the island, cut off from resupply by air or sea. What the Allies did to Rabaul set the pattern for the "island-hopping" strategy in the Pacific.

BATTLES IN THE CENTRAL PACIFIC On June 15, 1944, just days after the D-day invasion, U.S. forces liberated Tinian, Guam, and Saipan, three Japanese-controlled islands. Saipan was strategically important because it allowed the new American B-29 "Superfortress" bombers to strike Japan itself. The struggle for the island lasted three weeks. Some 20,000 Japanese were killed compared to 3,500 Americans. But 7,000 more Japanese soldiers committed suicide upon the order of their commanding general, who killed himself with his sword.

General MacArthur's forces invaded the Japanese-held Philippines on October 20. The Japanese, knowing that the loss of the Philippines would cut them off from essential raw materials, brought in warships from three directions to battle the U.S. fleet.

The four battles fought in the Philippine Sea from October 23 to October 26, 1944, came to be known collectively as the Battle of Leyte Gulf, the largest naval engagement in history and the worst Japanese defeat of the war. Some 216 U.S. warships converged to engage 64 Japanese ships. By the end of the first day, 36 Japanese warships, including 4 aircraft carriers, had been destroyed.

The Battle of Leyte Gulf included the first Japanese *kamikaze* ("divine wind") attacks, in which young suicide pilots deliberately crashed their bomb-laden planes into American warships. From the fall of 1944 to the war's end in the summer of 1945, an estimated 4,000 kamikaze pilots died on suicide missions. One in seven hit an American ship, thirty-four of which were sunk.

WORLD WAR II IN THE PACIFIC, 1942–1945

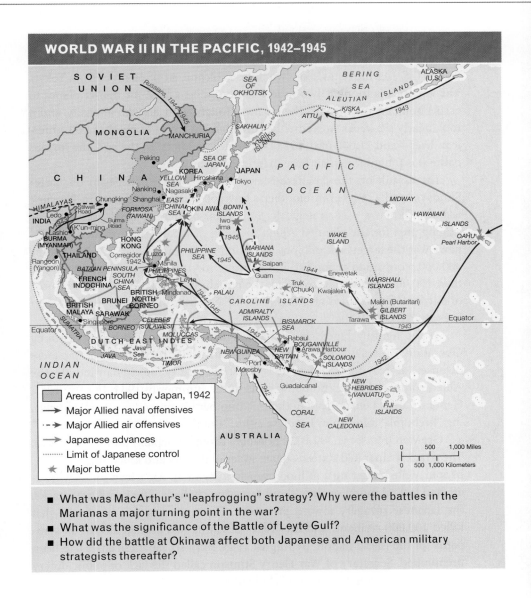

- What was MacArthur's "leapfrogging" strategy? Why were the battles in the Marianas a major turning point in the war?
- What was the significance of the Battle of Leyte Gulf?
- How did the battle at Okinawa affect both Japanese and American military strategists thereafter?

"Kamikazes just poured at us, again and again," a sailor remembered. "It scared the shit out of us."

As MacArthur waded ashore with the U.S. troops liberating the Philippines, he reminded reporters of his 1942 pledge—"I shall return"—when he was evacuated from the islands in the face of the Japanese invasion. Now he announced with great fanfare: "People of the Philippines, I have returned! The hour of your redemption is here. . . . Rally to me."

A WAR TO THE DEATH The closer the Allied forces got to Japan, the fiercer the resistance they encountered. While fighting continued in the Philippines, 30,000 U.S. Marines landed on Iwo Jima, a volcanic atoll 760 miles from Tokyo. The Americans thought Iwo Jima was needed as a base for fighter planes to escort bombers over Japan. The Japanese fought with suicidal intensity, and it took nearly six weeks to secure the tiny island at a cost of nearly 7,000 American lives—and 21,000 of the 22,000 Japanese soldiers. In the end, the furious battle was fought for an air base that never materialized.

The assault on the Japanese island of Okinawa, which began on Easter Sunday, April 1, was even bloodier. Only 360 miles from the main Japanese islands, Okinawa was strategically important because it would serve as the staging area for the planned Allied invasion of Japan. The conquest of Okinawa was the largest amphibious operation of the Pacific war, involving some 300,000 troops and requiring almost three months of brutal fighting. More than 150,000 Japanese were killed; the remaining 7,871 were either captured or surrendered. A third of U.S. pilots and a quarter of submariners lost their lives at Okinawa.

As the fighting raged on Okinawa, Allied commanders began planning Operation Downfall—the invasion of Japan itself. To weaken the Japanese defenses, destroy their war-related industries, and erode civilian morale, the Allied command began bombing raids in the summer of 1944. In early 1945, General Curtis Lemay, head of the U.S. Bomber Command, ordered devastating "firebomb" raids upon Japanese cities: "Bomb and burn 'em till they quit."

On March 9, some 300 B-29 bombers dropped napalm bombs on Tokyo. The attack incinerated sixteen square miles of the city and killed some 100,000 people while rendering a million homeless. By then, American military leaders had lost all moral qualms about targeting civilians. The kamikaze attacks, the Japanese savagery toward prisoners of war, the burning of Manila that killed 100,000 civilians, and the "rape" of China had eroded almost all sympathy for the island nation. By August 1945, sixty-six Japanese cities had been firebombed. Secretary of War Henry Stimson called the lack of public outcry in the United States over the raids "appalling."

THE ATOMIC BOMB Still, the Japanese leaders showed no willingness to surrender. In early 1945, new U.S. president Harry S. Truman learned of the first successful test of an atomic bomb in New Mexico. Now that military planners knew the bomb would work, they selected two Japanese cities as targets. The first was **Hiroshima**, a port city and army headquarters in southern Japan. On July 25, 1945, Truman, who knew nothing about the devastating effects of

The aftermath of Little Boy This image shows the wasteland that remained after the atomic bomb "Little Boy" decimated Hiroshima, Japan, on August 6, 1945.

radiation poisoning, ordered that the atomic bomb be used if Japan did not surrender before August 3.

Although an intense debate emerged over the decision to drop the bomb—spurred by Truman's chief of staff, Admiral William D. Leahy, who argued that the "Japanese were already defeated and ready to surrender"—Truman said that he "never had any doubt that it should be used." He later recalled that "we faced half a million casualties trying to take Japan by land. It was either that or the atom bomb, and I didn't hesitate a minute, and I've never lost any sleep over it since."

To Truman and others, the use of atomic bombs seemed a logical next step to end the war. As it turned out, scientists greatly underestimated the physical effects of the bomb. Their prediction that 20,000 people would be killed proved much too low.

In mid-July 1945, the Allied leaders met in Potsdam, Germany, near Berlin. There they issued the Potsdam Declaration. In addition to outlawing Nazism, it demanded that Japan surrender by August 3 or face "prompt and utter destruction." Truman left Potsdam optimistic about postwar relations with the

Bombing of Nagasaki A 20,000-foot tall mushroom cloud enveloped the city of Nagasaki after the atomic bombing on August 9, 1945.

Soviet Union. "I can deal with Stalin," he wrote. "He is honest—but smart as hell." (Truman would soon change his mind about Stalin's honesty.)

The deadline calling for Japan's surrender passed, and on August 6, 1945, a B-29 bomber named *Enola Gay* (after the pilot's mother) took off at 2:00 a.m. from the island of Tinian and headed for Hiroshima. At 8:15 a.m., flying at 31,600 feet, the *Enola Gay* released the five-ton, ten-foot-long uranium bomb nicknamed "Little Boy."

Forty-three seconds later, the bomb exploded at an altitude of 1,900 feet, creating a blinding flash of light followed by a fireball towering to 40,000 feet. The tail gunner on the *Enola Gay* described the scene: "It's like bubbling molasses down there . . . the mushroom is spreading out . . . fires are springing up everywhere . . . it's like a peep into hell."

The bomb's incredible shock wave and firestorm killed some 78,000 people, including thousands of Japanese soldiers and 23 American prisoners of war housed in the city. By the end of the year, the death toll would reach 140,000, as people died of injuries or radiation poisoning. In addition, of the city's 76,000 buildings, only 6,000 were left standing, and four square miles of the city were turned to rubble.

President Truman was aboard the battleship *Augusta* returning from the Potsdam conference when news arrived that the atomic bomb had been dropped. "This is the greatest thing in history!" he exclaimed. In the United States, Americans greeted the news with similar joy. To them, the atomic bomb promised a quick end to the long nightmare of war. "No tears of sympathy will be shed in America for the Japanese people," the *Omaha World-Herald* predicted. "Had they possessed a comparable weapon at Pearl Harbor, would they have hesitated to use it?" Others reacted more soberly when they considered the implications of atomic warfare. "Yesterday," journalist Hanson Baldwin wrote in the *New York Times*, "we clinched victory in the Pacific, but we sowed the whirlwind."

Two days after the Hiroshima bombing, an opportunistic Soviet Union, hoping to share in the spoils of victory, hastened to enter the war in the Pacific by sending hundreds of thousands of troops into Japanese-occupied Manchuria along the border between China and the Soviet Union. Truman and his aides, frustrated by the stubborn refusal of Japanese leaders to surrender and fearful that the Soviet Union's entry would complicate negotiations, ordered a second atomic bomb ("Fat Man") to be dropped on Japan. On August 9, the city of Nagasaki, a shipbuilding center, experienced the same nuclear devastation that had destroyed Hiroshima. Five days later, on August 14, 1945, the Japanese emperor accepted the terms of surrender. The formal surrender ceremony occurred on an American warship in Tokyo Bay on September 2, 1945.

Upon learning of the unexpected Japanese decision to surrender, Paul Fussell, one of the American soldiers preparing for the dreaded invasion of Japan, said he went into his tent and pulled the zipper closed. "And I sat there in silence for at least a full day before I could compose myself because my joy was such that I knew I couldn't survive it in public." Then he came out and cheered and danced with everyone else.

A NEW AGE IS BORN

Thus ended the costliest war in history. It was a *total* war in its scope, intensity, and numbers. Including deaths from war-related disease and famine, some 50 million civilians and 22 million combatants died.

The Second World War was more costly for the United States than any other foreign war: 292,000 combat deaths and 114,000 noncombat deaths among soldiers, sailors, airmen, and marines. A million more were wounded, with half of them seriously disabled. In proportion to its population, however, the United States suffered far fewer losses than did the other major Allies or their enemies, and American territory escaped the devastation suffered in so many parts of the world. For every American killed in the Second World War, for example, some fifty-nine Soviets died.

The war was the pivotal event of the turbulent twentieth century. It engulfed five continents, leveled cities, reshaped societies, and transformed international relations. German and Italian fascism as well as Japanese militarism were destroyed. The war set in motion the fall of China to communism in 1949 and the outbreak of the Korean War a year later. Colonial empires in Africa and Asia rapidly crumbled as the conflict unleashed independence movements. The Soviet Union emerged from the war as a new global superpower, while the United States, as Winston Churchill told the House of Commons, stood "at the summit of the world."

WHY DID THE ALLIES WIN? Many factors contributed to the Allied victory. Roosevelt and Churchill were better at coordinating military efforts and maintaining national morale than were Hitler, Mussolini, and the Japanese emperor, Hirohito. By 1944, Hitler had grown increasingly unstable and unpredictable and more withdrawn from the German people, especially after a failed attempt by high-ranking officers to assassinate him that July.

In the end, however, what turned the tide was the awesome productivity of American industry and the ability of the Soviet Union to absorb the massive German invasion and then push back all the way to Berlin. By the end of the war, Japan had run out of food and Germany had run out of fuel. By contrast, the United States was churning out more of everything. As early as 1942, just a few weeks after the attack on Pearl Harbor, Fritz Todt, a Nazi engineer, told Hitler that the war against the United States was already lost because of America's ability to out-produce all the other warring nations combined.

A TRANSFORMATIONAL WAR Like the First World War, the Second World War had far-reaching effects. It shattered the old world order and created a new international system, and nations such as France, Germany, Great Britain, and Japan were left devastated or impoverished. Henry Luce, the powerful publisher of *Time* magazine, said that the war had demonstrated the "moral and practical bankruptcy of all forms of Isolationism." Internationalism was now the dominant outlook, as most Americans acknowledged that the United States had profound responsibilities for global stability and security. It had emerged from the war with the most powerful military in the world—and as the only nation with atomic weapons.

The expansion of the federal government spurred by the war effort continued after 1945, and presidential authority increased enormously at the expense of congressional and state power. The war also ended the Great Depression and launched a long period of unprecedented prosperity and global economic domination. Big businesses grew into gigantic corporations as a result of huge government contracts for military weapons and supplies. New technologies and products developed for military purposes—radar, computers, electronics, plastics and synthetics, jet engines, rockets, atomic energy—transformed the private sector, as did new consumer products generated from war-related innovations. And the opportunities created by the war for women as well as for African Americans, Mexican Americans, and other minorities set in motion major social changes that would culminate in the civil rights movement of the 1960s and the feminist movement of the 1970s.

In August 1945, President Truman announced that the United States had "emerged from this war the most powerful nation in this world—the most powerful nation, perhaps, in all history." But the Soviet Union, despite its profound human losses and physical destruction, had gained much new territory, built massive armed forces, and enhanced its international influence, making it the greatest power in Eurasia. A little over a century after Frenchman Alexis de Tocqueville had predicted that Europe would eventually be overshadowed by the United States and Russia, his prophecy had come to pass.

CHAPTER REVIEW

SUMMARY

- **Fascism and the Start of the War**   In Italy, Benito Mussolini assumed control by promising law and order. Adolf Hitler rearmed Germany in defiance of the Treaty of Versailles. By March 1939, Nazi Germany had annexed Austria and seized Czechoslovakia. Hitler then invaded Poland with the *blitzkrieg* strategy in September 1939, after signing a non-aggression pact with the Soviet Union. The British and French governments declared war.

- **America Goes to War**   The United States issued *"neutrality laws"* to avoid being drawn into wars in Europe and Asia, but with the fall of France, Roosevelt accelerated military aid to Great Britain through the *Lend-Lease Act.* In 1941, the United States and Great Britain signed the *Atlantic Charter,* announcing their aims in the war. After Japan joined with Germany and Italy to form the *"Axis" alliance,* President Roosevelt froze Japanese assets in the United States and restricted oil exports to Japan, which frustrated the Japanese, who decided to launch a surprise attack at *Pearl Harbor,* Hawaii.

- **The Second World War and American Society**   The war had profound social effects. Americans—white, black, and brown—migrated west to take jobs in defense industry factories; unemployment was soon a thing of the past. Farmers recovered, supported by Mexican labor through the *bracero program.* The federal government, through agencies such as the *War Production Board,* took control of managing the economy. Many women took nontraditional jobs. About 1 million African Americans served in the military in segregated units. More than 100,000 Japanese Americans were forcibly interned in *"war relocation camps."*

- **Road to Allied Victory in Europe**   By 1943, the Allies had defeated the German and Italian armies occupying North Africa. From there, they launched attacks on Sicily and then the mainland of Italy. Stalin, meanwhile, demanded a full-scale Allied attack on the Atlantic coast of France to ease pressure on the Russian Front, but *Operation Overlord* was delayed until June 6, 1944. German resistance slowly crumbled. The "Big Three" Allied leaders—Roosevelt, Churchill, and Stalin—met at the *Yalta Conference* in February 1945, where they decided that a conquered Germany would be divided into four occupation zones. In May, Soviet forces captured Berlin, and Germany surrendered. After the war, Allied forces discovered the extent of the *Holocaust*—the Nazis' systematic effort to exterminate the Jews.

- **The Pacific War**   The Japanese advance across the Pacific was halted in June 1942 with the *Battle of Midway.* Fierce Japanese resistance at Iwo Jima and Okinawa and Japan's refusal to surrender after the firebombing of Tokyo led the new president, Harry S. Truman, to order the use of atomic bombs on the cities of *Hiroshima* and Nagasaki.

- **Postwar World**   The Soviet Union and the United States emerged from the war as global superpowers, with the United States possessing the world's strongest economy. The opportunities for women and minorities during the war also increased their aspirations and would contribute to the emergence of the civil rights and feminist movements.

CHRONOLOGY

1933	Adolf Hitler becomes chancellor of Germany
1937	War between China and Japan begins
1939	Non-Aggression pact between Germany and the Soviet Union
September 1939	German troops invade Poland
1940	Battle of Britain
June 1941	Germany invades Soviet Union
August 1941	United States and Great Britain sign the Atlantic Charter
December 7, 1941	Japanese launch surprise attack at Pearl Harbor, Hawaii
June 1942	Battle of Midway
January 1943	Roosevelt and Churchill meet at Casablanca
November 1943	Roosevelt and Churchill meet Stalin in Tehran
June 6, 1944	D-day
February 1945	Yalta Conference
April 1945	Roosevelt dies; Hitler commits suicide
May 8, 1945	Nazi Germany surrenders; V-E day
August 1945	Atomic bombs dropped on Hiroshima and Nagasaki
September 2, 1945	Japan surrenders; V-J day

KEY TERMS

fascism p. 1152

"neutrality laws" p. 1156

"Axis" alliance p. 1157

Lend-Lease Act (1941) p. 1166

Atlantic Charter (1941) p. 1167

Pearl Harbor p. 1172

War Production Board p. 1173

Women's Army Corps (WAC) p. 1175

Tuskegee Airmen p. 1179

bracero program p. 1179

"war relocation camps" p. 1181

Operation Overlord p. 1187

Yalta Conference (1945) p. 1193

Holocaust p. 1196

Battle of Midway p. 1199

Hiroshima p. 1202

 INQUIZITIVE

Go to InQuizitive to see what you've learned—and learn what you've missed—with personalized feedback along the way.

part seven

THE AMERICAN AGE

The United States emerged from the Second World War as the dominant nation on the planet. It was the world's preeminent military and economic power, and the only nation to possess atomic weapons. The war changed things in ways no one could have imagined. Some changes came immediately; others emerged more slowly. But their combined effect was truly transformational.

While much of Europe and Asia struggled to recover from the devastation of the war, the United States was virtually unscathed, its economic infrastructure intact and operating at peak efficiency. Jobs that had been scarce in the 1930s were now available for the taking. By 1955 the United States, with only 6 percent of the world's population, was producing half of the world's goods. American capitalism became a dominant cultural force as U.S. products, fashion, and forms of entertainment attracted international attention.

In 1941, Henry Luce, the publisher of *Time* and *Life* magazines, proclaimed that the twentieth century had become the "American century." The ideal of America, he explained, included "a love of freedom, a feeling for the equality of opportunity, a tradition of self-reliance and independence." America seemed free and unshackled, its potential unlimited.

The deepening cold war between democratic and Communist nations cast a cloud over the postwar world. The tense ideological contest with the Soviet Union produced numerous crises and sparked a witch hunt for Communists in the United States. After 1945, Republican and Democratic presidents aggressively sought to "contain" the spread of communism. This bedrock assumption embroiled the United States in costly wars in Korea and in Southeast Asia.

A backlash against the Vietnam War (1964–1973) also inflamed a rebellious "countercultural" movement at home in which young idealists not only opposed the war but also provided much of the energy for many overdue social reforms, including racial equality, gay rights, feminism, and environmentalism. The anti-war movement destroyed Lyndon Johnson's presidency in 1968 and provoked a conservative counterattack. President Richard Nixon's paranoid reaction to his critics led to the Watergate affair and the destruction of his presidency.

Through all of this turmoil, however, the expanding role of the federal government that Franklin Roosevelt and his New Deal programs had initiated remained essentially intact. With only a few exceptions, both Republicans and Democrats after 1945 acknowledged that the federal government must assume greater responsibility for the welfare of individuals. This fragile consensus, however, had largely broken down by the late 1980s amid stunning international developments and social changes at home. The surprising collapse of the Soviet Union in 1989 and the disintegration of European communism left the United States as the only superpower.

The end of the cold war and the dissolution of the Soviet Union lowered the threat of nuclear war and reduced public interest in foreign affairs. Yet numerous ethnic, nationalist, and separatist conflicts brought constant international instability. The United States found itself drawn into political and military crises in faraway lands such as Bosnia, Somalia, Afghanistan, Iraq, Ukraine, and Syria.

Throughout the 1990s, the United States waged a difficult struggle against many groups engaged in organized terrorism. The challenges of tracking the movements of foreign terrorists became tragically evident in 2001. At 8:46 on the morning of September 11, 2001, the world watched in horror as hijacked commercial airplanes slammed into the World Trade Center in New York City.

Officials identified the hijackers as members of al Qaeda (Arabic for "The Base"), a well-financed network of Islamic terrorists led by a wealthy Saudi renegade, Osama bin Laden. President George W. Bush responded by declaring a "war on terror." With the passage of the so-called Patriot Act, Congress gave the president authority to track down

and imprison terrorists at home and abroad. The "war on terror" began with assaults first on terrorist bases in Afghanistan and then on Saddam Hussein's dictatorship in Iraq ("Operation Iraqi Freedom"). Yet terrorism proved to be an elusive and resilient foe, and the war in Iraq and the ensuing U.S. military occupation was much longer, more expensive, and less successful than Americans had expected.

The surprising victory of Barack Obama in the 2008 presidential election resulted from people embracing his theme of "hope and change." He pledged to end the wars in Iraq and Afghanistan, unite the nation, and provide jobs to the growing numbers of unemployed. As the first African American president, Obama symbolized the societal changes transforming national life.

Yet no sooner was Obama inaugurated than he inherited the worst economic slowdown since the Great Depression. What came to be called the Great Recession dominated the Obama presidency and, indeed, much of American life, bringing with it a prolonged sense of uncertainty and insecurity. For all of its economic power and military might, the United States in the twenty-first century has not eliminated the threat of terrorism or unlocked the mystery of sustaining prosperity and reducing economic inequality.

27

The Cold War and the Fair Deal

1945–1952

Duck and cover A "duck-and-cover" air-raid drill in 1951 that was commonplace in schools across the country during the cold war. The drills began in 1949, when the Soviet Union set off its first nuclear weapon. Pictured above are American schoolchildren practicing ducking and covering in February 1951.

No sooner did the Second World War end than a prolonged "cold war" between communism and capitalism began. The awkward wartime alliance between the United States and the Soviet Union collapsed during the spring and summer of 1945. With the elimination of their common enemy, Nazism, the two nations became intense global rivals who could not bridge their ideological differences over basic issues such as human rights, individual liberties, democratic elections, and religious freedom.

Mutual suspicion and a race to gain influence over "nonaligned" nations in Asia, Africa, the Middle East, and Central and South America further distanced the two former allies. The defeat of Japan and Germany had created power vacuums in Europe and Asia that sucked the Soviet Union and the United States into an unrelenting war of words fed by clashing strategic interests and political ideologies.

The postwar era also brought anti-colonial liberation movements in Asia, Africa, and the Middle East that would soon strip Great Britain, France, the Netherlands, and the United States of their global empires. The Philippines, for example, gained its independence from America in 1946. The next year, Great Britain withdrew from Hindu-dominated India after carving out two new Islamic nations, Pakistan and Bangladesh (originally called East Pakistan). The emergence of Communist China (the People's Republic) in 1949 further complicated global politics.

The mere possibility of nuclear holocaust also cast a cloud of anxiety over the postwar era. The advent of atomic weapons made the very idea of warfare

focus questions

1. Why and how did the cold war between the United States and the Soviet Union develop after the Second World War?

2. What was the impact of American efforts to contain the Soviet Union and the expansion of communism during Truman's presidency?

3. How did Truman expand the New Deal? How effective was his own "Fair Deal" agenda?

4. What were the major international developments during 1949–1950, and how did they alter U.S. foreign policy?

5. How did the Red Scare emerge after the Second World War? How did it impact American politics and society?

unthinkably horrific, which in turn made national leaders more cautious in handling disputes.

TRUMAN AND THE COLD WAR

In April 1945, less than three months after Harry S. Truman had begun his new role as vice president, Eleanor Roosevelt calmly informed him, "Harry, the President is dead." When Truman asked what he could do to help her, the First Lady replied: "Is there anything we can do for *you*? For you are the one in trouble now." Truman was largely unknown outside of Washington. What everyone did know, however, was that he was not Franklin Delano Roosevelt. Truman had no wealthy family, had not traveled the world, and had not attended Harvard or Columbia. In fact, he had not gone to college.

Born in 1884 in western Missouri, Truman grew up in Independence, near Kansas City. Bookish and withdrawn, he was, he recalled, a bit of "a sissy" as a boy. He moved to his grandmother's farm after high school, spent a few years working in Kansas City banks, and grew into an outgoing young man.

During the First World War, Truman served in France as captain of an artillery battery. Afterward, he and a partner started a clothing business, but it failed miserably in the recession of 1922, leaving him in debt for the next twenty years. Truman then entered local politics under the tutelage of Kansas City's Democratic machine. In 1934, Missouri sent him to the U.S. Senate, where he remained obscure until he chaired a committee investigating fraud in the war-mobilization effort.

Truman was a plain, decent, lovable man who lacked Roosevelt's dash, charm, brilliance, and creativity. On his first full day as president, Truman was awestruck. "Boys, if you ever pray, pray for me now," he told reporters. "I don't know whether you fellows ever had a load of hay fall on you, but when they told me yesterday what had happened, I felt like the moon, the stars and all the planets had fallen on me."

Washington politicos had low expectations of Roosevelt's successor. As Truman was seated waiting to be sworn in as the grieving nation's new president, a Democratic official said "he looked to me like a very little man as he sat" in a huge leather chair. An unreflective man whose famed decisiveness was rarely troubled by doubts or moral ambiguities, Truman was famously short-tempered, profane, and dismissive, and was notorious for his scrappy press conferences. ("If you ask smart-aleck questions, I'll give you smart-aleck answers.") He called publisher William Randolph Hearst "the No. 1 whore monger of our time," columnist Westbrook Pegler "the greatest character assassin in the United States," and Richard Nixon "a shifty-eyed god-damned liar."

The plain-speaking man from Missouri resembled his hero Andrew Jackson in his decisiveness, bluntness, folksy manner, salty language, and raw courage. Despite his lack of executive experience, Truman was confident and self-assured—and he needed to be. Managing the transition from war to peace both at home and abroad was a monumental task. He was expected to lead America into a postwar era complicated by the cold war and the need to rebuild Europe and Asia.

He ended up doing better than anyone expected. A common man who became president at an uncommon time, Truman rose above his limitations to do extraordinary things. He never pretended to be something he was not; as he admitted, he was "an ordinary human being who has been lucky." During a visit in 1952, British leader Winston Churchill confessed to Truman that initially he had held him "in very low regard. I loathed your taking the place of Franklin Roosevelt. I misjudged you badly. Since that time, you, more than any other man, have saved Western civilization."

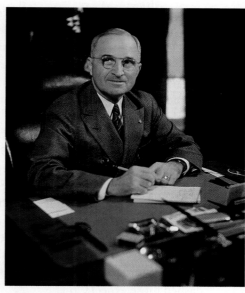

Harry S. Truman The successor to Franklin Roosevelt who led the United States out of the Second World War and into the Cold War.

ORIGINS OF THE COLD WAR Historians have long debated the unanswerable question: Was the United States or the Soviet Union more responsible for the onset of the cold war? The conventional view argues that the Soviets, led by Josef Stalin, a ruthless Communist dictator, set out to dominate the globe after 1945. The United States had no choice but to defend democratic capitalist values. By contrast, "revisionist" historians insist that instead of continuing Roosevelt's efforts to collaborate with the Soviets, President Truman pursued a confrontational foreign policy that aggravated tensions. Yet such an interpretation fails to recognize that Truman inherited a deteriorating relationship with the Soviets. Both sides in the postwar world were captives of a nuclear nightmare of fear, suspicion, and posturing.

In retrospect, the onset of the cold war seems to have been inevitable. America's commitment to capitalism, political self-determination, and religious freedom conflicted dramatically with the Soviet Union's preference for controlling its neighbors, enforcing ideological conformity, and prohibiting religious practices. Insecurity, as much as Communist ideology, drove much of Soviet behavior after the Second World War. Russia, after all, had been invaded by Germany twice in the first half of the twentieth century, and some 23 million people died as a result. Soviet leaders were determined to create loyal nations on their borders for protection. The people of Eastern Europe were caught in the middle.

CONFLICTS WITH THE SOVIETS The wartime military alliance against Nazism disintegrated after 1945 as the Soviet Union violated the promises it had made at the Yalta Conference and imposed military control and the Communist political system on the nations of Eastern Europe it had liberated. On May 12, 1945, four days after victory in Europe, Winston Churchill asked Truman: "What is to happen about Europe? An **iron curtain** is drawn down upon [the Russian] front. We do not know what is going on behind [it]." Churchill and Truman wanted to lift the "iron curtain" and help those nations develop democratic governments. But events during the second half of 1945 dashed those expectations.

As early as the spring of 1945 and continuing for the next two years, the Soviet Union systematically imprisoned half of the European continent. The Red Army ran amok, raping and killing the "liberated" citizens of Eastern Europe. Thereafter, the Soviets systematically installed "puppet" governments across central and Eastern Europe (Albania, Bulgaria, Czechoslovakia, East Germany, Hungary, Poland, Romania, and Yugoslavia). Totalitarian regimes essentially turned once-proud nations into Soviet colonies. In their ruthless pursuit of total control, the Soviets eliminated all political parties except the Communists, created secret police forces, took control of intellectual and cultural life (including the mass media), undermined the Roman Catholic Church, and organized a process of ethnic cleansing whereby whole populations—12 million Germans, as well as Poles and Hungarians—were relocated from their homes in Eastern Europe, usually to West Germany or to prisons. More than 500,000 of the refugees died in the process. Anyone who opposed the Soviet-installed regimes was exiled, silenced, executed, or imprisoned.

Stalin's promises at the Yalta Conference to allow open elections in the nations of Eastern Europe controlled by Soviet armies had turned out to be lies. In a fit of candor, he admitted that "a freely elected government in any of these countries would be anti-Soviet, and that we cannot allow."

U.S. secretary of state James F. Byrnes tried to use America's monopoly on atomic bombs to pressure the Soviets to abide by the Yalta accords. In April 1945, he suggested to President Truman that nuclear weapons "might well put us in position to dictate our own terms [with the Soviets] at the end of the war." The Soviets, however, paid little attention, in part because their spies had kept them informed of what American scientists had been doing and in part because they were developing their own atomic bombs.

Throughout the spring of 1945, the Soviets created "friendly governments" in Eastern Europe, arguing that the United States had done the same in Italy and Japan after those nations had surrendered. The difference was that the Soviets prevented non-Communists from participating in the political process.

A few days before the opening of the conference to organize the United Nations in April, Truman met with Soviet foreign minister Vyacheslav Molotov. The Soviets had just put in place a pro-Communist government in Poland in violation of Stalin's pledge at Yalta to allow free elections. Truman directed Molotov to tell Stalin that the United States expected the Soviet leader to live up to his agreements. "I have never been talked to like that in my life," Molotov angrily replied. "Carry out your agreements," Truman snapped, "and you won't get talked to like that."

Later, in July 1945, when Truman met Stalin at the Potsdam Conference, he wrote his mother that he had never seen "such pig-headed people as are the Russians." He later acknowledged that the Soviets broke their promises "as soon as the unconscionable Russian Dictator [Stalin] returned to Moscow!" Truman added, with a note of embarrassment, "And I liked the little son of a bitch."

THE CONTAINMENT POLICY

By the beginning of 1947, relations with the Soviet Union had grown ice cold. A year before, in February 1946, Stalin had proclaimed the superiority of the Soviet Communist system of government and declared that peace was impossible "under the present capitalist development of the world economy." His provocative statement suggesting an inevitable war between communism and capitalism led the State Department to ask for an analysis of Soviet communism from forty-two-year-old George Frost Kennan, the best-informed expert on the Soviet Union, then working in the U.S. embassy in Moscow.

Kennan responded on February 22, 1946, with a famous 5,000-word "Long Telegram"—the longest in the history of the State Department. He included considerable detail about Russian history, the pillars of Soviet policy, Stalin's "neurotic view of world affairs," and Russia's historic determination to protect its western border with Europe.

Kennan explained that the Soviet Union was founded on a rigid ideology (Marxism-Leninism), which saw a fundamental global conflict between Communist and capitalist nations and helped Soviet rulers justify their amoral

George F. Kennan A specialist in the history and behavior of the Soviet Union, American diplomat George Kennan developed the rationale for containment at the heart of the Truman Doctrine.

actions. They could not imagine "permanent peaceful coexistence" with capitalist nations and were "fanatically" committed to the necessity of perpetual tension and conflict. In this regard, Kennan implied, Franklin Roosevelt had mistakenly assumed that his personal diplomacy with Stalin would ensure that the Soviets behaved. Kennan insisted instead that Stalin needed external enemies to maintain his totalitarian power at home.

The Soviet goal, according to Kennan, was to build military strength while subverting the stability of the capitalist democracies. The best way for the United States to deal with such an ideological foe, he advised, was through patient, persistent, and firm "strategic" efforts to "contain" Soviet expansionism, without resorting to war. The economic power of capitalist democracies was their greatest asset. Creating "unalterable counterforce" to Communist expansionism, Kennan predicted, would eventually cause "either the breakup or the gradual mellowing of Soviet power" because communism, in Kennan's view, was an inherently unstable system that would eventually collapse.

New secretary of state George C. Marshall, the austere but much revered commander of the U.S. armed forces during the war, was so impressed by Kennan's analysis that he put him in charge of the State Department's Policy Planning office. No other American diplomat at the time forecast so accurately what would happen to the Soviet Union some forty years later. As Kennan recalled, "my reputation was made. My voice now carried."

Kennan later acknowledged that his "Long Telegram" suffered from excessive optimism and occasional vagueness. In its broadest dimensions, its call for "firm and vigilant **containment**" echoed the outlook of Truman and his advisers and would guide U.S. foreign policy for decades.

But how exactly were the United States and its allies to "contain" the Soviet Union's expansionist tendencies? How should the United States respond to

Soviet aggression around the world? Kennan left the task of "containing" communism to Truman and his advisers, most of whom, unlike Kennan, considered containment to be as much a *military* doctrine as a *political* strategy.

In 1946, civil war broke out in Greece between an authoritarian monarchy backed by the British and a Communist-led insurgency supported by the Soviets. On February 21, 1947, the financially strapped British informed the U.S. government that they could no longer provide economic and military aid to Greece and would withdraw in five weeks. Truman quickly conferred with congressional leaders, one of whom, Republican senator Arthur Vandenburg of Michigan, warned the president that he would need to "scare the hell out of the American people" about the menace of communism to gain public support for his aid program. Truman was eager to do so, for he had grown tired of "babying the Russians."

THE TRUMAN DOCTRINE On March 12, 1947, President Truman gave a national radio speech in which he asked Congress for $400 million for economic and military assistance for Greece and Turkey. More important, the president announced what came to be known as the **Truman Doctrine**. To ensure congressional support, he intentionally exaggerated the danger of a Communist takeover in Greece. Like a row of dominoes, Truman predicted, the fall of Greece would topple the other nations of the eastern Mediterranean, then Western Europe. To prevent such a catastrophe, he said, the United States must "support free peoples who are resisting attempted subjugation by armed minorities or by outside pressures."

In this single sentence, the president established the foundation of U.S. foreign policy for the next forty years. In essence, he was declaring war on communism everywhere. In Truman's view, shared by later presidents, the assumptions of the "domino theory" made an aggressive "containment" strategy against communism a necessity.

Truman's speech generated widespread public support. The *New York Times* said that his message was clear: "The epoch of isolation is ended. It is being replaced by an epoch of American responsibility." At the State Department, Secretary of State Marshall announced that "we are now concerned with the peace of the entire world."

Still, Marshall and others feared that Truman's speech was unnecessarily provocative. George Kennan cringed at the president's "grandiose" commitment to "contain" communism *everywhere*. In Kennan's view, Truman's "militarized view of the Cold War" was a foolish *crusade*, an open-ended ideological confrontation without limits rather than a *policy* with an accompanying program of steps capable of implementation. Efforts to "contain" communism needed to

"It's the same thing" The Marshall Plan, which distributed massive amounts of economic aid throughout postwar Europe, is represented in this 1949 cartoon as a modern tractor driven by a prosperous farmer. In the foreground a poor, overworked man is yoked to an old-fashioned "Soviet" plow, forced to go over the ground of the "Marshal Stalin Plan," while Stalin himself tries to persuade others that "it's the same thing without mechanical problems."

be selective rather than universal, political and economic rather than military; the United States could not intervene in every "hot spot" around the world. Walter Lippmann, the nation's leading political journalist, characterized Truman's policy of global anti-communism as a "strategic monstrosity" that would entangle the United States in endless international disputes and force it to partner with right-wing dictatorships—as turned out to be the case. Truman and his advisers rejected such concerns. In 1947, Congress approved the president's request for economic and military assistance to Greece and neighboring Turkey.

THE MARSHALL PLAN In the spring of 1947, most of postwar Europe remained broke, shattered, and desperate. Factories had been bombed to rubble; railroads and bridges had been destroyed; millions were homeless, starving, and jobless; and political unrest was growing. By 1947, Socialist and Communist parties were emerging in many European nations, including Italy, France, and Belgium. The crises among the struggling European democracies required bold action.

The United States stepped into the breach. In May 1947, Secretary of State George C. Marshall delivered a speech at Harvard University in which he outlined America's policy toward Europe in nonideological terms. Building upon suggestions given him by George Kennan and others, he called for massive financial and technical assistance to rescue Europe, including the Soviet Union.

What came to be known as the **Marshall Plan** was intended to reconstruct the European economy, neutralize Communist insurgencies, and build up foreign markets for American products. As Truman said, "the American [capitalist] system can survive only if it is part of a world system." But the Marshall Plan was also part of Truman's effort to contain the expansionist tendencies of the Soviet Union by reestablishing a strong Western Europe anchored in American values. The Americans, said a British official, "want an integrated Europe looking like the United States of America."

In December 1947, Truman submitted Marshall's proposal to Congress. Initially, Republican critics dismissed it as "New Dealism" for Europe. However, two months later, on February 25, 1948, a Communist-led coup in Czechoslovakia, the last nation in Eastern Europe with a democratic government, ensured the Marshall Plan's passage.

From 1948 until 1951, the Marshall Plan provided $13 billion to sixteen European nations. The Soviet Union, however, refused to participate and forced the Eastern European countries under its control—Albania, Bulgaria, Poland, Romania, Yugoslavia—to refuse to participate as well.

The Marshall Plan (officially called the European Recovery Plan) worked as hoped. By 1951, Western Europe's industrial production had soared to 40 percent above prewar levels, and its farm output was larger than ever. England's *Economist* magazine called the Marshall Plan "an act without peer in history." It became the most successful peacetime diplomatic initiative in American history.

DIVIDED GERMANY Although the Marshall Plan drew the nations of Western Europe closer together, it increased tensions with the Soviet Union, as Stalin saw it as a way to weaken Soviet influence in the region. The breakdown of the wartime alliance between the United States and the Soviet Union also left the problem of postwar Germany unsettled. In 1945, Berlin, the German capital, had been divided into four sectors, or zones, each governed by one of the four principal allied nations—the United States, France, Great Britain, and the Soviet Union.

The devastated German economy continued to languish, requiring the U.S. Army to provide food and basic necessities to millions of civilians. Slowly, the Allied occupation zones evolved into functioning governments. In 1948, the British, French, and Americans united their three administrative zones into one and developed a common currency to be used in West Germany as well as in West Berlin, a city of 2.4 million people, which was more than 100 miles inside the Soviet occupation zone of East Germany. The West Germans also organized state governments and began drafting a federal constitution.

The political unification of West Germany and its economic recovery infuriated Stalin, who was determined to keep Germany weak. And the status of divided Berlin had become a powder keg. In March 1948, Stalin prevented the new West German currency from being delivered to Berlin. Then, on June 23, he ordered the Soviet army occupying eastern Germany to stop all road and

Family reunion A girl gives her grandmother a kiss through the barbed wire fence that divides the Dutch-German frontier in 1947.

rail traffic into West Berlin. The blockade, he hoped, would force the United States and its allies to leave the divided city.

The Americans interpreted Stalin's blockade as a tipping point in the cold war. "When Berlin falls," predicted General Lucius D. Clay, the U.S. Army commander in Germany, "western Germany will be next. Communism will run rampant." The United States thus faced a dilemma: risk a third world war by using force to break the Soviet blockade or begin a humiliating retreat from West Berlin, leaving the residents to be swallowed up by communism.

Truman, who prided himself on his decisiveness ("the buck stops here"), made clear his stance: "We stay in Berlin—period." The United States announced an embargo against all goods exported from Soviet-controlled eastern Germany and began organizing a massive airlift to provide food and supplies to West Berliners.

By October 1948, the U.S. and British air forces were flying in 7,000 tons of food, fuel, medicine, coal, and equipment to Berlin each day. To support the airlift and prepare for a possible war, thousands of former military pilots were called back into service. Truman revived the military draft, and Congress provided emergency funds to increase military spending.

Through the iron curtain German children greet a U.S. cargo plane as it flies into West Berlin to drop off much-needed food and supplies.

At times it seemed that the two superpowers were on the verge of war. For all the threats and harsh words, however, the **Berlin airlift** went on for eleven months without any shots being fired. Finally, on May 12, 1949, the Soviets lifted their blockade, in part because bad Russian harvests had made them desperate for food grown in western Germany. The Berlin airlift was the first major "victory" for the West in the cold war, and the unprecedented efforts of the United States and Great Britain to supply West Berliners transformed most of them from defeated adversaries into devoted allies. In May 1949, as the Soviet blockade was ending, the Federal Republic of Germany (West Germany) was founded. In October, the Soviet-controlled German Democratic Republic (East Germany) came into being.

FORMING ALLIANCES The Soviet blockade of Berlin convinced the United States and its allies that they needed to act together to stop further Communist expansion into Western Europe. On April 4, 1949, the North Atlantic Treaty was signed by twelve nations: the United States, Great Britain, France, Belgium, the Netherlands, Luxembourg, Canada, Denmark, Iceland, Italy, Norway, and Portugal. Greece and Turkey joined the alliance in 1952, West Germany in 1955, and Spain in 1982.

The **North Atlantic Treaty Organization (NATO)**, the largest defensive alliance in the world, declared that an attack against any one of the members would be considered an attack against all. The creation of NATO marked the high point of efforts to "contain" Soviet expansion. In 1949, Congress provided $1 billion in military equipment to NATO members. By joining NATO, the United States— for the first time since its alliance with France during the Revolutionary War— committed itself to go to war on behalf of its allies. Isolationism was dead.

THE OCCUPATION OF GERMANY AND AUSTRIA

French zone · British zone · U.S. zone · Soviet zone

- How did the Allies decide to divide postwar Germany at the Yalta Conference?
- What was the "iron curtain"?
- Why did the Allies airlift supplies to West Berlin?

REORGANIZING THE MILITARY The onset of the cold war and the emergence of nuclear weapons led Truman to restructure the way the U.S. armed forces were managed. In 1947, Congress passed the **National Security Act**, which created a Department of Defense to oversee the three military branches—the Army, Navy, and Air Force—and the National Security Council (NSC), an advisory group of the government's top specialists in international relations. The act made permanent the Joint Chiefs of Staff, a wartime innovation bringing together the leaders of all branches of the armed forces. It also established the Central Intelligence Agency (CIA) to coordinate global intelligence-gathering activities.

In 1952, Truman created the National Security Agency (NSA) within the Defense Department. Its charge was to "encrypt" government communications to ensure their privacy and to intercept the communications of other nations. The NSA also provided surveillance of Americans targeted as potential threats.

A JEWISH NATION: ISRAEL At the same time that the United States was helping to form new alliances, it was helping to form a new nation. Palestine, the biblical Holy Land, had been a British protectorate since 1919. For hundreds of years, Jews throughout the world had dreamed of returning to their ancestral homeland of Israel and its ancient capital Zion, a part of Jerusalem. Many Zionists—Jews who wanted a separate Jewish nation—had migrated there. More arrived during and after the Nazi persecution of European Jews. Hitler's effort to exterminate the Jews convinced many that their only hope for a secure future was to create their own nation.

Late in 1947, the United Nations voted to divide ("partition") Palestine into separate Jewish and Arab states. The Jews readily agreed, but the Arabs were fiercely opposed. Palestine was their ancestral home, too; Jerusalem was as holy to Muslims as it was to Jews and Christians. Arabs viewed the creation of a Jewish nation in Palestine as an act of war, and they attacked Israel in early 1948. Hundreds were killed before the Haganah (Jewish militia) won control of most of Palestine. When British oversight of Palestine officially expired on May 14, 1948, David Ben-Gurion, the Jewish leader in Palestine, proclaimed Israel's independence. President Truman officially recognized the new Israeli nation within minutes, as did the Soviet Union.

One million Jews, most of them European immigrants, now had their own nation. Early the next morning, however, the Arab League nations—Lebanon, Syria, Iraq, Jordan, and Egypt—invaded Israel, beginning a period of nearly constant warfare in the Holy Land. Mediators from the UN gradually worked out a truce agreement, restoring an uneasy peace by May 11, 1949, when Israel joined the United Nations. Israel was allowed to keep all its conquered territories, including the whole Palestine coast.

The Palestinian Arabs lost everything. Most of them became stateless refugees who scattered into neighboring Lebanon, Jordan, and Egypt. Stored-up resentments and sporadic warfare between Israel and the Arab states have festered ever since, complicating U.S. foreign policy, which has tried to maintain friendships with both sides but has usually tilted toward Israel.

Expanding the New Deal

For the most part, Republicans and Democrats in Congress cooperated with President Truman on issues related to the cold war, though often grudgingly. Senator Claude Pepper, a liberal Democrat from Florida, insisted that if Franklin Roosevelt were still alive, "we'd be getting on better with Russia." Republican senator Robert A. Taft of Ohio accused Truman of "appeasing Russia, a policy which has sacrificed throughout Eastern Europe and Asia the freedom of many nations and millions of people." On domestic issues, however, Truman faced widespread opposition. The cost-cutting Republicans in Congress hoped that they could end the New Deal as the war drew to a close.

FROM WAR TO PEACE In September 1945, Truman called Congress into a special emergency session at which he presented a twenty-one-point program to guide the nation's "reconversion" from wartime back to peacetime. Massive government spending during the war had ended the Great Depression and brought about full employment, but Truman's postwar challenge was to ensure that the peacetime economy absorbed the millions of men and women who had served in the armed forces and were now seeking civilian jobs. During the second half of 1945 and throughout 1946, some 700,000 people in uniform, mostly men, returned to civilian life. By 1947, the armed forces had shrunk from 12 million to 1.5 million.

Fears of massive unemployment in defense-related industries led people to worry about another depression. A *New York Times* headline predicted: "5,000,000 EXPECTED TO LOSE ARMS JOBS!" Truman called for unemployment insurance to cover more workers, a higher minimum wage, construction of massive low-cost public housing projects, regional development projects to put military veterans to work, and much more. A powerful Republican congressman named Joseph W. Martin was stunned by the scope of Truman's proposals. "Not even President Roosevelt," he gasped, "ever asked for so much at one sitting."

Drugstore in Bronxville, NY America quickly demobilized after the long war effort, turning its attention to the pursuit of abundance.

Truman's primary goal was to "prevent prolonged unemployment" while avoiding the "bitter mistakes" that had produced wild price inflation and a recession after the First World War. He also wanted to retain, for a while, the wartime controls on wages, prices, and rents, as well as the rationing of scarce food items. Most of all, he wanted to minimize unemployment as workers in defense plants were laid off and millions of military veterans went looking for civilian jobs. Truman called on Congress to *guarantee* every American a job.

Congress refused to go that far. Instead, it approved the Employment Act of 1946, which authorized Truman and the federal government "to promote maximum employment, production, and purchasing power." Liberals were disappointed by the new president's inability to win over legislators. "Alas for Truman," said the *New Republic*, there was "no bugle note in his voice" to rally public opinion. "What one misses," said Max Lerner, an influential journalist, "is the confident sense of direction that Roosevelt gave, despite all the contradictions of his policy."

Throughout 1946, Republicans and conservative southern Democrats in Congress balked at most of Truman's efforts to revive or expand New Deal programs. The Great Depression was over, critics stressed. Different times demanded different programs—or none at all.

The end of the war caused short-term economic problems but not the postwar depression many had feared. Many women who had been recruited to work in defense industries were shoved out as men took off uniforms and looked for jobs. At a shipyard in California, the foreman gathered the women workers and told them to go welcome the troop ships as they pulled into port. The next day, all of the women were let go to make room for male veterans.

Still, several shock absorbers cushioned the economic impact of demobilization. They included federal unemployment insurance (and other Social Security benefits) and the Servicemen's Readjustment Act of 1944, known as the GI Bill of Rights, under which the federal government spent $13 billion on military veterans for education, vocational training, medical treatment, unemployment insurance, and loans for building houses and starting new businesses.

WAGES, PRICES, AND LABOR UNREST The most acute economic problem Truman faced was the postwar spike in prices charged for consumer goods. During the war, the government had frozen wages and prices and banned strikes by labor unions. When wartime economic controls were removed, prices for scarce consumer items shot up, spurring labor unions to demand pay increases. When raises were not provided, a record number of postwar strikes erupted in 1945–1946, exacerbating the shortages of consumer goods. Workers at General Motors went on strike for almost four months, making it much more difficult for people to buy a car. Never before or since had so many American workers walked off the job in one year.

Labor disputes crippled the crucial coal and railroad industries. Like Theodore Roosevelt before him, Truman grew frustrated with the stubbornness of both management and labor leaders. He took federal control of the coal mines, whereupon the mine owners agreed to union demands. In May 1946, Truman threatened to draft striking railroad workers into the military if they did not go back to work. His threat, probably illegal, did the trick, but it embittered many workers who had long voted Democratic. A leading union official announced that organized labor "is through with Truman."

Truman's efforts to control rising prices were equally controversial. On June 30, 1946, he lifted wartime controls on consumer prices. Within days, prices for groceries skyrocketed, rising in two weeks as much as they had risen in the previous three years. So Truman restored price controls. Ranchers were so upset by the president's change of course that they refused to sell their cattle for slaughter. Suddenly, there was a "beefsteak" crisis as consumers complained that the supply of food was worse than it had been during the war.

Time magazine's Washington-based political reporter alerted his editor that Truman was so unpopular "he could not carry Missouri now."

On October 14, just three weeks before the midterm congressional elections, Truman announced that he was removing price controls on meat. Steaks and hamburger meat soon appeared on grocery shelves, but prices again soared. A Republican political strategist loved the turn of events, telling his colleagues that "the tide is sweepin' our way." And it was.

POLITICAL COOPERATION AND CONFLICT During the congressional election campaigns in 1946, Republicans adopted a simple, four-word slogan: "Had Enough? Vote Republican!" Using loudspeakers, Republicans drove through city streets saying, "Ladies, if you want meat, vote Republican." A union leader tagged Truman "the No. 1 Strikebreaker," while much of the public, upset by the unions, price increases, food shortages, and the scarcity of automobiles and affordable housing, blamed the strikes on the White House.

Labor unions had emerged from the war with more power than ever before. Some 14.5 million workers, more than a third of the workforce, were now unionized. Members had tended to vote Democratic, but not in the 1946 elections, which gave the Republicans majorities in both houses of Congress for the first time since 1928. "The New Deal is kaput," one newspaper editor crowed. The *Chicago Tribune* claimed that Americans had "won the greatest victory for the Republic since Appomattox." The president, taunted the *United States News*, "is a one-termer." Even many Democrats had soured on Truman, circulating a slogan that expressed their frustration: "I'm just Mild about Harry."

The new Republican Congress that convened in early 1947 reflected the national discontent. It curbed the power of unions by passing the **Taft-Hartley Labor Act** of 1947 (officially called the Labor-Management Relations Act). The law allowed employers to campaign against efforts to form unions and outlawed unions from coercing workers to join or refusing to negotiate grievances.

The Taft-Hartley Act also required union leaders to take "loyalty oaths" declaring that they were not members of the Communist party, banned strikes by federal employees, and imposed a "cooling-off" period of eighty days on any strike that the president deemed dangerous to the public welfare. Yet the most troubling element of the new bill was a provision that allowed state legislatures to pass "right-to-work" laws that ended the practice of forcing all wage workers at a company to join a union once a majority voted to unionize.

In a show of support for organized labor, Truman vetoed the Taft-Hartley bill, which unions called "the slave-labor act." He denounced the "shocking" bill as "bad for labor, bad for management, and bad for the country." Working-class

Fight for desegregation Demonstrators led by activist A. Philip Randolph (left) picket the Democratic National Convention on July 12, 1948, calling for racial integration of the armed forces.

Democrats were delighted. Many unionists who had gone over to the Republicans in 1946 returned to the Democrats because of Truman's strong support. Journalist James Wechsler reported that "Mr. Truman has reached the crucial fork in the road and turned unmistakably to the left."

Congress, however, overturned the president's veto, and Taft-Hartley became law. The number of strikes dropped sharply thereafter, and representatives of management and labor learned to work together. At the same time, by 1954, fifteen state legislatures, mainly in the South and West, had used the Taft-Hartley Act to pass "right-to-work" laws forbidding union-only workplaces. Those states thereafter recruited industries to relocate because of their low wages and "nonunion" policies.

CIVIL RIGHTS Another of Truman's challenges was the bigotry faced by returning African American soldiers. When one black veteran arrived home in a uniform decorated with combat medals, he was welcomed by a white neighbor who said: "Don't you forget . . . that you're still a nigger."

The Second World War had changed America's racial landscape in important ways, however. As a *New York Times* editorial explained in early 1946, "This is a particularly good time to campaign against the evils of bigotry, prejudice, and race hatred because we have witnessed the defeat of enemies who tried to found a mastery of the world upon such cruel and fallacious policy."

African Americans had fought in large numbers to overthrow the Nazi regime of government-sponsored racism, and returning veterans were unwilling to put up with racial abuse at home. The cold war also gave political leaders added incentive to improve race relations. The Soviets often compared racism in the United States to the Nazis' brutalization of the Jews. In the ideological contest against capitalism, Communists highlighted examples of American racism to win influence among the newly emerging nations of Africa.

Black veterans who spoke out against racial bigotry often risked their lives. In 1946, two African American couples in rural Georgia were gunned down by a white mob. One of the murderers explained that George Dorsey, one of the victims, was "a good nigger" until he went into the army. "But when he came out, he thought he was as good as any white people."

In the fall of 1946, a delegation of civil rights activists urged President Truman to condemn the Ku Klux Klan and the lynching of African Americans. The delegation graphically described incidents of torture and intimidation against blacks in the South. Truman was horrified: "My God! I had no idea that it was as terrible as that! We've got to do something."

Truman thereupon appointed a Committee on Civil Rights to investigate violence against African Americans. A year later, with Truman's endorsement, the commission issued a report, "To Secure These Rights," which called for a federal anti-lynching bill, abolition of the poll tax designed to keep poor blacks from voting, a voting rights act, an end to racial segregation in the armed forces, and a ban on racial segregation in public transportation. Southern Democrats were furious. South Carolina governor J. Strom Thurmond warned Truman that the southern Democratic vote was no longer "in the bag." Thurmond would soon leave the party to form the Dixiecrats in opposition to Truman.

On July 26, 1948, Truman took a bolder step when he banned racial discrimination in the federal government. Four days later, he issued an executive order ending racial segregation in the armed forces. The air force and navy quickly complied, but the army dragged its feet until the early 1950s. By 1960, however, the armed forces were the most racially integrated of all national organizations. Desegregating the military was, Truman claimed, "the greatest thing that ever happened to America."

JACKIE ROBINSON Meanwhile, racial segregation was being dismantled in a much more public area: professional baseball. In April 1947, the Brooklyn Dodgers roster included the first African American to play major

Jackie Robinson Robinson's unfaltering courage and superior athletic skills prompted the integration of sports, drawing African American and Latino spectators to the games. Here, he greets his Dominican fans at Trujillo High School in Santo Domingo.

league baseball: Jack Roosevelt "Jackie" Robinson. He was born in 1919 in a Georgia sharecropper's cabin, the grandson of slaves. Six months later, his father left town with a neighbor's wife, never to return. Robinson's mother moved the family to Pasadena, California, where Jackie became a marvelous all-around athlete. At UCLA, he was the first athlete in school history to letter in four sports: baseball, basketball, football, and track. After serving in the army during World War II, he began playing professional baseball in the so-called Negro Leagues. He did so well that major league scouts reported that he could play in the big leagues.

At that point, Branch Rickey, the president and general manager of the Brooklyn Dodgers, interviewed Robinson for three hours on August 28, 1945. Rickey asked Robinson if he could face racial abuse without losing his temper. Robinson was shocked: "Are you looking for a Negro who is afraid to fight back?" Rickey replied that he needed a pathbreaking "Negro player" with "guts enough *not* to fight back." Robinson assured him he was the best candidate to integrate baseball: "If you want to take this gamble, I will promise there will be no incident." He then signed Robinson to a contract for $600 a month. Rickey explained to his critics that he had found a terrific player who was a strong, quiet warrior of incomparable courage capable of looking the other way when provoked. And he was often provoked.

Soon after Robinson arrived for preseason practice, many of his white Dodger teammates refused to take the field with him. Manager Leo Durocher would have none of that. As he told the team, "I don't care if the guy is yellow or black, or if he has stripes . . . I'm the manager of this team, and I say he plays."

During the 1947 season, teammates and opposing players viciously baited Robinson. Pitchers hit him, base runners spiked him, and spectators booed him and drenched him in beer, even as he led the Dodgers to the National League championship and eventually six World Series appearances. In Cincinnati, Reds fans posted a sign reading: "Robinson: We are going to kill you if you attempt to enter a ball game as Crosley Field." Hotels refused him rooms, and restaurants denied him service. Hate mail arrived by the bucketful. One sportswriter called Robinson "the loneliest man I have ever seen in sports."

On the other hand, black spectators were electrified by Robinson's courageous example and turned out in droves to watch him play. A headline in a Boston newspaper expressed the prevailing sentiment: "Triumph of Whole Race Seen in Jackie's Debut in Major League Ball." As time passed, Robinson won over many fans and players with his courage, wit, grit, and talent. As sportswriter Red Smith observed, Robinson was an example of "the unconquerable doing the impossible." During his first season with the Dodgers, Robinson stole twice as many bases as anyone else in the National League, and he was named Rookie of the Year. Between 1949 and 1954, Robinson had a batting average of .327, among the best in baseball. Yankees catcher Yogi Berra said "he could beat you in a lot of ways."

Robinson's very presence on the field with lily-white teams forced spectators sitting in racially divided bleachers to confront the hypocritical reality of segregation. Other teams soon began signing black players. Racial attitudes were changing—slowly. In 1947, Robinson was voted the second most popular American, behind singer Bing Crosby. "My life," Robinson remembered, "produced understanding among whites, and it gave black people the idea that if I could do it, they could do it, too, that blackness wasn't subservient to anything."

MEXICAN AMERICANS In the Far West, Mexican Americans (often grouped with other Spanish-speaking immigrants as *Hispanics* or *Latinos*) continued to experience ethnic prejudice. Schools in Arizona, New Mexico, Texas, and California routinely segregated Mexican American children from whites. The 500,000 Latino veterans were especially frustrated that their efforts in the war were not rewarded with equality at home. They were frequently denied access to educational, medical, and housing benefits available to white servicemen. Some mortuaries even denied funeral services to Mexican Americans killed in combat. As a funeral director in Texas explained, "the Anglo people would not stand for it."

To fight such prejudicial treatment, Mexican American war veterans led by Dr. Hector Perez Garcia, a U.S. Army major who had served as a combat surgeon, organized the American GI Forum in Texas in 1948. Soon there were branches across the nation. Garcia, born in Mexico in 1914 and raised in Texas, stressed the importance of formal education to Mexican Americans. The organization's motto read: "Education Is Our Freedom and Freedom Should Be Everybody's Business."

At a time when Mexican Americans in Texas averaged no more than a third-grade education, Garcia and five of his siblings had completed medical school and become physicians. Yet upon his return from the war, he encountered "discrimination everywhere. We had no opportunities. We had to pay [poll taxes] to vote. We had segregated schools. We were not allowed to go into public places."

Garcia and the GI Forum initially focused on veterans' issues but soon expanded the organization's scope to include fostering equal opportunities and equal treatment for all people. The GI Forum lobbied to end poll taxes, sued for the right of Latinos to serve on juries, and developed schools for jobless veterans. In 1984, Garcia received the Presidential Medal of Freedom, the nation's highest civilian honor.

SHAPING THE FAIR DEAL   During 1947, after less than three years in the White House, Truman had yet to shake the widespread impression that he was not up to the job. Critics proclaimed that "to err is Truman." The editors of *Time* magazine reflected the national sentiment when they wrote, "Mr. Truman has often faced his responsibilities with a cheerful, dogged courage. But his performance was almost invariably awkward, uninspired, and above all, mediocre." Voters, they added, believed that Truman "means well, but he doesn't do well." Most political analysts assumed that the president would lose his effort to win another term.

Truman, too, feared that he would lose. In July 1947, he met with General Dwight D. Eisenhower as he was preparing to retire as chairman of the Joint Chiefs of Staff. Worried that General Douglas MacArthur, a self-described "right-wing Republican," might be the Republican presidential nominee in 1948, Truman urged Eisenhower to run as the Democratic nominee and even offered to be his vice-presidential running mate. Eisenhower declined, explaining that he was going to become president of Columbia University in New York City.

With the president's popularity sinking, the Democratic party was about to split in two. Southern conservatives resented Truman's outspoken support of civil rights, while the left wing of the party resented the firing of Secretary of Commerce Henry A. Wallace for publicly criticizing the administration's anti-Soviet policies. "Getting tough [with the Soviet Union]," Wallace had argued, "never brought anything real and lasting—whether for schoolyard bullies or world powers. The tougher we get, the tougher the Russians will get."

Wallace had said that the United States had "no more business in the *political affairs* of Eastern Europe than Russia has in the *political affairs* of Latin America." The danger of another world war, he said, "is much less from communism than it is from [American] imperialism." Wallace's comments so outraged the leaders of the State Department that Truman felt he had no choice but to get rid of him.

Despite the gloomy predictions for 1948, Truman mounted an intense reelection campaign. His first step was to shore up the major elements of the New Deal coalition of working-class voters: farmers, labor unionists, and African Americans.

In his 1948 State of the Union message, Truman announced that the programs he would later call his "**Fair Deal**" (to distinguish them from Roosevelt's New Deal) would build upon the efforts of the New Deal to help all Americans. The first goal, Truman said, was to ensure civil rights for all Americans. He added proposals to increase federal aid to education, expand unemployment and retirement benefits, create a comprehensive system of national health insurance, enable more rural people to connect to electricity, and increase the minimum wage.

THE ELECTION OF 1948 The Republican-controlled Congress dismissed Truman's proposals, an action it would later regret. At the Republican convention, New York governor Thomas E. Dewey won the presidential nomination on the third ballot. While the platform endorsed most of the New Deal reforms and approved the administration's bipartisan foreign policy, Dewey promised to run things more efficiently.

In July, glum Democrats gathered for their convention in Philadelphia. Everyone assumed a Republican victory in November. A reporter wrote that they behaved "as though they [had] accepted an invitation to a funeral." Some party leaders, including Roosevelt's son James, a California congressman, tried to convince Dwight Eisenhower to accept the Democratic nomination, and many others joined his "dump Truman" effort. The popular war hero declined, however, explaining that his refusal was "final and complete."

Delegates who expected to do little more than go through the motions of nominating Truman were doubly surprised, first by the battle on the conven-

Birth of the Dixiecrats Alabama delegates stand to boo Truman's call for civil rights before they walked out of the 1948 Democratic National Convention.

tion floor over civil rights and then by Truman's endorsement of civil rights for African Americans in his acceptance speech. Liberal Democrats led by Minnesota's Hubert Humphrey commended Truman "for his courageous stand on the issue of civil rights" and declared that the "time has arrived for the Democratic party to get out of the shadow of civil rights." White segregationist delegates from Alabama and Mississippi walked out in protest. The solidly Democratic South had fractured over race.

On July 17, a group of rebellious southern Democrats met in Birmingham, Alabama. While waving Confederate flags and singing "Dixie," they nominated South Carolina's segregationist governor, Strom Thurmond, on a States' Rights Democratic party ticket, quickly dubbed the "Dixiecrat party." The **Dixiecrats** denounced Truman's "infamous" civil rights initiatives and championed states' rights against federal efforts to change the tradition of white supremacy in the South.

A few days later, on July 23, the left wing of the Democratic party gathered in Philadelphia to form a new Progressive party and nominate for president Henry A. Wallace, Roosevelt's former secretary of agriculture and vice president, whom Truman had fired as secretary of commerce. One Democratic leader asked Truman to withdraw from the race to help the party's chances. He replied: "I was not brought up to run from a fight."

The splits in the Democratic ranks seemed to spell the final blow to Truman, but he refused to give in. He was finally renominated long after midnight. By the time he entered the auditorium, it was 2 A.M., but he aroused the faithful by promising that "I will win this election and make the Republicans like it!" He pledged to bring Congress into special session and demand that it confront the housing crisis and boost the minimum wage.

Within days, an invigorated Truman set out on a 22,000-mile "whistle-stop" train tour, making ten speeches a day scolding the "do-nothing" Eightieth Congress. The plain-talking president attracted huge crowds. The Republicans,

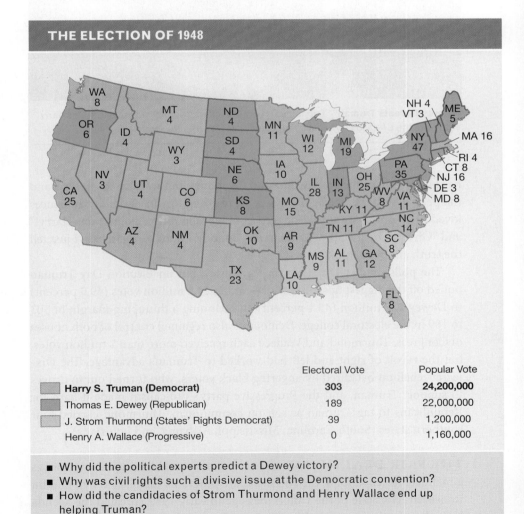

THE ELECTION OF 1948

	Electoral Vote	Popular Vote
Harry S. Truman (Democrat)	**303**	**24,200,000**
Thomas E. Dewey (Republican)	189	22,000,000
J. Strom Thurmond (States' Rights Democrat)	39	1,200,000
Henry A. Wallace (Progressive)	0	1,160,000

- Why did the political experts predict a Dewey victory?
- Why was civil rights such a divisive issue at the Democratic convention?
- How did the candidacies of Strom Thurmond and Henry Wallace end up helping Truman?

"Dewey Defeats Truman" Truman's victory in 1948 was such a surprise that this early edition of the *Chicago Daily Tribune* reported that Dewey had won.

he charged, "have the propaganda and the money, but we have the people, and the people have the votes. *That's* why we're going to win." Friendly audiences loved his fighting spirit and dogged courage, shouting, "Pour it on, Harry!" and "Give 'em hell, Harry." Truman responded: "I don't give 'em hell. I just tell the truth and they think it's hell."

The polls predicted a sure win for Dewey, but on Election Day Truman pulled off the biggest upset in history, taking 24.2 million votes (49.5 percent) to Dewey's 22 million (45.1 percent) and winning a thumping margin of 303 to 189 in the electoral college. Democrats also regained control of both houses of Congress. Thurmond and Wallace each received more than 1 million votes, but the revolt of right and left had worked to Truman's advantage. The Dixiecrat rebellion backfired by angering black voters, who turned out in droves to support Truman, and the Progressive party's radicalism made it hard for Republicans to tag Truman as soft on communism. Thurmond carried four southern states (South Carolina, Mississippi, Alabama, and Louisiana).

THE FAIR DEAL REJECTED Truman viewed his surprising victory as a mandate for expanding the social welfare programs established by Franklin Roosevelt. His State of the Union message in early 1949 repeated the agenda he had set forth the year before. "Every segment of our population and every individual," he declared, "has a right to expect from our government a *fair deal*."

Truman's Fair Deal promised "greater economic opportunity for the mass of the people."

Most of the Fair Deal proposals that gained congressional approval were extensions or enlargements of New Deal programs: a higher minimum hourly wage, expansion of Social Security coverage to 10 million workers not included in the original 1935 bill, and a large slum-clearance and public-housing program. Despite enjoying Democratic majorities in Congress, however, Truman ran up against the same alliance of conservative southern Democrats and Republicans who had worked against Roosevelt in the late 1930s. The bipartisan conservative coalition nixed most of Truman's new programs. Congress rejected several civil rights bills, national health insurance, federal aid to education, and a new approach to subsidizing farmers. It also turned down Truman's requested repeal of the anti-union Taft-Hartley Act. Yet the Fair Deal was not a complete failure. It laid the foundation for programs that the next generation of reformers would promote.

THE COLD WAR HEATS UP

As during Harry Truman's first term, global concerns during his second term would again distract him from domestic issues. In his 1949 inaugural address, Truman called for a vigilant anti-Communist foreign policy resting on three pillars: the United Nations, the Marshall Plan, and NATO. None of them could help resolve the civil war in China, however.

"LOSING" CHINA One of the thorniest postwar problems, the Chinese civil war, was fast coming to a head. Chinese Nationalists, led by Chiang Kai-shek, had been fighting Mao Zedong and the Communists since the 1920s. After the Second World War, the Communists won over most of the peasants. By the end of 1949, the Nationalist government was forced to flee to the island of Formosa, which it renamed Taiwan. Truman's critics—mostly Republicans—asked bitterly, "Who lost China to communism?" What they did not explain was how Truman could have prevented a Communist victory without a massive U.S. military intervention, which would have been risky, unpopular, and expensive. After 1949, the United States continued to recognize the Nationalist government on Taiwan as the official government of China, delaying formal relations with "Red China" (the People's Republic of China) for thirty years.

THE SOVIETS DEVELOP ATOMIC BOMBS As the Communists were gaining control of China, news that the Soviets had detonated a nuclear weapon in 1949 frightened people around the world and led Truman to speed

Mao Zedong Chairman of the Chinese Communist Party and the founder of the People's Republic of China.

up the design of a hydrogen "super-bomb," a weapon far more powerful than the atomic bombs dropped on Japan. That the Soviets now possessed atomic weapons greatly intensified every cold war confrontation. "There is only one thing worse than one nation having an atomic bomb," said Nobel Prize–winning physicist Harold C. Urey. "That's two nations having it." The fear of nuclear annihilation joined the fear of communism in deepening the Red Scare.

NSC-68 In January 1950, President Truman grew so concerned about the Soviets possessing atomic weapons that he asked the National Security Council to assess America's changing role in the cold war world. Four months later, the Council submitted a top-secret report, **NSC-68**. The document called for an even more robust effort to "contain" the spread of communism. In alarmist tones, NSC-68 revealed the major assumptions that would guide U.S. foreign policy for the next twenty years: "The issues that face us are momentous, involving the fulfillment or destruction not only of this Republic but of civilization itself."

NSC-68 endorsed George Kennan's "containment" strategy. But where he had focused on political and economic counterpressure, the report's tone was global and militaristic, calling for "a policy of calculated and gradual coercion" against Soviet expansionism—everywhere.

Paul Nitze, Kennan's successor as director of policy planning for the State Department, was the report's primary author. He claimed that the Soviets, driven to impose their will "on the rest of the world," were becoming increasingly "reckless" and would invade Western Europe by 1954, by which time they would have enough nuclear weapons to destroy the United States.

By signing NSC-68, Truman explained that it would mean "doubling or tripling the budget, increasing taxes heavily, and imposing various kinds of economic controls. It meant a great change in our normal peacetime way of doing things." NSC-68 became the guidebook for future American policy,

Shelter for sale On display in a 1950s showroom is a basement fallout shelter, complete with a television, library, and exercise bike, intended to help a family survive a nuclear attack.

especially as the United States became involved in an unexpected war in Korea that ignited into open combat the smoldering animosity between communism and capitalism around the world.

WAR IN KOREA

By the mid-1950s, tensions between the United States and the Soviet Union in Europe had temporarily eased as a result of the "balance of terror" created by both sides having atomic weapons. In Asia, however, the situation remained turbulent. The Communists had gained control of mainland China and were threatening to destroy the Chinese Nationalists, who had taken refuge on Taiwan.

Japan, meanwhile, was experiencing a dramatic recovery from the devastation caused by U.S. bombing raids during the Second World War. Douglas MacArthur showed deft leadership as the consul in charge of U.S.-occupied Japan. He oversaw the disarming of the Japanese military, the drafting of a democratic constitution, and the nation's economic recovery, all of which were turning Japan into America's friend.

To the east, however, tensions between North and South Korea threatened to erupt into civil war. The Japanese had occupied the Korean Peninsula since 1910, but after they were defeated and withdrew in 1945, the victorious Allies had faced the difficult task of creating an independent Korean nation.

A DIVIDED KOREA Complicating that effort was the presence of Soviet troops in northern Korea. They had accepted the surrender of Japanese forces above the 38th parallel, which divides the Korean Peninsula, while U.S. forces had overseen the Japanese surrender south of the line. The Soviets quickly organized a Communist government, the Democratic People's Republic of Korea (North Korea). The Americans countered by helping to establish a democratic government in the more populous south, the Republic of Korea (South Korea). By the end of 1948, separate regimes had appeared in the two sectors, Soviet and American forces had withdrawn, and some 2 million North Koreans had fled to South Korea.

WAR ERUPTS On January 12, 1950, Secretary of State Dean Acheson gave a speech to the National Press Club in Washington, D.C., in which he said he was often asked, "Has the State Department got an Asian policy?" He stressed that the United States had assumed "the necessity of . . . the military defense of Japan." He then added that America had created a "defensive perimeter" running along the Aleutian Islands off the coast of Alaska to Japan to the Ryukyu Islands to the Philippines. Where "other areas in the Pacific are concerned," Acheson added, "it must be clear that no person can guarantee these areas against military attack."

Acheson's statement came back to haunt him. On June 24, 1950, the secretary of state telephoned President Truman: "Mr. President," he reported, "I have very serious news. The North Koreans have invaded South Korea." With the encouragement of the Soviet Union and Communist China, the Soviet-equipped North Korean People's Army had rapidly forced the South Korean forces into a headlong retreat. Within three days, Seoul, the South Korean capital, was captured, and only 22,000 of the 100,000 South Korean soldiers were still capable of combat. People then and since have argued that Acheson's clumsy reference to the "defensive perimeter" in Asia may have convinced the North Koreans and Soviets that the United States would not resist an invasion of South Korea.

When reporters asked Truman how he would respond to the invasion, the president declared: "By God, I'm going to let them have it!" He assumed, correctly, that the North Korean attack had been encouraged by the Soviets. "There's no telling what they'll do if we don't put up a fight right now," Truman predicted. He then made a critical decision: without consulting the Joint

Fight and flight American soldiers and Korean civilian refugees march into the Nakdong River region in the south.

Chiefs of Staff or the Congress, he decided to wage war through the backing of the United Nations rather than by seeking a declaration of war from Congress. He knew that a congressional debate over a war in Korea would take so long that it may then be too late to stop the Communists.

An emergency meeting of the UN Security Council in late June 1950 censured the North Korean "breach of peace." By sheer coincidence, the Soviet delegate, who held a veto power, was at the time boycotting the council because it would not seat Communist China in place of Nationalist China. On June 27, the Security Council called on UN members to "furnish such assistance to the Republic of Korea as may be necessary to repel the armed attack and to restore international peace and security in the area."

Truman then ordered U.S. air, naval, and ground forces into action and appointed seventy-year-old Douglas MacArthur supreme commander of the UN forces. The attack on South Korea, Truman said, made "it plain beyond all doubt that the international Communist movement is prepared to use armed invasion to conquer independent nations." Truman's decisive steps gained strong bipartisan approval, but neither the nation nor the administration were united on the objectives of the war or its conduct.

The Korean conflict was the first military action authorized by the United Nations, and some twenty other nations participated. The United States provided the largest contingent by far, some 330,000 troops. The American defense of South Korea set a worrisome precedent: war by order of a president—rather than by a vote of Congress, which the U.S. Constitution requires. Truman dodged the issue by officially calling the conflict a "police action" rather than a war. Critics labeled it "Mr. Truman's War."

TURNING THE TABLES The Korean War featured brutal combat in terrible conditions punctuated by heavy casualties and widespread destruction on both sides. For the first three months, the fighting in Korea went badly for the Republic of Korea (ROK) and the UN forces. By September 1950, the decimated South Korean troops were barely hanging on at Pusan, at the southern tip of the Korean Peninsula. Then, in a brilliant maneuver on September 15, General MacArthur staged a surprise amphibious landing behind the North Korean lines at Inchŏn, the port city for Seoul, some 150 miles north of Pusan. UN troops drove a wedge through the North Korean army, only a quarter of whom (some 25,000 soldiers) managed to flee across the border. Days later, South Korean troops recaptured Seoul.

At that point, the vainglorious MacArthur became overconfident and persuaded Truman to allow U.S. troops to push across the 38th parallel into North Korea. Containment of communism was no longer enough; MacArthur now sought to rid North Korea of the "red menace," even if this meant expanding the war into China to prevent the Chinese from resupplying their North Korean allies.

THE CHINESE INTERVENE By October 1950, UN forces were about to capture the North Korean capital, P'yŏngyang. President Truman, concerned that MacArthur's move would provoke Communist China to enter the war, repeatedly asked the U.S. commander to meet with him in Washington, D.C., only to be rebuffed. Finally, the president flew 7,000 miles to Wake Island to meet with MacArthur, who contemptuously refused to salute his commander in chief.

At the meeting on October 15, MacArthur dismissed Chinese threats to intervene, even though they had massed troops on the Korean border. That same day, the Communist government in Beijing announced that China "cannot stand idly by" as its North Korean allies were humiliated. On October 20, UN forces entered the North Korean capital, and on October 26, advance units reached Ch'osan on the Yalu River, North Korea's border with China.

MacArthur predicted total victory by Christmas. Instead, he blundered into a catastrophe. On the night of November 25, some 300,000 Chinese "volunteers"

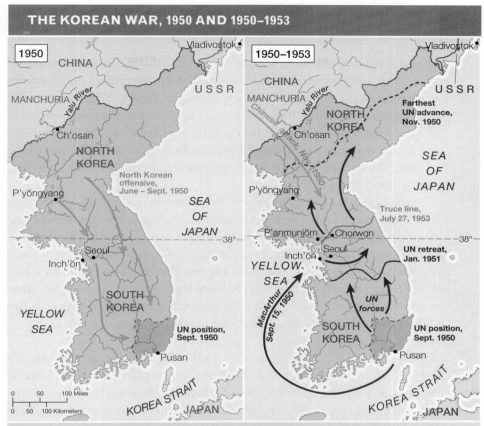

THE KOREAN WAR, 1950 AND 1950–1953

1950

CHINA
MANCHURIA
Yalu River
Ch'osan
NORTH KOREA
P'yŏngyang
North Korean offensive, June – Sept. 1950
Vladivostok
USSR
SEA OF JAPAN
38°
Seoul
Inch'ŏn
SOUTH KOREA
YELLOW SEA
UN position, Sept. 1950
Pusan
KOREA STRAIT   JAPAN

0   50   100 Miles
0   50   100 Kilometers

1950–1953

CHINA
MANCHURIA
Yalu River
Chinese attack, Nov. 1950
Ch'osan
NORTH KOREA
Farthest UN advance, Nov. 1950
P'yŏngyang
Vladivostok
USSR
SEA OF JAPAN
Truce line, July 27, 1953
P'anmunjŏm
Chorwon
38°
Inch'ŏn
Seoul
UN retreat, Jan. 1951
YELLOW SEA
MacArthur Sept. 15, 1950
UN forces
SOUTH KOREA
UN position, Sept. 1950
Pusan
KOREA STRAIT   JAPAN

- How did the surrender of the Japanese in Korea during 1945 set up the conflict between Soviet-influenced North Korea and U.S.-influenced South Korea?
- What was General MacArthur's strategy for winning the Korean conflict?
- Why did President Truman remove General MacArthur from command?

counterattacked, sending U.S. forces into a desperate retreat. "We ran like antelopes," said an American soldier. At the Chosin Reservoir, the First Marine Division was surrounded by seven Chinese divisions. Their desperate situation was worsened by minus-40-degree cold nights. When asked how the U.S. retreat was going, Marine general Oliver P. Smith replied: "Retreat, hell! We're not retreating, we're just advancing in a different direction." Smith eventually directed an ingenious breakout by the Marines that saved the division from total destruction.

Still, the UN forces were in retreat. By January 15, the Communist Chinese and North Koreans had recaptured Seoul. What had started as a defensive war against North Korean aggression had become an unlimited war against the North Koreans and China's People's Liberation Army.

MacARTHUR CROSSES THE LINE The Chinese intervention caught MacArthur wholly unprepared. He now asked for thirty-four atomic bombs and proposed air raids on China, explaining to President Truman and the Joint Chiefs of Staff that "If we lose the war to communism in Asia, the fall of Europe is inevitable." His plans horrified the military leadership in Washington, D.C. It would be, said General Omar Bradley, chairman of the Joint Chiefs of Staff, "the wrong war at the wrong place at the wrong time with the wrong enemy." Truman agreed.

In late 1950, the UN forces rallied. By January 1951, they had secured their lines below Seoul and launched a counterattack. When Truman began negotiations with North Korea to restore the prewar boundary, MacArthur undermined the president by issuing an ultimatum for China to make peace or suffer an attack. On April 5, on the floor of Congress, the Republican minority leader read a letter from MacArthur that criticized the president and said that "there is no substitute for victory." Such open insubordination left Truman only two choices: he could accept MacArthur's aggressive demands, or fire him.

SACKING A HERO On April 11, 1951, with civilian control of the military at stake, Truman removed MacArthur and replaced him with General Matthew B. Ridgway, a commander who better understood how to conduct a modern war in pursuit of limited objectives. "I believe that we must try to limit the war to Korea," Truman explained. "A number of events have made it evident that General MacArthur did not agree with that policy. I have therefore considered it essential to relieve General MacArthur so that there would be no doubt or confusion as to the real purpose and aim of our policy."

Truman's sacking of MacArthur, the army's only five-star general, divided the nation. Dean Acheson, the secretary of state, had warned the president that "if you relieve MacArthur, you will have the biggest fight of your administration." *Time* magazine reported that "seldom had a more unpopular man fired a more popular one." Senator Joseph McCarthy called the president a "son of a bitch" for sacking MacArthur. In his diary, Truman noted the ferocious backlash against him: "Quite an explosion. . . . Letters of abuse by the dozens." Sixty-six percent of Americans initially opposed Truman's decision.

Douglas MacArthur was a larger-than-life military hero and was greeted by adoring crowds upon his return to the United States. Republicans in Congress protested his removal, but Truman stood firm: "I fired him because he wouldn't respect the authority of the President. I didn't fire him because he was a dumb son of a bitch, although he was, but that's not against the law for generals. If it was, half to three-quarters of them would be in jail." That all of the top military leaders supported Truman's decision deflated much of the criticism. "Why, hell, if MacArthur had had his way," the president warned, "he'd have had us in the Third World War and blown up two-thirds of the world."

A CEASE-FIRE On June 24, 1951, the Soviet representative at the United Nations proposed a cease-fire in Korea along the 38th parallel, the original dividing line between North and South. Secretary of State Acheson accepted the cease-fire (armistice) with the consent of the United Nations. China and North Korea responded favorably.

Firing of MacArthur In this 1951 cartoon by L. J. Roche, President Harry Truman, Secretary of State Dean Acheson, and the Pentagon dance in the American public's proverbial frying pan for the removal of General Douglas MacArthur from his post as the supreme commander of U.N. forces in Korea.

Truce talks started on July 10, 1951, at Panmunjŏm, only to drag on for two years while sporadic fighting continued. The chief snags were exchanges of prisoners (many captured North Korean and Chinese soldiers did not want to go home) and South Korea's insistence on unification of the two rival Koreas. Syngman Rhee, the South Korean leader, explained that "an armistice without national unification [is] a death sentence without protest."

By the time a truce was reached, on July 27, 1953, Truman had retired and Dwight D. Eisenhower was president. No peace treaty was ever signed, and Korea, like Germany, remained divided. The inconclusive war, incredibly mindless in the way it began, often reckless in the way it was managed, and largely fruitless in the way it ended, cost the United States more than 33,000 battle deaths and 103,000 wounded or missing. South Korean casualties were about 2 million, and North Korean and Chinese casualties were an estimated 3 million.

THE IMPACT OF THE KOREAN WAR To most Americans, the North Korean attack on South Korea provided concrete proof that there was an international Communist conspiracy guided by the Soviet Union to control the world.

Truman's assumption that Stalin and the Soviets were behind the invasion of South Korea led him to deepen the American commitment to stop communism. "The interests of the United States are global in character," he explained. "A threat to the peace of the world *anywhere* is a threat to our security." Fearful that the Soviets would use the Korean conflict as a diversion to invade Western Europe, he ordered a major expansion of U.S. military forces in Europe—and around the world. Truman also increased assistance to French troops fighting a Communist independence movement in the French colony of Indochina (which included Vietnam), starting America's deepening military involvement in Southeast Asia.

ANOTHER RED SCARE

The Korean War excited another Red Scare at home, as people grew fearful that Communists were infiltrating American society. Since 1938, the **House Committee on Un-American Activities (HUAC)** had kept up a drumbeat of accusations about supposed Communist agents in the federal government.

On March 21, 1947, President Truman signed an executive order (also known as the Loyalty Order) requiring federal government workers to undergo a background investigation to ensure they were not Communists or even associated with Communists (or other "subversive" groups).

Truman knew that the "loyalty program" violated civil liberties, but he felt he had no choice. He was responding to pressure from FBI director J. Edgar Hoover and Attorney General Tom Clark, both of whom were convinced that there were numerous spies working inside the federal government. Truman was also eager to blunt criticism that he was not doing enough to ensure that Soviet sympathizers were not working in government.

Truman thought that the fear about Communist subversives was misplaced. "People are very much wrought up about the communist 'bugaboo,'" he wrote to Pennsylvania governor George Earle, "but I am of the opinion that the country is perfectly safe so far as Communism is concerned." By early 1951, the federal Civil Service Commission had cleared more than 3 million people, while only 378 had been dismissed for doubtful loyalty. Others, however, had resigned for fear they would be dismissed. In 1953, President Dwight D. Eisenhower revoked the Loyalty Order.

THE HOLLYWOOD TEN Charges that Hollywood was a "hotbed of communism" led the House Committee on Un-American Activities to launch a full-blown investigation of the motion-picture industry. The HUAC subpoenaed dozens of actors, producers, and directors to testify at its hearings, held in Los Angeles in October 1947. Ten witnesses refused to testify, arguing that

The Red Scare and Hollywood Several courageous movie stars attended the HUAC hearings to support their friends and colleagues who were accused of being Communists. Left to right: Danny Kaye, June Havoc, Humphrey Bogart, and Lauren Bacall (seated).

the questioning violated their First Amendment rights. When asked if he were a member of the Communist party, screenwriter Ring Lardner Jr. replied: "I could answer, but I would hate myself in the morning." Another member of the so-called Hollywood Ten, screenwriter Dalton Trumbo, shouted as he left the hearings, "This is the beginning of an American concentration camp." All ten were cited for contempt, given prison terms, and blacklisted (banned) from the film industry.

The witch hunt launched by the HUAC inspired playwright Arthur Miller, who himself was blacklisted, to write *The Crucible*, an award-winning play produced in 1953. It is a dramatic account of the notorious witch trials in Salem, Massachusetts, at the end of the seventeenth century, intended to alert audiences about the dangers of the anti-Communist hysteria.

ALGER HISS The spy case most damaging to the Truman administration involved Alger Hiss, president of the Carnegie Endowment for International Peace, who had served in several government agencies. Whittaker Chambers, a former Soviet spy and later an editor of *Time* magazine who reversed himself and became an informer testifying against supposed Communists in the government, told the HUAC in 1948 that Hiss had given him secret documents ten years earlier, when Chambers was spying for the Soviets and Hiss was working in the State Department. Hiss sued for libel, and Chambers produced microfilms of the State Department documents that he said Hiss had passed to him. Although Hiss denied the accusation, he was indicted and, after one mistrial, convicted in 1950. The charge was perjury, but he was convicted of lying about espionage, for which he could not be tried because the statute of limitations on the crime had expired.

More cases of Communist infiltration surfaced. In 1949, eleven top leaders of the Communist party of the United States were convicted under the Smith Act of 1940, which outlawed any conspiracy to advocate the overthrow of the government. The Supreme Court upheld the law under the doctrine of a "clear and present danger," which overrode the right to free speech.

ATOMIC SPYING In 1950, the FBI unearthed a spy network involving both American and British Communists who had secretly passed information about the development of the atomic bomb to the Soviet Union. The disclosure led to the arrest of Klaus Fuchs, a German-born English nuclear physicist who had worked in the United States during the war and helped to develop the atomic bomb.

As it turned out, a New York couple, former Communists Julius and Ethel Rosenberg, were part of the same Soviet spy ring. Their claims of innocence were undercut by the confession of Ethel's brother, who admitted he was a spy along with his sister and brother-in-law.

The convictions of Fuchs and the Rosenbergs fueled Republican charges that Truman's administration was not doing enough to hunt down Communist agents. The Rosenberg case, called the crime of the century by J. Edgar Hoover, also heightened fears that a vast Soviet network of spies and sympathizers was operating in the United States—and had "given" Stalin the secret of building atomic weapons. Irving Kaufman, the federal judge who sentenced the Rosenbergs to death, explained that "plain, deliberate murder is dwarfed . . . by comparison with the crime you have committed." They were the first Americans executed for spying.

McCARTHY'S WITCH HUNT Evidence of Soviet spying encouraged some to exploit fears of the Communist menace. Early in 1950, a little-known Republican senator, Joseph R. McCarthy of Wisconsin, surfaced as the most ruthless manipulator of anti-Communist anxieties.

McCarthy, eager to attract media attention through his "bare-knuckle" tactics, took up the cause of anti-communism with a fiery speech to a women's Republican club in Wheeling, West Virginia, on February 9, 1950, in which he charged that the State Department was infested with Communists. He claimed to have their names, although he never provided them.

McCarthy's stunt got him what he wanted most: publicity. As the *New York Times* said, "It is difficult, if not impossible, to ignore charges made by Senator McCarthy just because they are usually proved exaggerated or false." During the next four years, McCarthy made more wild accusations, initially against many Democrats, whom he smeared as "dupes" or "fellow travelers" of the "Commies," then against officers in the U.S. Army.

Truman privately denounced McCarthy as "just a ballyhoo artist who has to cover up his shortcomings with wild charges," but McCarthy was not so easily dismissed. He enjoyed the backing of fellow Republicans eager to hurt Democrats in the 1950 congressional elections by claiming they were not being tough enough in fighting communism. Senator Lyndon B. Johnson of Texas said McCarthy was "the sorriest senator" in Washington. "But he's riding high now, he's got people scared to death. . . ."

By the summer of 1951, however, **McCarthyism** had gotten out of control. McCarthy's feverish excesses were revealed for all to see when he outrageously accused George Marshall, the former secretary of state and war hero, of making "common cause with Stalin" by "being an instrument of the Communist conspiracy." Concerns about truth or fair play did not faze McCarthy; his focus was on creating a reign of terror through groundless accusations. Truman called him a "pathological character assassin."

However sincere McCarthy's desire was to purify America of Communist sympathizers, his unholy war never uncovered a single Communist agent. But his relentless smear campaign, which tarnished many lives and reputations and had a chilling effect on free speech, went largely unchallenged until the end of the Korean War. During the Red Scare, thousands of left-wing Americans were "blacklisted" from employment because of past political associations, real or rumored. Movies with titles like "I Married a Communist" fed the hysteria, and magazine stories warned of "a Red under every bed."

Joseph R. McCarthy The crusading senator who was determined to identify any Communists serving in the federal government.

THE McCARRAN ACT Fears of Soviet spies working with American sympathizers led Congress in 1950 to pass the McCarran Internal Security Act over President Truman's veto, making it unlawful "to combine, conspire, or agree with any other person to perform any act which would substantially contribute to . . . the establishment of a totalitarian dictatorship." Communist organizations had to register with the attorney general. Would-be immigrants who had belonged to totalitarian parties in their home countries were barred from entering the United States. And during any future national emergencies, American Communists were to be herded into concentration camps. The McCarran Internal Security Act, Truman said in his veto message, would "put the government into the business of thought control."

THE RED SCARE AND THE COLD WAR Playing upon the fears of the American public did not make for good policy in 1919, nor did it work well in the early fifties. Both Red Scares ended up violating the civil liberties of innocent people.

President Truman may have erred in 1947 by creating a government loyalty program that aggravated the anti-Communist hysteria. Truman's own attorney general, Tom Clark, contended that there were "so many Communists in America" that they "were everywhere—in factories, offices, butcher shops, on street corners, in private businesses—and each carries with him the germs of death for society."

Truman also overstretched American resources when he pledged to "contain" communism everywhere. Containment itself proved hard to contain amid the ideological posturing of Soviet and American leaders. Its chief theorist, George F. Kennan, later confessed that he was partly to blame because he had failed at the outset to clarify the limits of the containment policy and to stress that the United States needed to prioritize its responses to Soviet adventurism.

A COLD WAR GOVERNMENT The years after the Second World War were unlike any other postwar period in American history. Having taken on global burdens, the United States became committed to a permanently large national military establishment, along with shadowy new government agencies such as the National Security Council (NSC), the National Security Agency (NSA), and the Central Intelligence Agency (CIA).

The federal government—and the presidency—grew larger, more powerful, and more secretive, fueled by the actions of both major political parties as well as by the intense lobbying efforts of what Dwight D. Eisenhower would later call the *military-industrial complex*.

Fears of communism and concerns about a Soviet spy network in the United States mushroomed into politically motivated paranoia. Long-standing prejudices against Jews fed the hysteria; indeed, many Communist sympathizers were Jews from Eastern Europe.

The Red Scare also provided a powerful tool for Republicans to claim that Democrats were "soft on Communism." One of the worst effects of the Red Scare was to encourage widespread conformity of thought and behavior. By 1950, it had become dangerous to criticize anything associated with the American way of life.

ASSESSING HARRY TRUMAN On March 30, 1952, Harry Truman announced that he would not seek another presidential term, in part because it was unlikely he could win. Less than 25 percent of voters surveyed said that he was doing a good job, the lowest presidential approval rating in history. Although Americans applauded Truman's integrity and courage, the unrelenting war against communism, at home and abroad, led people to question his strategy. Negotiations to end the war in Korea had bogged down, the "red-baiting" of McCarthyism was expanding, and conservative southern Democrats, members of Truman's own party, had defeated most of his Fair Deal proposals. The war had also brought higher taxes and higher prices for American consumers, many of whom blamed the president. Only years later would people (and historians) fully appreciate how effectively Truman had dealt with so many complex problems.

To the end of his presidency, Truman, a plainspoken man who made decisions based on his "gut-feeling" about what was "right," viewed himself as an ordinary person who had been given opportunities to do extraordinary things. "I have tried my best to give the nation everything I have in me," Truman told reporters at one of his last press conferences. "There are a great many people . . . who could have done the job better than I did it. But I had the job and had to do it." And it was not a simple job, by any means. At the end of one difficult day in the White House, Truman growled while sipping a bourbon and water: "They [his critics] talk about the power of the President, how I can just push a button to get things done. Why, I spend most of my time kissing somebody's ass."

By the time Truman left the White House in early 1953, the cold war had become an accepted part of the American way of life. But fears about the spread of communism were counterbalanced by the joys of unexpected prosperity. Toward the end of Truman's presidency, the economy began to grow at what would become the fastest rate in history, transforming social and cultural life and becoming the marvel of the world. The booming economy brought with it the "nifty" fifties.

CHAPTER REVIEW

SUMMARY

- **The Cold War** The cold war was an ideological contest between the Western democracies (especially the United States) and the Communist countries. At the end of the Second World War, the Soviet Union established "friendly" governments in the Eastern European countries it occupied behind an *iron curtain* of totalitarian control and secrecy.

- **Containment** President Truman responded to the Soviet occupation of Eastern Europe with the policy of *containment*, the aim of which was to halt the spread of communism by opposing it wherever it emerged. With the *Truman Doctrine* (*1947*), he proposed giving economic and military aid to countries facing Communist insurgencies, such as Greece and Turkey; he also convinced Congress to approve the *National Security Act*, which reorganized the U.S. armed forces and created the Central Intelligence Agency. With the *Marshall Plan*, Truman offered redevelopment aid to all European nations. In 1948, the *Berlin airlift* overcame a Soviet blockade of supplies to West Berlin. In 1949, the United States became a founding member of the *North Atlantic Treaty Organization* (*NATO*), a military alliance of Western democracies united primarily against the Soviet Union.

- **Truman's Fair Deal** Truman's *Fair Deal* was proposed to expand the New Deal despite intense Republican opposition in Congress. Truman could not stop the *Taft-Hartley Act*, a Republican-backed measure to curb the power of labor unions. Truman was more successful in expanding Social Security and, through executive orders, desegregating the military and banning racial discrimination in the hiring of federal employees. After winning a second term in 1948, he proposed a civil rights bill, national health insurance, federal aid to education, and new farm subsidies. Despite the Democrats' majority in Congress, however, conservative Republicans and southern Democrats (*Dixiecrats*) joined forces to defeat these initiatives.

- **The Korean War** Containment policies proved less effective in East Asia, as Communists won a long civil war in China in 1949 and ignited a war in Korea. In response, Truman authorized *NSC-68*, a comprehensive blueprint for American foreign and defense policies that called for a dramatic increase in military spending and nuclear arms. When North Korean troops invaded South Korea in June 1950, Truman quickly decided to go to war under the auspices of the United Nations. After a year of major gains and reverses by both sides and then two years of stalemate, a truce, concluded in July 1953, established a demilitarized zone in Korea.

- **The Red Scare** The onset of the cold war inflamed another Red Scare. Investigations by the *House Committee on Un-American Activities* (*HUAC*) sought to find "subversives" within the federal government. Starting in 1950, Senator Joseph R. McCarthy exploited fears of Soviet spies infiltrating the highest levels of the U.S. government.

McCarthyism flourished in the short term because the threat of a world dominated by Communist governments seemed all too real to many Americans.

CHRONOLOGY

November 1946	Republicans win control of both houses of Congress
February 1946	George Kennan urges a containment policy toward the Soviet Union
March 1947	The Truman Doctrine promises financial and military assistance to countries resisting Communist takeover
May 1947	The Marshall plan provides massive financial assistance to European nations
June 1947	Congress passes the Taft-Hartley Labor Act over Truman's veto
July 1947	National Security Council (NSC) is established
May 1948	Israel is proclaimed an independent nation
July 1948	Truman's executive order ends segregation in the U.S. armed forces
October 1948	United States and Great Britain airlift supplies to West Berlin
November 1948	Truman defeats Dewey in the presidential election
April 1949	North Atlantic Treaty Organization (NATO) is created
October 1949	China "falls" to communism
February 1950	Senator Joseph McCarthy begins his crusade against suspected Communists in the federal government
June 1950	United States and other UN members go to war in Korea

KEY TERMS

iron curtain p. 1218

containment p. 1220

Truman Doctrine (1947) p. 1221

Marshall Plan (1948) p. 1222

Berlin airlift (1948) p. 1225

North Atlantic Treaty Organization (NATO) p. 1226

National Security Act p. 1227

Taft-Hartley Labor Act (1947) p. 1231

Fair Deal (1949) p. 1237

Dixiecrats p. 1238

NSC-68 (1950) p. 1242

House Committee on Un-American Activities (HUAC) p. 1250

McCarthyism p. 1253

 INQUIZITIVE

Go to InQuizitive to see what you've learned—and learn what you've missed—with personalized feedback along the way.

28 Cold War America
1950–1959

The Art of Consumerism The United States experienced tremendous prosperity after the Second World War, giving many Americans the unprecedented opportunity to engage in carefree consumption during the 1950s—and personal indebtedness. The Pop Art movement reflected the era's materialism. Its artists made use of mass-produced and advertised products to celebrate American consumer culture. One such artist was Tom Wesselmann, whose 1962 collage *Untitled (Still-Life No. 20)* is shown above.

In the summer of 1959, two young newlyweds spent their honeymoon in an underground bomb shelter in the backyard of their home. *Life* magazine showed them in their twenty-ton, steel and concrete bunker stocked with enough food and water to survive an atomic attack. The image of newlyweds seeking sheltered security in a new age of nuclear terror symbolized how America in the 1950s was awash in contrasting emotions.

The deepening cold war with the Soviet Union cast a frightening shadow over the nation's traditionally sunny optimism. In 1959, two out of three Americans listed the possibility of atomic war as the nation's most urgent threat. Still, Americans emerged from the Second World War proud of their military strength, international stature, and industrial might. It was a time rich with possibilities. As the editors of *Fortune* magazine proclaimed in 1946, "This is a dream era. . . . The Great American Boom is on."

So it was, at least for white, middle-class Americans. During the late 1940s and throughout the 1950s, the United States enjoyed unprecedented economic growth, and most Americans were content. Divorce and homicide rates fell, and people lived longer, on average, thanks in part to medical breakthroughs, including new antibiotics and the vaccine invented by Dr. Jonas Salk that ended the menace of polio. The "happy days" image of America in the fifties as an innocent, prosperous nation awash in good times and enlivened by teenage energies has a kernel of truth. But life was actually much more complicated, even contradictory and hypocritical at times, as many Americans worried about what seemed an uncontrollable future.

focus questions

1. What were President Eisenhower's political philosophy and priorities?

2. What factors contributed to postwar prosperity? To what extent did all Americans benefit from it?

3. What were the criticisms of postwar American society and culture? What were the various forms of dissent and anxiety?

4. What were the goals and strategies of the civil rights movement that emerged in the 1950s? What was its impact?

5. What were President Eisenhower's priorities in conducting the nation's foreign policy? What was his influence on global affairs?

MODERATE REPUBLICANISM

Dwight David Eisenhower dominated the political landscape during the 1950s. The military hero of the Second World War was a model of moderation, stability, and optimism. He was a soldier who hated war, a politician who hated politics. Committed to what he called **moderate Republicanism**, Eisenhower promised to restore the authority of state and local governments and restrain the federal government from engaging in political and social "engineering." In the process, he sought to renew traditional virtues and inspire Americans with a vision of a brighter future.

"TIME FOR A CHANGE" By 1952, the Truman administration was the target of growing public criticism. The conflict in Korea had stalled, the economy was sputtering, and Truman was put on the defensive by the disclosure that corrupt lobbyists had rigged military contracts. The scandal led Truman to fire nearly 250 employees of the Internal Revenue Service, but doubts lingered that he would ever finish the housecleaning. Critics charged that the slogan for his administration was "plunder at home, blunder abroad."

Dwight D. Eisenhower His many supporters wore "I Like Ike" hats, pins, and even nylon stockings, speaking to the powerful consumer culture's impact on politics.

It was, Republicans claimed, "time for a change," and public sentiment turned their way as the 1952 election approached. Beginning in the late 1940s, both Republican and Democratic leaders, including Truman, recruited Eisenhower to be their presidential candidate. The affable Eisenhower, known as "Ike," had displayed remarkable organizational and diplomatic skill in coordinating the Allied invasion of Nazi-controlled Europe. In 1952, after serving as president of Columbia University, he had moved to Paris to become supreme commander of NATO forces in Europe. His decision to run for president as a Republican was wildly popular with voters. Bumper stickers announced simply: "I Like Ike."

Eisenhower was nominated on the first ballot. Republican leaders then tried to reassure party conservatives by balancing the ticket with a youthful, fiercely ambitious running mate: Richard M. Nixon, a thirty-nine-year-old California senator distinctive for his shrewd opportunism and combative temperament. Nixon was an aggressive anti-Communist focused on exposing left-wing "subversives" in the Truman administration. His dogged pursuit of the Alger Hiss spying case had brought him national prominence. The Republican platform declared that the Democratic emphasis on "containing" communism was "negative, futile, and misguided." If elected, Eisenhower would roll back the Communist threat by bringing "genuine independence" to the "captive peoples" of Eastern Europe.

THE ELECTION OF 1952 The presidential campaign featured contrasting personalities. Eisenhower was an international figure and a man of readily acknowledged decency and integrity. His beaming smile and humble greatness won over the masses. Illinois governor Adlai Stevenson, the Democratic candidate, was hardly known outside his home state. Eisenhower pledged to clean up "the mess in Washington." Then, late in the campaign, he promised to travel to Korea to secure "an early and honorable" end to the prolonged conflict.

Stevenson was outmatched. Although brilliant and witty, he came across to most voters as more an "intellectual" than a "leader." Republicans labeled him an "egghead" (meant to suggest a balding professor with more intellect than common sense). Even Truman grumbled that Stevenson "was too busy making up his mind whether he had to go to the bathroom or not."

On election night, Eisenhower triumphed in a landslide, gathering nearly 34 million votes to Stevenson's 27 million. The electoral vote was much more lopsided: 442 to 89. Stevenson even failed to win his home state of Illinois. More important, by securing four southern states, Eisenhower had cracked the solidly Democratic South.

Yet voters liked Eisenhower more than they liked other Republican candidates. In the 1952 election, Democrats kept control of most governorships, lost control in the House by only eight seats, and broke even in the Senate. Throughout his second presidential term, Eisenhower would have to work with a Democratic Congress.

A "MIDDLE WAY" PRESIDENCY Eisenhower was the first professional soldier elected president since Ulysses S. Grant in 1868. He promised to pursue a "middle way between untrammeled freedom of the individual and the demands of the welfare of the whole nation." He saw no need to dismantle all New Deal and Fair Deal programs. Instead, he wanted to end the "excesses"

THE ELECTION OF 1952

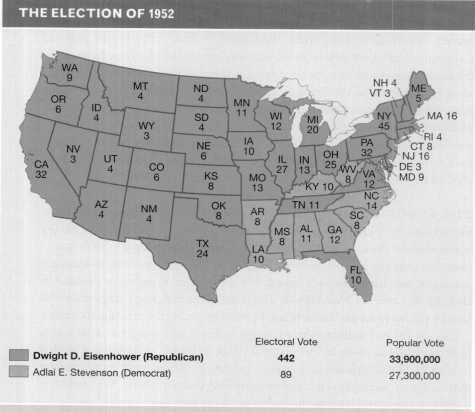

	Electoral Vote	Popular Vote
Dwight D. Eisenhower (Republican)	**442**	**33,900,000**
Adlai E. Stevenson (Democrat)	89	27,300,000

- Why was the contest between Adlai Stevenson and Dwight D. Eisenhower so lopsided?
- Why was Eisenhower's victory in several southern states remarkable?

that had resulted from twenty years of Democratic control of the White House. He pledged to shrink the federal bureaucracy and make it more efficient while restoring the balance between the executive and legislative branches.

Eisenhower also promised to reduce the national debt, cut military expenses, balance the federal budget, and trim taxes. At the same time, however, he insisted that workers had a right to form unions and bargain with management. He added that employees needed to be paid enough to afford the comforts of a good life. "We all—workers and farmers, foremen and financiers, technicians and builders—all must produce, produce more, and produce yet more," he said, to make the American Dream a reality and to ensure global stability. Peace would be maintained "not by weapons of war but by wheat and cotton, by milk and wool, by meat and by timber and by rice." He hated the growing arms race because "every gun that is made, every warship launched, every rocket fired signifies, in the final sense, a theft from those who hunger and are not fed, those who are cold and are not clothed."

Eisenhower's cautious personality and genial public face fit the prevailing mood of most voters. He was a unifier, not a divider; he inspired trust, sought consensus, and avoided confrontation. He also championed the nineteenth-century view that Congress should make policy and the president should carry it out.

"DYNAMIC CONSERVATISM" AT HOME   Eisenhower labeled his domestic program "dynamic conservatism," by which he meant being "conservative when it comes to money and liberal when it comes to human beings." He kept intact the basic structure of the New Deal, even convincing Congress to establish a new federal Department of Health, Education and Welfare and working with Democrats in Congress to extend Social Security benefits to millions of workers formerly excluded: white-collar professionals, maids and sales clerks, farmworkers, and members of the armed forces. Eisenhower also approved increases in the minimum wage and additional public-housing projects for low-income occupants. Conservative Republicans charged that he was being too liberal. He told his brother Edgar in 1954 that if the "stupid" right wing of the Republican party tried "to abolish Social Security and eliminate labor laws and farm programs, you would not hear of that party again in our political history."

TRANSPORTATION IMPROVEMENTS   Under Eisenhower, the federal government launched two huge construction projects: the St. Lawrence Seaway and the Interstate Highway System, both of which resembled the huge public works projects constructed under the New Deal during the 1930s. The St. Lawrence Seaway project (in partnership with Canada) opened the Great Lakes to oceangoing ships.

The **Federal-Aid Highway Act** (1956) created a national network of interstate highways to serve the needs of commerce and defense, as well as the public. The interstate highway system, funded largely by federal gasoline taxes, took twenty-five years to construct and was the largest federal project in history. It stretched for 47,000 miles and required 55,512 bridges.

Highway construction generated what economists call "multiplier effects": it created jobs; stimulated economic growth; and spurred the tourism, motor hotel ("motel"), billboard, fast-food, and long-haul trucking industries. Interstates transformed the way people traveled and where they lived, and it

Drive in, cash in Founded by brothers Maurice and Richard McDonald in southern California, this hugely successful fast food chain started as a carhop drive-in and did not have customer seating until the 1960s.

even created a new form of middle-class leisure—the family vacation by car. In 1956, writer Bernard De Voto exclaimed that "a new highway is not only a measure of progress, but a true index of our culture."

THE CAR CULTURE "The American," the Mississippi writer William Faulkner observed in 1948, "really loves nothing but his automobile." Americans had always cherished personal freedom and mobility, rugged individualism and masculine force. Automobiles embodied these qualities and more. Thanks to the highway system, said President Eisenhower, cars would provide "greater convenience, greater happiness, and greater standards of living." By 1958, 57 million Americans out of the national population of 175 million owned an automobile.

Cars became much more than a form of transportation; they provided social status and personal freedom. They granted more people a wider range of choices—where to travel, where to work and live, where to seek pleasure and recreation. The "car culture" soon transformed social behavior, prompting the creation of "convenience stores," drive-in movies, and fast-food restaurants.

THE END OF MCCARTHYISM Republicans thought their presidential victory in 1952 would curb the often unscrupulous efforts of Wisconsin senator Joseph R. McCarthy to ferret out Communist spies in the federal government. Instead, the publicity-seeking senator's behavior grew even more outlandish, in part because reporters were dazzled by his theatrics. President Eisenhower despised McCarthy but refused to criticize him in public, explaining that he did not want to "get into a pissing contest with that skunk." In March 1954, the president indirectly chastised McCarthy when he told a press conference that "we are defeating ourselves if we use methods [in opposing communism] that do not conform to the American sense of justice."

McCarthy finally committed political suicide when he made the absurd charge that the U.S. Army itself was "soft" on communism. For thirty-six days in the spring of 1954, the Army-McCarthy hearings provided 80 million television viewers with a fantastic spectacle. McCarthy was at his worst, hounding witnesses, seeking publicity, and producing little evidence to back up his charges. He was finally outwitted by the deliberate, reasoned counterattacks of the army's legal counsel, Joseph Welch. When McCarthy tried to smear one of Welch's associates, the attorney was outraged: "Until this moment, Senator, I think I never really gauged your cruelty or your recklessness. . . . Have you no sense of decency, sir, at long last?" When the audience burst into applause, the confused senator was reduced to whispering, "What did I do?"

On December 2, 1954, the Senate voted 67 to 22 to "condemn" McCarthy. Soon thereafter, his political influence collapsed. His crusade against Communists in government had catapulted him into the limelight and captured the nation's attention, but in the process he had trampled upon civil liberties. Now, with unexpected suddenness, his crusade was over. His rapid demise helped the Democrats capture control of both houses of Congress in the 1954 elections. In 1957, at the age of forty-eight, he died of liver inflammation brought on by years of alcohol abuse. His successor, William Proxmire, declared that McCarthy was "a disgrace to Wisconsin, to the Senate, and to America."

A PEOPLE OF PLENTY

What most distinguished the United States from the rest of the world after the Second World War was what one journalist called America's "screwball materialism." After a brief postwar recession in 1945–1946, the economy soared to record heights as businesses shifted from wartime production to the construction of new housing and the manufacture of mass-produced consumer goods. In 1953, Eisenhower's first year in office, the United States, with 6 percent of the world's population, was producing two-thirds of the world's manufactured goods. In 1957, *U.S. News and World Report* magazine declared that "never had so many people, anywhere, been so well off."

POSTWAR PROSPERITY

Several factors created the nation's prosperity. First, huge federal expenditures during the Second World War and Korean War propelled the economy out of the Great Depression. High government spending continued in the 1950s, thanks to the relentless construction of highways, bridges, airports, and ports, and the global arms race. The military budget after 1945 represented the single most important stimulant to the economy.

The superior productivity of American industries also contributed to economic growth. No sooner was the war over than the federal government turned over to civilian owners many war-related plants, giving them a boost as they retooled for peacetime manufacturing. Military-related research helped stimulate new glamour industries: chemicals (including plastics), electronics, and aviation. By 1957, the aircraft industry was the nation's largest employer.

Postwar consumerism Booming chain stores, such as the Super Giant Supermarket shown above, began to dot the suburbs of 1950s America, offering an outlet for the pent-up consumerism of the postwar years.

The economy also benefited from the emergence of new technologies, including the first generation of computers. Factories and industries became increasingly "automated." At the same time, the oil boom in Texas, Wyoming, and Oklahoma continued to provide low-cost fuel to heat buildings and to power cars and trucks.

Another reason for the record-breaking economic growth was the lack of foreign competition. Most of the other major industrial nations—Great Britain, France, Germany, Japan, and the Soviet Union—had been physically devastated during the Second World War, leaving American manufacturers with a virtual monopoly on international trade that lasted well into the 1950s.

THE CONSUMER CULTURE

The major catalyst for economic expansion after 1945, however, was the unleashing of pent-up consumer demand from the Depression and the war years. What differentiated the postwar era from earlier periods of prosperity was the large number of people who shared in the rising standard of living. Between

1947 and 1960, the average income for the working class increased by as much as it had in the previous *fifty* years.

More and more blue-collar Americans, especially automotive and steel workers, moved into the middle class. George Meany, the leading union spokesman during the 1950s, declared in 1955 that his members "never had it so good." Americans had money to spend during the fifties, and they did so with gusto, becoming famous around the world for their carefree consumption. In 1955, a marketing consultant stressed that the nation had come to view "*consumption* a way of life." The new economy required "that we convert the buying and use of goods into [religious] rituals, that we seek our spiritual satisfaction, our ego satisfaction, in consumption."

A BUYING SPREE Innovations in financing made it easier to buy things. The first credit card appeared in 1949; soon, "buying with plastic" had become the new norm for millions of people. Personal indebtedness doubled, in part because people were so confident about their economic future. Frugality became unpatriotic. As television personality Hugh Downs remembered, "those were exciting days . . . of hope and optimism . . . when the sky was the limit."

What most Americans wanted to buy after the Second World War was a new house. In 1945, only 40 percent of Americans owned homes; by 1960, the

Family, modified The dynamics of American family life changed with the onslaught of new, affordable products. In this 1959 advertisement for TV dinners, the family eats out of disposable containers in front of the television.

number had increased to 60 percent. New homes featured the latest electrical appliances—refrigerators, dishwashers, washing machines, vacuum cleaners, electric mixers, carving knives, even shoe polishers.

The use of electricity tripled, in part because of the popularity of television, which quickly displaced listening to the radio or going to the movies as the most popular way to spend free time. Between 1948 and 1952, the number of homes with TV sets jumped from 172,000 to 15.3 million. In 1954, grocery stores began selling frozen "TV dinners" to be heated and consumed while watching popular shows such as *Father Knows Best*, *I Love Lucy*, and *The Adventures of Ozzie and Harriet*, all of which idealized the child-centered world of suburban white families. In 1955, *U.S. News and World Report* magazine noted that the "biggest of the new forces in American life today is television."

The popularity of television provided a powerful new medium for advertisers to promote a powerful new phase of the consumer culture that reshaped the contours of postwar life: the nature of work, where people lived and traveled, how they interacted, and what they valued. It also affected class structure, race relations, and gender roles. Jack Metzgar, the son of a Pennsylvania steelworker, remembered that in 1946 "we did not have a car, a television set, or a refrigerator. By 1952, we had all those things."

THE GI BILL OF RIGHTS   In 1944, as Americans grew confident of victory in the Second World War, fear that a sudden influx of veterans into the civilian workforce would produce widespread unemployment led Congress to pass the Servicemen's Readjustment Act, also called the Veterans Act and nicknamed the **GI Bill of Rights**. ("GI" meant "government issue," a phrase stamped on military uniforms and equipment that became slang for "serviceman.")

The GI Bill boosted upward social mobility in postwar America. Its package of benefits for veterans included unemployment pay for one year, preference to those applying for federal government jobs, loans for home construction or starting a business, access to government hospitals, and generous subsidies for education. Some 5 million veterans bought homes with the assistance of GI Bill mortgage loans, which required no down payment. Almost 8 million took advantage of $14.5 billion in GI Bill benefits to attend college or enroll in job-training programs.

Before the Second World War, about 160,000 Americans had graduated from college each year. By 1950, the figure had risen to 500,000. In 1949, veterans accounted for 40 percent of college enrollments, and the United States could boast the world's best-educated workforce, largely because of the GI Bill. One example: Joe Shi, an army veteran from Macon, Georgia, was able to attend graduate school at the University of Pennsylvania thanks to the GI Bill.

Overall, the GI Bill was one of the most successful federal programs in history. For African American veterans, however, most colleges and universities remained racially segregated and refused to admit blacks. Those that did often discriminated against them. African Americans attending white colleges or universities were barred from playing on athletic teams, attending social events, and joining fraternities or sororities. Black veterans were also often prevented from buying homes in white neighborhoods. Although women veterans were eligible for GI Bill benefits, there were so few of them that the program had the unintended effect of widening the income gap between men and women.

THE SUBURBAN FRONTIER The second half of the twentieth century brought a mass migration to a new frontier—the suburbs. The acute postwar housing shortage (98 percent of cities reported shortages of houses and apartments in 1945) sparked the suburban revolution. People were eager to escape from inner cities to the sprawling suburbs emerging in the countryside, just outside of city or town limits. Of the 13 million homes built between 1948 and 1958, there were 11 million constructed in the suburbs. Many among the exploding middle-class white population moved to what were called the Sunbelt states—California, Arizona, Florida, Texas, and the southeast region, where rapid population growth and new highways generated an economic boom. As air conditioning became common in the Sunbelt, it greatly enhanced the appeal of living in warmer climates. California led the way. In 1940, it was the fifth most populous state; by 1963, it was first.

Suburbia met an acute need (affordable housing) and fulfilled a common dream—personal freedom and family security within commuting distance of cities. In the half century after the Second World War, the suburban "good life" included a big home with a big yard on a big lot accessed by a big car—or two. During the 1950s, suburbs grew six times as fast as cities, and by 1970 more people lived in suburbs than in cities.

A brassy New York real estate developer, William Levitt, led the suburban revolution. He had made a fortune during the war building housing units on new navy bases and around defense plants, and after the war he put his

Levittown Identical mass-produced houses in Levittown, New York, and other suburbs across the country provided veterans and their families with affordable homes.

expertise to use in the suburbs. Between 1947 and 1951, on 6,000 acres of Long Island farmland forty miles east of New York City, he built 17,447 small (750 square feet), sturdy, two-bedroom homes to house more than 82,000 mostly lower-middle-class people. Levitt believed he was enabling the American Dream. "No man who owns his own lot and his own house can be a communist," he said.

The planned community, called Levittown, included schools, swimming pools, shopping centers, and playing fields. Levitt encouraged and even enforced uniformity and conformity. The lookalike houses came in different colors but only three styles—the Cape Cod, the Rancher, and the Colonial. All sold for the same low price—$6,990, with no down payments for veterans—and featured the same floor plan and accessories. Each had a living room with a picture window and a television set, a bathroom, two bedrooms, and a kitchen equipped with an electric refrigerator, oven, and washing machine. Trees were planted every twenty-eight feet in the former potato fields; homeowners were required to cut their grass once a week and prohibited from hanging laundry on outside clothes lines during weekends.

When the first houses in Levittown went on sale, people stood in long lines to buy one. In seven days, Levitt sold 707 houses. He soon built three more Levittowns in Pennsylvania, New Jersey, and Puerto Rico. They and other planned suburban communities benefited greatly from government assistance. Federal and state tax codes favored homeowners over renters, and local governments paid for the infrastructure the subdivisions required: roads, water and sewer lines, fire and police protection. By insuring loans for up to 95 percent of the value of a house, the Federal Housing Administration (FHA) made it easy for builders to construct low-cost homes and for people to purchase them.

Levitt and other suburban developers created lily-white communities outside mostly black-populated cities. Initially, the contracts for houses in Levittown specifically excluded "members of other than the Caucasian race." As Levitt explained, "We can solve a housing problem or we can try to solve a racial problem. But we can't combine the two." It wasn't long, however, before the U.S. Supreme Court ruled in *Shelley v. Kraemer* (1948) that such racial restrictions were illegal.

The Court ruling, however, did not end segregated housing practices; it simply made them more discreet. In 1953, when Levittown's population reached 70,000, it was the largest community in the nation without a single African American resident. Although Jewish himself, Levitt also discouraged Jews from living in his communities. "As a Jew," he explained, "I have no room in my heart for racial prejudice. But the plain fact is that most whites prefer not to live in mixed communities. This attitude may be wrong morally, and someday it may change. I hope it will."

Other developers across the country soon mimicked Levitt's efforts, building suburban communities with rustic names such as Lakewood, Streamwood,

The Second Great Migration African American families, such as the New Jersey–bound family pictured here, moved to northern urban centers in droves following the end of World War II.

Elmwood, Cedar Hill, Park Forest, and Deer Park. In 1955, *House and Garden* magazine could declare that suburbia had become the "national way of life." By 1960, however, only 5 percent of African Americans lived in suburbs.

MINORITIES ON THE MOVE The mass migration of rural southern blacks to the urban North, Midwest, and West after the Second World War was much larger than the migration that occurred after the First World War, and its social consequences were even more dramatic. After 1945, more than 5 million blacks left the South in search of better jobs, higher wages, decent housing, and greater civil rights.

By 1960, for the first time in history, more African Americans were living in urban areas than in rural areas. As blacks moved into northern cities, many white residents moved to the suburbs, leaving behind racial ghettos. Between 1950 and 1960, some 3.6 million whites left the nation's largest cities for suburban neighborhoods, while 4.5 million blacks moved into the cities.

Deeply entrenched racial attitudes outside the South forced blacks to work to counter the hostility they confronted. Through organizations such as the National Association for the Advancement of Colored People (NAACP), the Congress of Racial Equality (CORE), and the National Urban League, they sought to change the hearts and minds of their white neighbors. However, for all of the racism that black migrants encountered, most found their new lives preferable to the enforced segregation and often violent racism in the South. Southern blacks still faced voting discrimination and segregation in theaters, parks, schools, colleges, hospitals, buses, cinemas, libraries, restrooms, beaches, bars, and prisons.

Just as African Americans were on the move, so, too, were Mexicans and Puerto Ricans. Congress renewed the *bracero* program, begun during the Second World War, which enabled Mexicans to work as wage laborers in the United States, often as migrant workers moving from farm to farm as needed. Mexicans streamed across the nation's southwest border. By 1960, Los Angeles had the largest concentration of Mexican Americans in the nation.

Mexican Americans, Puerto Ricans, and other Hispanic/Latino minorities who served in the military also benefited from the GI Bill. Many of them—and their families—were able to relocate to the mainland United States because of the educational and housing programs provided veterans through the federal government. Between 1940 and 1960, nearly a million Puerto Ricans, mostly small farmers and agricultural workers, moved into American cities, especially New York City. By the late 1960s, more Puerto Ricans lived in New York City than in San Juan, the capital of Puerto Rico.

SHIFTING WOMEN'S ROLES   During the Second World War, millions of women had assumed traditionally male jobs in factories and mills. After the war, those women were encouraged to return to their traditional roles as loving wives, caring mothers, and happy homemakers. A 1945 article in *House Beautiful* magazine informed women that the returning war veteran was "head man again. . . . Your part in the remaking of this man is to fit his home to him, understanding why he wants it this way, forgetting your own preferences."

Advertisements in popular magazines often targeted middle-class women, depicting them happily bound to the house, at work in the kitchen in dresses adorned with jewelry (usually pearl necklaces) and high heel shoes, conversing with children, serving dinner, cleaning, and otherwise displaying the joy of a clean home or the latest kitchen appliance.

The prevailing images of middle-class life featured tree-lined suburban streets, kids riding their bikes through beautiful neighborhoods, and women as devoted servants to their husbands. Idealized images of "the happy homemaker" and suburban life in popular television programs like *The Donna Reed Show* or *Leave It to Beaver* also supported the cold war campaign to portray the superiority of capitalism, democracy, freedom, and religion over communism. Russian women were depicted toiling in drudgery in drab factories or on government farms.

The new household A Tupperware party in a middle-class suburban home.

During the fifties, the U.S. marriage rate reached an all-time high, and the average age of marriage for women plummeted to nineteen. There was enormous social pressure on teenaged girls to get married quickly; if a woman wasn't engaged or married by her early twenties, she was in danger of becoming an "old maid." In 1956, one-fourth of all white college women wed while still enrolled in school, and most dropped out before receiving a degree. A common joke was that women went to college to get an "M.R.S. degree"—that is, a husband.

Female college students were encouraged to take such courses as home economics, interior decoration, and family finance. Lynn White, president of Mills College, argued that "the curriculum for female students should prepare women to foster the intellectual and emotional life of her family and community."

Despite this version of the nineteenth century's "cult of domesticity," many women did work outside the home, usually out of necessity. In 1950, women comprised 29 percent of the workforce, and that percentage rose steadily throughout the decade. Some 70 percent of employed women worked in clerical positions—as secretaries, bank tellers, or sales clerks—or on assembly lines or in the service industry (waitresses, laundresses, maids). Less than 15 percent were employed in a professional capacity (teachers, nurses, accountants, social workers). Women represented only 3.5 percent of attorneys and 6 percent of physicians. African American and other minority women had even fewer

Hollywood homemakers TV shows, movies, and plays in the fifties were outlets for homemakers' anxieties and fantasies. Top: *Father Knows Best* was a popular comedy about a middle-class family in the Midwest. Jane Wyatt portrayed the clan's matriarch Margaret, the unflappable voice of reason who oversaw an idealized suburban home life. Bottom: Domestic bliss was never in reach for African American female characters. In the award-winning Broadway production of *Porgy and Bess* (1959), Dorothy Dandridge plays an addict so lost in the vice of New Orleans that even her self-sacrificing disabled lover (Sidney Poitier) cannot save her.

vocational choices and were mostly delegated to low-paying service jobs such as maids and cooks.

THE CHILD-CENTERED FIF-TIES With the war over, millions of military veterans eagerly returned to schools, jobs, wives, and babies. The record number of Americans born during the postwar period (roughly 1941–1964) composed what came to be known as the "**baby boom** generation," which would shape the nation's social and cultural life throughout the second half of the twentieth century and after.

The fifties was the ideal decade to be a child. The horrors of the Second World War were over, the economy was surging, and social life became centered on the needs of children—because there were so many of them. Between 1946 and 1964, the birth of 76 million Americans reversed a century-long decline in the nation's birthrate and created a demographic upheaval whose repercussions are still being felt. The baby boom peaked in 1957, when a record 4.3 million births occurred, one every seven seconds.

A majority of brides during the fifties were pregnant within seven months of their wedding, and they didn't stop at one child. From 1940 to 1960, the number of families with three children doubled, and the number with four quadrupled. Dr. Benjamin Spock's *The Common Sense Book of Baby and Child Care* sold more than a million copies per year during the fifties.

Postwar babies initially created a surge in demand for diapers, washing machines, and baby food, then required the construction of thousands of new schools—and the hiring of teachers to staff them. Children's needs drove much of the economy's growth, creating a huge market for toys, candy, gum, records, clothes, and other items. In 1958, *Life* magazine reported that four-year-olds were causing a "backlog of business orders that will take two decades to fulfill."

That so many women were having babies and raising children necessarily shaped societal attitudes toward them—and vice versa. A special issue of *Life* in 1956 featured the "ideal" middle-class woman: a thirty-two-year-old "pretty and popular" white suburban housewife, mother of four, who had married at age sixteen. She was described as an excellent wife, mother, volunteer, and "home manager" who preferred marriage and child-rearing to a career outside the home. She made her own clothes, hosted dozens of dinner parties each year, sang in her church choir, and was devoted to her husband. "In her daily round," *Life* reported, "she attends club or charity meetings, drives the children to school, does the weekly grocery shopping, makes ceramics, and is planning to study French."

The soaring birthrate reinforced the notion that a woman's place was in the home. "Of all the accomplishments of the American woman," *Life* proclaimed, "the one she brings off with the most spectacular success is having babies."

A RELIGIOUS NATION

After the Second World War, Americans joined churches and synagogues in record numbers. In 1940, less than half the adult population belonged to a church; by 1960, more than 65 percent were members of churches or synagogues. The cold war provided a direct stimulant to Christian evangelism. A godly nation, it was widely assumed, would better withstand the march of "godless" communism.

President Eisenhower promoted a patriotic religious crusade. "Recognition of the Supreme Being," he declared, "is the first, the most basic, expression of Americanism. Without God, there could be no American form of government, nor an American way of life." In 1954, Congress added the phrase "[one nation] under God" to the Pledge of Allegiance. In 1956, it made the statement "In God We Trust" the nation's official motto. Eisenhower ordered that the motto be displayed on all currency. "Today in the United States," *Time* magazine claimed in 1954, "the Christian faith is back at the center of things."

The prevailing tone of the religious revival was upbeat and soothing. As the Protestant Council of New York City explained to its radio and television presenters, their on-air broadcasts "should project love, joy, courage, hope, faith, trust in God, goodwill. . . . In a very real sense we are 'selling' religion, the good news of the Gospel."

Roadside service Drive-in churches offered their members the comfort of listening to Sunday Mass from their cars. Here, the pastor of New York's Tremont Methodist Church greets a member of his car-centered congregation.

The best salesman for this "good news" was the Reverend Norman Vincent Peale. No speaker was more in demand, and no writer was more widely read. Peale's book *The Power of Positive Thinking* (1952) was a phenomenal best seller—and for good reason. It offered a simple how-to course in personal happiness, which Peale called Practical Christianity. "Flush out all depressing, negative, and tired thoughts," he advised. "Start thinking faith, enthusiasm, and joy." By following this simple formula, he pledged, each American could become "a more popular, esteemed, and well-liked individual." At the height of Peale's popularity, he was reaching 30 million people each week through radio, television, and his weekly newspaper columns.

CRACKS IN THE PICTURE WINDOW

In contrast to Peale's feel-good religion, the fifties also experienced growing anxiety, dissent, and diversity. In *The Affluent Society* (1958), for example, economist John Kenneth Galbraith attacked the prevailing notion that sustained economic growth was solving social problems. He reminded readers that the nation had yet to eradicate poverty, especially among minorities in inner cities; female-led households; Mexican American migrant farmworkers; Native Americans; and rural southerners, both black and white.

POVERTY AMID PROSPERITY Uncritical praise for the "throwaway" culture of consumption masked the chronic poverty amid America's mythic plenty. In 1959, a quarter of the population had *no* financial assets, and more than half had no savings accounts or credit cards. Poverty afflicted nearly half of the African American population, compared to only a quarter of whites. Although by 1950 blacks were earning on average more than four times their 1940 wages, they and other minority groups lagged well behind whites in their *rate* of improvement. At least 40 million people remained "poor" during the 1950s, but their plight was largely ignored.

Family on relief Many black families who migrated from the South to the Midwest became a part of a marginalized population in Chicago, dependent on public housing and experiencing the North's forms of racism.

The "promised land" in the North was not perfect. Because those who left the South were often undereducated, poor, and black, they were regularly denied access to good jobs, good schools, and good housing. Although states in the North, Midwest, and Far West did not have the same blatant forms of racial discrimination as the South, African Americans still encountered prejudice and discrimination in workplace hiring, housing, schools, and social life.

LITERATURE AS SOCIAL CRITICISM One of the most striking aspects of the fifties was the sharp contrast between the happy public mood and the increasingly bitter social criticism from intellectuals, theologians, novelists, playwrights, poets, and artists who questioned the prevailing attitude about the superiority of the American way of life. Playwright Thornton Wilder labeled the young adults of the fifties the "Silent Generation" because of the smug complacency prevalent among upper-middle-class whites. Writer Norman Mailer was equally disdainful. He said the 1950s was "one of the worst decades in the history of man."

Mailer was one of many social critics who challenged what they viewed as the decade's moral complacency and bland conformity. For all of America's

Ralph Ellison Ellison is best remembered for his 1952 novel *Invisible Man*.

mythic devotion to rugged individualism, the nation during the cold war celebrated conformity. As novelist John Updike observed, he and other writers felt estranged "from a government that extolled business and mediocrity." The most enduring novels of the postwar period emphasized the individual's struggle for survival amid the smothering forces of mass society. The characters in books such as James Jones's *From Here to Eternity* (1951), Ralph Ellison's *Invisible Man* (1952), Saul Bellow's *Seize the Day* (1956), J. D. Salinger's *Catcher in the Rye* (1951), William Styron's *Lie Down in Darkness* (1951), and John Updike's *Rabbit, Run* (1961) are restless, tormented souls who can find neither contentment nor respect in an uninterested world.

The upper-middle-class white suburbs and the culture of comfortable conformity they created were frequent literary targets. Writer John Cheever located most of his short stories in suburban neighborhoods—"cesspools of conformity" where democratic equality created a social life that was mindless and hollow. The typical suburban dweller, one critic charged in 1956, "buys the right car, keeps his lawn like his neighbor's, eats crunchy breakfast cereal, and votes Republican."

In his vicious satire of affluent suburbia, *The Crack in the Picture Window* (1956), John Keats charged that "miles of identical boxes are spreading like gangrene" across the nation, producing a runaway consumerism, "haggard" businessmen, "tense and anxious" housewives, and "the gimme kids" who, after unwrapping the last Christmas gift, "look up and ask whether that is all." He dismissed the Levittowns of America as residential "developments conceived in error, nurtured by greed, corroding everything they touch. They destroy established cities and trade patterns, pose dangerous problems for the areas they invade, and actually drive mad myriads of housewives shut up in them."

THE BEATS A small but highly visible and controversial group of young writers, poets, painters, and musicians rejected the consumer culture and the traditional expectations and responsibilities of middle-class life. They were known as the **Beats**, a term with multiple meanings: to be "beat" was likened to being "upbeat" and even "beatific," as well as being "on the beat" in "real cool" jazz music. But the Beats also liked the name because it implied "weariness," being "exhausted" or "beaten down," qualities which none of them actually exhibited.

Jack Kerouac, Allen Ginsberg, William Burroughs, Neal Cassady, Gary Snyder, and other Beats rebelled against conventional literary and artistic expression and excelled at outrageous, often purposeless and even criminal behavior, like stealing cars and cash or, in the case of Burroughs, shooting an apple off his wife's head—for the fun of it, even though the woman was killed in the process. Intensely self-absorbed to the point of ruthlessness, the mostly male Beats celebrated, even embodied, lives of breathtaking risk, fueled by feverish spontaneity and raw energy. They pursued reckless alcohol- and drug-induced ecstasies and sexual excesses. (Many of them were gay or bisexual during an era when homosexuality was considered a form of deviance requiring psychotherapy.)

The Beats viewed getting high as first-class trips and seducing women as second-class accessories; they were serial misogynists. Carolyn Cassady said her husband Neal's approach to making love was "rape." She added that Neal and "the boys didn't know where they were going. . . . They just knew they wanted to *go*."

The Beat hipsters emerged from the bohemian underground in New York City's Greenwich Village. Enlivened by tequila, marijuana, amphetamines, and heroin, the male Beats were essentially apolitical and self-indulgent chauvinists, more interested in transforming themselves than in reforming the world. Kerouac and the other Beats wanted their art and literature to change consciousness rather than address social ills.

During three feverish weeks, Kerouac typed nonstop (dictated by the "Holy Ghost") the manuscript of his remarkable novel *On the Road* (1957), an account of a series of frenzied cross-country trips he and others made between 1948 and 1950. Kerouac and the Beats were nomadic hipsters, restless

Art ache The Beat community fostered in its members a frenzied desire to experience life in all of its intensity, including the cultural realm. In this 1959 photograph, poet Tex Kleen reads in a bathtub at Venice Beach, California, while artist Mad Mike paints trash cans.

and tormented souls whose road to salvation lay in hallucinogenic drugs and lots of alcohol, casual sex, petty crime, gratuitous violence, a passion for up-tempo jazz ("bebop"), fast cars, the street life of urban ghettos, an affinity for Buddhism, and a vagabond spirit. At heart, the Beats were romantics search-ing for an authentic sense of self in a nation absorbed in consumerism, con-formism, and anti-communism. Their tortured rebelliousness set the stage for the more widespread youth revolt of the 1960s.

ROCK 'N' ROLL The millions of children making up the first wave of the baby boomers became adolescents in the 1950s. There were so many of them that people began calling them teenagers. A distinctive teen subculture began to emerge, as did a wave of juvenile delinquency. By 1956, more than a mil-lion teens were being arrested each year. One contributing factor was access to automobiles, which enabled teens to escape parental control and, in the words of one journalist, provided "a private lounge for drinking and for pet-ting [embracing and kissing] or sex episodes."

Many blamed teen delinquency on rock 'n' roll, a new form of music that emerged during the 1950s. Alan Freed, a Cleveland disc jockey known as "Moondog," coined the term *rock 'n' roll* in 1951. He had noticed that white teenagers buying rhythm and blues (R&B) records preferred the livelier recordings by African Americans and Hispanic Americans. Freed began play-ing R&B records on his radio show, but he called the music "rock 'n' roll" (a phrase used in African American communities to refer to dancing and sex). By 1954, Freed had moved to New York City, where his popular program helped bridge the gap between "white" and "black" music.

African American singers such as Chuck Berry, Little Richard, and Ray Charles, as well as Hispanic American performers such as Ritchie Valens (Richard Valenzuela), captivated young, white, middle-class audiences. At the same time, Sam Phillips, a radio disk jockey in Memphis, Tennessee, was searching for a particular type of pop singer. "If I could find a white man with a Negro sound," Phillips said, "I could make a billion dollars."

He found his singer in Elvis Presley, the lanky son of poor Mississippi farm-ers. In 1956, the twenty-one-year-old Presley, by then a regional star famous for his long, unruly hair, sullen yet sensual sneer, and swiveling hips, released his smash-hit recording "Heartbreak Hotel." Over the next two years, he emerged as the most popular musician in American history, carrying rock 'n' roll across the race barrier and assaulting the bland conformity of fifties culture. Presley's gyrat-ing performances (his nickname was "Elvis the Pelvis") and incomparably rich and raw baritone voice drove young people wild and earned him millions of fans around the world. His movements, said one music critic, "suggest, in a word, sex."

Cultural conservatives were outraged and urged parents to destroy Presley's records because they promoted "a pagan concept of life." A Roman Catholic official denounced Presley as a vile symptom of a teenage "creed of dishonesty, violence, lust and degeneration." Patriotic groups claimed that rock 'n' roll music was part of a Communist plot to corrupt America's youth. Writing in the *New York Times*, a psychiatrist characterized rock 'n' roll as a "communicable disease." The U.S. Senate subcommittee tasked with investigating juvenile delinquency warned that Presley was threatening "to rock-n-roll the juvenile world into open revolt against society. The gangster of tomorrow is the Elvis Presley type of today."

Elvis Presley Hysterical girls grab at him from all angles, but the "King of Rock and Roll" stays cool, crooning into the camera while performing in Miami in 1956.

Yet rock 'n' roll flourished in part because it was so controversial. It gave teenagers a self-conscious sense of belonging to a tribal social group. More important, it brought together, on equal terms, musicians (and their audiences) of varied races and backgrounds.

THE CIVIL RIGHTS MOVEMENT

Soon after the cold war began, Soviet diplomats began to use America's racial discrimination against African Americans as a propaganda tool to illustrate the defects of the American way of life. Under the Jim Crow system in the southern states, blacks still risked being lynched if they registered to vote. They were forced to use separate facilities—water fountains, restrooms, hotels, theaters, parks—and to attend segregated schools. In the North, discrimination was not as "official," but it was equally real, especially in housing and employment. President Eisenhower had an opportunity to exercise transformational leadership in race relations; his unwillingness to do so was his greatest failure. As *Time* magazine noted in 1958, Eisenhower "overlooked the fact that the U.S. needed [his] moral leadership in fighting segregation."

EISENHOWER AND RACE Eisenhower had entered the White House committed to civil rights in principle, and he pushed for improvements in some areas. During his first three years, public facilities (parks, playgrounds, libraries, restaurants) in Washington, D.C., were desegregated, and he intervened to end discrimination at military bases in Virginia and South Carolina. He also appointed the first African American to an executive office: E. Frederic Morrow, who was named Administrative Officer for Special Projects. Beyond that, however, Eisenhower refused to make civil rights for African Americans a moral crusade. Pushing too hard, he believed, would "raise tempers and increase prejudices," doing more harm than good.

Two aspects of Eisenhower's political philosophy limited his commitment to racial equality: his preference for state or local action over federal involvement and his doubt that laws could change attitudes. "I don't believe you can change the hearts of men with laws or decisions," he insisted. His passive attitude meant that governmental leadership on civil rights would come from the judiciary more than from the executive or legislative branches.

In 1953, Eisenhower appointed former Republican governor Earl Warren of California as chief justice of the U.S. Supreme Court, a decision he later said was the "biggest damn fool mistake I ever made." Warren, who had seemed safely conservative while in elected office, displayed a social conscience and a streak of libertarianism on the bench. Under Warren's leadership (1953–1969), the Supreme Court became a powerful force for social and political change.

AFRICAN AMERICAN ACTIVISM The most-crucial leaders of the civil rights movement came from those whose rights were most often violated: African Americans, Hispanic Americans, Asian Americans, and other minorities. Courageous blacks led what would become the most important social movement in twentieth-century American history. With intelligence, bravery, and dignity, they fought in the courts, at the ballot box, and in the streets.

Although many African Americans moved to the North and West during and after the Second World War, a majority remained in the South, where they still faced a rigidly segregated society. In the 1952 presidential election, for example, only 20 percent of eligible African Americans were registered to vote. In addition, the public schools, especially in the South, were supposedly racially separate but equal in quality. In fact, however, many all-black schools were underfunded, understaffed, and overcrowded.

In the mid-1930s, the National Association for the Advancement of Colored People (NAACP) challenged the **separate-but-equal** judicial doctrine that had preserved racial segregation since the *Plessy* decision by the Supreme Court in 1896. It took almost fifteen years, however, to convince the courts that racial segregation must end. Finally, in *Sweatt v. Painter* (1950), the Supreme Court ruled that a separate black law school in Texas was *not* equal in quality to the

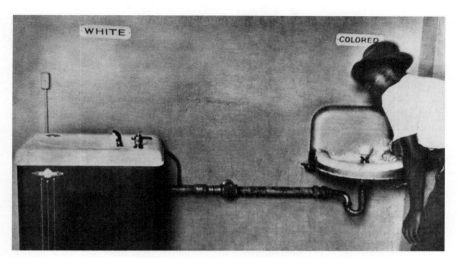

Fountains of truth An Alabama motel offers its white patrons chilled water from a cooler, while its African American guests must use a simple drinking fountain.

state's whites-only schools. The Court ordered the state to remedy the situation. It was the first step toward dismantling America's tradition of racial segregation.

THE *BROWN* DECISION By the early 1950s, people were challenging state laws mandating racial segregation in the public schools. Five such cases, from Kansas, Delaware, South Carolina, Virginia, and the District of Columbia—usually cited by reference to the first, ***Brown v. Board of Education of Topeka, Kansas***—went to the Supreme Court in 1952. President Eisenhower told the attorney general that he hoped the justices would postpone dealing with the explosive case "until the next Administration took over." When it became obvious that the Court was moving forward, Eisenhower urged Chief Justice Warren to side with segregationists. Warren was not swayed: "You mind your business," he told the president, "and I'll mind mine."

Warren wrote the pathbreaking opinion, delivered on May 17, 1954, in which the Court declared that "in the field of public education the doctrine of 'separate but equal' has no place." The justices used a variety of sociological and psychological findings to show that even if racially separate schools were equal in quality, the very practice of separating students by race caused feelings of inferiority among black children. A year later, the Court directed that the process of racial *integration* should move "with all deliberate speed."

Eisenhower refused to endorse or enforce the Court's ruling. Privately, he grumbled "that the Supreme Court decision set back progress in the South at least fifteen years." Anyone who thinks "you can do these things by force is just plain nuts," he said. Eisenhower had "little faith in the ability of law to change the human heart or eliminate prejudice."

While token racial integration began as early as 1954 in Kentucky and Missouri, hostility mounted in the Lower South and Virginia. The Alabama State Senate and the Virginia legislature both passed resolutions "nullifying" the Supreme Court's decision, arguing that racial integration was an issue of states' rights. Arkansas governor Orval Faubus insisted that the "federal government is a creature of the states. . . . We must either choose to defend our rights or else surrender."

In 1954, Harry F. Byrd, a Virginia senator and former governor, supplied a rallying cry for diehard white racists when he called for "**massive resistance**" against federal efforts to enforce integration in the South. Senator James O. Eastland of Mississippi, a state where African Americans made up 45 percent of the population, pledged that "integration will never come to Mississippi" and denounced the *Brown* decision as an "illegal, immoral, and sinful doctrine." He told the Senate that "the Negro race is an inferior race" and that the South was determined to maintain "white supremacy."

The grassroots opposition among southern whites to the *Brown* case was led by newly formed Citizens' Councils, middle-class versions of the Ku Klux Klan

Separate, but not equal African American children pose outside their segregated schoolhouse in Selma, Alabama, in 1965.

that spread quickly and eventually enrolled 250,000 members. Instead of physical violence, the Councils used economic coercion against blacks who crossed racial boundaries. The Citizens' Councils grew so powerful in some communities that membership became almost a necessity for an aspiring white politician.

The opponents of court-ordered integration were militantly defiant. In 1956, a Declaration of Constitutional Principles ("Southern Manifesto") was signed by 101 members of Congress, deploring the *Brown* decision as "a clear abuse of judicial power" that had created an "explosive and dangerous condition" in the South. Only three southern Democrats refused to sign. One of them, Senator Lyndon B. Johnson of Texas, would become president seven years later. In six southern states at the end of 1956, two years after the *Brown* ruling, no black children attended school with whites. Some southern politicians threatened to shut down white schools rather than allow racial integration.

THE MONTGOMERY BUS BOYCOTT The *Brown* case did much more than mobilize white resistance. It inspired many blacks (and white activists) by suggesting that the federal government was finally beginning to confront racial discrimination. Yet the essential role played by the NAACP and the courts in the civil rights movement often overshadows the courageous contributions of individual African Americans who took great personal risks to challenge segregation.

For example, in Montgomery, Alabama, on December 1, 1955, Mrs. Rosa Parks, a forty-two-year-old black seamstress who was a fiercely determined activist for racial justice, refused to give up her seat on a city bus to a white man. By doing so, she launched the modern civil rights movement.

Like many southern communities, Montgomery, the "Cradle of the Confederacy," required blacks to sit in the rear seats of buses or trains. They could sit in the front seats designated for whites only if there were empty seats. If a white rider asked a black to move, they were expected to go "to the back of the bus." Parks, however, was "tired of giving in." When the bus driver told her that "niggers must move back" or he would have her arrested, she replied, with quiet courage, "You may do that." Police then arrested her.

The next night, black community leaders met at Dexter Avenue Baptist Church to organize a long-planned boycott of the city's bus system, most of whose riders were African Americans. Student and faculty volunteers from Alabama State University stayed up all night to distribute 35,000 flyers denouncing the arrest of Rosa Parks and urging support for the **Montgomery bus boycott**.

MARTIN LUTHER KING JR. In the Dexter Avenue church's twenty-six-year-old pastor, Martin Luther King Jr., the boycott movement found a

Rosa Parks Parks is fingerprinted by a Montgomery policeman on February 22, 1956, along with about 100 others who joined the bus boycott.

brave and charismatic leader. Born in Atlanta, the grandson of a slave and son of a prominent minister, King was intelligent, courageous, and an eloquent and passionate speaker. "We must use the weapon of love," King told supporters. "We must realize so many people are taught to hate us that they are not totally responsible for their hate."

To his foes, King warned, "We will soon wear you down by our capacity to suffer, and in winning our freedom we will so appeal to your heart and conscience that we will win you in the process." King preached **nonviolent civil disobedience**, the tactic of defying unjust laws through peaceful actions, but he also valued militancy, for without crisis and confrontation with those in power there would be no negotiation or progress.

The Montgomery bus boycott was a stunning success—but it was not easy. For 381 days, African Americans, women and men, organized carpools, used black-owned taxis, hitchhiked, or simply walked. White supporters also provided rides. A few boycotters rode horses or mules to work. The unprecedented mass protest infuriated many whites; police harassed and ticketed black carpools, and white thugs attacked black pedestrians. Ku Klux Klan members burned black churches and bombed houses owned by King and other boycott leaders. King himself was arrested twice. In trying to calm an angry black crowd, he urged restraint: "Don't get panicky. Don't get your weapons. We want to love our enemies."

On December 20, 1956, the Montgomery boycotters won a federal case they had initiated against racial segregation on public buses. The Supreme Court affirmed that "the separate but equal doctrine can no longer be safely followed as a correct statement of the law." The next day, King and other African Americans boarded the city buses. The success of the boycott showed that well-coordinated, nonviolent black activism could trigger major changes in public policy. Among African Americans, hope replaced resignation, and action supplanted passivity. The boycott also catapulted King into the national spotlight.

And what of Rosa Parks? She and her husband lost their jobs, and hate mail as well as death threats and firebombings forced them to leave Alabama eight months after her arrest. They moved to Detroit, where they remained fully engaged in the evolving civil rights movement.

THE CIVIL RIGHTS ACTS OF 1957 AND 1960 President Eisenhower's timidity in the area of race relations emerged again when he was asked to protect the right of African Americans to vote. In 1956, hoping to exploit

Civil disobedience Martin Luther King Jr. is roughly arrested for "loitering" in 1958. He would be arrested thirty times in his life for defying racist laws.

divisions between northern and southern Democrats and reclaim some of the black vote for Republicans, congressional leaders agreed to support what became the Civil Rights Act of 1957.

The first civil rights law passed since 1875, it finally got through the Senate, after a year's delay, with the help of majority leader Lyndon B. Johnson, a Texas Democrat who knew that he could never be elected president if he was viewed as just another racist white southerner. The bill was intended to ensure that all Americans, regardless of race or ethnicity, were allowed to vote. Johnson won southern acceptance of the bill by watering down its enforcement provisions. Eisenhower reassured Johnson that the final version represented "the mildest civil rights bill possible."

The Civil Rights Act established the Civil Rights Commission and a new Civil Rights Division in the Justice Department intended to prevent interference with the right to vote. Yet by 1959, the law had not resulted in a single southern black voter being added to the rolls. Neither did the Civil Rights Act of 1960, which provided for federal courts to register African Americans to vote in districts where there was a "pattern and practice" of racial discrimination. This bill, too, lacked teeth and depended upon vigorous presidential enforcement to achieve any tangible results.

DESEGREGATION IN LITTLE ROCK   A few weeks after the Civil Rights Act of 1957 was passed, Arkansas's Democratic governor, Orval Eugene Faubus, a rabid segregationist eager to win a third term, called a special session of the state legislature to pass a series of bills designed to give him sweeping new powers to close public schools threatened with integration and to transfer funds from public schools facing federally enforced integration to private "segregation academies." Faubus defied a federal court order by using the state's National Guard to prevent nine black students from enrolling at Little Rock's Central High School. The National Guard commander's orders were explicit: "No niggers in the building." When one of the students, fifteen-year-old Elizabeth Eckford, tried to enter the school, a surging mob of jeering whites shrieked, "Lynch her! Lynch her!"

Local authorities removed the black students, and the mayor of Little Rock frantically called the White House to request federal troops, explaining that Faubus was creating "tensions where none existed." At that point, Eisenhower, who had resisted all appeals for federal action, reluctantly dispatched 1,000 army paratroopers of the 101st Airborne Division to protect the brave black students as they entered the school. "Mob rule," he told the nation, "cannot be allowed to overrule the decisions of our courts."

It was one of the nation's most painful and momentous confrontations, the first time since the 1870s that federal troops had been sent to the South to protect

"Lynch her!" Fifteen-year-old Elizabeth Eckford endures the hostile screams of future classmates as she enters Central High School in Little Rock, Arkansas.

the rights of African Americans. Dunbar Ogden, a Presbyterian minister in Little Rock, found a ray of hope in the ugly confrontation: "This may be looked back upon by future historians as the turning point—for good—of race relations in this country." Faubus claimed that Arkansas was now "an occupied territory."

With television cameras sending images across the country, seasoned paratroopers used bayonets and rifle butts to disperse the angry crowd. Inside Central High School, the nine black students attended their first classes with soldiers patrolling the halls. During lunch hour, two white pupils saw a black student eating alone. They asked: "Would you like to come over to our table?" The grateful boy replied: "Gosh, I'd love to."

The soldiers stayed in Little Rock through the school year. To a man, unyielding southern governors and congressmen furiously lashed out at Eisenhower, charging that he was violating states' rights. Eisenhower had "lit the fires of hate," claimed Senator James Eastland. A South Carolina moderate took a different tack: "Those who believed that integration could be accomplished gradually and peacefully are now convinced that Eisenhower will have to use force all the way."

Eisenhower was quick to stress that his use of federal troops had little to do with "the integration or segregation question" and everything to do with maintaining law and order. In his view, the gleaming bayonets in Little Rock showed that the United States was a government of law, that the Constitution remained the supreme law of the land, and that the U.S. Supreme Court was the final interpreter of the Constitution. Martin Luther King Jr., who had earlier criticized Eisenhower's tepid support of civil rights, told the president that the "overwhelming majority of southerners, Negro and white, stand behind your resolute action to restore law and order in Little Rock." Many southern politicians called for the president's impeachment and removal.

In the summer of 1958, Governor Faubus, supported by the state legislature, closed the Little Rock high schools rather than allow racial integration. The governor of Virginia did the same in his state. Their actions led Jonathan Daniels, editor of the Raleigh, North Carolina, *News & Observer*, to write that closing public schools is "something beyond secession from the Union; [it] is secession from civilization."

Court proceedings in Arkansas dragged into 1959 before the schools reopened. Resistance to integration in Virginia collapsed when state and federal courts struck down state laws that had cut off funds to integrated public schools. Thereafter, massive resistance to racial integration was confined mostly to the Lower South, where five states—from South Carolina westward through Louisiana—still opposed even token integration. Faubus went on to serve six terms as governor of Arkansas.

SOUTHERN CHRISTIAN LEADERSHIP CONFERENCE After Little Rock, progress toward greater civil rights seemed agonizingly slow. Frustrated African Americans began blaming the NAACP for relying too much on the courts. "The Negro masses are angry and restless, tired of prolonged legal battles that end in paper decrees," reported black journalist Louis Lomax.

The widespread sense of disappointment gave Martin Luther King's nonviolent civil rights movement even greater visibility. As King explained, "We were confronted with blasted hopes, and the dark shadow of a deep disappointment settled upon us. So we had no alternative except that of preparing for direct action, whereby we would present our very bodies as a means of laying our case before the conscience of the local and national community."

On January 10, 1957, Dr. King invited about sixty black ministers and leaders to Ebenezer Church in Atlanta. Their goal was to form an organization to coordinate and support nonviolent direct action as a method of desegregating bus systems across the South. After a follow-up meeting in New Orleans on February 15, a new organization emerged: the **Southern Christian Leadership Conference (SCLC)**, with Dr. King as its president. Unlike the NAACP, which recruited individual members, SCLC coordinated activities on behalf of a cluster of organizations, mostly individual churches or community groups. Because Dr. King pushed for direct action against the segregated South, only a few African American ministers were initially willing to affiliate with SCLC, for fear of a white backlash.

King persisted, however, and over time SCLC grew into a powerful organization. The activists knew that violence awaited them. Roy Wilkins, head of the NAACP, noted that "the Negro citizen has come to the point where he is not afraid of violence. He no longer shrinks back. He will assert himself, and if violence comes, so be it." Thus began the second phase of the civil rights movement, a phase that would come to fruition in the 1960s as King and other African American activists showed the nation the courage to resist injustice, the power to love everyone, and the strength to endure discouragement and opposition.

FOREIGN POLICY IN THE FIFTIES

The Truman administration's commitment to "contain" communism focused on the Soviet threat to Western Europe. During the 1950s, the Eisenhower administration, especially Secretary of State John Foster Dulles, expanded America's objective in the cold war. "Containment" was no longer enough; the United States must develop a "dynamic" foreign policy that would "roll back" communism around the world.

Dulles's goal was to "liberate" those people under Communist rule rather than merely contain Communist expansion. As a cold warrior, Dulles expected every nation to choose sides. "For us," he said, "there are two kinds of people in the world. There are those who are Christians and support free enterprise, and there are the others." He soon discovered, however, that the complexities of world affairs and the realities of Soviet and Communist Chinese power made his moral commitment to manage the destiny of the world unrealistic—and costly.

CONCLUDING AN ARMISTICE In Korea, Eisenhower, who had a unique understanding of the relationship between diplomacy and military force, faced three choices: increase the war effort, continue the military

"Don't Be Afraid—I Can Always Pull You Back" Secretary of State John Foster Dulles pushes a reluctant America to the brink of war.

stalemate, or pursue a negotiated settlement. Eisenhower chose the third option, but he first had to convince Dulles that negotiations were warranted. Dulles did not want peace until the Chinese had suffered "one hell of a licking" and the two Koreas had been reunited. In April 1953, Eisenhower told Dulles that he was not willing to prolong the military effort, but he was comfortable using the threat of nuclear weapons and other actions to break the impasse in the stalled negotiations.

In May 1953, Eisenhower took the bold step of intensifying the aerial bombardment of North Korea. The president let it be known that he would use nuclear weapons if a truce were not forthcoming. Thereafter, negotiations moved quickly toward a cease-fire agreement (called an armistice) on July 26, 1953. It ended "all acts of armed force" and reaffirmed the historical border between the two Koreas just above the 38th parallel until both sides could arrive at a "final peaceful settlement." Other factors in bringing about the armistice were China's rising military losses in the conflict and the spirit of uncertainty and caution felt by the Soviet Communists after the death of Josef Stalin on March 5, 1953, six weeks after Eisenhower's inauguration.

The Korean War had effects far beyond the divided nation's borders. It was the first war in which helicopters were used in combat and it ushered in the era of jet fighters. The conflict transformed the United States into the world's policeman by convincing American political and military leaders that communism was indeed a global threat. Within a few years, the United States would create scores of permanent military bases around the world and organize a permanent "national security" apparatus in Washington to manage its new responsibilities, not the least of which was a growing stockpile of nuclear weaponry.

DULLES AND MASSIVE RETALIATION Like Woodrow Wilson, Secretary of State Dulles was a Presbyterian minister's son whose favorite hymn was "Onward, Christian Soldiers." Self-righteous and humorless, he believed that the United States was "born with a sense of destiny and mission" to defeat communism. His British counterparts, however, were not impressed with his sermonizing monologues, calling them "dull, duller, Dulles."

Dulles insisted that the Democratic policy of "containing" communism was "immoral" because it did nothing to free people from oppression. America, he argued, should work toward the "liberation" of the "captive peoples" of Eastern Europe and China. When State Department analyst George F. Kennan, architect of the containment doctrine, dismissed Dulles's rhetoric as lunacy, Dulles fired him.

Eisenhower, however, understood Kennan's objections. He was quick to explain that the "liberation" doctrine would not involve military force. Instead, he would promote the removal of Communist control "by every peaceful means, but only by peaceful means." Yet he did nothing to temper Dulles's rhetoric and praised his secretary of state's moral fervor.

Dulles and Eisenhower knew that the United States could not win a ground war against the Soviet Union or Communist China, whose armies had millions more soldiers than did the United States. Nor could the administration afford—politically or financially—to sustain military expenditures at the levels required during the Korean War. So Dulles and Eisenhower crafted a strategy that came to be called "**massive retaliation**," which meant using the threat of nuclear warfare ("massive retaliatory power") to prevent Communist aggression. The strategy, they argued, would provide a "maximum deterrent at bearable cost."

Massive retaliation had major weaknesses, however. By the mid-1950s, both the United States and the Soviet Union had developed hydrogen bombs, which were 750 times as powerful as the atomic bombs dropped on Japan in 1945. A single hydrogen bomb would have a devastating global impact, yet war planners envisioned using hundreds of them. "The necessary art," Dulles explained, was in the brinkmanship, "the ability to get to the verge without getting into war. . . . If you are scared to go to the brink, you are lost." The *Milwaukee Journal* found Dulles's "brinkmanship" strategy terrifying: "It is like saying that the closer you get to war the better you serve peace. It is like saying that the destiny of the human race is something to gamble with."

THE CIA'S FOREIGN INTERVENTIONS While Eisenhower and Dulles were publicly promoting the "liberation" of Communist nations and massive retaliation as a strategy against the Soviets, they were secretly using the new **Central Intelligence Agency (CIA)** to manipulate world politics in covert ways that produced unintended consequences—all of them bad.

The anti-colonial independence movements unleashed by the Second World War placed the United States in the awkward position of watching nationalist groups around the globe revolt against British and French rule. In Iran in May 1951, the parliament seized control of the nation's British-run oil industry. The following year, a newly elected prime minister, Mohammed Mossadegh, cut all diplomatic ties with Great Britain and insisted that Iran, not Britain, should own, sell, and profit from Iranian oil. Dulles predicted that Iran was on the verge of falling under Communist control. The CIA and the British intelligence service, MI6, then launched Operation Ajax, designed, in the words of the agency's head, Allen Dulles (the secretary of state's brother), to "bring about the fall of Mossadegh."

In 1954, the CIA bribed Iranian army officers and hired Iranian agents to arrest Mossadegh, who was convicted of high treason. He was imprisoned for three years, then put under house arrest until his death in 1967. In return for access to Iranian oil, the U.S. government thereafter provided massive support for the anti-Communist and increasingly authoritarian regime of the shah (king) of Iran, Mohammad Reza Pahlavi, who consolidated power after the removal of Mossadegh. In the end, Operation Ajax proved to be a disaster by reinstating the incompetent and indecisive shah.

The success of the CIA-engineered coup in Iran emboldened Eisenhower to authorize other secret operations to undermine "unfriendly" government regimes, even if it meant aligning with corrupt dictatorships. In 1954, the target was Guatemala, a desperately poor Central American country led by Colonel Jacobo Arbenz Guzman. Arbenz's decision to take over U.S.-owned property and industries convinced Dulles that Guatemala was falling victim to "international communism." Dulles persuaded Eisenhower to approve a CIA operation to organize a secret Guatemalan army in Honduras. On June 18, 1954, aided by CIA-piloted warplanes, 150 paid "liberators" crossed the border and forced Arbenz Guzman into exile in Mexico. The United States then installed a new ruler in Guatemala who eliminated all political opposition.

By secretly overthrowing elected governments to ensure that they did not join the Soviet bloc, however, the CIA operations destabilized Iran and Guatemala and created problems in the Middle East and Central America that would eventually come back to haunt the United States.

INDOCHINA   During the 1950s, the United States also became embroiled in Southeast Asia. Indochina, created by French imperialists in the nineteenth century out of the old kingdoms of Cambodia, Laos, and Vietnam, offered a distinctive case of anti-colonial nationalism. During the Second World War, after Japanese troops occupied the region, the Viet Minh (League for the Independence of Vietnam) waged a guerrilla resistance movement led by Ho Chi Minh, a seasoned revolutionary and passionate nationalist.

"Uncle Ho," a wispy man weighing barely 100 pounds, worked sixteen hours each day toward a single goal: independence for his country. At the end of the war against Japan, the Viet Minh controlled part of northern Vietnam. On September 2, 1945, Ho Chi Minh proclaimed the creation of a Democratic Republic of Vietnam, with its capital in Hanoi.

The French, like the Americans would later, underestimated the determination of Ho and the Vietnamese nationalists to maintain their independence. In 1946, the First Indochina War began when Ho's fighters resisted French efforts to restore the colonial regime. French forces quickly regained control of the cities, while the Viet Minh controlled the countryside. Ho predicted that his forces would absorb more losses, but the French would give in first. When the Korean War ended, the United States continued its efforts to strengthen French control of Vietnam.

Ho Chi Minh Though a ruthless leader, he cultivated a public image of himself as the humble, gentle Uncle Ho, a man of the people.

By the end of 1953, the Eisenhower administration was paying nearly 80 percent of the cost of the French military effort.

In December 1953, some 12,000 French soldiers parachuted into **Dien Bien Phu**, a cluster of villages in a valley ringed by mountains in northwestern Vietnam. Their plan was to build a well-fortified base to lure Viet Minh guerrillas into the open and then overwhelm them with superior firepower. The French assumed that the surrounding forested hills were impassable. But slowly, more than 55,000 Viet Minh fighters equipped with Chinese Communist weapons took up positions atop the ridges overlooking the French military base. They laboriously dismantled cannons and carried them in pieces up the hills, then dug trenches and tunnels down into the valley. By March 1954, the French paratroopers found themselves surrounded.

As the weeks passed, the French government pleaded with the United States to relieve the pressure on Dien Bien Phu. The National Security Council—Dulles, Vice President Nixon, and the chairman of the Joint Chiefs of Staff—urged Eisenhower to use atomic bombs to aid the trapped French force.

Dien Bien Phu Viet Minh soldiers march French captives to a prisoner camp in Dien Bien Phu on May 7, 1954.

Eisenhower snapped back: "You boys must be crazy. We can't use those awful things against Asians for the second time in less than ten years. My God!"

The president opposed U.S. intervention unless the British joined the effort. When they refused, Eisenhower told the French that U.S. military action in Vietnam was "politically impossible." On May 7, 1954, the Viet Minh fighters overwhelmed the last French resistance. The catastrophic defeat caused the collapse of the French government and signaled the end of French colonial rule in Asia.

On July 20, 1954, representatives of France, Britain, the Soviet Union, the People's Republic of China, and the Viet Minh signed the Geneva Accords, which gave Laos and Cambodia their independence and divided Vietnam in two at the 17th parallel. The Geneva Accords gave the Viet Minh Communists control in the North; the French would remain south of the line until nationwide

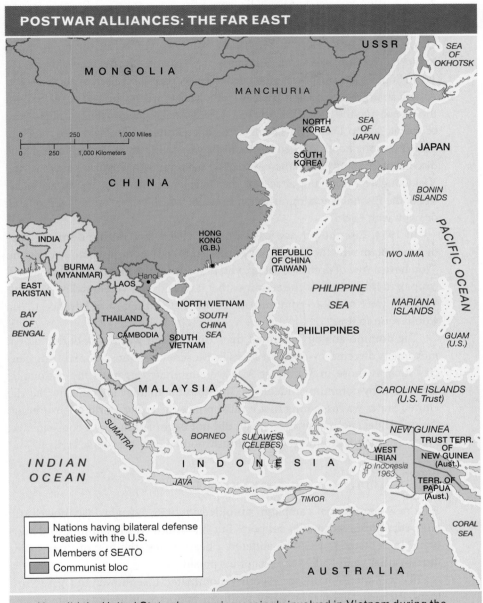

POSTWAR ALLIANCES: THE FAR EAST

Nations having bilateral defense treaties with the U.S.

Members of SEATO

Communist bloc

- How did the United States become increasingly involved in Vietnam during the fifties?
- Why did the installation of Ngo Dinh Diem by the French and the Americans backfire and generate more conflict in Vietnam?

elections in 1956. American and South Vietnamese representatives refused to sign the Geneva Accords, arguing that the treaties legitimized the Communist victory. After 1954, Ho Chi Minh took complete control of the government in North Vietnam, executing thousands of Vietnamese he deemed opponents.

In South Vietnam, power gravitated to a new premier chosen by the French at American urging: Ngo Dinh Diem, a Catholic nationalist who had opposed both the French and the Viet Minh. In 1954, Eisenhower began providing military and economic aid to Diem. Yet Diem's autocratic efforts to eliminate all opposition played into the hands of the Communists, who found eager recruits among the discontented South Vietnamese. By 1957, Communist guerrillas known as the **Viet Cong** were launching attacks on the Diem government. As the warfare intensified, the Eisenhower administration concluded that its only option was to "sink or swim with Diem."

In 1954, Eisenhower had used what he called the **"falling domino" theory** to explain why the United States needed to fight communism in Vietnam: "You have a row of dominos set up, you knock over the first one, and what will happen to the last one is the certainty that it will go over very quickly." If South Vietnam were to fall to communism, he predicted, the rest of Southeast Asia would soon follow.

The domino analogy assumed that communism was a monolithic global movement directed by Soviet leaders in Moscow. Yet anti-colonial insurgencies such as those in Southeast Asia were animated as much by nationalist motives as by communist ideology. The domino analogy also meant that the United States was assuming that it must police the entire world to ensure that the dominoes, no matter how small, did not begin falling. As a consequence, every insurgency around the world mushroomed into a strategic crisis.

REELECTION AND FOREIGN CRISES

As a new presidential campaign unfolded in 1956, Dwight Eisenhower still enjoyed widespread public support. But his health was beginning to deteriorate. In September 1955, he suffered a heart attack, the first of three major illnesses that would affect the rest of his presidency.

In 1956, the Republicans eagerly renominated Eisenhower and Vice President Richard Nixon. The party platform endorsed Eisenhower's moderate Republicanism, meaning balanced budgets, reduced government intervention in the economy, and an internationalist foreign policy. The Democrats turned again to the liberal Illinois leader, Adlai Stevenson.

REPRESSION IN HUNGARY During the last week of the presidential campaign, fighting erupted along the Suez Canal in Egypt and in the streets of

Budapest, Hungary. On October 23, 1956, Hungarian nationalists, encouraged by American propaganda broadcasts through Radio Free Europe, revolted against Communist troops in Budapest. The Soviets responded with a massive attack, killing 2,000 Hungarian "freedom fighters" and forcing nearly 200,000 more to flee before installing a new puppet government. The revolution had been smothered in twelve days.

Eisenhower offered his sympathy for the Hungarian people, but nothing more. His strategy in dealing with such crises was, as he later said, "Take a hard line—and bluff." Although he avoided war over Hungary, Eisenhower had allowed administration officials, especially Dulles, to make reckless pledges about "rolling back" communism and "liberating" Eastern Europe. "To all those suffering under Communist slavery," Dulles promised, "let us say you can count on us."

In Hungary, the Soviets called the Eisenhower administration's bluff. The Hungarian freedom fighters, having been led to expect U.S. support, paid with their lives. As the Soviets crushed the uprising, Hungarian rebels asked, "When are the Americans coming?" Richard Nixon cynically reassured Eisenhower that the Soviet crackdown would be beneficial in showing the world the ruthlessness of communism. The president, however, felt guilty, telling Dulles that "we have excited Hungarians for all these years" and are "now turning our backs on them when they are in a jam." Dulles showed little concern, reminding the president that "we always have been against violent rebellion."

THE SUEZ WAR Eisenhower was more successful in handling an unexpected international crisis in Egypt. In 1952, an Egyptian army officer, Gamal Abdel Nasser, had overthrown the monarchy of King Farouk and set out to become the leader of the Arab world. To do so, he promised to destroy the new Israeli nation, created in 1948, and vowed to end British and French imperialism in the region. Nasser, with Soviet support, first sought to take control of the Suez Canal, the internationally managed waterway in Egypt connecting the Mediterranean and Red Seas.

The canal had opened in 1869 as a joint French–Egyptian venture. From 1882 on, British troops had protected the canal as the British Empire's "lifeline" to oil in the Middle East and to India and its other Asian colonies. When Nasser's regime pressed for the withdrawal of the British forces, Eisenhower and Dulles supported the demand. In 1954, an Anglo–Egyptian treaty provided for the withdrawal of British troops within twenty months.

In 1955, Nasser, adept at playing both sides in the cold war, announced a huge arms deal with the Soviet Union. The United States countered by offering to help Egypt finance a massive hydroelectric dam at Aswan on the Nile River. In 1956, when Nasser increased trade with the Soviet bloc and recognized the People's Republic of China, Dulles abruptly cancelled the Aswan Dam offer.

Unable to retaliate directly against the United States, Nasser seized control of the French-based Suez Canal Company and denied Israel-bound ships access through the canal. The British and French were furious, but they needed a pretext for military action. Israel soon provided one. On September 30, 1956, Israeli, British, and French officials secretly hatched a plan: Israel would invade Egypt and race west to the Suez Canal. The French and British would then send troops to the canal zone, posing as peacekeepers to keep Egypt and Israel separated.

On October 29, 1956, Israeli paratroopers dropped into Egypt. The British and French governments then issued an ultimatum demanding that the fighting cease. When Egypt rejected the ultimatum, British warplanes began bombing Egyptian airfields. On November 5, British and French soldiers invaded the canal zone. Nasser responded by sinking all forty of the international ships then in the Suez Canal. A few days later, Anglo-French commandos and paratroopers took control of the canal.

Eisenhower was furious that the three nations had hatched their scheme and attacked Egypt without informing the American government. He bluntly told Anthony Eden, the British prime minister, that he "flatly reject[ed] the thought of using force" in Egypt. And he resolved to put a stop to the invasion. "How could we possibly support Britain and France," he asked, "if in doing so we lose the whole Arab world?"

Eisenhower demanded that the British and French withdraw and that the Israelis evacuate the Sinai Peninsula—or face severe economic sanctions. That the three aggressor nations grudgingly complied on November 7 testified to Eisenhower's strength, influence, and savvy. The Suez debacle caused the downfall of the British government and hastened the process of independence among its remaining colonies. But perhaps its major result was that the British government realized that never again would it be able to act independently of the United States. Egypt reopened the Suez Canal, and, as Eisenhower had predicted, operated it in a professional, nonpolitical manner.

The **Suez crisis** and the Hungarian revolt led Democrat Adlai Stevenson to declare the administration's foreign policy "bankrupt." Eleanor Roosevelt complained that Eisenhower's opposition to "our oldest and strongest allies . . . is an ironic, strange, and horrible situation."

Most Americans, however, reasoned that the crises actually affirmed the nation's status as *the* global superpower. Voters handed Eisenhower an even more lopsided victory than the one in 1952. In carrying Louisiana, Eisenhower became the first Republican to win a Lower South state since Reconstruction; nationally, he carried all but seven states and won the electoral vote 457 to 73. Eisenhower's decisive victory, however, failed to swing a congressional majority for his party in either house.

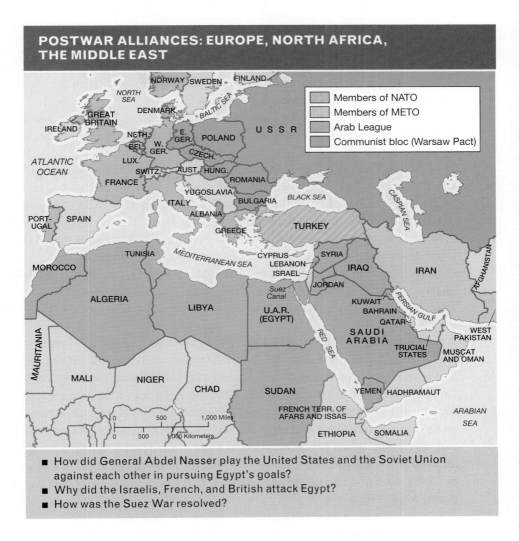

POSTWAR ALLIANCES: EUROPE, NORTH AFRICA, THE MIDDLE EAST

Legend:
- Members of NATO
- Members of METO
- Arab League
- Communist bloc (Warsaw Pact)

- How did General Abdel Nasser play the United States and the Soviet Union against each other in pursuing Egypt's goals?
- Why did the Israelis, French, and British attack Egypt?
- How was the Suez War resolved?

SPUTNIK On October 4, 1957, the Soviets shocked the United States by launching the first communications satellite, called *Sputnik*, a polished aluminum sphere the size of a beach ball. Americans panicked at the news, believing that if the Soviets could put a satellite in orbit, they could also fire a rocket with a nuclear warhead across the Pacific Ocean and detonate it on the West Coast. "It was a frightful blow," said a radio commentator. America had grown "soft and complacent," assuming that it was "Number One in everything." Yet now the United States had been bested in space by its Soviet rival. Senator Lyndon B. Johnson warned that the Russians would soon be "dropping bombs on us from space like kids dropping rocks on cars from freeway overpasses."

The Soviet success in space dealt a severe blow to the prestige of American science and technology, which had seemed unquestionably preeminent since the Second World War. It also changed the military balance of power. If the Soviets were so advanced in rocketry, many people reasoned, then perhaps they could hit U.S. cities with nuclear missiles.

Democrats charged that the Soviets had "humiliated" the United States and launched a congressional investigation to assess the new threat to the nation's security.

"*Sputnik*-mania" led the United States to increase defense spending and establish a crash program to enhance science education. In 1958, Congress created the National Aeronautics and Space Administration (NASA) to coordinate research and development related to outer space. The same year, Congress, with Eisenhower's support, enacted the National Defense Education Act (NDEA), which authorized large federal grants to colleges and universities to enhance education and research in mathematics, science, and modern languages, as well as for student loans and fellowships. The NDEA provided more financial aid to higher education than any other previous legislation.

THE EISENHOWER DOCTRINE In the aftermath of the Suez crisis, Eisenhower decided that the United States must replace Great Britain and France as the guarantor of Western interests in the Middle East. In 1958, Congress approved what came to be called the Eisenhower Doctrine, a resolution that promised to extend economic and military aid to Arab nations and to use armed force if necessary to assist any such nation against Communist aggression. When Lebanon appealed to the United States to help fend off an insurgency, Eisenhower ordered 5,000 marines into the country. In October 1958, once the situation had stabilized, U.S. forces (up to 15,000 at one point) withdrew.

CRISIS IN BERLIN Since the Second World War, West Berlin had become an oasis of Western democracy and prosperity in Communist East Germany, while East Berlin continued to be administered by the Soviet Union. West Berlin also served as an enticing alternative to life behind the "iron curtain." Each year, thousands of East Germans escaped to West Berlin. Nikita Khrushchev, the unpredictable Soviet leader, called West Berlin a "bone in my throat."

On November 10, 1958, Khrushchev threatened to give East Germany control of East Berlin and of the air lanes into West Berlin. After the deadline he set (May 27, 1959), Western authorities would have to deal with the Soviet-controlled East German government, in effect officially recognizing it, or face the possibility of another blockade of the city.

Nikita Khruschev A fiery speaker, the Soviet premier addresses journalists at a press conference in 1959.

Eisenhower told Khrushchev that he "would hit the Russians" with every weapon in the American arsenal if they persisted in their efforts to intimidate West Berlin. At the same time, however, Eisenhower also sought a settlement. There was little hope of resolving the conflicting views on Berlin, but the negotiations distracted attention from the May 27 deadline, which passed almost unnoticed. In September 1959, Khrushchev and Eisenhower agreed that the time was ripe for a summit meeting.

THE U-2 SUMMIT The summit meeting literally crashed and burned, however, when on Sunday morning, May 1, 1960, a Soviet rocket brought down a U.S. spy plane (called the U-2) flying over the Soviet Union. Khrushchev, embarrassed by the ability of American spy planes to enter Soviet airspace, then sprang a trap on Eisenhower. The Soviets announced only that the plane had been shot down. The U.S. government, not realizing that the Soviets had captured the pilot, said it was missing a weather plane over Turkey. It was a lie. Khrushchev announced that the Soviets had American pilot Francis Gary Powers "alive and kicking" and also had the photographs Powers had taken of Soviet military installations.

On May 11, Eisenhower abandoned U.S. efforts to cover up the incident. Rather than blame others, he took personal responsibility for the spying

Fidel Castro Castro (center) became Cuba's Communist premier in 1959 after three years of guerrilla warfare that overthrew the Batista regime.

program, explaining that such illegally obtained intelligence information was crucial to national security. At the testy summit meeting in Paris five days later, Khrushchev lectured Eisenhower for forty-five minutes before walking out. The U-2 incident set back efforts to reduce cold war tensions. Later, in 1962, Francis Gary Powers would be exchanged for a captured Soviet spy.

COMMUNIST CUBA Of all of Eisenhower's crises in foreign affairs, the greatest embarrassment was Fidel Castro's new Communist regime in Cuba, which came to power on January 1, 1959, after two years of guerrilla warfare against the corrupt U.S.-supported dictator, Fulgencio Batista. Castro, a fiery young lawyer, readily embraced Soviet support, leading a CIA agent to predict, "We're going to take care of Castro just like we took care of Arbenz [in Guatemala]." The Soviets warned that any American intervention in Cuba would trigger a military response. One of Eisenhower's last acts as president, on January 3, 1961, was to suspend diplomatic relations with Castro's Cuba. Eisenhower also set in motion a secret CIA operation to train a force of Cuban refugees to oust Castro. It would be up to Eisenhower's successor, John F. Kennedy, to launch the invasion.

EVALUATING THE EISENHOWER PRESIDENCY

During President Eisenhower's second term, Congress added Alaska and Hawaii as the forty-ninth and fiftieth states (1959), while the nation experienced its worst economic slump since the Great Depression. Volatile issues such as civil rights, defense policy, and corrupt aides, including White House chief of staff Sherman Adams, compounded the administration's troubles. The president's desire to avoid divisive issues and maintain public goodwill led him at times to value harmony and popularity over justice. One observer called the Eisenhower years "the time of the great postponement" during which the president left domestic and foreign policies "about where he found them in 1953."

Opinion of Eisenhower's presidency has improved with time, however. He presided with steady self-confidence over a prosperous nation. In dealing with crises, he displayed unusually good judgment and firmness of purpose. He fulfilled his pledge to end the war in Korea, refused to intervene militarily in Indochina, and maintained the peace in the face of explosive global tensions. Eisenhower's greatest decisions were the wars he chose to avoid. After the truce in Korea, not a single American soldier died in combat during his two administrations, something no president since has achieved. For the most part, he acted with poise, restraint, and intelligence in managing an increasingly complex cold war.

If Eisenhower refused to take the lead in addressing social and racial problems, he did balance the budget while sustaining the major reforms of the New Deal. If he tolerated unemployment of as much as 7 percent, he saw to it that inflation remained minimal. Even Adlai Stevenson admitted that Ike's victory in 1952 had been good for America. "I like Ike, too," he said.

Eisenhower's January 17, 1961, farewell address focused on the threat posed to government integrity by "an immense military establishment and a large arms industry." It was all the more striking for Eisenhower, a celebrated military leader, to highlight the dangers of a large "military-industrial complex" exerting "unwarranted influence" in Congress and the White House. "The potential for the disastrous rise of misplaced power exists and will persist," he warned.

Eisenhower confessed that his greatest disappointment was that he could affirm only that "war has been avoided," not that "a lasting peace is in sight." Despite the combative language of Secretary of State John Foster Dulles, Eisenhower never promoted warfare as an instrument of foreign policy. Instead, he pledged to "do anything to achieve peace within honorable means. I'll travel anywhere. I'll talk to anyone." His successors were not as successful in keeping war at bay.

CHAPTER REVIEW

SUMMARY

- **Eisenhower's Dynamic Conservatism**   President Eisenhower promoted *moderate Republicanism*, or "dynamic conservatism." While critical of excessive government spending on social programs, he expanded Social Security coverage and launched ambitious public works programs, such as the *Federal-Aid Highway Act* that constructed the Interstate Highway System.

- **Growth of the U.S. Economy**   High levels of federal government spending continued during the postwar period. The *GI Bill of Rights* boosted home buying and helped many veterans attend college and enter the middle class. Consumer demand for homes, cars, and household goods fueled the economy.

- **Critics of Mainstream Culture**   The *Beats* and many other writers and artists rebelled against what they claimed was the suffocating conformity of middle-class life. Adolescents rebelled through acts of juvenile delinquency and a new form of sexually provocative music called rock 'n' roll. Pockets of chronic poverty persisted despite record-breaking economic growth, and minorities did not prosper to the extent that white Americans did.

- **Civil Rights Movement**   During the early 1950s, the NAACP mounted legal challenges in federal courts to states requiring racially segregated public schools. In *Brown v. Board of Education (1954)*, the U.S. Supreme Court nullified the *separate-but-equal* doctrine. Many white southerners adopted a strategy of *"massive resistance"* against court-ordered desegregation. In response, civil rights activists used *nonviolent civil disobedience* to force local and state officials to allow integration, as demonstrated in the *Montgomery bus boycott* in Alabama and the forced desegregation of public schools in Little Rock, Arkansas. Martin Luther King organized the *Southern Christian Leadership Conference (SCLC)* after white violence against activists in Little Rock. In 1957, the U.S. Congress passed a Civil Rights Act intended to stop discrimination against black voters in the South, but it was rarely enforced.

- **American Foreign Policy in the 1950s**   Eisenhower's first major foreign-policy accomplishment was to end the fighting in Korea. Thereafter, he kept the United States out of war and relied on secret *Central Intelligence Agency (CIA)* intervention, financial and military aid, and threats of *massive retaliation* to stem the spread of communism. Though American aid was not enough to save the French at *Dien Bien Phu*, Eisenhower's belief in the *"falling domino" theory* deepened U.S. support for the government in South Vietnam in its war with North Vietnam and the Communist *Viet Cong* insurgents.

CHRONOLOGY

1944	Congress passes the Servicemen's Readjustment Act (GI Bill of Rights)
1951	Alan Freed coins the term *rock 'n' roll*
1952	Eisenhower wins the presidency
July 1953	Armistice is reached in Korea
1954	*Brown v. Board of Education of Topeka, Kansas*
July 1954	Geneva Accords adopted
December 1955	Montgomery, Alabama, bus boycott begins
1956	Congress passes the Federal-Aid Highway Act
	Soviets suppress Hungarian revolt
	In Suez War, Israel, Britain, and France attack Egypt
1957	Federal troops sent to protect students attempting to integrate Central High School in Little Rock, Arkansas
	Soviet Union launches *Sputnik 1* satellite
1960	U-2 incident reveals that the United States is flying spy planes over the Soviet Union

KEY TERMS

 INQUIZITIVE

Go to InQuizitive to see what you've learned—and learn what you've missed—with personalized feedback along the way.

29 A New Frontier and a Great Society
1960–1968

The Dove (1964) African American artist Romare Bearden's collage presents a disjointed vision of a contemporary urban street scene: fragments of black bodies appear in a surreal clash of flesh and pavement, reflecting the upheaval and violence of African American life in the 1960s. At the same time, though, the titular dove presides over the scene, suggesting that a life of peace could still be in reach.

For those who considered the social and political climate of the fifties dull, the following decade provided a striking contrast. The sixties were years of extraordinary social turbulence and liberal activism, tragic assassinations and painful trauma, cultural conflict and youth rebellion. Assassins killed four of the most important leaders of the time: John F. Kennedy, Malcolm X, Martin Luther King Jr., and Robert F. Kennedy.

The "politics of expectation" that a British journalist said shone brightly in Kennedy's short tenure as president did not die with him in November 1963. Instead, Kennedy's idealistic commitment to improving America's quality of life—for everyone—was given new meaning and momentum by his successor, Texan Lyndon B. Johnson, whose war on poverty and Great Society programs outstripped Franklin Roosevelt's New Deal in their scope and promises.

Johnson's energy and legislative savvy resulted in a blizzard of new federal programs as many social issues that had been ignored or postponed for decades—civil rights for minorities, equality for women, gay rights, medical insurance, federal aid to the poor—forced their way to the forefront of national concerns.

In the end, however, Johnson promised too much. The Great Society programs fell victim to unrealistic hopes, poor execution, and the nation's deepening involvement in Vietnam. The deeply entrenched assumptions of the cold war led the nation into the longest, most controversial, and least successful war in its history to that point.

focus questions

1. What were President John F. Kennedy's efforts to contain communism abroad and pursue civil rights and other social programs at home?

2. What were the strategies and achievements of the civil rights movement in the 1960s? What divisions emerged among its activists during the decade?

3. What were Lyndon B. Johnson's major war on poverty and Great Society initiatives? How did they impact American society?

4. What were Presidents Kennedy and Johnson's motivations for deepening America's military involvement in the Vietnam War?

5. What were the issues that propelled Richard Nixon to victory in the 1968 presidential election?

THE NEW FRONTIER

In his 1960 speech accepting the Democratic presidential nomination, John F. Kennedy showcased the muscular language that would characterize his campaign and his presidency: "We stand today on the edge of a **New Frontier**—the frontier of unknown opportunities and perils—a frontier of unfulfilled hopes and threats." Kennedy and his staff fastened upon the frontier metaphor as the label for their proposed domestic program because they believed that Americans had always been adventurers, eager to conquer and exploit new frontiers. Kennedy promised that if elected he would get the country "moving again" and be a more aggressive cold warrior than Dwight Eisenhower.

KENNEDY VERSUS NIXON In 1960, the presidential election featured two candidates—Vice President Richard M. Nixon and Massachusetts senator John F. Kennedy (JFK)—of similar ages but contrasting personalities and backgrounds. As Eisenhower's partner over successive terms, Nixon was assured the Republican nomination in 1960, although President Eisenhower himself had grave misgivings. When asked by reporters to name a single major accomplishment of his vice president, Ike replied: "If you give me a week, I might think of one."

The president's snide comment undercut Nixon's claim of significant executive experience as vice president. The two Republicans had long had a testy relationship. Nixon once called his presidential boss "a goddamned old fool," while Eisenhower dismissed his fiercely ambitious vice president as a man who couldn't "think of anything but politics." On more than one occasion, Eisenhower clumsily sought to dump his vice president in favor of other Republicans whom he respected.

A native of California, the forty-seven-year-old Nixon had come to Washington after the Second World War eager to reverse the tide of New Deal liberalism. His visibility among Republicans benefited from his leadership of the anti-Communist hearings in Congress during the McCarthy hysteria. All his life, Nixon had clawed and struggled to reach the top. Now he had the presidency within his grasp. But Nixon, graceless, awkward, and stiff, proved to be one of the most complicated and most interesting political figures in American history. Kennedy told an aide that "Nixon doesn't know who he is . . . so every time he makes a speech he has to decide which Nixon he is, and that will be very exhausting."

Forty-three-year-old John Kennedy had not distinguished himself in the House or the Senate. More pragmatic than principled, he was handsome, articulate, and blessed with energy and wit. Friends said his charisma was magical.

The Kennedy–Nixon debates Nixon's decision to debate his less prominent opponent on television backfired.

"One of life's great pleasures," his brother-in-law said, "was spending time with that man."

Kennedy lit up a room with his inviting smile, athletic presence, and infectious zest for life. Coolly analytical and dangerously self-absorbed, he was a contradictory and elusive personality. Even his wife Jacqueline was unsure about him. "He may be a fine politician," she told a dinner guest, "but do we know if he's a fine person?"

This much is certain: Kennedy had a bright, agile mind, a quick wit, a Harvard education, a record of heroism in the Second World War, a rich and powerful Roman Catholic family, and a beautiful and accomplished young wife. In the words of a southern senator, Kennedy combined "the best qualities of Elvis Presley and Franklin D. Roosevelt"—a combination that played well in the first-ever televised presidential debate, as he began the process of seducing a nation.

Some 70 million people tuned in to the debate and saw an obviously uncomfortable Nixon perspiring heavily and looking pale. By contrast, Kennedy looked tanned and confident. He offered crisp answers that made him appear to be qualified for the nation's highest office. The morning after the debate, his approval ratings skyrocketed.

Kennedy's political rise owed much to the public relations campaign engineered by his father, Joseph, a self-made tycoon with a genius for promotion. In Joseph Kennedy's view, *image* was much more important than substance. "Can't you get it into your head," he told John, "that it's not important what you *really* are? The only important thing is what people *think* you are." He assured family and friends that he would "sell Jack like soap flakes" to jump-start his political career. The elder Kennedy hired talented writers to produce his son's two books, paid a publisher to print them, purchased tens of thousands of copies to make them "best sellers," and helped engineer his son's elections to the House and Senate.

John Kennedy was a relentless presidential campaigner, traveling 65,000 miles, visiting twenty-five states, and making more than 350 speeches, including an address to Protestant ministers in Texas in which he neutralized concerns about his being a Roman Catholic by stressing that the pope in Rome would never "tell the President—should he be a Catholic—how to act." In speech after speech, Kennedy said he was tired of waking up and reading about what Soviet and Cuban leaders were doing. Instead, he wanted to read about what the U.S. president was doing to combat communism. He wanted to develop a foreign policy that would break out of the confining assumptions of the Cold War, but as yet had no clear plan for doing so.

Kennedy also worked to increase the registration of African American voters across the nation. His response to the growing civil rights movement was ambivalent, however. Like Eisenhower, Kennedy believed racial unrest needed to be handled with caution rather than boldness. To him, racial justice was less an urgent moral crusade than a potential barrier to his election. He understood the injustices of bigotry and segregation, but he needed the votes of southern whites to win the presidency.

During the campaign, Kennedy won the hearts of many black voters by helping to get Martin Luther King Jr. out of a Georgia jail after King had been unjustly convicted of "trespassing" in an all-white restaurant. "I've got a suitcase of votes," said King's appreciative father, "and I'm going to take them to Mr. Kennedy and dump them in his lap." On the Sunday before Election Day, a million leaflets describing Kennedy's effort to release King from prison were distributed in African American churches across the nation.

In November, Kennedy and his running mate, powerful Texas senator Lyndon B. Johnson, won one of the closest presidential elections in history. Their

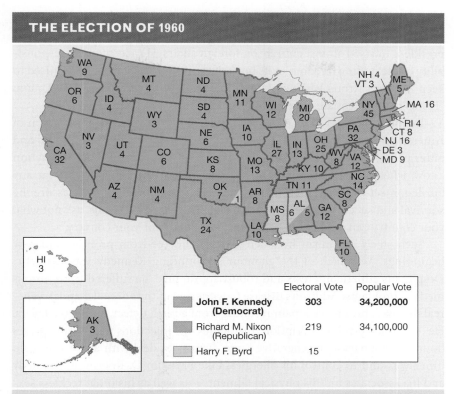

THE ELECTION OF 1960

	Electoral Vote	Popular Vote
John F. Kennedy (Democrat)	**303**	**34,200,000**
Richard M. Nixon (Republican)	219	34,100,000
Harry F. Byrd	15	

- How did the election of 1960 represent a sea change in American presidential politics?
- How did John F. Kennedy win the election in spite of winning fewer states than Richard M. Nixon?

margin was only 118,574 votes out of more than 68 million cast. Nixon won more states than Kennedy, but the Democrat captured 70 percent of the black vote, which proved decisive in at least three key states.

A VIGOROUS NEW ADMINISTRATION John F. Kennedy was the youngest person and first Roman Catholic elected president. He had promised "to get America moving again," and he was eager to begin that effort. At times, he seemed self-assured to the point of cockiness. "Sure it's a big job," he told a reporter. "But I don't know anybody who can do it any better than I can." That he had been elected by the narrowest of margins and had no working majority in Congress did not faze him. In his mind, he was destined to be a great president.

Kennedy's inauguration ceremony on a cold, sunny, blustery January day introduced the nation to his distinctive elegance and flair. In his speech, the new president focused almost entirely on foreign affairs. He accepted the responsibility of "defending freedom in its hour of maximum danger" and promised to keep America strong while seeking to reduce friction with the Soviet Union: "Let us never negotiate out of fear, but let us never fear to negotiate."

Kennedy claimed "that the torch has been passed to a new generation of Americans—born in this century, tempered by war, disciplined by a hard and bitter peace," and he dazzled listeners with uplifting words: "Let every nation know, whether it wishes us well or ill, that we shall pay any price, bear any burden, meet any hardship, support any friend, oppose any foe, to assure the survival and success of liberty. . . . And so, my fellow Americans: ask not what your country can do for you—ask what *you* can do for your country."

Such steely optimism heralded a presidency of fresh promise and new beginnings. Yet much of the glamour surrounding Kennedy was cosmetic. Despite his athletic interests and robust appearance, he suffered from serious medical problems: Addison's disease (a withering of the adrenal glands), venereal disease, chronic back pain resulting from a birth defect, and fierce fevers. He took powerful prescription medicines or injections daily, sometimes hourly, to manage a degenerative bone disease, to deal with anxiety, to help him sleep, and to control his allergies. Like Franklin D. Roosevelt, Kennedy and his associates hid his physical ailments—as well as his often reckless sexual dalliances in the White House with a galaxy of women, including actress Marilyn Monroe and Judith Campbell Exner, the girlfriend of a Chicago mob boss. When Kennedy met British prime minister Harold Macmillan, he told him that "I don't know about you, Harold, but if I don't have a woman every three days, I get these terrible headaches. How about you?"

Kennedy was determined to bring together the "best and the brightest" minds to fashion a "vigorous" new era in political achievement. He represented a new generation of political figures who had fought in the Second World War. Known as the "pragmatic generation," they were decisive and bold and prized the "manly" virtues, especially courage and conviction in the face of the Cold War and the threat of nuclear conflict. The new secretary of defense, Robert McNamara, the whiz-kid president of Ford Motor Company, displayed the cult of activism surrounding the Kennedy administration when he stressed that it was better to "have a wrong decision made than no decision at all." With at times an almost dismissive arrogance, Kennedy frequently complained about "academics" who spent all their time criticizing statesmen without exercising responsibility themselves. In the White House, he observed, he and others could not afford to be professorial. The Oval Office was "where decisions have to be made."

Jack and Jackie Young, dashing, wealthy, and culturally sophisticated, the Kennedys were instant celebrities. Women imitated the First Lady's famous hairdo, while men craved JFK's effortless "cool" and youthful energy.

Yet Kennedy had a difficult time launching his New Frontier domestic program. His narrow election victory gave him no mandate, and he faced a congressional roadblock in the form of conservative southern Democrats who joined with Republicans to oppose his efforts to increase federal aid to education, provide medical insurance for the aged, and create a cabinet-level department of urban affairs and housing to address inner-city poverty. In his first year, Kennedy submitted 355 legislative requests; Congress approved only half of them. He suffered so many defeats that he complained he "couldn't get a Mother's Day resolution through the goddamned Congress."

Legislators did approve increasing the minimum wage, a Housing Act that earmarked nearly $5 billion for new public housing projects in poverty-stricken inner-city areas, the Peace Corps, created in 1961 to recruit idealistic young volunteers who would provide educational and technical service abroad, and the Alliance for Progress, a financial assistance program to Latin American countries intended to blunt the appeal of communism in those nations. But the president's efforts to provide more assistance for educational programs and medical care for the elderly never got out of committees.

Perhaps Kennedy's greatest legislative success was in convincing Congress to commit $40 billion to put an American on the moon within ten years.

(It would happen in 1969.) What spurred the start of the program was the news that the Soviets had launched the first manned space flight in 1961. Former president Eisenhower said that Kennedy's "race to the moon for national prestige is nuts." But Vice President Lyndon Johnson assured the president that "dramatic accomplishments in space are being increasingly identified as a major indicator of world leadership." Kennedy explained that he had decided to shoot for the moon not because it is "easy, but because it is hard, because that goal will serve to organize and measure the best of our energies and skills."

CIVIL RIGHTS   The most important developments in domestic life during the sixties occurred in civil rights. Throughout the South, racial segregation remained firmly in place. Signs outside public restrooms distinguished between "whites" and "colored"; restaurants declared "Colored Not Allowed," or "Colored Served Only in Rear." Stores prohibited African Americans from trying on clothes before buying them. Despite the *Brown v. Board of Education* ruling in 1954, many public schools across the South remained segregated and unequal in quality.

Like Franklin D. Roosevelt, President Kennedy celebrated racial equality but did little to promote it until forced to do so. His caution reflected his narrow election margin in 1960. He was reluctant to challenge conservative southern Democrats on the explosive issue of segregation. Both he and his brother Robert ("Bobby"), the attorney general and his closest adviser, had to be dragged into actively supporting the civil rights movement. After appointing Harris Wofford, a white law professor and experienced campaigner for racial equality, as the special presidential assistant for civil rights, President Kennedy told him "to make substantial headway against . . . the nonsense of racial discrimination," but to do so with "minimum civil rights legislation [and] maximum Executive action." Such actions led Martin Luther King Jr. to comment that Kennedy had great political skill but no "moral passion" about the need to end racial injustice.

CATASTROPHE IN CUBA   Kennedy's performance in foreign relations was spectacularly mixed. Although he had told a reporter that he wanted to "break out of the confines of the Cold War," he quickly found himself reinforcing its confining assumptions. While still a senator, Kennedy had blasted President Eisenhower for not being tough enough with the Soviets and for allowing Fidel Castro and his Communist followers to take over Cuba, just ninety miles from the southern tip of Florida.

Soon after his inauguration, Kennedy learned that a secret CIA operation, which had been approved by Eisenhower, was training 1,500 anti-Castro Cubans in Guatemala, Texas, and Florida to invade their homeland in hopes

Walk of shame Captured anti-Castro Cubans after the failed invasion at the Bay of Pigs.

of triggering a mass uprising against Castro. U.S. military leaders assured Kennedy that the invasion plan (Operation Trinidad) was feasible; CIA analysts predicted that news of the invasion would inspire anti-Castro Cubans to rebel against their Communist dictator.

In reality, the covert operation had little chance of succeeding. Its assumptions were flawed, its strategy faulty, its tactics bungled, and the forces and weapons used inadequate. Kennedy seemed to realize it might fail when he callously said, "If we have to get rid of those 800 men [actually 1,400], it is much better to dump them in Cuba than in the United States."

When the ragtag force of right-wing Cubans, transported on American ships, landed before dawn at the **Bay of Pigs** on Cuba's south shore on April 17, 1961, Castro's forces were waiting for them. Kennedy panicked when he realized the operation was failing and refused desperate pleas from the rebels for "promised" support from U.S. warplanes. General Lyman Lemnitzer, chair of the Joint Chiefs of Staff, said that Kennedy's "pulling out the rug [on the Cuban invaders] was . . . absolutely reprehensible, almost criminal." Some 1,200 rebels were captured; the rest were killed. (Kennedy later paid $53 million to ransom the captured rebels).

The clumsy effort to overthrow the Cuban government was a complete failure. It humiliated Kennedy and elevated Castro in the eyes of the world. To his credit, Kennedy admitted that the Bay of Pigs invasion was a "colossal mistake." Only later did he learn that the planners of the operation had assumed that he would commit American forces once the invasion effort had failed. He said that after the initial disastrous reports from the Bay of Pigs, "we all looked at each other and asked, 'How could we have been so stupid?'" After the failed invasion, Kennedy never again trusted his trigger-happy military and intelligence leaders.

THE VIENNA SUMMIT   Just weeks after the Bay of Pigs invasion, Kennedy met Soviet premier Nikita Khrushchev at a summit conference in Vienna, Austria. Khrushchev badgered and bullied the young president, bragged about the superiority of communism, and threatened to take control of all of Berlin, the divided city inside Communist East Germany. A stunned Kennedy told the British prime minister that Khrushchev was "much more of a barbarian" than he had expected. He confided to a journalist that the summit "was awful. Worst thing of my life. He rolled right over me—he thinks I'm a fool—he thinks I'm weak." When asked what he planned to do next, Kennedy replied: "I have to confront them [the Soviets] someplace to show that we're tough."

The first thing Kennedy did upon returning to the White House was to request an estimate of how many Americans might be killed in a nuclear war with the Soviet Union. The answer was chilling: 70 million. Kennedy, desperate not to appear weak in the face of Khrushchev's aggressive actions in Germany, asked Congress for additional spending on defense and called up 156,000 members of the Army Reserve and National Guard to protect West Berlin. He also ordered an armed military convoy to travel from West Germany across East Germany to West Berlin to show the Soviets that he would protect the city with force.

The Soviets responded on August 13, 1961. They stopped all traffic between East and West Berlin and began erecting the twenty-seven-mile-long **Berlin Wall** to separate East Berlin from West Berlin, where thousands of refugees were fleeing communism each week, many of them the best and the brightest: engineers, doctors, scientists, and writers. For the United States, the wall became a powerful propaganda weapon in the Cold War. As Kennedy said, "Freedom has many difficulties and democracy is not perfect, but we have never had to put up a wall to keep our people in."

The Berlin Wall demonstrated the Soviets' willingness to challenge American resolve in Europe. In response, Kennedy and Secretary of Defense Robert McNamara embarked upon the most intensive arms race in history, increasing the number of nuclear missiles fivefold, adding 300,000 men to the armed

Severed ties Two West Berliners climb the newly constructed Berlin Wall to talk with a family member at an open window.

forces, and creating the U.S. Special Forces (Green Berets), an elite group of commandos who specialized in guerrilla warfare and could provide a "more flexible response" than nuclear weapons to "hot spots" around the world.

THE CUBAN MISSILE CRISIS Soon after taking office, President Kennedy predicted that "we shall have to test anew" whether a nation "such as ours can endure." It was an accurate prediction. In the fall of 1962, Nikita Khrushchev and the Soviets decided to challenge Kennedy again. To protect Communist Cuba from another American-backed invasion and to show critics at home that he was not afraid of the Americans, Khrushchev approved the secret installation of Soviet missiles on the island nation. The Soviets felt they were justified in doing so because Kennedy, after the Bay of Pigs invasion, had ordered that U.S. missiles with nuclear warheads be installed in Turkey, along the Soviet border.

On October 16, 1962, Kennedy learned that photos taken two days earlier by U.S. spy planes showed some forty Soviet missile sites and twenty-five jet bombers in Cuba. "We have some big trouble," he alerted his brother Bobby by phone.

Over the next thirteen days, perhaps the most dangerous two weeks in history, Kennedy and the National Security Council (NSC) considered several possible responses, ranging from doing nothing to invading Cuba. The world held its breath as the NSC discussed the unthinkable possibility of a nuclear exchange with the Soviets. The commander of the U.S. Marines at one point reminded the group that the missiles in Cuba were not a true strategic threat; the Soviet Union, he said, "has a hell of a lot better way to attack us than to attack us from Cuba." Secretary of Defense Robert McNamara agreed, noting that "it makes no difference whether you are killed by a missile fired from the Soviet Union or from Cuba." Yet the group insisted that the missiles be removed for symbolic reasons.

Eventually, the NSC fastened on two options: (1) a "surgical" air strike on the missiles, followed, if necessary, by an invasion, or (2) a naval blockade of Cuba in which U.S. warships would stop Soviet vessels and search them for missiles. Although most of the military advisers supported the first option, Kennedy chose the blockade, prompting a general to shout, "You're screwed! You're screwed!"

Kennedy, however, had been burned by overconfident military advisers during the Bay of Pigs operation and was not going to let it happen again. He also feared that an American attack on Cuba would give the Soviets an excuse to take control of West Berlin.

On Monday night, October 22, a grim Kennedy delivered a televised speech of the "highest national urgency" to the world, announcing that the U.S. Navy was establishing a "quarantine" of Cuba to prevent Soviet ships from delivering more weapons to the island nation. Kennedy added that he had "directed the armed forces to prepare for any eventuality." He closed by urging the Soviets to "move the world back from the abyss of destruction." The world watched as tensions grew, and some 200,000 U.S. soldiers made their way to southern Florida.

Khrushchev replied that Soviet ships would ignore the quarantine and accused Kennedy of "an act of aggression propelling humankind into the abyss of a world nuclear-missile war." Despite such rhetoric, however, on Wednesday, October 24, five Soviet ships, presumably with more missiles aboard, stopped well short of the quarantine line.

Two days later, Khrushchev, knowing that the United States still enjoyed a 5 to 1 advantage in nuclear weapons, offered a deal. The Soviets would agree to remove the missiles already in Cuba in return for a *public* pledge by the United States never to invade Cuba—and a *secret* agreement to remove U.S. missiles from Turkey. Kennedy agreed. Secretary of State Dean Rusk stressed to a newscaster, "Remember, when you report this, [say] that eyeball to eyeball, they [the Soviets] blinked first." The air force chief of staff, General Curtis Lemay, who had urged an air attack on Cuba, called the deal "the greatest defeat in our history."

In the aftermath of the **Cuban missile crisis**, tensions between the United States and the Soviet Union subsided, in part because of several symbolic steps: an agreement to sell the Soviet Union surplus American wheat, the installation of a "hotline" telephone between Washington and Moscow to provide instant contact between the heads of government, and the removal of U.S. missiles from Turkey, Italy, and Britain.

"PEACE FOR ALL TIME" Going to the edge of nuclear war led Kennedy and others in the administration to soften their Cold War rhetoric and pursue other ways to reduce the threat of atomic warfare. As Kennedy told his advisers, "It is insane that two men, sitting on opposite sides of the world, should be able to decide to bring an end to civilization." He told an audience at American University on June 10, 1963, that his new goal was "not merely peace in our time, but peace for all time," which would require reducing the risk of nuclear warfare. "We all inhabit this small planet," he explained. "We all breathe the same air."

What kind of peace did he seek? "Not the peace of the grave or the security of the slave. I am talking about . . . the kind of peace that makes life on earth worth living, the kind that enables men and nations to grow, and to hope,

The Cuban missile crisis Photographs taken from a U.S. surveillance plane on October 14, 1962, revealed both Soviet missile launchers and missile shelters near San Cristóbal, Cuba.

and build a better life for their children—not merely peace for Americans but peace for all men and women, not merely peace in our time but peace for all time."

Soon after delivering this speech, the president began discussions with Soviet and British leaders to reduce the risk of nuclear war. The discussions resulted in the Test Ban Treaty, ratified in September 1963, which banned the testing of nuclear weapons in the atmosphere. It was the first joint agreement of the Cold War and an important move toward improved relations with the Soviet Union. As Kennedy put it, using an ancient Chinese proverb, "A journey of a thousand miles begins with one step."

VIETNAM As tensions with the Soviet Union eased, a new crisis was growing in Southeast Asia, where events were moving toward what would eventually become the greatest American foreign-policy calamity of the century. Throughout the fifties, U.S. officials increasingly came to view the preservation of South Vietnam as the critical test of American willpower in the Cold War. In 1956, then senator John F. Kennedy described South Vietnam as the "cornerstone of the free world in Southeast Asia."

Yet the situation in South Vietnam had worsened under the corrupt leadership of Premier Ngo Dinh Diem and his family. Diem had backed away from promised social and economic reforms, and his repressive tactics, directed not only against Communists but also against the Buddhist majority and other critics, played into the hands of his enemies.

President Eisenhower had provided over $1 billion in aid to Diem's government during the late fifties. Kennedy sent even more weapons, money, and some 16,000 military advisers to South Vietnam to help shore up the government. (They were called "advisers" to avoid the impression that U.S. soldiers were doing the fighting.) In the countryside of South Vietnam, the National Liberation Front (NLF), a left-wing nationalist movement backed by Communist Vietnam, had launched a violent insurgency in which guerrilla fighters known as the Viet Cong (VC), were winning the fight against the South Vietnamese government. American military advisers began relocating Vietnamese peasants to "strategic hamlets"—new villages ringed by barbed wire—where the VC could not receive assistance.

By the fall of 1963, Kennedy agreed with his top advisers that Diem was "out of touch with his people" and had to be removed—in large part because he refused to follow American orders. On November 1, Vietnamese generals, with the approval of U.S. officials, took control of the Saigon government. They then took a step that Kennedy had neither intended nor expected: they murdered Diem and his brother. The rebel generals, however, soon fell to fighting one another, leaving Vietnam even more vulnerable to the Communist insurgency. Thereafter, unstable South Vietnam essentially became an American colony. The United States put the generals in power, gave the orders, and provided massive financial support, much of which was diverted into the hands of corrupt politicians.

By September 1963, Kennedy had developed doubts about the ability of the United States to defend the South Vietnamese. "In the final analysis," he told aides, "it's their war. They're the ones who have to win it or lose it. We can help them as advisers but they have to win it." Yet only a week later, in a televised interview, Kennedy reiterated the domino theory endorsed by Presidents Truman and Eisenhower, saying that if South Vietnam fell to communism, the rest of Southeast Asia would soon follow. He stressed that "we should stay [in South Vietnam]. We should use our influence in as effective a way as we can, but we should not withdraw."

KENNEDY'S ASSASSINATION What Kennedy would have done in Vietnam has remained a matter of endless discussion, because on November 22, 1963, while riding in an open car through Dallas, Texas, he was shot and killed by Lee Harvey Oswald, a twenty-four-year-old ex-Marine turned Communist. Oswald, who had lived for a time in the Soviet Union, idolized Fidel Castro and hated the United States and its capitalist system. As he fled the scene after shooting Kennedy, he also shot and killed a Dallas policeman.

Debate still swirls about whether Oswald acted alone or as part of a conspiracy because he did not live long enough to tell his story. As he was being transported to a court hearing, Jack Ruby, a Dallas nightclub owner distraught over Kennedy's death, shot and killed the handcuffed Oswald as a nationwide television audience watched.

Kennedy's shocking assassination and heartrending funeral enshrined the president in the public imagination as a martyred leader cut down in the prime of his life. He came to have a stronger reputation after his death than he enjoyed in life. "That debonair touch, that shock of chestnut hair, that beguiling grin, that shattering understatement—these are what we shall remember," wrote newspaper columnist Mary McGrory. Kennedy's drama-filled, thousand-day presidency had flamed up and out like a comet hitting the earth's atmosphere. Americans wept in the streets, and the world was on edge as the wounded nation buried its fallen president. Roy Wilkins, a prominent civil rights leader, noted that "the bullet that killed Kennedy paralyzed the civil rights movement" as the world welcomed a new and very different president, Lyndon Johnson.

"President Shot Dead" Commuters react to the news of President Kennedy's assassination on November 22, 1963.

CIVIL RIGHTS

After the Montgomery bus boycott of 1955–1956, Martin Luther King Jr.'s philosophy of militant nonviolence stirred others to challenge the deeply entrenched patterns of racial segregation in the South. During the sixties, King became the face and heart of the civil rights movement. His goal was integration and equality, and he was an uplifting example of fortitude and dignity in confronting brutality and oppression. By nature, he was inspirational and courageous, with an astonishing capacity for forgiveness and a deep understanding of the dynamics of political power and social change. Yet he was also immensely complicated and contradictory, even hypocritical, as the FBI discovered by subjecting him to relentless electronic surveillance and even blackmail.

King was neither a genius nor a saint, but his shortcomings pale into insignificance when compared to his achievements. He was one of the world's most inspiring examples of courage, conviction, and dignity in the face of often violent prejudice and persecution. With the help of those he led and inspired,

King changed the trajectory of American history—for the better. Alas, he did not live to see the promised land made possible by his actions.

SIT-INS The civil rights movement gained momentum when four brave African American college students sat down and ordered coffee and dough-nuts at an "all-white" Woolworth's lunch counter in Greensboro, North Car-olina, on February 1, 1960. The clerk refused to serve them, explaining that blacks had to eat standing up or take their food outside.

The Greensboro Four, as the students came to be called, waited forty-five minutes and then returned the next day with two dozen more students. As they sat for hours, fruitlessly waiting to be served, some read Bibles; others read Henry David Thoreau's famous essay on civil disobedience. They returned every day for a week, patiently tolerating being jeered at, jostled, and spat upon by white hooligans.

Within two months, similar sit-ins—involving 50,000 blacks and whites, men and women, young and old—had occurred in more than 100 cities. Black comedian Dick Gregory participated in several sit-ins at whites-only restau-rants. When the managers told him, "We don't serve Negroes," he replied: "No problem, I don't eat Negroes." Some 3,600 people were arrested nationwide, but the sit-ins worked. By the end of July 1960, officials in Greensboro lifted the whites-only policy. The civil rights movement had found an effective new, nonviolent tactic against segregation.

In April 1960, some 200 student activists, black and white, converged in Raleigh, North Carolina, to form the **Student Nonviolent Coordinat-ing Committee** (**SNCC**—pronounced "snick"). The goal of what they called "the movement" was to intensify the effort to dismantle segregation. SNCC expanded the sit-ins to include "kneel-ins" at all-white churches and "wade-ins" at segregated public swimming pools. In many communities, demonstra-tors were pelted with rocks, burned with cigarettes, and even killed by white racists. As a Florida hog farmer named Holstead "Hoss" Manucy told a jour-nalist, "I ain't got no bad habits. Don't smoke. Don't cuss. My only bad habit is fightin' niggahs."

FREEDOM RIDES In 1961, civil rights leaders decided to focus on inte-grating public transportation: buses and trains. Their larger goal was to force the Kennedy administration to engage the cause of civil rights in the South. On May 4, the New York–based Congress of Racial Equality (CORE), led by James Farmer, decided to put "the civil rights movement on wheels" when a courageous group of eighteen black and white **Freedom Riders**, as they were

Civil rights and its peaceful warriors The Greensboro Four—(listed from left) Joseph McNeil, Franklin McCain, Billy Smith, and Clarence Henderson—await service on day two of their sit-in at the Woolworth's in Greensboro, North Carolina.

called, boarded two public buses traveling from Washington, D.C., through the Lower South to New Orleans. They wanted to test a federal court ruling that banned racial segregation on buses and trains, and in terminals.

On May 14, a mob of white racists in rural Alabama, many of them members of the Ku Klux Klan, surrounded the Greyhound bus carrying the "Freedom Riders." After throwing a firebomb into the bus, the Klan members barricaded its door. "Burn them alive," one of them yelled. "Fry the damned niggers." The riders were able to escape, only to be battered with metal pipes, chains, and clubs.

A few hours later, Freedom Riders on a second bus were beaten after entering whites-only waiting rooms at the bus terminal in Birmingham, Alabama. The police, as it turned out, had encouraged the beatings. Alabama's governor complained that the Freedom Riders were violating "our law and customs," but the brutality displayed on television caused national outrage. The next day, the Freedom Riders wanted to continue their trip, but the bus drivers refused.

Freedom Riders On May 14, 1961, a white mob in Alabama assaulted a Freedom Bus, flinging fire bombs into its windows and beating the activists as they emerged. Here, the surviving Freedom Riders sit outside the burnt shell of their bus.

When Diane Nash, a fearless black college student and SNCC leader in Nashville, Tennessee, heard about the violence in Birmingham, she recruited new riders. President Kennedy called her, warning that she would "get killed if you do this," but she refused to back down. "It doesn't matter if we're killed," she told the president. "Others will come—others will come."

On May 17, Nash and ten other students took a bus to Birmingham, where they were arrested. While in jail, they sang "freedom songs": "We'll Never Turn Back," "Ain't Gonna Let Nobody Turn Me Around," "We Shall Overcome." Eugene "Bull" Connor, the city's notoriously racist police chief, grew so frustrated at their joyous rebelliousness that he drove them in the middle of the night to the Tennessee state line and dropped them off to walk. Instead of going back to Nashville, however, the gutsy students returned to Birmingham.

President Kennedy was not inspired by the Freedom Riders. To him, they were a "pain in the ass" threatening to embarrass him and the United States on the eve of his summit meeting with Soviet leader Nikita Khrushchev. After dismissing them as "publicity seekers" who were putting the administration in "a politically painful spot," he grabbed a telephone and ordered Harris Wofford, his special assistant on civil rights, to end the freedom rides. "Can't you get your goddamned friends off those buses? Stop them!"

When Kennedy suggested to several civil rights leaders that they allow things to "cool off," James Farmer replied that blacks had been "cooling off for a hundred years. . . . If we got any cooler, we'd be in the deep freeze." Louis Martin, an influential black newspaper publisher, explained that "Negroes are getting ideas [about securing equal rights] they didn't have before." Kennedy asked where they were getting such ideas. Martin replied: "From you!"

The activists finally forced the president to provide another bus, which enabled them to renew the journey to New Orleans. When the new group of riders reached Montgomery, the capital of Alabama, they too were attacked. The next night, civil rights activists, including Martin Luther King Jr., gathered at a Montgomery church to honor the Freedom Riders. But their meeting was interrupted by a rampaging mob of whites armed with rocks and firebombs.

Ministers made frantic appeals to the White House. Kennedy responded by urging the Alabama governor to intervene. After midnight, national guardsmen arrived to disperse the mob. The Freedom Riders continued into Mississippi, where they were jailed. They never made it to New Orleans.

Still, the courage and principled resistance of the Freedom Riders—and of federal judges whose rulings supported integration efforts—prompted the Interstate Commerce Commission (ICC) in September 1961 to order that all interstate transportation facilities be integrated. Equally important, the Freedom Riders kindled the growth of civil rights groups. The experience of being assaulted and jailed galvanized the participants to become full-time members while attracting more recruits. The freedom rides were thus a crucial turning point in the civil rights movement.

White segregationists, however, remained violently opposed to racial equality. In Birmingham in September 1962, Dr. King was speaking at the annual meeting of the Southern Christian Leadership Conference when a white member of the American Nazi party jumped to the stage and punched him in the face. King simply dropped his hands and allowed the man to punch him again. "Don't touch him," King yelled. "We have to pray for him." His self-control and composure were as remarkable as his bravery. King was determined, as an aide said, to "love segregation to death." His home was bombed three times, and he was arrested fourteen times, yet he kept telling people to use "the weapon of nonviolence, the breastplate of righteousness, the armor of truth, and just keep marching" toward justice.

JAMES MEREDITH   In the fall of 1962, James Meredith, an African American student and air force veteran whose grandfather had been a slave, tried to enroll at the all-white University of Mississippi in Oxford. Ross Barnett, the governor of Mississippi, described by *Time* magazine as "bitter a racist as inhabits the nation," refused to allow Meredith to register for classes. The militantly stubborn Barnett breathed scorching defiance: he vowed "to rot in jail before he will let one Negro ever darken the sacred threshold of our white schools." Attorney General Robert F. Kennedy then dispatched federal marshals to enforce the law.

When the marshals were assaulted with bricks, bottles, and steel pipes by a white mob shouting "Go to Hell, JFK," President Kennedy sent National Guard troops. Their arrival ignited rioting that left two dead and dozens injured. Once the violence subsided, however, Meredith was registered at the university. "Only in America," a reporter noted, "would the federal government send thousands of troops to enforce the right of an otherwise obscure citizen to attend a particular university."

BIRMINGHAM In early 1963, in conjunction with the celebration of the hundredth anniversary of Abraham Lincoln's Emancipation Proclamation, Martin Luther King Jr. defied President Kennedy's wishes by organizing a

Bull's dogs Eugene "Bull" Connor ordered Birmingham police to unleash their dogs and clubs on civil rights demonstrators in May 1963.

massive series of demonstrations in Birmingham. Alabama was now led by George Wallace, a feisty racist governor who had vowed to protect "segregation now, segregation tomorrow, segregation forever!" King knew that weeks of public demonstrations would result in thousands of arrests and would likely provoke violence, but a hard-won victory, he felt, would "break the back of segregation all over the nation" by revealing southern "brutality openly—in the light of day—with the rest of the world looking on" through television cameras.

The Birmingham campaign began with sit-ins at restaurants, picket lines at segregated businesses, and a march on city hall. The police arrested and jailed hundreds of activists. Each day, however, more demonstrators, black and white, joined in the efforts. As King and others led 2,500 demonstrators through Birmingham streets on May 7, the all-white police force led by "Bull" Connor used snarling dogs, tear gas, electric cattle prods, and high-pressure fire hoses on the protesters. Millions of Americans were outraged when they saw the ugly confrontations on television. "The civil rights movement," President Kennedy observed, "owes Bull Connor as much as it owes Abraham Lincoln." It also owed a lot to the power of television.

More than 3,000 demonstrators were arrested, including Dr. King and several white ministers, both men and women, who were rushing to the cause of civil rights. While in jail, King was inspired to write a "Letter from Birmingham Jail," a stirring defense of "**nonviolent civil disobedience**" that has become a classic document of the civil rights movement. "One who breaks an unjust law," King stressed, "must do so openly, lovingly, and with a willingness to *accept the penalty*." In a reference to President Kennedy's timid support, King wrote that the most perplexing foe of equal justice was not the southern white bigot but "the white moderate, who is more devoted to 'order' than to justice . . . who constantly says, 'I agree with you in the goal you seek, but I cannot agree with your methods.'"

King's efforts prevailed when Birmingham officials finally agreed to end their segregationist practices. White racists did not change overnight, however. One angry Alabaman sent a letter to King: "This isn't a threat but a promise—your head will be blown off as sure as Christ made green apples."

Throughout 1963, whites in the Lower South continued to defy efforts at racial integration, while blacks and white liberals organized demonstrations in cities and towns across the nation. On June 11, 1963, Alabama governor George Wallace theatrically blocked the door at the University of Alabama as African American students tried to register for classes. Wallace finally stepped aside in the face of insistent federal marshals.

That night, President Kennedy finally decided he needed to lead. In a hastily arranged televised speech, he announced that he would soon submit to Congress a major new civil rights bill that would remove race as a consideration "in American life or law." He stressed that "a great change is at hand," and he was determined to make "that change, that [civil rights] revolution" peaceful and constructive. "We are confronted primarily with a moral issue," the president said. "It is as old as the Scriptures and is as clear as the American Constitution. The heart of the question is whether all Americans are to be afforded equal rights and equal opportunities." He asked "every American, regardless of where he lives," to "stop and examine his conscience," for America, "for all its hopes and all its boasts, will not be fully free until all its citizens are free."

That night, in Mississippi, a 37-year-old African American civil rights activist, Medgar Evers, listened to the president's speech in his car. He was so excited by Kennedy's new commitment to civil rights that he turned the car around and went home so that he could discuss the speech with his children. When Evers arrived at his house in Jackson at midnight, he was shot in his driveway by a white racist lying in ambush. He staggered to the carport and collapsed in front of his horrified wife and children. He died before reaching a hospital. Such violence aroused the nation's indignation and reinforced Kennedy's commitment to make civil rights America's most pressing social issue. The killing of Medgar Evers led the president to host his first meeting of civil rights leaders in the White House and helped spur plans for a massive demonstration on the Mall in Washington, D.C.

"I HAVE A DREAM!"   For weeks, southern Democrats in the House of Representatives blocked Kennedy's civil rights bill. The standoff in Congress led African American leaders to take a bold step. On August 28, some 250,000 blacks and whites, many of them schoolchildren brought in on buses, marched arm-in-arm down the Mall in Washington, D.C., chanting "Equality Now!" and singing "We Shall Overcome."

The **March on Washington** for Jobs and Freedom was the largest political demonstration in American history. "When you looked at the crowd," remembered a U.S. Park Service ranger, "you didn't see blacks or whites. You saw America." For almost six hours, prominent entertainers sang protest songs, and civil rights activists gave speeches calling for racial justice.

Then something remarkable happened. Standing on the steps of the Lincoln Memorial, thirty-four-year-old Martin Luther King Jr. came to the podium, the tenth and last speaker of the day. The crowd roared as he prepared

"I Have a Dream," August 28, 1963 Protesters in the massive March on Washington make their way to the Lincoln Memorial, where Martin Luther King Jr. delivered his now-famous speech.

to speak. He started awkwardly. Noticing his nervousness, someone urged him to "tell 'em about the dream, Martin."

As if suddenly inspired, King set aside his prepared remarks and delivered an extraordinary improvised speech that resonated around the world. He started slowly and picked up speed, as if he were speaking at a revival, giving poetic voice to the hopes of millions as he stressed the "fierce urgency of now" and the unstoppable power of "meeting physical force with soul force."

King then shared his dream for America:

In spite of the difficulties and frustrations of the moment, I still have a *dream*. It is a *dream* deeply rooted in the American dream. I have a *dream* that one day this nation will rise up and live out the true meaning of its creed: 'We hold these truths to be self-evident; that all men are created equal.' I have a *dream* that one day . . . the sons of former slaves and the sons of former slaveowners will be able to sit together at the table of brotherhood.

As if at a massive church service, many in the crowd began shouting "Amen!" as King summoned a flawed nation to justice: "So let freedom ring!" he shouted, for "when we allow freedom to ring from every town and every hamlet, from every state and every city, we will be able to speed up the day when *all* God's children—black men and white men, Jews and Gentiles, Protestants and Catholics—will be able to join hands and sing in the words of the old Negro spiritual, *Free at last, free at last, thank God Almighty, we are free at last!*"

As King finished, there was a startling hush, then a deafening ovation. The crowd spontaneously joined hands and began singing "We Shall Overcome." "I have never been so proud to be a Negro," said baseball superstar Jackie Robinson. "I have never been so proud to be an American." President Kennedy, who had tried to convince organizers to call off the march, was watching on TV at the White House, just a mile away. As King spoke, the president told an aide that "he's damn good."

But King's dream remained just that—a dream. Eighteen days later, four Klansmen in Birmingham detonated a bomb in a black church, killing four young girls. The murders sparked a new wave of indignation across the country and the world. The editors of the *Milwaukee Sentinel* stressed that the bombing "should serve to goad the conscience. The deaths . . . in a sense are on the hands of each of us."

THE WARREN COURT The civil rights movement depended as much on the courts as it did on the leadership of Dr. King and others, and federal judges kept forcing states and localities to integrate schools and other public places. Under Chief Justice Earl Warren, the U.S. Supreme Court also made landmark decisions in other areas of American life.

In 1962, the Court ruled that a school prayer adopted by the New York State Board of Regents violated the constitutional prohibition against government-supported religion. In *Gideon v. Wainwright* (1963), the Court required that every felony defendant be provided a lawyer regardless of the defendant's ability to pay. In 1964, the Court ruled in *Escobedo v. Illinois* that a person accused of a crime must be allowed to consult a lawyer before being interrogated by police.

Two years later, in *Miranda v. Arizona* (1966), the Court issued a bitterly criticized ruling when it ordered that an accused person in police custody be informed of certain basic rights: the right to remain silent; the right to know that anything said to authorities can be used against the individual in court; and the right to have a defense attorney present during interrogation; since then, these requirements have been known as "Miranda rights." In addition, the Court established rules for police to follow in informing suspects of their legal rights before questioning could begin.

FREEDOM SUMMER During late 1963 and throughout 1964, the civil rights movement grew in scope, visibility, and power. Racism, however, remained entrenched in the Lower South, as blacks continued to be excluded from the political process. White officials kept African Americans from voting by charging them expensive poll taxes, forcing them to take difficult literacy tests, making the application process inconvenient, and intimidating them through the use of arson, beatings, and lynchings.

In early 1964, Harvard-educated Robert "Bob" Moses, a black New Yorker who had resigned from the SCLC to head the Student Nonviolent Coordinating Committee (SNCC) office in Mississippi, decided it would take "an army" to force the state to give voting rights to blacks. So he set about recruiting an army of black and white volunteers who would live with rural African Americans, teach them in "freedom schools," and help them register to vote.

Most of the recruits for what came to be called "Freedom Summer" were idealistic white college students, many of whom were Jewish. Mississippi's white leaders prepared for "the nigger-communist invasion" by doubling the state police force and stockpiling tear gas, electric cattle prods, and shotguns. Writer Eudora Welty reported from her hometown of Jackson, Mississippi, that she had heard that "this summer all hell is going to break loose."

It did. In mid-June, the volunteer activists met at an Ohio college to learn about southern racial history, nonviolent civil disobedience, and the likely abuses they would suffer. On the final evening of the training session, Moses

A freedom school in Jackson, Mississippi A volunteer from Brooklyn, New York, instructs young black students on the arts, African American history, and civil rights at a freedom school as part of the "Mississippi Summer Project" in August 1964.

pleaded with anyone who feared heading to Mississippi to go home; several did. The next day, the remaining volunteers boarded buses and headed south, fanning out across the state.

In all, forty-one "freedom schools" taught thousands of children math, writing, and history. They also tutored black adults about the complicated process of voter registration. Stokely Carmichael, an African American student from Howard University, wrote that black Mississippians "took us in, fed us, instructed and protected us, and ultimately civilized, educated, and inspired the smartassed college students."

Forty-six-year-old Fannie Lou Hamer was one of the local blacks who worked with the SNCC volunteers during Freedom Summer. The youngest in a household of twenty children, she had spent most of her life working on local cotton plantations. During the Freedom Summer of 1963 and after, she led gatherings of volunteers in freedom songs and excelled as a lay preacher. "God is not pleased," she said, "at all the murdering, and all of the brutality, and all the killings for no reason at all. God is not pleased at the Negro children in the State of Mississippi, suffering from malnutrition. God is not pleased because we have to go raggedy each day. God is not pleased because we have to go to the field and work from ten to eleven hours for three lousy dollars." In response, the Ku Klux Klan, local police, and other white racists harassed, arrested, and assaulted many of the volunteers.

On June 21, 1964, just two days after Congress approved the Civil Rights Act, three young SNCC workers—James Earl Chaney, Andrew Goodman, and Michael "Mickey" Schwerner—disappeared after going to investigate the burning of an African American church. Their decomposed, bullet-riddled bodies were found two months later buried in a dam at a cattle pond. They had been abducted and murdered by Klan members. While searching for the missing men, authorities found the bodies of eight black males in rivers and swamps who also had been killed. The murders, said one volunteer, were "the end of innocence," after which

White terror Young men cruise through a riot zone in Chicago in 1966, brandishing a Confederate flag and racist signs.

"things could never be the same." A growing number of blacks began to call into question Martin Luther King's nonviolent strategy.

BLACK POWER Racism in America was not limited to the South. By the mid-sixties, about 70 percent of the nation's African Americans were living in blighted urban areas, and many young blacks in the large cities were losing faith in the strategy of Christian nonviolence employed by King and others in the South. Inner-city poverty and frustration cried out for its own social justice movement.

The fragmentation of the civil rights movement was tragically evident on August 11, 1965, when Watts, the largest black ghetto in Los Angeles, exploded in rioting and looting that left thirty-four dead, almost 4,000 in jail, and widespread property damage. Dozens of other large cities experienced similar riots in the summer of 1966. Between 1965 and 1968, nearly 300 racial uprisings shattered the peace of urban America.

The violence revealed the growing civil war within the civil rights movement. As Gil Scott-Heron, a black musician, sang: "We are tired of praying and marching and thinking and learning / Brothers want to start cutting and shooting and stealing and burning." What came to be called "black power" began to compete with the integrationist, nonviolent philosophy espoused by Dr. King and the SCLC.

MALCOLM X The most visible spokesman for the **black power movement** was Malcolm X, born in 1925 in Omaha, Nebraska, as Malcolm Little. His father, a Baptist minister, and his mother, a West Indian, were supporters of Marcus Garvey's crusade for black nationalism in the 1920s, and his childhood home was burned to the ground by white racists. His father was killed when Malcolm was six, perhaps the victim of white supremacists. After her husband's death, Louise Little suffered a breakdown and was institutionalized for the rest of her life. Young

Malcolm X The black power movement's most influential spokesman.

Malcolm was placed in foster care but became an unruly rebel. After being expelled from school in the ninth grade, he drifted from Detroit to New York City to Boston.

By age nineteen, Malcolm, now known as Detroit Red, had become a thief, drug dealer, and pimp. He spent seven years in Massachusetts prisons, where he experienced a conversion and joined a small Chicago-based religious sect, the Nation of Islam (NOI), whose members were called Black Muslims. The organization had little to do with Islam and everything to do with its domineering leader, Elijah Muhammad, and the cultlike devotion he required. Muhammad dismissed whites as "devils" and championed black nationalism, racial pride, self-respect, and self-discipline. By 1953, a year after leaving prison, Malcolm Little was calling himself Malcolm X in tribute to his lost African name, and he had become a full-time NOI minister famous for electrifying speeches attacking white racism and black powerlessness.

Malcolm X dismissed Martin Luther King and other mainstream civil rights leaders as "nothing but modern Uncle Toms" who "keep you and me in check, keep us under control, keep us passive and peaceful and nonviolent." He insisted that there "was no such thing as a nonviolent revolution." His militant speeches inspired thousands of mostly urban blacks to join the Nation of Islam.

More than most black leaders, Malcolm X expressed the emotions and frustrations of the inner-city African American working poor. Yet at the peak of his influence, and just as he was moderating his militant message, he became embroiled in a conflict with Elijah Muhammad that proved fatal. NOI assassins killed Malcolm X in Manhattan on February 21, 1965.

Black militancy did not end with Malcolm X, however. By 1966, "black power" had become a rallying cry for many young militants. When Stokely Carmichael became head of the Student Nonviolent Coordinating Committee (SNCC), he ousted whites from the organization. "When you talk of black power," Carmichael shouted, "you talk of bringing this country to its knees, of building a movement that will smash everything Western civilization has created." Having been beaten by whites and having seen fellow volunteers killed, Carmichael rejected the nonviolent philosophy of the mainstream civil rights movement and urged blacks to defend themselves.

Where Martin Luther King spoke to white America's moral conscience, Carmichael and other firebrands spoke to the seething rage of the young black underclass. Soon Carmichael would move on to the Black Panther party, a group of leather-jacketed black revolutionaries founded in Oakland, California, that promoted incendiary strategies and cultural pride. H. Rap Brown, who succeeded Carmichael as head of SNCC in 1967, urged blacks to "get you some guns" and "kill the honkies [whites]."

THE EFFECT OF BLACK POWER   Although widely covered in the media, the black power movement never attracted more than a small minority of African Americans. Still, it forced King and other mainstream black leaders and organizations to shift their focus from the rural South to inner-city ghettos in the North and West. Legal access to restaurants, schools, and other public accommodations, King pointed out, meant little to people mired in chronic poverty. They needed jobs and decent housing.

The time had come, King declared while launching his "Poor People's Campaign" in December 1967, for radical new measures "to provide jobs and income for the poor." Yet as he and others stressed, the war in Vietnam was taking funds away from federal programs serving the poor, and black soldiers were dying in disproportionate numbers in Southeast Asia.

The black power movement also motivated African Americans to take greater pride in their racial heritage by pushing for black studies programs in schools and colleges, the celebration of African cultural and artistic traditions, the organizing of inner-city voters to elect black mayors, laws forcing landlords to treat blacks fairly, and the creation of grassroots organizations and

Panther power   Black Panthers issue a black power salute outside a San Francisco Liberation School, where activists raised awareness and appreciation of African American history, a topic ignored by white, mainstream curriculum.

community centers in black neighborhoods. It was Malcolm X who insisted that blacks call themselves *African Americans* as a symbol of pride in their roots and as a spur to learn more about their history. As the popular singer James Brown urged, "Say it loud—I'm black and I'm proud."

THE GREAT SOCIETY

Growing federal support for civil rights came from an unlikely source: a drawling white southerner who succeeded John F. Kennedy in the White House. A stunned Lyndon Baines Johnson, the towering Texan known as LBJ, took the presidential oath of office on board the plane that brought Kennedy's body back to Washington from Dallas.

The fifty-five-year-old Johnson, the first southern president since Woodrow Wilson, had excelled as Senate majority leader before becoming vice president. His transition to the presidency was not easy, however. He inherited a

The oath of office Less than 90 minutes after Kennedy's death, Johnson took the presidential oath aboard Air Force One between his wife, Lady Bird (left), and Jacqueline Kennedy (right), before flying out of Dallas for Washington, D.C.

political deadlock between the White House and a congressional alliance of Democratic and Republican conservatives that had blocked most of Kennedy's legislative proposals. Johnson had also been kept out of the inner circle of power in the Kennedy White House. The Kennedy brothers despised Johnson and excluded him from key decisions. Robert Kennedy described Johnson as "vicious, an animal in many ways." Johnson, in turn, dismissed "all those Bostons and Harvards" who knew less about the legislative process "than an old maid does about fucking."

Like Kennedy, Johnson was one of the most complex and inexplicable men to occupy the White House. Unlike the wealthy, aristocratic Kennedy, however, Johnson was a rags-to-riches story. With almost superhuman effort and ambition, he had worked his way out of rural Texas poverty during the Great Depression to become one of the Senate's dominant figures.

LBJ's ego and insecurities were as massive as his vanity and ambition; he could not stand being alone; he insisted on being the center of attention wherever he went. Johnson personalized the presidency; in press conferences, he referred to "my Vietnam policy," "my Security Council," "my Cabinet," "my legislation," and "my boys" fighting in Southeast Asia. George Reedy, the president's press secretary, said that Johnson was a "man of too many paradoxes." Ruthless and often bullying, needy and warmhearted, he was a contradictory whirlwind of workaholic energy and inspiring hopes, a crude idealist and a brutal optimist so thin-skinned that he took all criticism personally. In his view, people were either with him or against him. There was no middle ground.

Johnson yearned to be loved and respected as a transformational leader. And, like Kennedy, he had a weakness for both political power and attractive women. (His wife, Lady Bird, acknowledged that "Lyndon loved the human race, and half of the human race are women.")

Few leaders had ever dreamed as big as Lyndon Johnson. His outlook was grandiose. He wanted to be the greatest American president, the one who did the most good for the most people by creating the most new programs and agencies. He promised to "help every child get an education, to help every Negro and every American citizen have an equal opportunity, to help every family get a decent home, and to help bring healing to the sick and dignity to the old."

Those who dismissed Johnson as a traditional southern conservative failed to appreciate his genuine concern for the poor and his embrace of civil rights. "I'm going to be the best friend the Negro ever had," Johnson bragged to a member of the White House staff. His commitment to civil rights was in part motivated by politics, in part by his desire to bring the South into the mainstream of American life, and in part by his life experiences. His first teaching job after college was at an elementary school in Texas serving Mexican-American children. They created in him a lifelong desire to help "those poor little kids. I saw hunger in their eyes and pain in their bodies. Those little brown bodies had so little and needed so much." He grew determined to "fill their souls with ambition and interest and belief in the future."

POLITICS AND POVERTY

Johnson managed legislation through Congress better than any president in history. As a woman in Hawaii said, "Johnson is a mover of men. Kennedy could inspire men, but he couldn't move them." LBJ was the consummate wheeler-dealer on Capitol Hill. "It is the politician's task," he asserted, "to pass legislation, not to sit around saying principled things."

In 1964, he set about doing just that, taking advantage of widespread public support to push through Congress Kennedy's stalled measures for tax reductions and civil rights. He later said that he wanted to take Kennedy's incomplete program "and turn it into a martyr's cause."

The Revenue Act of 1964 provided a 20 percent reduction in tax rates. (The top rate was then a whopping 91 percent, compared to 39.6 today.) It was intended to give consumers more money to spend so as to boost economic growth and create new jobs, and it worked. Unemployment fell from 5.2 percent in 1964 to 4.5 percent in 1965 and 3.8 percent in 1966.

THE CIVIL RIGHTS ACT   Long thwarted by southern Democrats in Congress, the **Civil Rights Act of 1964** finally became law on July 2. It guaranteed equal treatment under the law for *all* Americans and outlawed discrimination in public places on the basis of race, sex, or national origin. It also prohibited discrimination in the buying, selling, and renting of housing, as well as the hiring and firing of employees.

The civil rights movement set the stage and provided the momentum for the new law, but Johnson pursued its passage with an urgent sense of purpose. He lobbied key legislators one-on-one; one senator who survived the "Johnson treatment," as it came to be called, said that the president would "twist your arm off at the shoulder and beat your head with it" if you did not agree to vote as he wanted.

Soon after becoming president, Johnson hosted Georgia senator Richard Russell, his close friend and an arch-segregationist. Over lunch, the president warned Russell that "you've got to get out of my way. I'm going to run over you" to pass the Civil Rights Act. "You may do that," Russell replied. "But by God, it's going to cost you the South and cost you the election of 1964." Johnson answered: "If that's the price I've got to pay, I'll pay it gladly." Soon thereafter, Johnson told Congress that "we have talked long enough in this country about equal rights. . . . It is time now to write the next chapter, and to write it in the book of law." He added that it would be the best way to honor Kennedy's memory.

Many others helped Johnson convince Congress to pass the Civil Rights Act—Senator Hubert Humphrey, congressional committee chairs (both Republicans and Democrats), labor unions, church leaders, and civil rights organizations. Their collective efforts produced what is arguably the single most important piece of legislation in the twentieth century. The passage of the Civil Rights Act after more than a year of congressional delays marked one of those extraordinary moments when the ideals of democracy, equal opportunity, and human dignity are affirmed by action.

The Civil Rights Act of 1964 dealt a major blow to the deeply entrenched system of racial segregation while giving the federal government new powers to bring lawsuits against organizations or businesses that violated constitutional rights. It also established the Equal Employment Opportunities Commission to ensure that employers treated job applicants equally, regardless of race, gender, or national origin.

Down with segregation A worker removes a sign from a Greensboro, North Carolina, bus that reads: "White Patrons Please Seat from Front. Colored Patrons Please Seat from Rear."

On the night after signing the bill, Johnson knew that conservative white southerners would be furious. He correctly predicted that "we have just delivered the South to the Republican party for a long time to come."

A WAR ON POVERTY In addition to fulfilling President Kennedy's legislative priorities that had been stalled in Congress, Lyndon Johnson launched an elaborate legislative program of his own by declaring "unconditional war on poverty in America." Americans had "rediscovered" poverty in 1962 when social critic Michael Harrington published a powerful exposé, *The Other America,* in which he revealed that more than 40 million people were mired in an invisible "culture of poverty." Poverty led to poor housing conditions, which in turn led to such problems as poor health, poor attendance at school or work, alcohol and drug abuse, unwanted pregnancies, and single-parent families. Harrington added that poverty was much more extensive than people realized because much of it was hidden from view in isolated rural areas or inner-city slums. He urged the United States to launch a "comprehensive assault on poverty."

President Kennedy had read Harrington's book and asked his advisers in the fall of 1963, just before his assassination, to investigate the problem and suggest solutions. Upon becoming president, Johnson announced that he wanted an anti-poverty legislative package "that would hit the nation with real impact." He was determined to help the "one-fifth of all American families with incomes too small to even meet their basic needs." They needed better homes, better schools, better medical care, and better job training. Money for the program would come from the tax revenues generated by corporate profits made possible by the tax reduction of 1964, which had led to one of the longest sustained economic booms in history. Johnson knew that the "war" on poverty would be long and costly. He said he did not expect to "wipe out poverty" in "my lifetime. But we can minimize it, moderate it, and in time eliminate it." And he pledged that his war on poverty would not be "a struggle to support people" by giving them handouts but by opening "the door of opportunity" for them.

The **Economic Opportunity Act** of 1964 was the primary weapon in the "War on Poverty." It created an Office of Economic Opportunity (OEO) to administer eleven new community-based programs, many of which still exist. They included a Job Corps training program for inner-city youths ages sixteen to twenty-one; a Head Start educational program for disadvantaged preschoolers; a Legal Services Corporation to provide legal assistance for low-income Americans; financial-aid programs for low-income college students; grants to small farmers and rural businesses; loans to businesses that hired the chronically unemployed; the Volunteers in Service to America program (VISTA) to combat inner-city poverty; and the Community Action Program, which would allow the poor "maximum feasible participation" in organizing and directing their own neighborhood programs. In 1964, Congress also approved the Food Stamp Act, a program to help poor people afford to buy groceries.

THE ELECTION OF 1964   Johnson's successes aroused a conservative Republican counterattack. Arizona senator Barry Goldwater, a wealthy department-store owner, emerged as the blunt-talking leader of the growing right wing of the Republican party. He was one of only six Republican senators to vote against the Civil Rights Act of 1964 and warned that the bill would lead to a "federal police state."

In his best-selling book *The Conscience of a Conservative* (1960), Goldwater had called for ending the income tax and drastically reducing federal entitlement programs such as Social Security. Conservatives controlled the Republican Convention when it gathered in San Francisco in the early summer of 1964, and they ensured Goldwater's nomination. "I would remind you," Goldwater told the delegates, "that extremism in the defense of liberty is no vice." He later explained that his objective was like that of Calvin Coolidge in the 1920s: "to reduce the size of government. Not to pass laws, but repeal them."

As a candidate, Goldwater frightened many voters when he urged wholesale bombing of North Vietnam and even suggested using atomic weapons. He criticized Johnson's war on poverty as a waste of money, told students that the federal government should not provide any assistance for education, and opposed the nuclear test ban treaty. To Republican campaign buttons that claimed, "In your heart, you know he's right," Democrats responded, "In your guts, you know he's nuts."

Johnson, by comparison, portrayed himself as a responsible centrist. He chose as his running mate Hubert H. Humphrey of Minnesota, a prominent liberal senator who had long promoted civil rights. In contrast to Goldwater's aggressive rhetoric, Johnson pledged that he was "not about to send American boys nine or ten thousand miles from home to do what Asian boys ought to be doing for themselves."

The election was not close. Johnson won 61 percent of the popular vote and dominated the electoral vote by 486 to 52. Goldwater captured only Arizona and five states in the Lower South. In the Senate, the Democrats increased their majority by two (68 to 32) and in the House by thirty-seven (295 to 140). But Goldwater's success in the Lower South accelerated the region's shift to the Republican party, and his candidacy proved to be a turning point in the development of the national conservative movement by inspiring a generation of young activists and the formation of conservative organizations that would transform the dynamics of American politics during the 1970s and 1980s.

Their success would culminate in the presidency of Ronald Reagan, the Hollywood actor who co-chaired the California for Goldwater campaign in 1964.

THE GREAT SOCIETY

Lyndon Johnson misread his lopsided victory in 1964 as a mandate for massive changes. He knew, however, that his popularity could quickly fade. "Every day I'm in office," he told his aides, "I'm going to lose votes. I'm going to alienate somebody. . . . We've got to get this legislation fast. You've got to get it during my honeymoon."

As Johnson's war on poverty gathered momentum, his already-outsized ambitions grew even larger. In May 1964, he announced his intention to develop an array of programs intended to "move not only toward the rich society and the powerful society, but upward to the **Great Society**" which would end poverty and racial injustice and provide "abundance and liberty for all."

It soon became clear that Johnson viewed the federal government as the magical lever for raising the quality of life for all Americans—rich and poor. He would surpass Franklin Roosevelt's New Deal in expanding the goals and scope of the federal government to ensure that Americans were a people of plenty. "Hell, we're the richest country in the world, the most powerful," Johnson told an aide. "We can do it all." Soon, Johnson was working full-time to gain congressional approval for dozens of new bills and federal programs. LBJ, said an aide, became a "great, hurtling locomotive running down the track."

**HEALTH INSURANCE, HOUSING, AND HIGHER EDU-
CATION** Johnson's first priorities among his "Great Society" programs were federal health insurance and aid for young people to pursue higher education—"liberal" proposals that had first been suggested by President Truman in 1945. For twenty years, the steadfast opposition of the physicians making up the American Medical Association (AMA) had stalled a comprehensive medical-insurance program. Now that Johnson and the Democrats had the votes to pass the measure, however, the AMA joined Republicans in supporting a bill serving those over age sixty-five.

The act that finally emerged created not just a **Medicare** health insurance program for the elderly but also a **Medicaid** program of federal grants to states to help cover medical expenses for the poor of all ages. Johnson signed the bill on July 30, 1965, in Independence, Missouri, with eighty-one-year-old Harry Truman looking on.

The Higher Education Act of 1965 increased federal grants to universities, created scholarships for low-income students, provided low-interest loans for students, and established a National Teachers Corps. "Every child," Johnson

War on Poverty In 1964, President Johnson visited Tom Fletcher, a father of eight children living in a tar-paper shack in rural Kentucky. Fletcher became a "poster father" for the War on Poverty, though, as it turned out, his life benefited little from its programs.

asserted, "must be encouraged to get as much education as he has the ability to take."

The momentum generated by the Higher Education and Medicare acts helped carry 435 more Great Society bills through Congress. Among them was the Appalachian Regional Development Act of 1966, which allocated $1 billion for programs in impoverished mountain areas. The Housing and Urban Development Act of 1965 provided $3 billion for urban renewal projects in inner-city ghettoes. Funds to help low-income families pay their rent followed in 1966, and the same year a new Department of Housing and Urban Development appeared, headed by Robert C. Weaver, the first African American cabinet member.

In implementing the many different Great Society programs, Lyndon Johnson had, in the words of one Washington reporter, "brought to harvest a generation's backlog of ideas and social legislation." No president, reported *Time* magazine, was "more passionately, earnestly, and all-encompassingly dedicated to and consumed by his work."

THE IMMIGRATION ACT Little noticed in the stream of Great Society legislation was the Immigration and Nationality Services Act of 1965, which Johnson signed in a ceremony on Liberty Island in New York Harbor. It abolished the discriminatory annual quotas based upon an immigrant's national origin and treated all nationalities and races equally. The old system greatly favored immigrants from Great Britain and the countries of western and northern Europe over those from southern and eastern Europe, Asia, and Africa. In place of quotas, it created hemispheric ceilings on visas issued: 170,000 for persons from outside the Western Hemisphere, 120,000 for persons from within. It also stipulated that no more than 20,000 people could come from any one country each year.

VOTING RIGHTS LEGISLATION Building upon the successes of "Freedom Summer," Martin Luther King Jr. organized an effort in early 1965 to register the 3 million unregistered African American voters in the South. On February 6, the White House announced that it would urge Congress to enact a voting rights bill.

To keep the pressure on the president and Congress, activists converged on Selma, Alabama, where only 250 of the 15,000 blacks of voting age were registered voters. King told his staff on February 10 that to get the voting rights bill passed, "we need to make a dramatic" statement. That drama occurred three weeks later.

On Sunday, March 7, some 600 black and white civil rights protesters assembled near the Edmund Pettus Bridge to begin a fifty-four-mile march to the state capitol in Montgomery. Before reaching the bridge, however, the marchers were assaulted by 500 state troopers and local police using billy clubs, tear gas, and bullwhips. In what came to be called "Bloody Sunday," the violence was televised for all to see. Fifty injured marchers were hospitalized. "The news from Selma," reported the *Washington Post*, "will shock and alarm the whole nation." It did. Dr. King, torn between congressional appeals to call off the march and the demands of militants that it continue, announced that a second march would be held. A federal judge agreed to allow the marchers to continue once President Johnson agreed to provide soldiers and federal marshals for their protection.

By March 25, when the demonstrators reached Montgomery, some 25,000 people were with them, and King delivered a rousing address in which he said, "the battle is in our hands. And we can answer with creative nonviolence the call to higher ground to which the new directions of our struggle summons us."

Several days earlier, on March 15, Johnson had urged Congress to "overcome the crippling legacy of bigotry and injustice" by making the cause of civil rights "our cause too." He concluded by slowly speaking the words of the movement's hymn: "And we *shall* overcome."

The resulting **Voting Rights Act of 1965** was one of the most momentous legislative accomplishments of the twentieth century. It ensured *all* citizens the right to vote. It authorized the attorney general to send federal officials to register voters in areas that had long experienced racial discrimination. In states or counties where fewer than half the adults had voted in 1964, the act banned the various ways, like literacy tests, that local officials used to keep blacks and Hispanics from voting.

By the end of the year, some 250,000 African Americans were newly registered to vote in several southern states. By 1968, an estimated 53 percent of blacks in Alabama were registered to vote, compared to 14 percent in 1960. In this respect, the Voting Rights Act was even more important than the Civil Rights Act because it empowered black voters in the South, thereby transforming the white-dominated politics in the region and making possible the election of black public officials. Yet by enabling southern blacks—most of whom preferred Democratic candidates—to vote, it also helped turn the once-solidly Democratic South into a Republican stronghold, as many white voters switched parties.

THE GREAT SOCIETY IN PRACTICE   Lyndon B. Johnson sought to give Americans a sense of forward movement in troubled times and show them that he could create a "great society" whereby people would be "more concerned with the quality of their goals than the quantity of their goods."

Franklin Roosevelt passed fifteen major bills in his First Hundred Days, Johnson told an aide in 1966, whereas he had "passed two hundred in the last two years." A *New York Times* columnist joked that LBJ was "getting everything through the Congress but the abolition of the Republican party, and he hasn't tried that yet."

The scope of Johnson's Great Society programs exceeded Roosevelt's New Deal in part because of the nation's booming prosperity during the mid-1960s. "This country," Johnson proclaimed, "is rich enough to do anything it has the guts to do and the vision to do and the will to do." That proved *not* to be the case, however. As *Time* magazine reported, "No matter how much Lyndon gets, he asks for more." Yet soon there was no more money to spend. In 1966, Johnson warned Congress that if taxes were not raised, the economy would suffer a "ruinous spiral of inflation" and "brutally higher interest rates."

The Great Society and war on poverty never lived up to Johnson's grandiose goals, in part because the Vietnam War soon took priority and siphoned away funding, and in part because neither Johnson nor his congressional supporters understood the stubborn complexity of chronic poverty. In many respects, the Great Society generated its own downfall by inspiring a conservative Republican backlash that would gain political control during the eighties. In the congressional elections of 1966, only 38 of the 71 Democrats elected to the House in 1964 won reelection. The political tide was running against Johnson.

The Great Society programs did, however, include several triumphs. Infant mortality has dropped, college completion rates have soared, malnutrition has virtually disappeared, and far fewer elderly Americans live below the poverty line and without access to health care. The federal guarantee of civil rights and voting rights remains in place. Medicare and Medicaid have become two of the most appreciated government programs. Consumers now have a federal agency protecting them. Head Start programs providing preschool enrichment activities for poor students have produced long-term benefits. The federal food stamp program has improved the nutrition and health of children living in poverty. Finally, scholarships for low-income college students have been immensely valuable providing access to higher education.

Several of Johnson's most ambitious programs, however, were ill-conceived, others were vastly underfunded, and many were mismanaged and even corrupt. Some of the problems they were meant to address actually worsened. Medicare, for example, removed incentives for hospitals to control costs, so medical bills skyrocketed—for everyone. In addition, food stamp fraud occurred as people took selfish advantage of a program intended to ensure healthy nutrition.

Overall, Great Society programs helped reduce the population living in poverty from 19 percent in 1964 to 10 percent in 1973, but it did so largely by providing federal welfare payments, not by finding people decent jobs. In 1966, middle-class resentment over the cost and excesses of the Great Society programs generated a conservative backlash that fueled the Republican resurgence in Congress. By then, however, the Great Society had transformed public expectations of the power and role of the federal government.

THE TRAGEDY OF VIETNAM

In foreign affairs, Lyndon Johnson was, like Woodrow Wilson, a novice. And, again like Wilson, his presidency would become a victim of his crusading idealism. As racial violence erupted in America's cities, the war in Vietnam reached new levels of intensity and destruction. With weapons and supplies from China and the Soviet Union, North Vietnam provided massive support to the Viet Cong (VC), the guerrillas fighting in South Vietnam to overthrow the U.S.-backed government and unify the divided nation under Communist control.

Johnson inherited a long-standing U.S. commitment to prevent a Communist takeover in Vietnam. Beginning with Harry S. Truman, U.S. presidents

U.S. air strikes Sustained bombing of Vietnam left 30- to 50-foot-wide craters that can still be seen today.

had done just enough to avoid being charged with having "lost" Vietnam. Johnson initially sought to do the same, fearing that any other course of action would jeopardize his Great Society programs in Congress. His path, however, took the United States into a deeper military commitment.

In November 1963, when President Kennedy was assassinated, there were 16,000 U.S. military "advisers" in South Vietnam. Early in his presidency, Johnson doubted that Vietnam was worth a more extensive military involvement. In May 1964, he told his national security adviser, McGeorge Bundy, that he had spent a sleepless night worrying about Vietnam: "It looks to me like we are getting into another Korea. . . . I don't think it's worth fighting for. And I don't think we can get out. It's just the biggest damned mess that I ever saw."

Yet Johnson's fear of appearing weak abroad outweighed his misgivings. By the end of 1965, there were 184,000 U.S. troops in Vietnam; in 1966, there were 385,000; and by 1969, at the height of the war effort, 542,000.

ESCALATION IN VIETNAM   The official justification for the military *escalation*—a Defense Department term favored in the Vietnam era—was the **Tonkin Gulf Resolution**, passed by the Senate on August 7, 1964. On that day, President Johnson, unknowingly acting on false information provided by the secretary of defense, reported that on August 2 and 4, North Vietnamese torpedo boats had attacked two U.S. warships in the Gulf of Tonkin, off the coast of North Vietnam. As it turned out, the American vessels had actually fired first in support of South Vietnamese attacks against two North Vietnamese islands—attacks planned by American advisers. (Whether the American warships were actually fired upon remains in dispute).

The Tonkin Gulf Resolution empowered the president to "take all necessary measures to repel any armed attack against the forces of the United States and to prevent further aggression." Only two senators voted against the Tonkin Gulf Resolution, which Johnson interpreted as equivalent to a congressional declaration of war, since it allowed him to wage war as he saw fit.

In early 1965, Johnson made the crucial decisions that committed America to full-scale war in Vietnam. On February 5, 1965, Viet Cong (VC) guerrillas attacked a U.S. base near Pleiku, in South Vietnam, killing and wounding more than 100 Americans. More attacks that week led Johnson to approve Operation Rolling Thunder, the first sustained U.S. bombing of North Vietnam. Thereafter, there were essentially two fronts in the war: one, in North Vietnam, where U.S. warplanes continued a massive bombing campaign, and the other, in South Vietnam, where nearly all the ground combat occurred.

In March 1965, the U.S. commander, General William C. Westmoreland, greeted the first American combat troops in Vietnam. His strategy was focused not on capturing territory but on waging a war of attrition, using overwhelming U.S. firepower to cause so many casualties that the Viet Cong and North Vietnamese would give up their effort to undermine the South Vietnamese government.

Soon, U.S. forces launched "search and destroy" operations against VC guerrillas throughout South Vietnam, reporting the "body count" on the evening newscasts. But the Viet Cong, made up of both men and women, wore no uniforms and dissolved by day into the villages, hiding among civilians. Their elusiveness exasperated American soldiers, most of whom were not trained for such unconventional warfare in Vietnam's dense jungles and intense heat and humidity. The escalating war brought rising U.S. casualties (the number of killed, wounded, and missing), which were announced each week on the television news. Criticism of the war grew, but LBJ stood firm. "We will not be defeated," he told the nation. "We will not grow tired. We will not withdraw."

THE CONTEXT FOR POLICY President Johnson's decision to "Americanize" the war flowed directly from the assumptions that had long guided U.S. foreign policy during the Cold War. The commitment to "contain" the spread of communism, initiated by Harry Truman and continued by Dwight Eisenhower and John Kennedy, guided Johnson as well. "Why are we in Vietnam?" the president asked during a speech in 1965. "We are there because we have a promise to keep. . . . To leave Vietnam to its fate would shake the confidence of all these people in the value of American commitment." What Johnson did not say was that he dreaded being blamed for "losing Vietnam" to communism as Truman had been accused by Republicans of "losing China" to Communists led by Mao Zedong.

Hidden A Vietnamese mother hides her son and herself in the bushes near My Lai in 1965 after U.S. Marines murdered Vietnamese villagers.

Johnson and his advisers also believed that U.S. military force would defeat the Viet Cong fighting in South Vietnam. Yet the president insisted that the American war effort not reach levels that would cause the Chinese or Soviets to become involved—which meant, as it turned out, that a military victory was never possible. The United States was not fighting to "win" the war but to prevent the North Vietnamese and Viet Cong from winning and, eventually, force them to sign a negotiated settlement. This meant that the United States would have to maintain a military presence as long as the enemy retained the will to fight.

As the war ground on, opposition at home grew fierce. In 1965, three dozen college campuses began hosting "teach-ins" critical of the war effort. Professors would gather in classrooms or outside on the grass to discuss with students "a better policy" in Vietnam. "The times must be a-changing," wrote the Michigan State student newspaper. In April, 1965, some 20,000 students from campuses across the nation converged on Washington, D.C., where they picketed the White House before moving to the Washington Monument, where they carried signs saying: Get Out of Saigon and into Selma, Freedom Now in Vietnam, War on Poverty Not People. The crowd then went to the Capitol, where it presented Congress with a petition demanding that the legislators "end, not extend, the war in Vietnam."

The following year, Senator J. William Fulbright of Arkansas, chairman of the Senate Foreign Relations Committee, began congressional investigations into American policy in Vietnam. George F. Kennan, the former State Department diplomat who had inspired the "containment" policy, told the committee that the containment doctrine was appropriate for Europe but not for Southeast Asia, which was not vital to American security. Such opposition to the war effort brought out the worst in Johnson. He labeled his political critics and antiwar protesters "Communists" and used government agencies to punish them.

Still, the resistance to the escalating war grew. By 1967, anti-war demonstrations were commonplace. Americans began dividing into "hawks" who supported the war and "doves" who opposed it. Nightly television accounts of the fighting—Vietnam was the first war to receive extended television coverage and hence was dubbed the "living-room war"—called into question the accuracy of statements by military and government officials claiming the Americans were winning. Johnson admitted that the situation was "a mess. There is no question about that. I wish it was better, too." But he dug in his heels and insisted that there would be no withdrawal from Vietnam.

Between 1965 and 1968, U.S. warplanes dropped more bombs on Vietnam than had fallen on all enemy targets in the Second World War. But Johnson and his advisers badly underestimated the strength and determination of the North Vietnamese and Viet Cong. While the United States fought a limited war for limited objectives, the Vietnamese Communists, aided by the Soviets and Chinese, fought an all-out war for their very survival.

Johnson became preoccupied with the day-to-day conduct of the war, insisting on giving the final approval to bombing targets, fretting over logistical details, demanding information about enemy movements. As Westmoreland requested more and more soldiers, Johnson found it impossible to turn him down, explaining that doing so would be like "hearing the call from the Alamo for help and answering that we're not coming." Yet spending so much time dealing with the war was bitterly frustrating to Johnson. How could he be expected to "help every child get an education, to help every Negro and every American citizen have an equal opportunity, to help every family get a decent home, and to help bring healing to the sick and dignity to the old" if the war kept siphoning away the nation's resources?

THE TET OFFENSIVE On January 31, 1968, the first day of the Vietnamese New Year (Tet), the Viet Cong unleashed surprise attacks on U.S. and South Vietnamese forces throughout South Vietnam. Within a few days, American firepower turned the tables, but the damage had been done. Although General Westmoreland proclaimed the **Tet offensive** a major defeat for the Viet Cong, the *political* impact of the surprise attack in the United States was dramatic; it decisively turned Americans against the war. The scope and intensity of the Tet offensive contradicted upbeat claims by U.S. commanders. "What the hell is going on?" CBS newscaster Walter Cronkite demanded. "I thought we were winning this war." After the Tet offensive, Johnson's popularity plummeted, as did the president's confidence in his Vietnam policy. "The country is demoralized," he admitted. "Most of the press is against us. . . . We have no support for the war."

VIETNAM, 1966

Why did the United States intervene militarily in South Vietnam?

What was the Ho Chi Minh Trail?

What was the Tet Offensive?

Civil rights leaders and social activists felt betrayed as they saw federal funds earmarked for the war on poverty spent on Vietnam. By 1968, the United States was spending some $2 billion each month on the war, about $322,000 for every VC killed; anti-poverty programs at home received only $53 per person. As Martin Luther King Jr. pointed out, "the bombs in Vietnam explode at home—they destroy the hopes and possibilities for a decent America."

President Johnson, under constant assault by critics, grew increasingly embittered and isolated. The president who had accomplished so much could now do nothing right. Anti-war protesters chanted, "Hey, Hey, LBJ, how many kids [in Vietnam] have you killed today?" Johnson suffered from depression and paranoia as he realized how much "that bitch of a war" was dividing the nation, gobbling up its resources, and killing its young men. Clark Clifford, Johnson's new secretary of defense, reported in 1968 that a task force of experts had concluded that the United States could not "win" the war. It was not what Johnson wanted to hear.

Robert F. Kennedy, now a New York senator, began exploring a run for the presidency to challenge Johnson's Vietnam policy. Senator Eugene McCarthy of Minnesota had already announced his own campaign as an anti-war candidate. In New Hampshire's Democratic primary in March 1968, McCarthy won a stunning 42 percent of the vote to Johnson's 48 percent. "Dove bites Hawk," one reporter quipped. Johnson now seemed mortally wounded, and the results in New Hampshire convinced Bobby Kennedy to enter the race. LBJ hated Kennedy, dismissing him as a "grandstanding little runt."

Being challenged for reelection by members of his own party devastated Johnson. The growing opposition to the Vietnam War was even a worse blow. During a private meeting with military leaders, the president acknowledged that "the country is demoralized. . . . Most of the press is against us. . . . We have no support for the war." On March 31, 1968, a weary Johnson appeared on national television to announce a limited halt to the bombing of North Vietnam to enable a negotiated cease-fire agreement with the Communists. Then, he made an astounding announcement: "I shall not seek, and I will not accept, the nomination of my party for another term as your President." As his daughter explained, the "agony of Vietnam" had engulfed her father.

Johnson had become a tragic victim of his grandiose ambitions: by promising far more than he could accomplish, he raised false hopes, stoked violent resentments, and fractured society. Although U.S. troops would remain in Vietnam for five more years, the quest for military victory ended with Johnson's presidency.

America tried to fight a "limited war" in Vietnam. The problem with the strategy was that the Vietnamese Communists fought an absolute war in defense of their country. Among other things, the war revealed that the

Whose war? President Johnson lowers his head in disappointment as he listens to a commander's report from Vietnam in 1968.

resources of the United States, including its military power, were limited; the nation could not have its way around the world.

Now there were three candidates for the Democratic nomination: McCarthy, Kennedy, and Vice President Hubert Humphrey. Many antiwar Democrats expected McCarthy to drop out in favor of Kennedy, but the Minnesota senator, buoyed by his success and convinced of his moral superiority, refused to leave the race. For his part, Bobby Kennedy, with long hair and a boyish faith, appealed to the idealism of America's youth, promising them an end to the Vietnam War and a more inclusive and transparent presidency: "Some men see things as they are and ask, Why? I dream things that never were and say, why not?"

THE TURMOIL OF THE SIXTIES

By the late 1960s, traditional notions of authority were under attack as an angry spirit of rebelliousness expanded into a powerful cultural movement. The spirit of resistance was especially evident among disaffected youth who called into question not only the Vietnam War and the credibility of the Johnson administration but virtually every aspect of mainstream life, including the traditional family structure, the middle-class work ethic, universities, religion, and the nonviolent integrationist philosophy underpinning the civil rights movement. Many alienated young Americans, often lumped together as "hippies," felt that they were part of "the Revolution," a magical force that would overthrow a corrupt and outdated way of life.

1968: A TRAUMATIC YEAR   All of the turbulent elements affecting American life came to a head in 1968, the most traumatic year in a traumatic decade. As *Time* magazine reported, "Nineteen sixty-eight was a knife blade that severed past from future." It was "one tragic, surprising, and perplexing thing after another."

On April 4, James Earl Ray, a petty thief, drifter, and white racist, shot and killed Martin Luther King Jr. as the black leader stood outside the Lorraine Motel in Memphis, Tennessee. Ray had earlier vowed that he was going "to get the big nigger."

King's murder ignited a wave of violence. Riots erupted in more than 100 cities. Forty-six people died, all but five of them black. Some 20,000 army troops and 34,000 national guardsmen were mobilized across the country, and 21,000 people were arrested.

The night that King died, Robert Kennedy was in Indianapolis, Indiana. Upon hearing the news, he stood on a flatbed truck to speak to a grieving crowd of African Americans. "Those of you who are black can be filled with hatred, with bitterness and a desire for revenge," he said. "We can move toward further polarization. Or we can make an effort, as Dr. King did, to understand, to reconcile ourselves and to love."

Love was hard to find in 1968. Two months after King's death, after midnight on June 6, 1968, Robert Kennedy appeared at the Ambassador Hotel in Los Angeles to celebrate his victory over Eugene McCarthy in the California presidential primary. Kennedy closed his remarks by pledging that "we can end the divisions within the United States, end the violence."

After the applause subsided, Kennedy walked through the hotel kitchen on his way to the press room for interviews. Along the way, a Jordanian Arab named Sirhan Sirhan, resentful of the senator's strong support of Israel, pulled out a pistol and fired eight shots, hitting Kennedy in the head and wounding three others. Kennedy died the next morning. Only forty-two years old, Kennedy was buried beside his brother John in Arlington National Cemetery outside of Washington, D.C.

The assassinations of the Kennedys, Martin Luther King, and Malcolm X came to frame the sixties. With their deaths, a wealth of idealism died too— the idealism that Bobby Kennedy had hoped would put a fragmented America back together again. A growing number of young people felt orphaned from the political system. Having lost the leading voices for real change, many of them lost hope in democracy and turned to radicalism and violence—or dropped out of society.

CHICAGO AND MIAMI In August 1968, the nation's social unrest came to a head at the **Chicago Democratic National Convention**, where delegates gathered inside a convention hall to nominate Johnson's faithful vice president, Hubert H. Humphrey, as the party's candidate for president.

Outside, almost 20,000 police officers and national guard soldiers confronted thousands of passionate anti-war protesters who taunted the police with obscenities. Richard J. Daley, Chicago's gruff Democratic mayor, warned that he would not tolerate disruptions. Nonetheless, riots broke out and were televised nationwide. It was war in the streets. As police used tear gas and clubs to pummel the demonstrators, others chanted, "The whole world is watching." As the *New York Times* reported, "Those were our children in the streets, and the Chicago police beat them up." Nationally, the Democratic party began to fragment as a result of the chaos in Chicago.

Three weeks earlier, the Republicans had gathered in Miami Beach to nominate Richard Nixon. In 1962, after losing the California governor's race, Nixon had vowed never again to run for public office. By 1968, however, he had changed his mind and become a self-appointed spokesman for the values

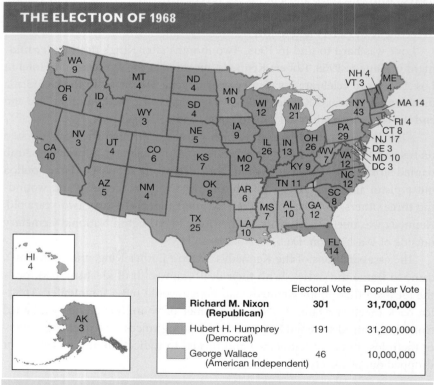

THE ELECTION OF 1968

		Electoral Vote	Popular Vote
■	**Richard M. Nixon** **(Republican)**	**301**	**31,700,000**
■	Hubert H. Humphrey (Democrat)	191	31,200,000
■	George Wallace (American Independent)	46	10,000,000

- How did the riots at the Chicago Democratic National Convention affect the 1968 presidential campaign?
- What does the electoral map reveal about the support for each of the three major candidates?
- How was Richard Nixon able to win enough electoral votes in such a close, three-way presidential race?
- What was George Wallace's appeal to 10 million voters?

of "middle America." He and the Republicans promised they would bring "law and order" to the nation's streets. Nixon appealed to what he called the "**silent majority**," those who viewed the "rabble rousing" street protesters with contempt. In accepting the nomination, Nixon promised to listen to "the voice of the great majority of Americans, the forgotten Americans, the non-shouters, the non-demonstrators, that are not racists or sick, that are not guilty of the crime that plagues the land."

Former Alabama governor George Wallace, an outspoken segregationist, dismissed both Democrats and Republicans as too liberal and ran on the American Independent party ticket, a party he formed to defend racial segregation. Wallace promised to get tough on "scummy anarchists" and bring stability to the nation. He appealed even more forcefully than Nixon to voters' concerns about anti-war protesters, the mushrooming federal welfare system, the growth of the federal government, forced racial integration, and rioting in urban ghettos.

Wallace displayed a savage wit, once saying that the "only four-letter words that hippies did not know were w-o-r-k and s-o-a-p." He predicted that on Election Day, the nation would realize that "there are a lot of rednecks in this country." His candidacy generated considerable appeal outside his native South, especially among white working-class communities, where resentment of Johnson's Great Society liberalism flourished. Wallace hoped to deny Humphrey and Nixon an electoral majority and thereby throw the choice into the House of Representatives.

NIXON TRIUMPHANT   George Wallace's hopes were dashed on Election Day, however, as Richard Nixon and his acid-tongued running mate, Governor Spiro Agnew of Maryland, won a narrow victory. Nixon claimed 302 electoral votes to 191 for Hubert Humphrey. Wallace's 46 electoral votes all came from the Lower South. So at the end of the century's most turbulent year, a divided society looked to Richard Nixon to fulfill his promises to bring "peace with honor" in Vietnam and to "bring us together" as a nation.

CHAPTER REVIEW

SUMMARY

- **Kennedy's New Frontier**   President John F. Kennedy promised a *"New Frontier"* in 1961, but many of his domestic policies stalled in Congress. The *Bay of Pigs* fiasco led the Soviet premier, Nikita Khrushchev, to test American resolve by erecting the *Berlin Wall* and installing nuclear-armed missiles in Cuba, which provoked the *Cuban missile crisis*. Determined to stand up to the Soviets, in October 1962 Kennedy ordered a naval "quarantine" of Cuba that led Khrushchev to withdraw the missiles. During his presidency, Kennedy deepened America's commitment in Vietnam.

- **Civil Rights' Achievements**   At the beginning of the decade, growing numbers of African Americans and whites staged acts of *nonviolent civil disobedience* to protest discrimination in the South. In 1960, activists formed the *Student Nonviolent Coordinating Committee (SNCC)* to intensify efforts to dismantle desegregation. In 1961, courageous *"Freedom Riders"* attempted to integrate bus and train stations in the South. The high point of the early phase of the civil rights movement was the 1963 *March on Washington* for Jobs and Freedom, at which Martin Luther King Jr. delivered his famous "I Have a Dream" speech. Later on, the *black power movement* emerged and emphasized militancy, black nationalism, separatism, and, often, violence.

- **Johnson's Great Society**   Lyndon Johnson began his presidency committed to social reform, especially civil rights. He forced the *Civil Rights Act of 1964* through Congress and then declared "war" on poverty by persuading Congress to pass the *Economic Opportunity Act*. After his resounding victory in the 1964 presidential election, he pushed his vision for a *Great Society*. Hundreds of initiatives expanded federal social welfare programs, most noticeably the *Voting Rights Act of 1965*, *Medicare*, and *Medicaid*.

- **1968 Presidential Election**   Frustrated by his failures in Vietnam and aware that he had lost public support, Johnson chose not to seek reelection in 1968. Anti-war Democrats rallied around Senators Eugene McCarthy and Robert Kennedy. In April, Martin Luther King Jr. was assassinated, setting off violent riots in urban ghettos across the country. Then Robert Kennedy was assassinated in June. Ultimately, the Democrats selected Johnson's loyal vice president, Hubert Humphrey, as their nominee, provoking angry protests by anti-war demonstrators at the *1968 Chicago Democratic National Convention*. As they had in 1960, the Republicans nominated Richard Nixon, who claimed to represent the *"silent majority."* In the end, Nixon narrowly bested Humphrey, while Wallace made one of the best showings ever by a third-party candidate.

CHRONOLOGY

KEY TERMS

New Frontier p. 1310

Bay of Pigs (1961) p. 1317

Berlin Wall p. 1318

Cuban missile crisis (1962) p. 1321

Student Nonviolent Coordinating Committee (SNCC) p. 1325

Freedom Riders p. 1325

nonviolent civil disobedience p. 1330

March on Washington (1963) p. 1331

black power movement p. 1336

Civil Rights Act of 1964 p. 1341

Economic Opportunity Act (1964) p. 1343

Great Society p. 1345

Medicare and Medicaid p. 1345

Voting Rights Act of 1965 p. 1348

Tonkin Gulf Resolution (1964) p. 1350

Tet offensive (1968) p. 1353

1968 Chicago Democratic National Convention p. 1357

silent majority p. 1359

 INQUIZITIVE

Go to InQuizitive to see what you've learned—and learn what you've missed—with personalized feedback along the way.

30 Rebellion and Reaction

1960s and 1970s

Rebels with a Cause Established in 1967, the Vietnam Veterans Against the War (VVAW) grew quickly during the sixties and early seventies. Here, a former Marine throws his service uniform jacket and medals onto the Capitol steps on April 23, 1971, as part of a five-day protest against the U.S. invasion of Laos.

A
s Richard M. Nixon entered the White House in early 1969, he took charge of a nation whose social fabric was in tatters. The traumatic events of 1968 had been like a knife cutting the past away from the future, revealing how deeply divided American society had become and how difficult a task Nixon faced in carrying out his campaign pledge to restore social harmony.

Ironically, many of the same forces that had contributed to the complacent prosperity of the crew-cut fifties—the baby boom, the cold war, and the growing consumer culture—helped generate the social upheaval of the sixties and early seventies. The civil rights movement promoting equality for African Americans inspired efforts to ensure equal treatment for other minorities, including women, gays, Native Americans, and Hispanics. It was one of the most turbulent and significant periods in American history.

Despite Nixon's promise to restore the public's faith in the integrity of its leaders, he ended up aggravating the growing cynicism about the motives and methods of government officials. During 1973 and 1974, the Watergate scandal resulted in the greatest constitutional crisis since the impeachment of President Andrew Johnson in 1868, and it ended with the first resignation of a U.S. president.

focus questions

1. What were the origins of the youth revolt? How did it manifest in the New Left and the counterculture?

2. How did the youth revolt and the early civil rights movement influence other protest movements? How did new protest movements affect social attitudes and public policy?

3. How did the political environment of the late sixties shape Richard Nixon's election strategy and domestic policy?

4. How and why did Richard Nixon and Henry Kissinger change military and political strategies to end America's involvement in the Vietnam War?

5. What was the international strategy brought about by Richard Nixon's and Henry Kissinger's diplomacy and foreign policy during the 1970s?

6. How did the Watergate scandal unfold? What was its political significance?

"Forever Young": The Youth Revolt

The Greensboro sit-ins in 1960 not only launched a decade of civil rights activism but also signaled an end to the carefree complacency that had characterized the fifties. Rennie Davis, a sophomore at Ohio's Oberlin College in 1960, remembered that the Greensboro student activists inspired him and many others to work for social reform and political change: "Here were four students from Greensboro who were suddenly all over *Life* magazine. There was a feeling that they were us and we were them, and a recognition that they were expressing something we were feeling as well."

The sit-ins, marches, protests, ideals, and sacrifices associated with the civil rights movement inspired other minority groups—women, Native Americans, Hispanics, gays, and the disabled—to demand justice, freedom, and equality. Many idealistic young people decided that they could no longer turn a blind eye to the growing evidence of injustice and inequality staining the American dream.

A full-fledged youth revolt erupted during the mid-sixties. "Your sons and your daughters are beyond your command," sang Bob Dylan in "The Times They Are a-Changin'." By 1970, more than half of Americans were under thirty years of age, and almost 8 million of them were attending college. The baby boomers, who unlike their parents had experienced neither an economic depression nor a major war during their young lifetimes, were now attending colleges and universities in record numbers; enrollment quadrupled between 1945 and 1970.

Many universities had become gigantic institutions dependent upon huge research contracts from corporations and the federal government, especially the Defense Department. As these "multiversities" grew larger and more bureaucratic, they became targets for a generation of students wary of involvement in what President Dwight D. Eisenhower had labeled "the military-industrial complex." As criticism of U.S. military involvement in Vietnam mounted, young people disillusioned with the government and "authority" of all kinds flowed into two distinct yet frequently overlapping movements: the New Left and the counterculture.

THE NEW LEFT The political arm of the youth revolt originated when Tom Hayden and Alan Haber, two University of Michigan students, formed Students for a Democratic Society (SDS), a campus-based organization influenced by the tactics and successes of the civil rights movement. In 1962, Hayden and Haber called a meeting of sixty young men and women activists at Port Huron, Michigan. Their goal was to remake the United States into a more democratic society. Several of the participants were the children of former leftists or Communists; even more were Jewish.

Hayden drafted an impassioned document known as the Port Huron Statement. It began: "We are the people of this generation, bred in at least moderate comfort, housed in universities, looking uncomfortably to the world we inherit." Only by giving power to "the people," the manifesto insisted, could America restore its founding principles. Hayden called for political reforms, racial equality, and workers' rights. Inspired by the example of African American civil rights activists, Hayden declared that college students should engage in "participatory democracy" by snatching "control of the educational process from the administrative bureaucracy."

Hayden and others adopted the term **New Left** to distinguish their efforts at grassroots democracy from those of the "Old Left" of the thirties, which had embraced an orthodox Marxism. SDS grew quickly, forming chapters on more than 1,000 campuses.

In the fall of 1964, students at the University of California at Berkeley took Hayden's New Left program to heart. Several had spent the summer working with the Student Nonviolent Coordinating Committee's (SNCC) voter-registration project in Mississippi, where three volunteers had been killed and

The free-speech movement Mario Savio, a founder of the free-speech movement, speaks at a rally at the University of California at Berkeley.

many others arrested or harassed. They were eager to bring changes to campus life. When the university's chancellor announced that political demonstrations would no longer be allowed on campus, thousands of students staged a sit-in. After a tense thirty-two-hour standoff, the administration relented. Student groups then formed the free-speech movement (FSM).

Led by Mario Savio, who had participated in Freedom Summer in Mississippi, the FSM became the first major student revolt of the sixties. The FSM initially protested on behalf of students' rights, but it quickly mounted more general criticisms of the university and what Savio called the "depersonalized, unresponsive bureaucracy" smothering American life. In 1964, Savio led hundreds of students into Sproul Hall, UC Berkeley's administration building, and organized another sit-in. At 4 A.M., 600 state police arrested the protesters. But their example lived on. Some 7,000 students filled Sproul Plaza that morning, circulating leaflets and joining folk singer Joan Baez in singing "We Shall Overcome." Finally, the university's president gave in and revoked the ban on political demonstrations. The FSM succeeded, Savio explained, because "it was so obvious to everybody that it was right."

All that rises must converge This protester's sign at a Washington, D.C., demonstration bridged the civil rights and anti-war movements, which pursued many of the same racial and political goals.

ANTI-WAR PROTESTS The goals and tactics of FSM and SDS soon spread across the country. By 1965, however, the growing U.S. involvement in Vietnam had changed the rebellious students' agenda. Millions of young men suddenly faced the grim prospect of being drafted to fight in the increasingly unpopular conflict.

The Vietnam War was primarily a poor man's fight. Most college students were able to postpone military service until they received their degree or reached the age of twenty-four; in 1965–1966, college students made up only 2 percent of military inductees. African Americans and Hispanics were twice as likely to be drafted as whites.

As the war dragged on, Americans divided into "hawks" and "doves," those who supported the war and those who opposed it. Some 200,000 young men ignored their draft notices, and some 4,000 served prison sentences for doing so. Another 56,000 qualified for conscientious objector status. Others ceremoniously burned their draft cards in front of television cameras while shouting "Hell No, We Won't Go!" Still others fled to Canada or Sweden to avoid military service. The most popular means of escaping the draft was to find a way to flunk the physical examination. Whatever the method, many college students succeeded in avoiding military service. Of the 1,200 men in Harvard's class of 1970, only 56 served in the military, and just 2 of them went to Vietnam.

RISING VIOLENCE Throughout 1967 and 1968, the anti-war movement grew more violent as inner-city ghettos in Cleveland, Detroit, Newark, and other large cities were exploding in flames fanned by racial injustice. Frustration over deeply entrenched patterns of discrimination in employment and housing, as well as staggering rates of joblessness among inner-city African American youths, ignited the rage. "There was a sense everywhere, in 1968," journalist Garry Wills wrote, "that things were giving way. That man had not only lost control of his history, but might never regain it."

During the eventful spring of 1968—when Lyndon Johnson announced that he would not run for reelection and Martin Luther King Jr. and Robert F. Kennedy were assassinated—campus unrest boiled over. The turmoil reached a climax at Columbia University, where SDS student radicals and black militants occupied the president's office and classroom buildings. They renamed the administration building Malcolm X Hall. Mark Rudd, the campus SDS leader, called his parents to report that "we took a building." His father, Jacob Rudd, a retired army officer and a real estate investor, replied: "Well, give it back." He did not, and, after a failed attempt by professors to negotiate an end to the takeover, the university's president cancelled classes and called in the New York City police. More than 100 students were injured, 700 were arrested, and the leaders of the uprising were expelled.

Part of the problem with SDS and other militant organizations is that they were much more effective at criticizing the status quo than they were at creating a blueprint for an alternative future. "If there is a road to power," SDS president Todd Gitlin acknowledged, "we have no map for it."

The events at Columbia inspired similar clashes at Harvard, Cornell, and San Francisco State, among dozens of other universities. Student radicals adopted a tough, macho style, dismissing traditional approaches to reform and protest as "wimpy" and rooted in "white skin privilege."

Columbia riots Mark Rudd, leader of SDS at Columbia University, speaks to the media during student protests on campus in April 1968.

Most Americans viewed the student radicals with fear and loathing. Vice President Spiro Agnew dismissed them as "impudent snobs who characterize themselves as intellectuals." Richard Nixon declared that the campus unrest represented "the first major skirmish in a revolutionary struggle to seize the universities."

THE WEATHER UNDERGROUND A small group of radical militants called the Revolutionary Youth Movement (RYM) surged into prominence during the summer of 1969. They wanted to move political radicalism from "protest to resistance." At the SDS convention in Chicago on June 18, 1969, RYM members distributed a position paper titled "You don't need a weatherman / To know which way the wind blows," a line from Bob Dylan's song "Subterranean Homesick Blues" (1965).

The document called for a "white fighting force" to ally with the Black Panthers and other radical movements to pursue "the destruction of U.S. imperialism and achieve a classless world: world communism." By embracing revolutionary violence, however, the so-called Weathermen essentially committed revolutionary suicide. They killed SDS by abandoning the pacifist principles that had originally inspired participants and given the movement moral legitimacy.

Members of the Weather Underground took to the streets of Chicago in October 1969 to assault police and trash the city. Their goal was "to lead white kids into armed revolution." Almost 300 were arrested. During the so-called Days of Rage between September 1969 and May 1970, there were 250 bombings of draft board offices, ROTC buildings providing military training on university campuses, federal government facilities, and corporate headquarters. In March 1970, three members of the Weather Underground in New York City died when a bomb they were making exploded prematurely.

The Weathermen and other radical groups were forced underground by the aggressive efforts of federal law enforcement agencies, and their energy diminished as Nixon ended the draft and withdrew U.S. troops from Vietnam. Mark Rudd, one of the organizers of the Weather Underground, later confessed that their "totally failed strategy" was designed to destroy SDS "because it wasn't revolutionary enough for us. I am not proud of this history." His own conversion to revolutionary violence, he explained, "had something to do with an exaggerated sense of my own importance. I wanted to prove myself as a man—a motive exploited by all armies and terrorist groups." Rudd called the intentional destruction of SDS by the Weathermen a "crime." Their "hyper-militancy" and bombings weakened "the larger anti-war movement and demoralized many good people." Blowing things up "got us isolated" by the media and "smashed" by the FBI.

THE COUNTERCULTURE Looking back over the 1960s, Tom Hayden, the founder of SDS, recalled that most rebellious young Americans "were not narrowly political. Most were not so interested in attaining [elected] office but in changing lifestyles. They were not interested in being opinion makers as in changing the climate of opinion." Hayden acknowledged that the shocking events of 1968 led disaffected young rebels—so-called hippies—to embrace the **counterculture**, an unorganized rebellion against mainstream institutions, values, and behavior that focused more on cultural change than political activism.

Hippies rejected the pursuit of wealth and careers and embraced plain living, authenticity, friendship, peace, and, especially, *freedom*. In a 1967 cover story, the editors of *Time* magazine suggested that "in their independence of material possessions and their emphasis on peacefulness and honesty, hippies lead considerably more virtuous lives than the great majority of their fellow citizens. . . . In the end, it may be that the hippies have not so much dropped out of American society as given it something to think about."

Flower power Hippies let loose at a 1967 love-in, one of many such gatherings that celebrated peace, free love, and nontheological spirituality, often as a gesture of protest.

Both the counterculture and the New Left fiercely rejected the status quo, but most hippies preferred to "drop out" of mainstream society rather than try to change the political system. Their preferred slogan was "Make Love, Not War." Like the Beats of the fifties, hippies created their own subculture that promoted personal freedom from virtually all traditional constraints. They were at once defiant, innocent, egalitarian, optimistic, and indulgent as they rejected the authority of the nation's core institutions: the family, government, political parties, corporations, the military, and colleges and universities. The "idea was to liberate yourself from the confining conventions of life and to celebrate the irrational side of your nature, kind of let yourself go," explained a student at the University of Chicago. "Do Your Own Thing" became the unofficial motto of the counterculture.

The counterculture lifestyle included an array of popular ideals and activities: peace, love, harmony, rock music, mystical religions, mind-altering drugs, casual sex, and communal living. Hippie fashion featured defiantly long hair for both women and men and clothing that was striking, unusual, or, God forbid, comfortable: flowing cotton dresses, granny gowns, ragged bell-bottom blue jeans, tie-dyed T-shirts, love beads, Tibetan bells, peace symbols, black

Flower power Author Ken Kesey and his posse, the Merry Pranksters, held Acid Test Graduation parties throughout the San Francisco area that celebrated the psychedelic drug LSD (also known as "acid").

boots, or sandals. Young men grew beards, and women stopped wearing makeup.

Underground newspapers celebrating the counterculture appeared in every large city, many of them with defiant names such as *Fuck You: A Magazine of the Arts*. A hippie magazine published in Boston in 1967–1968 called *Avatar* asked, "Who is the underground?" Its answer was "You are, if you think, dream, work, and build towards the improvements and changes in your life, your social and personal environments, towards the expectations of a better existence. . . . Think, look around, maybe in a mirror, maybe inside."

DO YOUR OWN THING The countercultural rebels were primarily middle-class whites deeply alienated by the Vietnam War, racism, political corruption, and parental authority. They were determined to break away from conventional behavior. For many, the preferred pathway to freedom was that recommended by former Harvard psychology professor Timothy Leary: "Tune in, turn on, drop out." He added that "your only hope is dope." If it had not been for marijuana, said one hippie, "I'd still be wearing a crew cut and saluting the flag."

"EIGHT MILES HIGH" Illegal drugs—marijuana, amphetamines, cocaine, peyote, hashish, heroin, and LSD, the "Acid Test"—were common within the counterculture. Said Todd Gitlin, a former SDS president, "More and more, to get access to youth culture" in the late 1960s, "you had to get high." The Byrds sang about getting "Eight Miles High," and Bob Dylan proclaimed that "everybody must get stoned!"

In fact, getting stoned was one of the favorite activities of the millions who participated in the 1967 "Summer of Love," a series of events protesting the Vietnam War and celebrating the youth revolt. The initial event was actually held April 15, when a peace march in New York City attracted 300,000 participants, the most ever assembled for a single event up to that time.

Perhaps the most publicized activity of the "Summer of Love" occurred in San Francisco, where more than 100,000 hippies ("flower children") converged. The loosely organized "Council for the Summer of Love" intended the gathering to be the first step in a grassroots revolution opposing the war by celebrating alternative lifestyles—listening to rock music, experimenting with mind-altering drugs, wearing "psychedelic" clothing, and indulging in casual sex.

THE YIPPIES The countercultural alternative to SDS and the New Left was the zany Youth International party, better known as the Yippies, founded by two irreverent pranksters, Jerry Rubin and Abbie Hoffman. Often calling themselves Groucho Marxists, the Yippies were bent on thumbing their noses at conventional laws and behavior and mocking capitalism and the consumer culture.

Abbie Hoffman explained that their "conception of revolution is that it's fun." They wanted to form an alliance between hippies and Weathermen, a "blending of pot and politics," and to overthrow the power structure. Rubin claimed that "the first part of the Yippie program is to kill your parents," since they are "our first oppressors." He added that the widespread use of "psychedelic" drugs among young Americans "signifies the total end of the Protestant ethic: screw work, we want to know ourselves." The Yippie platform called for peace in Vietnam, absolute personal freedom, free birth control and abortions, and legalization of marijuana and LSD.

Hoffman had no interest in making the Yippies a traditional political organization. "We shall not defeat *Amerika* by organizing a political party," he declared. "We shall do it by building a new nation—a nation as rugged as the marijuana leaf." The anarchistic Yippies organized marijuana "smoke-ins," threw pies in the faces of political figures, nominated a squealing pig for the presidency, urged voters to cast their ballots for "None of the Above," and threatened to put LSD in the city of Chicago's water supply during the 1968 Democratic National Convention.

COMMUNES For some, the counterculture involved experimenting with alternative living arrangements, especially "intentional communities" or "communes." Communal living in urban areas such as San Francisco's Haight-Ashbury district, New York's Greenwich Village, Chicago's Uptown, and Atlanta's 14th Street neighborhood were popular for a time, as were rural communes. Thousands of hippie romantics flocked to the countryside, eager to liberate themselves from parental and institutional restraints, live in harmony with nature, and coexist in love and openness.

The participants in the back-to-the-land movement, as it became known, were seeking to deepen their sense of self and forge authentic community ties. "Out here," one of the rural communalists reflected, "we've got the

Little house on the commune This photograph of the members of the Family of the Mystic Arts commune in Oregon was featured on the cover of *Life* magazine's July 18, 1969, edition.

earth and ourselves and God above. . . . We came for simplicity and to rediscover God."

Yet all but a handful of the back-to-the-land experiments collapsed within a few months or years. Almost none of those attracted by rural life actually knew how to farm, and many were not willing to do the hard work that living off the land required. "The hippies will not change America," a journalist predicted, "because change means pain, and the hippie subculture is rooted in the pleasure principle." *Newsweek* magazine reported "Trouble in Hippieland" in 1968, noting that most of the flower children were "seriously disturbed youngsters" incapable of sustaining an alternative to mainstream life. In a candid reflection, a young hippie confessed that "we are so stupid, so unable to cope with anything practical." A resident of Paper Farm in northern California, which started in 1968 and collapsed a year later, said of its participants: "They had no commitment to the land—a big problem. All would take food from the land, but few would tend it. . . . We were entirely open. We did not say no [to anyone]. We felt this would make for a more dynamic group. But we got a lot of sick people."

WOODSTOCK The sixties counterculture thrived on music—initially folk "protest" songs and later psychedelic rock music. During the early sixties, Pete Seeger, Joan Baez, Peter, Paul, and Mary, and Bob Dylan, among others, produced powerful songs intended to spur social reform. In Dylan's "The Times They Are a-Changin'," first sung in 1963, he warns: "There's a battle outside and it's ragin' / It'll soon shake your windows and rattle your walls / For the times, they are a-changin'."

Within a few years, however, the hippies' favorite performers were those under the influence of mind-altering drugs, especially the San Francisco–based "acid rock" bands: Jefferson Airplane, Big Brother and the Holding Company, and the Grateful Dead.

Huge outdoor concerts were wildly popular. The largest was the sprawling Woodstock Music and Art Fair ("Aquarian Exposition"). In mid-August 1969, more than 400,000 mostly young people converged on a 600-acre farm near the tiny rural town of Bethel, New York, for what was called the world's "largest happening," three days "of peace and music."

The festival boasted an all-star cast of musicians, among them Jimi Hendrix, the Jefferson Airplane, Janis Joplin, Santana, the Who, Joan Baez, and Crosby, Stills & Nash. For three days amid heat, rain storms, and rivers of mud, the assembled "flower children" "grooved" on good music, beer and booze, cheap marijuana, and casual sex. There were overdoses ("bad trips"), but no robberies, assaults, or rapes. Baez said that Woodstock was a "technicolor, mud-splattered reflection of the 1960s."

Bob Dylan Born Robert Allen Zimmerman in northern Minnesota, Dylan helped transform the New York folk music scene, penning the anti-war movement anthem "Blowin' in the Wind."

Woodstock's carefree "spirit of love" was short-lived, however. Just four months later, when other concert promoters tried to replicate the

"Woodstock Nation" experience at the Altamont Speedway Free Festival near San Francisco, the counterculture fell victim to the criminal culture.

The Rolling Stones hired the Hells Angels motorcycle gang to provide "security" for their show. During the band's performance of "Under My Thumb," a drunken Hells Angel stabbed to death an eighteen-year-old African American man wielding a gun in front of the stage. Three other spectators were accidentally killed. Much of the vitality and innocence of the counterculture died with them. After 1969, the hippie phenomenon began to fade as the spirit of liberation ran up against the hard realities of growing poverty, drug addiction, crime, and mental and physical illness among the "flower children."

SOCIAL ACTIVISM SPREADS

The same liberationist ideals that prompted young people to revolt against mainstream values and to protest against the Vietnam War also led many of them to embrace other causes. The success of the civil rights movement inspired other groups—women; Mexican Americans and Native Americans; gays; the elderly; and the physically and mentally disabled—to demand equal opportunities and equal rights. Still others joined the emerging environmental movement or groups working on behalf of consumers.

THE NEW FEMINISM

The women's movement in the late nineteenth and early twentieth centuries had focused on gaining the right to vote. The feminist movement of the sixties and seventies aimed to challenge the conventional ideal of female domesticity and ensure that women were treated equally in the workplace.

Most women in the early sixties, however, did not view gender equality as possible or even desirable. In 1962, more than two-thirds of women surveyed agreed that the most important family decisions "should be made by the man of the house." Although the Equal Pay Act of 1963 had made it illegal to pay women less than men for doing the same job, discrimination and harassment continued in the workplace and throughout society. Women, who were 51 percent of the nation's population and held 37 percent of the jobs, were paid 42 percent less than men.

Betty Friedan, a forty-two-year-old journalist and mother of three from Peoria, Illinois, emerged as the leader of the **women's movement**. Her influential book *The Feminine Mystique* (1963) helped launch the new phase of female protest. Friedan claimed that "something was very wrong with the way American women are trying to live their lives today." Her generation

Betty Friedan Author of *The Feminine Mystique* and the first president of NOW.

of white, college-educated women (she did not discuss working-class or African American women) had actually lost ground after the Second World War, when many left wartime employment and settled in suburbia as full-time wives and mothers, only to suffer from the "happy home-maker" syndrome which undermined their intellectual capacity and public aspirations. College-educated women, she observed, "seemed suddenly inca-pable of any ambition, any vision, any passion, except the pursuit of a wedding ring."

Friedan blamed a massive propa-ganda campaign by advertisers and women's magazines for brainwashing women to embrace the "feminine mys-tique" of blissful domesticity in which fulfillment came only with marriage and motherhood. Women, Friedan claimed, "were being duped into believing homemaking was their natural destiny."

The Feminine Mystique, an immediate best seller, forever changed Amer-ican society by defining "the problem that has no name." Friedan's analysis of the "feminine mystique" inspired many well-educated, unfulfilled middle- and upper-class white women who felt trapped by a suffocating suburban ideal of household drudgery.

Moreover, Friedan discovered that there were far more women working outside the home than she had assumed. Many of them were frustrated by the demands of holding "two full-time jobs instead of just one—underpaid cleri-cal worker and unpaid housekeeper." Perhaps most important, Friedan helped empower women to achieve their "full human capacities"—in the home, in schools, in offices, on college campuses, and in politics.

In 1966, Friedan and other activists founded the National Organization for Women (NOW). They chose the acronym NOW because it was part of a pop-ular civil rights chant: "What do you want?" protesters yelled. "FREEDOM!" "When do you want it?" "NOW!"

NOW was formed to promote "true equality for all women in America . . . as part of the world-wide revolution of human rights now taking place." It sought to end gender discrimination in the workplace and spearheaded efforts to legalize abortion and obtain federal and state support for child-care centers. Change came slowly, however. By 1970, there was still only one woman in the U.S. Senate, ten in the House of Representatives, and none on the Supreme Court or in the president's cabinet.

In the early seventies, members of Congress, the Supreme Court, and NOW advanced the cause of gender equality. Title IX of the Educational Amendments of 1972 barred discrimination on the basis of sex in any "education program or activity receiving federal financial assistance." Most notably applied to athletics, Title IX has enabled female participation in high school sports to increase nearly tenfold and almost double at the college level.

Congress also overwhelmingly approved an equal-rights amendment (ERA) to the U.S. Constitution, which, if ratified by the states, would have required equal treatment for women throughout society and politics. By mid-1973, twenty-eight states had approved the amendment, ten short of the thirty-eight needed for approval.

In 1973, the Supreme Court, in its **Roe v. Wade** decision, made history by striking down state laws forbidding abortions during the first three months of pregnancy. The Court ruled that women have a fundamental "right to choose" whether to bear a child or not, since pregnancy necessarily affects a woman's health and well-being. The *Roe v. Wade* decision and the ensuing success of NOW's efforts to liberalize local and state abortion laws generated a powerful conservative backlash, especially among Roman Catholics and evangelical Protestants, who mounted a potent "right-to-life" crusade that helped fuel the conservative political resurgence in the seventies and thereafter.

RADICAL FEMINISM During the late sixties, a new wave of younger and more radical feminists emerged. They sought "women's liberation" from all forms of "sexism" (also called "male chauvinism" or "male oppression").

The new feminists, often called "women's libbers," were more militant than those who had established NOW. Many were veterans of the civil rights movement and the anti-war crusade who had come to realize that male revolutionaries could be sexists, too. The women began meeting in small groups to discuss their opposition to the war and racism, only to discover at such "consciousness-raising" sessions that what bound them together was their shared grievances as women in a "man's world."

To gain true liberation, many of them decided, required exercising "sexual politics" whereby women would organize into a political movement based on their common problems and goals. Writer Robin Morgan captured this newly politicized feminism in the slogan, "The personal is political," a radical notion that Betty Friedan rejected. When lesbians demanded a public role in the women's movement, Friedan deplored the "lavender menace" of lesbianism as a divisive distraction that would only enrage their opponents. By 1973, however, NOW had endorsed gay rights.

Friedan could not dampen or deflect the younger generation of women activists, just as Martin Luther King Jr. had failed to control the Black Power movement. The goal of the women's liberation movement, said Susan Brownmiller, was to "go beyond a simple concept of equality. NOW's emphasis on legislative change left the radicals cold."

For women to be truly equal, Brownmiller and others believed, required transforming *every* aspect of society: child rearing, entertainment, domestic duties, business, and the arts. Feminists demanded that their "hidden history," the story of women's rights advocates over the centuries, be taught in schools and colleges. They also took direct action, such as picketing the 1968 Miss America Pageant, burning copies of *Playboy* and other men's magazines, and tossing their bras and high-heeled shoes into "freedom cans."

They also formed militant organizations like WITCH (Women's International Terrorist Conspiracy from Hell), WRAP (Women's Radical Action Project), Keep on Truckin' Sisters, and the Redstockings, whose manifesto proclaimed that they were tired of being exploited by men "as sex objects, breeders, domestic servants, and cheap labor." Members sported buttons proclaiming their collective nickname: "Uppity Women."

What women want The Women's Strike for Equality brought tens of thousands of women together on August 26, 1970, to march for gender equality and celebrate the fiftieth anniversary of the Nineteenth Amendment.

FRACTURED FEMINISM By the end of the seventies, sharp disputes between moderate and radical feminists had fractured the women's movement in ways similar to the fragmentation experienced by civil rights organizations a decade earlier. The movement's failure to broaden its appeal much beyond the confines of the white middle class also caused reform efforts to stall.

Ratification of the Equal Rights Amendment, which had once seemed a straightforward assertion of equal opportunity ("Equality of rights under the law shall not be denied or abridged by the United States or by any State on account of sex"), was stymied in several state legislatures by conservative groups. By 1982, it had died, three states short of ratification.

Yet the successes of the women's movement endured. The women fighting for equal rights focused on several basic issues: gender discrimination in the workplace; equal pay for equal work; an equal chance at jobs traditionally reserved for men; the availability of high-quality, government-subsidized child-care centers; and easier access to birth-control devices, prenatal care, and abortion. Feminists also helped win improvements in divorce laws.

Conservative women speak The antifeminist campaign, STOP ERA ("Stop Taking Our Privileges, Equal Rights Amendment"), found its most outspoken activist in Phyllis Schlafly, a constitutional lawyer and staunch conservative.

Feminists called attention to issues long hidden or ignored. In 1970, for example, 36 percent of the nation's "poor" families were headed by women, as were most urban families dependent on federal welfare services. Nearly 3 million poor children needed access to day-care centers, but there were places for only 530,000.

The feminist movement helped women achieve mass entry into the labor market and enjoy steady improvements toward equal pay and treatment. In 1960, some 38 percent of women were working outside the home; by 1980, some 52 percent were doing so.

Their growing presence in the labor force brought women a greater share of economic and political influence. By 1976, more than half of married women, and nine of ten female college graduates, were employed outside the home, a development that one economist called "the single most outstanding phenomenon of this century." Women also enrolled in graduate and professional schools in record numbers. During the 1970s, women began winning elected offices at the local, state, and national levels.

THE SEXUAL REVOLUTION AND THE PILL The feminist movement coincided with the so-called sexual revolution. Americans became more tolerant of premarital sex, and women became more sexually active. Between

Birth control To spread the word about birth-control options, Planned Parenthood in 1967 displayed posters like this one in New York City buses.

1960 and 1975, the number of college women engaging in sexual intercourse doubled, to 50 percent. Enabling this change, in large part, was a scientific breakthrough: the birth-control pill, approved for public use by the Food and Drug Administration in 1960.

Widespread access to the pill gave women a greater sense of sexual freedom and led to more-open discussion of birth control, reproduction, and sexuality in general. By 1990, the world would have 400 million fewer people as a result of the pill.

Although the birth-control pill contributed to a rise in sexually transmitted diseases, many women viewed it as an inexpensive, nonintrusive way to gain better control over their bodies and their futures. "It was a savior," recalled Eleanor Smeal, president of the Feminist Majority Foundation.

HISPANIC RIGHTS

The activism of student revolts, the civil rights movement, and the crusade for women's rights soon spread to various ethnic minority groups. The word *Hispanic*, referring to people who trace their ancestry to Spanish-speaking Latin America or Spain, came into increasing use after 1945 in conjunction with growing efforts to promote economic and social justice. (Although frequently used as a synonym for Hispanic, the term *Latino* technically refers only to people of Latin American descent.)

Labor shortages during the Second World War had led defense industries to offer Hispanic Americans their first significant access to skilled-labor jobs. And as with African Americans, service in the military helped to heighten an American identity among Hispanic Americans and increase their desire for equal rights and social opportunities.

Social equality, however, remained elusive. After the Second World War, Hispanic Americans still faced widespread discrimination in hiring, housing, and education, and in 1960, the median income of a Mexican American family was only 62 percent of the national average. Hispanic American activists denounced segregation, called for improved public schools, and struggled to increase Hispanic political influence, economic opportunities, and visibility in the curricula of schools and colleges.

Hispanic civil rights leaders also faced an awkward dilemma: What should they do about the continuing stream of undocumented Mexican immigrants flowing across the border into the United States? Many Mexican Americans argued that their hopes for economic advancement and social equality were threatened by the influx of Mexican laborers willing to accept low-paying jobs. Mexican American leaders thus helped end the *bracero* program in 1964 (which trucked in contract day-laborers from Mexico during harvest season).

THE UNITED FARM WORKERS In the early sixties, Mexican American workers formed their own civil rights organization, the **United Farm Workers (UFW)**. Its founder was the charismatic Cesar Chavez. Born in 1927 in Yuma, Arizona, the son of Mexican immigrants, Chavez served in the U.S. Navy during the Second World War, and afterward worked as a migrant laborer and community organizer focused on registering Latinos to vote.

Then, along with Dolores Huerta, he created the UFW, a union for migrant lettuce workers and grape pickers, many of them undocumented immigrants who could be deported at any time. Up and down California, Chavez led non-violent protest marches that had the energy of religious pilgrimages. He staged hunger strikes and managed nationwide boycotts.

Cesar Chavez The usually energetic Chavez is visibly weakened from what would be a twenty-five-day hunger strike in support of the United Farm Workers Union in March 1968. Robert F. Kennedy, a great admirer of Chavez, is seated to his right.

The United Farm Workers gained national attention in September 1965 when the union organized a strike (*la huelga*) against the corporate grape growers in California's San Joaquin Valley. As Huerta explained, "We have to get farmworkers the same type of benefits, the same type of wages, and the respect that they deserve because they do the most sacred work of all. They feed our nation every day."

Chavez's relentless energy and deep Catholic faith, his insistence upon nonviolent tactics, his reliance upon college-student volunteers, his skillful alliance with organized labor and religious groups, and the life of poverty he chose for himself—all combined to attract media interest and popular support.

However, the chief strength of the Hispanic rights movement lay less in the tactics of sit-ins and protest marches than in the rapid growth of the Hispanic American population. In 1970, Hispanics in the United States numbered 9 million (4.8 percent of the total population); by 2000 their numbers had increased to 35 million (12.5 percent); and in 2015, they numbered 55 million, making them the nation's largest minority group (17 percent). The voting power of Hispanics and their concentration in states with key electoral votes has helped give the Hispanic point of view significant political clout.

NATIVE AMERICAN RIGHTS

American Indians—many of whom had begun calling themselves *Native Americans*—also emerged as a political force in the late sixties. Two conditions combined to make Indian rights a priority. First, many whites felt guilty for the destructive actions of their ancestors toward a people who had, after all, been here first. Second, Native Americans faced desperate times: Indian unemployment was ten times the national rate, life expectancy was twenty years lower than the national average, and the suicide rate was a hundred times higher than the rate for whites.

Although President Lyndon Johnson attempted to funnel federal anti-poverty-program funds to reservations, militants within the Indian community grew impatient with the pace of change. Those promoting "**Red Power**" organized protests and demonstrations against local, state, and federal agencies.

On November 20, 1969, fourteen Red Power activists occupied Alcatraz Island near San Francisco, which until 1963 had hosted a federal prison. Over the next several months, they were joined by hundreds of others, mostly students. The Nixon administration responded by cutting off electrical service and telephone lines. Stranded without electrical power and fresh water, most of the protesters left the island. Finally, on June 11, 1971, the government removed the remaining fifteen Native Americans from the island.

In 1968, the year before the Alcatraz occupation, two Chippewas (or Ojibwas) living in Minneapolis, George Mitchell and Dennis Banks, founded the American Indian Movement (AIM). In October 1972, AIM organized the Trail of Broken Treaties caravan, which traveled by bus and car from the West Coast to Washington, D.C., drawing attention to the federal government's broken promises. When Nixon administration officials refused to meet with them, the protesters occupied the federal Bureau of Indian Affairs. The sit-in ended when government negotiators agreed to renew discussions of Native American grievances about the government programs intended to improve their quality of life.

In 1973, AIM led 200 Sioux in the occupation of the tiny South Dakota village of Wounded Knee, where the U.S. Seventh Cavalry had massacred a Sioux village in 1890. Outraged by the light sentences given a group of local whites who had killed a Sioux in 1972, the organizers sought to draw attention to the plight of the Indians. After the militants took eleven hostages, federal marshals and FBI agents surrounded the encampment.

When AIM leaders tried to bring in food and supplies, a shoot-out erupted, with one Indian killed and another wounded. The confrontation ended with a government promise to reexamine Indian treaty rights.

Standoff at Wounded Knee After occupying Wounded Knee and taking eleven hostages, members of the American Indian Movement and the Oglala Sioux stand guard outside of the town's Sacred Heart Catholic Church.

Indian protesters subsequently discovered a more effective tactic: they went into federal courts armed with copies of old treaties and demanded that the documents become the basis for financial restitution for the lands taken from them. In Alaska, Maine, South Carolina, and Massachusetts, they won substantial settlements that officially recognized their tribal rights and awarded monetary compensation at levels that upgraded the standard of living on several reservations.

GAY RIGHTS

The liberationist impulses of the sixties also encouraged homosexuals to assert their right to equal treatment. Throughout the sixties, gay men and lesbians were treated with disgust, cruelty, and violence. On Saturday night, June 28, 1969, New York City vice police raided the Stonewall Inn, a popular gay bar in Greenwich Village. Instead of dispersing, the patrons fought back, and the struggle spilled into the streets. Hundreds of other gays and their supporters joined the fracas.

The **Stonewall riots** lasted throughout the weekend, during which the Stonewall Inn burned down. When the turmoil ended, gays had forged a sense

Gay Pride in the Seventies Gay rights activists march in the Fifth Annual Gay Pride Day demonstration, commemorating the fifth anniversary of the Stonewall riots which jumpstarted the modern gay rights movement in the United States.

of solidarity embodied in two new organizations, the Gay Liberation Front and the Gay Activists' Alliance, both of which focused on ending discrimination and harassment against gay and transgender people. "Gay is good for all of us," proclaimed one of its members. "The artificial categories 'heterosexual' and 'homosexual' have been laid on us by a sexist society."

As news of the Stonewall rebellion spread, the gay rights movement grew. By 1973, almost 800 gay organizations had been formed across the country. That year, the American Psychiatric Association removed homosexuality from its official manual of "mental illnesses." Colleges and universities began offering courses and majors in "Gay Studies" (also called Queer Studies), and groups began pushing for official government recognition of same-sex marriages. As with the civil rights and women's movements, however, the campaign for gay rights soon suffered from internal divisions and a conservative counterattack.

NIXON AND THE REVIVAL OF CONSERVATISM

The turmoil of the sixties spawned a cultural backlash among what Richard Nixon called the "great silent majority" of middle-class Americans that propelled him to a narrow election victory in 1968. He had been elected president as the representative of middle America—voters fed up with liberal politics, hippies, radical feminism, and **affirmative-action** programs giving preferential treatment to minorities and women to atone for past injustices.

THE CONSERVATIVE BACKLASH Alabama's Democratic governor, George Wallace, led the conservative counterattack. He was a fierce champion of states' rights and the voice of the white backlash against civil rights and cultural rebellion. "Liberals, intellectuals, and long hairs," he shouted, "have run the country for too long." Wallace repeatedly lashed out at "welfare queens," unmarried women he claimed "were breeding children as a cash crop" to receive federal child-support checks. Wallace became the voice for many working-class whites fed up with political liberalism and social radicalism.

All in the Family, the most popular television show in the 1970s, was created to showcase the decade's cultural wars. In the much-celebrated situation comedy, the Bunker family lived in a state of perpetual conflict in a working-class suburb of New York City. Semi-literate Archie Bunker (played by Carroll O'Connor), a Polish-American loading-dock worker, was the gruff but lovable head of the family, a proud Republican, Nixon supporter, and talkative member of the "silent majority" who was a bundle of racial, ethnic, and political prejudices.

Enthroned in his easy chair, Archie railed against blacks, Jews, Italians, gays, feminists, hippies, and liberals (including his live-in daughter and her hippie husband). At one point, he says: "I ain't no bigot. I'm the first guy to say, 'It ain't your fault that youse are colored.'" The producer of the series, Norman Lear, sought to provoke viewers to question their own prejudices. In fact, however, many of the 50 million people watching each Saturday night identified *with* Archie's narrow-minded values.

RICHARD NIXON   Richard Nixon appealed to the working- and middle-class whites who feared that America was being corrupted by permissiveness, anarchy, and the tyranny of the rebellious minority. He explicitly appealed to voters "who did not break the law, people who pay their taxes and go to work, people who send their children to school, who go to their churches, people who are not haters, people who love this country." Above all, he promised to restore "law and order."

In 1952, Senator Robert A. Taft of Ohio, known as "Mr. Republican," had characterized young Senator Nixon as a "little man in a big hurry" with "a mean and vindictive streak." A grocer's son from Whittier, California, Nixon was a humorless man of fierce ambition and extraordinary perseverance. Raised in a family that struggled with poverty, he had to claw and struggle to the top, and he nursed a deep resentment of people who had an easier time of it (the "moneyed class").

Nixon was smart, shrewd, cunning, and doggedly determined to succeed in politics. He was also famously hard to get to know. Republican senator Barry Goldwater described Nixon as "the most complete loner I've ever known." Throughout his career, Nixon displayed violent mood swings punctuated by raging temper tantrums, profanity, and anti-Semitic outbursts. He was driven as much by anger and resentment as by civic duty. Critics nicknamed him "Tricky Dick" because he was a good liar. In his speech accepting the Republican nomination in 1968, Nixon pledged "to find the truth, to speak the truth, and live with the truth." In fact, however, he often did the opposite. One of his presidential aides admitted that "we did often lie, mislead, deceive, try to use [the media], and to con them."

NIXON'S APPOINTMENTS   In his first term, Nixon selected for his cabinet and staff only white men who would blindly carry out his orders. John Mitchell, the gruff attorney general who had been a senior partner in Nixon's

New York law firm, was his closest confidant. H. R. (Bob) Haldeman, a former advertising executive, served as chief of staff. As Haldeman explained, "Every President needs a son of a bitch, and I'm Nixon's." John Ehrlichman, a Seattle attorney and college schoolmate of Haldeman, was chief domestic-policy adviser. John W. Dean III, an associate deputy in the office of the U.S. Attorney General, became the White House legal counsel.

Nixon tapped as secretary of state his old friend William Rogers, who had served as attorney general under Dwight D. Eisenhower. Nixon, however, had no intention of making Rogers the nation's chief diplomat. Instead, the president virtually ignored Rogers while forging an unlikely partnership with Dr. Henry Kissinger, a brilliant German-born Harvard political scientist who had become the nation's leading foreign-policy expert. Kissinger's thick accent, owlish appearance, and outsized ego had helped to make him an international celebrity, courted by presidents of both parties. In 1969, Nixon named Kissinger his National Security Adviser, and in 1973 Kissinger became secretary of state.

Nixon and Kissinger formed an odd but effective diplomatic team. Both were outsiders who preferred operating in secret; both were insecure and even paranoid at times; and both mistrusted and envied the other's power and prestige. Nixon would eventually grow tired of Kissinger's efforts at self-promotion and his frequent threats to resign if he did not get his way.

For his part, Kissinger lavished praise on Nixon in public, while in private dismissing the president's "meatball mind" and criticizing his excessive drinking. Yet for all of their differences, they worked well together, in part because they both loved intrigue, power politics, and diplomatic flexibility, and in part because of their shared vision of a multipolar world order beginning to replace the bipolar cold war as the United States slowly withdrew from Vietnam.

THE SOUTHERN STRATEGY A major reason for Nixon's election victories in 1968 and 1972 was his shrewd southern strategy, designed to win over white southern Democrats upset by the civil rights revolution. Of all the nation's regions, the South had long been the most conservative. The majority of white southern voters were religious and patriotic, fervently anti-Communist and anti-union, and skeptical of social-welfare programs.

For a century, whites in the "Solid South" had steadfastly voted for Democrats. This trend reflected lingering resentments, dating to the Civil War and Reconstruction, against Abraham Lincoln and his Republican successors for imposing northern ways of life on the South, including racial integration. During the late sixties and seventies, however, a surging economy and a spurt of population growth transformed the South.

Between 1970 and 1990, the South's population grew by 40 percent, more than twice the national average. The region's warm climate, low cost of living, absence of labor unions, low taxes, and government incentives for economic development convinced waves of businesses to relocate there. During the seventies, job growth in the South was seven times greater than in New York and Pennsylvania.

Southern "redneck" culture suddenly became all the rage, as the nation embraced stock car racing, cowboy boots, pickup trucks, barbecue, and country music. Rapid population growth—and the continuing spread of air-conditioning—brought the sunbelt states of the South, the Southwest, and California more congressional seats and more electoral votes. Every president elected between 1964 and 2008 had roots in the sunbelt.

Nixon's favorite singer, country star Merle Haggard, crooned in his smash hit, "Okie from Muskogee": "We don't smoke marijuana in Muskogee / We don't take our trips on LSD / We don't burn our draft cards down on Main Street / We like livin' right and bein' free." Haggard's conservative working-class fans bristled at anti-war protesters, hippies, rising taxes, social-welfare programs, and civil rights activism. The alienation of many blue-collar whites from the Democratic party, the demographic changes transforming sunbelt states, and the white backlash against court-ordered integration created an opportunity to gain southern votes that the Republican party eagerly exploited.

In the 1968 presidential campaign, Nixon's southern strategy won over traditionally Democratic white voters. He shrewdly "played the race card," assuring white conservatives that he would appoint justices to the Supreme Court who would undermine federal enforcement of civil rights laws, such as mandatory school busing to achieve racial integration and affirmative-action programs that gave minorities priority in hiring decisions and the awarding of government contracts. Nixon also appealed to the economic concerns of middle-class southern whites by promising lower tax rates and less government regulation.

In the 1972 election, Nixon carried every southern state by whopping majorities. The Republican takeover of the once "solid" Democratic South was the greatest realignment in American politics since Franklin D. Roosevelt's election in 1932.

NIXON'S DOMESTIC AGENDA As president, Richard Nixon shared with his predecessors John Kennedy and Lyndon Johnson an urge to increase presidential power. They believed that the presidency had become the central source of governmental action, that foreign policy should be managed from the White House rather than the State Department, and that the president had the authority to wage war without a congressional declaration of war.

Nixon was less a rigid conservative ideologue than a crafty politician. Forced to deal with a Congress controlled by Democrats, he chose his battles carefully and showed surprising flexibility, leading journalist Tom Wicker to describe him as "at once liberal and conservative, generous and begrudging, cynical and idealistic, choleric and calm, resentful and forgiving."

Nixon's focus during his first term was developing policies and programs that would help him be reelected. To please Republicans and recruit conservative Democrats, he touted his New Federalism, whereby he sent federal monies to state and local governments to spend as they saw fit. He also disbanded the core agency of Lyndon Johnson's war on poverty—the Office of Economic Opportunity—and cut funding to several Great Society programs.

At the same time, the Democrats in Congress passed significant legislation that Nixon signed: the right of eighteen-year-olds to vote in national elections (1970) and in all elections under the Twenty-Sixth Amendment (1971); increases in Social Security benefits and food-stamp funding; the Occupational Safety and Health Act (1970) to ensure safer workplace environments; and the Federal Election Campaign Act (1971), which modified the rules governing corporate financial donations to political campaigns.

NIXON AND CIVIL RIGHTS During his first term, President Nixon followed through on campaign pledges to blunt the momentum of the civil rights movement. He appointed no African Americans to his cabinet and refused to meet with the all-Democratic Congressional Black Caucus. "We've had enough social programs: forced integration, education, housing," he told his chief of staff. "People don't want more [people] on welfare. They don't want to help the working poor, and our mood needs to be harder on this, not softer."

Nixon also launched a concerted effort to block congressional renewal of the Voting Rights Act of 1965 and to delay implementation of federal court orders requiring the racial desegregation of school districts in Mississippi. Sixty-five lawyers in the Justice Department signed a letter protesting Nixon's stance. The Democratic-controlled Congress then extended the Voting Rights Act over Nixon's veto.

The Supreme Court also thwarted Nixon's efforts to slow desegregation. In its first decision under the new chief justice, Warren Burger—a Nixon appointee—the Court ordered the racial integration of the Mississippi public schools in *Alexander v. Holmes County Board of Education* (1969). During Nixon's first term, more schools were desegregated under court order than

Off to school Because of violent protests by whites against forced desegregation, school buses in South Boston are escorted by police in October 1974.

in all the Kennedy–Johnson years combined.

Nixon's efforts to block desegregation in urban areas also failed. The Burger Court ruled unanimously in *Swann v. Charlotte-Mecklenburg Board of Education* (1971) that school systems must bus students out of their neighborhoods if necessary to achieve racially integrated schools. Protests over busing erupted in the North, the Midwest, and the Southwest, as white families denounced the destruction of "the neighborhood school." Angry white parents in Pontiac, Michigan, were so determined to stop mandatory busing that they firebombed empty school buses.

NIXON AND ENVIRONMENTAL PROTECTION During the seventies, dramatic increases in the price of oil and gasoline fueled a major energy crisis in the United States. Natural resources grew limited—and increasingly precious. Nixon recognized that the public mood had shifted in favor of greater federal environmental protections, especially after two widely publicized environmental events in 1969.

The first was a massive oil spill off the coast of Santa Barbara, California, when an enormous slick of crude oil contaminated 200 miles of California beaches, killing thousands of sea birds and marine animals. Six months later, on June 22, 1969, the Cuyahoga River, an eighty-mile-long stream that slices through Cleveland, Ohio, spontaneously caught fire. Fouled with oil and grease, bubbling with subsurface gases, and littered with debris, the river burned for five days, its flames leaping fifty feet into the air. As with the Santa Barbara oil spill, the images of the burning river helped raise environmental awareness. A 1969 survey of college campuses by the *New York Times* revealed that many young people were transferring their attention and idealism from the anti-war movement to the environmental movement.

Nixon knew that if he vetoed legislative efforts to improve environmental quality, the Democratic majorities in Congress would overrule him, so he chose not to stand in the way. In late 1969, he signed the amended Endangered Species Preservation Act and the National Environmental Policy Act. The latter became effective on January 1, 1970, the year that environmental groups established an annual Earth Day celebration.

In 1970, Nixon by executive order created two new federal environmental agencies, the **Environmental Protection Agency (EPA)** and the National Oceanic and Atmospheric Administration (NOAA). The same year, he signed

Environmental awareness An Earth Day demonstration dramatizing the dangers of air pollution, April 1972.

the Clean Air Act. Two years later, he vetoed a new clean water act, only to see Congress override his effort. He also undermined many of the new environmental laws by refusing to spend money appropriated by Congress to fund them.

"STAGFLATION" The major domestic development during the Nixon administration was a floundering economy. The accumulated expense of the Vietnam War and the Great Society programs helped quadruple the annual inflation rate from 3 percent in 1967 to 12 percent in 1974. Meanwhile, unemployment, at 3.3 percent when Nixon took office, nearly doubled to 6 percent by the end of 1970. Economists coined the term "**stagflation**" to describe the simultaneous problems of stalled economic growth (stagnation), rising inflation, and high unemployment. Consumer prices usually rose with a rapidly growing economy and rising employment. Now it was just the reverse, and there were no easy ways to fight the unusual combination of recession and inflation.

Stagflation had at least three deep-rooted causes. First, the Johnson administration had financed both the Great Society social-welfare programs and the Vietnam War without a major tax increase, thereby generating larger federal deficits, a major expansion of the money supply, and price inflation. Second, U.S. companies were now facing stiff international competition from West Germany, Japan, and other emerging international industrial powers. The

Oil crisis, 1973 The scarcity of imported Arab oil forced the rationing of gasoline. Gas stations, such as this one in Colorado, closed on Sundays to conserve supplies.

technological and economic superiority that the United States had enjoyed since the Second World War was no longer unchallenged. Third, America's prosperity since 1945 had resulted in part from the ready availability of cheap sources of energy. No other nation was more dependent upon the automobile and the automobile industry, and no other nation was more wasteful in its use of fossil fuels. During the seventies, however, oil and gasoline became scarcer and costlier. High energy prices and oil shortages took their toll on the economy.

Just as domestic petroleum reserves began to dwindle and dependence upon foreign sources increased, the Organization of Petroleum Exporting Countries (OPEC) decided to use its huge oil supplies as a political and economic weapon. In 1973, the United States sent massive aid to Israel after a devastating Syrian-Egyptian attack launched on Yom Kippur, the holiest day on the Jewish calendar. OPEC responded by announcing that it would not sell oil to nations supporting Israel and that it was raising its oil prices by 400 percent.

The Arab oil embargo caused gasoline shortages and skyrocketing prices. American motorists suddenly faced mile-long lines at gas stations, and factories cut production because of spiking fuel costs.

Another condition leading to stagflation was the flood of new workers—mainly baby boomers and women. From 1965 to 1980, the workforce grew by almost 30 million, a number greater than the total labor force of France or West Germany. The number of new jobs could not keep up with the growth of the workforce, leaving many unemployed.

The Nixon administration responded erratically and ineffectively to stagflation. First, the president sought to reduce the federal deficit by raising taxes and cutting the budget. When the Democratic Congress refused to cooperate, he encouraged the Federal Reserve Board to reduce the nation's money supply by raising interest rates. The stock market immediately nose-dived, and the economy plunged into the "Nixon recession."

"Peace with Honor": Ending the Vietnam War

By the time Richard Nixon entered the White House in January 1969, he and Henry Kissinger had developed a comprehensive vision of a new world order. The result was a dramatic transformation of U.S. foreign policy. Since 1945, the United States had lost its monopoly on nuclear weapons, its overwhelming economic dominance, and much of its geopolitical influence. The rapid rise of competing power centers in Europe, China, and Japan further complicated the cold war as well as international relations in general.

Nixon and Kissinger envisioned defusing the cold war by pursuing peaceful coexistence with the Soviets and Chinese. After a "period of confrontation," Nixon explained in his 1969 inaugural address, "we are entering an era of negotiation." Preoccupied with secrecy, Nixon and Kissinger bypassed the State Department and Congress in their efforts to take advantage of shifting world events.

Their immediate task was ending the war in Vietnam. Until all troops had returned home, the nation would find it difficult to achieve the social harmony that Nixon had promised. Privately, he had decided "there's no way to win the war," so he sought what he called "peace with honor." That is, the United States needed to withdraw in a way that upheld the credibility of its military alliances around the world. Peace, however, was long in coming, not very honorable, and shockingly brief.

GRADUAL WITHDRAWAL The Vietnam policy implemented by President Nixon and Henry Kissinger moved along three fronts. First, U.S. negotiators in Paris demanded the withdrawal of Viet Cong forces from South Vietnam and the preservation of the U.S.-backed government of President Nguyen Van Thieu. The North Vietnamese and Viet Cong negotiators, for their part, insisted on retaining a Communist military presence in the south and reunifying the Vietnamese people under a government dominated by the Communists. Hidden from public awareness and from America's South Vietnamese allies were secret meetings between Kissinger and the North Vietnamese.

On the second front, Nixon sought to defuse the anti-war movement by reducing the number of U.S. troops in Vietnam, justifying the reduction as the natural result of "**Vietnamization**"—the equipping and training of South Vietnamese soldiers and pilots to assume the burden of combat. The president began withdrawing troops while expanding the American bombing of North Vietnam to buy time for the transition. From a peak of 560,000 troops in January 1969, only 50,000 remained in Vietnam by 1973.

In 1969, Nixon also established a draft lottery whereby the birthdates of nineteen-year-old men were randomly selected and assigned a number between 1 and 366. Those with low lottery numbers would be the first drafted into military service. The lottery system eliminated many inequities and clarified the likelihood of being drafted. Four years later, in 1973, the president did away with the draft altogether by creating an all-volunteer military.

These initiatives, coupled with the troop withdrawals, defused the antiwar movement. Opinion polls showed strong support for Nixon's war policies. "We've got those liberal bastards on the run now," the president gloated, "and we're going to keep them on the run."

On the third front, Nixon and Kissinger greatly expanded the bombing of North Vietnam in hopes of pressuring the Communist leaders to end the war. Kissinger felt that "a fourth-rate power" like North Vietnam must have a "breaking point." Nixon agreed, suggesting that they let the North Vietnamese leaders know that he was so "obsessed about Communism" that he might use the "nuclear button" if necessary.

In March 1969, the United States began a fourteen-month-long bombing campaign aimed at Communist forces using neighboring Cambodia as a base for raids into South Vietnam. The total tonnage of bombs dropped was four times that dropped on Japan during the Second World War. Still, Hanoi's leaders did not flinch.

Then, on April 30, 1970, Nixon announced an "incursion" into "neutral" Cambodia to "clean out" hidden Communist military bases. Privately, Nixon told Kissinger, who strongly endorsed the decision, "If this doesn't work, it'll be your ass, Henry." Nixon knew that sending troops into Cambodia would reignite the anti-war movement. Secretary of State William Rogers predicted that "this will make the [anti-war] students puke."

DIVISIONS AT HOME Strident public opposition to the war and Nixon's slow withdrawal of combat forces had a devastating effect on the military's morale and reputation. "No one wants to be the last grunt to die in this lousy war," said one soldier. Between 1969 and 1971, there were 730 reported fragging incidents (efforts by troops to kill or injure their own officers). Drug abuse became a major problem; in 1971, four times as many troops were hospitalized for drug overdoses as for combat-related wounds.

Revelations of atrocities committed by U.S. soldiers caused even the staunchest supporters of the war to wince. Late in 1969, the story of the My Lai Massacre plunged the country into two years of exposure to the tale of William L. "Rusty" Calley, a twenty-six-year-old army lieutenant who ordered the murder of 347 Vietnamese civilians in the village of My Lai in 1968. One soldier described it as "point-blank murder, and I was standing there watching it." As newsmagazines published gruesome photos of the massacre, Americans debated the issues it raised. A father in northern California grumbled that Calley "would have been a hero" in the Second World War. His son shot back: "Yeah, if you were a Nazi." Twenty-five army officers were charged with complicity in the massacre and subsequent cover-up, but only Calley was convicted. Nixon later granted him parole.

Just as Nixon had expected, the escalation of the air war in Vietnam and the extension of the war into Cambodia triggered widespread anti-war demonstrations. The president, however, was unmoved. "As far as this kind of activity is concerned," he gruffly explained, "we expect it; however, under no circumstances will I be affected whatever by it."

In the spring of 1970, news of the secret Cambodian "incursion" by U.S. forces set off explosive demonstrations on college campuses. At Kent State University, the Ohio National Guard was called in to control rioting on May 4. As radicals hurled insults and rocks at the soldiers, the poorly trained guardsmen panicked and opened fire. Thirteen students were hit, and four of them, all bystanders, were killed.

The killings at Kent State added new fury to the anti-war and anti-Nixon movements. That spring, demonstrations occurred on more than 350 campuses. A presidential commission charged with investigating the Kent State shootings concluded that they were "unnecessary and unwarranted." Not all agreed. A resident of Kent told a reporter that "anyone who appears on the streets of a city like Kent with long hair, dirty clothes, or barefooted deserves to be shot. . . . It would have been better if the Guard had shot the whole lot of them." Singer Neil Young had a different view. Shortly after the killings, he composed a song called "Ohio":

> Tin soldiers and Nixon's coming.
> We're finally on our own.
> This summer I hear the drumming.
> Four dead in Ohio.

The Ohio governor banned radio stations from playing the song, which only made it more popular.

America again seemed at war with itself. Eleven days after the Kent State tragedy, on May 15, Mississippi highway patrolmen riddled a dormitory at Jackson State College with bullets, killing two students who were protesting the war. In New York City, anti-war demonstrators who gathered to protest the student deaths and the invasion of Cambodia were attacked by conservative "hard-hat" construction workers shouting "America, Love It or Leave It,"

Shooting at Kent State Mary Ann Vecchio, a teenage runaway participating in the anti-war demonstration, decries the murder of a Kent State student after the National Guard fired into the crowd.

who forced the protesters to disperse, and then marched on City Hall to raise the U.S. flag, which had been lowered to half-staff in mourning for the Kent State victims. "Thank God for the hard hats," Nixon exclaimed.

The following year, in June 1971, the *New York Times* began publishing excerpts from *The History of the U.S. Decision-Making Process of Vietnam Policy*, a secret Defense Department study commissioned by Robert McNamara before his resignation as secretary of defense in 1968.

The so-called Pentagon Papers, leaked to the press by Daniel Ellsberg, a former Defense Department official who had been one of Henry Kissinger's students at Harvard, confirmed what many critics of the war had long suspected: Congress and the public had not received the full story about the Gulf of Tonkin incident of 1964, and contingency plans for U.S. entry into the war were being drawn up even as President Johnson was promising that combat troops would never be sent to Vietnam.

Although the Pentagon Papers dealt with events only up to 1965, the Nixon administration blocked their publication, arguing that their release would endanger national security and prolong the war. By a vote of 6 to 3, the Supreme Court ruled against the government. Newspapers throughout the country began publishing the documents the next day. Nixon was furious. He ordered the FBI to find out who had leaked the Pentagon Papers to the media. When the agency identified Ellsberg as the culprit, the president launched a crusade to destroy him, including a botched effort to break in to his psychiatrist's office.

WAR WITHOUT END In the summer of 1972, Henry Kissinger renewed private meetings with the North Vietnamese negotiators in Paris. He now dropped his insistence upon the removal of all North Vietnamese troops from South Vietnam before the withdrawal of the remaining U.S. troops. On October 26, only a week before the U.S. presidential election, Kissinger announced that "Peace is at hand."

As it turned out, however, this was a cynical ploy to win votes. Several days earlier, the Thieu regime in South Vietnam had rejected the Kissinger plan for a cease-fire, fearful that allowing North Vietnamese troops to remain in the south would virtually guarantee a Communist victory. The peace talks broke off on December 16, and two days later the newly reelected Nixon ordered massive bombings of Hanoi and Haiphong, the two largest cities in North Vietnam. Nixon told Kissinger that he now would "stop at nothing to bring the enemy to his knees. . . . We have the power. The only question is whether we have the will to use that power. What distinguishes me from Johnson is that I have the will in spades."

The so-called Christmas bombings and the simultaneous U.S. mining of North Vietnamese harbors aroused worldwide protest. Yet the talks in Paris soon resumed, and on January 27, 1973, the United States, North and South Vietnam, and the Viet Cong signed an "agreement on ending the war and restoring peace in Vietnam," known as the Paris Peace Accords.

In fact, it was a carefully disguised surrender that enabled the United States to end its combat role. While Nixon and Kissinger claimed that the bombings had brought North Vietnam to its senses, in truth the North Vietnamese never altered their basic stance; they kept 150,000 troops in South Vietnam and remained committed to the reunification of Vietnam under one government. What had changed was the willingness of the South Vietnamese, who were never allowed to participate in the negotiations, to accept the agreement on the basis of Nixon's promise that the United States would respond "with full force" to any Communist violation of the agreement.

By the time the Paris Peace Accords were signed in 1973, another 20,000 Americans had died since Nixon had taken office in 1969, the morale of the U.S. military had been shattered, and millions of Southeast Asians had been killed or wounded. Fighting soon broke out again in both Vietnam and Cambodia. In the end, Nixon and Kissinger's diplomatic efforts gained nothing the president could not have accomplished in 1969 by ending the war on similar terms.

THE COLLAPSE OF SOUTH VIETNAM On March 29, 1973, the last U.S. combat troops left Vietnam. The same day, almost 600 American prisoners of war, most of them downed pilots, were released from Hanoi. Within months, however, the cease-fire collapsed, the war between North and South resumed, and Communist forces gained the upper hand. In Cambodia (renamed the Khmer Republic after a 1970 military coup) and Laos, where fighting had been sporadic, a Communist victory also seemed inevitable.

In 1975, the North Vietnamese launched a full-scale invasion of South Vietnam, sending the South Vietnamese army and civilians into headlong panic. President Thieu desperately appealed to Washington for the U.S. assistance promised in the Paris Peace Accords. But Congress, weary of spending dollars and lives in Vietnam, refused. On April 21, Thieu resigned and flew to Taiwan.

In the end, "peace with honor" had given the United States just enough time to remove itself before the collapse of the South Vietnamese government. On April 30, 1975, Americans watched on television as North Vietnamese tanks rolled into Saigon, soon to be renamed Ho Chi Minh City, and military helicopters lifted desperate U.S. embassy and South Vietnamese officials and their families to warships waiting offshore.

The longest, most controversial, and least successful war in American history to that point was finally over. It left a bitter legacy. During the period of U.S. involvement, the combined death count for combatants and civilians reached nearly 2 million. North Vietnam absorbed incredible losses—some 600,000 soldiers and countless civilians. South Vietnam lost 240,000 soldiers, and more than 500,000 Vietnamese became refugees in the United States. More than 58,000 Americans died in Vietnam; another 300,000 were wounded, 2,500 were declared missing, and almost 100,000 returned missing one or more limbs. The United States spent more than $699 billion on the war.

The Vietnam War was the defining life event for the baby boomers, the generation that provided most of the U.S. troops as well as most of the antiwar protesters. The controversial war divided them in ways that would be felt for years. The "loss" of the war, combined with news of atrocities committed by American soldiers, eroded respect for the military so thoroughly that many young people came to regard military service as corrupting and dishonorable.

Vietnam combat veterans (average age nineteen, compared to twenty-six among servicemen in the Second World War) had "lost" a war in which their country had lost interest. When they returned, many found that even their families were unwilling to talk about what the soldiers had experienced,

Leave with honor Hundreds of thousands of terrified South Vietnamese tried to flee the Communist forces with evacuating Americans. Here, a U.S. official punches a Vietnamese man trying to join his family in an overflowing airplane at Nha Trang.

or were embarrassed about their involvement in the war. "I went over there thinking I was doing something right and came back a bum," said Larry Langowski from Illinois. "I came back decked with medals on my uniform, and I got spit on by a hippie girl."

The Vietnam War, initially described as a crusade for democratic ideals, revealed that democracy was not easily transferable to regions of the world that lacked any historical experience with democratic government. Fought to contain the spread of communism, the war instead fragmented the national consensus that had governed foreign affairs since 1947, when President Truman developed policies to "contain" communism around the world.

As opposition to the war undermined Lyndon B. Johnson's presidency, it also created enduring fractures within the Democratic party. Said George McGovern, the anti-war senator and 1972 Democratic presidential nominee, "The Vietnam tragedy is at the root of the confusion and division of the Democratic party. It tore up our souls."

Not only had a decade of American effort in Vietnam proved futile, but the Khmer Rouge, the insurgent Cambodian Communist movement, had also won a resounding victory over the government of the U.S.-backed Khmer Republic, plunging that country into a bloodbath. The maniacal Khmer Rouge leaders renamed the country Kampuchea and organized a genocidal campaign to destroy all of their opponents, killing almost a third of the total population.

The Nixon Doctrine and a Thawing Cold War

Despite the frustrations associated with his efforts to end the Vietnam War, Richard Nixon, like John F. Kennedy, greatly preferred foreign policy over domestic policy (which he compared to building "sewer projects"), and his greatest successes were in international relations. Nixon was an expert in foreign affairs and had traveled abroad frequently as Dwight Eisenhower's vice president during the 1950s.

As president, Nixon benefited greatly from the expertise and strategic vision of Henry Kissinger. Their grand design for U.S. foreign policy after the Vietnam War centered on developing friendly relations with the Soviet Union and Communist China. Nixon envisioned a post–cold war world, "an era of negotiation rather than confrontation." He and Kissinger pressed for a return to an Eisenhower-era approach that entailed reducing large-scale military interventions around the world and using the Central Intelligence Agency (CIA) to pursue America's strategic interests covertly.

THE CIA IN CHILE Ever since Fidel Castro and his supporters gained control of Cuba in 1959, American presidents had been determined to prevent any more Communist insurgencies in the Western Hemisphere. In 1970, Salvador Allende, a Marxist, Socialist party leader, and friend of Castro, was a leading presidential candidate in Chile, on the southwest coast of South America. President Nixon and Henry Kissinger knew that, if elected, Allende planned to "nationalize" Chilean industries, including those owned by U.S. corporations. They did not want "another Castro" in Latin America.

In September 1970, Nixon urged the CIA to do anything to prevent an Allende presidency. Although CIA agents provided campaign funds to his opponents, Allende was elected on October 24, 1970. The CIA then encouraged Chilean military leaders to oust him. In September 1973, the army took control, Allende either committed suicide or was murdered, and General Augusto Pinochet, a ruthless military dictator supposedly friendly to the United States, declared himself head of the government.

In consolidating control over Chile, Pinochet executed thousands. It was yet another example of the United States being so obsessed by anti-communism and protecting American business interests that it was willing to interfere in the democratic process of other nations.

THE NIXON DOCTRINE In July 1969, while announcing the first troop withdrawals from Vietnam, President Nixon unveiled what came to be called the Nixon Doctrine, a new approach to America's handling of international crises. Unlike John F. Kennedy, who had declared that the United States would "pay any price, bear any burden" to win the cold war, Nixon explained that "America cannot—and will not—conceive *all* the plans, design *all* the programs, execute *all* the decisions, and undertake *all* the defense of the free nations of the world." Those nations experiencing Communist insurgencies must in the future assume primary responsibility for their own defense. The United States would provide weapons and money but not soldiers.

At the same time, Nixon announced that the United States would pursue partnerships with Communist countries in areas of mutual interest. That Nixon, a Republican with a history of rabid anti-communism, would pursue such a policy of **détente** (a French word meaning "easing of relations") with America's Communist archenemies shocked many and demonstrated yet again his pragmatic flexibility.

THE PEOPLE'S REPUBLIC OF CHINA Richard Nixon had a genius for surprise. In 1971, without informing Secretary of State William Rogers, Nixon told Henry Kissinger to make a secret trip to Beijing to explore the possibility of U.S. recognition of Communist China, the most populous nation in the world, with over 800 million people. Kissinger was flabbergasted. He had earlier told his staff that "our leader has taken leave of reality. He thinks this is the moment to establish normal relations with Communist China." Since 1949, when Mao Zedong's revolutionary movement established control, the United States, with Richard Nixon's hearty support, had refused even to recognize the People's Republic of China, preferring to regard Chiang Kai-shek's exiled regime on Taiwan as the legitimate Chinese government.

Now, however, the time seemed ripe to Nixon for a bold renewal of ties. Both the United States and Communist China were exhausted from intense domestic strife (anti-war protests in America, the Cultural Revolution in China), and both were eager to resist Soviet expansionism. Nixon also relished the shock effect of his action. His reaching out to Communist China, he told aide John Ehrlichman, would "discombobulate" the "god-damned liberals." It would "just kill them" for him to be the one reaching out to a Communist enemy.

Nixon's bombshell announcement on July 15, 1971, that Kissinger had just returned from Beijing and that the president himself would be going to China

Nixon goes to China President Nixon and Chinese premier Zhou Enlai toast each other at the lavish farewell banquet in Shanghai celebrating the historic visit.

the following year sent shock waves around the world. Nixon became the first U.S. president to use the term *People's Republic of China*, an important symbolic step in normalizing relations. The Nationalist Chinese on Taiwan felt betrayed, and the Japanese, historic enemies of China, were furious. In October 1971, the United Nations voted to admit the People's Republic of China and expel Taiwan.

On February 21, 1972, during the "week that changed the world," President Nixon arrived in Beijing with almost a hundred journalists to report on his dramatic visit to Communist China. Americans watched on television as the president shook hands and drank toasts with Prime Minister Zhou Enlai and Communist party Chairman Mao Zedong. In one simple but astonishing stroke, Nixon and Kissinger had ended two decades of diplomatic isolation of the People's Republic of China.

During the president's week-long visit, the two nations agreed to scientific and cultural exchanges, steps toward resuming trade, and the eventual reunification of Taiwan with the mainland. A year after Nixon's visit, "liaison offices" that served as unofficial embassies were established in Washington and Beijing. In 1979, diplomatic recognition was formalized.

As a conservative anti-Communist, Nixon had accomplished a diplomatic feat that his Democratic predecessors could not have attempted for fear of being branded "soft" on communism. Nixon and Kissinger's bold move had the added benefit of giving them leverage with the Soviet Union, which was understandably nervous about a U.S.–Chinese alliance.

EMBRACING THE SOVIET UNION In truth, China welcomed the breakthrough in relations because of tensions with the Soviet Union, with which it shared a long but contested border. By 1972, the Chinese leadership had become more fearful of the Soviet Union than the United States.

The Soviets, troubled by the agreements between China and the United States, were also eager to ease tensions with the Americans. Once again, President Nixon surprised the world by announcing that he would visit Moscow in

1972 for discussions with Leonid Brezhnev, the Soviet premier. The high drama of the China visit was repeated in Moscow, with toasts and elegant dinners attended by world leaders who had previously regarded each other as incarnations of evil.

What became known as détente with the Soviets offered the promise of less intense competition between the superpowers. Nixon and Brezhnev signed the pathbreaking **Strategic Arms Limitation Treaty (SALT I)**, which negotiators had been working on since 1969. The SALT agreement did not end the nuclear arms race, but it did limit the number of missiles with nuclear warheads and prohibited the construction of missile-defense systems. The Moscow summit also produced new trade agreements, including an arrangement whereby the United States sold almost a quarter of its wheat crop to the Soviets at a favorable price. (Critics called it the Great Grain Robbery.)

The summit resulted in the dramatic easing of tensions between the two superpowers. As Nixon told Congress upon his return, "never before have two adversaries, so deeply divided by conflicting ideologies and political rivalries, been able to limit the armaments upon which their survival depends."

For Nixon and Kissinger, the agreements with China and the Soviet Union represented monumental changes in the global order. Over time, détente with the Soviet Union would help end the cold war altogether by lowering Soviet hostility to Western influences, which in turn slowly eroded Communist rule from the inside.

SHUTTLE DIPLOMACY The Nixon–Kissinger initiatives in the Middle East were less dramatic and less conclusive than those in China and the Soviet Union, but they did show that the United States at last recognized the legitimacy of Arab interests in the region and its own dependence upon Middle Eastern oil. In the Six-Day War of 1967, Israeli forces had routed the armies of Egypt, Syria, and Jordan, and seized territory from all three nations. Moreover, the number of Palestinian refugees, many of them homeless since the creation of Israel in 1948, increased after the Israeli victory.

The Middle East remained a tinderbox of tensions. On October 6, 1973, the Jewish holy day of Yom Kippur, Syria and Egypt, backed by Saudi Arabia and armed with Soviet weapons, attacked Israel, igniting what became the Yom Kippur War. It created the most dangerous confrontation between the United States and the Soviet Union since the Cuban missile crisis.

When the Israeli army, with weapons supplied by the United States, launched a fierce counterattack that appeared likely to overwhelm Egypt, the Soviets threatened to intervene militarily. Nixon, whose presidency was at risk because of the ongoing Watergate investigations, was bedridden because he was drunk, according to Henry Kissinger and other aides, so Kissinger, as secretary of state, presided over a National Security Council meeting that placed America's military forces on full alert.

On October 20, Kissinger flew to Moscow to meet with Soviet premier Brezhnev. Kissinger skillfully negotiated a cease-fire agreement and exerted pressure on the Israelis to prevent them from taking additional Arab territory. In an attempt to broker a lasting settlement, Kissinger made numerous flights among the capitals of the Middle East. His "shuttle diplomacy" won acclaim from all sides, though he failed to find a comprehensive formula for peace. He did, however, lay the groundwork for an important treaty between Israel and Egypt in 1977.

WATERGATE

Nixon's foreign policy achievements allowed him to stage the presidential campaign of 1972 as a triumphal procession. Early on, the main threat to his reelection came from George Wallace, who had the potential as a third-party candidate to deprive the Republicans of conservative southern votes and thereby throw the election to the Democrats. That threat ended, however, on May 15, 1972, when Wallace was shot in an assassination attempt. Although he survived, he was left paralyzed below the waist and had to withdraw from the campaign.

Meanwhile, the Democrats nominated Senator George McGovern of South Dakota, an anti-war liberal who had been a decorated bomber pilot during the Second World War. Bobby Kennedy once called McGovern "the most decent man in the Senate." Yet he was a poor campaigner. One journalist mused that the Democratic campaign was so inept that it must have been planned by the Republicans. A growing number of voters viewed McGovern as a left-wing extremist whose campaign speeches seemed lifeless. His high school debate coach acknowledged that "George's colorfulness was his colorlessness." On Election Day, McGovern was trounced. Nixon won the greatest victory of any Republican presidential candidate in history, capturing 520 electoral votes to only 17 for McGovern. The popular vote was equally decisive: 46 million to 28 million, a proportion of the total vote (60.8 percent) that was second only to Lyndon Johnson's victory over Barry Goldwater in 1964.

For all of his abilities and accomplishments, however, Nixon was chronically insecure. He nursed grudges and took politics personally, and he could be ruthless in attacking his opponents. As president, he began keeping a secret "enemies list" and launched numerous efforts to embarrass and punish those on the list. Little did he know that such behavior would bring him crashing down.

"DIRTY TRICKS" By the spring of 1972, senior Nixon aide John Ehrlichman was overseeing a secret team of agents who performed various acts of sabotage against Democrats, such as falsely accusing Democratic senators Hubert H. Humphrey and Henry Jackson of sexual improprieties, forging press releases, setting off stink bombs at Democratic campaign events, and planting spies on George McGovern's campaign plane. Charles "Chuck" Colson, one of the most active "dirty tricksters," admitted that "we did a hell of a lot of things and never got caught."

During the campaign, McGovern had complained about the "dirty tricks" orchestrated by members of the Nixon administration. Nixon, it turned out, had ordered illegal wiretaps on his opponents (as well as on his own aides), tried to coerce the Internal Revenue Service to intimidate Democrats, and told his chief of staff, Bob Haldeman, to break into the safe at the Brookings Institution, a Washington research center with Democratic ties.

McGovern was especially disturbed by an incident on June 17, 1972, when five men were caught breaking into the Democratic National Committee headquarters in the exclusive **Watergate** apartment and office complex in Washington, D.C. Four of the burglars were right-wing Cuban exiles who had worked for the CIA, and one, James W. McCord, worked for Nixon's campaign. At the time, McGovern's complaints about the break-in seemed like sour grapes from a candidate running far behind in the polls. Few people paid any attention to the burglary.

Nixon denied any involvement in this "very bizarre incident." Privately, however, he and his senior aides began feverish efforts to cover up the Watergate affair. The president told Alexander Haig, his chief of staff, that "we will cover up until hell freezes over." They secretly provided $400,000 to the jailed burglars to buy their silence and tried to keep the FBI out of the investigation. They also discussed using the CIA to derail the Justice Department's investigation. They lied to journalists and destroyed evidence related to the case. Bob Haldeman, Nixon's chief of staff, developed a plan for the jailed Cubans to take the fall, suggesting that they claim they acted solely on their own. He also told the FBI to quit investigating the incident because it involved a super-secret CIA operation (a lie). Nixon encouraged such efforts, stressing that "the main concern is to keep the White House out of it."

What Nixon and his aides failed to account for was the dogged efforts of two *Washington Post* reporters, Carl Bernstein and Bob Woodward, to uncover the facts of the Watergate break-in. On September 16, 1972, they reported that a grand jury was about to indict the Watergate burglars along with two other men, Gordon Liddy and Howard Hunt, who had been connected to the scheme. Liddy would be the first White House aide ever indicted. Then, on October 10, Bernstein and Woodward revealed that the FBI had discovered a direct connection between the Watergate burglary and the Committee to Re-Elect the President. Seventeen days later, CBS's Walter Cronkite, the nation's most popular news reporter, announced that "Watergate has escalated into charges of a high-level campaign of political sabotage and espionage apparently unparalleled in American history."

UNCOVERING THE COVER-UP During the trial of the accused Watergate burglars in January 1973, relentless questioning by federal judge John J. Sirica led one of the accused to tell the full story of the Nixon administration's involvement. James W. McCord, security chief of the Committee to Re-Elect the President (CREEP), was the first in what would become a long line of informers to reveal the systematic efforts of Nixon and his aides to create an "imperial presidency." By the time of the Watergate break-in, money to finance "dirty tricks" was being illegally collected through CREEP and controlled by the White House staff.

The trail of evidence pursued first by Sirica, then by a grand jury, and then by a Senate committee headed by Democrat Samuel J. Ervin Jr. of North Carolina, led directly to what White House legal counsel John Dean called a "cancer close to the Presidency." Nixon was personally involved in the cover-up, using his power to discredit and block the investigation. He ordered the CIA to keep the FBI off the case and even coached his aides how to lie under oath. Most alarming, as it turned out, the Watergate burglary was merely part of a larger pattern of corruption and criminality sanctioned by the Nixon White House.

The cover-up unraveled further later that year when L. Patrick Gray, acting director of the FBI, resigned after confessing that he had destroyed several incriminating documents. On April 30, 1973, Ehrlichman and Haldeman resigned (they would later serve time in prison), as did Attorney General Richard Kleindienst. A few days later, Nixon nervously assured the public in a television address, "I am not a crook." Then Dean, whom Nixon had dismissed because of his cooperation with prosecutors, shocked the nation by testifying before the Ervin committee that there had been a cover-up approved by the president.

Nixon thereafter became preoccupied with legal self-defense and political survival. He refused to provide Ervin's committee with documents it requested, citing "executive privilege" to protect national security. In another shocking disclosure, a White House aide told the committee that Nixon had installed a secret taping system in the White House, and that many of the conversations about the Watergate burglary and cover-up had been recorded.

The bombshell news set off a legal battle for the "Nixon tapes." Harvard law professor Archibald Cox, whom Nixon's new attorney general, Elliot Richardson, had appointed as special prosecutor to investigate the Watergate case, took the president to court in October 1973 to obtain the tapes. Nixon refused to release the recordings and ordered Cox fired.

On October 20, in what became known as the "Saturday Night Massacre," Richardson and Deputy Attorney General William Ruckelshaus resigned rather than fire Cox. (Solicitor General Robert Bork finally fired him.) Cox's dismissal produced a firestorm of public indignation. Numerous newspaper and magazine editorials, as well as a growing chorus of legislators, called for

John Ehrlichman Ehrlichman, aide to President Nixon, addresses the Senate Watergate committee on July 24, 1973.

the president to be impeached for obstructing justice. A Gallup poll revealed that Nixon's approval rating had plunged to 17 percent, the lowest level any president had ever received.

The new special prosecutor, Leon Jaworski, also took the president to court. In March 1974, the Watergate grand jury indicted Ehrlichman, Haldeman, and former attorney general John Mitchell for obstruction of justice and named Nixon an "unindicted co-conspirator."

On April 30, Nixon, still refusing to turn over the actual tapes, released 1,254 pages of transcribed recordings that he had edited himself, often substituting the phrase "expletive deleted" for his vulgar language and anti-Semitic rants. The transcripts revealed a president whose Oval Office conversations were so petty, self-serving, bigoted, and profane that they degraded the stature of the office and fueled growing demands for Nixon to resign.

By the summer of 1974, Nixon was in full retreat. He became alternately combative, melancholy, and petty. Henry Kissinger found him increasingly unstable and drinking heavily. Nixon's efforts to orchestrate the cover-up obsessed, unbalanced, and unhinged him. After meeting with the president, Senator Barry Goldwater reported that Nixon "jabbered incessantly, often incoherently." He seemed "to be cracking."

Americans watched the Ervin committee hearings as if they were episodes in a soap opera. On July 24, 1974, the Supreme Court ruled unanimously, in *United States v. Richard M. Nixon*, that the president must surrender *all* of the tape recordings. A few days later, the House Judiciary Committee voted to recommend three articles of impeachment: obstruction of justice through the payment of "hush money" to witnesses and the withholding of evidence; abuse of power through the use of federal agencies to deprive citizens of their constitutional rights; and defiance of Congress by withholding the tapes.

V for "Victory" Before boarding the White House helicopter following his resignation, Nixon flashes a bright smile and his trademark V-for-Victory sign to the world on August 9, 1974.

Before the House of Representatives could vote on impeachment, Nixon grudgingly handed over the complete set of White House tapes. The drama continued, however, when investigators learned that sections of certain key recordings were missing, including eighteen minutes of a conversation in June 1972 during which Nixon first mentioned the Watergate burglary.

The president's loyal secretary took the blame for the erasure, claiming that she had accidentally pushed the wrong button, but technical experts later concluded that the missing segments had been intentionally deleted. The other recordings, however, provided more than enough evidence of Nixon's involvement in the cover-up. At one point, he had yelled at aides who were asking what they and others should say to Watergate investigators: "I don't give a shit what happens. I want you all to stonewall it, let them plead the Fifth Amendment, cover up or anything else."

The recordings led Republican leaders to urge Nixon to quit rather than face an impeachment trial in the Senate. On August 9, 1974, the embattled president resigned from office, the only president to do so. In 1969, he had begun his presidency hoping to heal America, to "bring people together." Now he left the White House for a self-imposed exile at his home in San Clemente, California, having deeply wounded the nation.

Nixon was one of the strangest, most complicated, and most interesting political figures in American history. He never understood why the Watergate affair could have ended his presidency; in his view, his only mistake was getting caught. Nixon claimed that a president's actions could not be "illegal." He was wrong. The Watergate affair's clearest lesson was that not even a president is above the law. But the fact that the system worked by calling a president to justice did not prevent many Americans from losing faith in the credibility of elected officials. The *New York Times* reported that people across the country "think and feel differently from what they once did" as a result of the Watergate crisis. "They ask questions, they reject assumptions, they doubt what they are told."

WATERGATE AND THE PRESIDENCY If there was a silver lining in the dark cloud of Watergate, it was the vigor and resilience of the institutions that had brought a rogue president to justice—the press, Congress, the courts, and public opinion.

In the aftermath of the scandal, Congress passed several pieces of legislation designed to curb executive power. Nervous about possible efforts to renew military assistance to South Vietnam, the Democratic Congress passed the **War Powers Act** (1973), which requires a president to inform Congress within forty-eight hours if U.S. troops are deployed in combat abroad and to withdraw troops after sixty days unless Congress specifically approves their stay.

To correct abuses in the use of campaign funds, Congress enacted legislation in 1974 that set new ceilings on political contributions and expenditures. And in reaction to the Nixon claim of "executive privilege" as a means of withholding evidence, Congress strengthened the 1966 Freedom of Information Act to require prompt responses to requests for information from government files and to place on government agencies the burden of proof for classifying information as secret.

AN UNELECTED PRESIDENT During Richard Nixon's last year in office, the Watergate crisis so dominated national politics that major domestic and foreign problems received little attention. Vice President Spiro Agnew had himself been forced to resign in October 1973 for accepting bribes from contractors before and during his term in office. The vice president at the time of Nixon's resignation was Gerald Rudolph Ford, a square-jawed, plain-speaking former House minority leader from Michigan whom Nixon had appointed to succeed Agnew under the provisions of the Twenty-Fifth Amendment. An honest, decent man, Ford had played football at the University of Michigan before getting a law degree at Yale. But none of his accomplishments had prepared him for his unexpected role as an accidental president called upon to restore stability to a nation reeling from one crisis after another.

On August 9, 1974, Ford was sworn in as the nation's first politically appointed chief executive, the only person in history to serve as both vice president and president without having been elected to those offices. "I am acutely aware that you have not elected me as your President by your ballots," Ford said in a nationally televised address. "So I ask you to confirm me as your President with your prayers." He then assured the people that "our long national nightmare [Watergate] is over."

But it wasn't. Restoring public confidence in elected leaders was not easy. Less than a month after taking office, Ford reopened the wounds of Watergate by issuing Nixon a "full, free, and absolute pardon" for any crimes he may have committed while in office. Many Americans were not in a forgiving mood, and

Ford's pardon unleashed a storm of controversy. He was grilled by a House subcommittee wanting to know whether Nixon had made a secret deal for the pardon. Ford vigorously denied the charge, but the pardon hobbled his presidency. Doing what he had thought was the right thing made him suspect in the eyes of many voters. His approval rating plummeted from 71 percent to 49 percent in one day, the steepest drop ever recorded. Even his press secretary resigned in protest of the "Nixon pardon."

THE FORD YEARS As president, Gerald Ford soon adopted the posture he had developed as the minority leader in the House of Representatives: naysaying head of the opposition who believed that the federal government exercised too much power. In his first fifteen months as president, he vetoed thirty-nine bills passed by the Democratic-controlled Congress, outstripping Herbert Hoover's all-time veto record in less than half the time.

By far the most important development during Ford's brief presidency was the struggling economy. During the fall of 1974, the nation had entered its deepest recession since the Great Depression. Unemployment jumped to 9 percent in 1975, the annual rate of inflation reached double digits, and the federal budget deficit soon hit a record. Ford announced that inflation had become "Public Enemy No. 1," but instead of taking bold action, he launched a timid public relations campaign featuring lapel buttons that simply read WIN, symbolizing the administration's determination to "Whip Inflation Now."

Gerald Ford The 38th president listens apprehensively to news of rising rates of unemployment and inflation in 1974.

The WIN buttons became a national joke and a symbol of Ford's ineffectiveness. He later admitted that they were a failed "gimmick." Ford initially supported increasing taxes to fight inflation, then reversed himself. By 1975, when he delivered his State of the Union address, he lamely conceded that "the state of the union is not good." In March 1975, Ford signed a tax reduction bill that failed to stimulate economic growth. The federal budget deficit grew from $53 billion in 1975 to $74 billion in 1976.

In foreign policy, Ford retained Henry Kissinger as secretary of state (while stripping him of his dual role as national security adviser) and pursued Nixon's goals of stability in the Middle East, friendly relations with China, and détente with the Soviet Union. Kissinger's tireless Middle East diplomacy produced an important agreement: Israel promised to return to Egypt most of the Sinai territory captured in the 1967 war, and the two nations agreed to rely on negotiations rather than force to settle future disagreements.

These limited but significant achievements should have enhanced Ford's image, but they were drowned in the criticism over the collapse of the South Vietnamese government in the face of the North Vietnamese invasion. At the same time, conservative Republicans led by Ronald Reagan lambasted Ford and Kissinger for their policy of détente toward the Soviet Union. Reagan argued that the efforts of Nixon, Kissinger, and Ford were helping to ensure the continued existence of the Soviet Union rather than accelerating its self-destruction.

THE ELECTION OF 1976 Both political parties were in disarray as they prepared for the 1976 presidential election. At the Republican convention, Gerald Ford had to fend off a powerful challenge from the darling of the party's growing conservative wing, Ronald Reagan, a former two-term California governor and Hollywood actor.

The Democrats chose James Earl Carter Jr., who had served one term as governor of Georgia. A former naval officer and engineer turned peanut farmer, Carter was one of several Democratic southern governors who sought to move their party away from its traditional "tax and spend" liberalism.

Carter capitalized on post-Watergate cynicism by promising that he would "never tell a lie to the American people." He also trumpeted his status as a political "outsider" whose inexperience in Washington politics would be an asset. Carter was certainly different from conventional candidates. Reporters covering the campaign marveled at a Southern Baptist candidate who was a "born again" Christian.

To the surprise of many, Carter revived the New Deal voting alliance of southern whites, blacks, urban labor unionists, and ethnic groups like Jews and Hispanics to eke out a narrow win, receiving 41 million votes to Ford's 39 million. A heavy turnout of African Americans in the South enabled Carter to sweep every state in the region except Virginia. He also benefited from the appeal of Walter F. Mondale, his liberal running mate and a favorite among blue-collar workers and the urban poor.

The most significant story of the election, however, was the low voter turnout. Almost half of eligible voters, apparently alienated by Watergate, the stagnant economy, and the two lackluster candidates, chose to sit out the election. It was not a good omen for the incoming Democratic president.

CHAPTER REVIEW

SUMMARY

- **Youth Revolt**   Civil rights activism inspired a heightened interest in social causes during the sixties, especially among the young. Students for a Democratic Society (SDS) embodied the *New Left* ideology, and their ideas and tactics spread to many other campuses. By 1970, a distinctive *counterculture* had emerged among disaffected youth, and attracted young people ("hippies") alienated by mainstream American values and institutions.

- **The Inspirational Effects of the Civil Rights Movement**   The energy, ideals, tactics, and courage of the civil rights movement inspired many other social reform movements during the sixties and seventies, including the *women's movement*, the *Red Power* movement among Native Americans, and the *United Farm Workers* (*UFW*). The *Stonewall riots* in New York City in 1969 marked a militant new era for gay rights.

- **Reaction and Domestic Agenda**   Richard Nixon's "southern strategy" drew conservative southern white Democrats into the Republican party. As president, he sought to slow the momentum of the civil rights movement, including *affirmative action* programs giving special treatment to minorities, and vetoed the extension of the Voting Rights Act of 1968, but Congress overrode his veto. Nixon did grudgingly support new federal environmental policies such as the creation of the *Environmental Protection Agency* (*EPA*).

- **End of the Vietnam War**   In 1968, Nixon campaigned for the presidency pledging to secure "peace with honor" in Vietnam, but years would pass before the war ended. Nixon implemented what was called the *Vietnamization* of the war, which involved increasing economic and military aid to the South Vietnamese, reducing U.S. ground forces, and escalating the bombing of North Vietnam (and Cambodia), while attempting to negotiate a cease-fire agreement. The publication of the Pentagon Papers in 1971 and the intense bombing of North Vietnam in December 1972 aroused more protests, but a month after the bombings began, North and South Vietnam agreed to a cease-fire called the Paris Peace Accords.

- **Détente**   Nixon's greatest accomplishments were in foreign policy. He opened diplomatic relations with Communist China and pursued *détente* with the Soviet Union. He and Henry Kissinger also helped ease tensions in the Middle East.

- **Watergate**   During the 1972 presidential campaign, burglars were caught breaking into the Democratic party's national campaign headquarters at the *Watergate* complex in Washington, D.C. Nixon tried to block congressional investigations, which eventually led to calls for his impeachment for obstruction of justice. Nixon resigned in 1974 to avoid being impeached. He was succeeded by Vice President Gerald Ford, whose presidency was undermined by economic struggles, international incidents, and his controversial decision to pardon Nixon.

Chronology

Key Terms

 INQUIZITIVE

Go to InQuizitive to see what you've learned—and learn what you've missed—with personalized feedback along the way.

31 Conservative Revival

1977–1990

Feels good to be Right This proud Republican and Reagan supporter lets his cowboy hat adorned with campaign buttons speak for him at the 1980 Republican National Convention. Held in Detroit, Michigan, the convention nominated former California governor Ronald Reagan, who promised to "make America great again."

D uring the seventies, the United States lost much of its self-confidence as it confronted difficult lessons about its power and resources and the pitfalls of greed and corruption. The Vietnam War, the Watergate scandal, and the spike in world oil prices, interest rates, and consumer prices revealed the limits of American power, prosperity, and virtue. For a nation accustomed to economic growth and spreading prosperity, the frustrating persistence of stagflation and gasoline shortages undermined national optimism. In July 1976, as the United States celebrated the bicentennial of its independence, many people were downsizing their expectations of the American Dream.

Jimmy Carter, the first president from the Lower South, took office in 1977 promising a government that would be "competent" as well as "decent, open, fair, and compassionate." But after four years as president, Carter had little to show for his efforts. The economy remained sluggish, consumer prices continued to increase at historic levels, and failed efforts to free Americans held hostage in Iran prompted critics, including Democrats, to denounce the administration as indecisive and inept. In the end, Carter's inability to mobilize national support for an ill-fated energy program and his call for "a time of national austerity" revealed both his ineffective legislative skills and his misreading of the public mood.

The Republicans capitalized by electing Ronald Reagan president in 1980. Where Carter had denounced the evils of unregulated capitalism, Reagan

focus questions

1. Why did Jimmy Carter have such limited success as America's thirty-ninth president?

2. What were the factors that led to the election of Ronald Reagan, the rise of the conservative movement, and the resurgence of the Republican party?

3. What is "Reaganomics"? What were its effects on American society and economy?

4. How did Reagan's Soviet strategy help end the cold war?

5. What were the social and economic issues and innovations that emerged during the 1980s?

6. What was the impact of the end of the cold war and the efforts of President George H. W. Bush to create a post–cold war foreign policy?

promised to unleash the capitalist spirit, restore national pride, and regain international respect. He did all of that and more. During his two terms as president, he inspired a conservative resurgence in politics, helped restore prosperity and raise the nation's morale, and accelerated the forces that would cause the collapse of the Soviet Union and the end of the cold war.

THE CARTER PRESIDENCY

James (Jimmy) Earl Carter Jr. won the 1976 election because he convinced voters that he was a common man of pure motives who would restore integrity and honesty to the presidency in the aftermath of the Watergate scandal. He represented a new generation of "moderate" southern Democrats who were committed to restraining "big-government" spending. In his inaugural address, Carter stressed America's limitations rather than its power: "We have learned that 'more' is not necessarily 'better,' that even our great nation has its recognized limits, and that we can neither answer all questions nor solve all problems." That may have been true, but it was not what many Americans wanted to hear.

JIMMY WHO?

Like Gerald Ford before him, Jimmy Carter was honest and forthright. But his public modesty masked a complex and at times contradictory personality. No modern president was as openly committed to his Christian faith as Carter. At the same time, few presidents were as tough on others as Carter.

The former governor of Georgia who came out of nowhere to win the presidential campaign ("Jimmy Who?") was both blessed and cursed by a surplus of self-confidence. All his life, he had displayed a fierce determination to succeed. He expected those around him to show the same tenacity. "I am pretty rigid," Carter admitted. As he entered the White House in early 1977, Carter, the former naval officer, nuclear engineer, efficiency expert, and business executive, stressed that he wanted to be a "strong, aggressive president" who would reshape the federal government by eliminating waste and providing expert management.

Carter faced difficult economic problems and formidable international challenges. He was expected to cure the stubborn recession and reduce inflation at a time when industrial economies around the world were struggling. Carter was also expected to restore U.S. stature abroad and lift the national spirit in the wake of the Watergate scandal. Meeting such expectations would be miraculous, but Carter displayed a sunburst smile, flinty willpower, and an "almost arrogant self-confidence," as *Time* magazine described it. As it turned out, however, he was no miracle worker.

EARLY SUCCESS During the first two years of his presidency, Carter enjoyed several successes, both symbolic and real. He reduced the size of the White House staff by a third and told cabinet officers to give up their government cars. His administration included more African Americans and women than any before. He fulfilled a controversial campaign pledge by offering amnesty (forgiveness) to the thousands of young men who had fled the country rather than serve in Vietnam. He reorganized the executive branch and reduced government red tape.

Carter also pushed through the Democratic-controlled Congress sev-

The Carters After his inauguration in 1977, President Jimmy Carter forgoes the traditional limousine and walks down Pennsylvania Avenue with his wife, Rosalynn.

eral significant environmental initiatives, including stricter controls over the strip-mining of coal, the creation of a $1.6 billion "Superfund" to clean up toxic chemical waste sites, and a bill protecting more than 100 million acres of Alaskan land from development. At the end of his first 100 days in office, Carter enjoyed a 75 percent public approval rating.

CARTER'S LIMITATIONS But President Carter's successes were short-lived. More than most presidents, he faced difficulties beyond his control, including ongoing inflation and a global energy crisis. Carter, however, contributed to the perception that he was not up to the challenges by failing to display two qualities necessary for presidential success: forcefulness and optimism. He was less an inspiring leader than an efficiency-minded bureaucrat, a compulsive micromanager who failed to establish a compelling vision for the nation's future. Carter tried to do too much too fast, deciding disastrously that he needed no chief of staff to help manage his schedule and implement his decisions. His senior aides were often more a burden than a blessing. The "outsider" president saw little need to consult with Democratic leaders in

Congress, which helps explain why many of his legislative requests were voted down.

Ultimately, Carter's mismanagement of the economy crippled his presidency. He first tried to attack unemployment, authorizing some $14 billion in federal spending to trigger job growth while cutting taxes by $34 billion. His actions helped generate new jobs but also caused a spike in inflation. Annual inflation (increases in consumer prices) jumped from 5 percent when he took office to as much as 13 percent during 1980. The result was a deepening recession and rising unemployment.

What made Carter's efforts to restore prosperity more challenging was the worsening global "energy crisis." Since the Arab oil embargo in 1973, the price of imported oil had doubled, while U.S. dependence on foreign oil had grown from 35 percent to 50 percent of its annual needs. In April 1977, Carter presented Congress with a comprehensive energy proposal designed to cut oil consumption. However, the final energy bill, the National Energy Act of 1978, was so gutted by oil, gas, and automobile industry lobbyists that one presidential aide said it looked like it had been "nibbled to death by ducks."

In 1979, the energy crisis grew more troublesome when Islamic fundamentalists took over the government in oil-rich Iran and shut off the supply of Iranian oil to the United States, creating shortages of gasoline and much higher prices. Warning that the "growing scarcity in energy" would paralyze the U.S. economy, Carter asked the Democratic-controlled Congress for a new and much more comprehensive energy bill. But legislators again turned down its most important energy conservation provisions intended to reduce dependence on foreign oil.

A "CRISIS OF CONFIDENCE" By July 1979, Carter had grown so discouraged by his failures that he took an unusual step: for two weeks he holed up at Camp David, the presidential retreat in the Maryland mountains. There he met privately with leaders from all walks of life—business, labor, education, religion, even psychiatry. Then, on July 15, he returned to the White House and delivered a televised speech in which he admitted that the people had lost confidence in his leadership.

Carter then made a crucial mistake when he blamed Americans for the nation's problems. "All the legislation in the world can't fix what's wrong with America," he said, sounding more like an angry preacher than an uplifting president. People had become preoccupied with "owning and consuming things" at the expense of "hard work, strong families, close-knit communities, and our faith in God." The nation was at a crossroads, he concluded. Americans could choose continued self-indulgence and political stalemate, or they could revive traditional values such as thrift, mutual aid, simple living, and spirituality. "We can take the first step down that path as we begin to solve our energy problem. Energy will be the immediate test of our ability to unite this nation."

Americans were not inspired by the president's "sad and worried" speech. An Arizona newspaper expressed the feelings of many when it said that "the nation did not tune in Carter to hear a sermon. It wanted answers. It did not get them." Carter's new energy proposals got nowhere in Congress, and by the end of the summer, his negative ratings were the highest in history. "Our greatest single failure," said Hamilton Jordan, Carter's chief of staff, "is that we have not communicated effectively a description of the country's problems or a pertinent solution to those problems." It did not help matters when Carter took the unusual step two days after the speech of asking over thirty government officials, including his entire cabinet, to resign. He accepted the resignations of five cabinet officers. In doing so, he reinforced the public image of a White House out of control.

CARTER'S FOREIGN POLICY

Carter's greatest success was facilitating a 1978 peace agreement between Prime Minister Menachem Begin of Israel and President Anwar Sadat of Egypt. When negotiations between the enemies stalled, Carter invited Begin and Sadat to Camp David. For twelve days in September, the three leaders engaged in non-stop discussions.

At times the discussions to end the thirty-year state of war between the two nations grew so heated that the talks seemed doomed to fail. Thanks to Carter's tireless efforts, however, the two sides persevered. The U.S. president played a crucial role in coaxing Sadat and Begin to compromise on key issues. Their efforts resulted in two landmark treaties, thereafter called the **Camp David Accords**. The first provided the framework for an eventual peace treaty. The Israelis pledged to end their military occupation of the Sinai region of Egypt, and the Egyptians promised to restore Israeli access to the Suez Canal. The second treaty called for a comprehensive settlement of the Arab-Israeli tensions based on Israel's willingness to allow the Palestinians living in the Israeli-controlled West Bank and Gaza Strip to govern themselves.

Sadat's willingness to recognize the legitimacy of the Israeli nation and sign the two treaties sparked waves of violent protests across the Arab world. The Arab League expelled Egypt and announced an economic boycott, and the Israelis later backtracked on aspects of the agreements. Sadat, however, paid the highest price. Most Arab nations condemned him as a traitor, and Islamic extremists assassinated him in 1981. Still, Carter's high-level diplomacy made an all-out war between Israel and the Arab world less likely.

The Camp David Accords Egyptian president Anwar el-Sadat (left), Jimmy Carter (center), and Israeli prime minister Menachem Begin (right) at the announcement of the Camp David Accords, September 1978.

Carter was also caught in a political crossfire when he vowed that "the soul of our foreign policy" should be an absolute "commitment to human rights" abroad, drawing a direct contrast between his international "idealism" and the geopolitical "realism" practiced by Richard Nixon and Henry Kissinger. Carter created an Office of Human Rights within the State Department and selectively cut off financial assistance to some repressive governments. "America did not invent human rights," he stressed. "In a very real sense, human rights invented America."

Critics, however, noted that the United States had its own human rights issues, including the plight of Native Americans and African Americans, and that Carter ignored abuses occurring among key allies, such as the shah of Iran. Others asserted that Carter's definition of human rights was so vague and sweeping that few nations could satisfy it. Critics on the right argued that he was sacrificing America's global interests to promote an impossible standard of international moral purity, while critics on the left highlighted his seeming hypocrisy in pursuing human rights in a few nations but not everywhere.

Similarly, Carter's controversial decision to turn over control of the ten-mile-wide Panama Canal zone to the Panamanian government aroused intense criticism. The president argued that Panama's deep resentment of

America's having taken control of the Canal Zone during the presidency of Theodore Roosevelt left him no choice but to transfer management of the canal to Panama.

Conservatives blasted Carter for surrendering U.S. control of such a strategic asset. Former California governor and presidential candidate Ronald Reagan repeatedly lambasted Carter's "giveaway," claiming that the canal was America's forever: "We bought it, we paid for it, it's ours." Legal scholars and the Panamanian government disagreed, however. No Panamanian had ever signed the 1903 document granting the United States perpetual control of the strategic waterway (instead, a French engineer signed it). The new agreement between Panama and the United States called for the Canal Zone to be transferred to Panama at the end of 1999. Carter said the exchange reflected the American belief that "fairness, not force, should lie at the heart of our dealings with the world."

In late December 1979, Carter faced another crisis when 100,000 Soviet soldiers invaded Afghanistan, a remote, mountainous country where a faltering Communist government was being challenged by Islamist *jihadis* ("holy warriors") and ethnic warlords. It was the first Soviet army deployment outside of Europe since the Second World War, and the forces soon found themselves mired in what some called the Soviet Vietnam. "They have taken the ultimate step," said a U.S. diplomat. "They've finally grasped the tar baby."

President Carter responded with a series of steps: in January 1980, he refused to sign a Strategic Arms Limitation Talks treaty with the Soviets (SALT II), suspended grain shipments to the Soviet Union, began supplying Afghan "freedom fighters" with weapons smuggled through Pakistan, requested large increases in military spending, required all nineteen-year-old men to register for the military draft, and called for an international boycott of the 1980 Olympic Games, which were to be held that summer in Moscow. Some sixty nations joined the United States in boycotting the Olympic games. Still, the Soviets persisted in their intervention for nine years. It ultimately cost 15,000 Soviet lives.

The Soviet invasion of Afghanistan also prompted Carter to announce what came to be called the Carter Doctrine, in which he threatened to use military force to prevent any nation from gaining control of the Persian Gulf waterways, through which most of the oil from the Middle East made its way to foreign ports.

CRISIS IN IRAN Then came the **Iranian hostage crisis**, a series of dramatic events that illustrated the inability of the United States to control world affairs. In January 1979, Islamic revolutionaries had ousted the pro-American government led by the shah of Iran, Mohammad Reza Pahlavi, who owed his rule to a CIA intervention in 1953 that overthrew the elected Iranian government.

The rebel leaders executed hundreds of the shah's former officials. Thousands more Iranians were imprisoned, tortured, or executed for refusing to abide by strict Islamic social codes. The turmoil led to a sharp drop in oil production, driving gasoline prices up worldwide. By the spring of 1979, Americans were again waiting in long lines to pay record prices for limited amounts of gas.

In October, the Carter administration allowed the deposed shah to receive medical treatment for cancer at an American hospital. This "humanitarian" decision enraged Iranian revolutionaries, millions of whom took to the streets to demand that the United States return the shah to Iran. On November 4, 1979, a frenzied mob stormed the U.S. embassy in Tehran and seized sixty-six diplomats and staff, including fifty-two American citizens. Iranian leader Ayatollah Ruhollah Khomeini endorsed the mob action and demanded the return of the hated shah (along with all his wealth) in exchange for the release of the hostages. Nightly television coverage of the taunting Iranian rebels generated among viewers a near obsession with the fate of the hostages.

A king's ransom An Iranian militant holds a group of U.S. embassy staff members hostage in Tehran, Iran, in 1979.

Angry Americans, including many in Congress, demanded a military response to the kidnappings. Carter, however, believed his options were limited; he wanted to keep the hostages alive. He appealed to the United Nations, but Khomeini scoffed at UN efforts. Carter then froze all Iranian financial assets in America and asked Europe to join the United States in a trade embargo of Iran, including its oil. The trade restrictions were only partially effective because America's allies were not willing to lose access to Iranian oil.

As the crisis continued and gasoline prices rose to record levels, Carter authorized a risky rescue attempt by U.S. commandos on April 24, 1980. (His decision caused his secretary of state, Cyrus Vance, to resign in protest.) The raid had to be cancelled when three of the eight helicopters developed

Ayatollah Khomeini Religious figure and leader of the Iranian Revolution who overthrew the Iranian monarchy in 1979.

mechanical problems; it ended with eight U.S. deaths when a helicopter collided with a transport plane in the Iranian desert.

For fourteen months, the Iranian hostage crisis paralyzed Carter's ability to lead the nation. For many, the prolonged standoff became a symbol of his failed presidency. "For the first time in its history," *Business Week* magazine's editors observed, "the United States is no longer growing in power and influence among the nations of the world." The crisis finally ended after 444 days, on January 20, 1981, when Carter, just hours before leaving office, released several billion dollars of Iranian assets to ransom the hostages.

THE RISE OF RONALD REAGAN

No sooner had Carter been elected in 1976 than conservative Republicans (the "New Right") began working to ensure that he would not win a second term. Their plans centered on the popularity of tall, square-shouldered, plain-speaking Ronald Reagan, the Hollywood actor, two-term California

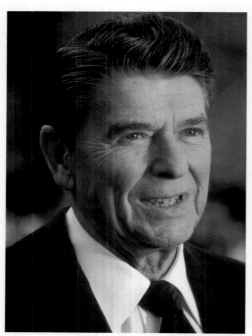

Ronald Reagan The "Great Communicator" flashes his charming, trademark smile.

governor, and prominent political commentator. Reagan was not a deep thinker, but he was a superb reader of the public mood, an outspoken patriot, and a committed champion of conservative principles.

THE ACTOR TURNED PRESIDENT

Born in the town of Tampico, Illinois, in 1911, the son of an often-drunk, Irish Catholic shoe salesman and a devout, Bible-quoting mother who preached a prairie Protestantism centered on individual freedom, Ronald Reagan grew up in a household short of money and frequently on the move. A football scholarship enabled him to attend tiny Eureka College during the Great Depression; he washed dishes in the dining hall to pay for his meals. After graduation, Reagan worked as a radio sportscaster before starting a movie career in Hollywood. He served three years in the army during the Second World War, making training films. At that time, as he recalled, he was a Democrat, "a New Dealer to the core" who voted "blindly" for Franklin D. Roosevelt four times.

After the war, Reagan became president of the acting profession's union, the Screen Actors Guild (SAG), where he honed his negotiating skills and fended off Communist efforts to infiltrate the union. Reagan supported Democrat Harry S. Truman in the 1948 presidential election, but during the fifties he decided that federal taxes were too high. In 1960, he campaigned as a Democrat for Richard Nixon, and two years later he joined the Republican party. Reagan achieved political stardom in 1964 when he delivered a rousing speech on national television on behalf of Barry Goldwater's presidential candidacy. Wealthy admirers convinced him to run for governor of California in 1966, and he won by a landslide.

As the Republican presidential nominee in 1980, Reagan set about drawing a vivid contrast between his optimistic vision of America's future and Jimmy Carter's bleak outlook. Reagan insisted that there was "nothing wrong with the American people" and that there were "simple answers" to the complex problems facing the country, although they were not *easy* answers. He pledged to slash social-welfare programs, increase military spending to "win" the cold war, dismantle the "bloated" federal bureaucracy, restore states' rights, reduce taxes and government regulation of businesses ("get the government off our backs and release the energies of free enterprise"), and appoint conservative judges to the federal courts. He also promised to affirm old-time religious values by banning abortions and reinstituting prayer in public schools. (He ended up achieving neither.)

Reagan's popularity resulted in part from his skill as a speaker (journalists dubbed him the "Great Communicator") and his steadfast commitment to a few basic principles and simple themes. Blessed with a reassuring baritone voice and a wealth of entertaining stories, he charmed audiences while rejecting Carter's assumption that Americans needed "to start getting along with less, to accept a decline in our standard of living." He instead promised boundless economic expansion.

THE RISE OF THE "NEW RIGHT"

By 1980, social developments had made Ronald Reagan's anti-liberal stance a major asset. An increase in the number of senior citizens, a group that tends to be more politically and socially conservative, and the steady migration of people—especially older Americans—to the conservative sunbelt states were shifting the political balance of power. Fully 90 percent of the nation's population growth during the eighties occurred in southern or western sunbelt states, while the Northeast and industrial states of the Midwest—Ohio, Michigan, and Illinois (called the "rust belt")—experienced economic decline and population losses.

A related development was a growing grassroots tax revolt. As consumer prices and home values rose, so did property taxes. In California, Reagan's home state, skyrocketing property taxes threatened to force many working-class people from their homes. This led to efforts to cut back on the size and cost of government to enable reductions in property taxes. In June 1978, tax rebels, with Reagan's support, succeeded in putting an initiative known as Proposition 13 on the state ballot. An overwhelming majority of voters approved the measure, which slashed property taxes by 57 percent and amended the state constitution to make it more difficult to raise taxes. The "Prop 13" tax revolt soon spread across the nation, leading the *New York Times* to call it a "modern Boston Tea Party."

THE RELIGIOUS RIGHT The California tax revolt fed into a national conservative resurgence led by the "religious Right." Religious conservatives pushing a faith-based political agenda formed the strongest grassroots movement of the late twentieth century. By the eighties, Catholic conservatives and Protestant evangelicals owned television and radio stations, operated their own schools and universities, and organized "mega churches" from which such "televangelists" as the Reverend Jerry Falwell launched a cultural crusade against the "demonic" forces of liberalism at home and communism abroad.

In 1979, Falwell formed a group he called the **Moral Majority** (later renamed the Liberty Alliance) to campaign for the major political and social goals of the religious Right: the economy should operate without "interference" by the government, which should be reduced in size; the Supreme Court decision in *Roe v. Wade* (1973) legalizing abortion should be reversed; Darwinian evolution should be replaced in school textbooks by the biblical story of creation; prayer should return to public schools; women should submit to their husbands; and, communism should be opposed as a form of pagan totalitarianism.

That Ronald Reagan became the hero of the religious Right was a tribute to his political skills, for he rarely attended church and had no strong religious affiliations. President Carter, though famous as a born-again Baptist Sunday School teacher, lost the support of religious conservatives because he was not

Look on the Right side The rise of the religious right saw protests against Supreme Court rulings that reinforced the separation of church and state. Here, in a 1984 rally organized by the Moral Majority, students chant "Kids want to pray!" in support of an amendment to reinstate prayer in public schools. (The effort failed.)

willing to ban abortions or restore prayers in public schools. His push for state ratification of the equal-rights constitutional amendment (ERA) also cost him the support of anti-feminist conservatives.

ANTI-FEMINIST BACKLASH By the late seventies, a well-organized and well-financed backlash against the feminist movement reinforced the rise of the "New Right." Activists like Republican Phyllis Schlafly, a conservative Catholic attorney from Illinois, campaigned successfully to keep the ERA from being ratified by the required thirty-eight states. Schlafly's STOP (Stop Taking Our Privileges) ERA organization warned that the ERA would allow husbands to abandon their wives, force women into military service, and give gay "perverts" the right to marry. She and others stressed that the gender equality promised by the proposed amendment violated biblical teachings about women's "God-given" roles as nurturers and helpmates. By the late seventies, the effort to gain ratification of the ERA had failed, largely because no states in the conservative South and West had ratified it.

Many of Schlafly's supporters also participated in the growing anti-abortion, or "pro-life," movement. The National Right to Life Committee, supported by the National Conference of Catholic Bishops, denounced abortion as murder, and the emotional intensity of the issue made it a powerful political force. Reagan highlighted his support for traditional "family values," gender roles, and the "rights" of the unborn, which helped persuade many northern Democrats—mostly working-class Catholics—to support him.

FINANCING CONSERVATISM The business community as well had become a source of revitalized conservative activism. In 1972, the leaders of the nation's largest corporations formed the Business Roundtable to promote their interests in Congress. Within a few years, many of them had created political action committees (PACs) to distribute money to pro-business political candidates. Corporate donations also helped fund conservative "think tanks," such as the American Enterprise Institute, the Cato Institute, and the Heritage Foundation. By 1980, the conservative insurgency had become a powerful political force with substantial financial resources, carefully crafted ideas, and grassroots energy.

THE ELECTION OF 1980 Ronald Reagan's supporters during the 1980 campaign loved his simple solutions, upbeat personality, and folksy humor, and they responded passionately to his recurring question: "Are you better off than you were four years ago?" Their answer was a resounding "No!" On Election Day, Reagan swept to a lopsided victory, with 489 electoral votes to 49 for Jimmy Carter, who carried only six states. (It was the second worst defeat of an incumbent president in the twentieth century behind William Howard Taft in 1912). The popular vote was 44 million (51 percent) for Reagan to Carter's 35 million (41 percent), with 7 percent going to John Anderson, a moderate Republican who ran as an independent. Reagan's resounding victory signaled a major realignment of voters in which many so-called Reagan Democrats— conservative white southern Protestants and blue-collar northern Catholics— crossed over to the Republican party. The Reagan era had begun.

THE REAGAN REVOLUTION

Democrats who dismissed sixty-nine-year-old Ronald Reagan, the oldest man to assume the presidency, as a third-rate actor and mental lightweight underrated his many virtues. Few people in public life had Reagan's stage presence— or confidence. He may have been a mediocre actor, but no one played the part of president better. His remarkable ability to make Americans believe again in the greatness of their country won him two presidential elections, in 1980 and 1984, and ensured the victory of his anointed successor, Vice President George H. W. Bush, in 1988. Just how revolutionary the "Reagan era" was remains a subject of debate, but it cannot be denied that Reagan's actions and beliefs set the tone for the decade's political and economic life.

REAGAN'S FIRST TERM

"Fellow conservatives," President Reagan said in a speech in 1981, "our moment has arrived." He and others were determined to "get America moving again." In his inaugural address, he promised to help Americans "renew our faith and hope" in their nation as a "shining city on a hill" for the rest of the world to emulate.

Reagan helped restore the prestige of the presidency through the force of his personality and the appeal of his ideas and ideals. He succeeded for three main reasons. First, he focused on a few priorities (slowing the rate of inflation, lowering tax rates, reducing the scope of the federal government, increasing military spending, and conducting an anti-Soviet foreign policy), and he pursued those goals with what an aide called a "warmly ruthless" intensity.

Second, Reagan, unlike Carter, was skilled at negotiating with congressional leaders and foreign heads of states. He also recognized that politics is a profession built on compromises. Because the Democrats controlled Congress, Reagan was forced to convince the public to pressure their legislators to support his initiatives. As a former union leader, Reagan was a masterful

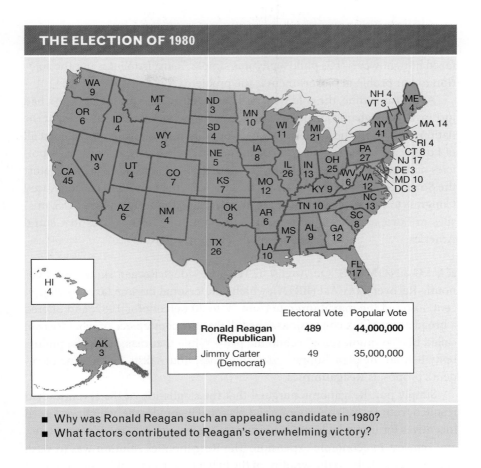

THE ELECTION OF 1980

	Electoral Vote	Popular Vote
Ronald Reagan (Republican)	**489**	**44,000,000**
Jimmy Carter (Democrat)	49	35,000,000

- Why was Ronald Reagan such an appealing candidate in 1980?
- What factors contributed to Reagan's overwhelming victory?

negotiator with Congress, willing to modify his positions while sustaining his overarching goals, accepting a partial success and then going back again and again for the rest of what he wanted.

Third, Reagan's infectious optimism gave people a sense of renewed confidence. Voters wanted to believe his insistent claim that America could do no wrong. An uncommon politician, he avoided both the arrogance and self-importance that often accompany the highest office.

Public affection for Reagan spiked just two months into his presidency when an assassination attempt left him with a punctured lung and a bullet lodged near his heart. The witty Reagan told doctors as they prepared for surgery: "Please tell me you're Republicans." His gritty response to his injuries created an outpouring of support that gave added momentum to his presidency. The Democratic Speaker of the House, Tip O'Neill, told colleagues that Reagan "has become a hero. We can't argue with a man as popular as he is."

Reagan inherited an economy in shambles: the annual rate of inflation had reached 13 percent, and unemployment hovered at 7.5 percent. None of this fazed him, however. His philosophy was simple: "Government is not the solution to our problem. Government *is* the problem."

At the same time, the cold war was heating up again. The Soviet Union had just invaded Afghanistan and had placed missiles with nuclear weapons in the nations of central and Eastern Europe under its control, which threatened all of Europe. But Reagan refused to be intimidated. He discarded the earlier policies of containment and détente in favor of a confrontational posture against the Soviet Union which he summarized as "We win, you lose." He convinced Congress to support a huge increase in the military budget, deployed U.S. missiles in Europe, and sought to root out Communist insurgencies in Central America.

REAGANOMICS On August 1, 1981, President Reagan signed the Economic Recovery Tax Act (ERTA), which cut personal income taxes by 25 percent, lowered the maximum rate from 70 to 50 percent for 1982, and offered a broad array of tax concessions. The bill was the centerpiece of what Reagan called his "common sense" economic plan. While theorists called the philosophy behind the plan "supply-side economics," journalists dubbed the president's proposals **Reaganomics**.

Simply put, Reaganomics argued that the stagflation of the seventies had resulted from excessive corporate and personal income taxes, which weakened incentives for individuals and businesses to increase productivity, save money, and reinvest in economic expansion. The Reaganomics solution was to slash tax rates, especially on the wealthy, in the belief that they would spend their tax savings on business expansion and consumer goods (the "supply side" of the economy). Such spending, advocates believed, would provide "trickle down" benefits to the masses. By generating economic growth, Reaganomics promised to produce enough new tax revenues from rising corporate profits and personal incomes to pay for the tax cuts. In the short term, however, ERTA did not work as planned. The federal budget deficit grew, and by November 1981, the economy was officially in recession.

MANAGING THE BUDGET To offset the loss of government tax revenues, David Stockman, President Reagan's budget director, proposed sharp reductions in federal spending, including Social Security and Medicare, the two most expensive—and most popular—federal programs. Liberal Democrats howled at Stockman's proposal, and Reagan responded that he was committed to maintaining the "safety net" of government services for the "truly

A miss for Reaganomics A throng of more than 5,000 senior citizens staged a demonstration in downtown Detroit against Reagan's decision to make cuts in Social Security and other federal programs supporting the elderly in 1982.

needy." According to Stockman, Reagan was "too kind, gentle, and sentimental" to make the drastic cuts needed to balance the budget.

The Reagan administration also continued huge federal subsidies to corporations and agribusinesses—what critics called "welfare for the rich." In the end, Reagan never dismantled the major New Deal programs that he had savagely criticized. Conservative political columnist George Will explained Reagan's failure to make substantial cuts in federal spending by noting that "Americans are conservative. What they want to conserve is the New Deal."

Within a year, Stockman realized that the cuts in domestic spending approved by Reagan had fallen far short of what would be needed to balance the budget in four years, as the president had promised. Massive increases in military spending greatly complicated the situation. In essence, Reagan gave the Defense Department a blank check. Over the next five years, the administration would spend some $1.2 *trillion* on military expenses. Something had to give.

In the summer of 1981, Stockman warned that "we're heading for a crash landing on the budget. We're facing potential deficit numbers so big that they could wreck the president's entire economic program." The fast-growing federal deficit, which had helped trigger the worst economic recession since the 1930s, was Reagan's greatest failure, as he himself admitted. During 1982, an estimated 10 million Americans were unable to find jobs. Stockman and other aides finally convinced the president that the government needed "revenue enhancements" (tax increases). With Reagan's support, Congress passed a tax bill in 1982 that would raise almost $100 billion, but the economic slump persisted for a time. In the 1982 congressional midterm elections, Democrats picked up twenty-six seats in the House of Representatives.

But Reagan's determination to "stay the course" with his economic program began to pay off. By the summer of 1983, a major economic recovery was under way, in part because of increased government spending and lower interest rates and in part because of lower tax rates. Inflation subsided, as did unemployment. Reaganomics was not helping to balance the budget, however. In fact, the federal deficits had grown larger—so much so that the president had in fact run up an accumulated debt larger than that of all his predecessors combined. Reagan was willing to tolerate the deficits in part because he believed that they would force more responsible spending behavior in Congress, and in part because he was so committed to increased military spending as a way to intimidate the Soviets.

REAGAN'S ANTI-LIBERALISM During Reagan's presidency, organized labor suffered severe setbacks, even though Reagan himself had been a union leader. In 1981, he fired members of the Professional Air Traffic Controllers Organization who had participated in an illegal strike intended to shut down air travel (air traffic controllers were deemed essential to public safety and therefore were prohibited from striking). Reagan's actions broke the political power of the American Federation of Labor–Congress of Industrial Organizations (AFL-CIO), the national confederation of labor unions that traditionally supported Democratic candidates. His criticism of unions reflected a general trend in public opinion. Although record numbers of jobs were created during the eighties, union membership steadily dropped. By 1987, unions represented only 17 percent of the nation's full-time workers, down from 24 percent in 1979.

Sandra Day O'Connor Her Supreme Court confirmation hearing in September 1981 was picketed by conservatives who decried her pro-abortion stance.

Reagan also went on the offensive against feminism. He opposed the Equal Rights Amendment, legal abortion, and proposals to require equal pay for jobs of comparable worth. He did name Sandra Day O'Connor as the first woman Supreme Court justice, but critics labeled it a token gesture. In addition, he cut funds for civil rights enforcement and the Equal Employment Opportunity Commission, and he opposed renewal of the Voting Rights Act of 1965 before being overruled by Congress.

THE ELECTION OF 1984 By 1983, prosperity had returned, the stock market was soaring, and President Reagan's "supply-side" economic program was at last working as advertised—except for the growing budget deficit. Like the liberal presidents he often criticized, Reagan was a big spender, especially when it came to military growth. At the same time, his decision to remove price controls on oil and natural gas and his efforts to pressure Saudi Arabia to increase oil production produced a decline in energy prices that helped to stimulate economic growth.

By 1984, reporters had begun to speak of the "Reagan Revolution." The slogan at the Republican National Convention was "America is back and standing tall." The Democrats' presidential nominee, Walter Mondale (Jimmy Carter's vice president), struggled to present a competing vision. Endorsed by the AFL-CIO, the National Organization for Women (NOW), and many prominent African Americans, Mondale was viewed as the candidate of liberal special-interest groups. He set a precedent by choosing as his running mate Geraldine Ferraro, a New York congresswoman, who was quickly placed on the defensive by the need to explain her husband's complicated business dealings.

A bit of frankness in Mondale's acceptance speech ended up hurting his campaign. "Mr. Reagan will raise taxes, and so will I," he told the convention. "He won't tell you. I just did." Reagan responded by vowing never to approve a tax increase (a promise he could not keep) and by chiding Mondale for his stance. Reagan also repeated a theme he had used against Carter: the future, according to Mondale and the Democrats, was "dark and getting darker." Reagan's vision of America's future, however, was bright. As his campaign ads claimed, "It's morning again in America," and record numbers of Americans were headed to work. In the end, Reagan took 59 percent of the popular vote and lost only Minnesota (Mondale's home state) and the District of Columbia.

REAGAN'S SECOND TERM

Spurred by his overwhelming victory, Ronald Reagan called for "a Second American Revolution of hope and opportunity." He dared Democrats to raise taxes; his veto pen was ready. "Go ahead and make my day," he said, echoing a popular line from a Clint Eastwood movie. Through much of 1985, the president drummed up support for a tax-simplification plan. After vigorous debate, Congress passed a comprehensive Tax Reform Act in 1986. The measure cut the number of federal tax brackets from fourteen to two and reduced rates from the maximum of 50 percent to 15 and 28 percent—the lowest since Calvin Coolidge was president in the twenties.

REAGAN'S HALF-HEARTED REVOLUTION Although Ronald Reagan had promised to "curb the size and influence of the federal establishment," the number of federal employees actually *grew* during his two terms as president. Neither the Social Security system nor Medicare, the two largest federal social programs, were overhauled, and the federal agencies that Reagan had threatened to abolish, such as the Department of Education, not only survived but saw their budgets grow.

The federal deficit almost tripled during Reagan's two terms. He blamed Congress for the problem, "since only Congress can spend money," but in fact the legislators essentially approved the budgets that Reagan submitted to them (and he never submitted a balanced budget). As Dick Cheney, a future Republican vice president, quipped, "Reagan showed that deficits don't matter."

The cost of Social Security, the most expensive "entitlement" program, grew by 27 percent under Reagan, as some 6,000 Americans each day turned 65. Moreover, Reagan failed to fulfill his campaign promises to the religious Right, such as reinstituting daily prayer in public schools and a ban on abortions. But he did follow through on his pledge to reshape the federal court system. He appointed 368 mostly conservative judges, three of them to the U.S. Supreme Court: Sandra Day O'Connor, Antonin Scalia, and Anthony Kennedy.

Martin Anderson, Reagan's domestic policy adviser, stressed that it was "a mistake to think that there ever was a Reagan Revolution, or that Reagan gave it life." It was the grassroots conservative revolution that "caused Reagan—and the same forces will continue to the end of the century." What Reagan did accomplish was to end the prolonged period of "stagflation" and set in motion what economists called "The Great Expansion," an unprecedented, twenty-year burst of productivity and prosperity. True, Reagan's presidency left the nation with a massive debt burden that would eventually cause major problems, but the "Great Communicator" also renewed the nation's strength, self-confidence, and soaring sense of possibilities.

Ronald Reagan was a transformational president. While restoring the stature of the presidency and reviving the economy, he transformed political life by accelerating the nation's shift toward conservatism and by revitalizing the Republican party. He put the Democrats on the defensive and forced conventional New Deal "liberalism" into a panicked retreat. For the next twenty years or so, Reagan's anti-government, anti-tax conservative agenda would dominate the national political landscape.

AN ANTI-SOVIET FOREIGN POLICY

On a flight to Detroit, Michigan, to accept the Republican party's presidential nomination in the summer of 1980, Ronald Reagan was asked why he wanted to be president. He answered: "To end the Cold War." As president, Reagan systematically promoted what he called his "peace through strength" strategy. Through a series of bold steps, he would build up U.S. military strength to the point it would overwhelm the Soviet Union, both financially and militarily.

Reagan also launched a "war of ideas" by charging that the Soviet Union was "the focus of evil in the modern world." What came to be called the Reagan Doctrine pledged to combat Soviet adventurism throughout the world, even if it meant partnering with brutal dictatorships. Reagan believed that aggressive CIA-led efforts to stymie Soviet expansionism would eventually cause the unstable Soviet system to implode "on the ash heap of history."

A MASSIVE DEFENSE BUILDUP Reagan's conduct of foreign policy reflected his belief that trouble in the world stemmed mainly from Moscow, the capital of what he called the "evil empire." Reagan had long believed that Nixon and Ford—following the advice of Henry Kissinger—had been too soft on the Soviets. Kissinger's emphasis on détente, he said, had been a "one-way street" favoring the Soviets. Reagan first wanted to reduce the risk of nuclear war by convincing the Soviets that they could not win such a conflict.

To do so, he and Secretary of Defense Caspar Weinberger embarked upon a major buildup of nuclear and conventional weapons. Under Reagan, defense spending came to represent a fourth of all federal government expenditures. Reagan claimed that the defense allocations had another purpose: to bankrupt the Soviets by forcing them to spend much more on their own military budgets. To critics who complained about the defense spending, Reagan replied, "It will break the Soviets first." It did.

"STAR WARS" On March 23, 1983, just two weeks after denouncing the Soviet Union as "the focus of evil in the modern world," Reagan escalated the nuclear arms race when he announced in a televised address that he was authorizing the Defense Department to develop the controversial **Strategic Defense Initiative (SDI)**. It featured a complex anti-missile defense system that would

Strategic Defense Initiative President Reagan addresses the nation on March 23, 1983, promoting the development of a space-age shield to intercept Soviet missiles.

make nuclear weapons "impotent and obsolete." He described a defensive shield provided by satellites equipped with laser weapons in outer space that would "intercept and destroy" all Soviet missiles in flight before they could harm the United States. The expensive program was controversial from the start because it relied upon untested technology and violated a 1972 U.S.–Soviet treaty banning such anti-missile defensive systems. Despite skepticism among the media, scientists, and even government officials that such a defense system (dubbed "Star Wars" by the media) could be built, Congress approved the first stage of funding, eventually allocating $30 billion to the fanciful program. In the end, SDI was never implemented, but it did fulfil Reagan's pledge to change "the course of history" because it forced the Soviets to launch an expensive research and development effort of their own, which helped bankrupt their economy.

CONFRONTING THE EVIL EMPIRE Reagan also borrowed the rhetoric of Harry S. Truman, John Foster Dulles, and John F. Kennedy to express resolve in the face of "Communist aggression anywhere in the world." When the Polish government declared martial law during the winter of 1981, Reagan forcefully protested and imposed economic sanctions against Poland's Communist government. He also worked behind the scenes to support the Polish protest movement, Solidarity, which sought independence from Soviet control.

THE AMERICAS President Reagan's foremost international concern, however, was Central America, where he detected the most serious Communist threat. The tiny nation of El Salvador, caught up since 1980 in a brutal struggle between Communist-supported revolutionaries and right-wing militants, received U.S. economic and military assistance. Critics argued that U.S. involvement ensured that the revolutionary forces would gain favor by capitalizing on "anti-Yankee" sentiment. Reagan's supporters countered that a victory by the revolutionaries would lead all of Central America into the Communist camp (a new "domino" theory). By 1984, the U.S.-backed government of President José Napoleón Duarte had brought some stability to El Salvador.

More troubling to Reagan was the situation in Nicaragua. The State Department claimed that the Cuban-sponsored Sandinista socialist government, which had seized power in 1979, was sending arms to leftist Salvadoran rebels. In response, the Reagan administration ordered the CIA to train anti-Communist Nicaraguans, or Contras (short for *contrarevolucionarios*, or counterrevolutionaries), who staged attacks on Sandinista bases from sanctuaries in Honduras. In supporting these "freedom fighters," Reagan sought not only to impede the traffic in arms to Salvadoran rebels but also to replace the Sandinistas with a democratic government. Critics accused the Contras of being mostly right-wing fanatics who killed indiscriminately. They also feared that the United States might eventually commit its own combat forces, leading to a Vietnam-like intervention. Reagan warned that if the Communists prevailed in Central America, "our credibility would collapse, our alliances would crumble, and the safety of our homeland would be jeopardized."

THE MIDDLE EAST The Middle East remained a tinderbox of conflict during the 1980s. No peaceable end seemed possible in the prolonged bloody Iran-Iraq War, entangled as it was with the passions of Islamic fundamentalism. In 1984 both sides began to attack tankers in the Persian Gulf, a major source of the world's oil. (The main international response was the sale of arms to both sides.) Nor was any settlement in sight in Afghanistan, where the Soviet occupation forces had bogged down as badly as the Americans had in Vietnam.

American administrations continued to see Israel as the strongest and most reliable ally in the volatile region, all the while seeking to encourage moderate Arab groups. But the forces of moderation were dealt a blow during the mid-1970s when Lebanon, long an enclave of peace despite its ethnic complexity, collapsed into an anarchy of warring groups. The capital, Beirut, became a battleground for Sunni and Shiite Muslims, the Druze, the Palestine Liberation

Organization (PLO), Arab Christians, Syrian invaders cast as peacekeepers, and Israelis responding to PLO attacks across the border.

In 1982, Israeli forces pushed the PLO from southern Lebanon all the way north to Beirut and then began shelling PLO strongholds in Beirut. The United States sent a special ambassador to negotiate a settlement. Israeli troops moved into Beirut and looked the other way when Christian militiamen slaughtered Muslim women and children in Palestinian refugee camps. French, Italian, and U.S. forces then moved into Lebanon as "peacekeepers," but in such small numbers as to become targets themselves. Angry Muslims kept them constantly harassed. American warships and planes responded by shelling and bombing Muslim positions in the highlands behind Beirut, thereby increasing Muslim resentment.

By 1983, Israel had driven the PLO from Beirut, but it made the capital city even more unstable. In April 1983, Islamic suicide bombers drove a truck laden with explosives into the U.S. embassy compound in Beirut, detonated it, and killed forty people, including seventeen Americans. On October 23, 1983, an Islamic suicide bomber attacked the U.S. Marine headquarters at the Beirut airport; the explosion left 241 Americans and 58 Frenchmen dead. In early 1984, Reagan announced that the U.S. Marines remaining in Lebanon would be "redeployed" to warships offshore. The Israeli forces pulled back to southern Lebanon, while the Syrians remained in eastern Lebanon. Bloody anarchy remained a way of life in a formerly peaceful country.

GRENADA Fortune, as it happened, presented Reagan the chance for an easy triumph closer to home, a "rescue mission" that eclipsed news of the debacle in Lebanon. On the tiny Caribbean island of Grenada, the smallest independent country in the Western Hemisphere, a leftist government had admitted Cuban workers to build a new airfield and signed military agreements with Communist countries. In 1983 an even more radical military council seized power. Appeals from the governments of neighboring islands led Reagan to order 1,900 marines to invade the island, depose the new government, and evacuate a small group of American students at Grenada's medical school. The UN General Assembly condemned the action, but it was popular among Grenadans and their neighbors and immensely popular in the United States. Although a lopsided affair, the decisive action served as notice to Latin American revolutionaries that Reagan might use military force elsewhere in the region.

THE IRAN-CONTRA AFFAIR During the fall of 1986, Democrats regained control of the Senate with a 55 to 45 majority. They also picked up 6 seats in the House to increase their already comfortable margin to 259 to 176.

These results were less a referendum on Reagan than they were a response to the qualities of the particular candidates and particular local and state issues. Whatever the reason, the 1986 elections meant that Reagan would face an oppositional Congress during the last two years of his presidency.

What boded worse, reports surfaced in late 1986 that the United States had been secretly selling arms to U.S.-hating Iran (which Reagan had called an "outlaw state") in the hope of securing the release of American hostages held in Lebanon by extremist groups sympathetic to Iran. Such action contradicted Reagan's insistence that his administration would never negotiate with terrorists. The disclosures angered America's allies as well as many Americans who vividly remembered the 1979 Iranian takeover of the embassy in Tehran. Over the next several months, revelations emerged of a complicated series of covert activities carried out by administration officials.

At the center of what came to be called the **Iran-Contra affair** was marine lieutenant colonel Oliver North, a National Security Council aide who specialized in counterterrorism. Working from the basement of the White House, North had been secretly selling military supplies to Iran and using the proceeds to support the Contra rebels in Nicaragua at a time when Congress had voted to ban such aid.

North's illegal activities, it turned out, had been approved by national security adviser Robert McFarlane; McFarlane's successor, Admiral John Poindexter; and CIA director William Casey. Both Secretary of State George Shultz and Secretary of Defense Caspar Weinberger criticized the arms sales to Iran, but their objections were ignored, and they were thereafter kept in the dark about what was going on—as was Reagan. After information about the secret dealings surfaced, North and others erased incriminating computer files and destroyed documents. McFarlane attempted suicide before being convicted of withholding information from Congress; Poindexter resigned; North, described by the White House as a "loose cannon," was fired. Casey, who denied any connection to the clumsy operation, left the CIA and died shortly thereafter from a brain tumor.

Facing a barrage of criticism, Reagan appointed a three-member commission, led by former Republican senator John Tower, to investigate the scandal. The Tower Commission issued a devastating report early in 1987 that placed much of the responsibility for

Iran-Contra hearings Admiral John Poindexter listens warily to a question from the Congressional investigation committee on July 21, 1987.

The Iran-Contra cover-up In Paul Szep's 1987 cartoon, political figures including President Ronald Reagan, Robert McFarlane, lieutenant colonel Oliver North, and Iran's Ayatollah Khomeini attempt to deflect blame for the Iran-Contra Affair.

the Iran-Contra affair on Reagan's loose management style. When asked if he had known of Colonel North's illegal actions, the president simply replied: "I don't remember." He was stunned that "for the first time in my life, people didn't believe me." During the spring and summer of 1987, a joint House-Senate committee began holding hearings into the Iran-Contra affair. In his own testimony, Oliver North claimed that he thought "he had received authority from the President."

The investigations led to six indictments in 1988. North was found guilty of three relatively minor charges but innocent of nine more serious counts, apparently reflecting the jury's reasoning that he acted as an agent of higher-ups. His conviction was later overturned on appeal. Of those involved, only John Poindexter received a jail sentence—six months for obstructing justice and lying to Congress.

A HISTORIC TREATY The most positive achievement at the end of Reagan's second term was a surprising arms-reduction agreement with the

Soviet government. Under the charming Mikhail Gorbachev, who came to power in 1985, the Soviets pursued three dramatic initiatives. They renewed the policy of détente, encouraging a reduction of tensions with the United States, so that they could reduce military spending and focus on more pressing problems, especially a notoriously inefficient economy and a losing war in Afghanistan. Gorbachev also instituted what he called *perestroika* (restructuring), an ambitious effort to streamline the clunky Soviet government bureaucracy and make it more efficient. And, third, Gorbachev encouraged *glasnost* (openness), a radical reappraisal of the Soviet system that allowed for open debate and shared information. In the end, however, the modernization forces that Gorbachev helped unleash would end up dismantling the Soviet Union itself.

THE REYKJAVIK SUMMIT In October 1986, Reagan and Gorbachev met for the first time in Reykjavik, Iceland, to discuss ways to reduce the threat of nuclear war. At one point during a private one-on-one meeting, Reagan shocked Gorbachev and the Soviets by saying, "It would be fine with me if we eliminated all nuclear weapons."

Equally shocking was Gorbachev's reply: "We can do that."

By the end of the meeting, however, the two sides were still far apart, and Gorbachev privately called Reagan a "feebleminded cave man." The main sticking point was Reagan's refusal to call off the Strategic Defense Initiative (SDI, or "Star Wars"). Reagan's arms control director, Kenneth Adelman, privately admitted that SDI was unworkable, "little more than pie in the colorful sky of Ronald Reagan's imagination." But it became a dazzling bluff in the standoff with the Soviet Union.

THE INF TREATY The logjam in the disarmament negotiations suddenly broke in 1987, when Gorbachev announced that he was willing to consider mutual reductions in nuclear weaponry. A member of the

Mikhail Gorbachev Deputy chairman, and later president, of the Soviet Union in 1988.

Soviet negotiating team acknowledged Reagan's role in the breakthrough. The U.S. president, he explained, "takes you by the arm, walks you to the cliff's edge, and invites you to step forward for the good of humanity."

After nine months of strenuous negotiations, Reagan and Gorbachev met amid much fanfare in Washington, D.C., on December 9, 1987, and signed the **Intermediate-Range Nuclear Forces (INF) Treaty**, an agreement to eliminate intermediate-range (300- to 3,000-mile) missiles. The treaty marked the first time that the two nations had agreed to destroy a whole class of weapons systems and produced the most sweeping cuts in nuclear weaponry in history.

Gorbachev's successful efforts to liberalize Soviet domestic life and improve East–West relations cheered Americans. In the Middle East, the Soviets urged the Palestine Liberation Organization, founded in 1964 to represent the Palestinian people, to recognize Israel's right to exist and advocated a greater role for the United Nations in the volatile Persian Gulf. Perhaps the most dramatic symbol of the thawing cold war was the phased withdrawal of 115,000 Soviet troops from Afghanistan, which began in 1988.

REAGAN'S GLOBAL LEGACY Ronald Reagan achieved the unthinkable by helping to end the cold war. Although his massive defense buildup almost bankrupted the United States, it forced the Soviet Union to the bargaining table. By negotiating the nuclear disarmament treaty and lighting the fuse of democratic freedom in Soviet-controlled East Germany, Hungary, Poland, and Czechoslovakia, Reagan set in motion events that would cause the collapse of the Soviet Union.

In June 1987, Reagan visited the Berlin Wall in East Germany and, in a dramatic speech, called upon the Soviet Union to allow greater freedom within the countries under its control. "General Secretary Gorbachev, if you seek peace, if you seek prosperity for the Soviet Union and Eastern Europe, if you seek liberalization: Come here to this gate! Mr. Gorbachev, open this gate! Mr. Gorbachev, tear down this wall!" It was great theater and good politics.

THE CHANGING ECONOMIC AND SOCIAL LANDSCAPE

During the eighties, the U.S. economy went through a wrenching transformation in adapting to an increasingly interconnected global marketplace. The nations that had been devastated by the Second World War—France, Germany, the Soviet Union, Japan, and China—had now developed formidable economies with higher levels of productivity than the United States. More and more American companies shifted their production overseas, accelerating the transition of the economy from its once-dominant industrial base to a more services-oriented approach. Driving all of these changes were the impact of the computer revolution and the development of the Internet.

THE COMPUTER REVOLUTION The idea of a programmable machine that would rapidly perform mental tasks had been around since the eighteenth century, but it took the Second World War to marshal the intellectual and financial resources needed to create such a "computer." In 1946, a team of engineers at the University of Pennsylvania developed ENIAC (electronic numerical integrator and computer), the first all-purpose, all-electronic digital computer. It was so primitive that it required 18,000 vacuum tubes to operate. The following year, researchers at Bell Telephone Laboratories invented the transistor, which replaced the bulky vacuum tubes and enabled much smaller, yet more powerful, computers—as well as new devices such as hearing aids and transistor radios.

The next major breakthrough was the invention in 1971 of the **microprocessor**—virtually a tiny computer on a silicon chip. Functions once performed by huge computers that filled entire rooms could now be performed by a microchip the size of a postage stamp. The microchip made possible the

"Introducing Macintosh. For the rest of us." Personal computers are introduced to the masses in this 1980s Apple advertisement.

personal computer. In 1975, an engineer named Ed Roberts developed the Altair 8800, the prototype of the personal computer. Its potential excited a Harvard University sophomore named Bill Gates, who improved the software of the Altair 8800, dropped out of college, and formed a company called Microsoft.

During the 1980s, IBM (International Business Machines), using a micro-processor made by the Intel Corporation and an operating system provided by Microsoft, had helped transform the personal computer into a mass con-sumer product. In 1963, a half-million computer chips were sold worldwide; by 1970, the number was 300 million. Computer chips transformed a variety of electronic products—televisions, calculators, wristwatches, clocks, ovens, and automobiles—while also facilitating American efforts to land astronauts on the moon and launch satellites in space. The development of the Internet, electronic mail (e-mail), and cell-phone technology during the eighties and nineties allowed for instantaneous communication, thereby accelerating the globalization of the economy and dramatically increasing productivity in the workplace.

DEBT AND THE STOCK MARKET PLUNGE In the late seventies, Jimmy Carter had urged Americans to lead simpler lives, cut back on conspic-uous consumption, reduce energy use, and invest more time in faith and fam-ily. During the eighties, Ronald Reagan promoted very different behavior: he reduced tax rates so people would have more money to spend. Americans pre-ferred Reagan's emphasis on prosperity rather than Carter's focus on propriety, for it endorsed entrepreneurship as well as an increasingly consumption-oriented and hedonistic leisure culture.

But Reagan succeeded too well in shifting the public mood back to the "more is more," "bigger is better" tradition of heedless consumerism. During the "age of Reagan," marketers and advertisers celebrated instant gratification at the expense of the future. Michelob beer commercials began assuring Amer-icans that "you can have it all," and many consumers went on a self-indulgent spending spree. The more they bought the more they wanted. In 1984, Hol-lywood producers launched a new TV show called *Lifestyles of the Rich and Famous* that exemplified the decade's runaway materialism. As the stock mar-ket soared, the number of multi-millionaires working on Wall Street and in the financial industry nationwide mushroomed. The money fever was contagious. Compulsive shoppers donned T-shirts proclaiming: "Born to Shop." By 1988, 110 million Americans had an average of seven credit cards each.

Money—lots of it—came to define the American Dream. In the hit movie *Wall Street* (1987), the high-flying land developer and corporate raider Gordon Gekko, played by actor Michael Douglas, announced that "greed . . . is good. Greed is right." During the eighties, many Americans caught up in the materialism of the times began spending more money than they earned. All kinds of debt—personal, corporate, and government—increased dramatically. Americans in the sixties had saved on average 10 percent of their income; in 1987 the figure was less than 4 percent. The federal debt more than tripled, from $908 billion in 1980 to $2.9 trillion at the end of the 1989 fiscal year.

Then, on October 19, 1987, the bill collector suddenly arrived at the nation's doorstep. On that "Black Monday," the stock market experienced a tidal wave of selling reminiscent of the 1929 crash as investors worried that the United States would never address the federal government's massive budget deficits. The Dow Jones industrial average plummeted an astounding 22.6 percent. The market plunge nearly doubled the record 12.8 percent fall on October 28, 1929. Wall Street's selling frenzy reverberated throughout the capitalist world, sending stock prices plummeting in Tokyo, London, Paris, and Toronto.

In the aftermath of the calamitous selling spree on Black Monday, fears of an impending recession led business leaders and economists to attack President Reagan for allowing such huge budget deficits. Reagan responded by agreeing to work with Congress to develop a deficit-reduction package. For the first time, the president indicated a willingness to include increased taxes in such a package to reduce the deficit. But the eventual compromise plan was so modest that it did little to restore investor confidence. As one Republican

Black Monday A 508-point plunge devastated the stock market on October 19, 1987, and sent traders on the floor of the New York Stock Exchange into a panic-selling frenzy.

senator lamented, "There is a total lack of courage among those of us in the Congress to do what we all know has to be done."

THE POOR The eighties were years of vivid contrast. Despite unprecedented prosperity, homelessness became the most acute social issue. A variety of causes had led to a shortage of low-cost housing. The government had given up on building public housing, urban-renewal programs had demolished blighted areas but provided no housing for those who were displaced, and owners had abandoned unprofitable buildings in poor neighborhoods or converted them into expensive condominiums, a process called gentrification. In addition, after new medications allowed for the release of some mentally ill patients from institutions, many of them ended up on the streets because the promised mental-health services failed to materialize. Drug and alcohol abuse were rampant among the homeless, mostly unemployed single adults. A quarter of them had spent time in mental institutions; some 40 percent had spent time in jail; a third were delusional.

Act Up! Members of the influential AIDS activist group Act Up! protest a New Orleans convention center where President Reagan was scheduled to speak in 1988. The protester in the front holds a sign which reads "He Kills Me."

THE AIDS EPIDEMIC Still another group of outcasts included those suffering from a newly identified disease called AIDS (acquired immunodeficiency syndrome). At the beginning of the eighties, public health officials had reported that gay men and intravenous drug users were especially at risk for developing AIDS. People contracted the human immunodeficiency virus (HIV), which causes AIDS, by coming into contact with the blood or body fluids of an infected person. Those infected with the virus showed signs of extreme fatigue, developed a strange combination of infections, and soon died.

The Reagan administration showed little interest in AIDS in part because it was initially viewed as a "gay" disease.

Patrick Buchanan, who served as Reagan's director of communications, said that homosexuals had "declared war on nature, and now nature is extracting an awful retribution." Buchanan and others convinced Reagan not to engage the **HIV/AIDS** issue. By 2000, AIDS had claimed almost 300,000 American lives. Nearly 1 million Americans were carrying the deadly virus, and it had become the leading cause of death among men ages twenty-five to forty-four.

THE PRESIDENCY OF GEORGE H. W. BUSH

During 1988, Ronald Reagan's final year in office, his influence waned. His claim that "government is the problem, not the solution" was losing its appeal, and people were ready for a new approach to governing. Kevin Phillips, a Republican strategist, explained that during the 1986 congressional elections, voters chose candidates who promised to "make the government work" for the public good. Even conservatives had come to realize that "Hey, we need something from government after all."

Reagan's two-term vice president, George H. W. Bush, won the Republican presidential nomination in 1988 because he pledged to insist on ethical government, be a more "hands on" president than Reagan and promote "a more compassionate conservatism." The prominent Republican mayor of Indianapolis, Indiana, William Hudnut, observed that Republicans were moving away from "the laissez-faire approach of Ronald Reagan to one that takes a more active, more compassionate approach to those in need." It was time to move away from self-congratulation and deal more seriously with the thorny problems of inner-city poverty, homelessness, and drug abuse.

Born into a prominent New England family, the son of a U.S. senator, George H. W. Bush had, at the age of eighteen, enlisted in the U.S. Navy at the start of the Second World War,

George H. W. Bush His son, George W. Bush, would also serve as president, making them the second father-son presidential duo in history (the first was John Adams and John Quincy Adams).

becoming America's youngest combat pilot. After his distinguished military service, Bush graduated from Yale University and became a wealthy oil executive in Texas before entering government service. He served first as a member of the U.S. House of Representatives, then as U.S. ambassador to the United Nations, chair of the Republican National Committee, a diplomat in China, and director of the CIA before becoming Reagan's loyal vice president, patiently waiting his turn.

In all of those roles, Bush had displayed intelligence, integrity, and courage. But he lacked Reagan's charm and eloquence. One Democrat described Bush as a man born "with a silver foot in his mouth." A centrist Republican who had never embraced right-wing conservatism, Bush promised to use the White House to fight bigotry, illiteracy, and homelessness. "I want a kinder, gentler nation," Bush said in accepting the Republican nomination. But his most memorable line in his acceptance speech was a defiant statement ruling out any tax increases: "The Congress will push me to raise taxes, and I'll say no, and they'll push, and I'll say no, and they'll push again. And I'll say to them: Read my lips. No new taxes."

In the end, Bush won a decisive victory over the Democratic nominee, Massachusetts governor Michael Dukakis. Dukakis carried only ten states plus the District of Columbia. Bush won with a margin of about 54 percent to 46 percent in the popular vote and 426 to 111 in the electoral college, but the Democrats retained control of the House and Senate.

Bush sought to consolidate the initiatives that Reagan had put in place rather than launch his own array of programs and policies. "We don't need to remake society," he announced. As an example of his compassionate conservatism, Bush supported the Democratic-proposed Americans with Disabilities Act (1990), which strengthened the civil rights of the physically or mentally disabled in areas such as employment, public transportation, and housing. The act also required organizations (for-profit, non-profit, and governmental) to ensure that people with disabilities could access facilities by providing amenities such as mechanized doors, wheelchair ramps, and elevators.

THE FEDERAL DEBT AND RECESSION The biggest problem facing the Bush administration was the huge national debt, which stood at $2.6 trillion in 1989, nearly three times its 1980 level. Bush's pledge not to increase taxes (mainly meaning income taxes) made it more difficult to reduce the deficit or trim the debt. Likewise, Bush was not willing to make substantial cutbacks in spending on defense or social-welfare programs like Social Security, Medicare, and food stamps. As a result, by 1990 the country faced "a fiscal mess."

During the summer of 1990, Bush agreed with congressional Democrats that the size of the deficit required "tax revenue increases," which he had sworn

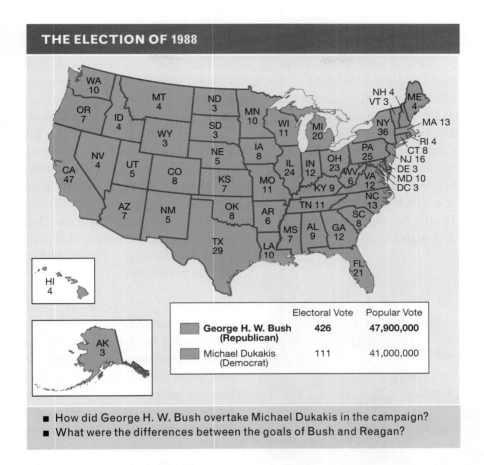

THE ELECTION OF 1988

	Electoral Vote	Popular Vote
George H. W. Bush (Republican)	426	47,900,000
Michael Dukakis (Democrat)	111	41,000,000

■ How did George H. W. Bush overtake Michael Dukakis in the campaign?
■ What were the differences between the goals of Bush and Reagan?

to avoid. His decision set off a revolt among conservative Republicans from which he never recovered. Increasing the top tax rate from 28 to 31 percent raised federal revenue but eroded Bush's political support, in part because the tax increases coincided with a prolonged economic recession. The economy barely grew at all during the first three years of the Bush administration—the worst record since the end of the Second World War.

THE DEMOCRACY MOVEMENT ABROAD George H. W. Bush entered the White House with more foreign-policy experience than most presidents, and, like Nixon before him, preferred to deal with international relations rather than the deficit, drug abuse, and the problems of the inner cities.

In the Soviet Union, amazing changes were under way. With his nation's economy failing, Mikhail Gorbachev accelerated the implementation of his policies designed to democratize Soviet life. And his foreign policy sought harmony and trade with the West, staking the Soviet Union's future on cooperation and trade with its cold war enemies.

Early in 1989, Soviet troops left Afghanistan after nine years. Gorbachev then renounced the right of the Soviet Union to intervene in the internal affairs of other Communist countries. His foreign minister, Eduard Shevardnadze, told the Soviet legislature that the nations of Eastern Europe had "absolute freedom" to choose their own form of governments. Soon thereafter, the Communist regimes in Eastern Europe fell with surprisingly little bloodshed, first in Poland and Hungary, then in Czechoslovakia and Bulgaria. In Romania, the year of peaceful revolution ended when the people joined the army in a bloody uprising against Nicolae Ceaușescu, the country's brutal dictator. He and his wife were captured and tried, then executed on Christmas Day. Although all of the new democratic governments faced immense economic and social challenges, Europe had at last been born anew.

A hammer to the Soviet Empire
A West German demonstrator pounds away at the Berlin Wall on November 11, 1989, while East German border guards look on. Two days later, all the crossings between East and West Germany were opened.

THE DESTRUCTION OF THE BERLIN WALL The most spectacular event in the collapse of the Soviet Empire came on November 9, 1989, when tens of thousands of East Germans gathered at the Berlin Wall and demanded that the border guards open the gates to West Berlin. Sensing the fierce determination of the crowds, the guards reluctantly did so, and soon Germans on both sides of the wall began tearing it down. Because the wall divided not only a city but a nation, its destruction symbolized a revolutionary change. What Germans called the "peaceful revolution" had occurred with dramatic suddenness. With the borders to West Germany now fully open, the Communist government of East Germany collapsed and Germans rushed to reunify their divided nation. On October 3, 1990, the five states of East Germany were united with West Germany.

The reform impulse that Gorbachev helped unleash in the Eastern-bloc countries sped out of control within the Soviet Union itself, however. Gorbachev had proven unusually adept at political restructuring and building a new presidential system that gave him, if anything, increased powers. His skills, however, could not salvage an antiquated economy that resisted change.

COMMUNIST COUP FAILS Gorbachev's popularity shrank in the Soviet Union as it grew abroad. Communist hard-liners saw in his reforms the unraveling of their bureaucratic and political empire. On August 18, 1991, a group of "old guard" political and military leaders accosted Gorbachev at his vacation retreat in Crimea and demanded that he proclaim a state of emergency and transfer his powers to them so that they could restore the supremacy of the Communist party. He replied, "Go to hell," whereupon he was placed under house arrest.

The coup, however, was poorly planned and clumsily implemented. The plotters failed to arrest popular leaders such as Boris Yeltsin, the feisty president of the Russian Republic. They also neglected to close the airports or cut off telephone and television communications, and they were opposed by key elements of the military and KGB (the Soviet secret police).

On August 20, President Bush responded favorably to Yeltsin's request for support and persuaded other leaders to join him in refusing to recognize the new Soviet government. The next day, word began to seep out that the plotters had given up and were fleeing. Several committed suicide, and a newly released Gorbachev ordered the others arrested. Although Gorbachev reclaimed the title of president, he was forced to resign as head of the Communist party and admit that he had made a grave mistake in appointing the men who had turned against him. Yeltsin emerged as the most popular political figure in the country.

What had begun as a reactionary coup turned into a powerful accelerant for astonishing changes in the Soviet Union, or the "Soviet Disunion," as one journalist termed it. Most of the fifteen republics proclaimed their independence from Russia, with the Baltic states of Latvia, Lithuania, and Estonia regaining the status of independent nations. The Communist party was dismantled, prompting celebrating crowds to topple statues of Lenin and other Communist heroes.

PANAMA The end of the cold war did not spell the end of international tensions, however. Since the collapse of the Soviet Union, the world has experienced numerous wars, violent turbulence, and fractious fundamentalisms of all sorts—religious, ethnic, and imperial. Before the close of 1989, U.S. troops were engaged in battle in Panama, where a petty tyrant provoked the first of America's military engagements under President Bush. In 1983, General Manuel Noriega had become the ruthless leader of the Panamanian Defense Forces, which made him head of the government in fact if not in title.

In 1988, federal grand juries in Florida indicted Noriega and fifteen others on charges of conspiring with Colombia's illegal drug lords to ship cocaine trough Panama to the United States. The next year, the Panamanian president tried to fire Noriega, but the National Assembly ousted the president instead and named Noriega "maximum leader." The legislators then declared Panama "in a state of war" with the United States. On December 16, 1989, a U.S. marine in Panama was killed. Bush thereupon ordered an invasion ("Operation Just Cause") to capture Noriega and install a government to be headed by Guill-ermo Endara, who had won the presidency in an election that was nullified by Noriega.

In the early morning of December 20, U.S. troops struck at strategic tar-gets. Noriega surrendered within hours. Twenty-three U.S. servicemen were killed; estimates of Panamanian casualties were as high as 4,000, including civilians. In April 1992, Noriega was convicted in the United States on eight counts of racketeering and drug distribution.

THE GULF WAR Months later, Saddam Hussein, dictator of Iraq, focused U.S. attention back upon the Middle East when his army suddenly invaded its tiny neighbor, Kuwait, on August 2, 1990. Kuwait had increased its production of oil, contrary to agreements with the Organization of the Petro-leum Exporting Countries (OPEC). The resulting drop in global oil prices offended the Iraqi regime, which was deeply in debt and heavily dependent upon oil revenues.

President Bush condemned Iraq's "naked aggression" and dispatched war-planes and troops to Saudi Arabia on a "wholly defensive" mission: to pro-tect Saudi Arabia. British forces soon joined in, as did Arab units from Egypt, Morocco, Syria, Oman, the United Arab Emirates, and Qatar. Iraq refused to yield, and on January 12, 1991, Congress authorized the use of U.S. armed forces. Four days later, more than thirty nations, including ten Islamic countries, launched **Operation Desert Storm**. During the next six weeks, Iraqi soldiers surrendered by the thousands, and on February 28, Bush called for a cease-fire. The Iraqis accepted. There were 137 American fatalities. The lowest estimate of Iraqi deaths, civilian and military, was 100,000. But although coalition forces occupied about a fifth of Iraq, Hussein's tyrannical regime remained intact.

What came to be called the First Gulf War was thus a triumph without vic-tory. Hussein had been defeated, but he was allowed to escape to foster greater

Operation Desert Storm Allied soldiers patrol the southern Iraqi town of Salman on February 27, 1991. On the side of a building is a propaganda mural of dictator Saddam Hussein in military uniform.

mischief. The consequences of the brief but intense war would be played out in the future, as Arabs humiliated by the American triumph began plotting revenge that would spiral into a new war of terrorism.

BUSH'S "NEW WORLD ORDER" For months after the First Gulf War, George Bush seemed unbeatable; his public approval rating soared to 91 percent. But the aftermath of Desert Storm was mixed, with Saddam Hussein's iron grip on Iraq still intact. The Soviet Union, meanwhile, stumbled to its surprising end. On December 25, 1991, the Soviet flag over the Kremlin was replaced by the flag of the Russian Federation. The cold war had ended with the dismemberment of the Soviet Union and its fifteen republics.

"Containment" of the communist Soviet Union, the bedrock of U.S. foreign policy for more than four decades, had suddenly become irrelevant. For all of its potential horrors, the cold war had brought stability; the two superpowers, the United States and the Soviet Union, had restrained themselves from an all-out war using nuclear weapons. Now the world would witness a growing number of unresolved crises and unstable regimes, some of which had access to weapons of mass destruction—nuclear as well as chemical and biological weapons.

Bush struggled to understand the fluid new international scene. He spoke of a "new world order" but never defined it, admitting he had trouble with "the vision thing." He faced a challenge in the Republican primary from Patrick Buchanan, the conservative commentator and former White House aide, who adopted the slogan "America First" and called on Bush to "bring home the boys."

The excitement over the victory in the Gulf War also gave way to anxiety over the depressed economy. In addressing the recession, Bush tried a clumsy balancing act, on the one hand acknowledging that "people are hurting" while on the other telling Americans that "this is a good time to buy a car." By 1991, the public approval rating of his economic policy had plummeted to 18 percent.

THE ELECTION OF 1992 At the 1992 Republican National Convention, Patrick Buchanan, who had won about a third of the votes in the party's primaries, blasted Bush for breaking his pledge not to raise taxes and for becoming the "biggest spender in American history." As the 1992 election unfolded, however, Bush's real problem proved to be his failed effort to improve the economy. A popular bumper sticker reflected the growing public frustration: "Saddam Hussein still has his job. What about you?"

In contrast, the Democrats at their convention presented an image of moderate forces in control. For several years, the Democratic Leadership Council, led by Arkansas governor William Jefferson Clinton, had been pushing the party from the liberal left to the center. The 1992 campaign also featured a third-party candidate, Texan H. Ross Perot, a puckish billionaire who found a large audience for his criticism of Reaganomics as "voodoo economics" (a phrase originally used by Bush in the 1980 Republican primary before he was named the vice-presidential candidate).

Born in 1946 in Hope, Arkansas, Bill Clinton never knew his biological father, a traveling salesman who died before his son was born. As a teen, Clinton yearned to be a political leader on a national scale. He attended Georgetown University in Washington, D.C., won a Rhodes Scholarship to Oxford University, and earned a law degree from Yale University, where he met his future wife, Hillary Rodham. Clinton returned to Arkansas and won election as the state's attorney general. By 1979, at age thirty-two, he was the youngest governor in the country. He served three more terms as Arkansas governor and emerged as a dynamic national leader of the **"New Democrats"** committed to winning back the middle-class whites ("Reagan Democrats") who had voted Republican during the 1980s.

In seeking the Democratic nomination, Clinton promised to cut the defense budget, provide tax relief for the middle class, and create a massive economic aid package to help the former republics of the Soviet Union forge democratic societies. Witty, intelligent, and charismatic, with an in-depth knowledge of public policy, Clinton projected energy, youth, and optimism, reminding many of John F. Kennedy, his boyhood hero.

But beneath Clinton's charisma and expertise were several flaws. The *New York Times* explained that Clinton was "emotionally needy, indecisive, and undisciplined." He had also earned a well-deserved reputation for half-truths, exaggerations, and talking out of both sides of his mouth. Clinton used opinion polls to shape his stances on issues, pandered to special-interest groups, and flip-flopped on controversial subjects, leading critics to label him "Slick Willie." Even more enticing

Bill Clinton and Al Gore The Democratic candidates celebrate the end of their presidential campaign in Clinton's hometown of Little Rock, Arkansas, on November 3, 1992.

to the media were charges that Clinton was a chronic adulterer and that he had manipulated the Reserve Officers' Training Corps (ROTC) program during the Vietnam War to avoid military service. Clinton's evasive denials could not dispel a lingering mistrust of his character.

After a series of bruising primaries, Clinton won the Democratic presidential nomination and promised to restore the "hopes of the forgotten middle class." He chose Senator Albert "Al" Gore Jr. of Tennessee as his running mate. Gore described himself as a "raging moderate." Flushed with their convention victory and sporting a ten-point lead over Bush in the polls, the Clinton-Gore team hammered the president on economic issues. Clinton pledged that, if elected, he would cut the federal budget deficit in half in four years while reducing taxes on middle-class Americans.

Such promises helped Clinton win with 370 electoral votes and about 43 percent of the vote. Bush received 168 electoral votes and 39 percent of the vote. Perot garnered 19 percent of the popular vote, more than any third-party candidate since Theodore Roosevelt in 1912. As 1992 came to an end, Bill Clinton, the "New Democrat," prepared to lead the United States through the last decade of the twentieth century. "The urgent question of our time," he said, "is whether we can make change our friend and not our enemy." Clinton would embrace unexpected changes while ushering America into the twenty-first century.

CHAPTER REVIEW

SUMMARY

- **The Carter Presidency** While Jimmy Carter had some notable achievements, such as the *Camp David Accords*, his administration suffered from legislative inexperience, a deepening economic recession, soaring inflation, and the *Iranian hostage crisis*. His sermonizing about the need for Americans to lead simpler lives compounded the public's loss of faith in his presidency.

- **The Rise of Conservatism** Ronald Reagan's charm, coupled with disillusionment over Carter's presidency, won Reagan the election in 1980. The Republican insurgency was dominated by Christian conservatives like those who made up the *Moral Majority*. The migration of older Americans and others to conservative southern and western states increased the voting power of the so-called sunbelt, where voters were socially conservative and favored lower taxes and a smaller, less intrusive federal government.

- **Reaganomics** Reagan introduced a "supply-side" economic philosophy, commonly called *Reaganomics*, that championed tax cuts for the rich, reductions in government regulations, cuts to social-welfare programs, and increased defense spending. Reagan was unable to cut domestic spending, however, and the tax cuts failed to pay for themselves as promised. The result was a dramatic increase in the national debt.

- **The End of the Cold War** Reagan's military buildup, including preliminary development of a space-based antiballistic-missile system called the *Strategic Defense Initiative (SDI)*, helped force the Soviets to the negotiating table to conclude the *Intermediate-Range Nuclear Forces (INF) Treaty*—the beginning of the end of the cold war. But Reagan's foreign-policy efforts were badly tarnished by the *Iran-Contra affair*, in which members of his administration sold American-made armaments to Iran in exchange for Iranian influence to secure the release of American hostages held in Lebanon (despite the president's public claims that he would never deal with terrorists).

- **America in the 1980s** Americans in the eighties not only experienced unprecedented prosperity but also rising poverty and homelessness. Conservatives condemned (and dismissed) *HIV/AIDS* as a "gay" disease. The development of the *microprocessor* paved the way for the computer revolution, which dramatically increased productivity and communications while generating whole new industries. Consumerism flourished all too well during the eighties, the result of which was massive public and private debt.

- **A New World Order** Toward the end of the 1980s, democratic political movements emerged in Eastern Europe. In the Soviet Union, Mikhail Gorbachev's steps to restructure the economy (*perestroika*) and promote more open policies (*glasnost*) led to further reform and the collapse of the Soviet Empire. But new trouble spots quickly emerged. Iraq, led by Saddam Hussein, invaded neighboring Kuwait in 1990. When Iraq did not withdraw, American-led allied forces launched *Operation Desert Storm*, and the Iraqis surrendered within six weeks.

CHRONOLOGY

1978	President Carter helps negotiate the Camp David Accords
	Tax revolt in California leads to the passage of Proposition 13
November 1979	Islamist militants storm the U.S. embassy in Tehran and take fifty-two Americans hostage
1980	Ronald Reagan elected president
1981	President Reagan enacts major tax cuts
1983	President Reagan authorizes development of the Strategic Defense Initiative (SDI)
1987	Reagan delivers his famous Berlin Wall speech
1988	George H. W. Bush is elected president
November 1989	Berlin Wall is torn down
December 1989	U.S. troops invade Panama and capture Manuel Noriega
1991	Iraq forced from Kuwait in the First Gulf War
	Breakup of the USSR
1992	Bill Clinton is elected president

KEY TERMS

Camp David Accords p. 1419

Iranian hostage crisis p. 1421

Moral Majority p. 1426

Reaganomics p. 1430

Strategic Defense Initiative (SDI) p. 1435

Iran-Contra affair p. 1439

perestroika p. 1441

glasnost p. 1441

Intermediate-Range Nuclear Forces (INF) Treaty (1987) p. 1442

microprocessor p. 1443

HIV/AIDS p. 1447

Operation Desert Storm (1991) p. 1452

"New Democrats" p. 1454

 INQUIZITIVE

Go to InQuizitive to see what you've learned—and learn what you've missed—with personalized feedback along the way.

32

Twenty-First-Century America
1993–Present

Youth speaks The Occupy Wall Street movement was born when thousands of protesters, many of them unemployed young adults, "occupied" Wall Street, the famous financial district in downtown Manhattan, to protest the "tyrannical" power of corporate America. The grassroots movement soon spread across the nation, then the world. Here, members of the movement stage a protest outside the New York Stock Exchange in September 2011.

T he United States entered the final decade of the twentieth century triumphant. American persistence in fighting and financing the cold war had contributed to the collapse of the Soviet Union and the birth of democracy and capitalism in Eastern Europe. By the end of the century, the United States was the world's only superpower.

Yet no sooner did the century come to an end than America's sense of physical security and material comfort was shattered by terrorist attacks in 2001 on New York City and Washington, D.C. The attacks killed thousands, plunged the economy into recession, and raised profound questions about national security.

In leading the fight against global terrorism, the United States became embroiled in long, costly, and controversial wars in Iraq and Afghanistan. Opposition to the wars would provide much of the momentum for Democrat Barack Obama to win election in 2008 as the nation's first African American president. Obama entered the White House at the same time that the United States and Europe were experiencing the Great Recession, a prolonged economic downturn that threatened the global banking system, caused widespread unemployment, and ignited social unrest and political tensions at home and abroad.

focus questions

1. What were the major population trends (demographics) in the United States during the twenty-first century? How did they impact the nation's politics?

2. What were the accomplishments and the setbacks of Bill Clinton's presidency?

3. What was the impact of global terrorism on the United States during the presidency of George W. Bush? How effective was his "war on terror?"

4. What were the issues and developments during Bush's second term that helped lead to Barack Obama's historic victory in the 2008 presidential election?

5. What were President Obama's priorities at home and abroad? How effective were his efforts to pursue them?

AMERICA'S CHANGING POPULATION

As the twenty-first century dawned, the United States began experiencing dramatic social changes. In 2015 the country's population surpassed 322 million, more than 80 percent of whom lived in cities or suburbs. Even more important, the nation's racial and ethnic composition was changing rapidly. In 1980, the population was 80 percent white. By 2015, that percentage had fallen below 63 percent.

In 2005, Hispanics became the nation's largest minority group. In 1980, Hispanics were 6 percent; in 2015, that number had tripled to 18 percent and was growing rapidly. More than 56 million Americans were Hispanic in origin, and a third of them were under the age of eighteen.

African Americans were at 13 percent, Asians about 8 percent, and Native Americans 1 percent. The rate of increase among those four groups was twice what it had been during the 1980s. Yet the fastest-growing group in the nation were the nearly 10 million who described themselves as "multiracial," representing more than 3 percent of the entire population.

The primary cause of this dramatic change in the nation's ethnic mix was a surge of immigration. In 2015, the United States had more foreign-born residents than ever before—more than 45 million, 11 million of whom were undocumented immigrants (formerly classified as "illegal aliens"). In the first decade of the twenty-first century, the United States became home to more than twice as many immigrants as *all* other countries combined. For the first time, the majority of immigrants came not from Europe but from other parts of the world: Asia, Latin America, and Africa. Mexicans made up the largest share of Hispanics, followed by Puerto Ricans and Cubans. Asian Americans increased their numbers at a faster rate than any other ethnic group, largely because of a surge in Chinese immigrants.

The nation's changing ethnic composition has had an increasingly significant impact on social life. In 1980, Hispanic Americans lived mainly in five states: California, Arizona, New Mexico, Texas, and Florida. By 2014, *every* state had a rapidly growing Hispanic population. Demographers projected that by 2044, whites would become a minority in the United States.

Immigration also is having potent political effects, as almost 1 million Hispanics reach voting age each year. Hispanics are usually Catholic and tend to vote Democratic. In 1980, there were six Hispanic Americans serving in the U.S. Congress. By 2010, there were more than five times as many. In 1992, Hispanics constituted only 2 percent of American voters; by 2014, they were 10 percent.

Over the quota, under the radar Large numbers of Chinese risked their lives to gain entry to the United States during the late twentieth century. A freighter carrying undocumented immigrants ran aground near Rockaway Beach, New York, in June 1993, forcing its undocumented passengers to swim ashore.

Only 23 percent of baby boomers born during and after the Second World War consider the surge in American diversity a "change for the better." They worry that Hispanics will always be a race apart from mainstream American culture, a permanent underclass of people tied closely to their ancestral homelands. Yet such concerns are countered by growing evidence that Hispanics are integrating themselves into American society and embracing its ideals. High school graduation and college enrollment rates among Hispanics are rising, teen pregnancy is falling, and more and more are learning English. In recent years, more than a quarter of Hispanic marriages have involved a non-Hispanic partner. Far from being a disaster, the growing Hispanic population is providing the nation with a surge of youthful energy and vitality—and demonstrating such traditional American attributes as self-reliance, rugged individualism, thrift, close family ties, strong religious beliefs, disproportionate participation in the military, and an ethic of hard work.

THE CLINTON PRESIDENCY

Bill Clinton arrived at the White House in 1993 with an almost legendary combination of strengths and weaknesses. At forty-six years old, he was the third youngest president in history, only slightly older than John Kennedy and Theodore Roosevelt. Like Ronald Reagan, Clinton charmed people, and his speeches inspired them. He was shrewdly smart, full of energy, resilient, persistent, and a self-described "policy wonk" who loved debating the fine points of new legislative ideas. Clinton resembled Jimmy Carter in his determination to be a "centrist" Democrat who reached out to working- and middle-class voters who no longer trusted liberals "to take their tax money and spend it with discipline."

Yet while graced with charm and a common touch with voters, as well as a commitment to fulfilling his campaign pledges, Clinton was also prone to self-absorption, self-deception, and self-inflicted wounds. A sucker for flattery with a compulsion to please and to be loved, he often seemed to decide his stances on issues by finding out what others believed, by studying the results of focus group interviews and public opinion surveys. A creature of both inspired leadership abilities and unruly passions, he at times seemed less a president than a flawed good ol' boy capable of self-righteous sleaziness and shameless misbehavior (he would dismiss his impeachment as "just a political deal"). In sum, Clinton was a bundle of warring impulses whose faults often confounded his talents. Yet he displayed legendary energy and "slick" resilience. (His nickname was the "Comeback Kid.") He thrived amid storms. One of his advisers predicted that Clinton would make every mistake possible, "but he will only make it once."

Like Jimmy Carter, Clinton's career as a governor did not prepare him well for some of his presidential duties. His inexperience in international affairs and congressional maneuvering led to several missteps in his first year as president. Like George H. W. Bush before him, he reneged on several campaign promises. In a bruising battle with Congress, he was forced to abandon his proposed middle-class tax cut to keep another campaign promise to reduce the federal deficit. Then he dropped his promise to allow gays to serve openly in the armed forces after military commanders expressed strong opposition. He later announced an ambiguous policy that came to be known as "don't ask, don't tell" (DADT), which allowed gays, lesbians, and bisexuals to serve in the military but only if they kept their sexual orientation secret.

"I got the worst of both worlds," Clinton later confessed. "I lost the fight, and the gay community was highly critical of me for the compromise." In his first two weeks in office, his approval rating dropped 20 percent. Throughout his presidency, however, he displayed a remarkable ability to manage crises and rebound from adversity.

THE ECONOMY As a candidate, Bill Clinton had pledged to reduce the federal deficit without damaging the economy or hurting the nation's most vulnerable people. To this end, he proposed $241 billion in higher taxes for corporations and for the wealthiest individuals (the top income tax rate rising from 33 to 39.6 percent) over four years, and $255 billion in spending cuts over the same period. The hotly contested bill passed the Democratic-controlled Congress by the slimmest of margins: 218 to 216 in the House and 51 to 50 in the Senate, with Vice President Al Gore providing the tie-breaking vote. In the end, the deficit-reduction effort worked as planned. It led to lower interest rates, which, along with low energy prices, helped spur dramatic economic growth.

NAFTA protesters Protesters going to a rally against NAFTA, the controversial free trade agreement for North America.

Equally difficult was gaining congressional approval of the **North American Free Trade Agreement (NAFTA)**, which the Bush administration had negotiated with Canada and Mexico. Clinton urged approval of NAFTA, which would make North America the largest free-trade zone in the world. Opponents favored tariffs to discourage the importation of cheaper foreign products, especially from Mexico. Yet Clinton prevailed with solid Republican support while losing a sizable minority of Democrats, mostly labor unionists and southerners, who feared that textile mills would lose business (and millions of jobs) to "cheap labor" countries—as they did.

HEALTH CARE REFORM Clinton's primary public-policy initiative was an ambitious plan to overhaul the nation's health care system. "If I don't get health care," he declared, "I'll wish I didn't run for president." Public support for government-administered health insurance had spread as annual medical costs skyrocketed and some 37 million Americans, most of them poor or unemployed, went without it.

The Clinton administration argued that providing medical insurance to everyone, regardless of income, would reduce the costs of health care to the nation as a whole, but critics questioned the savings as well as the ability of the federal government to manage such a huge program. The grand plan, known as the Health Security Act, called for large corporations to pay for most of the medical insurance expenses of their employees and required small businesses to form "health alliances" so that they, too, could provide subsidized health insurance to their workers.

By the summer of 1994, Clinton's 1,364-page health insurance plan, developed by a task force headed by the First Lady, Hillary Rodham Clinton, was doomed, in part because the president opposed any changes and in part because the report was impossibly complicated. Strenuously opposed by Republicans and health care interest groups, especially the pharmaceutical and insurance industries, Clinton's prized bill was voted down by Congress in August 1994.

LANDSLIDE REPUBLICAN VICTORY The health care bill disaster influenced the 1994 midterm elections. In the most stunning congressional victory of the twentieth century, the Republicans captured both houses of Congress and won 32 governorships, including the largest states of California, New York, and Texas, where George W. Bush, the son of the former president and a future president himself, won handily.

The Republican victory was led by a combative Georgia conservative named Newton ("Newt") Leroy Gingrich. In early 1995, he became the first Republican Speaker of the House in forty-two years. Gingrich, a former history professor with a lust for controversy and an unruly ego, was a superb tactician who had helped mobilize religious and social conservatives associated with the Christian Coalition.

The Christian Coalition, organized by television evangelist Pat Robertson in 1989 to replace Jerry Falwell's Moral Majority (which had disbanded that year), was pro–school prayer, anti-abortion, anti-feminist, and anti–gay rights. In addition to celebrating "traditional family values," it urged politicians to "radically downsize" government. Ralph Reed, a born-again Christian political activist who would head the Christian Coalition, declared that Christians needed "to take back this country." In many respects, the religious Right took control of the political and social landscape in the nineties.

In 1994, Gingrich and his fellow Republicans rallied conservative voters by promising a **Contract with America**, a pledge to dismantle the "corrupt liberal welfare state" created by Democrats. The ten-point, anti-big-government "contract" promised a smaller federal government by reducing the regulation of businesses, environmental protections, requiring term limits for members of Congress, slashing social-welfare programs, and passing a constitutional amendment requiring a balanced annual federal budget. As Texan Tom DeLay, a leading House Republican, explained, "You've got to understand, we are ideologues. We have an agenda. We have a philosophy." Yet the much-trumpeted Contract with America quickly fizzled. The conservatives pushed too hard and too fast, realizing too late that their slim majority in Congress could not launch a revolution. They were able to pass only four minor elements of their "contract."

Gingrich's heavy-handed methods contributed to the disintegration of the Contract with America. Republican senator Bob Dole said Gingrich was "a one-man band who rarely

Newt Gingrich Joined by 160 of his fellow House Republicans, Gingrich promotes the Contract with America in April 1995.

took advice." He was too ambitious, too abrasive, too divisive. When Clinton refused to go along with Republican demands for a balanced-budget pledge, Gingrich twice shut down the federal government during the fall of 1995. The tactic backfired. By 1996, Republicans abandoned the Contract with America, in part because Gingrich had higher negative ratings in public surveys than the president.

THE SUPREME COURT AND RACE The conservative mood also revealed itself in Supreme Court rulings that undermined affirmative-action programs, which gave African American students special consideration in college admissions and financial aid awards. Between 1970 and 1977, African American enrollment in colleges and universities doubled, even as white students and their parents complained about "reverse discrimination."

In 1996, two major rulings affected affirmative action in college admissions. In *Hopwood v. Texas*, a federal court ruled that race could not be used as a consideration for admission. Later that year, California voters passed Proposition 209 (also known as the California Civil Rights Initiative or CCRI), which ruled out preferential treatment ("affirmative action") in government hiring, government contracting, and public schools based on race, sex, ethnicity, or national origin. Similar complaints were directed against affirmative-action programs that awarded government contracts to minority-owned businesses. In 1995, the Court in *Adarand Constructors v. Peña* declared that affirmative-action programs had to be "narrowly tailored" to serve a "compelling national interest." The implication of such vague language was clear: the Court had come to share the growing public suspicion of the value and legitimacy of programs designed to benefit a particular race, gender, or ethnic group.

LEGISLATIVE BREAKTHROUGH   After the surprising 1994 Republican takeover of Congress, Bill Clinton shrewdly resolved to save his presidency by reinforcing his claim that he was a "centrist." He co-opted much of the energy of the conservative movement by announcing that "the era of big government is over" and by reforming the federal system of welfare payments to the poor, created during the 1930s under the New Deal.

Late in the summer of 1996, the Republican Congress passed a comprehensive welfare-reform measure that Clinton signed after some revisions. The **Personal Responsibility and Work Opportunity Act of 1996 (PRWOA)** illustrated Clinton's efforts to move the Democratic party away from the liberalism it had promoted since the 1930s. PRWOA abolished the Aid to Families with Dependent Children (AFDC) program, which provided poor families with almost $8,000 a year, and replaced it with the Temporary Assistance for Needy Families program, which limited the duration of welfare payments to two years in an effort to encourage unemployed people to get self-supporting jobs.

Liberal Democrats bitterly criticized Clinton's "welfare reform" deal. Yet the new approach to supporting the poor was a statistical success. Both the number of welfare recipients and poverty rates declined during the late nineties, leading the editors of the left-leaning *New Republic* to report that the PRWOA had "worked much as its designers had hoped."

THE 1996 CAMPAIGN   The Republican takeover of Congress in 1994 gave the party hope that they could prevent President Clinton's reelection. After clinching the Republican presidential nomination in 1996, Senate majority leader Bob Dole resigned his seat to devote his attention to the campaign. Clinton, however, maintained a large lead in the polls. With an improving economy and no major foreign-policy crises, cultural and personal issues surged into prominence.

Concern about Dole's age (seventy-three) and his gruff public personality, as well as tensions between economic conservatives and social conservatives over volatile issues such as abortion and gun control, hampered Dole's efforts to generate widespread support, especially among independent voters. Clinton was able to frame the election as a stark choice between Dole's desire to build a bridge to the past and Clinton's promise to build a bridge to the future.

On November 5, 1996, Clinton won a second term with an electoral vote victory of 379 to 159 and 49 percent of the popular vote. Dole received 41 percent of the popular vote, and third-party candidate Ross Perot got 8 percent.

THE "NEW ECONOMY" Bill Clinton's presidency benefited from a prolonged period of unprecedented economic prosperity. During his last three years in office (1998–2000), the federal government generated unheard-of budget *surpluses*. What came to be called the "new economy" featured high-flying electronics, computer, software, telecommunications (cellular phones, cable TV, etc.), and e-commerce Internet firms called "dot-com" companies.

These dynamic "tech" enterprises helped the economy set records in every area: low inflation, low unemployment, corporate profits, and personal fortunes. The stock-market value of U.S. companies nearly tripled, and people began to claim that the new economy defied the boom-and-bust cycles of the previous hundred years. Alan Greenspan, the Federal Reserve Board chairman, suggested that "we have moved beyond history" into an economy that seemed only to grow. He would be proven wrong.

GLOBALIZATION Another major feature of the new economy was **globalization**. The end of the cold war and the disintegration of the Soviet Union opened many new opportunities for U.S. companies in international trade. In addition, new globe-spanning communication technologies and massive new container-carrying ships and cargo jets shortened time and distance, enabling United States–based multinational companies to conduct more business abroad.

Bill Clinton accelerated the process of globalization. "The global economy," he said, "is giving more of our own people, and billions around the world, the chance to work and live and raise their families with dignity." He especially welcomed the World Wide Web, which opened the Internet to everyone, and, by doing so, greatly accelerated U.S. dominance of the international economy.

By 2000, more than a third of the production of U.S. multinational companies was occurring abroad, compared with only 9 percent in 1980. In 1970, there were 7,000 American multinational companies; by 2000, the number had soared to 63,000. Many U.S. multinational companies pursued controversial "outsourcing" strategies by which they moved their production "offshore" to nations such as Mexico and China to take advantage of lower labor costs and fewer workplace and environmental regulations. At the same time, many European and Asian companies, especially automobile manufacturers, built large plants in the United States to reduce the shipping expenses required to get their products to American markets. The U.S. economy had become internationalized to such an extent that global concerns exercised an ever-increasing influence on domestic and foreign policies.

FOREIGN POLICY IN THE NINETIES

Unlike George H. W. Bush, Bill Clinton had little interest in global politics. Untrained and inexperienced in international relations, he had to focus on creating opportunities around the world for U.S. business expansion. Yet, as international analyst Leslie Gelb cautioned the new president, "A foreign economic policy is not a foreign policy, and it is not a national security strategy." Events soon forced Clinton to intervene to help nations in crisis.

HAITI In 1990, the politically unstable Caribbean island nation of Haiti, the hemisphere's poorest country, had installed its first democratically elected president, a popular Catholic priest named Jean-Bertrand Aristide. When Haitian army officers ousted Aristide the following year, he and thousands of his supporters took up exile in America, most of them settling in south Florida, which upset many Floridians.

In 1994 President Clinton announced his intention to restore Aristide to power, in part to return the exiled "boat people" to their homeland. With drawn-out negotiations leading nowhere, Clinton asked in July for a UN resolution authorizing military intervention in Haiti. At that juncture, former president Jimmy Carter volunteered to help negotiate a last-minute settlement, and he convinced the military leaders to relinquish their control of the government and leave the nation. Clinton sent 20,000 U.S. troops to ensure a peaceful transfer of power. Aristide returned to Haiti on October 15, and on March 31, 1995, the U.S. peacekeeping troops left as a UN force commanded by an American general took over. But neither Aristide nor his successors were able to generate prosperity or stability.

THE MIDDLE EAST President Clinton continued George H. W. Bush's policy of orchestrating patient negotiations between the Arabs and the Israelis. A new development was the inclusion of the Palestinian Liberation Organization (PLO). In 1993, secret talks between Israeli and Palestinian representatives resulted in a draft agreement between Israel and the PLO that provided for the restoration of Palestinian self-rule in the occupied Gaza Strip and in Jericho, on the West Bank, in a "land for peace" exchange as outlined in United Nations Security Council resolutions. A formal signing occurred at the White House on September 13, 1993. With Clinton presiding, Israeli prime minister Yitzhak Rabin and PLO leader Yasir Arafat exchanged handshakes, and their foreign ministers signed the agreement.

The Middle East peace process suffered a terrible blow in early November 1995, however, when Rabin was assassinated by an Israeli zealot who

Clinton and the Middle East President Clinton presides as Israeli prime minister Yitzhak Rabin (left) and PLO leader Yasir Arafat (right) agree to a pathbreaking peace accord between Israel and the Palestinians, September 1993.

resented the efforts to negotiate with the Palestinians. Some observers feared that the assassin had killed the peace process as well when, seven months later, conservative hard-liner Benjamin Netanyahu narrowly defeated the United States–backed Shimon Peres in the Israeli national elections. Yet in October 1998, Clinton brought Arafat, Netanyahu, and King Hussein of Jordan together at a conference in Maryland, where they reached an agreement. Under the Wye River Accords, Israel agreed to surrender land in return for security guarantees by the Palestinians.

THE BALKANS Clinton also felt compelled to address turmoil in the Eastern European nations now free from Soviet domination. In 1991, Yugoslavia had disintegrated into ethnic warfare as four of its six multiethnic republics declared their independence. Serb minorities, backed by the new Republic of Serbia, stirred up civil wars in neighboring Croatia and Bosnia. In Bosnia, the conflict involved systematic efforts to eliminate Muslims. Clinton decided that the situation was "intolerable" because the massacres of tens of thousands of people "tore at the very fabric" of human decency. He ordered food and medical supplies sent to besieged Bosnian Muslims and dispatched warplanes to stop the massacres.

In 1995, U.S. negotiators finally persuaded the foreign ministers of Croatia, Bosnia, and Yugoslavia (by then a loose federation of the republics of Serbia and Montenegro) to agree to a comprehensive peace plan. Bosnia would remain

McRubble Pro-Milošević residents of Belgrade, Yugoslavia, destroy the storefront of a McDonald's restaurant in 1999 to protest NATO and the United States' airstrikes on their homeland.

a single nation but would be divided into two states: a Muslim-Croat federation controlling 51 percent of the territory, and a Bosnian-Serb republic controlling the rest. Basic human rights would be restored, and free elections would be held. To enforce the agreement, 60,000 NATO peacekeeping troops were dispatched to Bosnia.

In 1998, the Balkan tinderbox flared up again, this time in the Yugoslav province of Kosovo, which had long been considered sacred ground by Christian Serbs, although 90 percent of the 2 million Kosovars were in fact Albanian Muslims. In 1998, Yugoslav president Slobodan Milošević began a program of "**ethnic cleansing**" whereby Yugoslav forces burned Albanian villages, murdered men, raped women, and displaced hundreds of thousands of Muslim Kosovars.

On March 24, 1999, NATO, relying heavily upon U.S. military resources and leadership, launched air strikes against Yugoslavian military targets. After seventy-two days of bombardment, Milošević sued for peace on NATO's terms, in part because his Russian allies had finally abandoned him. An agreement was reached on June 3, 1999, and Clinton pledged extensive U.S. aid to help the Yugoslavs rebuild.

THE SCANDAL MACHINE

For a time, Clinton's preoccupation with foreign crises helped deflect attention from a growing number of investigations into his personal conduct. During his first term, he was dogged by old charges about investments he and his wife had made in Whitewater, a planned resort development in Arkansas. The project turned out to be a fraud and a failure, and the Clintons were accused of conspiring with the developer, although they lost $40,000 in the enterprise. In 1994, Kenneth Starr, a sanctimonious former judge and a conservative Republican, was appointed to investigate the Whitewater case.

Starr did not uncover any evidence that the Clintons were directly involved in the Whitewater fraud, but in the course of another investigation he happened upon evidence of a White House sex scandal. For years, rumors had circulated about the president's dalliances with women. James Carville, Clinton's political consultant, once asked Clinton about his sexual risk-taking. "Well," Clinton replied, "they haven't caught me." He spoke too soon.

MONICAGATE Between 1995 and 1997, Clinton had engaged in a sexual affair with a twenty-two-year-old White House intern, Monica Lewinsky. More disturbing, he had pressed her to lie about their relationship, even under oath. The news devastated the First Family and staggered the White House staff. Clinton's press secretary, Dee Dee Myers, could not believe that her boss would risk his presidency "for something so frivolous, so reckless, so small." Clinton initially denied the charges, telling the nation in late January 1998 that "I did not have sexual relations with that woman, Miss Lewinsky." Yet the scandal would not disappear.

For the next thirteen months, the media circus surrounding the "Monicagate" or "Zippergate" affair captured public attention. (After the Watergate affair in 1973–1974, journalists have loved to attach the suffix "-gate" to scandals.) Other women stepped forward to claim that Clinton had engaged in improper relations with them over the years, charges that the president denied.

The First Lady, Hillary Clinton, grimly stood by her husband amid his self-inflicted agony, declaring that the sexual rumors were the result of a "vast right-wing conspiracy" to bring him down. With the economy booming, Clinton's public approval ratings actually rose during 1998. In August, however, the scandal revived when Lewinsky agreed to provide a federal grand jury with a detailed account of her relationship with the president.

Soon thereafter, Clinton became the first president to testify before a grand jury. On August 17, the self-pitying, defiant president admitted having had "inappropriate, intimate physical contact" with Lewinsky that was "wrong." He also acknowledged that he had "misled" the American people. In his eagerness to keep himself in office, however, he insisted that he had done nothing *illegal*. Public reaction was mixed. A majority expressed sympathy for the president because of his public humiliation and because the Lewinsky affair was a private act of consensual sex. Others, however, were eager to see the president resign—or be impeached. Triumphant Republicans were convinced they could impeach the president.

THE IMPEACHMENT OF CLINTON On September 9, 1998, Kenneth Starr, the special prosecutor, submitted to Congress thirty-six boxes of documents that included a disturbingly graphic account of the president's White House encounters with Lewinsky. The report claimed that there was "substantial and creditable" evidence of presidential wrongdoing (perjury, obstructing justice, and abusing his presidential powers). The Starr report prompted the Republican-dominated House of Representatives on October 8 to begin a wide-ranging impeachment inquiry and led Bill Clinton to claim that he was the victim of a rogue prosecutor run amok. Starr "is evil," the president charged. "When this thing is over, there's only going to be one of us left standing. And it's going to be me."

On December 19, 1998, William Jefferson Clinton was impeached (charged with "high crimes and misdemeanors") by the House of Representatives. The House officially approved two articles of impeachment, charging Clinton with lying under oath to a federal grand jury and obstructing justice. He was the first elected president to be impeached. (Andrew Johnson was not elected; he became president upon the assassination of Abraham Lincoln.)

House Speaker Newt Gingrich, who been had censured (officially condemned) by his Republican colleagues in 1997 for several "serious violations" of House rules, led the effort to impeach the president, even though he himself was, at the time, secretly engaged in a six-year-long affair with a congressional staff member. (Gingrich resigned as speaker in November 1998 and left both the House and his wife, escaping with his new wife from politics altogether.) Journalists began calling Clinton's Senate trial the "soap opera" impeachment after Gingrich's successor as Speaker, Robert Livingston of Louisiana, suddenly resigned from Congress in late December after admitting that he, too, had engaged in adulterous affairs.

The impeachment trial began on January 7, 1999. Five weeks later, on February 12, a majority of senators, by a 55–45 vote, decided that Clinton's adultery and lies were not the "high crimes and misdemeanors" required to remove a president from office. The president was acquitted—much to the regret of many Republicans. The situation called to mind an old Texas saying: "We tried to hang him, but the rope broke." Arthur Schlesinger Jr., the distinguished scholar of the presidency, called the Clinton-Lewinsky affair "the weirdest episode in our political history." Though the impeachment effort failed, Clinton's final eighteen months in office were stained and distracted by the scandal and many Americans were exhausted by the partisan drama and disenchanted with politics and politicians. Clinton's last two years in office were anticlimactic.

ASSESSING THE CLINTON PRESIDENCY For all of his faults, Bill Clinton was the most compelling figure of his political generation. Both loved and hated, he presided over an unprecedented period of prosperity (115 consecutive months of economic growth and the lowest unemployment rate in 30 years), generated unheard-of federal budget surpluses, and passed a

Impeachment Representative Edward Pease, a member of the House Judiciary Committee, covers his face during the vote on the third of four articles of impeachment charging President Clinton with "high crimes and misdemeanors" in December 1998.

welfare-reform measure with support from both parties. In the process, he revitalized the Democratic party by moving it from the left to the "vital center" of the political spectrum. By 1998, it was the Democrats, not the Republicans, who were viewed as the party of fiscal responsibility. Clinton also helped bring peace and stability to the Balkans, one of the most violent regions of Europe.

At times, however, his boundless self-confidence led to arrogant reck-lessness. He debased the presidency with his sexual escapades, and his effort, undertaken with his wife, Hillary Rodham Clinton, to bring health insurance to the uninsured was a clumsy failure. Clinton was less a great statesman than a great escape artist. In 2000, his last year in office, he enjoyed a public approval rating of 65 percent, the highest end-of-term rating since President Dwight D. Eisenhower. Yet his popularity was not enough to ensure the election of his vice president, Al Gore, as his successor.

A Chaotic Start to a New Century

Wild celebrations around the world ushered in the year 2000, and Americans led the cheering. They greeted the new century with a sense of triumphalism. The Cold War was over, the United States was the world's only hyperpower, and the high-tech American economy dominated global trade. But the joyous mood did not last. Powerful and unstable new forces were emerging, the most dangerous of which were sophisticated global networks of menacing terrorists eager to disrupt and destroy American values and institutions.

A DISPUTED ELECTION

The presidential election of 2000 proved to be one of the closest and most controversial in history. The two major-party candidates, Vice President Albert Gore Jr., the Democrat, and Texas governor George W. Bush, son of the former Republican president, offered contrasting views on the role of the federal government, tax cuts, environmental policies, and the best way to preserve Social Security and Medicare.

Gore, a Tennessee native and Harvard graduate whose father had been a prominent senator, favored an active federal government that would do much

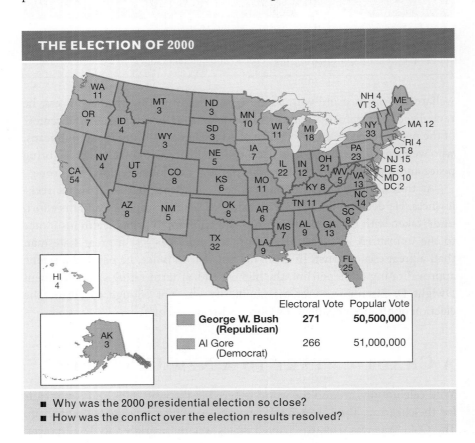

THE ELECTION OF 2000

	Electoral Vote	Popular Vote
George W. Bush (Republican)	271	50,500,000
Al Gore (Democrat)	266	51,000,000

■ Why was the 2000 presidential election so close?
■ How was the conflict over the election results resolved?

more to protect the environment. Bush campaigned on a theme of "compassionate conservatism," promised to restore "honor and dignity" to the White House, and proposed to transfer power from the federal government to the states. A "born-again" evangelical Christian with degrees from Yale University and Harvard Business School, Bush urged tax cuts and a more "humble" foreign policy that would end U.S. efforts to install democratic governments in undemocratic societies ("nation building").

The bitter tone of party politics (called *polarization*) continued to inspire candidates at the extremes to run as third-party candidates. Two independent candidates added zest to the 2000 presidential campaign: the colorful conservative commentator Patrick Buchanan, and the liberal consumer activist Ralph Nader, representing the Green party.

The November election created high drama. The television networks initially

The recount In yet another recount on November 24, 2000, Judge Robert Rosenberg examines a ballot with a magnifying glass. That Florida's voting machines were so unreliable introduced doubt about the legitimacy of the close results.

reported that Gore had narrowly won the state of Florida and its decisive twenty-five electoral votes. Later in the evening, however, they reversed themselves, saying that Florida was too close to call. In the chaotic early-morning hours, the networks declared that Bush had been elected president. The final tally showed Bush with a razor-thin lead, but Florida law required a recount. For the first time in 125 years, the results of a presidential election remained in doubt for weeks after the voting.

As a painstaking hand recount proceeded, supporters of Bush and Gore sparred in the courts. Each side accused the other of trying to steal the election. The political drama lasted for five weeks, until, on December 12, a bitterly divided U.S. Supreme Court decided, with a 5–4 majority ruling, that the recount was to be halted. Bush was declared the winner in Florida by 537 votes. Gore had amassed a 540,000-vote lead nationwide, but losing Florida meant he lost in the electoral college by two votes. Although Gore "strongly disagreed" with the

Supreme Court's decision, he asked voters to rally around President-elect Bush and move forward. "Partisan rancor," he urged, "must be put aside."

The ferocious sparring between the two national parties was not put aside, however, in part because Bush chose as key advisers men known for their brusqueness and strong ideological convictions. One of them, Richard "Dick" Cheney, a former Wyoming congressman and influential member of the Nixon, Ford, and Bush administrations, quickly became the most powerful vice president in history. Cheney, so secretive that he often appeared sinister, used his long experience with the government bureaucracy to fill the administration with like-minded associates who helped him control the flow of information to the president. He became a domineering influence on the inexperienced Bush.

A CHANGE OF DIRECTION

George W. Bush had promised to cut taxes for the wealthy, increase military spending, oppose strict environmental regulations, and "privatize" Social Security by investing workers' retirement pension funds in the stock market.

First, however, he had to deal with a sputtering economy. By March 2001, the economy was in recession for the first time in more than a decade. Bush decided that cutting taxes was the best way to boost economic growth. On June 7, 2001, he signed the Economic Growth and Tax Relief Act, which cut $1.35 trillion in taxes.

Instead of paying for themselves in renewed economic growth, however, the Bush tax cuts led to a sharp drop in federal revenue, producing in turn a fast-growing budget deficit as the Clinton surpluses were quickly used up. Huge increases in the costs of Medicare and Medicaid resulting from the aging of the baby boom generation contributed to the soaring deficits, as did military expenditures caused by an unexpected war.

Bush was also distracted by global crises. Islamic militants around the world bitterly resented what they viewed as the "imperial" globalization of U.S. culture and power. With increasing frequency, they used terrorism, including suicide bombings, to gain notoriety, exact vengeance, and generate fear and insecurity.

Throughout the nineties, the United States had fought a losing struggle against global terrorist groups, in part because terrorism thrives in nations with weak governments overwhelmed by rapid population growth, scarce resources, widespread poverty, and huge numbers of unemployed young men—symptoms many nations were suffering. The ineffectiveness of U.S. intelligence agencies in tracking the movements and intentions of militant extremists became tragically evident in the late summer of 2001.

9/11—A NEW DAY OF INFAMY At 8:45 A.M. on September 11, 2001, the continental United States was attacked for the first time since 1814 when a passenger airliner that had been hijacked by Islamist terrorists slammed into the north tower of the World Trade Center in New York City. Eighteen minutes later, a second hijacked jumbo jet crashed into the south tower. The twin towers, 110 stories tall and filled with 50,000 workers, burned fiercely, the infernos forcing hundreds of desperate people to jump to their deaths as thousands more on the floors below the points of impact struggled to evacuate. The steel structures quickly collapsed from the intense heat, destroying surrounding buildings and killing nearly 3,000 people, including more than 400 firefighters, police officers, and emergency responders. The southern end of Manhattan—"ground zero"—became a hellish scene of twisted steel, suffocating smoke, wailing sirens, and panicked people.

While the catastrophic drama in New York City was unfolding, a third hijacked plane crashed into the Pentagon in Washington, D.C. A fourth airliner,

September 11th Smoke pours out of the north tower of the World Trade Center as the south tower bursts into flames after being struck by a second hijacked airplane. Both iconic buildings would collapse within an hour.

probably headed for the White House, missed its mark when the passengers—who had heard reports of the earlier hijackings via their cell phones—assaulted the hijackers to prevent the plane from being used as a weapon. During the struggle, the plane went out of control and plummeted into the ground near Shanksville, Pennsylvania, killing all aboard.

Within hours of the hijackings, the nineteen dead terrorists were identified as members of al Qaeda (Arabic for "the Base"), a well-financed network of Islamic extremists led by a wealthy Saudi renegade, Osama bin Laden. Years before, bin Laden had declared *jihad* (holy war) on the United States, Israel, and the Saudi monarchy in his effort to create a single Islamist *caliphate* (global empire). He used remote bases in Sudan and war-torn Afghanistan as training centers for jihadist fighters. Collaborating with bin Laden's terrorist network was Afghanistan's ruling Taliban, a coalition of ultraconservative Islamists who provided bin Laden a safe haven.

THE "WAR ON TERROR"

The 9/11 assault on the United States, like the Japanese attack on Pearl Harbor on December 7, 1941, changed the course of modern life. People were initially paralyzed by grief, fear, and anger. The U.S. economy, already in decline, went into free fall. President Bush was thrust into the role of commander in chief of a nation eager for vengeance.

Bush said that he was going to launch a global **war on terror** "to answer these attacks and rid the world of evil." He warned other nations that "either you are with us or you are with the terrorists." A wave of patriotic fervor rolled across the nation. People formed long lines to donate blood, and many signed up for military service.

Bush demanded that Afghanistan's Taliban government surrender the al Qaeda terrorists or risk military attack. The Taliban refused, and on October 7, 2001, the United States and its allies launched Operation Enduring Freedom. After American and British cruise missiles and bombers destroyed Afghan military installations and al Qaeda training camps, ground troops from the United States and some of its NATO allies routed Taliban forces. On December 9, the Taliban regime collapsed. The war in Afghanistan then transitioned into a high-stakes manhunt for the elusive Osama bin Laden, who had escaped into the mountains of Pakistan.

FIGHTING TERROR AT HOME While the military campaign continued in Afghanistan, officials in Washington worried that terrorists might attack the United States with biological, chemical, or even nuclear weapons.

War fever President George W. Bush addresses members of the Special Forces in July 2002 as part of an appeal to Congress to increase defense spending after the September 11 terrorist attacks.

To address the threat and to help restore public confidence, President Bush, without Congressional approval, established the Office of Homeland Security and gave it sweeping authority to spy on Americans. Another new federal agency, the Transportation Security Administration, assumed responsibility for screening airline passengers for weapons and bombs.

At the same time, Bush and a supportive Congress created the **USA Patriot Act**, which gave government agencies the right to eavesdrop on confidential conversations between prison inmates and their lawyers and permitted suspected terrorists to be tried in secret military courts. Civil liberties groups voiced grave concerns that the measures jeopardized constitutional rights and protections, but most people supported these extraordinary steps.

What the public did not know was that Vice President Dick Cheney, Secretary of Defense Donald Rumsfeld, and other so-called neoconservatives ("neocons") in the departments of state and defense had convinced the president to authorize the use of torture ("enhanced interrogation techniques") in the CIA's and FBI's treatment of captured terrorist suspects. Such tactics violated international law and compromised the human rights ideals that had always been America's greatest strength. When asked about such activities, the shadowy Cheney scoffed that America sometimes had to work "the dark side": "We've got to spend time in the shadows in the intelligence world. . . ."

The Taliban A young woman shows her face in public for the first time in five years after Northern Alliance troops capture Kabul, the capital of Afghanistan, in November 2001. The strict sharia law enforced by the Taliban required that women be covered from head to foot.

THE BUSH DOCTRINE In the fall of 2002, President Bush unveiled a dramatic new national security policy. The **Bush Doctrine** said that the growing menace posed by "shadowy networks" of terrorist groups and unstable rogue nations with "**weapons of mass destruction**" (**WMDs**) required the United States at times to use preemptive military action. "If we wait for threats to fully materialize," or wait for allies to join America, he explained, "we will have waited too long. In the world we have entered, the only path to safety is the path of action. And this nation will *act*."

The dangerously sweeping Bush Doctrine promised to "extend the benefits of freedom across the globe . . . for all peoples everywhere," without reference to the potential human and financial cost of such an open-ended commitment.

THE SECOND IRAQ WAR During 2002 and 2003, Iraq emerged as the focus of the Bush administration's policy of "preemptive" military action. Three of the president's most influential advisers, all neocons, Vice President Cheney, Secretary of Defense Rumsfeld, and Deputy Defense Secretary Paul Wolfowitz, urged the president to use U.S. power to reshape the world in the American mold. This included sponsoring "regime change" in nations lacking "political and economic freedom" in order to create a new world order "friendly to our security, our prosperity, and our principles." They convinced Bush that the dictatorial regime of Saddam Hussein and his loyal Sunni faction of Muslims, who lorded over the nation's Shiite majority and the ethnic Kurds in the north, represented a "grave and gathering danger" because of its supposed possession of biological and chemical weapons of mass destruction. Some in Congress urged caution. Republican Senator Chuck Hagel of Nebraska, a Vietnam veteran, warned that "many of those who want to rush this country into war and think it would be so quick and easy don't know anything about war." The White House responded: "Trust us."

On March 17, 2003, Bush issued Hussein an ultimatum: he and his sons must leave Iraq within forty-eight hours or face a United States–led invasion. Hussein refused. Two days later, on March 19, American and British forces (the "coalition of the willing") attacked. France and Germany refused to participate in what they viewed as unnecessary American aggression. "Operation Iraqi Freedom," according to Bush and his advisers, would quickly topple Hussein with overwhelming military force and then usher in a new era of U.S.-style democracy in Iraq.

The Second Iraq War began with a massive bombing campaign, followed by a fast-moving invasion from bases in Kuwait. Some 250,000 American soldiers, sailors, and marines were joined by 50,000 British troops. On April 9, after three weeks of intense fighting amid sweltering heat and blinding sandstorms, U.S. forces captured Baghdad, the capital of Iraq. Saddam Hussein's regime and his inept, demoralized army collapsed a week later.

The six-week war came at a cost of fewer than 200 combat deaths among the 300,000 allied troops. More than 2,000 Iraqi soldiers were killed; civilian casualties numbered in the tens of thousands. President Bush staged a celebration on a U.S. aircraft carrier at which he announced victory under a massive banner proclaiming "MISSION ACCOMPLISHED." But he spoke too soon; the initial military triumph carried with it the seeds of deception and disaster, for no weapons of mass destruction were to be found in Iraq. Secretary of State Colin Powell later admitted that he had been misled about the issue. Bush said that the absence of WMDs in Iraq left him with a "sickening feeling," for he knew that his primary justification for the war had evaporated.

REBUILDING IRAQ It proved far easier to win the brief war than to rebuild Iraq in America's image. Unprepared U.S. officials faced the daunting task of installing a democratic government in a nation fractured by religious feuds and ethnic tensions made worse by the breakdown in law and order caused by the allied invasion. The successful invasion triggered a vicious civil war in Iraq and the disintegration of law and order. Looting and violence engulfed the war-torn country, large parts of which fell under the control of warlords and criminal gangs. In the process, the entire Middle East, already volatile, was further destabilized.

Within weeks, vengeful Islamic radicals streamed into the crippled nation to wage a merciless campaign of terror, sabotage, and suicide bombings against the U.S. forces. Bush's macho reaction to the insurgency—"Bring 'em on!"—revealed how uninformed he was about the fast-deteriorating situation. The leader of the new Iraqi government, Prime Minister Nouri al-Maliki, quickly imposed his own authoritarian, Shiite-dominated regime which discriminated against the Sunnis, the Kurds, and other ethnic and religious minorities.

Defense Secretary Rumsfeld greatly underestimated the difficulty and expense of occupying, pacifying, and reconstructing postwar Iraq. By the fall of 2003, Bush admitted that substantial numbers of American troops (around 150,000) would have to remain in Iraq much longer than anticipated. He also said that rebuilding Iraq would take years and cost almost a *trillion* dollars. Investigative reporter James Fallows concluded that the U.S. "occupation in Iraq is a debacle not because the government did no planning but because a vast amount of expert planning was willfully ignored by the people in charge."

Victory on the battlefields of Iraq did not bring victory in the "war on terrorism." Militant Islamist groups remained a global threat. Americans grew more and more dismayed as the number of casualties and the expense of the military occupation in Iraq soared. The nation became more alienated when journalists revealed graphic pictures of U.S. soldiers abusing and torturing Arab detainees in the Abu Ghraib prison near Baghdad. "When you lose the moral high ground," an army general sadly observed, "you lose it all."

President Bush urged Americans to "stay the course," insisting that a democratic Iraq would bring stability to the Middle East and thereby blunt the momentum of Islamic terrorism. Yet even though Saddam Hussein was captured in December 2003 and later hanged, Iraq seemed less secure than ever.

By the beginning of 2004, some 1,000 Americans had died in the conflict, and more than 10,000 had been wounded. The ethnic and religious tensions only worsened as violent Sunni jihadists allied with al Qaeda to undermine the new Iraqi government and assault U.S. forces.

The U.S. effort in Iraq was the wrong war in the wrong place fought in the wrong way. It forced Bush to spend government funds at a rate faster than any president since Lyndon Johnson, and it distracted attention from the revival of the Taliban and other terrorist groups in Afghanistan. "We thank God for appeasing us with the [U.S.] dilemmas in Iraq and Afghanistan," snickered bin Laden's deputy, Ayman al-Zawahiri. Journalist Roger Cohen distilled perhaps the most important lesson from the wars in Iraq and Afghanistan when

Freedom for whom? The American torture of Iraqis in Abu Ghraib prison only exacerbated the anger and humiliation that Iraqis experienced since the First Gulf War. In response to America's incessant promises of peace and autonomy, a Baghdad mural fires back: "That Freedom for B[u]sh."

he said that the American ideal of democracy "can still resonate" with people around the world, but U.S. leaders "must embody it rather than impose it."

THE ELECTION OF 2004 Growing public concern about Iraq complicated George W. Bush's campaign for a second presidential term in 2004. The Democratic nominee, Senator John Kerry of Massachusetts, condemned Bush for misleading the nation about weapons of mass destruction and for his slipshod handling of the reconstruction of postwar Iraq. Kerry also highlighted the Bush administration's record budget deficits. Bush countered that the tortuous efforts to create a democratic government in Iraq would enhance America's long-term security.

On Election Day, November 2, 2004, exit polls suggested a Kerry victory, but in the end the election hinged on the crucial swing state of Ohio. No Republican had ever lost Ohio and won the presidency. Despite early returns indicating a Kerry victory in Ohio, late returns tipped the balance toward Bush, even as rumors of electoral "irregularities" began to circulate.

THE ELECTION OF 2004

	Electoral Vote	Popular Vote
George W. Bush **(Republican)**	**286**	**60,700,000**
John Kerry (Democrat)	251	57,400,000

- How did the war in Iraq polarize American politics?
- In what ways did the election of 2004 give Republicans a mandate for change?

Nevertheless, Kerry conceded the election. "The outcome," he stressed, "should be decided by voters, not a protracted legal battle."

By narrowly winning Ohio, Bush captured 286 electoral votes to Kerry's 251. Yet in some respects, the election was not so close. Bush received 3.5 million more votes nationwide than Kerry, and Republicans increased their majorities in both houses of Congress. A reelected Bush pledged to bring democracy and stability to Iraq, trim the federal deficit, pass a major energy bill, create more jobs, and "privatize" Social Security funds by investing them in the stock market. "I earned capital in the campaign, political capital, and now I intend to spend it," he told reporters.

SECOND-TERM BLUES

George Bush's second term was beset by thorny political problems, a sluggish economy, and continuing turmoil in Iraq. In 2005, he pushed through Congress an energy bill and a Central American Free Trade Act. But his effort to privatize Social Security retirement accounts by enabling individuals to invest their accumulated pension dollars themselves went nowhere, and soaring budget deficits made many fiscal conservatives feel betrayed by the supposedly "conservative" Bush. The editors of the *Economist*, an influential conservative newsmagazine, declared that Bush had become "the least popular re-elected president since Richard Nixon."

HURRICANE KATRINA In 2005, President Bush's eroding public support suffered another blow. In late August, a killer hurricane named Katrina slammed into the Gulf coast, devastating large areas of Alabama, Mississippi, and Louisiana. Katrina left more than 1,000 dead and millions homeless and hopeless, especially in New Orleans. Local officials and the Federal Emergency Management Agency (FEMA) were caught unprepared as the catastrophe unfolded, and confusion and incompetence abounded. In the face of blistering criticism, Bush accepted responsibility for the balky federal response and accepted the resignation of the FEMA director. Rebuilding the Gulf coast would take a long time and a lot of money.

The backlash over the federal response to Katrina contributed to a devastating defeat for Republicans in the November 2006 congressional

The aftermath of Hurricane Katrina Two men use boards to paddle through high water in flood-devastated New Orleans.

Nancy Pelosi The first female Speaker of the House at a news conference on Capitol Hill.

elections. The Democrats capitalized on widespread public disapproval of the Bush administration to win control of the House of Representatives, the Senate, and a majority of governorships and state legislatures. Former Texas Republican congressman Dick Armey said that "the Republican Revolution of 1994 officially ended" with the 2006 election. The transformational election also included a significant milestone: Californian Nancy Pelosi, the leader of the Democrats in the House of Representatives, became the highest-ranking woman in the history of the U.S. Congress upon her election as House Speaker in January 2007.

THE "SURGE" IN IRAQ George W. Bush bore the brunt of public indignation over the bungled federal response to the Katrina disaster and the costs and casualties of the war in Iraq. Senator Chuck Hagel, a Nebraska Republican, declared in 2005 that "we're losing in Iraq." Throughout the fall of 2006, the violence in Iraq spiraled upward. Bush eventually responded to declining public and political support for the Iraq War by creating the Iraq Study Group, a bipartisan task force appointed by the president. It surprised the president by issuing a report recommending the withdrawal of combat forces from a "grave and deteriorating Iraq" by the spring of 2008.

Bush disagreed with those who urged a phased withdrawal. On January 10, 2007, he announced that he was sending a "surge" of 20,000 (eventually 30,000) more troops to Iraq, bringing the total to almost 170,000. From a military perspective, the "surge" succeeded. By the fall of 2008, violence in Iraq had declined dramatically, and the Iraqi government had grown in stature and confidence. The U.S. general who masterminded the increase in troops admitted that the gains were "fragile and reversible," however, and as the number of U.S. combat deaths in Iraq passed 4,000, Bush acknowledged that the conflict was "longer and harder and more costly than we anticipated." By 2008, more than 60 percent of Americans said that the war had been a mistake.

ECONOMIC SHOCK After the intense but brief 2001 recession, the boom/bust capitalist economy had begun another period of prolonged expansion. Between 1997 and 2006, home prices in the United States, especially in the fast-growing sunbelt states, rose 85 percent, leading to a frenzy of irresponsible mortgage lending—and a debt-financed consumer spending spree. Tens of millions of people bought houses they could not afford, refinanced their mortgages, or tapped home-equity loans to make discretionary purchases. The irrational confidence in soaring housing prices also led government regulatory agencies and mortgage lenders to ease credit restrictions so that unqualified people could buy homes without making any down payment.

The housing bubble burst in 2007, when home values and sales began a sharp decline. The loss of trillions of dollars in home values set off a seismic shock across the economy, as record numbers of borrowers defaulted on their mortgage payments. Foreclosures and bankruptcies soared, and banks lost billions, first on the shaky mortgages, then on most other categories of overleveraged debt: credit cards, car loans, student loans, and commercial mortgage-backed securities.

The sudden contraction of corporate spending and consumer purchases pushed the economy into a recession in 2008. Some of the nation's most prestigious banks, investment firms, and insurance companies went belly up. The price of food and gasoline spiked, and unemployment soared. What had begun as a sharp decline in home prices became a global economic meltdown.

The crisis demanded decisive action. On October 3, 2008, President Bush signed into law the Troubled Asset Relief Program (TARP), which called for the Treasury Department to spend $700 billion to keep big banks and other large financial institutions afloat. Yet the passage of the bill did little to restore confidence in the economy as a whole. In early October, stock markets around the world began to crash with the onset of what came to be called the **Great Recession**, which technically lasted from December 2007 to January 2009 and forced almost 9 million people out of work. Its effects would linger, however, and the economic recovery that began in June 2009 would be the weakest since the end of the Second World War.

The Great Recession had powerful political effects. Bush, who as governor of Texas had described himself as "a uniter, not a divider," became one of the least popular and most divisive presidents in American history. Just 29 percent of voters "approved" of his leadership, and more than 80 percent said that the nation was headed in the "wrong direction."

Kevin Phillips, a prominent Republican strategist, deemed Bush "perhaps the least competent president in modern history." Bush's failed presidency

Rio Vista, California With an $816,000 deficit, this northern California city filed for bankruptcy and pulled the plug on its massive, 750-home housing development in November 2008. Here, model homes stand eerily in a blank landscape of sidewalks and cul-de-sacs.

had weakened the Republican party, strained the nation's military, eroded American prestige, and created the largest budget deficits in history by cutting taxes while increasing spending. "I inherited a recession, and I'm ending on a recession," Bush admitted at one of his last press conferences.

A Historic New Presidency

George Bush's unpopularity excited Democrats about regaining the White House in 2008. The early front-runner for the nomination was New York senator Hillary Rodham Clinton, the spouse of ex-president Bill Clinton. Like her husband, she displayed an impressive command of policy issues and mobilized a well-funded campaign team. And, as the first woman with a serious chance of gaining the presidency, she had widespread support among voters eager for female leadership.

In the end, however, an overconfident Clinton was upset in the Democratic primaries and caucuses by Barack Obama of Illinois, a little-known first-term senator. Young, handsome, and intelligent, a vibrant mixture of idealism and pragmatism, coolness and passion, Obama was an inspiring speaker who attracted huge crowds by promising a "politics of hope." He mounted an innovative Internet-based campaign directed at grassroots voters, donors, and volunteers. In early June 2008, he gained enough delegates to secure the nomination, with Senator Joseph Biden of Delaware as his running mate.

The Clinton campaign Democratic presidential candidate Senator Hillary Rodham Clinton speaks at a rally in Fort Worth, Texas.

Obama was the first African American presidential nominee of either party, the gifted biracial son of a white mother from Kansas and a black father from Kenya who left the household and returned to Africa when Barack was a toddler. Obama eventually graduated from Columbia University before earning a law degree from Harvard. The forty-seven-year-old senator presented himself as a deal maker who could inspire, unite, and forge bipartisan collaborations.

Candidate Obama radiated poise, confidence, and energy. He told an aide that he didn't "need to be president. It turns out that being Barack Obama is a pretty good gig in and of itself." He and his strategists were able to turn his vitality and political inexperience into strengths at a time when voter disgust with politics was widespread. By contrast, his Republican opponent, seventy-two-year-old Arizona senator John McCain, was the oldest presidential candidate in history. As a twenty-five-year veteran of Congress and a leading senator, McCain had developed a reputation as a bipartisan "maverick" willing to work with Democrats to achieve key legislative goals.

Barack Obama The president-elect and his family wave to supporters in Chicago's Grant Park.

On November 4, 2008, Barack Obama made history by becoming the first person of color to be elected president. He won the popular vote by 53 percent to 46 percent, and the electoral

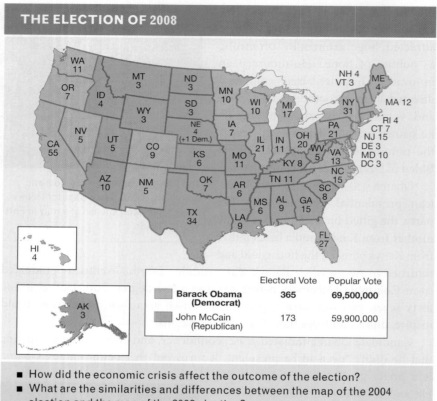

THE ELECTION OF 2008

	Electoral Vote	Popular Vote
Barack Obama (Democrat)	**365**	**69,500,000**
John McCain (Republican)	173	59,900,000

- How did the economic crisis affect the outcome of the election?
- What are the similarities and differences between the map of the 2004 election and the map of the 2008 election?

college 365 to 173. Obama also helped the Democrats win solid majorities in both houses of Congress.

Within days of his victory, Obama adopted a bipartisan approach in selecting his new cabinet members. He appointed Hillary Clinton secretary of state, retained Republican Robert Gates as secretary of defense, selected retired general James Jones, who had campaigned for McCain, as his national security adviser, and appointed Eric Holder as the nation's first African American attorney general. But picking a bipartisan cabinet proved easier than forging a bipartisan presidency.

OBAMA'S FIRST TERM President Obama and his administration inherited two unpopular wars and the worst economic situation in eighty years. His most pressing challenge was to keep the Great Recession from becoming a prolonged depression. Unemployment in early 2009 had passed 8 percent and was still rising. The financial sector remained paralyzed, and public confidence had plummeted.

One visible sign of the Great Recession's effects was the sharp decline in Mexicans emigrating to the United States. In 2000, some 700,000 Mexicans had crossed the Rio Grande, but by 2010, the number had dropped to less than 150,000, as it became easier for people to improve their quality of life in Mexico and harder to do so in the United States. By 2014, some experts believed that more Mexicans were leaving the U.S. than entering it.

To enable banks to start lending again, the new administration continued the TARP program that provided massive government bailouts to the largest banks and financial institutions. The bailouts were attacked by both the Left and the Right as deeply unfair to most struggling Americans. Treasury secretary Timothy Geithner later explained, "We had to do whatever we could to help people feel their money was safe in the [banking] system, even if it made us unpopular." Had they not saved the big banks, Obama and Geithner argued, the economy would have crashed.

Preserving the banking system did not create many jobs, however. To do so, in mid-February 2009, Congress passed, and Obama signed, an $832 billion economic-stimulus bill called the American Recovery and Reinvestment Act. The bill included cash distributions to states for construction projects to renew the nation's infrastructure (roads, bridges, levees, government buildings, and the electricity grid), money for renewable-energy systems, and $212 billion in tax reductions for individuals and businesses, as well as funds for food stamps and unemployment benefits. It was the largest government infusion of cash into the economy in history. In the end, however, it was not enough to generate a robust economic recovery, but Obama's actions did save the nation—and the world economy—from a financial meltdown.

HEALTH CARE REFORM The economic crisis merited Barack Obama's full attention, but he chose as his top legislative priority a controversial federal health insurance program. From his first day in office, Obama stressed his intention to reform a health care system that was "bankrupting families, bankrupting businesses, and bankrupting our government at the state and federal level." The United States, home to the world's costliest health system, was the only rich nation without a national health care program. Since 1970, the proportion of uninsured people had been steadily rising along with health care costs. In 2010, roughly 50 million Americans (16 percent of the population), most of them poor, young, or people of color, had no health insurance.

The president's goal in creating the Patient Protection and **Affordable Care Act (ACA)**, which Republican critics labeled "**Obamacare**," was to make health insurance more affordable and make health care accessible for everyone. The $940 billion law, proposed in 2009 and debated for a year, centered on the so-called *individual mandate*, which required uninsured adults to purchase an approved *private* insurance policy made available through state-run exchanges (websites where people could shop for insurance) or pay a tax penalty. Lower-income Americans could receive federal subsidies to help pay for their coverage, and insurance companies could no longer deny coverage to people with preexisting illnesses. Employers who did not offer health insurance would have to pay higher taxes, and drug companies and manufacturers of medical devices would have to pay annual government fees. Everyone, but especially the wealthy, would pay higher Medicare payroll taxes to help fund the changes.

The individual mandate was designed to ensure that all Americans had health insurance so as to reduce the skyrocketing costs of hospitals providing "charity care" for the uninsured. The ACA did not change the American tradition of employment-based health insurance provided by private companies. But the idea of *forcing* people to buy health insurance flew in the face of such ideals as individual freedom and personal responsibility. Critics questioned not only the individual mandate but the administration's projections that the program would reduce federal expenditures over the long haul.

Republicans mobilized to defeat the ACA. "If we're able to stop Obama on this it will be his Waterloo. It will break him," predicted South Carolina senator Jim DeMint. Despite heated opposition, however, the ACA passed with narrow party-line majorities in both houses of Congress. Obama signed it into law on March 23, 2010. Its complex provisions, to be implemented over a four-year period, would bring health insurance to 32 million people, half of whom would be covered by expanded Medicaid and the other half by the individual mandate. In its scope and goals, the ACA was a landmark in the history of health and social welfare—as well as the expansion of the federal government.

OBAMACARE AND THE COURTS   No sooner had President Obama pushed his health care plan through Congress than Republicans began challenging its constitutionality. On June 28, 2012, in the case of *National Federation of Independent Business v. Sebelius,* the Supreme Court surprised observers by ruling 5–4 that most of the new law was constitutional. Even more surprising was that the chief justice, John G. Roberts, a philosophical conservative who had never before voted with the four "liberal" justices on the Court, cast the deciding vote. Roberts upheld the ACA's individual mandate that required people to buy private health insurance or pay a tax, arguing that it was within Congress's power to impose taxes as outlined in Article 1 of the Constitution. Many conservatives, including the four dissenting justices, felt betrayed. The verdict led the *New York Times* to predict that the ruling "may secure Obama's place in history."

REGULATING WALL STREET The near collapse of the nation's financial system beginning in 2008 prompted calls for overhauling the financial regulatory system. On July 21, 2010, Obama signed the Wall Street Reform and Consumer Protection Act, also called the Dodd-Frank bill after its two congressional sponsors. It was the most comprehensive reform of the financial system since the New Deal in the thirties. The 2,319-page law required government agencies to exercise greater oversight over complex new financial transactions and protected consumers from unfair practices in loans and credit cards by establishing a new consumer financial-protection agency. President Obama predicted that the bill, despite its complexity, would "lift our economy," give "certainty to everybody" about the technical rules governing banking, and end "tax-funded bailouts—period." By 2010, however, the economy had not been "lifted" and many bankers remained confused about the new rules regulating the financial industry.

FOREIGN AFFAIRS

President Obama had more success in dealing with foreign affairs than in reviving the American economy. What journalists came to call the Obama Doctrine was very much like the Nixon Doctrine (1970), stressing that the United States could not continue to be the world's principal policeman. Yet the fate of America's economy and security was entangled more than ever with the fate of an unstable and often violent world.

THE OBAMA DOCTRINE The loosely defined Obama Doctrine grew out of efforts to end the expensive wars in Iraq and Afghanistan. In essence, the president wanted to replace confrontation and military intervention with a stance of cooperation and negotiation. The president told administration officials that his doctrine could be summed up in the phrase, "Don't do stupid stuff." On February 27, 2009, Obama announced that all 142,000 U.S. troops would be withdrawn from Iraq by the end of 2011, as the Iraqi government and the Bush administration had agreed in 2008. True to his word, the last U.S. combat troops left Iraq in December 2011.

Their departure marked the end of a bitterly divisive war that had raged for nearly nine years, killed more than 110,000 Iraqis, and left the nation shattered and unstable, despite Obama's upbeat claim that the departing U.S. forces were "leaving behind a sovereign, stable, and self-reliant Iraq with a representative government."

The war had cost more than 4,500 American lives, 30,000 wounded (many grievously so), and $2 trillion. Perhaps the greatest embarrassment was that the Iraqi government the United States left behind was inept and not even friendly to American interests. The long and chaotic war was an expensive mistake and a prolonged distraction for the government, the military, and the nation. As it turned out, there were no weapons of mass destruction, nor was there a direct link between the al Qaeda terrorists and Saddam Hussein. Al Qaeda, in fact, did not arrive in Iraq until *after* the American invasion. "The first Iraq war, in which I led a tank platoon, was necessary," said John Nagel, a retired army officer. "This one was not."

American efforts at nation building had failed. In June 2014, a journalist said that "it was time to admit that we cannot force a pluralistic society" on a dysfunctional Iraq torn by sectarian and ethnic violence into three rival regional states: one Shiite, one Sunni ("governed" by jihadists), and one Kurdish. Even Leon Panetta, who served as CIA director and secretary of defense under Obama, scolded the president for being so eager to withdraw U.S. forces that he failed to create the circumstances "that would preserve our influence and interests" in Iraq. Obama's hopes that the United States could get out of fighting wars in the Middle East and that the Iraqis could sustain a

Home from Iraq U.S. troops returned from Iraq to few celebrations.

stable and secure government in the face of terrorist incursions and sectarian fighting proved to be fantasies. Iraq's woeful self-government and the fractious nation's constant sectarian strife and disorder required continued infusions of U.S. military assistance, daily bombing raids, and massive economic aid.

"SURGE" IN AFGHANISTAN At the same time that President Obama was ending U.S. military involvement in Iraq, he dispatched 21,000 additional troops to Afghanistan in what was called a "surge." While doing so, however, he narrowed the focus of the U.S. mission to suppressing terrorists rather than transforming strife-torn Afghanistan into a stable capitalist democracy.

The surge worked. By the summer of 2011, Obama announced that the "tide of war was receding" and that the United States had largely achieved its goals in Afghanistan, setting in motion a substantial withdrawal of forces that lasted until 2014. Obama stressed that the Afghans must determine their country's future stability. "We will not try to make Afghanistan a perfect place," he said. "We will not police its streets or patrol its mountains indefinitely. That is the responsibility of the Afghan government."

As the troops came home, Americans quickly lost interest in what Obama had earlier called the "good war" in Afghanistan. In April 2014, despite threats by the Taliban to kill voters, Afghans turned out in huge numbers to choose a new president to lead them into the post-American era. But it was an expensive outcome for America's longest war. In the thirteen years since its 2001 invasion of Afghanistan, America had spent more than a trillion dollars there and lost 2,300 servicemen.

THE DEATH OF OSAMA BIN LADEN The crowning achievement of President Obama's anti-terrorism efforts was the discovery, at long last, of Osama bin Laden's hideout. Ever since the attacks of 9/11, bin Laden had eluded an intensive manhunt. In August 2010, however, U.S. intelligence analysts discovered his sanctuary in a walled residential compound outside of Abbottabad, Pakistan. On May 1, 2011, Obama authorized a daring night raid by a U.S. Navy SEAL team transported by helicopters from Afghanistan. After a brief firefight, the SEALs killed bin Laden. His death was a watershed moment, but it did not spell the end of Islamist terrorism.

THE "ARAB AWAKENING" In late 2010 and early 2011, spontaneous democratic uprisings erupted throughout much of the Arab world as long-oppressed peoples rose up against authoritarian regimes. Corrupt tyrants were forced out of power by a new generation of young activists inspired by democratic ideals and connected by social media on the Internet. What was soon dubbed

Arab Awakening Thousands of protesters converge in Cairo's Tahrir Square to call for an end to Mubarak's rule.

"the Arab Awakening" sent waves of youthful unrest across Tunisia, Algeria, Bahrain, Jordan, Morocco, Egypt, Oman, Yemen, Libya, Saudi Arabia, and Syria during what came to be called the Arab Spring of 2011. Dictators were toppled while democracy was embraced as the remarkable uprisings heralded a new era in the history of the Middle East. Yet the heroic days of revolutionary idealism soon gave way to the harsh reality that the rebels were so busy fighting among each other that they could not forge unified political alternatives. Building new democratic governments proved much harder than expected. The grassroots revolutionary movements in most Arab nations stumbled and stalled by 2014. Egypt reverted to an authoritarianism even harsher than that in place before the Arab Spring. Libya lapsed into chaos and Yemen exploded in civil war.

LIBYA OUSTS GADDAFI The pro-democracy turmoil in North Africa engulfed oil-rich Libya, long governed by the mercurial dictator Colonel Muammar Gaddafi, the Arab world's most violent despot. Anti-government demonstrations began on February 15, 2011, prompting Gaddafi to order Libyan soldiers and mercenaries (paid foreign soldiers) to suppress the rebellious "rats." By the end of February, what began as a peaceful pro-democratic uprising had turned into a full-scale civil war that provided the first real test of the Obama Doctrine.

True to his word, the president refused to act alone in helping the Libyan rebels (critics called it "leading from behind."). Instead, he encouraged European allies to take the lead. On March 19, France and Great Britain, with American support, launched a bombing campaign against Gaddafi's military strongholds. In late August, rebel forces captured the capital of Tripoli, scattering Gaddafi's government and marking the end of his forty-two-year dictatorship. On October 20, rebel fighters captured and killed Gaddafi. But the rebel militias that removed Gaddafi soon started shooting at each other, and stability remained elusive by the end of 2014.

THE CUBAN THAW At the end of 2014, President Obama surprised the world by announcing that the United States and Cuba were going to restore normal relations after more than fifty years of bitter hostility. As a first step, Obama relaxed restrictions on American tourists visiting Cuba. Six months later, in mid-2015, the two nations took a much more substantial step toward normalization when they reestablished embassies in each other's capital cities. The bold move was controversial, however. The powerful Cuban community in south Florida fiercely criticized Obama's decision, and Congressional Republicans threatened to block the appointment of a U.S. ambassador to Cuba because of its communist government. But the president persisted in his efforts, insisting that isolating Cuba had not worked. "Americans and Cubans alike are ready to move forward," he said in July 2015. "I believe it's time for Congress to do the same."

POLARIZED POLITICS

Barack Obama had campaigned in 2008 on the promise of bringing dramatic change to the federal government in a way that would reduce the partisan warfare between the two national parties. By the end of his first year in office, however, a Gallup poll found that he had become the most polarizing president in modern history. In part, the widening partisan divide resulted from Obama's aloof presidential style. Like Jimmy Carter, he does not like to lobby and horse-trade his way to legislative approval. Even Democrats criticized his growing "aloofness" from the messy business of working with legislators. Yet the standoff with Congress was not solely his fault. His Republican opponents had no interest in negotiating with him, and American political culture had become so polarized that it resembled two separate nations. Each party had its own cable-news station and rabidly partisan commentators, its own newspapers, its own think tanks, and its own billionaire donors. Governing, Obama quickly discovered, is far more difficult than campaigning.

THE TEA PARTY No sooner was Barack Obama sworn in than anti-government conservatives mobilized against him and the "tax-and-spend" liberalism he represented in their eyes. In January 2009, a New York stock trader named Graham Makohoniuk sent an e-mail message urging people to send tea bags to their congressional representatives to symbolize the Boston Tea Party of 1773, when American colonists protested against British tax policies.

Within a year or so, the tax revolt had become a national **Tea Party** movement, with groups in all fifty states. The Tea Party is not so much a cohesive political organization as it is a mood, an attitude, and an ideology,

The Tea Party movement Tea Party supporters gather outside the New Hampshire Statehouse for a tax day rally.

a diverse collection of self-described "disaffected," "angry," and "very conservative" activists, mostly white, male, married, middle-class Republicans over forty-five.

To the anti-tax rebels, the federal bailouts ordered by Presidents Bush and Obama in the wake of the 2008 economic meltdown were a form of "crony capitalism" whereby the "elite" rewarded the big companies that had funded their campaigns. Tea Party members demanded a radically smaller federal government (although most of them supported Social Security and Medicare, the two most expensive federal social programs). Democrats, including Obama, initially dismissed the Tea Party as a fringe group, but the 2010 election results proved them wrong.

Democratic House and Senate candidates (as well as moderate Republicans), including many long-serving leaders, were defeated in droves when conservative Republicans, many of them aligned with the Tea Party, gained sixty-three seats to recapture control of the House of Representatives. They won a near majority in the Senate as well. It was the most lopsided midterm election since 1938. Thereafter, the bickering between both parties prevented meaningful action on the languishing economy, chronic joblessness, and the runaway federal budget deficit. Neither party wanted to negotiate or compromise.

OCCUPY WALL STREET The emergence of the Tea Party was mirrored on the left by the Occupy Wall Street (OWS) movement, mobilized in the fall of 2011 when a call went out over the Internet to "Occupy Wall Street. Bring tent." Dozens, then hundreds, then thousands of people, many of them unemployed young adults, converged on Zuccotti Park in lower Manhattan. They formed tent villages and gathered to "occupy" Wall Street, protesting the "tyrannical" power of major banks and investment companies.

The protesters described themselves as the voice of the 99 percent of Americans who were being victimized by the 1 percent—the wealthiest and most politically connected Americans. Unlike the Tea Party, however, OWS did not have staying power. Within a year, its energies and visibility had waned, in part because of mass arrests, in part because it was an intentionally "leaderless" movement more interested in saying what it was *against* than explaining what it was *for*.

Occupy Wall Street The Manhattan-born grassroots movement grew rapidly from rallies to massive marches in financial districts nationwide, like this demonstration in downtown Los Angeles.

Bold Decisions

For all of the political sniping, however, attitudes toward "hot-button" cultural values were slowly changing. In December 2010, Congress repealed the "don't ask, don't tell" (DADT) military policy that, since 1993, had resulted in some 9,500 gay men and women being discharged from the armed forces. A year later, a report by army officers concluded that the repeal "had no overall negative impact on military readiness or its component dimensions, including cohesion, recruitment, retention, assaults, harassment, ormorale."

GAY MARRIAGE In May 2012, President Obama became the first sitting president to support the right of gay and lesbian couples to marry. That his statement came a day after the North Carolina legislature voted to ban all rights for gay couples illustrated how incendiary the issue was. While asserting that it was the "right" thing to do, Obama knew that endorsing **same-sex marriage** had powerful political implications. The gay community would play an energetic role in the 2012 presidential election, and the youth vote—the under-thirty electorate who most supported gay marriage—would be crucial. No sooner had Obama made his announcement than polls showed that American voters for the first time were evenly split on the charged issue, with Democrats and independent voters providing the bulk of support for same-sex marriage.

THE DREAM ACT In June 2012, Obama again made waves by issuing an executive order (soon labeled the DREAM Act) that allowed 1.5 million undocumented immigrants who had been brought to the United States as children to remain as citizens. His unanticipated decision thrilled Hispanic supporters who had lost heart over his failure to convince Congress to support more-comprehensive immigration reform. Congressional Republicans steadfastly opposed giving the estimated 12 million undocumented immigrants, 80 percent of whom were Latinos, a "pathway to citizenship" without first ensuring that the border with Mexico was secured.

The DREAM Act, however, had unexpected consequences. It excited masses of Central Americans willing to endure enormous risks to live in America. Panicked parents in El Salvador, Guatemala, and Honduras, worried about widespread drug-related gang violence, started sending their children through Mexico to the United States in hopes of connecting with relatives and being granted citizenship. During 2014, some 57,000 young migrants were caught along the nearly 2,000-mile-long border with Mexico, and communities across the nation rushed to find families to "sponsor" the unaccompanied children.

At the same time, the Obama administration was deporting record numbers of undocumented immigrants (more than 2 million by the end of 2014), some of whom had been working in the nation for decades, in what was called the "great expulsion." Obama, called the "Deporter in Chief" by critics, claimed that he was only following the laws written by anti-immigration Republicans. Others suggested that the harsh deportation policy was part of Obama's "grand strategy" to force Congress to pass a comprehensive immigration reform bill. Either way, the immigrants were caught in the middle.

THE SUPREME COURT IN THE TWENTY-FIRST CENTURY
The Supreme Court surprised observers in 2013 by overturning the Defense of Marriage Act (DOMA) of 1996, which had denied gay and lesbian couples

Refugees from gangland Braving hundreds of miles on foot, Honduran and Salvadorian children are sent off by their parents for a better life in the United States, away from the drug-dealing violence of Central America. Here, border guards stop a group of child refugees in Granjeno, Texas.

who married in states allowing such unions the right to federal benefits. In *United States v. Windsor* (2013), the Court voted 5–4 that the federal government could not withhold spousal benefits from same-sex couples who had been legally married. While restoring federal benefits, the Court did not rule that same-sex marriage was a *right* guaranteed under the Constitution. That issue would have to be resolved by a future Court decision, scheduled for the summer of 2015. In the meantime, each state could decide whether to allow such marriages. During 2014, however, federal courts repeatedly overturned state laws banning same-sex marriages, arguing that the right to marry *was* guaranteed by the Constitution.

While the Court disappointed social conservatives with its *Windsor* decision, its five conservative justices continued to make rulings intended to restrict the powers of the federal government. In June 2013, in *Shelby County v. Holder* (2013), the Court gutted key provisions of the 1965 Voting Rights Act (VRA), which had outlawed discrimination directed toward voters "on account of race or color." The majority opinion declared that in five of the six southern states originally covered by the VRA, black voter turnout now exceeded white turnout.

To the judges, this seemed to prove that there was no evidence of continuing racial discrimination. Today's laws "must be justified by current needs," Chief Justice John Roberts wrote. Soon after the Court's ruling, counties and states in the South pushed through new laws that had the effect of making it more difficult for minorities and poor people to vote by reducing voting hours or requiring that driver's licenses be shown on voting days.

THE 2012 ELECTION As the November 2012 presidential election approached, one thing was certain: it would be the most expensive election ever, in part because the Supreme Court ruled in *Citizens United v. Federal Elections Committee* (2010) that corporations could spend as much as they wanted in support of candidates.

After a divisive battle in the primaries, Mitt Romney, a former corporate executive and Massachusetts governor, won the Republican nomination. The main question for Romney was whether the still-powerful religious Right would allow him to sidestep tough social issues; the question for President Obama was whether he could sidestep his failure to restore prosperity.

Two factors injured Romney's candidacy toward the end of the most expensive campaign in history ($6 billion). The first was his decision to please right-wing voters by opposing immigration reforms that might allow undocumented immigrants a pathway to citizenship. The second was the disclosure that he had privately told a group of wealthy contributors that he "did not care" about the 47 percent of Americans who failed "to take personal responsibility and care for their lives." It was not his job "to worry about" those who did not pay federal income taxes because they were dependent on federal government programs. The Obama campaign seized on the impolitic statement and demonized the wealthy Romney as an uncaring elitist. On Election Day, Obama won with 66 million votes to Romney's 61 million, and 332 electoral votes to 206.

Nearly 60 percent of white voters chose Romney. But the nation's fastest growing groups—Hispanics, Asian Americans, and African Americans—voted overwhelmingly for Obama, as did college-educated women. David Frum, a prominent Republican speechwriter and columnist, confessed that his party was becoming "increasingly isolated and estranged from modern America."

Obama began his second term on an assertive note. In January 2013, the Defense Department lifted its ban on women serving in combat. The following month, Obama announced that more U.S. troops would be withdrawn from Afghanistan over the next year, leaving 34,000 by early 2014. It had become America's longest war.

OBAMACARE ON THE DEFENSIVE President Obama's proudest achievement, the Affordable Care Act, was so massive in its scope and complicated in its implementation that it took four years before it was ready to "roll out." In the fall of 2013, the federal online health insurance "exchange," where people without insurance could sign up, opened with great fanfare. Obama assured Americans that using the online registration system would be "real simple." It was not. On October 1, millions tried to sign up; only *six* succeeded. As it turned out, the website had never been properly tested, and it was hobbled with technical glitches. It also became evident that Obama had misled the nation about key elements of the plan. In campaigning for its passage in 2010, he had repeatedly told voters that if they liked their current health insurance plan, they could, under Obamacare, "keep that insurance. Period. End of story." As it turned out, however, many with substandard policies saw them canceled by insurers.

Congressional Republicans, as well as many Democrats, condemned the president for his misleading statements and inept management of his signature program. During the winter of 2013–2014, the Republican-led House of Representatives repeatedly tried—and failed—to overturn the ACA, at one point passing a federal budget that would have stripped the new health care program of its funding. When the president refused to sign the bill, the federal government (some 800,000 employees) shut down after the existing budget expired on September 30. For sixteen days, every nonessential federal agency was closed, costing the government $2 billion.

The Republicans' shutdown strategy failed, however, as it had in 1995, when citizen outrage was directed not at President Clinton, but at Republican legislators. In response to widespread criticism and the threat of global economic repercussions, House Republicans on October 16 passed a revised, Senate-approved budget that removed the anti-ACA provision. The conservative radio commentator Rush Limbaugh described the Republican shutdown as "one of the greatest political disasters I've ever seen."

Democrats had little time to celebrate, however. By November 2013, some 57 percent of voters said they opposed Obamacare, in part because the program benefited only a quarter of the population, the uninsured and the underinsured, and Obama's job approval ratings had plunged. It had taken the president weeks to acknowledge the botched roll-out of Obamacare: "We created this problem we didn't need to create," he said to aides. "And it's our own doing, and it's our most important initiative," and "nobody is madder than me."

Eventually, the ACA website was fixed, and by August 2014, more than 9 million people, well above the original target number, had signed up for health insurance. "The Affordable Care Act is here to stay," Obama said. But even though the sign-up system was fixed, public perception of the government's ability to manage the program never recovered.

NEW GLOBAL CHALLENGES IN AN AGE OF INSECURITY

In 2013, the United States held its first high-level talks with Iran since 1979, when Iranian militants took U.S. embassy employees in Tehran hostage. On November 23, Secretary of State John Kerry reached a multinational agreement with Iran to scale back its nuclear development program for six months as a first step toward a more comprehensive agreement not to develop nuclear weapons.

At the same time, an increasingly bloody civil war in Syria that had claimed 150,000 lives was beginning to have major international repercussions. In 2013, U.S. intelligence analysts confirmed that the Syrian government, ruled with an iron fist by Bashar al-Assad, on August 21 had used chemical weapons to kill 1,400 people, many of them children.

President Obama had repeatedly warned that such use of weapons of mass destruction was a "red line" that would trigger international military intervention of "enormous consequences." In late August, he (and the French government) hesitantly began preparing for a military strike, although Congress and most Americans opposed such action. It appeared that Obama had gotten cold feet about a military intervention. His former secretary of defense, Leon Panetta, argued that Obama's failure to follow through on his threat "was a blow to American credibility. When the president as commander in chief draws a red line, it is critical that he act if the line is crossed."

On September 9, Secretary of State Kerry defused the crisis by signing an agreement with Russia to dispose of Syria's chemical weapons. By the end of October, all the chemical weapon stockpiles had been destroyed or dismantled, but the civil war raged on.

UKRAINE As the Syrian civil war continued, a civil uprising occurred in Ukraine, the former Soviet republic of 46 million people that had gained its independence in 1991. For nearly a quarter of a century, Russian president Vladimir Putin had viewed the disintegration of the Soviet Union as the "greatest geopolitical catastrophe of the century." Like many Russian rulers before him, he developed an almost paranoid fear of being invaded from the west, either by armies or by democratic ideas. To restore Russian influence over its neighbors and to divide NATO and the European Union, he had exerted economic and political pressure on the republics of the former Soviet Union.

Civil war in Ukraine A protester in the Ukrainian capital of Kiev throws a Molotov cocktail during violent clashes with police on January 22, 2014. A month later, Russian President Vladimir Putin would use the unrest as an excuse to seize control of the Crimean region.

On February 27, Putin sent troops into the Crimea, a part of Ukraine along the Black Sea long claimed by Russia. A week later, the Crimean parliament voted to become part of the Russian Federation. Putin, claiming that Crimea had "always been an inseparable part of Russia," quickly made the illegal annexation official by positioning Russian troops there, while denying their presence.

The speed and ruthlessness with which Putin seized control of Crimea, mobilized 40,000 Russian troops on the Ukrainian border, and cut off Ukraine's crucial access to Russian natural gas surprised President Obama and European leaders. It may not have been the start of a new cold war, but it put an end to hope that Russia would become a cordial partner of the United States and the European democracies. By 2014 Putin had developed a raw and resentful anti-Americanism, fearful that the menacing United States (and NATO) was gaining influence in the former Soviet republics at the expense of Russia.

In response, the United States and the European Union hurriedly organized diplomatic efforts to "de-escalate the crisis." They refused to recognize the legitimacy of the annexation of Crimea and announced economic sanctions against Russia while pledging financial assistance to Ukraine. "If Russia continues to interfere in Ukraine, we stand ready to impose further sanctions," Obama said. By a vote of 100–11, the United Nations General Assembly also opposed the annexation.

In April 2014, heavily armed pro-Russian separatists, as many as a third of whom were Russian soldiers and agents, seized control of several cities in eastern Ukraine. They declared a "people's republic" and called for secession.

Pressure mounted to impose even more sanctions when a Malaysian passenger jet flying across eastern Ukraine was shot down by a Russian-made rocket in July 2014, killing all 298 on board. The United States and its allies slammed Russia with more economic sanctions, but the coldly calculating Putin showed no sign of backing away. In fact, his popularity in Russia had soared, leaving the United States once again in the position of containing Russia's expansionist ambitions.

THE BURDENS OF LEADERSHIP Rarely are presidents more popular than on their first day in office. To govern is to make decisions, and decisions in democratic nations inevitably produce disappointments, disagreements, and criticism. During his presidency, Barack Obama has discovered how hard it is to lead the world's economic and military superpower in the post–cold war era. He has struggled to stabilize a cluster of unstable nations—Iraq, Afghanistan, Libya, Ukraine, and Syria—that craved U.S. resources but resented American meddling.

What unites the crises in Ukraine and the Middle East is the seeming powerlessness of Obama, European leaders, and the United Nations to resolve them easily or quickly in an age of growing insecurity and turmoil. Overall, Obama adopted a posture of restraint in world affairs. He was determined to "avoid stupid errors," wind down the wars in Iraq and Afghanistan, stay aloof from the Arab Awakening, and reduce the use of U.S. military power abroad so as to concentrate on issues at home.

Yet he and others were naive to think that the United States could avoid the burdens of being the only superpower in a post–cold war world of growing anarchy and violence. There is no diplomatic solution to be found for groups seeking the total destruction of the American and European democracies. Democratic senator Diane Feinstein of California wondered out loud in September 2014 if Obama had become "too cautious" about the use of force in world affairs.

ISLAMISTS ON THE MOVE Unexpected events overseas during the summer of 2014 gave Obama the opportunity to take decisive action. In June, the volatile Middle East took a sudden turn for the worse when Sunni jihadists who had been fighting in Syria invaded northern Iraq and announced the creation of their own nation (caliphate), called the Islamic State (ISIS). With lightning speed, the Islamic State emerged as the largest, best-financed, most heavily-armed, and most brutal of the many jihadist terrorist groups, financing its far-flung operations and 40,000 fanatical fighters by selling captured oil and ransoming hostages.

ISIS was both the culmination of decades of Arab Islamist rage against Europe and the United States and the collapse of effective government and security in Syria and Iraq. Once American forces left Iraq and Sunnis grew frustrated with the Shia-dominated government, ISIS swept in, setting off a panic that helped topple the government. In the areas it captured, ISIS established its own tyrannical form of government based on what it called the "management of savagery."

In the face of the ISIS advance, many Iraqi government soldiers that the United States had spent billions of dollars training and equipping fled, leaving their valuable weapons and vehicles. Sadistic ISIS fighters seized huge tracts of territory in Syria and Iraq while enslaving, terrorizing, raping, massacring, crucifying, or beheading thousands of men, women, and children who in some way fell short of their ruthless version of the Sunni faith. In August 2014, after ISIS terrorists gruesomely beheaded two captured Americans, President Obama ordered "systematic" airstrikes, first in Iraq and later in Syria, to prevent genocide as ISIS fighters assaulted Christians, Yazidis, and Kurds in the region. Those airstrikes continue.

Obama pulled off a diplomatic coup by building a broad coalition of Arab and European partners, but U.S. warplanes bore the brunt of the action. Obama assured Americans that he would not "get dragged into another ground war," but the latest military intervention remained a bitter setback for a president committed to ending U.S. wars in the Middle East. If George W. Bush had plunged U.S. power too deeply into Iraq, Obama seemed to have withdrawn U.S. power too quickly. One over-reached, the other under-shot.

The stakes were high. Yousef al Otaiba, the ambassador of the United Arab Emirates to the United States, warned that the radical Islamist leaders of the Islamic State posed "an existential threat to those of us who believe in the true nature of Islam as a religion of peace." Although some criticized Obama's actions, he characterized the air campaign to slow the mass murder and mayhem by the Islamic State as "American leadership at its best." Preventing genocide and deterring the world's tyrants and terrorists from further mischief is not simply a burden of great power, he decided, it is a responsibility in an era burdened by constant warfare. During 2015, however, the stability and security in the Middle East desired and funded by the United States disintegrated. Civil wars between sectarian factions were engulfing Syria, Iraq, Libya, and Yemen.

In 2015 the United States remained the world's only superpower capable of projecting military power anywhere in the world. But the ill-considered wars in Afghanistan and Iraq had left many Americans deeply reluctant to support any use of extensive military power that might involve a long-term commitment. The painful lessons of Afghanistan and Iraq showed that no nation, not even a superpower, could easily impose its will and its democratic system on people with very different needs, beliefs, and traditions.

THE AGE OF GRIDLOCK

American politics has always been chaotic and combative; its raucous energy is one of its great strengths. During Barack Obama's two-term presidency, however, the emergence of the Tea Party and Occupy Wall Street symbolized how savage and unyielding political combat had become. *Compromise* and *moderation* had become dirty words. The scorched-earth tactics of Republicans in Congress were designed to protect the political status quo. "We're the party of 'Hell, no!'" cried Sarah Palin, the former Republican governor of Alaska who had run for vice president alongside John McCain in 2008 before becoming the darling of the Tea Party.

Intense partisanship dominated the 2014 congressional elections, when Republicans gained nine Senate seats, giving them control of the Senate for the first time since 2006. They also strengthened their hold on the House, added governorships, and tightened their control of state legislatures. Republicans campaigned on a single theme: the "failure" of President Obama and the "disaster" of Obamacare. Kentucky senator Rand Paul vowed that he and his colleagues would send "the president bill after bill until he wearies of it," including renewed efforts to repeal Obamacare.

Political moderates became a dying breed. By late 2014, the percentage of voters who described themselves as liberals or conservatives had doubled since 1994, and more than twice as many Democratic and Republican voters as in 1994 had a "very unfavorable" view of the other party. Congress included mostly Republicans on the far right, Democrats on the far left, and hardly anyone in the middle. "That alignment," said Gerald Seib of the *Wall Street Journal*, created a Congress "that does less, and does it less well, than any time in memory."

By 2014, six years after taking office on the promise of "hope and change," President Obama had discovered how difficult it is to preside over a polarized nation, much less bring it together. "You know I love this job," Obama told an adviser early in his presidency. "I love diving into problems. But dealing with some of the people you have to deal with . . . wears you out."

In the final two years of his presidency, Obama's greying hair and waning energy revealed a weariness that mirrored his public approval ratings, which were well below 50 percent. James Bennet, editor of the *Atlantic Monthly*, pointed out that every modern two-term president had experienced plummeting support. "If we weren't sick of the guy to start with, we certainly are by now. What once seemed like roguish charm, or bracing surety, or nuanced intelligence, has curdled into self-indulgence, or arrogance, or passivity."

Voters hoping for a more energetic and engaged Obama after his reelection were disappointed by his slow withdrawal from engaged leadership. He seemed disheartened by the troubling "gap between the magnitude of our challenges and the smallness of our politics." Critics savaged him for playing golf more often than any president since Eisenhower. Even prominent Democrats joined in the attacks. A successful presidency, former secretary of state Hillary Clinton said, needed "organizing principles, and 'Don't do stupid stuff' is not an organizing principle."

Obama repeatedly blamed Republicans for stalemating his second term, but the president was not blameless. Cabinet member Leon Panetta stressed that Obama's "most conspicuous weakness" was "a frustrating reticence to engage his opponents and rally support for his cause." While acknowledging that the president was "supremely intelligent," Panetta added that Obama "avoids the battle, complains, and misses opportunities."

Obama was a talented man drawn to political power but frustrated by horse-trading politics, a leader eager to have power but increasingly reluctant to exercise it. To many Americans, his naturally cautious and careful approach to foreign policy came across as indecisive and weak, and his coolness smacked of aloofness. "George W. Bush was a leader who didn't like to think," said Ian Bremmer, an international consultant. "Barack Obama is a thinker who doesn't like to lead."

RENEWED ENERGY Yet during the summer of 2015, in the sunset of his presidency, Obama regained his energy and momentum. While restoring normal relations with Cuba, he benefited from two surprising U.S. Supreme Court rulings in late June. For years, Republicans had waged all-out war on the Affordable Care Act (Obamacare). Unable to halt the implementation of the new program in Congress, the critics turned to the courts to challenge the "flawed" new health care law. In a surprising 6-3 decision in a case called *King v. Burwell*, the Supreme Court saved the controversial health care law that will define Obama's presidency for generations to come. Chief Justice Roberts explained in the majority opinion that some of the sloppy language in the original Congressional legislation should not be used to destroy the new program. "Congress passed the Affordable Care Act to improve health insurance markets, not to destroy them," Roberts stressed. "If at all possible, we must interpret the Act in a way that is consistent with the former, and avoids the

Married with pride A California couple pose in front of the United States Supreme Court building in Washington, D.C., while the Supreme Court justices hear arguments on the constitutional right for gay couples to wed in April 2015. On June 26, 2015, in a landmark 5-4 decision, the Court ruled in favor of upholding same-sex marriage in all fifty states.

latter." President Obama was overjoyed by the much-anticipated ruling. "Five years ago, after nearly a century of talk, decades of trying, a year of bipartisan debate, we finally declared that in America, health care is not a privilege for a few but a right for all," Obama said from the White House. "The Affordable Care Act is here to stay."

Then, just a day later, the U.S. Supreme Court issued another bombshell ruling when it announced a 5-4 decision in the *Obergefell v. Hodges* case, which banned states from preventing same-sex marriages. The landmark decision that same-sex couples had a constitutional right to marry infuriated the Religious Right. Rick Scarborough, a Baptist minister in Texas, vowed that he and others would "denounce this practice in our [religious] services, we will not teach it in our schools, we will refuse to officiate at this type of wedding, and we will not accept any encroachments on our First Amendment rights."

Yet the Supreme Court's affirmation of same-sex marriage reflected the profound change in public attitudes toward homosexual rights during the early twenty-first century. In 2008, presidential candidate Barack Obama had felt the need to disavow support for marriage equality. By 2012, he had reversed himself by embracing the right of same-sex marriage. His change of mind reflected a resurgent social transformation in American life. Cultural diversity, like Obamacare, was here to stay. Obama, for example, the nation's first African American president, had appointed two women to the U.S. Supreme Court, including the first Latina justice. He also ended the ban on open homosexuality in the military.

The unexpected momentum of the Court decisions in June 2015 bolstered Obama's efforts in another controversial arena: foreign policy. In his 2009 inaugural address, he had vowed to international enemies that "we will extend a hand if you are willing to unclench your fist." That effort finally paid off in 2015, not only with the normalizing of relations with Cuba but also when the United States and five other major world powers announced a draft treaty with Iran intended to thwart its efforts to develop a nuclear weapon. In exchange for ending the international trade embargo against Iran, the agreement called for the Iranians to dismantle much of their nuclear program and allow for international inspectors to confirm their actions. Obama warned Congressional critics that voting against such a treaty would mean "a greater chance of war in the Middle East."

A FADING AMERICAN DREAM?

When Barack Obama won the Democratic nomination for president in 2008, he and his supporters touted him as an uplifting example of the American Dream, a biracial man who had defied the odds and achieved great success. His inspiring story echoed one of the most powerful themes in the nation's history: America as a mythic land of unique opportunities for people from around the world. In 1811, former president John Adams marveled at the growth and prosperity of the young American republic: "There is no people on earth so ambitious as the people of America . . . because the lowest [poorest] can aspire [to wealth] as freely as the highest."

The ideal of equal opportunity has always been the engine of American distinctiveness. By the early twenty-first century, though, that ideal seemed increasingly out of reach to millions. The most striking change in modern life since 1980 was the *widening* inequality of income and wealth. Modern America had become a tale of two very different societies in which "the rich get richer and the poor get poorer," to quote a famous song. A rising wealth gap between rich and poor unfairly punishes those who have the bad luck to be born and raised in poverty, with little access to quality education, health care, and learning technologies. While the wealthy feel financially secure, the masses feel

Raising the minimum wage
Demonstrators rally in Albany, New York, for an increase to the minimum wage, a movement that gained national traction in 2014 and reflected the growing attention paid to wealth disparity in the country.

increasingly insecure against unexpected hardships and a rapidly changing high-tech economy that places a premium on higher education.

As Nobel Prize–winning economist Joseph Stiglitz said in 2012, "the United States has less equality of opportunity than almost any other advanced industrial country." The American dream of the poor having an equal chance to succeed economically, he said, was now more of a myth. Most of the economic benefits generated by the slow economic recovery under Obama were enjoyed by salaried executives and stockholders rather than the working and middle classes. Although unemployment dropped below 6 percent in 2015, wages had barely risen since 2007. In 1979, the richest 1 percent, mostly people engaged in global investment, banking, and business, controlled 9 percent of the nation's total income. By 2014, they controlled more than 20 percent.

The 46 million Americans living *below* the official poverty line in 2014 ($11,702 annual income for an individual, $23,850 for a family of four) were the most in history. One of every five children lived in poverty. At the other extreme, corporate executives were reaping an ever-higher percentage of national wealth. In 1993, the disparity in pay between corporate leaders and the average U.S. worker was 195 to 1; in 2012, it was 360 to 1. "Increasingly," journalist Hedrick Smith reported in 2012, America is becoming a society in which "privilege sustains privilege; poverty begets poverty," resulting in the "slow, poisonous polarization and disintegration of our great democracy."

Whatever its causes, what came to be called the "great divide" between the "1 percent" and the "99 percent" had profound social and political consequences, as well as moral dimensions. A nation founded on the idea that "All men are created equal" had become richer but less equal and less socially mobile than other advanced industrial nations. The true test of a capitalist democracy is not how wealthy the richest citizens are, but the quality of life of the average citizen.

The unresolved tension created by such inequality emerged as the foremost social issue of the twenty-first century. In an August 2014 national poll, 64 percent of Americans no longer believed that the nation offered everyone an equal chance to succeed, fewer than 10 percent trusted Congress, and 76 percent were not confident that the quality of life of their children's generation would be "better than it has been for us." Billionaire investor Bill Gross worried in 2014 that the new high-tech global economy was "producing one world for the rich and an entirely different world for the working class. It can't go on like this, either from the standpoint of the health of the capitalist system itself or the health of individuals and the family."

As the 2016 presidential campaign began in earnest, income inequality emerged as a major issue. Democratic frontrunner Hillary Clinton claimed she was reaching out to "everyday Americans" by calling for higher wages while criticizing the "bloated" salaries of corporate executives. Florida senator Marco Rubio urged his fellow Republicans to make their party "the champion of the working class."

The United States has so far survived its growing economic inequalities and social strife without serious upheavals. For all its diversity and divisions, the nation remains united under a common government and political system, something that few societies can claim. For centuries, Americans have also displayed a distinctively self-critical temperament, especially noticeable to foreign visitors. In the early nineteenth century, English writer Charles Dickens said that the American "always is depressed, and always is stagnated, and always is at an alarming crisis, and never was otherwise."

Perhaps that is why the nation always overcomes its greatest crises; Americans eventually summon the will and creativity to address their urgent problems. The nation has a remarkable genius for self-renewal and a confident ability to maneuver through the most difficult threats and challenges. It needs such innovative resilience today, for unless the entwined ideals of equal opportunity and fair reward are addressed, Americans may lose what has always united them and informed their sense of purpose: the widely shared hope, even expectation, of a better future for all based on hard work, ingenuity, and sacrifice.

CHAPTER REVIEW

SUMMARY

- **Changing Demographics**   From 1980 to 2010, the population of the United States grew by 25 percent, to 306 million. The nation was quickly becoming even more racially and ethnically diverse, and a wave of immigration from Latin America allowed Hispanics to surpass African Americans as the nation's largest minority. By 2012, the U.S. population included more foreign-born and first-generation residents than ever before.

- **Divided Government**   Just two years after the election of "New Democrat" Bill Clinton in 1992, Republican Speaker of the House Newt Gingrich crafted his *Contract with America* and achieved a Republican landslide in the midterm elections of 1994. Despite the bipartisan success of the 1993 *North American Free Trade Act (NAFTA)* and the *Personal Responsibility and Work Opportunity Act of 1996*—and a prosperous, high-tech "new economy" that helped balance the federal budget—Clinton's private life produced a sex scandal that resulted in impeachment proceedings against him. Clinton was ultimately acquitted and went on to intervene in the Balkans to stop *ethnic cleansing* and to broker the land-for-peace Wye River Accords in the Middle East.

- **Global Terrorism**   The 9/11 attacks led President George W. Bush to declare a *war on terror* that commenced with the U.S. invasion of Afghanistan to capture Osama bin Laden and oust the Islamist Taliban government. Through the *USA Patriot Act*, Congress authorized the federal government to monitor Americans for possible terrorist activities at home. The *Bush Doctrine* declared America's right to initiate preemptive military strikes against terrorists or rogue nations possessing *weapons of mass destruction (WMDs)*. In 2003, Bush invoked this doctrine against Saddam Hussein, the leader of Iraq. The ensuing second Iraq War removed Hussein from power but turned up no WMDs.

- **A Historic Election**   The 2008 presidential primary campaigns featured Democratic senators Hillary Rodham Clinton, the first formidable female candidate, and Barack Obama, the first truly contending African American candidate, as well as Republican senator John McCain, the oldest candidate in history. Obama won his party's nomination and went on to take the election, becoming the nation's first African American president. His victory resulted in large part from public dismay about the *Great Recession*, as well as voters' weariness with President Bush.

- **Obama's Priorities**   Obama's first priority was to shore up the failing economy, which he attempted through controversial Wall Street "bailouts" and a huge "economic stimulus" package. Yet the recovery remained slow and unequal, widening the economic divide and spawning the short-lived Occupy Wall Street movement. The *Affordable Care Act (Obamacare)* incited increasingly bitter opposition from the conservative *Tea Party*. Obama was more successful in winning public support to reduce American military deployment abroad, removing all combat troops from Iraq in 2011 and downsizing their presence in Afghanistan. Obama also intervened in the nation's culture wars, endorsing *same-sex marriage* and a path to citizenship for undocumented residents.

CHRONOLOGY

1992	Bill Clinton elected president
1993	Congress passes NAFTA
1995	The Contract with America
1996	Congress passes PRWOA
1998	President Clinton impeached and acquitted
2000	George W. Bush elected after controversial recount
September 11, 2001	Terrorists attack New York City
October 2001	Operation Enduring Freedom begins in Afghanistan
March 2003	Iraq War begins with Operation Iraqi Freedom
August 2005	Hurricane Katrina devastates Gulf coast
2008	Global financial markets collapse; Great Recession begins
2009	Barack Obama becomes the nation's first black president
2010	Congress passes the Affordable Care Act (Obamacare)
August 2011	Al Qaeda leader Osama bin Laden killed
2013	U.S. Supreme Court overturns the Defense of Marriage Act (DOMA) in *United States v. Windsor*
2015	U.S. Supreme Court upholds the Affordable Care Act and decides that same-sex couples have a constitutional right to marry

KEY TERMS

North American Free Trade Agreement (NAFTA) p. 1463

Contract with America p. 1464

Personal Responsibility and Work Opportunity Act of 1996 (PRWOA) p. 1466

globalization p. 1467

ethnic cleansing p. 1470

war on terror p. 1478

USA Patriot Act (2001) p. 1479

Bush Doctrine p. 1480

weapons of mass destruction (WMDs) p. 1480

Great Recession p. 1487

Affordable Care Act (ACA—also called Obamacare) p. 1491

Tea Party p. 1497

same-sex marriage p. 1500

 INQUIZITIVE

Go to InQuizitive to see what you've learned—and learn what you've missed—with personalized feedback along the way.

GLOSSARY

1968 Chicago Democratic National Convention The meeting of Democratic delegates in Chicago to nominate a candidate for the 1968 presidential elections, which were marred by violent anti-war protests.

36°30' According to the Missouri Compromise, any part of the Louisiana Purchase north of this line (Missouri's southern border) was to be excluded from slavery.

abolition In the early 1830s, the anti-slavery movement shifted its goal from the gradual end of slavery to the immediate end or abolition of slavery.

abolitionism Movement that called for an immediate end to slavery throughout the United States.

Abigail Adams (1744–1818) As the wife of John Adams, she endured long periods of separation from him while he served in many political roles. During these times apart, she wrote often to her husband; their correspondence has provided a detailed portrait of life during the Revolutionary War.

John Adams (1735–1826) He was a signer of the Declaration of Independence and a delegate to the First and Second Continental Congresses. A member of the Federalist Party, he served as the first vice president of the United States and the second president. As president, he passed the Alien and Sedition Acts and endured a stormy relationship with France, which included the XYZ affair.

John Quincy Adams (1767–1848) As secretary of state, he urged President Monroe to issue the Monroe Doctrine, which incorporated his belief in an expanded use of federal powers. As the sixth president, Adams's nationalism and praise of European leaders caused a split in his party, causing some Republicans to leave and form the Democrat party.

Samuel Adams (1722–1803) A genius of revolutionary agitation, he believed that English Parliament had no right to legislate for the colonies. He organized the Sons of Liberty as well as protests in Boston against the British.

Jane Addams (1860–1935) She founded and ran of one of the best known settlement houses, the Hull House. Active in the peace and suffragist movements, she established child care for working mothers, health clinics, job training, and other social programs.

affirmative action Programs designed to give preferential treatment to women and minorities as compensation for past injustices.

Affordable Care Act (ACA), or Obamacare (2010) Vast health care reform initiative signed into law and championed by President Obama and widely criticized by Republicans that aims to make health insurance more affordable and make health-care accessible to everyone, regardless of income or prior medical conditions.

Agricultural Adjustment Act (1933) Legislation that paid farmers to produce less in order to raise crop prices for all; the act was later declared unconstitutional by the U.S. Supreme Court in the case of *United States v. Butler* (1936).

Emilio Aguinaldo (1869?–1964) He was a leader in Filipino struggle for independence. During the Spanish-American War (the War of 1898), Commodore George Dewey brought Aguinaldo back to the Philippines from exile to help fight the Spanish. However, after the Spanish surrendered to Americans, America annexed the Philippines and Aguinaldo fought against the American military until he was captured in 1901.

Alamo, Battle of the Siege in the Texas War for Independence of 1836, in which the San Antonio mission fell to the Mexicans. Davy Crockett and Jim Bowie were among the courageous defenders.

Albany Plan of Union A failed proposal by the seven northern colonies in anticipation of the French and Indian War, urging the unification of the colonies under one Crown-appointed president.

Alien and Sedition Acts of 1798 Four measures passed during the undeclared war with France that limited the freedoms of speech and press and restricted the liberty of non-citizens.

alliance with France Critical diplomatic, military, and economic alliance between France and the newly independent United States, codified by the Treaty of Amity and Commerce and the Treaty of Alliance (1778).

Allied Powers The nations fighting the Central Powers during the First World War, including France, Great Britain, and Russia; later joined by Italy and, after Russia quit the war in 1917, the United States.

American Anti-Imperialist League Coalition of anti-imperialist groups united in 1899 to protest American territorial expansion, especially in the Philippine Islands; its membership included prominent politicians, industrialists, labor leaders, and social reformers.

American Colonization Society (ACS) Established in 1817, an organization whose mission was to return freed slaves to Africa.

American Federation of Labor (AFL) Founded in 1881 as a national federation of trade unions made up of skilled workers.

American Indian Movement (AIM) Fed up with the poor conditions on Indian reservations and the federal government's unwillingness to help, Native Americans founded the American Indian Movement in 1963. In 1973, AIM led 200 Sioux in the occupation of Wounded Knee. After a ten-week standoff with the federal authorities, the government agreed to reexamine Indian treaty rights and the occupation ended.

American Recovery and Reinvestment Act Hoping to restart the weak economy, President Obama signed this $787 billion economic stimulus bill in February 2009. The bill included cash distributions to states, funds for food stamps, unemployment benefits, construction projects to renew the nation's infrastructure, funds for renewable-energy systems, and tax reductions.

American System Economic plan championed by Henry Clay of Kentucky that called for federal tariffs on imports, a strong national bank, and federally-financed internal improvements—roads, bridges, canals—all intended to strengthen the national economy and end American dependence on Great Britain.

American Tobacco Company Business founded in 1890 by North Carolina's James Buchanan Duke, who combined the major tobacco manufacturers of the time, ultimately controlling 90 percent of the country's cigarette production.

Anaconda Plan Union's primary war strategy calling for a naval blockade of major southern seaports and then dividing the Confederacy by gaining control of the Tennessee, Cumberland, and Mississippi Rivers.

Antietam, Battle of (1862) Turning-point battle near Sharpsburg, Maryland, leaving over 20,000 soldiers dead or wounded, in which Union forces halted a Confederate invasion of the North.

anti-Federalists Opponents of the Constitution as an infringement on individual and states' rights, whose criticism led to the addition of a Bill of Rights to the document. Many anti-Federalists later joined Thomas Jefferson's Democratic-Republican party.

Anti-Masonic party This party grew out of popular hostility toward the Masonic fraternal order and entered the presidential election of 1832 as a third party. It was the first party to run as a third party in a presidential election, as well as the first to hold a nomination convention and announce a party platform.

Appomattox Court House Virginia village where Confederate general Robert E. Lee surrendered to Union general Ulysses S. Grant on April 9, 1865.

Arab Awakening A wave of spontaneous democratic uprisings that spread throughout the Arab world beginning in 2011, in which long-oppressed peoples demanded basic liberties from generations-old authoritarian regimes.

Armory show A divisive and sensational art exhibition in 1913 which introduced European-inspired modernism to American audiences.

Benedict Arnold (1741–1801) A traitorous American commander who planned to sell out the American garrison at West Point to the British, but his plot was discovered before it could be executed and he joined the British army.

Articles of Confederation The first form of government for the United States, ratified by the original thirteen states in 1781; weak in central authority, it was replaced by the U.S. Constitution in 1789.

Atlanta Compromise (1895) A speech by Booker T. Washington that called for the black community to strive for economic prosperity before attempting political and social equality.

Atlantic Charter (1941) Joint statement crafted by Franklin D. Roosevelt and British prime minister Winston Churchill that listed the war goals of the Allied Powers.

Crispus Attucks (1723–1770) During the Boston Massacre, he was supposedly at the head of the crowd of hecklers who baited the British troops. He was killed when the British troops fired on the crowd.

Stephen F. Austin (1793–1836) He established the first colony of Americans in Texas, which eventually attracted 2,000 people.

"Axis" alliance Military alliance formed in 1937 by the three major fascist powers: Germany, Italy, and Japan.

Aztec Empire Mesoamerican people who were conquered by the Spanish under Hernando Cortés, 1519–1528.

baby boom Markedly high birth rate in the years following World War II, leading to the biggest demographic "bubble" in U.S. history.

Bacon's Rebellion Unsuccessful 1676 revolt led by planter Nathaniel Bacon against Virginia governor William Berkeley's administration, which, Bacon charged, had failed to protect settlers from Indian raids.

Bank of the United States (1791) National bank responsible for holding and transferring federal government funds, making business loans, and issuing a national currency.

Bank War Political struggle in the early 1830s between President Jackson and financier Nicholas Biddle over the renewing of the Second Bank's charter.

Barbary pirates North Africans who waged war (1801–1805) on the United States after President Thomas Jefferson refused to pay tribute (a bribe) to protect American ships.

Bay of Pigs Failed CIA operation that, in April 1961, deployed a band of Cuban rebels to overthrow Fidel Castro's Communist regime.

Bear Flag Republic On June 14, 1846, a group of Americans in California captured Sonoma from the Mexican army and declared it the Republic of California, whose flag featured a grizzly bear. In July, the commodore of the U.S. Pacific Fleet landed troops on California's shores and declared it part of the United States.

Beats Group of bohemian, downtown New York writers, artists, and musicians who flouted convention in favor of liberated forms of self-expression.

Berlin airlift (1948) Effort by the United States and Great Britain to deliver massive amounts of food and supplies flown in to West Berlin in response to the Soviet land blockade of the city.

Berlin Wall Twenty-seven-mile-long concrete wall constructed in 1961 by East German authorities to stop the flow of East Germans fleeing to West Berlin.

Bessemer converter Apparatus which blasts air through molten iron to produce steel in very large quantities.

Nicholas Biddle (1786–1844) He was the president of the second Bank of the United States. In response to President Andrew Jackson's attacks on the bank, Biddle curtailed the bank's loans and exchanged its paper currency for gold and silver. In response, state banks began printing paper without restraint and lent it to speculators, causing a binge in speculating and an enormous increase in debt.

Bill of Rights First ten amendments to the U.S. Constitution, adopted in 1791 to guarantee individual rights and to help secure ratification of the Constitution by the states.

Osama bin Laden (1957–2011) The Saudi-born leader of al Qaeda, whose members attacked America on September 11, 2001. Years before the attack, he had declared *jihad* (holy war) on the United States, Israel, and the Saudi monarchy. In Afghanistan, the Taliban leaders gave bin Laden a safe haven in exchange for aid in fighting the Northern Alliance, who were rebels opposed to the Taliban. Following the Taliban's refusal to turn over bin Laden to the United States, America and a multinational coalition invaded Afghanistan and overthrew the Taliban. In May 2011, bin Laden was shot and killed by American special forces during a covert operation in Pakistan.

birth rate Proportion of births per 1,000 of the total population.

black codes Laws passed in southern states to restrict the rights of former slaves; to combat the codes, Congress passed the Civil Rights Act of 1866 and the Fourteenth Amendment and set up military governments in southern states that refused to ratify the amendment.

black power movement Militant form of civil rights protest focused on urban communities in the North and led by Malcolm X that grew as a response to impatience with the nonviolent tactics of Martin Luther King Jr.

James Gillepsie Blaine (1830–1893) As a Republican congressman from Maine, he developed close ties with business leaders, which contributed to him losing the presidential election of 1884. He later opposed President Cleveland's efforts to reduce tariffs, which became a significant issue in the 1888 presidential election. Blaine served as secretary of state under President Benjamin Harrison.

Bleeding Kansas (1856) A series of violent conflicts in the Kansas territory between anti-slavery and pro-slavery factions over the status of slavery.

blitzkrieg (1940) The German "lightning war" strategy characterized by swift, well-organized attacks using infantry, tanks, and warplanes.

Bolsheviks Under the leadership of Vladimir Lenin, this Marxist party led the November 1917 revolution against the newly formed provisional government in Russia. After seizing control, the Bolsheviks negotiated a peace treaty with Germany, the Treaty of Brest-Litovsk, and ended their participation in World War I.

Bonus Expeditionary Force (1932) Protest march on Washington, D.C., by thousands of World War I veterans and their families, calling for immediate payment of their service bonuses certificates; violence ensued when President Herbert Hoover ordered their tent villages cleared.

boomtown Town, often in the West, that developed rapidly due to the sudden influx of wealth and work opportunities; often male-dominated with a substantial immigrant population.

Daniel Boone (1734–1820) He found and expanded a trail into Kentucky, which pioneers used to reach and settle the area.

John Wilkes Booth (1838?–1865) He assassinated President Abraham Lincoln at the Ford's Theater on April 14, 1865. He was pursued to Virginia and killed.

Boston Massacre Violent confrontation between British soldiers and a Boston mob on March 5, 1770, in which five colonists were killed.

Boston Tea Party Demonstration against the Tea Act of 1773 in which the Sons of Liberty, dressed as Indians, dumped hundreds of chests of British-owned tea into Boston Harbor.

bracero program System created in 1942 that permitted seasonal farm workers from Mexico to work in the United States on year-long contracts.

Joseph Brant (1742?–1807) He was the Mohawk leader who led the Iroquois against the Americans in the Revolutionary War.

brinkmanship Secretary of State John Foster Dulles believed that communism could be contained by bringing America to the brink of war with an aggressive communist nation. He believed that the aggressor would back down when confronted with the prospect of receiving a mass retaliation from a country with nuclear weapons.

John Brown (1800–1859) In response to a pro-slavery mob's sacking of a free-state town of Lawrence, Kansas, Brown went to the pro-slavery settlement of Pottawatomie, Kansas, which led to a guerrilla war in the Kansas territory. In 1859, he attempted to raid the federal arsenal at Harpers Ferry, hoping to use the stolen weapons to arm slaves, but he was captured and executed.

Brown v. Board of Education **(1954)** Landmark Supreme Court case that struck down racial segregation in public schools and declared "separate-but-equal" unconstitutional.

William Jennings Bryan (1860–1925) He delivered the pro-silver "cross of gold" speech at the 1896 Democratic Convention and won his party's nomination for president. Disappointed pro-gold Democrats chose to walk out of the convention and nominate their own candidate, which split the Democratic party and cost them the White House. Bryan's loss also crippled the Populist movement that had endorsed him.

"Bull Moose" Progressive party *See* Progressive party

Bull Run, Battles of (First and Second Manassas) First land engagement of the Civil War took place on July 21, 1861, at Manassas Junction, Virginia, at which surprised Union troops quickly retreated; one year later, on August 29–30, Confederates captured the federal supply depot and forced Union troops back to Washington.

Martin Van Buren (1782–1862) During President Jackson's first term, he served as secretary of state and minister to London. In 1836, Van Buren was elected president, and he inherited a financial crisis. He believed that the government should not continue to keep its deposits in state banks and set up an independent Treasury, which was approved by Congress after several years of political maneuvering.

General John Burgoyne (1722–1792) He was the commander of Britain's northern forces during the Revolutionary War. He and most of his troops surrendered to the Americans at the Battle of Saratoga.

burial mounds A funeral tradition, practiced in the Mississippi and Ohio Valleys by the Adena-Hopewell cultures, of erecting massive mounds of earth over graves, often in the designs of serpents and other animals.

burned-over district Area of western New York strongly influenced by the revivalist fervor of the Second Great Awakening. Disciples of Christ and Mormons are among the many sects that trace their roots to the phenomenon.

Aaron Burr (1756–1836) Even though he was Thomas Jefferson's vice president, he lost favor with Jefferson's supporters who were Republicans. He sought to work with the Federalists and run as their candidate for the governor of New York. Alexander Hamilton opposed Burr's candidacy and his stinging remarks on the subject led to Burr challenging him to duel in which Hamilton was killed.

George H. W. Bush (1924–) He had served as vice president during the Reagan administration and then won the presidential election of 1988. His presidency was marked by raised taxes in the face of the federal deficit, the creation of the Office of National Drug Control Policy, and military activity abroad, including the invasion of Panama and Operation Desert Storm in Kuwait. He lost the 1992 presidential election to Bill Clinton.

George W. Bush (1946–) In the 2000 presidential election, Texas governor George W. Bush won as the Republican nominee against Democratic nominee Vice President Al Gore. After the September 11 terrorist attacks, he launched his "war on terrorism." President Bush adopted the Bush Doctrine, and United States invaded Afghanistan and Iraq with unclear outcomes, leaving the countries divided. In September 2008, the nation's economy nosedived as a credit crunch spiraled into a global economic meltdown. Bush signed into law the bank bailout fund called Troubled Asset Relief Program (TARP), but the economy did not improve.

***Bush v. Gore* (2000)** The close 2000 presidential election came down to Florida's decisive twenty-five electoral votes. The final tally in Florida gave Bush a slight lead, but it was so small that a recount was required by state law. While the votes were being recounted, a legal battle was being waged to stop the recount. Finally, the case, *Bush v. Gore*, was present to the Supreme Court who ruled 5–4 to stop the recount and Bush was declared the winner.

Bush Doctrine National security policy launched in 2002 by which the Bush administration claimed the right to launch preemptive military attacks against perceived enemies, particularly outlaw nations or terrorist organizations believed to possess weapons of mass destruction.

buying (stock) on margin The investment practice of making a small down payment (the "margin") on a stock and borrowing the rest of the money needed for the purchase from a broker who held the stock as security against a down market. If the stock's value declined and the buyer failed to meet a margin call for more funds, the broker could sell the stock to cover his loan.

Cahokia The largest chiefdom and city of the Mississippian Indian culture located in present-day Illinois, and the site of a sophisticated farming settlement that supported up to 15,000 inhabitants.

John C. Calhoun (1782–1850) He served in both the House of Representatives and the Senate for South Carolina before becoming secretary of war under President Monroe and then John Quincy Adams's vice president. Though he started his political career as an advocate of a strong national government, he eventually believed that states' rights, limited central government, and the power of nullification were necessary to preserve the Union.

California gold rush (1849) A massive migration of gold hunters, mostly men, who transformed the economy of California after gold was discovered in the foothills of the Sierra Nevada mountains in the Sacramento River Valley in northern California.

Camp David Accords Peace agreement in 1978 between Prime Minister Menachem Begin of Israel and President Anwar Sadat of Egypt, the first Arab head of state to officially recognize the state of Israel.

"Scarface" Al Capone (1899–1947) He was the most successful gangster of the Prohibition era whose Chicago-based criminal empire included bootlegging, prostitution, and gambling.

Andrew Carnegie (1835–1919) He was a steel magnate who believed that the general public benefited from big business even if these companies employed harsh business practices. This philosophy became deeply ingrained in the conventional wisdom of some Americans. After retiring, he devoted himself to philanthropy in hopes of promoting social welfare and world peace.

Carnegie Steel Company Corporation under the leadership of Andrew Carnegie that came to dominate the American steel industry.

Carolina colonies English proprietary colonies comprised of North and South Carolina, whose semitropical climate made them profitable centers of rice, timber, and tar production.

carpetbaggers Northern emigrants who participated in the Republican governments of the reconstructed South.

Jimmy Carter (1924–) Elected president in 1976, Jimmy Carter was an outsider to Washington. He created the departments of Energy and Education and signed into law several environmental initiatives. In 1978, he successfully brokered a peace agreement between Israel and Egypt called the Camp David Accords. However, his unwillingness to make deals with legislators caused other bills to be either gutted or stalled in Congress. His administration was plagued with a series of crises: a recession and increased inflation, a fuel shortage, the Soviet invasion of Afghanistan, and the overthrow of the Shah of Iran, leading to the Iran Hostage Crisis Carter struggled to get the hostages released and was unable to do so until after he lost the 1980 election to

Ronald Reagan. He was awarded the Nobel Peace Prize in 2002 for his efforts to further peace and democratic elections around the world.

Jacques Cartier (1491–1557) He led the first French effort to colonize North America and explored the Gulf of St. Lawrence and reached as far as present day Montreal on the St. Lawrence River.

Fidel Castro (1926–) In 1959, his Communist regime came to power in Cuba after two years of guerrilla warfare against the dictator Fulgenico Batista. He enacted land redistribution programs and nationalized all foreign-owned property. The latter action as well as his political trials and summary executions damaged relations between Cuba and America. Castro was turned down when he asked for loans from the United States. However, he did receive aid from the Soviet Union.

Carrie Chapman Catt (1859–1947) She was a leader of a new generation of activists in the women's suffrage movement who carried on the work started by Elizabeth Cady Stanton and Susan B. Anthony.

Central Intelligence Agency (CIA) Intelligence-gathering government agency founded in 1947; under President Eisenhower's orders, secretly undermined elected governments deemed susceptible to communism.

Central Powers One of the two sides during the First World War, including Germany, Austria-Hungary, the Ottoman Empire (Turkey), and Bulgaria.

Cesar Chavez (1927–1993) He founded the United Farm Workers (UFW) in 1962 and worked to organize migrant farm workers. In 1965, the UFW joined Filipino farm workers striking against corporate grape farmers in California's San Joaquin Valley. In 1970, the strike and a consumer boycott on grapes compelled the farmers to formally recognize the UFW. As the result of Chavez's efforts, wages and working conditions improved for migrant workers. In 1975, the California state legislature passed a bill that required growers to bargain collectively with representatives of the farm workers.

child labor The practice of sending children to work in mines, mills, and factories, often in unsafe conditions; widespread among poor families in the late nineteenth century.

Chinese Exclusion Act (1882) Federal law that barred Chinese laborers from immigrating to America.

Church of Jesus Christ of Latter-day Saints Founded in 1830 by Joseph Smith, the sect was a product of the intense revivalism of the burned-over district of New York; Smith's successor Brigham Young led 15,000 followers to Utah in 1847 to escape persecution.

Winston Churchill (1874–1965) The British prime minister who led the country during the Second World War. Along with Roosevelt and Stalin, he helped shape the post-war world at the Yalta Conference. He also coined the term "iron curtain," which he used in his famous "The Sinews of Peace" speech.

citizen-soldiers Part-time nonprofessional soldiers, mostly poor farmers or recent immigrants who had been indentured servants, who played an important role in the Revolutionary War.

Civil Rights Act of 1957 First federal civil rights law since Reconstruction; established the Civil Rights Commission and the Civil Rights Division of the Department of Justice.

Civil Rights Act of 1964 Legislation that outlawed discrimination in public accommodations and employment, passed at the urging of President Lyndon B. Johnson.

civil service reform An extended effort led by political reformers to end the patronage system; led to the Pendleton Act (1883), which called for government positions to be awarded based on merit rather than party loyalty.

Henry Clay (1777–1852) In the first half of the nineteenth century, he was the foremost spokesman for the American system. As Speaker of the House in the 1820s, he promoted economic nationalism, "market revolution," and the rapid development of western states and territories. A broker of compromise, he formulated the "second" Missouri Compromise and the Compromise of 1850. In 1824, Clay supported John Quincy Adams, who won the presidency and appointed Clay to secretary of state. Andrew Jackson claimed that Clay had entered into a "corrupt bargain" with Adams for his own selfish gains.

Clayton Anti-Trust Act (1914) Legislation that served to enhance the Sherman Anti-Trust Act (1890) by clarifying what constituted "monopolistic" activities and declaring that labor unions were not to be viewed as "monopolies in restraint of trade."

Bill Clinton (1946–) The governor of Arkansas won the 1992 presidential election against President George H. W. Bush. In his first term, he pushed through Congress a tax increase, an economic stimulus package, the adoption of the North America Free Trade Agreement, welfare reform, a raise in the minimum wage, and improved public access to health insurance. His administration also negotiated the Oslo Accord and the Dayton Accords. After his reelection in 1996, he was involved in two high-profile scandals: his investment in the fraudulent Whitewater Development Corporation (but no evidence was found of him being involved in any wrongdoing) and his sexual affair with a White House intern. His attempt to cover up the affair led to a vote in Congress on whether or not to begin an impeachment inquiry. The House of Representatives voted to impeach Clinton, but the Senate found him not guilty.

Hillary Rodham Clinton (1947–) In the 2008 presidential election, Senator Hillary Clinton, the spouse of former President Bill Clinton, initially was the front-runner for the Democratic nomination, which made her the first woman with a serious chance to win the presidency. However, Senator Barack Obama's Internet-based and grassroots-orientated campaign garnered him enough delegates to win the nomination. After Obama became president, she was appointed secretary of state. Clinton stepped down from her Cabinet position in 2013 and, in 2015, announced her second presidential bid.

clipper ships Tall, slender, mid-nineteenth-century sailing ships that were favored over older merchant ships for their speed, but ultimately gave way to steamships because they lacked cargo space.

Coercive Acts Four parliamentary measures of 1774 that required the colonies to pay for the Boston Tea Party's damages, imposed a military government, disallowed colonial trials of British soldiers, and forced the quartering of troops in private homes.

Columbian Exchange The transfer of biological and social elements, such as plants, animals, people, diseases, and cultural practices, among Europe, the Americas, and Africa in the wake of Christopher Columbus's voyages to the "New World."

Christopher Columbus (1451–1506) The Italian sailor who persuaded King Ferdinand and Queen Isabella of Spain to fund his expedition across the Atlantic to discover a new trade route to Asia. Instead of arriving at China or Japan, he reached the Bahamas in 1492.

Committee of Correspondence Group organized by Samuel Adams in retaliation for the *Gaspée* incident to address American grievances, assert American rights, and form a network of rebellion.

Committee to Re-elect the President (CREEP) During Nixon's presidency, his administration engaged in a number of immoral acts, such as attempting to steal information and falsely accusing political appointments of sexual improprieties. These acts were funded by money illegally collected through CREEP.

Common Sense Popular pamphlet written by Thomas Paine attacking British principles of hereditary rule and monarchical government, and advocating a declaration of American independence.

Compromise of 1850 A package of five bills presented to the Congress by Henry Clay intended to avoid secession or civil war by reducing tensions between North and South over the status of slavery.

Compromise of 1877 Deal made by a special congressional commission on March 2, 1877, to resolve the disputed presidential election of 1876; Republican Rutherford B. Hayes, who had lost the popular vote, was declared the winner in exchange for the withdrawal of federal troops from the South, marking the end of Reconstruction.

Comstock Lode Mine in eastern Nevada acquired by Canadian fur trapper Henry Comstock that between 1860 and 1880 yielded almost $1 billion worth of gold and silver.

Conestoga wagons These large horse-drawn wagons were used to carry people or heavy freight long distances, including from the East to the western frontier settlements.

Congressional Reconstruction A more radical phase of Reconstruction, beginning in 1867, in which Congress, over President Johnson's objections, passed the Military Reconstruction Act that abolished the new Southern state governments in favor of federal military control. In addition, the Act required each state to draft a new constitution that guaranteed voting rights to all adult males regardless of race or economic status.

conquistadores Spanish term for "conquerors," applied to Spanish and Portuguese soldiers who conquered lands held by indigenous peoples in central and southern America as well as the current states of Texas, New Mexico, Arizona, and California.

consumer culture A society in which mass production and consumption of nationally advertised products comes to dictate much of social life and status.

containment U.S. cold war strategy that sought to prevent global Soviet expansion and influence through political, economic, and, if necessary, military pressure as a means of combating the spread of communism.

Continental army Army authorized by the Continental Congress (1775–1784) to fight the British; commanded by General George Washington.

contrabands Slaves who sought refuge in Union military camps or who lived in areas of the Confederacy under Union control.

Contract with America A list of conservatives' promises in response to the supposed liberalism of the Clinton administration, that was drafted by Speaker of the House Newt Gingrich and other congressional Republicans as the GOP platform for the 1994 midterm elections. More a campaign tactic than a practical program, few of its proposed items ever became law.

Contras The Reagan administration ordered the CIA to train and supply guerrilla bands of anti-Communist Nicaraguans called Contras. They were fighting the Sandinista government that had recently come to power in Nicaragua. The State Department believed that the Sandinista government was supplying the leftist Salvadoran rebels with Soviet and Cuban arms. A cease-fire agreement between the Contras and Sandinistas was signed in 1988.

Calvin "Silent Cal" Coolidge (1872–1933) After President Harding's death, his vice president, Calvin Coolidge, assumed the presidency. Coolidge believed that the nation's welfare was tied to the success of big business, and he worked to end government regulation of business and industry as well as reduce taxes. In particular, he focused on the nation's industrial development.

Copperhead Democrats Democrats in northern states who opposed the Civil War and argued for an immediate peace settlement with the Confederates; Republicans labeled them "Copperheads," likening them to venomous snakes.

General Charles Cornwallis (1738–1805) He was in charge of British troops in the South during the Revolutionary War. His surrendering to George Washington at the Battle of Yorktown ended the Revolutionary War.

Corps of Discovery Meriwether Lewis and William Clark led this group of men on an expedition of the newly purchased Louisiana territory, which took them from Missouri to Oregon. As they traveled, they kept detailed journals and drew maps of the previously unexplored territory. Their reports attracted traders and trappers to the region and gave the United States a claim to the Oregon country by right of discovery and exploration.

"corrupt bargain" Scandal in which presidential candidate and Speaker of the House Henry Clay secured John Quincy Adams's victory over Andrew Jackson in the 1824 election, supposedly in exchange for Clay being named secretary of state.

Hernán Cortés (1485–1547) The Spanish conquistador who conquered the Aztec Empire and set the precedent for other plundering conquistadores.

cotton White fibers harvested from cotton plants, spun into yarn, and woven into textiles that made comfortable, easy-to-clean products, especially clothing; the most valuable cash crop driving the economy in the United States and Great Britain during the nineteenth century.

cotton gin Hand-operated machine invented by Eli Whitney in the late eighteenth century that quickly removed seeds from cotton bolls, enabling the mass production of cotton in nineteenth-century America.

Cotton Kingdom Cotton-producing region, relying predominantly on slave labor, that spanned from North Carolina west to Louisiana and reached as far north as southern Illinois.

counterculture "Hippie" youth culture of the 1960s, which rejected the values of the dominant culture in favor of illicit drugs, communes, free sex, and rock music.

"Court-packing" scheme President Franklin D. Roosevelt's failed 1937 attempt to increase the number of U.S. Supreme Court justices from nine to fifteen in order to save his Second New Deal programs from constitutional challenges.

crop-lien system Credit system used by sharecroppers and share tenants who pledged a portion ("share") of their future crop to local merchants or land owners in exchange for farming supplies and food.

"cross of gold" speech In the 1896 election, the Democratic Party split over the issue of whether to use gold or silver to back American currency. Significant to this division was the pro-silver "cross of gold" speech that William Jennings Bryan delivered at the Democratic convention, which was so well received that Bryan won the nomination to be their presidential candidate. Disappointed pro-gold Democrats chose to walk out of the convention and nominate their own candidate.

Cuban missile crisis Thirteen-day U.S.-Soviet standoff in October 1962, sparked by the discovery of Soviet missile sites in Cuba; the crisis was the closest the world has come to nuclear war since 1945.

cult of domesticity A pervasive nineteenth-century ideology that urged women to celebrate their role as manager of the household and nurturer of the children.

George A. Custer (1839–1876) He was a reckless and glory-seeking lieutenant colonel of the U.S. Army who fought the Sioux Indians in the Great Sioux War. In 1876, he and his detachment of soldiers were entirely wiped out in the Battle of Little Bighorn.

Dartmouth College v. Woodward **(1819)** Supreme Court ruling that enlarged the definition of *contract* to put corporations beyond the reach of the states that chartered them.

Daughters of Liberty Colonial women who protested the British government's tax policies by boycotting British products, such as clothing, and who wove their own fabric, or "homespun."

Dawes Severalty Act (1887) Federal legislation that divided ancestral Native American lands among the heads of each Indian family in an attempt to "Americanize" Indians by forcing them to become farmers working individual plots of land.

Jefferson Davis (1808–1889) He was the president of the Confederacy during the Civil War. When the Confederacy's defeat seemed inevitable in early 1865, he refused to surrender. Union forces captured him in May of that year.

death rate Proportion of deaths per 1,000 of the total population; also called *mortality rate*.

D-day June 6, 1944, when an Allied amphibious assault landed on the Normandy coast and established a foothold in Europe from which Hitler's defenses could not recover.

Eugene V. Debs (1855–1926) He founded the American Railway Union, which he organized against the Pullman Palace Car Company during the Pullman strike. Later he organized the Social Democratic party, which eventually became the Socialist Party of America. In the 1912 presidential election, he ran as the Socialist party's candidate and received more than 900,000 votes.

Declaration of Independence Formal statement, principally drafted by Thomas Jefferson and adopted by the Second Continental Congress on July 4, 1776, that officially announced the thirteen colonies' break with Great Britain.

Declaration of Rights and Sentiments Document based on the Declaration of Independence that called for gender equality, written primarily by Elizabeth Cady Stanton and signed by Seneca Falls Convention delegates in 1848.

Declaratory Act Following the repeal of the Stamp Act in 1766, Parliament passed this act that asserted Parliament's full power to make laws binding the colonies "in all cases whatsoever."

Deists Those who applied Enlightenment thought to religion, emphasizing reason, morality, and natural law rather than scriptural authority or an ever-present God intervening in human life.

détente Period of improving relations between the United States and Communist nations, particularly China and the Soviet Union, during the Nixon administration.

George Dewey (1837–1917) On April 30, 1898, Commodore George Dewey's small U.S. naval squadron defeated the Spanish warships in Manila Bay in the Philippines. This quick victory aroused expansionist fever in the United States.

John Dewey (1859–1952) He is an important philosopher of pragmatism. However, he preferred to use the term *instrumentalism*, because he saw ideas as instruments of action.

Dien Bien Phu Cluster of Vietnamese villages and site of a major Vietnamese victory over the French in the First Indochina War.

Ngo Dinh Diem (1901–1963) Following the Geneva Accords, the French, with the support of America, forced the Vietnamese emperor to accept Dinh Diem as the new premier of South Vietnam. President Eisenhower sent advisers to train Diem's police and army. In return, the United States expected Diem to enact democratic reforms and distribute land to the peasants. Instead, he suppressed his political opponents, did little or no land distribution, and let corruption grow. In 1956, he refused to participate in elections to reunify Vietnam. Eventually, he ousted the emperor and declared himself president.

Distribution Act (1836) Law requiring the distribution of the federal budget surplus to the states, creating chaos among state banks that had become dependent on such federal funds.

Dorothea Lynde Dix (1802–1887) She was an important figure in increasing the public's awareness of the plight of the mentally ill. After a two-year investigation of the treatment of the mentally ill in Massachusetts, she presented her findings and won the support of leading reformers. She eventually convinced twenty states to reform their treatment of the mentally ill.

Dixiecrats Breakaway faction of southern Democrats who defected from the national Democratic party in 1948 to protest the party's increased support for civil rights and to nominate their own segregationist candidates for elective office.

"dollar diplomacy" Practice advocated by President Theodore Roosevelt in which the U.S. government fostered American investments in less-developed nations and then used U.S. military force to protect those investments.

Donner party Forty-seven surviving members of a group of migrants to California were forced to resort to cannibalism to survive a brutal winter trapped in the Sierra Nevadas, 1846–1847; highest death toll of any group traveling the Overland Trail.

dot-coms In the late 1990s, the stock market soared to new heights and defied the predictions of experts that the economy could not sustain such a performance. Much of the economic success was based on dot-com enterprises, which were firms specializing in computers, software, telecommunications, and the Internet. However, many of the companies' stock market values were driven higher and higher by speculation instead of financial success. Eventually the stock market bubble burst.

Stephen A. Douglas (1812–1861) As a senator from Illinois, he authored the Kansas-Nebraska Act. Running for senatorial reelection in 1858, he engaged Abraham Lincoln in a series of public debates about slavery in the territories. Even though Douglas won the election, the debates gave Lincoln a national reputation.

Frederick Douglass (1818–1895) He escaped from slavery and become an eloquent speaker and writer against slavery. In 1845, he published his autobiography entitled *Narrative of the Life of Frederick Douglass* and two years later he founded an abolitionist newspaper for blacks called the *North Star*.

***Dred Scott v. Sandford* (1857)** U.S. Supreme Court ruling that slaves were not U.S. citizens and therefore could not sue for their freedom and that Congress could not prohibit slavery in the western territories.

W. E. B. Du Bois (1868–1963) He criticized Booker T. Washington's views on civil rights as being accommodationist. He advocated "ceaseless agitation" for civil rights and the immediate end to segregation and an enforcement of laws to protect civil rights and equality. He promoted an education for African Americans that would nurture bold leaders who were willing to challenge discrimination in politics.

John Foster Dulles (1888–1959) As President Eisenhower's secretary of state, he institutionalized the policy of containment and introduced the strategy of deterrence. He believed in using brinkmanship to halt the spread of communism. He attempted to employ it in Indochina, which led to the United States' involvement in Vietnam.

Dust Bowl Vast area of the Midwest where windstorms blew away millions of tons of topsoil from parched farmland after a long drought in the 1930s, causing great social distress and a massive migration of farm families.

Eastern Woodlands peoples Various Native American peoples, particularly the Algonquian, Iroquoian, and Muskogean regional groups, who once dominated the Atlantic seaboard from Maine to Louisiana.

Peggy Eaton (1796–1879) The wife of John Eaton, President Jackson's secretary of war, was the daughter of a tavern owner with an unsavory past. Supposedly her first husband had committed suicide after learning that she was having an affair with John Eaton. The wives of members of Jackson's cabinet snubbed her because of her lowly origins and past, resulting in a scandal known as the Eaton Affair.

Economic Opportunity Act (1964) Key legislation in President Johnson's "War on Poverty" which created the Office of Economic Opportunity and programs like Head Start and work-study.

Jonathan Edwards (1703–1758) New England Congregationalist minister, who began a religious revival in his Northampton church and was an important figure in the Great Awakening.

General Dwight D. Eisenhower (1890–1969) During the Second World War, he commanded the Allied Forces landing in Africa and was the supreme Allied commander as well as planner for Operation Overlord. In 1952, he was elected president on his popularity as a war hero and his promises to clean up Washington. His administration sought to cut the nation's domestic programs and budget, ended the fighting in Korea, and institutionalized the policies of containment and deterrence. He established the Eisenhower doctrine, which promised to aid any nation against aggression by a communist nation.

election of 1800 Presidential election between Thomas Jefferson and John Adams; resulted in the first Democratic-Republican victory after the Federalist administrations of George Washington and John Adams.

election of 1828 Highly contentious presidential election between Andrew Jackson and incumbent President John Quincy Adams; Jackson effectively campaigned as a war hero and champion of the "common man" to become the seventh president of the United States.

election of 1864 Abraham Lincoln's successful reelection campaign, capitalizing on Union military successes in Georgia, to defeat Democratic opponent, former general George B. McClellan, who ran on a peace platform.

election of 1912 The presidential election of 1912 featured four candidates: Wilson, Taft, Roosevelt, and Debs. Each candidate believed in the basic assumptions of progressive politics, but each had a different view on how progressive ideals should be implemented through policy. In the end, Taft and Roosevelt split the Republican party votes and Wilson emerged as the winner.

Queen Elizabeth I of England (1533–1603) The protestant daughter of Henry VIII, she was Queen of England from 1558–1603 and played a major role in the Protestant

Reformation. During her long reign, the doctrines and services of the Church of England were defined and the Spanish Armada was defeated.

Ellis Island Reception center in New York Harbor through which most European immigrants to America were processed from 1892 to 1954.

Emancipation Proclamation (1863) Military order issued by President Abraham Lincoln that freed slaves in areas still controlled by the Confederacy.

Embargo Act (1807) A law promoted by President Thomas Jefferson prohibiting American ships from leaving for foreign ports, in order to safeguard them from British and French attacks. This ban on American exports proved disastrous to the U.S. economy.

Ralph Waldo Emerson (1803–1882) As a leader of the transcendentalist movement, he wrote poems, essays, and speeches that discussed the sacredness of nature, optimism, self-reliance, and the unlimited potential of the individual. He wanted to transcend the limitations of inherited conventions and rationalism to reach the inner recesses of the self.

encomienda A land-grant system under which Spanish army officers (*conquistadores*) were awarded large parcels of land taken from Native Americans.

Enlightenment A revolution in thought begun in Europe in the seventeenth century that emphasized reason and science over the authority and myths of traditional religion.

Environmental Protection Agency (EPA) Federal environmental agency created in 1970 by Nixon to appease the demands of congressional Democrats for a federal environmental watchdog agency.

Erie Canal Most important and profitable of the many barge canals built in the early nineteenth century. It spanned 364 miles across New York state from west to east, connecting the Great Lakes to the Hudson River, and conveying so much cargo that it made New York City the nation's largest port.

ethnic cleansing The systematic removal of an ethnic group from a territory through violence or intimidation in order to create a homogenous society; the term was popularized by the Yugoslav policy brutally targeting Albanian Muslims in Kosovo.

Exodusters African Americans who migrated west from the South in search of a haven from racism and poverty after the collapse of Radical Republican rule.

Fair Deal (1949) President Truman's proposals to build upon the New Deal with national health insurance, the repeal of the Taft-Hartley Labor Act, new civil rights legislation, and other initiatives; most were rejected by the Republican-controlled Congress.

"falling domino" theory Theory that if one country fell to communism, its neighboring countries would follow suit.

Farmers' Alliances Like the Granger Movement, these organizations sought to address the issues of small farming communities; however Alliances emphasized more political action and called for the creation of a third party to advocate their concerns.

fascism A radical form of totalitarian government that emerged in Italy and Germany in the 1920s in which a dictator uses propaganda and brute force to seize control of all aspects of national life.

Federal-Aid Highway Act (1956) Largest federal project in U.S. history that created a national network of interstate highways and was the largest federal project in history.

Federal Deposit Insurance Corporation (FDIC) (1933) Independent government agency, established to prevent bank panics, that guarantees the safety of deposits in citizens' savings accounts.

Federal Reserve Act (1913) Legislation passed by Congress to create a new national banking system in order to regulate the nation's currency supply and ensure the stability and integrity of member banks who made up the Federal Reserve System across the nation.

Federal Trade Commission (FTC) (1914) Independent agency created by the Wilson administration that replaced the Bureau of Corporations as an even more powerful tool to combat unfair trade practices and monopolies.

Federal Writers' Project During the Great Depression, this project provided writers, such as Ralph Ellison, Richard Wright, and Saul Bellow, with work, which gave them a chance to develop as artists and be employed.

federalism Concept of dividing governmental authority between the national government and the states.

The Federalist Papers Collection of eighty-five essays, published widely in newspapers in 1787 and 1788, written by Alexander Hamilton, James Madison, and John Jay in support of adopting the proposed U.S. Constitution.

Federalists Proponents of a centralized federal system and the ratification of the Constitution. Most Federalists were relatively young, educated men who supported a broad interpretation of the Constitution whenever national interest dictated such flexibility. Notable Federalists included Alexander Hamilton and John Jay.

Geraldine Ferraro (1935–) In the 1984 presidential election, Democratic nominee Walter Mondale chose her as his running mate. As a member of the U.S. House of Representatives from New York, she was the first woman to be a vice-presidential nominee for a major political party. However, she was placed on the defensive because of her husband's complicated business dealings.

field hands Slaves who toiled in the cotton or cane fields in organized work gangs.

Fifteenth Amendment (1870) This amendment forbids states to deny any person the right to vote on grounds of "race, color or pervious condition of servitude." Former Confederate states were required to ratify this amendment before they could be readmitted to the Union.

"final solution" The Nazi party's systematic murder of some 6 million Jews along with more than a million other people including, but not limited to, gypsies, homosexuals, and handicap individuals.

First New Deal (1933–1935) Franklin D. Roosevelt's ambitious first-term cluster of economic and social programs designed to combat the Great Depression with a "new deal for the

American people;" the phrase became a catchword for his ambitious plan of economic programs.

First Red Scare (1919–1920) Outbreak of anti-Communist hysteria that included the arrest without warrants of thousands of suspected radicals, most of whom (mostly Russian immigrants) were deported.

flappers Young women of the 1920s whose rebellion against prewar standards of femininity included wearing shorter dresses, bobbing their hair, dancing to jazz music, driving cars, smoking cigarettes, and indulging in illegal drinking and gambling.

Food Administration After America's entry into World War I, the economy of the home front needed to be reorganized to provide the most efficient means of conducting the war. The Food Administration was a part of this effort. Under the leadership of Herbert Hoover, the organization sought to increase agricultural production while reducing civilian consumption of foodstuffs.

Force Bill (1833) Legislation, sparked by the nullification crisis in South Carolina, that authorized the president's use of the army to compel states to comply with federal law.

Gerald Ford (1913–2006) He was appointed to the vice presidency under President Nixon after the resignation of Spiro Agnew, and assumed the presidency after President Nixon's resignation. He resisted congressional pressure to both reduce taxes and increase federal spending, which sent the American economy into the deepest recession since the Great Depression. Ford retained Kissinger as his secretary of state and continued Nixon's foreign policy goals. He was heavily criticized following the collapse of South Vietnam.

Fort Laramie Treaty (1851) Restricted the Plains Indians from using the Overland Trail and permitted the building of government forts.

Fort Necessity After attacking a group of French soldiers, George Washington constructed and took shelter in this fort from vengeful French troops. Washington eventually surrendered to them after a day-long battle. This conflict was a significant event in igniting the French and Indian War.

Fort Sumter First battle of the Civil War, in which the federal fort in Charleston (South Carolina) Harbor was captured by the Confederates on April 14, 1861, after two days of shelling.

"forty-niners" Speculators who went to northern California following the discovery of gold in 1848; the first of several years of large-scale migration was 1849.

Fourteen Points (1918) President Woodrow Wilson's proposed plan for the peace agreement after the First World War that included the creation of a "league of nations" intended to keep the peace.

Fourteenth Amendment (1866) Guaranteed rights of citizenship to former slaves, in words similar to those of the Civil Rights Act of 1866.

Franciscan missions In 1769, Franciscan missionaries accompanied Spanish soldiers to California and over the next fifty years established a chain of missions from San Diego to San Francisco. At these missions, friars sought to convert Indians to Catholicism and make them members of the Spanish empire. The friars stripped the Indians of their native heritage and used soldiers to enforce their will.

Benjamin Franklin (1706–1790) A Boston-born American who epitomized the Enlightenment for many Americans and Europeans, Franklin's wide range of interests led him to become a publisher, inventor, and statesman. As the latter, he contributed to the writing of the Declaration of Independence, served as the minister to France during the Revolutionary War, and was a delegate to the Constitutional Convention.

Free-Soil party A political coalition created in 1848 that opposed the expansion of slavery into the new western territories.

Freedmen's Bureau Reconstruction agency established in 1865 to protect the legal rights of former slaves and to assist with their education, jobs, health care, and landowning.

Freedom Riders Activists who, beginning in 1961, traveled by bus through the South to test federal court rulings that banned segregation on buses and trains.

John C. Frémont, or "the Pathfinder" (1813–1890) He was an explorer and surveyor who helped inspire Americans living in California to rebel against the Mexican government and declare independence.

French and Indian War (Seven Years' War) The last—and most important—of four colonial wars fought between England and France for control of North America east of the Mississippi River.

French Revolution Revolutionary movement beginning in 1789 that overthrew the monarchy and transformed France into an unstable republic before Napoleon Bonaparte assumed power in 1799.

Sigmund Freud (1865–1939) He was the founder of psychoanalysis, which suggested that human behavior was motivated by unconscious and irrational forces. By the 1920s, his ideas were being discussed more openly in America.

frontier revivals Religious revival movement within the Second Great Awakening, that took place in frontier churches in western territories and states in the early nineteenth century.

Fugitive Slave Act (1850) Part of the Compromise of 1850, a provision that authorized federal officials to help capture and then return escaped slaves to their owners without trials.

fundamentalism Anti-modernist Protestant movement started in the early twentieth century that proclaimed the literal truth of the Bible; the name came from *The Fundamentals*, published by conservative leaders.

William Lloyd Garrison (1805–1879) In 1831, he started the anti-slavery newspaper *Liberator* and helped start the New England Anti-Slavery Society. Two years later, he assisted Arthur and Lewis Tappan in the founding of the American Anti-Slavery Society. He and his followers believed that America had been thoroughly corrupted and needed a wide range of reforms, embracing abolition, temperance, pacifism, and women's rights.

Marcus Garvey (1887–1940) He was the leading spokesman for Negro Nationalism, which exalted blackness, black cultural expression, and black exclusiveness. He called upon African Americans to liberate themselves from the surrounding white culture and create their own businesses, cultural centers, and newspapers. He was also the founder of the Universal Negro Improvement Association.

Citizen Genet (1763–1834) As the ambassador to the United States from the new French Republic, he engaged American privateers to attack British ships and conspired with frontiersmen and land speculators to organize an attack on Spanish Florida and Louisiana. His actions and the French radicals' excessive actions against their enemies in the new French Republic caused the French Revolution to lose support among Americans.

Geneva Accords In 1954, the Geneva Accords were signed, which ended French colonial rule in Indochina. The agreement created the independent nations of Laos and Cambodia and divided Vietnam along the 17th parallel until an election in 1956 would reunify the country.

Gettysburg, Battle of (1863) A monumental three-day battle in southern Pennsylvania, widely considered a turning point in the war, in which Union forces successfully countered a second Confederate invasion of the North.

Ghost Dance movement A spiritual and political movement among Native Americans whose followers performed a ceremonial "ghost dance" intended to connect the living with the dead and make the Indians bulletproof in battles intended to restore their homelands.

GI Bill of Rights (1944) Provided unemployment, education, and financial benefits for World War II veterans to ease their transition back to the civilian world.

***Gibbons v. Ogden* (1824)** Supreme Court case that gave the federal government the power to regulate interstate commerce.

Newt Gingrich (1943–) He led the Republican insurgency in Congress in the mid-1990s through mobilizing religious and social conservatives. Along with other Republican congressmen, he created the Contract with America, which was a ten-point anti–big government program. However, the program fizzled out after many of its bills were not passed by Congress.

Gilded Age (1860–1896) An era of dramatic industrial and urban growth characterized by widespread political corruption and loose government oversight over corporations.

The Gilded Age Mark Twain and Charles Dudley Warner's 1873 novel, the title of which became the popular name for the period from the end of the Civil War to the turn of the century.

glasnost Russian term for "openness"; applied to the loosening of censorship in the Soviet Union under Mikhail Gorbachev.

globalization An important, and controversial, transformation of the world economy whereby the Internet helped revolutionize global commerce by creating an international marketplace for goods and services. Led by the growing number of multinational companies and the Americanization of many foreign consumer cultures, with companies like McDonald's and Starbucks appearing in all of the major cities of the world.

Glorious Revolution Successful 1688 coup, instigated by a group of English aristocrats, which overthrew King James II and instated William of Orange and Mary, his English wife, to the British throne.

Barry Goldwater (1909–1998) He was a leader of the Republican right whose book, *The Conscience of a Conservative*, was highly influential to that segment of the party. He proposed eliminating the income tax and overhauling Social Security. In 1964, he ran as the Republican presidential candidate and lost to President Johnson. He campaigned against Johnson's war on poverty, the tradition of New Deal, the nuclear test ban and the Civil Rights Act of 1964. He advocated the wholesale bombing of North Vietnam.

Samuel Gompers (1850–1924) He served as the president of the American Federation of Labor from its inception until his death. He focused on achieving concrete economic gains such as higher wages, shorter hours, and better working conditions.

"good neighbor" policy Proclaimed by President Franklin D. Roosevelt in his first inaugural address in 1933, it sought improved diplomatic relations between the United States and its Latin American neighbors.

Mikhail Gorbachev (1931–) In the late 1980s, Soviet leader Mikhail Gorbachev attempted to reform the Soviet Union through his programs of *perestroika* and *glasnost* and pursued a renewal of détente with America, signing new arms-control agreements with President Reagan. Gorbachev allowed the velvet revolutions of Eastern Europe to occur without outside interference. Eventually the political, social, and economic upheaval he had unleashed would lead to the breakup of the Soviet Union.

Albert Gore Jr. (1948–) He served as a senator of Tennessee and then as President Clinton's vice president. In the 2000 presidential election, he was the Democratic candidate against Governor George W. Bush. The close election came down to Florida's electoral votes. While the votes were being recounted as required by state law, a legal battle was being waged to stop the recount. Finally, the case, *Bush v. Gore*, was presented to the Supreme Court who ruled 5–4 to stop the recount, and Bush was declared the winner.

Jay Gould (1836–1892) As one of the biggest railroad robber barons, he was infamous for buying rundown railroads, making cosmetic improvements, and then reselling them for a profit. He used corporate funds for personal investments and to bribe politicians and judges.

gradualism This strategy for ending slavery involved promoting the banning of slavery in the new western territories and encouraging the release of slaves from slavery. Supporters of this method believed that it would bring about the gradual end of slavery.

Granger Movement Began by offering social and educational activities for isolated farmers and their families and later started to promote "cooperatives" where farmers could join together to buy, store, and sell their crops to avoid the high fees charged by brokers and other middlemen.

Ulysses S. Grant (1822–1885) After distinguishing himself in the western theater of the Civil War, he was appointed general-in-chief of the Union army in 1864. Afterward, he defeated General Robert E. Lee through a policy of aggressive attrition. Lee surrendered to Grant on April 9, 1865 at the Appomattox Court House. His presidential tenure suffered from scandals and fiscal problems, including the debate on whether or not greenbacks, that is, paper money, should be removed from circulation.

Great Awakening Fervent religious revival movement that swept the thirteen colonies from the 1720s through the 1740s.

Great Compromise (Connecticut Compromise) Mediated the differences between the New Jersey and Virginia delegations to the Constitutional Convention by providing for a bicameral legislature, the upper house of which would have equal representation and the lower house of which would be apportioned by population.

Great Depression (1929–1941) Worst economic downturn in American history; it was spurred by the stock market crash in the fall of 1929 and lasted until the Second World War.

Great Migration Mass exodus of African Americans from the rural South to the Northeast and Midwest during and after the First World War.

Great Railroad Strike (1877) A series of demonstrations, some violent, held nationwide in support of striking railroad workers in Martinsburg, West Virginia, who refused to work due to wage cuts.

Great Recession Massive, prolonged economic downturn sparked by the collapse of the housing market and the financial institutions holding unpaid mortgages; it lasted from December 2007 to January 2009 and resulted in 9 million Americans losing their jobs.

Great Sioux War Conflict between Sioux and Cheyenne Indians and federal troops over lands in the Dakotas in the mid-1870s.

Great Society Term coined by President Lyndon B. Johnson in his 1965 State of the Union address, in which he proposed legislation to address problems of voting rights, poverty, diseases, education, immigration, and the environment.

Horace Greeley (1811–1872) In reaction to Radical Reconstruction and corruption in President Ulysses S. Grant's administration, a group of Republicans broke from the party to form the Liberal Republicans. In 1872, the Liberal Republicans chose as their presidential candidate Horace Greeley, who ran on a platform of favoring civil service reform and condemning the Republican's Reconstruction policy.

Greenback party Formed in 1876 in reaction to economic depression, the party favored issuance of unsecured paper money to help farmers repay debts; the movement for free coinage of silver took the place of the greenback movement by the 1880s.

greenbacks Paper money issued during the Civil War. After the war ended, a debate emerged on whether or not to remove the paper currency from circulation and revert back to hard-money currency (gold coins). Opponents of hard money feared that eliminating the greenbacks would shrink the money supply, which would lower crop prices and make it more difficult to repay long-term debts. President Ulysses S. Grant, as well as hard-money currency advocates, believed that gold coins were morally preferable to paper currency.

General Nathanael Greene (1742–1786) He was appointed by Congress to command the American army fighting in the South during the Revolutionary War. Using his patience and his skills of managing men, saving supplies, and avoiding needless risks, he waged a successful war of attrition against the British.

Sarah Grimké (1792–1873) and **Angelina Grimké (1805–1879)** These two sisters gave anti-slavery speeches to crowds of mixed gender that caused some people to condemn them for engaging in unfeminine activities. In 1840, William Lloyd Garrison convinced the Anti-Slavery Society to allow women equal participation in the organization.

Alexander Hamilton (1755–1804) His belief in a strong federal government led him to become a leader of the Federalists. As the first secretary of the Treasury, he laid the foundation for American capitalism through his creation of a federal budget, funded debt, a federal tax system, a national bank, a customs service, and a coast guard. His "Reports on Public Credit" and "Reports on Manufactures" outlined his vision for economic development and government finances. He died in a duel against Aaron Burr.

Alexander Hamilton's economic reforms Various measures designed to strengthen the nation's economy and generate federal revenue through the promotion of new industries, the adoption of new tax policies, the payment of war debts, and the establishment of a national bank.

Warren G. Harding (1865–1923) In the 1920 presidential election, he was the Republican nominee who promised Americans a "return to normalcy." Once in office, Harding's administration dismantled many of the social and economic components of progressivism and pursued a pro-business agenda. Harding appointed four pro-business Supreme Court Justices, cut taxes, increased tariffs, and promoted a lenient attitude toward regulation of corporations. However, he did speak out against racism and ended the exclusion of African Americans from federal positions.

Harlem Renaissance The nation's first self-conscious black literary and artistic movement; it was centered in New York City's Harlem district, which had a largely black population in the wake of the Great Migration from the South.

Hartford Convention A series of secret meetings in December 1814 and January 1815 at which New England Federalists protested American involvement in the War of 1812 and discussed several constitutional amendments, including limiting each president to one term, designed to weaken the dominant Republican Party.

Haymarket Riot (1886) Violent uprising in Haymarket Square, Chicago, where police clashed with labor demonstrators in the aftermath of a bombing.

headright A land-grant policy that promised fifty acres to any colonist who could afford passage to Virginia, as well as fifty more for any accompanying servants. The headright policy was eventually expanded to include any colonists—and was also adopted in other colonies.

Patrick Henry (1736–1799) He inspired the Virginia Resolves, which declared that Englishmen could only be taxed by their elected representatives. In March of 1775, he met with other colonial leaders to discuss the goals of the upcoming Continental Congress and famously declared "Give me liberty or give me death." During the ratification process of the U.S. Constitution, he became one of the leaders of the anti-federalists.

Hessians German mercenary soldiers who were paid by the royal government to fight alongside the British army.

Hiroshima Japanese port city that was the first target of the newly developed atomic bomb on August 6, 1945. Most of the city was destroyed.

Alger Hiss (1904–1996) During the second Red Scare, he served in several government departments and was accused of being a spy for the Soviet Union. He was convicted of lying about espionage. The case was politically damaging to the Truman administration because the president called the charges against Hiss a "red herring."

Adolf Hitler, or *"Führer" (1889–1945)* The leader of the Nazis who advocated a violent anti-Semitic, anti-Marxist, pan-German ideology. He started World War II in Europe and orchestrated the systematic murder of some 6 million Jews along with more than a million others.

HIV/AIDS Human immunodeficiency virus (HIV) transmitted via the bodily fluids of infected persons to cause acquired immunodeficiency syndrome (AIDS), an often-fatal disease of the immune system when it appeared in the 1980s.

holding company A corporation established to own and manage other companies' stock rather than to produce goods and services itself.

Holocaust Systematic racist attempt by the Nazis to exterminate the Jews of Europe, resulting in the murder of over 6 million Jews and more than a million other "undesirables."

Homestead Act (1862) Legislation granting "homesteads" of 160 acres of government-owned land to settlers who agreed to work the land for at least five years.

Homestead Steel strike (1892) Labor conflict at the Homestead steel mill near Pittsburgh, Pennsylvania, culminating in a battle between strikers and private security agents hired by the factory's management.

Herbert Hoover (1874–1964) Prior to becoming president, Hoover served as the secretary of commerce in both the Harding and Coolidge administrations. As president during the Great Depression, he believed that the nation's business structure was sound and sought to revive the economy through boosting the nation's confidence. He also tried to restart the economy with government constructions projects, lower taxes, and new federal loan programs, but nothing worked.

horizontal integration The process by which a corporation acquires or merges with its competitors.

horse A tall, four-legged mammal (*Equus caballus*), domesticated and bred since prehistoric times for carrying riders and pulling heavy loads. The Spanish introduced horses to the Americas, eventually transforming many Native American cultures.

House Committee on Un-American Activities (HUAC) Committee of the U.S. House of Representatives formed in 1938; it was originally tasked with investigating Nazi subversion during the Second World War and later shifted its focus to rooting out Communists in the government and the motion-picture industry.

Sam Houston (1793–1863) During Texas's fight for independence from Mexico, Sam Houston was the commander in chief of the Texas forces, and he led the attack that captured General Antonio López de Santa Anna. After Texas gained its independence, he was named its first president.

Jacob Riis' *How the Other Half Lives* Jacob Riis was an early muckraking journalist who exposed the slum conditions in New York City in his book *How the Other Half Lives*.

General William Howe (1729–1814) As the commander of the British army in the Revolutionary War, he seized New York City from Washington's army, but failed to capture it. He missed several more opportunities to quickly end the rebellion, and he resigned his command after the British defeat at Saratoga.

Saddam Hussein (1937–2006) The former dictator of Iraq who became the head of state in 1979. In 1980, he invaded Iran and started the eight-year-long Iran-Iraq War. In 1990, he invaded Kuwait, which caused the Gulf War of 1991. In 2003, he was overthrown and captured when the United States invaded. He was sentenced to death by hanging in 2006.

Anne Hutchinson (1591–1643) The articulate, strong-willed, and intelligent wife of a prominent Boston merchant, who espoused her belief in direct divine revelation. She quarreled with Puritan leaders over her beliefs, and they banished her from the colony.

Immigration Act of 1924 Federal legislation intended to favor northern and western European immigrants over those from southern and eastern Europe by restricting the number of immigrants from any one European country to 2 percent of the total number of immigrants per year, with an overall limit of slightly over 150,000 new arrivals per year.

Immigration and Nationality Services Act of 1965 Legislation that abolished discriminatory quotas based upon immigrants' national origin and treated all nationalities and races equally.

imperialism The use of diplomatic or military force to extend a nation's power and enhance its economic interests, often by acquiring territory or colonies and justifying such behavior with assumptions of racial superiority.

impressment The British navy used press-gangs to kidnap men in British and colonial ports who were then forced to serve in the British navy.

indentured servants Settlers who consented to a defined period of labor (often four to seven years) in exchange for having their passage to the New World paid by their "master."

Independent Treasury Act (1840) System created by President Martin Van Buren and approved by Congress in 1840 whereby the federal government moved its funds from favored state banks to the U.S. Treasury, whose financial transactions could only be in gold or silver coins of paper currency backed by gold or silver.

"Indian New Deal" This phrase refers to the reforms implemented for Native Americans during the New Deal era. John Collier, the commissioner of the Bureau of Indian Affairs (BIA), increased the access Native Americans had to relief programs and employed more Native Americans at the BIA. He worked to pass the Indian Reorganization Act. However, the version of the act passed by Congress was a much-diluted version of Collier's original proposal and did not greatly improve the lives of Native Americans.

Indian Removal Act (1830) Law permitting the forced relocation of Indians to federal lands west of the Mississippi River in exchange for the land they occupied in the East and South.

Indian wars Bloody conflicts between U.S. soldiers and Native Americans that raged in the West from the early 1860s to the late 1870s, sparked by American settlers moving into ancestral Indian lands.

Indochina This area of Southeast Asian consists of Laos, Cambodia, and Vietnam and was once controlled by France as a colony. After the Viet Minh defeated the French, the Geneva Accords were signed, which ended French colonial rule. The agreement created the independent nations of Laos and Cambodia and divided Vietnam along the 17th parallel until an election would reunify the country. Fearing a communist takeover, the U.S. government began intervening in the region during the Truman administration, which led to President Johnson's full-scale military involvement in Vietnam.

industrial war A new concept of war enabled by industrialization that developed from the early 1800s through the Atomic Age. New technologies, including automatic weaponry, forms of transportation like the railroad and airplane, and communication technologies such as the telegraph and telephone, enabled nations to equip large, mass-conscripted armies with chemical and automatic weapons to decimate opposing armies in a "total war."

industrialization Major shift in the nineteenth century from hand-made manufacturing to mass production in mills and factories using water-, coal-, and steam-powered machinery.

infectious diseases Also called contagious diseases, illnesses that can pass from one person to another by way of invasive biological organisms able to reproduce in the bodily tissues of their hosts. Europeans unwittingly brought many such diseases to the Americas, devastating the Native American peoples.

Alfred Thayer Mahan's *The Influence of Sea Power upon History, 1660–1783* **(1890)** Historical work in which Rear Admiral Alfred Thayer Mahan argues that a nation's greatness and prosperity comes from the power of its navy; the book helped bolster imperialist sentiment in the United States in the late nineteenth century.

Intermediate-Range Nuclear Forces (INF) Treaty (1987) Agreement signed by U.S. president Ronald Reagan and Soviet premier Mikhail Gorbachev to eliminate the deployment of intermediate-range missiles with nuclear warheads.

internal improvements Construction of roads, bridges, canals, harbors, and other infrastructural projects intended to facilitate the flow of goods and people.

Interstate Commerce Commission (ICC) An independent federal agency established in 1887 to oversee businesses engaged in interstate trade, especially railroads, but whose regulatory power was limited when tested in the courts.

interstate highway system In the late 1950s, construction began on a national network of interstate superhighways for the purpose of commerce and defense. The interstate highways would enable the rapid movement of military convoys and the evacuation of cities after a nuclear attack.

Iran-Contra affair Reagan administration scandal in 1987 over the secret, unlawful U.S. sale of arms to Iran in partial exchange for the release of hostages in Lebanon; the arms money in turn was used illegally to aid Nicaraguan right-wing insurgents, the Contras.

Iranian hostage crisis Storming of the U.S. embassy in Tehran in 1979 by Iranian revolutionaries, who held fifty-two Americans hostage for 444 days, despite President Carter's appeals for their release as well as a botched rescue attempt.

Irish Potato Famine In 1845, an epidemic of potato rot brought a famine to rural Ireland that killed over 1 million peasants and instigated a huge increase in the number of Irish immigrating to America. By 1850, the Irish made up 43 percent of the foreign-born population in the United States; in the 1850s, they made up over half the population of New York City and Boston.

iron curtain Term coined by Winston Churchill to describe the cold war divide between western Europe and the Soviet Union's Eastern European satellites.

Iroquois League An alliance of the Iroquois tribes, originally formed sometime between 1450 and 1600, that used their combined strength to pressure Europeans to work with them in the fur trade and to wage war across what is today eastern North America.

Andrew Jackson (1767–1837) As a major general in the Tennessee militia, he had a number of military successes. As president, he worked to enable the "common man" to play a greater role in the political arena. He vetoed the rechartering of the Second National Bank and reduced federal spending. When South Carolina nullified the Tariffs of 1828 and 1832, Jackson requested that Congress pass a "force bill" that would authorize him to use the army to compel the state to comply with the tariffs. He forced eastern Indians to move west of the Mississippi River so their lands could be used by white settlers. Groups of those who opposed Jackson came together to form a new political party called the Whigs.

Thomas "Stonewall" Jackson (1824–1863) He was a Confederate general who was known for his fearlessness in leading rapid marches, bold flanking movements, and furious assaults. He earned his nickname at the Battle of the First Bull Run for standing courageously against Union fire. During the battle of Chancellorsville, his own men accidently mortally wounded him.

William James (1842–1910) He was the founder of Pragmatism and one of the fathers of modern psychology. He believed that ideas gained their validity not from their inherent truth, but from their social consequences and practical application.

Jay's Treaty (1794) Agreement between Britain and the United States, negotiated by Chief Justice John Jay, that settled disputes over trade, prewar debts owed to British merchants, British-occupied forts in American territory, and the seizure of American ships and cargo.

"Jazz Age" Term coined by writer F. Scott Fitzgerald to characterize the spirit of rebellion and spontaneity among young Americans in the 1920s, a spirit epitomized by the hugely popular jazz music of the era.

Thomas Jefferson (1743–1826) He was a plantation owner, author, the drafter of the Declaration Independence, ambassador to France, leader of the Republican party, secretary of state, and the third president of the United States. As president, he purchased the Louisiana territory from France, withheld appointments made by President Adams leading to *Marbury v. Madison*, outlawed foreign slave trade, and was committed to a "wise and frugal" government.

Jeffersonian Republicans Political party founded by Thomas Jefferson in opposition to the Federalist Party led by Alexander Hamilton and John Adams; also known as the Democratic-Republican Party.

Jesuits A religious order founded in 1540 by Ignatius Loyola. They sought to counter the spread of Protestantism during the Protestant Reformation and spread the Catholic faith through work as missionaries. Roughly 3,500 served in New Spain and New France.

"Jim Crow" laws In the New South, these laws mandated the separation of races in various public places that served as a way for the ruling whites to impose their will on all areas of black life.

Andrew Johnson (1808–1875) He was elevated to the presidency after Abraham Lincoln's assassination. In order to restore the Union after the Civil War, he issued an amnesty proclamation and required former Confederate states to ratify the Thirteenth Amendment. After disagreements over the power to restore states' rights, the Radical Republicans attempted to impeach Johnson but fell short on the required number of votes needed to remove him from office.

Lyndon B. Johnson (1908–1973) Former member of the House of Representatives and the former Majority Leader of the Senate, Vice President Lyndon B. Johnson assumed the presidency after President Kennedy's assassination. During his presidency, he passed the Civil Rights Act of 1964, declared a "war on poverty" promoting his own social program called the Great Society, and signed the Immigration and Nationality Service Act of 1965. Johnson greatly increased America's role in Vietnam.

Johnson's Restoration Plan President Andrew Johnson's post–Civil War plan to readmit Confederate states into the Union; requirements included the appointment of a Unionist as a provisional governor in each southern state, ratification of the Thirteenth Amendment, and the extension of voting rights to "educated" blacks.

joint-stock companies Businesses owned by investors, who purchase shares of companies' stocks and share all the profits and losses.

Kansas-Nebraska Act (1854) Controversial legislation that created two new territories taken from Native Americans, Kansas and Nebraska, where residents would vote to decide whether slavery would be allowed (popular sovereignty).

Florence Kelley (1859–1932) As the head of the National Consumer's League, she led the crusade to promote state laws to regulate the number of working hours imposed on women who were wives and mothers.

George F. Kennan (1904–2005) While working as an American diplomat, he devised the strategy of containment, which called for the halting of Soviet expansion. It became America's choice strategy throughout the cold war.

John F. Kennedy (1917–1963) He was elected president in 1960. Despite the difficulties he had in getting his legislation through Congress, he established the Alliance for Progress programs to help Latin America, the Peace Corps, the Trade Expansion Act of 1962, and funding for urban renewal projects and the space program. His foreign political involvement included the failed Bay of Pigs invasion and the missile crisis in Cuba, as well as support of local governments in Indochina. In 1963, he was assassinated by Lee Harvey Oswald in Dallas, Texas.

Kent State During the spring of 1970, students on college campuses across the country protested the expansion of the Vietnam War into Cambodia. At Kent State University, the National Guard attempted to quell the rioting students. The guardsmen panicked and shot at rock-throwing demonstrators. Four student bystanders were killed.

Kentucky and Virginia Resolutions (1798–1799) Passed in response to the Alien and Sedition Acts, the resolutions advanced the state-compact theory that held states could nullify an act of Congress if they deemed it unconstitutional.

Francis Scott Key (1779–1843) During the War of 1812, he watched British forces bombard Fort McHenry, but fail to take it. Seeing the American flag still flying over the fort at dawn inspired him to write "The Star-Spangled Banner," which became the American national anthem.

Martin Luther King Jr. (1929–1968) A central leader of the civil rights movement, he urged people to use nonviolent civil disobedience to demand their rights and bring about change. He successfully led the Montgomery Bus Boycott. While in jail for his role in the demonstrations, he wrote his famous "Letter from Birmingham City Jail," in which he defended his strategy of nonviolent protest. In 1963, he delivered his famous "I Have a Dream" speech from the steps of the Lincoln Memorial as a part of the March on Washington. A year later, he was awarded the Nobel Peace Prize. In 1968, he was assassinated.

King Philip's War A bloody, three-year war in New England (1675–1678), resulting from the escalation of tensions between Indians and English settlers; the defeat of the Indians led to broadened freedoms for the settlers and their dispossessing the region's Indians of most of their land.

King William's War (War of the League of Augsburg) First (1689–1697) of four colonial wars between England and France.

Henry Kissinger (1923–) He served as the secretary of state and national security adviser in the Nixon administration. He negotiated with North Vietnam for an end to the Vietnam War, but the cease-fire did not last; South Vietnam fell to North Vietnam. He helped organize Nixon's historic trips to China and the Soviet Union. In the Middle East, he negotiated a cease-fire between Israel and its neighbors following the Yom

Kippur War and solidified Israel's promise to return to Egypt most of the land it had taken during the 1967 war.

Knights of Labor A national labor organization with a broad reform platform; reached peak membership in the 1880s.

Know-Nothings Nativist, anti-Catholic third party organized in 1854 in reaction to large-scale German and Irish immigration.

Ku Klux Klan (KKK) Organized in Pulaski, Tennessee, in 1866 to terrorize former slaves who voted and held political offices during Reconstruction; a revived organization in the 1910s and 1920s stressed white, Anglo-Saxon, fundamentalist Protestant supremacy; the Klan revived a third time to fight the civil rights movement of the 1950s and 1960s in the South.

Marquis de Lafayette (1757–1834) A wealthy French idealist excited by the American cause, he offered to serve in Washington's army for free in exchange for being named a major general. He overcame Washington's initial skepticism to become one of his most trusted aides.

laissez-faire (**"leave things alone"**) An economic doctrine holding that businesses and individuals should be able to pursue their economic interests without government interference.

Land Ordinance of 1785 Directed surveying of the Northwest Territory into townships of thirty-six sections (square miles) each, the sale of the sixteenth section of which was to be used to finance public education.

Bartolomé de Las Casas (1484–1566) A Catholic missionary who renounced the Spanish practice of coercively converting Indians and advocated their better treatment. In 1552, he wrote *A Brief Relation of the Destruction of the Indies*, which described the Spanish's cruel treatment of the Indians.

League of Nations Organization of nations formed in the aftermath of the First World War to mediate disputes and maintain international peace; despite President Wilson's intense lobbying for the League of Nations, Congress did not ratify the treaty and the United States failed to join.

Mary Elizabeth Lease (1850–1933) She was a leader of the farm protest movement who advocated violence if change could not be obtained at the ballot box. She believed that the urban-industrial East was the enemy of the working class.

Robert E. Lee (1807–1870) Even though he had served in the U.S. Army for thirty years, he chose to fight on the side of the Confederacy. Lee was excellent at using his field commanders and his soldiers respected him. However, General Ulysses S. Grant eventually wore down his army, and Lee surrendered to Grant at the Appomattox Court House on April 9, 1865.

Lend-Lease Act (1941) Legislation that allowed the president to lend or lease military equipment to any country whose own defense was deemed vital to the defense of the United States.

Levittown First low-cost, mass-produced development of suburban tract housing built by William Levitt on Long Island, New York, in 1947.

Lewis and Clark expedition (1804) Led by Meriwether Lewis and William Clark, a mission to the Pacific coast commissioned for the purposes of scientific and geographical exploration.

Lexington and Concord, Battle of The first shots fired in the Revolutionary War, on April 19, 1775, near Boston; approximately 100 Minutemen and 250 British soldiers were killed.

Liberator William Lloyd Garrison started this anti-slavery newspaper in 1831 in which he renounced gradualism and called for abolition.

Queen Liliuokalani (1838–1917) In 1891, she ascended to the throne of the Hawaiian royal family and tried to eliminate white control of the Hawaiian government. Two years later, Hawaii's white population revolted and seized power with the support of American marines.

Abraham Lincoln (1809–1865) Shortly after he was elected president in 1860, southern states began seceding from the Union, and in April 1861, he declared war on the seceding states. On January 1, 1863, Lincoln signed the Emancipation Proclamation. At the end of the war, he favored a reconstruction strategy for the former Confederate states that did not radically alter southern social and economic life. He was assassinated by John Wilkes Booth at Ford's Theater on April 14, 1865.

Lincoln-Douglas debates (1858) In the Illinois race between Republican Abraham Lincoln and Democrat Stephen A. Douglas for a seat in the U.S. Senate, a series of seven dramatic debates focusing on the issue of slavery in the territories.

John Locke (1632–1704) An English philosopher whose ideas were influential during the Enlightenment. He argued in his *Essay on Human Understanding* (1690) that humanity is largely the product of the environment, the mind being a blank tablet, *tabula rasa*, on which experience is written.

Henry Cabot Lodge (1850–1924) He was the chairman of the Senate Foreign Relations Committee who favored limiting America's involvement in the League of Nations' covenant and sought to amend the Treaty of Versailles.

de Lôme letter Private correspondence written in 1898 by the Spanish ambassador to the U.S., Depuy de Lôme, that described President McKinley as "weak"; the letter was stolen by Cuban revolutionaries and published in the *New York Journal*, deepening American resentment of Spain and moving the two countries closer to war in Cuba.

Lone Star Republic After winning independence from Mexico, Texas became its own nation and was called the Lone Star Republic. In 1836, Texans drafted themselves a constitution, legalized slavery, banned free blacks, named Sam Houston president, and voted for the annexation to the United States. However, quarrels over adding a slave state and fears of instigating a war with Mexico delayed Texas's entrance into the Union until December 29, 1845.

Huey P. Long (1893–1935) He began his political career in Louisiana where he developed a reputation for being an unscrupulous reformer. As a U.S. senator, he became a critic of President Roosevelt's New Deal Plan and offered his alternative: the Share-the-Wealth program. He was assassinated in 1935.

Lost Generation Label given to modernist writers and authors, such as F. Scott Fitzgerland and Ernest Hemingway, who had lost faith in the values and institutions of Western civilization in the aftermath of the Great War.

Louisiana Purchase (1803) President Thomas Jefferson's purchase of the Louisiana Territory from France for $15 million, doubling the size of U.S. territory.

Lowell girls Young female factory workers at the textile mills in Lowell, Massachusetts, which in the early 1820s provided its employees with prepared meals, dormitories, moral discipline, and educational opportunities.

Lowell system Model New England factory communities that during the first half of the nineteenth century provided employees, mostly young women, with meals, a boardinghouse, and moral discipline, as well as educational and cultural opportunities.

Loyalists Colonists who remained loyal to Great Britain before and during the Revolutionary War.

Lusitania British ocean liner torpedoed and sunk by a German U-boat; the deaths of nearly 1,200 of its civilian passengers, including many Americans, caused international outrage.

Martin Luther (1483–1546) A German monk who founded the Lutheran church. He protested abuses in the Catholic Church by posting his Ninety-five Theses, which began the Protestant Reformation.

General Douglas MacArthur (1880–1964) During World War II, he and Admiral Chester Nimitz dislodged the Japanese military from the Pacific Islands they had occupied. Following the war, he was in charge of the occupation of Japan. After North Korea invaded South Korea, Truman sent the U.S. military to defend South Korea under the command of MacArthur. Later in the war, Truman expressed his willingness to negotiate the restoration of prewar boundaries, which MacArthur attempted to undermine. Truman fired MacArthur for his open insubordination.

James Madison (1751–1836) He participated in the Constitutional Convention during which he proposed the Virginia Plan. He believed in a strong federal government and was a leader of the Federalists. However, he also presented to Congress the Bill of Rights and drafted the Virginia Resolutions. As secretary of state, he withheld a commission for William Marbury, which led to the landmark *Marbury v. Madison* decision. During his presidency, he declared war on Britain in response to violations of American shipping rights, which started the War of 1812.

maize (corn) The primary grain crop in Mesoamerica yielding small kernels often ground into cornmeal. Easy to grow in a broad range of conditions, it enabled a global population explosion after being brought to Europe, Africa, and Asia.

Malcolm X (1925–1964) The most articulate spokesman for black power. Originally the chief disciple of Elijah Muhammad, the black Muslim leader in the United States, Malcolm X broke away and founded his own organization committed to establishing relations between African Americans and the nonwhite peoples of the world. Near the end of his life, he began to preach a biracial message of social change. In 1964, he was assassinated by members of a rival group of black Muslims.

manifest destiny The widespread belief that America was "destined" by God to expand westward across the continent into lands claimed by Native Americans as well as European nations.

Horace Mann (1796–1859) He believed the public school system was the best way to achieve social stability and equal opportunity. As a reformer of education, he sponsored a state board of education, the first state-supported "normal" school for training teachers, a state association for teachers, and the minimum school year of six months. He led the drive for a statewide school system.

***Marbury v. Madison* (1803)** First Supreme Court decision to declare a federal law—the Judiciary Act of 1801—unconstitutional.

March on Washington Civil rights demonstration on August 28, 1963, on the National Mall, where Martin Luther King Jr. gave his famous "I Have a Dream" speech.

"March to the Sea" The Union army's devastating march through Georgia from Atlanta to Savannah, led by General William T. Sherman, intended to demoralize civilians and destroy the resources the Confederate army needed to fight.

market-based economy Large-scale manufacturing and commercial agriculture that emerged in America during the first half of the nineteenth century, displacing much of the premarket subsistence and barter-based economy and producing boom-and-bust cycles while raising the American standard of living.

George C. Marshall (1880–1959) As the chairman of the Joint Chiefs of Staff, he orchestrated the Allied victories over Germany and Japan in the Second World War. In 1947, he became President Truman's secretary of state and proposed the massive reconstruction program for western Europe called the Marshall Plan.

Chief Justice John Marshall (1755–1835) During his long tenure as chief justice of the Supreme Court (1801–1835), he established the foundations for American jurisprudence, the authority of the Supreme Court, and the constitutional supremacy of the national government over states.

Marshall Plan (1948) Secretary of State George C. Marshall's post–World War II program providing massive U.S. financial and technical assistance to war-torn European countries.

Massachusetts Bay Colony English colony founded by English Puritans in 1630 as a haven for persecuted Congregationalists.

massive resistance White rallying cry disrupting federal efforts to enforce racial integration in the South.

massive retaliation Strategy that used the threat of nuclear warfare as a means of combating the global spread of communism.

Mayflower Compact A formal agreement signed by the Separatist colonists aboard the *Mayflower* in 1620 to abide by laws made by leaders of their own choosing.

Senator Joseph R. McCarthy (1908–1957) In 1950, this senator became the shrewdest and most ruthless exploiter of America's anxiety of communism. He claimed that the U.S. government was full of Communists and led a witch hunt to find them, but he was never able to uncover a single communist agent.

McCarthyism Anti-Communist hysteria led by Senator Joseph McCarthy's "witch hunts" attacking the loyalty of politicians, federal employees, and public figures, despite a lack of evidence.

George B. McClellan (1826–1885) In 1861, President Abraham Lincoln appointed him head of the Army of the Potomac and, later, general-in-chief of the U.S. Army. He built his army into a well-trained and powerful force. After failing to achieve a decisive victory against the Confederacy, he was removed from command in 1862.

Cyrus Hall McCormick (1809–1884) In 1831, he invented a mechanical reaper to harvest wheat, which transformed the scale of agriculture. By hand, a farmer could only harvest half an acre a day, while the McCormick reaper allowed two people to harvest twelve acres of wheat a day.

McCormick reapers Mechanical reapers invented by Cyrus Hall McCormick in 1831 that dramatically increased the production of wheat.

***McCulloch v. Maryland* (1819)** A decision by the Marshall-led Supreme Court that ruled unanimously that Congress had the authority to charter the Bank of the United States and that states did not have the right to tax the national bank.

William McKinley (1843–1901) As a congressman, he was responsible for the McKinley Tariff of 1890, which raised the duties on manufactured products to their highest level ever. Voters disliked the tariff and McKinley, as well as other Republicans, lost his seat in Congress the next election. However, he won the presidential election of 1896 and raised the tariffs again. In 1898, he annexed Hawaii and declared war on Spain. The war concluded with the Treaty of Paris, which gave America control over Puerto Rico, Guam, and the Philippines. Soon America was fighting Filipinos, who were seeking independence for their country. In 1901, McKinley was assassinated.

Robert McNamara (1916–2009) He was the secretary of defense for both President Kennedy and President Johnson and a supporter of America's involvement in Vietnam.

Medicare and **Medicaid** Health care programs designed to aid the elderly and disadvantaged, respectively, as part of President Johnson's Great Society initiative.

Andrew W. Mellon (1855–1937) As President Harding's secretary of the Treasury, he sought to generate economic growth by reducing government spending and lowering taxes. However, he insisted that the tax reductions mainly go to the rich because he believed the wealthy would reinvest their money. In order to bring greater efficiency and nonpartisanship to the government's budget process, he persuaded Congress to created a new Bureau of the Budget and a General Accounting Office.

mercantilism Policy of Great Britain and other imperial powers of regulating the economies of colonies to benefit the mother country.

James Meredith (1933–) In 1962, the governor of Mississippi defied a Supreme Court ruling and refused to allow James Meredith, an African American, to enroll at the University of Mississippi. Federal marshals were sent to enforce the law, which led to clashes between a white mob and the marshals. Federal troops intervened and two people were killed and many others were injured. A few days later, Meredith was able to register at the university.

Metacomet (?–1676) or **King Philip** The chief of the Wampanoages, whom the colonists called King Philip. He resented English efforts to convert Indians to Christianity and waged a war against the English colonists, one in which he was killed.

Mexica Otherwise known as "Aztecs," a Mesoamerican people of northern Mexico who founded the vast Aztec Empire in the fourteenth century, later conquered by the Spanish under Hernán Cortés in 1521.

microprocessor An electronic circuit printed on a small silicon chip; a major technological breakthrough in 1971, it paved the way for the development of the personal computer.

Middle Passage The hellish and often deadly middle leg of the transatlantic "Triangular Trade" in which European ships carried manufactured goods to Africa, then transported enslaved Africans to the Americas and the Caribbean, and finally conveyed American agricultural products back to Europe; from the late sixteenth to the early nineteenth centuries, some 12 million Africans were transported via the Middle Passage, unknown millions more dying en route.

Midway, Battle of A 1942 battle that proved to be a turning point in the Pacific front during World War II; it was the Japanese navy's first major defeat in 350 years.

militant nonviolence After the success of the Montgomery bus boycott, people were inspired by Martin Luther King Jr.'s use of this nonviolent form of protest. Throughout the civil rights movement, demonstrators used this method of protest to challenge racial segregation in the South.

Militia Act (1862) Congressional measure that permitted freed slaves to serve as laborers or soldiers in the United States Army.

Ho Chi Minh (1890–1969) He was the Vietnamese communist resistance leader who drove France and the United States out of Vietnam. After the Geneva Accords divided the region into four countries, he controlled North Vietnam, and ultimately became the leader of all of Vietnam at the conclusion of the Vietnam War.

minstrelsy A form of entertainment that was popular from the 1830s to the 1870s. The performances featured white performers who were made up as African Americans, or blackface. They performed banjo and fiddle music, "shuffle" dances, and lowbrow humor that reinforced racial stereotypes.

Minutemen Special units organized by the militia to be ready for quick mobilization.

***Miranda v. Arizona* (1966)** U.S. Supreme Court decision required police to advise persons in custody of their rights to legal counsel and against self-incrimination.

Mississippi Plan Series of state constitutional amendments in 1890 which sought to severely disenfranchise black voters and was quickly adopted by other southern states.

Missouri Compromise (1820) Legislative decision to admit Missouri as a slave state and abolish slavery in the area west of the Mississippi River and north of the parallel 36°30'.

Model T Henry Ford developed this model of car so that it was affordable for everyone. Its success led to an increase in the production of automobiles, which stimulated other related industries such steel, oil, and rubber. The mass use of automobiles increased the speed goods could be transported, encouraged urban sprawl, and sparked real estate booms in California and Florida.

moderate Republicanism Promise to curb federal government and restore state and local government authority, spearheaded by President Eisenhower.

modernism An early-twentieth-century intellectual and artistic movement that rejected traditional notions of reality and adopted radical new forms of artistic expression.

"money question" Late-nineteenth-century national debate over the nature of U.S. currency; supporters of a fixed gold standard were generally money lenders, and thus preferred to keep the value of money high, while supporters of silver (and gold) coinage were debtors, they owed money, so they wanted to keep the value of money low by increasing the currency supply (inflation).

monopoly A corporation so large that it effectively controls the entire market for its products or services.

James Monroe (1758–1831) He served as secretary of state and war under President Madison and was elected president. As the latter, he signed the Transcontinental Treaty with Spain, which gave Florida to the United States and expanded the Louisiana territory's western border to the Pacific coast. In 1823, he established the Monroe Doctrine. This foreign policy proclaimed that the American continents were no longer open to colonization and America would be neutral in European affairs.

Monroe Doctrine (1823) U.S. foreign policy that barred further colonization in the Western Hemisphere by European powers and pledged that there would be no American interference with any existing European colonies.

Montgomery bus boycott Boycott of bus system in Montgomery, Alabama, organized by civil rights activists after the arrest of Rosa Parks.

Moral Majority Televangelist Jerry Falwell's political lobbying organization, the name of which became synonymous with the religious right; conservative evangelical Protestants who helped ensure President Ronald Reagan's 1980 victory.

J. Pierpont Morgan (1837–1913) As a powerful investment banker, he would acquire, reorganize, and consolidate companies into giant trusts. His biggest achievement was the consolidation of the steel industry into the United States Steel Corporation, which was the first billion-dollar corporation.

J. Pierpont Morgan and Company An investment bank under the leadership of J. Pierpont Morgan that bought or merged unrelated American companies, often using capital acquired from European investors.

Mormons Members of the Church of Jesus Christ of Latter-day Saints, which dismissed other Christian denominations, emphasizing universal salvation and a modest lifestyle; Mormons were often persecuted for their secrecy and clannishness.

Morrill Land Grant Act (1862) Federal statute that allowed for the creation of land-grant colleges and universities, which were founded to provide technical education in agriculture, mining, and industry.

Samuel F. B. Morse (1791–1872) In 1832, he invented the telegraph and revolutionized the speed of communication.

mountain men Inspired by the fur trade, these men left civilization to work as trappers and reverted to a primitive existence in the wilderness. They were the first white people to find routes through the Rocky Mountains, and they pioneered trails that settlers later used to reach the Oregon country and California in the 1840s.

muckrakers Writers who exposed corruption and abuses in politics, business, consumer safety, working conditions, and more, spurring public interest in progressive reforms.

Mugwumps Reformers who bolted the Republican party in 1884 to support Democratic Grover Cleveland for president over Republican James G. Blaine, whose secret dealings on behalf of railroad companies had brought charges of corruption.

mulattoes Mixed-race people who constituted most of the South's free black population.

Benito Mussolini, or "*Il Duce*" (1883–1945) The Italian founder of the Fascist party who came to power in Italy in 1922 and allied himself with Adolf Hitler and the Axis powers during the Second World War.

National Association for the Advancement of Colored People (NAACP) Organization founded in 1910 by black activists and white progressives that promoted education as a means of combating social problems and focused on legal action to secure the civil rights supposedly guaranteed by the Fourteenth and Fifteenth Amendments.

National Industrial Recovery Act (1933) Passed on the last of the Hundred Days, it created public-works jobs through the Federal Emergency Relief Administration and established a system of self-regulation for industry through the National Recovery Administration, which was ruled unconstitutional in 1935.

National Labor Union (NLU) A federation of labor and reform leaders established in 1866 to advocate for new state and local laws to improve working conditions.

National Recovery Administration (NRA) (1933) Controversial federal agency that brought together business and labor leaders to create "codes of fair competition" and "fair labor" policies, including a national minimum wage.

National Security Act Congressional legislation passed in 1947 that created the Department of Defense, the National Security Council, and the Central Intelligence Agency.

National Socialist German Workers' Party (Nazi) Founded in the 1920s, this party gained control over Germany under the leadership of Adolf Hitler in 1933 and continued in power until Germany's defeat at the end of the Second World War. It advocated a violent anti-Semitic, anti-Marxist, pan-German ideology. The Nazi party perpetrated the Holocaust.

National Trades' Union Formed in 1834 to organize all local trade unions into a stronger national association, only to be dissolved amid the economic depression during the late 1830s.

nativists Members of a reactionary conservative movement characterized by heightened nationalism, anti-immigrant sentiment, and the enactment of laws setting stricter regulations on immigration.

natural rights An individual's basic rights that should not be violated by any government or community.

Navigation Acts Restrictions passed by the British Parliament between 1650 and 1775 to control colonial trade and bolster the mercantile system.

Negro nationalism A cultural and political movement in the 1920s spearheaded by Marcus Garvey which exalted blackness, black cultural expression, and black exclusiveness.

Negrophobia A violent new wave of racism that spread in the late nineteenth century largely spurred by white resentment for African-American financial success and growing political influence.

"neutrality laws" Series of laws passed by Congress aimed at avoiding entering a Second World War; these included the Neutrality Act of 1935, which banned loans to warring nations.

"New Democrats" Centrist ("moderate") Democrats led by President Bill Clinton that emerged in the late 1980s and early 1990s to challenge the "liberal" direction of the party.

"new economy" Period of sustained economic prosperity during the nineties marked by budget surpluses, the explosion of dot.com industries, low inflation, and low unemployment.

New France The name used for the area of North America that was colonized by the French. Unlike Spanish or English colonies, New France had a small number of colonists, which forced them to initially seek good relations with the indigenous people they encountered.

New Freedom Program championed in 1912 by the Woodrow Wilson campaign that aimed to restore competition in the economy by eliminating all trusts rather than simply regulating them.

New Frontier Proposed domestic program championed by the incoming Kennedy administration in 1961 that aimed to jump-start the economy and trigger social progress.

"new immigrants" Wave of newcomers from southern and eastern Europe, including many Jews, who became a majority among immigrants to America after 1890.

New Jersey Plan The delegations to the Constitutional Convention were divided between two plans on how to structure the government: New Jersey wanted one legislative body with equal representation for each state.

New Left Term coined by the Students for a Democratic Society to distinguish their efforts at grassroots democracy from those of the 1930s Old Left, which had embraced orthodox Marxism.

New Mexico A U.S. territory and later a state in the American Southwest, originally established by the Spanish, who settled there in the sixteenth century, founded Catholic missions, and exploited the region's indigenous peoples.

New Nationalism Platform of the Progressive party and slogan of former President Theodore Roosevelt in the presidential campaign of 1912; stressed government activism, including regulation of trusts, conservation, and recall of state court decisions that had nullified progressive programs.

"New Negro" In the 1920s, a slow and steady growth of black political influence occurred in northern cities where African Americans were freer to speak and act. This political activity created a spirit of protest that expressed itself culturally in the Harlem Renaissance and politically in "new Negro" nationalism.

New Netherland Dutch colony conquered by the English in 1667 and out of which four new colonies were created: New York, New Jersey, Pennsylvania, and Delaware.

New Orleans, Battle of (1815) Final major battle in the War of 1812, in which the Americans under General Andrew Jackson unexpectedly and decisively countered the British attempt to seize the port of New Orleans, Louisiana.

New South *Atlanta Constitution* editor Henry W. Grady's 1886 term for the prosperous post–Civil War South: democratic, industrial, urban, and free of nostalgia for the defeated plantation South.

William Randolph Hearst's *New York Journal* In the late 1890s, the *New York Journal* and its rival, the *New York World*, printed sensationalism on the Cuban revolution as part of their heated competition for readership. The *New York Journal* printed a negative letter from the Spanish ambassador about President McKinley and inflammatory coverage of the sinking of the *Maine* in Havana Harbor. These two events roused the American public's outcry against Spain.

Joseph Pulitzer's *New York World* In the late 1890s, the *New York World* and its rival, *New York Journal*, printed sensationalism on the Cuban revolution as part of their heated competition for readership.

Admiral Chester Nimitz (1885–1966) During the Second World War, he was the commander of central Pacific. Along with General Douglas MacArthur, he dislodged the Japanese military from the Pacific Islands they had occupied.

Nineteenth Amendment Constitutional amendment that granted women the right to vote in 1920.

Richard M. Nixon (1913–1994) He first came to national prominence as a congressman involved in the investigation of Alger Hiss, and later served as vice president during the Eisenhower administration. After being elected president in 1968, he slowed the federal enforcement of civil rights and appointed pro-Southern justices to the Supreme Court. He began a program of Vietnamization of the war. In 1973, America, North and South Vietnam, and the Viet Cong agreed to end the war and the United States withdrew. However, the cease-fire was broken, and South Vietnam fell to North Vietnam. In 1970, Nixon declared that the America was no longer the world's policemen and he would seek some partnerships with Communist countries, historically travelling to China and the Soviet Union. In 1972, he was reelected, but the Watergate scandal erupted shortly after his victory. He resigned the presidency under threat of impeachment.

nonviolent civil disobedience Tactic of defying unjust laws through peaceful actions championed by Dr. Martin Luther King Jr.

Lord North (1732–1792) The first minister of King George III's cabinet whose efforts to subdue the colonies only brought them closer to revolution. He helped bring about the Tea Act of 1773, which led to the Boston Tea Party. In an effort to discipline Boston, he wrote, and Parliament passed, four acts that galvanized colonial resistance.

North American Free Trade Agreement (NAFTA) Agreement eliminating trade barriers that was signed in 1994 by the United States, Canada, and Mexico, making North America the largest free-trade zone in the world.

North Atlantic Treaty Organization (NATO) Defensive political and military alliance formed in 1949 by the United States, Canada, and ten Western European nations to deter Soviet expansion in Europe.

Northwest Ordinance (1787) Land policy for new western territories in the Ohio valley that established the terms and conditions for self-government and statehood while also banning slavery from the region.

NSC-68 (1950) Top-secret policy paper approved by President Truman that outlined a militaristic approach to combating the spread of global communism.

nullification The right claimed by some states to veto a federal law deemed unconstitutional.

Barack Obama (1961–) In the 2008 presidential election, Senator Barack Obama mounted an innovative Internet-based and grassroots-oriented campaign. As the nation's economy nosedived in the fall of 2008, Obama linked the Republican economic philosophy with the country's dismal financial state and promoted a message of "change" and "politics of hope," which resonated with voters. He decisively won the presidency and became America's first person of color to be elected president.

Occupy Wall Street A grassroots movement protesting a capitalist system that fostered social and economic inequality. Begun in Zuccotti Park, New York City, during 2011, the movement spread rapidly across the nation, triggering a national conversation about income inequality and protests of the government's "bailouts" of the banks and corporations allegedly responsible for the Great Recession.

Sandra Day O'Connor (1930–) She was the first woman to serve on the Supreme Court of the United States and was appointed by President Reagan. Reagan's critics charged that her appointment was a token gesture and not a sign of any real commitment to gender equality.

Ohio gang In order to escape the pressures of the White House, President Harding met with a group of people, called the "Ohio gang," in a house on K Street in Washington, D.C. Members of this gang were given low-level positions in the American government and they used their White House connection to "line their pockets" by granting government contracts without bidding, which led to a series of scandals, most notably the Teapot Dome Scandal.

Old Southwest Region covering western Georgia, Alabama, Mississippi, Louisiana, Arkansas, and Texas, where low land prices and fertile soil attracted hundreds of thousands of settlers after the American Revolution.

Open Door policy Official U.S. insistence that Chinese trade would be open to all nations; Secretary of State John Hay unilaterally announced the policy in 1899 in hopes of protecting the Chinese market for U.S. exports.

open shop Business policy of not requiring union membership as a condition of employment; such a policy, where legal, has the effect of weakening unions and diminishing workers' rights.

open range Informal system of governing property on the frontier in which small ranchers could graze their cattle anywhere on unfenced lands; brought to an end by the introduction of barbed wire, a low-cost way to fence off one's land.

Operation Desert Shield After Saddam Hussein invaded Kuwait in 1990, President George H. W. Bush sent American military forces to Saudi Arabia on a strictly defensive mission. They were soon joined by a multinational coalition. When the coalition's mission changed to the retaking of Kuwait, the operation was renamed Desert Storm.

Operation Desert Storm (1991) Assault by American-led multinational forces that quickly defeated Iraqi forces under Saddam Hussein in the First Gulf War, ending the Iraqi occupation of Kuwait.

Operation Overlord The Allies' assault on Hitler's "Atlantic Wall," a seemingly impregnable series of fortifications and minefields along the French coastline that German forces had created using captive Europeans for laborers.

J. Robert Oppenheimer (1904–1967) He led the group of physicists at the laboratory in Los Alamos, New Mexico, who constructed the first atomic bomb.

Oregon Country The Convention of 1818 between Britain and the United States established the Oregon Country as being west of the crest of the Rocky Mountains and the two countries were to jointly occupy it. In 1824, the United States and Russia signed a treaty that established the line of 54°40′ as the southern boundary of Russia's territorial claim in North America. A similar agreement between Britain and Russia finally gave the Oregon Country clearly defined borders, but it remained under joint British and American control.

Oregon fever The lure of fertile land and economic opportunities in the Oregon Country that drew thousands of settlers westward, beginning in the late 1830s.

Osceola (1804?–1838) He was the leader of the Seminole nation who resisted the federal Indian removal policy through a protracted guerilla war. In 1837, he was treacherously seized under a flag of truce and imprisoned at Fort Moultrie, where he was left to die.

Overland Trails Trail routes followed by wagon trains bearing settlers and trade goods from Missouri to the Oregon Country, California, and New Mexico, beginning in the 1840s.

A. Mitchell Palmer (1872–1936) As the attorney general, he played an active role in the government's response to the Red Scare. After several bombings across America, including one at Palmer's home, he and other Americans became convinced that there was a well-organized Communist terror campaign at work. The federal government launched a campaign of raids and deportations and collected files on radical individuals.

Panic of 1819 A financial panic that began a three-year-long economic crisis triggered by a reduced demand of American imports, declining land values, and reckless practices by local and state banks.

Panic of 1837 A financial calamity in the United States brought on by a dramatic slowdown in the British economy and exacerbated by falling cotton prices, failed crops, high inflation, and reckless state banks.

Panic of 1873 A major economic collapse caused by President Grant's efforts to remove greenbacks from circulation; the resultant depression, in which thousands of businesses closed and millions lost their jobs, was then the worst in the nation's history.

Panic of 1893 A major collapse in the national economy after several major railroad companies declared bankruptcy, leading to a severe depression and several violent clashes between workers and management.

panning A method of mining that used a large metal pan to sift gold dust and nuggets from riverbeds during the California gold rush of 1849.

Rosa Parks (1913–2005) In 1955, she refused to give up her seat to a white man on a city bus in Montgomery, Alabama, which a local ordinance required of blacks. She was arrested for disobeying the ordinance. In response, black community leaders organized the Montgomery bus boycott.

Parliament Legislature of Great Britain, composed of the House of Commons, whose members are elected, and the House of Lords, whose members are either hereditary or appointed.

party bosses Powerful political leaders who controlled a "machine" of associates and operatives to promote both individual and party interests, often using informal tactics such as intimidation or the patronage system.

paternalism A moral position developed during the first half of the nineteenth century which claimed that slaves were deprived of liberty for their own "good." Such a rationalization was adopted by some slave owners to justify slavery.

Patriots Colonists who rebelled against British authority before and during the Revolutionary War.

patronage An informal system (sometimes called the "spoils system") used by politicians to reward their supporters with government appointments or contracts.

Alice Paul (1885–1977) She was a leader of the women's suffrage movement and head of the Congressional Committee of National Women Suffrage Association. She instructed female suffrage activists to use more militant tactics, such as picketing state legislatures, chaining themselves to public buildings, inciting police to arrest them, and undertaking hunger strikes.

Norman Vincent Peale (1898–1993) He was a champion of the upbeat and feel-good theology that was popular in the 1950s religious revival. He advocated getting rid of any depressing or negative thoughts and replacing them with "faith, enthusiasm and joy," which would make an individual popular and well liked.

Pearl Harbor Surprise Japanese attack on the U.S. fleet at Pearl Harbor on December 7, 1941, which prompted the immediate American entry into the war.

"peculiar institution" A phrase used by whites in the antebellum South to refer to slavery without using the word slavery.

Pennsylvania English colony founded by William Penn in 1681 as a Quaker commonwealth, though it welcomed people of all religions.

Pentagon Papers Informal name for the Defense Department's secret history of the Vietnam conflict; leaked to the press by former official Daniel Ellsberg and published in the *New York Times* in 1971.

People's party (Populists) Political party largely made up of farmers from the South and West that struggled to gain political influence from the East. Populists advocated a variety of reforms, including free coinage of silver, a progressive income tax, postal savings banks, regulation of railroads, and direct election of U.S. senators.

Pequot War Massacre in 1637 and subsequent dissolution of the Pequot Nation by Puritan settlers, who seized the Indians' lands.

perestroika Russian term for "economic restructuring"; applied to Mikhail Gorbachev's series of political and economic reforms that included shifting a centrally planned Commmunist economy to a mixed economy allowing for capitalism.

Commodore Matthew Perry (1794–1858) In 1854, he negotiated the Treaty of Kanagawa, which was the first step in starting a political and commercial relationship between the United States and Japan.

John J. Pershing U.S. general sent by President Wilson to put down attacks on the Mexican border led by Francisco "Pancho" Villa.

Personal Responsibility and Work Opportunity Act of 1996 (PRWOA) Comprehensive welfare-reform measure, passed by a Republican Congress and signed by President Clinton, that aimed to decrease the size of the "welfare state" by limiting the amount of government aid provided to the unemployed so as to encourage recipients to find jobs.

"pet banks" During President Andrew Jackson's fight with the national bank, Jackson resolved to remove all federal deposits from it. To comply with Jackson's demands, Secretary of Treasury Taney continued to draw on government's accounts in the national bank, but deposit all new federal receipts in state banks. The state banks that received these deposits were called "pet banks."

Pilgrims Puritan Separatists who broke completely with the Church of England and sailed to the New World aboard the *Mayflower*, founding Plymouth Colony on Cape Cod in 1620.

Gifford Pinchot (1865–1946) As the head of the Division of Forestry, he implemented a conservation policy that entailed the scientific management of natural resources to serve the public interest. His work helped start the conservation movement.

Elizabeth Lucas Pinckney (1722?–1793) One of the most enterprising horticulturists in colonial America, she began managing her family's three plantations in South Carolina at the age of sixteen. She had tremendous success growing indigo, which led to many other plantations growing the crop as well.

Pinckney's Treaty Treaty with Spain negotiated by Thomas Pinckney in 1795; established United States boundaries at the Mississippi River and the 31st parallel and allowed open transportation on the Mississippi.

Francisco Pizarro (1478?–1541) In 1531, he led his Spanish soldiers to Peru and conquered the Inca Empire.

"plain white folk" Yeoman farmers who lived and worked on their own small farms, growing food and cash crops to trade for necessities.

plantation mistress Matriarch of a planter's household, responsible for supervising the domestic aspects of the estate.

planter Owner of a large farm in the South that was worked by twenty or more slaves and supervised by overseers.

political "machine" A network of political activists and elected officials, usually controlled by a powerful "boss," that attempts to manipulate local politics.

James Knox Polk, or **"Young Hickory" (1795–1849)** As president, his chief concern was the expansion of the United States. Shortly after taking office, Mexico broke off relations with the United States over the annexation of Texas. Polk declared war on Mexico and sought to subvert Mexican authority in California. The United States defeated Mexico, and the two nations signed the Treaty of Guadalupe Hidalgo, in which Mexico gave up any claims on Texas north of the Rio Grande River and ceded New Mexico and California to the United States.

Pontiac's Rebellion An Indian attack on British forts and settlements after France ceded to the British its territory east of the Mississippi River, as part of the Treaty of Paris in 1763, without consulting France's Indian allies.

popular sovereignty Legal concept by which the white male settlers in a new U.S. territory would vote to decide whether or not to permit slavery.

Pottawatomie Massacre In retaliation for the "sack of Lawrence," John Brown and his abolitionist cohorts hacked five men to death in the pro-slavery settlement of Pottawatomie, Kansas, on May 24, 1856, triggering a guerrilla war in the Kansas Territory that cost 200 settlers' lives.

Powhatan Confederacy An alliance of several powerful Algonquian tribes under the leadership of Chief Powhatan, organized into thirty chiefdoms along much of the Atlantic coast in the late sixteenth and early seventeenth centuries.

Chief Powhatan Wahunsonacock He was called Powhatan by the English after the name of his tribe, and was the powerful, charismatic chief of numerous Algonquian-speaking towns in eastern Virginia representing over 10,000 Indians.

professions Occupations requiring specialized knowledge of some field; the Industrial Revolution and its new organization of labor created an array of professions in the nineteenth century.

Progressive party In the 1912 election, Theodore Roosevelt was unable to secure the Republican nomination for president. He left the Republican party and formed his own party of progressive Republicans, called the "Bull Moose" party (later Progressive Party). Roosevelt and Taft split the Republican vote, which allowed Democrat Woodrow Wilson to win.

Prohibition National ban on the manufacture and sale of alcohol that lasted from 1920 to 1933, though the law was widely violated and proved too difficult to enforce effectively.

proprietary colonies A colony owned by an individual, rather than a joint-stock company.

Protestant Reformation Sixteenth-century religious movement initiated by Martin Luther, a German monk whose public criticism of corruption in the Roman Catholic Church, and whose teaching that Christians can communicate directly with God, gained a wide following and led to the Protestant Reformation.

public schools Elementary and secondary schools funded by the state and free of tuition.

pueblos The Spanish term for the adobe cliff dwellings of the indigenous people of the southwestern United States.

Pullman strike (1894) A national strike by the American Railway Union, whose members shut down major railways in sympathy with striking workers in Pullman, Illinois; ended with intervention of federal troops.

Puritans English religious dissenters who sought to "purify" the Church of England of its Catholic practices.

Quakers George Fox founded the Quaker religion in 1647. They rejected the use of formal sacraments and ministry, refused to take oaths, and embraced pacifism. Fleeing persecution, they settled and established the colony of Pennsylvania.

race-based slavery Institution that uses racial characteristics and myths to justify enslaving a people.

Radical Republicans Senators and congressmen who, strictly identifying the Civil War with the abolitionist cause, sought swift emancipation of the slaves, punishment of the rebels, and tight controls over the former Confederate states after the war.

railroads Steam-powered vehicles that improved passenger transportation, quickened western settlement, and enabled commercial agriculture in the nineteenth century.

Raleigh's Roanoke Island Colony English expedition of 117 settlers, including Virginia Dare, the first English child born in the New World; colony disappeared from Roanoke Island in the Outer Banks sometime between 1587 and 1590.

A. Philip Randolph (1889–1979) He was the head of the Brotherhood of Sleeping Car Porters who planned a march on Washington, D.C., to demand an end to racial discrimination in the defense industries. To stop the march, the Roosevelt administration negotiated an agreement with the Randolph group. The demonstration would be called off and an executive order would be issued that forbade discrimination in defense work and training programs and set up the Fair Employment Practices Committee.

range wars In the late 1800s, conflicting claims over land and water rights triggered violent disputes between farmers and ranchers in parts of the western United States.

Ronald Reagan (1911–2004) In 1980, the former actor and governor of California was elected president. In office, he reduced social spending, cut taxes, and increased defense spending. During his presidency, the federal debt tripled, the federal deficit rose, programs such as housing and school lunches were cut, and the HIV/AIDS crisis grew to prominence in the United States. He signed an arms-control treaty with the Soviet Union in 1987 and authorized covert CIA operations in Central America. In 1986 the Iran-Contra scandal was revealed.

Reaganomics President Reagan's "supply-side" economic philosophy combining tax cuts with the goals of decreased government spending reduced regulation of business, and a balanced budget.

Reconstruction Finance Corporation (RFC) (1932) Federal program established under President Hoover to loan money to banks and other corporations to help them avoid bankruptcy.

Red Power Activism by militant Native American groups to protest living conditions on Indian reservations through demonstrations, legal action, and, at times, violence.

Redeemers Post–Civil War Democratic leaders who supposedly saved the South from Yankee domination and preserved the primarily rural economy.

Dr. Walter Reed (1851–1902) His work on yellow fever in Cuba led to the discovery that the fever was carried by mosquitoes. This understanding helped develop more effective controls of the worldwide disease.

reform Darwinism A social philosophy developed by Lester Frank War that challenged the ruthlessness of social Darwinism by asserting that humans were not passive pawns of evolutionary forces. Instead, people could actively shape the process of evolutionary social development through cooperation, innovation, and planning.

Reformation European religious movement that challenged the Catholic Church and resulted in the beginnings of Protestant Christianity. During this period, Catholics and Protestants persecuted, imprisoned, tortured, and killed each other in large numbers.

religious right Christian conservatives with a faith-based political agenda that includes prohibition of abortion and allowing prayer in public schools.

reparations As a part of the Treaty of Versailles, Germany was required to confess its responsibility for the First World War and make payments to the victors for the entire expense of the war. These two requirements created a deep bitterness among Germans.

Alexander Hamilton's Report on Manufactures First secretary of the Treasury Alexander Hamilton's 1791 analysis that accurately foretold the future of American industry and proposed tariffs and subsidies to promote it.

Republican ideology Political belief in representative democracy in which citizens govern themselves by electing representatives, or legislators, to make key decisions on the citizens' behalf.

republican simplicity Deliberate attitude of humility and frugality, as opposed to monarchial pomp and ceremony, adopted by Thomas Jefferson in his presidency

Republicans First used during the early nineteenth century to describe supporters of a strict interpretation of the Constitution, which they believed would safeguard individual freedoms and states' rights from the threats posed by a strong central government. The idealist Republican vision of sustaining an agrarian-oriented union was developed largely by Thomas Jefferson.

"return to normalcy" Campaign promise of Republican presidential candidate Warren G. Harding in 1920, meant to contrast with Woodrow Wilson's progressivism and internationalism.

Paul Revere (1735–1818) On the night of April 18, 1775, British soldiers marched toward Concord to arrest American Revolutionary leaders and seize their depot of supplies. Paul Revere famously rode through the night and raised the alarm about the approaching British troops.

Roaring Twenties The 1920s, an era of social and intellectual revolution in which young people experimented with new forms of recreation and sexuality. The Eastern, urban cultural shift clashed with conservative and insular Midwestern America, which increased the tensions between the two regions.

Jackie Robinson (1919–1972) In 1947, he became the first African American to play major league baseball. He won over fans and players and stimulated the integration of other professional sports.

rock-and-roll music Alan Freed, a disc jockey, noticed white teenagers were buying rhythm and blues records that had been only purchased by African Americans and Hispanic Americans. Freed began playing these records, but called them rock-and-roll records as a way to overcome the racial barrier. As the popularity of the music genre increased, it helped bridge the gap between "white" and "black" music.

John D. Rockefeller (1839–1937) In 1870, he founded the Standard Oil Company of Ohio, which was his first step in creating his vast oil empire. He perfected the idea of a holding company.

***Roe v. Wade* (1973)** Landmark Supreme Court decision striking down state laws that banned abortions during the first trimester of pregnancy.

Roman Catholicism The Christian faith and religious practices of the Roman Catholic Church, which exerted great political, economic, and social influence on much of Western Europe and, through the Spanish and Portuguese Empires, on the Americas.

Romanticism Philosophical, literary, and artistic movement of the nineteenth century that was largely a reaction to the rationalism of the previous century; Romantics valued emotion, mysticism, and individualism.

Eleanor Roosevelt (1884–1962) She redefined the role of the presidential spouse and was the first woman to address a national political convention, write a nationally syndicated column, and hold regular press conferences. She travelled throughout the nation to promote the New Deal, women's causes, and organized labor, and to meet with African American leaders.

Franklin Delano Roosevelt (1882–1945) Elected during the Great Depression, Roosevelt sought to help struggling Americans through his New Deal programs that created employment and social programs, such as Social Security. After the bombing of Pearl Harbor, he declared war on Japan and Germany and led the country through most of the Second World War before dying of a cerebral hemorrhage.

Theodore Roosevelt (1858–1919) As the assistant secretary of the navy, he supported expansionism, American imperialism, and war with Spain. He led the Rough Riders, in Cuba during the War of 1898 and used the notoriety of this military campaign for political gain. As President McKinley's vice president, he succeeded McKinley after his assassination. His forceful foreign policy became known as "big stick diplomacy." Domestically, his policies on natural resources helped start the conservation movement. Unable to win the Republican nomination for president in 1912, he formed his own party of progressive Republicans: the "Bull Moose" party.

Roosevelt Corollary President Theodore Roosevelt's 1904 revision of the Monroe Doctrine (1823) in which he argued that the United States could use military force in Central and South American nations to prevent European nations from intervening in the Western Hemisphere.

Rough Riders The First U.S. Volunteer Cavalry, led in the War of 1898 by Theodore Roosevelt; they were victorious in their only engagement, the Battle of San Juan Hill near Santiago, Cuba, and Roosevelt was celebrated as a national hero, bolstering his political career.

Royal Proclamation of 1763 Statement issued by King George III in the wake of the Treaty of Paris which prohibited British colonists from settling any lands beyond the Appalachian mountains.

Nicola Sacco (1891–1927) In 1920, he and Bartolomeo Vanzetti were Italian immigrants who were arrested for stealing $16,000 and killing a paymaster and his guard. Their trial took place during a time of numerous bombings by anarchists and their judge was openly prejudicial; many liberals and radicals believe that their conviction was based on their political ideas and ethnic origin rather than the evidence against them.

Sacco and Vanzetti case The 1921 trial of two Italian immigrants that occurred at the height of Italian immigration and against the backdrop of numerous terror attacks by anarchists; despite a lack of clear evidence, the two defendants, both self-professed anarchists, were convicted of murder and were executed in 1927.

saloons Bars or taverns where mostly men would gather to drink, eat, relax, play games, and, often, to discuss politics.

salutary neglect Informal British policy during the first half of the eighteenth century that allowed the American colonies considerable freedom to pursue their economic and political interests in exchange for colonial obedience.

same-sex marriage The legal right for gay and lesbian couples to marry; it became the most divisive issue in the culture wars of the early 2010s as more and more court rulings affirmed this right in states and municipalities across the United States. In a landmark 2015 decision, the Supreme Court ruled in favor of legalizing same-sex marriage nationwide.

Sand Creek Massacre (1864) A brutal slaughter of unarmed Indian men, women, and children who had been promised protection by the territorial governor of Colorado; the massacre ignited warfare between Americans and Indians across the central plains for the next three years.

Sandinista Cuban-sponsored government that came to power in Nicaragua after toppling a corrupt dictator. The State Department believed that the Sandinistas were supplying the leftist Salvadoran rebels with Cuban and Soviet arms. In response, the Reagan administration ordered the CIA to train and supply guerrilla bands of anti-Communist Nicaraguans called Contras. A cease-fire agreement between the Contras and Sandinistas was signed in 1988.

Sandlot Incident Violence occurring during the Great Railroad Strike of 1877, when mobs of frustrated working-class whites in San Francisco attacked Chinese immigrants, blaming them for economic hardship.

General Antonio López de Santa Anna (1794–1876) In 1834, he seized political power in Mexico and became a dictator. In 1835, Texans rebelled against him and he led his army to Texas to crush their rebellion. He captured the missionary called the Alamo and killed all of its defenders, which inspired Texans to continue to resistance and Americans to volunteer to fight for Texas. The Texans captured Santa Anna during a surprise attack and he bought his freedom by signing a treaty recognizing Texas's independence.

Saratoga, Battles of Decisive defeat of 5,000 British troops under General John Burgoyne in several battles near Saratoga, New York, in October 1777; the American victory helped convince France to enter the war on the side of the Patriots.

scalawags White southern Republicans—some former Unionists—who served in Reconstruction governments.

Phyllis Schlafly (1924–) A right-wing Republican activist who spearheaded the anti-feminism movement. She believed feminists were "anti-family, anti-children, and pro-abortion." She worked against the equal rights amendment for women and civil rights protection for gays.

Scopes Trial Highly publicized 1925 trial of a high school teacher in Tennessee for violating a state law that prohibited the teaching of evolution; the trial was seen as the climax of the fundamentalist war on Darwinism.

Winfield Scott (1786–1866) During the Mexican War, he was the American general who captured Mexico City, which ended the war. Using his popularity from his military success, he ran as a Whig party candidate for President.

Sears, Roebuck and Company By the end of the nineteenth century, this company dominated the mail-order industry and helped create a truly national market. Its mail-order catalog and low prices allowed people living in rural areas and small towns to buy products that were previously too expensive or available only to city dwellers.

secession Shortly after President Abraham Lincoln was elected, southern states began dissolving their ties with the United States because they believed Lincoln and the Republican party were a threat to slavery.

Second Bank of the United States (B.U.S.) Established in 1816 after the first national bank's charter expired; it stabilized the economy by creating a sound national currency, by making loans to farmers, small manufacturers, and entrepreneurs, and by regulating the ability of state banks to issue their own paper currency.

Second Great Awakening Religious revival movement that arose in reaction to the growth of secularism and rationalist religion and spurred the growth of the Baptist and Methodist churches.

Second Industrial Revolution Beginning in the late nineteenth century, a wave of technological innovations, especially in iron and steel production, steam and electrical power, and telegraphic communications, all of which spurred industrial development and urban growth.

Second New Deal (1935–1938) Expansive cluster of legislation proposed by President Roosevelt that established new regulatory agencies, strengthened the rights of workers to organize unions, and laid the foundation of a federal social welfare system through the creation of Social Security.

second two-party system Domination of national politics by two major political parties, such as the Whigs and Democrats during the 1830s and 1840s.

Securities and Exchange Commission (1934) Federal agency established to regulate the issuance and trading of stocks and bonds in an effort to avoid financial panics and stock market "crashes."

Seneca Falls Convention (1848) Convention organized by feminists Lucretia Mott and Elizabeth Cady Stanton to promote women's rights and issue the pathbreaking Declaration of Sentiments.

"separate but equal" Principle underlying legal racial segregation, which was upheld in *Plessy v. Ferguson* (1896) and struck down in *Brown v. Board of Education* (1954).

separation of powers Strict division of the powers of government among three separate branches (executive, legislative, and judicial) which, in turn, check and balance each other.

September 11 On September 11, 2001, Islamic terrorists, who were members of the al Qaeda terrorist organization, hijacked four commercial airliners. Two were flown into the World Trade Center, a third into the Pentagon, and a fourth plane was brought down in Pennsylvania. In response, President George W. Bush launched his "war on terrorism." His administration assembled an international coalition to fight terrorism, which invaded Afghanistan after the country's government would not turn over Osama bin Laden. Bush and Congress passed the USA Patriot Act, which allowed government agencies to try suspected terrorists in secret military courts and eavesdrop on confidential conversations.

settlement houses Product of the late nineteenth-century movement to offer a broad array of social services in urban immigrant neighborhoods; Chicago's Hull House was one of hundreds of settlement houses that operated by the early twentieth century.

Seventeenth Amendment (1913) Constitutional amendment that provided for the direct election of senators rather than the traditional practice allowing state legislatures to name them.

Shakers Founded by Mother Ann Lee Stanley in England, the United Society of Believers in Christ's Second Appearing settled in Watervliet, New York, in 1774 and subsequently established eighteen additional communes in the Northeast, Indiana, and Kentucky.

share tenants Poor farmers who rented land to farm in exchange for a substantial share of the crop, though they would often have their own horse or mule, tools, and line of credit with a nearby store.

sharecroppers Poor, mostly black farmers who would work an owner's land in return for shelter, seed, fertilizer, mules, supplies, and food, as well as a substantial share of the crop produced.

Share-the-Wealth program Huey Long offered this program as an alternative to the New Deal. The program proposed to confiscate large personal fortunes, which would be used to guarantee every poor family a cash grant of $5,000 and every worker an annual income of $2,500. This program promised to provide pensions, reduce working hours, pay veterans' bonuses, and ensures a college education to every qualified student.

Shays's Rebellion Storming of the Massachusetts federal arsenal in 1787 by Daniel Shays and 1,200 armed farmers seeking debt relief from the state legislature through issuance of paper currency and lower taxes.

silent majority Term popularized by President Richard Nixon to describe the great majority of American voters who did not express their political opinions publicly—"the non-demonstrators."

Sixteenth Amendment (1913) Constitutional amendment that authorized the federal income tax.

slave codes Ordinances passed by a colony or state to regulate the behavior of slaves, often including brutal punishments for infractions.

Alfred E. Smith (1873–1944) In the 1928 presidential election, he won the Democratic nomination, but failed to win the presidency. Rural voters distrusted him for being Catholic and the son of Irish immigrants as well as for his anti-Prohibition stance.

Captain John Smith (1580–1631) A swashbuckling soldier of fortune with rare powers of leadership and self-promotion, he was appointed to the resident council to manage Jamestown.

Joseph Smith (1805–1844) In 1823, he claimed that the Angel Moroni showed him the location of several gold tablets on which the Book of Mormon was written. Using the Book of Mormon as his gospel, he founded the Church of Jesus Christ of Latter-day Saints, or Mormons. In 1839, they settled in Commerce, Illinois, to avoid persecution. In 1844, Joseph and his brother were arrested and jailed for ordering the destruction of a newspaper that opposed them. While in jail, an anti-Mormon mob stormed the jail and killed both of them.

social Darwinism The application of Charles Darwin's theory of evolutionary natural selection to human society; social Darwinists used the concept of "survival of the fittest" to justify class distinctions, explain poverty, and oppose government intervention in the economy.

social gospel Protestant movement that stressed the Christian obligation to address the mounting social problems caused by urbanization and industrialization.

social justice An important part of the Progressive's agenda, social justice sought to solve social problems through reform and regulation. Methods used to bring about social justice ranged from the founding of charities to the legislation of a ban on child labor.

Social Security Act (1935) Legislation enacted to provide federal assistance to retired workers through tax-funded pension payments and benefit payments to the unemployed and disabled.

Sons of Liberty First organized by Samuel Adams in the 1770s, groups of colonists dedicated to militant resistance against British control of the colonies.

Hernando de Soto (1500?–1542) A conquistador who explored the west coast of Florida, western North Carolina, and along the Arkansas river from 1539 till his death in 1542.

Southern Christian Leadership Conference (SCLC) Civil rights organization formed by Dr. Martin Luther King Jr. that championed nonviolent direct action as a means of ending segregation.

"southern strategy" This strategy was a major reason for Richard Nixon's victory in the 1968 presidential election. To gain support in the South, Nixon assured southern conservatives that he would slow the federal enforcement of civil rights laws and appoint pro-southern justices to the Supreme Court. As president, Nixon fulfilled these promises.

Spanish Armada A massive Spanish fleet of 130 warships that was defeated at Plymouth in 1588 by the English navy during the reign of Queen Elizabeth I.

Spanish flu Unprecedentedly lethal influenza epidemic of 1918 that killed more than 22 million people worldwide.

Herbert Spencer (1820–1903) As the first major proponent of social Darwinism, he argued that human society and institutions are subject to the process of natural selection and that society naturally evolves for the better. He was against any form of government interference with the evolution of society, like business regulations, because it would help the "unfit" to survive.

spirituals Songs with religious messages sung by slaves to help ease the strain of field labor and to voice their suffering at the hands of their masters and overseers.

spoils system The term—meaning the filling of federal government jobs with persons loyal to the party of the president—originated in Andrew Jackson's first term; the system was replaced in the Progressive Era by civil service.

Square Deal Roosevelt's progressive agenda of the "Three C's": control of corporations, conservation of natural resources, and consumer protection.

stagflation Term coined by economists during the Nixon presidency to describe the unprecedented situation of stagnant economic growth and consumer price inflation occurring at the same time.

Joseph Stalin (1879–1953) The Bolshevik leader who succeeded Lenin as the leader of the Soviet Union in 1924 and ruled the country until his death. During his totalitarian rule of the Soviet Union, he used purges and a system of forced labor camps to maintain control over the country, and claimed vast areas of Eastern Europe for Soviet domination.

Stalwarts Conservative Republican party faction during the presidency of Rutherford B. Hayes, 1877–1881; led by Senator Roscoe B. Conkling of New York, Stalwarts opposed civil service reform and favored a third term for President Ulysses S. Grant.

Stamp Act Act of Parliament requiring that all printed materials (e.g., newspapers, bonds, and even playing cards) in the American colonies use paper with an official tax stamp in order to pay for British military protection of the colonies.

Stamp Act Congress Twenty-seven delegates from nine of the colonies met from October 7–25, 1765 and wrote a Declaration of the Rights and Grievances of the Colonies, a petition to the King, and a petition to Parliament for the repeal of the Stamp Act.

Standard Oil Company Corporation under the leadership of John D. Rockefeller that attempted to dominate the entire oil industry through horizontal and vertical integration.

Elizabeth Cady Stanton (1815–1902) She was a prominent reformer and advocate for the rights of women, and she helped organize the Seneca Falls Convention to discuss women's rights. The convention was the first of its kind and produced the Declaration of Sentiments, which proclaimed the equality of men and women.

staple crops Profitable market crops, such as cotton, tobacco, or rice, that predominate in a given region.

state constitutions Charters that define the relationship between the state government and local governments and individuals, also protecting their rights from violation by the national government.

steamboats Ships and boats powered by wood-fired steam engines. First used in the early nineteenth century, they made two-way traffic possible in eastern river systems, creating a transcontinental market and an agricultural empire.

Thaddeus Stevens (1792–1868) As one of the leaders of the Radical Republicans, he argued that the former Confederate states should be viewed as conquered provinces, which were subject to the demands of the conquerors. He believed that all of Southern society needed to be changed, and he supported the abolition of slavery and racial equality.

Adlai E. Stevenson (1900–1965) In the 1952 and 1956 presidential elections, he was the Democratic nominee who lost to Dwight Eisenhower. He was also the U.S. Ambassador to the United Nations and is remembered for his famous speech in 1962 before the UN Security Council that unequivocally demonstrated that the Soviet Union had built nuclear missile bases in Cuba.

Stonewall Riots Violent clashes between police and gay patrons of New York City's Stonewall Inn in 1969; seen as the starting point of the modern gay rights movement.

Stono Rebellion A 1739 slave uprising in South Carolina that was brutally quashed, leading to executions as well as a severe tightening of the slave code.

Strategic Arms Limitation Treaty (SALT I) Agreement signed in 1972 by President Nixon and Secretary Brezhnev prohibiting the development of missile defense systems in the United States and Soviet Union and limiting the quantity of nuclear warheads for both.

Strategic Defense Initiative (SDI) (1983) Ronald Reagan's proposed space-based anti-missile defense system, dubbed "Star Wars" by the media, that aroused great controversy and escalated the arms race between the United States and the Soviet Union.

Levi Strauss (1829–1902) A Jewish tailor who followed miners to California during the gold rush and began making durable work pants that were later dubbed blue jeans or Levi's.

Student Nonviolent Coordinating Committee (SNCC) Interracial organization formed in 1960 with the goal of intensifying the effort to end racial segregation.

Students for a Democratic Society (SDS) Major organization of the New Left, founded at the University of Michigan in 1960 by Tom Hayden and Al Haber.

suburbia Communities formed from mass migration of middle-class whites from urban centers.

Suez crisis British, French, and Israeli attack on Egypt in 1956 after Nasser's seizure of the Suez Canal; President Eisenhower interceded to demand the withdrawal of the British, French, and Israeli forces from the Sinai peninsula and canal.

Sunbelt The label for an arc that stretched from the Carolinas to California. During the postwar era, much of the urban population growth occurred in this area.

the "surge" In early 2007, President Bush decided he would send a "surge" of new troops to Iraq and implement a new strategy. U.S. forces would shift their focus from offensive operations to the protection of Iraqi civilians from attacks by terrorist insurgents and sectarian militias. While the "surge" reduced the violence in Iraq, Iraqi leaders were still unable to develop a self-sustaining democracy.

Taft-Hartley Labor Act (1947) Congressional legislation that banned "unfair labor practices" by labor unions, required union leaders to sign anti-Communist "loyalty oaths," and prohibited federal employees from going on strike.

Taliban A coalition of ultraconservative Islamists who rose to power in Afghanistan after the Soviets withdrew. The Taliban leaders gave Osama bin Laden a safe haven in their country in exchange for aid in fighting the Northern Alliance, who were rebels opposed to the Taliban. After they refused to turn bin Laden over to the United States, America invaded Afghanistan.

Tammany Hall The "city machine" used by "Boss" Tweed to dominate politics in New York City until his arrest in 1871.

tariffs Taxes on goods imported from other nations, typically used to protect home industries from foreign competitors and to generate revenue for the federal government.

Tariff of 1816 A cluster of taxes on imports passed by Congress to protect America's emerging iron and textile industries from British competition.

Tariff of 1832 This tariff act reduced the duties on many items, but the tariffs on cloth and iron remained high. South Carolina nullified it along with the tariff of 1828. President Andrew Jackson sent federal troops to the state and asked Congress to grant him the authority to enforce the tariffs. Henry Clay presented a plan of gradually reducing the tariffs until 1842, which Congress passed and thereby ended the crisis.

Tariff of Abominations (1828) Tax on imported goods, including British cloth and clothing, that strengthened New England textile companies but hurt southern consumers, who experienced a decrease in British demand for raw cotton grown in the South.

tariff reform Effort led by the Democratic party to reduce taxes on imported goods, which Republicans argued were needed to protect American industries from foreign competition.

Zachary Taylor (1784–1850) During the Mexican War, he scored two quick victories against Mexico, which made him very popular in America. He used his popularity from his military victories to be elected the president as a member of the Whig party, but died before he could complete his term.

Taylorism Labor system based on detailed study of work tasks, championed by Frederick Winslow Taylor, intended to maximize efficiency and profits for employers.

Tea Party Right-wing populist movement, largely made up of middle-class, white male conservatives, that emerged as a response to the expansion of the federal government under the Obama administration.

Teapot Dome Affair Harding administration scandal in which Secretary of the Interior Albert B. Fall profited from secret leasing of government oil reserves in Wyoming to private oil companies.

Tecumseh (1768–1813) He was a leader of the Shawnee tribe who tried to unite all Indians into a confederation that could defend their hunting grounds. He believed that no land cessions could be made without the consent of all the tribes because they held the land in common. His beliefs and leadership made him seem dangerous to the American government and they waged war on him and his tribe. He was killed at the Battle of the Thames.

Tecumseh's Indian Confederacy A group of Native Americans under leadership of Shawnee leader Tecumseh and his prophet brother Tenskwatawa; its mission of fighting off American expansion was thwarted in the Battle of Tippecanoe (1811), when the confederacy fell apart.

Tejanos Texas settlers of Spanish or Mexican descent.

telegraph system System of electronic communication invented by Samuel F. B. Morse that could be transmitted instantaneously across great distances (first used in the 1840s).

Teller Amendment Addition to the congressional war resolution of April 20, 1898, which marked the U.S. entry into the war with Spain; the amendment declared that the United States' goal in entering the war was to ensure Cuba's independence, not to annex Cuba as a territory.

temperance A widespread reform movement, led by militant Christians, focused on reducing the use of alcoholic beverages.

tenements Shabby, low-cost inner-city apartment buildings that housed the urban poor in cramped, poorly ventilated apartments.

Tenochtitlán The capital city of the Aztec Empire. The city was built on marshy islands on the western side of Lake Tetzcoco, which is the site of present-day Mexico City.

Tet offensive Surprise attack by Viet Cong guerrillas and the North Vietnamese army on U.S. and South Vietnamese forces in 1968 that shocked the American public and led to widespread sentiment against the war.

Texas Revolution (1835–1836) Conflict between Texas colonists and the Mexican government that resulted in the creation of the separate Republic of Texas in 1836.

textile industry Commercial production of thread, fabric, and clothing from raw cotton in mills in New England during the first half of the nineteenth century, and later in the South in the late nineteenth century.

Thirteenth Amendment (1865) Amendment to the U. S. Constitution that freed all slaves in the United States.

Battle of Tippecanoe (1811) Battle in northern Indiana between U.S. troops and Native American warriors led by Tenskwatawa, the brother of Tecumseh, who had organized an anti-American Indian confederacy to fight American efforts to settle on Indian lands.

tobacco A cash crop grown in the Caribbean as well as the Virginia and Maryland colonies, made increasingly profitable by the rapidly growing popularity of smoking in Europe after the voyages of Columbus.

Gulf of Tonkin incident On August 2 and 4 of 1964, North Vietnamese vessels attacked two American destroyers in Gulf of Tonkin off the coast of North Vietnam. President Johnson described the attacks as unprovoked. In reality, the U.S. ships were monitoring South Vietnamese attacks on North Vietnamese islands that American advisers had planned. The incident spurred the Tonkin Gulf resolution.

Tonkin Gulf Resolution Congressional action that granted the president unlimited authority to defend U.S. forces abroad, passed in August 1964 after an allegedly unprovoked attack on American warships off the coast of North Vietnam.

Tories Term used by Patriots to refer to Loyalists, or colonists who supported the Crown after the Declaration of Independence.

Townshend Acts Parliamentary measures to extract more revenue from the colonies; the Revenue Act of 1767, which taxed tea, paper, and other colonial imports, was one of the most notorious of these policies.

Trail of Tears The Cherokees' eight-hundred mile journey (1838–1839) from the southern Appalachians to Indian Territory (in present-day Oklahoma); four thousand people died along the way.

transcendentalism Philosophy of a small group of New England writers and thinkers who advocated personal spirituality, self-reliance, social reform, and harmony with nature.

Transcontinental railroad First line across the continent from Omaha, Nebraska, to Sacramento, California, established in 1869 with the linkage of the Union Pacific and Central Pacific railroads at Promontory, Utah.

Transcontinental Treaty (Adams-Onís Treaty)(1819) Treaty between Spain and the United States that clarified the boundaries of the Louisiana Purchase and arranged the transfer of Florida to the United States in exchange for cash.

Treaty of Ghent (1814) Agreement between Great Britain and the United States that ended the War of 1812, signed on December 24, 1814.

Treaty of Guadalupe Hidalgo (1848) Treaty between United States and Mexico that ended the Mexican-American War.

Treaty of Paris Settlement between Great Britain and France that ended the French and Indian War.

Treaty of Versailles (1919) Peace treaty that ended the First World War, forcing Germany to dismantle its military, pay immense war reparations, and give up its colonies around the world.

trench warfare A form of prolonged combat between the entrenched positions of opposing armies, often with little tactical movement.

Trenton, Battle of A surprising and pivotal victory for General Washington and American forces in December 1776 that resulted in major British and Hessian losses.

triangular trade A network of trade in which exports from one region were sold to another region, which sent its exports to a third region, which exported its own goods back to the first country or colony.

Troubled Asset Relief Program (TARP) In 2008, President George W. Bush signed into law the bank bailout fund called Troubled Asset Relief Program (TARP), which required the Treasury Department to spend $700 billion to keep banks and other financial institutions from collapsing.

Harry S. Truman (1884–1972) As President Roosevelt's vice president, he succeeded him after his death near the end of the Second World War. After the war, Truman wrestled with the inflation of both prices and wages, worked with Congress to pass the National Security Act, and banned racial discrimination in the hiring of federal employees and ended racial segregation in the armed forces. In foreign affairs, he established the Truman Doctrine to contain communism, developed the Marshall Plan to rebuild Europe, and sent the U.S. military to defend South Korea after North Korea invaded.

Truman Doctrine (1947) President Truman's program of "containing" communism in Eastern Europe and providing economic and military aid to any nations at risk of Communist takeover.

trust A business arrangement that gives a person or corporation (the "trustee") the legal power to manage another person's money or another company without owning those entities outright.

Sojourner Truth (1797?–1883) She was born into slavery, but New York State freed her in 1827. She spent the 1840s and 1850s travelling across the country and speaking to audiences about her experiences as slave and asking them to support abolition and women's rights.

Harriet Tubman (1820–1913) She was born a slave, but escaped to the North. Then she returned to the South nineteen times and guided 300 slaves to freedom.

Frederick Jackson Turner An influential historian who authored the "Frontier Thesis" in 1893, arguing that the existence of an alluring frontier and the experience of persistent westward expansion informed the nation's democratic politics, unfettered economy, and rugged individualism.

Nat Turner (1800–1831) He was the leader of the only slave revolt to get past the planning stages. In August 1831, the revolt began with the slaves killing the members of Turner's master's household. Then they attacked other neighboring farmhouses and recruited more slaves until the militia crushed the revolt. At least fifty-five whites were killed during the uprising and seventeen slaves were hanged afterward.

Nat Turner's Rebellion (1831) Insurrection in rural Virginia led by black overseer Nat Turner, who killed slave owners and their families; in turn, federal troops indiscriminately killed hundreds of slaves in the process of putting down Turner and his rebels.

Tuskegee Airmen U.S. Army Air Corps unit of African American pilots whose combat success spurred military and civilian leaders to desegregate the armed forces after the war.

Mark Twain (1835–1910) Born Samuel Langhorne Clemens in Missouri, he became a popular humorous writer and lecturer and established himself as one of the great American satirists and authors. His two greatest books, *The Adventures of Tom Sawyer* and *The Adventures of Huckleberry Finn*, drew heavily on his childhood in Missouri.

William "Boss" Tweed (1823–1878) An infamous political boss in New York City, Tweed used his "city machine," the Tammany Hall ring, to rule, plunder, and sometimes improve the city's government. His political domination of New York City ended with his arrest in 1871 and conviction in 1873.

Twenty-first Amendment (1933) Repealed prohibition on the manufacture, sale, and transportation of alcoholic beverages, effectively nullifying the Eighteenth Amendment.

U-boats German military submarines (*Unterseeboot*) used during the First World War to attack enemy naval vessels as well as merchant ships of enemy and neutral nations.

Underground Railroad A secret system of routes and safe houses through which runaway slaves were led to freedom in the North.

Unitarians Members of the liberal New England Congregationalist offshoot, often well-educated and wealthy, who profess the oneness of God and the goodness of rational man.

United Farm Workers (UFW) Organization formed in 1962 to represent the interests of Mexican American migrant workers.

United Nations Security Council A major agency within the United Nations which remains in permanent session and has the responsibility of maintaining international peace and security. Originally, it consisted of five permanent members, (United States, Soviet Union, Britain, France, and the Republic of China), and six members elected to two-year terms. After 1965, the number of rotating members was increased to ten. In 1971, the Republic of China was replaced with the People's Republic of China, and the Soviet Union was replaced by the Russian Federation in 1991.

Universalists Members of a New England religious movement, often from the working class, who believed in a merciful God and universal salvation.

USA Patriot Act (2001) Wide-reaching Congressional legislation, triggered by the war on terror, which gave government agencies the right to eavesdrop on confidential conversations between prison inmates and their lawyers and permitted suspected terrorists to be tried in secret military courts.

U.S. battleship *Maine* American warship that exploded in the Cuban port of Havana on January 25, 1898; though later discovered to be the result of an accident, the destruction of the *Maine* was attributed by war-hungry Americans to Spain, contributing to the onset of the War of 1812.

utopian communities Ideal communities that offered innovative social and economic relationships to those who were interested in achieving salvation.

Valley Forge American military encampment near Philadelphia, where more than 3,500 soldiers deserted or died from cold and hunger in the winter of 1777–1778.

Cornelius Vanderbilt (1794–1877) In the 1860s, he consolidated several separate railroad companies into one vast entity, New York Central Railroad.

Bartolomeo Vanzetti (1888–1927) In 1920, he and Nicola Sacco were Italian immigrants who were arrested for stealing $16,000 and killing a paymaster and his guard. Their trial took place during a time of numerous bombings by anarchists and their judge was openly prejudicial. Many liberals and radicals believe that their conviction was based on their political ideas and ethnic origin rather than the evidence against them.

vertical integration The process by which a corporation gains control of all aspects of the resources and processes needed to produce and sell a product.

Amerigo Vespucci (1455–1512) Italian explorer who reached the New World in 1499 and was the first to suggest that South America was a new continent. Afterward, European mapmakers used a variant of his first name, America, to label the New World.

Vicksburg, Battle of (1863) A protracted battle in northern Mississippi in which Union forces under Ulysses Grant besieged the last major Confederate fortress on the Mississippi River, forcing the inhabitants into starvation and then submission.

Viet Cong Communist guerrillas in Vietnam who launched attacks on the Diem government.

Vietnamization Nixon-era policy of equipping and training South Vietnamese forces to take over the burden of combat from U.S. troops.

Francisco Pancho Villa (1877–1923) While the leader of one of the competing factions in the Mexican civil war, he provoked the United States into intervening. He hoped attacking the United States would help him build a reputation as an opponent of the United States, which would increase his popularity and discredit Mexican president Carranza.

Virginia Company A joint-stock enterprise that King James I chartered in 1606. The company was to spread Christianity in the New World as well as find ways to make a profit in it.

Virginia Plan The delegations to the Constitutional Convention were divided between two plans on how to structure the government: Virginia called for a strong central government and a two-house legislature apportioned by population.

Virginia Statute of Religious Freedom A Virginia law, drafted by Thomas Jefferson in 1777 and enacted in 1786, that guarantees freedom of, and from, religion.

virtual representation The idea that the American colonies, although they had no actual representative in Parliament, were "virtually" represented by all members of Parliament.

Voting Rights Act of 1965 Legislation ensuring that all Americans were able to vote; the law ended literacy tests and other means of restricting voting rights.

Wagner Act (1935) Legislation that guaranteed workers the right to organize unions, granted them direct bargaining power, and barred employers from interfering with union activities.

George Wallace (1919–1998) An outspoken defender of segregation. As the governor of Alabama, he once attempted to block African American students from enrolling at the University of Alabama. He ran as the presidential candidate for the American Independent party in 1968, appealing to voters who were concerned about rioting anti-war protesters, the welfare system, and the growth of the federal government.

war hawks In 1811, congressional members from the southern and western districts who clamored for a war to seize Canada and Florida were dubbed "war hawks."

War of 1812 Conflict fought in North America and at sea between Great Britain and the United States, 1812–1815, over American shipping rights and British efforts to spur Indian attacks on American settlements. Canadians and Native Americans also fought in the war.

war on terror Global crusade to root out anti-American, anti-Western Islamist terrorist cells launched by President George W. Bush as a response to the 9/11 attacks.

War Powers Act (1973) Legislation requiring the president to inform Congress within 48 hours of the deployment of U.S. troops abroad and to withdraw them after 60 days unless Congress approves their continued deployment.

War Production Board Federal agency created by President Roosevelt in 1942 that converted America's industrial output to war production.

"war relocation camps" Detention camps housing thousands of Japanese Americans from the West Coast who were forcibly interned from 1942 until the end of the Second World War.

Warren Court The U.S. Supreme Court under Chief Justice Earl Warren, 1953–1969, decided such landmark cases as *Brown v. Board of Education* (school desegregation), *Baker v. Carr* (legislative redistricting), and *Gideon v. Wainwright* and *Miranda v. Arizona* (rights of criminal defendants).

Booker T. Washington (1856–1915) He founded a leading college for African Americans in Tuskegee, Alabama, and become the foremost black educator in America by the 1890s. He believed that the African American community should establish an economic base for its advancement before striving for social equality. His critics charged that his philosophy sacrificed educational and civil rights for dubious social acceptance and economic opportunities.

George Washington (1732–1799) In 1775, the Continental Congress named him the commander in chief of the Continental Army which defeated the British in the American Revolution. He had previously served as an officer in the French and Indian War. In 1787, he was the presiding officer over the Constitutional Convention, but participated little in the debates. In 1789, the Electoral College chose Washington to be the nation's first president. Washington faced the nation's first foreign and domestic crises, maintaining the United States' neutrality in foreign affairs. After two terms in office, Washington chose to step down, and the power of the presidency was peacefully passed to John Adams.

Watergate (1972–1974) Scandal that exposed the criminality and corruption of the Nixon administration and ultimately led to President Nixon's resignation in 1974.

weapons of mass destruction (WMDs) According to the Bush Doctrine, these were in the hands of terrorist groups and rogue nations which required the United States to use preemptive military action in order to disable the threat.

Daniel Webster (1782–1852) As a representative from New Hampshire, he led the New Federalists in opposition to the moving of the second national bank from Boston to Philadelphia. Later, he served as representative and a senator for Massachusetts and emerged as a champion of a stronger national government. He also switched from opposing to supporting tariffs because New England had built up its manufactures with the understanding tariffs would protect them from foreign competitors.

Webster-Ashburton Treaty Settlement in 1842 of U.S.–Canadian border disputes in Maine, New York, Vermont, and in the Wisconsin Territory (now northern Minnesota).

Webster-Hayne debate U.S. Senate debate of January 1830 between Daniel Webster of Massachusetts and Robert Hayne of South Carolina over nullification and states' rights.

Western Front The contested frontier between the Central and Allied Powers that ran along northern France and across Belgium.

Whig party Political party founded in 1834 in opposition to the Jacksonian Democrats; Whigs supported federal funding for internal improvements, a national bank, and high tariffs on imported goods.

Whigs Another name for revolutionary Patriots.

Whiskey Rebellion (1794) Violent protest by western Pennsylvania farmers against the federal excise tax on corn whiskey, put down by a federal army.

Eli Whitney (1765–1825) He invented the cotton gin, which separated cotton from its seeds. One machine operator could separate fifty times more cotton than a worker could by hand, which led to an increase in cotton production and prices. These increases gave planters a new profitable use for slavery and a lucrative slave trade emerged from the coastal South to the Southwest.

Wilderness Road Originally an Indian path through the Cumberland Gap, it was used by over 300,000 settlers who migrated westward to Kentucky in the last quarter of the eighteenth century.

Roger Williams (1603–1683) Puritan who believed that the purity of the church required a complete separation between church and state and freedom from coercion in matters of faith. In 1636, he established the town of Providence, the first permanent settlement in Rhode Island and the first to allow religious freedom in America.

Wendell L. Willkie (1892–1944) In the 1940 presidential election, he was the Republican nominee who ran against President Roosevelt. He supported aid to the Allies and criticized the New Deal programs. Voters looked at the increasingly dangerous world situation and chose to keep President Roosevelt in office for a third term.

Wilmot Proviso (1846) Proposal by Congressman David Wilmot, a Pennsylvania Democrat, to prohibit slavery in any land acquired in the Mexican-American War.

Woodrow Wilson (1856–1924) In the 1912 presidential election, Woodrow Wilson ran under the slogan of New Freedom, which promised to improve of the banking system, lower tariffs, and break up monopolies. At the beginning of the First World War, Wilson kept America neutral, but provided the Allies with credit for purchases of supplies; however, the sinking of U.S. merchant ships and the Zimmermann telegram caused him to ask Congress to declare war on Germany. Wilson supported the entry of America into the League of Nations and the ratification of the Treaty of Versailles, but Congress would not approve the entry or ratification.

John Winthrop Puritan leader and Governor of the Massachusetts Bay Colony who resolved to use the colony as a refuge for persecuted Puritans and as an instrument of building a "wilderness Zion" in America.

woman suffrage Movement to give women the right to vote through a constitutional amendment, spearheaded by Susan B. Anthony and Elizabeth Cady Stanton's National Woman Suffrage Association.

Women Accepted for Voluntary Emergency Services (WAVES) During the Second World War, the increased demand for labor shook up old prejudices about gender roles in workplace and in the military. Nearly 200,000 women served in the Women's Army Corps or its naval equivalent, Women Accepted for Volunteer Emergency Service (WAVES).

Women's Army Corps (WAC) Women's branch of the United States Army; by the end of the Second World War nearly 150,000 women had served in the WAC.

women's movement Wave of activism sparked by Betty Friedan's *The Feminine Mystique* (1963); it argued for equal rights for women and fought against the cult of domesticity of the 1950s that limited women's roles to the home as wife, mother, and housewife.

women's work The traditional term referring to routine tasks in the house, garden, and fields performed by women. The sphere of women's occupations expanded in the colonies to include medicine, shopkeeping, upholstering, and the operation of inns and taverns.

Woodstock In 1969, roughly half a million young people converged on a farm near Bethel, New York, for a three-day music festival that was an expression of the flower children's free spirit.

Works Progress Administration (WPA) (1935) Government agency established to manage several federal job programs created under the New Deal; it became the largest employer in the nation.

Wounded Knee, Battle of Last incident of the Indians Wars took place in 1890 in the Dakota Territory, where the U.S. Cavalry killed over 200 Sioux men, women, and children who were in the process of surrender.

XYZ affair French foreign minister Tallyrand's three anonymous agents demanded payments to stop French plundering of American ships in 1797; refusal to pay the bribe led to two years of sea war with France (1798–1800).

Yalta Conference (1945) Meeting of the "Big Three" Allied leaders, Franklin D. Roosevelt, Winston Churchill, and Joseph Stalin, to discuss how to divide control of postwar Germany and eastern Europe

yellow journalism A type of news reporting, epitomized in the 1890s by the newspaper empires of William Randolph Hearst and Joseph Pulitzer, that intentionally manipulates public opinion through sensational headlines, illustrations, and articles about both real and invented events.

yeomen Small landowners (the majority of white families in the South) who farmed their own land and usually did not own slaves.

Yorktown, Battle of Last major battle of the Revolutionary War; General Cornwallis along with over 7,000 British troops surrendered to George Washington at Yorktown, Virginia, on October 17, 1781.

surrender at Yorktown Last battle of the Revolutionary War; General Lord Charles Cornwallis, along with over 7,000 British troops, surrendered at Yorktown, Virginia, on October 17, 1781.

Brigham Young (1801–1877) Following Joseph Smith's death, he became the leader of the Mormons and promised Illinois officials that the Mormons would leave the state. In 1846, he led the Mormons to Utah and settled near the Salt Lake. After the United States gained Utah as part of the Treaty of Guadalupe Hidalgo, he became the governor of the territory and kept the Mormons virtually independent of federal authority.

youth culture The youth of the 1950s had more money and free time than any previous generation and this allowed a distinct youth culture to emerge. A market emerged for products and activities that were specifically for young people such as transistor radios, rock records, *Seventeen* magazine, and Pat Boone movies.

Zimmermann telegram Message sent by a German official to the Mexican government in 1917 urging an invasion of the United States; the telegram was intercepted by British intelligence agents and angered Americans, many of whom called for war against Germany.

APPENDIX

THE DECLARATION OF INDEPENDENCE (1776)

When in the Course of human events, it becomes necessary for one people to dissolve the political bands which have connected them with another, and to assume among the powers of the earth, the separate and equal station to which the Laws of Nature and of Nature's God entitle them, a decent respect to the opinions of mankind requires that they should declare the causes which impel them to the separation.

We hold these truths to be self-evident, that all men are created equal, that they are endowed by their Creator with certain unalienable Rights, that among these are Life, Liberty and the pursuit of Happiness.—That to secure these rights, Governments are instituted among Men, deriving their just powers from the consent of the governed, —That whenever any Form of Government becomes destructive of these ends, it is the Right of the People to alter or to abolish it, and to institute new Government, laying its foundation on such principles and organizing its powers in such form, as to them shall seem most likely to effect their Safety and Happiness. Prudence, indeed, will dictate that Governments long established should not be changed for light and transient causes; and accordingly all experience hath shewn, that mankind are more disposed to suffer, while evils are sufferable, than to right themselves by abolishing the forms to which they are accustomed. But when a long train of abuses and usurpations, pursuing invariably the same Object evinces a design to reduce them under absolute Despotism, it is their right, it is their duty, to throw off such Government, and to provide new Guards for their future security.—Such has been the patient sufferance of these Colonies; and such is now the necessity which constrains them to alter their former

Systems of Government. The history of the present King of Great Britain is a history of repeated injuries and usurpations, all having in direct object the establishment of an absolute Tyranny over these States. To prove this, let Facts be submitted to a candid world.

He has refused his Assent to Laws, the most wholesome and necessary for the public good.

He has forbidden his Governors to pass Laws of immediate and pressing importance, unless suspended in their operation till his Assent should be obtained; and when so suspended, he has utterly neglected to attend to them.

He has refused to pass other Laws for the accommodation of large districts of people, unless those people would relinquish the right of Representation in the Legislature, a right inestimable to them and formidable to tyrants only.

He has called together legislative bodies at places unusual, uncomfortable, and distant from the depository of their public Records, for the sole purpose of fatiguing them into compliance with his measures.

He has dissolved Representative Houses repeatedly, for opposing with manly firmness his invasions on the rights of the people.

He has refused for a long time, after such dissolutions, to cause others to be elected; whereby the Legislative powers, incapable of Annihilation, have returned to the People at large for their exercise; the State remaining in the mean time exposed to all the dangers of invasion from without, and convulsions within.

He has endeavoured to prevent the population of these States; for that purpose obstructing the Laws for Naturalization of Foreigners; refusing to pass others to encourage their migrations hither, and raising the conditions of new Appropriations of Lands.

He has obstructed the Administration of Justice, by refusing his Assent to Laws for establishing Judiciary powers.

He has made Judges dependent on his Will alone, for the tenure of their offices, and the amount and payment of their salaries.

He has erected a multitude of New Offices, and sent hither swarms of Officers to harrass our people, and eat out their substance.

He has kept among us, in times of peace, Standing Armies without the Consent of our legislatures.

He has affected to render the Military independent of and superior to the Civil power.

He has combined with others to subject us to a jurisdiction foreign to our constitution, and unacknowledged by our laws; giving his Assent to their Acts of pretended Legislation:

For Quartering large bodies of armed troops among us:

For protecting them, by a mock Trial, from punishment for any Murders which they should commit on the Inhabitants of these States:

For cutting off our Trade with all parts of the world:

For imposing Taxes on us without our Consent:

For depriving us in many cases, of the benefits of Trial by Jury:

For transporting us beyond Seas to be tried for pretended offences

For abolishing the free System of English Laws in a neighbouring Province, establishing therein an Arbitrary government, and enlarging its Boundaries so as to render it at once an example and fit instrument for introducing the same absolute rule into these Colonies:

For taking away our Charters, abolishing our most valuable Laws, and altering fundamentally the Forms of our Governments:

For suspending our own Legislatures, and declaring themselves invested with power to legislate for us in all cases whatsoever.

He has abdicated Government here, by declaring us out of his Protection and waging War against us.

He has plundered our seas, ravaged our Coasts, burnt our towns, and destroyed the lives of our people.

He is at this time transporting large Armies of foreign Mercenaries to compleat the works of death, desolation and tyranny, already begun with circumstances of Cruelty & perfidy scarcely paralleled in the most barbarous ages, and totally unworthy the Head of a civilized nation.

He has constrained our fellow Citizens taken Captive on the high Seas to bear Arms against their Country, to become the executioners of their friends and Brethren, or to fall themselves by their Hands.

He has excited domestic insurrections amongst us, and has endeavoured to bring on the inhabitants of our frontiers, the merciless Indian Savages, whose known rule of warfare, is an undistinguished destruction of all ages, sexes and conditions.

In every stage of these Oppressions We have Petitioned for Redress in the most humble terms: Our repeated Petitions have been answered only by repeated injury. A Prince whose character is thus marked by every act which may define a Tyrant, is unfit to be the ruler of a free people.

Nor have We been wanting in attentions to our Brittish brethren. We have warned them from time to time of attempts by their legislature to extend an unwarrantable jurisdiction over us. We have reminded them of the circumstances of our emigration and settlement here. We have appealed to their native justice and magnanimity, and we have conjured them by the ties of our common kindred to disavow these usurpations, which, would inevitably interrupt our connections and correspondence. They too have been deaf to the voice of justice and of consanguinity. We must, therefore, acquiesce in the necessity, which denounces our Separation, and hold them, as we hold the rest of mankind, Enemies in War, in Peace Friends.

We, therefore, the Representatives of the united States of America, in General Congress, Assembled, appealing to the Supreme Judge of the world for the rectitude of our intentions, do, in the Name, and by Authority of the good People of these Colonies, solemnly publish and declare, That these United Colonies are, and of Right ought to be Free and Independent States; that they are Absolved from all Allegiance to the British Crown, and that all political connection between them and the State of Great Britain, is and ought to be totally dissolved; and that as Free and Independent States, they have full Power to levy War, conclude Peace, contract Alliances, establish Commerce, and to do all other Acts and Things which Independent States may of right do. And for the support of this Declaration, with a firm reliance on the protection of divine Providence, we mutually pledge to each other our Lives, our Fortunes and our sacred Honor.

Georgia
Button Gwinnett
Lyman Hall
George Walton

North Carolina
William Hooper
Joseph Hewes
John Penn

South Carolina
Edward Rutledge
Thomas Heyward, Jr.
Thomas Lynch, Jr.
Arthur Middleton

Massachusetts
John Hancock

Maryland
Samuel Chase
William Paca
Thomas Stone
Charles Carroll of
    Carrollton

Virginia
George Wythe
Richard Henry Lee
Thomas Jefferson
Benjamin Harrison
Thomas Nelson, Jr.
Francis Lightfoot Lee
Carter Braxton

Pennsylvania
Robert Morris
Benjamin Rush
Benjamin Franklin
John Morton
George Clymer
James Smith
George Taylor
James Wilson
George Ross

Delaware
Caesar Rodney
George Read
Thomas McKean

New York
William Floyd
Philip Livingston
Francis Lewis
Lewis Morris

New Jersey
Richard Stockton
John Witherspoon
Francis Hopkinson
John Hart
Abraham Clark

New Hampshire
Josiah Bartlett
William Whipple

Massachusetts
Samuel Adams
John Adams
Robert Treat Paine
Elbridge Gerry

Rhode Island
Stephen Hopkins
William Ellery

Connecticut
Roger Sherman
Samuel Huntington
William Williams
Oliver Wolcott

New Hampshire
Matthew Thornton

Articles of Confederation (1787)

TO ALL TO WHOM these Presents shall come, we the undersigned Delegates of the States affixed to our Names send greeting.

Whereas the Delegates of the United States of America in Congress assembled did on the fifteenth day of November in the Year of our Lord One Thousand Seven Hundred and Seventy-seven, and in the Second Year of the Independence of America agree to certain articles of Confederation and perpetual Union between the States of Newhampshire, Massachusetts-bay, Rhodeisland and Providence Plantations, Connecticut, New York, New Jersey, Pennsylvania, Delaware, Maryland, Virginia, North-Carolina, South-Carolina and Georgia in the Words following, viz.

Articles of Confederation and perpetual Union between the States of Newhampshire, Massachusetts-bay, Rhodeisland and Providence Plantations, Connecticut, New-York, New-Jersey, Pennsylvania, Delaware, Maryland, Virginia, North-Carolina, South-Carolina and Georgia.

Article I. The stile of this confederacy shall be "The United States of America."

Article II. Each State retains its sovereignty, freedom and independence, and every power, jurisdiction and right, which is not by this confederation expressly delegated to the United States, in Congress assembled.

Article III. The said States hereby severally enter into a firm league of friendship with each other, for their common defence, the security of their liberties, and their mutual and general welfare, binding themselves to assist each other, against all force offered to, or attacks made upon them, or any of them, on account of religion, sovereignty, trade or any other pretence whatever.

Article IV. The better to secure and perpetuate mutual friendship and intercourse among the people of the different States in this Union, the free inhabitants of each of these States, paupers, vagabonds and fugitives from justice excepted, shall be entitled to all privileges and immunities of free citizens in the several States; and the people of each State shall have free ingress and regress to and from any other State, and shall enjoy therein all the privileges of trade and commerce, subject to the same duties, impositions and restrictions as the inhabitants thereof respectively, provided that such restrictions shall not extend so far as to prevent the removal of property imported into any State, to any other State of which the owner is an inhabitant; provided also that no imposition, duties or restriction shall be laid by any State, on the property of the United States, or either of them.

If any person guilty of, or charged with treason, felony, or other high misdemeanor in any State, shall flee from justice, and be found in any of the United States, he shall upon demand of the Governor or Executive power, of the State from which he fled, be delivered up and removed to the State having jurisdiction of his offence.

Full faith and credit shall be given in each of these States to the records, acts and judicial proceedings of the courts and magistrates of every other State.

Article V. For the more convenient management of the general interests of the United States, delegates shall be annually appointed in such manner as the legislature of each State shall direct, to meet in Congress on the first Monday in November, in every year, with a power reserved to each State, to recall its delegates, or any of them, at any time within the year, and to send others in their stead, for the remainder of the year.

No State shall be represented in Congress by less than two, nor by more than seven members; and no person shall be capable of being a delegate for more than three years in any term of six years; nor shall any person, being a delegate, be capable of holding any office under the United States, for which he, or another for his benefit receives any salary, fees or emolument of any kind.

Each State shall maintain its own delegates in a meeting of the States, and while they act as members of the committee of the States.

In determining questions in the United States, in Congress assembled, each State shall have one vote.

Freedom of speech and debate in Congress shall not be impeached or questioned in any court, or place out of Congress, and the members of Congress shall be protected in their persons from arrests and imprisonments, during the time of their going to and from, and attendance on Congress, except for treason, felony, or breach of the peace.

Article VI. No State without the consent of the United States in Congress assembled, shall send any embassy to, or receive any embassy from, or enter into any conference, agreement, alliance or treaty with any king, prince or state; nor shall any person holding any office of profit or trust under the United States, or any of them, accept of any present, emolument, office or title of any kind whatever from any king, prince or foreign state; nor shall the United States in Congress assembled, or any of them, grant any title of nobility.

No two or more States shall enter into any treaty, confederation or alliance whatever between them, without the consent of the United States in Congress assembled, specifying accurately the purposes for which the same is to be entered into, and how long it shall continue.

No State shall lay any imposts or duties, which may interfere with any stipulations in treaties, entered into by the United States in Congress assembled, with any king, prince or state, in pursuance of any treaties already proposed by Congress, to the courts of France and Spain.

No vessels of war shall be kept up in time of peace by any State, except such number only, as shall be deemed necessary by the United States in Congress assembled, for the defence of such State, or its trade; nor shall any body of forces be kept up by any State, in time of peace, except such number only, as in the judgment of the United States, in Congress assembled, shall be deemed requisite to garrison the forts necessary for the defence of such State; but every State shall always keep up a well regulated and disciplined militia, sufficiently armed and accoutred, and shall provide and constantly have ready for use, in public stores, a due number of field pieces and tents, and a proper quantity of arms, ammunition and camp equipage.

No State shall engage in any war without the consent of the United States in Congress assembled, unless such State be actually invaded by enemies, or shall have received certain advice of a resolution being formed by some nation of Indians to invade such State, and the danger is so imminent as not to admit of a delay, till the United States in Congress assembled can be consulted: nor shall any State grant commissions to any ships or vessels of war, nor letters of marque or reprisal, except it be after a declaration of war by the United States in Congress assembled, and then only against the kingdom or state and the subjects thereof, against which war has been so declared, and under such regulations as shall be established by the United States in Congress assembled, unless such State be infested by pirates, in which case vessels of war may be fitted out for that occasion, and kept so long as the danger shall continue, or until the United States in Congress assembled shall determine otherwise.

ARTICLE VII. When land-forces are raised by any State of the common defence, all officers of or under the rank of colonel, shall be appointed by the Legislature of each State respectively by whom such forces shall be raised, or in such manner as such State shall direct, and all vacancies shall be filled up by the State which first made the appointment.

ARTICLE VIII. All charges of war, and all other expenses that shall be incurred for the common defence or general welfare, and allowed by the United States in Congress assembled, shall be defrayed out of a common treasury, which shall be supplied by the several States, in proportion to the value of all land within each State, granted to or surveyed for any person, as such land and the buildings and improvements thereon shall be estimated according to such mode as the United States in Congress assembled, shall from time to time direct and appoint.

The taxes for paying that proportion shall be laid and levied by the authority and direction of the Legislatures of the several States within the time agreed upon by the United States in Congress assembled.

ARTICLE IX. The United States in Congress assembled, shall have the sole and exclusive right and power of determining on peace and war, except in the cases mentioned in the sixth article—of sending and receiving ambassadors— entering into treaties and alliances, provided that no treaty of commerce shall be made whereby the legislative power of the respective States shall be restrained from imposing such imposts and duties on foreigners, as their own people are subjected to, or from prohibiting the exportation or importation of and species of goods or commodities whatsoever—of establishing rules for deciding in all cases, what captures on land or water shall be legal, and in what manner prizes taken by land or naval forces in the service of the United States shall be divided or appropriated—of granting letters of marque and reprisal in times of peace—appointing courts for the trial of piracies and felonies committed on the high seas and establishing courts for receiving and determining finally appeals in all cases of captures, provided that no member of Congress shall be appointed a judge of any of the said courts.

The United States in Congress assembled shall also be the last resort on appeal in all disputes and differences now subsisting or that hereafter may arise between two or more States concerning boundary, jurisdiction or any other cause whatever; which authority shall always be exercised in the manner following. Whenever the legislative or executive authority or lawful agent of any State in controversy with another shall present a petition to Congress, stating the matter in question and praying for a hearing, notice thereof shall be given by order of Congress to the legislative or executive authority of the other State in controversy, and a day assigned for the appearance of the parties by their lawful agents, who shall then be directed to appoint by joint consent, commissioners or judges to constitute a court for hearing and determining the matter in question: but if they cannot agree, Congress shall name three persons out of each of the United States, and from the list of such persons each party shall alternately strike out one, the petitioners beginning, until the number shall be reduced to thirteen; and from that number not less than seven, nor more than nine names as Congress shall direct, shall in the presence of Congress be drawn out by lot, and the persons whose names shall be so drawn or any five of them, shall be commissioners or judges, to hear and finally determine the controversy, so always as a major part of the judges who shall hear the cause shall agree in the determination: and if either party shall neglect to attend at the day appointed, without reasons, which Congress shall judge sufficient, or being present shall refuse to strike, the Congress shall proceed to nominate three persons out of each State, and the Secretary of Congress shall strike in behalf of such party absent or refusing; and the judgment and sentence of the court to be appointed, in the manner before prescribed, shall be final and conclusive; and if any of the parties shall refuse to submit to the authority of such court, or to appear or defend their claim or cause, the court shall nevertheless proceed to pronounce sentence, or judgment, which shall in like manner be final and decisive, the judgment or sentence and other proceedings being in either case transmitted to Congress, and lodged among the acts of Congress for the security of the parties concerned: provided that every commissioner, before he sits in judgment, shall take an oath to be administered by one of the judges of the supreme or superior court of the State where the case shall be tried, "well and truly to hear and determine the matter in question, according to the best of his judgment, without favour, affection or hope of reward:" provided also that no State shall be deprived of territory for the benefit of the United States.

All controversies concerning the private right of soil claimed under different grants of two or more States, whose jurisdiction as they may respect such lands, and the states which passed such grants are adjusted, the said grants or either of them being at the same time claimed to have originated antecedent to such settlement of jurisdiction, shall on the petition of either party to the Congress of the United States, be finally determined as near as may be in the same manner as is before prescribed for deciding disputes respecting territorial jurisdiction between different States.

The United States in Congress assembled shall also have the sole and exclusive right and power of regulating the alloy and value of coin struck by their own authority, or by that of the respective States—fixing the standard of weights and measures throughout the United States—regulating the trade and managing all affairs with the Indians, not members of any of the States, provided that the legislative right of any State within its own limits be not infringed or violated—establishing and regulating post-offices from one State to another, throughout all of the United States, and exacting such postage on the papers passing thro' the same as may be requisite to defray the expenses of the said office—appointing all officers of the land forces, in the service of the United States, excepting regimental officers—appointing all the officers of the naval forces, and commissioning all officers whatever in the service of the United States—making rules for the government and regulation of the said land and naval forces, and directing their operations.

The United States in Congress assembled shall have authority to appoint a committee, to sit in the recess of Congress, to be denominated "a Committee of the States," and to consist of one delegate from each State; and to appoint such other committees and civil officers as may be necessary for managing the general affairs of the United States under their direction—to appoint one of their number to preside, provided that no person be allowed to serve in the office of president more than one year in any term of three years; to ascertain the necessary sums of money to be raised for the service of the United States, and to appropriate and apply the same for defraying the public expenses—to borrow money, or emit bills on the credit of the United States, transmitting every half year to the respective States an account of the sums of money so borrowed or emitted,—to build and equip a navy—to agree upon the number of land forces, and to make requisitions from each State for its quota, in proportion to the number of white inhabitants in such State; which requisition shall be binding, and thereupon the Legislature of each State shall appoint the regimental officers, raise the men and cloath, arm and equip them in a soldier like manner, at the expense of the United States; and the officers and men so cloathed, armed and equipped shall march to the place appointed, and within the time agreed on by the United States in Congress assembled: but if the United States in Congress assembled shall, on consideration of circumstances judge proper that any State should not raise men, or should raise a smaller number of men than the quota thereof, such extra number shall be raised, officered, cloathed, armed and equipped in the same manner as the quota of such State, unless the legislature of such State shall judge that such extra number cannot be safely spared out of the same, in which case they shall raise officer, cloath, arm and equip as many of such extra number as they judge can be safely spared. And the officers and men so cloathed, armed and equipped, shall march to the place appointed, and within the time agreed on by the United States in Congress assembled.

The United States in Congress assembled shall never engage in a war, nor grant letters of marque and reprisal in time of peace, nor enter into any treaties or alliances, nor coin money, nor regulate the value thereof, nor ascertain the sums and expenses necessary for the defence and welfare of the United States, or any of them, nor emit bills, nor borrow money on the credit of the

United States, nor appropriate money, nor agree upon the number of vessels to be built or purchased, or the number of land or sea forces to be raised, nor appoint a commander in chief of the army or navy, unless nine States assent to the same: nor shall a question on any other point, except for adjourning from day to day be determined, unless by the votes of a majority of the United States in Congress assembled.

The Congress of the United States shall have power to adjourn to any time within the year, and to any place within the United States, so that no period of adjournment be for a longer duration than the space of six months, and shall publish the journal of their proceedings monthly, except such parts thereof relating to treaties, alliances or military operations, as in their judgment require secresy; and the yeas and nays of the delegates of each State on any question shall be entered on the Journal, when it is desired by any delegate; and the delegates of a State, or any of them, at his or their request shall be furnished with a transcript of the said journal, except such parts as are above excepted, to lay before the Legislatures of the several States.

ARTICLE X. The committee of the States, or any nine of them, shall be authorized to execute, in the recess of Congress, such of the powers of Congress as the United States in Congress assembled, by the consent of nine States, shall from time to time think expedient to vest them with; provided that no power be delegated to the said committee, for the exercise of which, by the articles of confederation, the voice of nine States in the Congress of the United States assembled is requisite.

ARTICLE XI. Canada acceding to this confederation, and joining in the measures of the United States, shall be admitted into, and entitled to all the advantages of this Union: but no other colony shall be admitted into the same, unless such admission be agreed to by nine States.

ARTICLE XII. All bills of credit emitted, monies borrowed and debts contracted by, or under the authority of Congress, before the assembling of the United States, in pursuance of the present confederation, shall be deemed and considered as a charge against the United States, for payment and satisfaction whereof the said United States, and the public faith are hereby solemnly pledged.

ARTICLE XIII. Every State shall abide by the determinations of the United States in Congress assembled, on all questions which by this confederation are submitted to them. And the articles of this confederation shall be inviolably observed by every State, and the Union shall be perpetual; nor shall any alteration at any time hereafter be made in any of them; unless such alteration be agreed to in a Congress of the United States, and be afterwards confirmed by the Legislatures of every State.

And whereas it has pleased the Great Governor of the world to incline the hearts of the Legislatures we respectively represent in Congress, to approve of, and to authorize us to ratify the said articles of confederation and perpetual union. Know ye that we the undersigned delegates, by virtue of the power and authority to us given for that purpose, do by these presents, in the name and in behalf of our respective constituents, fully and entirely ratify and confirm each and every of the said articles of confederation and perpetual union, and all and singular the matters and things therein contained: and we do further solemnly plight and engage the faith of our respective constituents, that they shall abide by the determinations of the United States in Congress assembled, on all questions, which by the said confederation are submitted to them. And that the articles thereof shall be inviolably observed by the States we respectively represent, and that the Union shall be perpetual.

In witness thereof we have hereunto set our hands in Congress. Done at Philadelphia in the State of Pennsylvania the ninth day of July in the year of our Lord one thousand seven hundred and seventy-eight, and in the third year of the independence of America.

THE CONSTITUTION OF THE UNITED STATES (1787)

We the People of the United States, in Order to form a more perfect Union, establish Justice, insure domestic Tranquility, provide for the common defence, promote the general Welfare, and secure the Blessings of Liberty to ourselves and our Posterity, do ordain and establish this Constitution for the United States of America.

ARTICLE. I.

SECTION. 1. All legislative Powers herein granted shall be vested in a Congress of the United States, which shall consist of a Senate and House of Representatives.

SECTION. 2. The House of Representatives shall be composed of Members chosen every second Year by the People of the several States, and the Electors in each State shall have the Qualifications requisite for Electors of the most numerous Branch of the State Legislature.

No Person shall be a Representative who shall not have attained to the Age of twenty five Years, and been seven Years a Citizen of the United States, and who shall not, when elected, be an Inhabitant of that State in which he shall be chosen.

Representatives and direct Taxes shall be apportioned among the several States which may be included within this Union, according to their respective Numbers, which shall be determined by adding to the whole Number of free Persons, including those bound to Service for a Term of Years, and excluding Indians not taxed, three fifths of all other Persons. The actual Enumeration shall be made within three Years after the first Meeting of the Congress of the United States, and within every subsequent Term of ten Years, in such Manner as they shall by Law direct. The Number of Representatives shall not exceed one for every thirty Thousand, but each State shall have at Least one Representative; and until such enumeration shall be made, the State of New Hampshire shall be entitled to chuse three, Massachusetts eight, Rhode-Island and Providence Plantations one, Connecticut five, New-York six, New Jersey four, Pennsylvania eight, Delaware one, Maryland six, Virginia ten, North Carolina five, South Carolina five, and Georgia three.

When vacancies happen in the Representation from any State, the Executive Authority thereof shall issue Writs of Election to fill such Vacancies.

The House of Representatives shall chuse their Speaker and other Officers; and shall have the sole Power of Impeachment.

SECTION. 3. The Senate of the United States shall be composed of two Senators from each State, chosen by the Legislature thereof for six Years; and each Senator shall have one Vote.

Immediately after they shall be assembled in Consequence of the first Election, they shall be divided as equally as may be into three Classes. The Seats of the Senators of the first Class shall be vacated at the Expiration of the second Year, of the second Class at the Expiration of the fourth Year, and of the third Class at the Expiration of the sixth Year, so that one third may be chosen every second Year; and if Vacancies happen by Resignation, or otherwise, during the Recess of the Legislature of any State, the Executive thereof may make temporary Appointments until the next Meeting of the Legislature, which shall then fill such Vacancies.

No Person shall be a Senator who shall not have attained to the Age of thirty Years, and been nine Years a Citizen of the United States, and who shall not, when elected, be an Inhabitant of that State for which he shall be chosen.

The Vice President of the United States shall be President of the Senate, but shall have no Vote, unless they be equally divided.

The Senate shall chuse their other Officers, and also a President pro tempore, in the Absence of the Vice President, or when he shall exercise the Office of President of the United States.

The Senate shall have the sole Power to try all Impeachments. When sitting for that Purpose, they shall be on Oath or Affirmation. When the President of the United States is tried, the Chief Justice shall preside: And no Person shall be convicted without the Concurrence of two thirds of the Members present.

Judgment in Cases of Impeachment shall not extend further than to removal from Office, and disqualification to hold and enjoy any Office of honor, Trust or Profit under the United States: but the Party convicted shall nevertheless be liable and subject to Indictment, Trial, Judgment and Punishment, according to Law.

SECTION. 4. The Times, Places and Manner of holding Elections for Senators and Representatives, shall be prescribed in each State by the Legislature thereof; but the Congress may at any time by Law make or alter such Regulations, except as to the Places of chusing Senators.

The Congress shall assemble at least once in every Year, and such Meeting shall be on the first Monday in December, unless they shall by Law appoint a different Day.

SECTION. 5. Each House shall be the Judge of the Elections, Returns and Qualifications of its own Members, and a Majority of each shall constitute a Quorum to do Business; but a smaller Number may adjourn from day to day, and may be authorized to compel the Attendance of absent Members, in such Manner, and under such Penalties as each House may provide.

Each House may determine the Rules of its Proceedings, punish its Members for disorderly Behaviour, and, with the Concurrence of two thirds, expel a Member.

Each House shall keep a Journal of its Proceedings, and from time to time publish the same, excepting such Parts as may in their Judgment require Secrecy; and the Yeas and Nays of the Members of either House on any question shall, at the Desire of one fifth of those Present, be entered on the Journal.

Neither House, during the Session of Congress, shall, without the Consent of the other, adjourn for more than three days, nor to any other Place than that in which the two Houses shall be sitting.

SECTION. 6. The Senators and Representatives shall receive a Compensation for their Services, to be ascertained by Law, and paid out of the Treasury of the United States. They shall in all Cases, except Treason, Felony and Breach of the Peace, be privileged from Arrest during their Attendance at the Session of their respective Houses, and in going to and returning from the same; and for any Speech or Debate in either House, they shall not be questioned in any other Place.

No Senator or Representative shall, during the Time for which he was elected, be appointed to any civil Office under the Authority of the United States, which shall have been created, or the Emoluments whereof shall have been encreased during such time; and no Person holding any Office under the United States, shall be a Member of either House during his Continuance in Office.

SECTION. 7. All Bills for raising Revenue shall originate in the House of Representatives; but the Senate may propose or concur with Amendments as on other Bills.

Every Bill which shall have passed the House of Representatives and the Senate, shall, before it become a Law, be presented to the President of the United States: If he approve he shall sign it, but if not he shall return it, with his Objections to that House in which it shall have originated, who shall enter the Objections at large on their Journal, and proceed to reconsider it. If after such Reconsideration two thirds of that House shall agree to pass the Bill, it shall be sent, together with the Objections, to the other House, by which it shall likewise be reconsidered, and if approved by two thirds of that House, it shall become a Law. But in all such Cases the Votes of both Houses shall be determined by yeas and Nays, and the Names of the Persons voting for and against the Bill shall be entered on the Journal of each House respectively. If any Bill shall not be returned by the President within ten Days (Sundays excepted) after it shall have been presented to him, the Same shall be a Law, in like Manner as if he had signed it, unless the Congress by their Adjournment prevent its Return, in which Case it shall not be a Law.

Every Order, Resolution, or Vote to which the Concurrence of the Senate and House of Representatives may be necessary (except on a question of Adjournment) shall be presented to the President of the United States; and before the Same shall take Effect, shall be approved by him, or being disapproved by him, shall be repassed by two thirds of the Senate and House of Representatives, according to the Rules and Limitations prescribed in the Case of a Bill.

SECTION. 8. The Congress shall have Power To lay and collect Taxes, Duties, Imposts and Excises, to pay the Debts and provide for the common Defence and general Welfare of the United States; but all Duties, Imposts and Excises shall be uniform throughout the United States;

To borrow Money on the credit of the United States;

To regulate Commerce with foreign Nations, and among the several States, and with the Indian Tribes;

To establish an uniform Rule of Naturalization, and uniform Laws on the subject of Bankruptcies throughout the United States;

To coin Money, regulate the Value thereof, and of foreign Coin, and fix the Standard of Weights and Measures;

To provide for the Punishment of counterfeiting the Securities and current Coin of the United States;

To establish Post Offices and post Roads;

To promote the Progress of Science and useful Arts, by securing for limited Times to Authors and Inventors the exclusive Right to their respective Writings and Discoveries;

To constitute Tribunals inferior to the supreme Court;

To define and punish Piracies and Felonies committed on the high Seas, and Offences against the Law of Nations;

To declare War, grant Letters of Marque and Reprisal, and make Rules concerning Captures on Land and Water;

To raise and support Armies, but no Appropriation of Money to that Use shall be for a longer Term than two Years;

To provide and maintain a Navy;

To make Rules for the Government and Regulation of the land and naval Forces;

To provide for calling forth the Militia to execute the Laws of the Union, suppress Insurrections and repel Invasions;

To provide for organizing, arming, and disciplining, the Militia, and for governing such Part of them as may be employed in the Service of the United States, reserving to the States respectively, the Appointment of the Officers, and the Authority of training the Militia according to the discipline prescribed by Congress;

To exercise exclusive Legislation in all Cases whatsoever, over such District (not exceeding ten Miles square) as may, by Cession of particular States, and the Acceptance of Congress, become the Seat of the Government of the United States, and to exercise like Authority over all Places purchased by the Consent of the Legislature of the State in which the Same shall be, for the Erection of Forts, Magazines, Arsenals, dock-Yards, and other needful Buildings;—And

To make all Laws which shall be necessary and proper for carrying into Execution the foregoing Powers, and all other Powers vested by this Constitution in the Government of the United States, or in any Department or Officer thereof.

SECTION. 9. The Migration or Importation of such Persons as any of the States now existing shall think proper to admit, shall not be prohibited by the Congress prior to the Year one thousand eight hundred and eight, but a Tax or duty may be imposed on such Importation, not exceeding ten dollars for each Person.

The Privilege of the Writ of Habeas Corpus shall not be suspended, unless when in Cases of Rebellion or Invasion the public Safety may require it.

No Bill of Attainder or ex post facto Law shall be passed.

No Capitation, or other direct, Tax shall be laid, unless in Proportion to the Census or enumeration herein before directed to be taken.

No Tax or Duty shall be laid on Articles exported from any State.

No Preference shall be given by any Regulation of Commerce or Revenue to the Ports of one State over those of another; nor shall Vessels bound to, or from, one State, be obliged to enter, clear, or pay Duties in another.

No Money shall be drawn from the Treasury, but in Consequence of Appropriations made by Law; and a regular Statement and Account of the Receipts and Expenditures of all public Money shall be published from time to time.

No Title of Nobility shall be granted by the United States: And no Person holding any Office of Profit or Trust under them, shall, without the Consent of the Congress, accept of any present, Emolument, Office, or Title, of any kind whatever, from any King, Prince, or foreign State.

SECTION. 10. No State shall enter into any Treaty, Alliance, or Confederation; grant Letters of Marque and Reprisal; coin Money; emit Bills of Credit; make any Thing but gold and silver Coin a Tender in Payment of Debts; pass any Bill of Attainder, ex post facto Law, or Law impairing the Obligation of Contracts, or grant any Title of Nobility.

No State shall, without the Consent of the Congress, lay any Imposts or Duties on Imports or Exports, except what may be absolutely necessary for executing it's inspection Laws: and the net Produce of all Duties and Imposts, laid by any State on Imports or Exports, shall be for the Use of the Treasury of the United States; and all such Laws shall be subject to the Revision and Controul of the Congress.

No State shall, without the Consent of Congress, lay any Duty of Tonnage, keep Troops, or Ships of War in time of Peace, enter into any Agreement or Compact with another State, or with a foreign Power, or engage in War, unless actually invaded, or in such imminent Danger as will not admit of delay.

ARTICLE. II.

SECTION. 1. The executive Power shall be vested in a President of the United States of America. He shall hold his Office during the Term of four Years, and, together with the Vice President, chosen for the same Term, be elected, as follows:

Each State shall appoint, in such Manner as the Legislature thereof may direct, a Number of Electors, equal to the whole Number of Senators and Representatives to which the State may be entitled in the Congress: but no Senator or Representative, or Person holding an Office of Trust or Profit under the United States, shall be appointed an Elector.

The Electors shall meet in their respective States, and vote by Ballot for two Persons, of whom one at least shall not be an Inhabitant of the same State with themselves. And they shall make a List of all the Persons voted for, and of the Number of Votes for each; which List they shall sign and certify, and transmit sealed to the Seat of the Government of the United States, directed to the President of the Senate. The President of the Senate shall, in the Presence of the Senate and House of Representatives, open all the Certificates, and the Votes shall then be counted. The Person having the greatest Number of Votes shall be the President, if such Number be a Majority of the whole Number of Electors appointed; and if there be more than one who have such Majority, and have an equal Number of Votes, then the House of Representatives shall immediately chuse by Ballot one of them for President; and if no Person have a Majority, then from the five highest on the List the said House shall in like Manner chuse the President. But in chusing the President, the Votes shall be taken by States, the Representation from each State having one Vote; A quorum for this purpose shall consist of a Member or Members from two thirds of the States, and a Majority of all the States shall be necessary to a Choice. In every Case, after the Choice of the President, the Person having the greatest Number of Votes of the Electors shall be the Vice President. But if there should remain two or more who have equal Votes, the Senate shall chuse from them by Ballot the Vice President.

The Congress may determine the Time of chusing the Electors, and the Day on which they shall give their Votes; which Day shall be the same throughout the United States.

No Person except a natural born Citizen, or a Citizen of the United States, at the time of the Adoption of this Constitution, shall be eligible to the Office of President; neither shall any Person be eligible to that Office who shall not have attained to the Age of thirty five Years, and been fourteen Years a Resident within the United States.

In Case of the Removal of the President from Office, or of his Death, Resignation, or Inability to discharge the Powers and Duties of the said Office, the Same shall devolve on the Vice President, and the Congress may by Law provide for the Case of Removal, Death, Resignation or Inability, both of the President and Vice President, declaring what Officer shall then act as President, and such Officer shall act accordingly, until the Disability be removed, or a President shall be elected.

The President shall, at stated Times, receive for his Services, a Compensation, which shall neither be increased nor diminished during the Period for which he shall have been elected, and he shall not receive within that Period any other Emolument from the United States, or any of them.

Before he enter on the Execution of his Office, he shall take the following Oath or Affirmation:—"I do solemnly swear (or affirm) that I will faithfully execute the Office of President of the United States, and will to the best of my Ability, preserve, protect and defend the Constitution of the United States."

SECTION. 2. The President shall be Commander in Chief of the Army and Navy of the United States, and of the Militia of the several States, when called into the actual Service of the United States; he may require the Opinion, in writing, of the principal Officer in each of the executive Departments, upon any Subject relating to the Duties of their respective Offices, and he shall have Power to grant Reprieves and Pardons for Offences against the United States, except in Cases of Impeachment.

He shall have Power, by and with the Advice and Consent of the Senate, to make Treaties, provided two thirds of the Senators present concur; and he shall nominate, and by and with the Advice and Consent of the Senate, shall appoint Ambassadors, other public Ministers and Consuls, Judges of the supreme Court, and all other Officers of the United States, whose Appointments are not herein otherwise provided for, and which shall be established by Law: but the Congress may by Law vest the Appointment of such inferior Officers, as they think proper, in the President alone, in the Courts of Law, or in the Heads of Departments.

The President shall have Power to fill up all Vacancies that may happen during the Recess of the Senate, by granting Commissions which shall expire at the End of their next Session.

SECTION. 3. He shall from time to time give to the Congress Information of the State of the Union, and recommend to their Consideration such Measures as he shall judge necessary and expedient; he may, on extraordinary Occasions, convene both Houses, or either of them, and in Case of Disagreement between them, with Respect to the Time of Adjournment, he may adjourn them to such Time as he shall think proper; he shall receive Ambassadors and other public Ministers; he shall take Care that the Laws be faithfully executed, and shall Commission all the Officers of the United States.

SECTION. 4. The President, Vice President and all civil Officers of the United States, shall be removed from Office on Impeachment for, and Conviction of, Treason, Bribery, or other high Crimes and Misdemeanors.

ARTICLE III.

SECTION. 1. The judicial Power of the United States shall be vested in one supreme Court, and in such inferior Courts as the Congress may from time to time ordain and establish. The Judges, both of the supreme and inferior Courts, shall hold their Offices during good Behaviour, and shall, at stated Times, receive for their Services a Compensation, which shall not be diminished during their Continuance in Office.

SECTION. 2. The judicial Power shall extend to all Cases, in Law and Equity, arising under this Constitution, the Laws of the United States, and Treaties made, or which shall be made, under their Authority;—to all Cases affecting Ambassadors, other public Ministers and Consuls;—to all Cases of admiralty and maritime Jurisdiction;—to Controversies to which the United States shall be a Party;—to Controversies between two or more States;— between a State and Citizens of another State,—between Citizens of different States,—between Citizens of the same State claiming Lands under Grants of different States, and between a State, or the Citizens thereof, and foreign States, Citizens or Subjects.

In all Cases affecting Ambassadors, other public Ministers and Consuls, and those in which a State shall be Party, the supreme Court shall have original Jurisdiction. In all the other Cases before mentioned, the supreme Court shall have appellate Jurisdiction, both as to Law and Fact, with such Exceptions, and under such Regulations as the Congress shall make.

The Trial of all Crimes, except in Cases of Impeachment, shall be by Jury; and such Trial shall be held in the State where the said Crimes shall have been committed; but when not committed within any State, the Trial shall be at such Place or Places as the Congress may by Law have directed.

SECTION. 3. Treason against the United States, shall consist only in levying War against them, or in adhering to their Enemies, giving them Aid and Comfort. No Person shall be convicted of Treason unless on the Testimony of two Witnesses to the same overt Act, or on Confession in open Court.

The Congress shall have Power to declare the Punishment of Treason, but no Attainder of Treason shall work Corruption of Blood, or Forfeiture except during the Life of the Person attainted.

ARTICLE. IV.

SECTION. 1. Full Faith and Credit shall be given in each State to the public Acts, Records, and judicial Proceedings of every other State. And the Congress may by general Laws prescribe the Manner in which such Acts, Records and Proceedings shall be proved, and the Effect thereof.

SECTION. 2. The Citizens of each State shall be entitled to all Privileges and Immunities of Citizens in the several States.

A Person charged in any State with Treason, Felony, or other Crime, who shall flee from Justice, and be found in another State, shall on Demand of the executive Authority of the State from which he fled, be delivered up, to be removed to the State having Jurisdiction of the Crime.

No Person held to Service or Labour in one State, under the Laws thereof, escaping into another, shall, in Consequence of any Law or Regulation therein, be discharged from such Service or Labour, but shall be delivered up on Claim of the Party to whom such Service or Labour may be due.

SECTION. 3. New States may be admitted by the Congress into this Union; but no new State shall be formed or erected within the Jurisdiction of any other State; nor any State be formed by the Junction of two or more States, or Parts of States, without the Consent of the Legislatures of the States concerned as well as of the Congress.

The Congress shall have Power to dispose of and make all needful Rules and Regulations respecting the Territory or other Property belonging to the United States; and nothing in this Constitution shall be so construed as to Prejudice any Claims of the United States, or of any particular State.

SECTION. 4. The United States shall guarantee to every State in this Union a Republican Form of Government, and shall protect each of them against Invasion; and on Application of the Legislature, or of the Executive (when the Legislature cannot be convened), against domestic Violence.

ARTICLE. V.

The Congress, whenever two thirds of both Houses shall deem it necessary, shall propose Amendments to this Constitution, or, on the Application of the Legislatures of two thirds of the several States, shall call a Convention for proposing Amendments, which, in either Case, shall be valid to all Intents and Purposes, as Part of this Constitution, when ratified by the Legislatures of three fourths of the several States, or by Conventions in three fourths thereof, as the one or the other Mode of Ratification may be proposed by the Congress; Provided that no Amendment which may be made prior to the Year One thousand eight hundred and eight shall in any Manner affect the first and fourth Clauses in the Ninth Section of the first Article; and that no State, without its Consent, shall be deprived of its equal Suffrage in the Senate.

ARTICLE. VI.

All Debts contracted and Engagements entered into, before the Adoption of this Constitution, shall be as valid against the United States under this Constitution, as under the Confederation.

This Constitution, and the Laws of the United States which shall be made in Pursuance thereof; and all Treaties made, or which shall be made, under the Authority of the United States, shall be the supreme Law of the Land; and the Judges in every State shall be bound thereby, any Thing in the Constitution or Laws of any State to the Contrary notwithstanding.

The Senators and Representatives before mentioned, and the Members of the several State Legislatures, and all executive and judicial Officers, both of the United States and of the several States, shall be bound by Oath or Affirmation, to support this Constitution; but no religious Test shall ever be required as a Qualification to any Office or public Trust under the United States.

ARTICLE. VII.

The Ratification of the Conventions of nine States, shall be sufficient for the Establishment of this Constitution between the States so ratifying the Same.

The Word, "the," being interlined between the seventh and eighth Lines of the first Page, the Word "Thirty" being partly written on an Erazure in the fifteenth Line of the first Page, The Words "is tried" being interlined between the thirty second and thirty third Lines of the first Page and the Word "the" being interlined between the forty third and forty fourth Lines of the second Page.

Attest William Jackson Secretary done in Convention by the Unanimous Consent of the States present the Seventeenth Day of September in the Year of our Lord one thousand seven hundred and Eighty seven and of the Independance of the United States of America the Twelfth In witness whereof We have hereunto subscribed our Names,

G°. Washington
Presidt and deputy from Virginia

Delaware	Geo: Read Gunning Bedford jun John Dickinson Richard Bassett Jaco: Broom	Massachusetts	Nathaniel Gorham Rufus King

		Connecticut	Wm. Saml. Johnson Roger Sherman

Maryland	James McHenry Dan of St Thos. Jenifer Danl. Carroll	New York	Alexander Hamilton

Virginia	John Blair James Madison Jr.		

		New Jersey	Wil: Livingston David Brearley Wm. Paterson Jona: Dayton

North Carolina	Wm. Blount Richd. Dobbs Spaight Hu Williamson		

		Pennsylvania	B Franklin Thomas Mifflin Robt. Morris Geo. Clymer Thos. FitzSimons Jared Ingersoll James Wilson Gouv Morris

South Carolina	J. Rutledge Charles Cotesworth Pinckney Charles Pinckney Pierce Butler		

Georgia	William Few Abr Baldwin		

New Hampshire	John Langdon Nicholas Gilman		

Amendments to the Constitution

The Bill of Rights: A Transcription

THE PREAMBLE TO THE BILL OF RIGHTS Congress of the United States begun and held at the City of New-York, on Wednesday the fourth of March, one thousand seven hundred and eighty nine.

THE Conventions of a number of the States, having at the time of their adopting the Constitution, expressed a desire, in order to prevent misconstruction or abuse of its powers, that further declaratory and restrictive clauses should be added: And as extending the ground of public confidence in the Government, will best ensure the beneficent ends of its institution.

RESOLVED by the Senate and House of Representatives of the United States of America, in Congress assembled, two thirds of both Houses concurring, that the following Articles be proposed to the Legislatures of the several States, as amendments to the Constitution of the United States, all, or any of which Articles, when ratified by three fourths of the said Legislatures, to be valid to all intents and purposes, as part of the said Constitution; viz.

ARTICLES in addition to, and Amendment of the Constitution of the United States of America, proposed by Congress, and ratified by the Legislatures of the several States, pursuant to the fifth Article of the original Constitution.

Note: The following text is a transcription of the first ten amendments to the Constitution in their original form. These amendments were ratified December 15, 1791, and form what is known as the "Bill of Rights."

Amendment I

Congress shall make no law respecting an establishment of religion, or prohibiting the free exercise thereof; or abridging the freedom of speech, or of the press; or the right of the people peaceably to assemble, and to petition the Government for a redress of grievances.

Amendment II

A well regulated Militia, being necessary to the security of a free State, the right of the people to keep and bear Arms, shall not be infringed.

AMENDMENT III

No Soldier shall, in time of peace be quartered in any house, without the consent of the Owner, nor in time of war, but in a manner to be prescribed by law.

AMENDMENT IV

The right of the people to be secure in their persons, houses, papers, and effects, against unreasonable searches and seizures, shall not be violated, and no Warrants shall issue, but upon probable cause, supported by Oath or affirmation, and particularly describing the place to be searched, and the persons or things to be seized.

AMENDMENT V

No person shall be held to answer for a capital, or otherwise infamous crime, unless on a presentment or indictment of a Grand Jury, except in cases arising in the land or naval forces, or in the Militia, when in actual service in time of War or public danger; nor shall any person be subject for the same offence to be twice put in jeopardy of life or limb; nor shall be compelled in any criminal case to be a witness against himself, nor be deprived of life, liberty, or property, without due process of law; nor shall private property be taken for public use, without just compensation.

AMENDMENT VI

In all criminal prosecutions, the accused shall enjoy the right to a speedy and public trial, by an impartial jury of the State and district wherein the crime shall have been committed, which district shall have been previously ascertained by law, and to be informed of the nature and cause of the accusation; to be confronted with the witnesses against him; to have compulsory process for obtaining witnesses in his favor, and to have the Assistance of Counsel for his defence.

AMENDMENT VII

In Suits at common law, where the value in controversy shall exceed twenty dollars, the right of trial by jury shall be preserved, and no fact tried by a jury, shall be otherwise re-examined in any Court of the United States, than according to the rules of the common law.

AMENDMENT VIII

Excessive bail shall not be required, nor excessive fines imposed, nor cruel and unusual punishments inflicted.

AMENDMENT IX

The enumeration in the Constitution, of certain rights, shall not be construed to deny or disparage others retained by the people.

AMENDMENT X

The powers not delegated to the United States by the Constitution, nor prohibited by it to the States, are reserved to the States respectively, or to the people.

AMENDMENT XI

Passed by Congress March 4, 1794. Ratified February 7, 1795.

Note: Article III, section 2, of the Constitution was modified by amendment 11.

The Judicial power of the United States shall not be construed to extend to any suit in law or equity, commenced or prosecuted against one of the United States by Citizens of another State, or by Citizens or Subjects of any Foreign State.

AMENDMENT XII

Passed by Congress December 9, 1803. Ratified June 15, 1804.

Note: A portion of Article II, section 1 of the Constitution was superseded by the 12th amendment.

The Electors shall meet in their respective states and vote by ballot for President and Vice-President, one of whom, at least, shall not be an inhabitant of the same state with themselves; they shall name in their ballots the person voted for as President, and in distinct ballots the person voted for as Vice-President, and they shall make distinct lists of all persons voted for as President, and of all persons voted for as Vice-President, and of the number of votes for each, which lists they shall sign and certify, and transmit sealed to the seat of the government of the United States, directed to the President of the Senate; — the President of the Senate shall, in the presence of the Senate and House of Representatives, open all the certificates and the votes shall then be counted; — The person having the greatest number of votes for President, shall be the President, if such number be a majority of the whole number of Electors appointed; and if no person have such majority, then from the persons having the highest numbers not exceeding three on the list of those voted for as President, the House of Representatives shall choose immediately, by ballot, the President. But in choosing the President, the votes shall be taken by states, the representation from each state having one vote; a quorum for this purpose shall consist of a member or members from two-thirds of the states, and a majority of all the states shall be necessary to a choice. [And if the House of Representatives shall not choose a President whenever the right of choice shall devolve upon them, before the fourth day of March next following, then the Vice-President shall act as President, as in case of the death or other constitutional disability of the President. —]* The person having the greatest number of votes as Vice-President, shall be the Vice-President, if such number be a majority of the whole number of Electors appointed, and if no person have a majority, then from the two highest numbers on the list, the Senate shall choose the Vice-President; a quorum for the purpose shall consist of two-thirds of the whole number of Senators, and a majority of the whole number shall be necessary to a choice. But no person constitutionally ineligible to the office of President shall be eligible to that of Vice-President of the United States.

AMENDMENT XIII

Passed by Congress January 31, 1865. Ratified December 6, 1865.

Note: A portion of Article IV, section 2, of the Constitution was superseded by the 13th amendment.

SECTION 1. Neither slavery nor involuntary servitude, except as a punishment for crime whereof the party shall have been duly convicted, shall exist within the United States, or any place subject to their jurisdiction.

SECTION 2. Congress shall have power to enforce this article by appropriate legislation.

Superseded by section 3 of the 20th amendment.

Amendment XIV

Passed by Congress June 13, 1866. Ratified July 9, 1868.

Note: Article I, section 2, of the Constitution was modified by section 2 of the 14th amendment.

SECTION 1. All persons born or naturalized in the United States, and subject to the jurisdiction thereof, are citizens of the United States and of the State wherein they reside. No State shall make or enforce any law which shall abridge the privileges or immunities of citizens of the United States; nor shall any State deprive any person of life, liberty, or property, without due process of law; nor deny to any person within its jurisdiction the equal protection of the laws.

SECTION 2. Representatives shall be apportioned among the several States according to their respective numbers, counting the whole number of persons in each State, excluding Indians not taxed. But when the right to vote at any election for the choice of electors for President and Vice-President of the United States, Representatives in Congress, the Executive and Judicial officers of a State, or the members of the Legislature thereof, is denied to any of the male inhabitants of such State, being twenty-one years of age,* and citizens of the United States, or in any way abridged, except for participation in rebellion, or other crime, the basis of representation therein shall be reduced in the proportion which the number of such male citizens shall bear to the whole number of male citizens twenty-one years of age in such State.

SECTION 3. No person shall be a Senator or Representative in Congress, or elector of President and Vice-President, or hold any office, civil or military, under the United States, or under any State, who, having previously taken an oath, as a member of Congress, or as an officer of the United States, or as a member of any State legislature, or as an executive or judicial officer of any State, to support the Constitution of the United States, shall have engaged in insurrection or rebellion against the same, or given aid or comfort to the enemies thereof. But Congress may by a vote of two-thirds of each House, remove such disability.

SECTION 4. The validity of the public debt of the United States, authorized by law, including debts incurred for payment of pensions and bounties for services in suppressing insurrection or rebellion, shall not be

---

Changed by section 1 of the 26th amendment.

questioned. But neither the United States nor any State shall assume or pay any debt or obligation incurred in aid of insurrection or rebellion against the United States, or any claim for the loss or emancipation of any slave; but all such debts, obligations and claims shall be held illegal and void.

SECTION 5. The Congress shall have the power to enforce, by appropriate legislation, the provisions of this article.

AMENDMENT XV

Passed by Congress February 26, 1869. Ratified February 3, 1870.

SECTION 1. The right of citizens of the United States to vote shall not be denied or abridged by the United States or by any State on account of race, color, or previous condition of servitude—

SECTION 2. The Congress shall have the power to enforce this article by appropriate legislation.

AMENDMENT XVI

Passed by Congress July 2, 1909. Ratified February 3, 1913.

Note: Article I, section 9, of the Constitution was modified by amendment 16.

The Congress shall have power to lay and collect taxes on incomes, from whatever source derived, without apportionment among the several States, and without regard to any census or enumeration.

AMENDMENT XVII

Passed by Congress May 13, 1912. Ratified April 8, 1913.

Note: Article I, section 3, of the Constitution was modified by the 17th amendment.

The Senate of the United States shall be composed of two Senators from each State, elected by the people thereof, for six years; and each Senator shall have one vote. The electors in each State shall have the qualifications requisite for electors of the most numerous branch of the State legislatures.

When vacancies happen in the representation of any State in the Senate, the executive authority of such State shall issue writs of election to fill such vacancies: *Provided*, That the legislature of any State may empower the executive thereof to make temporary appointments until the people fill the vacancies by election as the legislature may direct.

This amendment shall not be so construed as to affect the election or term of any Senator chosen before it becomes valid as part of the Constitution.

AMENDMENT XVIII

Passed by Congress December 18, 1917. Ratified January 16, 1919. Repealed by amendment 21.

SECTION 1. After one year from the ratification of this article the manufacture, sale, or transportation of intoxicating liquors within, the importation thereof into, or the exportation thereof from the United States and all territory subject to the jurisdiction thereof for beverage purposes is hereby prohibited.

SECTION 2. The Congress and the several States shall have concurrent power to enforce this article by appropriate legislation.

SECTION 3. This article shall be inoperative unless it shall have been ratified as an amendment to the Constitution by the legislatures of the several States, as provided in the Constitution, within seven years from the date of the submission hereof to the States by the Congress.

AMENDMENT XIX

Passed by Congress June 4, 1919. Ratified August 18, 1920.

The right of citizens of the United States to vote shall not be denied or abridged by the United States or by any State on account of sex.

Congress shall have power to enforce this article by appropriate legislation.

AMENDMENT XX

Passed by Congress March 2, 1932. Ratified January 23, 1933.

Note: Article I, section 4, of the Constitution was modified by section 2 of this amendment. In addition, a portion of the 12th amendment was superseded by section 3.

SECTION 1. The terms of the President and the Vice President shall end at noon on the 20th day of January, and the terms of Senators and Representatives at noon on the 3rd day of January, of the years in which such terms would have ended if this article had not been ratified; and the terms of their successors shall then begin.

SECTION 2. The Congress shall assemble at least once in every year, and such meeting shall begin at noon on the 3d day of January, unless they shall by law appoint a different day.

SECTION 3. If, at the time fixed for the beginning of the term of the President, the President elect shall have died, the Vice President elect shall become President. If a President shall not have been chosen before the time fixed for the beginning of his term, or if the President elect shall have failed to qualify, then the Vice President elect shall act as President until a President shall have qualified; and the Congress may by law provide for the case wherein neither a President elect nor a Vice President shall have qualified, declaring who shall then act as President, or the manner in which one who is to act shall be selected, and such person shall act accordingly until a President or Vice President shall have qualified.

SECTION 4. The Congress may by law provide for the case of the death of any of the persons from whom the House of Representatives may choose a President whenever the right of choice shall have devolved upon them, and for the case of the death of any of the persons from whom the Senate may choose a Vice President whenever the right of choice shall have devolved upon them.

SECTION 5. Sections 1 and 2 shall take effect on the 15th day of October following the ratification of this article.

SECTION 6. This article shall be inoperative unless it shall have been ratified as an amendment to the Constitution by the legislatures of three-fourths of the several States within seven years from the date of its submission.

Amendment XXI

Passed by Congress February 20, 1933. Ratified December 5, 1933.

SECTION 1. The eighteenth article of amendment to the Constitution of the United States is hereby repealed.

SECTION 2. The transportation or importation into any State, Territory, or Possession of the United States for delivery or use therein of intoxicating liquors, in violation of the laws thereof, is hereby prohibited.

SECTION 3. This article shall be inoperative unless it shall have been ratified as an amendment to the Constitution by conventions in the several States, as provided in the Constitution, within seven years from the date of the submission hereof to the States by the Congress.

AMENDMENT XXII

Passed by Congress March 21, 1947. Ratified February 27, 1951.

SECTION 1. No person shall be elected to the office of the President more than twice, and no person who has held the office of President, or acted as President, for more than two years of a term to which some other person was elected President shall be elected to the office of President more than once. But this Article shall not apply to any person holding the office of President when this Article was proposed by Congress, and shall not prevent any person who may be holding the office of President, or acting as President, during the term within which this Article becomes operative from holding the office of President or acting as President during the remainder of such term.

SECTION 2. This article shall be inoperative unless it shall have been ratified as an amendment to the Constitution by the legislatures of three-fourths of the several States within seven years from the date of its submission to the States by the Congress.

AMENDMENT XXIII

Passed by Congress June 16, 1960. Ratified March 29, 1961.

SECTION 1. The District constituting the seat of Government of the United States shall appoint in such manner as Congress may direct:

A number of electors of President and Vice President equal to the whole number of Senators and Representatives in Congress to which the District would be entitled if it were a State, but in no event more than the least populous State; they shall be in addition to those appointed by the States, but they shall be considered, for the purposes of the election of President and Vice President, to be electors appointed by a State; and they shall meet in the District and perform such duties as provided by the twelfth article of amendment.

SECTION 2. The Congress shall have power to enforce this article by appropriate legislation.

AMENDMENT XXIV

Passed by Congress August 27, 1962. Ratified January 23, 1964.

SECTION 1. The right of citizens of the United States to vote in any primary or other election for President or Vice President, for electors for President or Vice President, or for Senator or Representative in Congress, shall not be denied or abridged by the United States or any State by reason of failure to pay poll tax or other tax.

SECTION 2. The Congress shall have power to enforce this article by appropriate legislation.

AMENDMENT XXV

Passed by Congress July 6, 1965. Ratified February 10, 1967.

Note: Article II, section 1, of the Constitution was affected by the 25th amendment.

SECTION 1. In case of the removal of the President from office or of his death or resignation, the Vice President shall become President.

SECTION 2. Whenever there is a vacancy in the office of the Vice President, the President shall nominate a Vice President who shall take office upon confirmation by a majority vote of both Houses of Congress.

SECTION 3. Whenever the President transmits to the President pro tempore of the Senate and the Speaker of the House of Representatives his written declaration that he is unable to discharge the powers and duties of his office, and until he transmits to them a written declaration to the contrary, such powers and duties shall be discharged by the Vice President as Acting President.

SECTION 4. Whenever the Vice President and a majority of either the principal officers of the executive departments or of such other body as Congress may by law provide, transmit to the President pro tempore of the Senate and the Speaker of the House of Representatives their written declaration that the President is unable to discharge the powers and duties of his office, the Vice President shall immediately assume the powers and duties of the office as Acting President.

Thereafter, when the President transmits to the President pro tempore of the Senate and the Speaker of the House of Representatives his written declaration that no inability exists, he shall resume the powers and duties of his office unless the Vice President and a majority of either the principal officers of the executive department or of such other body as Congress may by law provide, transmit within four days to the President pro tempore of the Senate and the Speaker of the House of Representatives their written declaration that the President is unable to discharge the powers and duties of his office. Thereupon Congress shall decide the issue, assembling within forty-eight hours for that purpose if not in session. If the Congress, within twenty-one days after receipt of the latter written declaration, or, if Congress is not in session, within twenty-one days after Congress is required to assemble, determines by two-thirds vote of both Houses that the President is unable to discharge the powers and duties of his office, the Vice President shall continue to discharge the same as Acting President; otherwise, the President shall resume the powers and duties of his office.

Amendment XXVI

Passed by Congress March 23, 1971. Ratified July 1, 1971.

Note: Amendment 14, section 2, of the Constitution was modified by section 1 of the 26th amendment.

SECTION 1. The right of citizens of the United States, who are eighteen years of age or older, to vote shall not be denied or abridged by the United States or by any State on account of age.

SECTION 2. The Congress shall have power to enforce this article by appropriate legislation.

Amendment XXVII

Originally proposed Sept. 25, 1789. Ratified May 7, 1992.

No law, varying the compensation for the services of the Senators and Representatives, shall take effect, until an election of representatives shall have intervened.

PRESIDENTIAL ELECTIONS

Year	Number of States	Candidates	Parties	Popular Vote	% of Popular Vote	Electoral Vote	% Voter Participation
1789	11	**GEORGE WASHINGTON**	No party designations			69	
		John Adams				34	
		Other candidates				35	
1792	15	**GEORGE WASHINGTON**	No party designations			132	
		John Adams				77	
		George Clinton				50	
		Other candidates				5	
1796	16	**JOHN ADAMS**	Federalist			71	
		Thomas Jefferson	Democratic-Republican			68	
		Thomas Pinckney	Federalist			59	
		Aaron Burr	Democratic-Republican			30	
		Other candidates				48	
1800	16	**THOMAS JEFFERSON**	Democratic-Republican			73	
		Aaron Burr	Democratic-Republican			73	
		John Adams	Federalist			65	
		Charles C. Pinckney	Federalist			64	
		John Jay	Federalist			1	
1804	17	**THOMAS JEFFERSON**	Democratic-Republican			162	
		Charles C. Pinckney	Federalist			14	

Year	Number of States	Candidates	Parties	Popular Vote	% of Popular Vote	Electoral Vote	% Voter Participation
1808	17	**JAMES MADISON**	Democratic-Republican			122	
		Charles C. Pinckney	Federalist			47	
		George Clinton	Democratic-Republican			6	
1812	18	**JAMES MADISON**	Democratic-Republican			128	
		DeWitt Clinton	Federalist			89	
1816	19	**JAMES MONROE**	Democratic-Republican			183	
		Rufus King	Federalist	34			
1820	24	**JAMES MONROE**	Democratic-Republican			231	
		John Quincy Adams	Independent	1			
1824	24	**JOHN QUINCY ADAMS**	Democratic-Republican	108,740	30.5	84	26.9
		Andrew Jackson	Democratic-Republican	153,544	43.1	99	
		Henry Clay	Democratic-Republican	47,136	13.2	37	
		William H. Crawford	Democratic-Republican	46,618	13.1	41	
1828	24	**ANDREW JACKSON**	Democratic	647,286	56.0	178	57.6
		John Quincy Adams	National-Republican	508,064	44.0	83	

Year	Number of States	Candidates	Parties	Popular Vote	% of Popular Vote	Electoral Vote	% Voter Participation
1832	24	**ANDREW JACKSON**	Democratic	688,242	54.5	219	55.4
		Henry Clay	National-Republican	473,462	37.5	49	
		William Wirt	Anti-Masonic	101,051	8.0	7	
		John Floyd	Democratic			11	
1836	26	**MARTIN VAN BUREN**	Democratic	765,483	50.9	170	57.8
		William H. Harrison	Whig			73	
		Hugh L. White	Whig	739,795	49.1	26	
		Daniel Webster	Whig			14	
		W. P. Mangum	Whig			11	
1840	26	**WILLIAM H. HARRISON**	Whig	1,274,624	53.1	234	80.2
		Martin Van Buren	Democratic	1,127,781	46.9	60	
1844	26	**JAMES K. POLK**	Democratic	1,338,464	49.6	170	78.9
		Henry Clay	Whig	1,300,097	48.1	105	
		James G. Birney	Liberty	62,300	2.3		
1848	30	**ZACHARY TAYLOR**	Whig	1,360,967	47.4	163	72.7
		Lewis Cass	Democratic	1,222,342	42.5	127	
		Martin Van Buren	Free Soil	291,263	10.1		
1852	31	**FRANKLIN PIERCE**	Democratic	1,601,117	50.9	254	69.6
		Winfield Scott	Whig	1,385,453	44.1	42	
		John P. Hale	Free Soil	155,825	5.0		
1856	31	**JAMES BUCHANAN**	Democratic	1,832,955	45.3	174	78.9
		John C. Frémont	Republican	1,339,932	33.1	114	
		Millard Fillmore	American	871,731	21.6	8	

Year	Number of States	Candidates	Parties	Popular Vote	% of Popular Vote	Electoral Vote	% Voter Participation
1860	33	**ABRAHAM LINCOLN**	Republican	1,865,593	39.8	180	81.2
		Stephen A. Douglas	Democratic	1,382,713	29.5	12	
		John C. Breckinridge	Democratic	848,356	18.1	72	
		John Bell	Constitutional Union	592,906	12.6	39	
1864	36	**ABRAHAM LINCOLN**	Republican	2,206,938	55.0	212	73.8
		George B. McClellan	Democratic	1,803,787	45.0	21	
1868	37	**ULYSSES S. GRANT**	Republican	3,013,421	52.7	214	78.1
		Horatio Seymour	Democratic	2,706,829	47.3	80	
1872	37	**ULYSSES S. GRANT**	Republican	3,596,745	55.6	286	71.3
		Horace Greeley	Democratic	2,843,446	43.9	66	
1876	38	Rutherford B. Hayes	Republican	4,036,572	48.0	185	81.8
		Samuel J. Tilden	Democratic	4,284,020	51.0	184	
1880	38	**JAMES A. GARFIELD**	Republican	4,453,295	48.5	214	79.4
		Winfield S. Hancock	Democratic	4,414,082	48.1	155	
		James B. Weaver	Greenback-Labor	308,578	3.4		
1884	38	**GROVER CLEVELAND**	Democratic	4,879,507	48.5	219	77.5
		James G. Blaine	Republican	4,850,293	48.2	182	
		Benjamin F. Butler	Greenback-Labor	175,370	1.8		
		John P. St. John	Prohibition	150,369	1.5		
1888	38	**BENJAMIN HARRISON**	Republican	5,477,129	47.9	233	79.3
		Grover Cleveland	Democratic	5,537,857	48.6	168	
		Clinton B. Fisk	Prohibition	249,506	2.2		
		Anson J. Streeter	Union Labor	146,935	1.3		

Year	Number of States	Candidates	Parties	Popular Vote	% of Popular Vote	Electoral Vote	% Voter Participation
1892	44	**GROVER CLEVELAND**	Democratic	5,555,426	46.1	277	74.7
		Benjamin Harrison	Republican	5,182,690	43.0	145	
		James B. Weaver	People's	1,029,846	8.5	22	
		John Bidwell	Prohibition	264,133	2.2		
1896	45	**WILLIAM MCKINLEY**	Republican	7,102,246	51.1	271	79.3
		William J. Bryan	Democratic	6,492,559	47.7	176	
1900	45	**WILLIAM MCKINLEY**	Republican	7,218,491	51.7	292	73.2
		William J. Bryan	Democratic; Populist	6,356,734	45.5	155	
		John C. Wooley	Prohibition	208,914	1.5		
1904	45	**THEODORE ROOSEVELT**	Republican	7,628,461	57.4	336	65.2
		Alton B. Parker	Democratic	5,084,223	37.6	140	
		Eugene V. Debs	Socialist	402,283	3.0		
		Silas C. Swallow	Prohibition	258,536	1.9		
1908	46	**WILLIAM H. TAFT**	Republican	7,675,320	51.6	321	65.4
		William J. Bryan	Democratic	6,412,294	43.1	162	
		Eugene V. Debs	Socialist	420,793	2.8		
		Eugene W. Chafin	Prohibition	253,840	1.7		
1912	48	**WOODROW WILSON**	Democratic	6,296,547	41.9	435	58.8
		Theodore Roosevelt	Progressive	4,118,571	27.4	88	
		William H. Taft	Republican	3,486,720	23.2	8	
		Eugene V. Debs	Socialist	900,672	6.0		
		Eugene W. Chafin	Prohibition	206,275	1.4		

Year	Number of States	Candidates	Parties	Popular Vote	% of Popular Vote	Electoral Vote	% Voter Participation
1916	48	**WOODROW WILSON**	Democratic	9,127,695	49.4	277	61.6
		Charles E. Hughes	Republican	8,533,507	46.2	254	
		A. L. Benson	Socialist	585,113	3.2		
		J. Frank Hanly	Prohibition	220,506	1.2		
1920	48	**WARREN G. HARDING**	Republican	16,143,407	60.4	404	49.2
		James M. Cox	Democratic	9,130,328	34.2	127	
		Eugene V. Debs	Socialist	919,799	3.4		
		P. P. Christensen	Farmer-Labor	265,411	1.0		
1924	48	**CALVIN COOLIDGE**	Republican	15,718,211	54.0	382	48.9
		John W. Davis	Democratic	8,385,283	28.8	136	
		Robert M. La Follette	Progressive	4,831,289	16.6	13	
1928	48	**HERBERT C. HOOVER**	Republican	21,391,993	58.2	444	56.9
		Alfred E. Smith	Democratic	15,016,169	40.9	87	
1932	48	**FRANKLIN D. ROOSEVELT**	Democratic	22,809,638	57.4	472	56.9
		Herbert C. Hoover	Republican	15,758,901	39.7	59	
		Norman Thomas	Socialist	881,951	2.2		
1936	48	**FRANKLIN D. ROOSEVELT**	Democratic	27,752,869	60.8	523	61.0
		Alfred M. Landon	Republican	16,674,665	36.5	8	
		William Lemke	Union	882,479	1.9		
1940	48	**FRANKLIN D. ROOSEVELT**	Democratic	27,307,819	54.8	449	62.5
		Wendell L. Willkie	Republican	22,321,018	44.8	82	
1944	48	**FRANKLIN D. ROOSEVELT**	Democratic	25,606,585	53.5	432	55.9
		Thomas E. Dewey	Republican	22,014,745	46.0	99	

Year	Number of States	Candidates	Parties	Popular Vote	% of Popular Vote	Electoral Vote	% Voter Participation
1948	48	**HARRY S. TRUMAN**	Democratic	24,179,345	49.6	303	53.0
		Thomas E. Dewey	Republican	21,991,291	45.1	189	
		J. Strom Thurmond	States' Rights	1,176,125	2.4	39	
		Henry A. Wallace	Progressive	1,157,326	2.4		
1952	48	**DWIGHT D. EISENHOWER**	Republican	33,936,234	55.1	442	63.3
		Adlai E. Stevenson	Democratic	27,314,992	44.4	89	
1956	48	**DWIGHT D. EISENHOWER**	Republican	35,590,472	57.6	457	60.6
		Adlai E. Stevenson	Democratic	26,022,752	42.1	73	
1960	50	**JOHN F. KENNEDY**	Democratic	34,226,731	49.7	303	62.8
		Richard M. Nixon	Republican	34,108,157	49.5	219	
1964	50	**LYNDON B. JOHNSON**	Democratic	43,129,566	61.1	486	61.9
		Barry M. Goldwater	Republican	27,178,188	38.5	52	
1968	50	**RICHARD M. NIXON**	Republican	31,785,480	43.4	301	60.9
		Hubert H. Humphrey	Democratic	31,275,166	42.7	191	
		George C. Wallace	American Independent	9,906,473	13.5	46	
1972	50	**RICHARD M. NIXON**	Republican	47,169,911	60.7	520	55.2
		George S. McGovern	Democratic	29,170,383	37.5	17	
		John G. Schmitz	American	1,099,482	1.4		
1976	50	**JIMMY CARTER**	Democratic	40,830,763	50.1	297	53.5
		Gerald R. Ford	Republican	39,147,793	48.0	240	

Year	Number of States	Candidates	Party	Popular Vote	Percentage of Popular Vote	Electoral Vote	Percentage of Voter Participation
1980	50	**RONALD REAGAN**	Republican	43,901,812	50.7	489	52.6
		Jimmy Carter	Democratic	35,483,820	41.0	49	
		John B. Anderson	Independent	5,719,437	6.6		
		Ed Clark	Libertarian	921,188	1.1		
1984	50	**RONALD REAGAN**	Republican	54,451,521	58.8	525	53.1
		Walter F. Mondale	Democratic	37,565,334	40.6	13	
1988	50	**GEORGE H. W. BUSH**	Republican	47,917,341	53.4	426	50.1
		Michael Dukakis	Democratic	41,013,030	45.6	111	
1992	50	**BILL CLINTON**	Democratic	44,908,254	43.0	370	55.0
		George H. W. Bush	Republican	39,102,343	37.4	168	
		H. Ross Perot	Independent	19,741,065	18.9		
1996	50	**BILL CLINTON**	Democratic	47,401,185	49.0	379	49.0
		Bob Dole	Republican	39,197,469	41.0	159	
		H. Ross Perot	Independent	8,085,295	8.0		
2000	50	**GEORGE W. BUSH**	Republican	50,455,156	47.9	271	50.4
		Al Gore	Democrat	50,997,335	48.4	266	
		Ralph Nader	Green	2,882,897	2.7		
2004	50	**GEORGE W. BUSH**	Republican	62,040,610	50.7	286	60.7
		John F. Kerry	Democrat	59,028,444	48.3	251	
2008	50	**BARACK OBAMA**	Democrat	69,456,897	52.92	365	63.0
		John McCain	Republican	59,934,814	45.66	173	
2012	50	**BARACK OBAMA**	Democrat	65,915,795	51.1	332	54.9
		Mitt Romney	Republican	60,933,504	47.2	206	

Candidates receiving less than 1 percent of the popular vote have been omitted. Thus the percentage of popular vote given for any election year may not total 100 percent.

Before the passage of the Twelfth Amendment in 1804, the electoral college voted for two presidential candidates; the runner-up became vice president.

ADMISSION OF STATES

Order of Admission	State	Date of Admission	Order of Admission	State	Date of Admission
1	Delaware	December 7, 1787	26	Michigan	January 26, 1837
2	Pennsylvania	December 12, 1787	27	Florida	March 3, 1845
3	New Jersey	December 18, 1787	28	Texas	December 29, 1845
4	Georgia	January 2, 1788	29	Iowa	December 28, 1846
5	Connecticut	January 9, 1788	30	Wisconsin	May 29, 1848
6	Massachusetts	February 7, 1788	31	California	September 9, 1850
7	Maryland	April 28, 1788	32	Minnesota	May 11, 1858
8	South Carolina	May 23, 1788	33	Oregon	February 14, 1859
9	New Hampshire	June 21, 1788	34	Kansas	January 29, 1861
10	Virginia	June 25, 1788	35	West Virginia	June 30, 1863
11	New York	July 26, 1788	36	Nevada	October 31, 1864
12	North Carolina	November 21, 1789	37	Nebraska	March 1, 1867
13	Rhode Island	May 29, 1790	38	Colorado	August 1, 1876
14	Vermont	March 4, 1791	39	North Dakota	November 2, 1889
15	Kentucky	June 1, 1792	40	South Dakota	November 2, 1889
16	Tennessee	June 1, 1796	41	Montana	November 8, 1889
17	Ohio	March 1, 1803	42	Washington	November 11, 1889
18	Louisiana	April 30, 1812	43	Idaho	July 3, 1890
19	Indiana	December 11, 1816	44	Wyoming	July 10, 1890
20	Mississippi	December 10, 1817	45	Utah	January 4, 1896
21	Illinois	December 3, 1818	46	Oklahoma	November 16, 1907
22	Alabama	December 14, 1819	47	New Mexico	January 6, 1912
23	Maine	March 15, 1820	48	Arizona	February 14, 1912
24	Missouri	August 10, 1821	49	Alaska	January 3, 1959
25	Arkansas	June 15, 1836	50	Hawaii	August 21, 1959

POPULATION OF THE UNITED STATES

Year	Number of States	Population	% Increase	Population per Square Mile
1790	13	3,929,214		4.5
1800	16	5,308,483	35.1	6.1
1810	17	7,239,881	36.4	4.3
1820	23	9,638,453	33.1	5.5
1830	24	12,866,020	33.5	7.4
1840	26	17,069,453	32.7	9.8
1850	31	23,191,876	35.9	7.9
1860	33	31,443,321	35.6	10.6
1870	37	39,818,449	26.6	13.4
1880	38	50,155,783	26.0	16.9
1890	44	62,947,714	25.5	21.1
1900	45	75,994,575	20.7	25.6
1910	46	91,972,266	21.0	31.0
1920	48	105,710,620	14.9	35.6
1930	48	122,775,046	16.1	41.2
1940	48	131,669,275	7.2	44.2
1950	48	150,697,361	14.5	50.7
1960	50	179,323,175	19.0	50.6
1970	50	203,235,298	13.3	57.5
1980	50	226,504,825	11.4	64.0
1985	50	237,839,000	5.0	67.2
1990	50	250,122,000	5.2	70.6
1995	50	263,411,707	5.3	74.4
2000	50	281,421,906	6.8	77.0
2005	50	296,410,404	5.3	77.9
2010	50	308,745,538	9.7	87.4

IMMIGRATION TO THE UNITED STATES, FISCAL YEARS 1820–2013

Year	Number	Year	Number	Year	Number	Year	Number
1820–1989	**55,457,531**	**1871–80**	**2,812,191**	**1921–30**	**4,107,209**	**1971–80**	**4,493,314**
1820	8,385	1871	321,350	1921	805,228	1971	370,478
		1872	404,806	1922	309,556	1972	384,685
1821–30	**143,439**	1873	459,803	1923	522,919	1973	400,063
1821	9,127	1874	313,339	1924	706,896	1974	394,861
1822	6,911	1875	227,498	1925	294,314	1975	386,914
1823	6,354	1876	169,986	1926	304,488	1976	398,613
1824	7,912	1877	141,857	1927	335,175	1976	103,676
1825	10,199	1878	138,469	1928	307,255	1977	462,315
1826	10,837	1879	177,826	1929	279,678	1978	601,442
1827	18,875	1880	457,257	1930	241,700	1979	460,348
1828	27,382					1980	530,639
1829	22,520	**1881–90**	**5,246,613**	**1931–40**	**528,431**		
1830	23,322	1881	669,431	1931	97,139	**1981–90**	**7,338,062**
		1882	788,992	1932	35,576	1981	596,600
1831–40	**599,125**	1883	603,322	1933	23,068	1982	594,131
1831	22,633	1884	518,592	1934	29,470	1983	559,763
1832	60,482	1885	395,346	1935	34,956	1984	543,903
1833	58,640	1886	334,203	1936	36,329	1985	570,009
1834	65,365	1887	490,109	1937	50,244	1986	601,708
1835	45,374	1888	546,889	1938	67,895	1987	601,516
1836	76,242	1889	444,427	1939	82,998	1988	643,025
1837	79,340	1890	455,302	1940	70,756	1989	1,090,924
1838	38,914					1990	1,536,483
1839	68,069	**1891–1900**	**3,687,564**	**1941–50**	**1,035,039**		
1840	84,066	1891	560,319	1941	51,776	**1991–2000**	**9,090,857**
		1892	579,663	1942	28,781	1991	1,827,167
1841–50	**1,713,251**	1893	439,730	1943	23,725	1992	973,977
1841	80,289	1894	285,631	1944	28,551	1993	904,292
1842	104,565	1895	258,536	1945	38,119	1994	804,416
		1896	343,267	1946	108,721		

Year	Number	Year	Number	Year	Number	Year	Number
1843	52,496	1897	230,832	1947	147,292	1995	720,461
1844	78,615	1898	229,299	1948	170,570	1996	915,900
1845	114,371	1899	311,715	1949	188,317	1997	798,378
1846	154,416	1900	448,572	1950	249,187	1998	660,477
1847	234,968					1999	644,787
1848	226,527	1901–10	8,795,386	1951–60	2,515,479	2000	841,002
1849	297,024	1901	487,918	1951	205,717	2001–13	10,501,053
1850	369,980	1902	648,743	1952	265,520	2001	1,058,902
1851–60	2,598,214	1903	857,046	1953	170,434	2002	1,059,356
1851	379,466	1904	812,870	1954	208,177	2003	705,827
1852	371,603	1905	1,026,499	1955	237,790	2004	957,883
1853	368,645	1906	1,100,735	1956	321,625	2005	1,122,373
1854	427,833	1907	1,285,349	1957	326,867	2006	1,266,129
1855	200,877	1908	782,870	1958	253,265	2007	1,052,415
1856	200,436	1909	751,786	1959	260,686	2008	1,107,126
1857	251,306	1910	1,041,570	1960	265,398	2009	1,130,818
1858	123,126	1911–20	5,735,811	1961–70	3,321,677	2010	1,042,625
1859	121,282	1911	878,587	1961	271,344	2011	1,062,040
1860	153,640	1912	838,172	1962	283,763	2012	1,031,631
1861–70	2,314,824	1913	1,197,892	1963	306,260	2013	990,553
1861	91,918	1914	1,218,480	1964	292,248		
1862	91,985	1915	326,700	1965	296,697		
1863	176,282	1916	298,826	1966	323,040		
1864	193,418	1917	295,403	1967	361,972		
1865	248,120	1918	110,618	1968	454,448		
1866	318,568	1919	141,132	1969	358,579		
1867	315,722	1920	430,001	1970	373,326		
1868	138,840						
1869	352,768						
1870	387,203						

Source: U.S. Department of Homeland Security.

IMMIGRATION BY REGION AND SELECTED COUNTRY OF LAST RESIDENCE, FISCAL YEARS 1820–2013

Region and country of last residence	1820 to 1829	1830 to 1839	1840 to 1849	1850 to 1859	1860 to 1869	1870 to 1879	1880 to 1889	1890 to 1899
Total	128,502	538,381	1,427,337	2,814,554	2,081,261	2,742,137	5,248,568	3,694,294
Europe	99,272	422,771	1,369,259	2,619,680	1,877,726	2,251,878	4,638,677	3,576,411
Austria-Hungary	—	—	—	—	3,375	60,127	314,787	534,059
Austria	—	—	—	—	2,700	54,529	204,805	268,218
Hungary	—	—	—	—	483	5,598	109,982	203,350
Belgium	28	20	3,996	5,765	5,785	6,991	18,738	19,642
Bulgaria	—	—	—	—	—	—	—	52
Czechoslovakia	—	—	—	—	—	—	—	—
Denmark	173	927	671	3,227	13,553	29,278	85,342	56,671
Finland	—	—	—	—	—	—	—	—
France	7,694	39,330	75,300	81,778	35,938	71,901	48,193	35,616
Germany	5,753	124,726	385,434	976,072	723,734	751,769	1,445,181	579,072
Greece	17	49	17	32	51	209	1,807	12,732
Ireland	51,617	170,672	656,145	1,029,486	427,419	422,264	674,061	405,710
Italy	430	2,225	1,476	8,643	9,853	46,296	267,660	603,761
Netherlands	1,105	1,377	7,624	11,122	8,387	14,267	52,715	29,349
Norway-Sweden	91	1,149	12,389	22,202	82,937	178,823	586,441	334,058
Norway	—	—	—	—	16,068	88,644	185,111	96,810
Sweden	—	—	—	—	24,224	90,179	401,330	237,248
Poland	19	366	105	1,087	1,886	11,016	42,910	107,793
Portugal	177	820	196	1,299	2,083	13,971	15,186	25,874
Romania	—	—	—	—	—	—	5,842	6,808
Russia	86	280	520	423	1,670	35,177	182,698	450,101
Spain	2,595	2,010	1,916	8,795	6,966	5,540	3,995	9,189
Switzerland	3,148	4,430	4,819	24,423	21,124	25,212	81,151	37,020
United Kingdom	26,336	74,350	218,572	445,322	532,956	578,447	810,900	328,759
Yugoslavia	—	—	—	—	—	—	—	—
Other Europe	3	40	79	4	9	590	1,070	145

Asia	34	55	121	36,080	54,408	134,128	71,151	61,285
China	3	8	32	35,933	54,028	133,139	65,797	15,268
Hong Kong	—	—	—	—	50	166	247	102
India	9	38	33	42	—	—	—	102
Iran	—	—	—	—	—	—	—	—
Israel	—	—	—	—	138	193	1,583	13,998
Japan	—	—	—	—	—	—	—	—
Jordan	—	—	—	—	—	—	—	—
Korea	—	—	—	—	—	—	—	—
Philippines	—	—	—	—	—	—	—	—
Syria	—	—	—	—	—	—	—	—
Taiwan	—	—	—	—	—	—	—	—
Turkey	19	8	45	94	129	382	2,478	27,510
Vietnam	—	—	—	—	—	—	—	—
Other Asia	3	1	11	11	63	248	1,046	4,407
America	9,655	31,905	50,516	84,145	130,292	345,010	524,826	37,350
Canada and Newfoundland	2,297	11,875	34,285	64,171	117,978	324,310	492,865	3,098
Mexico	3,835	7,187	3,069	3,446	1,957	5,133	2,405	734
Caribbean	3,061	11,792	11,803	12,447	8,751	14,285	27,323	31,480
Cuba	—	—	—	—	—	—	—	—
Dominican Republic	—	—	—	—	—	—	—	—
Haiti	—	—	—	—	—	—	—	—
Jamaica	—	—	—	—	—	—	—	—
Other Caribbean	3,061	11,792	11,803	12,447	8,751	14,285	27,323	31,480
Central America	57	94	297	512	70	173	279	649
Belize	—	—	—	—	—	—	—	—
Costa Rica	—	—	—	—	—	—	—	—
El Salvador	—	—	—	—	—	—	—	—
Guatemala	—	—	—	—	—	—	—	—
Honduras	—	—	—	—	—	—	—	—
Nicaragua	—	—	—	—	—	—	—	—
Panama	—	—	—	—	—	—	—	—
Other Central America	57	94	297	512	70	173	279	649
South America	405	957	1,062	3,569	1,536	1,109	1,954	649
Argentina	—	—	—	—	—	—	—	1,389
Bolivia	—	—	—	—	—	—	—	—

Region and country of last residence	1820 to 1829	1830 to 1839	1840 to 1849	1850 to 1859	1860 to 1869	1870 to 1879	1880 to 1889	1890 to 1899
Brazil	—	—	—	—	—	—	—	—
Chile	—	—	—	—	—	—	—	—
Colombia	—	—	—	—	—	—	—	—
Ecuador	—	—	—	—	—	—	—	—
Guyana	—	—	—	—	—	—	—	—
Paraguay	—	—	—	—	—	—	—	—
Peru	—	—	—	—	—	—	—	—
Suriname	—	—	—	—	—	—	—	—
Uruguay	—	—	—	—	—	—	—	—
Venezuela	—	—	—	—	—	—	—	—
Other South America	405	957	1,062	3,569	1,536	1,109	1,954	1,389
Other America								
Africa								
Egypt	15	50	61	84	407	371	763	432
Ethiopia	—	—	—	—	4	29	145	51
Liberia	1	8	5	7	43	52	21	9
Morocco	—	—	—	—	—	—	—	—
South Africa	—	—	—	—	35	48	23	9
Other Africa	14	42	56	77	325	242	574	363
Oceania	3	7	14	166	187	9,996	12,361	4,704
Australia	2	1	2	15	—	8,930	7,250	3,098
New Zealand	—	—	—	—	—	39	21	12
Other Oceania	1	6	12	151	187	1,027	5,090	1,594
Not Specified	19,523	83,593	7,366	74,399	18,241	754	790	14,112

Total	8,202,388	6,347,380	4,295,510	699,375	856,608	2,499,268	3,213,749	6,244,379
Europe	7,572,569	4,985,411	2,560,340	444,399	472,524	1,404,973	1,133,443	668,866
Austria-Hungary	2,001,376	1,154,727	60,891	12,531	13,574	113,015	27,590	20,437
Austria	532,416	589,174	31,392	5,307	8,393	81,354	17,571	15,374
Hungary	685,567	565,553	29,499	7,224	5,181	31,661	10,019	5,063
Belgium	37,429	32,574	21,511	4,013	12,473	18,885	9,647	7,028
Bulgaria	34,651	27,180	2,824	1,062	449	97	598	1,124
Czechoslovakia	—	—	101,182	17,757	8,475	1,624	2,758	5,678
Denmark	61,227	45,830	34,406	3,470	4,549	10,918	9,797	4,847
Finland	—	—	16,922	2,438	2,230	4,923	4,310	2,569
France	67,735	60,335	54,842	13,761	36,954	50,113	46,975	32,066
Germany	328,722	174,227	386,634	119,107	119,506	576,905	209,616	85,752
Greece	145,402	198,108	60,774	10,599	8,605	45,153	74,173	37,729
Ireland	344,940	166,445	202,854	28,195	15,701	47,189	37,788	22,210
Italy	1,930,475	1,229,916	528,133	85,053	50,509	184,576	200,111	55,562
Netherlands	42,463	46,065	29,397	7,791	13,877	46,703	37,918	11,234
Norway-Sweden	426,981	192,445	170,329	13,452	17,326	44,224	36,150	13,941
Norway	182,542	79,488	70,327	6,901	8,326	22,806	17,371	3,835
Sweden	244,439	112,957	100,002	6,551	9,000	21,418	18,779	10,106
Poland	—	—	223,316	25,555	7,577	6,465	55,742	63,483
Portugal	65,154	82,489	44,829	3,518	6,765	13,928	70,568	42,685
Romania	57,322	13,566	67,810	5,264	1,254	914	2,339	24,753
Russia	1,501,301	1,106,998	61,604	2,463	605	453	2,329	33,311
Spain	24,818	53,262	47,109	3,669	2,774	6,880	40,793	22,783
Switzerland	32,541	22,839	31,772	5,990	9,904	17,577	19,193	8,316
United Kingdom	469,518	371,878	341,552	61,813	131,794	195,709	220,213	153,644
Yugoslavia	514	6,527	49,215	6,920	2,039	6,966	17,990	16,267
Other Europe	299,836	269,736	22,434	9,978	5,584	11,756	6,845	3,447
Asia	19,884	20,916	126,740	19,231	34,532	135,844	358,605	2,391,356
China	—	—	30,648	5,874	16,072	8,836	14,060	170,897
Hong Kong			—	—	—	13,781	67,047	112,132
India	3,026	3,478	2,076	554	1,692	1,850	18,638	231,649
Iran	—	—	208	198	1,144	3,195	9,059	98,141
Israel	—	—	—	—	98	21,376	30,911	43,669

Region and country of last residence	1820 to 1829	1830 to 1839	1840 to 1849	1850 to 1859	1860 to 1869	1870 to 1879	1880 to 1889	1890 to 1899
Japan	139,712	77,125	42,057	2,683	1,557	40,651	40,956	44,150
Jordan	—	—	—	—	—	4,899	9,230	28,928
Korea	—	—	—	—	83	4,845	27,048	322,708
Philippines	—	—	—	391	4,099	17,245	70,660	502,056
Syria	—	—	5,307	2,188	1,179	1,091	2,432	14,534
Taiwan	—	—	—	—	—	721	15,657	119,051
Turkey	127,999	160,717	40,450	1,327	754	2,980	9,464	19,208
Vietnam	—	—	—	—	—	290	2,949	200,632
Other Asia	9,215	7,500	5,994	6,016	7,854	14,084	40,494	483,601
America	277,809	1,070,539	1,591,278	230,319	328,435	921,610	1,674,172	2,695,329
Canada and Newfoundland	123,067	708,715	949,286	162,703	160,911	353,169	433,128	156,313
Mexico	31,188	185,334	498,945	32,709	56,158	273,847	441,824	1,009,586
Caribbean	100,960	120,860	83,482	18,052	46,194	115,661	427,235	790,109
Cuba	—	—	12,769	10,641	25,976	73,221	202,030	132,552
Dominican Republic	—	—	—	1,026	4,802	10,219	83,552	221,552
Haiti	—	—	—	156	823	3,787	28,992	121,406
Jamaica	—	—	—	—	—	7,397	62,218	193,874
Other Caribbean	100,960	120,860	70,713	6,229	14,593	21,037	50,443	120,725
Central America	7,341	15,692	16,511	6,840	20,135	40,201	98,560	339,376
Belize	77	40	285	193	433	1,133	4,185	14,964
Costa Rica	—	—	—	431	1,965	4,044	17,975	25,017
El Salvador	—	—	—	597	4,885	5,094	14,405	137,418
Guatemala	—	—	—	423	1,303	4,197	14,357	58,847
Honduras	—	—	—	679	1,874	5,320	15,078	39,071
Nicaragua	—	—	—	405	4,393	7,812	10,383	31,102
Panama	—	—	—	1,452	5,282	12,601	22,177	32,957
Other Central America	7,264	15,652	16,226	2,660	—	—	—	—

South America	15,253	39,938	43,025	9,990	19,662	78,418	250,754	399,862
Argentina	—	—	—	1,067	3,108	16,346	49,384	23,442
Bolivia	—	—	—	50	893	2,759	6,205	9,798
Brazil	—	—	4,627	1,468	3,653	11,547	29,238	22,944
Chile	—	—	—	347	1,320	4,669	12,384	19,749
Colombia	—	—	—	1,027	3,454	15,567	68,371	105,494
Ecuador	—	—	—	244	2,207	8,574	34,107	48,015
Guyana	—	—	—	131	596	1,131	4,546	85,886
Paraguay	—	—	—	33	85	576	1,249	3,518
Peru	—	—	—	321	1,273	5,980	19,783	49,958
Suriname	—	—	—	25	130	299	612	1,357
Uruguay	—	—	—	112	754	1,026	4,089	7,235
Venezuela	—	—	—	1,155	2,182	9,927	20,758	22,405
Other South America	15,253	39,938	38,398	4,010	7	17	28	61
Other America	—	—	29	25	25,375	60,314	22,671	83
Africa	6,326	8,867	6,362	2,120	6,720	13,016	23,780	141,990
Egypt	—	—	1,063	781	1,613	1,996	5,581	26,744
Ethiopia	—	—	—	10	28	302	804	12,927
Liberia	—	—	—	35	37	289	841	6,420
Morocco	—	—	—	73	879	2,703	2,880	3,471
South Africa	6,326	8,867	5,299	312	1,022	2,278	4,360	15,505
Other Africa	12,355	12,339	9,860	909	3,141	5,448	9,314	76,923
Oceania	11,191	11,280	8,404	3,306	14,262	11,353	23,630	41,432
Australia	—	—	935	2,260	11,201	8,275	14,986	16,901
New Zealand	1,164	1,059	521	790	2,351	1,799	3,775	6,129
Other Oceania	—	—	—	256	710	1,279	4,869	18,402
Not Specified	33,493	488	930	—	135	12,472	119	305,406

Region and country of last residence	1990 to 1999	2000 to 2009	2010	2011	2012	2013
Total	9,775,398	10,299,430	1,042,625	1,062,040	1,031,631	990,553
Europe	1,348,612	1,349,609	95,429	90,712	86,956	91,095
Austria-Hungary	27,529	33,929	4,325	4,703	3,208	2,061
Austria	18,234	21,151	3,319	3,654	2,199	1,053
Hungary	9,295	12,778	1,006	1,049	1,009	1,008
Belgium	7,077	8,157	732	700	698	803
Bulgaria	16,948	40,003	2,465	2,549	2,322	2,720
Czechoslovakia	8,970	18,691	1,510	1,374	1,316	1,258
Denmark	6,189	6,049	545	473	492	546
Finland	3,970	3,970	414	398	373	360
France	35,945	45,637	4,339	3,967	4,201	4,668
Germany	92,207	122,373	7,929	7,072	6,732	6,880
Greece	25,403	16,841	966	1,196	1,264	1,526
Ireland	65,384	15,642	1,610	1,533	1,694	1,765
Italy	75,992	28,329	2,956	2,670	2,946	3,233
Netherlands	13,345	17,351	1,520	1,258	1,294	1,376
Norway-Sweden	17,825	19,382	1,662	1,530	1,441	1,665
Norway	5,211	4,599	363	405	314	389
Sweden	12,614	14,783	1,299	1,125	1,127	1,276
Poland	172,249	117,921	7,391	6,634	6,024	6,073
Portugal	25,497	11,479	759	878	837	917
Romania	48,136	52,154	3,735	3,679	3,477	3,475
Russia	433,427	167,152	7,502	8,548	10,114	10,154
Spain	18,443	17,695	2,040	2,319	2,316	2,970
Switzerland	11,768	12,173	868	861	916	1,040
United Kingdom	156,182	171,979	14,781	13,443	13,938	15,321
Yugoslavia	57,039	131,831	4,772	4,611	4,488	4,445
Other Europe	29,087	290,871	22,608	20,316	16,865	17,839

Asia	389,301	416,488	438,580	410,209	3,470,835	2,859,899
China	68,410	78,184	83,603	67,634	591,711	342,058
Hong Kong	2,614	2,642	3,149	3,263	57,583	116,894
India	65,506	63,320	66,331	66,185	590,464	352,528
Iran	9,658	8,955	9,015	9,078	76,755	76,899
Israel	4,555	4,640	4,389	5,172	54,081	41,340
Japan	6,383	6,581	6,751	7,100	84,552	66,582
Jordan	5,949	7,014	8,211	9,327	53,550	42,755
Korea	22,937	20,802	22,748	22,022	209,758	179,770
Philippines	52,955	55,441	55,251	56,399	545,463	534,338
Syria	3,999	6,674	7,983	7,424	30,807	22,906
Taiwan	5,336	5,295	6,206	6,785	92,657	132,647
Turkey	7,189	7,362	9,040	7,435	48,394	38,687
Vietnam	26,578	27,578	33,486	30,065	289,616	275,379
Other Asia	107,232	122,000	122,417	112,320	745,444	637,116
America	399,380	409,664	423,277	426,981	4,441,529	5,137,743
Canada and Newfoundland	20,489	20,138	19,506	19,491	236,349	194,788
Mexico	134,198	145,326	142,823	138,717	1,704,166	2,757,418
Caribbean	121,349	126,615	133,012	139,389	1,053,357	1,004,687
Cuba	31,343	32,551	36,261	33,372	271,742	159,037
Dominican Republic	41,487	41,535	46,036	53,890	291,492	359,818
Haiti	20,083	22,446	21,802	22,336	203,827	177,446
Jamaica	19,052	20,300	19,298	19,439	172,523	177,143
Other Caribbean	9,384	9,783	9,615	10,352	113,773	181,243
Central America	44,056	39,837	43,249	43,597	591,130	610,189
Belize	969	875	933	997	9,682	12,600
Costa Rica	2,232	2,152	2,230	2,306	21,571	17,054
El Salvador	18,015	15,874	18,477	18,547	251,237	273,017
Guatemala	9,829	9,857	10,795	10,263	156,992	126,043
Honduras	8,795	6,773	6,053	6,381	63,513	72,880

Region and country of last residence	1990 to 1999	2000 to 2009	2010	2011	2012	2013
Nicaragua	80,446	70,015	3,476	3,314	2,943	2,940
Panama	28,149	18,120	1,627	1,447	1,363	1,276
Other Central America	—			—		-
South America	570,624	856,508	85,783	84,687	77,748	79,287
Argentina	30,065	47,955	4,312	4,335	4,218	4,227
Bolivia	18,111	21,921	2,211	2,113	1,920	2,005
Brazil	50,744	115,404	12,057	11,643	11,248	10,772
Chile	18,200	19,792	1,940	1,854	1,628	1,751
Colombia	137,985	236,570	21,861	22,130	20,272	20,611
Ecuador	81,358	107,977	11,463	11,068	9,284	10,553
Guyana	74,407	70,373	6,441	6,288	5,282	5,564
Paraguay	6,082	4,623	449	501	454	437
Peru	110,117	137,614	14,063	13,836	12,414	12,370
Suriname	2,285	2,363	202	167	216	170
Uruguay	6,062	9,827	1,286	1,521	1,348	1,314
Venezuela	35,180	82,087	9,497	9,229	9,464	9,512
Other South America	28	2	1	2	-	1
Other America	37	19	4			1
Africa	346,416	759,734	98,246	97,429	103,685	94,589
Egypt	44,604	81,564	9,822	9,096	10,172	10,719
Ethiopia	40,097	87,207	13,853	13,985	15,400	13,484
Liberia	13,587	23,316	2,924	3,117	3,451	3,036
Morocco	15,768	40,844	4,847	4,249	3,534	3,202
South Africa	21,964	32,221	2,705	2,754	2,960	2,693
Other Africa	210,396	494,582	64,095	64,228	68,168	61,455
Oceania	56,800	65,793	5,946	5,825	5,573	6,061
Australia	24,288	32,728	3,077	3,062	3,146	3,529
New Zealand	8,600	12,495	1,046	1,006	980	1,027
Other Oceania	23,912	20,570	1,823	1,757	1,447	1,505
Not Specified	25,928	211,930	5,814	6,217	9,265	10,127

—Represents zero or not available.

PRESIDENTS, VICE PRESIDENTS, AND SECRETARIES OF STATE

	President	Vice President	Secretary of State
1.	George Washington, Federalist 1789	John Adams, Federalist 1789	Thomas Jefferson 1789 Edmund Randolph 1794 Timothy Pickering 1795
2.	John Adams, Federalist 1797	Thomas Jefferson, Dem.-Rep. 1797	Timothy Pickering 1797 John Marshall 1800
3.	Thomas Jefferson, Dem.-Rep. 1801	Aaron Burr, Dem.-Rep. 1801 George Clinton, Dem.-Rep. 1805	James Madison 1801
4.	James Madison, Dem.-Rep. 1809	George Clinton, Dem.-Rep. 1809 Elbridge Gerry, Dem.-Rep. 1813	Robert Smith 1809 James Monroe 1811
5.	James Monroe, Dem.-Rep. 1817	Daniel D. Tompkins, Dem.-Rep. 1817	John Q. Adams 1817
6.	John Quincy Adams, Dem.-Rep. 1825	John C. Calhoun, Dem.-Rep. 1825	Henry Clay 1825
7.	Andrew Jackson, Democratic 1829	John C. Calhoun, Democratic 1829 Martin Van Buren, Democratic 1833	Martin Van Buren 1829 Edward Livingston 1831 Louis McLane 1833 John Forsyth 1834
8.	Martin Van Buren, Democratic 1837	Richard M. Johnson, Democratic 1837	John Forsyth 1837
9.	William H. Harrison, Whig 1841	John Tyler, Whig 1841	Daniel Webster 1841

	President	Vice President	Secretary of State
10.	John Tyler, Whig and Democratic 1841	None	Daniel Webster 1841 Hugh S. Legaré 1843 Abel P. Upshur 1843 John C. Calhoun 1844
11.	James K. Polk, Democratic 1845	George M. Dallas, Democratic 1845	James Buchanan 1845
12.	Zachary Taylor, Whig 1849	Millard Fillmore, Whig 1848	John M. Clayton 1849
13.	Millard Fillmore, Whig 1850	None	Daniel Webster 1850 Edward Everett 1852
14.	Franklin Pierce, Democratic 1853	William R. King, Democratic 1853	William L. Marcy 1853
15.	James Buchanan, Democratic 1857	John C. Breckinridge, Democratic 1857	Lewis Cass 1857 Jeremiah S. Black 1860
16.	Abraham Lincoln, Republican 1861	Hannibal Hamlin, Republican 1861 Andrew Johnson, Unionist 1865	William H. Seward 1861
17.	Andrew Johnson, Unionist 1865	None	William H. Seward 1865
18.	Ulysses S. Grant, Republican 1869	Schuyler Colfax, Republican 1869 Henry Wilson, Republican 1873	Elihu B. Washburne 1869 Hamilton Fish 1869
19.	Rutherford B. Hayes, Republican 1877	William A. Wheeler, Republican 1877	William M. Evarts 1877

	President	Vice President	Secretary of State
20.	James A. Garfield, Republican 1881	Chester A. Arthur, Republican 1881	James G. Blaine 1881
21.	Chester A. Arthur, Republican 1881	None	Frederick T. Frelinghuysen 1881
22.	Grover Cleveland, Democratic 1885	Thomas A. Hendricks, Democratic 1885	Thomas F. Bayard 1885
23.	Benjamin Harrison, Republican 1889	Levi P. Morton, Republican 1889	James G. Blaine 1889 John W. Foster 1892
24.	Grover Cleveland, Democratic 1893	Adlai E. Stevenson, Democratic 1893	Walter Q. Gresham 1893 Richard Olney 1895
25.	William McKinley, Republican 1897	Garret A. Hobart, Republican 1897 Theodore Roosevelt, Republican 1901	John Sherman 1897 William R. Day 1898 John Hay 1898
26.	Theodore Roosevelt, Republican 1901	Charles Fairbanks, Republican 1905	John Hay 1901 Elihu Root 1905 Robert Bacon 1909
27.	William H. Taft, Republican 1909	James S. Sherman, Republican 1909	Philander C. Knox 1909
28.	Woodrow Wilson, Democratic 1913	Thomas R. Marshall, Democratic 1913	William J. Bryan 1913 Robert Lansing 1915 Bainbridge Colby 1920
29.	Warren G. Harding, Republican 1921	Calvin Coolidge, Republican 1921	Charles E. Hughes 1921
30.	Calvin Coolidge, Republican 1923	Charles G. Dawes, Republican 1925	Charles E. Hughes 1923 Frank B. Kellogg 1925

	President	Vice President	Secretary of State
31.	Herbert Hoover, Republican 1929	Charles Curtis, Republican 1929	Henry L. Stimson 1929
32.	Franklin D. Roosevelt, Democratic 1933	John Nance Garner, Democratic 1933 Henry A. Wallace, Democratic 1941 Harry S. Truman, Democratic 1945	Cordell Hull 1933 Edward R. Stettinius, Jr. 1944
33.	Harry S. Truman, Democratic 1945	Alben W. Barkley, Democratic 1949	Edward R. Stettinius, Jr. 1945 James F. Byrnes 1945 George C. Marshall 1947 Dean G. Acheson 1949
34.	Dwight D. Eisenhower, Republican 1953	Richard M. Nixon, Republican 1953	John F. Dulles 1953 Christian A. Herter 1959
35.	John F. Kennedy, Democratic 1961	Lyndon B. Johnson, Democratic 1961	Dean Rusk 1961
36.	Lyndon B. Johnson, Democratic 1963	Hubert H. Humphrey, Democratic 1965	Dean Rusk 1963
37.	Richard M. Nixon, Republican 1969	Spiro T. Agnew, Republican 1969 Gerald R. Ford, Republican 1973	William P. Rogers 1969 Henry Kissinger 1973
38.	Gerald R. Ford, Republican 1974	Nelson Rockefeller, Republican 1974	Henry Kissinger 1974
39.	Jimmy Carter, Democratic 1977	Walter Mondale, Democratic 1977	Cyrus Vance 1977 Edmund Muskie 1980

	President	Vice President	Secretary of State
40.	Ronald Reagan, Republican 1981	George H. W. Bush, Republican 1981	Alexander Haig 1981 George Schultz 1982
41.	George H. W. Bush, Republican 1989	J. Danforth Quayle, Republican 1989	James A. Baker 1989 Lawrence Eagleburger 1992
42.	William J. Clinton, Democratic 1993	Albert Gore, Jr., Democratic 1993	Warren Christopher 1993 Madeleine Albright 1997
43.	George W. Bush, Republican 2001	Richard B. Cheney, Republican 2001	Colin L. Powell 2001 Condoleezza Rice 2005
44.	Barack Obama, Democratic 2009	Joseph R. Biden, Democratic 2009	Hillary Rodham Clinton 2009 John Kerry 2013

FURTHER READINGS

CHAPTER 1

A fascinating study of pre-Columbian migration is Brian M. Fagan's *The Great Journey: The Peopling of Ancient America*, rev. ed. (2004). Alice B. Kehoe's *North American Indians: A Comprehensive Account*, 2nd ed. (1992), provides an encyclopedic treatment of Native Americans. See also Charles Mann's *1491: New Revelations of the Americas before Columbus* (2005) and *1493: Uncovering the New World that Columbua Created* (2011), and Daniel K. Richter, *Before the Revolution: America's Ancient Pasts* (2011). On North America's largest Native American city, see Timothy R. Pauketat, *Cahokia* (2010).

The conflict between Native Americans and Europeans is treated well in James Axtell's *The Invasion Within: The Contest of Cultures in Colonial North America* (1986) and *Beyond 1492: Encounters in Colonial North America* (1992). Colin G. Calloway's *New Worlds for All: Indians, Europeans, and the Remaking of Early America* (1997) explores the ecological effects of European settlement.

Laurence Bergreen examines the voyages of Columbus in *Columbus: The Four Voyages* (2011). To learn about the queen who sent Columbus to the New World, see Kristin Downey's *Isabella: The Warrior Queen* (2014). For sweeping overviews of Spain's creation of a global empire, see Hugh Thomas's *Rivers of Gold: The Rise of the Spanish Empire, from Columbus to Magellan* (2004) and Robert Goodwin, *Spain: The Center of the World, 1519–1682* (2015). David J. Weber examines Spanish colonization in *The Spanish Frontier in North America* (1992). For the French experience, see William J. Eccles's *France in America*, rev. ed. (1990). For an insightful comparison of Spanish and English modes of settlement, see J. H. Elliott, *Empires of the Atlantic World: Britain and Spain in America, 1492–1830* (2006).

CHAPTER 2

Two excellent surveys of early American history are Peter C. Hoffer's *The Brave New World: A History of Early America*, 2nd ed. (2006), and William R. Polk's *The Birth of America: From before Columbus to the Revolution* (2006).

Bernard Bailyn's *The Barbarous Years: The Peopling of British North America: The Conflict of Civilizations, 1600–1675* (2013) tells the often brutal story of British settlement in America during the seventeenth century. Jack P. Greene offers a brilliant synthesis of British colonization in *Pursuits of Happiness: The Social Development of Early Modern British Colonies and the Formation of American Culture* (1988). On the impact of the American environment on colonial settlement, see Malcolm Gaskill's *Between Two Worlds: How the English Became Americans* (2015). The best overview of the colonization of North America is Alan Taylor's *American Colonies: The Settling of North America* (2001). On the interactions among Indian, European, and African cultures, see Gary B. Nash's *Red, White, and Black: The Peoples of Early North America*, 5th ed. (2005).

A good overview of the founding of Virginia and Maryland is Jean and Elliott Russo's *The Early Chesapeake in British North America* (2012). For information regarding the Puritan settlement of New England, see David D. Hall's *A Reforming People: Puritanism and the Transformaiton of Public Life in New England* (2013). The best biography of John Winthrop is Francis J. Bremer's *John Winthrop: America's Forgotten Founding Father* (2003). On Roger Williams, see John M. Barry's *Roger Williams and the Creation of the American Soul* (2012).

The pattern of settlement in the middle colonies is illuminated in Barry Levy's *Quakers and the American Family: British Settlement in the Delaware Valley* (1988). On the early history of New York, see Russell Shorto's *The Island at the Center of the World: The Epic Story of Dutch Manhattan and the Forgotten Colony That Shaped America* (2004). Settlement of the areas along the Atlantic in the South is traced in James Horn's *Adapting to a New World: English Society in the Seventeenth-Century Chesapeake* (1994).

On shifting political life in England, see Steve Pincus, *1688: The First Modern Revolution* (2009). For a study of race and the settlement of South Carolina, see Peter H. Wood's *Black Majority: Negroes in Colonial South Carolina from 1670 through the Stono Rebellion* (1974). On the flourishing trade in captive Indians, see Alan Gallay's *The Indian Slave Trade: The Rise of the English Empire in the American South, 1670–1717* (2002). On the Yamasee War, see Steven J. Oatis's *A Colonial Complex: South Carolina's Frontiers in the Era of the Yamasee War, 1680–1730* (2004).

CHAPTER 3

The diversity of colonial societies may be seen in David Hackett Fischer's *Albion's Seed: Four British Folkways in America* (1989). John Frederick Martin's *Profits in the Wilderness: Entrepreneurship and the Founding of New England Towns in the Seventeenth Century* (1991) indicates that economic concerns rather than spiritual motives were driving forces in many New England towns.

Bernard Rosenthal challenges many myths concerning the Salem witch trials in *Salem Story: Reading the Witch Trials of 1692* (1993). Mary Beth Norton's *In the Devil's Snare: The Salem Witchcraft Crisis of 1692* (2002) emphasizes the role of Indian violence.

Discussions of women in the New England colonies can be found in Laurel Thatcher Ulrich's *Good Wives: Image and Reality in the Lives of Women in Northern New England, 1650–1750* (1980), and Mary Beth Norton, *Separated by Their Sex: Women in Public and Private in the Colonial Atlantic World* (2011). On women and religion, see Susan Juster's *Disorderly Women: Sexual Politics and Evangelicalism in Revolutionary New England* (1994). John Demos describes family life in *A Little Commonwealth: Family Life in Plymouth Colony*, new ed. (2000).

For an excellent overview of Indian relations with Europeans, see Colin G. Calloway's *New Worlds for All: Indians, Europeans, and the Remaking of Early America* (1997). For analyses of Indian wars, see Alfred A. Cave's *The Pequot War* (1996) and Jill Lepore's *The Name of War: King Philip's War and the Origins of American Identity* (1998). The story of the Iroquois is told well in Daniel K. Richter's *The Ordeal of the Longhouse: The Peoples of the Iroquois League in the Era of European Colonization* (1992). Indians in the southern colonies are the focus of James Axtell's *The Indians' New South: Cultural Change in the Colonial Southeast* (1997). On the fur trade, see Eric Jay Dolan, *Fur, Fortune, and Empire: The Epic Story of the Fur Trade in America* (2010).

For the social history of the southern colonies, see Allan Kulikoff's *Tobacco and Slaves: The Development of Southern Cultures in the Chesapeake, 1680–1800* (1986). On the interaction of the cultures of blacks and whites, see Mechal Sobel's *The World They Made Together: Black and White Values in Eighteenth-Century Virginia* (1987). On the slave trade, see William St. Clair's *The Door of No Return* (2007). African Americans during colonial settlement are the focus of Timothy H. Breen and Stephen Innes's *"Myne Owne Ground": Race and Freedom on Virginia's Eastern Shore, 1640–1676*, new ed. (2004). David W. Galenson's *White Servitude in Colonial America: An Economic Analysis* (1981) looks at the indentured labor force.

Henry F. May's *The Enlightenment in America* (1976) and Donald H. Meyer's *The Democratic Enlightenment* (1976) examine intellectual trends in eighteenth-century America. On the Great Awakening, see Frank Lambert's *Inventing the "Great Awakening"* (1999), and Thomas S. Kidd's *The Great Awakening: The Roots of Evangelical Christianity in Colonial America* (2007). Excellent biographies of the key revivalists are Phillip F. Gura's *Jonathan Edwards: A Life* (2003) and Thomas S. Kidd's *George Whitefield* (2015).

CHAPTER 4

A good introduction to the imperial phase of the colonial conflicts is Douglas Edward Leach's *Arms for Empire: A Military History of the British Colonies in North America, 1607–1763* (1973). Also useful is Brendan Simms's *Three Victories and a Defeat: The Rise and Fall of the Fiurst British Empire* (2008). Fred Anderson's *Crucible of War: The Seven Years' War and the Fate of Empire in British North America, 1754–1766* (2000) is the best history of the Seven Years' War. For the implications of the British victory in 1763, see Colin G. Calloway's *The Scratch of a Pen: 1763 and the Transformation of North America* (2006). On the French colonies in North America, see Allan Greer's *The People of New France* (1997).

For a narrative survey of the events leading to the Revolution, see Edward Countryman's *The American Revolution,* rev. ed. (2003). For Great Britain's perspective on the imperial conflict, see Ian R. Christie's *Crisis of Empire: Great Britain and the American Colonies, 1754–1783* (1966). Also see Jeremy Black's *George III: America's Last King* (2007) and David Preston's *Braddock's Defeat* (2015). For the British perspective, see Nick Bunker's *An Empire on the Edge: How Britain Came to Fight America* (2015).

The intellectual foundations of revolt are traced in Bernard Bailyn's *The Ideological Origins of the American Revolution* (1992). To understand how these views were connected to organized protest, see Jon Butler's *Becoming America: The Revolution before 1776* (2000) and Kevin Phillips's *1775: A Good Year for a Revolution* (2012). On the first major battle, see Nathaniel Philbrick's *Bunker Hill: A City, A Siege, A Revolution* (2013).

On the efforts of colonists to boycott the purchase of British goods, see T. H. Breen's *The Marketplace of Revolution: How Consumer Politics Shaped American Independence* (2004). For the events during the summer of 1776, see Joseph J. Ellis's *Revolutionary Summer: The Birth of American Independence.* Pauline Maier's *American Scripture: Making the Declaration of Independence* (1997) remains the best analysis of the framing of that document. The best analysis of why Americans supported independence is Thomas Slaughter's *Independence: The Tangled Roots of the American Revolution* (2014).

CHAPTER 5

Military affairs in the early phases of the Revolutionary War are handled in John W. Shy's *Toward Lexington: The Role of the British Army in the Coming of the American Revolution* (1965). The Revolutionary War is the subject of Gordon S. Wood's *The Radicalism of the American Revolution* (1991) and Jeremy Black's *War for America: The Fight for Independence, 1775–1783* (1991). John Ferling's *Setting the World Ablaze: Washington, Adams, Jefferson, and the American Revolution* (2000) highlights the roles played by key leaders. For a splendid account of Washington's generalship, see Robert Middlekauf's *Washington's Revolution: The Making of America's First Great Leader* (2015).

On the social history of the Revolutionary War, see John W. Shy's *A People Numerous and Armed: Reflections on the Military Struggle for American Independence*, rev. ed. (1990). Colin G. Calloway tells the neglected story of the Indian experiences in the Revolution in *The American Revolution in Indian Country: Crisis and Diversity in Native American Communities* (1995).

Why some Americans remained loyal to the Crown is the subject of Thomas B. Allen's *Tories: Fighting for the King in America's First Civil War* (2010) and Maya Jasanoff's *Liberty's Exiles: American Loyalists in the Revolutionary War* (2011). A superb study of African Americans during the Revolutionary era is Douglas R. Egerton's *Death or Liberty: African Americans and Revolutionary America* (2009).

Carol Berkin's *Revolutionary Mothers: Women in the Struggle for America's Independence* (2005) documents the role that women played in securing independence. A superb biography of Revolutionary America's most prominent woman is Woody Holton's *Abigail Adams* (2010). A fine new biography of America's commander in chief is Ron Chernow's *Washington: A Life* (2010). The best analysis of the British side of the war is Andrew Jackson O'Shaughnessy's *The Men Who Lost America: British Leadership, the American Revolution, and the Fate of Empire* (2013).

CHAPTER 6

A good overview of the Confederation period is Richard B. Morris's *The Forging of the Union, 1781–1789* (1987). Another useful analysis of this period is Richard Buel Jr.'s *Securing the Revolution: Ideology in American*

Politics, 1789–1815 (1972). David P. Szatmary's *Shays's Rebellion: The Making of an Agrarian Insurrection* (1980) covers that fateful incident. For a fine account of cultural change during the period, see Joseph J. Ellis's *After the Revolution: Profiles of Early American Culture* (1979).

An excellent overview of post-Revolutionary life is Joyce Appleby's *Inheriting the Revolution: The First Generation of Americans* (2000). On the political philosophies contributing to the drafting of the Constitution, see Ralph Lerner's *The Thinking Revolutionary: Principle and Practice in the New Republic* (1987). For the dramatic story of the framers of the Constitution, see Richard Beeman's *Plain, Honest Men: The Making of the American Constitution* (2009). Woody Holton's *Unruly Americans and the Origins of the Constitution* (2007) emphasizes the role of taxes and monetary policies in the crafting of the Constitution. The complex story of ratification is well told in Pauline Maier's *Ratification: The People Debate the Constitution, 1787–1788* (2010). An excellent study of James Madison's development as a political theorist is Michael Signer's *Becoming Madison* (2015).

The best introduction to the early Federalists remains John C. Miller's *The Federalist Era, 1789–1801* (2011). Other works analyze the ideological debates among the nation's first leaders. Richard Buel Jr.'s *Securing the Revolution: Ideology in American Politics, 1789–1815* (1972), Joyce Appleby's *Capitalism and a New Social Order: The Republican Vision of the 1790s* (1984), and Stanley Elkins and Eric McKitrick's *The Age of Federalism: The Early American Republic, 1788–1800* (1993) trace the persistence and transformation of ideas first fostered during the Revolutionary crisis. The best study of Washington's political career is John Ferling's *The Ascent of George Washington: The Hidden Political Genius of an American Icon* (2009). For compelling portraits of four key leaders, see Joseph J. Ellis's *The Quartet: Orchestrating the Second American Revolution, 1783–1789* (2015).

The 1790s may also be understood through the views and behavior of national leaders. See the following biographies: Richard Brookhiser's *Founding Father: Rediscovering George Washington* (1996), *Alexander Hamilton, American* (1999), and *James Madison* (2013), and Joseph J. Ellis's *Passionate Sage: The Character and Legacy of John Adams* (1993).

On the formation of the federal government and its economic policies, see Thomas K. McCraw's *The Founders and Finance* (2012). Federalist foreign policy is explored in Jerald A. Comb's *The Jay Treaty: Political Battleground of the Founding Fathers* (1970) and William Stinchcombe's *The XYZ Affair* (1980).

CHAPTER 7

Marshall Smelser's *The Democratic Republic, 1801–1815* (1968) presents an overview of the Republican administrations. Even more comprehensive is Gordon S. Wood's *Empire of Liberty: A History of the Early Republic, 1789–1815* (2010). The best treatment of the election of 1800 is Edward J. Larson's *A Magnificent Catastrophe: The Tumultuous Election of 1800* (2008).

The standard biography of Jefferson is Joseph J. Ellis's *American Sphinx: The Character of Thomas Jefferson* (1996). A more recent analysis is Andrew Burstein's *Democracy's Muse* (2015). On the life of Jefferson's friend and successor, see Drew R. McCoy's. *The Last of the Fathers: James Madison and the Republican Legacy* (1989). Joyce Appleby's *Capitalism and a New Social Order: The Republican Vision of the 1790s* (1984) minimizes the impact of Republican ideology.

Linda K. Kerber's *Federalists in Dissent: Imagery and Ideology in Jeffersonian American* (1970) explores the Federalists while out of power. The concept of judicial review and the courts can be studied in Cliff Sloan and David McKean's *The Great Decision: Jefferson, Adams, Marshall, and the Battle for the Supreme Court* (2009). Liff Sloan and David McKean's *The Great Decision: Jefferson, Adams, Marshall, and the Battle for the Supreme Court* (2009). Milton Lomask's two volumes, *Aaron Burr: The Years from Princeton to Vice President, 1756–1805* (1979) and *The Conspiracy and the Years of Exile, 1805–1836* (1982), trace the career of that remarkable American.

For the Louisiana Purchase, consult Jon Kukla's *A Wilderness So Immense: The Louisiana Purchase and the Destiny of America* (2003). For a captivating account of the Lewis and Clark expedition, see Stephen Ambrose's *Undaunted Courage: Meriwether Lewis, Thomas Jefferson, and the Opening of the American West* (1996).

Burton Spivak's *Jefferson's English Crisis: Commerce, Embargo, and the Republican Revolution* (1979) discusses Anglo-American relations during Jefferson's administration; Clifford L. Egan's *Neither Peace Nor War: Franco-American Relations, 1803–1812* (1983) covers America's relations with France. An excellent revisionist treatment of the events that brought on war in 1812 is J. C. A. Stagg's *Mr. Madison's War: Politics, Diplomacy, and Warfare in the Early American Republic, 1783–1830* (1983). See also Paul A. Gilje's *Free Trade and Sailors' Rights in the War of 1812* (2013). The war itself is the focus of Donald R. Hickey's *The War of 1812: A Forgotten Conflict* (1989). For the perspective of those who fought in the war, see A. J. Langguth's *Union 1812: The Americans Who Fought the Second War of Independence* (2007). See also Alan Taylor's award-winnning *The Civil War of 1812: American Citizens, British Subjects, Irish Rebels, and Indian Allies* (2011).

CHAPTER 8

The best overview of the second quarter of the nineteenth century is Daniel Walker Howe, *What Hath God Wrought: The Transformation of America, 1815–1845* (2007). The classic study of transportation and economic growth is George Rogers Taylor's *The Transportation Revolution, 1815–1860* (1951). A more recent treatment is Sarah H. Gordon's *Passage to Union: How the Railroads Transformed American Life, 1829–1929* (1996). On the Erie Canal, see Carol Sheriff's *The Artificial River: The Erie Canal and the Paradox of Progress, 1817–1862* (1996). See also John Lauritz Larson's *Internal Improvement: National Public Works and the Promise of Popular Government in the Early United States* (2001).

Several books focus on social issues of the post-Revolutionary period, including *Keepers of the Revolution: New Yorkers at Work in the Early Republic* (1992), edited by Paul A. Gilje and Howard B. Rock; Ronald Schultz's *The Republic of Labor: Philadelphia Artisans and the Politics of Class, 1720–1830* (1993); and Peter Way's *Common Labor: Workers and the Digging of North American Canals, 1780–1860* (1993).

On the industrial revolution, see Charles R. Morris's *The Dawn of Innovation: The First American Industrial Revolution* (2013). The impact of technology is traced in David J. Jeremy's *Transatlantic Industrial Revolution: The Diffusion of Textile Technologies between Britain and America, 1790–1830s* (1981). On the invention of the telegraph, see Kenneth Silverman's *Lightning Man: The Accursed Life of Samuel F. B. Morse* (2003). For the story of steamboats, see Andrea Sutcliffe's *Steam: The Untold Story of America's First Great Invention* (2004).

The outlook of the working class during this time of transition is surveyed in Edward E. Pessen's *Most Uncommon Jacksonians: The Radical Leaders of the Early Labor Movement* (1967). Detailed case studies of working communities include Anthony F. C. Wallace's *Rockdale: The Growth of an American Village in the Early Industrial Revolution* (1978), Thomas Dublin's *Women at Work: The Transformation of Work and Community in Lowell, Massachusetts, 1826–1860* (1979), and Sean Wilentz's *Chants Democratic: New York and the Rise of the American Working Class, 1788–1850* (1984).

For a fine treatment of urbanization, see Charles N. Glaab and A. Theodore Brown's *A History of Urban America* (1967). On immigration, see Jay P.

Dolan's *The Irish Americans* (2008) and John Kelly's *The Graves Are Walking: The Great Famine and the Saga of the Irish People* (2012).

CHAPTER 9

The standard overview of the Era of Good Feelings remains George Dangerfield's *The Awakening of American Nationalism, 1815–1828* (1965). A classic summary of the economic trends of the period is Douglass C. North's *The Economic Growth of the United States, 1790–1860* (1961). An excellent synthesis of the era is Charles Sellers's *The Market Revolution: Jacksonian America, 1815–1846* (1991).

On diplomatic relations during James Monroe's presidency, see William Earl Weeks's *John Quincy Adams and American Global Empire* (1992). For relations after 1812, see Ernest R. May's *The Making of the Monroe Doctrine* (1975). The campaign that brought Andrew Jackson to the White House is analyzed in Robert Vincent Remini's *The Election of Andrew Jackson* (1963).

CHAPTER 10

The best comprehensive surveys of politics and culture during the Jacksonian era are Daniel Walker Howe's *What Hath God Wrought: The Transformation of America, 1815–1848* (2007) and David S. Reynolds's *Waking Giant: America in the Age of Jackson* (2008). A more political focus can be found in Harry L. Watson's *Liberty and Power: The Politics of Jacksonian America* (1990). On the rise of urban political machines, see Terry Golway's *Machine Made: Tammany Hall and the Creation of Modern American Politics* (2014).

For an outstanding analysis of women in New York City during the Jacksonian period, see Christine Stansell's *City of Women: Sex and Class in New York, 1789–1860* (1986). In *Chants Democratic: New York City and the Rise of the American Working-Class, 1788–1850* (1984), Sean Wilentz analyzes the social basis of working-class politics. More recently, Wilentz has traced the democratization of politics in *The Rise of American Democracy: Jefferson to Lincoln* (2009).

The best biography of Jackson remains Robert Vincent Remini's three-volume work: *Andrew Jackson: The Course of American Empire, 1767–1821* (1977), *Andrew Jackson: The Course of American Freedom, 1822–1832* (1981), and *Andrew Jackson: The Course of American Democracy, 1833–1845* (1984). A more critical study of the seventh president is Andrew Burstein's *The Passions of Andrew Jackson* (2003).

On Jackson's successor, consult John Niven's *Martin Van Buren: The Romantic Age of American Politics* (1983) and Ted Widmer's *Martin Van Buren* (2005). Studies of other major figures of the period include John Niven's *John C. Calhoun and the Price of Union: A Biography* (1988), Merrill D. Peterson's *The Great Triumvirate: Webster, Clay, and Calhoun* (1987), and Robert Vincent Remini's *Henry Clay: Statesman for the Union* (1991) and *Daniel Webster: The Man and His Time* (1997).

The political philosophies of Jackson's opponents are treated in Michael F. Holt's *The Rise and Fall of the American Whig Party: Jacksonian Politics and the Onset of the Civil War* (1999) and Harry L. Watson's *Andrew Jackson vs. Henry Clay: Democracy and Development in Antebellum America* (1998). The outstanding book on the nullification issue remains William W. Freehling's *Prelude to Civil War: The Nullification Controversy in South Carolina, 1816–1836* (1965). John M. Belohlavek's *"Let the Eagle Soar!": The Foreign Policy of Andrew Jackson* (1985) is a thorough study of Jacksonian diplomacy. A. J. Langguth's *Driven West: Andrew Jackson and the Trail of Tears to the Civil War* (2010) analyzes the controversial relocation policy.

CHAPTER 11

Three efforts to understand the mind of the Old South and its defense of slavery are Eugene D. Genovese's *The Slaveholders' Dilemma: Freedom and Progress in Southern Conservative Thought, 1820–1860* (1992), William W. Freehling's *The Road to Disunion: Secessionists Triumphant, 1854–1861* (2007), and Walter Johnson's *River of Dark Dreams: Slavery and Empire in the Cotton Kingdom* (2013). Stephanie McCurry's *Masters of Small Worlds: Yeoman Households, Gender Relations, and the Political Culture of the Antebellum South Carolina Low Country* (1995) describes southern households, religion, and political culture. The best recent book on the role of slavery in creating the cotton culture is Edward E. Baptist's *The Half Has Never Been Told: Slavery and the Making of American Capitalism* (2014).

Other essential works on southern culture and society include Bertram Wyatt-Brown's *Honor and Violence in the Old South* (1986), Elizabeth Fox-Genovese's *Within the Plantation Household: Black and White Women of the Old South* (1988), Catherine Clinton's *The Plantation Mistress: Woman's World in the Old South* (1982), Joan E. Cashin's *A Family Venture: Men and Women on the Southern Frontier* (1991), and Theodore Rosengarten's *Tombee: Portrait of a Cotton Planter* (1986).

John W. Blassingame's *The Slave Community: Plantation Life in the Antebellum South*, rev. and enlarged ed. (1979), Eugene D. Genovese's *Roll, Jordan,*

Roll: The World the Slaves Made (1974), and Herbert G. Gutman's *The Black Family in Slavery and Freedom, 1750–1925* (1976) all stress the theme of a persisting and identifiable slave culture. On the question of slavery's profitability, see Robert William Fogel and Stanley L. Engerman's *Time on the Cross: The Economics of American Negro Slavery* (1974), and Edward E. Baptist's *The Half Has Never Been Told* (2014). Charles Joyner's *Down by the Riverside: A South Carolina Slave Community* (1984) offers a vivid reconstruction of one community.

CHAPTER 12

Russel Blaine Nye's *Society and Culture in America, 1830–1860* (1974) provides a wide-ranging survey of the Romantic movement. On the reform impulse, consult Ronald G. Walter's *American Reformers, 1815–1860*, rev. ed. (1997). Revivalist religion is treated in Nathan O. Hatch's *The Democratization of American Christianity* (1989), Christine Leigh Heyrman's *Southern Cross: The Beginnings of the Bible Belt* (1997), and Ellen Eslinger's *Citizens of Zion: The Social Origins of Camp Meeting Revivalism* (1999). On the Mormons, see Alex Beam's *American Crucifixion: The Murder of Joseph Smith and the Fate of the Mormon Church* (2014).

The best treatments of transcendentalist thought are Paul F. Boller's *American Transcendentalism, 1830–1860: An Intellectual Inquiry* (1974) and Philip F. Gura's *American Transcendentalism: A History* (2007). On Henry D. Thoreau, see Michael Sims's *The Adventures of Henry Thoreau* (2014). Edgar Allan Poe is the subject of Jerome McGann's *The Poet Edgar Allan Poe: Alien Angel* (2015). For the war against alcohol, see W. J. Rorabaugh's *The Alcoholic Republic: An American Tradition* (1979) and Barbara Leslie Epstein's *The Politics of Domesticity: Women, Evangelism, and Temperance in Nineteenth-Century America* (1981). On prison reform and other humanitarian projects, see David J. Rothman's *The Discovery of the Asylum: Social Order and Disorder in the New Republic*, rev. ed. (2002), and Thomas J. Brown's biography *Dorothea Dix: New England Reformer* (1998).

Useful surveys of abolitionism include Seymour Drescher's *Abolition: A History of Slavery and Antislavery* (2009), James Brewer Stewart's *Holy Warriors: The Abolitionists and American Slavery*, rev. ed. (1997), and Julie Roy Jeffrey's *The Great Silent Army of Abolitionism: Ordinary Women in the Antislavery Movement* (1998). For the pro-slavery argument as it developed in the South, see Larry E. Tise's *Proslavery: A History of the Defense of Slavery in America, 1701–1840* (1987) and James Oakes's *The Ruling Race: A History of American Slaveholders* (1982). The problems southerners had in justifying slavery are explored in Kenneth S. Greenberg's *Masters and Statesmen: The Political Culture of American Slavery* (1985). For the dramatic story of the role of the Underground Railroad in freeing slaves, see Eric Foner's *Gateway to Freedom: The Hidden History of the Underground Railroad* (2015).

CHAPTER 13

For background on Whig programs and ideas, see Michael F. Holt's *The Rise and Fall of the American Whig Party: Jacksonian Politics and the Onset of the Civil War* (1999). On John Tyler, see Edward P. Crapol's *John Tyler: The Accidental President* (2006). On the expansionist impulse westward, see Thomas R. Hietala's *Manifest Design: Anxious Aggrandizement in Late Jacksonian America* (1985), Walter Nugent's *Habits of Empire: A History of American Expansionism* (2008) and Richard White's *"It's Your Misfortune and None of My Own": A New History of the American West* (1991).

For the expansionism of the 1840s, see Steven E. Woodworth's *Manifest Destinies: America's Westward Expansion and the Road to the Civil War* (2010). The movement of settlers to the West is ably documented in John Mack Faragher's *Women and Men on the Overland Trail,* 2nd ed. (2001), David Dary's *The Santa Fe Trail: Its History, Legends, and Lore* (2000), and Rinker Buck's *The Oregon Trail* (2015).

Gene M. Brack's *Mexico Views Manifest Destiny, 1821–1846: An Essay on the Origins of the Mexican War* (1975) takes Mexico's viewpoint on U.S. designs on the West. For the American perspective on Texas, see Joel H. Silbey's *Storm over Texas: The Annexation Controversy and the Road to Civil War* (2005). On the siege of the Alamo, see William C. Davis's *Three Roads to the Alamo: The Lives and Fortunes of David Crockett, James Bowie, and William Barret Travis* (1998) and James Donovan's *The Blood of Heroes* (2012). An excellent biography related to the emergence of Texas is Gregg Cantrell's *Stephen F. Austin: Empresario of Texas* (1999).

On James K. Polk, see Robert W. Merry's *A Country of Vast Designs: James K. Polk, the Mexican War, and the Conquest of the American Continent* (2009). The best survey of the military conflict is John S. D. Eisenhower's *So Far from God: The U.S. War with Mexico, 1846–1848* (1989). The Mexican War as viewed from the perspective of the soldiers is ably described in Richard Bruce Winders's *Mr. Polk's Army: American Military Experience in the Mexican War* (1997). On the diplomatic aspects of Mexican-American relations, see David M. Pletcher's *The Diplomacy of Annexation: Texas, Oregon, and the Mexican War* (1973).

CHAPTER 14

The best surveys of the forces and events leading to the Civil War include James M. McPherson's *Battle Cry of Freedom: The Civil War Era* (1988), Stephen B. Oates's *The Approaching Fury: Voices of the Storm, 1820–1861* (1997), James Oakes's *The Scorpion's Sting: Antislavery and the Coming of the Civil War* (2015), and Bruce Levine's *Half Slave and Half Free: The Roots of Civil War* (1992). The most recent narrative of the political debate leading to secession is Michael A. Morrison's *Slavery and the American West: The Eclipse of Manifest Destiny and the Coming of the Civil War* (1997).

Mark J. Stegmaier's *Texas, New Mexico, and the Compromise of 1850: Boundary Dispute and Sectional Crisis* (1996) probes that crucial dispute, while Michael F. Holt's *The Political Crisis of the 1850s* (1978) traces the demise of the Whigs. See also Fergus M. Bordewich's *America's Great Debate: Henry Clay, Stephen A. Douglas, and the Compromise That Preserved the Union* (2012). Eric Foner, in *Free Soil, Free Labor, Free Men: The Ideology of the Republican Party before the Civil War* (1970), shows how events and ideas combined in the formation of a new political party. The pivotal *Dred Scott* case is ably assessed in Earl M. Maltz's *Dred Scott and the Politics of Slavery* (2007).

On the role of John Brown in the sectional crisis, see Robert E. McGlone's *John Brown's War Against Slavery* (2009). A detailed study of the South's journey to secession is William W. Freehling's *The Road to Disunion*, vol. 1, *Secessionists at Bay, 1776–1854* (1990), and *The Road to Disunion*, vol. 2, *Secessionists Triumphant, 1854–1861* (2007). Robert E. Bonner traces the emergence of southern nationalism in *Mastering America: Southern Slaveholders and the Crisis of American Nationhood* (2009).

On the Buchanan presidency, see Jean H. Baker's *James Buchanan* (2004). Maury Klein's *Days of Defiance: Sumter, Secession, and the Coming of the Civil War* (1997) treats the Fort Sumter controversy. An excellent collection of interpretive essays is *Why the Civil War Came* (1996), edited by Gabor S. Boritt.

CHAPTER 15

On the start of the Civil War, see Adam Goodheart's *1861: The Civil War Awakening* (2011). The best one-volume overview of the Civil War period is James M. McPherson's *Battle Cry of Freedom: The Civil War Era* (1988). A more recent synthesis of the war and its effects is David Goldfield's *America*

Aflame: How the Civil War Created a Nation (2011). A good introduction to the military events is Herman Hattaway's *Shades of Blue and Gray: An Introductory Military History of the Civil War* (1997). The outlook and experiences of the common soldier are explored in James M. McPherson's *For Cause and Comrades: Why Men Fought in the Civil War* (1997. For the global dimensions of the conflict, see Don H. Doyle's *The Cause of All Nations: An International History of the American Civil War* (2015).

The northern war effort is ably assessed in Gary W. Gallagher's *The Union War* (2011). For emphasis on the South, see Gallagher's *The Confederate War* (1997). A sparkling account of the birth of the Rebel nation is William C. Davis's *"A Government of Our Own": The Making of the Confederacy* (1994). On the president of the Confederacy, see James M. McPherson's *Embattled Rebel: Jefferson Davis as Commander in Chief* (2014). . On two of the leading Confederate commanders, see Michael Korda's *Clouds of Glory: The Life and Legend of Robert E. Lee* (2014) and S. C. Gwynne's *Rebel Yell: Stonewall Jackson* (2014). On the key Union generals, see Lee Kennett's *Sherman: A Soldier's Life* (2001) and Josiah Bunting III's *Ulysses S. Grant* (2004). The controversy over Sherman's March to the Sea is the focus of Matthew Carr's *Sherman's Ghosts: Soldiers, Civilians, and the American Way of War* (2015).

The history of the North during the war is surveyed in Philip Shaw Paludan's *A People's Contest: The Union and Civil War, 1861–1865*, 2nd ed. (1996), and J. Matthew Gallman's *The North Fights the Civil War: The Home Front* (1994). See also Jennifer L. Weber's *Copperheads: The Rise and Fall of Lincoln's Opponents in the North* (2006). The central northern political figure, Abraham Lincoln, is the subject of many books. See James McPherson's *Abraham Lincoln* (2009) and Ronald C. White Jr., *A. Lincoln: A Biography* (2009).

The experience of the African American soldier is surveyed in Joseph T. Glatthaar's *Forged in Battle: The Civil War Alliance of Black Soldiers and White Officers* (1990) and Ira Berlin, Joseph P. Reidy, and Leslie S. Rowland's *Freedom's Soldiers: The Black Military Experience in the Civil War* (1998). For the African American woman's experience, see Jacqueline Jones's *Labor of Love, Labor of Sorrow: Black Women, Work and the Family, from Slavery to the Present* (1985). On Lincoln's evolving racial views, see Eric Foner's *The Fiery Trial: Abraham Lincoln and American Slavery* (2010). The war's impact on slavery is the focus of James Oakes's *Freedom National: The Destruction of Slavery in the United States, 1861–1865* (2013) and Bruce Levine's *The Fall of the House of Dixie* (2013). On the emancipation proclamation, see Louis P. Masur's *Lincoln's Hundred Days: The Emancipation Proclamation and the War for the Union* (2012). For a sensory perspective on the fighting, see Mark M. Smith's *The Smell of Battle, the Taste of Siege: A Sensory History of the Civil War* (2014).

Recent gender and ethnic studies include Nina Silber's *Gender and the Sectional Conflict* (2008), Drew Gilpin Faust's *Mothers of Invention: Women of the Slaveholding South in the American Civil War* (1996), George C. Rable's *Civil Wars: Women and the Crisis of Southern Nationalism* (1989), and William L. Burton's *Melting Pot Soldiers: The Union's Ethnic Regiments*, 2nd ed. (1998). What Civil War veterans experienced after the conflict ended is the subject of Brian Matthew Jordan's *Marching Home* (2015) and Gregory P. Downs's *After Appomattox: Military Occupation and the Ends of War* (2015).

CHAPTER 16

The most comprehensive treatment of Reconstruction is Eric Foner's *Reconstruction: America's Unfinished Revolution, 1863–1877* (1988). On Andrew Johnson, see Hans L. Trefousse's *Andrew Johnson: A Biography* (1989) and David D. Stewart's *Impeached: The Trial of Andrew Johnson and the Fight for Lincoln's Legacy* (2009). An excellent brief biography of Grant is Josiah Bunting III's *Ulysses S. Grant* (2004).

Scholars have been sympathetic to the aims and motives of the Radical Republicans. See, for instance, Herman Belz's *Reconstructing the Union: Theory and Policy during the Civil War* (1969) and Richard Nelson Current's *Those Terrible Carpetbaggers: A Reinterpretation* (1988). The ideology of the Radicals is explored in Michael Les Benedict's *A Compromise of Principle: Congressional Republicans and Reconstruction, 1863–1869* (1974). On the black political leaders, see Phillip Dray's *Capitol Men: The Epic Story of Reconstruction through the Lives of the First Black Congressmen* (2008).

The intransigence of southern white attitudes is examined in Michael Perman's *Reunion without Compromise: The South and Reconstruction, 1865–1868* (1973) and Dan T. Carter's *When the War Was Over: The Failure of Self-Reconstruction in the South, 1865–1867* (1985). Allen W. Trelease's *White Terror: The Ku Klux Klan Conspiracy and Southern Reconstruction* (1971) covers the various organizations that practiced vigilante tactics. On the massacre of African Americans, see Charles Lane's *The Day Freedom Died: The Colfax Massacre, the Supreme Court, and the Betrayal of Reconstruction* (2008).

The difficulties former slaves had in adjusting to the new labor system are documented in James L. Roark's *Masters without Slaves: Southern Planters in the Civil War and Reconstruction* (1977). Books on southern politics during Reconstruction include Michael Perman's *The Road to Redemption: Southern*

Politics, 1869–1879 (1984), Terry L. Seip's *The South Returns to Congress: Men, Economic Measures, and Intersectional Relationships, 1868–1879* (1983), and Mark W. Summers's *Railroads, Reconstruction, and the Gospel of Prosperity: Aid under the Radical Republicans, 1865–1877* (1984).

Numerous works study the freed blacks' experience in the South. Start with Leon F. Litwack's *Been in the Storm So Long: The Aftermath of Slavery* (1979). The Freedmen's Bureau is explored in William S. McFeely's *Yankee Stepfather: General O. O. Howard and the Freedmen* (1968). The situation of freed slave women is discussed in Jacqueline Jones's *Labor of Love, Labor of Sorrow: Black Women, Work and the Family, from Slavery to the Present* (1985).

The politics of corruption outside the South is depicted in William S. McFeely's *Grant: A Biography* (1981). The political maneuvers of the election of 1876 and the resultant crisis and compromise are explained in Michael Holt's *By One Vote: The Disputed Presidential Election of 1876* (2008).

CHAPTER 17

For masterly syntheses of post–Civil War industrial development, see Walter Licht's *Industrializing America: The Nineteenth Century* (1995) and Maury Klein's *The Genesis of Industrial America, 1870–1920* (2007). On the growth of railroads, see Richard White's *Railroaded: The Transcontinentals and the Making of Modern America* (2011) and Albro Martin's *Railroad Triumphant: The Growth, Rejection, and Rebirth of a Vital American Force* (1992).

On entrepreneurship in the iron and steel sector, and Thomas J. Misa's *A Nation of Steel: The Making of Modern America, 1865–1925* (1995). The best biographies of the leading business tycoons are Ron Chernow's *Titan: The Life of John D. Rockefeller, Sr.* (1998), David Nasaw's *Andrew Carnegie* (2006), and Jean Strouse's *Morgan: American Financier* (1999). Nathan Rosenberg's *Technology and American Economic Growth* (1972) documents the growth of invention during the period.

For an overview of the struggle of workers to organize unions, see Philip Bray's *There Is Power in a Union: The Epic Story of Labor in America* (2010). On the 1877 railroad strike, see David O. Stowell's *Streets, Railroad, and the Great Strike of 1877* (1999). For the role of women in the changing workplace, see Alice Kessler-Harris's *Out to Work: A History of Wage-Earning Women in the United States* (1982) and Susan E. Kennedy's *If All We Did Was to Weep at Home: A History of White Working-Class Women in American* (1979). On

Mother Jones, see Elliott J. Gorn's *Mother Jones: The Most Dangerous Woman in America* (2001). To trace the rise of socialism among organized workers, see Nick Salvatore's *Eugene V. Debs: Citizen and Socialist* (1982). The key strikes are discussed in Paul Arvich's *The Haymarket Tragedy* (1984) and Paul Krause's *The Battle for Homestead, 1880–1892: Politics, Culture, and Steel* (1992).

CHAPTER 18

The classic study of the emergence of the New South remains C. Vann Woodward's *Origins of the New South, 1877–1913* (1951). A more recent treatment of southern society after the end of Reconstruction is Edward L. Ayers's *Southern Crossing: A History of the American South, 1877–1906* (1995). A thorough survey of industrialization in the South is James C. Cobb's *Industrialization and Southern Society, 1877–1984* (1984).

On race relations, see Howard N. Rabinowitz's *Race Relations in the Urban South, 1865–1890* (1978). Leon F. Litwack's *Trouble in Mind: Black Southerners in the Age of Jim Crow* (1998) treats the rise of legal segregation, while Michael Perman's *Struggle for Mastery: Disfranchisement in the South, 1888–1908* (2001) surveys efforts to keep African Americans from voting. An award-winning study of white women and the race issue is Glenda Elizabeth Gilmore's *Gender and Jim Crow: Women and the Politics of White Supremacy in North Carolina, 1896–1920* (1996). On W. E. B. Du Bois, see David Levering Lewis's *W. E. B. Du Bois: Biography of a Race, 1868–1919* (1993). On Booker T. Washington, see Robert J. Norrell's *Up from History: The Life of Booker T. Washington* (2009).

For stimulating reinterpretations of the frontier and the development of the West, see William Cronon's *Nature's Metropolis: Chicago and the Great West* (1991), Patricia Nelson Limerick's *The Legacy of Conquest: The Unbroken Past of the American West* (1987), Richard White's *"It's Your Misfortune and None of My Own": A New History of the American West* (1991), and Walter Nugent's *Into the West: The Story of Its People* (1999). An excellent overview is James M. McPherson's *Into the West: From Reconstruction to the Final Days of the American Frontier* (2006).

The role of African Americans in western settlement is the focus of William Loren Katz's *The Black West: A Documentary and Pictorial History of the African American Role in the Westward Expansion of the United States*, rev. ed. (2005), and Nell Irvin Painter's *Exodusters: Black Migration to Kansas after Reconstruction* (1977).

The best account of the conflicts between Indians and whites is Robert M. Utley's *The Indian Frontier of the American West, 1846–1890* (1984). For the Sand Creek massacre, see Ari Kellman's *A Misplaced Massacre: Struggling over the Memory of Sand Creek* (2013). On the Battle of the Little Bighorn, see Nathaniel Philbrick's *The Last Stand: Custer, Sitting Bull, and the Battle of the Little Bighorn* (2010). On Crazy Horse, see Thomas Powers's *The Killing of Crazy Horse* (2010).

For a presentation of the Native American side of the story, see Peter Nabokov's *Native American Testimony: A Chronicle of Indian-White Relations from Prophecy to the Present, 1492–2000*, rev. ed. (1999). On the demise of the buffalo herds, see Andrew C. Isenberg's *The Destruction of the Bison: An Environmental History, 1750–1920* (2000).

CHAPTER 19

For a survey of urbanization, see David R. Goldfield's *Urban America: A History* (1989). Gunther Barth discusses the emergence of a new urban culture in *City People: The Rise of Modern City Culture in Nineteenth-Century America* (1980). John Bodnar offers a synthesis of the urban immigrant experience in *The Transplanted: A History of Immigrants in Urban America* (1985). See also Roger Daniels's *Guarding the Golden Door: American Immigration Policy and Immigrants since 1882* (2004). Walter Nugent's *Crossings: The Great Transatlantic Migrations, 1870–1914* (1992) provides a wealth of demographic information and insight. Efforts to stop Chinese immigration are described in Erika Lee's *At America's Gates: Chinese Immigration during the Exclusion Era* (2003).

On urban environments and sanitary reforms, see Martin V. Melosi's *The Sanitary City: Urban Infrastructure in America from Colonial Times to the Present* (2000), Joel A. Tarr's *The Search for the Ultimate Sink: Urban Pollution in Historical Perspective* (1996), and Suellen Hoy's *Chasing Dirt: The American Pursuit of Cleanliness* (1995).

For the growth of urban leisure and sports, see Roy Rosenzweig's *Eight Hours for What We Will: Workers and Leisure in an Industrial City, 1870–1920* (1983) and Steven A. Riess's *City Games: The Evolution of American Urban Society and the Rise of Sports* (1989). Saloon culture is examined in Madelon Powers's *Faces along the Bar: Lore and Order in the Workingman's Saloon, 1870–1920* (1998).

On the impact of Darwin's theory of evolution, see Barry Werth's *Banquet at Delmonico's: Great Minds, the Gilded Age, and the Triumph of Evolution in America* (2009). On the rise of realism in thought and the arts during the second half of the nineteenth century, see David E. Shi's *Facing Facts: Realism in American Thought and Culture, 1850–1920* (1995). The rise of pragmatism is the focus of Louis Menand's *The Metaphysical Club: A Story of Ideas in America* (2001).

Two good overviews of the Gilded Age are Sean Cashman's *America in the Gilded Age: From the Death of Lincoln to the Rise of Theodore Roosevelt* (1984) and Mark Summers's *The Gilded Age or, The Hazard of New Functions* (1996). Nell Irvin Painter's *Standing at Armageddon: The United States, 1877–1919* (1987) focuses on the experience of the working class.

For a stimulating overview of the political, social, and economic trends during the Gilded Age, see Jack Beatty's *Age of Betrayal: The Triumph of Money in America, 1865–1900* (2007). On the development of city rings and bosses, see Kenneth D. Ackerman's *Boss Tweed: The Rise and Fall of the Corrupt Pol Who Conceived the Soul of Modern New York* (2005). Excellent presidential biographies include Hans L. Trefousse's *Rutherford B. Hayes* (2002), Zachary Karabell's *Chester Alan Arthur* (2004), Henry F. Graff's *Grover Cleveland* (2002), and Kevin Phillips's *William McKinley* (2003). On the political culture of the Gilded Age, see Charles Calhoun's *Minority Victory: Gilded Age Politics and the Front Porch Campaign of 1888* (2008).

A balanced account of Populism is Charles Postel's *The Populist Vision* (2007). The election of 1896 is the focus of R. Hal Williams's *Realigning America: McKinley, Bryan, and the Remarkable Election of 1896* (2010). On the role of religion in the agrarian protest movements, see Joe Creech's *Righteous Indignation: Religion and the Populist Revolution* (2006). The best biography of Bryan is Michael Kazin's *A Godly Hero: The Life of William Jennings Bryan* (2006).

CHAPTER 20

An excellent survey of the diplomacy of the era is Charles S. Campbell's *The Transformation of American Foreign Relations, 1865–1900* (1976). For background on the events of the 1890s, see David Healy's *U.S. Expansionism: The Imperialist Urge in the 1890s* (1970). The dispute over American policy in Hawaii is covered in Thomas J. Osborne's *"Empire Can Wait": American Opposition to Hawaiian Annexation, 1893–1898* (1981).

Ivan Musicant's *Empire by Default: The Spanish-American War and the Dawn of the American Century* (1998) is the most comprehensive volume on the conflict. A colorful treatment of the powerful men promoting war is Evan Thomas's *The War Lovers: Roosevelt, Lodge, Mahan, and the Rush to Empire,*

1898 (2010). For the war's aftermath in the Philippines, see Stuart Creighton Miller's *"Benevolent Assimilation": The American Conquest of the Philippines, 1899–1903* (1982). On the Philippine-American War, see David J. Silbey's *A War of Frontier and Empire: The Philippine-American War, 1899–1902* (2007).

A good introduction to American interest in China is Michael H. Hunt's *The Making of a Special Relationship: The United States and China to 1914* (1983). John Taliaferro's *All the Great Prizes: The Life of John Hay* (2013) examines the role of this key secretary of state in forming policy.

For U.S. policy in the Caribbean and Central America, see Walter LaFeber's *Inevitable Revolutions: The United States in Central America*, 2nd ed. (1993). David McCullough's *The Path between the Seas: The Creation of the Panama Canal, 1870–1914* (1977) presents an admiring account of how the United States secured the Panama Canal. A more sober assessment is Julie Greene's *The Canal Builders: Making America's Empire at the Panama Canal* (2009). For a detailed treatment of Theodore Roosevelt's diplomacy as president, see James Bradley's *The Imperial Cruise: A Secret History of Empire and War* (2009).

CHAPTER 21

Splendid analyses of progressivism can be found in John Whiteclay Chambers II's *The Tyranny of Change: America in the Progressive Era, 1890–1920*, rev. ed. (2000), Steven J. Diner's *A Very Different Age: Americans of the Progressive Era* (1997), Maureen A. Flanagan's *America Reformed: Progressives and Progressivisms, 1890–1920* (2006), Michael McGerr's *A Fierce Discontent: The Rise and Fall of the Progressive Movement in America* (2003) and David Traxel's *Crusader Nation: The United States in Peace and the Great War, 1898–1920* (2006). On Ida Tarbell and the muckrakers, see Steve Weinberg's *Taking on the Trust: The Epic Battle of Ida Tarbell and John D. Rockefeller* (2008).

The evolution of government policy toward business is examined in Martin J. Sklar's *The Corporate Reconstruction of American Capitalism, 1890–1916: The Market, the Law, and Politics* (1988). Mina Carson's *Settlement Folk: Social Thought and the American Settlement Movement, 1885–1930* (1990) examines the social problems in the cities. Robert Kanigel's *The One Best Way: Frederick Winslow Taylor and the Enigma of Efficiency* (1997) highlights the role of efficiency and expertise in the Progressive Era.

An excellent study of the role of women in progressivism's emphasis on social justice is Kathryn Kish Sklar's *Florence Kelley and the Nation's Work: The Rise of Women's Political Culture, 1830–1900* (1995). On the tragic fire at the Triangle Shirtwaist Company, see David Von Drehle's *Triangle: The*

Fire That Changed America (2003). The best study of the settlement house movement is Jean Bethke Elshtain's *Jane Addams and the Dream of American Democracy: A Life* (2002).

On Theodore Roosevelt and the conservation movement, see Douglas Brinkley's *The Wilderness Warrior: Theodore Roosevelt and the Crusade for America* (2009) The pivotal election of 1912 is covered in James Chace's *1912: Wilson, Roosevelt, Taft, and Debs—The Election That Changed the Country* (2004) and Sidney M. Milkis's *TR, the Progressive Party, and the Transformation of Democracy* (2009). Excellent biographies include Kathleen Dalton's *Theodore Roosevelt: A Strenuous Life* (2002) and A. Scott Berg's *Wilson* (2013). The racial blind spot of Progressivism is assessed in David W. Southern's *The Progressive Era and Race: Reform and Reaction, 1900–1917* (2006).

CHAPTER 22

A lucid overview of international events in the early twentieth century is Robert H. Ferrell's *Woodrow Wilson and World War I, 1917–1921* (1985). For a vivid account of U.S. intervention in Mexico, see Frederick Katz's *The Life and Times of Pancho Villa* (1999). On Wilson's stance toward war, see Robert W. Tucker's *Woodrow Wilson and the Great War: Reconsidering America's Neutrality, 1914–1917* (2007). An excellent biography is John Milton Cooper Jr.'s *Woodrow Wilson: A Biography* (2010).

For the European experience in the Great War, see Adam Hochschild's *To End All Wars: A Story of Loyalty and Rebellion, 1914–1918* (2011), Margaret MacMillan's *The War That Ended Peace* (2013), and William Philpott's *Attrition: Fighting the First World War* (2015). Edward M. Coffman's *The War to End All Wars: The American Military Experience in World War I* (1968) is a detailed presentation of America's military involvement. See also Gary Mead's *The Doughboys: America and the First World War* (2000).

For a survey of the impact of the war on the home front, see Meirion Harries and Susie Harries's *The Last Days of Innocence: America at War, 1917–1918* (1997). Maurine Weiner Greenwald's *Women, War, and Work: The Impact of World War I on Women Workers in the United States* (1980) discusses the role of women in the war effort while Sara Hunter Graham's *Woman Suffrage and the New Democracy* (1996) traces the movement during the war to give women the vote. Ronald Schaffer's *America in the Great War: The Rise of the War Welfare State* (1991) shows the effect of war mobilization on business organization. Richard Polenberg's *Fighting Faiths: The*

Abrams Case, the Supreme Court, and Free Speech (1987) examines the prosecution of a case under the 1918 Sedition Act. See also Ernest Freeberg's *Democracy's Prisoner: Eugene V. Debs, the Great War, and the Right to Dissent* (2009).

How American diplomacy fared in the making of peace has received considerable attention. Thomas J. Knock connects domestic affairs and foreign relations in his explanation of Wilson's peacemaking in *To End All Wars: Woodrow Wilson and the Quest for a New World Order* (1992). See also John Milton Cooper Jr.'s *Breaking the Heart of the World: Woodrow Wilson and the Fight for the League of Nations* (2002), and Adam Tooze's *The Deluge: The Great War, America, and the Remaking of the Global Order* (2014).

The problems of the immediate postwar years are chronicled by a number of historians. The best overview is Ann Hagedorn's *Savage Peace: Hope and Fear in America, 1919* (2007). On the Spanish flu, see John M. Barry's *The Great Influenza: The Epic Story of the Deadliest Plague in History* (2004). Labor tensions are examined in David E. Brody's *Labor in Crisis: The Steel Strike of 1919* (1965) and Francis Russell's *A City in Terror: Calvin Coolidge and the 1919 Boston Police Strike* (1975). On racial strife, see Jan Voogd's *Race Riots and Resistance: The Red Summer of 1919* (2008). The fear of Communists is analyzed in Robert K. Murray's *Red Scare: A Study in National Hysteria, 1919–1920* (1955).

CHAPTER 23

For a lively survey of the social and cultural changes during the interwar period, start with William E. Leuchtenburg's *The Perils of Prosperity, 1914–32*, 2nd ed. (1993). Even more comprehensive is Michael E. Parrish's *Anxious Decades: America in Prosperity and Depression, 1920–1941* (1992). The best introduction to the culture of the 1920s remains Roderick Nash's *The Nervous Generation: American Thought, 1917–1930* (1990). See also Lynn Dumenil's *The Modern Temper: American Culture and Society in the 1920s* (1995).

The impact of woman suffrage is treated in Kristi Anderson's *After Suffrage: Women in Partisan and Electoral Politics before the New Deal* (1996). The best study of the birth-control movement is Ellen Chesler's *Woman of Valor: Margaret Sanger and the Birth Control Movement in America* (1992).

On the African American migration from the South, see James N. Gregory's *The Southern Diaspora: How the Great Migrations of Black and White Southerners Transformed America* (2005). See Charles Flint Kellogg's *NAACP: A History of the National Association for the Advancement of Colored People* (1967) for his analysis of the pioneering court cases against racial discrimination. Nathan Irvin Huggins's *Harlem Renaissance* (1971) assesses the cultural impact of the Great Migration on New York City. The emergence of jazz is ably documented in Burton W. Peretti's *The Creation of Jazz: Music, Race, and Culture in Urban America* (1992). Scientific breakthroughs are analyzed in Manjit Kumar's *Quantum: Einstein, Bohr, and the Great Debate about the Nature of Reality* (2010). See also Steven Gimbel's *Einstein: His Space and Times* (2015). The best overview of cultural modernism in Europe is Peter Gay's *Modernism: The Lure of Heresy from Baudelaire to Beckett and Beyond* (2009). On southern modernism, see Daniel Joseph Singal's *The War Within: From Victorian to Modernist Thought in the South, 1919–1945* (1982). Stanley Coben's *Rebellion against Victorianism: The Impetus for Cultural Change in 1920s America* (1991) surveys the appeal of modernism among writers, artists, and intellectuals. See also Charles J. Shindo's *1927 and the Rise of Modern America* (2010).

CHAPTER 24

On Harding, see Robert K. Murray's *The Harding Era: Warren G. Harding and His Administration* (1969). On Coolidge, see Amith Shlaes's *Coolidge* (2013). On Hoover, see Martin L. Fausold's *The Presidency of Herbert C. Hoover* (1985). The influential secretary of the Treasury during the 1920s is ably analyzed in David Cannadine's *Mellon: An American Life* (2006).

John Higham's *Strangers in the Land: Patterns of American Nativism, 1860–1925,* 2nd ed. (2002) details the story of immigration restriction. The controversial Sacco and Vanzetti case is the focus of Moshik Temkin's *The Sacco-Vanzetti Affair: America on Trial* (2009). For analysis of the revival of Klan activity, see Thomas R. Pegram's *One Hundred Percent American: The Rebirth and Decline of the Ku Klux Klan in the 1920s* (2011). The best analysis of the Scopes trial is Edward J. Larson's *Summer for the Gods: The Scopes Trial and America's Continuing Debate over Science and Religion* (1997). On Prohibition, see Daniel Okrent's *Last Call: The Rise and Fall of Prohibition* (2011). For the story of the invention of the airplane, see David McCullough's *The Wright Brothers* (2015).

On the stock market crash in 1929, see Maury Klein's *Rainbow's End: The Crash of 1929* (2000). Overviews of the depressed economy are found in Charles P. Kindleberger's *The World in Depression, 1929–1939,* rev. and enlarged ed. (1986) and Peter Fearon's *War, Prosperity, and Depression: The U.S. Economy, 1917–1945* (1987). On the removal of the Bonus Army, see Paul Dickson and Thomas B. Allen's *The Bonus Army: An American Epic* (2004).

CHAPTER 25

Two excellent overviews of the New Deal are Ira Katznelson's *Fear Itself: The New Deal and the Origins of Our Time* (2013) and David M. Kennedy's *Freedom from Fear: The American People in Depression and War, 1929–1945* (1999). A lively biography of Roosevelt is H. W. Brands's *Traitor to His Class: The Privileged Life and Radical Presidency of Franklin Delano Roosevelt* (2009). The Roosevelt marriage is well described in Hazel Rowley's *Franklin and Eleanor: An Extraordinary Marriage* (2011).

The busy first year of the New Deal is ably detailed in Anthony J. Badger's *FDR: The First Hundred Days* (2008). Perhaps the most successful of the early New Deal programs is the focus of Neil M. Maher's *Nature's New Deal: The Civilian Conservation Corps and the Roots of the American Environmental Movement* (2008). On the political opponents of the New Deal, see Alan Brinkley's *Voices of Protest: Huey Long, Father Coughlin, and the Great Depression* (1982). Roosevelt's battle with the Supreme Court is detailed in Jeff Shesol's *Supreme Power: Franklin Roosevelt vs. The Supreme Court* (2010). The actual effects of the New Deal on the economy are detailed in Elliot A. Rosen's *Roosevelt, the Great Depression, and the Economics of Recovery* (2005).

A critical assessment of Roosevelt and the New Deal is Amity Schlaes's *The Forgotten Man* (2007). James N. Gregory's *American Exodus: The Dust Bowl Migration and Okie Culture in California* (1989) describes the migratory movement. The dramatic Scottsboro court case is the focus of James Goodman's *Stories of Scottsboro* (1995). On the environmental and human causes of the dust bowl, see Donald Worster, *Dust Bowl: The Southern Plains in the 1930s* (1979). On cultural life during the 1930s, see Morris Dickstein's *Dancing in the Dark: A Cultural History of the Great Depression* (2009).

The best overview of diplomacy between the world wars remains Selig Adler's *The Uncertain Giant, 1921–1941: American Foreign Policy between the Wars* (1965). Robert Dallek's *Franklin D. Roosevelt and American Foreign Policy, 1932–1945* (1979) provides a judicious assessment of Roosevelt's foreign policy initiatives during the 1930s.

On Roosevelt's war of words with isolationists, see Lynne Olsen's *Those Angry Days: Roosevelt, Lindbergh, and America's Fight over World War II, 1939–1942* (2013), David Kaiser's *No End Save Victory: How FDR Led the Ntion into War* (2014), and Nicholas Wapshott's *The Sphinx: Franklin Roosevelt, the Isolationists, and the Road to World War II* (2015). See also David Reynolds's *From Munich to Pearl Harbor: Roosevelt's America and the Origins of the Second World War* (2001). For the Japanese perspective, see Eri Hotta's

Japan 1941: Countdown to Infamy (2014). On the surprise attack on Pearl Harbor, see Gordon W. Prange's *Pearl Harbor: The Verdict of History* (1986). Japan's perspective is described in Akira Iriye's *The Origins of the Second World War in Asia and the Pacific* (1987).

CHAPTER 26

For a sweeping survey of the Second World War, consult Anthony Roberts's *The Storm of War: A New History of the Second World War* (2011). The best detailed treatment of U.S. involvement is Rick Atkinson's multivolume Pulitzer prize–winning series, *An Army at Dawn* (2007), *The Day of Battle* (2008), and *The Guns at Last Light* (2013). Roosevelt's wartime leadership is analyzed in Eric Larrabee's *Commander in Chief: Franklin Delano Roosevelt, His Lieutenants, and Their War* (1987).

Books on specific European campaigns include Anthony Beevor's *D-Day: The Battle for Normandy* (2010) and Charles B. MacDonald's *A Time for Trumpets: The Untold Story of the Battle of the Bulge* (1985). On the Allied commander, see Carlo D'Este's *Eisenhower: A Soldier's Life* (2002). Richard Overy assesses the controversial role of air power in *The Bombing War: Europe, 1939–1945* (2013).

For the war in the Far East, see John Costello's *The Pacific War, 1941–1945* (1981), Ronald H. Spector's *Eagle against the Sun: The American War with Japan* (1985), John W. Dower's award-winning *War without Mercy: Race and Power in the Pacific War* (1986), and Dan van der Vat's *The Pacific Campaign: The U.S.-Japanese Naval War, 1941–1945* (1991).

An excellent overview of the war's effects on the home front is Michael C. C. Adams's *The Best War Ever: America and World War II* (1994). On the transformation to the wartime economy, see Arthur Herman's *Freedom's Forge: How American Business Produced Victory in World War II* (2012) and Maury Klein's *A Call to Arms* (2013). Susan M. Hartmann's *The Home Front and Beyond: American Women in the 1940s* (1982) treats the new working environment for women. Kenneth D. Rose tells the story of problems on the home front in *Myth and the Greatest Generation: A Social History of Americans in World War II* (2008). Neil A. Wynn looks at the participation of blacks in *The Afro-American and the Second World War* (1976). The story of the oppression of Japanese Americans is told in Greg Robinson's *A Tragedy for Democracy: Japanese Confinement in North America* (2009). On the development of the atomic bomb, see Jim Baggott's *The First War of Physics: The Secret History of the Atomic Bomb* (2010). The devastation caused by the atomic bomb is the focus of Susan Southard's *Nagasaki: Life after Nuclear War* (2015). For the controversy over America's policies towards the Holocaust, see Richard Breitman and Alan J. Lichtman's *FDR and the Jews* (2013).

A detailed introduction to U.S. diplomacy during the conflict can be found in Gaddis Smith's *American Diplomacy during the Second World War, 1941–1945* (1965). To understand the role that Roosevelt played in policy making, consult Warren F. Kimball's *The Juggler: Franklin Roosevelt as Wartime Statesman* (1991). The most important wartime summit meeting is assessed in S. M. Plokhy's *Yalta: The Price of Peace* (2010). The issues and events that led to the deployment of atomic weapons are addressed in Martin J. Sherwin's *A World Destroyed: The Atomic Bomb and the Grand Alliance* (1975).

CHAPTER 27

The cold war remains a hotly debated topic. The traditional interpretation is best reflected in John Lewis Gaddis's *The Cold War: A New History* (2005). Both superpowers, Gaddis argues, were responsible for causing the cold war, but the Soviet Union was more culpable. The revisionist perspective is represented by Gar Alperovitz's *Atomic Diplomacy: Hiroshima and Potsdam: The Use of the Atomic Bomb and the American Confrontation with Soviet Power,* 2nd ed. (1994). Also see H. W. Brands's *The Devil We Knew: Americans and the Cold War* (1993) and Melvyn P. Leffler's *For the Soul of Mankind: The United States, the Soviet Union, and the Cold War* (2007). On the architect of the containment strategy, see John L. Gaddis, *George F. Kennan: An American Life* (2011).

Frank Constigliola assesses Franklin Roosevelt's role in the start of the cold war in *Roosevelt's Lost Alliances: How Personal Politics Helped Start the Cold War* (2013). Arnold A. Offner indicts Truman for clumsy statesmanship in *Another Such Victory: President Truman and the Cold War, 1945–1953* (2002). For a positive assessment of Truman's leadership, see Alonzo L. Hamby's *Beyond the New Deal: Harry S. Truman and American Liberalism* (1973) and Robert Dallek's *The Lost Peace: Leadership in a Time of Horror and Hope, 1945–1953* (2010). The domestic policies of the Fair Deal are treated in William C. Berman's *The Politics of Civil Rights in the Truman Administration* (1970), Richard M. Dalfiume's *Desegregation of the U.S. Armed Forces: Fighting on Two Fronts, 1939–1953* (1969), and Maeva Marcus's *Truman and the Steel Seizure Case: The Limits of Presidential Power* (1977). The most comprehensive biography of Truman is David McCullough's *Truman* (1992).

For an introduction to the tensions in Asia, see Akira Iriye's *The Cold War in Asia: A Historical Introduction* (1974). For the Korean conflict, see Callum A. MacDonald's *Korea: The War before Vietnam* (1986) and Max Hasting's *The Korean War* (1987).

The anti-Communist crusade is surveyed in David Caute's *The Great Fear: The Anti-Communist Purge under Truman and Eisenhower* (1978). Arthur Herman's *Joseph McCarthy: Reexamining the Life and Legacy of America's Most Hated Senator* (2000) covers McCarthy himself. For a well-documented account of how the cold war was sustained by superpatriotism, intolerance, and suspicion, see Stephen J. Whitfield's *The Culture of the Cold War*, 2nd ed. (1996).

CHAPTER 28

Two excellent overviews of social and cultural trends in the postwar era are William H. Chafe's *The Unfinished Journey: America since World War II*, 6th ed. (2006), and William E. Leuchtenburg's *A Troubled Feast: America since 1945*, rev. ed. (1979). For insights into the cultural life of the 1950s, see Jeffrey Hart's *When the Going Was Good! American Life in the Fifties* (1982) and David Halberstam's *The Fifties* (1993).

The baby boom generation and its impact are vividly described in Paul C. Light's *Baby Boomers* (1988). The emergence of the television industry is discussed in Erik Barnouw's *Tube of Plenty: The Evolution of American Television*, 2nd rev. ed. (1990), and Ella Taylor's *Prime-Time Families: Television Culture in Postwar America* (1989).

On the process of suburban development, see Kenneth T. Jackson's *Crabgrass Frontier: The Suburbanization of the United States* (1985). Equally good is Tom Martinson's *American Dreamscape: The Pursuit of Happiness in Postwar Suburbia* (2000).

The middle-class ideal of family life in the 1950s is examined in Elaine Tyler May's *Homeward Bound: American Families in the Cold War Era*, rev. ed. (2008). Thorough accounts of women's issues are found in Wini Breines's *Young, White, and Miserable: Growing Up Female in the Fifties* (1992). For an overview of the resurgence of religion in the 1950s, see George M. Marsden's *Religion and American Culture*, 2nd ed. (2000).

The origins and growth of rock and roll are surveyed in Carl Belz's *The Story of Rock*, 2nd ed. (1972). The colorful Beats are brought to life in Steven Watson's *The Birth of the Beat Generation: Visionaries, Rebels, and Hipsters, 1944–1960* (1995).

Scholarship on the Eisenhower years is extensive. A balanced treatment is Jean Edward Smith's *Eisenhower in War and Peace* (2012). For the manner in which Eisenhower conducted foreign policy, see Evan Thomas's *Ike's Bluff: President Eisenhower's Secret Battle to Save the World* (2012).

The best overview of American foreign policy since 1945 is Stephen E. Ambrose and Douglas G. Brinkley's *Rise to Globalism: American Foreign Policy since 1938* 9th ed. (2011). For the buildup of U.S. involvement in Indochina, consult Fredrik Logevall's *Embers of War: The Fall of an Empire and the Making of America's Vietnam* (2012). The Cold War strategy of the Eisenhower administration is the focus of Chris Tudda's *The Truth Is Our Weapon: The Rhetorical Diplomacy of Dwight D. Eisenhower and John Foster Dulles* (2006). To learn about the CIA's secret activities in Iran, see Ervand Abrahamian's *The Coup: 1953, the CIA, and the Roots of Modern U.S.-Iranian Relations* (2013).

The impact of the Supreme Court during the 1950s is the focus of Archibald Cox's *The Warren Court: Constitutional Decision as an Instrument of Reform* (1968). A masterly study of the important Warren Court decision on school desegregation is James T. Patterson's *Brown v. Board of Education: A Civil Rights Milestone and Its Troubled Legacy* (2001).

For the story of the early years of the civil rights movement, see Taylor Branch's *Parting the Waters: America in the King Years, 1954–1963* (1988), Robert Weisbrot's *Freedom Bound: A History of America's Civil Rights Movement* (1990), and David A. Nicholas's *A Matter of Justice: Eisenhower and the Beginning of the Civil Rights Revolution* (2007). On Rosa Parks, see Jeanne Theoharis's *The Rebellious Life of Mrs. Rosa Parks* (2013). On the testy relationship of Eisenhower and his vice president, Richard Nixon, see Jeffrey Frank's *Ike and Dick: Portrait of a Strange Political Marriage* (2013).

CHAPTER 29

A superb analysis of John Kennedy's life is Thomas C. Reeves's *A Question of Character: A Life of John F. Kennedy* (1991). The 1960 campaign is detailed in Gary A. Donaldson's *The First Modern Campaign: Kennedy, Nixon, and the Election of 1960* (2007). The best study of the Kennedy administration's domestic policies is Irving Bernstein's *Promises Kept: John F. Kennedy's New Frontier* (1991). See also Robert Dallek's *Camelot's Court: Inside the Kennedy White House* (2013), Thurston Clarke's *JFK's Last Hundred Days* (2013), and Ira Stoll's *JFK, Conservative* (2013). For details on the still swirling conspiracy theories about the assassination, see David W. Belin's *Final Disclosure: The Full Truth about the Assassination of President Kennedy* (1988).

On LBJ, see the magisterial multivolume biography by Robert Caro's titled *The Years of Lyndon Johnson*. On the Johnson administration, see Vaughn Davis Bornet's *The Presidency of Lyndon B. Johnson* (1984). For an insider's perspective, see Joseph A. Califano's *The Triumph and Tragedy of Lyndon Johnson* (2015).

Among the works that interpret liberal social policy during the 1960s, John E. Schwarz's *America's Hidden Success: A Reassessment of Twenty Years of Public Policy* (1983) offers a glowing endorsement of Democratic programs. For a contrasting perspective, see Charles Murray's *Losing Ground: American Social Policy, 1950–1980* (1994). Also see Martha J. Bailey and Sheldon Danzinger's *Legacies of the War on Poverty* (2015).

On foreign policy, see *Kennedy's Quest for Victory: American Foreign Policy, 1961–1963* (1989), edited by Thomas G. Paterson, and Patrick J. Sloyan's *The Politics of Deception* (2015). To learn more about Kennedy's problems in Cuba, see Mark J. White's *Missiles in Cuba: Kennedy, Khrushchev, Castro and the 1962 Crisis* (1997). See also Aleksandr Fursenko and Timothy Naftali's *"One Hell of a Gamble": Khrushchev, Castro and Kennedy, 1958–1964* (1997).

American involvement in Vietnam has received voluminous treatment from all political perspectives. For an excellent overview, see Larry Berman's *Planning a Tragedy: The Americanization of the War in Vietnam* (1983) and *Lyndon Johnson's War: The Road to Stalemate in Vietnam* (1989), as well as Stanley Karnow's *Vietnam: A History*, 2nd rev. ed. (1997). An analysis of policy making concerning the Vietnam War is David M. Barrett's *Uncertain Warriors: Lyndon Johnson and His Vietnam Advisors* (1993). A fine account of the military involvement is Robert D. Schulzinger's *A Time for War: The United States and Vietnam, 1941–1975* (1997). On the legacy of the Vietnam War, see Arnold R. Isaacs's *Vietnam Shadows: The War, Its Ghosts, and Its Legacy* (1997).

Many scholars have dealt with various aspects of the civil rights movement and race relations in the 1960s. See especially Carl M. Brauer's *John F. Kennedy and the Second Reconstruction* (1977), David J. Garrow's *Bearing the Cross: Martin Luther King, Jr., and the Southern Christian Leadership Conference* (1986), and Adam Fairclough's *To Redeem the Soul of America: The Southern Christian Leadership Conference and Martin Luther King, Jr.* (1987). William H. Chafe's *Civilities and Civil Rights: Greensboro, North Carolina, and the Black Struggle for Freedom* (1980) details the original sit-ins. An award-winning study of racial and economic inequality in a representative American city is Thomas J. Sugrue's *The Origins of the Urban Crisis: Race and Inequality in Postwar Detroit* (1996).

CHAPTER 30

An engaging overview of the cultural trends of the 1960s is Maurice Isserman and Michael Kazin's *America Divided: The Civil War of the 1960s,* 3rd ed. (2007). The New Left is assessed in Irwin Unger's *The Movement: A History of the American New Left, 1959–1972* (1974). On the Students for a Democratic Society, see Kirkpatrick Sale's *SDS* (1973) and Allen J. Matusow's *The Unraveling of America: A History of Liberalism in the 1960s* (1984). Also useful are Todd Gitlin's *The Sixties: Years of Hope, Days of Rage,* rev. ed. (1993) and Bryan Burrough's *Days of Rage* (2015). For a focused study, see James T. Patterson's *The Eve of Destruction: How 1965 Transformed America* (2013). On the popularity of folk music and the role of Greenwich Village, see Stephen Petrus and Ronald D. Cohen's *Folk City* (2015).

For insights into the black power movement, see Peniel E. Joseph's *Stokely: A Life* (2014), and Joshua Bloom and Waldo E. Martin Jr.'s *Black against Empire: The History and Politics of the Black Panther Party* (2013).

Two influential assessments of the counterculture by sympathetic commentators are Theodore Roszak's *The Making of a Counter-Culture: Reflections on the Technocratic Society and Its Youthful Opposition* (1969) and Charles A. Reich's *The Greening of America: How the Youth Revolution Is Trying to Make America Livable* (1970). A good scholarly analysis that takes the hippies seriously is Timothy Miller's *The Hippies and American Values* (1991). A more recent assessment of the "culture wars" since the Sixties is Andrew Hartman's *A War for the Soul of America* (2015).

The best study of the women's liberation movement is Ruth Rosen's *The World Split Open: How the Modern Women's Movement Changed America,* rev. ed. (2006). The organizing efforts of Cesar Chavez are detailed in Ronald B. Taylor's *Chavez and the Farm Workers* (1975). See also Miriam Pawel's *The Crusades of Cesar Chavez: A Biography* (2014). The struggles of Native Americans for recognition and power are sympathetically described in Stan Steiner's *The New Indians* (1968).

The best overview of the 1970s and 1980s is James T. Patterson's *Restless Giant: The United States from Watergate to Bush v. Gore* (2005). On Nixon, see Melvin Small's thorough analysis in *The Presidency of Richard Nixon* (1999). A good slim biography is Elizabeth Drew's *Richard M. Nixon* (2007). A massive biography is Evan Thomas's *Being Nixon* (2015). An especially critical approach is Tim Weiner's *One Man Against the World: The Tragedy of Richard Nixon* (2015). For an overview of the Watergate scandal, see Stanley I. Kutler's *The Wars of Watergate: The Last Crisis of Richard Nixon* (1990). For the way the Republicans handled foreign affairs, consult Tad Szulc's *The Illu-*

sion of Peace: Foreign Policy in the Nixon Years (1978). The Nixon White House tapes make for fascinating reading. See *The Nixon Tapes* (2014), ed. by Douglas Brinkley and Luke Nichter. Rick Perlstein traces the effects of Nixon's career on the Republican party and the conservative movement in two compelling books: *Nixonland: The Rise of a President and the Fracturing of America* (2007) and *The Invisible Bridge: The Fall of Nixon and the Rise of Reagan* (2014).

The Communist takeover of Vietnam and the end of American involvement there are traced in Larry Berman's *No Peace, No Honor: Nixon, Kissinger, and Betrayal in Vietnam* (2001). William Shawcross's *Sideshow: Kissinger, Nixon and the Destruction of Cambodia*, rev. ed. (2002), deals with the broadening of the war, while Larry Berman's *Planning a Tragedy: The Americanization of the War in Vietnam* (1982) assesses the final impact of U.S. involvement. The most comprehensive treatment of the anti-war movement is Tom Wells's *The War Within: America's Battle over Vietnam* (1994).

A comprehensive treatment of the Ford administration is contained in John Robert Greene's *The Presidency of Gerald R. Ford* (1995). The best overview of the Carter administration is Burton I. Kaufman's *The Presidency of James Earl Carter, Jr.*, 2nd rev. ed. (2006). A work more sympathetic to the Carter administration is John Dumbrell's *The Carter Presidency: A Re-evaluation*, 2nd ed. (1995). Gaddis Smith's *Morality, Reason, and Power: American Diplomacy in the Carter Years* (1986) provides an overview. Background on how the Middle East came to dominate much of American policy is found in William B. Quandt's *Decade of Decisions: American Policy toward the Arab-Israeli Conflict, 1967–1976* (1977). For a biography of Carter, see Randall Balmer, *Redeemer: The Life of Jimmy Carter* (2014).

CHAPTER 31

The rise of modern political conservatism is well told in Patrick Allitt's *The Conservatives: Ideas and Personalities throughout American History* (2009) and Michael Schaller's *Right Turn: American Life in the Reagan-Bush Era, 1980–1992* (2007).

On Reagan, see John Patrick Diggins's *Ronald Reagan: Fate, Freedom, and the Making of History* (2007), Richard Reeves's *President Reagan: The Triumph of Imagination* (2005), Sean Wilentz's *The Age of Reagan: A History, 1974–2008* (2008), and Thomas C. Reed's *The Reagan Enigma: 1964–1980* (2015). The best political analysis is Robert M. Collins's *Transforming America: Politics and Culture during the Reagan Years* (2007). For insights into the

1980 election, see Andrew E. Busch's *Reagan's Victory: The Presidential Election of 1980 and the Rise of the Right* (2005). On Reaganomics, see David A. Stockman's *The Triumph of Politics: Why the Reagan Revolution Failed* (1986).

For Reagan's foreign policy in Central America, see James Chace's *Endless War: How We Got Involved in Central America—and What Can Be Done* (1984) and Walter LaFeber's *Inevitable Revolutions: The United States in Central America*, 2nd ed. (1993). On Reagan's second term, see Jane Mayer and Doyle McManus's *Landslide: The Unmaking of the President, 1984–1988* (1988). For a masterly work on the Iran-Contra affair, see Theodore Draper's *A Very Thin Line: The Iran Contra Affairs* (1991). Several collections of essays include varying assessments of the Reagan years. Among these are *The Reagan Revolution?* (1988), edited by B. B. Kymlicka and Jean V. Matthews; *The Reagan Presidency: An Incomplete Revolution?* (1990), edited by Dilys M. Hill, Raymond A. Moore, and Phil Williams; and *Looking Back on the Reagan Presidency* (1990), edited by Larry Berman.

The 41st president is the focus of Timothy Naftali's *George H. W. Bush* (2007). On the 1988 campaign, see Sidney Blumenthal's *Pledging Allegiance: The Last Campaign of the Cold War* (1990). For a social history of the decade, see John Ehrman's *The Eighties: America in the Age of Reagan* (2005). On the Persian Gulf conflict, see Lester H. Brune's *America and the Iraqi Crisis, 1990–1992: Origins and Aftermath* (1993).

CHAPTER 32

Analysis of the Clinton years can be found in Joe Klein's *The Natural: The Misunderstood Presidency of Bill Clinton* (2002). Clinton's impeachment is assessed in Richard A. Posner's *An Affair of State: The Investigation, Impeachment, and Trial of President Clinton* (1999). The conflict between Clinton and Ginrich is explained in Elizabeth Drew's *The Struggle between Gingrich and the Clinton White House* (1996).

On changing demographic trends, see Sam Roberts's *Who We Are Now: The Changing Face of America in the Twenty-First Century* (2004). For a textured account of the exploding Latino culture, see Roberto Suro's *Strangers among Us: How Latino Immigration Is Transforming America* (1998). On social and cultural life in the 1990s, see Haynes Johnson's *The Best of Times: America in the Clinton Years* (2001). Economic and technological changes are assessed in Daniel T. Rogers's *Age of Fracture* (2011). The onset and growth of the AIDS epidemic are traced in *And the Band Played On: Politics, People, and the AIDS Epidemic*, 20th anniversary ed. (2007), by Randy Shilts.

On the religious right, see George M. Marsden's *Understanding Fundamentalism and Evangelicalism,* new ed. (2006) and Ralph E. Reed's *Politically Incorrect: The Emerging Faith Factor in American Politics* (1994).

On the invention of the computer and the Internet, see Paul E. Ceruzzi's *A History of Modern Computing,* 2nd ed. (2003), Janet Abbate's *Inventing the Internet* (1999), and Michael Lewis, *The New New Thing: A Silicon Valley Story* (1999). The booming economy of the 1990s is well analyzed in Joseph E. Stiglitz's *The Roaring Nineties: A New History of the World's Most Prosperous Decade* (2003).

For further treatment of the end of the cold war, see Michael R. Beschloss and Strobe Talbott's *At the Highest Levels: The Inside Story of the End of the Cold War* (1993) and Richard Crockatt's *The Fifty Years War: The United States and the Soviet Union in World Politics, 1941–1991* (1995).

On the transformation of American foreign policy, see James Mann's *Rise of the Vulcans: The History of Bush's War Cabinet* (2004), Claes G. Ryn's *America the Virtuous: The Crisis of Democracy and the Quest for Empire* (2003), and Stephen M. Walt's *Taming American Power: The Global Response to U.S. Primacy* (2005).

The disputed 2000 presidential election is the focus of Jeffrey Toobin's *Too Close to Call: The Thirty-Six-Day Battle to Decide the 2000 Election* (2001). On the Bush presidency, see *The Presidency of George W. Bush: A First Historical Assessment,* edited by Julian E. Zelizer (2010). See also Fred H. Israel and Jonathan Mann's *The Election of 2000 and the Administration of George W. Bush* (2003). Also see Dick Cheney's illuminating, if self-serving, account of his service as Bush's vice president in *In My Time: A Personal and Political Memoir* (2011).

On the attacks of September 11, 2001, and their aftermath, see *The Age of Terror: America and the World after September 11,* edited by Strobe Talbott and Nayan Chanda (2001). For a devastating account of the Bush administration by a White House insider, see Scott McClellan's *What Happened: Inside the Bush White House and Washington's Culture of Deception* (2008). On the historic 2008 election, see Michael Nelson's *The Elections of 2008* (2009). The best biography of Obama is David Maraniss's *Barack Obama: The Story* (2012). A conservative critique is provided in Edward Klein's *The Amateur: Barack Obama in the White House* (2012). For an insider's account of the Obama administration, see David Axelrod's *Believer: My Forty Years in Politics* (2015).

The Great Recession is explained in Alan S. Blinder's *After the Music Stopped: The Financial Crisis, the Response, and the Work Ahead* (2013). The Tea Party movement is assessed in Theda Skocpol and Vanessa Williamson's

The Tea Party and the Remaking of Republican Conservatism (2012) and Elizabeth Price Foley's *The Tea Party: Three Principles* (2012). The polarization of politics is the focus of Russell Muirhead's *The Promise of Party in a Polarized Age* (2015). The partisan gridlock in Congress is the focus of Thomas E. Mann and Norman J. Ornstein's *The Broken Branch: How Congress Is Failing America and How to Get it Back on Track* (2012). The tension between the conservative majority on the U.S. Supreme Court and the Obama administration is examined in Jeffrey Toobin's *The Oath: The Obama White House and the Supreme Court* (2012). On the growing economic inequality in America, see Joseph Stiglitz's *The Price of Inequality: How Today's Divided Society Endangers Our Future* (2013).

The emergence of Islamist radicalism is well analyzed in Michael Weiss and Hassan Hassan's *ISIS: Inside the Army of Terror* (2015) and Jesssica Stern and J. M. Berger's *ISIS: The State of Terror* (2015). The conflicts in the Middle East are the focus of Dominic Tierney's *The Right Way to Lose a War: America in an Age of Unwinnable Conflicts* (2015).

CREDITS

PART 1: p. 1: Werner Forman/Art Resource, NY; **p. 2**: British Museum/Art Resource.

CHAPTER 1: p. 4: bpk, Berlin/Kunstbibliothek, Staatliche Museen/Knud Petersen/Art Resource; **p. 8**: Bettmann/Corbis; **p. 9**: Library of Congress; **p. 13**: Bettmann/Corbis; **p. 15**: Richard A. Cooke/Corbis; **p. 17**: MPI/Getty Images; **p. 21**: Bettmann/Corbis; **p. 31**: The Benson Latin American Collection, University of Texas; **p. 35**: Atlantide Phototravel/Corbis; **p. 38**: Granger Collection; **p. 41**: The Royal Library of Copenhagen; **p. 44**: Werner Forman/Art Resource, NY; **p. 49**: Bettmann/Corbis.

CHAPTER 2: p. 54: British Library, London, UK/© British Library Board. All Rights Reserved/Bridgeman Images; **p. 57**: Granger Collection; **p. 63**: Granger Collection; **p. 66**: Bettmann/Corbis; **p. 67**: Granger Collection; **p. 72**: Granger Collection; **p. 74**: Granger Collection; **p. 75**: Granger Collection; **p. 77**: Granger Collection; **p. 82**: The Mariners' Museum/Corbis; **p. 83**: Granger Collection; **p. 86**: Museum of the City of New York/Corbis; **p. 87**: Bettmann/Corbis; **p. 90**: Stapleton Collection/Corbis; **p. 93**: Granger Collection; **p. 96**: Library of Congress; **p. 98**: Granger Collection; **p. 99**: British Museum/Art Resource; **p. 101**: The Swem Library, the College of William & Mary; **p. 103**: Granger Collection; **p. 104**: Granger Collection.

CHAPTER 3: p. 108: Granger Collection; **p. 111**: Granger Collection; **p. 113**: Connecticut Historical Society Museum; **p. 117**: Granger Collection; **p. 118**: North Wind Picture Archive; **p. 120**: Granger Collection; **p. 123**: Granger Collection; **p. 130**: Granger Collection; **p. 132**: Collection of the New-York Historical Society/Bridgeman Images; **p. 133**: Library Company of Philadelphia; **p. 136**: Stock Montage/Getty Images; **p. 137**: Granger Collection; **p. 138**: Granger Collection; **p. 139**: National Portrait Gallery, London; **p. 140**: North Wind Picture Archive/Alamy.

CHAPTER 4: p. 146: Granger Collection; **p. 148**: Snark/Art Resource, NY; **p. 151**: Wikimedia Commons, pd; **p. 153**: I.N. Phelps Stokes Collection, Miriam and Ira D. Wallach Division of Art, Prints and Photographs, New York Public Library, Astor, Lenox and Tilden Foundations. Art Resource, NY; **p. 159**: Library of Congress; **p. 161**: Collection of the New-York Historical Society/Bridgeman Images; **p. 162**: Granger Collection; **p. 170**: Library of Congress; **p. 171**: Library of Congress; **p. 174**: Library of Congress; **p. 176**: Library of Congress; **p. 178**: Library of Congress; **p. 181**: Granger Collection; **p. 183**: Granger Collection; **p. 184**: Library of Congress; **p. 187**: Courtesy of the Historical Society of Pennsylvania Collection, Atwater Kent Museum of Philadelphia; **p. 188**: National Archives; **p.190**: North Wind Picture Archives/Alamy.

PART 2: p. 197: Granger Collection; **p. 198**: Granger Collection.

CHAPTER 5: p. 200: Francis G. Mayer/Corbis; **p. 204**: US Senate Collection; **p. 208**: (left): Private Collection/Photo © Christie's Images/The Bridgeman Art Library; (right): Granger Collection; **p. 213**: Anne S.K. Brown Military Collection, Brown University Library; **p. 214**: Granger Collection; **p. 217**: Granger Collection; **p. 219**: Granger Collection; **p. 228**: Library of Congress; **p. 230**: Granger Collection; **p. 234**: MPI/Getty Images; **p. 235**: Granger Collection; **p. 239**: Granger Collection.

CHAPTER 6: p. 244: Granger Collection; **p. 252**: Print Collection, Miriam and Ira D. Wallach Division of Art, Prints, and Photographs, The New York Public Library; Astor, Lenox, and Tilden Foundations; **p. 254**: Granger Collection; **p. 256**: Library of Congress; **p. 257**: Granger Collection; **p. 260**: Independence National Historical Park; **p. 262**: Granger Collection; **p. 265**: Granger Collection; **p. 268**: Library of Congress; **p. 270**: Library of Congress; **p. 274**: Independence National Historical Park; **p. 278**: The New York Public Library/Art Resource, NY; **p. 280**: Historical Society of Pennsylvania; **p. 281**: Granger Collection; **p. 284**: Granger Collection; **p. 287**: Granger Collection; **p. 290**: Art Resource, NY; **p. 291**: Granger Collection; **p. 293**: Image copyright © The Metropolitan Museum of Art/Art Resource, NY; **p. 294**: Granger Collection; **p. 295**: Granger Collection.

CHAPTER 7: p. 302: Photography by Erik Arnesen © Nicholas S. West; **p. 305**: Library of Congress; **p. 307**: Library of Congress; **p. 311**: Collection of the New-York Historical Society/Bridgeman Art Library; **p. 315**: Copyright American Philosophical Society; **p. 317**: Photo by EncMstr/Wikimedia Commons; https://creativecommons.org/licenses/by-sa/3.0/deed.en; **p. 320**: New Jersey Historical Society; **p. 321**: Library of Congress; **p. 323**: Granger Collection; **p. 326**: Library of Congress; **p. 329**: American Antiquarian Society, Worcester, Massachusetts/Bridgeman Images; **p. 336**: Granger Collection; **p. 339**: Library of Congress.

PART 3: p. 347: Saint Louis Art Museum, Gift of Bank of America; **p. 348**: Yale University Art Gallery/Wikimedia, pd; **p. 349**: The Walters Art Museum, Baltimore.

CHAPTER 8: p. 350: Granger Collection; **p. 357**: Minnesota Historical Society; **p. 358**: © Collection of the New-York Historical Society/Bridgeman Images; **p. 361**: Fenimore Art Museum; **p. 366**: Granger Collection; **p. 369**: Official catalogue Great Exhibition, Crystal Palace, London 1851, pd; **p. 370**: Granger Collection; **p. 371**: Maryland Historical Society 1934.2.1; **p. 372**: Granger Collection; **p. 376**: The New York Public Library/Art Resource, NY; **p. 377**: Board of Trustees, National Gallery of Art, Washington 1980.62.9.(2794) PA; **p. 378**: Library of Congress; **p. 382**: National Park Service, Ellis Island Collection; **p. 383**: American Antiquarian Society; **p. 384**: Library of Congress; **p. 386**: The New York Public Library/Art Resource, NY; **p. 387**: John W. Bennett Labor Collection, Special Collections and University Archives, W. E. B. Du Bois Library, University of Massachusetts Amherst.

CHAPTER 9: p. 392: Photo © Christie's Images/Bridgeman Images; **p. 397**: Library of Congress; **p. 398**: Image copyright © The Metropolitan Museum of Art. Image source: Art Resource, NY; **p. 401**: Granger Collection; **p. 404**: Wikimedia Commons, pd; **p. 407**: Granger Collection; **p. 408**: Yale University Art Gallery/Wikimedia, pd; **p. 412**: Library of Congress; **p. 414**: Image copyright © The Metropolitan Museum of Art. Image source: Art Resource, NY; **p. 416**: Collection of the New-York Historical Society/Bridgeman Images.

CHAPTER 10: p. 422: Museum of the City of New York/Art Resource, NY; **p. 426**: Library of Congress; **p. 429**: Library of Congress; **p. 433**: Granger Collection; **p. 434**: Granger Collection; **p. 436**: Library of Congress; **p. 439**: National Portrait Gallery, Smithsonian Institution/Art Resource, NY; **p. 440**: Courtesy Boston Art Commission 2014; **p. 442**: Library of Congress; **p. 444**: Saint Louis Art Museum, Gift of Bank of America; **p. 446**: Courtesy of the Richland County Public Library, SC; **p. 452**: Corbis; **p. 454**: Library of Congress; **p. 455**: Library of Congress; **p. 458**: Library of Congress.

CHAPTER 11: p. 464: Universal History Archive/UIG/Bridgeman Images; **p. 469**: Paul Verkin/National Geographic Society/Corbis; **p. 475**: Bettmann/Corbis; **p. 478**: Fotosearch/Getty Images; **p. 483**: © Atwater Kent Museum of Philadelphia/Courtesy of Historical Society of Pennsylvania Collection/The Bridgeman Art Library; **p. 484**: Courtesy of The Charleston Museum, Charleston, South Carolina; **p. 485**: Private Collection/Courtesy of Swann Auction Galleries/Bridgeman Images; **p. 490**: 2006 Harvard University, Peabody Museum Photo 35-5-10/53044T1874; **p. 491**: Private Collection/Peter Newark American Pictures/Bridgeman Art Library; **p. 494**: The Historic New Orleans Collection/Bridgeman Images; **p. 499**: Library of Congress.

Chapter 12: p. 504: Munson-Williams-Proctor Arts Institute/Art Resource, NY; **p. 508**: Mary Evans Picture Library/Alamy; **p. 510**: Granger Collection; **p. 512**: Image copyright © The Metropolitan Museum of Art. Image source: Art Resource, NY; **p. 516**: Lordprice Collection/Alamy; **p. 519**: Wikimedia Commons; pd; **p. 520**: Bettmann/Corbis; **p. 522**: Bettmann/Corbis; **p. 524**: Wikimedia Commons, pd: **p. 526**: Wikimedia Commons, pd; **p. 527**: The Walters Art Museum, Baltimore; **p. 529**: Library of Congress; **p. 531 (left)**: Library of Congress; **(right)**: Private Collection/J. T. Vintage/Bridgeman Images; **p. 534**: Granger Collection; **p. 539**: Granger Collection; **p. 542 (left and right)**: Library of Congress; **p. 544 (left)**: Granger Collection; **(right)**: Library of Congress.

Part 4: p. 551: The Stapleton Collection/The Bridgeman Art Library; **p. 552**: Civil War Archive/ The Bridgeman Art Library.

Chapter 13: p. 554: The Oregon Trail, 1869 (oil on canvas), Bierstadt, Albert (1830–1902)/Butler Institute of American Art, Youngstown, OH, Gift of Joseph G. Butler III 1946/Bridgeman Images; **p. 558**: Library of Congress; **p. 560**: Library of Congress; **p. 561**: Image copyright © The Metropolitan Museum of Art. Image source: Art Resource, NY; **p. 563**: Kansas State Historical Society; **p. 567**: Library of Congress; **p. 569**: Private Collection/Peter Newark American Pictures/Bridgeman Art Library; **p. 573**: MPI/Getty Images; **p. 576**: National Archives; **p. 580**: Granger Collection; **p. 584**: American Antiquarian Society/Bridgeman Images; **p. 588**: National Portrait Gallery, Smithsonian Institution/Art Resource; **p. 592**: Granger Collection; **p. 593**: Library of Congress.

Chapter 14: p. 598: Granger Collection; **p. 600**: American Antiquarian Society/Bridgeman Art Library; **p. 603**: The Long Island Museum of American Art, History & Carriages, Stony Brook N.Y., Gift of Mr. and Mrs. Ward Melville, 1955; **p. 604**: Art Resource; **p. 607**: Granger Collection; **p. 609**: Granger Collection; **p. 611**: Library of Congress; **p. 613**: Granger Collection; **p. 615**: Granger Collection; **p. 618**: akg-images/The Image Works; **p. 619**: Wikimedia, pd; **p. 622**: Art Resource, NY; **p. 625**: Art Resource; **p. 627**: Private Collection/Peter Newark American Pictures/Bridgeman Art Library; **p. 629**: Private Collection/Peter Newark American Pictures/Bridgeman Art Library; **p. 632**: Granger Collection.

Chapter 15: p. 638: Chicago Historical Museum; **p. 643**: Bettmann/Corbis; **p. 644**: Buyenlarge/ Getty Images; **p. 649**: Bettmann/Corbis; **p. 651**: Private Collection/The Stapleton Collection/Bridgeman Art Library; **p. 658**: Library of Congress; **p. 660**: Library of Congress; **p. 661**: Bettmann/Corbis; **p. 662**: Library of Congress; **p. 663**: Library of Congress; **p. 668**: Beinecke Rare Book and Manuscript Library, Yale University/Wikimedia Commons; **p. 669**: Library of Congress; **p. 670**: Boston Athenaeum/ Bridgeman Art Library; **p. 672**: Granger Collection; **p. 674**: Library of Congress; **p. 675**: Library of Congress; **p. 679**: Library of Congress; **p. 683**: Library of Congress; **p. 687**: Massachusetts Commandery Military Order of the Loyal Legion and the U.S. Army Military History Institute; **p. 688**: Library of Congress; **p. 689**: National Archives; **p. 690**: Corbis.

Chapter 16: p. 700: Smithsonian American Art Museum, Washington, DC/Art Resource; **p. 703**: Granger Collection; **p. 707**: Library of Congress; **p. 708**: Corbis; **p. 710**: Bettmann/Corbis; **p. 711**: Library of Congress; **p. 713**: Library of Congress; **p. 717**: Library of Congress; **p. 720**: Granger Collection; **p. 722**: Library of Congress; **p. 723**: Bettmann/Corbis; **p. 724**: Granger Collection; **p. 726**: Granger Collection; **p. 728**: Library of Congress; **p. 731**: Library of Congress; **p. 736**: Granger Collection; **p. 740**: Library of Congress.

Part 5: p. 745: Walter P. Reuther Library, Wayne State University; **p. 746**: David J. & Janice L. Frent Collection/Corbis.

Chapter 17: p. 748: Granger Collection; **p. 752**: Granger Collection; **p. 753**: Granger Collection; **p. 756**: Bettmann/Corbis; **p. 760**: National Archives; **p. 764**: Wikimedia, pd; **p. 765**: American Petroleum Institute Historical Photo Collection; National Museum of American History, Smithsonian Institution; **p. 767**: Library of Congress; **p. 768**: Library of Congress; **p. 770**: Granger Collection; **p. 771**: Special Collections Research Center, Earl Gregg Swem Library, The College of William & Mary; **p. 773**: Private

Collection/Peter Newark American Pictures/Bridgeman Images; **p. 774**: © Museum of the City of New York/Bridgeman Images; **p. 776**: Special Collections, Vassar College Libraries; **p. 777**: Library of Congress; **p. 778**: The New York Public Library/Art Resource, NY; **p. 780**: Bettmann/Corbis; **p. 783**: Private Collection/Peter Newark American Pictures/Bridgeman Images; **p. 785**: T.V. Powderly Photographic Collection, The American Catholic History Research Center University Archives, The Catholic University of America, Washington, D.C.; **p. 789**: Bettmann/Corbis; **p. 793**: PhotoQuest/Getty Images; **p. 794**: Bettmann/Corbis.

CHAPTER 18: p. 798: Granger Collection; **p. 802**: The New York Public Library/Art Resource, NY; **p. 804**: Library of Congress; **p. 810**: Corbis; **p. 811**: Corbis; **p. 813**: Special Collections, University of Chicago Library; **p. 814**: Library of Congress; **p. 815**: Library of Congress; **p. 820**: Kansas State Historical Society; **p. 822**: National Archives; **p. 825**: Corbis; **p. 828**: Keystone View Company/National Geographic Society/Corbis; **p. 830**: Western Historical Collections, University of Oklahoma Library; **p. 835**: Library of Congress; **p. 836**: Stapleton Collection/Corbis; **p. 838**: Library of Congress.

CHAPTER 19: p. 846: © 2015 Delaware Art Museum/Artist Rights Society (ARS), New York *Wet Night on the Bowery,* 1911 (oil on canvas), Sloan, John (1871–1951)/Delaware Art Museum, Gift of the John Sloan Memorial Fund/Bridgeman Images; **p. 852**: Bettmann/Corbis; **p. 853**: William Williams Papers, Manuscripts and Archives Division, The New York Public Library, Astor, Lenox and Tilden Foundations, Art Resource, NY; **p. 855**: Library of Congress; **p. 856**: Granger Collection; **p. 857**: Bettmann/Corbis; **p. 859**: © Museum of the City of New York/Bridgeman Images; **p. 860**: Bettmann/Corbis; **p. 863**: *Stag at Sharkey's,* 1909 (oil on canvas), Bellows, George Wesley (1882–1925)/Cleveland Museum of Art/Hinman B. Hurlbut Collection/Bridgeman Images; **p. 865**: Library of Congress; **p. 867**: Granger Collection; **p. 869**: Library of Congress; **p. 873**: Library of Congress; **p. 874**: Bettmann/Corbis; **p. 877**: Wikimedia, pd; **p. 878**: Bettmann/Corbis; **p. 881**: Library of Congress; **p. 884**: Kansas State Historical Society; **p. 885**: Nebraska State Historical Society; **p. 886**: Library of Congress; **p. 888**: Bettmann/Corbis; **p. 889 (top and bottom)**: David J. & Janice L. Frent Collection/Corbis.

PART 6: p. 895: Bettmann/Corbis; **p. 897**: From the Collections of The Henry Ford Museum.

CHAPTER 20: p. 898: Frederic Remington Art Museum; **p. 903**: Granger Collection; **p. 904**: Corbis; **p. 906**: Wikimedia, pd; **p. 909**: Corbis; **p. 911**: Bettmann/Corbis; **p. 915**: National Archives; **p. 917**: Corporal George J. Vennage c/o Ohio State University Rare Books and Manuscripts Library; **p. 919**: Granger Collection; **p. 921**: Bettmann/Corbis; **p. 926**: Bettmann/Corbis; **p. 927**: Granger Collection; **p. 929**: Corbis; **p. 932**: Granger Collection.

CHAPTER 21: p. 936: Granger Collection; **p. 941**: Granger Collection; **p. 944**: University of Illinois at Chicago Library; **p. 945**: Library of Congress; **p. 951**: Wikimedia, pd; **p. 952**: Corbis; **p. 954**: Library of Congress; **p. 955**: Library of Congress; **p. 957**: Library of Congress; **p. 960 (top)**: Collection of the New-York Historical Society/Bridgeman Images; **(bottom)**: Library of Congress; **p. 961**: New York Public Library/Art Resource; **p. 962**: Granger Collection; **p. 964**: Culver Pictures/The Art Archive at Art Resource, NY; **p. 966**: Library of Congress; **p. 968**: Library of Congress; **p. 969**: Donald C. & Elizabeth M. Dickinson Research Center, National Cowboy & Western Heritage Museum; **p. 971**: Library of Congress; **p. 978**: Corbis; **p. 980**: Granger Collection.

CHAPTER 22: p. 986: Library of Congress; **p. 991**: Galerie Bilderwelt/Getty Images; **p. 993**: Granger Collection; **p. 995**: Granger Collection; **p. 998**: Bettmann/Corbis; **p. 1000**: Library of Congress; **p. 1002**: Bettmann/Corbis; **p. 1003**: Library of Congress; **p. 1004**: Library of Congress; **p. 1006**: Bettmann/Corbis; **p. 1008**: US Army Signal Corps/Education Images/UIG via Getty Images; **p. 1009**: National Archives; **p. 1011**: Google Art Project/Wikimedia, pd; **p. 1013**: Granger Collection; **p. 1021**: Bettmann/Corbis; **p. 1022**: Bettmann/Corbis; **p. 1023**: Bettmann/Corbis; **p. 1025**: Hulton-Deutsch Collection/Corbis.

CHAPTER 23: p. 1028: Granger Collection; **p. 1033**: Granger Collection; **p. 1035**: Bettmann/Corbis; **p. 1037**: Schlesinger Library, Radcliffe Institute, Harvard University/Bridgeman Images; **p. 1038**: From the Collections of The Henry Ford Museum; **p. 1040**: National Baseball Hall of Fame Library/MLB Photos via Getty Images; **p. 1042**: Bettmann/Corbis; **p. 1043**: Wikimedia, pd; **p. 1045**: Bettmann/Corbis; **p. 1046**: Snark/Art Resource, NY; **p. 1049**: (2015) The Jacob and Gwendolyn Knight Lawrence Foundation, Seattle/Artist Rights Society (ARS), New York. Photo: Granger Collection; **p. 1051**: Art © Heirs of Aaron Douglas/Licensed by VAGA, New York, NY. Photo: National Gallery of Art, DC; **p. 1052**: Andrew Herman, photographer. Federal Art Project, pd, Photographic Division collection, Archives of American Art, Smithsonian Institution; **p. 1053**: AP Photo; **p. 1054**: Ferdinand Schmutzer/Wikimedia, pd; **p. 1057**: Max Weber (American, born Russia, 1881–1961). Russian Ballet, 1916. Oil on canvas, 30 x 36 in. (76.2 x 91.4 cm). Brooklyn Museum, Bequest of Edith and Milton Lowenthal, 1992.11.29.

CHAPTER 24: p. 1062: Corbis; **p. 1065**: Bettmann/Corbis; **p. 1067**: Bettmann/Corbis; **p. 1070**: Everett Collection/Alamy; **p. 1073**: Hulton-Deutsch Collection/Corbis; **p. 1076**: Corbis; **p. 1079**: Bettmann/Corbis; **p. 1084**: Granger Collection; **p. 1086**: Library of Congress; **p. 1089**: Kirn Vintage Stock/Corbis; **p. 1091**: David J. & Janice L. Frent Collection/Corbis; **p. 1092**: Herbert Hoover Presidential Library; **p. 1095**: OFF/AFP/Getty Images; **p. 1098**: Corbis; **p. 1100**: Bettmann/Corbis.

CHAPTER 25: p. 1104: Granger Collection; **p. 1107**: Museum of History and Industry/Corbis; **p. 1108**: Corbis; **p. 1110**: Joe Costa/NY Daily News Archive via Getty Images; **p. 1115**: Corbis; **p. 1116**: Granger Collection; **p. 1119**: Bettmann/Corbis; **p. 1122**: Library of Congress; **p. 1123**: Berenice Abbot/Getty Images; **p. 1125**: Everett Collection/Alamy; **p. 1127**: Margaret Bourke-White/Time & Life Pictures/Getty Images; **p. 1129**: Bettmann/Corbis; **p. 1132**: © 2015 Estate of Reginald Marsh/Arts Students League, New York/Artist Rights Society (ARS), New York. A Paramount Picture, 1934 (tempera on masonite), Marsh, Reginald (1898–1954)/Cleveland Museum of Art, OH, USA/Leonard C. Hanna, Jr. Fund/Bridgeman Images; **p. 1133**: Bettmann/Corbis; **p. 1135**: Bettmann/Corbis; **p. 1137**: The Art Archive at Art Resource, NY; **p. 1139**: Library of Congress; **p. 1140**: American Stock/Getty Images; **p. 1142**: Corbis; **p. 1146**: Bettmann/Corbis.

CHAPTER 26: p. 1150: Corbis; **p. 1153**: Imagno/Getty Images; **p. 1154**: Hugo Jaeger/Getty Images; **p. 1156**: Granger Collection; **p. 1159**: AF archive/Alamy; **p. 1162**: Library of Congress; **p. 1163**: Granger Collection; **p. 1165**: Bettmann/Corbis; **p. 1169**: Kyodo/Landov; **p. 1171**: National Archives; **p. 1173**: National Archives; **p. 1176**: Library of Congress; **p. 1177**: Granger Collection; **p. 1178**: AP Photo/U.S. Army Signal Corps, file; **p. 1180**: Corbis; **p. 1181**: Bettmann/Corbis; **p. 1182**: National Archives; **p. 1184**: AP Photo; **p. 1188**: National Archives; **p. 1190**: Adoc-photos/Art Resource, NY; **p. 1194**: HIP/Art Resource, NY; **p. 1196**: National Archives; **p. 1197**: dpa/Corbis; **p. 1199**: National Archives; **p. 1203**: Bettmann/Corbis; **p. 1204**: Corbis.

PART 7: p. 1211: JP Laffont/Sygma/Corbis; **p. 1213**: Reuters/Corbis.

CHAPTER 27: p. 1214: Bettmann/Corbis; **p. 1217**: Bettmann/Corbis; **p. 1220**: AP Photo/John Rooney; **p. 1222**: Library of Congress; **p. 1224**: Hulton-Deutsch Collection/Corbis; **p. 1225**: Bettmann/Corbis; **p. 1229**: ClassicStock/Alamy; **p. 1232**: Bettmann/Corbis; **p. 1234**: Bettmann/Corbis; **p. 1238**: Francis Miller/The LIFE Picture Collection/Getty Images; **p. 1240**: Bettmann/Corbis; **p. 1242**: Hulton-Deutsch Collection/Corbis; **p. 1243**: Pictorial Parade/Getty Images; **p. 1245**: Bettmann/Corbis; **p. 1249**: Granger Collection; **p. 1251**: Martha Holmes/Life Picture Collection/Getty Images; **p. 1253**: J. T. Vintage/Bridgeman Images.

CHAPTER 28: p. 1258: Art © Estate of Tom Wesselmann/Licensed by VAGA, New York, NY. Photo: Albright-Knox Art Gallery/Art Resource, NY; **p. 1260**: Corbis; **p. 1264**: Everett Collection Inc/Alamy; **p. 1266**: John Dominis/Time Life Pictures/Getty Images; **p. 1267**: Lake County Discovery Museum/UIG/Bridgeman Images; **p. 1269**: Hulton Archives/Getty Images; **p. 1271**: Corbis; **p. 1273**: Harvard Art Museums/Fogg Museum, Transfer from the Carpenter Center for the Visual Arts, American Professional Photographers Collection, 4.2002.3. Photo: Imaging Department © President and Fellows of Harvard College; **p. 1274 (top)**: Courtesy Everett Collection; **(bottom)**: Mondadori via Getty Images;

p. 1276: Three Lions/Getty Images; **p. 1277**: Library of Congress; **p. 1278**: Bernard Gotfryd/Getty Images; **p. 1279**: Allan Grant/The LIFE Picture Collection/Getty Images; **p. 1281**: Don Wright/The LIFE Images Collection/Getty Images; **p. 1283**: Elliott Erwitt/Magnum Photos; **p. 1284**: Bruce Davidson/Magnum Photos; **p. 1286**: Granger Collection; **p. 1287**: Charles Moore/Black Star; **p. 1289**: Bettmann/Corbis; **p. 1292**: Herb Block Foundation; **p. 1295**: Bettmann/Corbis; **p. 1296**: AFP/Getty Images; **p. 1303**: Howard Sochurek/The LIFE Picture Collection/Getty Images; **p. 1304**: Andre St. George/Corbis.

Chapter 29: p. 1308: Art © Romare Bearden Foundation/Licensed by VAGA, New York, NY. Digital Image © The Museum of Modern Art/Licensed by SCALA/Art Resource, NY; **p. 1311**: Granger Collection; **p. 1315**: Bettmann/Corbis; **p. 1317**: Granger Collection; **p. 1319**: Bettmann/Corbis; **p. 1321**: National Archives; **p. 1324**: Carl Mydans/The LIFE Picture Collection/Getty Images; **p. 1326**: Jack Moebes/Corbis; **p. 1327**: Granger Collection; **p. 1329**: AP Photo/Bill Hudson; **p. 1332**: Hulton Archives/Getty Images; **p. 1334**: AP Photo/BH, File; **p. 1335**: AP Photo; **p. 1336**: Bettmann/Corbis; **p. 1338**: Bettmann/Corbis; **p. 1339**: Corbis; **p. 1342**: Jack Moebes/Corbis; **p. 1346**: Bettmann/Corbis; **p. 1350**: Tim Page/Corbis; **p. 1352**: Bettmann/Corbis; **p. 1356**: Jack Kightlinger, Lyndon Baines Johnson Library and Museum.

Chapter 30: p. 1362: Bettmann/Corbis; **p. 1365**: Ted Streshinsky/Corbis; **p. 1366**: Leif Skoogfors/Corbis; **p. 1368**: AP Photo; **p. 1370**: Henry Diltz/Corbis; **p. 1371**: Ted Streshinsky/Corbis; **p. 1373**: John Olson/The LIFE Picture Collection/Getty Images; **p. 1374**: 91040/dpa/Corbis; **p. 1376**: Globe Photos/ZUMAPRESS.com; **p. 1378**: JP Laffont/Sygma/Corbis; **p. 1379**: Bettmann/Corbis; **p. 1380**: H. William Tetlow/Getty Images; **p. 1381**: Michael Rougier/The LIFE Picture Collection/Getty Images; **p. 1383**: Bettmann/Corbis; **p. 1384**: Fred W. McDarrah/Getty Images; **p. 1390**: Lee Lockwood/The LIFE Images Collection/Getty Images; **p. 1391**: AP Photo; **p. 1392**: Bettmann/Corbis; **p. 1396**: Howard Ruffner/Time & Life Pictures/Getty Images; **p. 1399**: Bettmann/Corbis; **p. 1402**: John Dominis/Getty Images; **p. 1407**: AP Photo; **p. 1408**: Bettmann/Corbis; **p. 1410**: Dirck Halstead/Time Life Pictures/Getty Images.

Chapter 31: p. 1414: Diego Goldberg/Sygma/Corbis; **p. 1417**: Corbis; **p. 1420**: AP Photo; **p. 1422**: Mohsen Shandiz/Sygma/Corbis; **p. 1423**: Bettmann/Corbis; **p. 1424**: Francois Lochon/Gamma-Rapho via Getty Images; **p. 1426**: Bettmann/Corbis; **p. 1431**: Bettmann/Corbis; **p. 1432**: Wally McNamee/Corbis; **p. 1436**: Bettmann/Corbis; **p. 1439**: Bettmann/Corbis; **p. 1440**: © Paul Szep; **p. 1441**: Bisson-Orban/Sygma/Corbis; **p. 1443**: Image Courtesy of The Advertising Archives; **p. 1445**: AP Photo/Peter Morgan; **p. 1446**: Jerry Cleveland/The Denver Post via Getty Images; **p. 1447**: Bill Nation/Sygma/Corbis; **p. 1450**: Reuters/Corbis; **p. 1453**: Mike Nelson/AFP/Getty Images; **p. 1455**: Chris Wilkins/Getty Images.

Chapter 32: p. 1458: Brendan McDermid/Reuters/Corbis; **p. 1461**: AP Photo/Mike Albans; **p. 1463**: AP Photo/James Finley; **p. 1465**: Richard Ellis/AFP/Getty Images; **p. 1469**: AP Photo/Ron Edmonds; **p. 1470**: Elmer Davez/epa/Corbis; **p. 1473**: AP Photo/Doug Mills; **p. 1475**: Robert King/Newsmakers/Getty Images; **p. 1477**: Sean Adair/Reuters/Corbis; **p. 1479**: Reuters/Corbis; **p. 1480**: Reuters/Corbis; **p. 1483**: Ali Jasim/Reuters/Corbis; **p. 1485**: Mario Tama/Getty Images; **p. 1486**: AP Photo/Pablo Martinez Monsivais; **p. 1488**: Justin Sullivan/Getty Images; **p. 1489 (top)**: Michael Ainsworth/Dallas Morning News/Corbis; **(bottom)**: AP Photo/Jae C. Hong, file; **p. 1494**: AP Photo/Erich Schlegel, File; **p. 1496**: Jeff J Mitchell/Getty Images; **p. 1498**: Darren McCollester/Getty Images; **p. 1499**: AP Photo/Ringo H.W. Chiu; **p. 1501**: AP Photo/Eric Gay; **p. 1505**: AP Photo/Efrem Lukatsky, file; **p. 1510**: Antonov Mladen/AFP/Getty Images; **p. 1512**: AP Photo/Mike Groll, file.

INDEX

Page numbers in *italics* refer to illustrations.

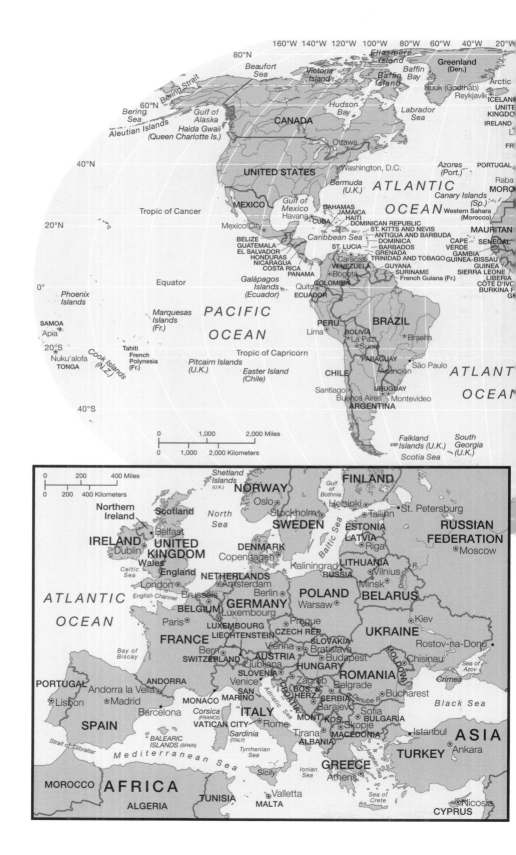